the Pharmer's Almanac

•

Andy Bernstein, Lockhart Steele,
Larry Chasnoff, & Brian Celentano

•

Berkley Boulevard Books, New York

The Pharmer's Almanac

A Berkley Boulevard Book / published by arrangement with Melting Media, Inc.

PRINTING HISTORY
Berkley Boulevard trade paperback edition / September 1998

For information address: The Berkley Publishing Group, a member of Penguin Putnam Inc.,
200 Madison Avenue, New York, New York 10016.

The Penguin Putnam World Wide Web site address is http://www.penguinputnam.com

To learn more about *The Pharmer's Almanac*, e-mail us at apharmers@aol.com,
or check out our Web site at www.pharmers.com.

ISBN: 0-425-16356-3

BERKLEY BOULEVARD
Berkley Boulevard Books are published by The Berkley Publishing Group,
a member of Penguin Putnam Inc.,
200 Madison Avenue, New York, New York 10016.
BERKLEY BOULEVARD and its logo are trademarks belonging to Berkley Publishing Corporation.

Book Design and Composition by Pauline Neuwirth, Neuwirth & Associates, Inc.

Printed in the United States of America

10 9 8 7 6 5 4 3 2 1

Contents

• Introduction •

If you've been to even one Phish concert, then you know it's about more than just hearing a band play music. It's about the Phish *experience*—you are not a consumer of the sound, instead you find yourself interacting with it and everything around you.

For most of us, Phish is not something you hear, it's something you listen to. And going to a concert does not mean pulling into the parking lot just before showtime and rushing to your seat; it's about new friends and old, and being part of an extended family. Even away from the venues, the process continues, with tape trading and reflections shared by fans.

The Pharmer's Almanac seeks to document and be a companion to every facet of the Phish experience. Whether you are a taping connoisseur, a history buff, or you just enjoy hearing the voices of fellow phans, *The Pharmer's Almanac* will offer you a journey into the Phish world that nothing other than the music itself can equal.

In the pages you will find:

- A continually expanding table of setlists, dating back to 1983.
- A comprehensive history of the band.
- The insights of over a dozen friends and collaborators of the band who were interviewed for this book.
- Stories written by fans—ranging from amusing to poignant—about show and touring experiences.
- Statistics, cross-referencing data, and show details—everything a taper needs to make sense of a collection.
- A top-to-bottom look at Phish side projects and guest appearances.
- Features on VIPs and active members of the Phish community.
- Reader's survey results.
- Photos, memorabilia, artifacts.

If it sounds like we went overboard, that's the idea. Our goal is to look at the band from every conceivable angle and to offer a little something to the many different types of Phish enthusiasts. Every time you pick up the *Almanac* you will undoubtedly find something new. That's what makes it, as our motto says, "The Ultimate Toilet Reading for Phans."

Key to this endeavor are the more than two hundred contributors to *The Pharmer's Almanac*. When four of us conceived the idea for the *Almanac* in the summer of 1995, our goal was to create a truly collective project, one which would incorporate the voices and knowledge of phans from all over the country.

We are proud to say that this volume indeed represents the work of hundreds of fans from dozens of states. Whether it be simple setlist corrections or in-depth show reviews, every page of this book represents the efforts and expertise of many, and we hope the *Almanac* as a whole speaks with a sort of collective voice which represents diverse facets of the Phish community.

Also essential to the compilation of this book were the voluminous online resources compiled by an even broader base of fans, including "The Helping Phriendly Book," the original compilation of setlists which served as a primary source and springboard to further research for the *Almanac*.

Piecing together the *Almanac* over the last three years (this is our fifth volume; it began in 1995 as ninety-six pages stapled together and sold at shows) has been a rewarding and challenging adventure. It has been our profound pleasure to get to know and learn from so many members of the Phish community. Our goal is to offer something which enhances the enjoyment of the band for each and every one of you.

photo courtesy of Jessica Fausty.

1

A Phish Story

Photo courtesy of Jay Archibald.

A PHISH STORY:

An Unlikely Journey from Dorm Room to Destiny

By Andy Bernstein and Lockhart Steele

DURING A 1991 INTERVIEW, PHISH guitarist Trey Anastasio told a reporter that the band's main goal was to make enough money to have separate rooms on the road.

Phish already had a devoted following, and was a sure draw at places like the Campus Club in Providence, RI, and the Somerville Theater outside of Boston—small halls that had played host to many big-money acts on their way to the top, and a bunch more who never made it past doubling-up at Motel 6.

For a band like Phish, which was still without a major-label record contract and had labored seven years just to achieve solid regional recognition, simple comforts appeared to be a reasonable set of goals. After all, a pair of band members were essentially homeless, having given up their apartments before the 1991 fall tour to save rent money.

Less than two years later, the band sold out the 17,000 capacity Great Woods Amphitheater in Mansfield, MA. And several years after that, they blew the doors off their own attendance records by attracting a city's worth of followers to the Clifford Ball in Plattsburgh, NY, and the Great Went in Limestone, ME. And yet, when journalists and music pontifs attempt to tell the band's oddly anachronistic story—which is void of MTV propulsion, hit songs, or genius marketing wizards—it is the roots of the band and the small bars of New England that form the crux of every narrative.

In this rags to riches story, the rags have always been more intriguing than the riches.

While the majority of fans cannot claim to have been initiated in the days of small clubs and shoestring-budget tours, it's places like the Stone Church in Newmarket, NH, and, of course, Nectar's in Burlington, VT, that are forever encrusted as part of the band's identity. For now at least, the colossal masses that squeeze (or break) their way into concerts remain an oddity, even to the fans who form them.

Phish, having made the transition to arena rock so seamlessly, still manages to emit the homey, detailed essence of the bar band they once were. The story of their ascension, powered by word-of-mouth hysteria and tape-trading dementia, is the same as it was when they made the then miraculous leap from part-time lounge act to small-time headliner. The band's exponential growth in popularity only serves as incentive to look back, as the music remains inextricably linked with its shadowy roots.

TREY HAD BEEN WRITING songs with friends since junior high school, often going off to fields near his home in New Jersey and writing nonsense lyrics which, speculation has it, never quite managed to impress the chicks. Although a teacher at the Princeton Day School called Trey an "excellent musician" on his report card, he failed music class because of poor behavior. In fact, his delinquency would continue to frustrate his parents, especially after he crashed the family car into a firetruck, just a month after being grounded for nearly running over his own father.

For the tenth grade, Trey packed up and headed off to The Taft School, a boarding school in Watertown, CT. An avowed Led Zeppelin fan, he was skilled at playing the drums but had never really picked up a guitar. Trey's only involvement with a band came as a cameo vocalist for the group Red Tide, an outfit of older Taft students who named their group after a bacteria that was striking fear into the nation at the time.

Trey performed the Traffic song "Low Spark of High-Heeled Boys" as his first ever performance with a rock band.

It was not until his junior year that Trey began playing guitar, but his virtuosity was immediately apparent.

"Within like a month, he was just whaling on that thing," remembers Rob Florence, a friend from Taft. "He was constantly playing it. It was pretty remarkable just how quickly he was able to play just anything."

By his senior year, a new band was formed. Dubbed "Space Antelope" by friend and occasional vocalist Steve Pollak (better known as the Dude of Life), the group featured Trey on

Phish on VERMONT

Trey: "Vermont has everything to do with who we are. Simplicity and slowness. And cold. People here are in no rush to get anywhere. And neither is Phish."
—to Charles Hirshberg, Life *(June 1996)*

Page: "We just really like it up here. It's out of the way and has a small town feeling to it. It definitely feels like a community. And where else would we go? I can't imagine us moving to Boston or Los Angeles. We're on the road a lot—eight or nine months last year—so why not spend the rest of our time in a beautiful place like Vermont?"
—to Steve Morse, Boston Globe *(March 27, 1994)*

Trey: "The only time we hear anything about Vermont is during the election. During the last primary, the newscasters were wondering aloud how to pronounce the capital of Vermont. It's pronounced 'mont-PEE-lee-yer.'"
—to Bill Locey, Los Angeles Times *(April 16, 1992)*

Mike: "Had we not come from Burlington we wouldn't have made it as a band. There would have been pressure to play other kinds of music, to do certain kinds of gigs. . . We've found all these people in Burlington and in the outskirts of Burlington, a community of musicians."
—to Steve Rosenfeld, Vermont Times *(March 12, 1992)*

rhythm guitar. The following September, Trey, the Dude, and Rob Florence all headed off to the University of Vermont. Upon arrival, one of Trey's first priorities was to assemble a real college band.

In his first month at UVM, Trey hitched up with fellow frosh Jonathan Fishman (Fish) when Trey heard drumming through his dormitory walls and investigated the source of the sublime rhythms. Listening to each other play, the two immediately knew they had found a good match. As Fishman later related to the *Boston Globe*, "As soon as I heard him [Trey] play guitar, then after I heard some of the songs he'd written, I was like, 'This is it. I'll play drums to this guy's music.' I could see immediately that he thought in a really original way and was into writing his own stuff."

Photo courtesy of Jay Archibald.

Trey, now proficient at lead guitar, found rhythm guitarist Jeff Holdsworth in much the same way. Walking by Jeff's dorm room, Trey heard Jeff playing and liked what he heard. The three began jamming together in the rec room of a dormitory called Wing-Davis-Wilke. It began not really as a band rehearsal, just a sort of rolling improv. Seeking a bass player to turn their gathering into a group, Trey hung signs around campus, drawing the interest of fellow freshman Mike Gordon.

Mike, too, arrived at UVM itching to play. He had played in a cover band in high school named the Tombstone Blues Band, as well as a new wave outfit called The Edge. An introverted youth who preferred building gadgets and starting projects to playing with toys, Mike was pretty much a loner until music broke him out of his shell in high school. Early that first semester at UVM, he joined the other three in the rec room and their first series of notes together attracted about 25 fellow students who heard the sounds coming through the hallways and came out and danced. When the jam wound down, Mike turned to the others and asked, "So, do I get the job?" He did.

As it turned out, Jeff knew someone who needed a band for an ROTC Halloween dance to be held in the basement of a campus dorm. The band volunteered to take the gig. Even though they had been playing together for only a few weeks, they had assembled a play list of cover tunes and made a demo tape. The foursome played under the temporary name Blackwood Convention.

That the ROTC dance represented a rookie outing was clear: in lieu of microphone stands, the band relied on hockey sticks duct-taped to a table to support their mikes. There wasn't a stage either, so the band set up on one side of the dark basement room, playing classic rock standards such as "Heard It through the Grapevine" to the apparently unimpressed (and overdressed) crowd. When they stepped aside for a breather, somebody put Michael Jackson's *Thriller* on over the sound system, and taking the hint, the band that would become Phish packed it in. Their first gig had been a bomb. [See sidebar for more on the first show.]

The group retooled for several more gigs that fall, including some better-received performances in Slade Hall, an environmental cooperative house on the UVM campus.

The new band faced a potentially devastating obstacle that winter when Trey undertook a prank of the highest order and had to pay the

TIMELINE

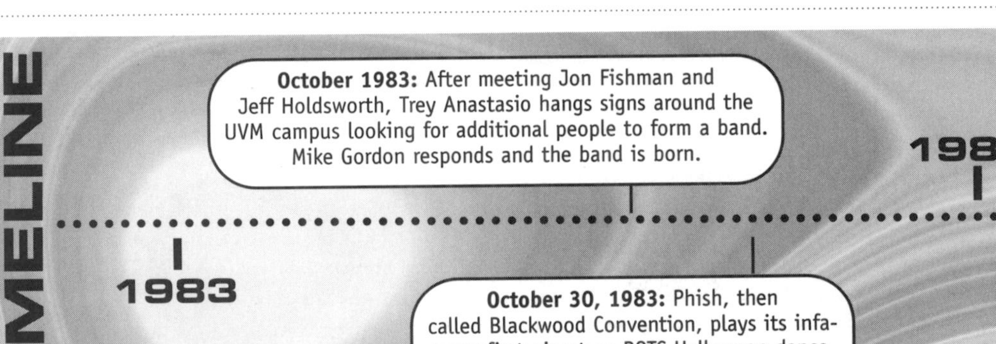

The FIRST Gig

If they ever turn the Phish story into a movie, a hilarious opening scene is ready-made, one that truly proves just how humble the beginnings were.

After practicing together for several weeks in a dorm lounge, the band that would become Phish—then comprised of Trey, Mike, Fish, and Jeff Holdsworth on rhythm guitar—landed their first gig at an ROTC formal on October 30, 1983.

Trey negotiated the band's fee, said to be $250, and didn't flinch when organizers told him they were looking for a band that could "play the hits." What he didn't mention was that while Jeff Holdsworth was well versed in rock standards, none of them had a clue how to play anything from *Thriller* or *Born in the USA*, the hot albums of the time.

Rob Florence, a friend from high school who also attended UVM, accompanied the band to the gig, along with the Dude of Life and Trey's then girlfriend. He remembers it was one of the funnier but more uncomfortable nights he spent at college. "It was kind of weird and a little awkward. There were all these people there and they had rented tuxedos," he says. "All the girls had corsages. This was something these people had planned for a long time and put a lot of time into."

When the band, playing under the temporary name Blackwood Convention, launched into the Hollies' "Long Cool Woman in a Black Dress," the conservative crowd was less than impressed. Everyone sat in their chairs, while Florence and the Dude, dressed in jeans and T-shirts, peeked over at each other in amused silence. "The vibe I got from the people there was that they weren't pleased," Florence says.

When the band veered into "Your Momma Don't Dance and Your Daddy Don't Rock 'n' Roll," and a stretched out version of "Heard It through the Grapevine," things only got worse. The guy who was running the formal gave the band a stern look from the audience. One intrepid couple made it to the dance floor, but no one else followed.

But for Trey and the rest, it was a chance to have some fun. "There came a point in the evening where they launched into these jam songs," says Florence. "I remember they played 'Whipping Post' that night, and they absolutely tore it up. I may be getting a little exaggerated in my memory, but I remember this thing was like 30 or 40 minutes long. They just went on and on and on just jamming and jamming, and that I think is what tried these people's patience."

No one quite remembers whether it was before or after the band left the stage, but when *Thriller* came over the loudspeaker, the band packed it up and called it a night. At that point, the audience immediately left their seats. "The minute that pop music came on, the dance floor was swarmed immediately," Florence says.

You have to wonder if anyone in attendance that night knows what they were a part of.

Phish on DRUGS

Mike: "Our fans like to alter their consciousness. Hopefully, the music, independent of the Drug, is a conscious altering thing."

—*to Nate Eaton,* The Best of High Times *#18*

Mike: "I smoke pot from time to time. Not regularly, though I really like to play music after smoking pot. I don't do it very often; I save it as a sort of ritual. It's pretty rare that I do. And I haven't tried any other drugs. That's it for me. Not everyone who experiments with drugs is a drug addict."

—*to* The Onion *(www.theonion.com)*

Fish: "I was never heavily into drugs. My drug is music.

I ended up stopping quickly because I would have one experience or another where drugs would end my ability to play. Of course my first experiences inspired me to play. When you're high, your playing seems to sound better, but when you listen back to the tapes, it sucks."

—*to Christopher Rossi,* Relix *(October 1996)*

price. Engaged in a game of one-upsmanship with a high school friend who'd headed out west to Colorado, Trey and the Dude of Life snuck into the cadaver storage area at a UVM research facility and stole a human hand and heart. They then packaged the two souvenirs and prepared to send them to their friend with a note reading, "I've got to hand it to you—you've really got heart!"

The prank would have just been a good laugh if not for one damning error and another mortal coincidence. Trey and the Dude didn't mail the package themselves—instead, they enlisted Rob Florence, who stupidly included a return address on the package.

When their target received the little surprise, he was a good sport about it, but didn't want the decaying human body parts to stink up his house. So he simply left the box out on his lawn and went out for the day. It also happened to be the day that the local firemen were walking around collecting gifts and donations from the townsfolk. One of the brave firefighters came upon the box, and thinking it was a present, opened it.

When Trey's friend returned that day, he was greeted by the flashing lights of police cars, investigating what they thought was a murder. Quick detective work traced the package and the body parts back to UVM and Florence, and ultimately to Trey and the Dude, who stepped forward and shared the rap. In a sense, it was Trey's first brush with fame. Although his name never actually appeared in the newspaper, it was a major scandal in Burlington, and even made national news. The culprits were sus-

December 1, 1984: Back together again, Phish plays its first show in the upstairs space at Nectar's in downtown Burlington. The Dude of Life sits in for the concert debut of "Fluffhead."

Summer 1985: Trey and Fish spend part of the summer together traveling in Europe, where Trey writes a number of future Phish songs, including "You Enjoy Myself."

1985

May 3, 1985: Page McConnell sits in with Phish at Goddard Springfest.

Fall 1985: Trey and Fish return from Europe to find that Mike has invited Page to join the band despite their earlier protests. Phish is now a five-piece group.

pended for a semester and the band took an involuntary hiatus.

During his time away from UVM, Trey attended classes at Mercer Community College near his home in New Jersey. One day, he ran into old friends Tom Marshall and Marc Daubert, who also were at Mercer for the semester. Marshall and Daubert helped Trey set up a recording studio in his basement, where they recorded a four-track project called *Bivouac Jaun*, pieces of which would later find their way onto Phish's "white tape."

Meanwhile, Fish and Mike played together in another campus band called the Dangerous Grapes, which covered tunes by the Grateful Dead and the Allman Brothers Band, as well as some blues standards. When Trey returned to UVM in the fall of 1984, Fish and Mike faced a decision: stay with the Grapes, or re-form with Trey? For Fish, the decision wasn't hard: he knew he wanted to play with Trey and he liked Trey's vision for the future, which included playing all original material.

The decision wasn't as easy for Mike, who later told *Relix*, "When we first started jamming together in dorm rooms, I actually thought that we really didn't click together in terms of how we sounded." Fish's certainty helped solidify Mike as a member of the group, but Mike decided to rejoin the band only on the condition they also could play cover songs. Trey agreed.

Around this time the band christened itself Phish. Numerous stories swirl around the origin of the band's name, but the most believable is that they simply came up with a silly variation on Fishman's last name while hanging around the UVM student center.

Rob Dasaro, the keyboardist from another Burlington band, The Joneses, was actually on hand when the decision was made. "I don't know how I became part of it, but I vividly remember those guys sitting in the Billings Dining Hall, which, if you went upstairs, kind of had this reading place," says Dasaro. "I remember the band sitting around a table coming up with the name Phish off of Jon Fishman's name. Like right then just going, 'Phish—yeah, that's it!' and going 'Wow! That's cool.'"

That fall, the foursome played for the first time under the name Phish in the basement of Slade Hall in a gig the band still recalls fondly. In December, the band made its debut on the

Phish on GROWING UP

Mike: "I was a very strange kid. I never played any sports, ever, and I spent much of my time alone. I didn't want to be a kid—I wanted to be an adult. I spent a lot of time planning projects; when I was nine I planned a full-length feature film, and I also put together these clubs that never existed. . . .

I was completely introverted; even when I was one or two, I'm told, I never played with toys. I preferred things in the real world, like going through the stuff in my mom's purse. I always needed to be building something, like a little-kid mad scientist. Finally, in high school, I came out of my shell, and music started to become this thing I cared about more and more."
—*to Karl Coryat,* Bass Player *(September 1996)*

Trey: "Growing up, I was always getting into trouble—serious trouble. I remember in the fifth grade taking a big black magic marker and writing on walls. I defaced a kid's painting and tried to lie my way out of it. My parents so drilled it into me not to lie that now I don't know how to lie."
—*to Lynn Minton,* Parade Magazine *(February 6, 1997)*

Fish: "There were times when I caught my dad saying to my mom, 'We should never have gotten that kid a drum set.'"
—*to Lynn Minton,* Parade Magazine *(February 6, 1997)*

Trey: "Starting in about sixth grade I had this group of friends who are very musical. We would just hang out and write songs constantly. . . . When we would go out, it was usually five or six people, we'd go to this rhombus in Princeton. We still do—at the age of almost 30, on Tom's wedding night; it's this weird thing. We just call everybody up, people we haven't seen in years. We say, 'Rhombus, half an hour.' Everybody will show up there. It's a big black rhombus in the middle of a green field. You climb up on top of it. It's kind of a magical place for us."
—*to Bob Doran,* Edge City Magazine *(March 1993)*

Mike: "We have close family ties, family values. We're not angst-ridden. We're rebellious in certain ways. We rebel against the norm. But we're not rebelling necessarily against our parents. They all have parent laminates, and they come to see us a lot. Every single parent we have a great relationship with."
—*to Robin Caudell,* Plattsburgh Press-Republican *(August 17, 1996)*

Page: "Both my parents are very giving people who feel it's important to give back to the community. Their lives make me feel good about what we're doing—trying to bring happiness and joy into people's lives."
—*to Lynn Minton,* Parade Magazine *(February 6, 1997)*

They Found Goddard

When writing about Phish, some mainstream media publications simplify the band members' history and say they all graduated from the University of Vermont. But that's only true for Mike Gordon, because Page, Fish, and Trey all graduated from tiny Goddard College in Plainfield, VT.

Goddard is an alternative college based on the theories of philosopher John Dewey, and prides itself on its experimental nature. The curriculum is created anew at the start of every semester as each student works with faculty advisers to create a study plan unique to their interests. At the end of the semester, professors give their students evaluations of their work and effort in lieu of letter grades—the focus clearly is on personal development. In addition, every senior must undertake a senior project in an area of particular interest to them. For Page, this turned into a study of musical improvisation. For Trey, it was the writing and production of "The Man Who Stepped into Yesterday."

During the early 1980s, Goddard's undergraduate enrollment had dropped below 50 students, so Page received $50 each for recruiting Fish and Trey to his school. Now, though, enrollment has rebounded to over 200 undergrads. Those seeking more information can reach Goddard at (802) 454-8311.

November 23, 1985: Mike experiences an intensely spiritual moment playing with Phish in the Goddard cafeteria. He later recalls it as one of the most important moments in his life.

Spring 1986: After graduating from UVM, Jeff quits the band. Rumors that he "discovered Christ" will circulate for the next decade.

1986

Fall 1986: Paul Languedoc joins on as the band's soundman and jack-of-all-trades. Phish plays its first of four Halloween concerts at Goddard College, where Trey and Fish had enrolled in September.

upstairs stage at Nectar's on Burlington's main drag, a nightspot that has offered many local area bands their first shot.

While their technical accomplishment was still lacking, Trey and the band managed to do something few in the history of rock and roll have ever done. Some of the very first songs they composed were classics. Tunes such as "Slave to the Traffic Light" and "Fluffhead"—albeit without most of the complexity the four-part "Fluff's Travels" brings to the song—found their way into the setlist at Nectar's that night, along with a few Grateful Dead covers. "Slave" and "Fluffhead" remain two of the most adored tunes in the band's repertoire, proving that, although it would be another decade before most Phish fans would hear these songs, Phish's creative acumen was present at the band's genesis.

In early 1985, Phish signed a five-week contract to play Thursday night happy hours at Doolin's, a notorious frat bar in Burlington. The Doolin's shows, running from 5:00 to 6:00 p.m., didn't attract big crowds, but they did attract loyal ones. Amy Skelton, the famous "phirst phan," and Brian Long showed up each week and danced like crazy. They didn't know it—or each other—at the time, but they were grooving their way into Phish history.

Amy would go on to serve as the band's on-tour merchandise manager. She also played host to the Amy's Farm free concert in 1991. Brian, meanwhile, moved in with the band a short time later in a red house on King Street in Burlington, across from a Hood milk factory. It was there that he helped pen some of the lyrics to "Harry Hood."

In the spring of 1985, Brian helped Phish arrange a gig at Goddard College's annual Springfest. The organizer of the Springfest, a Goddard student originally from Basking Ridge, NJ, by the name Page McConnell, liked Phish so much he volunteered to join, in the manner an overzealous little leaguer "volunteers" to bat first. Phish watched Page's band at Springfest and liked his style, and invited him to jam with them during their set.

That summer, Trey and Fish headed to Europe with several other friends where they played as vagabonds while Trey composed pieces including the epic "You Enjoy Myself" and the music to "Harry Hood." Telephoning Mike in Burlington, Trey and Fish voiced their belief that Page shouldn't join Phish, but Mike spent much of the summer teaching Page early Phish compositions including "Slave" and "Fluffhead," and by the time autumn rolled around, Page was in.

Marc Daubert, a percussionist and close friend of Trey's, also popped up in the early days, but by 1986 the lineup was solidified when Jeff supposedly "discovered Christ" and left the band. Others say Jeff simply left to pursue different interests after graduating that spring, including a trip to Alaska, but the "discovering Christ" story still circulates. (Versions of this Phishy folklore include everything from his playing in Jimmy Swaggart's church band to returning to Burlington years later in hopes of converting the rest of Phish to recognize Christ as their savior.)

The band's commitment to composing and performing original music also played a role in their original separation. Trey later told California-based *Edge City Magazine*, "Myself and Jon had gone to Europe, and we were playing street music. While we were there I wrote this thing, 'You Enjoy Myself.' I brought it back to the band when we got back and I said, 'Let's learn this.' That was it—the tension started with Jeff. It was like beating his head against the wall. He thought it was stupid. My whole goal was, 'as different as possible.' That was the beginning of the end for him. He left the band and I started working with Ernie [Stires] and writing even more."

Page, however, loved the new direction of the band's music, and he worked to convince them to play jazz standards as well. A series of trade-offs ensued when Mike, who disliked jazz, agreed to play it if the band would cover some bluegrass songs, even though both Trey and Fish professed to hate country music. In the grand art of compromise, Phish agreed to do it all; the band members later would surprise themselves by each learning to enjoy parts of these varied musical styles.

The fall of 1986 saw Trey and Fish transfer to

Phish on INFLUENCES

Trey: "The thing about the influence question is understanding how many there are. All I do is listen to music. We have thousands of albums."
—*to Paul Robicheau,* Boston Globe *(September 20, 1990)*

Fish: "We all have a certain desire to honor the roots and traditions of music, but there's also this persistent desire to find out what else we can do rather than the common forms, the things you always hear."
—*to Parke Puterbaugh,* Rolling Stone *(February 20, 1997)*

Trey: "You have to at least familiarize yourself with Jazz if you're going to be an American band. That's something we think about a lot. I think Phish is a really American kind of thing."
—*to Keith Sperar,* Times-Picayune *(April 26, 1996)*

Trey: "There's a kind of competitive edge in the band where we hear somebody and we think 'I want to be able to do that.'"
—*to Marek Kohn,* The Independent *(June 25, 1992)*

Fish: "Well of course [the Grateful Dead were an influence], along with a zillion other bands that were a huge influence. The Grateful Dead did pave the way for improvisational playing in the context of rock music and arena rock. So in that way, yeah, they really opened the doors for bands like us, and any other bands that jam. The Allmans kind of did too, but the Grateful Dead had the highest exposure. That's definitely an influence. In the structure of the shows and the whole approach, I think there are more similarities. I don't think the actual music sounds the same."
—*to Paul Robicheau,* Boston Globe *(December 22, 1996)*

Trey [on practicing to The Meters]: "We knew it was the only way we were ever going to even resemble playing with a groove. We'd try to be as far back on the beat as they would be, knowing that we were going to speed up—there was no way to lay back as far as those guys. It was like going to school."
—*to Keith Spera,* Times-Picayune *(April 26, 1996)*

Fish: "Sun Ra said he had two rules for his band: expect the unexpected and play with urgency, and I think the playing with urgency is to live as much as you can in the moment. . . . You step foot on stage and that's who you are."
—*to Paul Robicheau,* Boston Globe *(December 22, 1996)*

Trey: "I try to think of music the way the big bands thought of it. They'd take a popular song, and you'd be able to listen to it on every level. Someone who likes show tunes would be able to dance to it. But someone whose ear was more trained would notice the arrangement was pushing the limits of musical language."
—*Elektra band bio (February 1992)*

1987

Fall 1987: Phish enters a Boston recording studio for the first time, recording a three-song demo tape.

Summer 1987: Phish starts drawing its first real crowds to its shows in Burlington and environs. Nectar's remains a favorite spot.

1988

Courtesy of Katie McConnell.

Spring 1988: Phish plays its first paid out-of-state gigs in New Hampshire; Amherst, MA; and at Kenny's Castaways in New York City.

Phish on EACH OTHER

Mike: "Because Fish isn't concerned with demonstrating his technical skill at all times, you can sometimes forget what a great player he is."
—*to William F. Miller,* Modern Drummer *(September 1995)*

Fish: "Mike is probably the worst drummer out of all of us in the band."
—*to Chriss Gill,* Guitar Player *(Vol. 28, No. 9)*

Fish: "The first time Trey saw me, I was walking past the library. He and a friend were having a conversation about who looked like they belonged there and who didn't. I came walking by and they both fell down laughing. They pegged me from a hundred yards in a crowd of people, going, 'He doesn't look like he belongs here.'"
—*to Parke Puterbaugh,* Rolling Stone *(February 20, 1997)*

Trey: "For a long time, Fish had a personal rule that he'd never play the same drumbeat twice. It was a great idea, but it got to be a pain in the ass after a while."
—*to Mac Randall,* Musician *(December 1996)*

Page: "It's been a many-year process to get to where I am today, which I feel like we're all equal members and we converse. There always was that feeling, but . . . I mean, I don't really know how to describe it except it's kind of like a marriage except you're married to three other guys and everybody's married to everybody. I can honestly say we're getting along better now than we ever have."
—*to Michael Goldberg,* Addicted to Noise *(www.atn.com, February 1997)*

Mike: "We're pretty much lucky to have someone like Trey. I just wouldn't have the patience and the stamina to make all the decisions, to write the song lists and plan our songs, even though we don't usually stick to it. My personality is much better suited to being in the engine room, making things work from that level.

Page and Fish—I was looking at them sitting next to each other and thinking they're sort of opposites. . . . Page is really level-headed. He's a very reliable guy. Fish can be very disciplined. He probably practices more than any of us, but you can't count on him to be somewhere on time or that sort of thing. Fish is the most willing to do something crazy. He's the least wanting of control."
—*to Robin Caudell,* Plattsburgh Press-Republican *(August 17, 1996)*

Photo courtesy of Kelley Thomas.

Goddard College. Mike, the most serious student of the group, stayed behind at UVM, majoring in film and electrical engineering. But Trey was all too happy to get out of UVM's music department, which he thought focused too much on making students into music teachers, not musicians.

To supplement what UVM hadn't been teaching him, he had already taken music lessons from the classically trained theorist Ernie Stires, who helped teach him the art of composition. Goddard offered him college credit to continue studying with Stires, and Stires became Trey's mentor. Stires didn't have a taste for rock music, but he got Trey to focus on composition theory, using big band music, classical music, and jazz as jumping-off points. He gave Trey compositional exercises to work on, several of which planted seeds for future Phish songs. The eager student devoured it all.

Although stationed an hour down the road in Plainfield, VT, the band became regulars at Nectar's and other small bars in Burlington—including Hunt's and Finbar's—making the rounds and playing several nights a week, while also gigging at several colleges around Vermont. "A lot of who we are developed playing three sets a night at Nectar's," Trey later told *Guitar World*. "You can really do anything you wanted within reason. And we pushed reason. We tried everything including doing musical plays. There was no cover so there was always a crowd hanging at the bar drinking, whether they thought we sucked or not. Slowly but surely people actually started coming."

Eliminating the Dead covers along the way, they began filling their sets with more originals, most of which were written by Trey with lyrics often supplied by Tom Marshall. During this period, several more of the most popular Phish songs were completed, including "David Bowie," "Divided Sky," and "Harry Hood." Gordon contributed "Mike's Song" to the group's repertoire, and the Dude of Life supplied "Suzie Greenberg," giving Phish a solid list to choose from for any occasion.

IN THE FALL OF 1986, Phish gained a permanent soundman in Paul Languedoc, who met the band while working at Time Guitars in Burlington. Paul became the band's Mr. Everything, building custom guitars and speaker cases, carrying equipment, keeping the books, all while running the sound and monitors. He would later limit his duties to the soundboard as Phish's touring entourage swelled in size, but throughout the 1980s and into the 1990s, he was the heart and soul of the Phish crew.

Mike and Page graduated in 1987, and Mike then took part of the summer off with Trey to practice in a secluded cabin in the woods. Trey's graduation came in 1988 (Fish wouldn't don a graduate's cap until 1990). As they kept playing, word of their epic jams and quirky sense of onstage fun spread around Vermont. A devoted following could be found at Goddard and at schools like Johnson State College in Johnson, VT, which later became the first place to ban Phish from playing because of the unwelcomed convergence of VW buses that accompanied

Summer 1988: Phish graduates from Nectar's in July and heads west on its first real tour, a week's worth of shows at the tiny Roma in Telluride, Colorado.

1989

1989: Katie McConnell and Kristy Anastasio create the first Phish newsletters.

each appearance. Ironically, Phish still struggled for popularity in Burlington.

"They never got much recognition in the local papers—I remember that being kind of an issue," recalls Jamie Masefield, a fellow musician who entered UVM around the same time as Phish band members, and would later form the side project Bad Hat with Trey. "They were really weird, they were totally different. And now, everyone says, 'Oh, that's so cool, they were so weird.' But at the time, it wasn't a cool weird, necessarily, it was just weird."

But as they caught on in other portions of Vermont, Burlington music fans woke up to the Phish phenomenon. "They had a really unique following, a small but very loyal following, and I think a lot of them came from Goddard. It was the weirdest looking crowd," Masefield says. "I think that one of the keys for those guys was that they worked at developing it in other places, and people in Burlington started hearing, 'Wow, people really liked them at Goddard.' I think that was one of their initial jumping steps, and then, 'Wow, they liked them at UNH,' and that really helped to improve their image in Burlington."

In March of 1988, the band clued their fans into Gamehendge, the magical musical tale of the Lizard people and their enslavement at the hands of the evil King Wilson. Songs from Gamehendge had been in the band's repertoire since 1986, but they had never performed them as a group or with a narration until the "Story Time at Nectar's" show on March 12. Few of their fans even knew there was any relationship between the songs, but during this period Trey was putting the finishing touches on the recorded version of the saga, which was called "The Man Who Stepped into Yesterday" and served as his senior thesis at Goddard.

The early spring of 1988 also saw a student from Amherst College in Western Massachusetts take a break from a ski trip to catch a band his friends had raved about. The student was John Paluska and his impression of Phish was so strong that he immediately booked them to play three weeks later at the Zoo, a cooperative theme house at Amherst where he was social director.

That period saw Phish playing their first paying out-of-state shows. On March 31, they conquered New York City for the first time, playing the Greenwich Village club Kenny's Castaways with plenty of friends in attendance. Three days later, they hit Paluska's Zoo. And Amy Skelton, who had by this time moved to New Hampshire, secured them a show at the Steak House at Squam Lake, NH. It was Phish's first "spring tour." The foundation for a professional band was beginning to be set.

Paluska was so excited with the band that he called his friend Ben Hunter, a student at Boston University and a childhood chum from Maine, and convinced him to drive out for the Zoo show on April 2. Hunter, like Paluska, was blown away by the band's musical prowess and the two later co-founded Dionysian Productions to manage Phish. Paluska's love for Phish never faded—he still manages the band (Hunter left Dionysian in the early 1990s to pursue a career in music journalism).

In August, the band hit the road for two weeks' worth of shows at a tiny club in Telluride, CO. By the time they returned to Burlington in September, they graduated from the 200-person capacity Nectar's, which had "never a cover charge" as its motto, to The Front, which held about twice as many people.

The change was not welcomed by all. Mike still tells the story of a woman sitting at the bar at The Front wailing, "They're not our band anymore!" But, as he later recounted to the *Plattsburgh Press-Republican*, "She might have been turned off, but she kept coming. She probably discovered we were pretty similar at The Front."

Times were good in Burlington, but gigs in Boston—the cultural epicenter of New England—remained elusive. Ben Hunter, still at Boston University, offered to help, landing the band a gig at a club called Molly's and plastering the area with posters. The show that November was a success (Hunter booked them again at Molly's in early December).

Still, demo tapes the band mailed to the larger and more prestigious nightclub The Paradise were never reviewed by the club's booking

Phish on THE SHOWS

Mike [on playing in Germany]: "It's just kind of like another day at the office or something, so it's a lot more low-key and we get on stage and people are drinking, you can hear glasses clinking and all that. So it's kind of fun. Maybe we sort of let loose in a different kind of way. There's less pressure to be something, which is good, because probably the best stuff happens when you're not trying to be something."

—*to Parke Puterbaugh,* *(Phish. Com September 7, 1997)*

Trey: "It's the experience at the concerts. There's a real feeling between us. I don't feel like I'm performing at the audience. It's like a party. Or it's like some night in high school, where you blew off some plans and, instead, you and your friends stayed out all night. You went to the lake and watched the sun rise. It was a spontaneous bonding experience that you remember all of your life. That's how I feel at a show when everything goes right. It's much more powerful."

—*to Michael Snyder,* San Francisco Chronicle *(May 1994)*

Trey: "If there's anything I'm thinking about before I go on stage, it's 'What are we going to do tonight that we've never done before?' And hopefully I won't know what that is until it happens."

—*to Larry Nager,* Commercial Appeal *(June 11, 1995)*

Mike: "We do really weird stuff onstage sometimes, and we have a group of people listening who'd rather we did that than play the same thing each night. It's so much fun to know we can take chances and that there are people willing to come along and listen and dance.

These great journeys are the ideal, but there's another side. Sometimes we get off the stage and fight with each other about who wasn't concentrating.

It always comes down to hooking up."

—*to Karl Coryat,* Bass Player *(September 1996)*

Trey: "I still look down on the front row now and can probably name or recognize a third of the people there. It's weird. I feel like I'm playing in a room full of buddies."

—*to Brian McCollum,* Tampa Tribune *(November 10, 1995)*

Trey: "[Our strangest gig ever] would have to be this gig we played at this sex commune in Vermont. It was run by this old guy named Irving who had to be about 80 years old. They were a bunch of old hippies with gardens and kids running around everywhere, and they intermingled their lovemaking . . . Irving showed up at the gig with a beautiful young woman on each arm. . . . They cooked us an incredible meal, too."

—*to Bill Locey,* Los Angeles Times *(April 16, 1992)*

Courtesy of Katie McConnell.

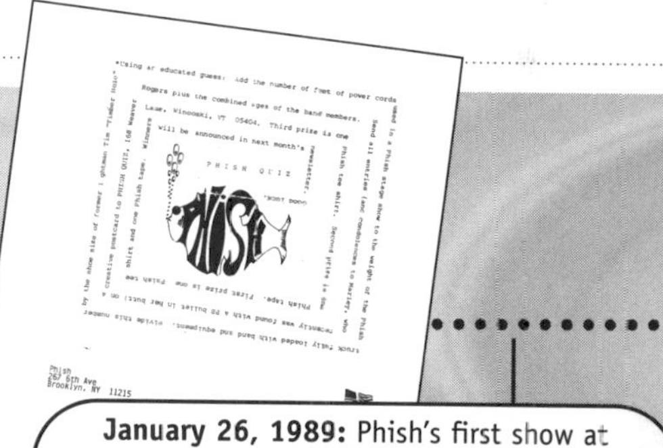

January 26, 1989: Phish's first show at the Paradise in Boston is a success, as fans travel from Vermont and New Hampshire to sell out the 650-person club.

Phish on MUSICAL PROCESS

Fish: "I feel that the inspiration and the new directions you can achieve by opening yourself up to the other styles far outweighs anything you might lose.

No matter how straight a thing might be, you can still find some different way to play it and still be true to the basic groove of the song."
—*to William F. Miller,* Modern Drummer *(September 1995)*

Trey: "The way I look at it, the music exists in the universe, and if you're lucky enough, or strong enough, to get your ego out of the way, the music comes through you. The audience that we have is open to that, and they understand that conversational transfer of energy."
—*to Steve Silberman,* San Diego Reader *(December 22, 1994)*

Mike: "If you were actually flying, your inner ear would be giving you information about balance, there'd be wind rushing past your face, and there'd be pressure from the altitude. All of those senses come into your brain, which perceives that you're flying. My theory is that by standing completely still, you can create not only a feeling similar to flight but the exact feeling of flight. When music is great, that's how it is for me—and the bass is the vehicle for that to happen."
—*to Karl Coryat,* Bass Player *(September 1996)*

Trey: "It's like you're surfing: The wave is stronger than you. If you relax and have no fear, and you're with the flow of the wave, you can ride it. But if you try to fight it, you'll wipe out. The same wave can be a source of pain, or beautiful flowing grace—it's just a matter of how you respond to it."
—*to Kevin Ransom,* Detroit News *(October 26, 1995)*

Mike: "When I'm playing, there are times when a note can be completely thrilling in a way I couldn't even imagine when I'm not in that state, and there are other times when I play that same note and think, 'When am I going to get some food?'

For me, playing music isn't about creating art that will stand the test of time; it's about performing a ritual."
—*to Paul Alan,* Guitar World *(December 1996)*

Trey: "Music is sort of the last pure thing on earth. We've kind of always seen it as a thing where it's an escape. You can go with the music and lose yourself."
—*to David Goldberg,* Worcester Telegram & Gazette *(January 1, 1994)*

Fish: "If you're taking a risk you've really got nothing to lose."
—*to Paul Robicheau,* Boston Globe *(December 22, 1996)*

agents. So, in what the band often points to as a major turning point, Phish rented out the club in January 1989 to stage their own show. They expected to lose a chunk of money, but they were willing to invest in making a larger Boston inroad.

To their great surprise, the show sold out. Burlington friend Tom Baggott organized a giant bus trip down to Boston, and many more loyal fans drove down from Burlington to show their support. Hunter also brought out the Boston crowd, and snide comments by Paradise bouncers who asked Phish if they were "a real band" were silenced.

The winter and spring of 1989 marked one of the most important periods in the band's development. They finished recording an album at Euphoria Studios in Revere, MA, laying down six new tracks after putting four on tape back in the fall of 1987. The cassette was released in May, and wrapped in artwork by Jim Pollock, a former teacher of Page's at Goddard. The album took its title, *Junta*, from a mispronunciation of Ben Hunter's nickname (hunt-ah).

Meanwhile, the band's behind-the-scenes personnel also was shifting. Longtime "roadie extraordinaire" Del Martin called it quits that year. But Chris Kuroda, a guitar student of Trey's, took a job with the band moving equipment. Then, at a March show at the Stone Church in Newmarket, NH, Kuroda stepped behind the lightboard while the band's light guy of the moment took a bathroom break. Later, Trey remarked that he liked the light work during "Famous Mockingbird," and Chris told him he was responsible. One week later, Kuroda was named Phish's lighting director, a post he still holds.

In April, Phish competed in the Rock Rumble held at The Front. Facing off against contemporary Burlington bands like the Hollywood Indians and Screaming Broccoli (who many Vermont music fans considered to be superior), Phish won over the diverse crowd. That performance reportedly marked the first time Fish ever attempted a vacuum cleaner solo before an audience. The effort failed—Fish lowered himself onto the stage, stark naked, but the vacuum malfunctioned—but the band won the Rumble and its prize, free recording time at Archer Studios.

By the summer, Phish had an entire staff in place, which would remain with them through their ascent into arenas in the mid-1990s. Languedoc relinquished control of Phish's books when Paluska graduated from Amherst College in May and took on the job of managing Phish full-time, creating Dionysian Productions with Hunter. The team of Paluska, Kuroda, and Languedoc, in time, would be credited with much of the band's success. While each were relative neophytes at first—only Languedoc had past experience in the role he served with Phish—they developed along with the band until they were known as masters in their field (Kuroda would later receive repeated offers to join the Grateful Dead's lighting staff).

The band's audience steadily grew during this period, packing hundreds into a Halloween gig at Goddard, and hundreds more at their first New Year's Eve show in Boston to welcome in the new decade. The Halloween show proved to be another turning point for the band, as folks marveled at Phish's ability to draw so many fans to the Goddard campus on Halloween night. The show was videotaped and later broadcast on public access television in Burlington.

But a stronger network—word-of-mouth—propelled the band. Fans were already trading Phish concert tapes, and the scene at the soundboard each night was growing more chaotic as people arrived with tape decks to patch in. Everyone in Burlington, it seemed, wanted a piece of the action.

Despite the strong support at home, the band used the early part of 1990 to build audiences in more unknown regions. February saw Phish make their first run to the Southeast in a series of "gig trades" Paluska arranged with Widespread Panic, whom Phish opened for south of the Mason-Dixon Line before Widespread made it up north supporting Phish.

As sales of *Junta* helped fund the band's exploits (and they dipped into family capital to upgrade their equipment), they also took advantage of the free studio time they'd won from the Rock Rumble to record songs that would eventually form the album *Lawn Boy*. Recorded off and on from May through December 1989 and originally released as a

March 30, 1989: Chris Kuroda works his first show as the band's lighting designer, and the Phish concert experience leaps forward again.

April 22, 1989: Phish wins the Rock Rumble at the Front in April, then releases *Junta* in May. The trampolines make their stage debut.

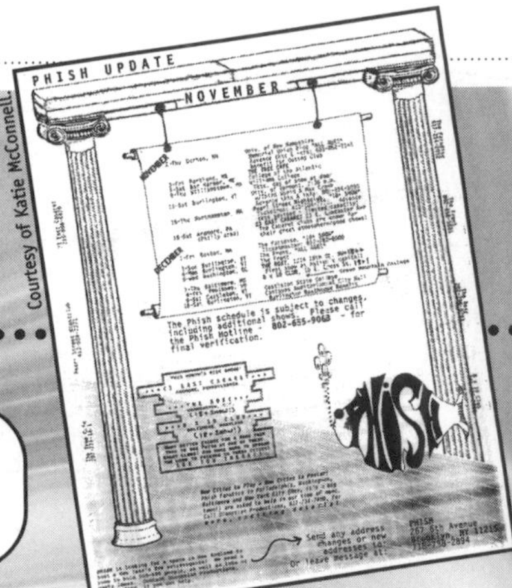

Courtesy of Katie McConnell.

cassette tape in the spring of 1990 (which made its way to only a few hundred lucky fans), *Lawn Boy* was officially released that September with a new album cover on vinyl, cassette, and CD on independent Absolute A-Go-Go records. *Lawn Boy* sold out its 10,000 copy run shortly after its release, but Rough Trade Records, the distributing company, went out of business, and the band never saw a cent from the deal.

Still, word about their live shows continued to spread throughout New England. The band's policy of allowing tapers to plug directly into the soundboard to make high-quality concert recordings meant thousands of crystal-clear reproductions of the Phish live experience were winding their way around college campuses and frequently could be heard in parking lots at Grateful Dead shows.

With the reputation of offering "the fabulous jam for the thinking man," Phish not only attracted a loyal team of Deadheads but also a road-hungry troupe of college students who began to catch multiple shows. Hives of Phish fans seemed to be developing in places like Amherst, MA, Ithaca, NY, and Boston, where even suburban high school students were catching on.

When Phish made their second and third trips to Colorado in 1990, a small fan base was waiting for them, familiarized through the tapes that had made their way across the continent. Fans who had been indoctrinated at Telluride in 1988 could finally show their peers what they had been talking about.

The earnings that year were humble but consistent, and Phish even managed to find their way onto industry top concert-earners charts, after being omitted initially when someone thought the concert gross reports on the band might be some sort of hoax. "Phish who?" reacted music executives who, of course, had never heard of the band.

But as early as December 1990, the record companies were on to Phish. Elektra Records A&R person Sue Drew caught Phish at several shows that month, including the band's December 28 show at the Marquee in New York City, and was stunned by the loyalty she saw from the fans.

Phish put that loyalty to the test when they left New England for their first true tour in February of 1991, snaking around the country over a two-month span and making it all the way to California, where they secured gigs at solid starter venues like The Catalyst in Santa Cruz and the DNA Lounge in San Francisco.

Returning from the tour, the band played their last show at The Front in May. Then, still without a recording contract, though beginning to see a deal with Elektra on the horizon, they headed into Burlington's White Crow Studios at their own expense to begin recording the album that would become *A Picture of Nectar*. The sessions took them off the road in June, but they gave their fans a summer to remember, hitting the road for the first and only tour with the Giant Country Horns in July. Phish had come to know Burlington musicians Dave "The Truth" Grippo, Carl "Gears" Gearhard, and Russ Remington through the local music scene and a club called Sneakers in Winooski, VT. Phish began checking out the Sneakers Jazz Club there years earlier, and actually spent a year gigging with musicians at the club every Monday night under the name The Johnny B. Fishman Jazz Ensemble.

Phish and the Horns hit the road together for over a dozen legendary shows, the most popular of which came at a two-day stop at Arrowhead Ranch in upstate New York. There, they invited fans to join them several weeks later for a free show at Amy Skelton's farm in Maine, a thank-you for eight years of support. They also sent out personal invitations to fans on their mailing list, and thousands of folks made the trek to Auburn, ME, on August 3. One fan even traveled 3,000 miles to catch the Amy's Farm show, which included three sets performed on the back of a platform truck. The band honored him a month later at a show in Buffalo, NY.

August also marked the formal beginnings of the Phish.Net, an Internet mailing list launched by a fan named Matt Laurence and sent to 13 people. It grew to become a Usenet bulletin board with over 30,000 daily readers. The growth of the Internet would contribute significantly to the band's explosion in the years

Phish on THE ESTABLISHMENT

Fish: "We're already successful, and on our terms. Not everybody needs MTV. We definitely don't and I'm proud of that."
—*to Peter Castro,* People *(June 6, 1994)*

Trey: "MTV is fucking up music."
—*to Nate Eaton,* The Best of High Times #18

Mike: "A hit single—that's the fear, because that hit single can sometimes be the curse of death."
—*to Michael Mehle,* Rocky Mountain News *(June 9, 1995)*

Trey: "You have to be a very strong person not to cave in to the pressures of trying to recreate another hit. And the music that's trying to be a hit often sounds a little stale."
—*to Larry Nager,* Commercial Appeal *(June 11, 1995)*

Mike: "We've spent more time avoiding growth than seeking it."
—*to Jeff Gordinier,* Entertainment Weekly *(November 1, 1996)*

Trey: "I think the luckiest thing for us was to be ignored for 11 years. It was bliss."
—*to Vic Garbarini,* Guitar World *(August 1997)*

Trey: "We never made any money off Gamehendge, and that's what kept it a cool thing. We made a vow that we will never make money off any of those songs. So we canceled the CD ROM."
—*to Mac Randall,* Musician *(December 1996)*

Trey: "When we first came to the awareness of the media, it would always be the Dead or Zappa they'd compare us to, all of these bands I love you know? But I got very sensitive about it.

So if you've never seen the band, and you're reading that 'new Grateful Dead' stuff, it doesn't really matter in my life. Because all that matters is my personal life with my family, and my musical life interacting with the people who actually come."
—*to J. D. Considine,* Baltimore Sun *(November 22, 1995)*

Fish: "The Grateful Dead has been part of all of our interviews for the last 12 years—why is that going to change?"
—*to Paul Robicheau,* Boston Globe *(December 22, 1996)*

Page: "We've been compared to more bands than any other band. It all depends what track was playing when they hear it."
—*to Marek Kohn,* The Independent *(June 25, 1992)*

Fish: "There was one critic who ragged on us really creatively. I used to save her articles because her adjectives were so good."
—*to Peter Castro,* People *(June 6, 1994)*

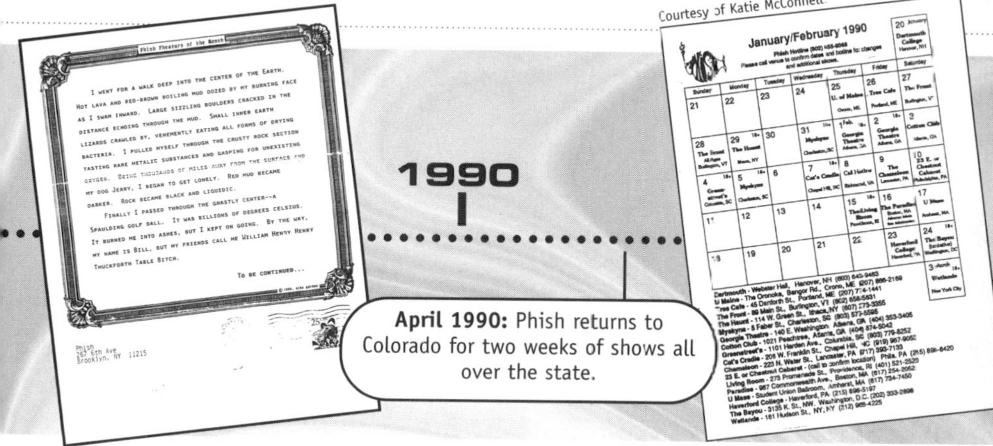
Phish Pheature of the Month

I WENT FOR A WALK DEEP INTO THE CENTER OF THE EARTH. HOT LAVA AND RED-BROWN BOILING MUD OOZED BY MY BURNING FACE AS I SWAM INWARD. LARGE SIZZLING BOULDERS CRACKED IN THE DISTANCE ECHOING THROUGH THE MUD. SMALL INNER EARTH LIZARDS CRAWLED BY, VEHEMENTLY EATING ALL FORMS OF DRYING BACTERIA. I PULLED MYSELF THROUGH THE CRUSTY ROCK SECTION TASTING RARE METALIC SUBSTANCES AND GASPING FOR UNEXISTING OXYGEN. BEING THOUSANDS OF MILES AWAY FROM THE SURFACE AND MY DOG JERRY, I BEGAN TO GET LONELY. RED MUD BECAME DARKER. ROCK BECAME BLACK AND LIQUIDIC.

FINALLY I PASSED THROUGH THE GHASTLY CENTER--A SPAULDING GOLF BALL. IT WAS BILLIONS OF DEGREES CELSIUS. IT BURNED ME INTO ASHES, BUT I KEPT ON GOING. BY THE WAY, MY NAME IS BILL, BUT MY FRIENDS CALL ME WILLIAM HENRY HENRY THUCKFORTH TABLE BITCH.

TO BE CONTINUED...

Phish
267 6th Ave
Brooklyn, NY 11215

Courtesy of Katie McConnell

January/February 1990

Phish Hotline (802) 455-8068
Please call venue to confirm dates and hotline for changes and additional shows.

20 January Dartmouth College Hanover, NH

Sunday	Monday	Tuesday	Wednesday	Thursday	Friday	Saturday
21	22	23	24	25 U. of Maine Orono, ME	26 Tree Cafe Portland, ME	27 The Front Burlington, VT
28 The Front All Ages Burlington, VT	29 18+ The Haunt Ithaca, NY	30	31 18+ Myskyne Charleston, SC	1 Feb. 18+ Georgia Theatre Athens, GA	2 18+ Georgia Theatre Athens, GA	3 Cotton Club Atlanta, GA
4 18+ Greenstreet's Columbia, SC	5 18+ Myskyne Charleston, SC	6	7 18+ Cat's Cradle Chapel Hill, NC	8 Call Hotline Richmond, VA	9 The Chameleon Lancaster, PA	10 23 E. or Chestnut Cabaret Philadelphia, PA
11	12	13	14	15 18+ The Living Room Providence, RI	16 The Paradise Boston, MA	17 U Mass Amherst, MA
18	19	20	21	22	23 Haverford College Haverford, PA	24 18+ The Bayou (tentative) Washington, DC

3 March 18+ Wetlands New York City

Dartmouth - Webster Hall, Hanover, NH (603) 643-9463
U Maine - The Oronoka, Bangor Rd., Orono, ME (207) 866-2169
Tree Cafe - 45 Danforth St., Portland, ME (207) 774-1441
The Front - 89 Main St., Burlington, VT (802) 658-5631
The Haunt - 114 W. Green St., Ithaca, NY (607) 273-3355
Myskyne - 5 Faber St., Charleston, SC (803) 577-5595
Georgia Theatre - 140 E. Washington, Athens, GA (404) 353-3405
Cotton Club - 1021 Peachtree, Atlanta, GA (404) 874-5042
Greenstreet's - 1101 Harden Ave., Columbia, SC (803) 779-8252
Cat's Cradle - 206 W. Franklin St., Chapel Hill, NC (919) 967-9053
Chameleon - 223 N. Water St., Lancaster, PA (717) 393-7133
23 E. or Chestnut Cabaret - (call to confirm location) Phila. PA (215) 896-6420
Living Room - 273 Promenade St., Providence, RI (401) 521-2520
Paradise - 967 Commonwealth Ave., Boston, MA (617) 254-2052
U Mass - Student Union Ballroom, Amherst, MA (617) 734-7450
Haverford College - Haverford, PA (215) 896-5197
The Bayou - 3135 K. St., NW. Washington, D.C. (202) 333-2898
Wetlands - 161 Hudson St., NY, NY (212) 966-4225

1990

April 1990: Phish returns to Colorado for two weeks of shows all over the state.

Phish on PHANS

Trey: "[Our fans] keep you on your toes. You have to play different songs every night, and you know they're paying attention to every single little thing you do. You don't get lazy then."
—*to J. D. Considine,* Baltimore Sun *(November 22, 1995)*

Page: "A lot of Americans never get a chance to see the rest of the U.S. When kids are 18-24, following a band is a good opportunity to travel and see the rest of the country."
—*to Dan Glaister,* The Guardian *(July 5, 1996)*

Mike: "We're very thankful for the people that follow us around. They listen to whatever we play—even if it's strange, even if we're taking risks."
—*to Jeff Gordinier,* Entertainment Weekly *(November 1, 1996)*

Trey: "There's a song we did last night, 'Stash,' where the audience does this clapping thing. They just started doing it one night and it worked its way into the song. The audience wrote it. No matter where we go, our audience knows to do that."
—*to Chris Gill,* Guitar Player *(September 1994)*

Mike: "[Our fans] are critical even when we're playing well. They pay attention, and they're aware of what's going on. If we have a bad gig, people backstage say, 'You guys were great'—but we know that means it was a bad show. If we have a good show, the fans might say, 'This was the best day of my whole life.'"
—*to Karl Coryat,* Bass Player *(September 1996)*

Trey: "God's honest truth is that they can be vicious. We have created a situation where they expect a lot from us."
—*to Jeff Gordinier,* Entertainment Weekly *(November 1, 1996)*

Mike: "Every time we make a new album, we get someone who calls up and says: 'How could you do it? You were the center of my universe, and I'm never going to see you again.'"
—*to Scott Sutherland,* New York Times *(July 1995)*

Mike: "The worst thing for your career is to be considered Godlike by your fans. First, it's impossible to live with those expectations, and the flip side is you can't do anything wrong."
—*to Dean Johnson,* Boston Herald *(December 26, 1996)*

Page: "We walk even a different line, which is trying to please the hardcore fans, of which there's a certain percentage that's following us around. And then there's the people in Phoenix who get to see us when we come to Phoenix. Now who am I playing my show for? I'm playing it for both of them."
—*to Michael Goldberg,* Addicted to Noise *(www.atn.com, February 1, 1997)*

ahead, as setlists and concert stories were instantly devoured by online readers. More importantly, perhaps, the Internet facilitated tape trades, allowing Phish's music to fly across the continent just days after a gig.

That fall, back on the road, Phish became the first unsigned act to sell out San Francisco's Great American Music Hall, while negotiations with Elektra kicked into high gear. Despite the fact that Gordon wore a silly wig to the final hashing out of the contract, an agreement was signed on November 22, 1991, calling for *Picture of Nectar* to be released on a major label. *Junta* and *Lawn Boy* would go into wide distribution sometime after *Nectar*'s release, assuming all went well.

The band had never sought a record contract—Elektra had, quite literally, come to them—so the band had some room to work during the negotiations. Phish insisted that the live tapers who'd played such an instrumental role in their growth still be allowed to tape their concerts. And they got Elektra to change contract wording that stipulated their albums had to be "commercially satisfactory" to "technically satisfactory," freeing them from a possible commitment to produce only radio-friendly songs.

With *Nectar* landing in record stores on February 18, 1992, Phish hit the road in March with excitement at an all-time high. The tour marked their last hurrah at many of the small New England theaters they'd called home over the previous years—like the Portsmouth Music Hall in Portsmouth, NH, and the Colonial Theater in Keene, NH—and the beginning of Phish's "secret language," an interactive game played with the audience using musical signals from the band.

When *Nectar* was released, it immediately became one of the top-selling albums in Boston and sold out its initial 35,000-copy pressing in the spring of '92, but it never approached gold record status. It became clear that Phish was a tough sell commercially, and not radio-friendly, although "Chalkdust Torture" did get airtime from some scattered stations.

But several other relatively obscure touring bands, such as Spin Doctors and Blues Traveler, were also starting to release records and get national attention at the time, and the bands seemed to feed off each other's fan bases. The summer of 1992 began with a write-up for the groups in *Rolling Stone* and Phish's trip to Europe opening up for The Violent Femmes.

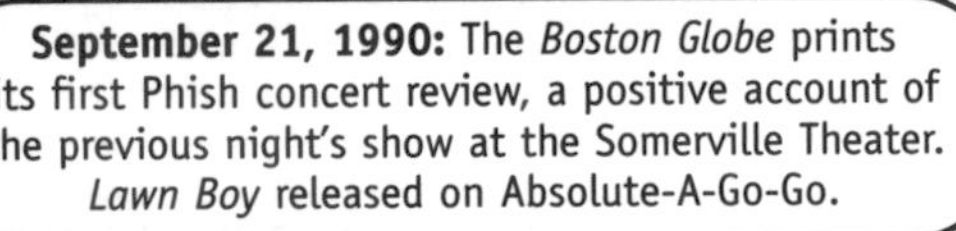

September 21, 1990: The *Boston Globe* prints its first Phish concert review, a positive account of the previous night's show at the Somerville Theater. *Lawn Boy* released on Absolute-A-Go-Go.

June 16, 1990: Phish closes out the spring with a three-set outdoor show, then takes the summer off to rehearse.

Courtesy of Katie McConnell.

Then came the first HORDE Tour, the brainchild of Blues Traveler's John Popper, featuring his band along with Phish, Spin Doctors, Widespread Panic, and Aquarium Rescue Unit at four northern venues. It brought Phish to huge stages such as the 12,000-seat Jones Beach Amphitheater in Long Island, NY, where they played one set as a headliner.

Four HORDE shows down south lost Phish from the package, but the band had another commitment—opening for rock legend Carlos Santana. The band had previously received invitations to open for acts like the Allman Brothers and had turned them down, but the chance to spend time on the road with Santana—one of the band's heroes and major influences—proved too good to pass up. Though they generally played to small crowds, Phish was frequently invited by Carlos to jam with him on stage during his set, and he also sat in with the boys at their hometown gig in Stowe, VT.

But the national exposure did not make Phish an overnight sensation. Spin Doctors became MTV prodigies and sold millions of records, almost instantly alienating their core fans. It would take a few years, but Blues Traveler would also achieve hit-single success. Meanwhile, the musical and journalistic establishment continued to ignore Phish, so it was underground communication—often via the Phish.Net—that added the most fans during this period. MTV apparently wasn't interested, and albums more or less stayed on record store shelves. But Phish tapes continued to fly around college campuses at a furious pace, beckoning even those behind on their cable bills and too broke to replace busted CD players.

New Year's Eve 1992 attracted a record 6,000 fans to a sold-out Matthews Arena in Boston, and a radio audience the next day on big Boston FM station WBCN. Proving they could remain intimate with even a small town's worth of devotees, the band went without a microphone for an *a cappella* encore, showing off the product of barbershop quartet lessons they took in Burlington that year.

The winter and spring of 1993 followed with the release of *Rift* in early February and a 70-plus show tour. Some, like an April gig at the 4,000-seat University of Hartford Sports Arena, were solid sellouts. Others, like the show in Bangor, ME, a week later, were played before ample empty seats.

Like *Nectar*, *Rift* was a limited commercial success. But with a famed Muscle Shoals producer producing the album in lieu of the band itself, it turned a corner for the band in terms of production value and emphasis on the recorded product. The title track served as the centerpiece, with each ensuing tune loosely tied into themes it laid out.

That summer, the band made one of its odder, but more magnanimous decisions. Rather than hit mid-sized stages for sure sellouts on the summer tour—which would have meant less pressure and kept the veteran fans satisfied that Phish wasn't growing away from them—the band booked almost every major amphitheater on the East Coast. The brave decision meant there would be a good number of $5 tickets going around in the parking lots, but everyone who wanted to would get a chance to see the band.

Of course, the tale at that juncture could be told a different way: that Phish jumped on their first chance to hit the big leagues, ready or not. The guy who shouted "Remember Nectar's?" when Phish cut short a rain-soaked gig in Stowe, VT, probably felt that way. But that summer, the band proved they could turn their late-night, indoor shtick into an outdoor, all-ages spectacle, and still hold on to the character so precious to their longtime fans.

Following many gigs on that now-classic string of shows, Trey, Mike, Fish, and Page wandered into the parking lots. The band took the time to know many of the fans who, for the first time ever, were going cross-continent on their quest to hear the perfect show. Even as the band left the East Coast, and slipped back into smaller halls and fields, about 50 vanguards carried a flourishing "lot scene" as far south as Florida and as far west as Vancouver.

Back north for New Year's after spending the fall in Los Angeles recording their next album, Phish sold out mid-sized and large arenas for a four-show run—including the 14,500-seat

Phish on the FUTURE

Trey: "We won't be hitting RFK Stadium. It's too big; it's just a stupid place to have a concert. The only reason to play a room like that is because you make a whole lot of money."
—*to Richard Leiby,* Washington Post *(October 16, 1994)*

Fish: "We've already had discussions about this—if anyone in the band goes, that it's over. The other three can continue to play together, but they've got to change the name. It's stupid [otherwise], change the name and get on with it. The only reasons to stick with the names is marketing."
—*to Paul Robicheau,* Boston Globe *(December 22, 1996)*

Page: "Our popularity will wane. It's on the rise now and has been. At a certain point, there will be a media backlash and then there will be sort of a social backlash and this sort of improvisational band thing, which is pretty popular right now, won't be as popular. And then if we can make it through that, eventually it will come back up again, I think if we stick around long enough."
—*to Michael Goldberg,* Addicted to Noise *(www.atn.com, February 1997)*

Fish: "We're never going to make some ultimate song. The goals of the band aren't commercial. We are as intent as intent can be on staying together. We realize that the only thing standing between us and the record for the band with the exact same lineup staying together the longest in rock history is our getting along."
—*to Peter Richmond,* GQ *(January 1997)*

Mike: "I want us to be able to play in concert as sparsely as we do at soundcheck. We all want that. . . . If we could do that, a lot of the time, then we would be a great band. But it's something to overcome."
—*to Robin Caudell,* Plattsburgh Press-Republican *(August 17, 1996)*

Trey: "Moving into the next millennium, I'm kind of visualizing this whole new way of playing live. The Clifford Ball was the first step to that. Next summer, I'd like to do two shows like that. Because everything was different. We completely reworked the whole experience.

There are a lot of different paths you can take. What would happen if we locked ourselves in a room for six months and just completely rewrote the entire live Phish? . . . Or what if you did a thing where you did a tour where the tour was four theaters across the country? . . . I just don't want to get trapped in every year for 20 years we do a fall tour, then we do a spring tour, then we do a summer tour and play the arenas that everybody plays."
—*to Michael Goldberg,* Addicted to Noise *(www.atn.com, December 1996)*

1991

Amy's Farm
August 3rd 1991

Driving along in the love van a short time ago, it suddenly dawned on us that we were only a few months away from our eighth anniversary as a band. We started thinking about all of the friends we'd met over the years, and we realized that it would be great to throw a party to thank everyone for all the good times. So we went and talked to the one person we knew could help, Amy Skelton. Amy is our first fan. We began a regular weekly bar gig in Burlington in 1984, and Amy would show up every week and dance with Brian Long, our other first fan. A number of weeks went by where we played to a two person audience. When Amy moved to New Hampshire a couple years later, she helped set up gigs for us at Nick's, the Stone Church, and UNH, introducing us to many friends from the New Hampshire area who has stuck around through the years. Amy now runs a 255 acre horse farm in Maine, and together we want to throw a party to thank you all for eight years of memories. This will be a free concert on Saturday August 3rd, which will run from early afternoon till early evening. Amy's house is in Auburn Maine and there will be free camping and ... The only expense will be a minimal charge (a buck or two) ... the fields that people will park on. There will be food ...ailable, as well as information booths, swimming and ...iful camping space. Hope to see you there.

Trey, Mike, Page, and Fish.

Rules for Amy's Farm

...allowed (due to dry climate)
...stubbly hay field
...everything with you when you arrive (food, water, etc...)
...n't have to drive under the influence.
...don't feed horses, cross fence lines, or go off Amy's land.
Please take your garbage with you.

August 3, 1991: Lured by the promise of a free three-set show on a horse ranch, thousands of fans trek to Auburn, ME, for the legendary Amy's Farm show.

October 17–18, 1991: Phish becomes the first unsigned band to sell out San Francisco's Great American Music Hall for two consecutive nights.

November 22, 1991: After months of negotiations, Phish and Elektra sign a six-album deal.

Phish and COLORADO

If Phish has a home away from home, it's the great state of Colorado. No locale other than Burlington can claim such a special place in Phish history, or has been witness to so many unforgettable shows.

The legacy began in 1988 when a friend booked Phish a few dates in the mining village/ski mecca of Telluride. But just days before loading up the van for the journey west, they learned the gigs had fallen through. Undeterred, they made the trek anyway, and managed to land themselves a nine-night engagement at a tiny restaurant named the Roma, playing for door earnings.

The pattern that spurred Phish's growth in the Northeast—word-of-mouth and tape trading—proved valuable in Colorado, too. "We met everybody in town and the same 20 people were coming down to see us every night. And that started off this whole Colorado thing. The next time we went back there, they each kind of brought one friend," Trey recalled to *Addicted to Noise* years later.

Their first return visit came two years later, when Phish came west for two weeks of shows. The crowds were still small, but enough tape-trading students and transplanted Easterners had spread the word to make the shows a success. And one intrepid taper brought a recording and mixing rack to the April 22 show and a string of shows during Phish's fall 1990 Colorado run, starting the "Colorado Collection" of digitally recorded concerts that rank among the best-sounding Phish tapes in existence.

From there on, Colorado Phish tours would be more spread out. But in 1993, they booked the Red Rocks Amphitheater for the first time, beginning a whole new era of legendary Phish visits that would continue through 1996, when Phish became the only band other than Huey Lewis and the News to play a four-night stand there.

They managed to grab the attention of the entire state when an incident in nearby Morrison led to a police-phan riot and newspaper headlines. Red Rocks promoter Barry Fey declared that Phish had outgrown the venue.

Phish continues to play larger venues in Colorado, but in some ways, the fairy tale story that started at the Roma came to a strange end on that mysterious night.

Worcester Centrum in less than a day—and did more of the same the next spring. But the band continued to be an accessible presence before and after each gig.

The following spring tour coincided with the release of *Hoist,* the band's fifth album. It received mixed reviews from fans who questioned the compact format into which each song was neatly placed, and wondered if epic jams would ever be a part of

the band's new tunes. The Phish newsletter included letters from fans bemoaning the release of a video for the first single off *Hoist*, "Down with Disease," even though none other than Mike Gordon—fulfilling a dream when a film major at UVM—directed it.

Of course, Phish had their own concerns about the video. They'd had plenty of conversations and arguments about making a video before, but, already committed to making an album that would have several radio-friendly songs, they decided to do a video for a song from *Hoist* to finally "see how it feels," as Trey later put it. "What worried us about doing a video was the thought of, 'What if we suddenly have this big success?'" he told *People* magazine.

That needn't have been a concern, as the "Down with Disease" video received scant MTV airplay, mostly in the middle of the night. And as it turned out, the band didn't like making the video—all, that is, except Mike, who enjoyed the chance to run a camera crew and mix the video in a high-tech Boston studio. The other band members said they felt silly acting in the video, and none of them really appeared pleased with the results. "We did it, and I didn't like it," Trey told the *Washington Post* six months later. "It's too commercial."

But while *Hoist* missed by some accounts, the live shows of 1994 did not. Songs that seemed too radio-packaged on the album, like "Down with Disease," opened up in concert. And during this period, Phish first began to employ the "throw the setlist to the wind" philosophy, which would become standard fare in later years. At a sparsely attended show in Dallas on May 7, the band went into "Tweezer" three songs into the second set, and they never quite found their way out. The 72-minute jam included slices of seven other tunes, all of it improvised. Although Phish had never made a habit of sticking to their pre-planned setlists, this was a giant step in an entirely new direction. Trey's resolve to break the rules, so strong in the band's early days, was busting out again.

When the band returned to the Northeast that summer, the largest crowds ever awaited, and the band proved capable of switching from small theaters to spacious amphitheaters from one week to the next. Capped by an acclaimed performance halfway up a mountain at the Sugarbush ski area in July, Phish continued to prove that new, large venues gave a novel, larger-than-life feel to both old and new songs.

A marathon Halloween show in Glens Falls, NY, was remarkable not only for the much-discussed rendition of The Beatles' *White Album* and Fish's naked run across the stage, but for the unexpectedly generous and furious third set, which stretched into the wee hours of the morning. The inaugural "musical costume," the first of three straight years in which Phish would perform an album by another artist in its

1992

February 18, 1992: Phish's major-label debut, *A Picture of Nectar*, is released by Elektra.

March 22, 1992: Phish plays a short set on National Public Radio's "MountainStage Live" program, which is broadcast nationally several weeks later.

April 1992: A letters column debuts in the Phish newsletter and includes the first "What are you saying in 'You Enjoy Myself'?" question. Mike's response: "Wasohbf woeh ejwro jeeef je ei Fndsbid."

Summer 1992: Phish plays on the first HORDE tour, then spends the summer opening for Carlos Santana on his U.S. tour.

entirety, attracted an unprecedented horde of ticketless fans, who were outside waving $50 and $100 bills to no avail.

Glens Falls also marked the first time Phish and Phish management realized the band was getting so popular that the size of the fan base alone could be a problem. After his Halloween experience, Paluska wrote a 30-page manual for security personnel on how to handle Phish fans, and band representatives began pleading with fans to not come to shows without a ticket.

Musically, the band was turning another corner. Excited by the levels achieved during the May "Tweezerfest" in Dallas, the band began to experiment even more with protracted versions of songs, which often veered off into improvised tangents that had little to do with the original tune. Half-hour-long "Tweezer"s popped up semi-regularly. During a December show in Providence, RI, "David Bowie" took a turn on the lab table, turning in to a thirty-minute platform for beautiful compositions made up on the spot. It was the highlight of a splendid New Year's run that included the band's first show at Madison Square Garden in New York and New Year's Eve at the legendary Boston Garden.

A prolonged break followed, during which the band's popularity only increased as the tape lists continued to fly across the Internet and cassettes buzzed through the mail.

But among the devoted there remained a dirty, avoided topic. Just as Congress danced around the issue of Medicare cuts, Phish fans had to take the same verbal care in addressing the fact that almost all the most popular songs were at least five years old. The true crowd pleasers, to both veterans and newcomers, were mostly from early recordings or the pre-album era. "Antelope," "Slave," "You Enjoy Myself," "Harry Hood," "Fluffhead," "Harpua," "Mike's Groove"—the songs that could carry a show on their backs—were born of another time.

While the band's broad playlist could surely guarantee fresh shows into the next century, their recent offerings failed to equal the favor garnered by the Phish classics. Whether Trey could write songs on a plush touring bus as well as he could in a beat-up van was a question that had to be asked, and had seemingly been answered.

But on a warm May night in Lowell, MA, Phish took the stage for a rare benefit show and whipped out a half-dozen new songs. There may not have been a "Mike's Groove" among them, but tunes such as "Theme from the Bottom" and "Free" managed to combine all the elements that had vaulted the band to its current level of semi-stardom. The psychedelic abandon, the open-ended jamming, the delicate vocalization, the sound that thousands had come to know as Phish, had rarely before been realized in such a distinct manner.

The 1995 summer and fall tours saw the band fill large venues from coast to coast. The regionalism apparent two years earlier, when New England audiences numbered about 10 times the size of crowds in other time zones, was lessening. The band's first show at the 20,000-seat Deer Creek Music Center in Noblesville, IN, that June and their Halloween show at the 18,300-seat Rosemont Horizon near Chicago demonstrated the coming-of-age of Phish in the Midwest.

Phish's first live album, *A Live One*, was released that June and received respectable airplay. Even *The New York Times* devoted a full page in the Sunday Arts & Leisure section to the band, terming Phish one of the hottest acts of the summer. The secret was starting to get out. The year climaxed with two sold-out gigs at Madison Square Garden. The strong finish propelled them up *Pollstar*'s ratings of the highest-grossing concert acts of the year, landing them at number 15 with a gross of $15.2 million. In 1991, they'd grossed just over $200,000.

Then, when it seemed Phish couldn't climb any higher, they once again defied gravity. After

SAY "HEY"

WHEN NOT TOURING, Phish usually practices together five hours a day, five days a week at a studio in Paul Languedoc's home (only Trey and Fish practice while on the road). To make the most of that time, the band has created several exercises to encourage improvisation. "We've decided that it's important to tune up our ears so that when we're on stage jamming, we don't go off in our own world," Mike told the *Sacramento Bee*. Several of their jamming exercises include the following:

Including Your Own Hey (also called "Hey"). This practice routine grew out of the fact that when playing, Fish usually only followed Trey. So the band decided that they should learn to all follow each other, and this drill helped teach them how to do it. The drill progresses in the band's stage order (Page > Trey > Mike > Fish), where the first guy starts a groove, and the next guy joins in, and so on, until everyone thinks everyone else is locked in together (they say "hey" to indicate this). Then it's up to the next guy in line to initiate a change.

Filling the Hey Hole. Each band member plays part of the beat not occupied by others. No one plays at the same time.

Mimicking Hey. Two people mimic and the other two specifically do not mimic the mimickers. When the mimicker matches the originator, the originator says "hey," and everyone rotates one position.

Have the drills paid off? The band sure thinks so. "We've played so much together that we've got this thing going now that we can read each other's minds," Trey told the *Commercial Appeal*. "I mean it's scary. We actually, in the practice room, sit around practicing musical communication exercises for hours and hours, so we can read each other's minds better."

1993

February 1993: The Phish newsletter contains the first published letter from a fan urging the band to "remain as 'small' as possible."

February 3, 1993: *Rift* released. The album hits the Boston charts at number 7.

April 7, 1993: More than a year after its release, *A Picture of Nectar* wins best debut album on a major label at the Boston Music Awards.

Fall 1993: Phish spends the fall in Los Angeles recording *Hoist*, and the Phish newsletter is rechristened *Doniac Schvice*.

How the CREW Does It

When the house lights come up at the end of another Phish show, the road crew swings into action, breaking down the stage and light and sound systems and packing them into the trucks, which will cart them to the next venue.

While this is going on, the band hangs out backstage and then boards their tour bus, where on a typical night they might play chess or relax until checking into a hotel in the vicinity of their next show. There, they generally sleep until mid-afternoon—except Mike, who adheres to a strict sleep and exercise schedule even on rigorous tour legs.

Meanwhile, the crew has slept through the night on bunkbeds in their bus, and they arrive at the next venue by 9:00 a.m. to begin setting the show up. First, riggers locate and mark reference points for the set, lights, and speakers. The lighting crew assembles the light show and raises it into position. Then the sound crew assembles the sound system and raises it above the stage and soundboard. Chris then updates the light positions so specific lights correspond with the placement of the band's equipment on stage and with the venue's unique layout. Following this, Paul checks the house sound, correcting any obvious problems.

Sometime in the late afternoon, if all has gone well, or the early evening, if there have been snafus, the band takes the stage for their soundcheck. A couple of hours later, fans file into the venue and the show gets under way, while the crew prepares again for the show's end and the beginning of their daily tour cycle.

Photo courtesy of Jason Gleason.

spending the winter and spring of 1996 recording the album that would become *Billy Breathes*—a studio experience the band thought to be their most pleasurable since *Junta*—Phish played one set at the New Orleans Jazz & Heritage Festival on the festival's opening day, April 26. An influx of Phish fans took New Orleans by storm.

In a city that regularly absorbs Mardi Gras and the Super Bowl, the attack of the Phishheads was front-page news, and caused a panic that led JazzFest organizers to say Phish would not be welcomed back to the festival, despite a giant turnout of over 60,000 people. Though Phish's management later disputed the statement and JazzFest apologized, Phish's drawing power—and the related problems that it caused—was clearly continuing to grow.

At the opposite end of the spectrum, Phish played to only a few hundred fans at a surprise gig in Woodstock, NY, in early June. Although news of the show was leaked to just a few of the band's close friends, the tiny Joyous Lake Club was packed to the hilt for a show that saw Phish play several *Billy Breathes* tracks live for the first time.

The summer of 1996 saw the band spend the month of July in Europe, frequently opening for Carlos Santana and pushing a European compilation album of their recorded work titled *Stash*.

Back in the United States in August for two weeks' worth of shows stretching from Utah to New York, Phish's popularity reached new heights. The number of fans on tour with the band had been growing since the death of Jerry Garcia and the end of the Grateful Dead the summer before. It reached critical mass in August 1996 when an alleged altercation between fans and police near the Red Rocks Amphitheater in Morrison, CO, led the local promoter to declare Phish had outgrown the venue.

But it was the apex of the tour in upstate New York that pushed Phish to the top of yet another plateau and earned them only accolades. The Clifford Ball, named for an obscure airmail aviator of the same name, drew almost 80,000 fans to a decommissioned Air Force Base outside of Plattsburgh, NY, for two days of camping, activities galore, and six sets of Phish.

The Ball was a Phish creation in the truest sense of the word—every detail revealed the band's fingerprints from the Clifford Ball Town Square (complete with a 35-foot statute of the aviator himself) to the late-night Phish jazz jam performed on the back of a flatbed truck that circled through the campground. The level of

New Year's Eve With PHISH

CENTRUM

December 31 • 9 pm

All Seats Reserved $22.50

Tickets On Sale Saturday November 6 10am

December 1993: A reserved-seating tapers section debuts in New Haven on December 29, then Phish closes the year at the 14,500-seat Centrum in Worcester, MA.

March 15, 1994: "Down with Disease" released as a single to radio stations; a week later, MTV airs the video in the wee hours of the night.

1994

March 29, 1994: *Hoist* released. It enters the *Billboard* charts at number 34.

organization was impeccable, drawing praise from the many fans who feared chaos. The event was later recognized as the largest concert in North America in 1996.

The television media that had been so quick to report the goings-on at Red Rocks, though, were nowhere to be found in Plattsburgh. But several magazine journalists would offer long stories on "Phish Nation" to their readers soon after.

Fall of 1996 offered another national tour, again in major-league venues from coast to coast, in support of *Billy Breathes*. Well received by fans, *Billy Breathes* also caught the attention of the national media like never before. *Entertainment Weekly* went as far as to declare Phish "the biggest band in America, no bones about it."

Articles appeared in *GQ*, countless local newspapers, and later *Rolling Stone*, which ran its first full Phish feature in the winter of 1997. Each article suggested that Phish was ready to break through to the mainstream, and was in for another explosion in popularity. And though the band continued to pick up steam—receiving a reported 300,000 mail-order requests for New Year's Eve tickets for the show at the FleetCenter in Boston—the crossover predicted by the media never came to pass. The album debuted on the *Billboard* charts all the way up at number seven, but dropped steadily thereafter. To most fans, and perhaps to the band who spoke of how hard they tried to avoid producing a hit single, it was a welcome relief.

The winter of 1997 saw Phish's first ever headlining tour in Europe, a month-long affair in venues about the size of halls Phish played in the Northeast in 1991. It was almost as if they were trying to do it all over again, prove they could rise to the top simply through the power of the music and word-of-mouth. The music on the Europe tour certainly was powerful—one of the last shows of the tour, a gig in Hamburg, Germany, would later become Phish's second live album, *Slip Stitch and Pass*.

The band seemed to relish the intimate venues, and they would later tell friends that the experience absolutely rejuvenated them as performers. Trey began to take less of a central role, opening up doors for the rest of the band while also rediscovering some of their core roots in American music forms like soul, blues, and funk. The band returned for another European tour in early summer. By then they had nearly 20 new songs at their disposal, including several that lent themselves to long, improvisational jams. It was just what the hardcore fans were looking for, and something the mainstream fans Phish was supposedly about to lure in wouldn't quite understand.

By the time they returned to the United States, they had turned another corner musically, delving into a tighter, funkier sound with less soloing and broader use of electronic effects. The new sound turned once-short and seldom played tunes like "Gumbo" and "Wolfman's Brother" into show stoppers.

The month-long U.S. summer tour ended with another grand two-day finale, the Great Went in far-off Limestone, ME. A town so far north that Phish flew in through Canada and temperatures dropped into the 40s in the middle of August, Limestone grew to become the largest city in Maine for the weekend, as close to 65,000 people made the trek. The spiritual heir of the previous summer's Clifford Ball, the Went matched the Ball in offering six sets of Phish spread over two days, camping, and a surprise pre-dawn set, this time with the band members deejaying a disco-rave affair.

In a seminal moment during the final show of the summer, the band took turns painting on stage, and then pointed to a large, towering sculpture in the midst of the crowd, which fans had been building throughout the weekend. Phish proceeded to pass their creations through the crowd and had them tacked to the sculpture—a gesture of making art with the audience.

Trey then asked Chris Kuroda to shut off all the stage lights and allow the band to jam beneath the light of the moon, breaking into an emotional "Harry Hood." Audience members near the stage hurled neon necklaces and lightsticks into the air by the dozen, creating a light show of their own. A misty-eyed Trey closed the set by asking fans to "get more of those, they look cool from up here."

During the encore, the art sculpture was set ablaze, and as the last notes of the summer's final song, "Tweezer Reprise," soared above the assembled mass, the tower crumbled into embers, glowing brightly for the rest of the night.

When Phish headed back to the arena circuit for the fall tour, they were simply on fire. The many musical pieces they'd tinkered with throughout the year were finally locked in place, and longtime fans were leaving every show astounded. Most of the second sets during the tour featured only four or five songs, and stretched-out funk jams became standard fare for every tune. The band seemed to be amazing themselves, and they celebrated with marathon shows and setlist surprises (such as opening first sets with "Tweezers" and "Mike's Groove").

Ironically, the cataclysmic growth of the band's fan base seemed to subside a bit during this period, perhaps even to level off. Fans were pleased to notice that Phish tickets in the Northeast weren't as impossible to get a hold of as they had been. And while the band was adding new fans every day, many old ones had stopped coming for one reason or another.

But perhaps it's fitting that as Phish found a musical path that produced some of their best-ever performances as a band, it wasn't immediately recognized by any mass audience. In the end, the Phish story is not about how many people hear the music, it's about the music they hear.

Throughout Phish's steady rise, the band has never lost its widely recognized ability to be personal with what, to any other band, could have been a faceless mass. Phish has proven they can maintain their identity, even if the forums in which they exercise their craft are antithetical to that persona.

Even if Phish leaves the stage for good tomorrow, the band will have left its legacy—proof that whatever the forum, inspired music can resist corporate mutation. And most of all, the thousands who came to know the band through everything but music videos and the radio will remain an undying testament to the fact that music's power can operate outside the confines of the modern business juggernaut it created.

Even in the 1990s, art will find its audience.

June 6, 1994: *People* magazine devotes two pages to Phish. "I think Phish will have a double-platinum record in a year or two," the chairman of Elektra says.

October 31, 1994: The band performs The Beatles' *White Album* in its entirety as its first "musical costume." The show ends at 3:20 a.m.

December 4, 1994: Tickets go on sale for Phish's December 30 show at Madison Square Garden and sell out in four hours; tickets for the New Year's Eve show at Boston Garden disappear within 50 minutes.

December 30, 1994: Appearing for the first time on "Late Night with David Letterman," the band plays an awkward "Chalkdust Torture."

A WALKING TOUR OF BURLINGTON

Places and Points of Interest from Phish's Green Mountain Past

WING-DAVIS-WILKE

Every college in America has dorm lounges that look like this one. But it was in this room that history unfolded when Trey, Fish, Jeff Holdsworth, and later, Mike Gordon, had their first jam sessions.

SLADE HALL

Phish's first successful performances took place in the basement of Slade Hall, UVM's environmental cooperative dorm. On October 1, 1996, Mike Gordon returned there for a performance with Gordon Stone.

Photo © 1997 by Pete Bershon.

NECTAR'S

Immortalized forever in the liner notes to *A Picture of Nectar,* this club and eatery still gives many up-and-coming bands their first shot in Burlington. Phish played at Nectar's regularly from 1984 through 1988, when they moved over to the now-defunct Club Toast.

10
Miner Danl E Rte 7 Mil ---------- 8
Miner David R N Ferrisburg Vt ------ 4
Miner Edith M Panton Vt -------- 475-
Miner EN Scale Sales & Service
Maplewood Av Mil ---------- 893-7
Miner Floyd 156 King Burl --------- 862-7
Miner G E St George ---------- 482-2
Miner H M Colchester Vt -------- 878-
Miner John Panton ---------- 47
Miner John L E Charlotte Vt --------
Miner Keith H & Sherrie G
117 Cherry Ln Burl --------
Miner Kenneth Maplewood A
Miner Kim & David Kienl
Miner L C 132 Villag
Miner Lawrence Fer

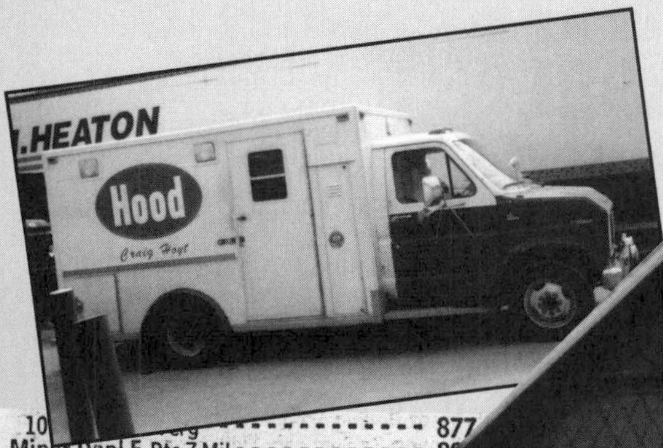

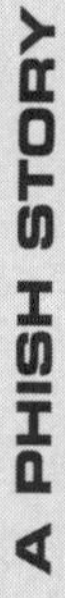

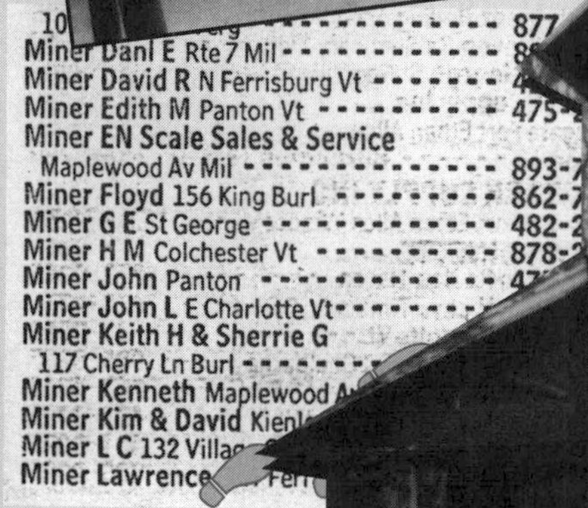

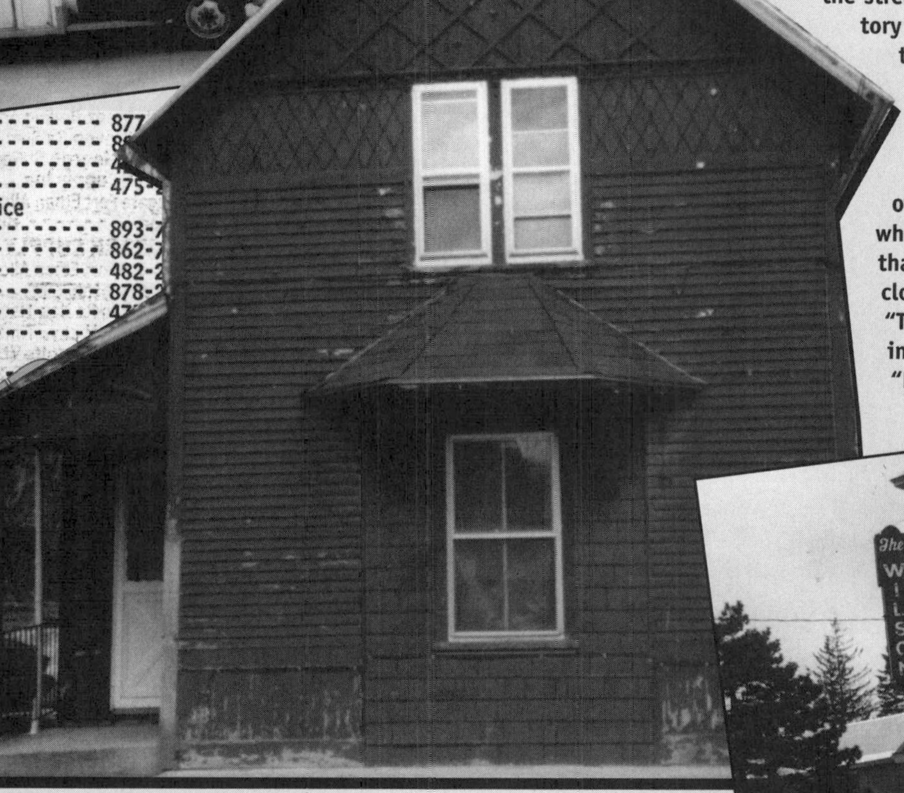

353 KING STREET

Several band members lived in this house in the mid-1980s. Its location, across the street from the Hood milk factory and down the block from the ominous hotel the Wilson, helped inspire several Phish lyrics and songs. The house was also the former residence of a man named Floyd Miner, who still received junk mail at that address. One letter closed with the sentence "Thank You, Mr. Miner," inspiring that lyric for "Harry Hood."

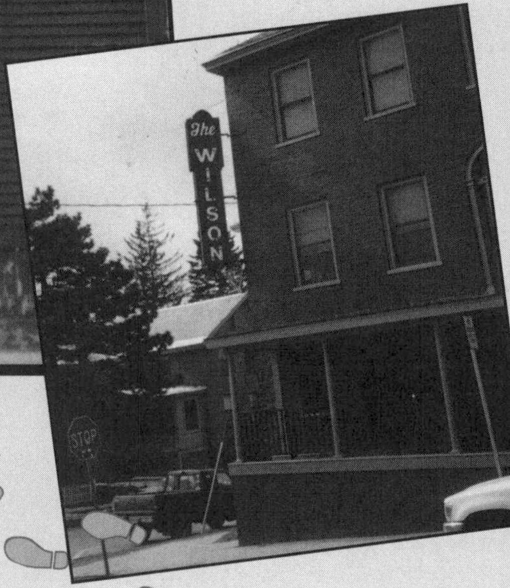

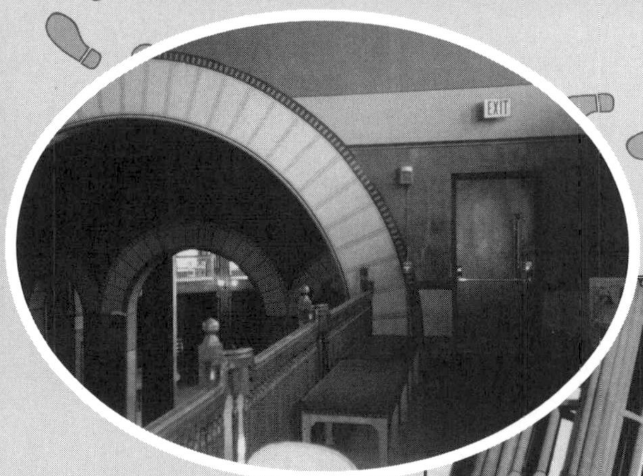

BILLINGS HALL

One day in the fall of 1984, Phish band members huddled in an upstairs alcove of Billings Hall on the UVM campus, and came up with the name Phish.

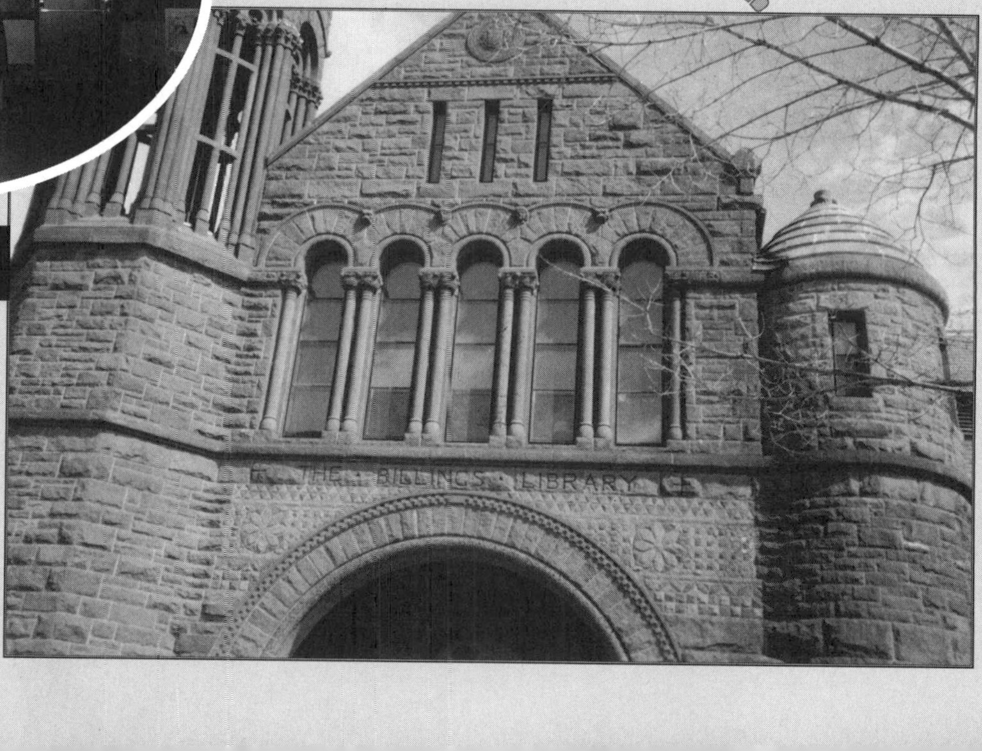

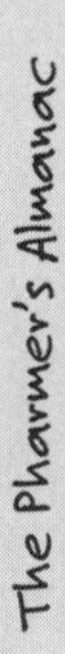

• Dionysian Productions •

Phish's business office, Dionysian Productions, is probably unlike any major rock act's management. Dionysian has just one client, and is as homegrown as the band itself, while still winning respect throughout the music industry.

Led by John Paluska and flanked by assistant managers Shelly Culbertson and Jason Colton, Dionysian has a small staff based in Burlington and is responsible for everything from tickets by mail to issuing the newsletter.

In the early years, Mike and Paul Languedoc shouldered much of the behind-the-scenes responsibilities of keeping Phish's house in order. Katie McConnell and Kristy Anastasio, sisters of Page and Trey, created the first Phish newsletters, which were mailed from Brooklyn, NY. Phish didn't have a true management company until Dionysian was formed by Paluska and his friend Ben Hunter after Paluska graduated from Amherst College in 1989 (about a year after first seeing the band). At the time, Phish commanded about $1,000 per gig.

Hunter did not stay on long as Phish's co-manager (instead, he helped form the magazine *Swing* with David Lauren, the son of clothing designer Ralph. Originally meant to be a music magazine devoted to bands like Phish and Blues Traveler, *Swing* became a Gen-X lifestyle rag instead).

Paluska, however, had found his calling.

He set up a home office at 505 Main Street in Watertown, MA, and immediately began working on ways to help the band grow. "For a long time, in terms of what we did, how I managed was dictated by necessity, it was pretty hand to mouth," Paluska told the *Maine Times* in 1995. "We were trying to get started and I did everything myself—keeping the books, selling merchandise, booking concerts, writing ads, trying to get record companies interested." It was around this time that Phish really began to take off and by 1991, although he still worked out of the tiny Watertown office, Paluska had helped turn Phish into a growing and financially stable operation.

"John did whatever he needed to do to keep Phish the tightest ship in the business. And it always was, even back then," says John Greene, who helped computerize the Phish mailing list (around 15,000 names in 1991) and the on-tour operation.

The organization grew to include assistant manager Marni Davis, a college friend of Ben Hunter, and several part-timers like Greene. Davis then departed and was replaced by Culbertson, one of the earliest Phish.Netters, around 1992. (She remains the band's unofficial liaison to the Net.)

Dionysian later took up larger offices in Lexington, MA, and negotiated Phish's recording contract with Elektra.

As soon as it was financially possible, the band and Dionysian made sure that the entire organization was treated well. Both the road crew and office staff received full salaries and health benefits. Although the faces changed a bit over the years (road manager Andrew Fishbeck left the band and was replaced down the line by former roadie Brad Sands), Dionysian created a solid foundation based on internal trust and respect, and kept the music industry's well-known dark side out of its dealings as much as possible.

It was also the unseen force behind Phish's ascent. From making tough decisions on how much to charge per ticket (Paluska went by the credo of never increasing prices by more than $2 when returning to a venue) to convincing Elektra that fans should be allowed to tape shows, the organization shepherded Phish to the next level without forgetting what got them there.

By 1993, when the band first began to headline major amphitheaters, the organization took on a whole new set of challenges. No longer would a manager's basic edicts (grow the fan base and make money for the client) apply. The band members, all of whom came from well-to-do families and had simple tastes as individuals, were not focused on the millions that were now obviously soon to come their way.

Instead, one of Dionysian's main directives became to preserve sanity, along with Phish's pristine image as an undercommercialized band that cared about its audience.

After a while, Paluska actually downsized the behind-the-scenes staff, which was composed mostly of hardcore fans who'd hopped on at one point or another.

"The one mistake the Grateful Dead made was becoming too in-house," he explained to the *Maine Times*. "All of a sudden they had sixty to seventy people relying on them for a living. They couldn't afford to be off the road too long. We have this incredible luxury of seeing what worked for them and what didn't."

In late 1995, Dionysian moved into offices on Pine Street in Burlington, and most of the staff moved along with them. Soon Kevin Shapiro, the band's archivist, would be added to the payroll, and he would eventually be joined by Shane Johnson, a former tour-head who ran the Green Crew.

Although the organization has several key business partners (Chip Hooper of California-based Monterey Artists handles booking, Time Warner–owned Giant Merchandising has played a key role in Phish's merchandise sales and production, Connecticut-based Snow Sound handles the band's speaker setup, and Great Northern Entertainment staged the Great Went), it's the crew of trusted friends at Dionysian who really get the band from show to show. This tight-knit group, which also includes Amy Skelton and Cynthia Brown (who handle different areas of merchandising and Vermont Dry Goods) continue to see Phish through mega-events and mail-order rushes, all while maintaining a hometown family feeling. And oh yes, each of them still loves Phish's music, Paluska especially.

Spring 1995: Phish Tickets-by-Mail debuts for the summer tour.

June 27, 1995: *A Live One* is released. The double live album enters the *Billboard* charts at number 18 after selling almost 50,000 copies in its first week.

December 1995: *A Live One* sales top 270,000 copies, giving the album gold record status as a double CD. But a later article in *Rolling Stone* refers to the poor sales of live albums throughout the music industry, and cites *A Live One* as an example.

1995

May 16, 1995: Phish plays a benefit show for Voters For Choice in Lowell, MA, raising over $30,000 for the organization while debuting a crop of new songs.

July 30, 1995: *The New York Times* Sunday arts section devotes an entire page to Phish, calling it "one of the summer's most talked-about bands."

Photo courtesy of Alison Offerman.

Photo courtesy of Jay Archibald.

Ernest J. "Trey" Anastasio

Personal: Born September 30, 1964, in Fort Worth, TX; before his second birthday, his family moved to Princeton, NJ, where Trey grew up. • Mother, Diane Anastasio, writes and illustrates children's books (Trey has collaborated on some of them); previously, she worked as editor of *Sesame Street Magazine*. • Father, Ernie Anastasio, is Executive Vice President of Educational Testing Services—the SAT people—in Princeton, NJ. Trey also has one sister. • Trey married longtime girlfriend Susan Eliza Stateser on August 13, 1994, in Stowe, VT. His first daughter, Eliza Jean Anastasio, was born August 21, 1995. His second daughter, Isabella Anastasio, was born April 22, 1997.

Education: Trey attended the Taft School, a private preparatory high school in Connecticut, after spending junior high at Princeton Day School • Enrolled at the University of Vermont in September 1983, but transferred to Goddard College by fall 1986 after growing discontented with the music department at UVM. • Graduated from Goddard in spring 1988, where he wrote "The Man Who Stepped into Yesterday" as his senior thesis.

Musical Notes: Trey began drum lessons when he was seven years old, but switched to the guitar in high school, and played in the band Space Antelope at Taft with the Dude of Life. • At UVM, he hosted an early-morning radio show on student radio called the Ambient Alarm Clock. • During his college career, he took guitar lessons from Paul Asbell and composition lessons from neo-classical composer Ernie Stires. • Considers Sun Ra, Miles Davis, and the Velvet Underground big musical influences (among many others); also credits friend Dave Grippo as an important teacher.

In the band: Trey is the closest thing Phish has to a leader, composing most of the band's music and selecting the setlist for shows with help from Page. • Golden retriever Marley has served as "director of security" at many Phish gigs.

1996

December 31, 1995: Phish plays Madison Square Garden on New Year's Eve; the concert is still ranked by fans as the band's best ever.

Winter–Spring 1996: Phish records *Billy Breathes* in Bearsville, NY, taking a break from the studio to play the New Orleans Jazz & Heritage Festival on April 26.

August 1996: A disturbance near Red Rocks during Phish's four-night stand there draws bad press in Denver and beyond.

Rocky Mountain News
DENVER
Tuesday, August 6, 1996 www.denver-rmn.com ★ 35¢ (50¢ in Designated Areas)

Rock fans battle police

12 arrested, Morrison shut down after Phish crowd refuses to leave. 5A

Photo courtesy of Alison Offerman.

Photo courtesy of Jay Archibald.

Page McConnell

Personal: Born May 17, 1963, in Philadelphia, PA, Page grew up in Basking Ridge, NJ. • His father, Dr. Jack McConnell, a big Dixieland jazz fan, helped develop Tylenol at McNeil Laboratories and later founded a health clinic on Hilton Head Island in South Carolina. His mother, Mary Ellen McConnell, also is a musician. • He has an older brother and younger sister. • Married longtime girlfriend Sofi Dillof—who has appeared onstage with Phish, most recently at Amy's Farm—in September 1995.

Education: Attended one year of private high school at Lawrence Academy in Groton, MA, which he graduated from in 1982. • Enrolled at college at Southern Methodist University in Dallas, TX, but after two years there, he transferred to Goddard College where he started classes in September 1984. • Received a $50 per person "finder's fee" for convincing Trey and Fish to transfer to Goddard in 1986. • While at Goddard, he studied with advisor Karl Boyle and wrote his senior thesis, "The Art of Improvisation," about his experiences with music and Phish. • Graduated from Goddard College in December 1987.

Musical Notes: Started playing piano in his childhood. • Considers Fats Waller, James P. Johnson, Art Tatum, Thelonius Monk, Lou Reed, his father, and Burlington pianist Lar Duggan as influences (among many others). • Composed the movie soundtrack for a friend's feature film, *Only in America*, which features "Cars Trucks Buses" and several other original songs.

In the band: Page holds down the calm center of the group, often functioning as a primary decision maker with Trey. He's probably the most wary of rock-star fame of anyone in the group, and is said to be very laid back. Helps put together show setlists with Trey, usually serving as the proofreader of Trey's song lists. • Nicknames include "The Chairman of the Boards" and "Leo." ■

August 16–17, 1996: The Clifford Ball draws over 75,000 fans to Plattsburgh, NY, making it the largest concert event in North America in 1996, but receives scant media coverage.

October 15, 1996: *Billy Breathes* released to a four-star album review in *Rolling Stone*. Though the album debuted at number 7 on the *Billboard* charts, it never becomes the runaway hit some expected.

December 6, 1996: Phish plays Las Vegas for the first time, a wild affair that features appearances by most of Primus and four Elvis impersonators.

1997

February 20, 1997: Ben & Jerry's releases Phish Food ice cream, and Phish pledges its portion of the proceeds to help clean up Lake Champlain.

February–March 1997: Phish returns to Europe for three weeks of sol shows at small clubs and theaters.

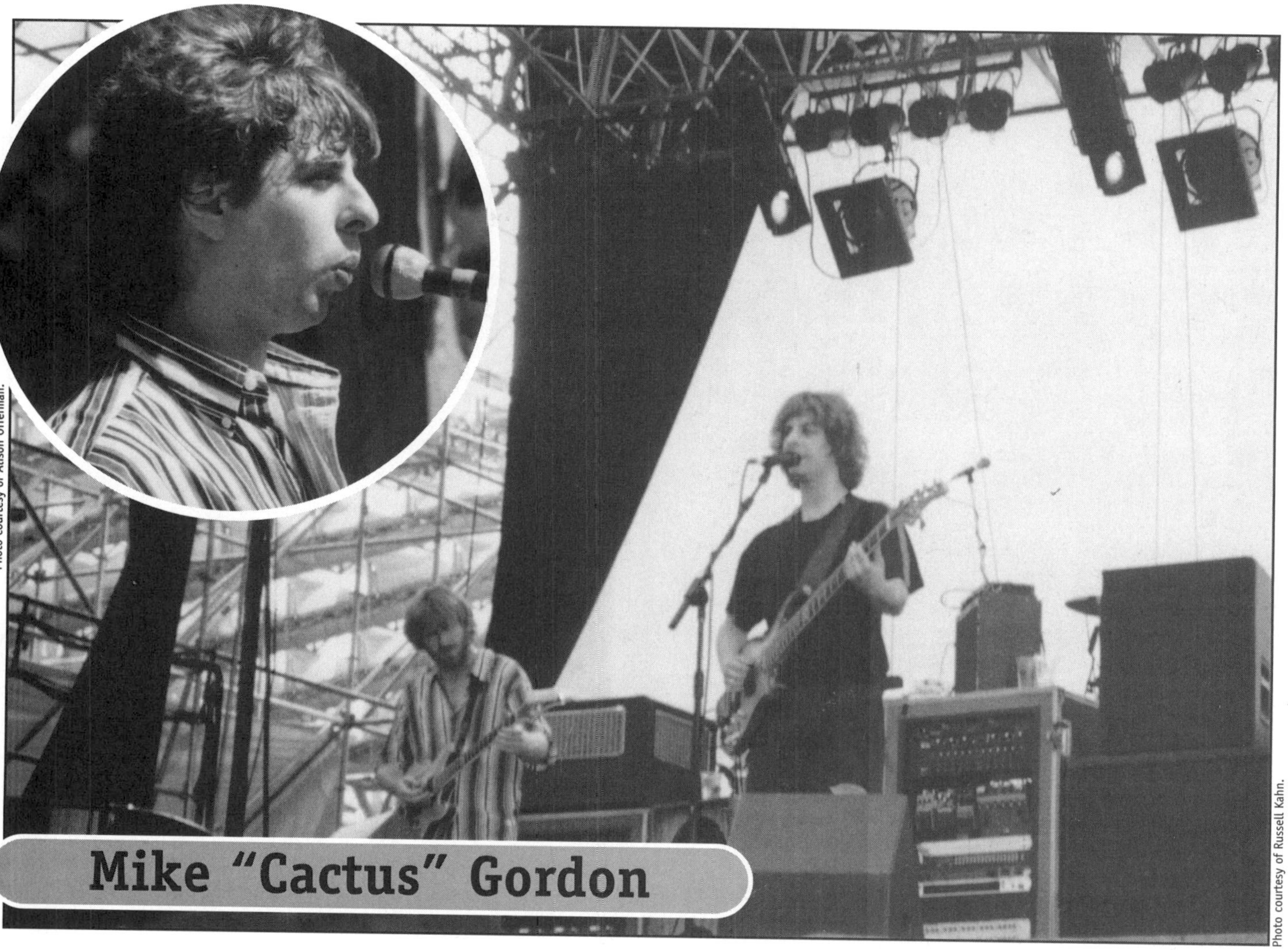

Photo courtesy of Alison Offerman.

Photo courtesy of Russell Kahn.

Mike "Cactus" Gordon

Personal: Born June 3, 1965, in Boston, MA. Grew up in nearby Sudbury, MA, where he attended the Jewish Solomon Schecter Day School. • Father founded the very successful Store 24 convenience-store chain. • Mother, Marjorie (Marge) Minkin, is an artist who has painted several of Phish's set backdrops, known as "Minkins." • One brother. • Engaged at presstime to Cilla Foster.

Education: Mike attended local high school near his home in Sudbury. • Enrolled at UVM in the fall of 1983. • During his time at UVM, he studied electrical engineering for two and a half years before switching his major to Film and Communications. He produced a film for his senior project called "TVF," which apparently is about the evils of television. • Graduated from UVM in the spring of 1987.

Musical Notes: Became attracted to the bass in 1979 after hearing reggae group the Mustangs play poolside in the Bahamas on a family vacation and recognizing the instrument's ability to "vibrate people."• Played in several bands in high school: the Tombstone Blues Band, which played blues and 1960s rock, and The Edge, a new-wave outfit that covered bands including the Talking Heads and the Pretenders and performed some original music. • Took bass classes from teacher Jim Stinnette during his time at college. • Considers bluegrass music, Phil Lesh, the Grateful Dead, Bootsy Collins, and the Mustangs as primary influences (among many others).

In the band: The band member most likely to disagree with the other three, Mike is nevertheless content to not play a primary role in all decision making. But when he disagrees, he lets them know it. • Nicknamed "Cactus." • Gets at least eight hours of sleep a night on tour. • *Mike's Corner*, a collection of his eclectic tales, was published in May 1997.

June 13–14, 1997: Back in Europe again, Phish gives Dublin audiences two shows packed with all-new material, most of which would be heavily played throughout the summer.

Photo courtesy of Anthony Euchla.

August 16–17, 1997: Nearly 65,000 fans trek to far northern Maine for the Great Went, 1997's spiritual heir to the Clifford Ball.

October 28, 1997: Live album *Slip Stitch and Pass,* recorded in Hamburg on March 1, 1997, is released.

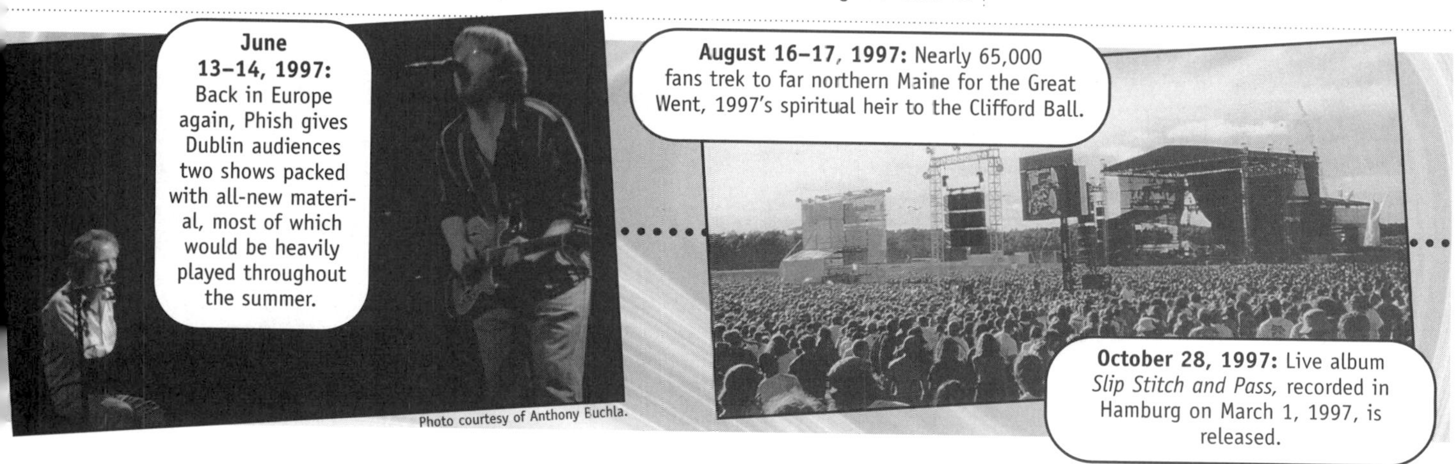

Photo courtesy of Alison Offerman.

Photo courtesy of George Lyons.

Jonathan "Fish" Fishman

Personal: Born February 19, 1965, in Philadelphia, PA. • Grew up in Syracuse, NY. • Father, Len Fishman, works as an orthodontist and also as a sculptor. • Mother, Mimi, has become renowned as a follower of New York-area jam bands, and has appeared on stage with Phish on numerous occasions. • Has one brother and one sister; all of them (including Fish) are adopted. • Married Pam Tengiris in Las Vegas on September 28, 1997.

Education: Attended Moses Dewitt high school near his home in Syracuse. • Enrolled at UVM in September 1983, where he spent one year. • Transferred to Goddard by the fall of 1986. After taking some time off he graduated from Goddard in 1990. • Wrote his senior thesis at Goddard, "A Self-Teaching Guide to Drumming Written in Retrospect," on his experiences with music and with drumming.

Musical Notes: Started playing drums at eight years old when he played along to Led Zeppelin albums. • Took three formal drum lessons at age 13, when he learned to read music, but didn't take another lesson until several years ago when he had a session with Joe Morello. • At Goddard he was said to practice playing the drums as much as eight hours a day. • Considers King Crimson, Yes, early Genesis, Frank Zappa's band, Sun Ra, and the Velvet Underground as major influences (among many others).

In the Band: Fish is the band member most likely to try anything, as his vacuum-cleaner solos and occasional naked exploits have demonstrated. Content to not be a primary decision maker in the group dynamic. • Numerous nicknames include Henrietta, Zero Man (accompanied by a costume now worn since Amy's Farm), Moses Brown, Moses Dewitt, Moses Heaps, Tubbs (circa *Rift*), Greasy Fizeek (circa *Hoist*), and Norton Charleton Heston (circa fall 1996). • Wears a frock on stage, a habit begun in the late 1980s, but ended the habit temporarily in 1997. During the summer 1997 tour, he fashioned a sleek black outfit, and in the fall tour that followed, he was seen in the frock with pants underneath (a new display of modesty) and a Philadelphia Flyers jersey.

FISH Tools

NO ONE IN PHISH can claim the wide array of musical skills that Fishman can. During his appearances as Henrietta (and other alter egos) over the years, Fish has mastered some of the strangest instruments:

Vacuum. His trademark piece, Fish first played the vacuum at a party in the late 1980s when Sofi Dillof (now Page's wife) asked him if he knew any instruments besides the drums. Fish replied, "Of course," and proceeded to play the house's vacuum cleaner. He subsequently translated the skill to concert.

Trombone. As the "fourth member of the Giant Country Horns," Henrietta's trombone skill has improved steadily over the years.

Madonna Washboard. So named for its conical breast features, the washboard debuted in 1992 and has been used for solos and during acoustic sets.

Cymbals. His instrument of choice for "Cracklin' Rosie," the cymbals held up together spell out the word "BAH."

Plastic. For part of the 1993 spring tour, Fish shook a piece of plastic to produce noise. He also "played" a cardboard picture of Otis Redding the same way on February 5, 1993.

Vacuum bagpipes. This strange device surfaced for the early half of the 1992 spring tour, and featured bagpipes attached to the vacuum to produce a new sucking/droning noise. The contraption gave out by May 1, 1992.

Photo courtesy of Jay Archibald.

PRESSED PHISH

The White Album

An unofficial demo tape never officially titled, the "White Album" (also referred to as the "white tape") is mostly comprised of short pieces recorded separately by Trey and Mike on four-track equipment. Only a few of the songs feature all four of the band members; friends played various instruments on some tracks. Many of the songs are abridged versions.

Recorded: Throughout the mid-1980s (1986 and 1987 in particular). Never officially released, tapes circulate among fans and for a while in the late 1980s, the tape could be found on sale at Phish shows. Some versions of the "White Album" have the entire tape of material abridged to fit on one 45-minute side.

Track List: (A:) Alumni Blues > Steve Reich, And So to Bed, You Enjoy Myself, AC/DC Bag, Fuck Your Face, Divided Sky, Slave to the Traffic Light, Aftermath, Ingest; (B:) N2O, Fluff's Travels, Dog Log, Hamburger, Run Like an Antelope, Minkin, Letter to Jimmy Page.

The Man Who Stepped into Yesterday

Also known as Gamehendge, Trey's senior thesis at Goddard College was the recording of a musical fairy tale that he originally intended to be staged as a musical. For much of the 1990s, the band toyed with the idea of re-recording TMWSIY as an interactive CD-ROM, but decided before recording *Billy Breathes* that they would never record Gamehendge and hence, never profit from it.

Recorded: As Trey's senior thesis, 1987 to 1988. Never officially released; tapes that circulate among fans have the narration on one track and the music on the other.

Track List: Wilson Chant > narrative > Lizards > Tela > narrative > Wilson > narrative > AC/DC Bag > narrative> Colonel Forbin's Ascent > Famous Mockingbird > narrative > The Sloth > narrative > Possum.

Junta

Phish's first studio-recorded and released album, *Junta*—named after friend Ben Hunter's nickname, which was mispronounced JOON-ta—could only be bought at Phish shows and by mail order from the band on cassette until its re-release by Elektra on CD in 1992. The album, which includes some acoustic playing, features many of the band's most popular epics.

The band now says that in some ways *Junta* is their purest album, and some longtime fans consider it Phish's best studio effort to date. In weekly record store sales, it sold better than any other Phish album prior to the release of *Billy Breathes*.

Junta was recorded during two separate sessions. The first, in 1987, was a three-day stint in Euphoria Studios in Revere, MA, for the purpose of cutting a demo tape.

Gordon Hookailo, whose name was later misspelled on the album, served as engineer. "The first tune we recorded was 'Fluffhead.' I remember we were setting up for and running a soundcheck on them, and everyone in the control room's jaws just dropped to the ground as these kids started whaling out this music," remembers Hookailo. "It was just incredible."

During the first day of the session, the band ran through "Fluffhead," "Fee," and "Golgi Apparatus." The versions that appear on the album are single performances of each song played straight through, without any splicing from one take to another (considered rare, especially for a song as long as "Fluffhead"). The next day was spent adding sound effects to "Fee," and the third day was devoted to mixing.

"Back then they were a bunch of kids. They literally didn't look any older than teens when they walked into the studio," Hookailo says. When they returned to the studio during the winter of 1989 to cut the rest of the album, they stayed for a longer period but still got the job done at breakneck speed by modern standards (a little over two weeks, Hookailo says). They experimented more in the studio, especially on the vocal tracks to "Esther," and added some sound effects to "David Bowie," an overdub to "You Enjoy Myself," and a glockenschpiel to "Divided Sky." "This was total fun," Hookailo quips.

In the end, the band spent just around $5,000 to create a masterpiece.

After its initial release on cassette tape, *Junta* got a second life as an Elektra re-release. In 1992, when planning the two-disc Elektra version, Phish considered making one of the discs an interactive compact disc and including an animated "Esther" video (shown during setbreak at the Somerville Theater on July 19, 1991). But they decided that CD-I technology had not been standardized enough to make it worthwhile. So with extra space to play with to fill the second disc, they decided to include three live tracks from the era when they recorded *Junta*. The versions of "Sanity" and "Icculus" are from the show at Nectar's on July 24, 1988, not May 3, 1988, as the album liner notes state. "Union Federal" comes from a fabled annual jam session known as the "Oh Kee Pa" Ceremony, recorded at one of the band member's homes in 1989.

Recorded: At Euphoria Sound Studios, Revere, MA, in two separate sessions, one during the fall of 1987 and one during the winter of 1988 to 1989. Produced by Phish. Left on the cutting room floor: "Alumni Blues" and possibly others.

Released: By Phish (cassette only) in May 1989, with the Jim Pollock artwork that still graces it today. Re-released by Elektra on a double-CD set (featuring new Pollock longbox artwork that can no longer be found) in November 1992.

Track List [1989]: [A:] Fee, You Enjoy Myself, Esther, Golgi Apparatus, Foam, Dinner and a Movie; [B:] Divided Sky, David Bowie, Fluffhead, Fluff's Travels (Part 1: Fluff's Travels,

Phish Sampler CDs

***Phish: A Sampler* [1993]**

Released for Phish's national tour in summer 1993, the CD is, as the promotional copy on the back states, "intended to always be around, sort of like Phish. . . . Play it in your store, play it in your room, wherever you want Phish." The CD came with an insert listing Phish's 1993 North American summer tour dates.

Track List: (from *Rift*) Fast Enough for You, The Wedge; (from *Picture of Nectar*) Chalkdust Torture, Cavern, Stash; (from *Lawn Boy*) Bouncing around the Room; (from *Junta*) Fee, Golgi Apparatus

***Stash* [1996]**

Released in Europe for Phish's July 1996 tour, *Stash* is another greatest hits compilation.

Track List: Down with Disease, If I Could, You Enjoy Myself (*Junta* version), Fast Enough for You, Scent of a Mule, Maze, Split Open and Melt, Sample in a Jar, Bouncing around the Room, Stash (*A Live One* version), Gumbo

***Free* (single) [1997]**

Released in Europe for Phish's 1997 winter tour, the disc contains the *Billy Breathes* versions of "Free" and "Theme," plus the previously unreleased "Strange Design" studio track.

Unreleased Studio

Like most bands, Phish has an array of studio material that's never been officially released. (Though the *White Album* technically falls under this category, it's covered in Pressed Phish—the main album section—because it was sold at Phish shows in the late 1980s.) Here's a sampling of these unreleased gems:

Bivouac Jaun

Recorded: Spring 1984 on four-track in Trey's basement at his home in New Jersey. Features collaborations with Marc Daubert and Tom Marshall, who helped record it. Includes early versions of "Slave," "Antelope," and "I Am Hydrogen." Impossible to find.

Untitled 4-Track Project

Recorded: December 1985. "Fluffhead" is a live concert version featuring the Dude of Life on vocals. Copies are impossible to find.

Track List: And So To Bed, You Enjoy Myself, Green Dolphin Street, Harry Hood, Slave to the Traffic Light, Run Like an Antelope, Divided Sky, Letter to Jimmy Page, Fluffhead

1987 Promo Tape

Recorded: Exact dates unclear, the tape circulates with a "©1987 Ernest Anastasio III" tagline. Labeled simply "Phish," the tape list is grouped by "Covers" and "Originals." This tape was sent to prospective bars and clubs where the band hoped to play through 1988. All songs are in-studio versions, and the originals are the versions that eventually ended up on *Junta*.

Track List: I Know a Little, Sneakin' Sally through the Alley, Golgi Apparatus, Fee, David Bowie, Fluffhead

Wendell Studio Sessions

Recorded: Summer 1990 at Wendell Studios in Boston, MA. The band entered the studio soon after the June 16, 1990, Townshend Family Park show, but elected not to release any of the material recorded. Tapes of the sessions circulate among phans; the first tape is more difficult to track down than the second tape.

Track List (tape one): Dog Log, Uncle Pen, Suzie Greenberg, Caravan, Alumni Blues, Take the A-Train, In a Mellow Tone, Possum, Mike's Song, I am Hydrogen

(tape two): TMWSIY, Avenu Malkenu, TMWSIY, Tweezer, Possum, Harry Hood, Rift (slow version), Runaway Jim (with alternate lyrics about Jim's death)

***Billy Breathes* Sessions**

Recorded: Spring 1996 in Bearsville, NY, for possible inclusion on *Billy Breathes*. Tapes of songs cut from the final album circulate among phans.

Track List: All of *Billy Breathes*, Glide II (instrumental), Strange Design, Grind (thirty-six-second Trey song, jazzy with lyrics), Waitin' Time (Mike song, funky)

—thanks to Dan Gibson, Tony Hume, Michael Shtadthender, Butch Weiss

Part 2: The Chase, Part 3: Who Do We Do, Part 4: Clod, Part 5: Bundle of Joy, Part 6: Arrival), Contact.

Track List [1992]: [Disc 1:] Fee, You Enjoy Myself, Esther, Golgi Apparatus, Foam, Dinner and a Movie, Divided Sky, David Bowie; [Disc 2:] Fluffhead, Fluff's Travels (Part 1: Fluff's Travels, Part 2: The Chase, Part 3: Who Do We Do, Part 4: Clod, Part 5: Bundle of Joy, Part 6: Arrival), Contact, Union Federal, Sanity, Icculus.

Lawn Boy

Phish's second studio effort got under way soon after the release of *Junta* in May 1989, when the band won some free recording time at Vermont's Archer Studios for taking first place at the Rock Rumble. They cashed in the prize by laying down "Split Open and Melt," with the help of a horn section, and "Bathtub Gin." From the outset, they planned to include mostly new material on the CD rather than recording some of their older concert favorites like "Mike's Song" or "Suzie Greenberg."

Work on *Lawn Boy* did not really hit full swing until the following January, when they went back into Archer Studios, this time on their own tab, to cut the rest of the album.

"I think we did all the recording in ten days to two weeks," remembers Dan Archer, the studio owner who also engineered the album. "This was back in the old days. They were just a local bar band. But I remember getting them all set up in different rooms with headphones on, but it sounded like they were playing in front of ten thousand people. I could not believe the energy."

The band also opted to include the *Junta* version of "Fee" as the final song on the album, although they later decided to cut it from the Elektra re-release of *Lawn Boy* in 1992.

More than any other Phish album, *Lawn Boy* suffered a number of quirky problems in its postproduction phase. The Absolute A-Go-Go release switched the printed order of "Reba" and "My Sweet One" on the album case, a problem corrected for the Elektra re-release. But Elektra inadvertently slowed down the title track, "Lawn Boy," on its re-release. More horribly, independent record distributor Rough Trade Records signed to distribute the album but went bankrupt by the end of 1990, taking any potential profits for Phish from the Absolute A-Go-Go release with it and even swallowing the studio masters.

Recorded: At Archer Studios, Winooski, VT, May through December 1989. Produced by Phish. Guest Artists: Horn section (Joseph Somerville Jr., trumpet; Dave Grippo, alto sax; Russell Remington, tenor sax) on "Split Open and Melt"; Christine Lynch (vocals on "Split Open and Melt").

Released: On Absolute A-Go-Go Records, in September 1990, in CD, cassette, and vinyl editions. Re-released on Elektra (CD and cassette only) on June 29, 1992.

Track List: The Squirming Coil, Reba, My Sweet One, Split Open and Melt, Oh Kee Pa Ceremony, Bathtub Gin, Run Like an Antelope, Lawn Boy, Bouncing around the Room, [Fee].

A Picture of Nectar

By the time Phish entered the studio to record their third album in the summer of 1991, the record companies were circling. The album that would become *A Picture of Nectar* would give the studio execs a taste of Phish's breadth because the album spans a huge number of musical genres. The album also includes the only studio version of a cover song—Dizzy Gillespie's "Manteca"—on any Phish album. Although band members say it happened as much by chance as for any other reason, the album switches styles with virtually every track, a fact that later led Phish to conclude that the album lacked cohesion.

The album is named after and dedicated to Nectar Rorris (whose likeness appears in shadow on the album's citrus cover). Nectar, of course, ran the Burlington bar Nectar's.

Recorded: At White Crow Studios, Burlington, VT, in June, July, and August 1991. Produced by Phish (with help from Kevin Halpin). Guest Artist: Gordon Stone (pedal steel guitar on "Poor Heart"). Left on the cutting room floor: "Runaway Jim," "Memories."

Released: On Elektra, February 18, 1992. Single released to radio: "Chalkdust Torture."

Track List: Llama, Eliza, Cavern, Poor Heart, Stash, Manteca, Guelah Papyrus, Magilla, The Landlady, Glide, Tweezer, The Mango Song, Chalkdust Torture, Faht, Catapult, Tweezer Reprise.

Rift

After the musical melange of *A Picture of Nectar,* the band decided to make their next studio effort a more focused affair, an album that would be more cohesive than their previous studio efforts. The result was *Rift*, a concept album in which each song represents a dream by a man in the course of one night of restless sleep.

In the year prior to the recording of the album, Tom Marshall had been undergoing a series of changes and challenges in his relationship, and wrote lyrics that reflected his situation (the best example being "Fast Enough for You"). The band members found that Marshall's words also reflected some of their own struggles to carry on relationships while spending large amounts of time on the road. They selected the songs for *Rift* with this theme in mind; the name of the album refers to the rift between the fictional couple.

The contract with Elektra afforded the band the chance to work with their first producer—Muscle Shoals veteran Barry Beckett. Beckett helped the band create the arrangement on "Fast Enough for You," which had never been performed live before the recording sessions, but most other songs appeared on the album in their previous concert incarnations.

The final addition to the disc was "The Wedge," which Trey wrote after the recording sessions in Burlington and the band recorded at The Castle in Nashville during the mixing of the album.

Though the band initially said they were pleased with how *Rift* came out, they later came to see *Rift*'s concept as too much of a forced effort. "I look back at *Rift* with a lot of dismay because it was a really fertile time for us—the music was just pouring out—but we were so excited about this conceptual thing that we beat it into the ground," Trey told *Guitar World* in 1996.

Recorded: At White Crow Studios, Burlington, VT, in September and October 1992; additional recording and mixing at The Castle, Nashville, TN, in October and November 1992. Produced by Barry Beckett. Guest Artist: Gordon Stone (pedal steel guitar on "Fast Enough for You").

Released: On Elektra, February 2, 1993. Singles released to radio: "Fast Enough for You," "Maze" (abridged version).

Track List: Rift, Fast Enough for You, Lengthwise, Maze, Sparkle, Horn, The Wedge, My Friend My Friend, Weigh, All Things Reconsidered, Mound, It's Ice, Lengthwise, The Horse, Silent in the Morning.

Hoist

After *Rift*, Phish planned to do an album of more singable, less lyrically depressing songs. The band's idea also was to take songs they generally hadn't performed live into the studio, because they wanted the album to sound less live than *Rift* and less similar to their live concerts. Their Elektra A&R person, Nancy Jeffries, also urged them to make an album that sounded less like their live style (in hopes of netting that elusive hit single).

"We were definitely out to make this one more accessible," Page told Steve Morse of the *Boston Globe* at the time of *Hoist*'s release. "We wanted an album that didn't have as many silly lyrics or as many fantasy-oriented lyrics."

Indeed, the album followed a conscious effort by Elektra to convince Phish to put out an album with several radio-friendly songs and to make their first rock video for MTV. Paul Fox, whose producing credits included 10,000 Maniacs, Sugar Cubes, and XTC, wasn't the band's first choice as a producer, but he ultimately filled that role. He used his connections to lure many guest artists into the studio.

Taking advantage of the Hollywood climate, the band did several photo sessions, which resulted in the images used in the booklet accompanying the CD and promotional materials. After considering calling the album *Hung Like a Horse* (inspired by the photo that appears on the back of the case), the idea evolved into hoisting (a common way of examining horses) Amy Skelton's horse Maggie. Maggie, in hoist, appears on the album's cover.

Recorded: At American Recording Co., Woodland Hills, CA, in October and November 1993. Mixed at Can-Am Studios, Tarzana, CA, in December 1993. Produced by Paul Fox. Recorded and mixed by Ed Thacker. Guest Artists: Rickey Grundy Chorale ("Julius"), Tower of Power Horn Section ("Julius," "Wolfman's Brother"), Alison Krauss (vocals on "If I Could"), Morgan Fichter (violin on "Lifeboy"), Rose Stone and Jean McClain (backing vocals on "Julius" and "DWD"), Bela Fleck (banjo on "Lifeboy," "Riker's Mailbox," "Scent of a Mule"), The Richard Green Fourteen (strings on "If I Could"), and Jonathan Frakes (trombone on "Riker's Mailbox"). Left on the cutting room floor: "Simple," "Buffalo Bill" (part of the song was remastered backwards, creating the "Riker's Mailbox" track), Frakes's trombone on "Julius" and long "If I Could" intro.

Released: On Elektra on March 29, 1994. Singles released to radio: "Down with Disease," "Sample in a Jar." Video: "Down with Disease."

Track List: Julius, Down with Disease, If I Could, Riker's Mailbox, Axilla (Part II), Lifeboy, Sample in a Jar, Wolfman's Brother, Scent of a Mule, Dog Faced Boy, Demand.

A Live One

Before *Hoist* even hit stores, Phish settled on doing a live album as their next Elektra release. Climbing concert revenues in 1994 helped sell Elektra on the idea.

To solve the dilemma of self-imposed pressure that comes from recording a select show for a live disc, Phish recorded their entire fall tour in 1994. On that tour, the band members kept journals and wrote in them after each show, describing their feelings about that night's songs and experiences. After the tour ended, they compared notes, and shows mentioned by at least two band members went on a master list.

All told, they chose from 45 shows recorded on 32-track A-DAT machines run by Paul at the soundboard. They also had access to FM recordings from Red Rocks on June 11, Great Woods on July 8 and 9, and the Centrum on New Year's Eve 1993. The band initially considered 560 songs, roughly half of the total number they had available. They cut that group to 100, then to 30, from which they decided on the final 12. They looked mainly for great performances, and strove to get some sort of mix between songs that had previously been released and those that had not. And, before making the final cut, they also solicited the opinions of the Phish.Net community.

The Bangor "Tweezer" was a favorite of Page's, which he worked to sell the rest of the band on, and the Great Woods "Stash" came to the band's attention thanks to Phish.Net suggestions (Trey later called "Stash" "maybe my favorite thing on the album").

The final challenge was setting an affordable price, which would not only draw old fans but also attract new listeners. They persuaded Elektra to retail the two-disc set for the low price of $19.95. The band considered naming the album *Phish*, because they felt it was the closest they had come to capturing their sound on a recording, but settled on the slightly punny *A Live One*. The band also balked at the idea of listing the venues from which the performances were taken (reputedly because not all of them had signed off on allowing the material to appear on an album), and instead simply put "Recorded Live at Clifford Ball, 1994."

Recorded: Live in the summer and fall 1994.

Released: On Elektra as a two-disc set with booklet of band and tour photos on June 27, 1995. Singles released to radio: "Bouncing," "Simple."

Track List: [Disc 1:] Bouncing around the Room (12/31/94 Boston, MA), Stash (7/8/94 Mansfield, MA), Gumbo (12/2/94 Davis, CA, with horns), Montana (actually a snippet from Tweezer 11/28/94 Bozeman, MT), You Enjoy Myself (12/7/94 San Diego, CA), Chalkdust Torture (11/16/94 Ann Arbor, MI), Slave to the Traffic Light (11/26/94 Minneapolis, MN); [Disc 2:] Wilson (12/30/94 New York, NY), Tweezer (11/2/94 Bangor, ME), Simple (12/10/94 Santa Monica, CA), Harry Hood (10/23/94 Florida), The Squirming Coil (10/9/94 Pittsburgh, PA).

Billy Breathes

With about a dozen new songs already tested on stage, Phish recorded their sixth album in February 1996. But their sojourn in upstate New York at Bearsville Studios wasn't just a studio session—it was a chance for Phish to get back to their roots as a band after feeling like things had gotten too big by the end of their 1995 fall tour. Trey told *Entertainment Weekly* in the fall of 1996, "We fulfilled this need to be completely alone, recording again and hanging out. Because things had gotten so big, we needed to get our feet back on the ground."

The recordings began with something the band called "The Blob of Music," with each member taking turns recording single notes on a variety of instruments, in hopes of creating a more textural, organic sound that got down to the roots of Phish's musical process. After almost 20 minutes' worth of Blob had been recorded, the band took turns removing portions of the recording. The band also spent time recording more recognizable songs, but faced burnout as Trey and Page spent countless hours trying to produce the album. They hoped to have the album done by early April, but they left the studio for a month to prepare for their Jazzfest appearance in late April.

When they headed back to the studio at Bearsville, NY, they decided they needed an outside producer. After calling former U2 producer Steve Lillywhite, he showed up two days later, and the band and Lillywhite spent six weeks re-recording and creating the album that would become *Billy Breathes*. The band later called this period one of its most pleasurable experiences as a group.

Trey told *Musician*, "This work with Steve feels like it was meant to be. I don't mean to talk in clichés, but it's been like one long party, during which some recording happened to take place. I've begun to realize that on our previous albums, we really tied the producers' hands. We were such control freaks, me particularly. Now we're loosening up."

Avoiding the endless brigade of guest and backup musicians, which marked the production of *Hoist*, the band limited *Billy Breathes* to the members of Phish themselves, laying down the tracks in a studio in a barn by a stream and going so far as even doing the album artwork themselves. The result was a highly emotional work remarkable for its consistency. Trey wrote "Bliss," an acoustic instrumental, for a fan who was shot on his way to a show in Philadelphia the previous winter. "Steep" was composed of two parts of the Blob spliced together.

On tour in Europe in July 1996, the band made the painful decision to drop "Strange Design"—which was supposed to close the album—from the disc. They'd tried recording it several different ways in the studio, but never quite got it right, yet they feared the song could produce the dreaded "hit single." So it was axed.

The album received four stars in *Rolling Stone*, the first time a Phish album garnered that treasured rating. And "Free," the single, received solid radio airplay before the album was released.

Recorded: At Bearsville Studios, Bearsville, NY, February through June 1996. Produced by Steve Lillywhite and Phish. Left on the cutting room floor: "Strange Design," "Glide II" (instrumental), "Spock's Brain," "Ha Ha Ha," plus two untitled songs (one by Trey and one by Mike).

Released: On Elektra, October 15, 1996. Singles released to radio: "Free," "Character Zero."

Track List: Free, Character Zero, Waste, Taste, Cars Trucks Buses, Talk, Theme from the Bottom, Train Song, Bliss, Billy Breathes, Swept Away, Steep, Prince Caspian.

Slip Stitch and Pass

Phish made its next release another live album, the first in what the band says will be a series of "more experimental" live material to complement studio albums (the next studio album is tentatively due out in the fall of 1998). Drawing the entire album from one show—Hamburg, Germany, on March 1, 1997—Phish chose material from a night that spotlighted the band's new jam style—in Trey's words, "Slower, funkier, more group-oriented and less guitar-solo-oriented"—that evolved on the European tour that winter.

Besides opting to include numerous cover songs for the first time ("Cities," "Jesus Left Chicago," "Hello My Baby"), the band picked one of its strangest Mike's Grooves ever—mixing intense jamming with trademark Phish musical humor. Mike was excited that they were able to include the cover tunes. "Actually, I think it's significant to note that we have three covers on this album. I was really happy about that. I think it shows we're trying to put out a fun album and we're not trying to show what we can do as much as provide fun," he told Parke Puterbaugh in an interview that appeared on the Phish web site. "Playing covers, for me, has always had that role. It takes some of the ego away, when you haven't written the song."

Released: On Elektra, October 28, 1997. Singles released to radio: "Cities."

Track List: Cities, Wolfman's Brother, Jesus Left Chicago, Weigh, Mike's Song, Lawn Boy, Weekapaug Groove, Hello My Baby, Taste.

PHISH ON VIDEO

A quick look at some of the snippets of Phish on video that circulate among fans or could surface in the future:

1993 Elektra promotional video: A peek into the Phish world geared toward outsiders, mainly the music media. It includes the band explaining the concept behind *Rift*, fans explaining what it means to be a Phish fan, and some concert footage from Port Chester on November 27 to 28, 1992, including brief concert shots of "Maze" and "YEM." This tape is frequently circulated among fans despite its short (under 15 minute) length.

"Down with Disease" video: The Amelia Earhardt of Phish history. Unless you stayed up late watching MTV in April of 1994, or have a rare copy on tape, you've probably never seen this little Phish venture into corp-o-rama. Directed by Mike Gordon, it features some trampoline footage and jamming from New Year's Eve 1993, a shot of a real Phish tank with the bandmembers swimming and Trey's dog Marley watching them, and a cartoon moving Phish logo in front of the stage. If you really want to see it, it's occasionally shown on the big screen TV at New York's Irving Plaza between sets of shows.

Tracking: A behind-the-scenes look at the recording and mixing of *Hoist*, this Mike Gordon-directed collectible was the subject of some derision in previous Almanacs, especially for the minimum amount of time you actually hear the band talking or singing. But Gordon later explained that he found footage of the Phish talking about their own music to be boring, and that he was trying to create a more "emotive" texture to the video.

"Late Show" and "Late Night": The boys have appeared on "The Late Show" with David Letterman three times, December 30, 1994 ("Chalkdust Torture," played at Letterman's request); July 15, 1995 ("Julius," with horns) and March 7, 1997 ("Character Zero"). They also debuted "Farmhouse" on "Late Night" with Conan O'Brien on November 7, 1997. Although Phish heads were stopped from getting standby tickets for some of the Letterman gigs, the audience was filled with fans for the Conan appearance.

Professionally shot concert videos: Several concert videos from venues that film performances circulate among fans. The most widespread is from Waterbury, CT, on April 29, 1990; it's shot from two angles and uses a straight soundboard feed for audio but strains to look professional. This video was legally taped at the venue and is still marketed, making it the only legal Phish concert video for sale—though Phish management cringes at the thought. Another video often sold illegally as "Phish: Live in a Maze" is from the Shoreline Amphitheater when Phish opened for Santanta on August 21, 1992; it's the venue video cameras that broadcast images to the lawn at Shoreline.

There's also an interesting video from the band's last Halloween show at Goddard College on October 31, 1989, clearly done with the band's cooperation, which was broadcast on public-access cable in Burlington. Look for Page's old-school haircut, Trey's devil-with-

JAM Tricks

Get Back. Used primarily from 1991 through 1993 as a way of hopping between jams, "Get Back" is a brief jam Trey would play (from the Beatles' song) to send the band immediately back into the song they were playing previously. Check out Antelope from 3/13/92 or Manteca/Tweezer from 8/12/93 for good examples of this one.

Hand Signals. It's not exactly a subtle trick, but keep your eyes on Trey when you're at a show. He'll often signal the other band members when he wants to jump into a new song, or stop a jam dead in its tracks.

Musical Signals. The signals that are now well known to many phans, like the Simpsons' "D'oh!" and All Fall Down, were first created for the band's exclusive use. After popping up in concert from 1990 on, the band finally let the audience in on the secret for the first time on 3/6/92 in Portsmouth, NH.

Starts and Stops. A new addition to the repertoire on the 1997 fall tour, Phish would come to a dead stop in the midst of a crazy jam, then start the jam back up again. Often, this would happen a number of times in the course of the same jam. Weekapaug from Las Vegas on 12/6/96 is sometimes credited as the first start-and-stop jam of this type.

Wait. The early kin of starts and stops, this annoying little trick was used on the fall tour in 1991. After playing an It's Ice-like riff, Trey would yell, "Wait!" and the band would wait—often several minutes—before resuming the jam.

Telepathy. Okay, we've got no official proof of this, but what other good explanation is there? You gotta believe.

Phish and MTV

Phish has often been referred to as a band that made it big with no help from the radio industry or MTV. Indeed, MTV virtually ignored the band (and vice-versa) through 1995. In 1996 and 1997, however, MTV hopped on the Phish bandwagon, twice airing a half-hour Clifford Ball special and dispatching MTV news crews to the band's 1996 Halloween show at the Omni in Atlanta. Here's a guide to Phish spottings on MTV:

- A spring 1992 edition of Cindy Crawford's brilliantly obtuse "House Of Style" uses "The Landlady" as background music.
- Phish appears as the house band on "Hangin' with MTV" on July 23, 1992, almost by mistake. Surprised fans who catch the show see a snippet of "Divided Sky" and Fish on vacuum. The hosts and studio audience appear befuddled, and ask Phish after their trampoline routine whether the Grateful Dead or Mary Lou Retton were a bigger influence on their band.
- The "Down with Disease" video was shown late at night on MTV for much of spring 1994; by that fall, a snippet from the video appears on "Beavis and Butt-Head," who joke about the video's aquarium, equating it to a toilet.
- A summer 1994 MTV special on "Sex in the '90s" uses the "Down with Disease" intro as background music. It was also heard on "Road Rules" and "Real World IV."
- In their 1995 "Year In Review," MTV finally caves and devotes about a minute of footage to Phish. John Popper is shown calling Phish the greatest band in the world, and a few fans from a HORDE show talk about their Phish bootleg collections. A snippet of the "Down with Disease" video (look quick!) also makes it in, as does a mention of the flying hot dog.
- Missing a story that was practically under their noses, MTV fails to send cameras or reporters to the Clifford Ball. To atone for the oversight, the station twice airs a half-hour, Dionsyian-produced video narrative on the Ball in November. Though there's precious little actual Phish performance in the show, it does include several minutes of "Free" from the first night of the Ball.

breasts costume, and some funny crowd shots. (Note that the video mixes up the song order and doesn't include all the songs played.) Finally, Phish's show in Cologne, Germany on February 16, 1997, was broadcast on German TV and now circulates along with the June 22, 1997, broadcast on the same show.

Bootleg concert videos: The band has long begged fans not to bring video cameras into shows, but in the last several years the practice has spread. The quality of the videos ranges from passable to unwatchable, mainly depending on whether the rogue cameraman used a tripod. There are a number of these amateur videos in circulation, the most popular of which seems to be October 31, 1994, the Halloween show in Glens Falls, which is shot from a tripod and includes most of the show, except a portion of the third set. Other amateur videos making the rounds include December 29, 1993, December 31, 1995, and November 15, 1996.

The Esther Video: Shown between sets at the July 19, 1991 show at the Somerville Theater, this animation combined still sketches from an artist named Scott Nybakken with computer-generated graphics developed by a company called CoSa, whose owner Greg DeoCampo was a friend of the band and John Paluska's. The video, directed in part by John Greene, has not been aired since the July 19 show and was considered to be very much a work-in-progress at the time. The only places it has ever been seen were on the band's bus several hours before the show, on a large screen on the stage during the show, and on bootleg videos of the entire concert, which circulate among fans. CoSa, driven by DeoCampo's vision that soon all computers would have CD-ROM drives, was planning to produce a full-length CD-ROM version of Gamehendge, but could not get the funding needed to complete the project. Later, the band would decide not to go ahead with any multi-media project in the name of keeping capitalism out of the magical land of Gamehendge.

American Road: Before twentysomething Peter Shapiro became the new owner of New York's Wetlands Preserve, he directed and produced "American Road," a short montage of images from all 50 states, shot beautifully on a single road trip around the country. The background music for the film is "You Enjoy Myself." "American Road" has been shown at the Sundance Music Festival and on MSNBC.

In the vaults: Phish has tons of video footage at its disposal should it ever want to release a documentary or film project. In 1991, John Greene shot hours of concert and audience snippets for what was supposed to be the Gamehendge CD-ROM. Then the band did a lot of its own video taping in 1993. In recent years, every show has been videotaped from the soundboard by a band employee. And then there's the miles of footage taken by film crews at the Great Went and Clifford Ball.

Choose YOUR Weapon

Everyone knows that Fishman has mastered more instruments than most mere mortals would ever attempt. But who said anyone else in the band is a mere mortal? Here's a guide to some of the other crazy instruments sometimes seen on the Phish stage, courtesy of Trey, Mike, and Page.

Accordion. Played by Mike Gordon in Contact on 3/13/92 at Providence, RI, this instrument apparently didn't catch on. A shame, considering the Klezmer feel it could bring to a good Scent of a Mule jam.

Banjo. Mike's "other instrument"; he's proven himself as a solid bluegrass banjoist, especially during the 1994 fall tour.

Beer Bottle. Used as a guitar slide by Trey in BBFCM at the Joyous Lake show on 6/6/96. Brand is believed to be Rolling Rock.

Bell. Look down at Mike Gordon's feet during a show and you'll see a shiny, metallic sphere. It's Mike's bell, which he rings with his right foot when the occasion calls for it. It makes a quick, high "ding!" noise, just what you'd expect from a bell.

Drill. One of Mike's stranger toys, the electric drill surfaced in the midst of some songs, including I Didn't Know on 6/15/95 in Atlanta and It's Ice on 7/1/95 at Great Woods, but hasn't been seen onstage since summer 1995.

Drum Kit. Added to Phish's stage setup between Page's piano and Trey in 1995, the drum kit allowed Trey to space out in jams, creating a more textural feel. Often used in Free, and sporadically in jams in songs including YEM, Weekapaug, Simple, Down with Disease, and Runaway Jim, the drum kit allowed Fishman to explore more complex drumbeats while Trey held down the groove. After the funk-jam style evolution on the 1997 winter European tour gave Trey a different way to fade to the back of jams, his drum kit was retired.

Drumsticks. Before he had his drum kit, one of Trey's favorite jam tricks was to grab a pair of drumsticks, sling his guitar behind his back, and drum on any surface on the stage. This was often done when there were special guests, like at Albany on 5/6/93.

Fiddle. During the "bluegrass tour" with Jeff Mosier in November 1994, Trey picked up the fiddle on several nights for Butter Them Biscuits, first on 11/18/94 in East Lansing, MI.

Megaphone. Every show, it sits silently atop Trey's amp, waiting for Fee or BBFCM to jar it loose. It's Trey's megaphone, used to sing the verses of Fee through, or to sling around in violent fashion in the midst of BBFCM jams. Trey has also at times used his megaphone to create feedback effects, like during David Bowie from Minneapolis on 11/26/94.

Mouth Piano. Page's first acoustic instrument, the mouth piano was used for much of the 1994 spring and summer tours when the band moved to the front of the stage for acoustic numbers. A plastic instrument, the piano worked by blowing air into it (much like a trumpet) and playing the mini piano on the side of the instrument. You might have gotten one for your fifth birthday.

Telephone. Sure, it's not technically an instrument, but that didn't stop Trey from picking it up in the middle of jams on the 1997 summer tour. Resting on top of Page's piano, and apparently not even plugged in, the telephone inspired spurious theories that Trey was calling his kids to wish them good night—either that, or 900 numbers.

Theremin. An instrument played by Page for songs like Somewhere over the Rainbow. Notes are based on how high the player holds his or her hands above the instrument.

Upright Bass. Another acoustic instrument, the upright bass (also called the stand-up bass) has been used by Mike Gordon as his acoustic instrument of choice in summer 1993 and spring/summer 1994, and by Page in fall 1994 and summer/fall 1995.

HOLLYWOOD HONCHOS

Look for Phish band members to start popping up on the silver screen. Jon Fishman did a cameo role in a Martin Guigui film with the working title *The Wedding Band*. It reportedly was filmed at the Basin Harbor Club on Lake Champlain, and Fish plays the drummer in the band. Members of Spastic and the Dude of Life band also reportedly appear, and famed portly actor Dom Deluise is in the cast.

Mike Gordon, meanwhile, teamed up with friend and fellow musician Col. Bruce Hampton to make a full-feature film about a bass instructor which was expected to be called *Outstructional*. There are also rumors that Mike is appearing in another movie being filmed in Vermont in which he plays a washed-up rock star.

And then there's Page, who supposedly wrote a score for a friend's film, from which "Cars Trucks Buses" was extracted.

PHOLKLORE

• Secret Language •

"This is a very interesting sociological experiment to find out how quickly word can spread." —Trey, March 13, 1992

The French phrase, "Langue D'oc" refers to an old dialect of Southern France ("Language of the 'oc'") but more importantly, this dialect implies a secret language used by the troubadours, poets, and knights from the era of Courtly Love (11th century, Southern France) to woo their mistress without the husband finding out. It was a language for the poets of Arthurian Legend to enchant and enrapture, entrance and entice married ladies to the world of adulterous pleasures.

Photo courtesy of George Lyons.

Phish's musical language, also can enchant and enrapture. Perhaps then it is best if we call it mere coincidence that Phish's sound engineer's last name is spelled "Languedoc." Truth be told, it doesn't really matter one way or the other—Phish's secret language has little to do with Arthurian Legends and Courts of Love and everything to do with mad science and participatory experimentation.

On March 6, 1992, at the Portsmouth Music Hall in Portsmouth, NH, the band interrupted its second set to let the audience in on a secret. Phish had been using musical signals on stage with each other for many years, but decided to cue the audience in for the first time, even making up new crowd participation signals, like "all fall down," on the spot.

Phish would give a number of tutorials through 1992, informing audiences in Providence, RI (3/13/92), Binghamton, NY (3/20/92), Atlanta, GA (3/28/92), Eugene, OR (4/22/92), Minneapolis, MN (4/29/92), and Port Chester, NY (5/14/92). More than five years later, the experiment was still continuing, though the band hasn't offered a formal lesson since its first trip to Florida on February 22, 1993.

The signals sometimes feel like the most inside of inside jokes to those who don't catch a signal at a show, but this is not a joke. This is an experiment. This is an ongoing conversation between band and audience. It is a language comprised of a musical call and a verbal or physical response.

The conversation begins by two musical cues that the band may play in any song or jam at any given time. The first cue is always the same: a high-pitched trill, usually played on guitar by Trey, or sometimes on piano by Page or on bass by Mike. The second cue varies, depending on what the band wants to "say." There are five options:

Simpson's "D'oh." Easily the most well-known and perhaps easiest of all the language signals. When Trey plays a quick riff of the Simpson's theme song, the knowing audience yells "D'oh!"

All Fall Down. The band announces this signal by playing a series of four "falling," descending notes, each note bent down from the previous one. When the listeners hear this, they are being told to fall down, along with the band. No one is to stand until the music resumes.

Turn, Turn, Turn. A take on the song by the Byrds. When the band plays the melody line to the chorus, the audience is supposed to turn around and pretend that the band is playing at the back of the venue as opposed to the stage. (Phish has pretty much left this trick in the bag since first teaching it to the audience.)

Sing a Random Note. This one is marked by the band playing a circus-like theme, after which participants are to sing a random note. Most audience members generally imitate the high-pitched "lahh" favored by the band.

Ah Fuck! The only part of the language not explained to the audience at the first lesson, this was officially introduced on May 14, 1992. This involves Trey making a muted brushing sound against the strings of his guitar, followed by the music stopping and the entire crowd and band yelling "Ah Fuck!" as Trey lifts his hand to the crowd while holding one finger back, as if the end of it was cut off.

The Rhombus. When Trey was growing up, he and his friends spent time by a rhombus in a field in Princeton, New Jersey. They even returned there on the eve of Tom Marshall's wedding to remember the old times. The rhombus has also become a mysterious part of Phish folklore, and is referenced in several shows, as far back as December 7, 1989.

About six years later, on December 1, 1995, Trey sent phans on a wild goose chase by offering what he termed "the best clue" as to the whereabouts of the Rhombus, insisting that it was in King of Prussia, PA. He even gave directions: "Go to King of Prussia. Go to Wilson street and walk up the hill. When you think you're there, keep going. You'll know when you're there."

Trampolines. If you were lucky enough to see them in your first show, it was probably the thing you walked out remembering most: the trampolines. The original tramps were purchased by Page way back in the eighties. Early on, Trey and Mike hopped on them on many different tunes, including Divided Sky and Runaway Jim. Later on, the bouncing would be limited to YEM and Mike's song. As of the fall of 1995, the trampolines were dropped from Mike's jam.

Mike got another set of trampoline partners during the fall tour of 1994, after Trey fell in a

Phish on HALLOWEEN

Phish's Halloween antics began long before they donned their first musical costume. The tradition began back in the Sculpture Room at Goddard College in 1986, where the band put on one of the few shows from that era for which bootlegs survive.

During two of the Goddard Halloween shows, Phish switched off sets with Burlington contemporaries The Joneses.

"There was this building that wasn't in use anymore because it wasn't engineered approved. But the architectural design of it was intense," remembers Rob Dasaro, the keyboardist for the Joneses. "There were stairways going up to these little cubicles. It was a great place. People would be drinking mushroom tea, or dosing. And we were both there, just playing for hours. It was definitely something that came close to whatever the Dead did in the Bay Area back in their day."

In 1989, Halloween marked Phish's final show at Goddard College, a marathon affair in which the band wore different costumes during each set, including pajamas in the third set, and pulled their first macaroni stunt, leading into "Bowie" as the crowd shook macaroni boxes to the rhythm. The next two years, Phish brought the party to Colorado, where they played Halloween gigs in Colorado Springs both times.

Then came a Halloween hiatus of sorts. The closest thing they came to a Halloween gig in 1992 was an October 30 shared-bill gig at the Boston Garden, and they took the entire fall off in 1993 to record *Hoist*.

But Phish turned the world upside down on October 31, 1994. The anticipation began when the fall newsletter asked fans to send in postcards voting on a "musical costume" for Phish—an album for the band to learn and play in its entirety.

The winner was officially a secret, but most fans had heard it would be The Beatles' *White Album*. And thousands drove to tiny Glens Falls, NY, for the historic gig. Phish did not take the stage

continued

hole and broke his ankle (barely averting a more serious injury). Not to be deterred, the band invite crew member Brad Sands to stand in for Trey on April 11, a flawless performance during YEM. A few days later an audience member tried, resulting in a complete disaster. Brad made one more appearance, and then long-time phan Big Phil took the stage during Mike's on April 18. To close off the trampoline cameo tour, Dave Matthews took turns on back-to-back nights.

Trampoline Guest Appearance:
4/11/94 Brad Sands on YEM
4/14/94 Audience member on YEM
4/16/94 Brad Sands on YEM
4/18/94 Big Phil on Mike's
4/20/94 Dave Matthews on YEM
4/21/94 Dave Matthews on Mike's

The frequency of Secret Language signals has diminished considerably in recent years. While they surfaced regularly in 1992 and 1993, by 1994 they qualified as a special treat, and an absolute rarity thereafter. But it would seem that in the signal's relative absence, their recognition by the audience has only grown.

In the secret laboratories of the Phish.Net, fans have started creating their own signals, like the "Hood!" chant in "Harry Hood," without informing the band beforehand. What started off as a "sociological experiment" has turned into an unstoppable beast. The lab animals have escaped and now may show up, unannounced, at any given moment in any Phish jam. The experiment has won. **—Benjy Eisen**

Benjy Eisen is a roller-coaster engineer and one of the inventors of the "Hood!" chant.

• Fun and Games •

From Chess to Gliders, Phish's concerts have offered more than just music.

Phish shows have always been defined almost as much by the band's onstage antics as by the music. Though the band has cut back on antics in recent years, putting more focus on the music, crowd-participation games and zany tricks remain part of the folklore.

Crowd-Participation Games

Besides the Secret Language, Phish has created several other games that involve the crowd, showing the band's willingness to forge new ties to their audience as venue sizes swelled in recent years.

Big Ball Jam: Officially introduced at St. Mike's College outside of Burlington, VT, on November 19, 1992, the "Big Ball Jam" involves three beach balls—each corresponding to Page, Trey, and Mike—being thrown into the audience. As people bat the balls around, each band member plays when his ball is hit or held by the crowd. In this way, the crowd "jams the band."

The Big Ball Jams usually ended with Trey, Page, and Brad Sands forming a giant hoop at the front of the stage while audience members tried to shoot the balls into the hoop. When the audience scored a basket, giant cheers usually erupted, a phenomenon that can be heard on many concert tapes that include a Big Ball Jam. The big balls haven't been used since the fall tour in 1994, reportedly because of larger venue sizes. Or maybe the band just got bored of the game.

Chess: After years of chess tournaments in the tour bus (several Fishman-McConnell matches were detailed in the *Schvice*) the band challenged the audience to a match during the 1995 fall tour. A giant chessboard hung behind the band starting at Shoreline on September 30, 1995, with the band making a move at the beginning of the show and the audience responding at the start of the second set via a representative selected at the Greenpeace table during setbreak, when the audience chess move decisions were reached.

The band won the first game easily, checkmating the audience, but blew a late lead in the second game. During the show at Lake Placid, NY, on December 17, 1995, the band and audience traded moves throughout the setbreak via walkie-talkies at the Greenpeace table and backstage, but the game was not resolved. It resumed on the New Year's Run, and the band resigned on NewYear's Eve. Investigations continue into whether the band threw the second game to even the score at the end of 1995 at 1 to 1.

Onstage Antics

Even a rookie generally walks into a show knowing about the trampolines and the vacuum cleaner, but here are some more subtle yet equally geeky tricks the band has invented over the years to get a little exercise while on stage.

Acoustic Switcheroo: Used in 1993, Trey would start "The Horse" or "My Friend My Friend" with his electric guitar slung over his back and an acoustic propped up on a stand. He played the first part of the song on the acoustic, then Brad Sands would run out from behind the stage and grab the acoustic from him so Trey could finish the song on his electric guitar.

Creature Freak: Trey and Mike have used BBFCM as an excuse to move around the stage in dramatic and sometimes odd fashions. For parts of 1992, Trey would climb onto Page's monitors. During 1993, Trey and Mike would lie down at the front of the stage or twist their microphone stands into strange shapes.

Going Nowhere Fast: Another 1993 creation, Trey and Mike slide from side to side on a slippery board speed-skating style during "Glide" or the middle segment of "It's Ice."

Guelah Hop: Trey and Mike sway their legs to the music in an awkward dance during "Guelah Papyrus."

Hydrogen Ride: At times in 1992 and 1993, Trey and Mike would lie down at the front of the stage during "I Am Hydrogen," pedaling their feet in the air as though riding a bicycle.

Landlady Shuffle: By far the band's most ambitious foray into busting out the moves, a quick dance to the rapid beat of "Landlady" always gets a rise from the crowd—listen to the tapes from the Roseland Ballroom (February 5, 1993) at which Trey tries to teach the dance to the New York City crowd. This one is alive and well, but Michael Jackson has nothing to fear.

Light Stick Shtick: During an intense jam, Trey will whisper "Topher" into the microphone, a signal to light man Chris "Topher" Karoda to bring the stage lights down. Then, phans begin hurling neon glow sticks into the air, which circulate in a symphony of orange and green until all the sticks litter the stage.

The tradition began in the summer of 1997, marking an emotional highlight of the Great Went.

Megaphone Mayhem: Employed frequently on fall tour 1994 and at times in 1995 and 1996, Trey runs around the stage with his megaphone, pointing it at the audience and whipping the crowd into a frenzy.

Robot Waltz: During "Stash," Trey and Mike walk back and forth on stage in an emotionless walk, facing each other and then turning toward the back of the stage.

Vacuum Freeze: Used in 1992 and a few times in 1993, Page, Trey, and Mike "freeze" in a position, often during a song, while Fish comes forward for a vacuum solo. When Fish returns to his drum set, the song resumes.

Photo courtesy of Jessica Fausty.

• Who's Who in Gamehendge •

It's not always easy to piece together who's who in Gamehendge from the songs Phish scatters throughout its shows. So herewith, The *Pharmer's Almanac* presents character profiles of the main characters in the Gamehendge song cycle. Those wishing to discover the full story of the mythical land of Gamehendge should consult the texts of live versions, or the ultimate Bible, "The Man Who Stepped into Yesterday" recording.

The AC/DC Bag: The electronic robotic hangman of Wilson; has a black bag over its head and wheels in place of feet. Ordered by Wilson to carry out the execution of Mr. Palmer.

Colonel Forbin: A retired American Colonel who, while walking his dog one morning, steps through a mysterious portal and follows a long, narrow passage that leads him to Gamehendge. After meeting Rutherford the Brave upon his arrival in Gamehendge, and soon thereafter the beautiful Tela with whom he falls in love, Forbin decides to help the revolutionaries regain their freedom. He climbs the mountain in search of Icculus, seeking help in defeating Wilson.

Errand Woolfe: The leader of the revolutionaries; the song "Wilson" is sung from his point of view. (The character's name is a play on a childhood friend of Trey's, Aaron Woolfe).

The Famous Mockingbird: A friend of Icculus sent to retrieve the Helping Friendly Book from the tallest tower of Wilson's castle and return it to its rightful owners, the Lizards.

Icculus: The great and knowledgeable prophet of the land who, eons ago, wrote the Helping Friendly Book. According to legend, he lives atop a great mountain, which is sacred ground to the Lizards. For thousands of years, prior to Col. Forbin's climb, no one had sought out Icculus in person.

Kayak Guy: From far north (the land where

more

HALLOWEEN

until just before 10 p.m. (the last of their late-late-night performances) and played into the wee hours of the morning, sandwiching an expertly played *White Album* between two brilliant sets. During the encore, fans paraded on stage for a costume contest, won by "Mounds" candy bar Skip MacFarland.

The next year, the Rosemont Horizon near Chicago played host. Frank Zappa's *Joe's Garage* was the actual winner in the vote (due in part to light voter turnout). But the band chose the number two vote-getter, The Who's *Quadrophenia*. They capped off the show by destroying acoustic equipment on stage.

In 1996, the band decided to select an album entirely on their own, choosing a favorite of all four members, *Remain in Light* by the Talking Heads. (Tom Marshall later joked to phan Dan Gladman that the band considered having fans vote on the album again, until the first vote arrived for Alanis). Each fan at Atlanta's Omni was handed a "Phishbill" on their way in, which included hilarious phony ads (Fishman modeled on behalf of the men's fragrance "Scent of a Fool") and an article about how much *Remain in Light* meant to the band.

the oceans freeze), he arrives in Gamehendge on his kayak and is captured by Wilson. "Punch You in the Eye" is sung from his perspective and shows Wilson's xenophobic side.

Llamas: In the later years of Gamehendge—a part of the legend that has yet to be translated from oral tradition to music—the revolutionaries apparently ride llamas, the better to escape on after triggering blatoplasts (explosive devices).

The Lizards: The peaceful, loving residents of the lush, green fields of Gamehendge. After thousands of years of peace, they are enslaved by Wilson after he steals the Helping Friendly Book, which possesses the knowledge the Lizards need to survive. They aren't the brightest race of people, which has put them close to extinction, and they are oppressed under Wilson's dictatorship.

Multibeasts: Giant mottled, hairy, four-legged creatures used as transport by both Wilson's men and the revolutionaries.

McGrupp: Colonel Forbin's faithful and watchful dog.

Mr. Palmer: Wilson's accountant; helps fund the revolutionaries by stealing funds from Wilson and funneling them to Woolfe and others. When Wilson discovers Palmer's deceit, he orders him assassinated by the AC/DC Bag as a warning to other revolutionaries.

The Possum: Seen by Icculus from his mountain perch, serves as a reminder of the base level of mortal existence.

Rutherford the Brave: A slightly dim-witted knight in shining armor whom Colonel Forbin meets when he steps through the tunnel into Gamehendge. Rutherford, once a member of Wilson's army, works as a secret agent for the revolutionaries.

The Shepherd: Tends his flock by the shores of the Baltic Sea; "McGrupp" and the "Watchful Hosemasters" is sung from his perspective.

The Sloth: The mercenary hit man from the ghetto hired by Errand Woolfe to kill Wilson. The meanest, ugliest guy in all of Gamehendge.

Tela: The beautiful revolutionary whom Colonel Forbin falls in love with, as chronicled in the song "Tela," which is sung from Forbin's perspective. She is a highly placed member of the revolutionaries, but circumstantial evidence points to the fact that she might be a traitor (Trey has termed her a spy in several Gamehendge performances).

Unit Monster: Tela's sidekick; a huge, strong beast who rescues Rutherford from the river after he falls in, as chronicled in "Lizards."

Wilson: Arrives in Gamehendge as a traveler from another country and becomes King of Prussia—Gamehendge's main city—and the land after stealing the Helping Friendly Book from the Lizards and enslaving them. Wilson is universally despised for his tyrannical and unjust leadership, and is apparently unable to still have fun (if he ever was).

Phish on NEW YEAR'S

If you haven't had the privilege of seeing Phish on New Year's Eve, then you'd better practice your mail-ordering technique and start finding transportation to the East Coast. New Year's Eve always promises to be the most impossible ticket of the year, and to this point has never ventured away from the Eastern Seaboard.

The tradition began at the World Trade Center in Boston in 1989. Phish rang in the new decade with Mike, Trey, and Page, all in full tuxedos. When they started singing "I Didn't Know," Fish emerged wearing nothing but a top hat and tails.

Phish returned to the World Trade Center in 1990, and then moved about an hour west to the New Aud in Worcester, MA, in 1991. Close to 4,000 fans made their way into the sold-out theater that night, marking the largest Phish show up to that point. That record was eclipsed in 1992 when Phish filled Northeastern University's Matthews Arena to capacity, the site of their first ever New Year's prank when Brad Sands flew over the stage dressed as the Famous Mockingbird and the band used a special "secret language" created just for the show.

From there, the stunts grew even more elaborate. In 1993, Phish played in a "Phish tank" set. To mark the New Year, they lowered themselves from the ceiling in scuba gear and climbed into a giant clam at the rear of the stage before the clam counted off to midnight and fired confetti into the crowd as giant balloons dropped from above.

Then came 1994 and the most daring feat ever, as they all boarded a giant hot dog—while still playing miniature instruments—and floated through Boston Garden as fans peppered the ship with ping-pong balls tossed out by the band.

The 1995 show stands out not for its comparatively ordinary prank—in which Phish entered the Gamehendge "time lab" and Fish emerged from a floating casket as the Baby New Year—but for being simply one of the most splendid musical performances ever mustered. In surveys conducted by *The Pharmer's Almanac* it easily ranks as the most popular Phish show of all time.

Phish returned to Boston and its new Fleet Center in 1996. Considered one of the less spectacular New Years shows, the gig's prank came in the form of tens of thousands of balloons, which began falling from the ceiling at the stroke of midnight, and didn't stop for most of a marathon "Down with Disease." The real zaniness came when Phish broke into Queen's "Bohemian Rhapsody" and a (barely audible) gospel choir joined the band onstage.

On the heels of their highly successful Fall 1997 tour, Phish set up shop for three holiday shows at New York's Madison Square Garden, including New Year's Eve. On that night, a large inverted dome was hung from the ceiling, and images were projected on it by four video projectors. The graphics corresponded to Trey's Harpua rap from the night before—a story involving a ball with udders, olives and fried eggs. At midnight, the dome opened and hundreds of balloons painted like those images fell to the floor below.

Of course, no one can predict what the future will hold for Phish and New Year's Eve, or what tricks they'll pull from their sleeves. But those looking to predict the pranks get one steady hint: the themes of the pranks are always represented on New Year's T-shirts and mail-order tickets.

Gamehendge LIVE

There was a time when Phish was actively planning to create a Gamehendge CD-ROM. In fact, way back in 1991 they sent a cameraman to a series of shows to record band and fan images for eventual inclusion in the project. But delays turned into introspection and by 1996, the band had decided never to record Gamehendge in any form. The reason? Trey felt that the songs from his original thesis, "The Man Who Stepped into Yesterday," were special because the band had never earned any income from them. He wanted to keep it that way, and vowed to make Gamehendge a commercial-free zone for eternity.

However, Gamehendge does make an occasional appearance onstage in its entirety. Following is a recap of every song through which the band has brought audiences to the magical land of Colonel Forbin, Tela, Rutherford the Brave, and the evil King Wilson.

It's like a baseball pitcher's perfect game, or the landing of a meteorite—a live performance of Gamehendge. You never know when it's going to happen. Only five times in Phishtory has the blessed event occurred, each in a unique setting, sometimes feeling planned, other times spontaneous. A recap:

3/12/88 Nectar's, Burlington, VT

This historical event can best be visualized through the eyes of an ancient black and white reel-to-reel projector. Those who attended were not the Gamehendge-craving folks we know today. But the audience seemed quite receptive as they interacted with "yeahs" and "boos" as Trey spoke of both the good and bad characters of his tale. As "Mockingbird" ends, Trey notes that Nectar's has emptied out, saying they'll continue "for those of you who are still here."

10/13/91 Surf Club, Olympia, WA

The beautiful and pristine surroundings seemed to play a huge part in Trey's decision to play Gamehendge. After opening the first set with "Wilson," they went into "Reba" and "Landlady," apparently harboring no intention of stepping into yesterday. But then something just gave. Like the original live performance, much of the crowd had yet to be exposed to such a thing. But Trey proudly acknowledged the diehards who were well aware of what was going on.

3/22/93 Crest Theater, Sacramento, CA

This second set begins like any other, but as we get to the middle part of "It's Ice," Trey tells the audience that they are the most quiet and receptive group he's seen in years. One can never be sure, but it seems Trey made the decision to do Gamehendge right then onstage. He effectively uses the Ice imagery to take us into the land of the Lizards. Trey's narration flows more smoothly and he jokes around less. Gamehendge is now serious business.

6/26/94 Municipal Theater, Charleston, WV

It's fairly obvious that Phish planned to do Gamehendge on this particular evening prior to hitting the stage. The "Kung Chant" served as the set opener and acted as a vehicle to bring the crowd to Gamehendge. This Gamehendge is capped off by "Divided Sky," an important cousin of the Gamehendge family. The second set was a complete rendition of *Hoist*. Gamehendge vs. *Hoist*, hmmm, tough choice.

7/8/94 Great Woods, Mansfield, MA

Perhaps the boys felt bad that each previous Gamehendge was in such an out-of-the-way place. The Great Woods Gamehendge served as a giant thank you to the New England fans who were the first to embrace the band. Coming only weeks after the GameHoist show, some thought Gamehendge might become a semi-regular part of Phish's repertoire. Not so.

For all the rumors of "Gamehendge in London!" and "Gamehendge at Clifford Ball!" the saga as a whole remains, for now, safely stored in another time.

2

Musical Conspirators

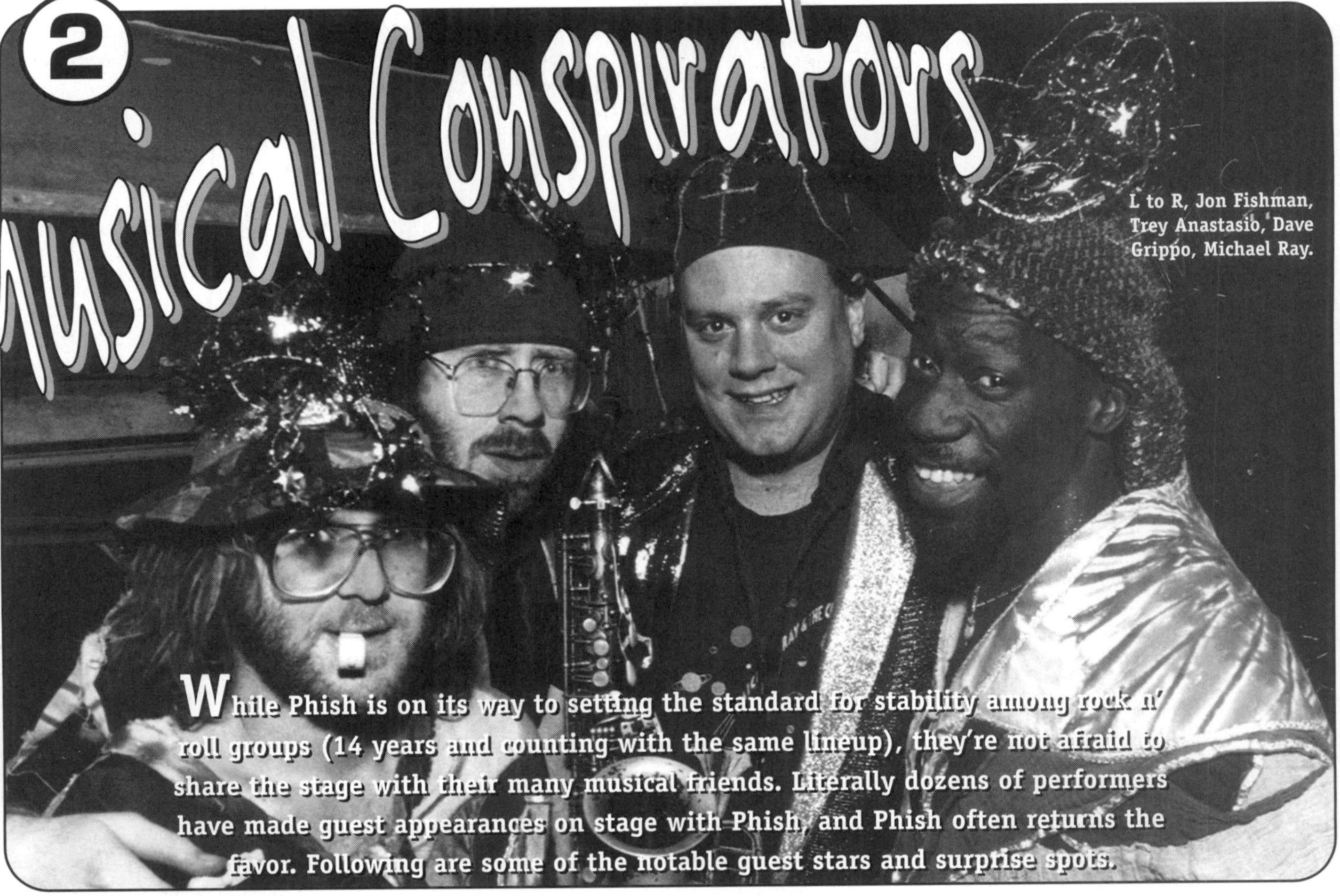

L to R, Jon Fishman, Trey Anastasio, Dave Grippo, Michael Ray.

Photo by Jeff Clarke/courtesy of Michael Ray & Rhythm and Muse

While Phish is on its way to setting the standard for stability among rock n' roll groups (14 years and counting with the same lineup), they're not afraid to share the stage with their many musical friends. Literally dozens of performers have made guest appearances on stage with Phish, and Phish often returns the favor. Following are some of the notable guest stars and surprise spots.

MUSICAL CONSPIRATORS

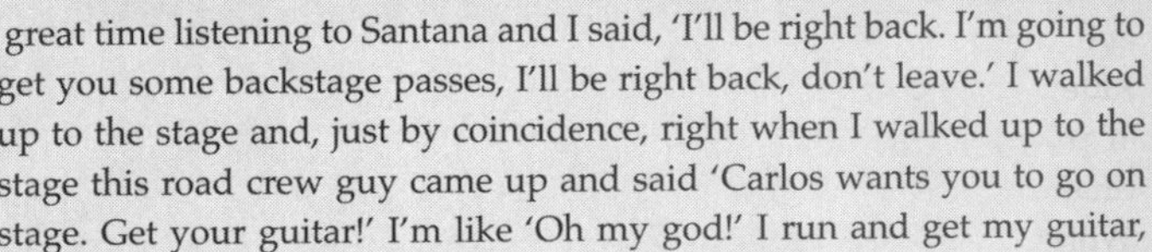

Phish and Santana

There's only one artist Phish has ever served as an opening act for on an extended basis: Santana, who they supported during the summer of 1992 and again in Europe in the summer of 1996. Carlos Santana has long been an inspiration for Phish, and they frequently reference his belief that all music already exists in the universe and the musician is merely a funnel, a conduit, to bring the sound into this dimension.

Admiration turned into lifelong friendship during the summer of 1992, when Santana not only offered Phish the largest audiences they'd ever played in front of, but also invited Phish band members on stage to jam with him almost on a nightly basis.

Carlos' guest spot with Phish, on July 25, 1992 at Stowe, has become legendary, and recordings of that show are some of the heaviest circulated Phish tapes. But what many do not realize is that Phish also popped up on stage during practically every Santana performance that summer.

Trey remembers the story of how he first received an unexpected invite to join the legendary guitarist on stage: "I didn't know it was going to happen until, like, five minutes before it happened. It was all coincidence," he told William Bengle of the University of Delaware student newspaper in a radio interview in 1994. "I was out in the crowd with some friends of mine, who I hadn't seen since high school. We were hanging out, partying, having a great time listening to Santana and I said, 'I'll be right back. I'm going to get you some backstage passes, I'll be right back, don't leave.' I walked up to the stage and, just by coincidence, right when I walked up to the stage this road crew guy came up and said 'Carlos wants you to go on stage. Get your guitar!' I'm like 'Oh my god!' I run and get my guitar, went out on stage and did that whole thing. Then I got offstage and grabbed a couple of backstage passes and ran back out. When I got up to [my friends] I said, 'Did I miss anything?'"

It was that night, at the Garden State Arts Center, that Carlos coined the phrase "The Hose" to describe the Phish concert experience. "He had said something to me before we'd walked off stage," Trey shared with Bengle. "[Carlos] was standing in the wings and said, 'I really like your band! When I listen to your band I picture the crowd as a sea of flowers, the music is the water and you guys are the hose.' That was the night he said that."

Following that summer's tour, Trey visited Carlos at his home in the San Francisco Bay Area. Early one morning, Carlos woke Trey from a sound sleep to—of all things—help take out the garbage. As Trey dragged himself to the alley, Carlos told Trey that he was about to become a big star, but he should never forget the kind of person he is, never put himself above anyone else, and always take out his own trash. It was a lesson Trey never forgot.

Special thanks to A.J. Fucile's research for this section.

Tom Marshall

Trey's friend (and eventual full-time lyricist) Tom Marshall first sang with Phish in a basement back in the 1980s. While Trey was jamming out to a new song he'd written called "Run Like an Antelope," he excitedly commanded Tom to "say something" into the microphone. What came out was something sort of like "Rye, Rye, roccco. . . ." He then looked over at their friend Marc Daubert and shouted, "Marco Escuandoles!"

About a decade later, on New Year's Eve in 1993, Trey invited Tom onstage to sing "the first lyric he ever wrote." It began a New Year's tradition of sorts. He made a return appearance on "Antelope" next year. Then, in 1995, Marshall bellowed the Collective Soul song "Shine" during "Col. Forbin's Ascent."

Things changed around again in 1996 as Marshall, who works as a computer programmer in Princeton, NJ, when not writing Phish lyrics, stayed close to home and only made it to the Philadelphia shows that preceded New Year's. His surprise appearance came on December 29 when he sang another pop classic, Oasis's "Champagne Supernova."

Marshall made his stage appearance in 1997 at the epic 12/30 show. It began with a long monologue by Trey in the middle of "Harpua," when he told a convoluted tale involving television, various food items, and a pentagonal triangle. Then the story came to a part where Trey, who was in the fourth grade when the story took place, saw his future: It included images of Page, Mike, and Fish, whom he did not recognize, and the grown up Tom Marshall. At that point, Tom appeared from a cloud of smoke and began singing the Proclaimers' song "500 Miles," complete with an Irish accent.

Before there was Phish, there was a band called Space Antelope, and before there was Space Antelope, there was a curly-haired wild man by the name of Steve Pollak, otherwise know as the Dude of Life.

Steve and Trey first met while students at the Taft School in Watertown, CT, and Steve came up with the name Space Antelope for the band Trey had formed with lead guitarist Rob Gordon (Trey handled rhythms; he was just a beginner at the time), bassist Doug Taft, and drummer Doug Parsons. Steve would make special "Dude" appearances at certain points during each performance.

While Space Antelope was short-lived, they managed to gain a sort of cold following at their small New England prep school. Their semi-original song "Fire at the Taft School" was among the crowd favorites. Their greatest achievement came in the form of a full performance of Pink Floyd's *Animals*, played flawlessly during rehearsal but botched in front of a crowd.

Rob "Flash" Gordon went on to become an accomplished guitarist and perform with several successful alternative bands in Seattle, while Trey and the Dude scampered off to the University of Vermont.

When Trey formed a then-unnamed band with Jeff Holdsworth, Jon Fishman, and Mike Gordon, Steve was on hand at their first-ever gig at an ROTC formal. He was also a fixture at the few gigs which followed in the fall of 1983, but Trey and the Dude were then more partners in crime than in music, when they fessed up to being the culprits behind a human hand and heart somehow making their way to Colorado. They were suspended for a semester.

Upon their return, Trey's band reformed, and dubbed themselves Phish. Although "Lacking a playlist long enough to fill three sets," according to *A Picture of Nectar*'s liner notes, they were offered a gig at the upstairs room of the bar and music club called Nectar's. And the Dude was there.

Lending his vocal talents to the since-retired "Skippy the Wondermouse" and "Fluffhead," two songs for which he wrote the lyrics, Steve appeared behind the microphone in what is the oldest recorded Phish gig.

He left UVM not long after that, but was still a frequent onstage collaborator of the band. One summer, he showed up in Burlington with a pair of new songs he'd written, "Sanity" and "Suzie Greenberg."

"Suzie Greenberg" was about a real person he'd met in a film class while attending college in Purchase, NY. "I had a crush on her and we got together very quickly but we were only together for a month. We had a lot of good times in that month, but then after that, I was totally in love with her but then she broke up with me at that time and I was kind of heartbroken. It was during that time that I wrote the song."

The Dude of Life tied the knot with the Wife of Life, Kathy, on September 30, 1990. Phish performed at the wedding, one of two matrimonials for which Phish served as the house band.

A year later, Steve's collaborations with Phish took another turn when they served as his backup band for an album of Steve Pollak's original songs. *Crimes of the Mind* was finally released by Phish's record company, Elektra, in 1994.

He would go on to perform the album's title song during five different Phish performances. Six other Dude originals were performed with Phish, including the song "Self," which has appeared four times.

His most acclaimed performance may have been the New Year's Eve cameo in 1992, when he belted out Traffic's "Diamond Girl" while wearing one of his trademark silly outfits.

Just over a year later, in the wake of the Elektra rerelease, Steve hit the road for a series of Northeast gigs with Jon Fishman on drums and Dan Archer (who owns the studio where *Crimes* and *Lawnboy* were recorded) on guitar. Trey also made a guest appearance with the band. Later, the Dude would appear on the small stage at HORDE festivals with former members of the Burlington band Shockra.

His last performance with Phish came on July 10, 1994, at Saratoga Springs. Since then, Steve (whose lyric credits also include "Dinner and a Movie" and "Slave to the Traffic Light") has written a bevy of new tunes, and can now be heard performing them with backup band Great Red Shark. Trey helped him record some new tracks for a forthcoming album.

On December 13, 1997, in Albany, Phish seemed to be calling the Dude out on stage during a spacey Mike's Groove, but Steve, who was in attendence, did not make an appearance.

Two weeks later following Phish's epic December 30 show at New York's Madison Square Garden, Fishman played drums during the latter half of a Dude show at the small New York club Downtime.

The Dude of Life means many things to many Phish fans. To some, he represents the zanier, unpredictable side of the band. To others, he represents an easy target of derision, as the same sort of online pundits who critique every facet of Phish performances have never been kind to the Dude. But to anyone who has seen him perform with his new band, he is a talented musician and a creative lyricist, who has given Phish and music fans a whole new set of choices.

And remember, Let the Dude Sing!

The Dude of Life, fully costumed, gets down with Trey.

Photo courtesy of the Dude of Life.

Dude of Life Appearances with Phish

12/1/84— Sings on "Fluffhead" and "Skippy the Wondermouse."

9/13/90 Wetlands—The Dude of Life sings his songs "I Don't Care," "Dahlia," and "The Revolution's Over."

5/12/91 The Front—David Gavidpor on "Magilla," "AC/DC Bag," and "Rocky Top." The Dude of Life sings on "Mike's Song."

8/3/91 Auburn, ME—The Dude of Life sings on "YEM," "I Dont Care," "She's Bitching Again," and "Crimes of the Mind." Sofi Dillof sings on "She's Bitching" and "Crimes."

11/8/91 Tuscaloosa, AL—The Dude of Life sings "I Don't Care," "Life Is a TV Show," "Family Picture," and "Crimes of the Mind."

11/20/92 Albany, NY—The Dude of Life sings "I Don't Care."

12/31/92 Boston, MA—The Dude of Life sings "Diamond Girl."

5/5/93 Albany, NY—Col. Bruce and ARU plays on the jam out of "YEM." The Dude of Life also adds some vocals on the jam.

8/9/93 Toronto, ON—The Dude of Life sings on "Crimes of the Mind."

8/28/93 Berkeley, CA—The Dude of Life sings on "Crimes of the Mind."

7/10/94 Saratoga Springs, NY—The Dude of Life sings "Crimes of the Mind."

To find out more about the Dude of Life, call (212) 501-0584, or check out the Dude's Web site at www.dudeoflife.com.

Burlington Friends

DURING THE EARLY YEARS, many of the band's friends and peers took a turn on stage with Phish. All the way back on December 1, 1984, at Phish's first gig, the Dude of Life was there to take over vocals on "Skippy the Wondermouse" and "Fluffhead," while Trey's boyhood pal Marc Daubert added percussion. The Dude and Daubert would both be frequent on-stage guests through the early years.

As Phish became better known in Burlington, more locals began popping up in their sets. Members of the reggae group Lamb's Bread were known to join Phish for tunes like "Fire Up the Ganja" and "Scarlet Begonias." The Joneses, a Grateful Dead–oriented band Phish often shared the bill with, joined Phish on stage on April 1, 1986 to perform "Not Fade Away." During the previous summer, while Trey was out of town, members of The Joneses and Phish formed a hybrid group under the name The Phoneses, and relived the combination again on Halloween in 1987 and 1988.

Another Burlington musician who can be heard on early Phish tapes is Jah Roy, who frequently invited himself up to add a little reggae rap to the Phish sound (October 31, 1986, May 25, 1988, June 20, 1988). "Ninja Mike" Billington, of the Ninja Custodian, also used to make cameo appearances (March 26, 1987, May 29, 1989).

Phish friends Tim Rogers, Tom Baggott, Pete Danforth, and Nancy Taube also had their turn on the stage from time to time.

WHETHER YOU PREFER Phish with horns or without, there's no doubt that catching a Phish show with The Giant Country Horns is a special treat, and almost always a surprise.

The roots of GCH can be traced back to the 1980s when they first met local saxaphone player Dave "The Truth" Grippo.

"The first time I saw Trey play was at a jazz festival in Burlington, and he really impressed me because he could play jazz pretty well and there aren't too many jazz guitarists in Burlington," remembers Grippo. "He was a young kid at the time, the new kid on the block, and I was really impressed by his band. He used to come with Phish to see the Sneakers Jazz Band at a club called Sneakers in Winooski, VT. The Sneakers Jazz Band was a seven-piece jazz group which had a three-piece horns section, which later became members of the Giant Country Horns, along with some other key people."

Horns

Phish actually formed a jazz outfit of their own, playing at Sneakers under the name The Johnny B. Fishman Jazz Ensemble. And as early as November 11, 1988, Phish began toying with incorporating horns into their regular shows. On November 11, future Giant Country Horns members Russ Remington and Carl "Gears" Gerhard sat in on several tunes including "Timber Ho."

But it was not until recording *Lawn Boy* close to a year later that the Phish with horns combination really began to take hold. Grippo, Gerhard, and Remington all went into the studio to perfrom "Split Open and Melt." The new team made its first performance on stage at The Front on October 20.

Phish didn't have a horn relapse until close to two years later. Gerhard performed several times with the band during winter and spring of 1991, and then they got the idea for a 17-day Phish with Horns tour, which included a legendary stop at Arrowhead Ranch. The Giant Country Horns, as we know them today, were born.

"I was pretty much a jazz and R&B player and hadn't had much experience with their style of music before, so it was a great experience," says Grippo. "And the tour was right before they got really big. When we toured with them, the horns section traveled in Fishman's Caravan, which was a risk to say the least. The car overheated many a time, and I remember having to drive with the heat on in 100-degree weather just to cool the engine and keep it from overheating. That part of it wasn't so pleasurable, but the music was always great and meeting people across the country, I always enjoy that."

Since then, appearances by Grippo and the horns have come roughly once a year, the last (as of this printing) on March 18, 1997 in Burlington. The previous Halloween, Grippo and trumpeter Gary Gazaway played backup for Phish's rendition of Talking Heads' *Remain in Light* album. Grippo also played with Phish the Halloween before during the band's rendition of The Who's *Quadrophenia*, along with Don Glasgo on trombone, Joe Sommerville on trumpet, and Alan Parshley on french horn.

Over the years, The Giant Country Horns has included many faces. Sun Ra veteran Michael Ray (his band the Cosmic Krewe also incorporates Grippo and bassist Stacey Starkweather, another Phish collaborator) played trumpet as part of GCH at a pair of California gigs in December of 1994. Peter Apfelbaum and James Harvey were also part of that lineup.

While relatively few Phish tunes have been played with horns, it seems that the band has tried every different type of song with horn accompaniment. From epic jams like "Mike's Song" or "YEM" or "Slave," to quick-hitters like "Cavern," they've found a way to give it a whirl with GCH. Several songs, however, are really known as horn favorites. "Suzie Greenberg" is probably the tune most frequently performed with GCH, although the horn section seemed to lay back a bit on their most recent rendition on Halloween in 1996. "Gumbo" is another horn favorite.

Fans wanting to get the best taste of Phish with horns should look for tapes from the July 21, 1991 Arrowhead show. It ranks as one of the best circulated and most popular tapes of all time.

Phish Appearances With Horns

11/11/88 Newmarket, NH—Carl Gerhard and Russ Remmington appeared on various tunes.

10/20/89 Burlington, VT—Russ Remmington and Dave Grippo on horns for most of the second set.

3/9/90 Burlington, VT—Dave Grippo on sax for "Caravan," "Ya Mar," and "Donna Lee."

2/8/91 Portsmouth, NH—Carl Gerhard on trumpet for "Landlady" and "La Grange."

5/17/91 Providence, RI—Carl Gerhard on trumpet on "A-Train," "Magilla," "Cavern," and "Lawn Boy."

Summer 1991 Giant Country Horns appearances: 7/11/91, 7/12/91, 7/13/91, 7/14/91, 7/15/91, 7/18/91, 7/19/91, 7/20/91, 7/21/91, 7/23/91, 7/24/91, 7/25/91, 7/26/91, 7/27/91
line-up:
Dave Grippo, alto sax
Russ Remmington, tenor sax
Carl Gerhard, trumpet

9/25/91 Keene, NH—Carl Gerhard on trumpet on "Cavern" and "Jesus Left Chicago."

11/20/91 Providence, RI—Carl Gerhard on trumpet on "Magilla" and "Brother."

11/23/91 Barre, VT—Dave Grippo on sax on "Jesus Left Chicago" and "BBFCFM."

3/24/92 Richmond, VA—Carl Gerhard on trumpet on "Brother" and "Cavern."

3/3/93 New Orleans, LA—Carl Gerhard on trumpet on "Lawn Boy" and "Cavern."

4/4/94 Burlington, VT—Six-piece GCH: Carl Gerhard on trumpet, Dave Grippo on alto sax, Chris Peterman on tenor sax, Mike Hewitt on baritone sax, Don Glasgow on trombone, and Joey Sommerville Jr. on trumpet. The GCH played the entire second set after and including "Buried Alive," excluding "Oh Kee Pah." "Cavern" featured Carl Gerhard on trumpet.

4/15/94 New York, NY—GCH, with same lineup as 4/4/94, played the entire second set after and including "Suzie Greenburg" as well as on the "Magilla" encore.

5/4/94 New Orleans, LA—The Cosmic Country Horns (Carl Gerhard on trumpet, Michael Ray on trumpet, Tony Tate on tenor sax, Dave Grippo on alto sax, Jerome Theriot on baritone sax, and Rick Trolsen on trombone) played on "YEM," "Landlady," "Julius," "Wolfman's Brother," "Magilla," "Suzie Greenburg," and "Caravan."

10/14/94 New Orleans, LA—Michael Ray and Carl Gerhard played trumpet on "Nellie Cane," "Beaumont Rag," and "Foreplay/Longtime."

12/2/94 Davis, CA—The Giant Country Horns (Dave Grippo on alto sax, Carl Gerhard on trumpet, Michael Ray on trumpet, Peter Apflebaum on baritone and tenor sax, and James Hardy on trombone) played the entire second set starting with "David Bowie."

12/3/94 San Jose, CA—The Giant Country Horns (same lineup as the night before) played the entire second set.

10/31/95 Chicago, IL—On the second set, The Who's *Quadrophenia*, a horn section (featuring Dave Grippo on sax, Don Glasgo on trombone, Joey Sommerville Jr. on trumpet, and Alan Parshley on french horn) joined the band. Dave Grippo also played on "Jesus Left Chicago" in the third set, and was joined by Don Glasgo and Joey Sommerville, Jr. on "Suzie Greenburg."

4/26/96 New Orleans, LA—Michael Ray played trumpet on "Cars Trucks Buses."

11/18/96 Memphis, TN—Gary Gazaway played trumpet on "Tweezer," "Hello My Baby," "Tweezer Reprise," "Llama," and "Johnny B. Goode."

3/18/97 Burlington, VT—Dave Grippo and James Harvey played on "Cars Trucks Buses," "Suzy Greenburg," "Character Zero," and "Funky Bitch." Tammy Fletcher of the Disciples sang on "Reconsider Baby" and "Love Me Like a Man."

Jamie Janover

An occasionally overlooked guest performer is didgeridoo and hammer dulcimer master Jamie Janover. He met the band in 1991 after standing in the front row at shows for about two years, watching Fishman closely (Janover is also a drummer). He then told Fishman about the didgeridoo, a now-popular aboriginal instrument which none of the band members had heard of at the time.

Fish told Janover to bring it to a show sometime, which he did at the Chance on May 2, 1991. Upon hearing the instrument's enticing springy sound backstage, Trey immediately decided to have Janover play onstage during "Famous Mockingbird" that night. He also deemed it appropriate that Janover wear Fishman's dress (at the time, Fish and Trey were the only mortals ever to wear it) and sling his ponytail over his face.

Although the performance is barely audible on tape because the microphones had not been set up to handle the didgeridoo's unique low-end tone, Janover made his debut that night, to the surprise of his friends in the audience.

That summer, Janover made another appearance, this time playing "Buried Alive" at the famed Amy's Farm show. Again, the microphones had trouble picking up the sound.

"I think I blew out Mike's monitor," Janover remembers. "On the tape it's really distorted. It was hard because it was cued for Mike's vocals and here I come with this low-end, giant sound."

A respected hammer dulcimer player, Janover made a solo appearance between sets of the Phish show in Springfield 12/30/92. "That was the best," he says. "I was on the side of the stage and Trey says, 'Now our friend Jamie Janover is going to play some hammer dulcimer for you.' It was a 2,600-person show, one of the biggest of the time."

Janover has since recorded with Phish friends the Jazz Mandolin Project and continues to compose his own material.

John Popper

Blues Traveler and its front man John Popper may have lost some credibility among Phish fans when they became MTV sensations back in 1994, but you have to give the big guy some credit. He has never stopped declaring Phish to be the greatest band in the world (on an MTV talk show once, various guests were asked what other musicians excited them. Popper immediately answered Phish, saying they were "like Mozart." A writer for *Spin* then said "I still like Madonna," and the conversation never came back to Phish.)

Popper is also a favorite guest star of the band. His earliest cameo on record came on December 15, 1989, when the bands shared a double bill at the Ukrainian National Home in New York, and Popper played harmonica for "Jesus Left Chicago" and "Funky Bitch."

Popper would make a grand total of ten more surprise appearances through 1997. In fact, he and Trey would pen a song together called "Don't Get Me Wrong." Lifting music from an abandoned section of "Reba," "Don't Get Me Wrong" was performed by Phish and Popper on October 6 and 8, 1990, and then again on December 28, 1990. After 1990, his appearances came less frequently ("Don't Get Me Wrong" was never played again).

Popper's appearance on March 14, 1992 in New York ranks as a musical highlight of his cameos, as he wailed on harmonica for "Sleeping Monkey" and "Good Times, Bad Times." On February 6 of the following year, he shared the stage with not only Phish, but Noel Redding, the bass player for The Jimi Henrix Experience. They jammed out on "Fire." Popper last appeared with Phish in St. Louis for the famous "Letter M Show" on November 15, 1996. He played harmonica on "Weekapaug Groove" and "Funky Bitch."

The Family

If you ever have trouble selling your family on Phish, just tell them that every Phish parent has a laminate that allows them unfettered access to Phish concerts and backstage, and the 'rents often come up on stage to make guest appearances.

Every member of the band has had a family member join them on stage at one time or another. It all began on October 29, 1989, when Trey's mother, Diane Anastasio, joined Phish to sing "No Dogs Allowed," a relic of a musical the Anastasio family had written together. Trey also danced with his grandmother onstage at Portchester, NY, for "Contact" ("her favorite song") on November 28, 1992.

Page McConnell's father, Jack, the most musically accomplished of the Phish progenitors, first joined his son on stage on July 28, 1993, in Charlotte, NC. They sat together at the piano to perform a tune dubbed by tapers as "Father/Son Boogie" along with the standard "Bill Bailey." Dr. McConnell rose to the front of the stage to bellow out the "Bill Bailey vocals." He would make repeat appearances on April 22, 1994 and November 18, 1995.

Mike's grandmother walked across the stage at Boston Garden waving a shoe during "Chalkdust Torture" on December 31, 1994. She died less than a month later, and Mike wrote a poignant piece in the *Schvice* talking about how she equated her on-stage appearance to her wedding night.

And then of course, there's Mimi Fishman. Although she now seems to pop up more at moe. shows than at Phish, she occasionally has shown off her own vaccuum cleaner skill next to her son. Her debut came on July 19, 1991 at the Sommerville Theater near Boston, when she played the Electrolux on "I Didn't Know." In all, Mimi has made eight appearances with the band, the most recent being April 8, 1994. Songs she has played on include "Terrapin," "Lengthwise" (twice), "Purple Rain," "Whipping Post," and "I Didn't Know" (three times).

Names YOU Know

WHAT'S BETTER THAN seeing Phish? Seeing Phish with another musician whom, on any other night, you also would have paid money to see. Phish has treated their fans to many cameo appearances by musicians that their fans have always enjoyed. Bands like Aquarium Rescue Unit, Bela Fleck and the Flecktones, The Dave Matthews Band, Medeski, Martin & Wood, and the Allman Brothers have all seen their members find their way into Phish concerts. ARU's first guest appearance on record came on November 7, 1991 in New Orleans. Col. Bruce or other members of ARU could also be heard in shows from February 19, 1993, May 5, 1993, April 23, 1994, May 2, 1994, and November 28, 1995. (Col. Bruce just sat on stage while Fishman sang "Wind Beneath My Wings.") Bela Fleck made his first appearance with Phish in Salt Lake City on August, 21, 1993. Others followed on October 18, 1994, November 29, 1995, and in Europe on July 9, 1997.

Before they were a mega-popular radio hit, The Dave Matthews Band were known as Phish prodigies of sorts. They opened up several shows for Phish back in the spring of 1994, and they first appeared with the band on April 20, 1994 of that year when Matthews did the "YEM" trampoline routine for Trey. They played again with Phish the following night. Other surprise appearances by Dave Matthews or members of his band include October 15, 1994, June 16, 1995, June 17, 1995, and July 21, 1997.

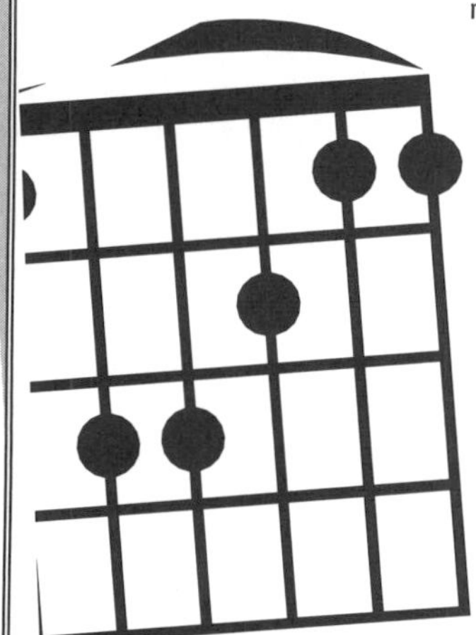

Medeski, Martin & Wood, who also opened for Phish at select shows, appeared with the band in Texas on October 14 and 17, 1995.

Old Jerry Garcia pal Merle Saunders has made it on stage with Phish, first on April 23, 1994 in Atlanta, and appearing again with Buddy Miles in New York on October 22, 1996. Butch Trucks was the first member of the Allman Brothers Band to appear with Phish, playing drums while Jimmy Buffet took lead vocals on "Brown Eyed Girl" on November 16, 1995. Warren Haynes played guitar on "Funky Bitch" and "While My Guitar Gently Weeps" in Portland, ME, on December 12.

Of another genre entirely, Les Claypool of Primus played bass on "YEM" at Laguna Seca Daze on May 28, 1994. He and bandmate Larry LaLonde would make a return appearance on December 6, 1996 in the famous Las Vegas show, which also featured Elvis impersonators and yodelers.

Now just to clear things up, Gene Simmons of KISS never did appear with Phish, although the band did acknowledge someone—audience member Jay Von Lehe—dressed up as Simmons during the Atlanta show on February 20, 1993.

Do you want a totally weird celebrity appearance? Take comedian Steven Wright playing the triangle during "Scent of a Mule" in Boston on December 30, 1996. A few weeks before, Wright had appeared on the Conan O'Brien Show and, when asked if he was promoting an album, held up a copy of *Billy Breathes*.

Bluegrass

MIKE GORDON'S INTEREST in bluegrass almost predates his association with Phish. In fact, he played in a bluegrass trio several times during his early days at UVM, alongside Jamie Masefield. Phish has played many bluegrass songs on their own, and the band seems to add a new one to their repertoire almost every year. But they've also gotten a few hints from many of the best bluegrass musicians in the world, who have joined Phish on stage.

On February 21, 1993, the Rev. Jeff Mosier played banjo with Phish on "Good Times, Bad Times," "Paul and Silas," and "Pig in a Pen." Later, Mosier would join Phish for a sort of mini bluegrass tour, which began on November 16, 1994 in Ann Arbor, MI, and spanned five shows, winding down in Madison, WI on November 20, 1994. Mosier appeared on about three or four songs per show.

Other bluegrass performers to take the stage with Phish include Dick Solberg (The Sun Mountain Fiddler), who played on "Lawn Boy," "Why You Been Gone So Long," "Tennessee Waltz," and "Fast Train" in Albany, NY, on May 6, 1993 (Jeff Walton played acoustic guitar during those tunes); good friend Gordon Stone, who appeared with Phish on November 19, 1992 at St. Michael's College in Vermont and at Stowe, VT. on July 22 of the next year; Steve Cooley, who played banjo on "My Old Home Place," "Ginseng Sullivan," and "Nellie Cane" on October 10, 1994 in Louisville, KY; Tim O'Brien, who played mandolin, acoustic guitar, and sang on "99 Years," "Ode to a Dream," and "Doin' My Time" at Red Rocks on August, 7, 1996; and John McEuen, who played on several tunes (along with Peter Apflebaum on tenor sax) on November 30, 1996, in Sacramento, CA.

Burlington Musicians Family Tree

Phish is sort of like a 1970s-style open marriage: They stay together forever, but they're allowed to get some variety on the side. Phish band members have participated in a variety of side projects over the years, and helped make celebrities of many of the ultratalented Burlington-area musicians with whom they've teamed up. Here is a look at the incestuous lot known as the Burlington Music Scene.

Blackwood Convention 1983

TREY ANASTASIO GUITAR · J. HOLDSWORTH GUITAR · MIKE GORDON BASS · JON FISHMAN DRUMS

Phish 1984

TREY ANASTASIO GUITAR · J. HOLDSWORTH GUITAR · JON FISHMAN DRUMS · MIKE GORDON BASS · MARC DAUBERT PRECUSSION · STEVE POLLAK VOCALS

Bluegrass Trio 1985

MIKE GORDON BASS · JAMIE MASEFIELD MANDOLIN · BRUCE CAITLIN GUITAR

Phish 1985

TREY ANASTASIO GUITAR · JON FISHMAN DRUMS · MIKE GORDON BASS · PAGE MCCONNELL KEYBOARDS · J. HOLDSWORTH GUITAR

Phish 1986-

TREY ANASTASIO GUITAR · JON FISHMAN DRUMS · MIKE GORDON BASS · PAGE MCCONNELL KEYBOARDS

Phish & The Giant Country Horns Summer 1991

CARL GERHARD TRUMPET · DAVE GRIPPO SAX · JON FISHMAN DRUMS · PAGE MCCONNELL KEYBOARDS · TREY ANASTASIO GUITAR · MIKE GORDON BASS · RUSS REMINGTON SAX

Jazz Trio (6-8-93, 9-10-93)

TREY ANASTASIO GUITAR · JAMIE MASEFIELD MANDOLIN · MIKE GORDON BASS

Jazz Combo (7-9-93, 9-3-93)

MIKE GORDON BASS · TREY ANASTASIO GUITAR · JAMIE MASEFIELD MANDOLIN · NOEL SAGERMAN DRUMS

Phish & G.C.H. 4-4-94, 4-15-94

TREY ANASTASIO GUITAR · MIKE GORDON BASS · JON FISHMAN DRUMS · PAGE MCCONNELL KEYBOARDS · CARL GERHARD TRUMPET · DAVE GRIPPO SAX · CHRIS PETERMAN SAX · MIKE HEWITT SAX · DON GLASCO TROMBONE · JOE SOMERVILLE TRUMPET

Phish & The Cosmic Country Horns 5-4-94

TREY ANASTASIO GUITAR · MIKE GORDON BASS · JON FISHMAN DRUMS · PAGE MCCONNELL KEYBOARDS · CARL GERHARD TRUMPET · DAVE GRIPPO SAX · MICHAEL RAY TRUMPET · TONY TATE SAX · RICK THERIOT SAX · RICK TROLSEN TROMBONE

Phish & G.C.H.12-2-94, 12-3-94

P. APFLEBAUM SAX · DAVE GRIPPO SAX · CARL GERHARD TRUMPET · PAGE MCCONNELL KEYBOARDS · MIKE GORDON BASS · JON FISHMAN DRUMS · TREY ANASTASIO GUITAR · JAMES HARVEY TROMBONE · MICHAEL RAY TRUMPET

Phish performs *Quadrophenia* 10-31-95

TREY ANASTASIO GUITAR · MIKE GORDON BASS · JON FISHMAN DRUMS · PAGE MCCONNELL KEYBOARDS · DAVE GRIPPO SAX · CARL GERHARD TRUMPET · ALAON PARSHLEY FRENCH HORN · JOE SOMERVILLE TRUMPET

Phish performs *Remain In Light* 10-31-96

TREY ANASTASIO GUITAR · MIKE GORDON BASS · JON FISHMAN DRUMS · PAGE MCCONNELL KEYBOARDS · DAVE GRIPPO SAXR · GARY GAZAWAY TRUMPET · KARL PERRAZO PRECUSSION

Phish

TREY ANASTASIO GUITAR · JON FISHMAN DRUMS · MIKE GORDON BASS · PAGE MCCONNELL KEYBOARDS

Option Anxiety 1997-

DAVE GRIPPO SAX · JAMES HARVEY TROMBONE · S. STARKWEATHER BASS · DAVE ELLIS TRUMPET · GABE JARRETT DRUMS

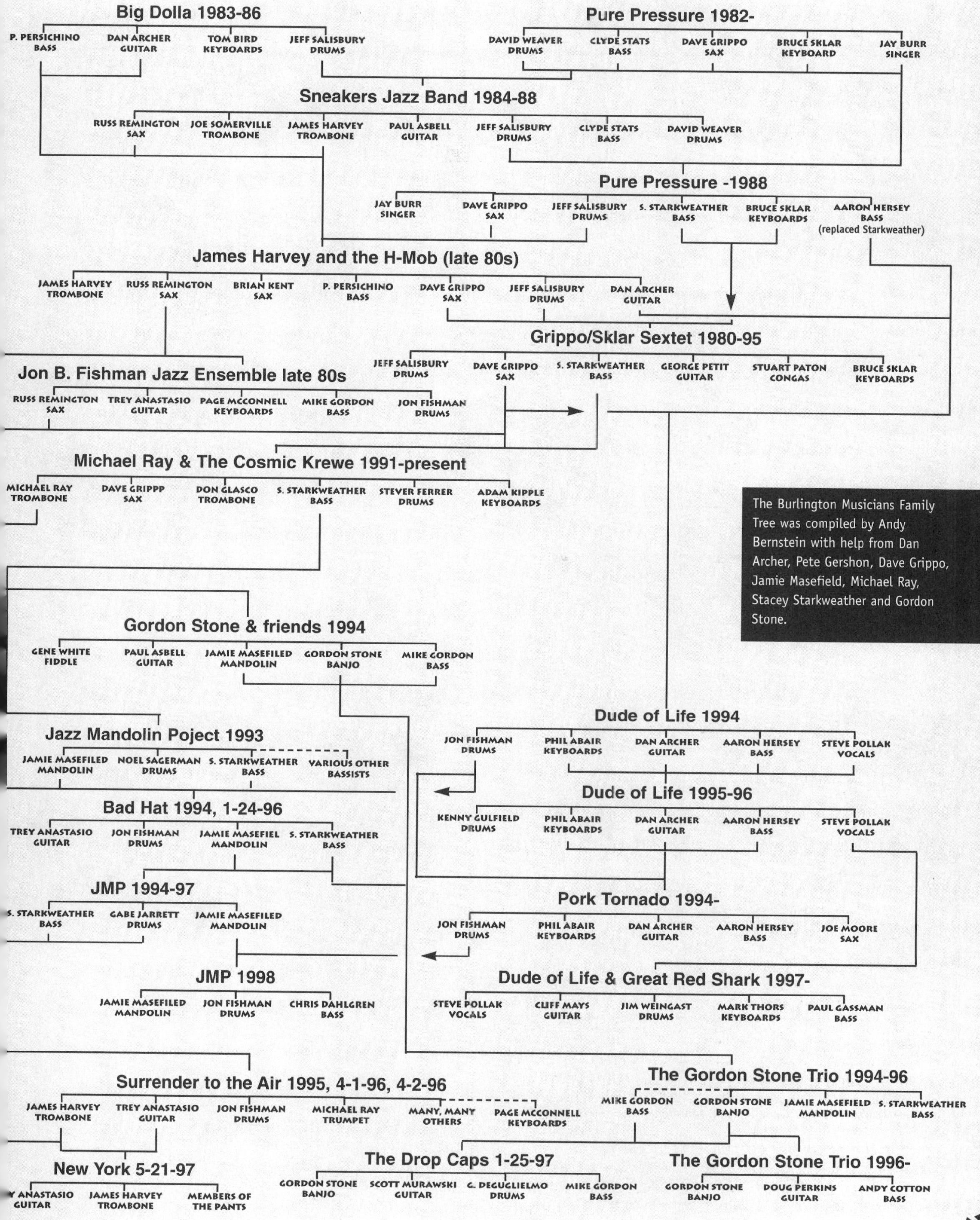

Big Dolla 1983-86

P. PERSICHINO BASS · DAN ARCHER GUITAR · TOM BIRD KEYBOARDS · JEFF SALISBURY DRUMS

Pure Pressure 1982-

DAVID WEAVER DRUMS · CLYDE STATS BASS · DAVE GRIPPO SAX · BRUCE SKLAR KEYBOARD · JAY BURR SINGER

Sneakers Jazz Band 1984-88

RUSS REMINGTON SAX · JOE SOMERVILLE TROMBONE · JAMES HARVEY TROMBONE · PAUL ASBELL GUITAR · JEFF SALISBURY DRUMS · CLYDE STATS BASS · DAVID WEAVER DRUMS

Pure Pressure -1988

JAY BURR SINGER · DAVE GRIPPO SAX · JEFF SALISBURY DRUMS · S. STARKWEATHER BASS · BRUCE SKLAR KEYBOARDS · AARON HERSEY BASS (replaced Starkweather)

James Harvey and the H-Mob (late 80s)

JAMES HARVEY TROMBONE · RUSS REMINGTON SAX · BRIAN KENT SAX · P. PERSICHINO BASS · DAVE GRIPPO SAX · JEFF SALISBURY DRUMS · DAN ARCHER GUITAR

Grippo/Sklar Sextet 1980-95

JEFF SALISBURY DRUMS · DAVE GRIPPO SAX · S. STARKWEATHER BASS · GEORGE PETIT GUITAR · STUART PATON CONGAS · BRUCE SKLAR KEYBOARDS

Jon B. Fishman Jazz Ensemble late 80s

RUSS REMINGTON SAX · TREY ANASTASIO GUITAR · PAGE MCCONNELL KEYBOARDS · MIKE GORDON BASS · JON FISHMAN DRUMS

Michael Ray & The Cosmic Krewe 1991-present

MICHAEL RAY TROMBONE · DAVE GRIPPP SAX · DON GLASCO TROMBONE · S. STARKWEATHER BASS · STEVER FERRER DRUMS · ADAM KIPPLE KEYBOARDS

The Burlington Musicians Family Tree was compiled by Andy Bernstein with help from Dan Archer, Pete Gershon, Dave Grippo, Jamie Masefield, Michael Ray, Stacey Starkweather and Gordon Stone.

Gordon Stone & friends 1994

GENE WHITE FIDDLE · PAUL ASBELL GUITAR · JAMIE MASEFILED MANDOLIN · GORDON STONE BANJO · MIKE GORDON BASS

Dude of Life 1994

JON FISHMAN DRUMS · PHIL ABAIR KEYBOARDS · DAN ARCHER GUITAR · AARON HERSEY BASS · STEVE POLLAK VOCALS

Jazz Mandolin Poject 1993

JAMIE MASEFILED MANDOLIN · NOEL SAGERMAN DRUMS · S. STARKWEATHER BASS · VARIOUS OTHER BASSISTS

Dude of Life 1995-96

KENNY GULFIELD DRUMS · PHIL ABAIR KEYBOARDS · DAN ARCHER GUITAR · AARON HERSEY BASS · STEVE POLLAK VOCALS

Bad Hat 1994, 1-24-96

TREY ANASTASIO GUITAR · JON FISHMAN DRUMS · JAMIE MASEFIEL MANDOLIN · S. STARKWEATHER BASS

JMP 1994-97

S. STARKWEATHER BASS · GABE JARRETT DRUMS · JAMIE MASEFILED MANDOLIN

Pork Tornado 1994-

JON FISHMAN DRUMS · PHIL ABAIR KEYBOARDS · DAN ARCHER GUITAR · AARON HERSEY BASS · JOE MOORE SAX

JMP 1998

JAMIE MASEFILED MANDOLIN · JON FISHMAN DRUMS · CHRIS DAHLGREN BASS

Dude of Life & Great Red Shark 1997-

STEVE POLLAK VOCALS · CLIFF MAYS GUITAR · JIM WEINGAST DRUMS · MARK THORS KEYBOARDS · PAUL GASSMAN BASS

Surrender to the Air 1995, 4-1-96, 4-2-96

JAMES HARVEY TROMBONE · TREY ANASTASIO GUITAR · JON FISHMAN DRUMS · MICHAEL RAY TRUMPET · MANY, MANY OTHERS · PAGE MCCONNELL KEYBOARDS

The Gordon Stone Trio 1994-96

MIKE GORDON BASS · GORDON STONE BANJO · JAMIE MASEFIELD MANDOLIN · S. STARKWEATHER BASS

New York 5-21-97

Y ANASTASIO GUITAR · JAMES HARVEY TROMBONE · MEMBERS OF THE PANTS

The Drop Caps 1-25-97

GORDON STONE BANJO · SCOTT MURAWSKI GUITAR · G. DEGUGLIELMO DRUMS · MIKE GORDON BASS

The Gordon Stone Trio 1996-

GORDON STONE BANJO · DOUG PERKINS GUITAR · ANDY COTTON BASS

• Pop-up Phish •

PHISH BAND MEMBERS frequently make surprise appearances with many other bands. The lists goes on and on, and it's happened so frequently over the years that no absolutely comprehensive list of Phish pop-ups will probably ever exist. But some of the highlights include occasional Trey cameos with the Aquarium Rescue Unit (at Burlington's Club Metronome on 3/11/94, for example), Widespread Panic (11/11/93 in Los Angeles), and Blues Traveler (1/16/91 in Burlington). He and Jon Popper also helped out Jamie Notarthomas on the album *Heads or Tales*. While many of Trey's guest appearances have been with his contemporaries, he also jammed with classic rocker Steve Winwood in Burlington in the fall of '97, after the two became friends while appearing in the same festivals in Europe. A guest spot with Medeski, Martin & Wood from October 14, 1995, is a popular bootleg tape.

Page has become a sort of regular with the Allman Brothers Band during their New York City runs, appearing with them in both 1996 and 1997. He also produced and played on a song by the New England band Uproot.

Mike is a familiar sight with Max Creek, for whom he occasionally plays guitar. He also appeared onstage once with the obscure act Rugby Road, along with ARU, following a Phish gig in Philadelphia.

Fishman has appeared with the Burlington jazz/soul combo Belizbeha, as well as the Phish cover band Stash ("I was drunk, it seemed like fun," Fish supposedly explained afterwards), and the New Orleans funk band Galactic, along with Col. Bruce Hampton's Zambieland Orchestra, which included over 60 musicians during its sole appearance in Atlanta in December of 1997.

the Pants

Burlington rock group the Pants has become a Phish protégé of sorts. While laying the finishing touches on *Billy Breathes*, Trey also helped produce a three-song demo for the Pants. A year later, in May 1997, Trey would appear with members of the Pants and trombonist James Harvey (an occasional Giant Country Horns conspirator) under the name "New York" at Burlington's Club Toast. That night Trey debuted several new tunes which would become part of the Phish repertoire, including "I Saw It Again" and "Dirt." The highlight of the set, however, was probably Trey leading the vocals on a rendition of Sly and the Family Stone's song "Stand!" Tapes of this performance are in wide circulation among fans.

Who WAS That?

SOME OF THE RANDOM faces which have popped up on the stage with Phish over the years:

The boys with Sidney Ellis.

7/21/91 Parksville, NY—Steve-O Nelson on washboard for the encores.
3/2/93 New Orleans, LA—Bruce Barnes played washboard, harmonica, and sang on "It's My Life," "Luke-a-Roo," and "Choo Choo Cha Boogie."
3/14/93 Gunnison, CO—Cameron McKenney added vocals to "Reba."
4/10/93 Chicago, IL—Sugar Blue played harmonica and sang on "Help Me Baby," "Hoochie Coochie Man," and "Cavern."
8/2/93 Tampa, FL—Joe Rooney lended vocals (screams) on the jam out of "Mike's Song."
8/25/93 Seattle, WA—Baby Gramps joined in on the "YEM" vocal jam then took the lead for "Bats & Mice."
8/26/93 Portland, OR—"Bats & Mice" again featured Baby Gramps.
5/3/94 Antioch, TN—Alison Krauss sang on "If I Could," just as she did on *Hoist*.
5/27/94 San Francisco, CA—Morgan Fitcher played fiddle on "Nellie Cane" and "My Minds Got a Mind"; Andrea Baker of the San Francisco Opera Co. took lead vocals on "O Mio Bambino Caro."
10/8/94 Fairfax, VA—During "Mike's" a local girls soccer team came up and led a "We Are the Muppets" cheer.
11/28/94 Bozeman, MT—Youngster Cameron McKenney played (unmiked) sax on "Simple."
10/20/95 Cedar Rapids, IA—A guest performer played bagpipes on "Amazing Grace" jam.
12/29/95 Worcester, MA—Mike's bass teacher, Jim Stinnete, played on a bass jam with Mike as well as on "La Grange."
8/17/96 Plattsburgh, NY—Ben Cohen and Jerry Greenfield added vocals on "Brother"; during "Antelope" there was a trapeze artist flying around the stage from a rope that was dropped from the light rigging; during "Tweezer" on each side of the stage was a giant trampoline, one of which had a person on snow skis, the other with a person on a snowboard, both doing flips and other feats of acrobatics.
10/23/96 Hartford, CT—Bob Gullotti played drums throughout second set.
12/31/96 Boston, MA—The Boston Community Choir joined Phish for "Bohemian Rhapsody," "Julius," and "Amazing Grace."
2/25/97 Munich, Germany—Sydney Ellis sang on "One Meatball," "Little Red Rooster," and "Get Your Mojo Working."
3/18/97 Burlington, VT—Tammy Fletcher of the Disciples sang on "Reconsider Baby" and "Love Me Like a Man."
7/25/97 Dallas, TX—Bob Gullotti played drums throughout second set.
7/26/97 Austin, TX—Bob Gullotti played drums throughout the entire show.

Bad Hat and Jazz Mandolin Project

Photo by Lauren Stagnitti.

AMONG THE MANY side projects in which members of Phish have participated, the best known is probably Bad Hat, the jazz outfit which featured Trey and Fish along with Burlington musicians Jamie Masefield on mandolin and Stacey Starkweather on bass.

The seeds of Bad Hat were planted around 1993 when Trey and Jamie began sharing the stage for occasional jazz sets, often joined by Mike or Fishman. They played several times across the lake at JC's in Plattsburgh during the spring, and appeared at Burlington's tiny Last Elm Cafe as part of the Burlington Jazz Festival on June 10 of that year.

Masefield's collaborations with members of Phish stretched back a decade, when he was a resident at UVM's Slade Hall and began jamming with Mike in a bluegrass trio.

But Bad Hat didn't begin to truly take shape until early 1994, when Masefield began heading up an ever-changing outfit called the Jazz Mandolin Project. "I was playing in various bands and started booking gigs in town, finding people who wanted to play with me," says Masefield. "Jazz Mandolin Project was lacking a drummer, and I called Fish and asked him if he wanted to play. A night or two later, I went to Sneakers and Trey was playing there with those guys, and Fish had told them, and we talked it over."

On January 24, 1994, they all took the stage at the Last Elm, with Starkweather on bass. Although that gig was under the Jazz Mandolin Project moniker, they adopted the name Bad Hat and set off for a series of gigs around New England, making appearances at JC's, at Granny Killam's in Portland, ME, as well as in Middlebury, VT, Northhampton, MA, and at several places in Burlington.

The sets consisted of mostly jazz standards like "Jump Monk," "Take the A-Train," and "Donna Lee," songs which were part of many early Phish sets. "Magilla" was the lone Phish original to sneak out. "The music started out as basically being a handful of original tunes of mine and the rest were jazz standards, with our own twist on it, taking a right turn here and there, spending twenty minutes on it and then coming back, that kind of thing," Masefield says.

When the Bad Hat string ended, Jazz Mandolin Project was up and running again. Starkweather was slowly becoming Masefield's standard partner despite many other obligations, but the pair needed a drummer.

Through a strange set of circumstances involving a recommendation and a "what the hell" phone call down to the New School in New York City, they attracted 23-year-old virtuoso Gabe Jarrett. He moved back to Vermont (he had been a student at Goddard College) and JMP's lineup was set.

The band's popularity has gained steadily since then, in the vein of most Northeastern, grassroots-oriented touring bands. Their music, however, is cut from a different mold—not really rock but by no means traditional jazz, and all instrumental.

They recorded their first album in winter of 1996, during which time Bad Hat rejoined for a single gig at Burlington's Carmel Coffeehouse on January 24, 1996.

JMP's self-titled album debuted later that year, to rave reviews. The band continued to tour with that lineup until December of 1997, when Starkweather and Jarrett left the group. Then a brief tour ensued with Chris Dahlgren on upright bass and none other than Jon Fishman on drums.

Could a return of Bad Hat be in the cards?

"We've been talking about doing things all along, and there's nothing planned specifically at this point, but I feel pretty confident that at some point we'll do something really nice," Masefield says. "One of my dreams would be to have a small tour in a lot of really nice old historic theaters. The problem is, everyone wants to see a Bad Hat show, so it's not possible anymore to book a two-hundred-seat place and have another seven hundred people all pissed off outside because they can't get in. And then, I don't know if we want to get into playing these huge things, because it's really a quiet kind of intimate experience."

For more information on Jazz Mandolin Project, check out their website at www.netspace.org/jmp/music/

Bad Hat and related performances:

2/2/92 Trey Anastasio, Jamie Masefield duo: Queen City Tavern, Burlington

6/8/93 Trey Anastasio, Jamie Masefield, Mike Gordon: Vermont Public Radio broadcast

6/10/93 Trey Anastasio, Jamie Masefield, Mike Gordon: Last Elm Cafe, Burlington

7/9/93 Trey Anastasio, Jamie Masefield, Noel Sagerman (drums), Justin Rose (bass): JC's, Plattsburgh, NY

9/3/93 Trey Anastasio, Jamie Masefield, Noel Sagerman (drums), Stacey Starkweather (bass): JC's, Plattsburgh, NY

1/14/94 Bad Hat (Trey Anastasio, Jamie Masefield, Jon Fishman, Stacey Starkweather): Last Elm Cafe, Burlington

1/24/94 Bad Hat: Granny Killiam's, Portland, ME

1/28/94 Bad Hat: JC's, Plattsburgh, NY

2/16/94 Bad Hat: St. Michael's College, Colchester, VT

2/23/94 Bad Hat: Middlebury College, Middlebury, VT

2/24/94 Bad Hat: Last Elm Cafe, Burlington

2/25/94 Bad Hat: JC's, Plattsburgh, NY

3/4/94 Bad Hat (with special guest Dave Grippo): Metronome, Burlington, VT

9/10/94 Bad Hat: Portland Performing Arts Center, Portland, ME

9/11/94 Bad Hat: Iron Horse Cafe, Northampton, MA

9/19/94 Bad Hat: Flynn Theater, Burlington

1/24/96 Bad Hat: Carmel Coffeehouse, University of Vermont, Burlington

Stone Soup

GORDON STONE SHARES more than just a name with Mike Gordon. The banjo player and steel pedal guitarist first met Mike Gordon when he gave him banjo lessons in the mid 1980s. Although they had only a few instruction sessions, they became good friends and Stone went on to do studio work on two Phish albums, and also appeared onstage with the band twice.

Photo courtesy of Pete Gershaw.

Jon Fishman sits in with Gordon Stone (front, on pedal steel guitar) and Andy Cotton on bass.

In recent years, Stone and Mike have collaborated on various side projects—some planned and some unplanned—exploring bluegrass, folk, and various other musical genres.

The first installment came when Gordon Stone formed the Gordon Stone Trio, which had Stacey Starkweather on bass at the time (if it seems like Stacey Starkweather has been mentioned in about every piece in this section, that's why they call him "the busiest bassist in Burlington"). When Stacey couldn't make it to a gig, Stone was in a bind.

"I had to call around and I'm like, 'Jeez, I wonder if Mike's around,' so I called him," Stone remembers. He suggested that Mike just come over and jam, because the material was too complicated to learn in a day or two. But Mike not only agreed to join them, he insisted on learning each song backwards and forwards. "He said, 'No, give me the tape.' He learned the whole thing in two days," says Stone.

In the fall of 1996, Mike Gordon performed with the Gordon Stone Trio at a pair of shows in Burlington, one at the famed Slade Hall on UVM's campus, the site of Phish's second-ever gig.

The following winter, Stone and Mike teamed up again for a performance under the name the Drop Caps in a benefit for the Ann Arbor, MI, folk club ARC. They appeared with members of Max Creek in front of six thousand people, most of whom were Phish fans.

Stone appeared onstage with Phish on Nov. 19, 1992, when he performed "Poor Heart" and "Fast Enough for You"—the two songs on which he also appears in the album versions—along with "Rocky Top." The following summer, on July 22, 1993, he played steel pedal guitar for "Paul and Silas," "Avenu Malkenu," and "Rocky Top."

Following the release of his solo album, *Touch and Go*, on Alcazar Records in 1996, Stone has been performing around the country with various lineups that feature Doug Perkins on guitar and Andy Cotton on bass. The Gordon Stone Trio played on the small stage at both the Clifford Ball and the Great Went, and can be caught on a regular basis at small music clubs. For more information on Gordon Stone, check out his website at www.nemac.com/gstone.htm

Surrender to the Air

In 1995, Trey drew together a diverse array of musicians—a "dream team" of sorts—to record an experimental jazz album. Though it was billed as a "solo project," the album that came out of several days' worth of sessions didn't feature Trey prominently (though he did produce the effort). Instead, he blended his guitar into a mix that featured Marshall Allen (saxophone), Kofi Burbridge (flute), Oteil Burbridge (bass), Damon R. Choice (keyboards), Jon Fishman (drums), Bob Gullotti (drums), James Harvey (trombone), John Medeski (keyboards), Michael Ray (trumpet), and Marc Ribot (guitar).

"Trey said that it came to him in a dream," shares Michael Ray, the clown prince of the troupe. "We all got together, and there were some very magical moments at that recording session—the stuff that they put out was just the tip of the iceberg."

Key to the effort was that it was entirely improvised. "When I asked Trey, 'What do you want to do?' he said, 'I think that someplace in the cosmos there are no words, just music.' And we just rolled tape," remembers Ray. "The first song was like thirty-seven minutes, and then it was just to the next one, and two days of recording like that."

The album, titled *Surrender to the Air*, was released by Elektra in March 1996. In addition to the album, the *Surrender to the Air* crew played two live shows together on April 1 and 2, 1996. The shows were the last-ever played at the Academy in New York City, a Phish stomping ground circa '91, and included Page sitting in for the second night's second set. (Setlists from the show are easy to recall: Set I: Jam; Set II: Jam.)

Track List: Intro (Gulloti), And Furthermore, We Deflate, And Furthermore, Down (Ribot, Allen, Ray), Intro (Medeski, Ribot, Anastasio, Choice), And Furthermore, And Furthermore, Out (Allen, Choice, Ray, Fishman)

FISH Out Of Water

Has it always been your dream to hang out in a bar with Jon Fishman? Well, it's not that hard to do, because his side project, Pork Tornado, remains a frequent sight at Burlington's Club Toast. Often booking the club for weekly appearances a month at a time, Pork Tornado was still going strong in the fall of 1997, even stealing Trey for a guest appearance on October 19 (see photos).

Pork Tornado, which plays a sort of "cosmic disco," normally includes Dan Archer (of the famed Archer Studios) on guitar, Phil Abair on keyboards, Joe Moore on sax, Aaron Hersey on bass, and Fishman on drums. The lineup is almost identical to the Dude of Life band, which toured briefly with Fishman early in 1994.

Fishman has also played with the band Spastic, fronted by singer/songwriter/actor Martin Guigui. He would also go on to appear in Guigui's film *The Wedding Band*, in which he played, of all things, the drummer.

Trey sits in with Pork Tornado, October 1997.

Photos courtesy of A. J. Fucile.

FROM THE BOTTOM

So you didn't get to see Phish in the pre-arena era and are still kicking yourself for all the times you said "Phish, pish," when you saw the name posted at a local bar. Or maybe you were around for those glory days, and would do anything to feel that joy again.

Well, the magic of the midnight show may be gone for Phish, but not for dozens of other bands who are hitting stages today and testing the waters of twenty-minute improvisations and psychedelic harmonies. In the last couple of years a disparate but recognizable group of Phish-inspired bands has surfaced on the club scene, playing to loyal pockets of tourheads and college-age crunchies while hocking self-produced, self-financed albums and building up their mailing lists and Web sites.

It would be both an insult and an undue compliment to say that these bands sound like Phish—few of them do. But each taps a nerve similar to the one the Phish experience does, and each brings a Phish-inspired element to the stage. Loosely referred to as jam rock, this genre is emerging rapidly and may be the most remarkable phenomenon Phish has spawned.

Here's a partial summary of these road warriors.

moe.

Photo Credit: Jeff Tisman.

moe.

After years of toiling in bars and small clubs in the Northeast, moe. has suddenly burst into major theaters and three-thousand-seat venues, gaining popularity by the minute. Sound familiar?

The moe.-Phish parallel is similar, in many ways, to comparisons between Phish and the Dead. They are different musically, but seem to be tapped into the fan network created by the predecessor, while subscribing to the same sort of jam ethic which drives tapers and tour heads wild. It's a ripple effect which has turned moe.—and their major label debut album *No Doy!*—into absolute sensations. Fans are already starting to grumble that moe. has gotten "too big," (again, sound familiar?), a complaint that will probably be heard more and more. Powered by guitarists Chuck Garvey and Al Schnier's scintillating trade-offs on lead, and bassist Rob Derhak's slaphappy yet precise bass lines, moe. proves that trippy rock can have a razor-sharp edge.

Within that framework, moe. has found avenues for improvisation and mutation, learning to paint the edges of each song and stretch each composition out in a manner only certain types of music fans can appreciate. And moe. has stayed true to the tastes of those fans, not seeking radio play or mainstream acceptance, instead applying the Phishy formula to an even greater degree. Yeah, they released a single, but it was a forty-five-minute version of the song "Meat" (which has only one lyric). Heck, they even allow videotaping. Another album is due out sometime in 1998, one which could vault them over the top. If you haven't seen moe. yet, now is the time.

Albums: *Headseed* (1994); *Loaf* (1996); *No Doy* (1996)

Contact Info: phone: (212) 592-3542; Web: www.moe.org; e-mail: moe@moe.org

The Ominous Seapods

The veritable grandfathers of jam rock, the Ominous Seapods have nine years and three albums under their belt, and show no signs of slowing down. The recent *Jet Smooth Ride* underscores what Seapods fans have known for close to a decade—that lead guitarist Max Verna is simply a master songwriter, and rhythm guitarist Dana Monteith is no slouch either. Songs like "Some Days" and "Blackberry Brandy," on the previously released *Guide to Roadside Ecology*, are so memorable and enticing, that it makes one ask how a band this talented is still playing in bars after all this time.

Of course, real Seapods fans will tell you that the true gems can only be heard on those stages, as their most popular tunes have never been released on album.

Aside from strong songwriting ability, the appeal of the Seapods is in their iconoclasm and utter lack of pretension. Managing to be religiously unhip without being contrived—a narrow ledge to walk—the Seapods sing about television, make fun of the pope, and wear gas station uniforms onstage, but back their shenanigans with captivating jams and memorable guitar phrases.

Albums: *Econobrain* (1994); *Guide to Roadside Ecology* (1995); *Jet Smooth Ride* (1997)

Contact Info: phone: (518) 489-7466; Web: www.netspace.org/seapods; e-mail: pod.net.request@dartmouth.edu

Strangefolk

IF YOU BLINKED in the last year, you may have missed the fact that Strangefolk has become one of the most popular unsigned touring acts in America, and appears on the cusp of joining that elite group of jam bands who can claim to have "made it." While they may be another band which has to fight off Phish comparisons (they *are* a Burlington-based quartet), Strangefolk's unique approach to music demands a far more accurate analysis, and may even require a few listens to fully comprehend.

Combining the folky, acoustic flavor of rhythm guitarist Reid Genauer with the noodly, psychedelic precision of lead guitarist Jon Trafton, Strangefolk is irony incarnate, and creates an inherent tension and release in every tune. To some, Strangefolk represents a step away from jam rock as we know it—they've even been called mainstream or "poppy" by naysayers. But it comes down to what part of the music catches your ear. If you listen only to the acoustic side, you may end up thinking Eagles or worse. But try walking up to the speaker and letting the electric sounds blow you away. Quite simply, this is a very trippy band, and once you "get it," you'll never want to turn back.

Their new release, *Weightless in Water*, could prove to be a breakthrough and their last self-release as major labels come a-knockin'.

Albums: *Strangefolk* (1994, rereleased 1997); *Lore* (1996); *Weightless in Water* (1997)

Contact Info: phone: (802) 658-6453; Web: www.strangefolk.com; e-mail: yourparty@strangefolk.com

Percy Hill

GOOD NEWS: RUMORS OF Percy Hill's death were greatly exaggerated, though they will be touring a bit less, so band members can return to school. A victory for education is a loss for music, because Percy Hill makes every show count.

Clearly beyond their years in taste and sound, Percy Hill put out their first album just months after forming, when most of the band members were still shy of their twentieth birthdays. That work, *Setting the Boat Adrift* (1993), is anything but amateur, putting forth a unique sound which mixes diverse musical influences ranging from the Allman Brothers to Steely Dan. Their next release, 1995's addictive *Straight On 'til Morning*, does more of the same. In 1997, they released a two-disc live album called *Double Feature*. All of these discs are essential listening for any fan of improvisational music.

From the outset, Percy Hill brought an ironically mature, schooled combination of vocals and instrumentalization to the stage. Less guitar-driven and psychedelic than some of the bands with whom they frequently share bills, Percy Hill has still garnered a loyal, crunchy following. With an affinity toward both long improvisations and light, bouncy harmonies, Percy Hill knows how to play with and reward the audience.

Fans were disappointed, however, when rhythm guitarist and vocalist Tom Powley left the band in fall of 1997. Percy Hill still pushes onward as it adjusts to being a one-guitar outfit.

Albums: *Setting the Boat Adrift* (1993); *Straight On 'til Morning* (1995); *Double Feature* (1997)

Contact Info: phone: (603) 778-4242; Web: cbix.unh.edu/percy; e-mail: percyhill@aol.com

© 1995 Amazing Photography

OMINOUS SEAPODS

The Disco Biscuits

IF BANDS LIKE MOE. and the Ominous Seapods are the pioneers of the homespun jam rock scene, then the Disco Biscuits are what the scene created. Unapologetically tacking twenty-minute, multi-part jams onto every song and not afraid to conquer complexity, the Disco Biscuits first generated a buzz on the Philadelphia music scene before becoming a regular headliner at the Wetlands in New York City, and also a frequent topic of discussion on the Phish.Net.

Guitarist and frontman Jon Gutwillig serves as the band's anchor, while keyboardist Aaron Magner adds the virtuoso spice that makes a Biscuits jam a head-spinning, mind-altering experience.

Before anyone outside of the University of Pennsylvania had ever heard of the Disco Biscuits, Gutwillig caught the eye of Trey Anastasio during a Burlington guitar competition that Trey helped judge. With every progression in Gutwillig's one-man performance, Trey practically leapt out of his seat. And he did rise to his feet in appreciation when Gutwillig turned a tuning knob to create a desired sound in the middle of the piece. Trey later threw his arm around the kid and pronounced that he should be known as "Jon the Jet-setter."

Their latest album, *Uncivilized Area*, is a chilling and uplifting compilation of the Biscuits' most ambitious tunes, combining the epic, improvised feel of their live performances with the precision of the studio.

Albums: *Encephalous Crime* (1996); *Uncivilized Area* (1998)

STRANGEFOLK

Contact Info: phone: (215) 243-0410; Web: www.discobiscuits.com; e-mail: saltman@discobiscuits.com

Foxtrot Zulu

Go to any Foxtrot Zulu show, and you'll probably see a good number of college-aged "mainstream" music fans, and then a bunch of Phish-heads gyrating in a frenzy, literally pushing everyone else off the dance floor. The secret of Foxtrot is starting to get out.

While listening to Foxtrot Zulu and trying to identify their musical influences, one cannot avoid just giving up to bask in the pleasurable sound they've created. This band pulls off something that is seldom accomplished in today's jam rock—they've included horns, which not only serve to embellish, but actually to drive the groove and overall color of the music. What better to cap off a jam than a frenetic brass explosion?

The band's ability to satisfy the ears of audiences with various tastes can perhaps be attributed to the fact that Foxtrot has five songwriters, each with something different to offer. What they all have in common, however, is the unmistakable ability to mesh together, producing high-energy dance rock and funk grooves with no fear of improvised exploration. Foxtrot has two high-quality albums to its credit, *Moe's Diner* and the more recent *Burn Slow*. Remarkably, they're as good in the studio as they are onstage.

Albums: *Moe's Diner* (1995); *Burn Slow* (1997)

Contact Info: phone: (401) 377-4938; Web: www.foxtrotzulu.com; e-mail: zulucrew@aol.com

String Cheese Incident

Lactose intolerant or not, String Cheese Incident will make you laugh and dance simultaneously. The Telluride, CO, quintet hits you from all angles, mixing bluegrass at the forefront with calypso, salsa, afro-pop, funk, rock, and jazz. The collage of styles is created using the distinctive sounds of acoustic and electric mandolins, with which this band, like Leftover Salmon, is able to enter the depths of psychedelia while pumping out its bread and butter—high-energy bluegrass.

String Cheese Incident has been known to appear at a bluegrass festival or two as well as draw a sellout crowd at Boulder's Fox Theater. And word has spread quickly, making String Cheese a solid draw in almost every region of the country. But no matter where you see them, the Incident will leave you strung out and jonesing for more!

Albums: *Born on the Wrong Planet* (1996); *A String Cheese Incident* (1997)

Contact Info: phone: (303)417-8909; Web: www.stringcheeseincident.com; e-mail: sci@stringcheese.incident.com

ulu

Every now and again you'll stumble into a gig and find an unexpected surprise. But ulu, a five-piece instrumental outfit based in New York City, is a band that will downright shock you, forcing your feet to move and your jaw to drop. The "unlabelable" groove they have mastered is as pioneering, and difficult to classify, as those of bands such as Medeski, Martin & Wood, and the Greyboy Allstars. One may encounter a distorted clavinet solo that hooks a hard harmonic left turn and settles back down to melodic pockets off the saxophone or flute. This is all happening above a relentless bass and rhythm groove skillfully providing space in the backyard of the beat. In just a few short months on the scene, ulu has generated a strong buzz and admiration among peers. This is a band that's on the way up.

Contact Info: phone: (212) 533-1075

Everything

There was once this little band from Vermont that no one had ever heard of except for a few thousand diehards. Those diehards went and saw them so much that the band vaulted onto the industry charts of top concert draws. Then came the record company and the rest, as they say, was history. Washington D.C.–based Everything is holding out hope for the same story. The band has cracked the list of top fifty U.S. concert draws through its backbreaking tour schedule and enticing grooves of brass, winds, and guitar. Perhaps the only band with a guitarist, vocalist, clarinetist, and alto sax player—who's all one guy—Everything has been selling out shows along the strip of southern clubs which Phish conquered around 1991. A pair of April 1996 gigs at the Bayou in D.C. formed a self-titled live album. It led to their signing with Blackbird Sire records, for their most recent album, *Super Natural*.

Albums: *Labrador* (1994); *Everything* (1996); *Super Natural* (1998)

Contact Info: phone: (540) 987-9417; Web: www.ecolon.com; e-mail: everything@ecolon.com

Freebeerandchicken

Further proof that Albany, NY, may be the modern hotbed for jam-oriented music, Freebeerandchicken has taken its act beyond the Capital District and become a recognized name around the country. At first listen, the band sounds like many familiar performers, throwing in a touch of bluegrass, a nice mix of acoustic and electric, and solid jams. But you'll do a double take upon realizing that Freebeerandchicken's lead instrument is a saxophone, not a guitar, which opens the doors to a whole different dimension of musical adventure.

The band insists that its name is not a sleazy ploy to attract the cheap and hungry. Instead, it's an homage to the old John Lee Hooker tradition of letting people into shows for free if they brought along beer and chicken. The band cut a live album in 1995 called *Papa's Waltz*, available on cassette.

Album: *Papa's Waltz* (1995)

Contact Info: phone: (518) 438-9391; Web: members.aol.com/fb&c; e-mail: FBandC@aol.com

Schleigho

SCHLEIGHO (PRONOUNCED SHLAY-HO), has titillated audiences through thunderous jams fusing jazz, funk, and a variety of other unlikely styles which round out their heavy, yet accessible sound.

Schleigho's flawless transitions are so tight they seem virtually impossible to the naked eye (and ear). Many of their tunes aggressively and boldly take the listener down a dark and sinister path while others return to semireality with jazzy Latin rhythms that lighten things up—at least for a moment or two.

"The Gromlins"—from their self-titled debut album—is a classic example of what jam music is all about. Clocking in at over twenty-six minutes long, it begins with evil, heliumlike vocals that swerve, sway, and meander underneath a furious driving beat, into the bouillabaisse of sounds that you must taste to fully appreciate Schleigho. *[Reviewed by Greg Shanken.]*

Albums: *Schleigho* (1995); *Farewell to the Sun* (1996)

Contact Info: phone: (508) 544-5341; Web: www.ledfeather.com/shleigho; e-mail: schleigho @bigfoot.com

Jiggle the Handle

THE HANDLE ISN'T the only thing that'll jiggle while enjoying a show. Putting all the toilet humor aside, this band can move your feet along with everything else. The Massachusetts quartet settles into jams which build up ferociously throughout the night.

Guitarist Gary Backstrom is considered a true virtuoso, whirling through supersonic leads while also knowing when to hold back. Jiggle the Handle has managed to gain the attention of some pretty big names in the business. They've shared the stage with icons such as Widespread Panic, Merle Saunders, the Jerry Garcia Band, and a bass player by the name of Mike Gordon. Their album, *Mrs White's Party,* with an imitation hologram cover, is almost as fun to stare at as it is to hear.

Album: *Mrs. White's Party* (1997)

Contact Info: phone: (508) 429-5994; Web: www.moonsite.com/jiggle

Day by the River

A VETERAN OF THE 1997 HORDE tour, Athens, GA-based Day by the River has channeled band members' sophisticated musical backgrounds into soulful songwriting. Their music is marked by passionate southern-style choruses which explode into musically advanced, sectional arrangements opening the doors for wistful jamming. The quintet has been improving its sound steadily since its formation in Athens in 1990. Several years spent in Miami turned out to be DBR's proving ground as it built a solid fan base there before returning home in 1995.

DBR has been extensively touring the southeast since their move, now supporting its recent release *Fly* (which was mixed by John Altschiller, the engineer of Phish's *Picture of Nectar*). Along with its repertoire of original classics, DBR has been known to bust out some influential cover tunes such as "Cosmik Debris" by Frank Zappa and "You Enjoy Myself." You'll be soothed and pleasantly surprised if you spend a Day by the River.

Albums: *Shimmy* (1993); *Fly* (1996)

Contact Info: phone: (706) 208-8341; Web: www.daybytheriver.com; e-mail: info@dayby theriver.com

Grinch

GRINCH STARTED OUT five years ago as a bunch of guys with acoustic guitars jamming together for fun at University of Delaware parties. With the addition of drums, bass, and amplification, Grinch has steamrolled the Mid-Atlantic region as an ever-present energetic groove band. Their distinctive sound contains a fusion of rock, funk, jazz, and blues which has evolved toward a psychedelic, funky platform for ambitious experimentation. Make no mistake about it, Grinch is a jam band and proud of it.

Independent label Ground Zero Records plans to release their 1997 disc nationally. But until then, enjoy their self-titled live album and catch a show. And if their drummer looks familiar, it's because he used to rattle the hi-hat with moe.

Album: *Grinch* (1995)

Contact Info: phone: (717) 872-8999; e-mail: Grinch7777@aol.com

Photo Credit: Chris Goodyear.

EVERYTHING

Hose

THE ROANOKE COLLEGE music department prides itself in its world-renowned choir and in having spawned an incredibly talented jam band called Hose. Greatly inspired by Phish (which might explain why they decided to name the band after the famous Carlos Santana analogy of Phish being a "hose" that waters the "sea of flowers") each of the band's four members exhibits a remarkable sense of musicianship which has crystallized from a combination of their talent as individuals, their musical training at Roanoke, and a love for Phish and other influential musicians. Hose has the sound of a seasoned band with the precise ability to bring out the work of each musician while emitting impressive melodies and well-conceived songs.

Hose is still making the transition from frat house gigs to flooding the local bar and club scene of Roanoke. While jamming live, the band adventurously funnels music into a fresh new direction which gives their fans reason to keep coming back for more. Still relative unknowns beyond their home base, the secret of Hose is bound to get out with a big splash.

Contact Info: phone: (540) 389-3076; e-mail: hosers@juno.com

Agents of Good Roots

WHILE FIRMLY PLANTED in the Southeast's jam rock scene, word of Agents of Good Roots continues to spread on a broad geographic scale. The jazz/funk-based quartet refuses to lose sight of the groove even while immersed in the depths of their rich musicality. Theirs is a tightly wound, edgy, rhythmic sound with outstanding songmanship and arrangement. Their critically acclaimed studio album, *Where Did You Get That Vibe,* was considered to be among the best homespun albums of 1996.

But there's nothing like the Agents live! *Straightaround,* a live CD which paints an even more accurate picture of the band's electrifying concert performance, helped gain the attention of RCA Records, which recently signed the band to a recording contract. Also a veteran of several HORDE performances, Agents of Good Roots has established itself as a band with a present and a future.

Albums: *Where Did You Get That Vibe* (1996); *Straightaround* (1997)

Contact Info: phone: (804) 971-8117; Web: www.agentsofgoodroots.com; e-mail: Agents@redlt.com

Moon Boot Lover

SINCE ALL THE WAY back in 1992, Albany-based trio Moon Boot Lover has had fans gravitating to their gigs and sinking into the groove. Aside from becoming a strong fixture in the upstate New York music scene (where jam rock got its start), Moon Boot Lover has caught the attention of the mainstream music world by linking up with national touring acts such as Maceo Parker.

"Immensely boogieful" is how the *Village Voice* sums them up. Moon Boot produces a groove that slides from thunderous to delicate in one sitting. The funky rhythm is coupled with multidimensional keyboards and guitar that come up with improvisational inventions throughout their jams.

Albums: *Outer Space Action* (1995); *Live Down Deep* (1995)

Contact Info: phone (603) 778-4242; e-mail: GBEnt@aol.com; Web: www.moonbootlover.com

From the TOP

Of course, it's not only the more obscure bands that are tapping that Phishy nerve. Others which gained fame around the same time Phish did still promise to stretch your mind while displaying their commitment to the jam ethic.

There are the well-known, MTV-coopted varieties such as **Blues Traveler** and **the Dave Matthews Band**. Blues Traveler seems to have taken a Spin Doctor–esque fall from grace when they failed to produce a follow-up hit after "Runaway" hit the top ten. They are now back to playing small venues after a brief flirtation with superstar status. The Dave Matthews Band has also failed to produce a radio hit in a while, but their cross-sectional following seems to be as strong as ever.

Widespread Panic continues its ascension at a glacial pace. An original 1992 HORDE band, Widespread never received mainstream acceptance, but their national following is a loyal and growing one. It almost goes without saying that their live shows are absolutely phenomenal. **Bela Fleck and the Flecktones** can also be found playing great shows across the country, as well as on a series of outstanding studio albums and the double CD *Live Art*.

Virtuosos **Medeski, Martin, & Wood** have caught on big with the Phish audience, proving just how appreciative of good music and good musicians Phish fans can be. This jazz-fusion trio's 1996 release, *Shack-man*, continues to draw raves.

From the great state of Colorado, **Leftover Salmon** proves that more than one aquatic band can tingle the senses. The Cheech and Chong of rock and roll, these guys are the only band around that can take a mandolin, a banjo, and an irrepressible herbal theme and make an entire crowd sing, "You gotta wake and bake!"

Now with Mercury Records after a failed marriage with Geffen, **God Street Wine** still manages to pack small clubs in the Northeast.

The **Aquarium Rescue Unit**, another HORDE original but now minus Col. Bruce Hampton, still hits the stage, performing tighter shows than ever. And Col. Bruce can now be found jamming with his new brainchild, the **Fiji Mariners**—perhaps the world's ugliest band, with apologies to the Stones and Zeppelin.

Meanwhile, **Michael Ray and the Cosmic Krewe** are also the rage amongst many Phishheads, including Trey and Page, who appeared with them at a small club called Jimmy's during JazzFest '96. And don't forget Phish-friends **Jazz Mandolin Project** and the **Gordon Stone Trio**, both profiled elsewhere in the *Almanac*.

Finally, for those who can't quite break the tie, Phish cover bands are surfacing at a rapid rate. In fact, Fishman joined the band Stash in the spring of 1997. Since then, however, Stash has tried to make its mark playing originals.

Courtesy of Jeremy Sheely

3 People in the Neighborhood

Most people would agree that Phish is about more than just music. It is about community, togetherness. It is, as we like to say, about the scene. About creating something together that we can all feel proud of and, of course, about having an amazing time while doing it. Nothing comes without effort, though, and there are many people and organizations that work extremely hard to help make the scene a better place for everyone. We would now like to recognize some of these phriendly pholks for their efforts.

COMMUNITY CONNECTION

• The Waterwheel Foundation •

Fans walking around venue corridors in the fall of 1997 were surprised by the absence of the Greenpeace table, a fixture at Phish shows since the fall of 1992. In its place sits the Waterwheel Foundation, a Phish-led activist and charity organization headed up by the same people who sat in front of the Greenpeace banner for all those years.

The association between Phish and Greenpeace began when Mike Hayes, who had been working for Greenpeace on its Tour Project, met up with Phish when they were opening for Santana in 1992. The band gave Mike carte blanche for Greenpeace to bring its message to Phish fans the following fall. Fellow activist Henry Schwab soon joined Mike and the two would be seen at shows working the table for years to come, encouraging fans to write letters or sign petitions for a variety of causes, including the Arctic Refuge campaign and countless forest conservation issues.

"The Tour Project was able to raise as many names as a small office, and you get to be outside, with the people, not in some office behind a desk," says Hayes.

One way Greenpeace raised money was through a popular raffle: fans who bought bumper stickers at the table automatically had their names thrown in a hat. The person whose name was picked at the end of a show (and was there to claim the prize) received a free backstage pass. Due to cutbacks, Greenpeace pulled the plug on its Tour Project, and the Great Went was the last time Phish fans saw the table at a venue.

"Financially they screwed up. It's a shame. A lot of people who worked really hard are gone. But we'll keep going in one way or another. This is just another phase," said Hayes, just prior to the fall 1997 tour. At the time, it was unclear what the future would hold for the Greenpeace crew.

But by the time the band hit the road again, so did Mike and Henry. In fact, Phish had been planning to create a charitable foundation for some time, in order to give something back to communities and find an effective way to deal with the barrage of requests they receive from worthy causes.

A registered nonprofit organization, the Waterwheel Foundation will oversee and administer Phish's contributions toward causes such as the Lake Champlain cleanup (which

Waterwheel has replaced Greenpeace at Phish shows.

royalties from Ben & Jerry's Phish Food ice cream support).

"I'm excited by the opportunity that this gives us to pursue some new ideas," says Hayes. One such brainstorm was to include more local organizations from communities where Phish is performing.

The fall '97 tour saw a focus on local organizations that supply food and shelter for those in need, as well as groups working on clean water issues.

So while Greenpeace will no longer be represented at shows, the ability for people to get involved and help to improve the community has not been diminished, and Mike and Henry will still be seen in their familiar spot—manning the table, and making a difference.

Walk-About Campsite

Every summer since 1995, thousands of Phish-heads have touched down in rural Noblesville, IN, for the special fun which only shows at Deer Creek can offer. At Deer Creek, it's not just the concert; it's not just the parking lot . . . it's the dozens of makeshift campsites which dot the county highways as area residents set up tent cities in their backyards and offer fans an all-night party for about $5 a head. Most even adopt some sort of name, like "The Dancing Bear" campsite. While these locals are entrepreneurs as crafty as the best parking lot vendors, one such family has a hidden agenda: raising money for worthy causes, and giving their "kids" a safe place to stay.

Pat Ogborn and her husband, Ron, have been running the temporary Walk-About campsite since the Grateful Dead came to town in 1993. They donate all of their profits to local charities, such as the antidrug group DARE (ironic, Pat admits).

Close to five-hundred Phish-heads camp out in the Ogborns' backyard. The family even built a shed to house a temporary convenience store, complete with toothbrushes and cold soda. Mrs. Ogborn's children and grandchildren help keep things orderly, but she says there's never been any problems with any of the overnight tenants.

"You guys are all my kids as far as I'm concerned," she says. "I've never met a nicer bunch of people."

She proudly boasts that one night she stayed out until 4:30 in the morning dancing at a drum circle: "It was the best time I ever had."

• The • Phellowship

In an environment synonymous with drugs and alcohol, the Phellowship offers a supportive alternative. While the pressure to take drugs or drink can be tremendous, the Phellowship provides help and support to people in the environment where they may be most vulnerable, right at the show.

The origins of the Phellowship date back to the fall of '94 when Paige C. of Alabama, familiar with a sober group of Deadheads known as the Wharf Rats, recognized the need for a similar group within the Phish community. After contacting the band and being told that organization of such a group would have to be fan-based, she made efforts to contact other clean and sober Phish fans within her circle and via the Phish.Net.

Meanwhile, Keith B. and John P., two clean and sober fans from Michigan, were also working toward a similar goal. Things began to take form in the summer of 1996, when sober fans familiar with the Wharf Rats were beginning to hook up at shows in twos and threes using the unofficial calling card of the Yellow Balloon.

At the Clifford Ball, Paige posted a message with a yellow balloon for Wharf Rats/ Phellowship—a name she and a friend came up with—for people to leave notes and try to hook up with each other. While checking the board, Paige overheard someone saying, "Oh, they're calling it the Phellowship." It was John P. from Michigan, and the official roots of the organization were starting to take hold.

During that weekend a small group of clean and sober fans met one another in the sea of seventy-thousand fans and shared in the comfort, camaraderie, and phellowship of each other's company.

Shortly after that tour ended, John P. was put in touch with the nonprofit organizer at Dionysian Productions.

By this time, it had been decided that on a trial basis, Phish management—though taking a neutral stand on the issue—would allow a group of clean and sober Phish-heads to have a table set up at shows as a way of finding each other. Equipped with a banner and a bag of yellow balloons, Keith B. and John P. headed south to the Omni for Halloween for what would be the first official meeting of the Phellowship.

They were later invited to have a permanent table set up for the '97 summer tour. Since then, the group has grown by leaps and bounds.

Each meeting begins and ends with what is called the serenity prayer, a tradition that is followed at many twelve-step programs. The prayer does use the word *God*, but organizers point out that it is in no way meant to imply any religious affiliation whatsoever. Even Trey uses the word *God* onstage, though the serenity prayer doesn't follow it with the word *shit*.

"Meetings are certainly not very structured. It's a place where you can talk about your feelings and struggles, or just hang out and listen. People gain strength by knowing that they are not alone," says Paige. She goes on to explain part of the reason the Phellowship is needed on tour.

"Being on tour, going to a number of consecutive shows, it's hard to not feel threatened by the environment."

The only requirement for membership in the Phellowship is a desire to stay substance-free at shows. One is simply considered a member when he or she says so; there is no enrollment process. The group is open to all and does not exclude anyone, for whatever reason. In their words, "we do not give ourselves the power to kick anyone out."

For more information on the Phellowship, check out their site at
www.phellowship.org
It's a great resource, with listings of different contact groups and their phone numbers for each city on tour. You can also read up on the Phellowship in more detail or correspond with members.

A meeting of the Phellowship.

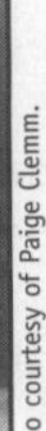

Karma Crew

You often will hear many longtime tour-heads lamenting the denigration of the scene. Litter, nitrous oxide salesmen, and drunk jerks often make Phish parking lots far from the utopia we sometimes make them out to be.

Jay Archibald, a fan who has spent many months of his life on the road with Phish, decided to do something about it. In the spring of 1996, he began pulling together the Karma Crew, a loose band of concerned citizens fighting for common sense and mutual respect while on tour.

The Karma Crew doesn't take a true stand on many things, other than being kind to your neighbors and ridding the scene of nitrous. Members are kept informed and strategize via a semiregular e-mail newsletter. For more information, contact Jay Archibald at Jarch420@aol.com.

• The Green Crew •

The Green Crew originated in the summer of '93 with just five people. Now it is one of the best-known Phish-related institutions, something recognized by fans and the outside world alike as the epitome of what the Phish community is all about.

Begun without a name as a loose group that spearheaded recycling efforts in the lot, the Crew now has nearly sixty members, each of whom can be seen cleaning up the parking lots after each show, picking up the pounds and pounds of trash which fellow fans foolishly leave behind.

In the early days, Mike Hayes, head of the since-dissolved Greenpeace Tour Project and now with the Waterwheel Foundation, was one of the leaders, along with Lisa Valdes and Shane Johnson, who would go on to become the official head of the Crew and eventually work for the band.

The Green Crew really began to take shape around the summer of 1994 when the band quietly supplied free tickets to some of the hard-core tour-heads who agreed to help clean up after shows. An occasional free dinner was thrown in and word began to spread.

Four years later, new fans are hoping to join the Green Crew at every single show.

"There's been a real population explosion recently," says Dave Madigan, a Massachusetts resident who joined the Green Crew in the summer of 1995.

The Crew has bulged so much, in fact, that the practice of giving free tickets to everyone who participates in the program can no longer be sustained. "This is an entirely volunteer commitment," says Madigan, "and is for people who want to keep the scene clean. We've lost enough venues due to post-show problems already."

The Crew meets before each show at 5:30, usually near the will-call window. That's when the game plan for that night is set, garbage bags are distributed, and new volunteers are able to join. The Crew generally sticks around in the parking lots for several hours after everyone has left, picking up trash and separating recyclables. How long the job takes depends on how many people pitch in and how messy the scene is.

For all that the Green Crew has done, the goals for the future are even more ambitious.

Madigan says that the idea is that the Green Crew can eventually be dissolved and replaced by an overall consciousness among everyone to help keep the scene clean and safe. "The scene keeps getting bigger . . . and messier! We want the Green Crew to become less of a group and more of a concept, and it starts with education and responsibility."

The recycling tower, which debuted in the summer of 1997 at Deer Creek, is one step in that direction. This twenty-foot-tall setup can be found at most venues, and is a centerpiece for the Green Crew and the whole recycling effort.

As Madigan says: "We'd like to see the Green Crew move from being diaper changers to potty trainers."

The Green Crew helps to maintain a recycling center at each show.

Photo courtesy of Paige Clemm.

Festival Forces

As the homespun jam rock scene continues to develop, three unique entities are shepherding it to the next level in different parts of the country. Connecticut's Terrapin Tapes, South Carolina's Homegrown Music Network, and Maryland's Walther Productions are all working overtime to bring great improvisational rock and jazz to music fans in their regions and beyond. Each stages several summer festivals that bring a who's who of the scene to weekend camping settings. Their goal: create a little slice of nirvana while helping expose the bands to larger audiences.

Terrapin Tapes is best known as a mail-order blank tape company, and continues to offer the Phish and Grateful Dead audiences some of the best prices out there on blank tapes and recording equipment. Founded several years ago by Ken Hays, Terrapin teamed up with *Dupree's Diamond News* in 1996 to stage the Deadhead Heaven, with bands like moe., Strangefolk, and the Jazz Mandolin Project. The company set out on its own the following summer and presented the Gathering of the Vibes, an equally successful affair.

In addition, Terrapin also produces some indoor shows and markets a Gathering of the Vibes double live CD, sold basically at cost for the purpose of getting the music out there. Terrapin-produced shows now have a broad awareness and following, and will probably expand to several dates and locations for 1998.

Similarly, the Homegrown Music Network is a multifaceted organization that markets albums and stages performances by the best up-and-coming bands out there—everyone from the Ominous Seapods to Foxtrot Zulu to the Disco Biscuits. Organizer Lee Crompton originally had the idea of offering fans one-stop-shopping for these bands' albums by setting up an 800-phone number and placing group advertisements in magazines like *Relix*. At the same time, Lee and Homegrown began setting up summer festivals for the many bands under Homegrown's umbrella, and also created a catalog and newsletter.

In the mid-Atlantic region, Tim Walther and Walther Productions are bringing the same energy to small clubs and large outdoor festivals as well. The various concerts held at Wilmer's Park in Brandywine, MD, have brought out such top names as Bela Fleck, God Street Wine, moe., and Everything, along with fantastic supporting lineups of some of the best unsigned acts out there.

These organizations—along with magazines like *Fantastic Voyage and Soundboard* and clubs such as the Wetlands in New York City—are making it their mission to help nourish today's emerging music scene.

Terrapin Tapes (800) 677-8650
Homegrown Music Network (800) 6LEEWAY
Walther Productions (410) 366-5483

MEDIA MIGHTIES

The *Pharmer's Almanac* is far from alone in the world of Phish scribes. Fanzine journalists, Dead-oriented magazines, established rock critics, and other fans have created a virtual library of Phish ink over the last few years, of varying quality and frequency. And a few intrepid radio disc jockeys have also tried to bring Phish and jam-oriented music to the airwaves.

• Book Nook •

The barrage of bound Phish literature began in October 1995, with the debut of *The Pharmer's Almanac*, then a 96-page, stapled-together collection of setlists and stories sold only in Phish parking lots. But now, the Almanac is only one of several Phish books on the shelves.

Longtime fan Dean Budnick authored the first Phish book ever produced by a major publisher. His work, *The Phishing Manual*, was released by Hyperion in the fall of 1996; it raised the bar concerning the level of detail in unearthing Phish history, and also includes the most in-depth look at Phish cover songs ever assembled.

The *Manual* almost immediately went into a third printing, and was a hit among Phish.Netters especially, who knew Dean Budnick as a familiar voice on rec.music.phish. Aside from authoring the Manual, Budnick's claim to fame is perhaps having the largest Phish tape collection in existence, outside of the band's own archives.

Rock writer Paul Thompson offered *Go Phish* in the fall of 1997, a biography-style account of the Phish story. Although the band's management was openly critical of the factual errors which riddled its pages (some of which, many pointed out, would never have been made by an experienced Phish fan) it still represents an interesting read from a historical standpoint, and offers many little facts which had not previously appeared in any work.

Of course, one cannot talk about Phish authors without mentioning Mike Gordon himself. *Mike's Corner*, a collection of odd ramblings from the *Doniac Schvice*, was published by Bullfinch Press in 1997. His fiancée, Cilla Foster, supplied the artwork.

Several other Phish books are expected to hit the streets in the coming years. The Mockingbird Foundation, a group of fans who met mostly via the Internet, are putting together a Phish guidebook which will support band-approved nonprofit causes. Meanwhile, another fan is trying to piece together a book of how people fell in love with Phish, under the title *Hooked*.

And then comes the officially sanctioned Phish biography by Richard Gehr, expected to be published in the fall of 1998. Rumor is it will play off a "Day in the Life" theme and tell the entire Phish history through tangents off the story of one particular show.

• The Pros at Prose •

At the top of the list among Phish writers, clearly, are rock critics Richard Gehr and Paul Robicheau. Gehr authored the *Spin* magazine feature on Phish in 1995, the *Rolling Stone* review of *Billy Breathes*, and is also behind a sanctioned Phish biography expected to be published in late 1998. Much to Gehr's credit, he has also been a staunch supporter of grassroots music and the emerging jam rock scene, penning features on moe., the Ominous Seapods and the rest of the genre in publications such as the *Village Voice* and *Guitar World*.

Robicheau, who writes regularly for the *Boston Globe*, was one of the first established rock journalists to discover Phish, writing a story for the *Globe* in September 1990. For the record, Robicheau was not responsible for the *Rolling Stone* New Year's review in 1994 which mistakenly claimed the band had played *The White Album* that night. While his name did appear next to the blurb, it was an ignorant *Rolling Stone* editor who was responsible for the gaffe, much to Paul's dismay.

What marks Robicheau's pieces on the band is a genuine understanding of and enthusiasm for the music. While a typical Phish review often has twelve Grateful Dead references and hopelessly tries to define the band to outsiders, Robicheau is way past that and actually reviews Phish in the context of other Phish shows. He also goes well beyond chronicling just Boston shows, popping up at Halloweens, the Clifford Ball, and the Great Went.

• The • 'zine Scene

Relix, Dupree's, and Unbroken Chain all trace their roots back to black-and-white, stapled-together "fanzines" put together on crude equipment with little possibility of ever making money. *Relix,* in fact, was first printed on stolen paper and intended as a communication tool for Grateful Dead tapers, well before the proliferation of the Internet.

Some Phish fans have concocted their own homespun fanzines, with varying degrees of longevity and ambition. The *Tackle Box,* a Chicago-based would-be quarterly, managed to get out a few issues starting in 1995, highlighted by original interviews with Dave Grippo, Nectar Rorris, and Bela Fleck. Its editors even commenced limited distribution to head shops and launched their own Web site. Yet, just as it seemed to be gaining momentum, it disappeared.

The summer of 1997 saw several makeshift fanzines surface on the lot scene, and even pop up in a few stores. One, called the *Helping Friendly Phanzine,* produced by Illinois resident Jason Kaczorowski, sold out a thousand-copy print run at $2 a pop. Although it had some clever ideas, such as directions to each summer show, most of it amounted to unholy copyright infringement, with lyrics and articles taken verbatim from various web sites.

It remains to be seen if any of the new fanzines will show any staying power. Several Phish-oriented ones have made their mark, however.

The *Fantastic Voyage System* (phone: (201) 795-4337) has been around since 1994, reviewing albums and shows from hundreds of jam rock, bluegrass, reggae, and jazz bands, and also devoting a monthly section to Phish. Music freak Paul Parietti produces this from-the-heart rag from his home in New Jersey, relying on a network of "Live Music Addicts" to report on shows from coast to coast.

Covering a similar batch of bands is the magazine *Soundboard* (phone: (802) 864-5552), which debuted with Jazz Mandolin Project on the cover in August 1997. It is available every other month at record shops throughout the Northeast. The brainchild of Burlington-based music writer Pete Gershon, it also includes ample Phish coverage and is far more professional in look and content than some of the other grassroots music rags. *Soundboard* could be on its way to establishing itself as a voice for the sort of music which often gets ignored by the mainstream press.

• Jerry's Kids •

Grateful Dead and sixties-oriented magazines *Relix, Dupree's Diamond News,* and the defunct *Unbroken Chain* have each brought a unique spin to Phish coverage (and also dealt with countless letters of complaint from longtime Deadhead readers who claim they are turning into "Phish" magazines).

The band first appeared in the ever-popular "Too New To Be Known" column in *Relix* in October 1989, and the magazine put Phish on the cover in 1995. *Relix,* which dates all the way back to 1974 and is credited with galvanizing the Grateful Dead tape trading scene, has also published interviews with Mike Gordon and Jon Fishman.

Claiming one of the most in-depth Trey interviews ever is *Dupree's Diamond News* (by Steve Silberman, in issue #31 in spring of '95) which first covered Phish in 1992. It began including a Phish section in every issue in 1995, a tradition which continues.

The smaller *Unbroken Chain* also offered ample Phish coverage in its brief heyday, but ceased publication early in 1997.

• Jam Rock Radio •

Improvisational rock and radio don't seem to mix. How can a jam band be expected to keep a tune under a time limit? But several independent and college stations are filling the void with regular jam rock radio shows. A few of note:

Every Sunday night from 7 P.M. to 9 P.M. "Space Jam" can be heard on WERS 88.9 FM in Boston, Emerson College's well-financed studio radio station. The show focuses on improvisational rock, and, to stay true to the genre, often features bands playing live in the WERS recording studio. Bands that have appeared live on the air include moe., Strangefolk, The Ominous Seapods, Aquarium Rescue Unit, Bela Fleck, the String Cheese Incident, and Jiggle the Handle, to name a few.

Jeff Waful created the show back in June of 1996 and handled host duties until his 1997 graduation. "When the show first started, I used to have my mother call so it seemed like a lot of

Jeff Waful of WERS with moe.

Photo courtesy Jeff Waful.

people were listening. Now, you can't even get through on the phone," Waful says. "We've developed a great relationship with these bands, and it's great to be able to help get this fantastic music out there."

You'll also hear Phish on WERS, and if there is one thing the station would love to do, it's get the Phab Phour into the studio. "Of course we would be thrilled if Phish would come down to the studio, jam a little, and talk with us on the air," Waful says. "We understand the time constraints that they must be under. They've gotten so big over the past few years, but if they are ever in town and have some spare time. . . ."

Another station to check out is WKWZ 88.5 FM Syosset, NY. Music Director J.T. Turret and crew present "From the Bottom" every Wednesday night from 9 P.M. to 11 P.M. From jam rock to jazz to ska, some of their favorites are the Ominous Seapods, Deep Banana Blackout, Yep, and the Scofflaws, to name a few. "There are a lot of bands that play this type of music and there's a huge audience out there. We've been able to reach this audience, and the response has been fantastic," says Turret.

In the Midwest, the state of Indiana boasts a couple of stations that are breaking some rules. WFHB 91.3 FM is a listener-supported community station that started up in the spring of 1997. The "FHB" stands for Firehouse Broadcasting, and it's not just a clever name. The station actually used to be a firehouse, and every Friday night Dave Weissman and Reid Olson turn on the hose and soak the airwaves. It's called the "Friday Night Sound Session" and can be heard from 1 A.M. to 3 A.M. More info can be found on their Web site at www.wfhb.org.

On Sunday nights, Dave and Reid take the sound session to the Indiana University station, WIUS 1570 AM from 10 P.M. to 12 A.M.

"We got involved in '94 when we saw a flyer posted and went to the meeting. Starting out we played mostly Dead, then eventually mixed in some Phish, but now we try to get a little more variety. We play Medeski, ARU, Bela Fleck," says Weissman. That station's Web site is wius@indiana.edu.

Aside from his on-air accomplishments, Dave also holds the honor of being hit in the eye by Trey's pick. "It was at the 11/22/94 Columbia show. Trey flicked something towards me. He was looking right at me, the way he often looks into the crowd, and then he flicked something that hit me in the eye. I was pissed, so I flipped him off. Later, some guy was all psyched because he had gotten Trey's pick. Then I realized what had hit me! I asked him for it, explaining how it rightfully belonged to me, but he wouldn't even let me touch it."

PHISHING THE NET

The online world is the backbone of the Phish community. While not everyone is touched by it directly, it remains the central conduit for information exchange among fans. When you hear a rumor in the parking lot, chances are it originated online. And when it seems that just about everyone knows the name of some new song, it's probably because someone posted it on the Internet and word spread from there.

The online world not only attracts some of the most knowledgeable and information-hungry fans (although not always the best dressers), it also claims some of the most dedicated. Many fans spend hours each week maintaining unique Phish Web pages and engaged in other Internet activity.

Interested in joining the cyber-Phish crowd, but don't know where to begin? To access the Phish.Net—also known by its Usenet name rec.music.phish—you'll need a subscription to an Internet provider that offers e-mail and, hopefully, Usenet access. (Usenet is the name for the section of the Internet which offers bulletin boards of information on thousands of topics.)

Accessing rec.music.phish directly via Usenet allows you to selectively read messages posted by other Phish.Netters. A lot of messages. More messages about Phish than you ever imagined possible. So many messages, in fact, that you may have to put the rest of your life on hold to read them.

It's the modern version of a communication and tape-trading network that dates back to long before the Internet became a modern buzzword.

The Phish.Net was founded in 1991 by Matt Laurence, who later became the bassist for Northeast touring band yeP!. He and fellow yeP! member John Greene were part of a small crew that became the first Net-heads, a group which has swelled to over forty-thousand posters and lurkers in recent years.

"I started noticing on Dead.Net threads of Phish-related conversation," remembers Laurence, who caught his first Phish show in 1989. "I posted a message to the Dead.Net saying 'Hey, is anyone interested in a Phish mailing list or something?' Thirteen people responded."

Laurence set up a mailing list for those thirteen and the Phish.Net, in its crudest form, was born. Of course, that group quickly expanded to include many who would play a key role in Phish's future. Shelly Culbertson, now the band's assistant manager, was introduced to Phish by John Greene, and later would be among the first to inform the band of the Net's existence during the fall of 1991. She and people like Kevin Shapiro, now the band's official archivist, and Lee Silverman, who created the official Phish Web site in 1996 after running the Phish.Net archives off a computer at Brown University during his time there as a student, set out on a mission to document the band's history.

Phish.Net took the unlikely step from a simple electronic mailing list to an official Usenet group in 1992. At the time, the only "rec.music" groups devoted to individual artists were rec.music.g-dead, and rec.music.beatles, and a vote of Usenet participants was required to create a new group. Some were aghast at the idea of an unheard-of band having its own discussion group. But Phish.Net advocates found support among users of rec.music.g-dead . . . who were sick of reading all the Phish discussion on their bulletin board. Phish.Net won the vote by an overwhelming margin.

Ellis Godard, who joined the Phish.Net when it was comprised of only about one hundred people, recalls that back then it had a markedly different tone than today. "It was a smaller group, much more cooperative. A grovel [a plea for tapes or tickets] was not a problem. Trees were small and quick." Now, many early veterans of the Phish.Net have opted out of the loop, unwilling to deal with the torrent of postings.

But even before the Net electronic mailing list grew to the many thousands, it clearly had its impact, becoming the conduit for transcontinental tape trading which paved the path for Phish's first national tours. "The band would play a song on one coast. By the time they got to the other coast everyone knew about it because of tape trading," Laurence says. "The Net facilitated that so much."

Much of this was spurred by tape trees. A tree is a system under which one taper agrees to make copies of a tape for, say, five people, and those five people agree to make copies for

another five. As the tree branches out, hundreds of people gain access to tapes very quickly. Several of Phish's more recent soundboard tape releases, including 12/30/93 and 5/7/94, were offered to the Net by the band and disseminated by tape trees.

A forum for rumors, debate, and information sharing, the Net has also taken an active role in documenting the band's history and influencing some of Phish's musical directions. Though the band has not heeded every request from the thousands who have posted over the years, Trey sometimes receives printouts from the Net at his home, and the band's management keeps tabs on Net chatter.

As the Phish.Net continues to grow, it has spawned various offshoots and side projects. On the 1996 summer tour, a group of Phish.Netters organized mass audience participation games, handing out flyers calling for everyone to sit down during the "Divided Sky" pregnant pause, and also to shout "Hood" back at the band after each chant of "Harry." Thousands of fans complied during the four-day Red Rocks run.

Today, the tone and subject matter of the Phish.Net varies greatly. "There's still plenty of the original spirit of cooperation and communal recreation. But with more people, there's plenty of flaming and antagonism and harassment," Godard says. "The other stuff has grown and that's a sociological inevitability, I suppose."

Basic tape trade requests and tapelists remain ever-present, as do simple requests for information or open-ended questions about band history. Debates on Phish fan ethics also volley back and forth, with a staunch group of fans often seen criticizing everything from trading tapes of shows not opened to recording (such as JazzFest), to ticketless fans, to the *Pharmer's Almanac*.

It happens that only a small percentage of fans frequently read the Net, as many remain without online access and a surprising number of fans who are hooked into the Internet still choose to get their Phish fixes elsewhere. But even those who don't participate can clearly recognize the impact Phish.Net has made. Much of the culture and knowledge shared by members of the Phish community originated online.

• Tangled in the Net •

The Web is awash in Phish pages, mostly vanity sites that offer tapelists and links to other Phish pages. But if you know what you're looking for, the Web is the greatest of tools for a fan. Here are some of the many notable Phish or Phish-related sites on the Web:

www.phish.com

Yup, the folks from Burlington got in the act in the summer of 1995 with the debut of the official Phish Web page. Besides offering updated ticket and touring information, phish.com has also offered goodies, including "This Month in Phish History" and excerpts from Mike Gordon's journal.

www.phishtapes.com

Launched in 1994, this site has developed into one of the central hubs of Phish trading on the Web. Users can post their tapelists and peruse the lists of other traders, then set up trades for the shows they've been seeking. There's also a tape trading message board for tape grovelers and traders.

www.tapetrading.com

Similar to the Trader's Corner, but wider in breadth, tapetrading.com allows users to post tapelists and trade tapes for all bands that encourage live concert taping. Over three thousand tapers have added their lists to the archive, making this site one of the largest tape-trading sites in existence.

http://www.tiac.net/users/swish/phish/

Maintained by the Swish, this site is another good resource for online traders. Visitors can post want ads for specific tapes, or make trade offers to the larger community.

ourworld.compuserve.com/homepages/ttphish/phishtap.htm (dubbed "The Helping Phriendly Program")

The official homesite of a freeware program written by Tom Torrillo. It allows you to create and maintain a database of all the Phish tapes you have.

Phish-Info (Mailing List)

This moderate mailing list e-mails all the essential Phish information to you—official tour dates, ticket release information, and setlists (usually within 24 hours of the show's completion). Since 1994, longtime Phish taper Mikey Perrott has handled the setlist responsibilities, making sure that subscribers stay up-to-date on what's happening on every Phish tour. To subscribe to Phish-Info, send an e-mail to phish-info-request@phish.net with the word "subscribe" on a line by itself.

www.bhm.tis.net/~rob/Digi-Phish.html

Now in its third year of operation, the low-volume Digital Phish Mailing List was created to facilitate communication between Phish DAT tapers and traders. Information about subscribing to the list can be found at www.bhm.tis.net/~rob/subscrib.html.

www.phish.net

The Phish Net

The official Phish.Net page, designed by Rosemary Mackintosh and maintained by Robert Johnson and Eddie Divel. It features lots of basic Phish information, and the ever-changing Frequently Asked Questions (FAQ) file.

www.newmarketproductions.com/phish/

Similar in overall concept to Andy Gadiel's page, "Bone's Phish Philes" is another frequently updated page of Phish information and links.

AOL Nightcrew

If you happen to venture into America Online's chat room "the Phish bowl" during the wee hours of the morning, well, we're sorry that you can't get to sleep, but you'll find that you are not alone. There is a group of phans who hang out in the Phish Bowl between 2 A.M. and dawn and they go by the name of the Night Crew.

Stacey Margolis remembers the first time she ventured into the land of the late-night Phish chatters. "I watched the dialogue scroll by for a little while, and realized that these kids all knew each other! They called each other by their first names, not their screen names. Everyone had something in common that allowed them to relate," she said.

One of the wonders of the Internet is how friendships can develop online. "It is a group of people who I can look forward to 'seeing' if I've had a bad night or can't sleep. We talk about meaningless things (rarely Phish)," Stacey says.

Among the hard-core members of the Night Crew are BENDEAD, CheekWeezl, CosmcChr1, Guavajelli, Iggy1977, KELTISCH, Lehigh98, Ryryrocco, Suzi3G, and Turtle1422. In all, about thirty people consider themselves members, and often meet in person at shows.

The crew is changing all the time, so by the time you read this there may be a whole new batch of names pecking the keys in the late-night hours. And if you ever find yourself up late at night with no place to go, you'll be sure to find a warm welcome in the Phish Bowl. Just be sure to get your eyes and fingers ready. Text tends to scroll quickly when the Night Crew is on.

www.mindspring.com/~pagey/phish
Bouncin's Phish Page
A good overall Phish site with lots of links, a tapelist, and an online version of the Gamehendge story. A phriendly place to be.

Compiled with help from Pharmer's Almanac Web master Matt Monaco.

Online Music

As Real Audio progresses as a standard for music on the Net, live broadcasts of music on the Net have become a reality. All you need is a 28.8k modem connection and the most recent version of Real Audio (www.realaudio.com). Several sites cater to the Phish crowd:

eyes.jeffdell.com/real.html
Sugarmegs
This "ecosystem of audio streams irrigates the ears of the net" with live music from the Grateful Dead, Phish, and other bands.

www3.bowdoin.edu/~msananto/shows/
Live Shows
A growing collection of Real Audio shows from jam bands including Phish, Bela Fleck, Strangefolk, and Percy Hill.

http://www.gadiel.com/phish
Among the thousands of Web pages related to Phish, Andy Gadiel's Phish Page clearly jumps out as one of the best.

Created by Gadiel in 1995, it was originally an effort on his part to make setlists more easily available to fans. "I remember that there were many people who didn't know how to get access to the setlists, or who didn't care to take the time to subscribe to Phish Info. I decided to put up a site where I could simplify the process and give people easy access to the information they wanted," says Gadiel.

Since then the site has grown, utilizing easily understandable tables and charts to give users access to setlists, articles, and interviews, links to other sites, as well as cool pictures, audio files, and tour info. There's even a section on the always popular "Phish rumors," confirmed and unconfirmed.

Gadiel says that he used his academic training to improve the site. "I was a computer science major at Michigan State, and as my love for Phish grew, and my knowledge of computers grew, the site really took off. I'd learn something new in school, and would implement it on the site."

All of his efforts have paid off for him, but mostly for the Phish community, as the site has become "self-sufficient," as Andy calls it. "I spend maybe two hours a day working on the page. Mostly people send in material and information and I work it into the page. It's a place where people in the community have an opportunity to speak freely about something they love so much."

http://www.nd.edu/~pjohnso8
The Helping Phriendly Book
In the early days of the Phish.Net, some of the original netters created a compilation of setlists that became the definitive Phish setlist collection of its day, and later served as primary source for the *Pharmer's Almanac*. Known as the "Helping Phriendly Book" (HPB), it was edited by phans Shelly Culbertson (who now works for Dionysian Productions), John Friedman, and Richard Stern. Dan Schoop, who later would design websites for moe. and the Wetlands Preserve, also played a key role. In the mid 1990s, the HPB passed through the hands of a string of administrators, and was updated only sporadically.

That changed when Pat Johnson, whose first show was the famous Carleton College "Prison Joke" gig in 1991, set up an interactive Web site for the HPB several years ago and began revising and updating the book. Now the HPB is the most current online archive of Phish setlists.

"I enjoy everything I can do for Phish and its fans, and I hope I can continue to help out in the future in any way," Johnson says. "The music is an inspiration, and I love everything about it." But he also acknowledges the many others who preceded him in working on the HPB. "I wouldn't feel right putting this on the Web without giving credit to the people who initially put the book together." A complete history of the HPB is available on Johnson's site.

www.oe.org
Operation Everyshow
Since the earliest days of the Phish.Net, tape trees have helped spread the wealth of Phish concert tapes far and wide. (A tree is an organized structure in which a taper agrees to copy a tape for, say, five people, and each of those five people agree to copy it for five more people, and so on. As the tree branches out, hundreds of people gain access to tapes in a very quick fashion.) Prior to 1995, tape trees were most often run on the Phish.Net for soundboards released by the band, including 5/7/94 Dallas, TX, and 12/30/93 Portland, ME. But in the summer of 1995, fan James Gray came up with an idea. What if a tape tree could be set up for every single Phish show? There were plenty of folks who wanted fast access to concert tapes who didn't tape live themselves, and Gray thought that a coordinated effort could ensure that dispersal of tapes from every show. In conjunction with that summer's tour, he launched Operation Everyshow.

Three years later, OE (as it is commonly known on the Net) is still going strong, and can claim responsibility for thousands of tapes in circulation. In a sense, it represents the complete evolution of the Phish taping phenomenon. There was a time when not even every show was taped; now, every show is taped and copied en masse, and never again will there be a show that isn't replicated in large numbers.

Of course, OE has faced its share of challenges. Anyone who has participated in a tape tree will tell you that they can be frustrating—all it takes is for one person along the way to ignore his or her duties, and an entire "branch" of the structure can fall apart. That's happened more than a few time to OE trees, resulting in some shows never getting dispersed in wide numbers.

So, for summer 1997, Gray limited OE to DAT tapers only, drawing fire from some analog folks who feared OE was becoming too exclusive. But OE DAT traders were encouraged to trade their tapes with analog tapers via the Phish.Net, ensuring that the music still got out. Indeed, many of the highest-quality audience tapes in circulation from recent years are a direct result of Gray and OE's efforts.

http://members.aol.com/im4hemp111
Becky's Schedule of Cool Music
Media, PA, resident Becky Stillwell is the force behind Becky's Schedule of Cool Music, a monthly schedule of, well, cool music that is mailed to over one thousand people via the Internet.

Becky's schedule includes Phish and many other bands, everyone from the Disco Biscuits to G Love. She includes only bands she's seen or heard perform and which she feels comfortable recommending.

"Over the past two years, I've seen over two hundred nights of live music, so I started a schedule to help keep track of all the shows. I sent it out to a few friends, who sent it out to a few friends, and then I started getting requests," says Stillwell. "Then I started keeping an eye out

AOL PHISH Forum

America Online users need only type [command] K and the word *Phish* to access the Phish Forum.

The Phish Forum grew out of the popular Grateful Dead Forum, which originally started as a folder inside Rock Link. There was a maximum space for five hundred messages, and the Deadheads were taking over too much of the room.

"The community wanted a place to communicate, and we were taking over the chat room," says Jeff Gould, who founded both the Phish and the Dead forums. In 1992, the GDF had launched primarily as a chat room. "There was a chat room, message board, download library, and some news items," Geoff said.

Eventually Phish began to emerge in earnest, and while there are many similarities between Phish-heads and Deadheads, the two groups were not always compatible. Geoff remembers that "there was some bickering that would go on. Despite the similarities, each group wanted their own area to communicate."

That led to creating the "Phish Bowl," a real-time chat room. "The Phish Bowl was really started in an attempt to kind of separate the Deadheads from the Phish-heads," Gould explains. That was in 1995. By 1996 the Phish Forum emerged as its own entity, including a messages section, great for ticket exchange connections, the tape trading den, and even a list of Phish-head favorite recipes. There is Phish news, info on upcoming shows, and links to other Phish sites.

Maintaining these sites takes a lot of work. "It's a full-time job. A lot of it is in place, and become automatic, but we do depend on volunteers to help maintain the sites," says Gould. Stephanie Finz is one of the main volunteers who helps out on the Phish Forum, helping in the upkeep of the message boards, and providing the true Phish insight. Gould admits, "I don't pretend to be a Phish-head, so her help is quite valuable."

But even if you won't find Gould at a Phish show, you may encounter him hanging out with Mike Gordon, a personal friend. In fact, Gould used to work for the bass company Modulus, which supplied instruments to Gordon and to Phil Lesh of the Grateful Dead.

for people who I thought would enjoy it, too."

Becky sometimes adds people to her mailing list if she sees their e-mail address pop up on pertinent newsgroups or Web pages. But many of the subscribers sought out Becky on their own.

In order to receive Becky's Schedule of Cool Music, just send Becky an e-mail at Im4hemp111@aol.com.

www.phish.net/discussion/benjys-digest/FAQ.html

Benjy's Digest

The Phish.Net can sometimes get you caught in the flow of an endless barrage of posts, of mixed value. When things sort of hit a breaking point in 1995, a fan by the name of Rosemary Macintosh set out to cut through the muck and create a "digest," an edited version of rec.music.phish which would include only key messages of interest to all. Of course, it was a controversial move, and Rosemary was the first to concede that the digest would represent only her opinion of what was noteworthy. But then again, no one was obligated to subscribe.

At its peak, Rosemary's Digest had about three thousand readers. When she stopped putting together the digest, which entailed many hours of work per day, the community was at a bit of a loss, and her readers loathed the idea of having to cut through the muck of Phish.Net once again.

That's when Wormleysburg, PA, resident Benjy Eisen stepped in. A longtime Phish.Netter who'd been seeing Phish since 1993, Eisen agreed to bear the load and get a digest going once again. When it was announced that Benjy would be handling the digest, over eight hundred people signed up within a matter of days. And the list continues to grow.

"I honestly don't know why I do it," Eisen says. "The value is anyone can get in on Phish discussion without having to go through millions of bullshit posts."

Anyone with Internet access who would like to receive Benjy's Digest should send an e-mail to Listserv@archive.phish.net with the line: subscribe benjys-digest [firstname, lastname].

www.Phish.net/Phish FAQ

Among the most popular and oldest fan-created Web sites is the Phish FAQ. (*FAQ* stands for "frequently asked questions.") It was created by Charlottesville, VA, resident Ellis Godard way back in 1992, when the Phish.Net and the Phish cyberworld were in their infancies.

Among the first eleven questions it answered were "What's the Helping Friendly Book?" and "What are they saying in 'You Enjoy Myself'?" Although updated infrequently and not always accurate, the FAQ remains an important resource for new fans just getting into the band.

Godard has also made other contributions to the Phish community, including the popular "Tank Talk Tapes," a pair of four-hour DAT tapes which include virtually every radio interview the band has ever done through 1994. He added a nice touch by splicing in music between each interview segment. Tank Talk Tapes I and II continue to circulate among fans.

Research on this section by Matt Monaco.

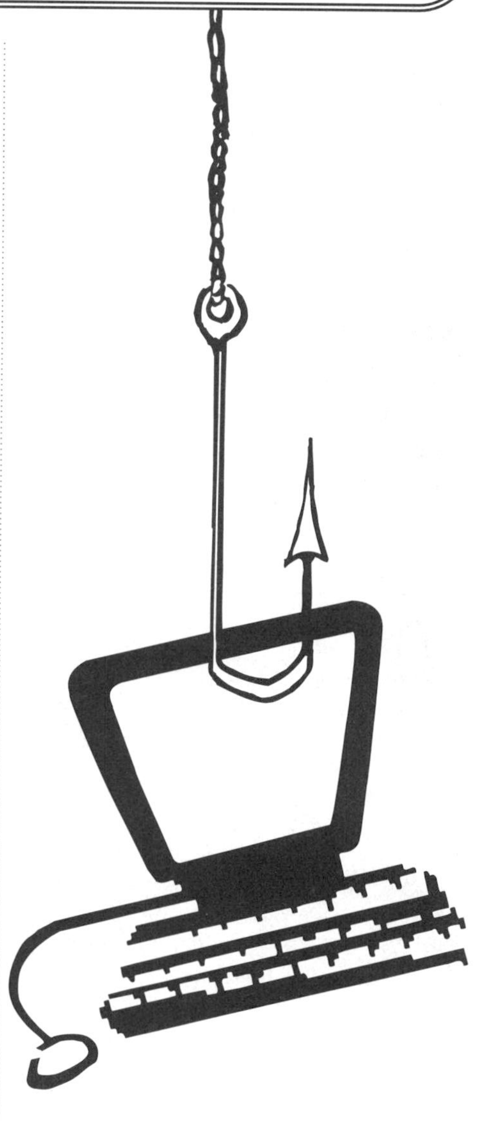

4

From the Fans

ON TOUR

• Up the Mountain •

LET ME TAKE YOU on a journey to Los Angeles, California. It could be anywhere, anytime, but this memory—this particular city—with its own particular vibration and unification, lingers deeply in my being.

I was on a California tour, like I usually am. My father, conveniently, lives in Sausalito, offering warmth and food in the middle of my travels. I had friends, tickets, and lodging planned for every show. I'm one of those creeps who must have an itinerary if I'm going to travel three hundred miles. So I was visiting Dad after Cal Expo Amphitheater and realizing I was about to miss a show in L.A. at the Greek Theater (9/29/95). I expressed my concern to my father. Probably growing tired of my incessant rattle about Phish's greatness, he graciously agreed to put me on a train south. Alone and knowing I was heading into a sold-out scene I smiled all the way to "Hell-A."

I sat on the train sipping juice and scoffing free peanuts, eyeing the beautiful woman seated across the aisle. She was reading the Bible. I wondered what her deal was. Striking up conversation, I learned she was the wife of a preacherman. Immediately, being the eclectic visionary that I am, I jumped back in my mind to the beginning of 1995, everyone's first show of the year. Lowell Auditorium 5/16/95. It opened with a traditional debut, "Missionary Sisters." This song definitely captured the experience I was having: The preacher's wife was sitting next to me rambling on about the church and her Christian family, and I was pondering my split-second decision to follow the tour south, feeling intense spiritual need to be there. The lyrics "C'mon, c'mon, c'mon, children, don't you want to go? Yes, I want to go" caught exactly how I was feeling.

I got off the train, entered a bus, and popped a hit of LSD. When I stepped off the bus there were twenty large L.A. residents and one short Phish-head with long hair awaiting my arrival. Together, the Phish-head and I trudged up the gigantic hill to the Greek. I wandered around aimless and happy for a while. I started to hallucinate and did not worry about getting into the venue (the key to getting into the venue of course is to ignore the urgency). Then a man literally walked up to me and sold me third row center for only ten dollars over face value, a true bargain for such a special place.

Here you must know something about my concert experience. Wherever I go at the start of a show, I am there until the end. Especially if I am in altered states, I have a very difficult time maneuvering through a crowd. When I station myself at an optimum spot, I own it and fear leaving. Well, this was my philosophy up until the fateful Greek Theater. I was third row center, made fun friends there and enjoyed the "AC/DC Bag." The "Sparkle" then touched a nervous vein and I sunk into some weird funk, whereby I decided I needed to leave my spot immediately. I struggled with this idea for quite some time. I was very worried about walking anywhere in the middle of a set. Worried I'd miss a note, get lost in a crowd, accidentally wander outside the gates and be shutout for the rest of the show (I've done that before). My mind told me to stay put but my soul told me to get out of there fast, so I left at the start of "Divided Sky."

I felt freer than I ever had. I had just broken a stagnant habit. I was wandering around the crowd with no particular means to an end and I felt great, free as a bird. I walked right, I walked left, I walked up, I walked down, I stopped to dance in the aisle, I moved on and danced next to sweet-looking girls and sweet-looking guys. Soon I tired of all this freedom and decided I'd better do something goal-oriented. I glanced upward at the very height of the venue, at a very large tree that shadowed the top of the surrounding wall, watching over all inside. I decided to go to that tree and give it a big hallucinogenic hug. So I pranced my way up the steps,

Courtesy of Jeremy Sheely.

widely smiling at hundreds of faces along the way. As I reached the top, so I reach the climax of this story, the issue at hand.

You know that silent part of "Divided Sky" where the band ceases all play and just stands there muted for an undisclosed period of time? Yes, yes, that part. Well, I was just prancing along honestly paying no attention at all to the music. In fact, for a moment I couldn't even have told you whose concert I was at had you asked and I approached the top. The tree was within arm's reach. For me this was a major accomplishment and my excitement increased exponentially with every final step. I could have been on Mars or Mt. Everest, as focused as my attention was on reaching my goal atop the Greek Theater. I stepped up to the tree, steadfastly hugging the thing, and noticed through peripheral vision that everyone sitting up there was intently staring at me. I cared not. I turned toward the stage, jumped one sturdy leap, and raised my arms high into the air, exactly like Rocky atop the Philadelphia Museum of Art staircase.

I performed this revelry at precisely the same moment Phish decided to sound their "diiiiiiiing" during their silent "Divided Sky" interlude.

Those people staring at me looked at each other in complete awe, then turned and continued staring at me as if I were definitely from Mars or else working for the band incognito. I think a few of them may have clapped in my direction. For them Christine Holbrook really was a special human being. I wish I could have introduced myself in glory. Instead I momentarily froze.

The ultimate synchronicity, drastically unintended. It was enough to tumult my soul as far out of my body as I've ever accomplished (which isn't really far but far enough at this point).

After working through this phantastic experience, using the bathroom during intermission and grounding myself on the toilet, I returned to third row center during the "2001." Here I believed I was a child of the future.

—Christine Holbrook

• The Journey •

"He doesn't know to behold what the cold frost can do."

THE 27TH AND 28TH of November will remain two of the worst days of my life, hopefully never to be matched again. The first snowstorm of the year landed in the Midwest at exactly the wrong time. I spent the first hours of the 27th waiting, watching The Weather Channel for a shift in weather patterns or a road closure. With a day off, and a fifteen-hour drive ahead of me, I figured I could wait until ten or eleven A.M. to leave Minneapolis. Equipped with a rear-wheel-drive car made more for California than Minnesota, I charged for Bozeman, Montana, blinded from all common sense and rationality in order to complete my mission: Phish in Montana.

By the time I left, the storm had hit the Twin Cities. Within five miles of my house, cars were already in the ditches and the roads were sloppy. Regardless, I did not return. If I missed the first leg of tour, I would have to miss the next three shows and skip to the Bay Area. Not happening.

About an hour into my venture, I come in contact with my first ditch. It's a graceful and quiet trip to the center of the roadway, no skidding tires or screeching brakes or broken glass. A quick and gentle lane shift into a pillow of snow and it's over.

I spun my tires for a minute or two and made my way out without having to get out of my car. Not too bad, I figured—at least the stuff doesn't dent! Traveling at about thirty five miles an hour in heavy snow was rough, but not too bad. At that rate I would still make Bozeman on time.

As I approached the North Dakota border things were looking good. The sky cleared and the sun poked through and, lo and behold, it started to rain. The gods were on my side, as I was able to speed up to sixty, even seventy. This seemed like great news, nothing to worry about because the rain was melting all the snow.

One lesson I learned that night, as I went into the ditch for the second time in East Fargo, North Dakota, was that as soon as the sun goes down, all water on the roads turns to ice. This time, I was facing perpendicular to the road, in the middle of a large ditch. Luckily, two locals pulled over in their truck to help push me out. They got out of their truck, looked at my California plates and said, "Boy, what in hell are you doing here?" I replied with, "Doing my best to get where I belong!" They laughed off the subtle insult and obvious self-acknowledgment of stupidity and ignorance of winter travel and pushed me on the road (in the other direction). As I was driving away they said, "And don't get back on these roads till they're clear, ya hear?"

I was pushing my luck and I knew it. I retreated to a twenty-dollar-a-night dive and went to bed at eight P.M., exhausted from nine hours of travel for a four-hour trip. I figured I'd wait until the next day to give them a chance to clear the roads. I woke up at 4:30 and was on the road by 5 A.M., unbeknownst to me the beginning of the worst day of my life. I was (seriously) the only car on the road until seven in the morning. I was averaging less than twenty-five miles an hour on a half-inch layer of ice and a top layer of snow, but figured it was better than making no ground at all. I stopped for gas, smokes, Mountain Dew, and took a piss, and that was it. For lunch I got some soup and fries at Perkins for twenty minutes and off again.

It was here where I realized I shouldn't be on the road. I saw the ice and snow on the ground and slipped on my ass twice in ten minutes. I also saw three tow trucks coming in from the ice rink known as I-94 with wrecked cars attached. Blinded from stupidity, still willing to put my life on the line for a concert, I decided to continue. Thirty minutes from here I was passed by a semitrailer truck going over forty miles an hour.

I had to slow down and downshift. I lost it and fumbled the downshift, giving it a bit too much gas, and finding myself spinning out of control. Just as I got some control back, I realized I was going to come to a stop, facing another oncoming semi. I thought fast and slammed on my brakes, knowing full well it would land me in the ditch, but deciding that it would be better to be there than attached to the Peterbuilt grill, eating a dashboard sandwich.

This time, I wasn't able to drive out or be pushed out; I actually had to climb out my window to get out of my car. A sheriff was called to help me out, which, given my situation and location, was not all that good. When he arrived, he got out of his car and came over to mine. No more than ten feet from his car, the local sheriff fell straight on his ass. This made me feel a bit better about my situation; even the locals couldn't keep their feet beneath them. He called a tow for me and about a half hour later the only tow truck within two hours came by to pull me out. He already had a car attached and figured he could stand to make a few extra bucks on the side without telling his boss. I figured this when he said he didn't take credit, so I played hippie and said I was out of money and only had nine dollars to my name. He said it was 150 dollars to get pulled out, but after realizing I had no money, he took the nine bucks. Not a bad tradeoff.

So I was off again, not smart enough to stop, still heading at a snail's pace to this now mystical place known as Bozeman. Traveling through the frozen tundra, one song seemed to come up more and more, taking on new meaning as I stared with an unrelenting gaze at the two black paths carved out of the whitewash of snow. "Mound." "The old man knows, very well." I didn't, so I kept driving. Heading back to Santa Barbara to return to school after spending my last long stay in Minnesota, it was time for the last rewind; nothing could stop me.

My saving grace was the fact that I crossed the border to Montana right around sunset. My friend Loomis, who went to school in Bozeman, told me that "you know when you're in Montana 'cause there's grass, green grass." Montana was also good in that they use salt on their roads, a policy South Dakotans shun with pride.

I was about twelve hours into my venture, and seven hours away from a show that started in two and a half hours. I was rather delerious; I stayed awake by playing a sick game of How Loud Can You Sing "Me and Bobby McGee" to Yourself?; drinking a case of Mountain Dew and three or four packs of Reds; taking multiple laps around the rest areas, running in snow without socks on; eating vitamin supplements, Snickers, and some NoDoze; and listening to a shitload of tapes.

Nineteen and one half hours after I left East Fargo, I arrived at Loomis's house in time only to hear the great stories of songs that "went on for a while." And that "a kid came out and played sax; they played a really long Tweezer too." I believe a Guyute and a yet-unseen-for-me-NICU also popped up as well. Hmmm, never heard it, never will. The only tape I know of that I really don't want.

Out of the twelve or so cars on that leg of tour, two made it to the show. Both left right after the show in Minneapolis. Two cars never made it out of South Dakota. Brother Rick slammed his car right into a cop car, totaling both, and abandoned his coach and jumped into his friend's bus. We all made it safely out of that adventure. Someone was looking out for us, I know it.

Not once again will I drive a snow tour. If I do drive for some reason, I will miss the show even if it means I have to get out of another person's car who is going to try to make it there. I realized from this rather adventurous yet pathetically rookie decision, my life is more important than seeing even one of the best Phish shows ever played.

—Jay Archibald

• You Enjoy My Coif •

I was heading down Third Avenue to get a haircut at my usual pretentious place (hey, they give a good haircut). The salon is typical of the Upper East Side in New York City; the decor is in the Louis XIV genre, the stylists wear either all black or puffy shirts (a lá *Seinfeld*), and everyone is sporting clunky black shoes. The background music is of the Parisian disco variety, with the occasional Gypsy Kings–esque ditty thrown in. This joint is trendy schmendy.

I stopped by HMV and finally picked up my copy of *Slip Stitch and Pass,* before heading over to get my hairs chopped, and I walked in with four-day-old road stubble and wearing old plaid flannel.

Upon entering the salon, I was greeted by my stylist, Franc, who noticed my HMV bag immediately. "Jonathan," he exclaimed in his French accent, "vat iz dis muuseek dat you haf?" I told him about Phish, which he had never heard of in his travels. "Oh . . . let's puut eet on!" Right there, my heart stopped. I didn't want to share my Phish with these people. They were going to ridicule them, turn up their noses, poo-poo my beloved band. I couldn't say no, and I reluctantly handed Franc the CD.

So there I was, sitting in the chair with butterflies in my stomach, waiting to hear the criticism of the yentas and the mod squad, when something wonderful happened . . . Cities.

As the band played, I noticed a sudden change in the salon's atmosphere. I glanced around the place (through my omnipotent mirror) and noticed that stylists too cool for the room were bobbing their heads, old women in the hair helmets were tapping their feet, the shampooers were massaging scalps in time to the music. It was truly a beautiful sight. The transition into Wolfman's, was just as cool, with everyone in the room movin' and groovin'.

Shortly into Wolfman's, I had to leave, and naturally I wanted to take my new CD with me. When they returned it and put on their standard fare, it was as if a switch had been flipped, Cinderella at the stroke of midnight. Everyone got tight—their faces, their bodies, the whole scene. During the Phishy interlude, it was as if the inhabitants had entered an alternate dimension, only to have no recollection of their experience when the music stopped.

The next time I get my hair cut, I plan to teach them the opening line to Destiny. Hey, you never know. . . .

—Jonathan Schwartz

Phish in Hamburg.

Photo courtesy of George Lyons.

• Ignorance Is, Sometimes, the Best of *Bliss!* •

In interviews about the live album Slip Stitch and Pass *that appeared on Phish's Web site, Trey and Mike elude to the fact that they were consciously attempting to change their sound on the winter 1997 Europe tour by making the guitar less of the main focus. Well, one fan found himself in the middle of this transition, and he may have played a tiny roll in history in the process.*

WHERE DO YOU START when you try to tell someone a story about one of the greatest musical experiences of your life? To tell Phish-heads about "their" band? Normally, one would be laughed out of a room for trying to pull such a crock! Well, I got one for y'all. I was there—3/1/97, Markthalle, Hamburg, Germany! This is the story about what led up to the show that, from what I understand, is one of the best Phish shows ever! That's me screaming on the *Slip Stitch and Pass* CD, telling Mike how much I enjoyed his bass sound that night, and *Oh, what a night it was!!!* This story is purely factual; it all really happened.

Being an old Deadhead, and one of the original tapers from that scene, I have a great appreciation for the "dedication" shown to Phish by their fans. Once again, we are taking it to a new level. And yes, I think I would have to include myself as part of the "we." After two Europe tours with Phish, and a few U.S. dates, I have officially grown gills. This band, put simply, is great!

I became aware of a band named Phish, in 1988 or 1989 from a friend, while attending a Grateful Dead show at the Greek Theater in Berkeley, CA. By this point I had heard the name, and seen the alternate spelling somewhere, but this particular set of shows at the Greek had Phil Lesh, the Grateful Dead's bassist, unveiling a new set of bass speakers and stage equipment. I asked my buddy what he thought the equipment changes entailed. He did not know what the new equipment was, but he had heard that the bass player for Phish had purchased Phil's old bass equipment. To this date, I don't know if this is fact or fiction, but I gained an immediate respect for Mike Gordon at that moment in time. I knew that anyone who bought Phil's old rig must be one hell of a player.

It wasn't until about six years later that I first really heard the band—in the parking lot at my last-ever Dead show (ironic, huh?).

I have some good friends that are past and present West Coast Phish phanatics, and they got me to go to the Greek Theater in Los Angeles a few months later, 9/29/95, and then Pauley Pavilion, 12/1/96. That show was great, and I decided to see them in Las Vegas, 12/6/96. Need I say more? My head had been opened up to Phish. These guys were doing it!

Around that time my friends had decided that they were going to do the Europe tour, and Phish and the Black Crowes were playing three consecutive nights at the Paradiso in Amsterdam! How could I pass up that kind of a party? Now, keep in mind that at this point in my life, I was thirty-seven years old and running a major Hollywood nightclub on the Sunset Strip, booking live bands for a living. But I decide to go to Europe for a two-week vacation that will have me seeing some shows here and there and relaxing. I never planned on jumping on Phish tour, but, then again, we never do! That's exactly how I ended up touring for fifteen years with the Dead!

After seeing one Phish show at Le Botanique, in Brussels, I was hooked like a guppy. My God! The Down with Disease was one of the greatest live songs I have ever seen played, by any band! Suddenly, what I did for a living was no longer on my list of priorities. This band was just frying my mind, and I knew right then and there that I was on the tour! I went on to Amsterdam, and saw two great Black Crowes shows, but my mind was on the next Phish show.

As the tour continued into Italy, I had begun to make friends with the small group of heads on tour, as well as the crew and band. The entire band hung out and talked with anyone that dared to talk to them. In my case, I was curious, and on the road with them . . . what did I have to lose?—they're just regular old nice guys!

By the time we got to Stuttgart, everybody

was pretty much on a first-name basis. I had bought Fishman a Swiss Army knife on my trip through the Alps and gave it to him as a way of saying thanks for all the cool vibes and sounds. He ended up placing me on his guest list for the last three shows, because I did not have tickets, and had not planned to stay. Suddenly, my plans had changed!

Now, Stuttgart was great. In fact, Fishman later told me that the band felt it was the best of the tour.

The scene was really something special too. The entire band was out talking to their fans, which gave me the chance to ask Mike about his "bass sound" and his "theory" behind it. It was obvious, after listening to him play, that he was not your "normal"-sounding low end of the band. This man has his shit together in a big way, and I wanted to find out what his deal was, so I did!

Now you must remember that at this point I had no idea what was going on with the band on any level. Historically, on tour, as friends, musical influences, nothing! I only knew that these four musicians I was listening to and getting to know in the past couple of weeks were totally cool. Hell, I work with musicians every day, so I'm not too intimidated to "talk shop" with them, and these guys were such a pleasure to be around. Mike, as I've come to learn, is probably the most accessible, and this particular night in Germany, he was more than happy to speak to me.

I asked him if we could talk about his "bass sound," and he looked at me very seriously and said, "I would like that very much!" I opened the discussion by asking him if he was influenced by Phil Lesh. He said, "Actually, yes, my other bass is a Modulus, like Phil plays." I asked who made his custom bass, and he told me that Paul Languedoc, their sound engineer, made both Trey's guitar and his bass guitar.

"So," I proceeded, "then you know that Phil played lead bass when he played. He did not sit back in the rear and simply hold down the bottom. Sometimes Jerry played the bass line while Phil was off in the 'Phil Zone' somewhere." Mike agreed wholeheartedly, with a look of "so what's your point?" I said, "You play with a pick most of the time, similar to the way Phil played." Mike continued to listen very intently, waiting to see what I had to say.

I proceeded to tell Mike what I was experiencing from his live sound. I told him that "I was not able to hear the entire note" that he was playing. By that, I meant that I could not hear his "lead bass line." I said, "When Phil played the notes, you heard every one of them with the strike of the pick!" That's one of the most unique stylings that he brought to the Grateful Dead's sound. Mike agreed. I said that I could feel his [Mike's] sound when he struck the string on his bass, but I could not hear the precision of his picking on some of the more intricate jams.

He looked at me with a very serious look at this point, and we were fully engulfed in this subject that was obviously of great concern for him, or so it seemed.

Jammin' in Amsterdam.

Photo courtesy of Anthony Buchla.

He asked, "So what do you think the problem is?"

I responded by saying and doing this: I placed my hands on his chest and said, "Your sound hits you right here as you play the notes, but I don't hear the pick strike the string. I need to hear you picking out the notes, as well as feel their impact. You're doing stuff up there that is mind-blowing. I'm watching you from the front rows every night, and I cannot hear your pick hit the string! Your sound needs to be more defined!"

I did not feel any pretentiousness at all between us. We were "talking shop," like I do at work every day.

Mike said, "The attack!" I said, "Yeah, I guess that's what you call the point where the pick strikes the string, the attack! Yes, I need to hear the attack, and I don't hear it now."

Mike said, "So what would you do about it?" I threw my hands up in the air and said, "Now you're asking me a technical question, and I'm not a soundman." Mike responded, "What would you do in your room in Hollywood?" I said, "In my room, if the bass player asked for my advice, I would tell him or her to turn up the high end on the amp, or equalizer." To this, Mike said, "One K," expecting me to agree. With a totally dumbfounded look, I replied, "Now you're really trying to get technical with me. I don't know where the pick strikes the string on the sound spectrum. It's somewhere on the high end of the spectrum, that's all I know for sure, maybe One K!" Mike is into his sound, that you can be sure of!

At this point, Mike looks me square in the

Photo courtesy of Anthony Buchla.

eye and asks me, "Would you tell Trey exactly what you just told me? I would really appreciate it if you would do that."

I must admit, I looked at Mike like he was crazy and said, "You must be joking!" He said, "No, this is a big point of contention in the band right now, and I would really appreciate it if Trey could hear what you just told me."

He said this with a totally straight face, and a very sincere way about it all. Being a person that deals with musicians on every level of the game, I knew this could be a touchy subject within any band. You never try to tell a musician, who does not want to hear it, about his or her sound. That's why I asked Mike first, before I just launched into my rap with him. His sound had been on my mind for a few shows, and I found an opportunity, an open mind, to speak to that night in Stuttgart.

I looked at Trey about ten feet away from me, just standing and talking to someone. I looked back at Mike and said, "Trey isn't going to pull a typical guitar player freak-out if I go and tell him what I told you?" Mike looked at me with a totally reassuring look and said, "No, he won't mind. Go tell him exactly what you told me before he leaves," and he points me in the direction of Trey, as I see Trey just finishing up a conversation.

I walked up to him and said "Trey," just as he was about to turn and leave. He looked back at me and said, "Yeah, George, what's up?" I said, bolstered by Mike's assurance, "Mike wanted me to tell you what I just told him about the way I was hearing his bass sound." Great opening line, huh? Trey kinda looked at me funny, and said, "What did you tell him?" Then I proceeded to place my entire leg into my mouth. "I told him that I was unable to really hear his pick striking the string" (oh no, it's coming out all wrong! I thought) "and Mike asked me to tell you that I think it's an equalization thing."

Trey's expression pulled an about-face, from really receptive to really annoyed, in about one second, and I just about lost my composure as a result. I said, "I knew I should not have said anything to you. You don't need to hear this crap. How about this, Trey? It sounds great every night, and I'm so happy to be able to enjoy it all. It's all good, and you don't need to worry about the way the bass sounds anyway. See you at the next show, and could you play Weekapaug one night!"

With that, his face became understanding, at which point he replied, "Oh, don't worry about it, George. That's a big point of contention in the band right now. You take care; I'm gonna go now. Good night." We shook hands, I bid him farewell, and we parted company for the evening. I felt like a total ass!

I turned back around, and Mike Gordon was nowhere to be seen. "Son of a bitch, I think. He set me up to do his dirty work! or so it seemed. As I looked around for Mike, I saw Page rapping with a fan, and I said to him, "Hey, Page, tell Mike I just made a complete ass of myself in front of Trey!" He looked at me, real curious, and asked, "What did you do?" With egg on my face, I repeated my conversation with Trey. Page's expression suddenly changed, and he said, "Oh that's a big point of contention in the band right now!" to which I responded, "So I've come to learn!"

At this point, I knew that *I had been had by Mike Gordon.*

Page continued, "I wouldn't worry about it. Have a good night, George." I did not then know the real magnitude of what had happened, but when we got to Berlin, then Hamburg, I would find out.

In Berlin, Mike pulled out the Modulus bass for the encore song, A Day in the Life. I spoke to him after the show, and commented that I could really notice the difference in the way it sounded. He replied that it was a "brighter sound," to which I agreed, and said that "I was able to hear the attack much better with that bass, and maybe the equalization was the key to the brighter sound." It was not a big deal, and we both moved on to the next subject and town.

After seeing one Phish show at Le Botanique, in Brussels, I was hooked like a guppy.

By the time the tour reached Hamburg, it was all just one big peak, and the music reflected the energy that was in that room. You can hear the excitement on the CD.

As I walked into the Markthalle that night, Mike was sitting at the T-shirt stand doing nothing. I walked right up to him, with my ticket stub in my hand and a pen, and I said, "Sorry, Mike, you're gonna have to sign before the show tonight!" They had been signing autographs for everyone after the shows almost every night on the tour. So cool! Mike looks at me and says, "Only on one condition: I get to play a new bass tonight." I said, "Oh, you're going to play the Modulus tonight?" He responded, "Yes, and I want you to tell me how it sounds. I think you'll be able to hear more of the attack with the pickups on that bass."

I was very surprised, and honored that he would trouble to tell me he was making an equipment change. I handed him the pen and said, "Condition met. You can play a new bass tonight. I was planning on standing in front of you anyway for tonight's show." He responded, "Oh, you'll be able to hear it no matter where you're standing!" I looked at him with a very excited look in my eye and said, "No, I'll be right in front of you, and I'll give you immediate feedback during the show! And, by the way, play Mike's Song tonight." He signed my ticket stub, and I hurried into the hall to take my place on the floor, five feet from Mike's monitors, in hopes that this would be "The Show." It was!

Now, what happened next was what I have to call the best Phish show I've ever seen or heard, on tape or live, before or since. I don't need to review the show, because that's been done, but I will tell you that Mike's sound was *so fat* from the first note of Cities. By the time he played the opening bass riff to Down With Disease the crowd was bubbling. It was obvious that Mike was making a change in his sound. When Trey takes a moment to tell us how "cool" the room is, I let loose with my overwhelming joy for what I consider to be Mike at his best. Hell, we all were screaming at that point. The whole band was on, but Mike was out of control.

What happened from there can all be heard on the CD. After Trey tells me, "O.K. O.K.," he turns to Mike and says "Mike, he likes the way it sounds!" to which Mike responds, "I know!" as he grinned and giggled like a kid with his favorite toy. Then Trey mouthed quietly to Mike, *"Now turn it down!"*

I was beside myself with excitement at that. Mike turned to his equipment rack and made some adjustments to his "new stage sound." By the time the second set rolled around, and they played the Mike's > Lawn Boy > Weekapaug, the entire room had peaked so hard, for so long, nothing else really seemed to compare on the entire tour! (Except Cortemaggiore!) Mike switched back to his custom bass for the encore song, Taste. Listen to the CD, and you will be able to hear the difference in bass sounds.

I asked him if we could talk about his "bass sound," and he looked at me very seriously and said, "I would like that very much!"

This band had risen to a new level in just under the three weeks that I was in Europe with them. I still did not know much about Phish, and that was just fine. All I needed to know was that this band had taken me to places that I had only visited in the most sacred of times. I rose to a new level that night, as a human being, through their music. It was wonderful! These men are "masters of their art." I had been turned on by the band themselves, and *I got it in a big way!*

In Copenhagen.

Photo courtesy of Jay Archibald.

When I spoke to Mike after the show in Hamburg, I told him that I could hear it all and that he should use the Modulus bass all the time. But I also told him that it was obvious that he felt more comfortable with his custom bass, to which he replied, "Well, I've been playing that instrument for eight years." He told me that he would probably have Paul build him a new bass that had some tonal qualities that the Modulus has, as he also liked the sound that night in Hamburg. I wished him "good luck" with his idea, and thanked him for a great musical experience. I walked away from that show with a little bit more added to my life.

Any way you cut it, that's the way it came down. I would never really believe that I actually had anything to do with Mike deciding to change instruments. And I don't know why they decided to keep the comments about the sound on the CD, other than that it adds to the excitement of the "live experience" while listening. But, since then, Mike has changed over to playing the Modulus bass on a regular basis, and continues to increase his presence onstage. I have no idea if Paul is working on a new instrument, or if Mike will change back to his other bass in the future. Intruments are like people; each has its own personality and sound. That tour through Europe, in the late days of February and for two days in March 1997, was magical. I discovered Phish by simply listening to the sounds and allowing them to sink in. My God! Ignorance is bliss!

—George Ove Lyons

EARLY PHISH SIGHTINGS

FROM THE FANS

Phish may be the only band in the world whose fans brag about how *small* audiences were for shows they've attended. Having seen Phish in a bar such as the Front or Nectar's is considered the holy grail of achievement—although most who had that experience didn't know they were having anything but a nice night out at the time.

The *Almanac* tracked down a few fans who began seeing Phish in the late 1980s and recorded some of their memories and observations. Interestingly, each painted some very different pictures of this magical period.

• Memories of the Scene •

THE PHISH SCENE, in the beginning, was never, dare I say, as tour-rat infested as it is now. It was always kind of come as you are, and as long as you are there, that's cool. There was never really a dress code, you didn't have to fly your colors, you know what I mean?

Short hair was cool, long hair was cool. Khakis and a polo shirt was cool, bell-bottoms were cool, or somebody who just pulled in off a Dead tour was cool. It really didn't matter. And the little family, which there was that early on, was really mellow and was really tight-knit. I wasn't necessarily as tight-knit in some of the families, but you knew who they were. It was so small that you could always count on seeing some of the same people at every East Coast show.

Back then, there was always an opportunity, one way or another, to get in to the show. I can remember my friends going down to see them at UMass at the University Ballroom. They went down there and they were all laughing their asses off the next day because they *were* security. They showed up there, the show was sold out, but the band took care of them and said, "Here, be security." So they were security and they were let in. In those days you could, during intermission, go outside and into your car and do whatever it is that you wanted to do and then go back in.

—Brendan McKenna

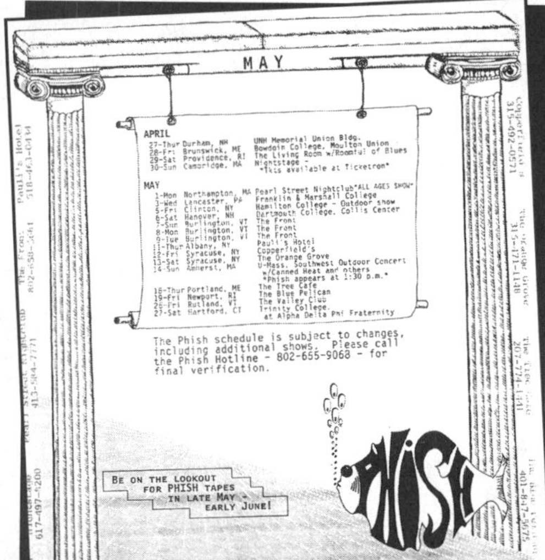

MAY

APRIL
27-Thur Durham, NH — UNH Memorial Union Bldg.
28-Fri Brunswick, ME — Bowdoin College, Moulton Union
29-Sat Providence, RI — The Living Room w/Roomful of Blues
30-Sun Cambridge, MA — Nightstage - *Tkts available at Ticketron*

MAY
1-Mon Northampton, MA — Pearl Street Nightclub *ALL AGES SHOW*
3-Wed Lancaster, PA — Franklin & Marshall College
5-Fri Clinton, NY — Hamilton College - Outdoor show
6-Sat Hanover, NH — Dartmouth College, Collis Center
7-Sun Burlington, VT — The Front
8-Mon Burlington, VT — The Front
9-Tue Burlington, VT — The Front
11-Thur Albany, NY — Paul's Hotel
12-Fri Syracuse, NY — Copperfield's
13-Sat Syracuse, NY — The Orange Grove
14-Sun Amherst, MA — U-Mass. Southwest Outdoor Concert w/Canned Heat and others *Phish appears at 1:30 p.m.*
18-Thur Portland, ME — The Tree Cafe
19-Fri Newport, RI — The Blue Pelican
26-Fri Rutland, VT — The Valley Club
27-Sat Hartford, CT — Trinity College. at Alpha Delta Phi Fraternity

The Phish schedule is subject to changes, including additional shows. Please call the Phish Hotline - 802-655-9068 - for final verification.

BE ON THE LOOKOUT FOR PHISH TAPES IN LATE MAY - EARLY JUNE!

Early Phish newsletters alerted phans of the band's hectic tour schedule.

THE ONLY T-SHIRT they had back then was green with a black logo on it, the classic Phish logo. I still have one of those T-shirts but it doesn't fit me very well anymore.

When I first started seeing them, you didn't even need tickets, you would just walk up and buy one at the door or give the guy five bucks a cover. I saw them at the Haunt in 1990, in Ithaca, a place, I remember, which is very narrow. God, I think it's only thirty feet wide or something like that, but it's pretty long. And the stage is only about six or seven inches high—and then there are wood beams, so they couldn't do their trampoline act in there or they would crack their heads on the wood beams. And then while we are sitting down drinking beers down at the bar, you can look up the stairs and see Mike and Trey drinking beers in the little musicians' lounge.

Most of the people that went to these shows were Deadheads. And when you are used to going to Dead shows, and you have all this entertainment before the concert and after the concert, and you go see a band like Phish—and Phish is totally different from the Dead, musically, philosophically, and stuff like that—but you can't help equate the scenes sometimes.

But the scene was a total letdown. The scene was like, you are used to going to these parking lot scenes and chilling out and drinking some beers or whatever, and you go up to the Haunt or something like that, or, for that matter, in 1991 at the Ithaca State Theater or the Somerville Theater in 1991 or '90, and there are fifteen people hanging around. And you show up an hour or two before the show and you would get totally bored because there was nothing happening. There was no scene, you know? The people who were going were basically Deadheads, you know, but the scene itself—I remember going outside the Somerville Theater, there were fifteen people sitting around. Not doing much. No guys playing hackysack. We got so bored that we went to a restaurant.

After the show was over, everybody left. There was no milling on the sidewalks or anything like that. People bolted. And I guess I just didn't notice that that was the thing to do or that you wanted to do it, you know? But when you got inside, there was the intensity, there was that electricity, there was that rare connection that a band can make with its audience.

—Mike Graff

IN THE EARLY DAYS it just seemed like Phish really gave a damn about the audience. There was this one night at UMass where they had sold the place out—it was a little ballroom in the middle

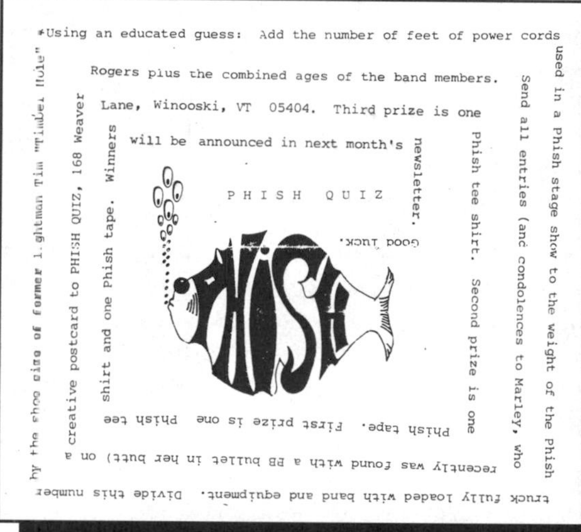

PHISH QUIZ

*Using an educated guess: Add the number of feet of power cords used in a Phish stage show to the weight of the Phish truck fully loaded with band and equipment. Divide this number by the shoe size of former lightman Tim "Timber Hole" Rogers plus the combined ages of the band members. Send all entries (and condolences to Marley, who recently was found with a BB bullet in her butt) on a creative postcard to PHISH QUIZ, 168 Weaver Lane, Winooski, VT 05404. Third prize is one Phish tee shirt. Second prize is one Phish tape. First prize is one Phish tee shirt and one Phish tape. Winners will be announced in next month's newsletter. Good luck.

of campus, and Fishman came out in the lobby, there were always, like, thirty of us who couldn't get in, but he came out and he walked us in, and he told a security guard, "It's cool, they're with me," and he walked us all in, little things like that, you got little things.

The audience used to be so much more focused on the music. It wasn't like you go and people would be talking beside you, and start packing a bowl; people would be going and be so focused, that was it, it was music lovers, that was the thing, it was about the music and only the music, and it was so important to people. It wasn't like, let's get our list out, and make the list, which there's nothing wrong with. I'm not against lists. My attitude on all that is that it's excellent to have, but there's people that were just so focused on the moment. I'm not knocking anything here. It's just an observation.

—Chad Garland

I'D SAY I WAS about average age for the group; I was twenty-three. It was mostly an of-age crowd, unlike now.

Maybe, in 1990, you saw a few more younger fans than in '89, like a few UVM undergrads or whatever, that had kinda got wind of Phish, but twenty, maybe thirty people at the most.

It was kind of like a young, kind of hippie, sort of very early stages of the grunge-type people. It was before grunge was a thing, or had a name yet. But you saw kind of like, hippies in their early twenties, people you'd normally maybe see at Dead shows. But it was a little younger than what you'd normally call the "hippie crowd." Everyone was pretty much the same age, between twenty-one and twenty-five at the shows, it was very homogeneous. You saw a lot of older college students or recent college graduates, that was the main crowd.

They usually had a few copies of *Junta* sitting around, and a really old Phish T-shirt where it's just green in the background, and it just says Phish across the chest and that's it. That's pretty much it, one T-shirt and one tape.

Nobody knew what Gamehendge was. In fact, I had never heard the word Gamehendge until, like, two years ago. I didn't know what it was, I didn't know who it was, was it a song or a concept? I'd heard "Lizards" and "Wilson", numerous times, but that whole kind of idea of it being this big, long, epic story was totally new to me, and I don't think I was the only clueless one, I think it was kind of news to everybody that this fit into some larger structure, this big epic tale. I had no idea.

—Charlene Smith

I'D SAY THAT THEY were largely prep school hippies. Just like the song. And that's partly why that song came about, because you'd look out into the crowd, you would be all white, all ages, seventeen to twenty-one. There weren't very many people at that time watching them that were out of college. It was all college-age, not even that many high-schoolers, it wasn't a young crowd. It was all college students, and they were all from the Northeast and they were all going to good schools in the Northeast and they all had money, so there were a lot of Saabs in the parking lot. It wasn't as diverse a scene as it is now, it was an East Coast, prep-school, you know, rich college-kid crowd, baseball caps.

—Jamie Janover

• Memories of the Band Members •

I REMEMBER THE FIRST-ever Wetlands show in '89. It was such a freeform show, my sister, who had probably way more beer than she should have had, got up on the stage and started jumping up and down on their trampolines. They tolerated her for about a song—I can't recall what song it was, but they allowed her just to sit there and jump up and down on this thing and then I think Mike went over and asked her to get off the stage.

What doesn't happen these days is that the band doesn't talk to the audience. But sometimes if somebody in the audience was making snide comments, somebody onstage would shoot their mouth off. Like Fishman would be like, "No way, man, you're totally wrong about that one." The band was so close and the band was so there that people would be having such a good time and, depending on what kind of recreations they were engaged in, would start making snide or sly comments at the band to try to get a rise out of them and the guys would respond back. But now, when you are in a big stadium or something, there is just such an overriding low noise that it is impossible to do that.

—Patrick Smith

IN THE SPRING OF '90 I saw them at the Wetlands and we got in beforehand. My friend Dan Talbot patched into the soundboard and recorded their soundcheck. And at the end of the soundcheck they came over, because this was before "Tweezer" was even a song. And they came over and they all took turns listening to "Tweezer" on the headphones, and in the meantime, Marnie [Davis] and my friend Dan and Trey sat down and Trey explained his guitar to my friend Dan, like "this does this and that does that and Paul built this," and so on and so forth.

Another story I remember is one cold winter's night, on route 15, coming home because my girlfriend at that time was going to school at UVM. So I went over to see her and I was coming home, and on the side of the road was this car, it had all kinds of Grateful Dead stickers all over the back of it, and they were a few hundred yards down and some guy had spun out. And it was cold and I usually don't do that and I was like, "Okay, I'll pick this guy up." So I pick this guy up and we start taking off and we're talking back and forth. He asked me if I had ever seen Phish before, and I was like, "Yes, yes," and we were talking about Phish and he asked me how big I thought they would get. I was like, "Well, I don't think they'll get that big, maybe like an Allman Brothers or something." And he says, "Oh, okay."

And I'm like, "Here, let me drive you to your house, where do you live?" He's like, "Jericho." I said, "Okay." So we drive and we drive and we drive and he says, "Well, can you take me to my driveway?" And I said, "Fine, why don't I take you to your house? It's really cold out." And he said, "I appreciate it. I might even need a ride back to my car." And I said, "Fine."

So I pull up to the house and there's all these Ryder rental trucks. And I'm thinking, "What the hell is going on?" And he says, "By the way, I do lights for Phish."

So I walk in the house and it's Chris Kuroda's house with Mike and Paul. The three of them, I think, shared a house at that time, I don't know. The downstairs, except for the kitchen, was all equipment as far as you could see. He ran upstairs to get money or something like that, because all he really needed was gas.

I started talking with Paul and Mike and Mike kept trying to sell me his bass amp. I don't play the bass, but he kept trying, over and over again, "Do you want my bass amp? Do you want my bass amp? Do you know anybody who would like to buy my bass amp?" He kept trying to sell me his bass amp but I was like, "I don't want your bass amp." But as it turns out, it was Michael's car that Chris had borrowed and I drove him back and dropped him off and that was that.

—Brendan McKenna

THEY'D TELL A LOT of jokes. There was a feel in the very beginning, the very first time I walked in the room, that there was some kind of inside joke, that you couldn't put your finger on, but somehow you played into it. I can't explain it really. It was definitely led by Trey, there's something going on with Trey that, he'd be making these comments between songs, he'd be saying funny little things that didn't make much sense, but everyone kinda got it. He did this incredible jam and they froze in the middle, like, stood still in time, and went right back into it, things like that. They did interesting stuff. There weren't any trampolines or anything like that at the time. And they weren't doing their little jigs, or whatever. There was just a lot going on onstage.

There was one night where Mike Gordon, they wouldn't let him in the front door. It was hilarious. Everyone in the audience was outside, it was a place that could only hold like five hundred, six hundred people tops, but we were all waiting to get in. It was a cold night, and I remember Mike was with some girl, and he was trying to get in, and this old man with a little walkie-talkie wouldn't let him in at the door. And everyone's going, "Hey, Mike, Mike, how ya doin," nothing too crazy, just asking how he's doing and patting him on the back. Security wouldn't let him in 'cause he's like, "Oh, yeah, that's what they all say, 'I'm with the band.' You know, like the cliché, I'm with the band. And he *was* with the fucking band, it was great. So finally the guy lets him in, he called some guy on the walkie-talkie. Meanwhile he's out here standing with all of these people, thoroughly ticked. You gotta understand that he had a good sense of humor about it the first couple of minutes, but he's up there for a few minutes, and they wouldn't let them in.

The Zero Man outfit was always there. Fish used to come out on stage with it. He had goggles on, swimming goggles. I think the cape was blue, it seemed to be like one huge outfit, pants and shirt, it was a complete outfit, and he wore all this stuff. He'd be barefoot with it on. I think the pants were red, the shirt was red, and the cape was darker blue. And he had this aviator cap that went all around and covered his entire head and covered his eyes, where he had the goggles, and his nose and his mouth, and you couldn't see anything else.

The big cape had a big zero, a huge zero in blue or black on the front of it. And he wore it all night. We would say, "He must be hotter than hell," 'cause we'd be sweating our nuts off, and he'd be up there in this spandex thing. I mean, he must have been dying in there. He'd be sitting back there with this crazy-looking outfit on, and then they used to always announce the band, but almost every time Trey would go, "This is Page McConnell, master of the boards, and this is Mike Gordon, and that's Greasy Fizeek." They'd also call him Tubbs. They had a few names for him, the Blue Zero Man, or something like that. So one day, he finally put that away, and he always wore the black skirt with the orange donuts on it, which is duct-taped together if you look at it. He'd rip his clothes onstage and duct-tape them back together.

> I CAN'T BELIEVE it's the same thing—the same dress, how could it possibly be the same dress? It's got to have a hole in the backside.
>
> There was a '91 show at the Ithaca State Theater where he took on this whole other persona, where he took on the persona of Captain Zero.
>
> He wore this giant jumpsuit leotard thing, man. And that was kind of interesting, you know? But I think the cape got in his way when he drummed. It must have been hot as hell to drum in that thing.
>
> **—Patrick Smith**

They were playing at Townsend, June 16, 1990. For anybody who's been to Townsend Family Park—another classic venue. This beautiful park with water and a stream, you had to go over a footbridge to get to the stage. Trey started the show with his big bushy red hair, and he was wearing a black tank top, and it had "#1" and "Harley Davidson", I don't know if it was a joke or whatever. He was so sunburned, he was like a lobster; they set the stage up directly in the sun. During the show, he went offstage, came back out, and he had shaved his head—there was no hair on his head! I don't think people caught it. I mean, I noticed immediately, you couldn't help it. I mean, he was bald. I mean, literally bald. And they didn't talk about it, they didn't say anything about it. He looked weird, he looked like he'd just gotten out of a concentration camp.

The big thing was, when you first saw them, I'd say that they really helped sell their own music, I don't mean sell as in money and all that, but they really sold it on people, because of the animation. Trey used to be so animated. Not that he isn't now, but he used to be so much more animated. He'd be doing these crazy things with his legs and arms while he'd be playing. Everyone used to love "Bathtub Gin", that was a great song. He'd get so excited during "Gin"; he'd be like, moving his whole body, he'd be swaying and moving. People can say what they want, nobody, nobody had seen a Trey-like guitar player. There's never been. I've heard music A to Z, everything in my collection. There's just no one like the guy. When he used to take it over the top, and then he'd take you over the top again, and then over that top, and you figured he couldn't get any more in, somehow, and some way on that guitar, he'd find another place to go, even higher, and then when you thought that was it, he'd go even higher.

Phish used to show up in the afternoon in a little white truck with "Winooski, Vermont" on the side of it. They'd pull up, and one of them would be driving, or Brad Sands, and one of the band members would be driving with him in the passenger seat or the lighting guy would be with him. They'd show up, they'd all, the band included, unload and set up, play all night, unpack and then drive all night, unload the truck and set it all up. People don't realize that, it's all pretty unbelievable to me.

At one point they sent out a letter inviting people to be a part of the road crew. It said, "Drugs and alcohol are not a part of this equation. We're trying to hire people to go on our crew, to go on the road." And I said to myself, "Why don't I?" I mean, if anyone did that, and they're still with them, what a great risk they took, because I'm sure they're being well taken care of.

—Chad Garland

> I HAD SIGNED MY NAME on the mailing list but I never got anything. So I called up the hotline one time to see when they were playing and Page answered the phone. So I'm like, "Uh. . . uh, I thought it was going to be a recording," and he's like, "Well, I can hang up and turn the recording on," and I'm like, "No, no, no, that's okay." So I said, "I never got any mail in the mail." And he was like, "Let me put your name on the mailing list right now." So he actually typed my name in personally. I know that for a fact.
>
> **—Rich Seaberg**

THEY DIDN'T HIRE ANY road crew at all really until after spring '92. So they were always more than happy to have somebody help them carry stuff. There were several shows where I helped them load up stuff after the show, they'd ask you if you were lingering around afterwards, kind of slow getting out. Not Paluska, who's the smaller guy? Is that Chris? There's another guy who was always with them, a smaller guy, he was kinda like the manager guy, you always saw him springing out the guest list and setting stuff up, and he usually came out and asked if anybody wanted to help load stuff up for a T-shirt or whatever.

It was never an announcement, it was more like, after the show, if you were hanging around and wanted to chip in.

At the Rink in Buffalo—it was a just a roller skating rink—I remember we were all sitting around outside and everybody was playing duck-duck-goose; there were about twenty people, and Fishman was out there, just in the circle with everybody playing duck-duck-goose. And this one girl tagged him, and I remember he was in bare feet, and he had his dress on, and he was running around trying to catch her, like he was goose. He did it hard, and he was running around and around trying to catch her before she would sit in his spot, and he just totally slipped out, and it was just so casual. I mean, that was before the show—everybody knew he was the drummer, he was kind of distinctive in a dress and bare feet—but it was still just so casual that he could sit down and play duck-duck-goose and everybody wasn't surrounding him or anything.

—Mike Graff

• Memories of The Front •

THE PLACE I USUALLY saw the band was the Front. It was always a last-minute type of deal, there was really no planning involved. You got there, you hopped in line, and you paid your five bucks and you're in. And it was that simple. And when you walked into the Front—which is now a bike shop—you would have to pass backstage. So as you walked in, here's this tiny little closet type of a room that the band would all be sitting in. So when they went on stage, they almost had to walk through the crowd to get onstage. I can remember if you got tired, you could sit down and many times I actually sat down around the soundboard. Not the soundboard itself, but on the staging it was on.

Everything was just very relaxed. Once the concert was done, band members would walk around; people weren't really bothering them, people would tape the show or whatever, but never were people really all over them like they seem to be nowadays.

The Front always had the eighteen-and-over shows and the twenty-one-plus shows. The Front was always pretty strict about the eighteen-and-over; many times friends got shut out from those shows because they were so strict. But if you were of age you could always get in.

A lot of cool things happened. I saw them one time—and I've never seen this setlist—but I saw them one time with a guy playing the fiddle.

I think that the last show at the Front was the spring of '91. I can remember I was standing at the urinal next to Paul and saying to Paul, "Jeez, this is going to be a real bummer. The Front is closing?" And he said, "Yeah, but they plan on making it a new Front." They were going to make a new place, or the guy that owned it was going to make a new place. It never happened. But I can remember that the very last show at the Front was even "get in line," it wasn't a sellout clearly. It was great because a friend of mine drove three hours and drove right up to the front of the place, right in front where he parked his car, got in line, and got in. That was the beauty of it.

—Brendan McKenna

I WENT TO GRADUATE school in Burlington from '89 until '92, so they were playing a lot of shows at the Front then. I'd say I probably saw more Phish shows at the Front than any other single venue.

It was a local bar, kind of medium-size. Different bands, small bands played there on a regular basis; probably two or three times a week they had live music. Black Dog was one of the larger bands that played there, but certainly not huge. Let's see, it sort of had a . . . not quite horseshoe, but more like a three-sided bar when you first walked in. There was a very low riser for the stage, probably about two feet. There was a dance floor that could accommodate, oh, probably about a hundred really squished people. But very seldom at the Phish shows that I went to was it packed to the gills. Very seldom. It was kind of like, people were just going to the bar saying, "Hey, there's some band there, they might be kind of cool." It wasn't like they were necessarily drawing tons of people that wouldn't have otherwise gone there.

I never remember seeing tapers there. I was surprised when I started seeing bootlegs from the Front and stuff. I was like, "Wow, people are taping this stuff?" I never remember having to dodge tapers or anything trying to get to the bar or anything.

There was no show at the Front that I went to, for example, where if I really wanted to talk to Trey or Mike or someone, that I couldn't have just walked up and with minimal effort had a conversation with either of them. I was kind of shy, but . . . [laughter] There was no show at the Front where that was impossible, where they were inaccessible. There was definitely a lot of contact between the band and the crowd. You know, between sets or after the show.

I really liked seeing them at the Front, it just seems like they were made for that location at the time, it was the perfect size for them and it was the perfect venue for that size band and that type of band. Although the dance floor was relatively small, there were just enough of us that we could feel comfortable, it didn't feel empty, it didn't feel vacuous in there. Another great thing about seeing them indoors in a small location is that they managed to get the whole place literally hopping, jumping up and down.

Yeah, it was kinda interesting, because even though it was all, well, not all Deadheads, but primarily people that you would associate with seeing at Dead shows, there was like a new way of dancing, and it was directly connected to those trampolines. Everyone would just hop, it was a much wilder kind of dancing than I saw at Dead shows, so that was sorta neat.

The interaction between the band and the crowd was pretty intense, a lot of it was probably off mikes, but if you shouted out "Fee" or something they would play it, pretty much right away. I mean, they could hear you, there weren't like, twenty thousand people screaming different things at them. But there were only about twenty of us at the most actively shouting out comments or suggestions or requests. So, if you yelled something to them, they would pretty much play it or make some comment back to you; there was heavy interaction with them.

—Charlene Smith

5 The Shows

New Year's Eve, 1996.

Here it is . . . every Phish show on record. The setlist section contains several elements, each of which is explained below.

The Setlists. It's the ever-expanding compilation of Phish setlists, dating all the way back to the band's inception. In the last three years, the *Almanac* has undertaken a research project to document setlists previously unavailable in the public sphere, and to correct erroneous setlists. Many *Almanac* readers have submitted previously undocumented setlists and setlist corrections, while *Almanac* research has also uncovered new setlists, show dates, and corrections. These additions have been combined with our earlier setlist archive—primarily public-domain setlist information contained in the Phish.Net archive—to create our current database. In this way, the *Almanac* setlist archive continues to mature.

Nitty-Gritty. Some setlists have descriptions written beneath them in italics. This information details guest spots, unusual performances, odd onstage antics, or other out-of-the-ordinary occurrences. We call it the nitty-gritty, and most of these were supplied by *Almanac* readers during our Phishtory '97 project. It's important to note that this is an incomplete compilation, as there are many onstage events which have never been documented. Our search continues for nitty-gritty, so please get in touch with us with any new info.

And of course, if you have setlists for any shows not included in the *Almanac*, or if you catch any errors, please contact us.

Phishtory Mini-Reviews. Setlists don't tell the whole story! That's why we have also added over five hundred show descriptions compiled from submissions from about two hundred fans.

This project, called Phishtory, began in January 1997 when we printed up thousands of flyers asking fans to write short reviews of any ten Phish shows. The responses created a library of close to three thousand reviews! We honed those down to create a collective work offering a lively and detailed account of every show of note.

Show Stories. Nothing livens up factual history like zany personal tales from fellow Phish fans of the wild things that happened to them at shows. Included in these pages are many such stories, positioned in close proximity to the setlist for the show where the adventure occurred. These stories were selected for their ability to cast light on the scene at a show, or on the general climate of Phish shows from an era. Again, this is an ever-changing piece of the *Almanac*, so if you have a few nutty tales from shows past, please feel free to send them on in.

In addition, several of the show stories and mini-reviews are the result of interviews we conducted with Phish fans who attended shows in the 1980s and early 1990s. Our thanks to Chad Garland, Mike Graff, Greg Kelly, Brendan McKenna, Rich Seaberg, and Patrick and Charlene Smith for sharing their memories.

Historical Reviews. To add yet another dimension, we selected roughly twenty shows that we identified as the most historic nights in Phish's rich concert history and researched the stories behind those shows. You'll also find these in the section that follows.

Accessibility Ratings. Wondering what your chances are of getting hold of a certain show on tape? The answer can be found in the accessibility rating next to each setlist. We compared fifty fans' tapelists to get an accurate sense of which shows are in heavy circulation and which are the hardest to find. The ratings are weighted based on year. If no one had a tape from the '80s, we assume it to be a pretty rare tape, otherwise hardcore tapers would have gone after it. However, there are many tapes from the '90s which are in reasonable circulation but do not find their way to many fans' collections simply because there are so many good shows from those years to choose from. Anyone wanting to get their hands on them might have a difficult time, but would not likely run into the same barriers as they would in looking for a rare '80s show. The accessibility ratings guidelines follow.

Accessibility Ratings Guidelines. Next to the date of a show is a bracketed accessibility rating of how hard or easy it is to track down tapes of that show. We surveyed fifty tape lists for our totally updated ratings:

❄ *So rare it's raw,* not appearing on any of the tapelists. Only shows from 1991 and before can get this rating.

- *Rare.* The tape appeared on only one of the tapelists (from 1991 or before) or on one or no tapelists if it's from 1992. This rating is not given to any show from 1993 on.
- •• *Medium rare.* Two to five lists claimed this one during 1992 or before. No more than three from 1993 on. A nice find.
- ••• *Medium.* Six to nine tapers had it on their lists. You may have to ask around to find this one, but it's definitely out there.
- •••• *Well done.* Ten to twenty-five tapers claimed this one. An easy find for anyone as long as you know more than a few tapers.
- ••••• *Singed to a crisp.* More than half the tapelists had this show. If you can't find it, you're just not looking in the right place.

Phishtory '97

PHISHTORY '97 IS THE MOST ambitious project yet undertaken by *The Pharmer's Almanac*—the documentation of Phish's concert history through the memories and concert reviews of hundreds of fans.

We distributed Phishtory forms over the first three months of 1997; the results can be seen throughout the setlists section in the mini-reviews that appear under most shows and the "nitty-gritty" notes in italics under most setlists. Everyone who contributed ten reviews was offered a free *Almanac*.

Phishtory contributors who did not request a taper listing are: Eric Acquafredda, M. N. J. Adams, Josh Albini, Jonathan Ardman, Matthew Ashenfelder, Lindsey Bates, Robyn Bayetis, Waylon Baynard, Connor Bergman, Adam Brilhante, David M. Brown, Emily Brown, Anthony Buchla, Angela Carrol, Bob Colby, Marcia Collins, Colm Connell, Mick Connor, Jos Conti, James Daly, Mike D'Amico, Mark Daniel, Ashley Davis, Dom DeLuca, Amy Duncan, David Eckers, Nancy Eddies, Pat Elkins, Tim Foisser, Mark Garofalow, Ernie Greene, Brian Gressler, Daniel Grilfand, Ric Hanna, Tyler Harris, Ryan Harsch, Jason Hedrington, Michelle Hirsch, Tricia Holmes, Andre Holton, Mike Hood, Tony Hume, Al Hunt, Jake Hunter, Julie Hunter, Mike Indgin, Davey Inkrea, Carri A. Johnson, Lee Johnston, Melissa Keller, Greg Kelly, James Kiddle, Langston Knipler, Richard Kot, Dan Kurtz, Shannon C. Lancaster, Russell Lane, Will Lehnert, Joseph LeRoy, Morgan Lester, Amanda Litton, Mike Livanos, Foster Lukas, Linda Mahdesian, Sarah Malo, Amy Manning, Dave Matson, Rich Mazer, Alexis Michael, Andrew Mitchell, Pete Morse, Charlie Murphy, Jefferson R. Musser, Mike Noll, Billy O'Malley, Kate O'Neil, Otis, Mike Palmer, Billy Jah Patrick, Nathaniel Peirce, Brett Pessin, Bob Peterson, Bruce A. Pickell, Tom Pinnick, Brian A. Rock, Andy Ross, Michael Rotkowitz, Hollis Rowan, Ian Rufe, Jeff Salvatore, Joseph A. Savino, Lee Schiller, Chrissy Schneider, Greg Schwartz, Mark Selby, Leah Shantz, Dave Sharpe, Scott Sifton, Ed Smith, J. J. Southard, Jen Spivey, Pat Stanley, Teddy Stuart, Ali Tariq, Melanie and Melita Terrell, Jen Verdon, Brian Watkins, Kevin Weise, Lara Wittels, Melissa Wolcott, and Joel Zeigler.

Our thanks to the entire Phishtory '97 team!

• Setlist • Team and Notes

Setlist Team (with Honors). The following people offered numerous setlist corrections and clarifications, and in some cases sent us tapes to help verify setlists. Many, many thanks to: Katie McConnell, A. J. Fucile, Otis from New York, John Nalbone, Adam Rizzuti, Brian Gressler, Ryan Harsch, Dave Schall, Pat Eagle, Howie Kopman, Don and the guys at Prime Cuts in Rockville Centre, NY, Tim King, Michael Shtadthender, and David Stockbridge.

Setlist Team. These amazing folks also offered setlist corrections and clarifications: Chuck Adams, Jeff Bergman, Chris Bertelsen, Brian Boehm, Rev. Darrin Barschdorf, Lee Boykoff, Ralph Branca, Brian Carrigan, Kevin Cassells, David Clement, Sam Cobb, Joey Conroy, Jamis Curran, Brian Daly, Adam Davidoff, Jeff Davis, Jason Deziel, James Dunnican, Steve Eisenhauer, K. C. Fisher, Dan Freeman, Dan Goldstein, Eli Hall, Bill Hance, Andrew Hayward, Will Herrmann, Gorey Hiles, Tony Hume, Ivan James, Haney Jones, Pete Jones, Andy Kahn, Brian Levine, Rob Livingston, Colin Malek, Stephen Mortlock, Nancy, Mike Noll, Dan O'Brien, Mark Pfister, Tom Pinnick, Andrew Potter, Todd Prusin, Mike Railey, Chad Redford, Peter Rocco, Greg Roth, Mike S., Lee Schaffler, Chad Shaw, Paul Sheets, Tom Smith, Paul Smiths, Len Stubbe Jr., Padraic Swanton, Gabe Tafoya, Bob Talatzko, Rob Thorne, Tinsley, Greg Vedder, Mike Waselus, Wayne, Kevin Weise, Greg Weiss, Katy Yaeland, Ross W. Yarrol, Mike Youngling, Nick Z., the crew at Prime Cuts, Dennis at Scarlet Begonias, and the many folks who have left information on our voicemail and others whose names we don't have. You know who you are. Because of the incredible efforts of all these people, the Phish community is better informed. A huge thank-you to you all!

Notes on Setlists and Nitty-Gritty

Segues. The *Almanac* policy on including segue notation (>) between songs in a setlist is to use an arrow any time there's no discernible pause between one song and the next. Segue corrections and additions are always welcomed.

Debuts. Concert debuts are noted in the nitty-gritty starting in 1989. Of course, the "unofficial" debut dates of earlier songs can easily be figured by referencing the "All the Songs" section, which begins on page 233.

Last Since. Any time Phish went more than fifty shows without playing a song, the lapse—counted in number of shows—is noted when it is finally played again.

Teases and Jams. In the nitty-gritty, we've listed some of the many times Phish has included teases or jams of other songs within the song they're playing, such as "Immigrant Song jam in YEM" or "Auld Lang Syne tease in Ya Mar." Roughly speaking, we define a "tease" as a quick reference of a song, maybe a few bars played by one band member. A "jam" is a

Photo courtesy of George Lyons.

longer, more developed take which usually includes several band members. We'd love to hear from *Almanac* readers who have identified additional teases or jams on their Phish tapes.

Phish Jams. We've limited the use of the word "Jam" in the actual setlists. Because so many Phish songs include long jams, it seems too arbitrary to assign a particular song a jam notation like Mike's > Jam > Weekapaug. "Jam" is used when Phish leaves one song completely behind, never to return, and embarks on a theme with no specific name.

Digital Delay Loop. Notation of the "digital delay loop" (known to some as "Trey's Big-Show Energy Jam") is included where applicable. Examples of this effect include the Bowie intro on 12/29/94 and the end of Mike's on 12/31/95.

Fish's Instruments. We've attempted to document every time Fish has played an instrument like the vacuum or trombone in the nitty-gritty. Separate notation is not made for versions of "Cracklin' Rosie," which have all featured Fishman on cymbals. We've also added listings of the "HYHU" (Hold Your Head Up) and "Cold as Ice" intros for Fishman songs in the setlists.

Phan Picks. A special "Phan Picks" logo accompanies the setlists to denote each of the top twenty-five shows of all time, as identified by *Almanac* readers in our readers' survey.

Bracketed Shows. Show dates that appear in brackets, such as [3/5/97], are not considered actual "concerts," so songs played in them are not included in the "All the Songs" section.

Pollstar Numbers. Where available, we list the total attendance at a show and the venue capacity in brackets, as tabulated by the trade magazine *Pollstar*.

Venue Sizes and Ticket Prices. New to this edition of the *Almanac* is crowd size, venue size, and ticket price information. Gathered primarily by *Pollstar* magazine starting with the New Year's Eve show in 1989, such data is spotty for much of the early 1990s and more reliable in recent years. ATTEN. is the paid attendance for that night's show; CAP. is the venue capacity, as reported by *Pollstar*; and TIX is the ticket price, also as reported by *Pollstar*. Note that venue sizes often change from performance to performance based on how much space is taken up by the stage, the soundboard and lightboard, and other factors. Also, Phish has at times played in partially blocked-off venues, then played the place again with no part of it blocked off, often more than doubling that venue's capacity. Similarly, ticket prices are not totally reliable; their inclusion here is intended to give a sense of what it cost to see a Phish show during certain eras. Also note that venue information marked by an asterisk (*) is not from *Pollstar* but from *Performance* magazine or based on *Almanac* research. Thanks to *Pollstar* and *Performance* for sharing their data with us.

Tapes 'R' Us

The amorphous, underground network of tape trading is what made Phish what it is today. But if you are not connected with the scene or lack Internet access, it's sometimes tough to get started. That's why several stores around the country have introduced their own low- or no-cost tape trading service.

Now, we've all probably walked into stores and seen CD bootlegs for sale or tapes for $10 or more. That's not what we're talking about. Instead, we refer to stores that keep a library of bootlegs on hand and allow you to select one and copy it in the store or pay a small fee to have someone make a copy for you. It should be noted that even this practice is controversial, and has been frowned on in some instances by management and fans alike. But it's a godsend for a newbie, and can be an excellent resource for even the most accomplished taper.

Prime Cuts in Rockville Centre, NY, claims the largest public access tape library in the country. Owner Don Kantor opened the doors in 1983 as a used and collectible record store. By 1987 he moved the direction of the store with the direction he felt inside, and made it a Grateful Dead–oriented ship. Three years later, right after Don went to his first Phish show at the Marquee, Prime Cuts had made its first Phish tapes available for trading.

The next summer, Don and his future wife worked part-time at Arrowhead Ranch, actually helping build the stage Phish performed on. By then, Don envisioned great things for Phish, and hoped to someday make Prime Cuts as focused on Phish as it was on the Grateful Dead.

Today they have over 5,000 hours' worth of Phish shows, and can claim to be the direct or indirect source for hundreds of thousands of tapes floating around Long Island and beyond. Assistant Manager Matt Bush and a dedicated staff work to snag high-quality tapes from tour, and immediately begin spinning copies for hungry customers. They charge the same price for a blank tape as they do for one with a Phish show recorded on it.

"We try to run the type of a store that I always wished had existed for me. We really make an effort to bring the parking lot to the store," says Kantor.

Now, Prime Cuts is trying to expand its identity to service the entire musical genre of improvisational rock. One of the first stores to carry moe. merchandise, a wide variety of signed and unsigned bands now grace the tape shelves.

Here is a list of stores which can assist you in expanding your tape collection:

Grateful Earth 149 College St., Lewiston, ME 04240; Phone (207) 783-6308; Approx. 1,000 hours. Give 3 blanks for 2 copies.

The Parking Lot 513 Davis St., Evanston, IL 60201; Phone (847) 866-8969; Approx. 4,500 hours. Free on-site self-service by appointment.

Prime Cuts 191A North Long Beach Rd., Rockville Centre, NY 11570; Phone (516) 678-0670; Approx. 5,000 hours. Buy blank tape or $1.

Starship 6243 North Teutonia Ave., Milwaukee, WI 53209 (ask about 3 other area locations); Phone (414) 466-7901; Approx. 2,000 hours. Free, limited to 3 tapes per person, tapes must be Maxell XLII 90.

Wild Man Steve's 114B West Magnolia, Auburn, AL 36830; Phone (334) 821-6622; Approx. 2,000 hours. Straight trades or 3 blanks for 2 copies.

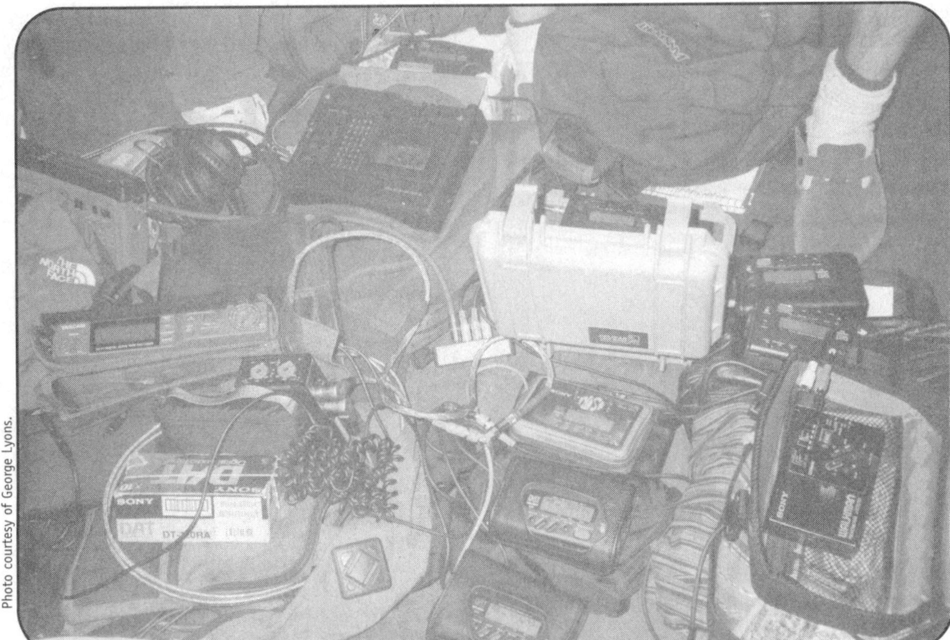

Photo courtesy of George Lyons.

• A Taping How-to •

You see them at shows, identifiable by the tall metal towers that sprout twenty feet into the air. They're the tapers, and most of them have live concert recording collections that would make your jaw drop. But let's say you're just starting to build your Phish tape collection. Here are a few things it might be helpful to know.

Taping Nuances. Tapes are either labeled SBD (for a soundboard recording; DSBD for a digital soundboard recording) or AUD (for audience recording; DAUD for a digital audience recording). Soundboard recordings come directly from the house sound, and although the sound quality is usually superior to that of audience recordings, certain instruments may sound too high or low depending on how the sound was mixed for the venue. Audience tapes are made by tapers who set up microphones at shows and capture the sound in the venue, resulting in more crowd noise and sometimes a "fuller" sound.

Many tapers record on DAT (digital audio tape), but dub their DATs to analog tapes to enjoy the music in cassette decks. What makes DATs so great, besides the fact that they can record up to three hours of consecutive music on one tape with no cuts, is that they can be digitally cloned with no generational loss of tape quality. With cassette tapes, as soon as you start making copies, you face generational loss—the hiss that gets introduced as tapes are passed along. This is why analog tape collectors label the generations of their tapes; a copy of a first-generation analog tape would be "2nd gen," a copy of a 2nd gen would be "3rd gen," and so on. Generally, the lower the generation number, the better the quality.

The tape's source also affects quality, obviously. Many people swear by soundboards, but Phish hasn't officially allowed tapers to patch directly into the soundboard since the summer of 1990. A good number of soundboard tapes still make it into general circulation [see "The Scoop on Soundboards" below].

According to some tapers, a good audience recording can better re-create the illusion of "being there" than a soundboard can. Recordings made from in front of the soundboard (FOB) sound best, but Phish asks tapers not to record from anywhere except the tapers' section (TS), so FOB tapes can be hard to come by. Most tapers will mark the type of microphones used to record shows—AKGs, B&Ks, Schoeps, and Neumanns are particularly good-sounding brands (again, generally speaking).

Starting a Collection. The best way to start a tape collection is to find a friend (or a friend of a friend) with a cache of tapes that you can raid. Once you've got a good base, you can hit the Internet and set up tape trades with others. Don't ever pay more than the price of blank tapes and postage for a tape of a show.

Another method is to ask tapers at shows to make you a copy of that night's show. If you want to go this route, there are a few points of etiquette: Put tapes (be on the safe side: use 100-minute ones) in a padded mailer, address it to yourself, and include the correct postage on the mailer. At the show, approach tapers with tact. Before the show, they'll be busy setting up and won't want to be disturbed, so it's often better to ask at setbreak or after the show. If you find a taper nice enough to take your envelope, you can reciprocate with a drink or equivalent thank-you. Then, be prepared to wait—for tapers who do a lot of trading, it can take a while to make copies.

Making Tapes. It's best if you have a three-head cassette deck to make copies—set the levels to peak at about +3, and have the levels hover between -4 and +2 otherwise. Dubbing decks are okay, but you can't set levels with them, and under no circumstances should you use high-speed dubbing to make copies (it really reduces the quality). Also, clean and demagnetize your decks religiously—cleaners and demagnetizers cost only a few bucks, and will hugely improve the quality of your recordings.

The 25 Most-Circulated Tapes

During the compilation of the tape accessibility ratings for Volume 4, we tabulated the twenty-five most-circulated Phish tapes. The number in the right column is the percentage of tapers surveyed that claimed that show.

1) 10/31/94	Glens Falls, NY	85%
2) 04/16/92	Santa Barbara, CA	75%
2) 10/31/95	Chicago, IL	75%
4) 12/31/93	Worcester, MA	70%
5) 07/21/91	Parksville, NY	68%
5) 12/31/95	New York, NY	68%
5) 08/16/96	Plattsburgh, NY	68%
5) 08/17/96	Plattsburgh, NY	68%
9) 07/25/92	Stowe, VT	60%
9) 02/20/93	Atlanta, GA	60%
11) 03/22/93	Sacramento, CA	58%
11) 12/30/95	New York, NY	58%
13) 08/21/87	Hebron, NY	55%
13) 08/03/91	Auburn, ME	55%
13) 03/13/92	Providence, RI	55%
13) 12/30/93	Portland, ME	55%
13) 05/07/94	Dallas, TX	55%
18) 08/20/93	Morrison, CO	53%
19) 03/12/88	Burlington, VT	50%
19) 10/20/89	Burlington, VT	50%
19) 10/31/96	Atlanta, GA	50%
22) 06/11/94	Morrison, CO	48%
22) 12/31/94	Boston, MA	48%
22) 06/06/96	Woodstock, NY	48%
25) 12/1/84, 11/4/90, 7/2/95, 12/29/95		45%

The Scoop on Soundboards

Soundman Paul Languedoc decided to end soundboard patches to most tapers after the Townshend Family Park show on June 16, 1990, because it was becoming too difficult for him to manage at shows; he was also apparently exasperated that some tapers were abusing the privilege by pulling cables out of the soundboard and plugging their decks in without asking his permission. A few longtime tapers continued to patch into the soundboard through most of 1991; the practice was all but halted by the end of that fall.

During contract negotiations with Elektra Records in 1991, the taping privilege proved to be a bit of a sticking point, but the band insisted that their contract stipulate that fans could continue to record Phish shows. By spring tour 1993, though, increasing venue sizes made it hard to manage the proliferation of tapers. The band and its management hoped to implement a designated tapers' section for summer tour 1993 but it proved too hard to organize on short notice with Ticketmaster. So mail-order ticketing for reserved seating shows debuted on the '93 New

The Phan 25

The results of our readers' survey yielded the "Phan 25," a rating of the best Phish shows of all time.

1) 12/31/95 New York, NY
2) 10/31/94 Glens Falls, NY
3) 02/20/93 Atlanta, GA
4) 08/16/96 Plattsburgh, NY
5) 05/07/94 Dallas, TX
6) 12/30/93 Portland, ME
7) 12/06/96 Las Vegas, NV
8) 07/16/94 Fayston, VT
9) 07/21/91 Parksville, NY (with horns)
10) 10/31/96 Atlanta, GA
11) 10/31/95 Chicago, IL
12) 08/17/96 Plattsburgh, NY
13) 12/31/96 Boston, MA
14) 03/13/92 Providence, RI
15) 12/30/95 New York, NY
16) 08/21/87 Hebron, NY
17) 12/29/95 Worcester, MA
18) 07/25/92 Stowe, VT (with Santana)
19) 03/22/93 Sacramento, CA
20) 12/01/84 Burlington, VT
21) 12/31/93 Worcester, MA
22) 08/20/93 Morrison, CO
23) 06/26/94 Charleston, WV
24) 05/25/88 Burlington, VT
25) 04/16/92 Santa Barbara, CA

Year's run, and has continued every tour since.

Finding soundboards from 1992 isn't tough—except for the Santana tour sets. By 1993, soundboards were released less liberally, as the band began a policy of distributing top shows on soundboard to the Phish.Net for dispersal. Releases included 3/22/93 Sacramento, 8/20/93 Red Rocks, and 12/30/93 Portland. The only show in 1994 released to the Phish.Net was the second set of 5/7/94 Dallas, which went through a cassette generation—designated as cDSBD, meaning it was originally recorded on DAT, then transferred to cassette, then back to DAT—as did the '93 boards. Apparently the distribution of the Dallas board irked one band member, and the soundboard release policy is currently under review. However, throughout 1994, a number of SBDs still made it into general release.

There are several illegally patched boards from 1994—Spreckels 12/8/94 and Erie 11/13/94 II. Paul was tipped off to the problem—people were plugging into the soundboard unknown to him. It hasn't happened since.

In a break with policy, Paul gave soundboard patches to the three tapers who made it to the Joyous Lake show—tapes now in circulation. Coupled with the FM broadcast tapes of the Clifford Ball, 1996 generated some exceptional-quality tapes.

• Song Title Abbreviations in the Setlists •

This edition of the *Almanac* has shortened many song names for ease of reading in the setlist section. In the left-hand column below are the song names as they appear in the setlist section, and the right-hand column shows the full titles of the songs.

A-Train	**Take the A-Train**	**Jesus Left Chicago**	**Jesus Just Left Chicago**
Adeline	**Sweet Adeline**	**Jimmy Page**	**Letter to Jimmy Page**
All Things	**All Things Reconsidered**	**Makisupa**	**Makisupa Policeman**
Also Sprach	**Also Sprach Zarathustra (a.k.a. 2001)**	**Mango**	**The Mango Song**
Alumni	**Alumni Blues**	**McGrupp**	**McGrupp and the Watchful Hosemasters**
Antelope	**Run Like an Antelope**	**Mike's**	**Mike's Song**
Avenu	**Avenu Malkenu**	**Melt**	**Split Open and Melt**
BBJ	**Big Ball Jam**	**Mockingbird**	**Fly Famous Mockingbird**
BBFCM	**Big Black Furry Creature from Mars**	**MSO**	**My Sweet One**
Bouncing	**Bouncing around the Room**	**My Friend**	**My Friend My Friend**
Bowie	**David Bowie**	**My Mind's**	**My Mind's Got a Mind of Its Own**
Brain	**If I Only Had a Brain**	**No Good Trying**	**It's No Good Trying**
Carini	**Carini Had a Lumpy Head**	**Oh Kee**	**Oh Kee Pa**
Caspian	**Prince Caspian**	**Peaches**	**Peaches En Regalia**
CTB	**Cars Trucks Buses**	**PYITE**	**Punch You in the Eye**
Chalkdust	**Chalkdust Torture**	**Sample**	**Sample in a Jar**
Do It in the Road	**Why Don't We Do It in the Road**	**Silent**	**Silent in the Morning**
FEFY	**Fast Enough for You**	**Slave**	**Slave to the Traffic Light**
Forbin's	**Colonel Forbin's Ascent**	**Sneaking Sally**	**Sneaking Sally through the Alley**
Golgi	**Golgi Apparatus**	**Suzie**	**Suzie Greenberg**
Great Gig	**Great Gig in the Sky**	**Theme**	**Theme from the Bottom**
GTBT	**Good Times Bad Times**	**Timber Ho**	**Timber (Jerry)**
Guelah	**Guelah Papyrus**	**TMWSIY**	**The Man Who Stepped into Yesterday**
Guitar Gently Weeps	**While My Guitar Gently Weeps**	**Weekapaug**	**Weekapaug Groove**
Halley's	**Halley's Comet**	**Wolfman's**	**Wolfman's Brother**
Hydrogen	**I Am Hydrogen**	**YEM**	**You Enjoy Myself**
HYHU	**Hold Your Head Up**	**Yerushalayim**	**Yerushalayim Schel Zahav**

Kevin's PICKS

Phish archivist Kevin Shapiro has a job to envy—listening to Phish tapes! The fruits of some of his efforts have been heard over Phish's radio stations at both the Clifford Ball and the Great Went, as he presented three "from the archives" shows.

Tapes of these shows—all gorgeous soundboard quality—are now in circulation among fans. Find 'em, and enjoy!

Clifford Ball Archives Show [8/15/96]: Brother (3/24/92 Richmond, VA), Catapult > Simple > Icculus (6/22/94 Columbus, OH), Setting Sail (7/15/94 Jones Beach, NY), Frankenstein (6/23/94 Pontiac, MI), Ride Captain Ride (12/12/92 Toronto, Ontario), Big Ball Jam, Split Open and Melt > Buffalo Bill > Makisupa (10/29/94 Spartanburg, SC), Cities (7/5/94 Ottawa, Ontario), PYITE (3/26/93 San Francisco, CA), Bathtub Gin > Ya Mar (8/13/93 Indianapolis, IN), Funky Bitch (2/19/93 Atlanta, GA), Curtis Lowe (2/9/90 Lancaster, PA), Landlady > Destiny Unbound (11/1/91 Denver, CO), Bowie > Timber Ho > Bowie (12/30/92 Springfield, MA), Magilla (7/14/91 Townshend, VT, with horns), Tube (6/26/94 Charleston, WV), Alumni Blues > Light Up or Leave Me Alone (5/25/88 Burlington, VT). *[Thanks to Paul Sheets.]*

Great Went Archives Show 1 [8/15/97]: Bathtub Gin (8/16/96 Plattsburgh, NY), Halley's Comet > Alumni Blues (8/17/89 Burlington, VT; Halley's Comet with Nancy Taube on vocals), Spock's Brain (5/16/95 Lowell, MA), Reba (5/16/95 Lowell, MA), Fixin' to Die (11/19/94 soundcheck, Bloomington, IN), Dog Log (10/14/95 soundcheck, Austin, TX), Swing Low Sweet Chariot (8/29/87 Shelburne, VT), The Curtain With (8/29/87 Shelburne, VT), Rhombus narration > Divided Sky (11/15/91 Charlottesville, VA), Camel Walk (7/25/88 Burlington, VT), Harry Hood (4/18/92 Palo Alto, CA).

Great Went Archives Show 2 [8/16/97]: Carini (3/1/97 Hamburg, Germany), Tela (8/27/88 State College, PA), Eliza (11/8/90 soundcheck, Madison, WI), Taste (11/30/96 Sacramento, CA; with Peter Apfelbaum), Hurricane (11/19/85 Burling-ton, VT; Bob Dylan cover, acoustic), Mike's Song > Simple > Mike's Song > I Am Hydrogen > Weekapaug (6/17/94 Milwaukee, WI, the "OJShow"), Shaggy Dog (10/31/86 Plainfield, VT), Fluffhead (10/31/86 Plainfield, VT), You Enjoy Myself (5/5/93 Albany, NY; with Col. Bruce Hampton and the Aquarium Rescue Unit, and the Dude of Life).

SETLISTS 1983–1998 and ANNUAL and LIFETIME STATS

1983–1988 The Early Years

In the formative years of the band, Phish played in and around Burlington as much as they could, often two or three times a week, and maintained a weekly stand at Nectar's before graduating to the Front in the fall of 1988. None of the shows from 1983 presently circulate, and the band went on hiatus during the spring of 1984 due to Trey's suspension from UVM. The 12/1/84 Nectar's show is the earliest Phish show fans will probably ever get to hear, though tapes apparently exist for the band's second show ever, in the Slade Hall basement.

During these early years, the band didn't have a tape deck rolling at most of their shows, so setlists and tapes from this era represent only a small portion of the shows which actually occurred. There are most likely hundreds of missing setlists for every one setlist included herein. Tapes from this era largely exist because of tapers who recorded Phish shows and copied the tapes for their friends. In the days before the tapers' section became a bevy of Phish experts intent on capturing every stray note in its pure digital glory, though, tapers would commit such foul acts as not recording songs they didn't like or leaving a show part way through the band's set.

1983

[10/30/83] Show not taped
ROTC Halloween Dance, University of Vermont, Burlington, VT
Heard It through the Grapevine, Long Cool Woman in a Black Dress

The famous "first show." The band claims its performance was so poor that when Phish took a break, the event organizers put Michael Jackson on over the PA, so Phish cut their performance short. Setlist is incomplete and probably inaccurate.

1984

12/1/84 [ACCESSIBILITY: ••••]
Nectar's, Burlington, VT
Scarlet Begonias > Fire > Fire on the Mountain, Slave > Makisupa, Spanish Flea, Don't Want You No More > Cities, Skippy, Fluffhead
E: Eyes of the World

The Dude of Life on vocals for Skippy and Fluffhead. Marc Daubert plays percussion; he was a member of Phish at this point.

This historic show is the first "official" Phish gig upstairs at Nectar's, without Page McConnell but with original band member Jeff Holdsworth on rhythm guitar. Things start off Dead, with an excellent cover of Scarlet busting into a zippy Fire and then into Fire on the Mountain (!). During an amusing Makisupa, Trey sings of how Jeff and Fishman's musical abilities are enhanced when they "go backstage and smoke a little herb." There's a garage-sounding, premature Slave as well as a cover of Herb Alpert's Spanish Flea, during which the Dude of Life introduces the band. Though their musical skills aren't as finely honed, this is interesting to hear. —Ryan Harsch

This was the first live tape I heard of Phish. Being a "big Deadhead," I thoroughly enjoyed Scarlet > Fire > Fire. It shows Phish's humor about music, which I have since found turns some people off. Still, I enjoy this. I like hearing the early roots of the band, and this tape is one of the best examples of that.—Kyle Niday

Mike sounds phat n' phunky, but Trey doesn't sound like himself on Scarlet Begonias (more like you-know-who . . .). Slave is pretty rough. It's just not the same without Page. This tape is definitely worth getting, if only for nostalgia. Everything sounds ancient, but you can also hear the beginnings of something very phresh . . . —Andrew Mitchell

1985

3/4/85 [ACCESSIBILITY: ••]
Hunt's, Burlington, VT

1980s

157 Total Show Dates
- **29** one-set shows
- **69** two-set shows
- **17** three-set shows
- **42** dates with no setlists

Phan Picks 1980s

SHOW	THE SKINNY
1) 08/21/87 Hebron, NY	Phish at their early best.
2) 12/01/84 Nectar's	First Nectar's gig; w/the Dude.
3) 05/25/88 Nectar's	Great WPost, Ya Mar w/Jah Roy.
4) 05/28/89 Hebron, NY	Best musical show of the '80s?
5) 09/24/88 Amherst, MA	Full Moon at the Zoo II.
6) 03/12/88 Nectar's	First live Gamehendge.
7) 08/27/88 Penn State, PA	Awesome Tela with long jam.
8) 05/15/88 Underhill, VT	Fun on the Pharm.
9) 10/20/89 Nectar's	Horns sit in for Melt and more.
10) 12/06/86 Shelburne, VT	Lots of rarities.

MUSICAL RECAP: The 1980s saw Phish traverse the wide range of styles that would become their hallmark, from rock to jazz to reggae and bluegrass. One of the pleasures of listening to older tapes is the looser, more wide-open jam style; unlike the focused jams of the early 1990s, the 1980s saw plenty of jam-happy sets.

REPRESENTATIVE JAMS: Whipping Post, 5/25/88; David Bowie, 10/31/86; Mike's Song > I Am Hydrogen > Weekapaug Groove, 5/28/89.

Dark Horses

SHOW	THE SKINNY
1) 04/01/86 Plainfield, VT	Help > Slip > AC/DC Bag.
2) 01/30/88 Waitsfield, VT	Very well played early show.
3) 03/04/89 New York, NY	First Phish show at Wetlands.
4) 04/20/89 Amherst, MA	Full Moon at the Zoo III.
5) 10/31/89 Plainfield, VT	Last Goddard Halloween show.

Most-Played Originals:		
1) You Enjoy Myself	76	48%
2) AC/DC Bag	66	42%
3) Golgi Apparatus	62	39%
4) Possum	60	36%
5) Lizards	50	32%
6) Alumni Blues	49	31%
7) Fluffhead	48	31%
8) Mike's Song	47	30%
9) Antelope	44	28%
9) Divided Sky	44	28%

Most-Played Covers:		
1) Good Times Bad Times	39	25%
2) Take the A-Train	37	24%
3) Peaches En Regalia	34	22%
3) Walk Away	34	17%
5) Ya Mar	27	17%
6) Fire	26	16%
7) Funky Bitch	25	16%
8) La Grange	24	15%
9) Bold as Love	23	15%
10) Sneaking Sally	18	12%

First-Set Openers:	
1) Golgi Apparatus	36
2) AC/DC Bag	8
3) I Didn't Know	6
4) Mike's Song	4
4) Oh Kee Pa	4
4) Funky Bitch	4

Second-Set Openers:	
1) Mike's Song	6
2) David Bowie	5
3) Alumni Blues	3
3) AC/DC Bag	3
3) Oh Kee Pa	3

Anarchy, Camel Walk, Fire up the Ganja, Skippy, Midnight Hour

African hunger relief benefit. Members of Lamb's Bread (a Burlington band) played on Fire up the Ganja.

5/3/85 [ACCESSIBILITY: •••]
Springfest, Goddard College, Plainfield, VT
Scarlet Begonias > Eyes of the World > Whipping Post > McGrupp > Makisupa > Antelope Jam > Other One **E:** Anarchy

Includes Page McConnell sitting in for the first time; he was not a member of Phish at this point.

Upstairs at Nectars

12/1/84

There are several places to turn when talking about Phish's first show. There's the infamous ROTC Dance in October '83, and the Slade Hall gig a few days later—neither was played under the "Phish" name, and neither is in circulation in the taping community.

Maybe that's why so many phans turn to Phish's show at Nectar's on December 1, 1984, as Phish's "first" show. It was, apparently, the first show played under the Phish name, and it marked the grand return of a band that had nearly broken up after Trey left UVM in the spring of '84 after his prank came back to haunt him. It's also the earliest-known Phish tape in general circulation, and their first show at Nectar's.

The funny thing is, the show wasn't really at Nectar's—at least, not the part of Nectar's where Phish would play so many shows in the 1985–1988 era. No, their first Nectar's gig was in the upstairs space, a smaller room than even the downstairs (which itself holds only 150 to 200 people). Nevertheless, the fact that they were given a slot at all was notable—as the band noted in the liner notes to *Picture of Nectar*, they didn't have a song list long enough to fill two sets. But Nectar gave them a shot, and the boys (including Marc Daubert on percussion and Jeff Holdsworth on rhythm guitar, with Page still about six months away from his Phish debut) took it and ran with it. Almost a decade later, PON would be dedicated to Nectar as the band's official "thank you."

Their set showed a lot of early influences, like the Dead and Hendrix, but in a way that made their sense of humor about the music abundantly clear—who would ever conceive of a Scarlet > Fire > Fire run? And of course the show featured The Dude of Life on vocals for two tunes he penned the lyrics to—Fluffhead and Skippy (which would later be stripped of its music for use in McGrupp). The performance was raw, but the passion—even way back then—was evident. They had taken the first step.

Page's first show. I have it on one tape that includes Scarlet Begonias into Eyes of the World, showing some major Jerry-fluence. Then comes the 25-minute Whipping Post. Oh my God—you gotta hear it to believe it! Next up is McGrupp, more spoken than played, then Makisupa and a jam that would later form into Antelope. This awesome show ends with The Other One. Man, for 1985, you gotta be kidding me! —Alex Banks

One of the finest early Phish shows, this one circulates also as 5/19/85. Whatever the date is, it's a lot of fun to hear Page's debut with the band. He's an obvious fit, though his contributions are obviously less pronounced than in later years (hey, whattya expect from a guest?). Soon after this gig, he talked his way into history. —Al Hunt

10/17/85 [ACCESSIBILITY: ••••]
Finbar's, Burlington, VT
Star Trek Jam, Alumni > Jimmy Page > Alumni, Mike's, Dave's Energy Guide, Revolution > Anarchy, Camel Walk, Antelope, McGrupp

10/30/85 [ACCESSIBILITY: •••]
Hunt's, Burlington, VT
Harry Hood, Dog Log, Possum, Slave, Sneaking Sally, I Wish, Revival, Alumni > Jimmy Page > Alumni, Prep School Hippie, Skippy

Mike is truly at his best. The bass throughout the show is direct and hard-driving. Harry Hood (the first one that exists on tape) is Mike and perfection intertwined. Prep School Hippie is always great to hear; Sneaking Sally gets weird; and the Alumni into Letter to Jimmy Page back to Alumni is an outstanding choice for breaking loose in an early show. Really, the whole show is a great part of early Phishtory. —Andy Kahn

11/23/85 [ACCESSIBILITY: ••]
Goddard College Cafeteria, Goddard College, Plainfield, VT
Mike's > Whipping Post > Antelope > Dave's Energy Guide

1986

[1/2/86]
Penn State University, State College, PA
Tapes that circulate with this date or "Penn State '86" are from 8/27/88.

4/1/86 [ACCESSIBILITY: ••]
Festival of Fools, Goddard College, Plainfield, VT
I: Quinn the Eskimo, Have Mercy > Harry Hood, Pendulum, Bob Dylan Band Jam, Icculus, YEM
II: Help on the Way > Slipknot! > AC/DC Bag, McGrupp > Alumni > Jimmy Page > Alumni, Dear Mrs. Reagan
E: Not Fade Away
Phish shared the bill with The Joneses; each band played two sets. Members of The Joneses played on NFA.

Phish sounded very young and inexperienced in 1986 compared to today, as well as different because of the two guitars (Trey and Jeff). Being a Deadhead, I like to hear the Help > Slip cover. YEM sounds great in its beginning stage but is not the powerhouse it is today. This sounds like it was a great fun festival. —Eric Higel

This old gem features Quinn the Eskimo with a nice guitar solo from Trey in the middle jam. Have Mercy has great piano from Page while Fishman keeps the reggae beat nicely. This flows into a very early rendition of Harry Hood, still a little rough in the transitional stages. Pendulum features a guest vocalist—I don't know who it is but he screams the lyrics "There's a war in the east! There's a war in the west! Which side are you on?" as Phish just rocks this song out. The Bob Dylan Band is Trey introducing Phish as the Bob Dylan Band while Phish plays some jazz—nothing too exciting, but kind of funny. Set II features an odd pairing of Help on the Way > Slipknot! > AC/DC Bag. This is pretty cool if you're someone who likes the Dead and Phish. This tape also features early versions of Icculus, YEM, and McGrupp. Well worth hearing. —Mike Noll

4/15/86 [ACCESSIBILITY: ••]
University of Vermont, Burlington, VT
AC/DC Bag, Dear Mrs. Reagan, Prep School Hippie, Quinn the Eskimo, Slave, Makisupa, Have Mercy, Dog Log, Possum, YEM, Anarchy, Camel Walk, Alumni > Jimmy Page > Alumni

10/15/86 [ACCESSIBILITY: ••]
Hunt's, Burlington, VT
Wilson, Slave, Quinn the Eskimo, Mike's, Have Mercy, Harry Hood, Peaches, Golgi, Swing Low Sweet Chariot, Camel Walk, Shaggy Dog, Mustang Sally, Fluffhead, Sneaking Sally
Paul Languedoc's first show as soundman. Often misdated 4/20/87.

10/31/86 [ACCESSIBILITY: •••]
Sculpture Room, Goddard College, Plainfield, VT
I: Mustang Sally, Camel Walk, Golgi, Slave, Melt the Guns, Dave's Energy Guide, Sneaking Sally, Halley's, Creek Jam, Shaggy Dog, Fluffhead
II: AC/DC Bag, Swing Low Sweet Chariot > Peaches > Bowie, Have Mercy > Harry Hood, Sanity, Skin It Back > Icculus, Alumni > Jimmy Page > Alumni
Jah Roy on vocals for Have Mercy. First of four Phish Halloween shows at Goddard College.

Phish knew how to jam right from their inception. Don't get this tape for the historical value—get it for the performance quality! The Bowie jam is something I'd be glad to hear in concert today, and Jah Roy puts in one of his many notable performances with the boys on the reggae tune Have Mercy. There's also a well-developed Hood, AC/DC Bag with a long intro jam before the current opening kicks in, and, in the comic relief department, Icculus! "This next song is the story of a great, great man," Trey says. "On Halloween, it's always important to remember this man because he was born on Halloween . . . in 1948 . . . in Ancient Greece." —Amy Manning

Halloween at Goddard! This was a period of transition, with Jeff having left the band in May and Trey and Fish transferring to Goddard, but their music soars. —Ernie Greene

12/6/86 [ACCESSIBILITY: ••••]
The Mead Ranch, Shelburne, VT
Mike's > Little Drummer Boy > Whipping Post, She Caught the Katy, AC/DC Bag, Bowie > Clod > Bowie, YEM, Dog Log, Tush, Sneaking Sally, Prep School Hippie, Jam > Icculus, McGrupp, GTBT, Skin It Back, Cities

This is a great show. For highlights, there's a long, drawn-out Whipping Post, the first Dog Log and some requests—a girl clearly asks if the band knows any Barry Manilow, to which Trey says yes, then whips into Tush by ZZ Top. But the Bowie in the set is quite lackluster, except for the neat Clod that's thrown in. —Jon Bahr

What went on before this show? Trey and Mike are all funked out. Mike forgets words, changes words, then just jams out. Not too many people at this show, but the crowd that's there is kind of rude. They keep talking! Is anyone paying attention? Anyway, you have to hear the old-school Phish style on tunes like She Caught the Katy, Dog Log, and Tush. —Josh Letourneau

Even though their music is not nearly as good as it is now, this show is great because you can tell by listening to it how much fun the band is having. Trey can be heard saying that there's a can in the bathroom for donations. Rare treats like Tush and Prep School Hippie make this tape a must-have. —Mike Jett

1987

3/6/87 [ACCESSIBILITY: •]
Cafeteria, Goddard College, Plainfield, VT
I: Funky Bitch, GTBT, Corrina, Golgi, Quinn the Eskimo, Sneaking Sally
II: Freebird, Harry Hood, Tell Me Something Good, Possum, Free World, Wilson

Ninja Mike Billington on vocals for Freebird. "Happy Birthday" sung before Harry Hood.

This is a fun-packed, funky-filled night of jams. Freebird is done with the coolest guitar trickery I've ever heard. You need to hear their performance of this song. The guy having his birthday must have laughed when Trey sang "Happy Birthday" to him because Trey makes fun of the guy's aging throughout the song. Also, when you hear this tape, you'll hear that everything is sung in a blues theme fashion. —Chad Mars

3/11/87 [ACCESSIBILITY: •]
Goddard College, Plainfield, VT
Corrina, Golgi, Quinn the Eskimo, Sneaking Sally, Freebird, Antelope, Flat Fee, YEM, Lushington, Possum, Sneaking Sally Reprise, Peaches, TMWSIY > Avenu > TMWSIY, Makisupa

Makisupa features a special guest on harmonica. All or part of this show may be from 5/11/87.

3/23/87 [ACCESSIBILITY: •]
Nectar's, Burlington, VT
I: Funky Bitch, Mike's, Alumni > Jimmy Page > Alumni, YEM > Sparks > Fluffhead, Peaches, Ride Captain Ride
II: Crimson Jam, Corrina, Why Don't You Love Me, Camel Walk, Golgi, Swing Low Sweet Chariot

4/24/87 [ACCESSIBILITY: •]
Billings Lounge, University of Vermont, Burlington, VT
Golgi, AC/DC Bag, Possum, Fluffhead, YEM, Dave's Energy Guide, Alumni > Jimmy Page > Alumni, Hydrogen, Bowie, Dear Mrs. Reagan, Slave

4/29/87 [ACCESSIBILITY: •••]
Nectar's, Burlington, VT
I: She Caught the Katy, Alumni > Jimmy Page > Alumni, Golgi, Swing Low Sweet Chariot, Fire > Skin It Back > Cities > Fuck Your Face
II: Lushington, Dog Log, Melt the Guns, Dave's Energy Guide, A-Train, Halley's, Quinn the Eskimo
III: Peaches > Fluffhead, GTBT, Anarchy, Makisupa, Antelope, Boogie On Reggae Woman, Timber Ho, Slave, Sparks, Jam, McGrupp, Curtis Lowe, Let the Good Times Roll, Hydrogen

Setlist for third set may be incomplete.

A good tape to have to chronicle how far the band has come. But even more important are the rare songs in this show full of hits. The first set contains only a few songs they still play today; most of the rest are extinct, at least for now. A ripping Lushington opens the second set, leading again into a set of almost all extinct songs. The third set is filled with tunes that seem like Phish wanted to play forever because they're classics today. If you get this show, you'll have a good idea about Phish "gems." —Brett Pessin

This three-set show contains some real diamonds. Golgi has a funk intro that was later dropped and A-Train has a horn player (who is that?) in honor of Duke Ellington's birthday. There are also many parts of the soon-to-be-epic Fluffhead throughout this show. Lushington contains (2) The Chase. The Fluffhead played includes (1) Fluff's Travels, back into the song, and finally (6) The Arrival, the jam at the end. Finally, I Am Hydrogen eventually jams into (3) Who Do? We Do! Add another 1980s tape with (4) The Clod and (5) Bundle of Joy and you have the whole shebang. —Brendan Neagle

5/11/87 [ACCESSIBILITY: ••]
Nectar's, Burlington, VT
Golgi, Corrina, Jimmy Page, YEM, Possum, Slave, Sneaking Sally, Clod, Peaches, TMWSIY > Avenu > TMWSIY, Makisupa, Ya Mar

8/9/87 [ACCESSIBILITY: •]
Nectar's, Burlington, VT
I: Fee, Harry Hood, Harpua, Suzie
II: Bowie, YEM, Ya Mar, Divided Sky, Fluffhead, McGrupp, Corrina

8/10/87 [ACCESSIBILITY: •]
Nectar's, Burlington, VT
I: Peaches, Alumni > Jimmy Page > Alumni, Golgi, Wilson, Quinn the Eskimo, Divided Sky, GTBT, Fire, AC/DC Bag, Possum, Fluffhead, Fee, Curtain
II: I Know a Little, Mustang Sally, YEM, La Grange, Icculus, Bowie, Jesus Left Chicago, Whipping Post, Anarchy, Tush, Dear Mrs. Reagan

8/21/87 [ACCESSIBILITY: •••••]
Ian McClain's Farm, Hebron, NY
I: Dog Log, Peaches, Divided Sky, Funky Bitch, Harry Hood, Clod, Curtain, Light Up or Leave Me Alone, Shaggy Dog, Wilson, Camel Walk
II: Mike's, Harpua > Bundle of Joy > Harpua > Golgi > Sparks, Flat Fee, Fee, Skin It Back > Low Rider/La Bamba/Low Rider > Creek Jam > Sloth
III: BBFCM, McGrupp > Stir It Up > "Mousehouse Rap"/Makisupa jam, Bowie, Sanity, Swing Low Sweet Chariot

Curtain "with" (slow jam at end with music that became Rift). "HYHU" jam in Mike's. Show is often misdated 8/27/87, and the third set circulates as 1/1/87 "Private Party at Page's House."

The two best Phish shows of the 1980s weren't really shows at all but informal affairs played before friends in Hebron, NY, right near the Vermont border. It's hard to say which show is "better," this show or their gig at Ian's place in May 1989, so I won't even try. I really think you ought to hear them both, as they are as "classic" as any Phish tapes you can get your hands on. This show is a little slower and goofier than 1989, as was Phish's style back then—I envision Marley and friends romping in the tall grass beneath a late-summer sun while the band weaves a complex tapestry of notes. —Melissa Wolcott

From the scattered barks on the tapes of this show, it sounds like there were more dogs

Friday, August 21, 1987 — IAN'S FARM, Hebron, NY

If you've heard a tape of the classic Ian's '87 show, you know dogs bark throughout it. The Almanac tracked down one of those pooches and asked him to review the show.

What a great, tail-waggin' time I had. Lots of other canines and butts to smell. There was this one Golden Retriever with a great-smelling butt, but she was all high and mighty and hanging out with these humans making weird noises on this platform. Every time I came close to them she'd growl. But the other dogs treated me better. We kept on barking at those humans, and they kept on making more noises, and so we kept on barking.

After a while I got to like some of the noises. At first they kept on singing "dog," which is one of those noises which I know has something to do with me. They also kept saying "log." I don't know that one. So I barked. Then there were more noises without any words, then a bunch of words, then some real pretty noises, and then they started saying "dog" again. So I kept on barking, and all the other guys joined in. The noises stopped for a while and there was a great barbecue with lots of scraps.

Then the noises started up again, and soon they were saying "dog" again, talking about someone named Harpua. I don't know him, but if I meet him, I'd like to smell his butt.

—Jim

in attendance than people. Appropriately enough, Phish starts off with Dog Log, kicking off the first of three amazing sets. Plenty of highlights here: a scorching Funky Bitch and a Harry Hood with at least five minutes of jamming before the lyrics; The Curtain, featuring the instrumental section that sounds like a slow Rift jam. Harpua is without narration, instead going into Bundle of Joy, back into a Harpua jam, then segueing smoothly into Golgi. Another highlight is a cover of Little Feat's Skin It Back, ending in squealing feedback from Trey that gives way to an amusing Low Rider. —Ryan Harsch

I have run across several versions of the famous 8/21/87 third set, and all of them have Mousehouse Rap listed before Makisupa. After Stir It Up, Trey yells, "Bass and drums! Bass and drums!" and Mike and Fish start a little reggae groove. Then, Trey spontaneously starts rapping: "You go to the house/See a little mouse/What can I do?/Go see you/Step in doggy-doo/And say pee-hew!" It goes on from there before he starts screaming, "Rasta! Jah!! Rasta is my savior! Jah is my savior!" played to a sort of Makisupa jam. Because it's an isolated incident, I think Mousehouse Rap should be given credit in the setlist for historical significance. —David Schall

This is the funniest, grooviest and coolest tape I own. Two paws up! —Amy Manning

8/22/87 ❄
WIZN Beach Party, Burlington, VT

8/29/87 [ACCESSIBILITY: ••••]
The Mead Ranch, Shelburne, VT
I: Alumni > Jimmy Page > Alumni, Curtis Lowe, Sneaking Sally, Makisupa, BBFCM, Flat Fee, Lushington, Suzie, Mustang Sally, Ya Mar, TMWSIY > Avenu > TMWSIY
II: Clod, Slave, Swing Low Sweet Chariot, Curtain, McGrupp, Possum, Harry Hood, Timber Ho, AC/DC Bag, Divided Sky, Harpua > Bundle of Joy > Harpua
"HYHU" teases in Suzie. Curtain "with."

My dream show! Beautiful, perfect, 1987-era Phish that kicks off with an Alumni > J. Page > Alumni opener. The rare Lushington, complete with The Chase, is sure to make you laugh, along with Suzie G., which sounds like Sweet Home Alabama at first until they keep teasing HYHU to spite Fishman. Ya Mar is dedicated to Marley, Trey's dog, and Trey acknowledges this by singing, "Ya Mar, you no good dog!" The set closes with The Man Who Stepped into a Pile of Yesterday, and Stopped in Jerusalem on the Way! The second set never fails to blow me away, too, beginning with Clod. Swing Low is one of my faves, followed by an unstoppable combination of: Curtain "with," McGrupp and Possum! But it doesn't stop there—Timber Ho, AC/DC Bag, and Divided Sky follow! And the set closer? Harpua > Bundle of Joy > Harpua! Best show of 1987? —Otis

This is without a doubt one of my favorite oldies. It opens with Alumni Blues, which appears on virtually all pre-1990s tapes. Then comes an unusually long Makisupa Policeman. The best song in the first set, though, is definitely Suzie. Whether or not this is their first time playing it, it sure sounds like it, mainly due to the fact that they seem to have real trouble getting it started. Once they do, it sounds great because it's much slower and less polished than it is now. —Jonathan Banco

9/3/87 ❄
Hunt's, Burlington, VT

9/12/87 [ACCESSIBILITY: •]
Nectar's, Burlington, VT
I: TMWSIY > Avenu > TMWSIY, Clod, Slave, Funky Bitch, Wilson, Dear Mrs. Reagan, Golgi, AC/DC Bag, Possum, YEM, Curtain, BBFCM
II: Suzie, Alumni > Jimmy Page, GTBT, Rocky Top, Sneaking Sally, Fee, Divided Sky, Dog Log, Curtis Lowe, Antelope, Makisupa, Fire, Terrapin, La Grange, Fluffhead
Curtain "with."

9/27/87 [ACCESSIBILITY: •]
Pledge Party, Burlington, VT
I: Bowie, Funky Bitch, Golgi, Peaches, A-Train, Possum, Phase Dance, GTBT, Skin It Back
II: Wilson, I Didn't Know, Fluffhead, Fire, Fee
Date uncertain and setlist likely incomplete.

Announcements made during the show include "The keg's back on tap in the basement," and "I hope all the pledges are feeling Irie," from a frat member. —AJ Fucile

10/14/87 [ACCESSIBILITY: •]
Hunt's, Burlington, VT
I: Peaches, A-Train, YEM > Golgi > Slave > Chase > Fluffhead > Possum
II: Bowie, AC/DC Bag > Divided Sky > McGrupp > Clod > Makisupa

This show—both sets of which fit comfortably onto a 90-minute tape—is littered with Fluffhead! The closing of Golgi slides into Slave, then the chords of The Chase emerge. It's almost unnerving to hear this part of Fluff's Travels merge into the opening "Fluffhead was a man . . . " refrain, but here it happens. As was standard on most early Fluffheads, the verses here are repeated at the end of the song. Clod—another future Fluff component, surfaces in the second set. Beyond Fluffhead, the second set starts immediately on my tape with Bowie—a solid portrait of the band's musicianship in late 1987. The grouping that follows would be great in concert today—AC/DC Bag into Divided Sky into McGrupp, although here the songs are shorter than their current incarnations.—Lock Steele

10/31/87
Sculpture Room, Goddard College, Plainfield, VT
Second annual Phish Halloween show at Goddard. Phish alternated sets with The Joneses.

11/18/87 ❄
Hunt's, Burlington, VT
I: Slave, TMWSIY, Flat Fee, Wilson > Peaches, A-Train, Golgi, Divided Sky, Alumni, GTBT
II: I Didn't Know, YEM, Fluffhead, AC/DC Bag

11/19/87 [ACCESSIBILITY: •]
Hunt's, Burlington, VT
I: McGrupp, Sparks, Funky Bitch, YEM, Sneaking Sally, Harry Hood, Fire
II: Timber Ho, Fluffhead, I Didn't Know, Fee, Corrina, Alumni > Jimmy Page > Alumni, Suzie, Possum, Divided Sky, BBFCM
III: Dinner and a Movie, Curtis Lowe, Whipping Post, Jimmy Page, A-Train, Camel Walk, La Grange, Bike, Slave

1988

1/30/88 [ACCESSIBILITY: ••]
Gallagher's, Waitsfield, VT
I: Funky Bitch, Mustang Sally, AC/DC Bag, Possum, Jesus Left Chicago, Sneaking Sally, Alumni, A-Train, GTBT
II: Wilson, Slave, Corrina, Fire, Fluffhead, Divided Sky, Curtis Lowe, YEM, Sloth, Whipping Post
III: Fee, Suzie, Lizards, Golgi, Bike, BBFCM, Camel Walk, Harry Hood
Show often misdated 1/27/88.

Musically speaking, this is simply my favorite 1980s Phish tape (and I've heard most of them). Besides offering a good view of what Phish was up to at the time—from an opening Funky Bitch to the blues of Jesus Left Chicago and Curtis Lowe to the humor of Pink Floyd's Bike—this show offers plenty of it. It's not as widely circulated as some other 1980s gigs like 10/20/89 and 8/21/87, but it's really worth seeking out. —Ernie Greene

2/7/88 [ACCESSIBILITY: •]
Nectar's, Burlington, VT
I: Fire, McGrupp, Shaggy Dog, Golgi, Alumni, Peaches, Phase Dance, Dear Mrs. Reagan
II: AC/DC Bag, Timber Ho, Flat Fee, Fee, Possum, Lizards, Mockingbird, Whipping Post
III: Suzy, TMWSIY, Clod, Bundle of Joy, Curtain, Curtis Lowe, GTBT

2/8/88 [ACCESSIBILITY: •]
Nectar's, Burlington, VT
II: Fluffhead, Wilson, Peaches, Divided Sky, Lizards, Antelope, Harry Hood, Mockingbird, TMWSIY > Avenu > TMWSIY
No first set available.

3/11/88 [ACCESSIBILITY: •]
Johnson State College, Johnson, VT
I: The Chicken, Funky Bitch, Sneaking Sally, A-Train, YEM, Wilson, Golgi, Slave, Flat Fee, Corrina, Lizards, Bowie
II: Fluffhead, Dinner and a Movie, Harry Hood, Curtis Lowe, Harpua, AC/DC Bag, Alumni > Jimmy Page > Alumni, Antelope

3/12/88 [ACCESSIBILITY: ••••]
Nectar's, Burlington, VT
Jump Monk > McGrupp > Lizards > Tela > Wilson > AC/DC Bag > Forbin's > Mockingbird > Sloth > Possum, Antelope
First live Gamehendge performance; Trey narrates between songs. Show billed as "Story Time at Nectar's."

This show was the first time Phish played Gamehendge live for an audience. Even if you never get into Gamehendge, you'll appreciate this tape. It's got the usual Gamehendge setlist with the exception of the Antelope and the first song, Jump Monk, a great jazz tune they don't play often. Unlike some Gamehendge performances, Trey tells the whole story, including Col. Forbin staring in the mirror shaving. If you see this tape, grab it and listen closely. —Matt Richardson

I really like the way they do this Gamehendge starting with McGrupp and ending with Possum, but what I enjoy most about this version is the intimacy of it. It's so much more personal in a small place like Nectar's rather than when I saw Gamehendge at Great Woods. It's hard to get the effect of the whole story in a big place, but every show I go to, I find myself begging for it. It's too phat to describe. —Nick Soricelli

The first Gamehendge show is a necessary part of any Phish collection! —Ed Smith

[3/20/88]
Nectar's, Burlington, VT
Tapes with this date are apparently from 5/9/89.

3/21/88 [ACCESSIBILITY: ••]
Nectar's, Burlington, VT
Suzie, Golgi, McGrupp, Sneaking Sally, Divided Sky, Boogie On Reggae Woman, Timber Ho, Lizards, Fire, AC/DC Bag, Possum, Dinner and a Movie, I Didn't Know, Forbin's > Mockingbird

3/31/88 [ACCESSIBILITY: •]
Kenny's Castaways, New York City, NY
I: I Didn't Know, Golgi, Fee > AC/DC Bag > Possum, Fluffhead
II: Alumni > Jimmy Page > Alumni, Lizards, Forbin's > Mockingbird, A-Train, Fire, YEM, Wilson
AC/DC Bag sung for Roger (the "crazy little kid"), who was in attendance. First Phish New York City show.

4/2/88 ❄
Full Moon at the Zoo, Humphries House, Amherst College, Amherst, MA
First Phish "Full Moon at the Zoo" show.

4/22/88 ❄
Billings Hall, UVM, Burlington, VT
I Didn't Know, Golgi, Lizards, Fee, Shaggy Dog, BBFCM, YEM, Suzie, Ya Mar, AC/DC Bag> Possum, Curtis Lowe, Bowie

Friday, April 2, 1988

"FULL MOON AT THE ZOO," Humphries House, Amherst, MA

The 1980s were probably the worst decade for rock music. Musicianship didn't seem to matter as long as you had one of those poofy hairdos and some flashy (aka cheesy) outfits that MTV execs seemed to go nuts for.

Fortunately there was always the good ol' Grateful Dead. In the spring of '88 I couldn't wait for them to come to New England and shake things up a bit. I had recently met this guy Ben in a music appreciation class at Boston University and upon discovering similar tastes in rock music, it was only natural that we jaunt off to a Dead show together in Hartford. A few days before the show (4/3/88), Ben asked if I wouldn't mind going out to his friend's dorm at Amherst College the night before the show because "he's having a cool party with some cool band playing." Sounded cool to me. Two days later we were off to Amherst playing Dead tapes and havin' a fine little road trip.

We got to the dorm, called "The Zoo," before most anyone else. There was just the band setting up and some really nice hippies who were playing hacky-sack on the other side of the room and who told me they'd come down from northern Vermont. It was just a small room with a sort of hallway leading to some stairs cutting through the middle. It was in this wooden-floored room—probably 25' x 65' at best—that I heard Phish for the first time. Before the show I met Ben's cool friend, John Paluska, who got the band down from Vermont to play their first Massachusetts show in his dorm. I also met Trey, who was noodling around with his guitar. I was intrigued, but a little skeptical and completely unprepared for the Phish onslaught. "So what kind of stuff do you guys play?" I asked, not at all thinking that I was about to be blown away.

Trey showed me a piece of paper with all the songs they play on it. Okay—first thing that jumped out at me was "Phase Dance" by Pat Metheny. Wow—this just may be really cool. "It says David Bowie. Which tune?"

"Uh . . . well, that's our tune. We can play it tonight if you want."

"All right, sure. You do 'Terrapin'!?"

"That's Syd Barrett's 'Terrapin.'"

"Wow—that's cool. If you're taking more requests, then play that too!"

Back down in the main room a bit later, the band started to tune up while a small crowd filed in. The room only needed about fifty people to feel stuffed and I'm sure there were a few more than that. Finally, at about 10 P.M. Phish started playing—with an energy that I hadn't seen live on stage (or floor, as was the case) in years. The opener—I'll never forget it—was "Golgi Apparatus." Looking back, it was a very appropriate first song to hear from those four lads. When you think about it, just about every element of Phish is in that song. Loud bursts, soft guitar lines, powerful vocals, tricky instrumental parts, thriving crescendos. All in a nice little package. You could hear their influences and yet experience something entirely new. In just a few short moments, I was an instant fan. I knew I wanted to hear everything they had to offer and see them many times, and I hadn't even heard the second song yet.

For a band that was still relatively "early" in their career, they certainly seemed like a well-oiled machine. Their playing was tight and the sound was really good, if somewhat loud for a small room. There was a mixer in the corner by the doorway and the sound-folks obviously knew what they were doing. No, there were no tapers that night, but I'm sure there must have been a board copy somewhere—though unfortunately, there's nothing in circulation.

I didn't even make it to the end of the show. Due to an early-morning class and rigorous halftime activities, by the third set I was curled up on a couch with a big smile on my face. I do remember many other phine moments, though. "Fee" was fun and the "Bowie" Trey promised me cracked me up and blew me away simultaneously. "Fluffhead" had me convinced that Prog-Rock would never die. As for covers, they did a killer "Good Times Bad Times" (from *Led Zep I*) and ended the second set with a scorching "Whipping Post."

I wish I remembered more, but it was all totally new to me. My mind was overloaded with incredibly cool new sounds, notes and ideas. I didn't even know the names to their originals until weeks later when John hooked us up with some studio stuff that ended up on the *Junta* album (plus some rare covers, too). It was strange to see them whipping up such a frenzy and then, just a few moments later, to be hanging out with them, conversing. An incredible night.

I became an early fan, but I soon graduated, toured Europe and moved out West. Ben took it one step further. He, along with John, eventually set up more New England gigs, and they soon became Phish's managers, establishing Dionysian Productions. Ben's last name was Hunter, by the way, and over time the Phish camp was calling him "Hunta" with a Bahston/New Hampsha type of accent. As Mike Gordon explained to me two springs later, somewhere along the line, someone wrote it down as JUNTA and then someone else read it and pronounced it phonetically. Apparently, this was funny as hell to everyone, and the rest is history.

Oh, and I'm still waiting for them to play "Phase Dance" . . .

—Daniel Gibson

5/14/88 [ACCESSIBILITY: •••]
Springfest, Goddard College, Plainfield, VT
II: Fire, I Didn't Know, Halley's, Light Up or Leave Me Alone, YEM, Lizards, BBFCM, Jesus Left Chicago, Fluffhead, Alumni > Jimmy Page > Alumni, A-Train
Nancy Taube on vocals for I Didn't Know and Halley's. Bobby Brown on horns for Jesus Left Chicago. Karl Boyle on saxophone for A-Train. "HYHU" jam before A-Train.

5/15/88 [ACCESSIBILITY: •••]
Vermont Farm Festival, Hinesburg, VT
Alumni > Jimmy Page > Alumni, Golgi, YEM, Suzie, GTBT, Fluffhead, Shaggy Dog, Lizards, Sneaking Sally, A-Train, Curtain, Flat Fee, Whipping Post, AC/DC Bag, Possum, Icculus, McGrupp, Wilson, Peaches, I Didn't Know, Sloth, Harpua
Party at Dan Lynch's house. Song order uncertain. Curtain "with."

My recollection of this show is sketchy. I do remember a tremendous Whipping Post. The rest of the show was a blur because there were several kegs sitting in the creek. I had also just gotten there after visiting Huntington Gorge and communing with the peace frog. Besides, it was senior week and I was graduating! —Dan Kurtz

A unique combination of Phish performing some rare tunes. A soothing McGrupp and spacey intro to Wilson add to this tape's pleasure. Concluding with Peaches, Sloth, and Harpua, I deem this tape my favorite and a necessity to all my phamily members. —Matthew Ashenfelder

5/19/88 ❄
Student Union, Goddard College, Plainfield, VT
II: Fire, I Didn't Know, Halley's, Light Up or Leave Me Alone, YEM, Lizards, BBFCM, Jesus Left Chicago, Fluffhead, Alumni > Jimmy Page > Alumni, A-Train

5/23/88 [ACCESSIBILITY: ••]
Nectar's, Burlington, VT
A-Train, Golgi, YEM, Rocky Top, Light Up or Leave Me Alone, I Didn't Know, Peaches, Possum, GTBT

5/25/88 [ACCESSIBILITY: ••••]
Nectar's, Burlington, VT
I: Curtain, Rocky Top, Funky Bitch, Alumni, Peaches, Golgi, Sneaking Sally, Suzie, Fire
II: Jesus Left Chicago, Fluffhead, Whipping Post
III: Sloth, I Didn't Know, Ya Mar > One Love, La Grange, Fee, I Know a Little, BBFCM, Corrina, Harpua, Antelope
Curtain "with." Jah Roy on vocals for Ya Mar and One Love. "Flintstones" jam in BBFCM.

Another crazy night at Nectar's. Fluffhead > Whipping Post to close the second set is awesome! Trey lights the Whipping Post on fire with crazy jamming throughout—it's killer. Ya Mar is helped out by Jah Roy doing a reggae rap along with the music. Rarities I Know a Little and Corrina bring us to an early but jam-filled Antelope, and don't forget to check out the Harpua. Still, if you're a fan of wackiness, the Ya Mar at this show is worth you finding this tape to enjoy! —Christopher Mills

The first set is led by superenergetic playing on Alumni Blues and Sneaking Sally. Trey's guitar dominates the entire show, which is about 90 percent devoted to the group's improvisation. For example, the second set opens with a 14-minute Jesus Left Chicago and closes with a 23-minute Whipping Post during which Trey pushes the envelope of guitar ability. But the show's standout is a 20-minute Ya Mar, which features Jah Roy on vocals. Phish jams into a reggae beat to which Jah Roy improvs. —Aaron Grossberg

There's a reason why the song order on most tapes of this show is a little mixed up: the original taper was smart enough to keep that incredible Whipping Post uncut! (Halley's Comet, which often appears in setlists in the third set following the Jah Roy jam, appears to be filler from a different show.) This is really just a great show, and both sets are unquestionably worth tracking down. —Ernie Greene

6/15/88 [ACCESSIBILITY: •••]
The Front, Burlington, VT
I: Suzie, Alumni, YEM, Wilson, Rocky Top, McGrupp, Fluffhead, Golgi, La Grange, Fee, Timber Ho, I Didn't Know
II: Lizards, AC/DC Bag, Sloth, Contact, Dinner and a Movie, A-Train, GTBT, Whipping Post, Dear Mrs. Reagan

6/18/88 [ACCESSIBILITY: •]
Nectar's, Burlington, VT
I: Curtain, Funky Bitch, Possum, Golgi, La Grange, Suzie, Big Leg Emma, YEM, GTBT, Cities
II: Alumni, BBFCM, Swing Low Sweet Chariot > Antelope, I Know a Little, Mike's, Corrina, Rocky Top, McGrupp, Jesus Left Chicago
Song order uncertain. Curtain "with."

6/20/88 [ACCESSIBILITY: ••]
Nectar's, Burlington, VT
I: Slave, Peaches, YEM, Fluffhead, AC/DC Bag, Lizards, Halley's, Wilson, Ya Mar
II: Jam, Sneaking Sally, Tela, Fee, Golgi, Satin Doll, A-Train, Curtis Lowe, Bowie
Jah Roy on vocals during the Jam to start the second set.

6/21/88 [ACCESSIBILITY: •]
Nectar's, Burlington, VT
I: Fluffhead, Rocky Top, Mustang Sally, Suzie, Curtain, Lizards, Forbin's > Mockingbird, Fire
II: Harpua, I Didn't Know, AC/DC Bag, Flat Fee, Alumni, Jesus Left Chicago, GTBT, Contact, Peaches, Golgi
Curtain "with."

7/11/88 [ACCESSIBILITY: •]
Sam's Tavern, Burlington, VT
I: Satin Doll, Suzie, Curtain, Funky Bitch, Fire, Bold as Love, Forbin's > Mockingbird, Golgi, Alumni

7/12/88 [ACCESSIBILITY: ••••]
Sam's Tavern, Burlington, VT
I: A-Train > Timber Ho, Fluffhead > Jesus Left Chicago, Makisupa, Slave, AC/DC Bag, Antelope
II: Cities, Lizards, Sneaking Sally, GTBT, Peaches, YEM, I Didn't Know
Antelope sung as "Roll Like a Cantaloupe."

7/23/88 [ACCESSIBILITY: ••••]
Pete's Phabulous Phish Phest, Peter Danforth's House, Underhill, VT
I: Jam, Forbin's > Mockingbird > Mike's > Hydrogen > Weekapaug, Lizards, On Your Way Down, AC/DC Bag, Possum, Walk Away, Bold as Love, No Dogs Allowed > Divided Sky Jam > No Dogs Allowed
II: Sloth, Fire, Curtain > Wilson, Terrapin, Antelope, Satin Doll, Blue Bossa, La Grange, Alumni, Peaches
III: YEM, Contact, Harry Hood, Dinner and a Movie, Slave, Curtis Lowe, GTBT
Fire featured Peter Danforth and Cameron McKinney. Slave featured a guest artist on saxophone. Dave's Energy Guide jam in the "with" of Curtain "with."

7/24/88 [ACCESSIBILITY: ••]
Nectar's, Burlington, VT
I: Walk Away, Golgi, Funky Bitch, Forbin's > Mockingbird, Sneaking Sally, Mike's > Hydrogen > Weekapaug, Bold as Love
II: Light Up or Leave Me Alone, Fluffhead, La Grange, Lizards, Alumni, On Your Way Down, Cities, Bowie
III: TMWSIY > Avenu > TMWSIY, Peaches, Jesus Left Chicago, McGrupp, Antelope

7/25/88 [ACCESSIBILITY: •]
Nectar's, Burlington, VT
II: Mike's > Hydrogen > Weekapaug, Bold as Love
III: Light Up or Leave Me Alone, Fluffhead, Skin It Back, Harpua, BBFCM, Sanity, Icculus, Camel Walk
The Sanity and Icculus from this concert appear on the Elektra re-release of Junta. *Last Nectar's show.*

7/30/88 ❄
Fly Me to the Moon Saloon, Telluride, CO
III: Harpua, Fluffhead, Anarchy, Dear Mrs. Reagan, Terrapin, Antelope
E: Fire

Anarchy played with Whipping Post bass line. Though tapes circulate with "Fly Me to the Moon Saloon" as the venue name, the location of this show was more likely the Roma in Telluride.

8/3/88 [ACCESSIBILITY: •••]
The Roma, Telluride, CO
I: I Know a Little, YEM, Jesus Left Chicago
II: Peaches, Mike's > Hydrogen, Fluffhead, Harry Hood, Satin Doll, Funky Bitch, Walk Away

The week of gigs in Telluride in late July and early August 1988 stands as a key historical signpost in the evolution of the band. The band had been booked for a week of shows in Telluride but found out the gigs had fallen through a few days before they were to depart for Colorado. After brief hesitation, however, they decided to go anyway, and took up residence as the house band at the Italian eatery and bar the Roma on Telluride's beautiful main street. No Phish collection is complete without a Telluride tape. —Pat Stanley

Plenty of funny banter on this tape. Page, after Jesus Left Chicago, says, "We're going to take a break now and come back and play a real long set. Well, it's not gonna be that long, but it's gonna be a real short break. Well, a medium-sized break." After Fluffhead, the band sings an a cappella Happy Birthday to Stacy, ending it with, "It's been a long time since you were born." Before Walk Away, the band gives last call and encourages big tips for Scott, the "only one working here tonight." —Bob Colby

I sometimes hear rumors that a few Telluride fans have this entire week's worth of shows on tape. If the few sets in circulation—plus the Jazz Odyssey comments made during set two on 3/17/91—are any indication, this is a treasure worth uncovering! (I've also heard that soundboard masters were stolen from a house in Telluride sometime around 1990, so we may never hear these lost shows. Damn.) —Ernie Greene

8/6/88 [ACCESSIBILITY: ••••]
The Roma, Telluride, CO
I: La Grange, YEM > Cities > Dave's Energy Guide > Cities, A-Train, Funky Bitch, Dinner and a Movie, Fire
II: Golgi, AC/DC Bag, Satin Doll, Sanity, BBFCM, Slave

London Bridge is Falling Down teases in A-Train. Jeopardy tease before Satin Doll. Fishman on trombone for Sanity.

If I could choose just one Phish tape from the 1980s for my collection, this would be it. Besides its historic value as part of Phish's week of gigs in Telluride, their first tour outside of New England, the music rocks. Cities > DEG > Cities is just phenomenal! Imagine walking down the steps into the tiny basement of the Roma and hearing a band you've never heard of playing this. No wonder the band made so many friends during their Telluride stay. —Scott Sifton

This show rolls along beautifully and has some really nice tunes. After an extremely slow but great YEM comes one of my favorite Cities in my collection. There are so many good songs on this tape it's unbelievable. Dave's Energy Guide is very good on this tape as well as Take the A-Train. Both sets of this show fit comfortably on one 90-minute tape, and anyone who doesn't have this tape should really try to get it. —Dave O'Connor

More humor on another night in Telluride. After they play AC/DC Bag with a strange intro and Page croons Satin Doll, Mike informs the minuscule crowd, "We're doing this song because Sting asked us to. I want you to know that Sting told you all to have a good time tonight." Sting's choice? Sanity. There's also the giveaway of a T-shirt from Baked in Telluride (a pasta and pizza joint a few blocks down from the Roma) to Tim Rogers, because as Trey says, "If anybody is baked in Telluride, it's Tim Rogers." —Amy Manning

8/27/88 [ACCESSIBILITY: ••••]
Penn State University, State College, PA
Satin Doll, YEM, Funky Bitch, Walk Away, Fluffhead, Mike's, A-Train, Golgi, Tela

Setlist may be incomplete. Show often circulates as 1/2/86 or "Penn State '86."

This has to be the funniest show I've ever heard. The guys obviously stopped at a bar on the way because Trey continually shouts inane ramblings and makes weird mouth noises. Another funny aspect is the lack of an audience. On one occasion I can hear *one person* clap. In response, Fish proclaims, "We're Phish . . . we're still Phish." Pick this one up for a great laugh and some good music. —Ben Ross

Even though the date and location are uncertain, the music quality and other virtues of this great show are known and acknowledged by those who own it. Satin Doll, a rare jazz treat, and A-Train give the set a good feel. But the true greatness lies in the Fluffhead and Tela. This Tela contains my personal favorite Phish jam and is an epic for all to enjoy. —Chip Croteau

After a Mike's Song that goes nowhere, A-Train and Golgi set the stage for one of the greatest treats of my tape collection. These really crisp chords emerge, coupled with a slick melody sung by Page—this is Tela in a different musical form with altered lyrics. The basic elements of the modern Tela progression are there, but this version is faster and more satisfying to the ear. Then comes a jam where Trey brilliantly flies around the neck and partially outlines the chords to the unique progression. The jam comes to a climax Harry Hood–style with Page banging and sustaining the implied chords while the band vocally harmonizes "Tela, Tela." This particular Tela is something every Phish fan should hear. —Larry Chasnoff

9/8/88 [ACCESSIBILITY: ••]
The Front, Burlington, VT
I: Peaches, Walk Away, Slave, Wild Child, AC/DC Bag, Forbin's > Mockingbird, Bold as Love
II: Possum, YEM, Cities, GTBT, On Your Way Down, Whipping Post

Home video played for audience during YEM.

This tape has popped into wide circulation, perhaps a "from the vault" find. It's obvious why this one made the rounds so quickly—the soundboard sound quality is perfect, and the band smokes! The short first set (fits on one side of a 45-minute tape) features Phish covering Lou Reed's Wild Child, and doing it justice. They also sound tight on the other first-set covers: Peaches, Walk Away, and Bold as Love. In the second set, Trey has the lights turned down at the start of YEM for some "home movie" screenings. (This YEM is great, by the way!) Out of that comes Cities, plus two more strong covers—On Your Way Down and the "real" (i.e., not Fishmanized) Whipping Post. —Ed Smith

9/12/88 [ACCESSIBILITY: •]
Sam's Tavern, Burlington, VT
Shaggy Dog, A-Train, Fee, Bold as Love, Timber Ho, Satin Doll, Lizards, TMWSIY > Avenu > Bundle of Joy > Camel Walk, The Practical Song, Harry Hood, Esther

Alternate lyrics in Esther.

9/13/88 [ACCESSIBILITY: •]
Sam's Tavern, Burlington, VT
I: Walk Away, Funky Bitch, YEM, Flat Fee > McGrupp > Wilson > Peaches, GTBT
II: Ride Captain Ride, Boogie on Reggae Woman > Cities, Antelope, Fluffhead

9/24/88 [ACCESSIBILITY: ••••]
Full Moon at the Zoo, Humphries House, Amherst College, Amherst, MA
I: Golgi, On Your Way Down, Alumni, YEM > Wilson > Peaches, La Grange, A-Train, Divided Sky, Bold as Love
II: Bowie, Lizards, Walk Away > Possum, Fee > Sparks, Whipping Post
III: GTBT, Fluffhead, Curtain, AC/DC Bag

Teases in AC/DC Bag include London Bridge is Falling Down and the Flintstones theme.

This show, Phish's second gig at Humphries House Full Moon at the Zoo party, is a classic. The show kicks off with YEM > Wilson. The YEMs from this time period are much simpler than those of the 1990s but are in my opinion much more pleasing to the ear, and the transition into Wilson is an interesting one. The other highpoint of this show is Fee > Sparks > Whipping Post. You can feel the excitement of the crowd by listening to Sparks, which is played about as well as The Who ever played it. —Ben Ross

Back when Phish still sounded amateur, but that's okay—they were still a little college band doing the New England circuit. All the soloing is simple, being that they were still at a very early stage in the great Phish experiment. Trey's guitar sounds a little bit tinny. Still, there's a great transition from YEM (no vocal jam) into Wilson and then Trey pushes into Peaches by singing the drum intro. —Scott Kushner

These tapes showed me an entirely new side of Phish. It's the way the songs are played that's so intriguing. Phish seems to have brought it down a notch for this show, with slower beats, less guitar, and vocal emphasis in Golgi, Wilson, Fluffhead, Lizards, and especially AC/DC Bag. Bag is played so slowly that it's transformed from an all-out jam into more of a lounge act song, allowing clear interpretation of the lyrics. Lizards has been slowed and put almost to a reggae beat. —Aaron Grossberg

10/12/88 [ACCESSIBILITY: ••••]
Red Barn, Hampshire College, Amherst, MA

I: I Didn't Know, Golgi, Bowie, Lizards, Foam, Fee, Mike's > Hydrogen > Weekapaug, Wilson, Forbin's > Mockingbird
II: Alumni, YEM, Contact, Sloth, AC/DC Bag > Possum, GTBT
E: Antelope
NORML benefit concert.

10/29/88 [ACCESSIBILITY: ••••]
Sculpture Room, Goddard College, Plainfield, VT
I: Suzie > Lizards, Time Loves a Hero, Golgi, Bold as Love, La Grange, Contact, Harry Hood
II: Halley's > Whipping Post, Fee, Alumni, Walk Away, Divided Sky, Curtis Lowe, Mike's, A-Train, Fire
III: Fluffhead, GTBT, YEM, Possum, AC/DC Bag, Foam, Terrapin, BBFCM, Timber Ho, Slave, Donna Lee, Antelope, I Didn't Know, Wilson > Peaches, Funky Bitch
Bobby Brown on harmonica for Curtis Lowe. Nancy Taube on vocals for Halley's. Russell Remington on saxophone for portions of the third set. Third annual Phish Halloween show at Goddard College.

Classic show—YEM is a killer, Possum is outstanding and they tear apart Bold as Love. The costume contest is great—Colonel Forbin and Tela both win dates with Fish. Harry Hood is the contest winner, though. The costume contest goes into a short but sweet Hood, ending the set on a fine note. —Kevin Weiss

After Contact, the audience cheers for the best costume. Trey comments that all of the finalists will be on the next album cover. I'm not sure what he's talking about, but it's pretty funny. —Jeffrey Ellenbogen

Set two of this Goddard show has my very favorite Halley's Comet, which I believe features Nancy Taube, followed by a great, extended Whipping Post with Trey on vocals and guitar. Fee seems to start off with different chords. Curtis Lowe is one of the best versions I've heard, and a nice A-Train follows a short Mike's Song. —Pat Elkins

[10/31/88]
Hamilton College, Clinton, NY
Tapes from this show are actually parts of the 10/29/88 Goddard show. Phish did not play Hamilton on this date.

11/3/88 [ACCESSIBILITY: •]
Molly's, Boston, MA
I: Fire, Golgi, Fluffhead, Possum, Fee, Alumni, GTBT, Time Loves a Hero, Walk Away, Lizards, Shaggy Dog, Foam
II: Whipping Post, Contact, Bold as Love, A-Train, Antelope, Suzie, I Didn't Know, BBFCM, Harpua, Bowie
Dave's Energy Guide jam in Whipping Post.

The band's first Boston show came three months before their more renowned debut at the Paradise. Performance-wise, little separates this show from other shows from this time period, but if you're a big fan of historical moments, you'll want to pick it up. Apparently Phish made such a big impression on the small crowd that they were immediately booked to play Molly's again in December. —Tricia Holmes

Another good one from the bar days. You can feel the diversity in cover tunes from early on, and this show has some good ones—Fire, GTBT, Time Loves a Hero (!), Walk Away, Whipping Post, and Bold as Love all sparkle with energy. Great early performance of Harpua, too. —Kyle Niday

11/5/88 [ACCESSIBILITY: ••]
Hamilton College, Clinton, NY
I: Slave, Time Loves a Hero, Fire, YEM, Possum, A-Train, Golgi, Walk Away, Fluffhead, Alumni, Bowie
II: Wilson, Peaches, Bold as Love, Lizards, AC/DC Bag, Fee, Mike's > Hydrogen > Weekapaug, I Didn't Know, GTBT
E: Suzie > Sparks, Divided Sky

11/11/88 [ACCESSIBILITY: ••]
The Stone Church, Newmarket, NH
I: Divided Sky, YEM, Slave, Foam, Possum, Forbin's > Mockingbird, Bowie
II: Mike's > Hydrogen > Weekapaug, M.P.C., Fee, Bold as Love, Timber Ho, Lizards, Whipping Post
E: Peaches, Funky Bitch, Donna Lee
Carl Gerhard on trumpet for the M.P.C., Timber Ho and encores.

This must have been an incredible show to attend. The second set starts with a half-hour-long Mike's > Weekapaug. Highlights include a great Bold as Love and Whipping Post, which is often performed by Fishman but here sung by Trey, featuring a monumental jam. And how about Peaches, Funky Bitch, and Donna Lee as an encore? —Jeff Salvatore

When talking about classic Phish venues of yesterday, you can't overlook the Stone Church in Newmarket, NH. Phirst Phan Amy Skelton moved to New Hampshire sometime around this time and proved instrumental in getting the band gigs at Granite State venues ranging from the Squam Lake Steak House to the Stone Church. You might want to add this tape, from what I consider a particularly strong night for the boys during one of their first Stone Church appearances. —Scott Sifton

12/2/88 [ACCESSIBILITY: ••]
Molly's, Boston, MA
I: Sloth, Golgi, Bold as Love, A-Train, Divided Sky, Contact, YEM
II: I Didn't Know, GTBT, Alumni > Jimmy Page, Lizards

[12/17/88]
The Stone Church, Newmarket, NH
Circulating tapes of this show are apparently from 11/11/88.

1989 Colonizing New England

After making their first real road trip as a band to Colorado in the summer of 1988, 1989 saw Phish spreading their roots further around the Northeast. While still playing frequently in and around Burlington—where they settled in at The Front after outgrowing Nectar's—frequent tour stops included small venues like the Living Room in Providence, RI, the Wetlands Preserve in New York City, and the Paradise in Boston.

By this time, Phish had achieved a level of success that allowed the band members to devote most of their time to music, as opposed to other jobs; the increased time spent practicing shows up in the music and in a series of newly penned songs. May 1989 saw the release of their first real album, *Junta*, and July found the band playing at the prestigious Montreal Jazz Festival. After taking the rest of the month off from playing live, the band resumed touring in August and didn't stop for the rest of the year. The year finished with the band's first New Year's show in Boston, a tradition that continued in various venues around Beantown for the next five years.

1/26/89 [ACCESSIBILITY: •]
The Paradise, Boston, MA
I Didn't Know, Golgi, Alumni, YEM, Lizards, A-Train, Divided Sky, Fee, GTBT, Wilson, Fluffhead, Icculus, Forbin's > Mockingbird, Sloth, Possum, Contact, BBFCM, Fire
Setlist may be incomplete. Phish's first show at the Paradise.

2/5/89 [ACCESSIBILITY: •••]
The Front, Burlington, VT
I: GTBT, Walk Away, Harry Hood, BBFCM, Curtis Lowe, Forbin's > Mockingbird, Whipping Post, Corrina, Bowie, La Grange, YEM
Though Phish played The Front on this date, the circulating setlist (above) is probably part of 2/6/89.

2/6/89 [ACCESSIBILITY: •••]
The Front, Burlington, VT
I: Suzie, Curtain > Wilson, Peaches > Fee > La Grange, YEM, All Blues > Sanity > A-Train, Golgi, Divided Sky, On Your Way Down, I Didn't Know
II: GTBT, Walk Away, Harry Hood, BBFCM, Curtis Lowe, Icculus > Whipping Post, Corrina
E: Bowie

Besides Ian's Farm 5/28/89, this is the show to pick up if you're looking for the "new" fast version of Sanity. The fast version was only played this spring; Phish shelved the song until spring tour 1992, when the original slow version made its famed comeback. As a bonus, this tape also features the only known version of Phish covering Miles Davis's All Blues. —Scott Sifton

2/7/89 [ACCESSIBILITY: ••]
The Front, Burlington, VT

"Paradise Found"

1/26/89 The Paradise, Boston, MA

Phish turned many tight corners on the way to the top, but it's the January 26, 1989, show at The Paradise in Boston that the band has always pointed to as its true "turning point."

While Phish's following in Burlington, VT, was well established in the late eighties, crowds and bookings outside the native state were hard to come by. Their first paying gig in Massachusetts didn't come until 1988—the Full Moon at the Zoo show in Amherst, arranged by eventual manager John Paluska. The first Boston appearance came in the fall of '88, at a club called Molly's, after Paluska's friend Ben Hunter rented out the club and hung flyers on all the buildings in the town, successfully attracting a crowd. On November 3, and then again on December 2 of that year, Phish played at the small club, filling it to the brim the second time around. The momentum was building.

But the real goal for Phish was to play The Paradise, a 650-person club where all of New England's up-and-coming bands could be found gigging regularly. The booking agents at The Paradise, however, had other things in mind. To them, Phish was just one of the hundreds of bands that sent in their demo tapes. And like most, the one marked "Phish" was never even listened to.

With the cooperation of Hunter and Paluska—who were planting the seeds that would grow into Phish's management company, Dionysian Productions—the band rented out The Paradise on its own. It was a risky, break-even-at-best sort of move, but considered necessary for Phish to make a name for itself in the hub of New England. Hunter went into action promoting the show, while Phish and friends were busy ensuring that a virtual army of faithful from Burlington made the trek.

Tom Baggott, a friend of the band's from the very first days at UVM, and Burlington resident "Brother Craig" organized a pair of buses that transported close to 100 Phish fanatics down to the club.

"It was a hair-brained scheme to get Phish's Burlington support down to the club," recalls Baggott, who now books rock acts for a living. Fans paid $20 each—which included transportation, the $6 show ticket, and a "fat tip" for the bus driver—and filled a pair of 47-seat luxury buses to the hilt.

"The bus was fucking insane. It was truly a magic bus," Baggott says. "The bus driver told me, 'I don't hear anything. I don't see anything. I don't smell anything.' The only rule was no glass bottles."

Many others caravaned in their own vehicles from Vermont, marking the true beginning of the era of Phishheads. And the club sold out. Paradise bouncers who asked if Phish was in fact a "real band" were silenced when some fans were even turned away at the door.

The show included most of the Phish repertoire from the time, from rockers like Good Times Bad Times and Fire, to Phish trademarks like YEM, Contact and Icculus. Sadly, most tapes of this show that now circulate among fans are incomplete and poor in quality.

Nevertheless, the band had done it. From there, the bookings would follow. In 1989 other key clubs like Wetlands in New York City and the 8 x 10 Club in Baltimore would also give the band a shot. They were off and running.

I: Esther, McGrupp, Foam, Sloth, Possum, Mike's > Hydrogen > Weekapaug, Golgi
II: Makisupa, Dinner and a Movie, AC/DC Bag, Lizards, Timber Ho, Contact, Alumni > Jimmy Page > Alumni, Fee, Antelope
III: Sanity, Fluffhead, Suzie, Slave, Bike, Whipping Post
E: Fire

2/17/89 [ACCESSIBILITY: •]
The Stone Church, Newmarket, NH
AC/DC Bag, YEM, Fee, Divided Sky, Melt, Golgi, A-Train, Alumni, Antelope, Fluffhead
Setlist may be incomplete.

2/18/89 [ACCESSIBILITY: •]
The Stone Church, Newmarket, NH
Forbin's > Mockingbird, Lizards, Walk Away, Possum, GTBT, Golgi, Wilson > Peaches, YEM, La Grange, Contact, Bowie
Setlist incomplete.

2/24/89 [ACCESSIBILITY: •]
The Front, Burlington, VT
I: TMWSIY > Avenu > TMWSIY, Curtain > Foam, Forbin's > Mockingbird, Antelope, On Your Way Down
II: AC/DC Bag, YEM, Camel Walk
Setlist for second set incomplete.

3/3/89 [ACCESSIBILITY: •••]
L&L Dorm, University of Vermont, Burlington, VT
I: Wilson, McGrupp, YEM > Foam, AC/DC Bag, Curtain, Antelope, I Didn't Know, Divided Sky, Alumni, GTBT
II: Mike's > Hydrogen > Weekapaug, Fee, Possum, Walk Away, Forbin's > Mockingbird, Lizards, Melt, A-Train, Bowie
Date uncertain. Fishman on trombone for I Didn't Know.

3/4/89 [ACCESSIBILITY: •]
Wetlands, New York, NY
I: A-Train, I Didn't Know, Mike's > Hydrogen > Weekapaug, Fee, Golgi, GTBT
II: Possum, Fluffhead, Lizards, Antelope, Contact
First Phish show at the Wetlands. Fishman on trombone for I Didn't Know.

Phish's first Wetlands show is a real tough tape to find—thanks to Dan Gibson for digging this one up! Even though it's the band's first time at the newly opened Wetlands, they obviously have a supportive crowd on hand—there are huge cheers when Trey introduces "Moses Brown, Moses Heaps and Moses Dewitt" for a little 'bone on I Didn't Know. After Mike's Groove, Mike tells the cheering crowd, "You're too kind." The sets are short—45 minutes each—and for historical value, check out the "upcoming band announcements" after the first set. On March 9, there's a tribute to Pig Pen, and on March 12, "Big Fat Love, back by popular demand." —Lock Steele

[3/17/89]
Bear Trap Road, VT
Tapes with this date are actually part of 7/23/88.

3/25/89 ❄
Tree Cafe, Portland, ME

3/30/89 [ACCESSIBILITY: •]
The Front, Burlington, VT
I: Bold as Love, McGrupp, Divided Sky, The Price of Love, On Your Way Down, Ya Mar, Fluffhead, Antelope
II: Mango, Mike's > Hydrogen > Weekapaug, YEM > You're No Good > Undone, La Grange, Golgi
III: Peaches, Foam, AC/DC Bag, BBFCM, Satin Doll, Rocky Top
E: Makisupa

3/31/89 ❄
The Front, Burlington, VT

4/1/89 ❄
U-Joint, Northampton, MA

4/2/89 ❄
Nightshift, Naugatuck, CT

4/7/89 ❄
Stone Church, Newmarket, NH

4/13/89 ❄
Valley Club, Rutland, VT

4/14/89 [ACCESSIBILITY: •]
Base Lodge, Johnson State College, Johnson, VT

TREE CAFE, Portland, ME

Saturday, March 25, 1989

The first time I saw Phish was at the Tree Cafe in Portland, ME, I think in the spring of 1989—my memory is a bit hazy. A guy I worked with named Mike had either seen them before or had heard word-of-mouth about them, and insisted that I had to see this band. We were both pretty much confirmed Deadheads at the time, and I asked Mike if Phish was a Dead cover band, which he hedged by saying, "sort of."

The Tree (now sadly defunct) was a pretty small place, capable of holding maybe 200 people if they ignored the fire codes. I can't remember much of what they played, other than the covers—La Grange was in there, and Peaches En Regalia, which fascinated me—you don't see a lot of bar bands covering Zappa. After the first set we went out to Mike's car, which, as I recall, was parked about eight feet from the door (that should give you an idea of the size of the crowd) to augment our already-altered perceptions.

The Tree got its name (after previous owners had called it Jim's Bar & Grille, Drew's Checkerboard Lounge, etc.) from its proximity to a huge, hundred-year-old oak in front of the entrance. Mike and I got out of the car, smoke billowing out the doors á la *Fast Times at Ridgemont High*, and ran into another Deadhead friend named Dennis, who greeted us with, "Hey, guys! Did you see the guitar player up in the tree?" We looked up and sure enough, there was Trey about ten feet over our heads, laughing his ass off.

The second set was notable for the appearance of the trampolines, which they used during Antelope (the only original song I can remember—the lyrics tend to stay with you). They encored with Rocky Top > Good Times Bad Times (how could I forget a medley that bizarre, yet strangely appropriate from this band). I was completely sold on this band, and persuaded my girlfriend (now my wife) to come see them the next time they played. I saw them at the Tree two or three more times after that, and within a couple of years they had outgrown bars.

—Bob Colby

I: YEM, Bold as Love, Lizards, Sloth, Possum
II: Brain, Mike's > Hydrogen > Weekapaug, Esther

Not too many folks have (or have heard) this tape; from what I've heard, there were only a few tapers there (only one or two SBDs). The band sounds excited and relaxed at the same time to be playing the Base Lodge (it's a small place). I know it's a contradiction, but the proof is in the tape. Keep your eyes peeled for this one—it's worth getting. —Mike D'Amico

4/15/89 [ACCESSIBILITY: •••]
Billings Hall, University of Vermont, Burlington, VT
I: Mike's > Hydrogen > Weekapaug, Esther, YEM, Wilson, Peaches, On Your Way Down, Alumni > Jimmy Page > Alumni, I Didn't Know, McGrupp, Foam, Bowie
II: Funky Bitch, Golgi, Slave, Mango, Divided Sky, Melt, Suzie, Fluffhead
E: GTBT
Soundcheck: Time Loves a Hero.

4/19/89 ❄
Johnny D's, Somerville, MA

4/20/89 [ACCESSIBILITY: ••]
Full Moon at the Zoo, Amherst College, Amherst, MA
I: AC/DC Bag, Fluffhead, You Shook Me All Night Long > Fluffhead, Fire, Esther, Suzie, Sloth, Possum, McGrupp, Foam, Bowie
II: Divided Sky, Walk Away, YEM, Melt, Lizards, Mike's > Hydrogen > Weekapaug, Love You, Harpua
Fire alarm went off during Fluffhead. After Phish returned, they started up You Shook Me, then segued back into the unfinished Fluffhead. Phish's final Full Moon at the Zoo show.

4/21/89–4/22/89 ❄
The Front, Burlington, VT
Rock Rumble with five bands, including Phish. Phish won the Rumble.

4/27/89 ❄
Memorial Union Building, University of New Hampshire, Durham, NH

4/28/89 ❄
Main Lounge, Moulton Union, Bowdoin College, Brunswick, ME

4/29/89 ❄
The Living Room, Providence, RI
Phish shared the bill with Roomful of Blues.

4/30/89 [ACCESSIBILITY: •]
Nightstage, Cambridge, MA
I: I Didn't Know, YEM, McGrupp, Lizards, Divided Sky, Wilson, Peaches, Antelope, Terrapin, Fluffhead
E: Possum
Setlist missing second set. Ben Hunter introduced Phish before I Didn't Know.

5/1/89 ❄
Pearl Street, Northampton, MA

5/3/89 ❄
Franklin & Marshall College, Lancaster, PA

5/5/89 [ACCESSIBILITY: •]
Hamilton College, Clinton, NY
I: Golgi, YEM, Ya Mar, Fluffhead, Alumni, Jazz Jam > Fee
II: Antelope, I Didn't Know, A-Train, GTBT
E: Esther

5/6/89 [ACCESSIBILITY: •]
Collis Center, Dartmouth College, Hanover, NH
I: YEM, I Didn't Know, Mike's > Hydrogen > Weekapaug, Esther, Sloth, Possum, Bold as Love, AC/DC Bag, Forbin's > Mockingbird, Bowie
II: Donna Lee, Suzie, Contact, Fire, Harry Hood, Golgi, Slave, Divided Sky, Antelope

5/7/89 ❄
The Front, Burlington, VT

5/8/89 ❄
The Front, Burlington, VT

5/9/89 [ACCESSIBILITY: ••]
The Front, Burlington, VT
I: Wilson > Peaches, Ya Mar, Mike's > Hydrogen > Weekapaug, Sloth, Possum, Divided Sky
II: YEM, La Grange, If I Don't Be There by Morning, Slave, Esther, Antelope, I Didn't Know > Nowhere Fast jam > I've Turned Bad jam > I Didn't Know, Lizards, Bold as Love, Harpua, Whipping Post
Junta release party. Sofi Dillof and Joe on vocals for Nowhere Fast and I've Turned Bad.

The band took the wraps off *Junta* on this night and made it available to the public, with the cassette wrapped in artwork by Jim Pollock. The Front hosted the *Junta* Release Party, though the band doesn't seem too concerned with selling albums—they're focused on the music. Check out this WILD Antelope with Trey saying, "Marco Esquandolis" in an eerie voice then asking the song's original question, "Bid you to have any spleef, man?" I Didn't Know (with a "pardon me Daubs" line) is also nuts as Sofi Dillof and Joe come on stage for a violent romp through Nowhere Fast and I've Turned Bad. ("When that angry side starts to show through, it feels so good to say 'fuck you,'" Sofi sings/yells at one point.) That leads to a drums and bass solo and then eventually back into I Didn't Know. Finally, the show is topped off by the hilarious "twice-shot ass" Harpua that includes a Poster Nutbag–like buildup for the announcement of Jimmy's name, and a rocking Whipping Post. —Melissa Wolcott

My favorite Front show! The second set has it all—jams, mayhem, and humor. Anyone

April 2 & May 27, 1989

NIGHTSHIFT CAFE and TRINITY COLLEGE

In the spring of 1989, a little tiny ad that ran in my local newspaper drew me to my first Phish show. The band played at this little tiny place called the Nightshift Cafe in Naugatuck, CT. It was a small bar—it's not even there anymore—and it cost five bucks to get in. There were ten people in the audience. Two or three dedicated fans had followed Phish down there but the band really wasn't that well known in Connecticut yet.

I remember them playing Fee, YEM and BBFCM. They also did the trampolines—I can't remember what song they did it in, though. (They didn't even tape the show—I asked Paul afterwards, and he's like, "No, we didn't tape it." I'm kind of bummed out about that.) They did two sets, and the show was great. I had a couple of tapes by then, so I knew the music but I had never seen them live before.

It was a fun night. The band came by and talked to us—they were nice guys, just regular guys, and they still are regular guys. Then I met Paul and I asked if he taped the show and he was like, "no," so he gave me his card and it had a phone number on it. I bought a red T-shirt—I still have it, my first Phish T-shirt, like a red or pink T-shirt with white letters on it. I've never even seen one like it since then. It's kind of weird.

The second show I saw is actually one of my favorites. I called up that hotline number and I heard that they were playing at Trinity College. So I called up Trinity College and nobody knew about it. And I was like, jeez, I don't know if they're really playing or not. But it said on the hotline recording that they were playing, so I went up there with my friend Jesse, real early, like one in the afternoon. I thought, maybe we'll hear something or we'll see somebody. And I was telling Jesse about the band and he was into it. So we're driving around, looking around, but we still weren't 21. I figured, what the hell. It seemed pretty hopeless until I heard this noise coming out of a building and I said, "Let's go over there and see what that is."

So we parked the car, walked in, and sure enough, there they are setting up. We walked in, didn't really say much to them—"How you doing?" that kind of thing. I remember they did a soundcheck with Sanity, they played that like four times, and then I remember playing pool with these guys. In the next room there was a pool table, and we were just hanging around until the evening when the show started. They were just regular guys and they weren't even famous. They were just good people—just a band.

It turned out to be a pretty good show. There was a $10 cover, which we never had to pay, and free beer. We wouldn't have gotten in anyway because you had to be 21 to get in. It was in the basement of a sorority house and they packed it in pretty well that night. There were a good 150 or 200 people there, and yes, they did tape this show.

—Rich Seaberg

who doesn't understand Phish's dark side has got to check out the bad craziness in the middle of I Didn't Know. Yikes! —Amy Manning

5/11/89 ❄
Pauli's Hotel, Albany, NY

5/12/89 ❄
Copperfield's, Syracuse, NY

5/13/89 [ACCESSIBILITY: ••]
The Orange Grove, Syracuse, NY
I: AC/DC Bag, Alumni > Jimmy Page > Alumni, YEM, Golgi, La Grange, Fluffhead, Possum, Foam, Walk Away, A-Train, Melt
II: Bowie, Suzie, Bold as Love, Lizards, Harry Hood, Brain, Contact
E: Fire, Whipping Post

5/14/89 ❄
University of Massachusetts, Amherst, MA
Southwest Outdoor Concert featured Canned Heat and other bands along with Phish.

5/18/89 ❄
Tree Cafe, Portland, ME

5/19/89 ❄
The Blue Pelican, Newport, RI

5/20/89 [ACCESSIBILITY: •]
Northfield Mt. Hermon School, Northfield, MA
I: AC/DC Bag, Alumni, YEM, Lizards, Wilson, Divided Sky, I Didn't Know, Possum
II: Bold as Love, Mike's > Hydrogen > Weekapaug, Foam, Contact, A-Train, Bowie, Golgi
E: GTBT

5/21/89 [ACCESSIBILITY: •]
The Front, Burlington, VT
Harry Hood, Foam, Contact, Mike's > Hydrogen > Weekapaug, Melt, Sloth, YEM, Ya Mar, AC/DC Bag, Divided Sky
Dazed and Confused jam between Melt and Sloth.

5/26/89 [ACCESSIBILITY: ••]
The Valley Club, Rutland, VT
I: Bold as Love, AC/DC Bag, Mike's > Hydrogen > Weekapaug, Sanity, Halley's, Sloth, YEM
II: Bowie, Mango, Melt, Bathtub Gin, Antelope, Golgi
III: Slave, Funky Bitch, Curtis Lowe, Possum, Jam
Bowie sung as "Lazy Lester." Jam at end of third set was an impromptu song the band created so they could play longer.

5/27/89 [ACCESSIBILITY: •]
Alpha Delta Phi Fraternity, Trinity College, West Hartford, CT
I: AC/DC Bag, Mike's > Hydrogen > Weekapaug, Funky Bitch, Fee, YEM, A-Train, Fluffhead, Bathtub Gin, GTBT
Setlist incomplete.

5/28/89 [ACCESSIBILITY: ••••]
Ian McClain's House, Hebron, NY
I: Divided Sky, Antelope, Forbin's > Mockingbird, Fee > Slave, Esther, Suzie, YEM
II: Fire, Mike's > Hydrogen > Weekapaug, Bathtub Gin, Sanity, Ride Captain Ride, Peaches, A-Train, Possum, Contact, Mike and Magoo Jam
III: Funky Bitch, La Grange, Sloth, Sneaking Sally > Vocal Jam, Ya Mar, Jesus Left Chicago, Melt, Mango, Harry Hood
Guest (Paul Ford?) on horns for A-Train. Merry Christmas singing after Possum. Auld Lang Syne jam in Contact. Ninja Mike Billington and Magoo (of Ninja Custodian) joined for the jam at the end of set II, with Fishman on trombone.

A three-set show packed with highlights. I love listening to early shows, hearing them talking and having a great time up on stage. This show has special guests and funny flavors in all the songs. The third set closes perfectly with Hood, then Trey says that the cops have arrived and the show's over. If you like to hear the band talking and having a wasted good time while on stage, you have to get all three sets! —Bill Patrick

Sanity in set II is a more upbeat, fast-paced version. Then Page sings Ride Captain Ride, one of the better Page-sung tunes. In between Possum and Contact, Trey says, "It's snowing—Merry Christmas!" Some people have been misled by this since the show took place in May—really it was just ashes from the fire blowing around. Then to end Contact, they play an Auld Lang Syne tease. Magoo and Mike take the stage for a phunny song to close the set. —Ryan Danyew

You have to love those Ninja Custodian guys. The jam that ends set two features Magoo and Mike ("from the 'where are they now' category," Trey quips) leading the boys through a fun, funky jam. —Tricia Holmes

Boy, Man, God, Shit, Poop—here's the best show of the 1980s, no question about it! Another party at Ian's house finds a pig over the flames and Phish kicking things off with a song Trey introduces as "Pighead" (Divided Sky). And what a set follows—Forbin/Mockingbird, Slave, Esther and a YEM in which they become fixated on the word "poop." (They actually chant "poop" in the song and the vocal jam.) When it's over, Trey says, "We'd like to take a break so we can poop." The second set is even better—there's hilarious dialogue about "getting it up" (Page's department), "keeping it up" (Mike's department) and "letting it back down again" (Johnny "The Turtle" Fishman's department). Mike's Groove rocks, with Trey yelling "Here comes the beer!" in the midst of a great jam.

There's also a "short visit to Weekapaug, Rhode Island," the "new" fast Sanity, a Ride Captain Ride by audience request, and a hilarious Trey ribbing of Fish during A-Train. Perhaps no Phish show better combines banter and music than this one. —Scott Sifton

They kick some fuckin' arse! —Jen Spivey

6/3/89 ❄
Wetlands, New York, NY

6/8/89 ❄
The Quad, Hobart and William Smith Colleges, Geneva, NY

6/10/89 ❄
The Living Room, Providence, RI

6/16/89 ❄
Tree Cafe, Portland, ME
Phish opened for Roomful of Blues.

6/17/89 ❄
Tree Cafe, Portland, ME
Phish opened for Roomful of Blues.

6/23/89 [ACCESSIBILITY: ••]
The Paradise, Boston, MA
I: AC/DC Bag, YEM, Wilson, Peaches, Donna Lee, Fee, Mike's > Hydrogen > Weekapaug, Lizards, Antelope
II: Sloth, Fluffhead, Harry Hood, Ya Mar, Melt, Possum, Bowie
E: Contact, GTBT

6/29/89 ❄
The Front, Burlington, VT
There may not have been a show at the Front on this date.

6/30/89 [ACCESSIBILITY: •]
Pearl Street, Northampton, MA
I: Funky Bitch, YEM, McGrupp, Possum, Donna Lee, Fluffhead, Antelope
II: Walk Away, AC/DC Bag, Curtain, Slave, Bathtub Gin, Mike's > Hydrogen > Weekapaug

7/1/89 ❄
Les Fou Founes Electriques, Montreal, QC
Phish played this show as part of the Montreal International Jazz Festival.

Wednesday, June 7, 1989

HOBART and WILLIAM SMITH COLLEGES, Geneva, NY

During our Senior Week, a couple of our friends got this band to come and play, and we didn't know anything about them. The only thing I remember about getting the band were people saying, 'Oh, well, Ross knows this band called Phish, so, you know, are you going to the Quad tonight to go listen to the Phish?" and I said, "On what the heck, I'll give it a try." So there were probably about maybe 75 to 100 people scattered around the Quad for that show, which probably started around 7:00 P.M. At most, there were maybe five people who didn't attend Hobart and William Smith at the show.

We were really surprised how good they were. People said things like, "Wow, this seems like a pretty good band, I wonder what they're doing bumming around on some college campus?" I don't really remember the setlist from that particular show, but it kind of set the tone for what I could expect from Phish shows after that. They pretty much always played the same songs at shows in '89 and '90—you expected to hear the same ten songs—Fee, Esther, YEM, AC/DC Bag, Lizards, Wilson, Mike's Song, Antelope, Contact and Alumni Blues. We pretty much heard that chunk of songs at every show in different kinds of orders.

—Charlene Smith

8/11/89 ❄
Tree Cafe, Portland, ME

8/12/89 [ACCESSIBILITY: ••]
Burlington Boat House, Burlington, VT
Blue Sky > Suzie, AC/DC Bag, Ya Mar, Rocky Top, On Your Way Down, Wonderful You, Swing Tune, I Didn't Know, YEM, Possum > Icculus > Antelope
Steve and Beth's wedding party. Fishman on trombone for Icculus.

For all of you who've dreamed of having Phish play at your wedding, this is a show to get. This wedding gig offers a nice setlist from top to bottom, including the only version of the Allman's Blue Sky and a couple of real dance tunes, as Trey puts it. And what wedding would be complete without the bride and groom bouncing on tramps during Suzie? —John Cunningham

8/13/89 ❄
The Atlantic Connection in Oak Bluffs, Martha's Vineyard, MA

8/17/89 [ACCESSIBILITY: •]
The Front, Burlington, VT
I: Ya Mar, Suzie, McGrupp, Sloth, Rocky Top, Harry Hood, Mike's > Hydrogen > Weekapaug
II: Walk Away, AC/DC Bag, Mango, Fee, YEM > Lizards
III: Oh Kee, Bold as Love, PYITE > Possum, Halley's, Alumni, Contact, Antelope
E: Golgi > Fire
Nancy Taube on vocals for Halley's.

There were plenty of Phishtorical shows at the Front over the years, but this might be the most meaningful of all—Nancy Taube's last performance singing the words he penned to Halley's. The jam in Halley's stretches out forever, with Fish yelling things like "This song sucks" and "I hate this song!" Because not only was this Nancy's last Halley's performance, this was Phish's last Halley's performance. They swore they'd never play it again, but four years later in Gunnison, CO, Halley's made its grand return. —Ed Smith

8/18/89 ❄
Pearl Street, Northampton, MA

8/19/89 [ACCESSIBILITY: ••]
Collis Center, Dartmouth College, Hanover, NH
I: Oh Kee > Suzie, TMWSIY > Avenu > TMWSIY, AC/DC Bag, PYITE, Rocky Top, Bold as Love, Mango, Lizards, Mike's > Hydrogen > Weekapaug
II: Melt, A-Train, Divided Sky, Bathtub Gin, Funky Bitch, Curtis Lowe, Bowie, Undone, Alumni > Jimmy Page > Alumni, YEM, Harry Hood

This show circulates as 8/18/87, 8/19/88, and its correct date, 8/19/89. Any way you date it, though, it's got a good selection of Phish party tunes. —Amy Manning

8/23/89 [ACCESSIBILITY: •]
The Living Room, Providence, RI
II: Antelope, Forbin's > Mockingbird, Ya Mar, YEM, AC/DC Bag, Foam, GTBT
Setlist missing first set.

8/25/89 ❄
The Blue Pelican, Newport, RI

8/26/89 [ACCESSIBILITY: ••]
Townshend Family Park, Townshend, VT
I: Fluffhead, Forbin's > Mockingbird, Harry Hood, Melt, Divided Sky, YEM > Possum
II: Bold as Love, Ya Mar, Slave, AC/DC Bag, Donna Lee, Funky Bitch, Foam, Bowie
III: TMWSIY > Avenu > TMWSIY, Suzie, Dinner and a Movie, Antelope
E: Contact, Lizards, La Grange
Odd Couple tease in Harry Hood. Show billed as "the ONLY outdoor show of the summer."

As far as sets go, set I is about as perfect as I could ask for. Start out with a classic early Fluffhead then coast into a Col. Forbin > Mockingbird that easily rivals those of today, not to mention the phatty Hood that featured an Odd Couple theme in the intro. Set II starts out with the band asking the phans to "snap your fingers together," followed by the Andy Griffith theme, which goes into Bold as Love! Set III is equally as impressive—TMWSIY opener is beautiful, played perfectly. Every time I hear it, I am transported to another dimension. Definitely check this one out—you'll be euphoric for the whole week. —David George

9/1/89
Bowdoin College, Brunswick, ME
Outdoor show.

9/2/89 ❄
Wetlands, New York, NY

9/7/89 ❄
University of Massachusetts, Amherst, MA
Outdoor show.

9/8/89 ❄
The Front, Burlington, VT

9/9/89 [ACCESSIBILITY: ••]
Bennington College, Bennington, VT
I: Foam, Oh Kee > Suzie, Divided Sky, AC/DC Bag, McGrupp > Makisupa, Bathtub Gin, PYITE, Wilson, MSO, Bowie
II: Ya Mar, YEM, Alumni, Melt, Harry Hood, Walk Away, Possum

9/21/89 [ACCESSIBILITY: •]
Pearl Street, Northampton, MA
I: Golgi, Ya Mar, AC/DC Bag, MSO, Fee, Alumni > McGrupp, Who Do We Do, Bowie
II: Divided Sky > The Chase > Dinner and a Movie > Bundle of Joy > Possum, Bathtub Gin, YEM, Brain, Antelope

10/1/89 [ACCESSIBILITY: ••]
The Front, Burlington, VT
I: Alumni, McGrupp > Jam, Golgi, Harry Hood > Wilson, Foam, Ya Mar, Oh Kee > Suzie, Antelope
II: AC/DC Bag > MSO, Reba, Dinner and a Movie, Fluffhead, Possum, YEM, Brain, Contact, Melt, Lizards
E: Highway to Hell
Concert debut: Reba. Reba includes extra verse and now-defunct section following lyrics. Sunday "All Ages" show at The Front.

The debut of Reba! It's a nice birth (they announce the debut, dedicated to the spirit of Nancy Taube), with the song in a bit of a different format than they play now. Other reasons to grab this tape include Ya Mar (I like the early short versions of Ya Mar like 3/1/90), Alumni, and McGrupp. There's also a classic Fishman performance of If I Only Had a Brain—do you think he's telling the truth? And there's an electric My Sweet One! I miss those. —Greg Marceau

10/6/89 ❄
The Paradise, Boston, MA
Timber Ho, Mike's > Hydrogen > Weekapaug, Sloth, Golgi, Bold as Love, Dinner and a Movie, Alumni > Jimmy Page, Harry Hood, Possum, Highway to Hell, BBFCM
E: GTBT
List may be incomplete.

10/7/89 [ACCESSIBILITY: ••]
Chase Hall, Bates College, Lewiston, ME
I: Golgi, Ya Mar, Mike's > Hydrogen > Weekapaug, Suzie, Fee, La Grange, Makisupa, Alumni > Jimmy Page > Alumni, GTBT
II: Dinner and a Movie, Possum, Happy Birthday Jam, Lizards, AC/DC Bag, Bowie, Contact > Highway to Hell
E: YEM
Date of show might be 11/7/89.

10/12/89 ❄
Keene State College, Keene, NH

10/13/89 ❄
Copperfield's, Syracuse, NY

10/14/89 [ACCESSIBILITY: •••]
The Barn, Hobart and William Smith Colleges, Geneva, NY
I: AC/DC Bag, Divided Sky, I Didn't Know, Golgi, Ya Mar, Melt, Fee, Alumni > Jimmy Page > Alumni, YEM, Makisupa, GTBT
II: Anarchy in the U.K., Highway to Hell, Possum, Harpua
Setlist may be incomplete. Fishman on vacuum for I Didn't Know. In-a-Gadda-Da-Vida jam in Harpua.

10/20/89 [ACCESSIBILITY: ••••]
The Front, Burlington, VT
I: Harpua > Bundle of Joy > Forbin's > Mockingbird, YEM, Oh Kee, Reba, Divided Sky, Golgi, Antelope
II: No Dogs Allowed, Walk Away, Dinner and a Movie, I Didn't Know, AC/DC Bag, Donna Lee, Melt, Melt, Harry Hood, Swing Low Sweet Chariot, Hole
E: La Grange, Slave
Reba includes extra verse and now-defunct section following lyrics. Entire second set after Dinner and a Movie featured Dave Grippo on alto saxophone and Russ Remington on tenor saxophone. Melt begun again after lighting problem. Odd Couple tease in Antelope and Hood. Spiderman tease in Antelope. Old Macdonald tease in Antelope.

This tape offers a great glimpse of Phish early on, but late enough that they really have their act together. The Split Open restarts after a lighting problem, but it's great and features horns guests including Dave "The Truth" Grippo. Harry Hood has an Odd Couple jam at the beginning, which is neat. Slave to the Traffic Light is one that must be heard—it's super-fast. There's also Antelope with the Spiderman jam. There are many hidden treats in this show, so keep your ears open. —Adam Davidoff

Amazing show! The horns sit in for most of the second set, which I find more enjoyable than many of the July 1991 gigs! An absolutely rocking show. —Tyler Harris

10/21/89 ❄
The Front, Burlington, VT
I: Fee, Ya Mar, Hole, McGrupp > Fluffhead, Foam, AC/DC Bag, Lizards, Dog Log, Bowie
II: Mike's > Hydrogen > Weekapaug, Oh Kee > Suzie, Wilson, Possum, Reba, Sloth, YEM, Highway to Hell
E: Antelope

I scored this one from a buddy—wow, what an eye-opener. Great quality for an old show. There's a very stripped-down Hole, McGrupp, AC/DC Bag, and of course, Dog Log. Sick, I tell you! If I could be at one show that I own tapes of from 1989, this would be it. Unfortunately, it's a rare tape and the setlist might be screwy. —Mark Daniel

10/22/89 [ACCESSIBILITY: •]
The Front, Burlington, VT
I: La Grange, Forbin's > Mockingbird, YEM > Oh Kee > Suzie, Ya Mar, Foam, Rocky Top, Melt, Tela, Divided Sky, I Didn't Know, GTBT
II: Harry Hood, Reba, Golgi, Hole, McGrupp, AC/DC Bag > MSO, Fee, Possum
E: Undone
Sunday "All Ages" show at The Front.

I own close to 500 Phish tapes, including all New Year's runs and most Halloween shows, but this is the best show I have on tape. It packs Phish's best-written songs into one show. The setlist is one beyond the dreams of fans, and the way they play the songs is flawless. The Forbin's > Mockingbird doesn't have a story and doesn't even need one. The show also contains the best Oh Kee Pa > Suzie I have ever heard. And as if that weren't enough, YEM and Divided Sky both appear in the first set. It's an excellent example of Phish's music in the late 1980s. —Adam Rizzuti

Anyone of any age could come to this show. Ninja Mike (of Ninja Custodians) ran from the bar up onto the stage, trying to bounce on his head while Phish's trampoline act was going on. He messed up and ended up running into Trey's guitar and amp. He landed behind the backdrop. He stayed there, hiding, as Fishman made cute comments. —Melissa Mixer

10/26/89 [ACCESSIBILITY: •••]
Wetlands, New York, NY
I: Oh Kee > Golgi, YEM, Fee > Divided Sky, I Didn't Know, Wilson, Lizards, Mike's > Hydrogen > Weekapaug

Saturday, October 14, 1989

THE BARN, Hobart and William Smith Colleges, Geneva, NY

The arrival of Phish at our campus on parents' weekend was our crazy secret. Only the "orphans" among us were at the show. No posters were put up and no one knew about it. Phish was brought on campus by two of my friends who also brought them to the colleges the previous spring. The day of the show we were so excited to get this band all for ourselves, we blew off classes to catch a buzz and prepare ourselves for a private party. The twilight came upon us and while we were at some off-campus house getting ready with a keg on a rather warm October night in upstate New York, Phish was having dinner at Farm House, a vegetarian co-op across the street from the Barn.

My friends and I arrived at the Barn and there was no line and, in fact, only about 50 people knew there was a concert that night. My friend who had brought the band to the colleges was collecting ticket money at the door—$2 each. Since many of us knew him personally we got in free. I was carrying a large backpack with a ten-liter bag of wine in it and once in the Barn, I looked for a place to hang the bag. I found what I was looking for—a coat hook on the wall of the dance area. I hung the bag upside down so the spigot poured strong, and went to get myself one of those VeryFine glass juice bottles out of the machine so I could drain it and use it for wine.

The Barn was a facility used for small concerts or indoor student parties. It was not used very often and only had a VeryFine juice machine and a Coke machine as amenities in the hallway, but that night we also sandwiched a keg between the juice machine and stairwell. The main hall was a large concrete slab laid in a modified barn, and it could hold 250 people. At about 10 P.M. Phish came to play. Trey and Mike were set up on a small, six-inch riser and Page and Fishman were on the concrete floor off in opposite corners flanking Trey and Mike.

They opened with a snappy version of AC/DC Bag and then proceeded to Divided Sky. People started drinking wine and frequent visits were also made to the keg using the dainty little VeryFine glass bottles or Coke cans as containers. Phish was here! Yes, our own little secret! Fishman graced us with an up-close lip-sucking on the vacuum cleaner during I Didn't Know. The show just kept rising through Golgi Apparatus, Ya Mar and Split Open and Melt. We cooled down with Fee, during which Trey skipped a line. We all knew the words and through crowd persuasion he was forced to admit his mistake by reciting the last verse—without music.

By this time the floor in front of the band was covered with broken glass, wine and beer. We all boogied in front of the six-foot-high box speakers, which were soaking up their fair share of puddles of vino and beer, and often someone wiped out on the slick floor. Because there was no real stage and no definitive line between performer and audience, we all were sweating together. The stench of wine started to float in the air; was it wine-sweat or was it from the floor? Again, a rockin' rise occurred when they kicked into a supreme Alumni Blues, in which I made a fool of myself by not realizing the band had stopped. I screamed, "Because I got . . . !" Then the humiliation set in. The band laughed and mocked me. Fishman went so far as to ask me, "You gotta what?"

The show must have been a disappointment to the band as far as attendance was concerned. Probably only about 75 people were there at the peak, and mostly there were people who wandered in and wanted to check out what all the noise was about since the Barn bordered some dorms. However, Phish just got more hyped up. The scene was so intimate and messy it drove them to a good old jamming show. At least that's what we all felt. They then broke into what back then could have been their hallmark song, You Enjoy Myself. Inspired by the arrival of Hobart security, which Trey announced to the crowd, the band eased into a nice little version of Makisupa Policeman and it was forever made Hobart's and William Smith's own when Trey replaced "my house" with "my barn" in the lyrics. This was quickly followed by Good Times Bad Times, which sent us all jumpin'.

Phish took a break and returned to the hallway with the keg, the coke machine and juice machine. I went over to Fishman as he was leaving and asked if he wanted some wine. He quickly replied "yes" and we went to suckle the wine tap. After a few minutes of quenching our thirst he went to find his fellow band members. I think the short second set was the direct result of the visit by security. I also believe Phish's frustration with security inspired a particularly apropos opening of the second set—Anarchy and Highway to Hell. After Possum, I saw my buddy talking with Page and then Trey, but I couldn't figure out about what. During Harpua I found out what it was, when Trey broke into a few bars of In-a-Gadda-Da-Vida, a special treat for some of us. In addition, obviously miffed by security, even though they left as quickly as they had come, Trey told a little story during Harpua about Jimmy, who wanted to grow up to be a Hobart security officer. Man, we loved this because Trey and the rest of the band shared the same indignation we students felt for security's intrusion on our fun.

The show was over and there was just the smelly, wine-slippery floor with broken glass and the sweaty people lingering and thanking the band not only with cheers but also with personal thanks. We invited them to our off-campus keg later that night, but they didn't show. Oh, well.

—Patrick Smith

II: Schoolgirl Jam > Dinner and a Movie > Who Do? We Do! > AC/DC Bag, Reba, Walk Away, Bathtub Gin, Sloth, The Chase, Possum, PYITE, Hole, "Sleepwalk," No Dogs Allowed, Bowie

Before PYITE, Trey clarifies that its correct title is "Punch Me in the Eye." Trey teases Space Oddity by Bowie while talking about the upcoming Goddard Halloween show, then the band goes into Bowie. Reba includes extra verse and now-defunct section following lyrics.

The second set of this show is a great one. A Little Schoolgirl jam kicks things off, into Dinner and a Movie. Clod follows with a slower AC/DC Bag. For all Reba fans, this tape is a must-hear: there is a currently omitted phrase in this early Reba (the third ever), which no longer exists, akin to the now-omitted Tela verse (see Penn State 1988). This is quite interesting and would be great to hear nowadays. Also, Trey introduces PYITE as "Punch Me in the Eye," then relatively new as well. —Adam Davidoff

Great show for some "old" Phish. Nice pieces of Fluff's Travels are added in between the songs, which keep flowing from one to the next. Several classic tunes are played that you don't see on current setlists, and a rare appearance is made by Trey's mom as they explain No Dogs Allowed. This is definitely one to get a hold of to listen to the differences in Phish between 1989 and 1997. —Tim Herrman

10/28/89 ❄

The Chance, Poughkeepsie, NY

10/31/89 [ACCESSIBILITY: ••]

Sculpture Room, Goddard College, Plainfield, VT

I: Oh Kee > Suzie, AC/DC Bag, Divided Sky, Fee, Walk Away, Bathtub Gin, Possum

II: YEM, Bowie, Wilson, Reba, Forbin's > Mockingbird, Alumni, Lizards, Highway to Hell

E: Contact > Antelope > Kung > Antelope

Final of four Phish Halloween shows at Goddard. Ninja Custodian opened. Reba includes extra verse and now-defunct section following lyrics. Band distributes macaroni and cheese boxes to the audience before David Bowie; the audience joins on percussion during Bowie. Concert debut: Kung. Portions of this show were later broadcast on public access cable TV in Burlington.

Halloween at Goddard was a huge costume party and a total blast. It was the largest Phish show I'd ever attended, but that's not saying much; there were probably two hundred people there. Everyone was dressed up, including the band. It was really dark, too—you couldn't really see anything in the crowd at this show. That was because of the not-very-well-lit room, which I think might have been some sort of barn. The show itself was really fun and was also a kind of a signal that Phish was getting a little bit bigger, that they could draw a few hundred people to this obscure Vermont town on Halloween night. A lot of people from Burlington, like myself, drove to Goddard for it. —Charlene Smith

The public access TV video of this show is out there, and it's hilarious! You can see the

Tuesday, October 31, 1989

SCULPTURE ROOM, Goddard College, Plainfield, VT

I saw my first Phish show on October 31, 1989, Halloween night, in what I believe was an art building (or something like that) at Goddard College. I kind of stumbled upon it.

I was going to school at Johnson State, which is on Route 15 in Vermont. My roommate talked me into driving to this concert and I didn't really want to go, but he told me it was kind of like a Grateful Dead cover band, so I said, "Oh, okay, what the hell."

To my surprise, Phish was much different and much to my liking. It was a really different situation—there were all kinds of people jam packed into a tiny little place. I'd never seen anything like it before in my life, and I thought, "This is really cool."

There were about three hundred people there. That's my guess. The room felt like a garage, and the people were packed in there. What really surprised me when I got there was the partying that was going on in the parking lot for this band I had never heard of before. And everybody was dressed in costume. Trey was wearing—well, they changed between sets—but during one set I can remember Trey wearing fake boobs with chains around them, and horns on his head. I can't remember what everybody else was wearing, but during another set, they came back and they were wearing pajamas.

I remember thinking to myself, "Wow, this is what the Grateful Dead used to be like in the good old days, and this is something that I can see, this is something of my own." And I can remember, it was Famous Mockingbird—that if I was to come away saying what tune really grabbed me, it was the Mockingbird.

At the beginning of one set, Phish just chucked all these boxes of macaroni and cheese into the crowd. Some of the students there were videotaping the show for public access TV in Burlington. So you had all kinds of people hanging from the rafters, people everywhere, and they just started chucking these macaroni and cheese boxes and everyone was getting hit by them. Then people started shaking them like they told us to, and then I think they went into David Bowie or something like that. The shaking dissipated very soon after the David Bowie intro, but it definitely got the crowd going.

Admission to the show was free but they gladly accepted donations at the end. As I was leaving, someone shook a coffee can in my direction. I can actually remember leaving the show early because it was just so late, and driving in the rain to go home because I was the only one able to drive. We lived an hour away from Goddard, and I remember pulling into home between four and five, so the show probably didn't end until 3 A.M.

—Brendan McKenna

costumes, the macaroni and cheese, and Page with really curly hair! It's obviously unprofessional, but man, does it make me laugh. —Ed Smith

11/2/89 [ACCESSIBILITY: ••••]
Memorial Union Building, University of New Hampshire, Durham, NH
I: Bathtub Gin, Foam, Mike's > Hydrogen > Weekapaug, Fee, Curtain, Reba, Melt, Esther, GTBT
II: Oh Kee > Golgi, YEM > Kung > Divided Sky, McGrupp > Who Do We Do > AC/DC Bag, MSO
E: Highway to Hell
Outing Club benefit. Reba includes extra verse and now-defunct section following lyrics.

A cafeteria-type room, approximate capacity 450 people. Mind-blowing first set during Reba's first tour. Reba has an extra verse, a harder-edge "bag it tag it" before the instrumental middle section. The Curtain is always a bonus, then during Divided Sky Trey speaks of the black rhombus. This was one hell of a first show for me—the band cruised around the crowd during set break. —Nathaniel Peirce

There are a few weird things about this show. First of all, it's one of the few early shows where good-sounding digital audience tapes can be found. Also, Phish must have been playing at a school dance or something, judging from their introduction. The jammy Mike's Groove sure caught people off-guard, judging from the crowd's reaction.
—Ben Ross

Quite a party at UNH this night. The start of Bathtub Gin drowned out the fire exit speech, and the show just took off from there. The YEM vocal jam was good clean fun. Our heros hammed it up and then segued straight into Kung. This was followed by a rhombus reference which gave way to Divided Sky which really moved. There have certainly been more experimental nights. This was pure fun. —Scott Kushner

11/3/89 [ACCESSIBILITY: •]
Tree Cafe, Portland, ME
I: Forbin's > Mockingbird, Bathtub Gin, MSO, Melt > Clod > Bundle of Joy, YEM, PYITE, Reba, Golgi
Reba includes extra verse and now-defunct section following lyrics.

11/4/89 ❄
College of the Atlantic, Bar Harbor, ME

11/9/89 [ACCESSIBILITY: •]
Mission Park Dining Hall, Williams College, Williamstown, MA
I: I Didn't Know, Golgi, Ya Mar, Curtain, MSO, Bathtub Gin, YEM, A-Train, GTBT
II: Oh Kee > AC/DC Bag, McGrupp > PYITE, Lizards, Mike's > Hydrogen > Weekapaug
E: Highway to Hell

11/10/89 [ACCESSIBILITY: ••••]
Sigma Phi Fraternity House, Hamilton College, Clinton, NY
I: Melt, Oh Kee > Suzie, Fee, Divided Sky > AC/DC Bag, MSO, YEM, My Girl > La Grange, Harry Hood, Bathtub Gin, Mike's > Hydrogen > Weekapaug
II: McGrupp > Fluff's Travels > Sloth, Lizards, Brain, Possum, Harpua, Highway to Hell, A-Train, Antelope

11/11/89 [ACCESSIBILITY: ••]
Patrick Gymnasium, University of Vermont, Burlington, VT
Oh Kee > Golgi, Bathtub Gin, AC/DC Bag, MSO, YEM, Brain, Frankenstein
Phish played one set; Max Creek and Third World played after Phish. Concert debut: Frankenstein.

11/16/89 [ACCESSIBILITY: •]
Pearl Street, Northampton, MA
I: Mike's > Hydrogen > Weekapaug, Bathtub Gin, Foam, Oh Kee > Suzie, MSO, Reba, YEM > Frankenstein
II: Sloth, AC/DC Bag, Tela, Bowie
Show ended after Bowie when a window broke in the club. Reba includes extra verse and now-defunct section following lyrics.

11/18/89 ❄
23 East Cabaret, Ardmore, PA

This was Phish's first Philadelphia-area show. To drum up fan support, the Phish newsletter advised, "These Cabaret clubs are known for their great atmosphere/good shows!" Elsewhere, the newsletter touted Phish's first show in Washington, D.C., on 12/6/89 and its show at the 8x10 Club in Baltimore the following day, saying, "What better excuse for a roadtrip than to see Phish at one of these great clubs! And make sure to spread the word to friends in these cities!" This is the famous word-of-mouth network that the band and its backers proved so good at coordinating into action. —Lock Steele

11/30/89 [ACCESSIBILITY: •]
The Paradise, Boston, MA
I: Bathtub Gin, Divided Sky, Ya Mar, Oh Kee > AC/DC Bag, Foam, Lizards, MSO, Antelope, Lawn Boy, Frankenstein
II: Reba, Possum, Forbin's > Mockingbird, Undone, Fee, Melt, A-Train, Suzie, Contact, Bowie
Date of show might be 12/1/89. Reba includes extra verse and now-defunct section following lyrics.

12/3/89 ❄
The Front, Burlington, VT
Sunday "All Ages" show at The Front.

12/4/89 ❄
The Front, Burlington, VT

12/6/89
The Roxy, Washington, DC

12/7/89 [ACCESSIBILITY: ••••]
8x10 Club, Baltimore, MD
I: I Didn't Know, YEM, A-Train, AC/DC Bag, Fee, Mike's > Hydrogen > Weekapaug, Alumni > Jimmy Page > Alumni, Divided Sky
II: Oh Kee > Suzie, Rocky Top, Ya Mar, Walk Away, Lizards, Antelope, Lawn Boy, Possum, Undone
E: Golgi

12/8/89 [ACCESSIBILITY: ••••]
Green Mountain College, Poultney, VT
I: Oh Kee > Suzie, Melt, Ya Mar, Reba, McGrupp > Who Do We Do > AC/DC Bag, MSO, Bathtub Gin, Antelope
II: Harry Hood, Tela, Timber Ho, Slave, I Didn't Know, YEM, Possum, Lawn Boy, Fire
Reba includes extra verse and now-defunct section following lyrics.

This tape is widely available but tends to be somewhat overlooked. I think set II contains some of the most perfectly balanced versions of Harry, Tela, and Slave I have from this era. But don't overlook the Antelope—it's not the best, but it's so, so crisp. —Justin Weiss

A good show from top to bottom. In the solo for Split Open, Trey sounds like a man possessed. Reba is average and so is Antelope. The boys make some funky aquatic sounds during the latter part of AC/DC Bag. Tela, Slave, and I Didn't Know are must-hears on this tape. They're phantastic! The vocal jam at the end of YEM is totally insane. Grab this tape if you can find it. —Tony Krupka

12/9/89 [ACCESSIBILITY: •]
Castleton State College, Bomeseen, VT
I: Dinner and a Movie, La Grange, Lizards, Foam, Hole, Rocky Top, Bowie, Lawn Boy, Bathtub Gin, Golgi
II: A-Train, Fluffhead, Esther, Alumni, Fee, Mike's > Hydrogen > Weekapaug, Contact, BBFCM

12/15/89 [ACCESSIBILITY: ••]
Ukranian National Home, New York, NY
I Didn't Know, Possum, Divided Sky, Antelope, Funky Bitch, Jesus Left Chicago, Contact, Bowie
Phish shared the bill with Blues Traveler and played one set. John Popper on harmonica for Funky Bitch and Jesus Left Chicago.

12/16/89 [ACCESSIBILITY: •]
Contois Auditorium at City Hall, Burlington, VT
Curtain > AC/DC Bag, Lawn Boy, Mike's > Hydrogen > Weekapaug, Lizards, Hole, Golgi
E: Possum
Burlington Boathouse benefit concert.

12/29/89 [ACCESSIBILITY: •]
23 East Cabaret, Ardmore, PA
I: Divided Sky, Ya Mar, Oh Kee > AC/DC Bag, Lizards, Lawn Boy, Mike's > Hydrogen > Weekapaug
Setlist incomplete.

12/30/89 ❄
Wetlands Preserve, New York, NY
Indecision opened.

12/31/89 ❄ [ATTEND. 1,678; CAP. 1,700] [TIX $13.50-$15]
Exhibition Hall, World Trade Center, Boston, MA
I: I Didn't Know, YEM, Oh Kee > AC/DC Bag, Auld Lang Syne, Antelope, Bathtub Gin, Lizards, Satin Doll, Highway to Hell
II: Mike's > Hydrogen > Weekapaug, Ya Mar, Melt, Divided Sky, Fee
E: Contact

UKRANIAN NATIONAL HOME, New York, NY

Friday, December 15, 1989

I sort of stumbled upon Phish by accident. I was maybe 16 or 17, hanging out with a friend on a street corner on a cold winter night in New York, looking for something to do. Someone heard that Blues Traveler was playing downtown with another band who "jumped up and down on mini-tramps while they played." So we hopped in a cab and headed downtown to the Village to a Ukranian Community Center someone rented out for the show. What a random place to see my first Phish show! What an odd place to go on a Saturday night!

I imagined that this center, with its pronounced Cyrillic signage on the building facade, was normally used for meetings, bake sales, folk-dance lessons or whatever else Ukranians might like to do. Upstairs was a recreation room with low ceilings, funny ceiling panel-tiles, and fluorescent lighting that, suffice to say, had been turned off. I don't think there was even a stage.

That night there was no folk dancing or potluck. I caught Phish in the middle of a set and I vaguely recall jamming to YEM, although that could be a wishful memory I've planted in my head. Alas, in those days of old I had a curfew and went home before the show ended, but I'm sure the party continued into the wee hours of the morning. Those New York Ukranian Phishheads, after all, sure know how to jam.

—Kirsti Scutt

The Ululators opened. Show billed as Phish's "1st annual New Year's Eve Extravaganza!"

In a small ballroom in Beantown, the Phish New Year's Eve tradition began. The November Phish newsletter noted, "Phish is looking for a space in New England to host a New Year's Eve extravaganza! We need a room to hold 500–800 people, as well as lots of party ideas." When the venue—Boston's World Trade Center Ballroom—had been confirmed, the December newsletter said, "Creative formal dress appreciated for this grand affair!" The band provided hors d'oeuvres (fruit) and champagne to the crowd, but also (in the first of what would become an increasingly elaborate series of New Year's Eve pranks) had a few tricks up their sleeves. When Page, Trey, and Mike appeared on stage in full tuxedo garb and started singing I Didn't Know, Fishman was nowhere to be seen. But when it came time for a vacuum solo in the middle of the song, Fish emerged wearing nothing but a top hat and g-string! —Lock Steele

1990 Mountains to Mountains

1990, the first year for which setlists are generally more accurate than inaccurate—although some of the setlists from this year likely have songs or encores missing—saw Phish touring as far south as Atlanta and as far west as Wisconsin. February led the band south (for several shows with Widespread Panic), then spring found them traveling across the Midwest and back to Colorado for the first time since their August 1988 Telluride sojourn. Phish took most of the summer off from gigging following a three-set show at Townshend Family Park on June 16, 1990. Starting things back up in September at the Wetlands, they unveiled a whole new slate of songs and were soon on their way west again for a run of fall shows in Colorado (including Halloween) that still rank among the most storied in Phishtory. After pressing northward to Wisconsin, the band trucked back across the country, finishing the year in the Mid-Atlantic and then the Northeast with another (somewhat less successful) New Year's Eve show in Boston.

Notable debuts in the spring of 1990 include Tweezer, Cavern, and Bouncing; the epic Wetlands show in September included more debuts than any show until Lowell in the spring of 1995. The year also saw frequent collaborations with Blues Traveler and especially their frontman, John Popper, with whom Trey co-wrote Don't Get Me Wrong. Excellent tapes from this year are in circulation, especially the Colorado run of 10/30–11/4 and the 4/22/90 show, for which digital soundboard/audience mixes can be found.

Though Paul stopped allowing soundboard patches for most tapers after the 6/16 Townshend show—he blamed sound difficulties

1990

103 Total Show Dates
- **7** one-set shows
- **74** two-set shows
- **2** three-set shows
- **20** dates with no setlists

Picks 1990

SHOW	THE SKINNY
1) 06/16/90 Townshend, VT	Three long sets in sunny VT.
2) 11/04/90 Ft. Collins, CO	The best of an amazing week.
3) 03/01/90 New Haven, CT	Widely available on bootleg CD.
4) 10/31/90 Colo. Springs, CO	First of two Halloweens in CO.
5) 11/02/90 Boulder, CO	The spirit of Glen Miller.
6) 11/03/90 Boulder, CO	Perhaps even better than 11/2.
7) 04/22/90 Colo. Springs, CO	Gorgeous Hood on perfect SBD.
8) 10/30/90 Crested Butte, CO	Another from a mystical week.
9) 04/29/90 Woodbury, CT	Find it on videotape.
10) 03/11/90 Burlington, VT	Roll like a cantaloupe!

MUSICAL RECAP: 1990 saw Phish honing their two-set live show format. Some of the long-winded craziness of the 1980s is already being toned down as more challenging compositional songs debut.
REPRESENTATIVE JAMS: Tweezer > Manteca > Tweezer, 12/28/90; Harry Hood, 11/4/90 and 4/22/90; David Bowie, 11/2/90 (w/tease medley).
ORIGINAL SONG DEBUTS: Asse Festival (9/13/90), Bouncing (1/20/90), Buried Alive (9/13/90), Cavern (3/28/90), Destiny Unbound (9/14/90), Don't Get Me Wrong (10/7/90), Eliza (11/17/90), Gumbo (9/28/90), Horn (5/24/90), Landlady (4/7/90), Magilla (9/13/90), Rift (slow version, 2/25/90), Runaway Jim (3/28/90), Squirming Coil (1/20/90), Stash (9/13/90), Tube (9/13/90), Tweezer (3/28/90).
COVER SONG DEBUTS: Caravan (1/20/90), Carolina (1/20/90), Communication Breakdown (1/27/90), Going Down Slow (9/13/90), Minute by Minute (9/13/90), It's No Good Trying (12/7/90), Paul and Silas (9/13/90), Sweet Adeline (3/28/90), Uncle Pen (3/28/90).

Dark Horse

SHOW	THE SKINNY
1) 12/28/90 New York, NY	John Popper joins and jams.
2) 09/13/90 New York, NY	Lots of debuts, plus the Dude.
3) 04/08-09/90 Telluride, CO	Tough to find, but worth it.
4) 11/24/90 Port Chester, NY	First Phish show at the Capitol.
5) 11/08/90 Madison, WI	Another one with Popper.

Most-Played Originals:		
1) Bouncing	58	56%
1) Possum	58	56%
3) You Enjoy Myself	57	55%
4) Mike's Song	54	52%
4) I Am Hydrogen	54	52%
4) Weekapaug Groove	54	52%
7) Oh Kee Pa	53	51%
8) Suzie Greenberg	48	47%
9) Divided Sky	42	41%
10) Reba	36	35%

Most-Played Covers:		
1) Uncle Pen	33	32%
1) Ya Mar	22	21%
3) Caravan	21	20%
3) La Grange	21	20%
3) Carolina	21	20%
6) Highway to Hell	17	17%
8) Funky Bitch	15	15%
8) Take the A-Train	15	15%
10) Donna Lee	11	11%
10) Fire	11	11%
10) Jesus Left Chicago	11	11%

First-Set Openers:	
1) Possum	9
2) Golgi Apparatus	8
3) Suzie Greenberg	7
4) The Landlady	6
5) Buried Alive	5

Second-Set Openers:	
1) Golgi Apparatus	7
2) The Landlady	6
3) Mike's Song	5
4) Buried Alive	3
4) Divided Sky	3
4) Suzie Greenberg	3

Henrietta Songs:	
1) If I Only Had a Brain	8
2) Love You	8
3) Terrapin	5
4) Bike	3
4) It's No Good Trying	3
6) Minute by Minute	2

A Cappella Songs:	
1) Carolina	21
2) Sweet Adeline	10
3) Memories	1

at the show on the tapers patched into his soundboard—many shows from this era can be found on soundboard tapes of varying quality.

1/20/90 [ACCESSIBILITY: ••]
Webster Hall, Dartmouth College, Hanover, NH
I: Carolina, Sloth, Bathtub Gin, YEM, Squirming Coil, Caravan, Lizards, Antelope
II: Oh Kee > Suzie, Bouncing, Reba, Tela > La Grange, Lawn Boy, Esther, Mike's > Hydrogen > Weekapaug
E: Harry Hood
Concert debuts: Bouncing, Carolina, Caravan, and Squirming Coil.

1/25/90 ❄
The Oronoko, University of Maine, Orono, ME

1/26/90 ❄
Tree Cafe, Portland, ME

1/27/90 [ACCESSIBILITY: •]
The Front, Burlington, VT
I: Carolina > Bathtub Gin, Ya Mar, Oh Kee > AC/DC Bag, MSO, Bouncing, Wilson, Reba, Funky Bitch, Mike's > Hydrogen > Weekapaug
II: Communication Breakdown, Caravan, YEM, Squirming Coil, Antelope, Terrapin, Divided Sky
E: La Grange
Concert debut: Communication Breakdown.

1/28/90 [ACCESSIBILITY: ••]
The Front, Burlington, VT
I: Suzie, Melt, Tela, Fluffhead, La Grange, Carolina, Forbin's > Mockingbird, Communication Breakdown
II: Wilson, Antelope, Bouncing, Caravan, Squirming Coil, YEM, Bathtub Gin, Mike's > Hydrogen > Weekapaug
E: Lawn Boy, BBFCM
Sunday "All Ages" show at The Front. Wilson played heavy-metal style.

Around this time, Phish experimented with a version of Wilson that has a distinctly heavy-metal feel to it. This show offers one of the rare performances of it, as well as the great Led Zep tune Communication Breakdown, which didn't last much longer in Phish setlists than the heavy-metal Wilson. —Ernie Greene

1/29/90 ❄
The Haunt, Ithaca, NY

2/1/90 ❄
Georgia Theater, Athens, GA

2/2/90 ❄
Georgia Theater, Athens, GA

2/3/90 ❄
Cotton Club, Atlanta, GA

2/4/90 ❄
Greenstreets, Columbia, SC

2/5/90 ❄
Myskyne, Charleston, SC

2/7/90 ❄
Cat's Cradle, Chapel Hill, NC

2/9/90 ❄
Chameleon Club, Lancaster, PA
I: Golgi, Oh Kee > Suzie, YEM, Walk Away, Bouncing, AC/DC Bag, Squirming Coil > Mike's > Hydrogen > Weekapaug, Carolina
II: Dinner and a Movie, Ya Mar, Reba, Wilson, A-Train, Alumni, Foam, Curtis Lowe, Bowie
E: I Didn't Know

2/10/90 [ACCESSIBILITY: •]
23 East Cabaret, Ardmore, PA
I: Dinner and a Movie, Oh Kee > Suzie, YEM, Bathtub Gin, Bouncing, Possum, Carolina, Contact, Bowie
II: La Grange, Esther, AC/DC Bag, Rocky Top, Donna Lee, Fee, Mike's > Hydrogen > Weekapaug
E: I Didn't Know, Highway to Hell

2/15/90 [ACCESSIBILITY: ••••] [ATTEND. 620; CAP. 620] [TIX $6]
The Living Room, Providence, RI
I: Carolina, Oh Kee > Suzie, Divided Sky, Dinner and a Movie, Caravan, Bathtub Gin, Mike's > Hydrogen > Weekapaug
Setlist missing second set and encore. Widespread Panic opened.

2/16/90 ❄ [ATTEND. 650; CAP. 650] [TIX $9.50]
The Paradise, Boston, MA
Widespread Panic opened.

2/17/90 ❄ [ATTEND. 1,000; CAP. 1,000] [TIX $7-$9]
Student Union Ballroom, University of Massachusetts, Amherst, MA
Oh Kee > Suzie, Dinner and a Movie, Caravan, Bathtub Gin, Mike's > Hydrogen > Weekapaug, Melt, Bouncing, Foam, Highway to Hell
Widespread Panic and Gene Matthews opened.

2/19/90 ❄
Student Union, Keene State College, Keene, NH
Date uncertain.

Monday, February 19, 1990

STUDENT UNION, Keene State, Keene, NH

I am not your typical Phish fan. I didn't have a high school or college friend who turned me on; rather, I came across Phish by a stroke of sheer luck. Let me explain.

It was the winter of 1990, and I had just finished graduate school and was starting my first "professional" career-type job in Keene, NH, working at a municipal planning consulting firm. This was a very difficult time for me. A relationship with the love of my life ended tragically; reality and idealism were clashing at work; the money sucked; I lived in a tiny one-room closet in downtown Keene; and the scene in the area was unbelievably boring. Thinking "Welcome to the rest of my life," I was severely depressed.

At that point, our office hired an intern—Stu Schwartz, I believe (anyone know him? I need to thank this man!) from local Antioch College. We got along quite well and shared a similar taste in music. Since he lived close by, I told him to come by my place sometime and we could roll up a couple of fat boys and play some music. Well, one cold night in February he did just that. Around 8 P.M. Stu told me there was this band at Keene State that I really should check out. I hemmed and hawed and said I was pretty comfortable right where I was, but Stu insisted: "No, Steve, you really need to see this band!" So he dragged me out into the cold winter night to the upstairs of the Keene State Student Union building. I walked up to the front of the stage and Phish began to play.

I absolutely flipped! This band was a blend of all my favorite bands and then some. At this time, my favorites included Zappa, Yes, King Crimson, Gentle Giant, Crack the Sky, Tull, old Genesis, and various jazz artists. They weren't aping any particular band's sound; rather, it seemed to me they were exploring uncharted territory, much like the above bands did in their primes. I remember thinking, "Oh my God . . . this is like seeing King Crimson before anyone knew about them!" I remember most of the songs they played: Fee, Wilson, Divided Sky, YEM, Bouncing and Lizards among them. I left that evening with much more than a shirt and a tape; I had a renewed sense that life was worth living. After two years of perpetual clouds, I felt like the sun was shining again.

—Steve Wallace

2/23/90 [ACCESSIBILITY: ••••]
Haverford College, Haverford, PA
I: Alumni, YEM, Possum, Foam, Carolina, Rocky Top, Dinner and a Movie, Ya Mar, Walk Away, Bouncing, Antelope
II: Golgi, Reba, Bathtub Gin, Jesus Left Chicago, Tela, Oh Kee > Suzie, Mike's > Hydrogen > Weekapaug, Highway to Hell
E: Contact, I Didn't Know, GTBT

The minute I picked up this tape I was blown away by the setlist. After listening to it, however, I'd say the setlist is probably the only thing this show has going for it. The only musical highlights for me are Walk Away and Page's playing during YEM. The disappointing playing is saved by crowd pleasers, though it sounds like there was virtually no one at this show. —Charlie Gubman

2/24/90 [ACCESSIBILITY: •]
The Bayou, Washington, DC
I: Carolina, YEM, Golgi, Divided Sky, Esther, Possum, I Didn't Know, A-Train, Antelope
II: Sloth, AC/DC Bag, Fee, Squirming Coil, La Grange, Bathtub Gin, Lawn Boy, Contact
E: Lizards, Caravan

2/25/90 [ACCESSIBILITY: ••]
The 8x10 Club, Baltimore, MD
I: Foam, MSO, Forbin's > Mockingbird, Funky Bitch, Squirming Coil, Bouncing, Bowie, Satin Doll, Rift, Possum
II: Reba, McGrupp, Makisupa, Lizards, Fluffhead, BBFCM
Soundcheck: Jessica, Donna Lee. Tweezer tease in Bowie. Jeopardy jam before Reba. Concert debut: slow version of Rift.

This tape is really nice if you're seeking some Phish rarities. Besides a really good version of Satin Doll, they play Rift for the first time. The older version of this song is light, jazzy and really interesting to hear. —Jen Spivey

If you see this show on someone's tape list, get it! A classic show from 1990. My tape starts with the soundcheck: Jessica and Donna Lee. The opener is Foam, dedicated to Nectar's french fries! A fun, early Forbin > Mockingbird is one of the highlights from set I. The Tweezer tease (Teezer!) before Bowie is very rare, given the fact that the Tweezer debut is still a month away. For me, the slow Rift is the highlight, and being the first one ever adds to the excitement. The second set starts out with a brief Jeopardy Theme jam, heading right into Reba. A great show indeed! —Otis

2/29/90
23 East Cabaret, Ardmore, PA
I: Divided Sky, Dinner and a Movie, Landlady, Ya Mar > Buried Alive, Bouncing, Possum, Magilla > Bowie
II: Squirming Coil, Tweezer, Gumbo, Uncle Pen, Stash, Mike's > Hydrogen > Weekapaug
E: Lawn Boy

3/1/90 [ACCESSIBILITY: •••]
Toad's Place, New Haven, CT
I: Golgi, Ya Mar, Divided Sky, I Didn't Know, YEM > Possum
II: Lizards, GTBT, Foam, Mike's > Hydrogen > Weekapaug
E: Carolina > Slave
E2: Fire
Fishman on vacuum for I Didn't Know. Bonanza tease in Weekapaug.

I remember hearing about this show on the radio, but I was only 15 years old at the time and had never heard of Phish. Oh well. I really like these old shows where things are just a little slower and more intimate. This night in New Haven served up a good setlist with YEM, Divided, and Possum in set one. During Lizards, Trey invites everyone along to Gamehendge and the crowd is so quiet. Nowadays, people would go nuts for an intro like this one, but seven years ago at a club, no one seemed to care. —Nick Soricelli

Quite a good show. Absolutely awesome Divided Sky during which Trey gives a neat introduction that takes the crowd off to Gamehendge. There's also a strong YEM, a vacuum solo, and a Mike's Groove. During the Weekapaug jam, Trey busts out the theme to Bonanza, which I find very amusing. —Pete Morse

I do enjoy the Mike's Groove, but I'm sorry to say the rest of this show isn't as good as it could be. A pretty average setlist that doesn't ever seem to take off. —Kyle Niday

3/2/90 ❄
The Chance, Poughkeepsie, NY

3/3/90 [ACCESSIBILITY: •] [ATTEND. 600; CAP. 600] [TIX $12]
Wetlands Preserve, New York, NY
I: Mike's > Hydrogen > Weekapaug, MSO, Squirming Coil, Lizards, Oh Kee > AC/DC Bag, Reba, Rocky Top, YEM, Possum
II: Dinner and a Movie, Caravan, Fluffhead, Esther, Funky Bitch, Carolina, Divided Sky
E: Suzie
MSO and Funky Bitch featured John Popper on harmonica. Soundcheck: Tweezer.

3/7/90 [ACCESSIBILITY: •]
University of New Hampshire, Durham, NH
I: Reba, Possum, Esther, A-Train, Lizards, Bowie
II: Oh Kee > AC/DC Bag, Squirming Coil, Bathtub Gin, Melt, Tela, Mike's > Hydrogen > Weekapaug
E: Whipping Post

3/8/90 [ACCESSIBILITY: ••••]
Aiko's, Saratoga, NY
I: Dinner and a Movie, YEM, Possum, Ya Mar, Foam, Carolina, Oh Kee > Suzie, A-Train, Antelope
II: Divided Sky, Bathtub Gin, MSO, AC/DC Bag, Caravan, I Didn't Know, Lizards, Mike's > Hydrogen > Weekapaug, Curtis Lowe, Golgi
E: Contact, GTBT
During MSO, Mike needed to change a bass string, so Fishman launched into a drum solo for about two minutes while Trey sang, "Music to change the bass string by."

3/9/90 [ACCESSIBILITY: ••]
The Front, Burlington, VT
I: TMWSIY > Avenu > TMWSIY, Caravan, Ya Mar, Bouncing, Forbin's > Mockingbird, Sloth, Possum, Donna Lee, Antelope, Reba, Oh Kee > AC/DC Bag
II: Curtain, Dog Log, Slave, Highway to Hell, YEM, La Grange, Contact, BBFCM
E: Whipping Post
Dave Grippo on saxophone for Caravan, Ya Mar, Donna Lee, and YEM. Frankenstein jam in YEM. Fishman on fretless guitar for Whipping Post.

With horn players (who would later help comprise the Giant Country Horns) sitting in, this is a jazzier than usual show. You Enjoy Myself is a particular highlight, with Dave Grippo whaling the riff from Frankenstein while Trey serves up a riff all his own. Is that the Andy Griffith Theme in BBFCM? —Russell Lane

Great early YEM on this tape, helped a whole lot by The Truth, who just rocks! After Trey drops some Hendrix licks, Grippo responds with Frankenstein and the whole band gets into it. There's also some Sunshine of Your Love teases in here as the band heads into a memorable vocal jam. —Amy Manning

3/11/90 [ACCESSIBILITY: ••••]
The Front, Burlington, VT
II: Carolina, Antelope, MSO, Bouncing, Dinner and a Movie, A-Train, Sloth, Ya Mar, Melt, Harpua, Slave, AC/DC Bag, Bowie
E: Tela
Setlist missing first set. Antelope sung as "Roll Like a Cantaloupe."

The setlist is packed from beginning to end on this night in Burlington, highlighted by Antelope (Cantaloupe). Trey builds up to the climax by describing heading down the aisles in a supermarket until reaching the fruit section, then declares, "You've got to roll like a cantaloupe, out of control!" Hilarious. Harpua with a Hendrix tease after they say "Jimi" is also cool. Otherwise, this is a fun early show to listen to, with their early talent almost ready to unfold into raging rock star level. —Bill Patrick

3/17/90 [ACCESSIBILITY: •]
23 East Cabaret, Ardmore, PA
I: Golgi, Esther, Dinner and a Movie > Bouncing > MSO > Divided Sky, Lizards > Antelope
II: "Killer Joe" jam, Bold as Love, Oh Kee > AC/DC Bag > Foam, YEM
E: GTBT

Before the second set begins, the emcee introduces the band and talks about it being set II on St. Patrick's Day. Then, before GTBT, Trey announces that this will be their final song in the Northeast before the band heads out for a Midwest tour and then a southern tour. (The first tune of the set is just about a two-minute jam with Fishman mumbling the words "Killer Joe.") —Chuck Smith

3/28/90 [ACCESSIBILITY: ••]
Beta Intramural Hockey Team Party, Denison University, Granville, OH
I: Possum, Ya Mar, Fee, Walk Away, Tweezer, Uncle Pen, Oh Kee > Suzie, A-Train, Runaway Jim, YEM, GTBT
II: Carolina, Adeline, Whipping Post, Funky Bitch, Mike's > Hydrogen > Weekapaug, Jesus Left Chicago, Lizards, Melt, Contact, La Grange, Rift, Cavern, Highway to Hell
Slow version of Rift. Concert debuts: Tweezer, Uncle Pen, Runaway Jim, Adeline, and Cavern.

Credit Dean Budnick with unearthing the actual date of this show, tapes for which circulated for years as Denison 1989 and Denison 1990. The significance of this date comes from the fact that this show marks the debut of a whole bunch of tunes—Tweezer, Uncle Pen, Runaway Jim, Sweet Adeline, and Cavern. Phish uses the informal atmosphere of an intramural team hockey party to give the new songs a go, and it's clear that they still need some work. They'd get it in Colorado, the tour's next stop. —Lock Steele

4/4/90 [ACCESSIBILITY: •]
Colorado University, Boulder, CO
I: Golgi, YEM, Walk Away, A-Train, Possum, Foam, Divided Sky, Carolina
II: Mike's > Hydrogen > Weekapaug, Lizards, Uncle Pen, Sloth, I Didn't Know, GTBT
E: Contact, Highway to Hell

4/5/90 [ACCESSIBILITY: ••]
J.J. McCabe's, Boulder, CO
I: Possum, Ya Mar, Bowie, Carolina, Oh Kee > Suzie, YEM, Lizards, Fire
II: Reba, Uncle Pen, Jesus Left Chicago, AC/DC Bag, Donna Lee, Tweezer, Fee, Cavern, Mike's > Hydrogen > Weekapaug, Brain, Contact, Golgi
Page on clarinet on Suzie, Cavern, and Contact. Fishman on vacuum for Brain.

4/6/90 [ACCESSIBILITY: •]
El Dorado Cafe, Crested Butte, CO
I: Cavern, YEM, Uncle Pen, Divided Sky, Ya Mar, Dinner and a Movie, Oh Kee > Suzie, Antelope
II: Carolina, La Grange, Esther, Sloth, Harry Hood, Caravan, Reba, I Didn't Know, Alumni, GTBT, Jesus Left Chicago
E: Jesus Left Chicago, Highway to Hell

4/7/90 [ACCESSIBILITY: •]
El Dorado Cafe, Crested Butte, CO
I: Bathtub Gin, Possum, Tweezer, Mike's > Hydrogen > Weekapaug, Bowie, MSO, Suzie, AC/DC Bag, Squirming Coil, Lizards, Landlady, Walk Away
II: Golgi, Forbin's > Mockingbird, Funky Bitch, A-Train, Bold as Love, Fee, Runaway Jim, Foam, YEM, Bike, Harpua
Concert debut: Landlady.

4/8/90 [ACCESSIBILITY: •]
Fly Me to the Moon Saloon, Telluride, CO
I: Divided Sky, Funky Bitch, YEM, Brain, Oh Kee > Suzie, Uncle Pen, Possum
II: Golgi, Walk Away, Lizards, Slave, Mike's > Hydrogen > Weekapaug, Fee, MSO, Antelope
E: Carolina, Fire

4/9/90 [ACCESSIBILITY: •]
Fly Me to the Moon Saloon, Telluride, CO
II: Funky Bitch, Esther, Uncle Pen, La Grange, Foam, Harry Hood, Jesus Left Chicago, Divided Sky, Love You, Tweezer, Whipping Post
Setlist missing first set.

4/10/90 ❄
Fly Me to the Moon Saloon, Telluride, CO
Date of the third Fly Me to the Moon show might have been 4/11/90.

4/12/90 [ACCESSIBILITY: •]
The Inferno, Steamboat Springs, CO
I: Golgi, Ya Mar, Walk Away, Uncle Pen, Possum, YEM, A-Train, Cavern, Jesus Left Chicago, Divided Sky, GTBT
Setlist missing second set.

4/13/90 [ACCESSIBILITY: •]
The Inferno, Steamboat Springs, CO
I: Funky Bitch, Dinner and a Movie, Bouncing, Fluffhead, Esther, La Grange, Oh Kee > AC/DC Bag, Reba, Fire
II: Antelope, Foam, YEM, Alumni, Curtis Lowe > Sloth, Harry Hood, Caravan, Possum, Highway to Hell

4/18/90 [ACCESSIBILITY: ••]
Herman's Hideaway, Denver, CO
I: Mike's > Hydrogen > Weekapaug, Uncle Pen, Curtain, Foam, YEM, MSO, A-Train, Possum
II: La Grange, Fee, Sloth, Funky Bitch, Reba, Walk Away, Oh Kee > Bold as Love, Lawn Boy, Bowie > Jaegermeister > Bowie
Lawn Boy tease in Bowie intro before "sexy lights" vocals and Jaegermeister.

The "sexy lights" show is your standard spring 1990 affair—the show fits on only a tape and a half—until the end of the second set. During the Bowie intro, Trey tells the small crowd, "We're trying to look for a date for our light person tonight. He wanted to make sure that we said that." Then: "We want to show you right now how sexy lights can be. Let's have a little light solo . . . . Chris Kuroda, he's right back there, go get him." Page quips, "Those are some hot lights from a hot guy." Then, before returning to Bowie, Trey says, "This next song is dedicated to those of you who have been drinking Jaegermeister tonight." They start up this wacky ditty that goes, "Gimme some Jaegermeister . . . Yaegermeister me, all night long!" —Amy Manning

4/19/90 ❄ [ATTEND. 930; CAP. 930] [TIX $6-$7]
Boulder Theater, Boulder, CO
The Circle opened.

4/20/90 [ACCESSIBILITY: •]
Ramskellar, Colorado State University, Fort Collins, CO
I: A-Train, Divided Sky, Alumni, Ya Mar, Cavern, Dinner and a Movie, Bouncing, Forbin's > Mockingbird, Possum
II: Caravan, Mike's > Hydrogen > Weekapaug, La Grange, Rift, Fee, Oh Kee > AC/DC Bag, Jesus Left Chicago, YEM

4/21/90 ❄
Lincoln Center, Canyon West, Fort Collins, CO
Common Ground opened.

4/22/90 [ACCESSIBILITY: ••••]
Cutler Quad, Colorado College, Colorado Springs, CO
I: Divided Sky, Uncle Pen, Oh Kee > Suzie, Possum, I Didn't Know, Cavern, MSO, Slave, Mike's > Hydrogen > Weekapaug
II: Dinner and a Movie, Bouncing, YEM, Fluffhead, How High the Moon, Esther, BBFCM, Harry Hood, Fire
E: Lawn Boy, Golgi
Free outdoor Earth Day show. Fishman on vacuum for I Didn't Know.

Picking the best Harry Hood from this era isn't easy when you're comparing the 11/4/90 masterpiece and the one from this Earth Day show. Do yourself a favor and pick up this tape for Hood and for the sound quality—this is the only spring 1990 show from the "Colorado Collection" of soundboard/audience mixed tapes; it's gorgeous. —Ernie Greene

4/25/90 [ACCESSIBILITY: ••••]
Notre Dame University, South Bend, IN
I: Brain, Divided Sky, MSO, Bowie
II: Foam, Adeline, Reba, Ya Mar, YEM, Esther, La Grange, Dinner and a Movie, Bouncing, Mike's > Hydrogen > Weekapaug
E: Contact

4/26/90 [ACCESSIBILITY: ••]
The 'Sco, Oberlin College, Oberlin, OH
I: Possum, Foam > YEM, Uncle Pen, Dinner and a Movie > Bouncing, I Didn't Know, Antelope, Lawn Boy

Thursday, April 19, 1990

BOULDER THEATER, Boulder, CO

"You gotta see these guys!"—I had heard that about Phish several times too many, but seeing how my friends in The Circle were going to be the opening band, a bunch of us decided to drive to Boulder from Colorado Springs to see our first Phish show.

The Boulder Theater was, at the time, *the* Boulder venue, with cool seating, micro-brews and southwestern murals on the walls. Getting the $6 tickets was no problem—call the venue and ask them to hold some. So, we all piled out of the car knowing that at least we were going to see The Circle in the nicest place they'd ever played.

My memory is fuzzy but I think Phish's opener was Good Times Bad Times. Doing Zeppelin covers is an automatic negative-point, but as the song progressed, it was obvious that not only could Phish legitimately play this song, but they were, more than anything, players. After the cheers died down, they made their way to an original composition. This being before the LP release of *Lawn Boy*, we thought the song was called, "Bag it, tag it." Reba, as we know it today, was the first time I ever entered that special place to which only Phish can take you. As they hit the jam, we saw the trampolines for the first time. Where would we have seen the combination of aerial stunts and precision playing before this night? As "the bass player" and "the guitar player" hit their strides, we did our best to keep up.

Their talents were laid bare on Joe Walsh's Walk Away. As with Good Times Bad Times, I had heard this song enough by the original artist, but Phish's attack on it was stellar.

As the evening progressed, it was impossible to count the number of songs they played as the jams seemed to indicate new tunes. We were sold. Phish was scheduled to do a free show in The Springs in a few days and all we could say to those who hadn't made the Boulder trip was, "You gotta see these guys!"

—Todd A. Prusin

II: How High the Moon, Esther, Bathtub Gin, Oh Kee > Suzie, Cavern, Adeline, Curtis Lowe, Mike's > Hydrogen > Weekapaug
E: Highway to Hell
Fishman on vacuum for I Didn't Know.

Even in 1990, Trey proves his worth as a guitar great. He's all over this show, with great solo work, especially in Possum, Antelope, and Bathtub Gin. His best is the great Oh Kee Pa > Suzie, a high-energy jam during which the boys are obviously having fun. YEM features a perfect early vocal jam and Suzie is full of screams and laughter. Foam and Dinner also shine. A great show from the early days! —Tim Foisser

4/28/90 [ACCESSIBILITY: •]
Strand Theater, Boston, MA
I: Adeline, Oh Kee > Suzie, Uncle Pen, Dinner and a Movie > Bouncing, Possum, YEM, Rift, Foam, Antelope
II: Cavern, Harry Hood, Caravan, I Didn't Know, Reba, MSO, Mike's > Hydrogen > Weekapaug
E: BBFCM
Slow version of Rift.

This beautiful small theater is just outside of Boston—excellent sound in this room. Phish opened with an unmiked Sweet Adeline. As the show heated up, many people jumped into the orchestra pit to dance, which left the rest of us with plenty of room. Very high energy during YEM, especially when Mike pulled out an extendo-jam solo that wouldn't quit. That was followed by a nice segue into a totally different version of Rift (also a good version). Mike led the way all night. —Nathaniel Peirce

4/29/90 [ACCESSIBILITY: ••]
Woodbury Ski and Racquet Club, Woodbury, CT
Carolina, Possum, Ya Mar, YEM, Dinner and a Movie > Bouncing, Uncle Pen, Divided Sky, Fluffhead, Walk Away, Love You, Lizards, Fire

My videotape of this concert shows a beautiful setting with not very many fans there. Nevertheless, Phish gave the small crowd a treat, offering up some of their best instrumental, improvisational, beautifully played tunes. YEM, Dinner and a Movie, and Divided Sky take flight and soar to new heights. A great Fishman intro gives me a smile, as does Trey's super guitar work throughout the show. —Andy Kahn

5/3/90 ❄
Somerville Theatre, Somerville, MA

5/4/90 [ACCESSIBILITY: •] [ATTEND. 813; CAP. 813] [TIX $9-$10]
Colonial Theater, Keene, NH
I: Whipping Post, Adeline, TMWSIY > Avenu > TMWSIY, Bouncing, Possum, Reba, MSO, YEM, Lizards
II: Runaway Jim, Sloth, Uncle Pen, Tweezer, Bathtub Gin, Oh Kee > Mike's > Hydrogen > Weekapaug, Caravan, Brain, Highway to Hell, Antelope
E: Contact

5/6/90 ❄
Toad's Place, New Haven, CT
I: Possum, Bouncing, Uncle Pen, Reba, Tweezer, Mike's > Hydrogen > Weekapaug
II: Fee, Harry Hood, Esther, Bowie, Terrapin, Jaegermeister, YEM
YEM halted before completion by club management.

5/7/90 ❄ [ATTEND. 330; CAP. 330] [$5.50-$7]
The Haunt, Ithaca, NY

5/10/90 ❄
Pearl Street, Northampton, MA
I: Suzie, Uncle Pen, Bouncing, Divided Sky, Tweezer, MSO, Bathtub Gin, Possum
II: Funky Bitch, Runaway Jim, Harry Hood, Caravan, Reba, Oh Kee > AC/DC Bag, GTBT
E: Whipping Post

5/11/90 ❄ [ATTEND. 671; CAP. 671] [TIX $7.50]
The Living Room, Providence, RI
I: Mike's > Hydrogen > Weekapaug > Uncle Pen, Bouncing, Possum, Reba, Highway to Hell
II: Oh Kee > AC/DC Bag, Lizards, Tweezer, Ya Mar, Love You, GTBT
E: BBFCM
Widespread Panic opened.

5/12/90 ❄
The Front, Burlington, VT

5/13/90 [ACCESSIBILITY: •]
The Front, Burlington, VT
I: Bathtub Gin, Oh Kee > AC/DC Bag, Dinner and a Movie, Bouncing, Runaway Jim, Uncle Pen, Divided Sky, Bowie
II: Mike's > Hydrogen > Weekapaug, Foam, Donna Lee, Tweezer, MSO, Reba, Funky Bitch, Adeline, La Grange, Foam, MSO, Reba
Possum tease between Adeline and La Grange. Second set setlist incomplete.

5/14/90 [ACCESSIBILITY: •]
McEwen Quad, Hamilton College, Clinton, NY
I: Fee, Reba, Alumni, Foam, Mike's > Hydrogen > Weekapaug, Uncle Pen, Bouncing, Runaway Jim, Squirming Coil, Lizards
Setlist missing second set. Second set played indoors due to inclement weather.

On this date, Phish had an outdoor gig scheduled at Hamilton College. But before the second set, as the skies opened and the rain poured, Trey and Co. apologized that the show would have to be unceremoniously canceled. Being good sports, the fellas agreed to spend the second set indoors in a dormitory lounge on our local college band's equipment. While sound quality suffered, the jams did not, and they completed the show. A bummer averted! —Chuck Smith

5/15/90 [ACCESSIBILITY: •]
The Front, Burlington, VT
I: Possum, Tela, Tweezer, Oh Kee > Suzie, Happy Birthday for Barbie, Harry Hood, Bike, Caravan, BBFCM
Setlist might be from 5/12/90; missing second set. Fishman on vacuum for Bike. Smoke on the Water jam in Tweezer.

There's definite confusion about the date of this show, but I believe I have a set I of either the 5/12/90 or 5/15/90 shows at The Front. I can't be sure which one because it was given to me labeled as "Phish at the Front, 5/90" by a buddy of mine who had the tape given to him by a friend of the band back in 1991. Since the 5/11 show in Providence includes Possum, Tweezer, and BBFCM I'm apt to believe that my tape is 5/15. During the set, between Possum and Tela, Fish tells Trey, "My kick drum is getting away," and then during Tweezer, Fish adds a line to the chorus at least three times as he sings, "My bass drum is getting away." Later in the set, he borrows duct tape to repair his drum kit. Tweezer contains a very nice, gritty Smoke on the Water guitar bit in the middle. I'm not sure who Barbie is, or why they decided to sing for her birthday, but Trey tells the crowd that everyone should buy Barbie a shot. Then during Bike, Fishman brings out his vacuum and proclaims, "While out west, I got a new vacuum. It's an Electrolux, like the old one, which blew a belt. This one has great sucking power." He sounds tipsy, and this song meanders until he's yelling into the microphone to the point where I have to fast-forward.—Tom Smith

5/19/90 [ACCESSIBILITY: •]
The Upper, St. Paul's School, Concord, NH
I: Golgi, Ya Mar, Alumni, Adeline, La Grange, YEM, Lizards, Highway to Hell
II: Possum, Reba, Oh Kee > Suzie, Fee, Dinner and a Movie > Bouncing, Rift, Jesus Left Chicago, GTBT
E: Contact
Slow version of Rift.

For prep schooler Trey Anastasio, playing a gig in the Upper Dining Room at New Hampshire prep school St. Paul's must have felt like a homecoming of sorts. Despite the weird wooden acoustics of this ancient dining room, with the names of graduates from the 1800s engraved on wooden panels lining the walls, the band treated the young crowd (which included several prep schoolers who had traveled up from Exeter for the show) to quite a night. Alumni Blues is dedicated to the graduating seniors, and Rift is played in the slow spring 1990 fashion. —Lock Steele

5/23/90 [ACCESSIBILITY: •]
The Library, Richmond, VA
I: Divided Sky, Ya Mar, YEM, Brain, Oh Kee > Suzie, Uncle Pen, Bouncing, Possum, Adeline
II: Squirming Coil, Reba, Tweezer, Lizards, La Grange, McGrupp, A-Train, Antelope, Mike's > Hydrogen > Weekapaug

5/24/90 [ACCESSIBILITY: ••]
The Brewery, Raleigh, NC
I: Sloth > Bouncing > Tweezer, Donna Lee, Reba, YEM > Oh Kee > AC/DC Bag, Golgi
II: Foam, Dinner and a Movie > Possum, I Didn't Know, MSO > Horn, Fee, Walk Away, Harry Hood, Highway to Hell > Contact
E: GTBT
Concert debut: Horn.

5/31/90 [ACCESSIBILITY: •]
Variety Playhouse, Atlanta, GA
Possum, YEM, Dinner and a Movie, Bouncing, Caravan, Esther, Tweezer, I Didn't Know, Uncle Pen, Divided Sky, Oh Kee > Suzie
E: GTBT
Phish opened for Aquarium Rescue Unit and played one set. Tapes of this show are sometimes misdated as 5/31/89.

6/1/90 ❄
The Cotton Club, Atlanta, GA
I: Bouncing, YEM, Divided Sky, Slave, Possum, Oh Kee > Suzie, Dinner and a Movie, Fee, Foam, Forbin's > Mockingbird
II: Rocky Top, Uncle Pen, Antelope, Mike's > Hydrogen > Weekapaug, Terrapin, Possum, Fee, BBFCM, Contact
Jeff Mosier on banjo for Rocky Top, Uncle Pen, and Antelope. Oteil Burbridge on bass for Antelope. Fee tease, with Fishman singing first verse, before Terrapin.

6/5/90 [ACCESSIBILITY: •••]
Cat's Cradle, Chapel Hill, NC
I: Squirming Coil, Uncle Pen, Mike's > Hydrogen > Weekapaug, Ya Mar, Oh Kee > Suzie, A-Train > Bowie, Lawn Boy, Possum
II: Adeline, Divided Sky, Caravan, Dinner and a Movie > Bouncing > MSO, Lizards, YEM > Curtis Lowe, GTBT
E: Whipping Post, Golgi
Fishman on vacuum for Whipping Post.

6/7/90 ❄ [ATTEND. 499; CAP. 500] [TIX $6]
The Bayou, Washington, DC
I: Suzie, Donna Lee, Possum, Fee, Reba, YEM, Lizards, GTBT
II: MSO, Dinner and a Movie > Bouncing, Tweezer, Uncle Pen, Divided Sky, Love You, Mike's > Hydrogen > Weekapaug
E: Lawn Boy, BBFCM
Col. Bruce Hampton and the Aquarium Rescue Unit opened.

6/8/90 ❄
23 East Cabaret, Philadelphia, PA
I: Possum, MSO, Bathtub Gin, Tweezer, I Didn't Know, Mike's > Hydrogen > Weekapaug, Foam, Bouncing, YEM, Divided Sky
Setlist missing second set.

6/9/90 [ACCESSIBILITY: ••] [ATTEND. 500; CAP. 500] [TIX $12]
Wetlands Preserve, New York, NY
I: Possum, Lawn Boy, Reba, Dinner and a Movie, Bouncing, Tweezer, Uncle Pen, Mike's > Hydrogen > Weekapaug
II: GTBT, Harry Hood, TMWSIY > Avenu > TMWSIY > La Grange, Fee > Foam, Oh Kee > Suzie, Antelope, Terrapin, Harpua
E: Landlady > Contact
Col. Bruce Hampton and the Aquarium Rescue Unit opened. Whole Lotta Love jam before GTBT.

The second set really shines, opening with a Whole Lotta Love jam and including great tunes such as TMWSIY, La Grange, and Terrapin. The reason I really enjoy this tape, though, is that it features one of my favorite Harpuas. The story wasn't any different than usual—in fact, it was a little short. But the way Trey over-over-overexaggerates on the little things (such as "Jimmy, furry little . . . " and the craziest, most insane introduction of Poster Nutbag I've ever heard) makes this set. —Chuck Adams

6/16/90 [ACCESSIBILITY: ••]
Townshend Family Park, Townshend, VT
I: AC/DC Bag, Divided Sky > Wilson, Reba, Horn, Uncle Pen, Bouncing, Timber Ho, Lawn Boy, Possum
II: Golgi, Esther, Tweezer, MSO, Bathtub Gin, YEM, Lizards, Antelope
III: La Grange, Ya Mar, Foam, Oh Kee > Suzie, Fee, Rocky Top, Caravan, HYHU > Brain > HYHU > Mike's > Hydrogen > Weekapaug
E: Contact, BBFCM
E2: GTBT
Soundcheck: Carolina, Funky Bitch. Fishman on vacuum for Brain. Trey shaves his head between sets. Show billed as "Phish's last show until the Fall."

If you look at the setlist to this tape, it appears to be the perfect show from this era—three sets, two encores. But I have never heard Trey sound worse. This show definitely has its good moments (AC/DC, Antelope), but the band sounds tired as the show wears on. What is Trey doing in Caravan? Fishman forgets the words in Brain, and Mike's Groove doesn't move mountains like it usually does. —Mike Garofalow

If Phish were to put together a greatest hits album, this could be it. —Adam Satz

I know a lot of people talk about this show, but perhaps it's worth a few more words. I think the fact that this show is so much fun to listen to is derived from all its offerings. Three sets gave the guys plenty of space to play some goodies—AC/DC Bag and Bathtub Gin both rocked more than usual. The Tweezer is my earliest recording of this song and it's nice to follow its musical evolution over the years. Mike's Groove is never a letdown, and GTBT is a great encore! —Daniel Paden

La Grange starts the third set, and Mike announces that some guy who hand-paints shirts lost one at a Max Creek show and would appreciate it if someone returned it. Trey then dedicates Ya Mar to Heather Paw because it's her birthday. Fish plays his vacuum and then does a pretty cool version of If I Only Had a Brain, telling about how his brain damage relates to the song. —Joseph South

[6/17/90] [ACCESSIBILITY: ••]
Wendell Studios, Boston, MA
Tape 1: Dog Log, Uncle Pen, Suzie, Suzie, Caravan, Alumni, A-Train, A-Train, In a Mellow Tone, Possum, Mike's > Hydrogen > Weekapaug
Tape 2: TMWSIY > Avenu > TMWSIY, Tweezer, Possum, Harry Hood, Rift, Runaway Jim
Unreleased studio session; date uncertain. Slow version of Rift. Alternate lyrics on Runaway Jim.

[9/90] *Lawn Boy* released on Absolute A-Go-Go Records.

9/13/90 [ACCESSIBILITY: ••••] [ATTEND. 450; CAP. 500] [TIX $10-$12]
Wetlands Preserve, New York, NY
I: Landlady, Divided Sky, Foam, Tube, Asse Festival, Antelope, Minute by Minute, Buried Alive, Paul and Silas, Bouncing, Possum
II: Mike's > Hydrogen > Weekapaug, Magilla, Stash, Going Down Slow, Oh Kee > AC/DC Bag > A-Train > Sparks > Reba, Self, Dahlia, Revolution's Over
E: Lizards, La Grange
Buried Alive jam between AC/DC Bag and A-Train. The Dude of Life on vocals for Self, Dahlia, and The Revolution's Over. Concert debuts: Tube, Asse Festival, Minute by Minute, Buried Alive, Paul and Silas, Magilla, Stash, Going Down Slow, Self, Dahlia, and Revolution's Over. Last Sparks, 11/5/88 Clinton, NY [164 shows].

This show is memorable for all the debuts, ten in all. I especially enjoy Tube, which is one of (if not the) most underrated and underplayed songs. It's kind of neat to hear the Asse Festival not in Guelah Papyrus. The only major downfall is Minute by Minute by the Doobie Brothers. Thank God they dropped it quickly. —Ric Hannah

A full show of new material packed with some old-time greats. Boy were they hot during this time period! Looking back, it seems as if they always played hot shows at the Wetlands Preserve. So if you need a show with a lot of song debuts, get wet at the Wetlands. (The Dude of Life was also at this show, contributing a bunch of his songs at the end of the second set.) —Bill Patrick

9/14/90 [ACCESSIBILITY: •] [ATTEND. 834; CAP. 834] [TIX $7.50]
The Living Room, Providence, RI
I: Suzie, Bouncing, Landlady, Reba, Paul and Silas, Stash, Dinner and a Movie, I Didn't Know

---

Friday, June 1, 1990

THE COTTON CLUB, Atlanta, GA

After two monstrous Colorado Phish shows the month before, I gathered a bunch of friends to go see Phish at the Cotton Club in Atlanta. This club would provide a nice small backdrop against which we could see the band. Little did I know the size of the place didn't matter—they could have been inside an enormo-dome or a closet, because nobody was there!

Phish's name had yet to arrive in Atlanta. There were about 20 people in front of the stage and we all pressed against the back wall for fear of standing alone in the middle of the dance floor.

Phish walked out on stage and greeted the Friday night concertgoers with their standard smile/wave combination. The bonus here was the added audible, non-miked, "Hello" from Trey as our clapping had died down to reveal the hum of the AC units above.

My friend Julie and I braved ridicule and went up to the stage to check out their chops. She was a student at Skidmore and had seen more shows than me. She knew all the songs and even kept a setlist.

The show was great. More people showed up and the trampolines even made their way out for a visit. The lack of attendance was fine but seemed to reduce the intensity of the event a bit. We had a blast, though, and the band seemed to be glad we hollered out the songs we did. Some guy kept calling for "Suzie Greenberg," or it may have been the question, "Do you like cheeseburgers?" in an effort to provoke "Halley's Comet." He went up and placed a quarter on a monitor speaker as a bribe . . . I think it worked.

—Todd A. Prusin

"The Wetlands"

9/13/90 Wetlands Preserve, New York, NY

From their first show at the Wetlands in March 1989, Phish made the TriBeCa club a frequent stopping-off point on their swings south of New England.

By the time of their fall 1990 tour, which came after the band took nearly three months off from gigging and spent some time in Boston's Wendell Studios, Phish had a solid New York City fanbase, and could expect a good reception during each visit to the Big Apple.

Or so they thought. In fact, the fall 1990 Phish newsletter didn't arrive in most fans' hands until mid-September, which made Phish's last-ever show at the Wetlands a less crowded affair than some of their earlier gigs. But perhaps the smaller audience size was a blessing in disguise, as the band used the show to introduce five new original songs, three new cover songs and three Dude of Life songs (written in conjunction with Trey and performed, of course, with the Dude himself, in his first formal appearance with Phish playing his own material).

Early in the show, Trey warned the crowd that the band would be exercising a lot of new material, starting with the opening Landlady, which Trey dedicated "to the spirit of Carlos." The first set also included the rollouts of Tube and the Asse Festival, as well as Fishman's take on the Doobie Brothers' Minute by Minute. Buried Alive and Paul and Silas rounded out the first-set debuts.

The second set saw more of the same, with a mid-set run of three new songs: Magilla, Stash and Going Down Slow. Then, jamming out on AC/DC Bag several songs later, the band whipped back around into a Buried Alive Reprise of sorts before taking that into Take the A-Train.

As the end of the set neared, The Dude of Life made his way on stage for the debut of three of his songs. He feigned vomiting with the dire warning, "Better get the bucket!" and assumed lead vocals for Self (his signature song, perhaps), Dahlia and The Revolution's Over. Self is notable for the guitar riff that Trey would later incorporate into Chalkdust Torture.

The show would be Phish's last-ever at the Wetlands, as the band graduated to the larger Marquee by early 1991 and then to the Roseland Ballroom by the spring of 1992.

The Wetlands still stands today, giving jam bands on their way up a firm foothold in New York City. For Phish, the Wetlands was a friendly home-away-from-home that is fondly remembered as another rung passed on their climb to the top.

II: Asse Festival, Squirming Coil, Buried Alive > Tweezer, Magilla, Cavern, Lizards, Destiny Unbound, Fire
E: Going Down Slow
Concert debut: Destiny Unbound.

9/15/90 [ACCESSIBILITY: •] [ATTEND. 825; CAP. 825] [TIX $10-$12]
Colonial Theater, Keene, NH
I: Buried Alive > Divided Sky, Paul and Silas, Landlady, Fee, Tube, Oh Kee > AC/DC Bag, Asse Festival, Bowie, Golgi, Stash, Magilla, Squirming Coil
II: Melt, Eliza, MSO, Bathtub Gin, Foam, Minute by Minute, Harry Hood > Possum
E: Communication Breakdown > YEM

9/16/90 [ACCESSIBILITY: ••••]
Wesleyan University, Middletown, CT
Dinner and a Movie, Bouncing, Sloth, Landlady, Reba, Ya Mar, Tube, Tweezer, Paul and Silas, Mike's > Hydrogen > Weekapaug, Magilla, Antelope
E: Contact

9/20/90 ❄
Somerville Theatre, Somerville, MA

9/21/90 ❄ [ATTEND. 889; CAP. 889] [TIX $10-$12]
Somerville Theatre, Somerville, MA
Release party for Lawn Boy *on Absolute A-Go-Go.*

9/22/90 [ACCESSIBILITY: •] [ATTEND. 1,000; CAP. 1,000] [TIX $10]
Student Ballroom, University of Massachusetts, Amherst, MA
I: Buried Alive, Horn, MSO, Divided Sky, Tela, Oh Kee > Suzie, Magilla, Wilson, Landlady, I Didn't Know, Bowie
II: Squirming Coil, Tweezer, Destiny Unbound, Fee, Uncle Pen, Bouncing, Stash, Lizards, Lawn Boy, Possum
E: Asse Festival, Golgi

9/28/90 ❄
The Chance, Poughkeepsie, NY
I: Landlady > Bouncing, Oh Kee > Suzie, Stash, MSO, Squirming Coil > Lizards, Asse Festival, Antelope
II: AC/DC Bag > Esther > Gumbo, Dinner and a Movie, YEM > Divided Sky
E: Paul and Silas
Concert debut: Gumbo. List may be incomplete.

9/29/90 ❄
23 East Cabaret, Ardmore, PA

[9/30/90]
The Dude of Life's Wedding
Phish played during the wedding reception of Steve and Kathy Pollak.

10/1/90 ❄
The Haunt, Ithaca, NY
I: Possum, Squirming Coil, Lizards, Landlady, Magilla, Dinner and a Movie, Bouncing, Tweezer, Oh Kee > Suzie
II: Lawn Boy, AC/DC Bag
Setlist for second set is incomplete.

10/4/90 [ACCESSIBILITY: •]
Field House, University of New Hampshire, Durham, NH
I: Golgi, Landlady, Esther, Possum, Squirming Coil, Lizards, Destiny Unbound, Sloth, Uncle Pen, Bowie
II: Reba, Bouncing, Foam, Tweezer, Magilla, Cavern, YEM
E: Divided Sky

10/5/90 [ACCESSIBILITY: •]
Skidmore College, Saratoga Springs, NY
I: I Didn't Know, Mike's > Hydrogen > Weekapaug, MSO, Landlady, Tela, Oh Kee > Suzie, Stash, Asse Festival, Bouncing, Antelope
II: Golgi > Curtain > Ya Mar, Alumni, Uncle Pen, Melt, Fee, Possum
E: GTBT

10/6/90 [ACCESSIBILITY: ••]
Capitol Theater, Port Chester, NY
Landlady, Squirming Coil, Dinner and a Movie, Bouncing, Foam, YEM, Oh Kee > Suzie, Esther, Possum, HYHU > Brain > HYHU, Bowie, Carolina
E: Don't Get Me Wrong
Concert debut: Don't Get Me Wrong, which featured John Popper on harmonica. Phish shared the bill with Blues Traveler and played one set.

10/7/90 ❄
Club Bene, Sayerville, NJ
I: Divided Sky, Uncle Pen, Stash, Landlady > Destiny Unbound, Forbin's > Mockingbird, Asse Festival, Squirming Coil, Mike's > Hydrogen > Weekapaug, A-Train, La Grange
II: Buried Alive, Bouncing, Tweezer, MSO, I Didn't Know, Lizards, GTBT, Golgi
E: Contact

10/8/90 [ACCESSIBILITY: •]
The Bayou, Washington, DC
I: Don't Get Me Wrong, Landlady > Bouncing, Foam, Cavern, Reba > MSO, YEM, Oh Kee > Possum
Setlist missing second set and encore. John Popper on harmonica for Don't Get Me Wrong.

10/12/90 ❄ **[ATTEND. 419; CAP. 550] [TIX $5]**
Cat's Cradle, Chapel Hill, NC
I: Suzie, YEM, Dinner and a Movie > Bouncing, Uncle Pen, Cavern, Esther, Tweezer, Golgi
II: Possum, Fee, Landlady, HYHU > Terrapin > HYHU, Divided Sky, Paul and Silas > Magilla, Mike's > Hydrogen > Weekapaug
E: Carolina, GTBT

10/13/90 ❄
Greenstreets, Columbia, SC

10/30/90 [ACCESSIBILITY: ••••] **[ATTEND. 211; CAP. 211] [TIX $5]**
El Dorado Cafe, Crested Butte, CO
I: Landlady > Bouncing, Donna Lee, Asse Festival > Suzie, Uncle Pen, Cavern, Squirming Coil, Possum
II: Mike's > Hydrogen > Weekapaug, Magilla, Foam, Reba > Llama, Curtis Lowe, Fluffhead, HYHU > Terrapin > HYHU, Buried Alive, Bowie
III: Paul and Silas, Lizards, GTBT, Contact, AC/DC Bag

Phish shows in Colorado have always been super-dank, and this show is no exception. Maybe it was Colorado's wide-open spaces or a relatively new audience to play for, but this show explodes from the Landlady opener to the AC/DC Bag closer three sets later. Landlady seamlessly crosses into a stellar, laid-back Bouncing that is one of the best I have heard. If you are a Mike's > Hydrogen > Weekapaug phan like myself then you will love this great version, similar to the one on 4/16/92. I wish that I could have been at this show—thank goodness for the tapes! —David George

This is one of those real jazzy shows. Most of the first half of the first set is instrumental, partly due to the sound troubles they have. It's pretty laid back and mellow, but still very nice. After getting the gremlins worked out, they roar back strong in the second. The Mike's Groove is definitely worth checking out, as well as an incredible Reba. Go find this tape if just for this song. The rest of the set is very similar to the first. Curtis Lowe, Terrapin, and Buried Alive keep the jazz mood going. —Brian Watkins

10/31/90 [ACCESSIBILITY: ••••] **[ATTEND. 850; CAP. 850] [TIX $7]**
Armstrong Hall, Colorado College, Colorado Springs, CO
I: Buried Alive > Possum, Squirming Coil, Lizards, Stash, Bouncing, YEM, Asse Festival, MSO, Cavern, Antelope
II: "Costume Contest," Landlady, Reba, Runaway Jim, Foam, Tweezer, Fee, Oh Kee > Suzie, HYHU > Love You > HYHU, Mike's > Hydrogen > Weekapaug
E: Uncle Pen, BBFCM
Fishman on vacuum for Love You. Heartbreaker teases in Tweezer.

Before the days of spectacular Halloween cover sets, there were just great shows. From the Buried Alive > Possum opener, you know it's going to be a smokin' show. Antelope is one of the best—very energetic. The BBFCM encore seemed appropriate, and Fish's Love You is hilarious, as usual. This is a true gem among older shows and is fairly easy to obtain. —Dave Matson

With so much talk about the 'Ween shows from 1994–1996, this one is often the forgotten gem. Very often after listening to a show people say, "Wow, Page was on tonight," or something like that, but this is one of those rare occasions that all four band members are in their zone. Just listen to the first four songs in the second set. I've never heard a show flow like this one does—a definite must for any collection. —Ben Ross

11/2/90 [ACCESSIBILITY: ••••]
Glen Miller Ballroom, University of Colorado at Boulder, Boulder, CO
I: Golgi, Landlady > Bouncing > Divided Sky, Sloth, Mike's > Hydrogen > Weekapaug, Esther, Cavern, Asse Festival, Possum > Buried Alive > Possum
II: Suzie Forbin's > Mockingbird, MSO, Foam, YEM, Lizards, I Didn't Know, Bowie
E: Lawn Boy, La Grange
Fishman on trombone for I Didn't Know. Tease medley, including teases from many other songs played at the show, in Bowie intro.

The emcee tells us that Phish broke up backstage before the show started, so instead we're gonna hear a new band, "Phish 2000." But when the sweet notes of Golgi begin, you know it's just a little fun from Trey. Two nights before the epic 11/4/90 show, this concert is one of the highlights from the 1990 Colorado run. The setlist really makes this show a must-have. —Charlie Gubman

This is nothing more than a solid Phish concert in the classic Phish tradition. There is nothing particularly outrageous about the show, but the boys are energetic and uncompromising from the opener to the encore. There's no low point in this performance. The first set (perfect for the car) features a great Mike's Groove and Possum. —Scott Kushner

There are two must-hear moments at this show (besides the outrageously wonderful Weekapaug jam); both come during the set-closers. During the Possum intro, without any warning, they're playing Buried Alive! Almost as suddenly, they're back into Possum, which rocks out. The second set closer, David Bowie, has its own craziness during the intro in the form of a tease medley that incorporates brief jams from many of the other songs played during the show. Like the Possum in the first set, the Bowie seems to draw on the strength of its intro to really soar. —Pat Stanley

11/3/90 [ACCESSIBILITY: ••••] **[ATTEND. 850; CAP. 850] [TIX $9-$10]**
Boulder Theater, Boulder, CO
I: Dinner and a Movie, Bouncing, Llama, Squirming Coil, Oh Kee > Suzie, Magilla, Foam, Runaway Jim, YEM, GTBT

Friday and Saturday, November 2 and 3, 1990

What a cool thing it is when Phish plays a show just a few blocks away from home. Home for me at this time was right in downtown Boulder and when I heard that the Vermonters were doing two nights here, at two different venues, I was ecstatic!

Although they had played Boulder the previous April—right before I saw them in Telluride—they really didn't have a big local following in the town (yet), save for some hardcores up on campus, where the first show was taking place. It was quite a struggle to get some of my "townie" friends to pay $12 to see a band they had never heard live before (I think my tape collection was up to four at this point, and mostly studio stuff) on "The Hill" with a bunch of college kids who collectively had a reputation for not holding their liquor as well as those of us "down the hill." So up the hill I peddled, alone, to see what still remains one of my favorite shows. It was cold and windy out, so I felt very cozy once I made it inside the charming Ballroom. A very cool crowd, and even a few friends whose curiosity led them to the right place at the right time. The Glen Miller Ballroom, about the size of two basketball courts, was an excellent venue for Phish in 1990. Lots of dancing space on hardwood floors, a big stage that was high enough for everyone to see the band clearly, and great acoustics. This was named for one of our greatest Big Band leaders, after all . . .

Kicking things off with Golgi and Landlady, the band rocked out from the get-go, playing tight and feeding off the good Colorado vibes bouncing around this room. The first set was just amazing, and I witnessed my very first trampoline exhibition during a rousing Mike's Song (my 2nd coming only two hours later, in the next set). The crowd, definitely appreciating all the room to dance, was also treated to The Asse Festival by itself, and a killer Possum that segued into a twisting Buried Alive then back again to our favorite road-kill song.

During the set break, I ran into my old college buddy Ben Hunter, who was videotaping the tour for the band (will we ever see these?). He knew the names to all the songs that I didn't and hooked me up with a ticket for the next night. Thanks again, Ben.

The next set proved transcendental for me. I heard my second Forbin's/Mockingbird, which was absolutely beautiful. They were really doing some cool things with dynamics, and Trey and Page were doing some lovely noodling, which actually spilled into the drum intro for My Sweet One. Page, whose keyboard work could be heard so distinctly (compared to his sound in a packed club), played some nice fills, continuing into a phat Foam. YEM was just fantastic.

Listening to the tape from this set, I can hear lots of whoops and hollers from the audience, and it now occurs to me that so many of these folks were probably at their very first show, being blown away by the band's skills and great, memorable melodies. The trampolines came back out and the crowd went even more ballistic. There was a funky . . . no, make that FUNKY! organ-based jam, and by the end of the tune the band swung into an all-out vocal assault, which evolved into an ol' Suthin' spiritual of sorts. The show ended with a tasty Lawn Boy and the rockin' La Grange, which fit in just fine in this Western town.

After the show, I asked Hunter ("Junta") if he wanted to go to a party a friend of mine told me about during the show. Ben said that would be cool, since we hadn't hung out in a while, and he didn't need to hang out with the band every night. When we got down the hill to this little soiree, there was the band, already there, Fishman controlling the stereo and playing Hendrix tapes. Small town, indeed.

The next day it was time for Phish to come down the hill to the downtown, less than a mile away, and to the newly renovated Boulder Theater, an attractive piece of real estate with two levels (18+ up top/21+ down on the floor), a bar with tables in the back, regular seating, and open space for dancing in front of the stage.

This time, I only walked three blocks to the show. I arrived a few hours early to interview the band for a CD-ROM article for a magazine that never really got going. Ben Hunter set up the interview and provided me with recording equipment (thanks again Ben, wherever you are—this was the last day I ever saw him), and the next thing I know, I'm in a room alone with Mike asking him how Phish songs are put together and about their brand-new album, *Lawn Boy*.

Everything went great with Mike, but Page didn't seem into it, and Jon was mostly upset about a review from a Denver newspaper comparing them to the Dead; he said (and I agree) that although the Dead were an influence, they were just as influenced by Coltrane, Mingus, and Zappa. Trey was too busy to be interviewed, but he took the time to apologize to me later.

It seemed as if it would be hard to top the previous night's show, but that doesn't seem to be a problem for these guys. Perhaps fueled by the negative press from the Denver paper, the band cooked all night. In fact, if you have any tapes of the Colorado part of the tour, you'll hear that they were in fine form throughout, as this was their second-friendliest turf after New England.

Early in the set we were presented with one of the very first Llamas that they ever played. Wow! What a rocker! A very cool new song. Next was Squirming Coil, which always adds a little spice to a great set, although here in 1990 it's in the middle of the set and has only a very short piano solo at the end. Oh Kee Pa had everyone doing a Rocky Mountain boogie. It led right into Suzie Greenberg, which, although it had been played the night before (as had a few others), no one seemed to mind since the Theater was one massive collection of high energy. We also got another new song, Page's Magilla, performed less than ten times by that point.

The second set was chock-full of goodies. Another Mike's Song (they loooove those trampolines), Paul and Silas, Stash (also brand new and quite the crowd pleaser) Uncle Pen, and the rare Love You. Possum was just incredible. Phish kept teasing us with the opening riff, then drifting off into something else, back to the opening, back to drifting, and then, just when you thought they weren't going to play it after all, they launch into a full-scale Possum attack! Even crazier than the night before.

The encore could not have been better. There was this very happy-go-lucky young scraggly guy wandering around all night putting out Fluffhead vibes, saying things like, "They just haaaaaaaaaaave to play it tonight!" and "Wouldn't it be just perfect if they did Fluffhead?" Well, his wish was granted because that's what they encored with, in all its glory. But wait kids—that's not all! Right when it ended they treated us to a bonus Fire that truly heated up the place before we poured back out into the cold. As the happy throngs left the theater, the first snow of the season lightly descended upon us—a wondrous sight after two great evenings of incredible music.

I can say in all honesty that Phish definitely left their mark on this Colorado town. Everyone in Boulder surely knew who they were by the end of this weekend.

—Dan Gibson

II: Landlady, Mike's > Hydrogen > Weekapaug, Paul and Silas, Stash, Fee, Uncle Pen, Reba, Possum, HYHU > Love You > HYHU, Antelope
E: Fluffhead, Fire

A classic Colorado show to acquire. The Boulder Theater is really small, with great acoustics. I have great soundboards from this show and every time I listen to it, I weep thinking about seeing these guys before 1992. Runaway, YEM, GTBT close the first set in a fierce way. In the second set, the band jumps right into an early Mike's > Hydrogen > Weekapaug. The rest of the set is what some people term SICK! Paul and Silas, Uncle Pen, Reba, Possum, and Antelope. Then, hello? Take a peek at the encore: Fluffhead, Fire. It would be an understatement to say that the band didn't want to get off the stage. —Brett Pessin

Set II features one of the best Magillas I have on tape. It's funny to hear the reaction of the crowd after each song back then—now, phans love every song, but it was different at this show. The crowd seemed so jumpy and pumped after Llama! I also like that they played all of their own music in this set, including the great Coil > Oh Kee Pa > Suzie combo. —Jason Mokhtarian

11/4/90 [ACCESSIBILITY: ••••]
Fort Ram Nightclub, Fort Collins, CO
I: Carolina, AC/DC Bag, Curtain, Bouncing, Tube, Harry Hood, Funky Bitch, Asse Festival, MSO, Bowie
II: Golgi, Rocky Top, Llama, Mike's > Hydrogen > Weekapaug, Manteca/Caravan/Manteca, Runaway Jim, Oh Kee > Suzie, Jesus Left Chicago, YEM
E: Contact, Highway to Hell
Caravan jammed in the midst of Manteca.

This is arguably the best Colorado show from this era. For some reason, the band keeps talking about a disco ball throughout the show. The first set is excellent—Tube is a welcome favorite, followed by a stellar Harry. It's not too often you get to hear Harry and Bowie together in a first set. The second set is good but not as exciting. —Ben Ross

Name the song, and this show probably has a good version of it. I love Harry Hood! This one really makes you feel good about Hood, too. Of course, any show with Mike's > Weekapaug is a good one. —Lindz Bryan

While this is popularly viewed as a great run of shows in the tour, this show stands out for its first set. A great AC/DC Bag > Curtain warms things up. Following a mellow Bouncin', things take off like we wish they always would. Tube, Harry Hood, and Funky Bitch constitute some of the most ferocious jams my ears have heard. The David Bowie to close the set is also about as good as they get. If only Phish would speed up the Tube jam more these days—it's something you must hear to believe. —Adam Davidoff

The band sounds like they are really trying hard to sound good during this show. The jamming is tight and the instruments are together, but they never really find that magic. Trey finally gets his groove going on Tube but things are not as energetic as other shows from 1990. Highlights are a great up-tempo, bluesy Funky Bitch and a spooky Harry. However, as I listen to this tape, I can't help but think of Phish on this night as a good cover band. Good, but not special. —Tim Foisser

11/8/90 [ACCESSIBILITY: ••]
The Great Hall, Madison, WI
I: Landlady, Possum, Lizards, Foam, Uncle Pen, Llama, Squirming Coil, Asse Festival, I Didn't Know, Mike's > Hydrogen > Weekapaug
II: Suzie, Divided Sky, Tweezer, Oh Kee > Dinner and a Movie, Bouncing, YEM, BBFCM
E: Jesus Left Chicago, Fire
John Popper on harmonica for YEM, BBFCM, and the encores.

Things really take off during this second set when John Popper comes to play. The YEM is one of my favorites, and John adds a lot to the vocal jam at the end. Who would have thought that BBFCM needed harmonica? Well, it sure sounds good. The Jesus Left Chicago is also awesome. —Kyle Niday

11/10/90 [ACCESSIBILITY: •]
Earlham College, Richmond, IN
I: Reba, Landlady > Bouncing, Runaway Jim, Cavern, MSO, Buried Alive > Lizards, Mike's > Hydrogen > Weekapaug
II: Suzie, YEM, Asse Festival, Fee, Llama, Divided Sky, HYHU > Bike > HYHU, Possum

11/16/90 [ACCESSIBILITY: •]
Campus Club, Providence, RI
I: Suzie, Buried Alive, Foam, YEM, Magilla, Llama, Divided Sky, Golgi
II: Landlady, Mike's > Hydrogen > Weekapaug, Lawn Boy, Tube, Paul and Silas, Lizards, Runaway Jim, I Didn't Know, Possum
E: Contact, Fire

11/17/90 [ACCESSIBILITY: •] [ATTEND. 860; CAP. 860] [TIX $10-$12]
Somerville Theater, Somerville, MA
I: Llama, Squirming Coil, Landlady, Runaway Jim, Bouncing, YEM, Cavern, Eliza, Oh Kee > Suzie, Bowie
II: Buried Alive, Fluffhead, Mike's > Hydrogen > Weekapaug, Esther, HYHU > Love You > HYHU, Possum, Lawn Boy, Rocky Top, Donna Lee, GTBT
E: Memories, Adeline
Concert debut: Eliza. Low Rider jams in Suzie and Bowie intro.

11/24/90 [ACCESSIBILITY: •••] [ATTEND. 1,735; CAP. 1,735] [TIX $16]
Capitol Theater, Port Chester, NY
I: Buried Alive > Possum, Foam, Mike's > Hydrogen > Weekapaug, Squirming Coil, Lizards, Oh Kee > Suzie, Bowie
II: Llama, Bouncing, Stash, Eliza, Landlady, Runaway Jim, YEM, HYHU > Love You > HYHU, GTBT, BBFCM
E: Lawn Boy, Divided Sky

11/26/90 ❄
The Haunt, Ithaca, NY
I: Landlady > Runaway Jim, Sloth > Reba > Buried Alive, YEM, Paul and Silas, Donna Lee, Bowie, Divided Sky, Makisupa, Llama
II: Uncle Pen, Forbin's > Mockingbird, Wilson, Mike's > Hydrogen > Weekapaug, HYHU > Whipping Post
E: Fire, Contact, Highway to Hell
Mainstreet and Down on Mainstreet teases in Weekapaug.

11/30/90 ❄
Colonial Theater, Keene, NH
I: Landlady, Mike's > Hydrogen > Weekapaug, Esther, Dinner and a Movie, Bouncing, Tweezer, MSO, Llama, Possum
II: Asse Festival, Squirming Coil, Runaway Jim, Stash, Lizards, Gumbo, Divided Sky, I Didn't Know, Sloth, Antelope
E: Caravan, Oh Kee > Suzie

12/1/90 ❄
The Front, Burlington, VT
I: Cavern, Landlady, Llama, Divided Sky, Foam, Tweezer, MSO, YEM, Runaway Jim
Setlist missing second set and encore.

12/3/90 ❄
The Front, Burlington, VT

12/7/90 ❄
Robert Crown Center, Hampshire College, Amherst, MA
I: Golgi, Stash, Bouncing, Landlady, YEM, Asse Festival, Runaway Jim, Foam, Llama
II: Mike's > Hydrogen > Weekapaug, Donna Lee, Cavern, Tweezer, Squirming Coil, Oh Kee > Suzie, HYHU > No Good Trying > HYHU, Bowie
E: Alumni
Concert debut: No Good Trying.

12/8/90 ❄
The Chance, Poughkeepsie, NY
I: Buried Alive > Runaway Jim, Foam, AC/DC Bag, Divided Sky, Cavern, Landlady, Mike's > Hydrogen > Weekapaug
II: Llama, Asse Festival, Dinner and a Movie, Bouncing, Antelope, Tela, Golgi, HYHU > No Good Trying > HYHU, YEM, Funky Bitch
E: Contact, Highway to Hell

12/28/90 [ACCESSIBILITY: ••••] [ATTEND. 947; CAP. 947] [TIX $13.50-$15]
The Marquee, New York, NY
I: Runaway Jim, Foam, Horn, Reba, Llama, Forbin's > Mockingbird, Mike's > Hydrogen > Weekapaug, Golgi
II: Landlady, Possum, Squirming Coil > Tweezer > Manteca > Tweezer, Oh Kee, MSO, Divided Sky, HYHU > No Good Trying > HYHU, Don't Get Me Wrong, Funky Bitch
E: Bouncing, Highway to Hell
John Popper on harmonica for No Good Trying, Don't Get Me Wrong, and Funky Bitch. Fishman on vacuum for No Good Trying.

A basic great Phish show that benefits from the addition of John Popper from Blues Traveler on Don't Get Me Wrong and Funky Bitch. Every time I listen to this show I feel the oneness that they must have felt on stage. Everything just phlows so nicely throughout the entire show. And Popper jammed out on his harmonica. —Bryan McCraner

Squirming Coil > Tweezer > Manteca > Divided Sky? What more do you need in a jam? The transitions between jams are barely noticeable. I love the band's willingness to combine such different song styles into one intense jam. —Ron Laurel

The second set of this show is perhaps the most popular Phish tape from 1990, helped by awesome soundboard quality, a killer setlist, great playing, and an appearance from John Popper. Early in the set, the band is on fire, swinging into Manteca in the midst of Tweezer, then returning to Tweezer for the closing jam. When Fish comes forward for Syd Barrett's No Good Trying, Popper does too, and there's a real good jam in the middle of the song. After that comes a rare performance of Don't Get Me Wrong (co-written by Trey and Popper), before a funky Funky Bitch closes the set. This apparently is the show that turned Elektra on to Phish; it's easy to see why. —Melissa Wolcott

12/29/90 ❄
Campus Club, Providence, RI
I: I Didn't Know, Llama, YEM, Esther, Bowie, Lawn Boy, Rocky Top, Horn > Oh Kee > Suzie
II: Buried Alive > Runaway Jim, Lizards, Cavern, Stash, Jesus Left Chicago, Dinner and a Movie > Bouncing, Destiny Unbound, Antelope
E: Donna Lee, AC/DC Bag

12/31/90 [ACCESSIBILITY: •]
Exhibition Hall, World Trade Center, Boston, MA
I: Suzie, Divided Sky, I Didn't Know, Landlady, Bouncing, MSO, Mike's > Hydrogen > Weekapaug > Auld Lang Syne, Buried Alive > Possum
II: Golgi, Stash, Squirming Coil, Runaway Jim, Magilla, YEM, Rocky Top, HYHU > Brain > HYHU, Antelope
Chucklehead opened. Venue management turned on the house lights while the band was deciding on an encore, ending the show prematurely.

1991 Sea to Shining Sea

During the year in which Phish would finally sign with a major record label, Elektra, and record the album that would become *A Picture of Nectar*, the band toured ferociously.

The 1991 spring tour brought the band to California and the Pacific Northwest for the first time, as well as points as far south as Mississippi. The end of the tour found the band in their last-ever gig at The Front in Burlington, and by the time they did a short summer tour with buddies the Giant Country Horns, Phish had comfortably settled in to the small theater circuit. Places like the Capitol Theatre in Port Chester, NY, the Colonial Theater in Keene, NH, and the Flynn Theater in Burlington, VT, would remain frequent stops over the next year.

Further south, the band became regulars at Trax in Charlottesville, VA, and Cat's Cradle in Chapel Hill, NC. The summer tour, shorter than usual to allow time for recording and mixing *Nectar*, saw less setlist craziness than the norm, but the presence of the horns for a sustained run of shows allowed for experimentation that had previously been impossible. The horns didn't make it to the legendary Amy's Farm show in early August, although thousands of fans who heard about the free outdoor gig on the horn tour or by a postcard-mailing from the band did make it.

The 1991 fall tour can, by most respects, be considered the first "real" tour in the way that most people now think of a Phish tour. Kicking off the tour in Keene with a bunch of first-time-played tunes, the band wound west, pulling out an unprepared Gamehendge in Olympia, WA, and digging in for a sold-out, two-night stand at the Great American Music Hall in San Francisco—impressive gigs for a band that still got by almost exclusively through word-of-mouth.

From there, the tour came back through Colorado for the now-traditional Halloween fête (this was its second year in Colorado after four years at Goddard) and then slowly back to the promised land of New England and Vermont where a record contract with Elektra awaited. . . .

2/1/91 [ACCESSIBILITY: •]
Alumnae Hall, Brown University, Providence, RI
I: MSO, Foam, Tweezer, Magilla, Guelah, Runaway Jim, Melt, Bouncing, Bowie
II: Reba, Landlady, Mango
Concert debut: Guelah. Show ended after Mango due to curfew. Last Mango, 8/19/89 Durham, NH [101 shows].

1991

127 Total Show Dates
- 5 one-set shows
- 97 two-set shows
- 2 three-set shows
- 23 dates with no setlists

Phan Picks 1991

SHOW	THE SKINNY
1) 07/21/91 Parksville, NY	With the horns at Arrowhead.
2) 08/03/91 Auburn, ME	Amy's Pharm, with phriends.
3) 11/30/91 Port Chester, NY	At the Capitol, a great Hood.
4) 10/19/91 Santa Cruz, CA	Very well played show & Mimi!
5) 10/13/91 Olympia. WA	First Gamehendge since '88.
6) 04/11/91 Northfield, MN	Comic relief: the Prison Joke.
7) 07/11/91 Burlington, VT	First show of the GCH tour.
8) 07/15/91 New York, NY	Only one set, but smoking.
9) 04/16/91 Ann Arbor, MI	Band and crew football songs.
10) 03/13/91 Boulder, CO	No gimmicks, just great music.

MUSICAL RECAP: By 1991, Phish's style had become even more refined, with sets often containing as many as a dozen songs. Though the songs are generally more compact versions than would be seen in later years, the band hadn't abandoned their jamming roots. Indeed, the shift in style allowed them to hone (or attempt to hone) their technical proficiency on new songs like All Things Reconsidered, while older favorites like YEM continued to receive star treatment. Though this year is often identified as the time when the band made its first real split from the style of an earlier era, there are arguably fewer "must-hear" musical moments from this year than most others. One obvious exception is the July tour with the Giant Country Horns that brought a new jazz sensibility to the Phish sound.
REPRESENTATIVE JAMS: Divided Sky, 7/21/91 (with horns); You Enjoy Myself, 11/16/91; Frankenstein, 7/12/91 (with horns).
ORIGINAL SONG DEBUTS: All Things Reconsidered (9/25/91), Brother (9/25/91), Chalkdust Torture (2/2/91), Glide (9/27/91), Guelah Papyrus (2/1/91), It's Ice (9/25/91), Poor Heart (4/22/91), Setting Sail (4/20/91), Sparkle (9/25/91), Tweezer Reprise (2/7/91).
COVER SONG DEBUTS: Touch Me (7/11/91), Moose the Mootche (7/12/91).

Dark Horses

SHOW	THE SKINNY
1) 04/27/91 Port Chester, NY	Probably the best show of '91.
2) 07/24/91 Charlottesville, VA	The hidden gem of the horn tour.
3) 03/16/91 Breckinridge, CO	Soft and sweet.
4) 12/05/91 Greenfield, MA	This whole week is pretty hot.
5) 05/03/91 Somerville, MA	Amazing second set.

Most-Played Originals:		
1) The Landlady	82	65%
2) Cavern	74	58%
3) My Sweet One	73	58%
4) Llama	69	54%
5) Bouncing	65	51%
5) The Squirming Coil	65	51%
7) Golgi Apparatus	64	50%
8) Chalkdust Torture	63	50%
9) Foam	61	48%
10) Runaway Jim	55	43%

Most-Played Covers:		
1) Rocky Top	36	28%
2) Uncle Pen	25	20%
3) Sweet Adeline	24	19%
4) Paul and Silas	23	18%
5) Love You	21	17%
6) Take the A-Train	14	11%
7) Terrapin	13	10%
8) Memories	12	9%
9) Ya Mar	11	9%
10) Three-way tie with	9	7%

First-Set Openers:	
1) Chalkdust Torture	13
2) Golgi Apparatus	7
2) The Landlady	7
2) Llama	7
2) Runaway Jim	7

Second-Set Openers:	
1) Llama	10
2) Chalkdust Torture	9
3) Golgi Apparatus	7
4) The Curtain	6
5) Brother	5
5) My Sweet One	5

Henrietta Songs:	
1) Love You	21
2) Terrapin	13
3) Touch Me	9
4) If I Only Had a Brain	4
5) Bike	2

A Cappella Songs:	
1) Sweet Adeline	24
2) Memories	12
3) Carolina	6

2/2/91 ❄
Bates College, Lewiston, ME
I: Oh Kee > Suzie, Guelah, Dinner and a Movie, Esther, Stash, Destiny Unbound, YEM, Chalkdust
II: Sloth, Antelope, Lawn Boy
Setlist for second set incomplete. Concert debut: Chalkdust.

2/3/91 [ACCESSIBILITY: ••]
The Front, Burlington, VT
I: Runaway Jim, Guelah > MSO > Tweezer > Esther, Destiny Unbound, Reba, Chalkdust, Foam, Golgi
II: Bowie, Squirming Coil, Landlady, Cavern, Mango, Melt, Bouncing, Oh Kee > Suzie
E: Jesus Left Chicago, BBFCM

2/7/91 [ACCESSIBILITY: •]
Pickle Barrel Pub, Killington, VT
I: Runaway Jim, Foam, MSO, Landlady, Mango, Melt, Bouncing, Possum, Squirming Coil, Golgi
II: Chalkdust, TMWSIY > Avenu > TMWSIY, Tweezer > Tweezer Reprise, Guelah, Uncle Pen, Cavern, HYHU > Love You > HYHU, Lizards > Sloth, Destiny Unbound, YEM
E: AC/DC Bag
Lizards aborted after Trey can't remember the lyrics. Concert debut: Tweezer Reprise.

2/8/91 [ACCESSIBILITY: ••] [ATTEND. 858; CAP. 858] [TIX $10-$12]
Portsmouth Music Hall, Portsmouth, NH
I: AC/DC Bag, Reba, Buried Alive, Forbin's > Mockingbird, MSO, Stash, Squirming Coil, Runaway Jim, Guelah, Bowie
II: Llama, Mango, Cavern, Lawn Boy, Mike's > Hydrogen > Weekapaug, Horn, Bouncing, Lizards, Antelope
E: Landlady, La Grange
Carl Gerhard on trumpet for Landlady and La Grange.

2/9/91 [ACCESSIBILITY: ••] [ATTEND. 1,458; CAP. 1,973] [TIX $12.50-$14]
John M. Greene Hall, Smith College, Northampton, MA
I: Mango > Sloth, TMWSIY > Avenu > TMWSIY, Runaway Jim, Foam, Guelah, MSO, Tweezer > Reba, Chalkdust
II: Golgi > Buried Alive > Fluffhead, Landlady > Bouncing, Harry Hood, Cavern, HYHU > Love You > HYHU, Squirming Coil, Llama
E: Lawn Boy, Suzie
E2: Contact, Rocky Top
Fishman on vacuum for Love You after his vacuum fails to work.

2/14/91 [ACCESSIBILITY: •]
State Theater, Ithaca, NY
I: MSO, McGrupp, Buried Alive, Reba, Destiny Unbound, Cavern, Mango, Stash, Lawn Boy, Oh Kee > Golgi
II: Mike's > Hydrogen > Weekapaug, Foam, Squirming Coil, Runaway Jim, Esther, Alumni, Bouncing, I Didn't Know, Landlady, Possum
E: Uncle Pen, La Grange
Car giveaway during I Didn't Know.

At my first Phish gig at the State Theater, the band gave away their car! During I Didn't Know in the second set, Fishman came out and they had a whole little ceremony about how they'd finally gotten enough money to purchase a blue minivan. They said something like, "We've finally got enough money to quit driving that junker that's parked right out front. . . . The pink slip's in the car, yell out for the keys." And so they tossed the keys out into the crowd. This kid that we were standing with, Toast, actually caught the keys and got to drive home Phish's car that night. Toast ended up selling the car for about two thousand dollars or something, and at my next show after that, which was the next time they came farther west in New York, on 4/20/91 at the University of Rochester, Fishman came out, and if you listen to tapes of the show, right at the beginning, they start talking about the car. Fishman said something like, "Maybe some of you were there." When people made it clear that they were, he said, "Yeah, well, I heard that guy sold it for like, two thousand dollars. If we knew it was worth that, we never would have given it away!" Then added, "He probably just used the money to buy dope anyway." Everybody cheered, so he yelled, "Oh yeah? Dope!" then chanted, "Dope, dope, dope" with us yelling along. —Mike Graff

2/15/91 [ACCESSIBILITY: •••] [ATTEND. 825; CAP. 825] [TIX $11]
Colonial Theater, Keene, NH
I: Curtain > Wilson, Divided Sky, Melt, Fee, Buried Alive, Mango, Sloth, Dinner and a Movie, Magilla, Llama
II: Bowie, Bathtub Gin, Ya Mar, Guelah, MSO, Oh Kee > AC/DC Bag, Harry Hood, HYHU > Terrapin > HYHU, Chalkdust
E: Caravan, BBFCM
E2: Contact, Golgi
Fishman on industrial-strength wet/dry vacuum for Terrapin.

2/16/91 ❄ [ATTEND. 852; CAP. 947] [TIX $15]
The Marquee, New York, NY
I: Sloth, MSO, Divided Sky, Cavern, A-Train, Landlady > Bouncing, Llama, Mango, Mike's > Hydrogen > Weekapaug
II: Chalkdust, Reba, Buried Alive, Runaway Jim, Guelah, Fluffhead, Rocky Top, HYHU > Love You > HYHU, Golgi
E: Lawn Boy, Fire
E2: Possum
Rocky Mountain Way jam in Possum.

2/19/91 ❄
The Bayou, Washington, DC
I: Llama, Curtain > Golgi, Reba, Dinner and a Movie > Sloth, Runaway Jim, Squirming Coil > Bowie
II: MSO, Mike's > Hydrogen > Weekapaug, Guelah, Landlady, Esther, Melt, Bouncing, Love You, Oh Kee > Suzie, Rocky Top
E: Magilla, Fire
Whole Lotta Love jam in Love You.

2/20/91 ❄
Kahootz, Richmond, VA

2/21/91 ❄
Trax, Charlottesville, VA
I: Reba, Dinner and a Movie, Melt, Fee, Llama, Lizards, Mike's > Hydrogen > Weekapaug
II: Golgi, Cavern, Landlady, Bouncing, Stash, Guelah, Uncle Pen, Asse Festival, Bowie
E: Suzie
The Jolly Llamas opened.

2/22/91 ❄
Cat's Cradle, Chapel Hill, NC
I: Golgi, Landlady > Cavern > Runaway Jim, Fluffhead > MSO, Sloth, Bouncing, Possum, Fire

2/23/91 ❄
1313 Club, Charlotte, NC

2/24/91 ❄
Trax, Charlottesville, VA

2/26/91 [ACCESSIBILITY: •]
Barrelhouse, Salem, VA
I: Foam > Squirming Coil, Llama, Guelah, MSO, Reba, Oh Kee > AC/DC Bag, Golgi, La Grange
II: Buried Alive > Runaway Jim, Dinner and a Movie, Stash, Bouncing, Landlady > Destiny Unbound, Possum, Lizards, Mike's > Hydrogen > Weekapaug
E: HYHU > Love You > HYHU, GTBT

2/27/91 ❄
Flamingo Cafe, Knoxville, TN
I: Golgi, Divided Sky, I Didn't Know, Landlady, YEM, Fee, MSO, Melt, Bouncing, Fire
II: Suzie > Buried Alive > Cavern, Squirming Coil, Bowie, Lawn Boy > Oh Kee > Sloth, HYHU > Love You > HYHU, Possum
E: Rocky Top

2/28/91 ❄
Sarrat Theater, Vanderbilt University, Nashville, TN
I: Landlady, Bouncing, Foam, Esther, Mike's > Hydrogen > Weekapaug, Cavern, TMWSIY > Avenu > TMWSIY, MSO, Golgi
II: Squirming Coil, Reba, Llama, Guelah, Divided Sky
Setlist for second set is likely incomplete.

3/1/91 [ACCESSIBILITY: ••••]
Georgia Theater, Athens, GA
I: Wilson, Foam, Divided Sky, Cavern, Squirming Coil, Tweezer, Dinner and a Movie, Bouncing, Buried Alive, Mike's > Hydrogen > Weekapaug
II: Golgi, Landlady, Reba, Llama, Guelah, Sloth, Possum, HYHU > Love You > HYHU, Bowie
E: Oh Kee > Suzie

3/2/91 ❄
Cotton Club, Atlanta, GA

3/6/91 ❄
Club 616, Memphis, TN
Golgi, YEM, Landlady, Squirming Coil, Possum, Cavern, Divided Sky, HYHU > Love You > HYHU, MSO, Bouncing, Bowie
E: Jesus Left Chicago
Setlist may be incomplete.

3/7/91 ❄
The Gim, Oxford, MS
II: Oh Kee > Landlady > Sloth, Runaway Jim, Reba, Possum, I Didn't Know, Mike's > Hydrogen > Weekapaug, Guelah, MSO, GTBT
E: Bathtub Gin
Setlist missing first set.

3/8/91 ❄
College Station Theater, Tuscaloosa, AL

3/9/91 ❄
Tipitina's, New Orleans, LA

3/13/91 [ACCESSIBILITY: ••••]
Boulder Theater, Boulder, CO
I: Fluffhead, Landlady, YEM, Cavern, Divided Sky, Esther, Llama, Squirming Coil, Bowie
II: Suzie, Melt, Bouncing, MSO, Guelah, Runaway Jim, Sloth > Reba > Tweezer, HYHU > Terrapin > HYHU, Oh Kee > Golgi
E: A-Train, BBFCM
Fishman on vacuum for Terrapin.

3/15/91 [ACCESSIBILITY: ••••]
Gothic Theater, Denver, CO
I: Llama, Foam, MSO, Stash, Dinner and a Movie, Bouncing, Oh Kee > AC/DC Bag, Lizards, Mike's > Hydrogen > Weekapaug
II: Buried Alive > Possum, Horn, Paul and Silas, Cavern, Destiny Unbound, I Didn't Know, Harry Hood, Chalkdust
E: Squirming Coil, Runaway Jim
Fishman on trombone for I Didn't Know.

I consider this one of the best shows of 1991, and it's definitely one of the best tapes I own (there are plenty of phatty soundboards of this one floating around). The second set is just vintage Phish, exactly how I like it. Buried > Possum are smooth while the Paul and Silas just flat out rocks. Harry is short but oh-so-sweet, then the Runaway Jim encore is the perfect way to show Colorado exactly how much Phish loves playing there. Excellent show. —Alex Banks

Horn is so soft it makes you melt—it's by far the most peaceful Horn I've heard to date; this is when the song was still relatively new. I Didn't Know features Fishman (as Moses Brown) contributing on trombone, and a terrifying scream from the audience accompanies him. —Matthew Ashenfelder

3/16/91 [ACCESSIBILITY: ••••]
The Ten Mile Room, Breckenridge, CO
I: TMWSIY > Avenu > TMWSIY, Golgi, Reba, Landlady, Bathtub Gin, Curtain, Rocky Top, Forbin's > Mockingbird, Oh Kee > Suzie, Antelope
II: Llama, Divided Sky, Guelah, MSO, Melt, Magilla > Buried Alive, Squirming Coil, Cavern, YEM
E: Manteca > Possum

Like the other shows that made up this notable week in Phishtory, the Ten Mile Room gig is a good example of Phish's evolving style during this period. In spring 1991, the band's magic comes not in the length of the jams but rather in the tight precision with which the band executed them. Listen to how excited Trey is to play compositional tunes like TMWSIY > Avenu > TMWSIY. In some ways, I think this period serves as a bridge between the looser, jammy 1980s Phish shows and their expansive, mind-blowing jams of the mid-1990s. Even if you prefer their current style, it's worth owning a few tapes from the Colorado shows of 1990 and 1991 to better appreciate the band's evolution.
—Tricia Holmes

Oh, to see Phish in a room this small—you can hear the tiny audience cheering between the songs. With plenty of Gamehendge and Lawn Boy, it's a treat for the ears. The encore is one of the most impressive I've heard: Manteca (jazz by Duke Ellington) and Possum (classic Elvis/JGB/Mystery Train by Phish). —Emily Binard

3/17/91 [ACCESSIBILITY: ••••]
Wheeler Opera House, Aspen, CO
I: Carolina, Bouncing, Landlady, Mike's > Hydrogen > Weekapaug, Foam, Fluffhead, Uncle Pen, Stash, Lizards, Bowie
II: Runaway Jim, Esther, MSO, Squirming Coil, Tweezer, Fee, "Fishman Story," Slave, "Colorado Story," Chalkdust
E: Lawn Boy, La Grange
Fishman tells a long narrative about his adventures in Telluride before Slave, and both Fishman and Trey tell stories about their adventures in Colorado after Slave. Last Slave, 4/22/90 Colorado Springs, CO [78 shows].

You can tell that the band loves their western U.S. fans. They take requests throughout the show and both Trey and Fish tell the crowd some long and interesting stories. Fish tells of his adventures with a Colorado bear and her cub, and Trey picks on Fish for missing a gig because he was lost in the woods (Fish denies that any illegal substances were involved). It's hilarious. The show is also highlighted by a good early version of Chalkdust and the best Trey vocals on La Grange that I've heard. —Tim Foisser

Besides the great stories, they also explain why they get off stage when they do, and why they don't stay on longer. This is a great tape for all who enjoy the talkative side of the band. —Matt Richardson

3/19/91 ❄
Fine Arts Auditorium, Fort Lewis College, Durango, CO

My first show—so many fond memories. It was in the Fine Arts Auditorium, with only about 250 people in attendance. I can say this is the smallest show I've seen. It only took this first experience for me to realize how special this group was, and I've been hooked ever since. Or maybe there was something on that animal cracker that guy gave me before the show. —Jeff Salvatore

3/22/91 [ACCESSIBILITY: ••••]
The Inferno, Steamboat Springs, CO
I: Llama, YEM, Landlady > Destiny Unbound, Bouncing, Melt, Squirming Coil, Buried Alive > Cavern, Reba, Fire
II: Oh Kee > Suzie, Antelope, Foam, Paul and Silas, Stash, Runaway Jim, Guelah, HYHU > Terrapin > HYHU, Mike's > Hydrogen > Weekapaug
E: Magilla, Golgi
Fishman on vacuum for Terrapin.

3/23/91 [ACCESSIBILITY: •]
The Inferno, Steamboat Springs, CO
I: Sloth, Divided Sky, Fee, Llama, I Didn't Know, Curtain > Possum, Forbin's > Mockingbird, Rocky Top
II: Chalkdust, Bathtub Gin, Oh Kee > AC/DC Bag, MSO, Tweezer, Lizards, Uncle Pen, Cavern, Bowie, Contact
E: A-Train, BBFCM

3/28/91 ❄ [ATTEND. 801; CAP. 801] [TIX $10-$12]
The Catalyst, Santa Cruz, CA

Golgi, Divided Sky, Cavern, Landlady > Bouncing, YEM, Guelah, MSO, Bowie, Squirming Coil, Oh Kee > Suzie, Magilla, Chalkdust
E: Lawn Boy, Fire
The Sky and Borneo Penguin opened. Phish played one set.

3/29/91 ❄
DNA Lounge, San Francisco, CA

3/31/91 ❄
Berkeley Square, Berkeley, CA

4/2/91 ❄
International Beer Garden, Arcata, CA

4/3/91 ❄
Southern Oregon State College, Ashland, OR

4/4/91 [ACCESSIBILITY: •]
Woodman of the World Union Trade Hall, Eugene, OR
I: Oh Kee > Suzie, YEM, Squirming Coil, Llama, Forbin's > Mockingbird, Possum, Carolina, Golgi
II: Curtain > Runaway Jim, Guelah, Bowie, Lawn Boy, Landlady, MSO, Divided Sky, HYHU > Love You > HYHU, BBFCM, Magilla, Highway to Hell
E: Contact, Uncle Pen

4/5/91 [ACCESSIBILITY: ••]
Starry Night, Portland, OR

Saturday, March 23, 1991

THE INFERNO, Steamboat Springs, CO

Phish and Colorado go way back. When a band is based in Ski-Country East, it's only natural that many from its fan base end up going to school somewhere in Ski-Country West. In the spring of '91, Phish returned to its loyal following out there for the fourth time, only now there were many new fans who knew them not from East Coast shows but solely from their regular appearances in the Mountain State over the years. By 1990, I found myself there, in Boulder, working with my own band. When Phish came to the Boulder Theater ("Cool, I can walk to a show!") on 3/13/91, I finally managed to drag my guitarist, Bruce, to see them, hoping this would help him understand what I hoped we could achieve. We sat in the balcony watching them, mesmerized (and admiring the Minkin backdrop, of course!)—the only time, I believe, that I sat for a Phish show.

Well, Bruce was blown away, just like we all were at one time or another. He insisted that we drag our bass player, John, who mostly listened to '80s new wave, to another Colorado show. As it turned out, the only one that all three of us could logistically make was all the way on the other side of the state (okay, neither place is at the extreme side, but it's on the other side of the Continental Divide—how's that?), perhaps four hours away, in Steamboat Springs, ten days later. This was to be the second night of a two-show run there, the last show in Colorado before their first trip to California—and boy, did we pick a winner!

It may have been two days after the start of spring, but traveling through the Rocky Mountains it was still the thick of winter—we nearly flew off Route 40 on an ice patch. What fun. We finally made it to Steamboat Springs, which isn't really a quaint ol' Western town but rather a highly developed, modern ski resort, complete with a newly built "old-looking" downtown, with bars named "Saloon." The Inferno was actually "out a ways" at the resorts. When we made it to the parking lot, there were already a few tour vehicles, some with plates from New England and southern states. After all, this was a Spring Break for many. The Inferno was actually in a complex of shops at the bottom of the slopes, but it was a rather cozy place (although no windows) and the last time I would see Phish in a room this small.

At the far end was a stage, small by today's Phish-show standards, but large enough to fit the band in its ever-popular "four across" set-up—the drums far right, facing the rest of the band. My pals and I (John also brought his housemate, Jane) arrived rather early in case we needed to scramble for tickets. There certainly was no need for that. We sat down for dinner in the back half of the room, and the admission (I think it was only about eight or ten bucks) was just added to the check. About half the room was full of tables and chairs, with a bar to the side, while the other half was the dance floor in front of the stage. The place was smaller than a basketball court.

The four of us were finishing up dinner and waiting for the show to begin, but that wasn't going to happen yet. First of all, only a few fans had started to trickle in, and second, Page walks up to our table with a plate full of chicken and asks if he can sit down and eat with us. Uh, gee, what do you think we said? We were all vegetarians, but certainly not stuck-up about it. Page remembered me from a few earlier shows out East and a rather brief interview I did with the band (but mostly with Mike and Jon) at the Boulder Theater in November 1990. He probably figured we wouldn't bother him too much before the show, and he was right. It was a pleasant dinner.

Eventually, the Inferno started to fill up, though I doubt there were more than 150 folks in that room. My friends and I moved right up to the stage and there was still some room to move around. As usual, I met a few nice people in my immediate surroundings. It was all so mellow, with little hint that we would soon be whipped up into such a frenzy.

The band hit the stage and promptly ripped into Sloth—a powerful start. Suddenly the Inferno was living up to its name. Everyone, save perhaps a few uninitiated who were still at the tables, whooped it up, having a grand ol' time. Next came, for the first time (I believe) what was to be a very popular future combination—like "I Know You Rider" after "China Cat" or "Livin' Lovin' Maid" after "Heartbreaker"—yep, the lovely and wondrous Divided Sky. Surprising at the time, but it somehow seemed natural. A beautiful rendition was on display and now a phull-on Phish show was in effect. Other first set highlights included I Didn't Know, The Curtain and—oh, the whole set was just awesome! Look at the setlist and you'll see what I mean. The boys were playing great as the audience fed them lots of positive, wild energy.

The second set just kept getting better as it went along. Happy spring-breakers and skiers passed their drinks around, so I never had to leave the front of the stage for refreshment. Chalkdust, still quite a new song and only the second time I had heard it, was fantastic. Oh Kee Pa was a great tune for these mountains and during AC/DC Bag, I bet the dance floor never felt such happy feet. If the set had ended after the gorgeous version of Lizards, I would have been content, but this was only the middle of one lonnnnng set. After the craziness of Bowie, perhaps Phish felt that we needed a set-closing Contact to bring us back to Earth.

It was not to last, though. For the encore, we were treated to a tasty "A-Train" for last call. Then came the monster of the show, so to speak. This was perhaps the most frantic, energetic and ferocious BBFCM this here body has ever witnessed. Fishman was eerie, the band was dead on, and we were one wet drippy blob of collective sweat. After the show, every wet one of us seemed to have a big Phish-eating grin on his or her face. This was definitely one of the "funnest" Phish shows I ever experienced.

That wasn't quite the end of the fun for the four of us from Boulder, though. We went out (into the c-c-c-cold) to an all-night diner down the road a piece with some of our new phriends and then sought out what the town was named after. Yes, in the 20-degree Colorado night, we made out way out to the hot springs, which weren't officially open yet at 5 A.M. But that didn't stop us from disrobing and sliding into the steamy sulfuric liquid. As the sun was rising, I thought that Phish should always play near a natural hot spring. Ahhhh . . . a great way to end an amazing evening.

—Dan Gibson

I: Landlady > Bouncing > Divided Sky, Cavern, Magilla > Reba, Chalkdust, Foam, Mike's > Hydrogen > Weekapaug
II: Rocky Top, Stash, Lizards, Sloth > Dinner and a Movie, Harry Hood, I Didn't Know, MSO, GTBT
E: Fee, Oh Kee > Suzie

4/6/91 [ACCESSIBILITY: •]
Campus Recreation Center, Evergreen College, Olympia, WA
I: Magilla, Llama, YEM, Bathtub Gin, Icculus, Antelope, Possum, Jesus Left Chicago, Alumni
Setlist missing second set. Last Icculus, 8/12/89 Burlington, VT [181 shows].

4/11/91 [ACCESSIBILITY: ••••]
The Cave, Carleton College, Northfield, MN
I: Runaway Jim, Cavern, Paul and Silas, Tweezer, Magilla, Dinner and a Movie, Bouncing, Foam, Carolina, YEM, Squirming Coil > Chalkdust
II: MSO, Reba, Llama, TMWSIY > Avenu > TMWSIY, Lizards, Melt, Lawn Boy, Landlady > Destiny Unbound, Mike's > Hydrogen > Weekapaug
E: Fee, HYHU > "The Prison Joke" > HYHU, Possum
Between Fee and Possum, the band convinces Fishman to tell "The Prison Joke." Soundcheck: Harpua jams, local radio station promo.

Ah, the (in)famous Prison Joke show. As the final notes of Fee die out, Trey encourages Henrietta to come forward, saying, "I think if you guys yell loud enough, he might be able to tell you a funny joke!" Fish responds, "I'm not telling any funny jokes. This isn't funny. There's nothing funny about this. This is serious as all hell." But Trey persists, "Maybe if you yell loud enough, Fish will tell the Prison Joke!" That gets a laugh out of Fishman, who goes on to explain how he bought a tape of dirty truckers' jokes for the band to listen to in their van. Then with no further prompting from Trey, he tells the Prison Joke—to a decidedly lukewarm audience response. Reflecting on the joke's failure, Fish laments, "It's all in the delivery. That's why I'm not a comedian." Like the music on this night, the whole joke sequence is a little messy. —Andre Holton

At first glance, all anyone sees when they look at this setlist is the Prison Joke. Although it is hilarious (with Fishman speaking in an almost surfer-dude accent), there is plenty more to this show. Lawn Boy is extra-long and lounge-lizardy, plus there's a great Reba and of course Landlady > Destiny. Boy, how great is Destiny? —Jon Bahr

4/12/91 [ACCESSIBILITY: •••] [ATTEND. 437; CAP. 750] [TIX $10-$12]
Barrymore Theater, Madison, WI
I: Llama, Uncle Pen, Divided Sky, Guelah, Oh Kee > Suzie, Stash, Rocky Top, Golgi
II: Landlady, Runaway Jim, YEM, Fluffhead, Cavern, Tela, Buried Alive, Reba, MSO, GTBT
E: Contact > BBFCM, Squirming Coil

Some of the band's parents were apparently in the crowd this night, which seems to make the show special for the boys. There's a really nice version of Tela, the Reba jam is very intense, and the YEM vocal jam is one of the best I've heard. I can definitely hear them say "Get your balls out of the butter" and "Come on, send your money." It's a totally hilarious part of a very cool show. —M.N.J. Adams

4/13/91 ❄
Biddy Mulligan's, Chicago, IL

4/15/91 [ACCESSIBILITY: •] [ATTEND. 400; CAP. 400] [TIX $3]
The Gathering Place, Northwestern University, Evanston, IL
I: Sloth, Ya Mar, Foam, Runaway Jim, Melt, Fee, Chalkdust, Forbin's > Mockingbird, Llama
II: Wipeout jam, Mike's > Hydrogen > Weekapaug, Horn, MSO, Landlady, Lizards, Possum, Magilla, Fire
E: Squirming Coil, Rocky Top

4/16/91 [ACCESSIBILITY: ••••]
Rick's American Cafe, Ann Arbor, MI
I: Golgi, YEM, Paul and Silas, Cavern, Mango, Oh Kee > AC/DC Bag, Tela, Bowie
II: MSO, Reba, Chalkdust, Magilla, Buried Alive, Uncle Pen, Tweezer, Runaway Jim, Carolina, Tweezer Reprise
E: HYHU > Brain > HYHU, GTBT
Ryth McFend opened. Crew Football Theme Song jam before MSO. Paul Gibbons on trombone for Magilla. Fishman on vacuum for Brain.

The band sounds like they took Valium before this show, which is understandable: Rick's is known for cheap drinks and BAD cover bands. The crowd is too busy swilling Jaegermeister to dig this show until the band busts into one of the first versions of Tweezer Reprise. But it's too late, because it closed the second set. For the encore, the band responds to the lousy crowd with a vacuum solo (let 'em figure that one out!) but caves in with a Zeppelin cover. Live and learn. —Paul Sheets

This show was at Rick's American Café, a tiny little bar in downtown Ann Arbor. Obviously it's a very intimate show. Some highlights include a solid Bowie first-set closer, Magilla with Paul Gibbons on trombone, and an If I Only Had a Brain encore! At the start of set II, the band mocks some of the audience by joking about football fans in the back of the bar. —Josh Halman

4/18/91 [ACCESSIBILITY: •]
Oberlin College, Oberlin, OH
II: Llama, Reba, Oh Kee Pa > Sloth, Paul and Silas, Horn, Suzie, Melt, Squirming Coil, Possum
E: Harpua
Setlist missing first set. Last Harpua, 6/9/90 New York, NY [81 shows].

4/19/91 ❄ [ATTEND. 473; CAP. 473] [TIX $6-$7]
Nietzche's, Buffalo, NY
I: Funky Bitch, Dinner and a Movie, Bouncing, Divided Sky, Cavern, Lizards, Stash, I Didn't Know, Rocky Top, Mike's > Hydrogen > Weekapaug, Adeline
II: Harry Hood, Curtain, Golgi, Landlady > Destiny Unbound, MSO, Squirming Coil, A-Train, Antelope
E: Paul and Silas, BBFCM
Last Adeline, 11/17/90 Somerville, MA [56 shows].

4/20/91 [ACCESSIBILITY: ••]
Cafeteria, University of Rochester, Rochester, NY
I: Runaway Jim, Reba, Llama, Fluffhead, MSO, Landlady, Esther, Chalkdust, Bouncing, YEM > Setting Sail
II: Sloth, Ya Mar, Melt, Squirming Coil, Paul and Silas, Cavern, TMWSIY > Avenu > TMWSIY, Tweezer, Oh Kee > Suzie, Adeline
E: Horn > Alumni
Concert debut: Setting Sail.

The show was in a cafeteria at the University of Rochester, so it only held two to three hundred people (including Fishman's parents). Tickets were $4 if you could find a Rochester student, and $6 to the public. (Even back then, it was a big thing to find a cheaper ticket. Now, a $6 ticket would be a dream.) They played a Bouncing in the first set, but between sets, the band threw out 300 super-bounce balls, and just filled this little tiny cafeteria with bouncy balls. It was hilarious. Everybody was bouncing these balls around, and when you've got a small little cafeteria like that and 45 minutes between sets to be throwing them around, well . . . I've still got my bounce ball from the show (a bunch of us held on to them). After that, it became a thing for about 30 of us from school to all throw in a buck or two whenever we went to see Phish, and we'd buy as many bouncy balls as we could. We'd all go in with our pockets full and just throw them. More than a couple of them made it onto the stage. Also, everybody says that the first Setting Sail was at Jones Beach on 7/15/94, but when I saw it at Jones Beach, I thought to myself, "I know this song." But I couldn't place where I knew it from—I thought it was a common tune, and everybody told me, "No, that was the first time." But sure enough, I went back and checked my tapes, and if you listen to the 4/20/91 YEM, they all start doing the vocal scat, and first they're doing the jumbled lyrics, so it wasn't very clear, but by the end, they're all singing the Setting Sail poem in unison. —Mike Graff

This show began the 4/20 tradition of opening shows on this date with Runaway Jim. The tradition continued in 1993 and 1994. —Michelle Hirsch

4/21/91 [ACCESSIBILITY: ••]
SUNY Potsdam, Potsdam, NY
I: Golgi, Rocky Top, Wilson, Divided Sky, Foam, Magilla, MSO, Oh Kee, AC/DC Bag, Tela, Mike's > Hydrogen > Weekapaug, Adeline
II: Possum, Fee, Landlady, Forbin's > Mockingbird, Llama, Uncle Pen, Harry Hood, Cavern, I Didn't Know, Bowie

4/22/91 ❄
Billy's, University of Vermont, Burlington, VT

Friday, April 26, 1991

PLYMOUTH STATE COLLEGE, Plymouth, NH

I was at college in the fall of 1990, and there was a little group of us who really liked Phish. We thought, "Why don't we get them to come play here? We can do it."

So (this was something you could do back then) I called John Paluska at Dionysian Productions. We spoke over and over—we practically talked every day. He told me what I had to do and he sent me some materials in the mail to present to the student board that decided on activities. He was the nicest guy to me—he was very decent and did everything he could. He wasn't like, "well," you know, "we want all this money." Instead, he said, "Thanks for calling, and I'm glad you guys have an interest in them. We'll work up for your interest, and we hope you'll try to work up for ours."

It wasn't like you called and he put you on hold for an hour, either—he always had the time to talk to me, he was always concerned, and he always answered all of our concerns. He baby-stepped me right through the whole process of trying to put on a Phish show at our school. It wasn't a big deal, but there were certain steps that had to be taken, and he was always there, calling me back when problems arose—which, of course, they did.

The student committee was talking about bringing Meatloaf to play on campus, but then Meatloaf couldn't make it so they started talking about Joan Jett and the Blackhearts as the main show for the semester. I said, "Well, there's no reason why we can't do another show. Why can't we just have a small show, too?" (There usually was one big concert a semester, as it was a small college.) They seemed skeptical, so I said, "We can use the fieldhouse," but they said no, there were reasons why we couldn't use the fieldhouse—it was too big, and they worried it would cost more to set up.

So I said, "Why don't we use the little activities room?"—the band I played in had played in there, and they used it for smaller sorts of gigs. We petitioned the board and they said, "Okay, we'll let you do this," and I had to call and find out how much Phish wanted for the show—originally it was $3,000 and then it was $3,500. Paluska and I agreed on $3,200.

To make it work, we had to sell 200 tickets for $20 a piece. But $20 for Phish was ridiculously high back then—they played UNH around this time for $7 a ticket. But we told everybody, "If you don't do this, if you don't fork over $20, they're not going to come here." The tickets were gone within a matter of days.

So Phish ended up coming and playing toward the end of April. It never made the newsletter for two reasons: one, it was a two-hundred-ticket show—they didn't want people just showing up because it was such a tiny room. The second reason was the show was scheduled too late. They did that a lot back then—many of the shows that they played never appeared in the newsletter.

The day of the show, Fishman and Page went to a party all day on Toby Road. You see, there was this house called Toby Road which is legendary up there, a red house, the only house on the street really, and everyone used to just call it "the Toby." It was the perfect college house, full of all old hippies, and it was always the place to go to make any connections or whatever, anything—just a great place.

There were always people passing through, just staying there for a couple of days on the couch, like a little Grand Central Station. They'd have parties, and a lot of bands who played would end up there late-night or before, like this reggae band from Jamaica who played. They were there for one night and ended up staying there for two days. So Fish and Page were hanging out, enjoying the barbecue and a couple of kegs.

The show that night was just tiny. It was very loud—the room actually had good acoustics, but it was so loud that the music would hit the back wall and come right back at us as though we were attending a concert in an echo chamber.

Phish played well, though, but the show was short—they got in there and they played, nothing special. Their approach was sort of businesslike: get in here, play, get out of here, move on. It seemed like it was just another stop right in the middle of their long tour. I think they left town that night.

—Chad Garland

I: Curtain > Runaway Jim, Sloth, Reba, Poor Heart, Llama, Guelah, Oh Kee > Suzie
II: Chalkdust, Bathtub Gin, Uncle Pen, Landlady > Destiny Unbound, Squirming Coil, Stash, MSO, Lizards, Highway to Hell
E: Lawn Boy, Rocky Top
E2: Tweezer, Tweezer Reprise
Concert debut: Poor Heart.

Billy's is a typical Old Campus building in one of those four really nice buildings on the crest of the hill, if you know the UVM campus. It's a splendid building—lots of wooden floors and really nice interior and exterior architecture. Phish played in a room students used to study, not a concert hall at all. They moved all the desks and chairs out of the room for Phish, and the band set up on a one-foot riser. It was pretty crowded, maybe a few hundred people in this long, narrow room that literally was a study "hall," so the crowd (made up almost entirely of UVM students) was squashed together. It was neat to see Phish in there because what was normally this dead silent library-type building suddenly had music booming and echoing off the walls and down through the corridors.
—Charlene Smith

4/25/91 ❄
Field House, University of New Hampshire, Durham, NH

4/26/91 [ACCESSIBILITY: •]
Plymouth State College, Plymouth, NH
I: Chalkdust, Squirming Coil, Sloth, Possum, Fluffhead, Poor Heart, Foam > YEM > Llama
II: Uncle Pen, Melt, Bouncing, MSO, Guelah, Landlady, I Didn't Know, Harry Hood, Harpua
E: Donna Lee > Fire
Soundcheck: Poor Heart, Paul and Silas, Funky Bitch. Last Donna Lee, 12/29/90 New York, NY [52 shows].

4/27/91 [ACCESSIBILITY: ••••]
Capitol Theater, Port Chester, NY
I: Adeline, Asse Festival, Runaway Jim, Cavern, Landlady, MSO, Reba, Llama, Lizards, Suzie, Stash, Golgi
II: Curtain > Possum, TMWSIY > Avenu > TMWSIY, Mike's > Hydrogen > Weekapaug, Fluffhead, Tweezer, Squirming Coil, Wipeout Jam, Tweezer Reprise
E: Bouncing, GTBT
Sweet Emotion teases in Tweezer. Fishman on vacuum for Wipeout jam. Last Asse Festival (separate from Guelah), 12/8/90 Poughkeepsie, NY [55 shows].

Even though the music isn't that great in the first set, all of the songs sound happy, especially Cavern, which is usually a darker song. Fish just goes crazy on the drums during the middle jam of Suzie, and when they go back into the verse he screams his head off. In the second set, the boys turn it on! They dish out everything from Curtain > Possum, Mike's Groove, the infamous Wipeout, Tweezer, and Fluffhead as highlights. GTBT encore isn't too shabby either. This show is out there, so get it! —Charlie Gubman

This is the way to see Phish—watching them run through a set without stopping and without turning every song into a 20-minute jam. Excellent songs during what I think was one of the best eras to see the band. The extra-funky show version of Cavern is one of the best ever —Daniel Grilfand

Maybe the perfect sound quality of these DSBDs biases me, but I think this show is easily the best of the year (horn shows aside—those are a different beast). Besides the strong setlist and very good playing, there's also a Good Times Bad Times encore to make up for the previous time the band played in Port Chester and botched it.
—Ed Smith

5/2/91 [ACCESSIBILITY: •]
The Chance, Poughkeepsie, NY
I: Rocky Top, drum solo > Foam, Bouncing, Landlady, Forbin's > Mockingbird, Llama, Squirming Coil, Cavern > Bowie, Adeline
II: Chalkdust, Poor Heart, Divided Sky, Fee > Melt > Tela, MSO > I Didn't Know, Buried Alive > Possum
E: Harry Hood
Drum solo before Foam while Mike repairs a bass string. Jamie Janover on didgeridoo during Forbin's rap. Tease medley in Bowie intro.

5/3/91 [ACCESSIBILITY: ••••]
Somerville Theater, Somerville, MA
I: Bouncing, Foam, Chalkdust, TMWSIY > Avenu > TMWSIY, Divided Sky, Fee, Paul and Silas, Tweezer, Lizards, Adeline
II: AC/DC Bag, Curtain > Sloth, Landlady, Runaway Jim, Tela, YEM, Harpua, Tweezer Reprise
E: A-Train, BBFCM
Col. Bruce Hampton and the Aquarium Rescue Unit opened. Sweet Emotion vocals in Tweezer.

The two-night stand at the Somerville Theater brought lots of good times—opening sets from the always-excellent ARU and spirited playing from Phish, who obviously didn't want to be upstaged by their friends from the South. They weren't—the second set of the first night's show is Phish at their best. A strong AC/DC Bag opener leads to an inspired pairing that sends chills down my spine every time I listen to it: The Curtain's fading beats build immediately back into the opening beats of The Sloth, as though Trey always meant it to be that way. The rest of the set is packed—Tela, YEM, and Harpua. This is also one of the earliest Tweezer Reps, a nice cap on a stellar set. —Richard Kot

Trey dedicates songs to Boston Bruins' living legend Cam Neely throughout the show. The second set makes this show. During Harpua, Jimmy is watching the NHL and Cam Neely and the Bruins win the Stanley Cup. —Brian Watkins

5/4/91 [ACCESSIBILITY: ••]
Somerville Theater, Somerville, MA
I: Oh Kee > Suzie, Cavern, Reba, MSO, Melt, Guelah, Fluffhead, Mike's > Hydrogen > Weekapaug
II: Dog Log, Llama, Forbin's > Mockingbird, Buried Alive, Harry Hood, Horn, Rocky Top, Possum
E: HYHU > Terrapin > HYHU, Runaway Jim, Golgi
Col. Bruce Hampton and Aquarium Rescue Unit opened. Last Dog Log, 3/11/90 Burlington, VT [129 shows].

5/9/91 ❄
Portland Performing Arts Center, Portland, ME

Held in a very unique 200-person-capacity theater, this show was added to the spring tour with only a few days' notice. The majority of the people there didn't start dancing until the third or fourth song. Trey tells everyone how he likes to dance and Page likes to sit. They call John Paluska's younger brother Peter to the stage. To get his wallet, he requests that Phish play Moby Dick backwards (they don't do it). This is a very rare tape, with only one taper in attendance! —Nathaniel Peirce

5/10/91 [ACCESSIBILITY: •••]
Student Center, Colby College, Waterville, ME
I: Bowie, Cavern, Ya Mar, Dinner and a Movie > Sloth, Landlady, Bathtub Gin, Buried Alive, Lizards, Possum, Stash
II: Harry Hood > Wilson, Poor Heart, Foam, McGrupp > Chalkdust, Love You, Mike's > Hydrogen > Weekapaug
E: A-Train, Highway to Hell

5/11/91 [ACCESSIBILITY: •]
The Front, Burlington, VT
II: Chalkdust, YEM, Poor Heart, Reba, Oh Kee > Suzie, Tweezer Reprise
E: BBFCM
Setlist missing first set.

5/12/91 [ACCESSIBILITY: ••]
The Front, Burlington, VT
I: Chalkdust, Bouncing, Dinner and a Movie, Stash, Lizards, Landlady > Destiny Unbound, Llama, Fee, Foam, Runaway Jim
II: Bowie, Bathtub Gin, Poor Heart, Curtain > Golgi > Magilla, Mike's > Hydrogen > Weekapaug, Squirming Coil, Oh Kee > AC/DC Bag, Rocky Top
E: Antelope, Fire
David Gavidpor on horn for Magilla, AC/DC Bag, and Rocky Top. Mike's featured the Dude of Life on vocals (including ad-libbed lyrics). Final Phish show at The Front.

5/16/91 [ACCESSIBILITY: •]
The Sting, New Britain, CT
I: Buried Alive, Golgi, Foam, Cavern, Divided Sky, Forbin's > Mockingbird, Chalkdust, YEM, Magilla, Llama
II: Runaway Jim, Dinner and a Movie, Bouncing, Landlady, Squirming Coil, Tweezer, MSO, Lizards, GTBT
E: Adeline
Brian Smith on trombone for Magilla.

5/17/91 ❄ [ATTEND. 914; CAP. 1,000] [TIX $9.50]
Campus Club, Providence, RI
I: Chalkdust, drum solo > Jam, Reba, Poor Heart, Oh Kee > Suzie, TMWSIY > Avenu > TMWSIY, Stash, I Didn't Know, Mike's > Hydrogen > Weekapaug, A-Train
II: Possum, Guelah, Rocky Top, Landlady > Fluffhead, Magilla, Cavern, HYHU > Bike > HYHU, BBFCM
E: Lawn Boy, Golgi
Drum solo followed a blackout in the club. Carl Gerhard on trumpet for A-Train, Magilla, Cavern, and Lawn Boy. The band delivered a birthday cake to Page during BBFCM. Last Bike, 11/10/90 Richmond, IN [73 shows].

5/18/91 ❄ [ATTEND. 947; CAP. 947] [TIX $15]
The Marquee, New York, NY
I: Buried Alive, Golgi, Chalkdust, YEM, Paul and Silas, Foam, Divided Sky, Cavern, Possum
II: Oh Kee > Suzie, Curtain > Stash, MSO, Guelah, Bowie, HYHU > Terrapin > HYHU, Lizards
E: Dinner and a Movie, Runaway Jim

5/25/91 [ACCESSIBILITY: •]
Salisbury School, Salisbury, CT
I: Divided Sky, Landlady, Chalkdust, Bouncing, YEM, Cavern, Squirming Coil, Llama, Oh Kee > AC/DC Bag > Fee, Foam, Reba, Dinner and a Movie > Sloth, McGrupp
II: I Didn't Know, Golgi
E: Possum
Fishman on vacuum for I Didn't Know. Second set cut short by school officials.

[6/91] White Crow Studios, Burlington, VT
Recording for *A Picture of Nectar*.

7/11/91 [ACCESSIBILITY: ••••]
Battery Park, Burlington, VT
I: Oh Kee > Suzie, Divided Sky, Flat Fee, MSO, Stash, Lizards, Landlady
II: Dinner and a Movie > Cavern > TMWSIY > Avenu > TMWSIY > Mike's > Hydrogen > Weekapaug, HYHU > Touch Me > HYHU, Frankenstein
E: Contact > BBFCM
With the Giant Country Horns: Dave Grippo, alto saxophone; Russ Remington, tenor saxophone; and Carl Gerhard, trumpet (the same lineup present at all shows this month). Concert debut: Touch Me.

Battery Park overlooks Lake Champlain on the west side of Burlington. It's a little outdoor park, and from time to time different bands played there, all for free. Phish's show there was in the daytime, with the Giant Country Horns, who they were playing with for one of the first times. I remember the Giant Country Horns were part of it, because that was something new, so we were all like, "Wow, fancy." There were a lot more people at this show, probably because it was summer and lots of people were visiting Burlington. It also seemed like there was a greater variety of people there—it wasn't just UVM students. It was a wider age range, including some curiosity seekers—people walking down the street who thought, "Hey what's going on over here?" It was definitely a signal to us that Phish was growing in terms of their audience. I think there were 400 or 500 people at the show. —Charlene Smith

Vermont rules! Battery Park is beautiful. It looks out across Lake Champlain, giving a great view of the Adirondacks. The Giant Country Horns added to the musical intensity of this hot show. Touch Me was both funny and entertaining—I still get Fishman's rendition in my head whenever I hear Jim Morrison crooning this classic on the radio. —Dan Kurtz

"A few hometown boys who made good," shouts an anonymous emcee. I'd say! This is a great tape. Oh Kee Pa > Suzie as an opener—they were made for each other! Flat Fee is a musical treat, horns and all. Landlady is tight, but the best is yet to come: a phat TMWSIY followed by one helluva Mike's Groove. And what better way to end a set than with Fishman doing his best Jim Morrison? —Carrie A. Johnson

7/12/91 [ACCESSIBILITY: ••••] [ATTEND. 850; CAP. 850] [TIX $12.50]
Colonial Theater, Keene, NH
I: Dinner and a Movie > Bouncing, Buried Alive, Flat Fee, Reba, Landlady, Bathtub Gin, Donna Lee, AC/DC Bag, Rocky Top, Cavern, Bowie
II: Golgi, Squirming Coil, Moose the Mootche, Tweezer > MSO, Gumbo > Mike's > Hydrogen > Weekapaug, HYHU > Touch Me > HYHU, Oh Kee > Suzie
E: Adeline, Frankenstein, Fee, Tweezer Reprise
With The Giant Country Horns. Concert debut: Moose the Mootche.

It must have been a hot night in Keene because before the set, Trey jokes about the availability of space heaters for those who want them. The set starts off in standard fashion with Golgi and Coil before the horns come out for Moose the Mootche, a great jazz song that Trey basically controls. The opening notes of Tweezer follow the closing of Moose, and absolute chaos breaks loose after the Uncle Ebeneezer verse with Phish and the horns combining in a wild, noisy free-for-all. The encore is a generous four songs, but listen to the crowd during Adeline—I'm not sure I've heard one louder. —Ed Smith

7/13/91 [ACCESSIBILITY: ••••]
Berkshire Performing Arts Center, Lenox, MA
I: Curtain > Runaway Jim, Foam, Llama, Oh Kee > Suzie, Alumni, TMWSIY > Avenu > TMWSIY, Melt, Bouncing, Frankenstein
II: Chalkdust, Guelah, Divided Sky, Flat Fee, Paul and Silas, Lizards, Stash, HYHU > Brain > HYHU, YEM
E: Landlady
With The Giant Country Horns.

7/14/91 [ACCESSIBILITY: ••••] [ATTEND. 1,735; CAP. 2,000] [TIX $12]
Townshend Family Park, Townshend, VT
I: Reba, Llama, Squirming Coil, Golgi, Guelah, MSO, Forbin's > Mockingbird, Sloth, I Didn't Know, Possum
II: Suzie, Caravan, Divided Sky, Gumbo, Dinner and a Movie, Bouncing, Melt, Magilla, Cavern, Antelope
III: AC/DC Bag, Landlady, Esther, Chalkdust, Bathtub Gin, Mike's > Hydrogen > Weekapaug, HYHU > Touch Me > HYHU, Harry Hood
E: Contact, BBFCM
With The Giant Country Horns. Jeopardy tease in Harry Hood. Last Caravan, 2.15/91 Keene, NH [59 shows].

Phish's last show at Townshend Family Park ended a glorious tradition that began in August 1989. For this grand event, Mother Nature treated us to a beautiful afternoon in the cradle of civilization and Phish provided the soundtrack. Horns and Phish—what bliss! Though Trey promised us at the end of the day that Phish would return to Townshend next year, fate had other plans in store for Vermont's Phinest. I'm glad I have my memories. —Ernie Greene

Townshend was another great show with the GCH. It has my favorite Antelope ("Hola mijetes, como estas?" is so funny). Then, in AC/DC Bag, Trey sounds like he's laughing during the "if you've got the time, I've got the inclination" line. Mike's Song is also really strong, and of course Touch Me is cool. After Weekapaug, Trey tells the crowd that Fish has gone to take a leak, and they stretch things out a bit while waiting for him to get back. There's also a taste of the Jeopardy Theme after Hood. —Chrissy Schneider

7/15/91 [ACCESSIBILITY: ••••] [ATTEND. 631; CAP. 1,000] [TIX $15]
The Academy, New York, NY
Oh Kee > Suzie, Landlady, Dinner and a Movie, Stash, Bouncing, Mike's > Hydrogen > Weekapaug, Flat Fee, Lizards, Cavern, Squirming Coil, Frankenstein
E: Caravan, Contact, Alumni
With The Giant Country Horns. The Ellen James Society and Yothu Yindi played before Phish. Phish played one set.

A great show—well, how could any show with the GCH be bad? The horns add a great sound to the best Lizards I have ever heard, and they're also an excellent addition to

TOWNSHEND FAMILY PARK, Townshend, VT

Saturday, July 14, 1991

My wife Charlene (who was my girlfriend back in '91) and I were driving up from Connecticut to see Phish, and all we knew was that they were playing at a place called Townshend State Park. So we got the map out, found the exit, and finally figured out where to park the car. (We had our dogs with us, too.)

Photo courtesy of Alison Offerman

When we got out of our car, we could see the band across a river—they had just started to play but we couldn't figure out how to get into this place. There were no signs. So we just waded across the river, lifted up a fishnet and just walked in. And there we were, standing with two hundred other people, jamming out with Phish.

We didn't pay a dime.

Nobody busted us. I saw that people had bracelets on, but we weren't worried about it because if somebody had come up and said, "Where's your bracelet?" I would have said, "Man, I'll be happy to give you fifteen—or whatever it was, seven bucks—but I couldn't find out how to get into this damn place. So I just walked across the river, man."

Photo courtesy of Alison Offerman

They had the Giant Country Horns there, and, if I recall correctly, it was somebody's birthday and they brought a cake out on stage with boobs on it. If my memory doesn't fail me, Trey played some of that set with an imitation breast plate on his chest. It was a great show. What made that show so special was the Giant Country Horns, and the fact that this was a joint effort.

We knew it was a joint effort when, at the beginning of the show, Trey said, "Hey, this is going to be a great show, we've got a lot of things planned, so everybody get settled in." We were all in it together, and it was a very intimate experience to have a band care so much about how much fun we were having.

—Patrick Smith

Photo courtesy of Alison Offerman

Frankenstein. Trey forgets the lines in the middle of Cavern and asks the crowd, "Does anyone know the words to this next part, 'cause I surely don't." This is a classic one-set show that all Phish fans should have. —Chris Black

Halfway through Oh Kee Pa, Trey announces: "Ladies and gentlemen, the Giant Country Horns," and we're on our way. An immediate segue into Suzie sustains the momentum. After a very technical Mike's Groove, Trey introduces the Horns. About 1:30 into Cavern, Trey stops rather suddenly and asks the audience for the lyrics. Someone reminds him and they finish the song without another glitch. As an encore, Caravan features powerful horns and Contact always enlightens with intrinsic intimacy. —Anthony Buchla

7/18/91 ❄ **[Attend. 1,061; Cap. 1,600] [TIX $12.50-$14.50]**
Casino Ballroom, Hampton Beach, NH
I: Chalkdust, Foam, Runaway Jim, Guelah, Suzie, Stash, A-Train, Cavern, Mike's > Hydrogen > Weekapaug
II: Llama, Reba, Poor Heart, Melt, Lizards, Landlady, I Didn't Know, Possum
With The Giant Country Horns.

7/19/91 [Accessibility: •••] [Attend. 873; Cap. 873] [TIX $12.50]
Somerville Theater, Somerville, MA
I: Golgi, Landlady, Bouncing, Bowie, Fee, Cavern, Squirming Coil, YEM, Gumbo, HYHU > Touch Me
II: Suzie, Divided Sky, I Didn't Know, MSO, Magilla, Tweezer, Mango, BBFCM
E: Lawn Boy, Runaway Jim
With The Giant Country Horns. Jeopardy tease in Bowie. Frankenstein tease in YEM. Runaway Jim sung as "Runaway Yim" for a fan whose birthday was on this day. Mimi Fishman on vacuum for I Didn't Know. Esther video produced by CoSA (including Phishhead John Greene) screened between sets.

This whole tour was cool. The Somerville Theater show was the first time with Mimi Fishman. I remember seeing her in the little parking lot after the show, yelling at people for playing the Grateful Dead. She said something like, "What are you playing the Grateful Dead for? Put on Phish!" because people were playing the Grateful Dead out of the back of their cars. Then, after leaving the parking lot, I took off for home in Vermont, heading up the Mass Pike. I stopped to grab a soda at the Burger King rest stop, and the next thing I know, I'm in line in between the horns—Grippo and so on—and Trey. I told Trey, "Good show," and I told the horn guys, "Good show." It came Trey's turn to order and the Burger King employee asked Trey what he wanted. In a low voice, he said, "A fish sandwich." She didn't hear him, so she said, "What?" "A fish sandwich." Again she said, "What?" Then Trey said, "A fish sandwich!" in a real loud voice, and she grabbed hold of the Burger King microphone and yelled, "Fish sandwich!" and all of us started cracking up. It was really funny because no one in there had any idea what we were all laughing at. Trey just shook his head. —Brendan McKenna

7/20/91 [Accessibility: ••]
Arrowhead Ranch, Parksville, NY
I: Chalkdust, Foam, Squirming Coil, Llama, Oh Kee > Suzie, Landlady, Bathtub Gin, MSO, Bowie
II: Buried Alive, Reba, Caravan, Dinner and a Movie, Flat Fee, Golgi, Stash, TMWSIY > Avenu > TMWSIY, YEM, Rocky Top
E: Possum
With The Giant Country Horns. Phish shared the bill with Spin Doctors and The Authority.

7/21/91 [Accessibility: •••••]
Arrowhead Ranch, Parksville, NY
I: Cavern, Divided Sky, Guelah, Poor Heart, Melt, Lizards, Landlady, Bouncing, Mike's > Hydrogen > Weekapaug
II: Tweezer, I Didn't Know, Runaway Jim, Lawn Boy, Sloth, Esther, AC/DC Bag, Contact > Tweezer Reprise
E: Gumbo, Touch Me
E2: Fee, Suzie
With The Giant Country Horns. Phish shared the bill with the Radiators and TR3. Fishman on vacuum for I Didn't Know and trombone for the end of Gumbo. Steve "Steve-O" Nelson on washboard for encores. Bonanza jam in Weekapaug.

I know, this show has been reviewed and praised so many times, but there's a reason. Set II of this show is possibly the best set with the GCH. "Gumbo, you guys remember that one?" From the sound of it, everyone on stage sure did. This show gets my vote for best Gumbo and Lawn Boy. —Justin Weiss

"Arrowhead"

7/20 & 21/91 Arrowhead Ranch, Parksville, NY

The summer of 1991 will long be remembered as the only all-out tour Phish ever did with The Giant Country Horns. And perhaps the highlight of that run was a two-night stand at Arrowhead Ranch. Without a doubt, it was the most historic.

At the time, Arrowhead served as a sort of summer getaway for the crunchy crowd—a vacation spot for those whose idea of a vacation was listening to great music and enjoying various pleasures of nature. Arrowhead owners Kenny and Michele Hoff started promoting concerts at the Ranch in the summer of 1990, hosting gigs by Hot Tuna, Max Creek and the New Riders of the Purple Sage.

The site drew the attention of legendary San Francisco promoter Bill Graham, who checked out Arrowhead and was so impressed that he told the Hoffs, "I want to create the Fillmore of the Catskills at Arrowhead." He took a stake in the venture. Graham's son, David, graduated from Columbia University in the spring of '91, and Bill put him in charge of promoting shows at Arrowhead.

The Arrowhead shows were, in part, orchestrated to capture and celebrate an emerging music scene which included bands like Blues Traveler (which had released just one album to date, a moderate success), Spin Doctors (still mostly unknown outside the club circuit), Widespread Panic (barely on the radar screen up North) and The Authority (a New York funk band which never achieved the level of success of its then-peers).

David—along with a group of his Columbia friends who were helping out—decided to host the Ranch's first small-scale festival of the summer, which was to include on-site camping and even horseback riding for those who dared, on the weekend of July 20 and 21. They faced a tough choice of which bands to book: Phish and Spin Doctors, or Bob Dylan and the Band. All of the groups were willing, but the youthful promoters picked the youthful bands, and the rest is history.

While Phish had played other outdoor gigs with nearby camping before, Arrowhead marked the first shows which seemed to tap into a crowd outside of the Vermont hardcores. About 1,000 to 1,500 fans—many of whom were seeing Phish for the first time—made it up to Arrowhead for the weekend. When, at the end of two days of great music, Trey made an announcement on stage about the upcoming Amy's Farm show to be held two weeks later, many instantly decided to make the trek to Maine. Phishheads were being born in every corner.

The Arrowhead shows themselves have stood the test of time as great performances. Though it may not be Phish's best pure-musical performance of the horn tour, it sounds unquestionably like the most fun. The weekend also featured one of the largest crowds, at the time, which Fishman had ever exposed himself to. That record has since been eclipsed, at a Halloween gig a little farther north in New York State.

Despite the promoters' foresight in booking Phish and the SD's, advance ticket sales were poor for the weekend and throughout the summer. In August, the promoters canceled a Little Feat concert, and eventually, Arrowhead closed down. The memories remain.

The horns at this show were the added touch it needed. —Hollis Rowan

A truly classic show. The first set is highlighted by an excellent Divided Sky featuring the horns, and the closing Mike's > Hydrogen > Weekapaug, which also benefited from the new sounds created by the GCH. The second set offers an interesting Tweezer and Lawn Boy. Contact > Tweezer Reprise is very good musically and is a great jam. The encores were unusual, too—a special guest showcased his skills on washboard. —Jay Green

You gotta love "Steve-O" from New Orleans on washboard, or "whatever the hell you call that thing," as Trey puts it. The encores of this show just rock!—Rich Mazer

Everyone has their own concept of Eden. For me, it's the Divided Sky that Phish played at Arrowhead ranch. There have been versions that peaked harder, or went on longer, but none that I have heard has soared to the same spiritual heights. The horns give the song a certain mythic texture, as though all that was "yes" in the universe came together that afternoon in Parksville. Listening to it now, I feel at peace with myself and the world. —Melissa Wolcott

7/23/91 [ACCESSIBILITY: ••]
The Bayou, Washington, DC
I: Chalkdust, Foam, Squirming Coil, MSO > Oh Kee > Suzie, Stash, Flat Fee, Bouncing, Mike's > Hydrogen > Weekapaug
II: Llama, Reba, Cavern, Lizards, Landlady > Tweezer, Adeline, Dinner and a Movie, Gumbo, HYHU > Touch Me
E: Caravan, Golgi
With The Giant Country Horns.

7/24/91 [ACCESSIBILITY: •••]
Trax, Charlottesville, VA
I: Golgi, Chalkdust, Squirming Coil > Buried Alive, Melt, Bathtub Gin, Landlady, Cavern, Tela, YEM
II: Possum, Guelah, Bowie, Jesus Left Chicago, MSO, Bouncing, Funky Bitch, I Didn't Know, Frankenstein, Suzie
E: Contact, BBFCM
With The Giant Country Horns. Fishman on vacuum for I Didn't Know. "I Love Lucy" jam in BBFCM.

7/25/91 [ACCESSIBILITY: •]
Cat's Cradle, Chapel Hill, NC
I: MSO, Sloth > Foam, Suzie, Divided Sky, Flat Fee, AC/DC Bag, Adeline, Cavern, Antelope
II: Landlady, Golgi, Squirming Coil, Llama, Poor Heart, Jesus Left Chicago, Lizards, Gumbo, HYHU > Touch Me > HYHU, Magilla, Mike's > Hydrogen > Weekapaug
E: Melt
With The Giant Country Horns.

7/26/91 [ACCESSIBILITY: ••]
Georgia Theater, Athens, GA
I: Chalkdust, Reba, MSO, Foam, Suzie, Cavern, TMWSIY > Avenu > TMWSIY, Buried Alive > Bouncing, Landlady, Golgi
II: Stash, Dinner and a Movie > YEM, Flat Fee > Funky Bitch, Squirming Coil, Tweezer, Adeline, Lizards, Happy Birthday jam, Tweezer Reprise
E: Lawn Boy, Frankenstein, Melt
With The Giant Country Horns. Happy Birthday jam (with horns) played for Chris Kuroda's 26th birthday.

It's really no surprise that the last few shows on the horns tour proved to be the best ones musically—after all, it took these guys a little while to find each other's grooves. But when they did, well, the results are something to see (or at least hear)! During the last two-set show of the GCH tour, the rapport between The Truth, Gears and Russell, and Phish is outstanding. Listen to their interplay in the second set, especially on Stash, Tweezer, and Melt. (Audience recordings of this show also reveal some poor soul screaming all night for Split Open and Melt. He finally got his wish.) —Andre Holton

7/27/91 [ACCESSIBILITY: •]
Variety Playhouse, Atlanta, GA
Llama, Foam, Oh Kee > Suzie, Cavern, Poor Heart, Stash, TMWSIY > Avenu > TMWSIY, Possum, I Didn't Know, Landlady, Mike's > Hydrogen > Weekapaug
E: Touch Me, Contact
With The Giant Country Horns. Phish shared the bill with Col. Bruce Hampton and the Aquarium Rescue Unit and played one set.

[8/91] White Crow Studios, Burlington, VT
Recording and mixing of *A Picture of Nectar*.

8/3/91 [ACCESSIBILITY: ••••]
Larabee (Amy Skelton's) Farm, Auburn, ME
I: Wilson, Foam, Runaway Jim, Guelah, Llama, Fee, Squirming Coil, Poor Heart, Sloth, Divided Sky, Golgi
II: Curtain, Reba, Chalkdust, Bouncing, Tweezer, Esther, Cavern, I Didn't Know, YEM, Rocky Top
III: Stash, Ya Mar, Fluffhead, Lawn Boy, MSO, Lizards, Buried Alive > Possum
E: Magilla, Self, She's Bitchin Again, Crimes of the Mind
E2: Harry Hood
Free outdoor concert. Jamie Janover on didgeridoo for Buried Alive. Self, She's Bitching Again, and Crimes of the Mind featured the Dude of Life on vocals. She's Bitching and Crimes featured Sofi Dillof on vocals. Concert debuts: She's Bitching Again, Crimes of the Mind. Fishman on vacuum for I Didn't Know. I Love Lucy jam in YEM and other places throughout the show.

This event sounded like a blast—camping and partying and a huge offering of tunes (three sets and five encore tunes!). They really changed pace a lot and switched up all the selections to create peaks and valleys of music. I usually don't much care for Dude of Life contributions, but this show was different. Listening to this show reminds me how down to earth and cool the band is. —Dave Matson

YEM, Ya Mar, Fluffhead, Lizards, Buried Alive > Possum, and Harry Hood? Are they trying to give me a heart attack? This show isn't musically perfect—they never really "got it right"—but it's a great one nevertheless. I love this tape. —Ron Lauer

Amy had her cowboy hat on—the whole nine yards. She was very, very visible throughout the whole thing, making announcements and jumping up and down on one of the trampolines. —Brendan McKenna

Amy's Farm is a show where every set is great. —Kevin M. Ward

This show includes a lot of incredible music. Sets I and II had standouts such as Llama, Fee, Curtain, YEM, and Divided Sky, but the highlight for me is Stash. Trey holds a single note longer than I've ever heard—I thought a smoke detector in my house was going off when I first played this tape. Check it out! —Michael Rambo

[8-9/91] White Crow Studios, Burlington, VT
Recording *Crimes of the Mind* with the Dude of Life.

9/25/91 [ACCESSIBILITY: •]
Colonial Theater, Keene, NH
I: Brother, Poor Heart > Foam, Llama, Tela > MSO, It's Ice, Landlady > Caravan > Reba > Possum
II: Squirming Coil, Stash, Sparkle, Cavern, Jesus Left Chicago, Runaway Jim, YEM, Chalkdust
E: All Things, BBFCM
Concert debuts: Brother, It's Ice, Sparkle, and All Things. Carl Gerhard on trumpet for Cavern and Jesus Left Chicago.

As was becoming the norm, the tour opener contained a bunch of new song debuts. The most difficult proved to be All Things Reconsidered, which the band didn't play again until spring 1992 because they weren't yet up to its technical demands. —Pat Stanley

This show marked the start of a very strong fall tour for Phish, the first tour that saw the level of musical innovation still present today. A lot of people overlook fall 1991 tapes, for no apparent reason, but you owe it to yourself to check a few out. —Ed Smith

9/26/91 [ACCESSIBILITY: •]
State Theater, Ithaca, NY
I: Llama, Bouncing, Divided Sky, Fee, It's Ice, MSO, Guelah, Lizards, Foam, Bowie
II: Golgi, Squirming Coil, Brother, Sparkle, Landlady > Destiny Unbound > Mike's > Hydrogen > Weekapaug, Lawn Boy, Chalkdust
E: Memories, Poor Heart, Adeline
"Dr. Seuss" sung as lyrics in Bowie.

There are really good tapes of this supposedly rare show circulating around Maine and New York. I'm doing my best to make sure everyone I trade with gets a copy of it . . . the Landlady > Destiny > Mike's > . . . is SO GOOD! —David Schall

At the State Theater show, they played the Dr. Seuss David Bowie, two days after Dr. Seuss had died. They sang, "Dr. Seuss" instead of "David Bowie." That was 9/26/91, and I think Dr. Seuss died 9/24/91 or 9/25/91. It was a great show. —Mike Graff

9/27/91 ❄
The Warehouse, Rochester, NY
I: Runaway Jim, Cavern, Reba, Buried Alive, Esther, Tweezer, Paul and Silas, It's Ice, I Didn't Know
II: Possum, Tela, Sparkle, Melt, Mango, Dinner and a Movie, Oh Kee > Suzie, YEM, Tweezer Reprise
E: Glide, Rocky Top
Concert debut: Glide. Setlist for first set may be incomplete.

8/3/91 Larabee Farm, Auburn, ME

"Amy's Farm"

It was only a postcard, but when it landed in the mailboxes of the thousands of people then on the Phish mailing list, its impact was most profound. A note from Trey, Mike, Page, and Fish said that as the band approached its eighth anniversary, they realized "it would be great to throw a party to thank everyone for all the good times." With that, the postcard went on to invite everyone to a free Phish concert in Auburn, ME, at the beginning of August.

The site? Larabee Farm, a 255-acre horse ranch owned by Amy Skelton, the acclaimed first fan who played a major role in helping Phish establish a New Hampshire fan base in the late 1980s when they were still mostly unknown outside of the Burlington, VT, area. The band had scouted the farm the previous fall—on horseback, no less, with Trey riding the famous Maggie, who would later be hoisted to appear on the cover of *Hoist*—and decided they'd found the perfect place to host a giant party.

Photo courtesy of Jong Chan Cho.

Word of the event spread fast. A makeshift map on the back of the postcard served as the directions, luring people from across the country. One fan, Henry Petras, traveled coast-to-coast for the event, a fact the band acknowledged at one of their first fall shows when they presented him an award for "the longest distanced traveled to attend a Phish show." About 2,000 fans (the most popular estimate) found their way that weekend to an open field, where Phish set up a makeshift stage on the back of a truck.

There were rules, of course, but they weren't tough to abide by—no campfires were allowed because it had been a dry summer in Maine, and everyone was asked to pick up after themselves. Beyond that, as Trey said at the end of the first set, "Go wild, because nobody's going to stop you here."

It seems that everyone who attended the Amy's Farm show returned with as much excitement about the scene as about the music. While no one complained about Phish's three-set marathon, along with a six-song encore with the Dude of Life, what stood out in most people's memories was the mellow but anything-goes atmosphere that pervaded the free event.

"There were literally naked women with bongs," remembers Jamie Janover, who played the didgeridoo during "Buried Alive" at Amy's Farm. "There was a woman absolutely naked holding a three-foot Grafix. And I was like, 'This is the ultimate.'"

There were lots of stories that would make Pat Robertson or Jerry Falwell cringe—public fornication, mind-altering substances—but lots more that would renew any cynic's faith in society. A schoolbus unloaded a pack of campers, brought by a pretty hip camp counselor. A true communal atmosphere, where people cleaned up after themselves and took care of each other in 100-degree heat, developed. As Trey remarked at the end of three long sets of music, "Have a good time tonight—we're going to be out there partying with you." It was one long raging party, which turned strangers into friends and for some marked the start of the real Phish explosion on the East Coast.

Behind a couple of Ryder trucks, an even more intense party raged in what was considered the "backstage area." Trey rode around on a Harley-Davidson. A gaggle of the band's friends were in attendance.

Photo courtesy of Jong Chan Cho.

For many, the highlight of the show was when Fishman appeared in the famed "Zero Man" outfit, the superhero getup that hadn't made an appearance in about a year and hasn't made it out since. There were also onstage collaborations with the Dude of Life, Sofi Dillof (then Page's girlfriend, now his wife, who claimed the role of the female singer on the Dude's classic "She's Bitching Again"), and Janover.

Although many fans would pay virtually anything to have shared in the Amy's Farm experience, many commented that not having to spend a cent to get in only added to the atmosphere.

"People don't realize, but when you take money out of a situation, it does beautiful things to people, and I never realized it till that day," comments fan Chad Garland. "There's no ticket, there's no 'I can't get in,' there's no 'I need a miracle,' none of that garbage. Everyone up there, the first thing you hear is 'Well, it's free!' It really brings the people together instead of putting them apart, so people were like 'Here, here,' because Phish was being so generous, it really trickled down."

Like so many of the stages and settings where Phish history was made, Amy's Farm is a place where the band will most likely never perform again (at least not in a concert open to the general public). And never again will an event of its intimate nature be possible. Still, the communal spirit of Amy's Farm unquestionably informed the later-year giant gatherings the Clifford Ball and the Great Went—events that have changed the very idea of what a rock concert can be.

While the Amy's Farm show is a popular and heavily circulated set of tapes, the band had certainly achieved grander musical heights before, and have since.

But the feelings of communality the show generated may never be equaled again, and that is why the Amy's Farm show holds what is perhaps an unrivaled spot in Phish folklore.

August 3, 1991

AMY'S FARM, Auburn, ME

We heard there was going to be a free Phish show, one celebrating their eighth anniversary, so my best buddy, Chris, and I decided to drive up to Maine from New Jersey. There were seven of us crammed into my little truck: I was driving, with Lou and Mikey in the front seat (Lou had just had a hernia operation and couldn't climb in the back of my covered pickup) and Chris, Master Chan, Brian, and Peter in the back. We set out at night and entered Maine with a glorious pastel sunrise—very tired but excited that Phish was so near. "Foouhledduh . . ." I exclaimed, too tired to know what I was saying, but sure it was something worthwhile.

We found Amy's Farm and drove across the huge field to park among the other heads. The dollar we paid went, I think, toward reseeding the field after Phish was done and gone.

What a glorious summer day! The perfect day for an outdoor show, with blue sky overhead, birds flying, the smell of fresh air, and the scent of fresh herb being smoked somewhere close by.

Everyone in our group went their separate ways for a while before the show. I tried to sleep and couldn't, while Chris and Mikey took a walk up the road to an old barn and walked in on Mike Gordon and a friend hanging out. I remember standing on the other side of the trees that separated the concert area from the camping area and listening to the soundcheck. Phish did a killer "Poor Heart." The buzz was on and the show was about to start!

The next eight hours or so were a frenzied, festive blur, but I remember the highlights. During the first set, we were all flying high, in the groove. The music was spectacular and I wasn't able to stop dancing. I danced until sweat was pouring down my body. A girl at the front of the stage stripped down and had everyone cheering and hollering. The sun was very hot and this very large guy was sweating so much as he danced that he was spraying everyone around him. It was music to dream by, and we were dreaming hard.

First set ended and I was lost all of a sudden. The band had hired a huge water truck to spray the crowd, and I wandered over to get hit by a cold wall of water being sprayed from the hoses.

So the band started again, and again I danced. I couldn't stop dancing around in circles and staring up at the sky, which had started to take on other colors than blue and was spinning in a curious bowl shape. But the music held me on, as weird as it got (and you know how it gets)—the band held my screaming soul and whipped it round and round. Trey's wailing stretched me up to the sky and just when I thought it was going too far, there was Mike or Page or Fish to anchor me again before doing it all over again. I found a sweaty, smelly piece of rainbow fabric and started dancing with it. I was reduced to my essence, no thought, just movement and music, sweat and sun. Then the second set break came.

I was feeling pretty spent at this point and I found my friends again. Chan and Peter and Brian and I exchanged knowing glances. We had been scoured clean by the music together. I grabbed my sketchbook from our stuff and sat on the side of the stage in the shade and "jammed out" with my pencil for the third set, the highlight being the Dude of Life coming out at the end. A couple of girls walked by and we talked for a bit about art. Needless to say it was a very interesting, though not very memorable, conversation.

So the show ended after something like six hours and some people drifted away, but a lot of people just hung out in this field to watch the sun set. I got a chance to talk to Trey while he was hanging around his motorcycle. I showed him some of my artwork, and he liked it. We just talked about music and art and the show. We were both just beaming and shook hands. At this point I pretty much couldn't even move, I was so exhausted, so I just lay down in the middle of the field and watched all the stars come out. I phased out for a while and woke in complete darkness except for the incredible starry display in the sky. It was magnificent. I was speechless and in utter peace watching the Milky Way, and satellites going past.

Then I heard a strange noise, like metal on metal, and I heard voices whispering to be quiet. It was so dark I couldn't see anything, but I was scared to move. There were a few different sets of voices and they were coming from near where the makeshift sound booth was during the show. They couldn't pry the lock off. They were breaking in! Uncool.

I didn't know what to do. I thought that if they knew I was there they would beat me up or something. So I started snoring. Really loud. Then pretended like I was just waking up. They got quiet and still. So I stood up and shuffled away, mumbling to myself. I found my way back to the campground and walked down the street to the house, where a party was going on and "guards" were at the door. I told them the deal. One guy looked like he didn't believe me and just blew me off. But a really nice lady there thanked me and offered me a drink. I could barely form words at this point so I said no and just walked out. I never found out what happened, if anything.

As I was walking back down the road, I saw Trey again. He was on his motorcycle in the parking lot, riding it around in circles, screaming really loudly, until he kind of toppled over. He stood up laughing and got back on again. I just kept walking back to the car and crashed in the back. I remember being really grouchy as we tried to load up in the middle of the night and head down to Arrowhead Ranch for a different show there the next night.

It is truly one of my best memories that I have of that time period. Phish holds a special place in my life that my friends and I share and continue to make memories with.

—Mike Ricci

Photo courtesy of Jong Chan Cho.

At the Warehouse in Rochester, during YEM, was the first time they started doing Homer Simpson's "D'oh!" During YEM, Trey started going "D'oh!" and then everybody joined in and they did an entire scat of them all going "D'oh!" "D'oh!" "D'oh!" They all really go off, all four of them trying to imitate Homer as best they could! I remember it as Phish's first "D'oh!" encounter. It was shortly after that—somewhere in the Midwest, I guess—that they developed their little "D'oh!" cue. Phish's show at the Warehouse was also the last show by any band there. The Warehouse changed ownership after that show; we were hanging out with the new owner at that show, and that was what pretty much made him want to buy the place when he saw how raging it was. But that may have been the high point of that place's history—they've changed its name a couple times since. The place had a low ceiling, it was like somebody had taken an antique shop or and old junk shop and glued it to the ceiling, there were hanging bathtubs and naked mannequins in cowboy boots hanging out of them, just inches above everybody's head. Once the new owner bought the place, he cleared all that out—I bet it was a fire hazard. But at the time of the Phish show there, the entire ceiling was covered with lamps and bikes and old machinery. —Mike Graff

9/28/91 [ACCESSIBILITY: •]
The Rink, Buffalo, NY

I: Landlady > Bouncing, Chalkdust, Squirming Coil, MSO, Stash, Foam, Brother, Golgi, Memories
II: Llama, Guelah, Sparkle, Cavern, Antelope, Lawn Boy, Lizards, Poor Heart, Mike's > Hydrogen > Weekapaug
E: Contact, BBFCM

Before Llama, Phish presented an award to fan Henry Petras for flying 3,000 miles to catch the Amy's Farm show—the longest distance then traveled to catch a Phish show. Trey solos through the crowd on rollerblades for Weekapaug. "I Love Lucy" tease in BBFCM.

When the band finished the song I Am Hydrogen, Trey took to his hockey roots and put on in-line skates and a wireless guitar. The song shifted into Weekapaug Groove and he skated into the crowd on his skates, jamming as he went. He took a solo and skated around the rink, inciting us all. —Melissa Mixer

9/29/91 ❄
Agora Theater-Bar, Cleveland, OH
Cavern, Divided Sky, I Didn't Know, It's Ice, Poor Heart, Landlady >YEM, Oh Kee >Suzie

Phish played one set.

This show wasn't actually at the Agora Theater—it was at the Agora theater-bar, the bar right across from the theater. The next time they played Cleveland was the first time they played the Agora Theater, on 5/7/92. It's actually the same building—the theater is on the right, and there's a little bar where bands can also play on the left. That's where Phish was this time. It was just a one-set show. —Mike Graff

10/2/91 ❄
The Cubby Bear, Chicago, IL
I: Llama, Foam, Squirming Coil, Poor Heart, Cavern, Reba, Brother > Bouncing, Chalkdust, Golgi
II: Landlady, YEM, MSO, Guelah, Runaway Jim, Lawn Boy, Stash, Oh Kee > Suzie
E: Possum, I Didn't Know, Rocky Top

10/3/91 [ACCESSIBILITY: •]
Mabel's, Champaign, IL
I: Chalkdust, Foam, Uncle Pen, It's Ice, Bouncing, Llama, Fee > Divided Sky, Cavern, Possum
II: Paul and Silas, Mike's > Hydrogen > Weekapaug, Esther, Landlady > Destiny Unbound, Buried Alive > Squirming Coil > Tweezer, Memories
E: HYHU > Terrapin > HYHU, Tweezer Reprise

10/4/91 [ACCESSIBILITY: •]
Barrymore Theater, Madison, WI
I: Memories, Chalkdust, Reba, Poor Heart, Cavern, Divided Sky, Guelah, Sparkle, Suzie, Magilla, Bowie
II: MSO, Brother, Bouncing, Foam, Runaway Jim, Lawn Boy, Stash, Squirming Coil, Mike's > Hydrogen > Weekapaug
E: Adeline, Golgi, Rocky Top, HYHU > Love You > HYHU, Llama

"Linus and Lucy" jam in Squirming Coil piano solo.

10/5/91 ❄
The Cabooze, Minneapolis, MN

10/6/91 ❄
Student Union, Macalester College, St. Paul, MN
I: Suzie, Foam, Divided Sky, Bouncing, Poor Heart, Oh Kee > AC/DC Bag, TMWSIY > Avenu, Brother, HYHU > Terrapin > HYHU, Golgi
II: MSO, Stash, Fee, Landlady > Destiny Unbound, Harry Hood, I Didn't Know, Cavern, Squirming Coil, Rocky Top
E: Adeline, Possum, Llama

Adeline performed from the balcony.

10/10/91 [ACCESSIBILITY: ••] [ATTEND. 903; CAP. 1,000] [TIX $10-$12]
EMU Ballroom, University of Oregon, Eugene, OR
I: Chalkdust, Foam, Paul and Silas, Melt, Bouncing, Landlady, Runaway Jim, It's Ice, Llama, Golgi, Alumni, Lizards
II: Brother, Reba, Poor Heart, Cavern, Antelope, I Didn't Know, Sparkle, Oh Kee > Suzie, Fee > Mike's > Hydrogen > Weekapaug
E: Squirming Coil, Fire

10/11/91 ❄ [ATTEND. 534; CAP. 534] [TIX $7.50-$10]
The Backstage, Seattle, WA
I: Landlady, MSO, Guelah, Chalkdust, YEM, Lizards, Llama, Bouncing, Runaway Jim
II: Curtain > Cavern, Foam, Bowie, Mango, Sloth, Poor Heart, Magilla, Possum
E: Adeline, BBFCM

Artis the Spoonman opened. Setlist for first set may be incomplete.

10/12/91 ❄ [ATTEND. 985; CAP. 1,120] [TIX $9-$11]
Roseland Theater, Portland, OR

Artis the Spoonman opened and played with Phish during the second set.

10/13/91 [ACCESSIBILITY: ••••] [ATTEND. 500; CAP. 500] [TIX $7.50-$10]
North Shore Surf Club, Olympia, WA
I: Runaway Jim, Wilson, Reba, Landlady, Forbin's > Mockingbird > Tela > AC/DC Bag > Sloth > McGrupp, Mike's > Hydrogen > Weekapaug
II: Llama, Bathtub Gin, Squirming Coil, It's Ice, MSO, Jesus Left Chicago, Bouncing, HYHU > Love You > HYHU, Bowie
E: Eliza, Uncle Pen
E2: Carolina

Artis the Spoonman opened. The first set features an almost complete Gamehendge saga, with narration by Trey, the second time ever performed live. Fishman on vacuum for Love You. A-Train jam in Bowie intro. Last complete Gamehendge, 3/12/88 Burlington, VT [316 shows].

Whatever compelled Trey to tell the crowd at a tiny bar in Olympia, WA, about the mystical, far-off land of Gamehendge for the first time since 1988 remains a mystery, but fast dispersal of these tapes in the early days of the Phish.Net created a far wider audience. Anyway, at least a few people in the crowd know they're witnessing history. This is the most incomplete version of the five live Gamehendge performances because Wilson had already been performed as the second song in the set before Trey decided to narrate, so Lizards (the usual starting point) had to be skipped. Still, it's obvious how excited Trey is to be telling the story—hard to believe he waited three and a half years between performances! —Scott Sifton

This is, of course, a Gamehendge show, but it's missing one of my favorites, Lizards. I'm also bothered by the slightly illogical Gamehendge order (I would've put a few songs before Forbin's > Mockingbird), but these are Gamehendge songs after all, making the set superb. —Andrew Mitchell

10/15/91 ❄
International Beer Garden, Humboldt Brewery, Arcata, CA
I: Chalkdust, Foam, Squirming Coil, Melt, Sparkle, Reba, Landlady > Destiny Unbound, YEM, Rocky Top
II: Brother, Bouncing, Runaway Jim, Poor Heart, Llama, Oh Kee > Suzie, HYHU > Love You > HYHU, Funky Bitch, Golgi
E: Memories, Harry Hood

Fishman on vacuum for Love You. Setlist for the second set is incomplete.

10/17/91 [ACCESSIBILITY: •] [ATTEND. 500; CAP. 500] [TIX $11]
Great American Music Hall, San Francisco, CA
I: Memories, Landlady > Bouncing, Divided Sky, Cavern, Poor Heart, Stash, Esther, Chalkdust, Golgi
II: Curtain, Oh Kee > Suzie, Bowie, Lawn Boy, Fluffhead, YEM, HYHU > Love You > HYHU, Possum
E: Magilla, Rocky Top

10/18/91 [ACCESSIBILITY: ••] [ATTEND. 500; CAP. 500] [TIX $11]
Great American Music Hall, San Francisco, CA
I: Runaway Jim, Foam, Paul and Silas, Reba, Wilson > Llama, Lizards, Adeline, Antelope
II: Brother, Uncle Pen, Guelah, Dinner and a Movie, Mike's > Hydrogen > Weekapaug, I Didn't Know, Fee > Melt, MSO, Cavern
E: Sparkle, Walk Away, Squirming Coil

Last Walk Away, 5/24/90 Raleigh, NC [137 shows].

Another Phish milestone—two sold-out shows at San Francisco's GAMH! As much a part of the folklore as the famous first Paradise gig in Boston, the band gained fame as the "first unsigned band to sell out GAMH for two nights." Get the tapes from the second night. —Amy Manning

This was the second of two nights at this classy little spot (500-person capacity). The

Walk Away encore was a real treat, though they soundchecked it the night previous. —Nathaniel Peirce

Trey's explanations of Brother, Uncle Pen, and Guelah add a little kick to the second set. He says Brother was played for Page's and Mike's brothers, who were in the audience, to "describe their personalities." He also talks about Guelah being his friend Dave's mom, and how she used to bust into his room while they wrote songs. Overall, this show gives a nice look into some early Phish tunes. Mike's > Hydrogen > Weekapaug was the set's musical highlight, followed closely by Dinner and a Movie. —Nick Soricelli

10/19/91 [ACCESSIBILITY: ••••] [ATTEND. 800; CAP. 800] [TIX $6-$7.50]
The Catalyst, Santa Cruz, CA
I: Landlady > Suzie, It's Ice, Runaway Jim, Foam, Chalkdust > Bouncing, MSO, Stash, Golgi
II: Llama, Bathtub Gin, Sparkle, Tweezer > Horn, Poor Heart, YEM, Oh Kee > HYHU > Terrapin > HYHU, Harry Hood
E: GTBT

Back to Back Blues Band opened. Mimi Fishman on vacuum for Terrapin. MSO performed a cappella, then electric (regular).

This was a very mellow show; the music was absolutely all over the place. Hold Your Head Up (which flowed into Terrapin, then back into HYHU) was played with Fishman as "Showboat Gertrude." Trey announced that Henrietta was dead ("You will never see Henrietta on the Phish stage again") and that Showboat Gertrude would take her place. The band was joined in Terrapin by Showboat Gertrude's mother, who whaled on the vacuum cleaner. —Matt Fitone

The setlist doesn't do this show justice. The band cooks through the entire second set at this great little restaurant/club in downtown Santa Cruz (if you ever get a chance to see a show at the Catalyst, go!). Besides the beautiful Harry Hood that closes the set, check out the "coughing and phlegm" YEM vocal jam, which might make you lose your lunch. Terrapin, with Mimi, is also hilarious as Fish improvises some lyrics in honor of his mother's appearance. —Andre Holton

10/23/91 ❄ [ATTEND. 363; CAP. 363] [TIX $5]
Chuy's, Tempe, AZ

10/24/91 [ACCESSIBILITY: ••]
Prescott College, Prescott, AZ
I: Oh Kee > Suzie, Foam, Poor Heart, Stash, Ya Mar, Divided Sky, I Didn't Know, TMWSIY > Avenu > TMWSIY, Bowie
II: Mike's > Hydrogen > Weekapaug, Lizards, Uncle Pen, Tube, Slave, Dinner and a Movie, Bouncing, HYHU > Terrapin > HYHU, Possum
E: Memories, Adeline, Rocky Top

10/26/91 ❄ [ATTEND. 450; CAP. 450] [TIX $5-$7]
Chez What, Santa Fe, NM

10/27/91 [ACCESSIBILITY: •] [ATTEND. 350; CAP. 350] [TIX $8-$10]
Elk Lodge, Telluride, CO
I: MSO, Chalkdust, Mango, Buried Alive, Guelah, Fluffhead, Brother, Bouncing, Harry Hood, Golgi
II: Llama, Forbin's > Mockingbird, Sparkle, It's Ice, Mike's > Hydrogen > Weekapaug, Tela, Landlady > Destiny Unbound, A-Train, Antelope
E: Glide > Possum

Soundcheck: La Bamba tease, Tube, It's Ice (3x).

This show was in the smallest venue I've ever seen Phish play—a room no bigger than a large living room. This was my second show and it further served to cement my appreciation of Phish. Standing only ten feet away from Trey and his newly shaven head, with no stage, he blew me away. All the classics were here: Mango Song, Mike's, Lizards, Antelope. Another highlight was walking down the hall between sets and saying "hi" to Trey. —Jeff Salvatore

10/28/91 [ACCESSIBILITY: ••] [ATTEND. 350; CAP. 350] [TIX $8-$10]
Elk Lodge, Telluride, CO
I: Curtain > Runaway Jim, Cavern, Poor Heart, Reba, I Didn't Know, Tube, Oh Kee > Foam, Fee, Bowie, Carolina
II: Divided Sky, Wilson > Dinner and a Movie > Stash, Paul and Silas, Bathtub Gin, YEM, Squirming Coil, Harpua, HYHU > Whipping Post > HYHU, Highway to Hell
E: Horn, Rocky Top

Whipping Post featured Mimi Fishman on vacuum and Fishman on slide guitar. Last Whipping Post. 10/28/91 Telluride, CO [140 shows].

10/30/91 ❄ [ATTEND. 885; CAP. 885] [TIX $11-$12]
Boulder Theater, Boulder, CO

10/31/91 [ACCESSIBILITY: ••]
Armstrong Hall, Colorado Springs, CO
I: Memories, Brother, Ya Mar, Sloth, Chalkdust, Sparkle, Foam, Bathtub Gin, Paul and Silas, YEM, Runaway Jim
II: Landlady, "Wait" > Llama, Fee > "Wait," MSO > "Wait" > Bowie, Horn, Dinner and a Movie, Tube, I Didn't Know, Harry Hood
E: Glide, Rocky Top

"Wait" indicates brief musical tease then a few minutes of silence after the band says, "wait." Female show-goer dressed as Mike started the second set on stage, with Mike playing from off stage. Costume Contest between Landlady and Llama. Fishman on vacuum for I Didn't Know.

11/1/91 [ACCESSIBILITY: ••••]
Gothic Theater, Denver, CO
I: AC/DC Bag > Sparkle, Landlady > Destiny Unbound, Squirming Coil, Melt, Fluffhead, Uncle Pen, Tube, Divided Sky, Adeline
II: Tweezer, MSO, It's Ice, Chalkdust, Eliza, Mike's > Hydrogen > Weekapaug, A-Train, Tela, Cavern, Poor Heart > Tweezer Reprise
E: HYHU > Love You > Pusher Man jam, Stash

Pusher Man replaced HYHU as the outro jam on Love You. Fishman on vacuum for Love You.

This show has become one of the best-circulated Phish tapes from 1991, I think more for the perfect digital soundboard sound quality than for the music. There are highlights—including a powerful Landlady > Destiny, a good Divided Sky and Tube during its prime—but no must-hear jams. The Phishtoric moments come during the encore after Love You, when Phish plays Pusher Man as the Henrietta theme because it's a song Fish likes in place of the Hold Your Head Up jam he hates. And Stash is a request from a group of Phish.Net phans standing close to the stage—it was around this time that the band learned of the Net's existence and Trey, for one, got pretty excited about it, even if he doesn't seem to quite understand how it works. —Al Hunt

11/2/91 [ACCESSIBILITY: •] [ATTEND. 1,002; CAP. 1,200] [TIX $10-$12]
Lory Theater, Fort Collins, CO
I: Suzie, Curtain > Llama, Reba, Paul and Silas, Foam, Bouncing, Forbin's > Mockingbird, Possum
II: Golgi, Antelope, TMWSIY > Avenu > TMWSIY, Sparkle, Guelah, Walk Away, Landlady, Runaway Jim, YEM
E: Contact, BBFCM

11/4/91 ❄
Rhythm Room, Dallas, TX

[11/5/91]
Liberty Lunch, Austin, TX
Show canceled.

11/7/91 [ACCESSIBILITY: ••]
Tipitina's, New Orleans, LA
I: Memories, Chalkdust, Foam, Sparkle, Cavern > It's Ice, YEM, Landlady > Runaway Jim, I Didn't Know, Llama
II: Brother, Bouncing, MSO, Reba, Tube, Horn, Bowie, A-Train, HYHU > Love You > HYHU
E: Fee, Rocky Top
E2: Lawn Boy > Fire

Col. Bruce Hampton and the Aquarium Rescue Unit opened, and they joined Phish for Bowie, A-Train, and Love You.

11/8/91 [ACCESSIBILITY: •]
The Ivory Tusk, Tuscaloosa, AL
I: Tube, Landlady > Dinner and a Movie, Stash, Poor Heart > Divided Sky, Mango, Brother > Eliza, Golgi
II: Sloth, Sparkle, Melt, Squirming Coil, I Didn't Know, Mike's > Hydrogen > Weekapaug, Jesus Left Chicago, Self, Life Is a TV Show, Family Picture > Crimes of the Mind
E: Fee > Suzie

Alternate lyrics in Weekapaug: "Bucket of lard," etc. The Dude of Life on vocals for Self, Life Is a TV Show, Family Picture, and Crimes of the Mind. Concert debuts: Life Is a TV Show, Family Picture.

11/9/91 ❄
Variety Playhouse, Atlanta, GA
I: Curtain, Runaway Jim, Foam, Sparkle, Llama, Reba, Tube, YEM, Horn, Brother, Adeline
II: Chalkdust, Fluffhead, Poor Heart, It's Ice, Tweezer, Tela, Landlady, HYHU > Terrapin > HYHU, MSO, Tweezer Reprise
E: Glide, Possum

11/10/91 ❄
Music Farm, Charleston, SC

11/12/91 [ACCESSIBILITY: •]
Georgia Theater, Athens, GA
I: Buried Alive > Golgi, Uncle Pen, Brother, Bouncing, Tube, Sloth, Harry Hood, Fee, Foam, Llama
II: Dinner and a Movie, Stash, Squirming Coil, Paul and Silas, Mike's > Hydrogen > Weekapaug, Guelah, Chalkdust, Magilla, Cavern, HYHU > Love You > HYHU, Antelope
E: Ya Mar, BBFCM
E2: Melt, Memories

11/13/91 [ACCESSIBILITY: •]
Love Auditorium, Davidson College, Davidson, NC
I: Landlady > Runaway Jim, It's Ice, Sparkle, Chalkdust, Esther, Cavern, Divided Sky, I Didn't Know, HYHU > Terrapin >HYHU, YEM
II: Bowie, Forbin's > Mockingbird, Golgi, Bathtub Gin, Squirming Coil, Llama, Possum
E: Horn, MSO, Adeline

11/14/91 [ACCESSIBILITY: ••]
Cat's Cradle, Chapel Hill, NC
I: Wilson, Uncle Pen, Llama, Reba, Foam, Tube, Sparkle, Brother, Mango, Golgi, Runaway Jim
II: Dinner and a Movie, Antelope, Fee, Paul and Silas, It's Ice, Glide, Tweezer > A-Train, HYHU > Brain > HYHU, Lizards > Tweezer Reprise
E: Bouncing, GTBT
E2: YEM
Antelope sung as "Roll Like a Cantaloupe." Smells Like Teen Spirit tease in Antelope. Frosty the Snowman tease in A-Train.

11/15/91 [ACCESSIBILITY: ••]
Trax, Charlottesville, VA
I: Chalkdust, Sparkle, Cavern, Curtain, Melt, Squirming Coil, MSO, Divided Sky, Lawn Boy, Golgi
II: Llama, Bathtub Gin, Poor Heart > Mike's > Hydrogen > Weekapaug, Eliza > Tube, Landlady > Destiny Unbound, Harry Hood, HYHU > Love You > HYHU, Bouncing > Possum
E: Highway to Hell, Suzie

When talking about superlative Phish shows, this one must be included. The second set alone is a dandy. Llama kicks things off and flows directly into an outstanding Bathtub Gin. While Mike's is always excellent, it is the Landlady > Destiny Unbound segue that gets me going (please bring it back, guys!). Finally, the concert is topped off by an awesome Possum. —Jonathan Banco

11/16/91 [ACCESSIBILITY: •]
The Bayou, Washington, DC
I: Landlady, Uncle Pen, Wilson, Runaway Jim, It's Ice > Sparkle > Fluffhead, Foam, Stash, Ya Mar, Cavern
II: Tube, MSO, Bathtub Gin, Brother, YEM, Horn > Chalkdust, HYHU > Terrapin > HYHU, Llama
E: Glide, Rocky Top
Fishman on vacuum for Terrapin.

A show ahead of its time, at least as far as YEM is concerned. The boys surf the waves of beauty and wonder on this night—this is the kind of music that can change the world! I hope some of our congressmen made it down to The Bayou, because they would have gotten to enjoy this hidden gem without the fifth-generation hiss of my analog tape. —Al Hunt

For some unknown reason, Trey got fixated on the phrase "Mrs. Pizza Shit" during this show. After Gin, in an attempt to one-up Trey, Fishman rechristened Phish "Mrs. Pizza Shit," a name change that Trey reiterates during the YEM intro. The YEM vocal jam then incorporates the "Mrs. Pizza Shit" theme. Hmmm. Maybe the presence of some Phishy friends in the audience—Tom Marshall, Trey's mom and his sister—inspired the weirdness. —Tricia Holmes

11/19/91 ❄ [ATTEND. 315; CAP. 1,200] [TIX $8-$10]
The Sting, New Britain, CT
I: Uncle Pen, Foam, Runaway Jim, Fee > Sparkle, Brother, Horn, Chalkdust, HYHU > Love You > HYHU, Wilson, Divided Sky
II: Tube, MSO, Mike's > Hydrogen > Weekapaug, Mango, Sloth, Reba, Dinner and a Movie, Cavern, Bowie
E: Glide, Rocky Top

11/20/91 [ACCESSIBILITY: •]
Campus Club, Providence, RI
I: Buried Alive > Possum, Forbin's > Mockingbird, Sparkle, Stash, Paul and Silas, Bathtub Gin, Squirming Coil, Llama, YEM
II: Golgi, It's Ice, MSO, Antelope, Tela, Landlady, HYHU > Bike > HYHU, Cavern
E: Magilla, Brother
Fishman on fretless guitar for Bike and Cavern. Carl Gerhard on trumpet for Magilla and Brother. Last Bike, 5/17/91 Providence, RI [56 shows].

11/21/91 [ACCESSIBILITY: ••]
Somerville Theater, Somerville, MA
I: Chalkdust, Bouncing, Poor Heart, Guelah, Reba, Foam, Horn, Melt, Esther, Mike's > Hydrogen > Weekapaug
II: Wilson, Harry Hood, It's Ice, Mango, Uncle Pen, Tweezer > TMWSIY > Avenu > TMWSIY, Runaway Jim
E: Memories, Adeline, Golgi
On Broadway jam in Weekapaug.

11/22/91 ❄
University of Southern Maine Gymnasium, Portland, ME
I: Possum, Cavern, Sparkle, Brother, Fee, Foam, Divided Sky, Lawn Boy, Dinner and a Movie, Stash, Rocky Top
II: Tube, MSO, Landlady, Bathtub Gin, Antelope, Squirming Coil, I Didn't Know, Llama, Lizards, YEM
E: Glide, Suzie

11/23/91 [ACCESSIBILITY: ••]
Barre Memorial Auditorium, Barre, VT
I: Llama, Reba, Foam, Runaway Jim, Guelah, Sparkle, Chalkdust, Uncle Pen, Brother, Bouncing, Golgi
II: Curtain > Mike's > Hydrogen > Weekapaug, Horn, Poor Heart, Tweezer, Eliza, Landlady, Fee, HYHU > Love You > HYHU, MSO, Tweezer Reprise
E: Jesus Left Chicago, BBFCM
Fishman on vacuum for Love You. Dave Grippo on alto sax for Jesus Left Chicago and BBFCM.

11/24/91 ❄
Webster Hall, Dartmouth College, Hanover, NH
I: Sloth, Paul and Silas, Stash, Landlady, Fluffhead, Sparkle, It's Ice, I Didn't Know, Bowie
II: Tube, Divided Sky, Cavern, Mango, Chalkdust, A-Train, YEM, Golgi
E: Adeline, Rocky Top
Bathrobes given to members of the crew during the Bowie intro.

11/30/91 [ACCESSIBILITY: ••••]
Capitol Theater, Port Chester, NY
I: Glide, Llama, Foam, Sparkle, Divided Sky, Cavern, Squirming Coil, Brother, Paul and Silas, Guelah, YEM
II: Chalkdust, Uncle Pen, Harry Hood, It's Ice, Bouncing, MSO, Horn, I Didn't Know, Antelope, Golgi

E: Contact, Rocky Top

Shockra opened. Fishman on trombone for I Didn't Know; he also played vacuum with Shockra.

I find myself listening to this show's second set more often than many others. Originally, this was due to the fact that there is one of the hottest Harrys included. But some shows just flow so well and this is definitely one of them. Ripping open the second set with a spectacular Chalkdust, things move cooly through Uncle Pen Then with one of the greatest intros ever (on my soundboard tape I can hear Trey call out to the rest of the guys, "Harry") they go into it—oh, feeling good about Hood! Later comes the other major highlight of the set—a near-perfect Antelope. Like I said, it just flows oh so well. —Peter Bukley

If you want to know why this tape is so well-circulated, I'll sum it up in two words: Harry Hood. This is one of the best versions of Harry from this era, a must-hear for all Hood aficionados. Beyond Hood, the second set is just good listening, a nice sampler of fall 1991 Phish, including "new tune" It's Ice and the still-developing Chalkdust Torture. —Linda Mahdesian

12/4/91 [ACCESSIBILITY: •]
Angell Ballroom, SUNY Plattsburgh, Plattsburgh, NY
I: Llama, Reba, Landlady > Runaway Jim, Cavern, Poor Heart, Brother, Squirming Coil, Dinner and a Movie, Bouncing, Bowie
II: MSO, Stash, Mango, Mike's > Hydrogen > Weekapaug, Sparkle, Lizards, Chalkdust, HYHU > Love You > HYHU, Golgi
E: Adeline, Suzie

12/5/91 [ACCESSIBILITY: ••••]
Greenfield Armory Castle, Greenfield, MA
I: Golgi, Paul and Silas, Melt, Ya Mar, Fluffhead, Llama, Bathtub Gin, It's Ice, Bouncing, Possum
II: Tweezer, Sparkle, Tube, Foam, Mike's > Hydrogen > Weekapaug, Fee, Sloth, Squirming Coil, I Didn't Know, MSO, Tweezer Reprise
E: Glide, Cavern

Fishman on vacuum for I Didn't Know.

12/6/91 [ACCESSIBILITY: ••••]
Middlebury College, Middlebury, VT
I: Memories, Foam, Reba, Uncle Pen, Squirming Coil, Magilla, Landlady, Guelah, I Didn't Know
II: It's Ice, Eliza, Sparkle, YEM, Horn, Divided Sky, Tela, Llama, HYHU > Whipping Post > HYHU, Possum > "Wait" > Possum
E: "Wait" > Lawn Boy, Rocky Top

Guelah abandoned after something goes wrong with Trey's guitar. Fishman on fretless guitar for Whipping Post; he intentionally smashes the guitar on stage after the song. "Wait," see note with 10/31/91 setlist. Soundcheck: Memories (2x), Dog Log, Blues jam, Shaggy Dog, Makisupa.

This show is a winner, but what's really worth hearing is the soundcheck, which has Trey offering some commentary on a Phish a cappella offering. After attempting Memories twice, he concludes that it's now "all the way up to the level of 'sucked.'" —Al Hunt

12/7/91 [ACCESSIBILITY: •••]
Portsmouth Music Hall, Portsmouth, NH
I: Wilson, Runaway Jim, Foam, Forbin's > Mockingbird, MSO, Stash, Curtain > Cavern > Mango, Antelope
II: Buried Alive, Reba, Chalkdust, Sparkle, Brother, Lizards, HYHU > Terrapin > HYHU, Harpua

"New Year's '91"

12/31/91 The New Aud, Worcester, MA

Phish's growth happened so gradually, spread over so many years of touring, that it's not always easy to find the milestone shows where they took a step up to the next level of popularity. But one clear marker is the band's New Year's Eve show in Worcester, which saw almost 4,000 fans come out for year-end festivities with Phish in by far the largest venue they'd headlined at that point in their careers.

As would be the case in subsequent years, the New Year's Eve appearance allowed the band to book themselves into a larger venue than they'd play on a regular night, figuring that enough people would be drawn by the aura of a special show that demand for tickets would be greater. Of course, they were right.

The '91 New Year's gig followed a fall tour that saw the band hit the Pacific coast for second time in the year—including a two-night sellout of the Great American Music Hall in San Francisco—and the signing of a record contract with Elektra. All signs pointed to the New Year's show as the chance to put an exclamation point on what had already been an incredible year for the band.

Realizing they'd outgrown the Exhibition Hall in Boston where they spent New Year's Eve in 1989 and 1990, the band looked an hour west of Boston to Worcester. One idea they considered was booking the 14,000-seat Centrum and hanging a huge sheet to block off most of the arena, creating a smaller "theater" at one end. But then the Worcester Aud—a smaller, 3,800-person room—came through, and the die was cast. Tickets would be $16.50, and the show a general-admission affair kicking off sometime around 10 P.M. For the first time on New Year's Eve, the band decided in advance to play three sets, a tradition that echoed that of the Grateful Dead's famed New Year's affairs and one that continues to this day.

Notification of the show came, like the Amy's Farm gig the summer before, by postcard. "The New Aud [has] a nice wrap-around balcony and huge dancefloor," the postcard advised. "Plan on getting tickets early, as last year's New Year's show sold out in advance." Fans who didn't heed that advice found themselves out of luck at the door—indeed, Phish drew more than 4,000 funseekers to the cold, industrial town of Worcester to ring in 1992.

The show marked the debut of the new multi-paneled Mirkin backdrops, painted by none other than Mike's mother, Marjorie. They served as the band's stage backdrop for the next several years, and proved particularly inviting for Chris Kuroda, who used the unique properties of the plastic and paint to create stunning visual effects.

Looking back on the Worcester show five years later, Kuroda termed the New Aud show a major sign to him that the band was growing beyond the bars. Little did anyone know that, two years later, they'd be back in town on New Year's Eve, headlining the Centrum, which sold out in less than a day.

Musically, the show was solid—certainly better than the 1990 New Year's gig, but not as vibrant as the shows on later New Year's Eve installments. There were some special moments, however, like Trey using a swearing keychain to produce a cacophony of "fuck yous" and "eat shits" during a very eerie Wilson. And there was the long jam session of the third set, which saw the band use Wilson as a springboard to a run of songs that segued from the Squirming Coil to Tweezer to the rare (even back then) McGrupp and then into a long (though mostly standard for the era) Mike's > Hydrogen > Weekapaug.

The show wasn't broadcast on the radio—that tradition wouldn't start until the next year's show at Matthews Arena in Boston—but a tape tree run on the nascent Phish.Net got the bootlegs out quickly.

Still, the show's lasting legacy, more than the music, was the feeling it sparked among fans that New Year's Eve had evolved from a "fun-to-attend" to a "must-attend" event. Subsequent years would see the evolution of the New Year's Eve prank and grander musical heights, but the New Aud show is remembered for laying the groundwork.

E: Adeline, Golgi

The band gave away their old trampolines before Adeline. "Merry Christmas" jam before and during Buried Alive. Fishman on vacuum for Terrapin.

This show was actually a reasonably tough ticket, at least as those things went in 1991. Wilson—perhaps the best Phish show opener—starts things off right before a standard Runaway > Foam. Things pick up again later in the set with a great Curtain > Cavern > Mango run topped by a strong Antelope closer. As second sets go, this one lacks places for wide-open jams but the Harpua at the end makes up for it. Prior to the encore, the band announces that they will give away their old trampolines. The apparent commotion in the audience leads Fishman to urge people to calm down a bit. Eventually things get quiet enough for an unmiked Adeline. —Ed Smith

12/31/91 [ACCESSIBILITY: ••••] [ATTEND. 3,870; CAP. 3,870] [TIX $16.50]
The New Aud, Worcester Memorial Auditorium, Worcester, MA
I: Possum, Foam, Sparkle, Stash, Lizards, Guelah, Divided Sky, Esther > Llama, Golgi
II: Brother, Bouncing > Buried Alive > New Year's Countdown > Auld Lang Syne, Runaway Jim, Landlady, Reba, Cavern, MSO, Antelope
III: Wilson > Squirming Coil > Tweezer > McGrupp > Mike's > Hydrogen > Weekapaug **E:** Lawn Boy, Rocky Top, Tweezer Reprise

Trey used an electronic keychain to make "Fuck you," "Eat shit," and "You're an asshole" noise effects during Wilson. "Wimoweh" jam in Weekapaug.

My first Phish show! I didn't intend to go, but an extra ticket was sent to me at Purdue by a buddy in Worcester. Since I had never seen Phish before, I was shocked. Opening with a fiery Possum into an extremely funky Foam set the mood for the night. The band didn't seem nervous or obligated to put on the "best" show they could do. At the New Year's countdown, I was lip-locked with a total stranger. Divided Sky, Reba, Runaway Jim, and Mike's Groove all jammed. —Rob Koeller

Crazy scene outside the New Aud—this was the first time I remember seeing ticketless fans trying to break into the show any way they could. At one point, a fire exit opened and a bunch of people scampered in, only to be removed by security a moment later. All this, just to see Phish? Well, little did we know. . . . The show was a lot of fun, everyone just having a great old time in a cool room. The show wasn't musical perfection, but that really wasn't the point. —Scott Sifton

Wow, a New Year's Eve show. This concert should be great, but unfortunately this show doesn't come close to Phish's normal high standards for this night. While the music is fine, it is the setlist that stands out as mediocre. Of course it's always nice to hear Brother and the third set Mike's Groove is nice, but nothing stands out that sets this night apart from any other regular Phish show. —Jonathan Banco

1992 SPRING California Dreamin'

With their first album on Elektra just hitting stores, Phish opened up their 1992 spring tour with a crop of new songs, most written by the Marshall / Anastasio songwriting duo. This spring tour still ranks in some fans' minds as one of the best to date by the band—almost every night saw long shows spiced with new songs and new arrangements, and the added element of the "secret language" that debuted on March 6. The California run, beginning with the band's first show in Los Angeles on April 15, is notable for a string of outstanding performances—one of which, the April 16 gig in Santa Barbara, remains among the most well-circulated Phish tapes. Although Phish had stopped soundboard patches for tapers long before the start of this tour, the majority of shows from this tour can be found on soundboards leaked by the band and friends.

[2/18/92] ***A Picture Of Nectar* released on Elektra.**

3/6/92 [ACCESSIBILITY: •••] [ATTEND. 850; CAP. 850] [TIX $13.50]
Portsmouth Music Hall, Portsmouth, NH
I: Rift, Cavern, Sparkle, It's Ice, Oh Kee > Divided Sky, Guelah, Maze, Reba, All Things, Bowie
II: My Friend, Poor Heart, "Language Lesson," Stash, Mound, Llama, Bouncing, NICU, Possum
E: Sleeping Monkey

Concert debuts: Rift (fast version), Maze, My Friend, Mound, NICU, and Sleeping Monkey. Also the debut of the "Language Lesson," an explanation of the band's secret language. "Bowie" jams during "Language Lesson." Last Rift (slow version), 5/19/90 Concord, NH [172 shows].

1992

121 Total Show Dates
- **40** one-set shows
- **79** two-set shows
- **1** three-set shows
- **1** date with no setlist

Phan Picks 1992

SHOW	THE SKINNY
1) 03/13/92 Providence, RI	Big Black Furry Antelope!
2) 07/25/92 Stowe, VT	Carlos Santana sits in.
3) 04/16/92 Santa Barbara, CA	Very widely circulated tape.
4) 03/20/92 Binghamton, NY	Terrific, jamming show.
5) 04/21/92 Redwood Acres, CA	Weirdness galore in set II.
6) 04/18/92 Palo Alto, CA	"Linus and Lucy" Hood.
7) 05/14/92 Port Chester, NY	Insane Antelope, "Aw fuck!"
8) 11/19/92 Colchester, VT	Fall tour opener just rocks.
9) 11/20/92 Albany, NY	Another all-around great show.
10) 04/17/92 San Francisco, CA	First time at the Warfield.

MUSICAL RECAP: Leaving the more controlled days of 1991 behind, the band starts opening up its jams, taking songs like Antelope, Possum, and Bowie to the edge while still retaining melodic themes. Jamming is still pretty straight-ahead, with "machine gun Trey" working the tension and release, especially on new songs like Maze.
REPRESENTATIVE JAMS: Possum, 5/17/92 and 4/5/92; Mike's Groove, 4/21/92 and 11/28/92; Antelope, 3/13/92; You Enjoy Myself, 7/25/92.
ORIGINAL SONG DEBUTS: Axilla (part one, 11/19/92), Big Ball Jam (11/19/92), Buffalo Bill (11/21/92); Faht (11/22/92), Fast Enough for You (11/19/92), The Horse (3/7/92), Lengthwise (11/19/92), Maze (3/6/92), Mound (3/6/92), My Friend My Friend (3/6/92), NICU (3/6/92), Rift (fast version, 3/6/92), "The Secret Language" (3/6/92), Sleeping Monkey (3/6/92), Silent in the Morning (3/7/92), Weigh (3/7/92).
COVER SONG DEBUTS: Blue Bayou (7/16/92), Cracklin' Rosie (3/7/92), Diamond Girl* (12/31/92), I Walk the Line (11/19/92), My Mind's Got a Mind of Its Own (3/7/92). (*only ever played this once)

Dark Horses

SHOW	THE SKINNY
1) 05/17/92 Schenectady, NY	Incredible Possum; lots more.
2) 12/29/92 New Haven, CT	Best of '92 New Year's run?
3) 04/19/92 Santa Cruz, CA	Another gem from a magic week.
4) 05/09/92 Syracuse, NY	Harpua and a great Tweezer.
5) 08/17/92 San Juan C., CA	Somewhere over the Rainbow.

Most-Played Originals:

1) Sparkle	64	53%
2) Llama	63	52%
3) Cavern	58	48%
4) Maze	55	45%
5) Rift	54	45%
6) Runaway Jim	54	45%
6) Stash	54	45%
8) Foam	53	44%
9) The Squirming Coil	52	43%
10) Poor Heart	47	39%
10) YEM	47	39%

Most-Played Covers:

1) Sweet Adeline	41	34%
2) Uncle Pen	38	31%
3) Rocky Top	29	24%
4) Cracklin' Rosie	25	21%
5) Love You	20	17%
6) Memories	17	14%
7) Carolina	15	12%
8) Take the A-Train	13	11%
9) Good Times Bad Times	12	10%
9) Paul and Silas	12	10%
9) Terrapin	12	10%

First-Set Openers:

1) The Landlady	17
2) Runaway Jim	16
2) Suzie Greenberg	13
2) Buried Alive	11
2) Chalkdust Torture	10

Second-Set Openers:

1) Glide	8
2) Mike's Song	6
2) Suzie Greenberg	6
4) The Curtain	5
5) The Landlady	4

Henrietta Songs:

1) Cracklin' Rosie	25
2) Love You	20
3) Lengthwise	6
4) Faht	4
5) Bike	3
5) Brain	3

A Cappella Songs:

1) Sweet Adeline	41
2) Memories	17
3) Carolina	15

A 900-seat theater, nice balcony, and the first show since New Year's. We saw many songs played for the first time: Knife (later My Friend), NICU, Sleeping Monkey, Maze, and the new Rift. Look for a video of this one floating around out there somewhere. —Nathaniel Peirce

The boys decided to let us in on something—The Secret Language. After an awesome My Friend (which also happens to be its debut), they laid out a nice groove and Trey started explaining the Language. If you don't know about it, don't wait any longer: get this tape and study it, because they will test you when you least expect it. —Michael Rambo

3/7/92 [ACCESSIBILITY: •••] [ATTEND. 850; CAP. 850] [TIX $13.50]
Portsmouth Music Hall, Portsmouth, NH
I: Brother, My Mind's, Foam, Runaway Jim, Horse > Silent, Maze, Mango, Landlady, Rift, Antelope
II: MSO, Tweezer, Squirming Coil, Weigh, Chalkdust, Horn, Mike's > Hydrogen > Weekapaug, Cold as Ice > Cracklin' Rosie > Cold as Ice, Tweezer Reprise
E: Adeline, Golgi
Concert debuts: My Mind's, Horse, Silent, Weigh, and Cracklin' Rosie (as well as the Cold as Ice intro and outro for Fishman, which replaced the traditional HYHU jam for most of spring 1992).

3/11/92 [ACCESSIBILITY: ••] [ATTEND. 840; CAP. 840] [TIX $13.50]
Colonial Theater, Keene, NH
I: Suzie, My Friend, Paul and Silas, Reba, Maze, Fee, Melt, Mound, Divided Sky, Cavern
II: Llama, NICU, Sloth, Lizards, Bathtub Gin, My Mind's, Brother, Cold as Ice > Baby Lemonade > Cold as Ice, All Things, Harry Hood, Rocky Top
E: Sanity, Memories, Carolina, Sleeping Monkey
Fishman on vacuum bagpipes for Baby Lemonade. Smoke on the Water jam before Llama. Sanity tease before All Things. Concert debut: Baby Lemonade. Last Sanity, 5/28/89 [232 shows].

Proof of the band's continued growth came this night, their last gig ever at Keene's Colonial Theater. Though the show itself wasn't one of the all-time greats, it had its moments—a strong Melt jam in the first set and then a hilarious moment during the quiet segment of Divided Sky. As Trey waited to play "the note," various audience members shouted out requests. So Trey steps up to his microphone and, in classic request-style, shouted, "Possum!!" To start the second set, there's a funny Smoke on the Water jam while Mike makes a no smoking announcement. Later, Fishman sings Syd Barrett's Baby Lemonade for the only time and introduces us to the weird vacuum bagpipes contraption he used for much of the spring tour. There's also the return of Sanity, which the band teases the crowd with before All Things, then plays during the encore. —Andre Holton

3/12/92 [ACCESSIBILITY: ••] [ATTEND. 1,323; CAP. 1,323] [TIX $10]
Flynn Theater, Burlington, VT
I: Runaway Jim, Foam, Sparkle, Stash, I Didn't Know, Reba, Buried Alive > Rift, Magilla, Llama, YEM
II: Golgi, Tweezer, Eliza, It's Ice, Bouncing, Squirming Coil, Uncle Pen, Bowie, Cold as Ice > Cracklin' Rosie > Cold as Ice, MSO, Cavern
E: Adeline, Weigh, Tweezer Reprise
Fishman on vacuum bagpipes for I Didn't Know. Brief tease medley in Bowie intro.

This show features what's in all likelihood the first Big Ball Jam. During a hot Tweezer, someone in the crowd lofted a giant beach ball and Trey got the idea to play a note every time someone in the audience hit the ball. Nine months later, just outside of Burlington at the Colchester show on 11/19/92, they unveiled BBJ in its "official" format. —Ed Smith

3/13/92 [ACCESSIBILITY: •••••]
Campus Club, Providence, RI
I: Curtain > Melt, Poor Heart, Guelah, Maze, Dinner and a Movie > Divided Sky, Mound, Fluffhead > Follow the Yellow Brick Road Jam > Antelope/BBFCM/Antelope
II: Wilson > Brother, Horse > Silent, Landlady, Lizards, My Mind's, Sloth, Rift, Cold as Ice > Love You > Cold as Ice, Possum > "Language Lesson" > Possum
E: Contact, Fire
There are several teases and jams on other songs in Antelope/BBFCM/Antelope, including Groove Is in the Heart, Lullabye of Birdland and several vocal jams. An Over the Rainbow jam leads into Wilson; Over the Rainbow is sampled again during the Wilson intro. Fishman on vacuum bagpipes and vacuum for Love You. Mike on accordion (his first appearance on that instrument) for Contact.

Fantastic show, totally hosed, every note is perfection and ecstasy. Great moments include two—count 'em—two, "d'oh" language signals and a full Language Lesson in set II; a Somewhere Over the Rainbow tease in both Fluffhead and Wilson; and of course the killer Run Like a Big Black Furry Antelope from Mars, which closes set I. —Jamis Curran

Everyone has talked a lot about this set and its legendary Antelope, but there are a few things that don't often get mentioned. How about Mike playing the bassline for Groove Is in the Heart (by early 1990s dance band Dee-Lite)? Or the Lullabye jam? Or Trey and Page sounding like they're shattering glass at one point? All of this takes place during the Antelope mayhem. I really wish this kind of thing occurred frequently! —Charlie Murphy

Man the band loves playing in Providence, that's for sure. It seems like every show here just rocks. The second set here is pretty sweet, since Brother's in its prime. But what makes this set totally awesome is the long, hilarious signal explanation by Trey before Possum—he laughs and jokes while explaining the basic signals to the small crowd. What follows is one of the tightest and sweetest-sounding Possums of 1992, which as we all know was an excellent year for Phish. —Alex Banks

3/14/92 [ACCESSIBILITY: ••••] [ATTEND. 3,200; CAP. 3,200] [TIX $16.50-$18]
Roseland Ballroom, New York, NY
I: Runaway Jim, Cavern, Reba, Sparkle, Foam, Rift, Stash, Fee, Chalkdust, A-Train, Mike's > Hydrogen > Weekapaug
II: Golgi, Llama, Squirming Coil, Melt, Bouncing, Oh Kee > Suzie, Harry Hood, Cold as Ice > Cracklin' Rosie > Cold as Ice, Possum
E: Sleeping Monkey, GTBT
John Popper on harmonica for Sleeping Monkey and GTBT. Funkytown jam in Reba. Somewhere Over the Rainbow tease in Horn.

3/17/92 [ACCESSIBILITY: •] [ATTEND. 921; CAP. 1,345] [TIX $12-$16]
Lisner Auditorium, Washington, DC
I: Buried Alive > Possum, Cavern, Sparkle, It's Ice, I Didn't Know, Divided Sky, Guelah, Rift, Bouncing, Antelope
II: Runaway Jim, Glide, Sloth, Poor Heart, Tweezer > Esther, Mike's > Hydrogen > Weekapaug, Cold as Ice > Love You > Cold as Ice, Llama
E: Memories, Adeline
Everything opened. Fishman on vacuum for I Didn't Know and vacuum bagpipes for Love You. Brief Poor Heart tease from Fishman before Sloth.

3/19/92 [ACCESSIBILITY: •••]
Palace Theater, New Haven, CT
I: Landlady, Rift, Melt, Sparkle, Golgi, Horse > Silent, Dinner and a Movie > Forbin's > Mockingbird, All Things, Bowie
II: Glide, Chalkdust, NICU, MSO, Stash, Oh Kee > Suzie, My Friend, Squirming Coil > Cold as Ice > Cracklin' Rosie > Cold as Ice, YEM
E: Sleeping Monkey, Rocky Top
E2: Adeline
Soundcheck: Shaggy Dog > Jam, Lullabye of Birdland, Mound, Maze. Michelle tease before Glide.

3/20/92 [ACCESSIBILITY: ••••] [ATTEND. 1,500; CAP. 1,500] [TIX $12-$14]
Broome County Forum, Binghamton, NY
I: Wilson, Reba, Brother, Glide, Rift, Fluffhead, Maze, Lizards, Mound, Antelope
II: Mike's > Hydrogen > Weekapaug, Sanity, Sloth, Mango, Cavern, Uncle Pen, Harry Hood, Cold as Ice > Terrapin > Cold as Ice, Possum > "Language Lesson" > Possum
E: Lawn Boy, Fire
Fishman on trombone for Antelope before the "Rye, rye, rocco," lyrics, and vacuum bagpipes for Terrapin. Roundabout tease before Mike's. Bowie and Possum jams during Language Lesson.

Phish played one of their best shows of the year on a Friday night in Binghamton. Though lacking the improvisational insanity of the previous week's Providence gig, this show shines with straight-ahead jams in the best Phish tradition. The first set highlight, besides the weirdness that erupts in Brother (Trey: "They're diving into the alligator pit!"), comes in a very well-jammed Antelope that sees Fishman grabbing his trombone. Mike's Groove is the best they'd done up to this point—Weekapaug traverses hard rock, spacy vocals, melodic jams, and even a few signals to reach an incredible climax. —Scott Sifton

I was a sophomore in high school when this "Phish group," as my friend called it, came to my hometown. Looking back, I wish I had gone. Playing in a venue of around 2,000 people, Phish treated the lucky ones to a great show. Highlights from the tapes include an early Maze, a Brother that I dearly wish I could have heard, and of course Mike's Song. Trey was "en fuego" that night, making some interesting comments throughout the show, providing band-audience humor and contact that I wish was more common today. —Daniel Paden

Besides being one of the hottest Phish sets from this era, set II is also one of the funniest. You know things are going to get interesting when Trey tells the crowd, "Help me,

I'm melting and I can't solidify!" to start the set. Sanity features lots of vocal play on Mike's nicknames then gives way to a vocal jam at the end. Before Terrapin, a chant for the Prison Joke (see 4/11/91) that Trey picks up leads Fish to declare, "You're dreaming, man. You're all dreaming!" —Amy Manning

3/21/92 [ACCESSIBILITY: ••••]
Chestnut Cabaret, Philadelphia, PA
I: Landlady, Runaway Jim, Foam, Sparkle, Melt, Horse > Silent, Dinner and a Movie, Squirming Coil, MSO, Stash, Golgi
II: Buried Alive, Oh Kee > Suzie, A-Train, My Friend, Poor Heart, All Things > Bowie, Weigh, Cold as Ice > Cracklin' Rosie > Cold as Ice, YEM
E: Bouncing, Rocky Top
Extended intro jam on MSO.

Don't let anyone tell you otherwise—these really were the days! Here's Phish, playing a tiny little Cabaret, perched on a low stage so close to the crowd that you could reach out and touch them! Thinking back, this was probably the last Northeast show in a tiny venue I caught—by the fall, they hit the theater circuit pretty much exclusively. It was a great last hurrah, with the boys treating us to a jazzy A-Train and the most outrageous Bowie I'd ever seen. A great show, a great tape. —Jos Conti

Phish must've been psyched to play Philly. This was one of those fun, playful concerts. The Suzie has an organ solo in the second slot, which was the habit at the time, and Page tosses the horn parts in over the final refrain. Silent has the original, cheesy ending with someone singing in an unmanly range. And My Sweet One features a long, improvised hoe-down intro. —Scott Kushner

[3/22/92] [ACCESSIBILITY: •••]
Cultural Center Auditorium, Charleston, WV
Sparkle, All Things, Foam, Landlady
Mountain Stage Live performance taped for nationwide broadcast on National Public Radio. Phish played four songs. Buckwheat Zydeco headlined, and Trey came out and jammed with them during the last song of their set, "Juke-Joint Johnny."

3/24/92 [ACCESSIBILITY: •]
Flood Zone, Richmond, VA
I: Stash, Poor Heart, Foam, Eliza, Rift, Golgi, Horse > Silent, Llama, Forbin's > Mockingbird, Landlady, Bowie
II: Curtain > Mike's > Hydrogen > Weekapaug, Guelah, Mango, Brother, Uncle Pen, I Didn't Know, Oh Kee > Suzie, Harry Hood, Cavern
E: Lawn Boy, Fire
Carl Gerhard on trumpet for Brother and Cavern.

3/25/92 [ACCESSIBILITY: ••]
Trax, Charlottesville, VA
I: Wilson > Sparkle > Melt, Rift, Fee > Maze, Glide > Runaway Jim, It's Ice > Antelope
II: Tweezer > Mound, Reba, All Things, Squirming Coil > YEM, Horn > MSO, Chalkdust, Cold as Ice > Cracklin' Rosie > Cold as Ice, Golgi
E: Sleeping Monkey > Tweezer Reprise

3/26/92 [ACCESSIBILITY: ••] [ATTEND. 650; CAP. 650] [TIX $8]
Ziggy's, Winston Salem, NC
I: Landlady, Runaway Jim, All Things, Foam, Sparkle, Stash, Fluffhead, Uncle Pen, NICU, Bowie
II: Buried Alive, Oh Kee > Suzie, Poor Heart, Brother, TMWSIY> Avenu > TMWSIY, My Friend, Lizards, Cavern, Cold as Ice > Cracklin' Rosie > Cold as Ice, Possum
E: Sleeping Monkey, Chalkdust, Harpua
Col. Bruce Hampton and the Aquarium Rescue Unit opened. Trey carries Marley out on stage during Harpua. Fire jam in Harpua.

3/27/92 [ACCESSIBILITY: ••]
1313 Club, Charlotte, NC
I: Llama, Reba, Paul and Silas, Sloth, Divided Sky, Guelah, Maze, Glide, Bouncing, Antelope
II: Mike's > Hydrogen > Weekapaug, Horse > Silent, MSO, Rift, Bathtub Gin, Dinner and a Movie, Magilla, Harry Hood, Cold as Ice > Love You > Cold as Ice, Golgi
E: Memories, Adeline
Extended intro jam on MSO.

3/28/92 [ACCESSIBILITY: •••]
Variety Theater, Atlanta, GA
I: Runaway Jim, Foam, Sparkle, Stash, Rift, Bouncing, Landlady, "Language Lesson," Bowie, Glide, Cavern
II: Memories, Carolina, I Didn't Know, Adeline
Lullabye of Birdland jam at end of Landlady. After a small flood in the theater threatened to short out the band's equipment, the abbreviated second set was performed a cappella. Fishman on trombone for I Didn't Know after his vacuum bagpipes failed because the power had been turned off. No encore.

3/30/92 [ACCESSIBILITY: ••••] [ATTEND. 752; CAP. 1,000] [TIX $7-$9]
Mississippi Nights, St. Louis, MO
I: Landlady, Llama, Foam, Guelah, Sparkle, Maze, I Didn't Know, All Things, Sloth, Runaway Jim, Cavern
II: Golgi, Uncle Pen, Tweezer, Mound, YEM, BBFCM, Squirming Coil, Weigh, Chalkdust, HYHU > Cracklin' Rosie > Cold as Ice, Bouncing, Tweezer Reprise
E: Sleeping Monkey, Oh Kee > Suzie
Fishman on vacuum for I Didn't Know. YEM vocal jam featured "Rock On" riffs, then Fishman on vacuum bagpipes leading into BBFCM. "We're Off to See the Wizard" jam in BBFCM.

3/31/92 [ACCESSIBILITY: •] [ATTEND. 438; CAP. 727] [TIX $6]
Blue Note, Columbia, MO
I: Wilson, Divided Sky, Glide, Melt, Rift, Reba, Llama, Forbin's > Mockingbird, Antelope
II: Mike's > Hydrogen > Weekapaug, Fee, Stash, Lizards, Cavern, Dinner and a Movie, My Friend, MSO, Cold as Ice > Love You > Cold as Ice, Possum
E: Adeline

If you haven't listened to this show, you really must. Phish just turns it up a notch when they play in Missouri. A mini-Gamehendge in the first set should be enough to make this show great, but then comes a truly epic Mike's Groove—one of my favorite versions ever. MSO starts off in "slow motion," then goes to new levels. Love You is also great—I think Fishman should do more Syd Barrett songs. —Tony Krupka

4/1/92 [ACCESSIBILITY: •]
Liberty Hall, Lawrence, KS
I: Golgi, Foam, Bouncing, Brother, All Things, Sparkle, Runaway Jim, I Didn't Know, Landlady, Bowie, Carolina
II: Llama, YEM, Horse > Silent, Uncle Pen, Tweezer, Horn, Chalkdust, Cold as Ice > Cracklin' Rosie > Cold as Ice, Squirming Coil, Tweezer Reprise, Contact, Rocky Top
E: Lawn Boy, GTBT

4/3/92 [ACCESSIBILITY: •]
Hyatt Regency Village Hall, Beaver Creek, CO
I: Landlady > Poor Heart, Stash, Rift, Guelah, Sparkle, Maze, Fluffhead, All Things, Melt, Golgi
II: Curtain > Sloth, Possum, Weigh, YEM, Mango, Llama, Harry Hood, Suzie
E: Rocky Top

4/4/92 [ACCESSIBILITY: •] [ATTEND. 2,439; CAP. 3,850] [TIX $12.50-$13.50]
CU Balch Fieldhouse, University of Colorado, Boulder, CO
I: Runaway Jim, Foam, Reba, Uncle Pen, Chalkdust, Bouncing, It's Ice, Sparkle, Lizards, I Didn't Know, Antelope
II: Mike's > Hydrogen > Weekapaug, Glide, MSO, Tweezer, Squirming Coil, Cold as Ice > Cracklin' Rosie > Cold as Ice, My Friend, Harpua, Cavern
E: Sleeping Monkey, Tweezer Reprise
Fishman on trombone for I Didn't Know, and on vacuum bagpipes for Harpua.

4/5/92 [ACCESSIBILITY: •••] [ATTEND. 512; CAP. 512] [TIX $12.50]
Fox Theater & Cafe, Boulder, CO
I: Llama, Guelah, Divided Sky, Wilson, Poor Heart, Stash, Rift, Horn, It's Ice, Possum, Adeline
II: Melt, All Things, YEM, Horse > Silent, Maze, Weigh, Landlady > Bowie, HYHU > Love You > Cold as Ice, A-Train > Runaway Jim
E: Lawn Boy, Rocky Top
Fishman on vacuum for Love You. Landlady jam in Possum intro. Dixie tease in A-Train.

I was lucky to catch this gig. They announced they'd be doing a show at the Fox the night before at the Fieldhouse show, and we were glad to have a chance to see Phish in this cool little theater. The Fox had only been open for about a month when Phish played here, and the show blew me away. A wild, wild Possum at the end of the first set (where did that Landlady jam come from?) led us to setbreak, then a strong Melt carried us back out into the second set. YEM featured a hilarious vocal jam with the boys chanting "reggae!" then "what?" followed by evil laughter. Later in the set, Landlady > Bowie and A-Train > Runaway Jim combos rocked! —Melissa Wolcott

Hey kids, you like the Possum, do you? Well then, you'll love the Fox. From the time Page strikes the first note until the time Mike steps up to sing "Come from top the mountain, baby," more than *five minutes* elapse. After the first lyric segment, Trey drives the jam up to the mountaintop. This version belongs in the Possum Pantheon with 5/17/92 Union College, 7/15/92 Trax, and 4/30/94 Orlando. Yum. —Ernie Greene

4/6/92 [ACCESSIBILITY: ••••] [ATTEND. 861; CAP. 1,000] [TIX $10-$12]
Western State College Gym, Gunnison, CO
I: Suzie, Foam, Sparkle, Reba, Brother, Esther, Chalkdust, Guelah, Squirming Coil, Antelope
II: Dinner and a Movie, Bathtub Gin, Paul and Silas, Mike's > Hydrogen > Weekapaug, NICU, Llama, Mound, Stash, Cold as Ice > Cracklin' Rosie > Cold as Ice, Uncle Pen, Cavern
E: BBFCM

Cavern features "yee-haw" yells, some bluegrass-style jamming, and "bluegrass" lyrics: "The foggy cavern's musty grime appeared within my palm/I saddled up horses and headed on down to the hoedown!"

This is absolutely one of my favorite shows of all time, mainly for the second set. Dinner and a Movie, Bathtub, and Mike's Groove are everything you'd expect them to be, but where this tape really gets me is the NICU, the early slow version that I think is far superior to the current one. It ends with the best-timed "D'oh!" I've ever heard. The other highlight is the bluegrass version of Cavern that follows Uncle Pen. It's a completely impromptu thing, just in the spirit of the moment, and is just hilarious. It ends with "Whatever you do, take care of your boots." Then the BBCFM encore has the band shouting "Guacamole!" throughout. This show is a perfect example of Phish using their skills to mix music and humor into one.—Andy Bernstein

4/7/92 [ACCESSIBILITY: ••]
Fine Arts Auditorium, Fort Lewis College, Durango, CO
I: Buried Alive > Possum, It's Ice, Fee, Divided Sky, Horse > Silent, Melt, Bouncing, Rift, Sloth, Runaway Jim
II: Poor Heart, All Things, Tweezer, Eliza, YEM, My Friend, Lizards, Maze, Cold as Ice > Bike > Cold as Ice, My Mind's, Golgi
E: Contact, Tweezer Reprise

Fishman on vacuum for Bike.

This was the second show at Fort Lewis, and once again there was a small crowd of about 300 people. There is nothing like seeing Phish in your school auditorium, and like always, the band won over the crowd, establishing many new converts with lots of new Rift material debuts. This was the last cheap Phish show for me—only $7 for three hours of bliss! —Jeff Salvatore

4/9/92 [ACCESSIBILITY: •]
El Ray Theater, Albuquerque, NM
I: Landlady, Sparkle, Foam, Guelah, Llama, Mound, Reba, Uncle Pen, Stash, Squirming Coil, Golgi
II: Oh Kee > Suzie, Bowie, TMWSIY > Avenu > TMWSIY, MSO, Mike's > Hydrogen > Weekapaug, Horse > Silent, Chalkdust, Cold as Ice > Terrapin > Cold as Ice, Cavern
E: Sleeping Monkey, Rocky Top

4/12/92 [ACCESSIBILITY: •] [ATTEND. 401; CAP. 970] [TIX $10-$12]
U. Of Arizona Ballroom, University of Arizona, Tucson, AZ
I: Suzie, Poor Heart, Guelah, Divided Sky, Horse > Silent, It's Ice, Sparkle, Maze, Reba, Antelope
II: Glide, Melt, Bouncing, Rift, YEM, Lawn Boy, NICU, Cold as Ice > Cracklin' Rosie > Cold as Ice, Harry Hood, Cavern
E: Adeline, Rocky Top

4/13/92 [ACCESSIBILITY: •••] [ATTEND. 447; CAP. 750] [TIX $10-$12]
After The Gold Rush, Tempe, AZ
I: Golgi, Uncle Pen, Stash, Lizards, Landlady, NICU, Fee, All Things, Foam, A-Train, Bowie
II: Llama, Fluffhead, Sparkle, Mike's > Hydrogen > Weekapaug, Magilla, Ya Mar, Squirming Coil, Cold as Ice > Love You > Cold as Ice, Possum
E: Memories, Fire

Fishman on vacuum for Love You. Smells Like Teen Spirit tease before Llama and in Mike's intro. We're Off to See the Wizard jam in Possum.

This is a tape swimming in teases. Set two begins with Trey mocking Nirvana's Smells Like Teen Spirit—the big hit at the time—and he even reprises the tease during Mike's big, bass-heavy intro to Mike's Song. It's a really funny poke at the rock n' roll mainstream. There's also a great Bundle of Joy during Fluffhead and a Wonderful Wizard of Oz guitar line in Possum. You know it's a really fun show when Fish stops his vacuum solo due to "not enough suction tonight." Lots of fun! —Tim Foisser

4/15/92 [ACCESSIBILITY: ••] [ATTEND. 689; CAP. 773] [TIX $14]
Variety Arts Theater, Los Angeles, CA
I: Oh Kee > Suzie, Foam, Guelah, Sparkle, Stash, Uncle Pen, Cavern, I Didn't Know, All Things, Runaway Jim
II: Chalkdust, YEM, Reba, Landlady, NICU, Cold as Ice > Cracklin' Rosie > Cold as Ice, MSO, Golgi
E: Memories, Adeline, Rocky Top

Widespread Panic opened. Tapers were inadvertently shut out from this show by venue management. Groove Is in the Heart and Funkytown jams in YEM. Fishman on vacuum for I Didn't Know.

4/16/92 [ACCESSIBILITY: •••••] [ATTEND. 492; CAP. 841] [TIX $12-$13.50]
Anaconda Theater, University of California at Santa Barbara, Santa Barbara, CA
I: Buried Alive > Possum, It's Ice, Bouncing, Melt, Rift, Fee > Maze, Forbin's > Icculus > Mockingbird, Antelope
II: Sanity, Llama, Lizards, Mike's > Hydrogen > Weekapaug, Horn, Poor Heart, Cold as Ice > Terrapin > Cold as Ice, Carolina, Memories, Adeline, Suzie
E: Sleeping Monkey

Widespread Panic opened. Fishman on vacuum for Terrapin. Last Icculus, 4/6/91 Olympia, WA [116 shows].

Both sets are full of timeless treats. In set I, Split Open and Melt is mind-blowing, the transition between Fee > Maze is short but interesting and Icculus makes an appearance between Forbin and Mockingbird. The second set is also solid, from Sanity to Suzie Greenberg. There's also a smokin' Mike's Groove and an a cappella suite to boot. —Chad Ashcraft

For no other reason, get the Anaconda show for the Buried Alive > Possum opener. The segue is smooth as silk and contains most of the secret language signals. Then get ready for one of the most over-the-top Possums ever. Trey layers theme upon bluesy theme to create a crescendo that always does it for me. The soundboard crispness makes this tape a joy. It's a roller coaster ride! —Paul Sheets

This is a great tape for times when people ask, "So which one of these tapes should be my first Phish tape?" It's also a great choice for those who have never heard Phish live—it hooks them every time! —Justin Weiss

4/17/92 [ACCESSIBILITY: •••]
Warfield Theater, San Francisco, CA
I: Runaway Jim, Foam, Sparkle, Stash, I Didn't Know > Cavern, Reba, Maze, Bouncing, Landlady > Bowie/Catapult/Bowie
II: Brother, YEM, Fluffhead, Squirming Coil, Tweezer, Uncle Pen, Cold as Ice > Cracklin' Rosie > Cold as Ice, Tweezer Reprise
E: Golgi

Widespread Panic opened. Fishman on vacuum for I Didn't Know. Brief "Doug" vocal jam in I Didn't Know. A bathtub was wheeled onto the stage before the start of the second set, and a parade of people walked across the stage and jumped in and out of it during Brother. Concert debut: Catapult.

Setlist-wise, this show looks middle-of-the-road. But don't be fooled—this is a show you really should hear. Set one features an incredible Reba (!) and a fantastic David Bowie that includes the concert debut of Catapult woven in it. Set two is a total jam-fest: Brother, YEM, and Tweezer are all strong versions, and the energy in Fluffhead is contagious. It's clear that the band enjoyed themselves, too. "We had an amazing time tonight. This is an incredible room," Trey says at the end of Golgi. The Warfield rocks. —Ed Smith

4/18/92 [ACCESSIBILITY: ••••]
Wilbur Field, Stanford University, Palo Alto, CA

I: Wilson, Divided Sky, Guelah, Poor Heart, Melt, Esther, Possum, It's Ice, Sparkle, All Things, Antelope
II: Glide, Oh Kee > Suzie, Rift, Manteca, Bathtub Gin > Manteca, Lizards, Mound, Llama, TMWSIY > Avenu > TMWSIY, Dinner and a Movie, Harry Hood, Cold as Ice > Love You > Cold as Ice, Rocky Top
E: Contact, BBFCM

Free outdoor show. Mind Left Body tease in Possum. Frere Jacques tease in Antelope intro. Linus and Lucy jam in Hood. Fishman on vacuum for Love You. Seven-year old Cameron McKenney played (unmiked) ukulele on BBFCM. Last Manteca, 3/16/91 Breckenridge, CO [130 shows].

This free afternoon show is a Phish classic. Divided Sky was beautifully hypnotic and took me to a higher ground; It's Ice was accompanied by a smooth breakdown with Trey and Page sounding off; and Antelope featured heavy jamming to end the first set. The second set has a good Oh Kee > Suzie transition, Harry Hood, and a Contact encore. —Jay Green

This show has gained fame as one of the most perfectly played Phish concerts ever. The second set is a masterpiece of musicianship from start to finish, including an outstanding Harry Hood with a Linus and Lucy (a.k.a. Peanuts) jam by Page during the quiet third segment of the song. A hot day in Palo Alto saw Trey calling for "squirt gun breaks" between songs (a roadie on the side of the stage had a SuperSoaker with him), and we're treated to a "happy Passover bass solo" from "Cactus" Gordon in Avenu. Other treats include a wonderfully playful Bathtub Gin and a double-dose of Manteca. —Tricia Holmes

Mike Gordon fans take notice! I don't know what was going on at the soundboard, but WOW is Mike prominent in the board mix. This tape makes up for all those times you've strained to make out Mike's bass in cavernous arenas and outdoor sheds. Happily, he's on fire throughout this show, a classic Phish concert if I ever heard one. —Pat Stanley

4/19/92 [ACCESSIBILITY: ••] [ATTEND. 800; CAP. 800] [TIX $10-$11.50]
The Catalyst, Santa Cruz, CA

I: Buried Alive > NICU, Stash, Paul and Silas, My Friend, Reba, Maze, Fee > Chalkdust, I Didn't Know, Golgi
II: Curtain > Mike's > Hydrogen > Weekapaug, Horse > Silent, MSO, Tube, Mango, Llama, Lawn Boy, Cold as Ice > Brain > Cold as Ice, Runaway Jim
E: Sleeping Monkey, Cavern

Fishman on trombone for I Didn't Know and vacuum for Brain.

Nearly lost among the other classic shows played this week, their return to Santa Cruz's tiny Catalyst features a great opening combo: Buried Alive > NICU. Unlike current versions of this song, NICU opens with Fish pounding out a beat (coming right out of Buried Alive) before Trey and Page drop in. By this point in the tour, NICU has already lost some of the reggae flavor apparent in March's versions but still has the "da-da-da-da" bridge to the final refrains. Hot! This show also offers a great Mike's Groove, Tube (as rare then as it is now), and a very jammy (not at all normal) Mango Song. —Jos Conti

4/21/92 [ACCESSIBILITY: ••••]
Redwood Acres, Eureka, CA

I: Suzie, Uncle Pen, Melt, Rift, Guelah, Possum, It's Ice, Eliza, NICU, Bouncing, Bowie
II: Dinner and a Movie, Forbin's > Mockingbird, Tweezer, Tela, Mike's > Hydrogen > Weekapaug, Weigh, Cold as Ice > Catapult > Cold as Ice, HYHU > Lively Up Yourself > HYHU, Sanity, Maze, Memories
E: Adeline, Cavern

Happy Birthday jam in Weekapaug. Fishman on bass, Trey on drums and Mike on guitar and vacuum for Lively Up Yourself. "Apology" vocal jam before Sanity. Concert debut: Lively Up Yourself.

What a second set! I don't know where to begin. First off, get this tape. Then check out Trey playing with echo effects during the Forbin's rap to repeat "evil King Wilson!" in a Darth Vader-like boom. Listen to Tweezer—the band finds an incredible groove and locks into it for about ten minutes of jamming that sounds so good I have to wonder if it's composed. Mike's Groove is also hot as hell, and the set continues with the famously mangled Lively Up Yourself and Sanity. This is one of the best sets of 1992. —Ed Smith

This Mike's Groove is one of the early greats—no weird shit, no spacey jams, no nonsense, just a wailed-on version of this amazing suite. Mike's Song really rocks, hard as a nail, but it's in Weekapaug that the band climbs to the next plateau. Following the Weekapaug opening, several "make" chants (similar to those on 3/20/92) lead to a melodic guitar line by Trey that's just beautiful, backed ferociously by Mike. Trey's guitar sings in here, and Mike is going crazy, too! The jam gives way to a bass-dominated segment that then builds back up into the Weekapaug theme. Trey takes the jam down a bit, wishes happy birthday to two friends, does a brief Happy Birthday tease and then roars into a closing Weekapaug jam that is simply stupendous. —Al Hunt

My vote for Phish's funniest on-stage moment comes in set II of this show. As Fishman comes to center stage for a song, someone in the crowd shouts out a request for Catapult. "That isn't my terrain," Fish says, but after a moment of contemplation he introduces Mike, who recites Catapult. That's followed by Cold as Ice, leading out of the Henrietta segment. But then Page and Trey start up the HYHU theme and Fish picks up Mike's bass. Somehow with this weird configuration the band manages to play a ridiculous version of Bob Marley's Lively Up Yourself, including Mike's debut performance on vacuum. "Thank you for tolerating that," Fish says when it's over. Suddenly everyone in the band wants to apologize, and their apologies create an odd vocal jam. —Andre Holton

4/22/92 [ACCESSIBILITY: •] [ATTEND. 1,023; CAP. 1,023] [TIX $11-$14]
Hilton Ballroom, Eugene, OR

I: Llama, Foam, Reba, Sparkle, Guelah, Divided Sky, Mound, Stash, All Things > Suzie
II: Glide, Antelope, Horse > Silent, Rift, Wilson > "Language Lesson" > Wilson > YEM, Poor Heart > Cold as Ice > Cracklin' Rosie > Cold as Ice, Harpua, Runaway Jim
E: A-Train, Rocky Top

Earth Day show.

It's cool to hear the first West Coast "secret language" explanation before Wilson, but Harpua is definitely the great reason to hear this tape. It's Earth Day, and Trey tells a story of Johnny, little Johnny Fishman. Trey tells Paul to turn off Fish's mike so he doesn't tell what hotel room he's staying in, but Fish, in true form, sneaks it in: "623, room 623." You've got to listen to it to get the whole story. —Ric Hannah

4/23/92 [ACCESSIBILITY: •] [ATTEND. 654; CAP. 654] [TIX $10-$12]
Oz Nightclub, Seattle, WA

I: Cavern, Curtain > Melt, Uncle Pen, Guelah, Squirming Coil, Llama, Bouncing, It's Ice, I Didn't Know, Possum
II: Landlady, Poor Heart, Mike's > Hydrogen > Weekapaug, Lizards, NICU, Horn, Tweezer, Fee, Maze, Cold as Ice > Cracklin' Rosie > Cold as Ice, Golgi
E: Sleeping Monkey, Tweezer Reprise

Fee lyrics: "Grab an espresso. . . " instead of "Grab a cup of coffee. . . "

4/24/92 [ACCESSIBILITY: •] [ATTEND. 1,120; CAP. 1,120] [TIX $12-$14]
Roseland Theater, Portland, OR

I: Runaway Jim, Forbin's > Icculus > Mockingbird, Uncle Pen, Sloth, Landlady, Fluffhead, Sparkle, Stash, Squirming Coil, Golgi
II: Bowie, Cavern, Ya Mar, Foam, Mike's > Hydrogen > Weekapaug > Mango, Horn, Cold as Ice > Love You > Cold as Ice, Glide, Llama
E: Contact, BBFCM

Jim opened. Fishman on vacuum and trombone for Love You. Vocal jam in Weekapaug led to an On Broadway jam and segued into Mango.

4/25/92 [ACCESSIBILITY: ••] [ATTEND. 820; CAP. 820] [TIX $12-$14]
Campus Recreation Center, Evergreen College, Olympia, WA

I: Suzie, My Friend, Paul and Silas, Reba, Brother, Tela, Chalkdust, Bouncing, Rift, Magilla, Antelope
II: Maze, Bathtub Gin, YEM, Horse > Silent, All Things, Dinner and a Movie, Harry Hood, Weigh
E: Cold as Ice > Terrapin > Cold as Ice, Poor Heart

Sprockets and Chariots of Fire themes in YEM vocal jam.

4/29/92 [ACCESSIBILITY: ••] [ATTEND. 879; CAP. 900] [TIX $7-$9]
First Avenue, Minneapolis, MN

I: Suzie, Foam, Sparkle, It's Ice, Runaway Jim, Guelah, Rift, Bouncing, A-Train, Bowie > "Language Lesson" > Bowie
II: Landlady > Possum, Mound, Oh Kee > Llama, Lizards, Mike's > Hydrogen > Weekapaug, Cold as Ice > Love You > Cold as Ice, Golgi
E: Horn, Rocky Top

Col. Bruce Hampton and the Aquarium Rescue Unit opened. Raspberry Beret jam in Weekapaug. Fishman on vacuum for Love You.

Welcome to Minneapolis, hometown of the Artist Who Was Still Called Prince in 1992. Trey pays tribute with a very pronounced Raspberry Beret jam in Weekapaug. This show is best known for its super-stoked Possum, though, which smokes. —Scott Sifton

4/30/92 [ACCESSIBILITY: ••] [ATTEND. 822; CAP. 822] [TIX $13-$15]
Barrymore Theater, Madison, WI

I: Curtain > Melt, Fee, Maze, Reba, Uncle Pen, Stash, Rift, Esther, Antelope
II: Glide, Tweezer, Squirming Coil, My Mind's, YEM, Horse > Silent, Chalkdust, Cold as Ice > Cracklin' Rosie > Cold as Ice, Harry Hood, Tweezer Reprise
E: Carolina, Cavern

Col. Bruce Hampton and the Aquarium Rescue Unit opened.

5/1/92 [ACCESSIBILITY: ••••] [ATTEND. 550; CAP. 1,200] [TIX $10-$12.50]
Rave at Central Park, Milwaukee, WI
I: Suzie, My Friend, Poor Heart, Landlady, NICU, Sloth, Divided Sky, Guelah, It's Ice, Horn, I Didn't Know, Possum
II: Sanity, Buried Alive > Wilson, All Things, MSO, Mike's > Hydrogen > Weekapaug, Mound, Lizards, Llama, Cold as Ice > Terrapin > Cold as Ice, Golgi
E: Lawn Boy, GTBT
E2: Rocky Top

Fishman on bagpipe reed (played like a kazoo) for I Didn't Know and vacuum for Terrapin.

5/2/92 [ACCESSIBILITY: ••••] [ATTEND. 1,000; CAP. 1,000] [TIX $13.50]
Cabaret Metro, Chicago, IL
I: Runaway Jim, Forbin's > Icculus > Mockingbird, Sparkle, Reba, Maze, Bouncing, Stash, Squirming Coil, Llama
II: Glide, Bowie, Tela, Foam, YEM, Chalkdust, Cold as Ice > Cracklin' Rosie > Cold as Ice, Cavern
E: Sleeping Monkey, BBFCM

Col. Bruce Hampton and the Aquarium Rescue Unit opened. Stash lyric: "Police pull you over, beat the shit out of you..." referencing the Rodney King verdict earlier in the week. Wicked Witch of the West jam before Bowie. Band Football Theme Song and Crew Football Theme Song jams in Bowie. Funky Bitch tease in YEM.

Phish hadn't hit the big-time yet: their show at the Metro had to be over by 10 p.m. so other bands could play later in the night. Despite the early start, Phish turned in another rocking show, with lots of stage humor that isn't attempted so much these days in arenas and amphitheaters. Mike and Trey videotaped each other bouncing on trampolines during YEM, and Mike pulled out his video camera again during BBFCM when Trey stood on Page's amp to play. Antics aside, check out this Bowie. —Mick Connor

In case you missed 4/16/91, here's another chance to get up to speed on the Band and Crew Football Theme Songs. The songs were written by Phish, one to represent their team and one for the crew's team. (Because the crew usually beats the band in their pickup football games, they made the band theme song really strong and powerful and the crew theme song kind of wimpy.) The tunes are dusted off in the midst of the Bowie jam—that's the band theme song first, followed by the crew theme song, then back into the band theme song. —Ernie Greene

5/3/92 [ACCESSIBILITY: •]
Student Union Ballroom, Michigan State University, East Lansing, MI
I: Landlady, Possum, It's Ice, Uncle Pen, Fee > All Things > Melt, I Didn't Know, Rift, Horn, Runaway Jim
II: Tweezer, Horse > Silent, Fluffhead, Guelah, Mike's > Hydrogen > Weekapaug, Mango, Cold as Ice > Cracklin' Rosie > Cold as Ice, Dinner and a Movie, Bouncing, Oh Kee > Suzie
E: Memories, Adeline, Tweezer Reprise

Fishman on vacuum for I Didn't Know.

5/5/92 [ACCESSIBILITY: •] [ATTEND. 1,124; CAP. 1,200] [TIX $8-$10]
Bogart's, Cincinnati, OH
I: Golgi, Curtain, Sparkle, Stash, Rift, Guelah, Divided Sky, I Didn't Know, It's Ice > Glide > Antelope
II: Chalkdust, Bouncing, All Things, Foam, Mike's > Hydrogen > Weekapaug, Horse > Silent, Poor Heart, Llama, Cold as Ice > Love You > Cold as Ice, Squirming Coil, Cavern
E: Contact, Rocky Top

Fishman on trombone for I Didn't Know and vacuum for Love You.

5/6/92 [ACCESSIBILITY: ••••]
St. Andrew's Hall, Detroit, MI
I: Llama, Foam, Reba, My Mind's, Maze, Tela, Brother, Forbin's > Mockingbird, Sparkle, Cavern
II: MSO, Stash, Squirming Coil, YEM, All Things, Bouncing, Uncle Pen, Chalkdust, HYHU > Terrapin > Cold as Ice, A-Train, Golgi
E: Carolina, GTBT

Shaggy Dog theme in YEM vocal jam. Cold as Ice tease before Chalkdust. Fishman on vacuum for Terrapin.

5/7/92 [ACCESSIBILITY: ••••] [ATTEND. 816; CAP. 1,000] [TIX $10-$12]
Agora Theater, Cleveland, OH
I: Suzie, Poor Heart, Buried Alive, My Friend, Foam, Runaway Jim, Esther, Melt, Rift, Guelah, Possum
II: Landlady, Sparkle, Tweezer, Fluffhead, Glide, Mike's > Hydrogen > Weekapaug, Fee, Cold as Ice > Bike > Cold as Ice, Squirming Coil, Tweezer Reprise
E: Adeline, Sleeping Monkey > Rocky Top

Fishman on vacuum for Bike. Banana tree prop lowered onto the stage during Fee.

Unremarkable first set, but the second set—after a standard Landlady/Sparkle opener—is a jamfest. Experimental Tweezer > Fluff > Glide, Mike's Groove just sparkles. Cold as Ice intro to Bike as Fish announces, "Ladies and gentlemen, this is Mike Gordon tuning his bass." An epic piano solo during Coil, then my tape runs out.—Bob Colby

5/8/92 [ACCESSIBILITY: ••] [ATTEND. 1,125; CAP. 1,125] [TIX $12-$14]
Riviera Theater, North Tonawanda (Buffalo), NY
I: Curtain > Cavern, Reba, Uncle Pen, It's Ice > Eliza, Llama, Mound, All Things, Bouncing, Bowie, Memories
II: Wilson, MSO, Stash, Magilla > Maze, YEM, Horse > Silent, Chalkdust, Cold as Ice > Terrapin > Cold as Ice, Harry Hood, Golgi
E: BBFCM

Fishman on vacuum for Terrapin. Brady Bunch and Popeye jams in BBFCM. House lights turned on by venue manager before BBFCM, and left on through the song.

The Curtain, always a strong opener, kicks things off, then Reba keeps the upbeat tempo going into the set. Bouncing > Bowie is an infallible connection as Phish enacts the secret language by all falling down at the end of Bouncing. Set II is musically wondrous. Magilla segues into Maze, which is spacey, and YEM traverses the outer limits of improvisational music and sound. Horse > Silent is very intimate, almost like Phish is simply having a conversation with the phans instead of singing to us. Golgi and BBFCM remind us to appreciate natural humor and the art of smiling. —Anthony Buchla

Friday, May 8, 1992

RIVIERA THEATER, Buffalo, NY

The Riviera Theater had just been restored—this was the first rock show they hosted there after putting a ton of money into it, and when Phish arrived, the venue staff and management thought all hell had broken loose. I asked this one old lady in the hallway what she thought of Phish's music, and her response was, and I quote, "That's what hell must sound like."

First, they didn't want to let Phish play the second set because so many people were smoking cigarettes and stuff. Page made a little announcement before Wilson, saying something like, "Please, please everybody, the fire marshall wants you to stop smoking."

Then they didn't want to let Phish do an encore. But the band was like, "We gotta do an encore." As they went to walk on the stage, the guy that owned the Riviera Theater tackled Mike to try to keep him from going on. But I guess they got on stage anyway, so the guy throws all the houselights on. Phish busted into Big Black Furry Creatures From Mars, as if these people didn't think hell had broken loose enough already. And Trey climbed on top of Page's piano, and played his whole solo behind his head, during which he played the Brady Bunch and the Popeye themes—everything behind his head. Mike, in the meantime, climbed the stacks next to Fishman and played his part from standing on top of the stacks with all the houselights on. The whole show was pretty hectic!

—Mike Graff

5/9/92 [ACCESSIBILITY: ••••]
Syracuse Armory, Syracuse, NY
I: Runaway Jim, Foam, Sparkle, Melt, Guelah, Rift, Fee, Maze, Squirming Coil, I Didn't Know, Antelope
II: Suzie, Divided Sky, Tela, Tweezer, Harpua, Llama, Cold as Ice > Cracklin' Rosie > Cold as Ice, Golgi
E: Poor Heart, Tweezer Reprise
Mimi Fishman and Fishman on vacuum for I Didn't Know, and Mimi on vocals for I Didn't Know. Smells Like Teen Spirit jam in Harpua.

5/10/92 [ACCESSIBILITY: •]
Spring Fling, University of Massachusetts, Amherst, MA
Landlady, Suzie, Sparkle, Stash, Uncle Pen, Cavern, Reba, I Didn't Know, YEM, Possum
Outdoor Spring Fling concert at which Phish played one set. The concert also featured sets by Rippopatamus and The Mighty, Mighty Bosstones, which played before Phish; and Firehose, Fishbone, and the Beastie Boys, which played after Phish.

5/12/92 [ACCESSIBILITY: ••••]
St. Lawrence University, Canton, NY
I: MSO, Reba, All Things, Sloth > Possum, It's Ice, Dinner and a Movie, Bouncing, Buried Alive, Uncle Pen, Horn, Bowie
II: Landlady, Bathtub Gin, YEM, Guelah, Chalkdust, Cold as Ice > Terrapin > Cold as Ice, Poor Heart, Llama, Cavern
E: Runaway Jim
Oye Como Va jam in YEM.

Although I only have set II, I can proudly say that this is my favorite tape—not because it's my best-sounding tape, but because of the killer playing (most obviously, Mike Gordon's bass)! The April-May 1992 soundboards have Gordon particularly fat in the mix. A great Landlady melts perfectly into a great Bathtub Gin. The YEM that follows is an all-time favorite! Nice SBDs of this show are out there. —Chris Mrachek

5/14/92 [ACCESSIBILITY: ••••] [ATTEND. 1,800; CAP. 1,800] [TIX $16-$18]
Capitol Theater, Port Chester, NY
I: Suzie, All Things, Sloth, Sparkle, Maze, Horn, Reba, Poor Heart, My Friend, Bouncing, Antelope > "Language Lesson" > Antelope
II: Glide, Cavern, Rift, Fluffhead, Eliza, Mike's > Hydrogen > Weekapaug, McGrupp, Stash, Cold as Ice > Cracklin' Rosie > Cold as Ice, Possum
E: Sleeping Monkey, Rocky Top
Spiderman jam in Antelope. "Wait" jam between Weekapaug and McGrupp.

Antelope, Antelope, Antelope—can't say enough about this Antelope. Trey jams on Spiderman! A new signal ("aw fuck!") is introduced! Phish rocks out! Hear it!—Ed Smith

5/15/92 [ACCESSIBILITY: •]
Lonestar Roadhouse, New York, NY
Golgi, Foam, Cavern, Sparkle, Stash, Bouncing, Cold as Ice > Love You > Cold as Ice, Chalkdust, YEM, Adeline, Rocky Top
Private party for recording and radio industry executives. Phish played one set.

5/16/92 [ACCESSIBILITY: •••] [ATTEND. 2,637; CAP. 2,637] [TIX $16.50]
Orpheum Theater, Boston, MA
I: Maze, Foam, Glide, Melt, Bouncing, MSO, Horn, Golgi, Lizards, Cavern, Bowie
II: Runaway Jim, It's Ice, Paul and Silas, Tweezer, Squirming Coil, YEM, Horse > Silent, Oh Kee > AC/DC Bag, Cold as Ice > Cracklin' Rosie > Cold as Ice, Poor Heart, Tweezer Reprise
E: Adeline, Suzie
Last AC/DC Bag, 11/1/91 Denver, CO [74 shows].

My first taste of Phish madness—the crowds swarming outside the run-down but majestic Orpheum blew my mind even before the music did. Where did all these people come from? It looked like a cross between a Dead tour and a prep school campus. Once we made it inside, diligent security guards kept us trapped near the back, but that didn't matter once the lights went out and the drummer emerged, wearing a dress, and tapped out a drum beat. One by one, the other band members came out and an incredible song materialized. Wow! Five years and many shows later, I still count this as one of my favorite Mazes. —Teddy Stuart

5/17/92 [ACCESSIBILITY: •••]
Achilles Rink, Union College, Schenectady, NY
I: Landlady, Llama, Forbin's > Mockingbird, MSO, Reba, I Didn't Know, Stash, Mango, Poor Heart, Chalkdust
II: Curtain > Possum, Guelah, Squirming Coil, All Things, Brother, Sanity, Cold as Ice > Love You > Cold as Ice, Sparkle, Harry Hood, Cavern
E: Lawn Boy, GTBT
Fishman on trombone for I Didn't Know and vacuum for Love You. Rocky Mountain Way, It's Ice and Divided Sky jams in Possum. Birthday cake brought to Page during Squirming Coil. Happy Birthday tease in Love You.

One of the most underrated shows out there, the band's Union College gig was a late but welcome addition to the tail end of the 1992 spring tour. Possum is incredible! The intro is practically its own song, as Trey is just off somewhere else (he gets a cool groove going). Once the song kicks in, they again wander, first into Rocky Mountain Way and then into It's Ice (not a simple little jam—I keep expecting Page to sing the lyrics!) When that's calmed down a bit, Trey plays the guitar line from Divided Sky for at least a minute—then tops off an over-the-top Possum jam in incredible fashion! This is wild! Not only that, but this show has the last Sanity for a while (and a loud one at that), plus a hilarious Fishman meditation on birthdays (it's Page's 28th) during Love You, including rare commentary from Paul at the soundboard. This set is other-worldly. —Mick Connor

5/18/92 [ACCESSIBILITY: ••]
Flynn Theater, Burlington, VT
I: Suzie, Maze, Bouncing, Divided Sky, Guelah, Foam, Poor Heart, Horn, Sparkle, Antelope
II: Glide, Llama, TMWSIY > Avenu > TMWSIY, Mike's > Hydrogen > Weekapaug, Fee, Rift, Cavern, Cold as Ice > Love You > HYHU, Runaway Jim
E: Rocky Top
Fishman on vacuum for Love You.

1992 SUMMER Europe

After taking a month off from touring, Phish jetted to Europe for a two-week stretch of shows at the end of June. Playing on various music festival bills and opening for an odd array of bands—primarily the Violent Femmes—the band got a taste of tour life overseas. Plans for European tours in the summers of 1993, 1994, and 1995 all failed to materialize, but summer 1996 and February 1997 took Phish back to Europe to work the connections made five years earlier.

6/19/92 [ACCESSIBILITY: ••]
Stadtpark/Freilichtbuhn, Hamburg, Germany
Landlady, Suzie, Stash, Squirming Coil, Sparkle, Cavern, YEM
Opened for the Violent Femmes. Soundcheck: MSO.

6/20/92 [ACCESSIBILITY: •]
Waldbuhn, Nordheim, Germany
Buried Alive, Bouncing, Foam, Runaway Jim, It's Ice, Horn, HYHU > Love You > HYHU, Llama
Opened for the Violent Femmes and Lou Reed. Fishman on vacuum for Love You.

6/23/92 [ACCESSIBILITY: •••]
Philipshalle, Dusseldorf, Germany
Chalkdust, Reba, Maze, Adeline, Uncle Pen, BBFCM, Brain, Golgi
Opened for the Violent Femmes. Fishman on vacuum for BBFCM.

6/24/92 [ACCESSIBILITY: •]
Resi, Nuremberg, Germany
Runaway Jim, Llama, Adeline, Uncle Pen, Guelah, I Didn't Know, Sparkle, Cavern, Rocky Top
Opened for the Violent Femmes.

6/27/92 [ACCESSIBILITY: •]
Roskilde Festival, Outside Copenhagen, Denmark
Runaway Jim, Foam, Sparkle, Reba, Maze, All Things, Chalkdust, Bouncing, Uncle Pen, Bowie
E: I Didn't Know, GTBT
Phish played as part of the annual four-day Roskilde Festival.

[6/30/92] Lawn Boy re-released on Elektra.

6/30/92 [ACCESSIBILITY: •]
Elysee Montmartre, Paris, France
Golgi, Divided Sky, Guelah, Possum, Adeline, YEM
Opened for the Violent Femmes. Frere Jacques jam in Possum.

7/1/92 [ACCESSIBILITY: •]
Ancienne Beguique, Brussels, Belgium
Curtain > Cavern, Rift, Horn, Melt, Adeline, Rocky Top
Opened for the Violent Femmes.

7/3/92 ❄
Brixton Academy, Radio One Music Festival, London, England
Opened for the Violent Femmes and Green on Red.

1992 SUMMER Santana

After returning from Europe, Phish played four concerts with Blues Traveler, Spin Doctors, Widespread Panic, and Aquarium Rescue Unit on the first leg of the first HORDE (Horizons of Rock Developing Everywhere) tour, then sneaked in a couple of solo concerts before spending the rest of the summer opening for Carlos Santana—a tour that became a major turning point for the band. It was Santana who described Phish as a "hose" watering the audience, a metaphor that has come to define the peak musical experience possible at a Phish concert. Besides the hose, the summer also saw the first "vacuum freeze"—Trey, Page, and Mike would freeze in position while Fishman came forward for a vacuum solo.

7/9/92 [ACCESSIBILITY: ••]
Cumberland County Civic Center, Portland, ME
Glide, Oh Kee > Suzie > Landlady, Sparkle, Stash, Squirming Coil, Runaway Jim, Guelah, Bowie, Glide Reprise
E: Rocky Top
HORDE show with Aquarium Rescue Unit, Widespread Panic, Spin Doctors, and Blues Traveler. Phish played one set, closing the show. Fishman on vacuum (vacuum freeze) during Bowie intro.

7/10/92 [ACCESSIBILITY: ••]
Empire Court, Syracuse, NY
Bouncing, Llama, Reba, Sparkle, Maze, Golgi, Lizards, Cavern, Antelope
E: MSO
HORDE show with Aquarium Rescue Unit, Widespread Panic, Spin Doctors, and Blues Traveler. Phish played one set. Fishman on vacuum (vacuum freeze) near the end of Cavern.

The first HORDE tour saw gem performances from Widespread, Col. Bruce & ARU, Spin Doctors, Blues Traveler and Phish. What more could you ask for? It rained all day, but I was under a tree and never noticed. Phish played a straight set with the jazz influences flying. Still, Col. Bruce and Blues Traveler blew them off the stage—well, third best isn't bad. This was a good exposure show for many "Who is this Phish band?" people. It starts getting bigger from here on. —David M. Brown

7/11/92 [ACCESSIBILITY: ••]
Garden State Arts Center, Holmdel, NJ
Landlady, Runaway Jim, Foam, Sparkle, Stash, Squirming Coil, Cavern, YEM, Suzie
HORDE show. Phish played one set. Fishman on vacuum (vacuum freeze) near the end of Cavern. Four female dancers boogied on stage with Trey and Mike during Landlady. John Popper came out to jump on trampoline during YEM, but in what turned out to be a rigged effect, the trampoline gave way under his weight.

7/12/92 [ACCESSIBILITY: ••]
Jones Beach Music Theater, Wantagh, NY
Adeline, Chalkdust, Bouncing, Divided Sky, Fluffhead, Uncle Pen, Maze, Glide, Possum
HORDE show. Phish played one set, closing the show. Fishman on vacuum (vacuum freeze) during Glide. But Anyway jam in Possum.

Phish was the last band to take the stage during the first HORDE visit to Jones Beach. Many people had already left. I sneaked up to front row center, where there was lots of dancing room available. Phish took the stage wearing Mardi Gras masks and dancing about. The setlist was good, but the quality of the music played was great. —Brian A. Rock

By far the largest audience Phish had played to at that point. The crowd was genuinely enthusiastic, and even those who weren't familiar with the band did a good job pretending. I know I did. —Andy Bernstein

7/14/92 [ACCESSIBILITY: •] [ATTEND. 862; CAP. 1,500] [TIX $8.50-$10]
The Boathouse, Norfolk, VA
I: Landlady, Rift, Guelah, Maze, Sparkle, It's Ice, Runaway Jim, Horn, Brother, I Didn't Know, Poor Heart, Cavern
II: Tweezer, Fee, All Things, Reba, Llama, Squirming Coil, Paul and Silas, YEM, A-Train, Tweezer Reprise
E: Sleeping Monkey

7/15/92 [ACCESSIBILITY: ••••]
Trax, Charlottesville, VA
I: Glide, Oh Kee > Suzie, Foam, My Friend, Uncle Pen, Melt, Horse > Silent, Chalkdust, Lizards, Antelope
II: Sloth, Divided Sky, Esther, MSO, Stash, McGrupp, All Things, Harry Hood, Golgi
E: Possum
Fishman on vacuum (vacuum freeze) in the middle of Possum.

7/16/92 [ACCESSIBILITY: ••]
The Flood Zone, Richmond, VA
I: Poor Heart, It's Ice, Sparkle, Wilson, Dinner and a Movie, Bouncing, Maze, Guelah, Rift, Bowie
II: Runaway Jim, Weigh, Landlady, Fluffhead, TMWSIY > Avenu > TMWSIY, Llama, Glide, Paul and Silas, Mike's > Hydrogen > Weekapaug
E: Blue Bayou, Squirming Coil
Concert debut: Blue Bayou.

7/17/92 ❄
Merriweather Post Pavilion, Columbia, MD
Chalkdust, Sparkle, Stash, Squirming Coil, Maze, Bouncing, Runaway Jim
Opened for Santana.

7/18/92 ❄
Mann Music Center, Philadelphia, PA
Suzie, Foam, Llama, Reba, Rift, Antelope
Opened for Santana.

7/19/92 ❄
Garden State Arts Center, Holmdel, NJ
Poor Heart, Maze, Runaway Jim, Bowie, Adeline
Opened for Santana. Trey joined Santana for one song during Santana's set.

7/21/92 [ACCESSIBILITY: •]
Great Woods, Mansfield, MA
All Things, Possum, It's Ice, Sparkle, Stash, Squirming Coil, Runaway Jim
Opened for Santana.

7/22/92 ❄
Holman Stadium, Nashua, NH
Reba, Poor Heart, Bouncing, Maze, Rift, Cavern, Bowie
Opened for Santana. Fishman on vacuum (vacuum freeze) near the end of Cavern. Trey joined Santana for a part of Santana's set.

7/23/92 [ACCESSIBILITY: •]
Hangin' with MTV, MTV Studios, New York, NY
Phish appeared as the "house band." Snippets from Buried Alive, Divided Sky, Stash, and Poor Heart, plus a Fishman vacuum solo and some trampoline action, were broadcast.

7/24/92 [ACCESSIBILITY: ••]
Jones Beach Music Theater, Wantagh, NY
MSO, Foam, Tweezer, Squirming Coil, YEM, Tweezer Reprise
Opened for Santana. Phish joined Santana for part of Santana's set.

7/25/92 [ACCESSIBILITY: •••••]
Stowe Performing Arts Center, Stowe, VT
Runaway Jim, Foam, Sparkle, Stash, Rift, YEM, Llama, Funky Bitch
Opened for Santana. YEM, Llama, and Funky Bitch featured Carlos Santana. Santana band percussionists Raul Rekow (on congas) and Karl Perazzo (on timbales) joined for YEM. Phish joined Santana for part of Santana's set. Last Funky Bitch, 7/26/91 Athens, CA [126 shows].

This was the hometown show on the Santana tour, and as a tribute, Carlos let the boys play a little longer than the normal 40-to-50-minute sets they played this summer. That was probably because Carlos joined them on stage during YEM and jammed out with Trey and the boys from YEM through Llama into Funky Bitch. The resulting music is an incredible confluence of rock's past, present and future, and is without question a seminal Phish event. No Phish tape collection is complete without a copy of this set. —Scott Sifton

My favorite tape in my collection! I love Santana jamming with them. This is the best Llama ever! I always listen to Trey and Carlos jam, and I don't know whose jam is better. The band seemed to be in total synch—every fan of Phish and Santana MUST own this show. Incredible! —Jason Mokhtarian

By the way, for those of you who care about this sort of thing, the Bowie > Catapult > Bowie that follows the Funky Bitch on most copies of this tape is actually from Phish's appearance at the Warfield Theater in San Francisco on 4/17/92. Phish's set on 7/25/92 ended with Funky Bitch—and what a Bitch it was! —Ernie Greene

7/26/92 ❄
Big Birch Concert Pavilion, Patterson, NY
Chalkdust, It's Ice, Divided Sky, Weigh, Melt, Lizards, Llama
Opened for Santana. Trey, Page, and Mike joined Santana for part of Santana's set.

7/27/92 [ACCESSIBILITY: •]
Saratoga Performing Arts Center, Saratoga Springs, NY
Golgi, All Things, Bowie, Horn, Suzie, Llama, Adeline
E: Rocky Top
Opened for Santana. Phish joined Santana for part of Santana's set. A cappella intro to Suzie.

7/28/92 ❄
Finger Lakes Performing Arts Center, Canandaigua, NY
Chalkdust, Bouncing, Uncle Pen, Squirming Coil, Tweezer, Runaway Jim
Opened for Santana. Phish joined Santana for part of Santana's set.

7/30/92 ❄
Meadow Brook Music Festival, Rochester Hills, MI
Rift, Horn, Sparkle, It's Ice > All Things, Maze, I Didn't Know, Possum
Opened for Santana. Phish joined Santana for part of Santana's set.

7/31/92 ❄
Blossom Music Center, Cayahoga Falls, OH
Suzie, Chalkdust, Bouncing, Oh Kee > YEM, GTBT
Opened for Santana. Trey joined Santana for part of Santana's set.

8/1/92 ❄
Poplar Creek Music Center, Hoffman Estates, IL
Golgi, Foam, Poor Heart, Stash, Squirming Coil, Horn, Llama
Opened for Santana. Phish joined Santana for part of Santana's set.

8/2/92 ❄
Riverport Performing Arts Center, Marilyn Heights, MO
Chalkdust, Guelah, Rift, Oh Kee > Suzie, Bowie, Cavern, Rocky Top
Opened for Santana.

8/13/92 [ACCESSIBILITY: •]
Greek Theater, Los Angeles, CA
Chalkdust, Foam, YEM
Opened for Santana.

8/14/92 [ACCESSIBILITY: •]
Greek Theater, Los Angeles, CA
Poor Heart, Stash, Squirming Coil, Llama, Adeline
Opened for Santana.

STOWE PERFORMING ARTS CENTER, Stowe, VT

Saturday, July 25, 1992

Is this the ultimate Phish experience? In a word, YES. In May 1992, I called a TicketMaster-type place for tickets to Santana at the Stowe Performing Arts Center, and the dude on the phone couldn't find such a show, much less a town called Stowe. Eventually he found it listed under another town's name and I ordered the tickets.

Two months later, it was a beautiful, warm Vermont summer day, and upon arriving at the venue we saw a little shack selling cassettes and stickers for a group called Phish. Having never heard of them, I figured they must be the opening group, and after asking a few questions, I found out they were local (meaning Vermont). From there, we went to check our seats—fourth row center, NO WAY!! I guess I had ordered REAL early. The seats went right to the stage so we were only about thirty feet from the musicians.

The "local group" came on early, and the drummer started tapping. I turned to my girlfriend and said, "Oh, this must be a folk group." The song—I'm convinced the tapes have it wrong—was Glide. Next was Runaway Jim, and I was thinking, boy these guys are good, but I was still stoked for Santana. Well, Trey launched into YEM and I was hooked for life. He nailed it, standing right on the edge of the stage and making ugly faces. As you all know, Santana literally jumped out in a bright yellow T-shirt and proceeded to give us the best show of our lives.

The part you NEVER hear about came near the end of Santana's set when Santana said, "Let's bring the local boys back out." With thirteen musicians on stage . . . . well, it just can't be put into words—solos everywhere, Fishman even soloed on a small hand-held drum he beat with a weird crooked stick.

My girlfriend always says that this was the best show she's ever seen, a tall order coming from a woman who's seen Jimi Hendrix, Led Zeppelin ('73) and Janis Joplin with the Tower of Power, and who went to a picnic at Greg Allman's house after being invited by Greg himself. I'm sorry to all the folks who missed it. This was the ultimate Phish experience, Santana was Santana and Phish was the best I've ever heard them—the best. The week after the show I asked the Vermont DMV for the Phish license plate—and got it!

—David Clement

8/15/92 [ACCESSIBILITY: •]
Greek Theater, Los Angeles, CA
Landlady, Sparkle, Guelah, Maze, Runaway Jim
Opened for Santana.

8/17/92 [ACCESSIBILITY: ••••] [ATTEND. 480; CAP. 480] [TIX $16.50]
The Coach House, San Juan Capistrano, CA
I: Buried Alive > Poor Heart, Landlady, Reba, Rift, Wilson, All Things, Foam, My Friend, Bouncing, Bowie
II: Suzie, It's Ice, Tweezer, Esther, Mike's > Hydrogen > Weekapaug, Horn, HYHU > Terrapin > HYHU, A-Train > Somewhere Over the Rainbow jam, Cavern
E: Squirming Coil
Ninja Custodian opened. Camel Walk jam at start of Wilson. A cappella intro to Suzie. Fishman on vacuum and Ninja Mike Billington on drums for Terrapin. Flintstones jams before and during A-Train. Somewhere Over the Rainbow jam in A-Train, followed by a separate SOTR jam after A-Train.

8/19/92 ❄
Pema County Fair, Tucson, AZ
Chalkdust, Landlady, Runaway Jim, Guelah, YEM, Uncle Pen, Llama
Opened for Santana. Trey, Page, and Mike joined Santana for part of Santana's set.

8/20/92 ❄
Pan American Center, Las Cruces, NM
Golgi, Foam, Stash, Squirming Coil > Bowie, Adeline
Opened for Santana. Phish joined Santana for part of Santana's set.

8/23/92 ❄
Colorado State Fair, Pueblo, CO
Chalkdust, Maze, Sparkle, Cavern, Foam, Runaway Jim, Stash
Opened for Santana.

8/24/92 ❄
Gerald Ford Amphitheatre, Vail, CO
Buried Alive > Poor Heart, All Things, Tweezer, Landlady, Reba, YEM
Opened for Santana. Phish joined Santana for part of Santana's set.

8/25/92 ❄
The Downs, Santa Fe, NM
Runaway Jim, It's Ice, Sparkle, Stash, Squirming Coil, Llama, Adeline
Opened for Santana.

8/27/92 ❄
Santa Barbara County Bowl, Santa Barbara, CA
Chalkdust, Bouncing, Landlady, Horn, Sparkle, YEM, Llama
Opened for Santana.

8/28/92 ❄
Concord Pavilion, Concord, CA
Poor Heart, Foam, Stash, Adeline, Squirming Coil, Runaway Jim, Rocky Top
Opened for Santana. Phish joined Santana for part of Santana's set.

8/29/92 **[ACCESSIBILITY: ••]**
Shoreline Amphitheatre, Mountain View, CA
Chalkdust, Rift, Bouncing, Maze, YEM
Opened for Santana. Oye Como Va jam in YEM. Phish joined Santana for part of Santana's set.

8/30/92 **[ACCESSIBILITY: •]**
Cal Expo Amphitheatre, Sacramento, CA
Uncle Pen, Landlady, Reba, Llama, Memories, Antelope, Adeline
Music festival featuring Santana, Los Lobos, and the Indigo Girls. Phish opened the festival, playing one set. Phish joined Santana for part of Santana's set.

🐟 Again, Santana and Phish rock and roll together during Santana's set. Carlos and Trey have a great time going back and forth. This show ended the six-week tour with these two artists playing together almost every night. Their guitars always seem to smoke when played together. —Leah Shantz

[9/7/92] White Crow Studios, Burlington, VT
Recording for *Rift* begins.

10/30/92 ❄
Boston Garden, Boston, MA
Runaway Jim, Maze, Bouncing, Rift, Cavern, Squirming Coil, Stash, Adeline, YEM
WBCN-FM new music concert featuring Spin Doctors and other groups. Phish headlined and played one set. Fishman on vacuum (vacuum freeze) near the end of Cavern.

[10/92-11/92] The Castle, Nashville TN
Additional recording and mixing for *Rift*.

1992 Fall Big Ball Fall

The band put the finishing touches on the album that would become *Rift* in early November, then headed out for a short fall tour that culminated in the band's first "official" New Year's Run of shows. The fall tour featured debuts of several of the new *Rift* songs and the premiere of the Big Ball Jam, a new interactive band-audience game. Soundboard tapes from this tour are tougher to come by than those for the spring tour, though a few fall 1992 boards (notably 11/27 and 11/28) have recently found their way into wider release.

11/19/92 **[ACCESSIBILITY: ••••]**
Ross Sports Center, St. Michael's College, Colchester, VT
I: Maze, Fee > Foam, Glide, Melt, Mound > Divided Sky, Esther, Axilla, Horse > Silent, Antelope
II: Mike's > Hydrogen > Weekapaug, Bouncing > It's Ice > I Walk the Line > Tweezer > BBJ, Poor Heart, FEFY, Llama, HYHU > Lengthwise > HYHU, Cavern
E: Bold as Love
Those Were the Days (All in the Family theme) teases in Divided Sky, Antelope (in the intro and again before "Rye, rye, rocco. . . "), and in Weekapaug. Price of Love jam in Weekapaug. I Walk the Line and BBFCM jams in Tweezer; Burning Ring of Fire vocal tease in Tweezer. Gordon Stone on pedal steel guitar for Poor Heart, FEFY, and Llama. Fishman on vacuum for Lengthwise. Concert debuts: Axilla, I Walk the Line, BBJ, FEFY, and Lengthwise. Last Mound, 5/8/92 Buffalo, NY [52 shows]. Last Bold as Love, 4/18/90 Denver, CO [285 shows].

🐟 This show is kind of comparable to a show like Lowell Auditorium from May 1995. Many of the songs Phish played were first-timers, among them Lengthwise, which I would consider special nowadays, so infrequently is it played. The entire setlist rocked. Mike's > I am Hydrogen > Weekapaug was very common at the time, but Phish still managed an excellent jam. The most exciting point for me was the Bold as Love encore, a comeback appearance of a song not seen since the 1980s. —Adam Rizzuti

🐟 This show really has a hometown feel to it. The Gordon Stone cameo adds to that, as does the debut of the Big Ball Jam. Trey explains that the big balls "let the audience jam the band," and when it's all done, Page says, "We hope you liked that as much as we did." This show also features a very rare reggae Lengthwise. When Fish finishes it, Page says, "He wrote that," and Trey adds, "We like that song so much, yes, it appears twice on the new album." —Andy Bernstein

🐟 Fans of Phish chaos, like Providence's 3/13/92 Run Like a Big Black Furry Antelope, might want to check out the St. Mike's Tweezer. After a jam sequence that includes I Walk the Line teases, the band turns a jam that didn't seem to be going anywhere into BBFCM. But then Mike starts singing I Walk the Line lyrics while Trey sings Burning Ring of Fire! Almost immediately, the band kicks back into the Tweezer theme, which peaks right away and then dies out. Trey introduces Pete Schall, who throws out the balls for the first official (and perhaps longest) Big Ball Jam. —Teddy Stuart

11/20/92 **[ACCESSIBILITY: •••] [ATTEND. 2,674; CAP. 2,674] [TIX $17]**
Palace Theater, Albany, NY
I: Axilla, All Things > Suzie, Rift, Sloth, Reba, Sparkle, Stash, Lizards, Memories, I Walk the Line, Bowie
II: Chalkdust, Fluffhead, Tube, YEM, FEFY, Dinner and a Movie > Harry Hood, HYHU > Terrapin, Lengthwise
E: Self
E2: Adeline, GTBT
Linus and Lucy jam in Stash. Bowie tease before I Walk the Line. Jimmy Olsen's Blues tease in Bowie (Bowie unfinished). Fishman on vacuum for Terrapin. Crowd sing-along on Lengthwise. The Dude of Life on vocals for Self. Last Tube, 4/19/92 Santa Cruz, CA [67 shows].

🐟 This show was two or three years ahead of its time. On first listening to it, I thought it sounded like a 1994 show. David Bowie is particularly exceptional. Granted, the I Walk the Line proceeding it was hokey, but the Bowie jam was tremendous. The boys got so wrapped up in it that they didn't even bother with the coda. It just sort of dissolved. Also, after hearing this show, I'm at a loss as to why they dropped Tube. —Scott Kushner

🐟 The scene was mellow, the theater was nice, and the show was phenomenal. There was ample dancing space, good sound, and the Dude of Life appeared, providing a nice twist to the show's conclusion. —Brian A. Rock

🐟 Everyone loves the Harry Hood from Stanford 4/18/92 with Page's jam on the Peanuts theme (Linus and Lucy). Less remarked upon is the Stash from this show at Albany's Palace Theater, which also features Page jamming on the Peanuts theme. And, like Stanford, this is a very well-played show—check out the outstanding jams on Stash, Bowie, and Hood. —Amy Manning

11/21/92 **[ACCESSIBILITY: ••] [ATTEND. 1,446; CAP. 1,446] [TIX $10-$16]**
Sports Complex, SUNY Stony Brook, Stony Brook, NY
I: Landlady, Runaway Jim, Foam, Glide, Poor Heart, It's Ice, Bouncing, Maze, Forbin's > Mockingbird, Possum
II: Carolina, Curtain > Mike's > Hydrogen > Weekapaug, Horse > Silent, Uncle Pen, Guelah, Squirming Coil, Love You, A-Train, Llama
E: Buffalo Bill, BBFCM
Concert debut: Buffalo Bill. Fishman on vacuum for Love You and Madonna washboard for Buffalo Bill. Last Carolina, 5/6/92 Detroit, MI [56 shows].

11/22/92 [ACCESSIBILITY: ••] [ATTEND. 1,821; CAP. 1,821] [TIX $10-$15]
Bailey Hall, Cornell University, Ithaca, NY
I: Buried Alive > Oh Kee > Suzie, Fee > Maze, Reba, Sparkle, Horn, All Things, Bathtub Gin, Adeline, Antelope
II: Axilla, My Friend, MSO, Tweezer > BBJ > Tweezer, Tela, YEM, Faht, Golgi
E: Bold as Love, Carolina, Tweezer Reprise

Jimmy Olsen's Blues jam in Suzie. Eleanor Rigby jam in YEM. Concert debut: Faht. Last Bathtub Gin, 5/12/92 Canton, NY [52 shows]. Last Tela, 5/9/92 Syracuse, NY [54 shows].

Hot hot, tasty tasty. Was that Eleanor Rigby I heard in YEM? Trey was electric at this show. I had side seats that sucked and I was still pulled into the magic. A heavy, heady show that lead to the following night's Forum show. Without speaking, Phish told a story of passion and feeling for their music. It was Eleanor Rigby—find the tape. —David M. Brown

This was the show that clinched my love for Phish. Antelope was stellar, taking me on an amazing trip (without any drugs). There were torrential downpours before the show and many people without tickets. A rumor went around that only a few tickets were left at the box office. I finagled my way inside, claiming that I had tickets at will-call and then I bought a ticket—there were plenty left! This was also the first time Faht was played, and the audience chimed in with our own jungle noises. —Brian A. Rock

11/23/92 [ACCESSIBILITY: ••••]
Broome County Forum, Binghamton, NY
I: Runaway Jim, Foam, Glide, Melt, Rift, Guelah, Divided Sky, Mound, Bouncing, Memories, Bowie
II: Poor Heart, Stash, Squirming Coil, I Walk the Line, Llama, Weigh, Mike's > Hydrogen > Weekapaug > BBJ > Weekapaug, Lengthwise, Cavern
E: Sleeping Monkey, Rocky Top

Vibration of Life in Bowie. Fishman on Madonna washboard for I Walk the Line. Mimi Fishman on vacuum for Lengthwise.

11/25/92 [ACCESSIBILITY: ••] [ATTEND. 1,267; CAP. 1,267] [TIX $14]
Keswick Theater, Glenside, PA
I: Buried Alive > Poor Heart, Landlady, Fee, Maze, Sparkle, It's Ice, Squirming Coil, Cavern > Adeline > Cavern, Antelope
II: Chalkdust, Foam, FEFY, YEM, Lizards, Tweezer > HYHU > Cracklin' Rosie > HYHU, MSO, Tweezer Reprise
E: Harry Hood, Carolina

Trey twice flubs lyrics during Lizards. Last Cracklin' Rosie, 5/16/92 Boston, MA [51 shows].

11/27/92 [ACCESSIBILITY: •••] [ATTEND. 1,800; CAP. 1,800] [TIX $18]
Capitol Theater, Port Chester, NY
I: Rift, Wilson > Divided Sky, Forbin's > Mockingbird, Melt, Lawn Boy, Reba, Llama > Mound, Memories, Runaway Jim
II: Axilla, Poor Heart, Possum, Glide > It's Ice, McGrupp > I Walk the Line > Bowie, Horse > Silent, Faht, A-Train, Cavern
E: Bold as Love

I Walk the Line jam in Bowie intro. Purple Haze jam in Cavern. Last Lawn Boy, 5/17/92 Schenectady, NY [51 shows].

11/28/92 [ACCESSIBILITY: ••••] [ATTEND. 1,800; CAP. 1,800] [TIX $18]
Capitol Theater, Port Chester, NY
I: MSO, Foam, Stash, Esther, Chalkdust, Sparkle, FEFY, All Things, Mike's > Hydrogen > Weekapaug
II: Suzie, Paul and Silas, Tweezer > BBJ, TMWSIY > Avenu > Maze > TMWSIY, Bouncing, Squirming Coil, HYHU > Love You > HYHU, Harpua, Golgi
E: Contact > Tweezer Reprise

Bass problems in MSO led to its interruption, a long pause, and then the song's finish. Walk this Way jam in Mike's. Jimmy Olsen's Blues jam in Harpua. Trey dances on stage with his grandmother during Contact. Last Contact, 5/5/92 Cincinnati, OH [62 shows]. Last Harpua, 5/9/92 Syracuse, NY [58 shows].

A nice place to see a show—the Capitol Theater has a cartoon feel to it. Many ticketless phans wandered outside, but I scored one and went inside for a show whose setlist speaks for itself. One especially funny moment came during Harpua when Trey said (mockingly), "Jimmy was listening to the number one hit," and then broke into Jimmy Olsen's Blues by the Spin Doctors. Supposedly, Phish later apologized to the SD's for making fun of them. —Brian A. Rock

During Mike's Song, the fog machines filled the stage with mist. From the front row, I couldn't see a thing. As the jam took Walk This Way around the chromatic scale, landing in many different keys, the fog cleared to show Trey standing on the very front of the stage leaning out over the audience three feet from me! Also worth noting about these shows is the continuation of a story taking place "inside Fish's head," from the Forbin's on 11/27 to the Harpua on 11/28! —Brendan Neagle

This two-night stand is legendary for both the music and the vibe—these were Phish's last shows ever at the Capitol in Port Chester, the historic 1,400-seat theater they'd played regularly for two years. The whole show was great, but I wouldn't see a Mike's Groove that topped the one at Port Chester for quite a while. During the fog that filled the theater for Mike's and Hydrogen, a giant gong was brought out to the center of the stage, and Trey faked us out by pretending to hit it but never making contact. People were flipping out! We spent the whole setbreak shaking our heads in amazement. There are fun Phish shows, and there are great Phish shows. This one was both. —Lock Steele

11/30/92 [ACCESSIBILITY: •] [ATTEND. 1,202; CAP. 1,202] [TIX $12-$14]
Metropol, Pittsburgh, PA
I: Llama, Foam, Bouncing, Poor Heart, Stash, Sparkle, It's Ice, I Didn't Know, Reba > Antelope
II: Buried Alive > Runaway Jim, Guelah, Maze, Glide, Uncle Pen, YEM, Squirming Coil, HYHU > Terrapin > HYHU, Cavern
E: Fee, Fire

No whistle jam at the end of Reba, apparently for the first time ever. Fishman on Madonna washboard for I Didn't Know and vacuum for Terrapin. Last Fire 4/13/92 Temple, AZ [79 shows].

12/1/92 [ACCESSIBILITY: ••]
Livingston Fieldhouse, Denison University, Granville, OH
I: Landlady > MSO, Melt, Bouncing, Rift, Cavern, Fluffhead, Maze, Adeline, Mike's > Hydrogen > Weekapaug
II: Axilla, Curtain, Chalkdust, My Friend, All Things, Uncle Pen, Llama, HYHU > Love You > HYHU, Dinner and a Movie, Bowie
E: GTBT

Peter and the Wolf jams in Bowie. Fishman on vacuum for Love You.

12/2/92 [ACCESSIBILITY: ••] [ATTEND. 1,398; CAP. 1,398] [TIX $12.75-$14]
Newport Music Hall, Columbus, OH
I: Suzie, Foam, Divided Sky, FEFY, Poor Heart, Stash, Lizards, Sparkle, Horn, YEM
II: Wilson > Possum, Mound, Tweezer > BBJ, Tela, Llama, Glide, HYHU > Lengthwise > HYHU, Squirming Coil, I Walk the Line, Runaway Jim
E: Golgi, Rocky Top

Fishman on vacuum for Lengthwise and Madonna washboard for I Walk the Line.

12/3/92 [ACCESSIBILITY: ••] [ATTEND. 1,250; CAP. 1,250] [TIX $11.50-$12.50]
Bogart's, Cincinnati, OH
I: Maze, Fee > All Things, Melt, Bouncing, Uncle Pen, Chalkdust, Horse > Silent, Reba, Adeline, Antelope
II: Rift, Guelah, Fluffhead, Mike's > Hydrogen > Weekapaug, Lawn Boy, It's Ice, MSO, BBJ, HYHU > Cracklin' Rosie > HYHU, A-Train, Cavern
E: Bold as Love

12/4/92 [ACCESSIBILITY: •] [ATTEND. 1,000; CAP. 1,000] [TIX $10-$12]
Mississippi Nights, St. Louis, MO
I: Llama, Foam, Poor Heart, Stash, Glide, Sparkle, FEFY, Maze, Forbin's > Mockingbird, Cavern
II: Suzie > Bowie, Esther, Possum, It's Ice, Squirming Coil, Carolina, Harry Hood, Faht, YEM
E: Fee, Rocky Top

12/5/92 [ACCESSIBILITY: ••] [ATTEND. 1,400; CAP. 1,400] [TIX $15]
Vic Theater, Chicago, IL
I: Landlady, Chalkdust, Bouncing, Rift, Guelah, Melt, Lizards, Mound, Divided Sky, Adeline, Uncle Pen, Golgi
II: Poor Heart, Tweezer, Reba > I Walk the Line > Reba, Sparkle, Maze, Lawn Boy, Mike's > Hydrogen > Weekapaug, HYHU > Whipping Post > HYHU, Tweezer Reprise
E: Memories, GTBT

Fishman on vacuum for Whipping Post.

12/6/92 [ACCESSIBILITY: ••] [ATTEND. 1,400; CAP. 1,400] [TIX $15]
Vic Theater, Chicago, IL

I: Runaway Jim, Foam, Fee, My Friend, MSO, Sloth, Squirming Coil, Llama, Fluffhead, Antelope
II: Suzie, Curtain > Stash, Paul and Silas, BBJ, Bathtub Gin, YEM, TMWSIY > Avenu > TMWSIY, HYHU > Lengthwise > HYHU, Carolina, Cavern
E: Possum
Vibration of Life during jam in Possum. Fishman on vacuum for Lengthwise.

12/7/92 [ACCESSIBILITY: ••] [ATTEND. 1,336; CAP. 1,336] [TIX $9-$11]
First Avenue, Minneapolis, MN
I: Axilla, Poor Heart, Maze, Glide, Sparkle, Foam, FEFY, Melt, Bouncing, YEM
II: Chalkdust, Reba > Llama, Horn, MSO, It's Ice, Fee, Bowie > HYHU > Love You > HYHU, Squirming Coil, Adeline
E: Runaway Jim
Oye Como Va jam in YEM. Vibration of Life between Horn and MSO. Fishman on vacuum for Love You.

12/8/92 [ACCESSIBILITY: •]
Barrymore Theater, Madison, WI
I: Rift, Wilson, Llama, Forbin's > Mockingbird, Uncle Pen, Guelah, Divided Sky, Mound, Adeline, Stash
II: Mike's > Hydrogen > Weekapaug, Horse > Silent, It's Ice, Lizards, Antelope, Lawn Boy, Sparkle, Suzie, HYHU > Lengthwise > HYHU, MSO > BBJ, Sleeping Monkey
E: Carolina, Fire
Fishman on vacuum for Lengthwise.

12/10/92 [ACCESSIBILITY: •] [ATTEND. 1,265; CAP. 1,700] [TIX $12.50-$14]
State Theater, Kalamazoo, MI
I: Golgi, Llama, Foam, Fee, Poor Heart, Melt, I Didn't Know, All Things, Reba, Adeline, Cavern
II: Rift, Tweezer > Tela, MSO > BBJ, Maze, Glide, YEM, HYHU > Love You > HYHU, I Walk the Line, Oh Kee > Suzie
E: Bold as Love, Carolina, Tweezer Reprise
Fishman on Madonna washboard for I Didn't Know and vacuum for Love You.

12/11/92 [ACCESSIBILITY: •••] [ATTEND. 1,663; CAP. 1,663] [TIX $12.50-$14.50]
Michigan Theater, Ann Arbor, MI
I: Runaway Jim, It's Ice, Uncle Pen, Stash, Lizards, Chalkdust, Guelah, Sparkle, My Friend, Memories, Bowie
II: Dinner and a Movie, Mike's > Hydrogen > Weekapaug, Esther, Axilla, Bouncing, Paul and Silas > BBJ, Squirming Coil, Faht, Possum
E: Contact, GTBT
Swing Low Sweet Chariot jam in Bowie intro and Moby Dick jam in Bowie closing jam. Bowie sung as "Dana Berie" in tribute to a Greenpeace staff member. Hydrogen contains The Vibration of Life.

12/12/92 [ACCESSIBILITY: •] [ATTEND. 1,030; CAP. 1,030] [TIX $11-$13]
The Spectrum, Toronto, ON
I: Llama, Foam, Sparkle, Cavern, Reba, Landlady, Melt, Poor Heart, All Things, Bouncing, Antelope
II: Maze, Glide, Curtain > Tweezer, Rift, Guelah, YEM, HYHU > Brain > HYHU, Squirming Coil, Golgi
E: Ride Captain Ride, Tweezer Reprise
Davy Crockett theme jams throughout second set; the theme is sung in the YEM vocal jam. Fishman on vacuum for Brain. Last Ride Captain Ride, 5/28/89 Hebron, NY [395 shows]. Last Brain, 6/23/92 Dusseldorf, Germany [60 shows].

One of the shows from 1992 that does it for me is this one—a fairly standard setlist enhanced by wild playing. The first set is real solid from the get-go: Llama, Foam, Sparkle, and Cavern sound pretty standard on paper, but I think the playing makes this set. The middle jam in Reba is sweet; Landlady and Melt make a nice pair; and Antelope is a good first-set closer. Maze starts off the second set—real nice, good and raw. Tweezer is crazy as always, then YEM stands up to the test. Then there's the break-out Ride Captain Ride encore! —Phil Valle

12/13/92 [ACCESSIBILITY: •]
Le Spectrum, Montreal, QC
I: Buried Alive > Wilson, Divided Sky, It's Ice, Fee, Uncle Pen, Stash, Rift, FEFY, I Didn't Know, Bowie
II: Suzie, Mound, Bouncing, Llama, Fluffhead, Chalkdust, TMWSIY > Avenu > TMWSIY, MSO > BBJ, HYHU > Cracklin' Rosie > HYHU, Harry Hood, Cavern
E: Adeline, Rocky Top
Fishman on vacuum for I Didn't Know.

1992 Holiday Tour

12/28/92 [ACCESSIBILITY: ••]
Palace Theater, New Haven, CT
I: Maze, Sparkle, Foam, Glide, It's Ice, Bouncing, Rift, Golgi, Adeline, Antelope
II: Poor Heart, Melt, Reba, Sloth, YEM, Lizards, HYHU > Bike > HYHU, Harry Hood, Cavern
E: Memories, Fire
Buried Alive jam before Glide during which Trey introduces some of his relatives in the audience. Fishman on vacuum for Bike. Last Bike, 5/7/92 Cleveland, OH [74 shows].

12/29/92 [ACCESSIBILITY: •••]
Palace Theater, New Haven, CT
I: Funky Bitch, Runaway Jim, Guelah, Llama, My Friend, Divided Sky, Wilson, Uncle Pen, Stash, Tela, Oh Kee > Suzie
II: Curtain, Tweezer, Horse > Silent, MSO > BBJ, FEFY, All Things, Mike's > Hydrogen > Weekapaug, HYHU > Terrapin > HYHU, Blue Bayou, Squirming Coil, Tweezer Reprise
E: Carolina, Rocky Top
On Broadway jam in Mike's and Maria jam in Weekapaug. Fishman on trombone for Terrapin, and unamplified Blue Bayou. Last Blue Bayou, 7/16/92 Richmond, VA [51 shows].

The best show of the 1992 New Year's Run, this show had a little of everything and a lot of jamming. The show rocks from the start with Funky Bitch; other great jams are heard in Mike's Song (with an On Broadway bit), Weekapaug (machine-gun Trey!), and of course Tweezer (probably my favorite version of the year). When Fishman comes forward for Terrapin, he tells the crowd, "I'm going to attempt a love solo on my trombone," drawing huge cheers. Trey chimes in, saying, "We will attempt now to do the slowest version of this song ever performed on the face of the Earth." They sure do! —Al Hunt

12/30/92 [ACCESSIBILITY: •••] [ATTEND. 2,457; CAP. 2,457] [TIX $17.50]
Symphony Hall, Springfield, MA
I: Landlady, Sparkle, Melt, Esther, Chalkdust, Fluffhead, Paul and Silas, Reba > I Walk the Line > Reba, I Didn't Know, Bowie > Timber Ho > Bowie
II: Axilla, Rift, Bathtub Gin, YEM, TMWSIY > Avenu > TMWSIY, Possum, BBJ > HYHU > Love You > HYHU, A-Train, Llama
E: Ride Captain Ride, Adeline
Jamie Janover played hammer dulcimer between sets. Fishman on trombone for I Didn't Know and vacuum for Love You. Auld Lang Syne tease in YEM. Last Timber Ho, 6/16/90 [275 shows].

Get this show for the rarities—one of only two Ride Captain Ride performances in the 1990s and the only Timber Ho until Sugarbush 1995 brought the song back into rotation. In Springfield, the band began the Bowie intro, then unexpectedly moved into the Timber Ho riff. In what turned out to be a totally unplanned move, they decided to play the whole song! This show also contains one of the funnier song dedications ever, a hilarious "cousins" send-off before TMWSIY. —Andre Holton

12/31/92 [ACCESSIBILITY: ••••] [ATTEND. 5,893; CAP. 5,893] [TIX $20]
Matthews Arena, Northeastern University, Boston, MA
I: Buried Alive > Poor Heart, Maze, Bouncing, Rift, Wilson, Divided Sky, Cavern, Foam, I Didn't Know, Antelope
II: Runaway Jim, It's Ice, Sparkle, Forbin's > Mockingbird, MSO > BBJ, Stash, Glide, GTBT
III: Mike's > New Year's Countdown > Auld Lang Syne > Weekapaug, Harpua > Kung > Harpua, Squirming Coil, Diamond Girl, Llama
E: Carolina, Fire
Jeopardy theme tease in Wilson. Fishman on vacuum for I Didn't Know. Brad Sands, dressed as the Mockingbird, flew over the stage during that song. Concert debut: Diamond Girl, with the Dude of Life on vocals. Last Kung, 11/2/89 Durham, NH [367 shows]. Show broadcast on WBCN-Boston on 1/1/93.

Though this show sold out weeks in advance, a good deal of tickets got into the hands of scalpers, who from what I could tell managed to get little more than face value outside the arena. Inside, the crowd milled around the hockey rink and Phish opened up in strong fashion with a great Buried Alive and then an absolutely tripping Maze. The second set was more uneven—the band never really sounded "on" until GTBT. But the energy resumed when Phish took the stage for the third set a little after 11:50 p.m. Leave it to Mike's Song to resuscitate a sagging show—the one that swung us into 1993 did the trick. The segue from Mike's into Auld Lang Syne into Weekapaug is amazing. —Ali Tariq

This show is a classic. This was my first live Phish tape, recorded off of WBCN's broadcast. Besides early show appearances of Rift and It's Ice, this show also has the best Squirming Coil I've ever heard—Page's solo is heavenly. The third set is definitely my favorite: Mike's > Auld Lang Syne > Weekapaug is awesome, as is Diamond Girl with the Dude. And there's a cool Kung and New Year's story in Harpua. —Greg Marceau

As we entered the arena, we were given flyers with a special secret language for the night. The show was taped for broadcast on WBCN and we were to mess with the listeners' heads. Trey held up signs and we reacted by doing things like snapping our fingers, stomping our feet, yeahs, boos, random screams, crying out "Eggplant!" and doing a lip-flop. It was so much fun!—Melissa Mixer

The day after Phish's Matthews Arena show, the *Boston Globe* reported on a small earthquake in Boston's North End on New Year's Eve. The article joked, "Was it an overly loud Phish concert at Matthews Arena?" Don't laugh—listen to Forbin's! —Ed Smith

1993 Spring A "Grand" Tour

The 1993 spring tour saw one major change to the band's on-stage setup: Page's baby grand piano debuted at Portland, ME, and the band celebrated with the breakout of Loving Cup. From there, the tour wound south, then west, then to the Pacific, and finally back again—a pattern becoming familiar to Phish and the band's fans. But for the first time, the band swung through Florida, a state that would become a familiar stomping ground over the next several years. The band played outstanding shows in Colorado and Ohio and finished the tour with panache in the Northeast. A summer tour of the outdoor sheds lay ahead.

[1/28/93] Hard Rock Cafe, Boston, MA
Amazing Grace
Rift release party. Fishman donated his 1967 Electrolux vacuum to the Cafe.

[2/2/93] *Rift* released on Elektra.

2/3/93 [ACCESSIBILITY: ••] [ATTEND. 2,700; CAP. 2,700] [TIX $16.50]
Portland Expo, Portland, ME
I: Loving Cup, Rift, Fee, Llama, Wedge, Divided Sky, I Didn't Know, My Friend, Poor Heart, Guelah, Bowie
II: Runaway Jim, It's Ice, Tweezer, Horse > Silent, Sparkle, YEM, Lifeboy, HYHU > Terrapin > HYHU > BBJ, Possum
E: Amazing Grace, Tweezer Reprise
Fishman on trombone for I Didn't Know, a piece of cardboard for Terrapin, and vacuum for BBJ. Trey on drums for BBJ. My Girl tease in YEM, which also featured the alternate lyrics "Water your team in a beehive, I'm a sent-you." Concert debuts: Loving Cup, Wedge, Lifeboy, and Amazing Grace. Also the debut of Page's baby grand piano and Trey's use of an acoustic guitar for The Horse and the pre-lyric segment of My Friend (this continued for the rest of 1993).

Newbies can debate the "YEM eternal question" because the old-school phans know. In old Phish newsletters, phans would write in asking the question "What are you saying in You Enjoy Myself?" and Mike would make up different answers. One of his responses, "Water your team in a beehive, I'm a sent you," was said very clearly during this YEM. I don't think that many people got the joke, but I thought it was pretty funny. Also, listen carefully while Fish is talking after Terrapin. The beach balls were sitting on the wings of the stage. Someone yelled out, "Give us the balls!" and Brad took the signal from Trey and right then threw them out to us! Everyone started freaking out, and Fish was running back and forth across the stage high-fiving the crowd. This is just an amazing show, one of the more underrated ever. —Mike D'Amico

2/4/93 [ACCESSIBILITY: •••] [ATTEND. 3,105; CAP. 3,105] [TIX $16.50]
Providence Performing Arts Center, Providence, RI
I: Axilla, Foam, Bouncing, Maze, FEFY, All Things, Stash, Lizards, Sample, Glide, Antelope
II: Chalkdust, Wedge, Mike's > TMWSIY > Avenu > TMWSIY > Weekapaug, Lawn Boy, Uncle Pen, BBJ, HYHU > Lengthwise > HYHU, Harry Hood, Cavern
E: Amazing Grace, GTBT

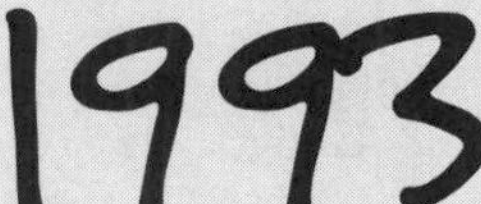

110 Total Show Dates
- **4** one-set shows
- **105** two-set shows
- **1** three-set show

Phan Picks 1993

SHOW	THE SKINNY
1) 02/20/93 Atlanta, GA	Mike's > Everything > Groove
2) 12/30/93 Portland, ME	Incredible from start to finish.
3) 03/22/93 Sacramento, CA	First Gamehendge since '91.
4) 12/31/93 Worcester, MA	A Peach(es) of a show.
5) 08/20/93 Morrison, CO	Incredibly well jammed show.
6) 08/07/93 Darien Center, NY	Wild second set.
7) 08/02/93 Tampa, FL	Breakouts in a tiny club.
8) 08/13/93 Indianapolis, IN	The famous Murat Gin.
9) 03/14/93 Gunnison, CO	First Halley's in the 1990s.
10) tie between 05/08/93 and 08/12/93	

MUSICAL RECAP: Still unwilling to fully abandon a setlist in progress, Phish nevertheless managed to stretch some songs past the 20-minute barrier in 1993. The band's improvising ability, aided by their "Hey!" exercises, can clearly be heard in great jams like the 8/13 Bathtub Gin.
REPRESENTATIVE JAMS: Bathtub Gin, 8/13/93; Split Open and Melt, 4/21/93 and 8/20/93; Antelope 8/20/93; Mike's Groove, 5/8/93.
ORIGINAL SONG DEBUTS: Leprechaun (7/15/93), Lifeboy (2/3/93); Sample in a Jar (2/4/93); The Wedge (2/3/93).
COVER SONG DEBUTS: Also Sprach Zarathustra (7/16/93), Amazing Grace (2/3/93), Bats and Mice (8/25/93), Choo Choo Ch'Boogie* (3/3/93), Crossroads (5/8/93), Daniel (7/15/93), Fast Train* (5/6/93), Freebird (a cappella version, 7/15/93), Ginseng Sullivan (8/11/93), Great Gig in the Sky (3/14/93), It's My Life* (3/3/93), Loving Cup (2/3/93), Luke-a-Roo* (3/3/93), Nellie Cane (2/23/93), Pig in a Pen (2/21/93); Purple Rain (7/16/93), Tennessee Waltz* (5/6/93), That's Alright Mama* (5/6/93), Why You Been Gone So Long* (5/6/93), Yerushalayim Schel Zahav (7/16/93).
(* only ever played once)

Dark Horses

SHOW	THE SKINNY
1) 08/06/93 Cincinnati, OH	See the city, see the zoo.
2) 08/09/93 Toronto, ON	Very well played show.
3) 02/19/93 Atlanta, GA	Moby Dick Bowie for Fish.
4) 08/14/93 Tinley Park, IL	Incredible Antelope.
5) 03/31/93 Portland, OR	Best of the West Coast run?

Most-Played Originals:		
1) Rift	68	62%
2) Big Ball Jam	64	58%
3) Sparkle	58	53%
4) Poor Heart	57	52%
5) Stash	56	51%
6) Bouncing	55	50%
6) It's Ice	55	50%
8) Maze	54	49%
9) You Enjoy Myself	53	48%
10) Chalkdust Torture	52	47%

Most-Played Covers:		
1) Amazing Grace	54	49%
2) Uncle Pen	33	30%
3) Sweet Adeline	25	23%
4) Paul and Silas	21	19%
5) Rocky Top	20	18%
6) Also Sprach	19	17%
6) GTBT	19	17%
8) Love You	17	15%
8) Ya Mar	17	15%
10) Nellie	15	14%
10) Purple Rain	15	14%
10) Lengthwise	15	14%

First-Set Openers:	
1) Buried Alive	16
2) Chalkdust Torture	13
2) Llama	12
2) Runaway Jim	10
2) Golgi Apparatus	7

Second-Set Openers:	
1) Also Sprach	19
2) Runaway Jim	8
2) Wilson	6
4) Chalkdust Torture	5
4) Llama	5
4) Rift	5

Top Henrietta Songs:	
1) Love You	17
2) Purple Rain	15
2) Lengthwise	15
4) Terrapin	11
5) Great Gig in the Sky	9

A Cappella Songs:	
1) Amazing Grace	54
2) Sweet Adeline	25
3) Freebird	14
4) Carolina	9
5) Memories	6

Fishman on vacuum for Lengthwise, which was performed regular and then reggae-style. Lengthwise jam in Harry Hood. Concert debut: Sample.

For a show that otherwise didn't let up from start to finish, this night offers one of the best-ever moments of comic relief. But in true Phish fashion, it was a moment that still made you want to boogie. Following a Big Ball Jam, Fishman appeared center stage and began crooning Lengthwise. Trey then whipped in with a reggae-ish drum beat, and Fishman gave it his best Jamaican-style bellow. As the beat sped up, it gained a sort of Elvis-ish sound. It wasn't just Lengthwise, it was "When you're gone, I sleep diagonally, in my . . . in my . . . in my bed. When you're there! When you're there! When you're there!" And the amazing thing was that it was fantastic musically—much better sounding than the similar version from 11/19/92. In fact, I once played the tape for a friend who didn't like Phish, and it was that performance that changed her mind. —Andy Bernstein

2/5/93 [ACCESSIBILITY: ••] [ATTEND. 3,203; CAP. 3,203] [TIX $16.50-$18]
Roseland Ballroom, New York, NY
I: Llama, Guelah, Rift, Melt, Sparkle, PYITE, I Didn't Know, Poor Heart, Reba, Bowie
II: Curtain > Tweezer, Horse > Silent, Paul and Silas, It's Ice, YEM, HYHU > Love You > HYHU, Squirming Coil, Tweezer Reprise
E: Amazing Grace, Loving Cup
Fishman on a portrait of Otis Redding for I Didn't Know and vacuum for Love You. Vibration of Life before Bowie. Funkytown tease in Tweezer. Last PYITE, 11/9/89 Williamstown, MA [367 shows].

2/6/93 [ACCESSIBILITY: ••••] [ATTEND. 3,203; CAP. 3,203] [TIX $16.50-$18]
Roseland Ballroom, New York, NY
I: Golgi, Foam, Wilson, My Friend, Maze, Horn, Divided Sky, Lawn Boy, Wedge, Bouncing, Antelope
II: Chalkdust, Mound, Stash, Adeline, All Things, Mike's > Hydrogen > Weekapaug, Lifeboy, Uncle Pen, BBJ, HYHU > Lengthwise > Buried Alive, Possum
E: Fire
Fishman on vacuum for Lengthwise. John Popper on harmonica for Buried Alive, Possum, and Fire. Noel Redding on bass for Fire, with Mike on organ.

I remember this night because it was so cold outside. My friend got mugged trying to sell an extra—scalpers suck, especially in NYC. Once inside, everything went real smooth. Mike sang his song in a very weird fashion, yelling and telling us how it was his song. The highlight was John Popper being wheeled out on stage for Buried Alive and Possum. It was the first appearance by him after his motorcycle wreck and he didn't disappoint, even standing up at one point. —Joshua Howley

One of the funniest Lengthwises features Fishman commenting on all the lighters being held up by people in the crowd: "When you're there/I'm burning my fingers/because I'm holding this lighter/on way too long." —Mick Connor

2/7/93 [ACCESSIBILITY: ••] [ATTEND. 1,450; CAP. 1,450] [TIX $18]
Lisner Auditorium, George Washington University, Washington, DC
I: Suzie, Buried Alive > Poor Heart, It's Ice, Sparkle, Forbin's > Mockingbird, Rift, I Didn't Know, Melt, Fee, Runaway Jim
II: Llama, FEFY, My Mind's, Reba, Tweezer > BBJ, Glide, YEM, Squirming Coil, HYHU > Brain > HYHU, Tweezer Reprise
E: Amazing Grace, Contact, BBFCM
Fishman on trombone for I Didn't Know and vacuum for Brain. Oh My Darling Clementine sung in YEM vocal jam. Last My Mind's, 5/6/92 Detroit, MI [83 shows].

2/9/93 [ACCESSIBILITY: ••]
Auditorium Theater, Rochester, NY
I: Bowie, Bouncing, Poor Heart, My Friend, Rift, Wedge, Chalkdust, Esther > Maze, Golgi
II: PYITE > Mike's > Hydrogen > Weekapaug > Weigh, MSO, Sample, BBJ, Stash > Lizards, HYHU > Bike > HYHU, Amazing Grace
E: Cavern, Rocky Top
Fishman on vacuum for Bike.

2/10/93 [ACCESSIBILITY: ••]
Smith Opera House, Geneva, NY
I: Loving Cup, Foam, Guelah, Reba, Sloth, Divided Sky, Tela, Llama, I Didn't Know, Catapult, Antelope
II: Runaway Jim, It's Ice, Squirming Coil, Tweezer, I Walk the Line, Sparkle, YEM, Horse > Silent, HYHU > Cracklin' Rosie > HYHU, Possum
E: Adeline, Amazing Grace, Tweezer Reprise

PROVIDENCE PERFORMING ARTS CENTER, Providence, RI

Thursday, February 4, 1993

Over seventy shows later and counting, I'm still not sure if I've ever seen one as spectacular as my first. Certainly I haven't had a show affect me as much as the one put on by four then-strangers at the Providence Performing Arts Center in February '93.

Your first time is supposed to be messy, a little uncomfortable, and you're not supposed to know what you're doing. Perhaps the latter applies. I did ask some dude who the opening act was, but the rest of the night was a smooth deliverance into audial heaven. Phish had me, owned me, right away.

I'll admit that I sometimes get a little bored at concerts. It's rare that I walk out of a place sure that I got my thirty bucks worth, and I'm usually fairly certain that I didn't have quite as good a time as everyone else. Not so, that night. The first time you hear Bouncing Around the Room, Maze, or Lizards, it's fucking candy. Sure, I'd outgrow those tunes—and then rediscover them—but in all my virginal naiveté, I could not escape the frank realization that I was experiencing the best music I'd ever heard.

Then came a second set that I'll still pit against any other ever played. The Wedge—which I wouldn't hear again until fifty-eight shows later—then Mike's Groove, with strobe in a fully darkened concert hall. "That's the trippiest thing I ever done seen," I turned to friends as mesmerized as I. Then in Weekapaug, there was some crazy sound, some shriek that was jabbing at me from the side. It was Mike, screaming. Just screaming. And it made perfect sense, musically and environmentally. I understood. There was this band, having more fun on stage than any I'd ever seen, and even cacophonous screams were perfectly placed.

Then came a moment of history. The thrice-performed reggae Lengthwise. Imagine my reaction when I see the guitarist start banging out the drums and the little drummer boy, whom I'd barely noticed, parade about in a dress and sing some insane chant with a reggae beat.

I was owned.

Harry, then Cavern. Toto, I don't think we're in Kansas anymore.

If there's one thing that stood out as much as the captivation of the music, it was the humor and attitude that surrounded the show. Therefore, it made no sense to me, and still doesn't, when people got really pissed off when a few others wouldn't quiet down during the micless a cappella tune.

"Shut the fuck up!" someone screamed. And it just made no sense to me. Yeah, I wanted to hear the band too, but nothing that night was worth getting upset over. How could there be anger when it seemed so clear that the dominant emotion was amusement? Well, I guess my friend was thinking the same thing I was because when everything finally quieted down, and there was dead silence, he let out this bellowing snort that filled the entire theater. It was the hardest I ever laughed at a show, and I've seen some really funny things at Phish concerts.

Now I know that the overwhelming majority of diehards hate people who make noise during the a cappella, and a good number do get angry. Still, after seventy-plus shows, I side with the snort.

Phish means as much to me as anyone I know. But it's never been more than a laugh. It can't be.

—David Porter

2/11/93 [ACCESSIBILITY: ••]
Haas Center for the Arts, Bloomsburg, PA
I: Suzie, Buried Alive > Poor Heart, Stash, Fee, Rift, Fluffhead > Llama, Lawn Boy, Bowie
II: Landlady, Wilson > Uncle Pen, Mike's > Hydrogen > Weekapaug, Mound, BBJ, Bouncing, HYHU > Love You > HYHU, Lizards, Cavern
E: Bold as Love, Amazing Grace
Fishman on vacuum for Love You.

2/12/93 [ACCESSIBILITY: •••]
Mid-Hudson Civic Center, Poughkeepsie, NY
I: Golgi, Maze, Guelah, Sparkle, Melt, Esther, Wedge, Chalkdust, I Didn't Know, A-Train, Antelope
II: My Friend, All Things, Reba, Poor Heart, BBJ, FEFY, YEM, Ya Mar, HYHU > Terrapin > HYHU, Harry Hood, Harpua
E: Amazing Grace, GTBT

Fishman on plastic for I Didn't Know and vacuum for Terrapin. Black or White jam in Harpua. Last Ya Mar, 4/24/92 Portland, OR [95 shows].

Very, very snowy night, with not many out-of-towners there. Fish played lots of strange instruments like a placard of Plexiglas and a washboard suite. The Harpua was really involved, and the Chalkdust Torture was hot. Just a big room, no chairs, with lots of freaks and Phish. That's how I like it. —Emily Brown

2/13/93 [ACCESSIBILITY: ••]
Bob Carpenter Center, Newark, DE
I: Bowie, Bouncing, Poor Heart, It's Ice, Glide, Rift, Stash, Lawn Boy, Maze, Golgi
II: Runaway Jim, Wilson, Uncle Pen, Tweezer, Lizards, Llama, YEM, BBJ, HYHU > Lengthwise, Squirming Coil, Cavern
E: Amazing Grace, Tweezer Reprise

Fishman on vacuum for Lengthwise. Wimoweh theme in YEM vocal jam.

2/15/93 [ACCESSIBILITY: ••]
Memorial Hall, University of North Carolina, Chapel Hill, NC
I: Amazing Grace, Suzie, Sparkle, Guelah, Divided Sky, Esther, Chalkdust, Mound, Stash, Guelah, I Didn't Know, Antelope
II: Rift, FEFY, Reba, Mike's > Hydrogen > Weekapaug, Wedge, Poor Heart > BBJ > HYHU > Bike > HYHU, Fee > Llama
E: Contact > Fire

Fishman on trombone for I Didn't Know and vacuum for Bike.

2/17/93 [ACCESSIBILITY: ••] [ATTEND. 2,048; CAP. 2,048] [TIX $12-$14]
Benton Convention Center, Winston-Salem, NC
I: Buried Alive > Possum, Weigh, All Things, Sloth, Runaway Jim, It's Ice, Bouncing, Fluffhead, Maze, Golgi
II: Axilla, Landlady, Bowie, Glide, My Friend, MSO > BBJ, Horn, YEM, HYHU > Lengthwise > HYHU, Squirming Coil
E: Carolina, GTBT

Fishman on vacuum for Lengthwise, which was performed reggae-style.

2/18/93 [ACCESSIBILITY: ••] [ATTEND. 1,030; CAP. 1,030] [TIX $15]
Electric Ballroom International, Knoxville, TN
I: Chalkdust, Guelah, Poor Heart, Tweezer > Foam, Sparkle, Cavern, Reba, Lawn Boy, Antelope
II: Rift, Stash, Lizards, PYITE, Mike's > Hydrogen > Weekapaug, Mound, Amazing Grace, Memories, Adeline, Rocky Top

Soundboard shorted out during Mound; rest of set played a cappella and, for Rocky Top, through monitors with Mike and Trey electric, Page acoustic, and Fish on trombone. No encore. Another One Bites the Dust jam in Weekapaug.

During Mound, you could hear the sound system start to fry, so Phish decided to go a cappella, plus a Rocky Top finale played through the monitors. Wild!—Jos Conti

2/19/93 [ACCESSIBILITY: ••••]
Roxy Theater, Atlanta, GA
I: Loving Cup, Rift, Melt, Fee > Maze, Forbin's > Mockingbird, Sparkle, My Friend, Poor Heart, Bowie
II: Runaway Jim, It's Ice, Paul and Silas, YEM, Ya Mar, BBJ, Lawn Boy, Funky Bitch, MSO, HYHU > Love You > HYHU, Llama, Amazing Grace
E: AC/DC Bag

Moby Dick jams during Bowie intro and outro. Bowie intro also featured Fish on vacuum and a Happy Birthday jam for Fish. Flavor-Flav clock presented to Fishman. Jimmy Herring on guitar for Lawn Boy, Funky Bitch, MSO, Love You, and Llama. Last AC/DC Bag, 5/16/92 Boston, MA [84 shows].

Fishman's birthday and the famous Moby Dick Bowie, which includes a Moby Dick jam in the intro and then again during the final coda. It's amazing! Jimmy Herring rocks the house in the second set. Perhaps because it falls under the shadow of the next night, this show tends to be overlooked by a lot of phans. I think it's one of the band's better shows of 1993. —Tricia Holmes

2/20/93 [ACCESSIBILITY: •••••]
Roxy Theater, Atlanta, GA
I: Golgi, Foam, Sloth, Possum, Weigh, All Things, Divided Sky, Horse > Silent, Fluffhead, Cavern
II: Wilson, Reba, Tweezer > Walk Away > Tweezer > Glide > Mike's > My Mind's > Mike's > Kung > Hydrogen > Weekapaug > Have Mercy > Rock and Roll All Night jam > Weekapaug > FEFY, BBJ, HYHU > Terrapin > HYHU, Harry Hood, Tweezer Reprise
E: Sleeping Monkey

Iron Man tease in Wilson. Iron Man and Woody Woodpecker teases in Reba. Tweezer teases in Glide and Mike's. Tease medley in Mike's includes teases of Wilson, Reba, Tweezer, Lizards, Wilson and Stash. Vibration of Life before Kung, including Nitrous lyrics from Mike. Fishman on vacuum for Terrapin. Last Walk Away, 11/2/91 Fort Collins, CO [158 shows]. Last Have Mercy, 10/31/86 Plainfield, VT [510 shows].

I'm not sure what was going on in Gamehendge this night, but something sure was crazy. The Wilson to start set II is weird—really, the whole show has a strange feel. Inside certain songs they reference other Phish songs. At one point, Glide segues into Mike's Song. Instead of the normal Mike's, it has a Tweezer bass line. The Mike's jam includes Fluffhead, Tweezer, Lizards, Stash, My Mind, Have Mercy, and Kung, plus H2 > Weekapaug, in which Fishman introduces Gene Simmons and they play "Rock and Roll All Night" by Kiss! —Jeffrey Ellenbogen

They weren't screwing around in the second set. After a heavy Wilson and an awe-inspiring Reba, they broke into one of THOSE Tweezers that last a whole set. Except it wasn't just Tweezer. After seguing into Walk Away and an amazing Glide, the first notes of Mike's Song were heard. This version had jams of Reba, Lizards, and My Mind's until they went into a Vibration of Life/Kung/H2/Weekapaug/Have Mercy/Rock and Roll All Night/Weekapaug! As if that weren't enough, they then busted into one of the best Hoods in my collection. Amazing set! —Seth Weinglass

I know, I know, but I had to mention this show. Not the usual praise of Mike's Groove, though, but praise for the unbelievable Tweezer. Right after the opening lyrics, Trey and Mike go on mumbling about something "coming straight from the sewer" and something about a freezer. The effect is awesome. I could listen to this Tweezer 100 times in a row and still love every minute of it! —Mike Jett

2/21/93 [ACCESSIBILITY: ••]
Roxy Theater, Atlanta, GA
I: Suzie, Buried Alive, PYITE, Uncle Pen, Horn, Chalkdust, Esther, Dinner and a Movie, Bouncing, Antelope
II: Axilla, Curtain > Stash > Manteca > Stash > Lizards, Bathtub Gin, HYHU > Cracklin' Rosie > HYHU, Squirming Coil, BBFCM
E: Adeline, GTBT > Paul and Silas > Pig in a Pen

Encores following Adeline featured the Reverend Jeff Mosier on banjo. A cappella intro to Suzie. GTBT performed bluegrass style. Concert debut: Pig in a Pen. Last Manteca, 4/18/92 Palo Alto, CA [107 shows].

2/22/93 [ACCESSIBILITY: ••]
The Moon, Tallahassee, FL
I: Rift, Guelah > "Language Lesson" > Guelah, Poor Heart, Maze, Fee, Sparkle, Foam, Cavern, I Didn't Know, Bowie
II: Runaway Jim, It's Ice, Uncle Pen, Tweezer, Glide, YEM, Oh Kee > Llama, HYHU > Love You > HYHU, Squirming Coil, Tweezer Reprise
E: Amazing Grace, Fire

Fishman on trombone for I Didn't Know and vacuum for Love You.

2/23/93 [ACCESSIBILITY: ••]
The Edge, Orlando, FL
I: Golgi, My Friend, Rift, Bouncing, Melt, Reba, Lawn Boy, Chalkdust, Wedge, Paul and Silas, Antelope
II: Axilla, MSO, Stash > Lizards, PYITE, All Things, Mike's > Hydrogen > Weekapaug > Nellie Cane > Weekapaug, HYHU > Terrapin > HYHU, Possum
E: Adeline, Poor Heart

Fishman on vacuum for Terrapin. Concert debut: Nellie Cane.

2/25/93 [ACCESSIBILITY: ••] [ATTEND. 1,151; CAP. 1,350] [TIX $13-$15]
Cameo Theater, Miami Beach, FL
I: Buried Alive > Poor Heart, Cavern, Maze, Forbin's > Mockingbird, Rift, Stash, Bouncing, I Didn't Know, Bowie

"Roxy 'n' Roll"

2/20/93 The Roxy, Atlanta, GA

When Phish visited Atlanta in the spring of 1992, their performance seemed a little soggy. That wasn't the band's fault, though—a broken water main in the venue had slowly covered the floor of the venue with water, and by the time Phish was due to come back out for their second set, the fear of electrocution loomed large. Hating to cut a gig short—what musician doesn't?—the band sang a few a cappella numbers and then did their best to apologize to the crowd. Trey in particular went out of his way to promise the crowd that the next time they played in Atlanta, they'd make sure everyone had a special time.

For some bands, such a promise might just be idle talk, a way of getting out of an awkward situation without pissing off the fans or inciting a riot. Phish, of course, wouldn't insult their fans' memories by not living up to their promise . . . would they?

The answer to that question came into focus on February 19, when they kicked off their first same-venue three-night stand in ages in Atlanta's intimate Roxy Theater. During the narration portion of Col. Forbin's Ascent, Trey spun a tale of the concert-goers being swept away by a flood, and invoked a chant: "We will make it up to you, we will make it up to you . . . " True to their word, Phish hadn't forgotten.

Now, the show on the 19th was, by almost all accounts, a hell of a good time—Fishman celebrated his birthday with a David Bowie that could have just as easily been labeled on a setlist as Moby Dick >Bowie >Dick >Bowie. So as the crowds headed back to the Roxy on Saturday night, most people no longer felt that Phish owed them anything except maybe your average great Phish show. The band had other ideas.

The first set was strong, packed with crowd-favorites including Possum and Fluffhead. But there was little hint of the madness that was to follow in the second set.

Some fans in attendance that night say they sensed musical tension between Trey and Mike (leading to Fishman's comment during Terrapin, "We're a mellow band.") But if Phish's music thrives on tension and release, then perhaps a momentary spat between the bandmates was just what the doctor ordered.

When the band dropped from there into Tweezer, things start getting nutty. "How's everyone feeling out there?" Trey yells in the midst of the jam, which eventually segues into Walk Away. The departure from Tweezer is only in name, though, as Trey sticks with the Tweezer riff even in Glide and then as Mike's Song opens. Then comes the part that makes this tape so desirable—the Mike's > everything > Groove that includes teases of numerous Phish songs, a Vibration of Life, and Kung. Then in Weekapaug, there's Have Mercy and an appearance by a person from the audience dressed as a member of Kiss for a brief jam on Kiss's "Rock and Roll All Night." This show really has it all.

II: Suzie, It's Ice, Sparkle, Wilson, YEM, Uncle Pen, BBJ, FEFY, HYHU > Brain > HYHU, Golgi, BBFCM
E: Amazing Grace, GTBT

Fishman on trombone for I Didn't Know and vacuum for Brain. Mimi Fishman on vacuum for Brain.

First off, Len and Mimi Fishman were grooving right above their son for the whole show. We were also delighted to have a bit of Mimi's vacuum-playing ability displayed during If I Only Had a Brain. And how about a little Jeopardy theme song during the Bowie? The Big Ball Jam and BBFCM were highlights for me. —Tony Hume

2/26/93 [ACCESSIBILITY: ••]
Ritz Theater, Ybor City (Tampa), FL
I: Runaway Jim, Foam, Fee, Melt, Fluffhead, Llama, Horn, Divided Sky, I Didn't Know, Cavern
II: Loving Cup, Paul and Silas, Tweezer, Glide, Chalkdust, Mound, BBJ, YEM, HYHU > Lengthwise > HYHU, Squirming Coil, Tweezer Reprise
E: Bold as Love, Adeline

Fishman on vacuum for Lengthwise.

2/27/93 [ACCESSIBILITY: ••]
Florida Theater, Gainesville, FL
I: Golgi, Rift, Guelah, Maze, Bouncing, It's Ice, Sparkle, PYITE, Lawn Boy, Antelope
II: Curtain > Stash, Poor Heart, Sample, BBJ, Ya Mar, Mike's > Hydrogen > Weekapaug, HYHU > Terrapin > HYHU, Fee, Llama
E: Sleeping Monkey, Amazing Grace, Rocky Top

Fishman on vacuum for Terrapin.

3/2/93 [ACCESSIBILITY: ••]
Tipitina's, New Orleans, LA
I: Buried Alive > Poor Heart, Stash, Reba, Sparkle, It's Ice, Fee, All Things, Chalkdust, Horse > Silent, I Didn't Know, Bowie
II: My Friend, Uncle Pen, Tweezer, Lizards, Llama, YEM, HYHU > Love You > HYHU, It's My Life, Luke-A-Roo, Choo Choo Ch'Boogie, Harry Hood, Amazing Grace
E: Golgi, Tweezer Reprise

Fishman on Madonna washboard for I Didn't Know and vacuum for Love You. Bruce "Sunpie" Barnes on washboard, harmonica, and vocals for It's My Life, Luke-A-Roo, and Choo Choo Ch'Boogie. Concert debuts: It's My Life, Luke-A-Roo, and Choo Choo Ch' Boogie.

3/3/93 [ACCESSIBILITY: ••]
Tipitina's, New Orleans, LA
I: Rift, Foam, Bouncing, Maze, Guelah, Paul and Silas, Sample, Runaway Jim, Lawn Boy, Cavern
II: Axilla, Curtain > Melt, Mound, Mike's > Hydrogen > Weekapaug, Glide, MSO, FEFY, HYHU > Terrapin > HYHU, Squirming Coil, Adeline
E: Fire

Carl Gerhard on trumpet for Lawn Boy and Cavern. Fishman on vacuum for Terrapin.

3/5/93 [ACCESSIBILITY: ••]
Deep Ellum Lodge, Dallas, TX
I: Buried Alive > Poor Heart, Cavern, Foam, Sloth, Rift, Stash, Sparkle, It's Ice, I Didn't Know, Possum
II: Landlady > Chalkdust, Guelah, Uncle Pen, Mike's > Hydrogen > Weekapaug, Jesus Left Chicago, MSO > BBJ, HYHU > Love You > HYHU, Squirming Coil, Amazing Grace
E: GTBT

Fishman on vacuum for Love You. Last Jesus Left Chicago, 11/23/91 Barre, VT [152 shows].

3/6/93 [ACCESSIBILITY: ••]
Liberty Lunch, Austin, TX
I: Llama, Horn, Curtain > Melt, Mound, PYITE, Bouncing, Maze, Golgi, Runaway Jim
II: Rift, Tweezer, Reba, Paul and Silas, BBJ, FEFY, YEM, HYHU > Cracklin' Rosie > HYHU, BBFCM
E: Adeline, Poor Heart, Tweezer Reprise

3/8/93 [ACCESSIBILITY: •] [ATTEND. 968; CAP. 1,150] [TIX $12-$14]
Sweeney Convention Center, Santa Fe, NM
I: Golgi, Rift, Guelah, Oh Kee > Llama, Forbin's > How High the Moon > Mockingbird, Sparkle, It's Ice, Glide, Bowie
II: Poor Heart, Cavern, Uncle Pen, Stash, BBJ, My Friend > Kung > YEM, Lizards, Amazing Grace
E: HYHU > Terrapin > HYHU, Chalkdust

Last How High the Moon, 4/26/90 Oberlin, OH [329 shows].

3/9/93 [ACCESSIBILITY: ••] [ATTEND. 1,721; CAP. 1,988] [TIX $10-$17]
Pike's Peak Center, Colorado Springs, CO
I: Runaway Jim, Foam, Bouncing, Maze, Esther, Divided Sky, Glide, PYITE, I Didn't Know, Antelope
II: Axilla, Rift, Tweezer, Reba, Lawn Boy, Mike's > Hydrogen > Weekapaug, Horse > Silent, BBJ, HYHU > Love You > HYHU, I Walk the Line, Squirming Coil, Tweezer Reprise **E:** Amazing Grace, Rocky Top

Fishman on trombone for I Didn't Know and vacuum for Love You. Before Amazing Grace, an audience member in the balcony sung an a cappella version of The Eleven.

3/12/93 [ACCESSIBILITY: •]
Daubson Arena, Vail, CO

I: Buried Alive > Poor Heart, Cavern, Possum, Guelah, Rift, Stash, Fluffhead, Horse > Silent, Bowie
II: AC/DC Bag, My Friend, Axilla, Sparkle, YEM, Mound, BBJ, Chalkdust, HYHU > Lengthwise > HYHU, Harry Hood, Golgi
E: Adeline, Carolina, Rocky Top

Fishman on vacuum for Lengthwise.

3/13/93 [ACCESSIBILITY: ••] [ATTEND. 3,788; CAP. 3,788] [TIX $15]
CU Balch Fieldhouse, University Of Colorado, Boulder, CO
I: Landlady, Funky Bitch, Bouncing, Maze, Fee, All Things, Melt, Contact, Llama, Wilson, Antelope
II: Suzie, Tweezer, Lizards, It's Ice, Glide, Uncle Pen, BBJ, Mike's > Hydrogen > Weekapaug, FEFY, HYHU > Love You > HYHU, Tweezer Reprise
E: MSO, Amazing Grace, BBFCM

Soundcheck: Dog Log, Halley's, Blues jam, Owner of a Lonely Heart. Fishman on vacuum for Love You.

3/14/93 [ACCESSIBILITY: ••••] [ATTEND. 1,545; CAP. 1,545] [TIX $11-$13]
Paul Wright Gym, Western State College, Gunnison, CO
I: Loving Cup, Foam, Guelah, Sparkle, Stash, Paul and Silas, Sample, Reba, PYITE, Runaway Jim
II: Halley's > Bowie, Curtis Lowe, YEM, Lifeboy, Rift, BBJ > Great Gig > HYHU, Squirming Coil
E: Memories, Adeline, Golgi

Soundcheck: Halley's, Curtis Lowe, Tales of Brave Ulysses > Sunshine of Your Love, Lifeboy. Indian War Dance jam before Reba whistle jam played by eight-year-old Cameron McKenney on piano. In order, jams in YEM were Owner of a Lonely Heart, (Trey on vocals), Low Rider, Spooky (Page on vocals), and Oye Como Va. YEM vocal jam included We Will Rock You and Welcome to the Machine vocal jams. Fishman on vacuum for Great Gig. Concert debut: Great Gig. Last Halley's, 8/17/89 Burlington, VT [418 shows]. Last Curtis Lowe, 10/30/90 Crested Butte, CO [296 shows].

After a good first set, with an always-welcome Punch and Paul & Silas, it happened. "It" being the first Halley's Comet of the 1990s. A great song finally revived. Then, Bowie or Possum? Bowie or Possum? Sounds like Possum, but no, a ripping, and I mean ripping, Bowie follows. Amazingly, it's outdone by a YEM with many pleasant teases and a great vocal jam—you can actually hear them laughing and cracking up as they chant the words. —Ric Hannah

Here's my pick for the best of 1993—the revival of Halley's Comet, plus Bowie, Big Ball Jam, the tease-filled YEM—what more could you ask from a Phish show? This is truly the band at its best and most playful, as the YEM vocal jam evolves spontaneously into the chorus of We Will Rock You and then Welcome to the Machine. Magnificent. —Jamis Curran

This is one of those shows where everyone in attendance has their own highlight. Not impressed by a first set featuring a Loving Cup opener and a killer Runaway Jim closer? Okay, how about the first Halley's in the 1990s, a song Phish swore they would never play live way back in 1989? Followed by a long Bowie? And that crazy YEM?—Linda Mahdesian

3/16/93 [ACCESSIBILITY: ••] [ATTEND. 938; CAP. 1,450] [TIX $14-$15]
Celebrity Theater, Phoenix, AZ
I: Adeline, Buried Alive > Poor Heart, It's Ice, Fee, Maze, I Didn't Know, Divided Sky, "Harry Jones' Song," McGrupp, Cavern
II: My Friend, Curtain > Tweezer > Bathtub Gin, Esther, Chalkdust, YEM, HYHU > Bike > Lengthwise > Bike > HYHU, Lawn Boy, Llama, Amazing Grace
E: Sparkle > Tweezer Reprise

Trey's grandfather Harry Jones came on stage and played on a song between Divided Sky and McGrupp. Sweet Emotion jam in Tweezer. Fishman on vacuum for Bike and Lengthwise (one verse).

3/17/93 [ACCESSIBILITY: ••] [ATTEND. 875; CAP. 1,100] [TIX $17.50]
The Palace, Hollywood, CA
I: Landlady > Runaway Jim, Foam, Bouncing, Stash, Amazing Grace, Paul and Silas, It's Ice, Oh Kee > Suzie, Antelope
II: Axilla, Glide, Reba, Jesus Left Chicago, Mound, Mike's > Hydrogen > Weekapaug, Horse > Silent, HYHU > Great Gig > HYHU, Golgi
E: Adeline, Rocky Top

Lively Up Yourself jam in Weekapaug. Fishman on vacuum for Great Gig.

3/18/93 [ACCESSIBILITY: ••] [ATTEND. 875; CAP. 1,100] [TIX $17.50]
The Palace, Hollywood, CA
I: Chalkdust, Guelah, Rift, Fee > Maze, Forbin's > Mockingbird, Sparkle, Horn, I Didn't Know, Bowie
II: My Friend, Poor Heart, Melt, Tela, YEM, Uncle Pen, BBJ, HYHU > Brain > HYHU, Squirming Coil, Cavern
E: GTBT

Little Drummer Boy jam in My Friend. Fishman on trombone for I Didn't Know and vacuum for Brain.

3/19/93 [ACCESSIBILITY: ••]
Greek Theater, University of Redlands, Redlands, CA
I: Suzie, Llama, Foam, Bouncing, Rift, Stash, Fluffhead, Cavern, Antelope
II: Runaway Jim, It's Ice, Uncle Pen, Sample, Lizards, Mike's > Hydrogen > Weekapaug > HYHU > Love You > HYHU, Golgi
E: Amazing Grace, Chalkdust

Soundcheck: Dog Log > Heartbreaker jam, Misty Mountain Hop, Get It On jam, Blues jam. Fishman on vacuum for Love You.

3/21/93 [ACCESSIBILITY: •] [ATTEND. 850; CAP. 850] [TIX $16.50]
Ventura Theater, Ventura, CA
I: Maze, Sparkle, Sloth, Divided Sky, Esther, All Things, Melt, Poor Heart, PYITE, Lawn Boy, Possum
II: Loving Cup, My Friend > Rift, Tweezer > Ya Mar, Llama, YEM, MSO, BBJ, HYHU > Cracklin' Rosie > HYHU, Harry Hood, Cavern
E: Sleeping Monkey, Adeline, Tweezer

3/22/93 [ACCESSIBILITY: •••••]
Crest Theater, Sacramento, CA
I: Chalkdust, Guelah, Uncle Pen, Stash, Bouncing, Rift, Weigh, Reba, Sparkle, Bowie
II: Golgi, It's Ice > Lizards > Tela > Wilson > AC/DC Bag > Forbin's > Mockingbird > Sloth > McGrupp, Mike's > Hydrogen > Weekapaug
E: Amazing Grace, Fire

Second set featured a full Gamehendge narration, beginning in the middle of It's Ice and continuing through McGrupp—third-ever live Gamehendge. Last live Gamehendge, 10/13/91 Olympia, WA [192 shows]. Last complete live Gamehendge, 3/12/88 Burlington, VT [508 shows]. Sundown jam in Weekapaug.

GAMEHENDGE—what a show! The best West Coast show I've heard, and definitely one of the top three of 1993. The band is mellow, tight, and tasteful and full of what they know best. This show highlights everyone doing everything right. Jon has some mighty rises, Trey takes your head off, Mike is a groovin' machine, and Page is a master of the keys. You all own it, so listen to it, cherish it—it's Phish, it's Gamehendge, and it's out of this world. —David M. Brown

I love this tape; it's just too perfect. Do you think maybe it was pre-planned, sort of? Maybe they had the idea in the back of their heads and were wondering when to unleash it. Anyway, this is one of the best live Gamehendges around (that's my thought). Then after all this splendor, they gave us a Mike's Groove. Wow. —Ron Lauer

3/24/93 [ACCESSIBILITY: ••] [ATTEND. 686; CAP. 1,400] [TIX $17.50-$19]
Luther Burbank Center for the Performing Arts, Santa Rosa, CA
I: Llama, Foam, Fee, Poor Heart, Maze, I Didn't Know, Sample, Amazing Grace, Cavern
II: Landlady, Melt, Sparkle, Tweezer, Mound, BBJ, FEFY, YEM, Horse > Silent, HYHU > Terrapin > HYHU, GTBT
E: Carolina, Squirming Coil

Fishman on trombone for I Didn't Know and vacuum for Terrapin. Before Terrapin, an audience member named Sam told The Prison Joke (see 4/11/91).

3/25/93 [ACCESSIBILITY: ••]
Santa Cruz Civic Auditorium, Santa Cruz, CA
I: Chalkdust, Guelah, It's Ice, Possum, Bouncing, Stash, Glide, Rift, Horn, Magilla, Antelope
II: Axilla > Curtain > Sample, Uncle Pen, Forbin's > Icculus > Kung > Mockingbird, Wedge, Mike's > Hydrogen > Weekapaug, Golgi
E: MSO, BBJ, Adeline

Ob-La-Di Ob-La-Da jam in Antelope intro and in Antelope jam; Ob-La-Di tease in Weekapaug. Last Icculus, 5/2/92 Chicago, IL [119 shows]. Last Magilla, 5/8/92 Buffalo, NY [114 shows].

Two nights after Gamehendge, and Icculus emerges! This show (along with 3/31) are the hidden gems of the 1993 spring West Coast tour. The second set of this show has the last Wedge until 1995; Trey quotes the Beatles, too, especially in Antelope! —Al Hunt

3/26/93 [ACCESSIBILITY: •••] [ATTEND. 2,175; CAP. 2,250] [TIX $16.50]
Warfield Theater, San Francisco, CA
I: Maze, Sparkle, Foam, Fee, PYITE, All Things, Melt, Fluffhead, Divided Sky, Cavern
II: Wilson, Runaway Jim, Mound, Tweezer, Horse > Silent, YEM, BBJ, Oh Kee > Suzie, HYHU > Great Gig > HYHU, Tweezer Reprise
E: Amazing Grace, Rocky Top
Fishman on vacuum for Great Gig.

3/27/93 [ACCESSIBILITY: •••] [ATTEND. 2,250; CAP. 2,250] [TIX $16.50]
Warfield Theater, San Francisco, CA
I: Llama, Guelah, Rift, Stash, Reba, My Friend, Uncle Pen, Sample, I Didn't Know, Bowie
II: Buried Alive > Halley's, It's Ice, Bouncing, Chalkdust, TMWSIY > Avenu > TMWSIY, Mike's > Hydrogen > Weekapaug, HYHU > Cracklin' Rosie > HYHU, Poor Heart, Golgi
E: Squirming Coil, Carolina
On Broadway jam in Weekapaug. Opening line of Suzie sung a cappella before Carolina.

3/28/93 [ACCESSIBILITY: ••]
East Gym, Humboldt State University, Arcata, CA
I: Landlady, Funky Bitch, Sparkle, Melt, Lizards, Sloth, Maze, Fee, It's Ice, Lawn Boy, Antelope
II: Walk Away, Runaway Jim, Mound, Bathtub Gin, YEM, Paul and Silas, BBJ, HYHU > Love You > HYHU, Possum
E: Contact, BBFCM
The Pez Song sung by Trey in YEM. Fishman on vacuum for Love You.

3/30/93 [ACCESSIBILITY: ••] [ATTEND. 1,500; CAP. 1,500] [TIX $15-$18.50]
Hilton Ballroom, Eugene, OR
I: Buried Alive > Poor Heart, All Things, Golgi, My Friend, Llama, Esther, Stash, Glide, Divided Sky, Cavern
II: Loving Cup, Rift, Tweezer, Lifeboy > BBJ, Weigh, Mike's > Hydrogen > Weekapaug, Horse > Silent, HYHU > Brain > HYHU, Tweezer Reprise
E: MSO, Amazing Grace
Soundcheck: She's So Cold, Funky Bitch, Theme to Sesame Street. Fishman on vacuum for Brain. Psycho Killer jam in Weekapaug.

3/31/93 [ACCESSIBILITY: •••] [ATTEND. 1,120; CAP. 1,120] [TIX $13.50-$16]
Roseland Theater, Portland, OR
I: Runaway Jim, Foam, Sparkle, Melt, Mound, PYITE, Sample, Reba, I Didn't Know, Bowie
II: Lengthwise > Maze, Bouncing, Uncle Pen, Harry Hood, BBJ, It's Ice, YEM, Harpua, Chalkdust
E: AC/DC Bag, Adeline
Soundcheck: Mango, Gumbo, Satisfaction. Fishman on Madonna washboard for I Didn't Know and on vacuum for YEM vocal jam. Axel F and She's So Cold jams in Harpua.

[4/1/93]
Ancient Forests Benefit, Portland, OR
Amazing Grace, I Didn't Know
Outdoor show with numerous other performers. Phish performed with no instruments.

4/1/93 [ACCESSIBILITY: ••] [ATTEND. 1,120; CAP. 1,120] [TIX $13.50-$16]
Roseland Theater, Portland, OR
I: Llama, Guelah, Rift, Stash, Squirming Coil, My Friend, Paul and Silas, Fluffhead, Lawn Boy, Antelope
II: Axilla, Curtain > Possum, Fee > Ya Mar, Tweezer, Poor Heart, BBJ, HYHU > Terrapin > HYHU, Cavern
E: Carolina, Tweezer Reprise
Heart of Gold tease before Llama. Heartbreaker tease in Antelope. April Fool's Day joke before Terrapin—a folding chair and acoustic guitar were set up and Trey announced, Ladies and gentlemen, Neil Young! Several audience members gave Fishman a pie in the face before Terrapin; Fishman on vacuum for Terrapin.

4/2/93 [ACCESSIBILITY: ••] [ATTEND. 1,408; CAP. 1,408] [TIX $10-$14]
Mount Baker Theater, Bellingham, WA
I: Buried Alive > Poor Heart, Foam, Bouncing, Divided Sky, I Didn't Know, Sparkle, Maze, Golgi
II: Runaway Jim, Sample, Uncle Pen, Llama, Horse > Silent, Mike's > Hydrogen > Weekapaug, Lizards > BBJ, HYHU > Bike > HYHU, Chalkdust
E: Amazing Grace, Rocky Top

4/3/93 [ACCESSIBILITY: ••] [ATTEND. 793; CAP. 793] [TIX $13.50]
86th Street Music Hall, Vancouver, BC
I: Landlady > Rift, Guelah, Sparkle, Melt, Squirming Coil, My Friend, Reba, Horn, Antelope
II: Suzie, Stash, Mound, All Things, Sloth, YEM, Jesus Left Chicago, MSO, HYHU > Love You > HYHU, Cavern
E: GTBT
Fishman on vacuum for Love You. My Girl theme in YEM vocal jam.

4/5/93 [ACCESSIBILITY: ••] [ATTEND. 1,623; CAP. 1,623] [TIX $11-$15]
H.U.B. Ballroom, Seattle, WA
I: Llama, It's Ice, Fee, Maze, Fluffhead, Paul and Silas, Stash, Forbin's > Mockingbird, Bowie
II: Axilla, Poor Heart, Caravan, PYITE, Tweezer, Glide, YEM, HYHU > Cracklin' Rosie > HYHU, Tweezer Reprise
E: Carolina, Fire
Last Caravan, 9/25/91 Keene, NH [216 shows].

4/9/93 [ACCESSIBILITY: ••] [ATTEND. 1,375; CAP. 1,375] [TIX $16.50]
State Theater, Minneapolis, MN
I: Chalkdust, Sparkle, Guelah, Stash, Horse > Silent, Maze, I Didn't Know, It's Ice, Divided Sky, Cavern
II: Buried Alive > Suzie, All Things, Llama, Mound, My Friend, YEM, MSO, HYHU > Love You > HYHU, Possum
E: Adeline, Golgi
Cookiehead theme in YEM vocal jam. Fishman on vacuum for Love You.

4/10/93 [ACCESSIBILITY: •••] [ATTEND. 5,000; CAP. 5,000] [TIX $16.50]
Aragon Ballroom, Chicago, IL
I: Runaway Jim, Weigh, Sparkle, Melt, Squirming Coil, My Friend, Uncle Pen, Chalkdust, Lawn Boy, Bowie
II: Lengthwise > Maze, Bouncing, Rift, Glide, BBJ, Mike's > Great Gig > Weekapaug, Funky Bitch, Help Me, Hoochie Coochie Man, Cavern
E: Amazing Grace, GTBT
Tease medley of songs played earlier in the set during Bowie intro. Miss You tease in Mike's. Sugar Blue on harmonica for Funky Bitch, Help Me, Hoochie Coochie Man, and Cavern. Fishman on vacuum for Great Gig. Concert debuts: Help Me, Hoochie Coochie Man.

The Aragon is a terrible place to see Phish—the place isn't acoustically well-developed. But with it being so echoey, Great Gig was totally amazing. The vacuum sounded just like the big woman on Dark Side of the Moon. I remember the smoke machine being used a few times, which completely filled the room and made it kind of mystical. —Rob Koeller

My recording of this show is not the best (tapes of most shows at the Aragon, unless they are soundboard dubs, usually suck), but the song selection and special guest Sugar Blue more than makes up for it. Several blues tunes played with Sugar Blue and an exceptional Cavern towards the end shine, thanks to the blues tinge of Sugar Blue's harmonica. Luckily I got to see this show, so the sound was as good as can be for us, although I'd love to hear a soundboard recording. —Daniel Grilfand

4/12/93 [ACCESSIBILITY: ••]
Student Union Ballroom, Iowa City, IA
I: Golgi, Tube, Bouncing, Poor Heart, Stash, Horse > Silent, Reba, Llama, Satin Doll, Antelope
II: Dinner and a Movie, Tweezer, Fee, Paul and Silas, It's Ice, BBJ, YEM, HYHU > Terrapin > HYHU, Tweezer Reprise
E: Amazing Grace, Highway to Hell
E2: Rocky Top
Fishman on vacuum for Terrapin. Gumbo (including a verse sung by Trey) and Honky Tonk Woman jams in YEM. New York New York and Swing Low Sweet Chariot themes in YEM vocal jam. Ina-Gadda-Da-Vida theme in YEM vocal jam. Last Tube, 11/20/92 Albany, NY [73 shows]. Last Highway to Hell, 11/15/91 Charlottesville, VA [184 shows]. Last Satin Doll, 2/25/90 Baltimore, MD [378 shows].

4/13/93 [ACCESSIBILITY: ••] [ATTEND. 1,845; CAP. 3,145] [TIX $9.89]
Memorial Hall, Kansas City, KS
I: Suzie, Foam, Sparkle, Possum, Forbin's > Mockingbird, Chalkdust, Guelah > Caravan, Cavern
II: My Friend, Rift, Sloth, Uncle Pen, FEFY, BBJ, Mike's > Hydrogen > Weekapaug, HYHU > Brain > HYHU, Squirming Coil
E: Bold as Love, Adeline
Fishman on vacuum for Brain.

4/14/93 [ACCESSIBILITY: •••] [ATTEND. 1,553; CAP. 1,600] [TIX $14-$16]
American Theater, St. Louis, MO
I: Buried Alive > Poor Heart, Maze, Bouncing, It's Ice, Stash > Kung > Stash > Kung > Horse > Silent, Divided Sky, I Didn't Know, Golgi
II: AC/DC Bag, MSO, Tweezer, Mound, BBJ, YEM > Harpua, Runaway Jim
E: Lengthwise, Contact, Tweezer Reprise
Fishman on Madonna washboard for I Didn't Know. At the beginning of the second set, Trey's childhood friend Roger gets on stage and asks his girlfriend to marry him. She accepts, the crowd cheers, and Phish plays AC/DC Bag ("just like Roger...") in tribute. Spooky jam (Page on vocals) in YEM. The End jam in Harpua.

The first set of this show features an incredible version of Stash with Kung in the middle. At the end of Stash, Trey starts up the acoustic beginning of The Horse, they whisper the lyrics to Kung again, then head into Silent. Before the second set, Trey's boyhood pal Roger asks his girlfriend Jen to marry him and the crowd screams when she says yes. Phish plays AC/DC Bag for Roger (a.k.a. "Just like Roger, he's a crazy little kid."). During the encore, they play Contact for "Roger and Jen on the road of life."—Mike Noll

This show offers an interesting "Dreampile" Harpua narration featuring the Jetsons and a spoof on the Doors' "And he walked on down the hall!" —Justin Weiss

During YEM, Trey yells the lyrics "BOY! MAN! GOD! SHIT!" with much more enunciation than usual. Jeopardy theme song during the vocal craziness following YEM. Then, a chunky Harpua with Trey telling us about his dreams and the dream bubbles we all have. Our dreams become bubbles and they float together into Gamehendge. Jimmy is apparently watching the Jetsons in this particular episode. —Russell Lane

4/16/93 [ACCESSIBILITY: ••] [ATTEND. 1,439; CAP. 1,439] [TIX $16.50-$17.50]
Macauley Theater, Louisville, KY
I: Chalkdust, Guelah, Sparkle, Melt, Esther, Llama, Sample, Rift, Harry Hood, Cavern
II: Axilla, Curtain > Maze, Lizards, Mike's > Hydrogen > Weekapaug, Horse > Silent, Uncle Pen > BBJ > HYHU > Bike > HYHU, Highway to Hell
E: Gumbo, Amazing Grace
Several hundred balloons were dropped from the balcony during Lizards. Fishman on vacuum for Bike. Last Gumbo, 7/25/91 Chapel Hill, NC [230 shows].

4/17/93 [ACCESSIBILITY: ••] [ATTEND. 1,580; CAP. 1,580] [TIX $15.50]
Michigan Theater, Ann Arbor, MI
I: Llama, Foam, Bouncing, Stash, It's Ice, Glide, My Friend, All Things, Golgi, Antelope
II: Wilson, Reba, Landlady, Halley's > YEM, Lifeboy, Oh Kee > Suzie, HYHU > Cracklin' Rosie > HYHU > BBJ, Squirming Coil
E: Adeline, BBFCM
Ob-La-Di Ob-La-Da jam in My Friend. I Wish jam in YEM. Fishman on vacuum and Trey on drums for BBJ. Extremely long silence in BBFCM while the band waited for Trey to start the song back up.

4/18/93 [ACCESSIBILITY: •••] [ATTEND. 1,580; CAP. 1,580] [TIX $15.50]
Michigan Theater, Ann Arbor, MI
I: Rift, Guelah, Melt, Sparkle, Divided Sky, Fee > Maze, Horn, I Didn't Know, Cavern
II: Poor Heart, Tweezer, Horse > Silent, Possum, Mound, BBJ, Mike's > Ya Mar, Walk Away, HYHU > Love You > HYHU, Tweezer Reprise
E: Amazing Grace, Rocky Top
During I Didn't Know, Page brought audience members on stage to give their opinions of the previous night's BBFCM encore and its long pause; Brad Sands, Paul, Chris, Mike, and Trey also weighed in with their opinions. Low Rider jam between Mike's and Ya Mar. Fishman on vacuum for Love You.

During the 4/17 BBFCM encore, Trey and Mike laid down on their backs at the front of the stage during one of the song's silent moments. Apparently, Trey forgot it was his turn to start the jam back up, so the band and the crowd sat there in silence for over five minutes. Finally, Mike got up and walked over to Trey to tell him it was his turn to play. This bizarre encore got special attention during their second show at Ann Arbor the next day. Page hosted a segment in the middle of I Didn't Know where audience members came up on stage and said what they were thinking during the long BBFCM silence. —Teddy Stuart

4/20/93 [ACCESSIBILITY: ••] [ATTEND. 1,400; CAP. 1,400] [TIX $14.75-$16]
Newport Music Hall, Columbus, OH
I: Runaway Jim, Weigh, Sparkle, Stash, Bouncing, It's Ice, Glide, Uncle Pen, Lawn Boy, Bowie
II: Chalkdust, Fluffhead, Sample, BBJ, TMWSIY > Avenu > TMWSIY, My Friend, Llama, YEM, HYHU > Whipping Post > HYHU, Golgi
E: Funky Bitch, Amazing Grace

4/21/93 [ACCESSIBILITY: •••] [ATTEND. 1,400; CAP. 1,400] [TIX $14.75-$16]
Newport Music Hall, Columbus, OH
I: Buried Alive > Poor Heart, Foam, Guelah, Maze, Forbin's > Mockingbird, Rift, PYITE, I Didn't Know, Antelope
II: Possum, Mound, Melt, Squirming Coil, Horse > Silent, BBJ, Mike's > Great Gig > Weekapaug > Gumbo
E: Adeline, Cavern
Fishman on trombone for I Didn't Know. A portion of Melt is featured in Demand on Hoist.

We made the short trip to Newport in a highly anxious state, having missed the prior evening's show. Little did we know the historic moment that lay ahead. Buried Alive started things off rather modestly, and an excellent Poor Heart followed. Then it drifted through some average songs until Col. Forbin/Mockingbird, which for me was the highlight of the first set. The second set was kick-ass, featuring the famed Split Open and Melt, which assuredly was one to remember! —Brian Hart

You probably own part of this show without knowing it—the jam from this Split Open and Melt is part of Demand on Hoist. On this night, after years of playing Melt, the band finally "got it right," taking the jam places it had never traveled before. When the song ended, they stood amazed on stage, like they did after the 12/29/94 Bowie. —Ernie Greene

4/22/93 [ACCESSIBILITY: ••]
Agora Theater, Cleveland, OH
I: Suzie, Sparkle, It's Ice, Reba, Chalkdust, Esther, Stash, Fee, Rift, Golgi
II: Llama, Bouncing, All Things, Tweezer, Lizards, BBJ, YEM, Uncle Pen, HYHU > Love You > HYHU, Tweezer Reprise
E: AC/DC Bag, Amazing Grace
Vibration of Life in YEM. Fishman on vacuum for Love You.

4/23/93 [ACCESSIBILITY: ••]
Reed Athletic Center, Colgate University, Clinton, NY
I: Runaway Jim, Weigh, Sparkle, Melt, Fluffhead > My Friend, Divided Sky, Guelah, Lawn Boy, Chalkdust
II: Golgi, Maze, Curtis Lowe, It's Ice, Paul and Silas, BBJ, Mike's > Hydrogen > Weekapaug, Lengthwise, Squirming Coil, Highway to Hell
E: Fire
Soundcheck: Horn, Funky Bitch, Buffalo Bill. Lengthwise featured Mimi Fishman on vacuum. Houselights turned on before encore, and left on through Fire.

4/24/93 [ACCESSIBILITY: ••]
Cheel Arena, Clarkson University, Potsdam, NY
I: Chalkdust, Guelah, Poor Heart, Stash, Horse > Silent, Rift, Caravan, Something Is Wrong with My Baby, Sparkle, Antelope
II: Llama, Foam, Bathtub Gin, Dinner and a Movie, Mound, BBJ, YEM, HYHU > Bike > HYHU, Harry Hood, Cavern
E: Amazing Grace, GTBT
Soundcheck: Something Is Wrong with My Baby. Fishman on vacuum for Bike. Concert debut: Something Is Wrong with My Baby.

4/25/93 [ACCESSIBILITY: ••] [ATTEND. 3,000; CAP. 3,000] [TIX $10-$16]
Kuhl Gym, SUNY Geneseo, Geneseo, NY
I: Landlady, Possum, Bouncing, It's Ice, Glide, Runaway Jim, Forbin's > Mockingbird, Maze, I Didn't Know, Golgi
II: Wilson, Curtain > Tweezer, Contact, Uncle Pen > BBJ, Mike's > Hydrogen > Weekapaug, Fee, Tweezer Reprise
E: Something Is Wrong with My Baby, Carolina, Rocky Top
Fishman on Madonna washboard for I Didn't Know.

4/27/93 [ACCESSIBILITY: ••] [ATTEND. 1,722; CAP. 1,722] [TIX $15.50-$17]
Concert Hall, Toronto, ON
I: Buried Alive > Poor Heart, Foam, Bouncing, Rift, Stash, Guelah, It's Ice, Sparkle, Bowie
II: Golgi, My Friend, All Things, Maze, Lizards, BBJ, YEM, Horse > Silent, HYHU > Love You > HYHU, Cavern
E: MSO, Amazing Grace
Sundown jam in YEM and in the YEM vocal jam. Fishman on vacuum for Love You.

4/29/93 [ACCESSIBILITY: •••]
Le Spectrum, Montreal, QC
I: Melt, Paul and Silas, Sloth, Runaway Jim, Horn, Llama, Glide, Rift, Fee, Oh Kee > Antelope
II: Chalkdust, It's Ice, Ya Mar, Mound, BBJ, Reba, Mike's > Hydrogen > Weekapaug > Makisupa > Weekapaug, HYHU > Terrapin > HYHU, Squirming Coil
E: My Friend, Adeline
I've Got Spurs jam in Hydrogen. Fishman on vacuum for Terrapin. Last Makisupa, 11/26/90 Ithaca, NY [319 shows].

4/30/93 [ACCESSIBILITY: ••••] [ATTEND. 4,095; CAP. 4,095] [TIX $16-$17]
Sports Center, University Of Hartford, West Hartford, CT
I: Lengthwise > Maze, Bouncing, Poor Heart, Stash, Horse > Silent, Divided Sky, Cavern, Lawn Boy, All Things, Possum
II: Wilson, Sparkle, Tweezer > Walk Away, Mound, BBJ, Harry Hood, HYHU > Brain > HYHU, YEM, Golgi
E: Something Is Wrong with My Baby, Amazing Grace, Tweezer Reprise
Fishman on vacuum for Brain.

5/1/93 [ACCESSIBILITY: ••••] [ATTEND. 2,993; CAP. 2,993] [TIX $16.50]
Tower Theater, Upper Darby, PA
I: Runaway Jim, Foam, Guelah, Melt, Fee, Rift, Sample, It's Ice, Glide, Bowie
II: Chalkdust, Fluffhead > My Friend, Squirming Coil, BBJ > Halley's > Paul and Silas, Mike's > Great Gig > Weekapaug, Cavern
E: Carolina, Rocky Top
Fishman on vacuum for Great Gig.

My first full Phish show (I had seen them open for Santana in Philly 7/15/92). Originally I only had a ticket for the next night, but I drove my friend down for the show. While hanging outside, everybody had tickets to unload for $5, but I didn't have any money. Then some guy who was drunk or just zoning on something starts yelling, "Who wants this ticket?" while holding it up in the air. I said, "Are you serious?" He said yes and gave it to me. He was in a big hurry to go in and just wanted to get rid of it. I knew this was the start of something good. I remember a good Mike's Song > Great Gig and Fluffhead. —Phil Valle

During most of 1993, Trey used an acoustic guitar for The Horse and the intro on My Friend, which often led to cool electric-into-acoustic-into-electric segues. At this Tower show, Trey brought his acoustic guitar forward near the end of Fluffhead and played the Fluffhead outro jam acoustic into My Friend. I remember thinking, this might be as close as I'll ever come to hearing Fluffhead acoustic-style like on *Junta*. These two Tower shows were both great; the tapes are worth owning. —Joe Conti

5/2/93 [ACCESSIBILITY: ••] [ATTEND. 2,993; CAP. 2,993] [TIX $16.50]
Tower Theater, Upper Darby, PA
I: Axilla, Sparkle, Divided Sky, Mound, Stash, Horse > Silent, Poor Heart, Maze, I Didn't Know, Golgi
II: Llama > PYITE, YEM > Lizards > BBJ, Uncle Pen, Bouncing > Antelope, HYHU > Cracklin' Rosie > HYHU, BBFCM
E: Sleeping Monkey, Amazing Grace
Fishman on Madonna washboard for I Didn't Know and vacuum for Love You.

5/3/93 [ACCESSIBILITY: ••] [ATTEND. 1,710; CAP. 1,710] [TIX $18.50-$20]
State Theater, New Brunswick, NJ
I: Buried Alive > Rift, Weigh, Chalkdust, Esther, Melt, Forbin's > Mockingbird, Possum, Lawn Boy, Cavern
II: AC/DC Bag > Curtain > Tweezer > Manteca > Tweezer > Contact, It's Ice, McGrupp, Runaway Jim > BBJ, HYHU > Love You > HYHU, MSO, Tweezer Reprise
E: Memories, Amazing Grace, Highway to Hell
I Feel the Earth Move jam in Tweezer. Fishman on vacuum for Love You. Last Manteca, 2/21/93 Atlanta, GA [51 shows].

5/5/93 [ACCESSIBILITY: ••••] [ATTEND. 2,674; CAP. 2,674] [TIX $17.50]
Palace Theater, Albany, NY
I: Rift, Guelah, Foam, Sparkle, Stash, Bouncing, It's Ice, Glide, Maze, Golgi
II: Runaway Jim > My Friend > Manteca > My Friend, Poor Heart, Weigh, BBJ, Ya Mar, YEM
E: Amazing Grace, Cavern > A-Train > Cavern
Two Princes jam in Ya Mar. Col. Bruce Hampton and the Aquarium Rescue Unit joined on YEM. The jam out of YEM also featured the Dude of Life on vocals and Fish on Madonna washboard and vacuum (at various times). Original extra verse sung in Cavern. Last A-Train, 2/12/93 Poughkeepsie, NY [59 shows].

My favorite tape as of late. It has a great live feel, as both the crowd and band have such incredible energy. It feels like you're dancing three rows back from Fish. The band is in a jammy kind of mood, and it shows, as the transitions like that from Runaway into My Friend is pure Phish magic. Trey dedicates a crazy good Ya Mar to then-girlfriend Sue on her birthday. The highlight, though, is the appearance by Col. Bruce and the ARU. Ten guys onstage jamming for 30 minutes. I love this tape! —Tim Foisser

After a weak first set, the magic started with a great Runaway Jim and a MFMF that segued in and out of Manteca. After special treats Weigh and Ya Mar (with Trey teasing the Spin Doctors hit of the moment, Two Princes) came one of the best Phish jams I've ever seen or heard—YEM with Col. Bruce and the ARU. The troops joined Phish for a long jam that (unlike some jams with special guests) never grew stale. The scene on stage was crazy—in the course of the jam, Trey grabbed a set of drumsticks and tapped on everything, the Dude of Life came out and shouted unintelligibly, Oteil gave one of his scats, singing along with the notes, Fishman donned his Madonna washboard, and everyone else played their hearts out. Wow! —Lock Steele

5/6/93 [ACCESSIBILITY: ••] [ATTEND. 2,674; CAP. 2,674] [TIX $17.50]
Palace Theater, Albany, NY
I: Chalkdust, Mound, Melt, Horse > Silent, All Things, Llama, Fluffhead, Possum, Lawn Boy, Why You Been Gone So Long, Tennessee Waltz, Fast Train
II: Suzie, Tweezer, Tela, Uncle Pen, BBJ, Squirming Coil, Mike's > Ob-La-Di Ob-La-Da jam > Bluegrass jam > Rocky Top, HYHU > Cracklin' Rosie > HYHU, That's All Right Mama
E: Adeline, Contact, Tweezer Reprise
Dick Solberg ("The Sun Mountain Fiddler") on fiddle for Lawn Boy and the rest of the first set, and Bluegrass jam to the end of the second set. Jeff Walton on acoustic guitar for Why You Been Gone So Long to the end of first set, and That's All Right Mama. Concert debut: Why You Been Gone So Long, Tennessee Waltz, Fast Train, That's All Right Mama.

We settled in for the second night at the beautiful Palace and Phish rocked from the get-go. After offering up Melt, Fluff, and Possum (!) all in the first set, the boys were joined by their friends Dick Solberg ("the Sun Mountain Fiddler") and Jeff Walton for a rocking bluegrass affair. Solberg had no problem jumping right in, offering up a gorgeous solo in Lawn Boy. Then Trey said, "I want to get Dick to sing one for us here," and for the rest of the set, Solberg gleefully took over. He sang lead vocals on the next three songs and had us in the palm of his hand—after all, here was an older guy with bright white hair rocking out with Phish and urging them along: "Come on, Page," and "How 'bout ya, Trey?" The boys returned for the second set without Solberg and Walton but proceeded to play what was arguably the best Tweezer of the year, a 20-minute version that brought the house down. The best musical moments were still to come: in the Mike's Song jam, Trey teased Ob-La-Di-Ob-La-Da and the crowd started singing along! Then, from out of the smoke that completely engulfed the stage during Mike's, we heard Solberg's telltale fiddle. The smoke lifted, there he was! A bluegrass jam developed and for a minute it sounded like they were heading into Sparkle, but then Mike stepped up and started Rocky Top. Closing the set, a rocking That's All Right Mama provided the final exclamation point. —Lock Steele

5/7/93 [ACCESSIBILITY: ••] [ATTEND. 2,703; CAP. 3,200] [TIX $16.50]
Bangor Auditorium, Bangor, ME
I: Buried Alive > Poor Heart, Melt, Sparkle, Caravan, Lizards, Horn, Divided Sky, I Didn't Know, Antelope
II: Rift, Bouncing, Maze, Fee > BBJ, YEM > Great Gig, Harry Hood, Harpua, Highway to Hell
E: Amazing Grace, Golgi
Bonanza theme in YEM vocal jam. Fishman on Madonna washboard for I Didn't Know and vacuum for Great Gig. An inflatable pig was lowered from rafters during Great Gig; Marley came onstage before the encore and sniffed it. Crossroads jam in Harpua.

I really got the sense that the band wanted to reward everyone who drove all the way up I-95 to Bangor. (No one had even heard of Limestone yet—I thought we were about as far up North as Phish or any sane human being would ever get.) This is a great show for non-Phish snobs. There are no amazing segues, breakouts, or crazy improvisations, just simply great songs and tight performances, with a healthy dose of humor. The highlights included a Great Gig in the Sky in which an inflatable pig was dropped from the rafters (with Marley brought out onstage to sniff it out), and an obviously unplanned Harpua that sampled Crossroads, a sign of things to come the next night down the road in Durham. —Andy Bernstein

5/8/93 [ACCESSIBILITY: •••] [ATTEND. 2,800; CAP. 2,800] [TIX $15.50-$17.50]
Field House, University of New Hampshire, Durham, NH
I: Chalkdust, Guelah, Rift, Mound, Stash > Kung > Stash, Glide, My Friend, Reba, Satin Doll, Cavern
II: Bowie > Have Mercy > Bowie, Horse > Silent, It's Ice > Squirming Coil > Jam > BBJ, Mike's > Crossroads > Mike's > Hydrogen > Weekapaug > Amazing Grace > Amazing Grace jam
E: AC/DC Bag

"Crew appreciation" before Satin Doll. Jessica jam in Bowie intro. Amazing Grace jam was electric with instruments. Concert debuts: Crossroads, Amazing Grace jam. Last Have Mercy, 2/20/93 Atlanta, GA [56 shows].

Our week of touring finished at the Fieldhouse, your typical college gym with bleachers against the back wall and a huge open floor. After spending the somewhat uneven first set about halfway between the soundboard and the stage, I decided to move further back for set II. The long Bowie intro mesmerized the crowd, making navigation easy, but I held my ground as Phish ripped into the song. Somewhere in the middle of the amazing jam, Trey started singing Have Mercy, but Page and Mike didn't pick up on it right away. Eventually they got the reggae groove going, sung Have Mercy, then swung back into Bowie for a climactic finale. I headed outside during Horse/Silent to cool off (there was a giant balcony off the left side of the venue) then came back in and climbed the mostly empty bleachers in back for the jam out of Page's Coil solo and a Mike's Groove that visited Eric Clapton (well, really Robert Johnston) and Weekapaug before arriving at one of the band's most beautiful jams—an electric Amazing Grace. It still gives me goose bumps. —Lock Steele

Anyone who doesn't have this tape in their collection is truly, truly missing out. With the possible exception of 12/29/94, this is simply the best David Bowie ever, complete with a Jessica tease, a wonderfully placed Have Mercy, and an insane heavy metalish jam that manages to be melodic at the same time. Do not forget the electric Amazing Grace in which Trey thanks the crew and the fans. This show really marked the end of the last Phish tour in which Phish played modest, makeshift Northeastern venues, giving Trey's thanks and farewells a special feel in retrospect. —Andy Bernstein

5/29/93 [ACCESSIBILITY: ••]
Laguna Seca Raceway, Monterey, CA
Chalkdust, Bouncing, Rift, Stash, Squirming Coil, Sparkle, Cavern, BBJ, YEM, Runaway Jim, Amazing Grace
E: GTBT

Laguna Seca Daze festival with Jeff Healey, Shawn Colvin, The Allman Brothers Band, and Blues Traveler. Phish played one set. Fishman on vacuum (vacuum freeze) near the end of Cavern.

5/30/93 [ACCESSIBILITY: ••]
Laguna Seca Raceway, Monterey, CA
Lengthwise, Maze, Guelah, Poor Heart, Foam, Ya Mar, Silent, Antelope, I Didn't Know, Melt, Contact, Llama, Golgi
E: Possum

Laguna Seca Daze festival with The Samples, 10,000 Maniacs, and Blues Traveler. Phish played one set. Fishman on Madonna washboard for I Didn't Know. First Silent without Horse.

1993 SUMMER Elbow Room

When the band solicited the Phish.Net community during the spring for suggestions on where to play on summer tour, no one really expected that they'd be making the leap to the amphitheatre circuit so soon—Great Woods? Jones Beach? These were 15,000-plus capacity venues, and Phish would fill them (or at least some of them) this summer. Out of the northeast, the band often found itself playing to vast expanses of empty seats, but that didn't seem to hurt the music.

Still, the musical highlights would come during August as the band swung back to smaller venues; the month is considered by many to be one of the hottest tour months the band has ever put on. Energized by the return of La Grange and Slave (among others), Phish played their hearts out at venues as small as Club Eastbrook in Grand Rapids, MI and as big as Berkeley's Greek Theatre.

7/15/93 [ACCESSIBILITY: •••]
Cayuga County Fairgrounds, Weedsport, NY
I: Rift, Sample, Divided Sky, Mound, Stash, Foam, I Didn't Know, My Mind's, Leprechaun > Runaway Jim
II: Bowie, Horse > Silent, Sparkle, It's Ice, Lifeboy, Possum, Faht, Lizards, Walk Away, Daniel
E: Chalkdust, Freebird

Little Drummer Boy jam in Stash. Fishman on Madonna washboard for I Didn't Know. Last My Mind's, 2/7/93 Washington, D.C. [69 shows]. Last Faht, 12/11/92 Ann Arbor, MI [80 shows]. Concert debuts: Leprechaun, Daniel, and Freebird (the a cappella version, as are all versions hereafter). Last My Minds, 2/7/93 Washington, DC [69 shows].

7/16/93 [ACCESSIBILITY: ••] [ATTEND. 6,356; CAP. 13,243] [TIX $14.50-$17.50]
Mann Music Center, Philadelphia, PA
I: Daniel, Golgi, My Friend, Ya Mar, Buried Alive, FEFY, All Things, Nellie Cane, Horn, Antelope
II: Also Sprach > Melt, Glide, Maze, Bouncing, YEM > Yerushalayim > YEM, Poor Heart, Purple Rain > HYHU, Harry Hood, Cavern
E: Llama, Freebird

Fishman on vacuum for Purple Rain. Concert debuts: Also Sprach, Purple Rain, and Yerushalayim.

7/17/93 [ACCESSIBILITY: ••] [ATTEND. 7,030; CAP. 7,030] [TIX $15-$18]
Filene Center at Wolf Trap, Vienna, VA
I: Landlady, Runaway Jim, Sample, My Mind's, Stash, Reba, Chalkdust, Horse > Silent, Oh Kee > Bowie
II: Also Sprach > Tweezer, Squirming Coil, It's Ice, Sparkle, BBJ, Mike's > Leprechaun > Weekapaug > HYHU > Faht, Rift, GTBT
E: Amazing Grace, Daniel, Tweezer Reprise

7/18/93 [ACCESSIBILITY: ••]
IC Light Amphitheatre, Pittsburgh, PA
I: Buried Alive > Rift, Foam, Guelah, Maze, Esther, Divided Sky, Uncle Pen, Cavern
II: Also Sprach > Poor Heart, Antelope, Mound, FEFY, Oh Kee > Fee, YEM, Purple Rain, Golgi
E: Rocky Top, Freebird

Soundcheck included Guyute. In order, jams in Antelope: Whole Lotta Love, fireworks jam, and Brother.

7/21/93 [ACCESSIBILITY: ••]
Orange County Fairgrounds, Middletown, NY
Also Sprach > Melt, Sparkle, Squirming Coil, Maze, Glide, Rift, Bouncing, Runaway Jim, BBJ, Purple Rain > HYHU, Daniel
E: Chalkdust

HORDE Festival. Phish played one set to close the show, coming on at about 1 a.m. Fishman on vacuum in Purple Rain. HYHU jam in Maze.

7/22/93 [ACCESSIBILITY: ••] [ATTEND. 5,306; CAP. 16,000] [TIX $16-$18.50]
Stowe Performing Arts Center, Stowe, VT
I: Llama, Foam, Horn, My Mind's, Sample, Divided Sky, Mound, Ya Mar, Poor Heart, Stash, Golgi
II: Also Sprach > Tweezer > Walk Away, Sparkle, It's Ice, Contact, Possum, Paul and Silas, TMWSIY > Avenu, Rocky Top
E: Freebird

Gordon Stone on pedal steel guitar for Paul and Silas, Avenu, and Rocky Top.

This was the worst experience with Phish I have ever had. Driving up from Middletown, it was beautiful out, but as soon as we got to the lot it started pouring down rain. It also got very cold, and they almost had to cancel the show. Before Llama, Trey said something like, "Yeah, they were gonna cancel the show, but I said, 'Fuck that, stick the plug up my ass and count out Llama!'" In retrospect, looking at the way they performed, they should have canceled the show. —Joshua Howley

Phish is God but they ain't Mother Nature. Hometown ambiance and a Gordon Stone appearance couldn't save this show from the weather. The only thing that made this rain-

Saturday, July 18, 1993

IC LIGHT AMPHITHEATER, Pittsburgh, PA

Pittsburgh has got to be the most underrated city in America. You think of Pittsburgh, you think of steel mills, labor strikes, and Franco Harris's breath visibly puffing out on a blustery day at Three Rivers Stadium. But the I.C. Light Amphitheater—which wasn't much of an amphitheater at all, just some makeshift bleachers between a couple sets of train tracks—managed to alter our perspective.

It was right at the confluence of the Allegeheny, Monongahela, and Ohio rivers, across from a modern, tasteful downtown that sparkled far behind the stage. In the other direction, hovering over the lot, was a cliff about 200 feet tall. That night, on a 100-yard ledge between a cliff and a river, facing a grand skyline, Phish would find ways to both accentuate and transcend the surroundings.

They didn't use a background curtain, so right behind the band there was that skyline. Something like that can add so much to a show. If your ears ever stop saying "wow," your eyes say it for them. The phrase "multi-sensory experience," which I think has been thrown around to describe Phish a few times, was made for this show.

Trey strolled out and shielded the sun from his eyes, and peered out over and past the audience. We turned around to see what he was looking at—about fifty people who had climbed the side of the cliff and were watching the show from little rock ledges. Trey seemed pleased.

After a few songs, the band whipped into Esther. As Page played the intro, one of those freight trains started rolling by. Chugga chugga chugga chugga. Chugga chugga chugga chugga. There was a rhythm to it. A distinct rhythm. The same rhythm as Esther. Exactly. Fish couldn't have done it better himself. Page just gave this sick little amazed smile. I just turned to Larry, my tourmate, and said, "The greatest band in the world." (Larry later asked Page if it was intentional, but Page said it was all just a coincidence. Great things happen to great bands).

A solid first set was followed by a spectacular second, anchored by an Antelope that still ranks as the best single-song performance I've ever seen. A sick, furious, but distinctly melodic jam that forged a new tune unto itself pounded on for about three minutes. It was so powerful that the crowd erupted right in the middle, not during any of the pauses or transitions but right in the goddamn middle. It was a jam that stretched you out so far you just couldn't contain yourself. And the band was just getting started.

It was nighttime now; the pleasant water and steel background had been replaced by the twinkle of city lights and their reflection in the river beneath. And as the jam continued, fireworks started going off at the point where the three rivers merged. The crowd was screaming again and the band didn't know why, but as the explosions continued, they turned around and saw what was happening.

It had nothing to do with the show, just something the chamber of commerce must do to keep the three tourists who visit each summer coming back. After shaking their heads a few times, the band didn't miss a beat. They started jamming to the fireworks. Big Ball jam style. With each burst, a chord. And it kept going on. Fishman tried to lead them back into Antelope a couple times but Trey was loving it, and wouldn't stop.

Every time another set went off, he'd smash the guitar in unison, followed by a thunder of applause. It never got boring. Finally, the band goes back into a tune—not Antelope, but Brother, just for a few bars. A tease. Then, after whipping the crowd up so high it almost hurt, Trey asked if we had any spike, or whatever the fuck he said that night. And there it was. The perfect climax. Unlimited tension and the ultimate relief. A time where a song was played so great, you almost want them to play a few shitty ones so you can catch your breath and get back to this planet.

Thankfully, they obliged, with Mound and Fast Enough For You, not among my favorites.

This interlude gave me the chance to listen to this dirtbag guy who pushed me out of my spot on the floor. He had just met this girl and offered to take her to the show. Apparently, they had never even heard of Phish but he had some cash and wanted to impress her. He was about twenty, missing a few teeth, and she was about thirty, and not looking much better. Then she started saying she had to leave, so he starts kissing her. Tonguing her down, ten feet in front of the stage, during Fast Enough For You. Really going at it. Cheap porno style.

The floor was crowded. There were some folding chairs in the mix that hadn't been tossed aside. There wasn't much room for this kind of spectacle. But not only did they find room to explore the inner reaches of each other's tonsils, but they managed to clear out a whole section of people behind them. No one wanted to look. A whole patch on the floor, a triangle stretching out around fifteen feet, ended up empty because it was too nasty a sight to behold, even with Phish and the skyscrapers behind them. Finally the guy extricated himself, and she said she had to leave. He asked a few people for a pen to get her phone number but couldn't find one, and then tried to memorize it by saying it out loud, and said goodbye. A strong YEM and a few more shenanigans, including a Purple Rain in which the band rigged the vacuum cleaner to blow out, closed the show.

Hours later, we found our way to the top of the cliff, and got pulled over because I had a busted taillight. And we weren't looking pretty. A clandestine swim in a hotel pool earlier in the day notwithstanding, we stank and the car was filled with garbage. We were just begging to get searched, ticketed and booked on whatever they could come up with. I talked a good game. "We're a little messy, but try to stay on the right side of things," I said. They ran a make on my license, and kept poking around the car with a flashlight. Finally the cop saw something and got all excited. "What's that?" she asked, pointing to a box of beer which, as she was unaware, we had been storing some food in.

Larry picked it up and pulled out a thing of mustard. She smiled. "Have a nice trip."

—Andy Bernstein

soaked gig entertaining were the fans climbing high up the ski hill to get around the fence, and then bolting down past guards busily intercepting anyone they could catch. —Andy Bernstein

7/23/93 [ACCESSIBILITY: ••••] [ATTEND. 8,273; CAP. 10,800] [TIX $19.50]
Jones Beach Music Theater, Wantagh, NY
I: Buried Alive > Rift, Caravan, Nellie Cane, Maze, Horse > Silent, PYITE, Runaway Jim, It's Ice, Lawn Boy, Cavern
II: Also Sprach > Poor Heart, Antelope, Faht > My Friend, Uncle Pen, BBJ, YEM > BBFCM > Chalkdust, Highway to Hell
E: Amazing Grace, Daniel

7/24/93 [ACCESSIBILITY: ••••] [ATTEND. 15,000; CAP. 15,000] [TIX $15-$19.50]
Great Woods Center for the Performing Arts, Mansfield, MA
I: Llama, Horn, Nellie Cane, Divided Sky, Guelah, Rift, Stash, Mango, Bouncing, Squirming Coil
II: Also Sprach > Melt, Fluffhead, Maze, Glide, Sparkle, Mike's > Yerushalayim > Weekapaug, Purple Rain > HYHU, Daniel, GTBT
E: Golgi, Freebird

"Also Sprach" jam in Maze. Fishman on vacuum for Purple Rain. Last Mango, 5/17/92 Schenectady, NY [150 shows].

I'd like to thank my former employer, Tower Records, for scoring me fifth row center tickets for this one. The first set was solid, but the second set is where it's at. Look at the setlist . . . wow. Glide stepped everything up a notch with Trey and Mike donning their slippy-slidy shoes to glide back and forth on stage. After the phat Mike's, Yerushalayim was about as beautiful, calming, and restful as you can get. In all of the excitement of one of my favorite Weekapaugs, I wrote down "Funky Bitch" for some reason on my setlist! Mike's bass intro matched the huge smile Trey was wearing. Then encore time, and immediately those of us who knew started a "Freebird" chant. They had done it two nights before in Stowe, VT, but we needed it here at one of their biggest sellouts to that day . . . and once again they did not disappoint! —Tony Hume

Trey later said this show and the Murat gig on August 13 were his favorite shows of the 1993 summer tour, and though the music on this night is not as incredible as the Murat's second set, it's still a great tape. Besides the Mango Song breakout in the first set, 2001 > SOAM and Mike's > Yerushalayim!! > Weekapaug are keepers. —Ed Smith

7/25/93 [ACCESSIBILITY: •••] [ATTEND. 5,427; CAP. 12,000] [TIX $20-$23]
Waterloo Village Music Center, Stanhope, NJ
I: Wilson, Foam, Mound, Stash, Fee, Rift, Sloth, My Mind's, I Didn't Know, Bowie
II: Also Sprach > Suzie, Tweezer > Horse > Silent, Maze, Lizards, Purple Rain > HYHU, Harpua > Tweezer Reprise
E: Cavern

Jeopardy jam before Foam. Donna Lee and Sounds of Silence teases in Bowie. Taxi theme jam in Harpua. Fishman on vacuum for Purple Rain.

7/27/93 [ACCESSIBILITY: ••]
Classic Amphitheatre, Richmond, VA
Also Sprach > Rift, Stash, Squirming Coil, Sparkle > It's Ice > Purple Rain > HYHU, YEM

HORDE festival. Phish played one set to close the show. Fishman on vacuum for Purple Rain. John Popper on harmonica and Chan Kinchla on guitar for YEM, along with other HORDE members.

During the jam in YEM, Trey, Mike and several stagehands brought a large (backyard-sized) trampoline out on stage. Then John Popper—in the midst of the jam—was wheeled back offstage in his wheelchair (this was after his motorcycle accident). A few minutes later, everyone looked up to see Popper (wheelchair and all) being lowered from above the stage by a rope. The rope snapped, Popper dropped through the trampoline, and the musicians still on stage took the jam up a notch. Turned out, the "Popper" lowered from above was a dummy. —Mick Connor

7/28/93 [ACCESSIBILITY: ••]
Grady Cole Center, Charlotte, NC
I: All Things, Runaway Jim, Ya Mar, Sample, Foam, Nellie Cane, Melt, Horse > Silent, Poor Heart, Cavern
II: Also Sprach > Axilla, MSO, Antelope, Lizards, Mound, My Friend, Harry Hood, Great Gig > HYHU, Chalkdust
E: Father/Son Boogie, Bill Bailey

Fishman on vacuum for Great Gig. Page's father, Dr. Jack McConnell, on keyboard for Father/Son Boogie and Bill Bailey, and vocals for Bill Bailey. Concert debuts: Father/Son Boogie and Bill Bailey.

7/29/93 [ACCESSIBILITY: ••] [ATTEND. 1,013; CAP. 1,400] [TIX $17-$18.50]
Tennessee Theater, Knoxville, TN
I: Funky Bitch, Divided Sky, Weigh, Rift, Landlady > FEFY, My Mind's, Forbin's > Mockingbird, Possum
II: Maze, Bouncing, It's Ice, Lifeboy, Sparkle, YEM, Purple Rain > HYHU, Daniel, GTBT
E: Rocky Top, Freebird

Fishman on vacuum on Purple Rain.

7/30/93 [ACCESSIBILITY: ••]
The Veranda at Starwood Amphitheater, Antioch, TN
I: Contact, Llama, Uncle Pen, Stash, Esther, Chalkdust, I Didn't Know, Reba, Cavern
II: Also Sprach > Tweezer, Horse > Silent, Poor Heart, Fluffhead > My Friend, Golgi, Squirming Coil, Bowie
E: Walk Away, Amazing Grace

Fishman on Madonna washboard for I Didn't Know.

The Tweezer jam begins with Trey scratching crazy rhythms on his strings, and moves to a jam on a theme that Page creates with the low keys of his piano. The jam builds to such a full sound, it's like a 1995 Free. Then Trey takes us acoustically into The Horse from the Tweezer breakdown, complete with a classical guitar solo. Later in the set, Trey segues the end of Fluffhead acoustically into My Friend My Friend. Acoustic Trey is really something. —Brendan Neagle

This had to be the oddest venue Phish has ever played. Starwood is a huge amphitheater, but they played at something called "The Veranda at Starwood"—a fancy way of saying the snack bar. The thing I'll never forget from this show is seeing Trey ride around the parking lot in a golf cart, surrounded by about 25 fans. Then a security guard pulled up on a golf cart of his own and stared Trey down, asking, "Where'd you get the golf cart?" Trey replied, "I'm the guitarist." —Andy Bernstein

7/31/93 [ACCESSIBILITY: ••]
Masquerade Music Park, Atlanta, GA
I: Rift, Sample, Ya Mar, Melt, Mound, Foam, Nellie Cane, Divided Sky, Cavern
II: Wilson, Runaway Jim, It's Ice, Maze, Sparkle, Mike's > Leprechaun > Weekapaug, Purple Rain > HYHU, Daniel, Highway to Hell
E: AC/DC Bag, Freebird

Heartbreaker and Black Dog jams in Mike's. Fishman on vacuum for Purple Rain.

8/2/93 [ACCESSIBILITY: ••••] [ATTEND. 1,260; CAP. 1,260] [TIX $13-$17]
Ritz Theater, Ybor City (Tampa), FL
I: Chalkdust, Guelah, Poor Heart, Brother, Oh Kee > Suzie, All Things, Bathtub Gin > Makisupa > My Mind's, Dog Log > La Grange
II: Also Sprach > Mike's > Sparks > Curtis Lowe, Rift, Squirming Coil > Weekapaug > HYHU > Bike > HYHU, Antelope > Makisupa Jam > Antelope
E: Sleeping Monkey, Amazing Grace

Soundcheck: Slave, Funky Bitch. Sweet Virginia jam in Bathtub Gin. Joe Rooney on (unintelligible) vocals during Mike's jam. Fishman on vacuum for Bike. Saints Go Marching In tease in Antelope intro. Last Brother, 7/14/92 Norfolk, VA [143 shows]. Last Dog Log, 5/4/91 Somerville, MA [280 shows]. Last La Grange, 3/17/91 Aspen, CO [307 shows].

The venue Phish was supposed to play had gone out of business a few days before, so it was moved to a small music club in Tampa, a hot, old, musty room. Yes, this was summer of 1993, and the band had sold out Great Woods about two weeks before, but it was also Florida, a state that Phish had yet to conquer. Everyone in that room walked out believers, and the band seemed to relish the atmosphere, busting out the oldies that had been created, and in some cases left behind, on stages like that one. Dog Log, Brother—songs which hadn't been played in eons and wouldn't surface again until more than two years later, as well as rarities La Grange (it hadn't been played in 307 shows) and Curtis Lowe (has it been played since?)—were only part of the story. The Bathtub Gin is one of the best ever, and the entire second set was pretty much one long jam with Makisupa in an Antelope closer, just to make sure everyone had gotten their fill of perfection. This was a show where you could just walk up to the stage and watch from the front row, which I did during set I, but I got so hot that I had to watch set II from the bar in the back, whipping out 50¢ every few songs to buy a cup of ice water. True nourishment would come later, when Mike emerged into the tiny parking lot with a platter of food. "Eat," he said, and the band fed the tourheads. —Andy Bernstein

Get this show if you don't already have it—the setlist is amazing. But the big treat of this show is what I refer to as Makisupelope. At the end of the Antelope, Mike throws the Makisupa bass line in, and the jam morphs into Makisupa. Trey sings, "Marco Policeman-Dolas," and the punchy jam moves with ease between Antelope and Makisupa before an Antelope closing. —Adam Davidoff

8/3/93 [ACCESSIBILITY: ••]
Bayfront Park Amphitheatre, Miami, FL
I: Runaway Jim, Nellie Cane, Foam, Fee > Rift, Stash, Horse > Silent, Ya Mar, Llama, Cavern
II: Lengthwise > Maze, Bouncing, It's Ice, YEM, Lizards, Sparkle, Purple Rain > HYHU, Golgi
E: Poor Heart, Freebird

Fishman on vacuum for Purple Rain.

8/6/93 [ACCESSIBILITY: ••••]
Cincinnati Zoo Peacock Pavilion, Cincinnati, OH
I: Melt, Poor Heart, Curtain > Sample, Rift, Horn, Divided Sky, Nellie Cane, Chalkdust, Suzie
II: Buried Alive > Tweezer, Guelah, Squirming Coil, Uncle Pen, YEM > Halley's > Slave, HYHU > Cracklin' Rosie > HYHU, Tweezer Reprise
E: Amazing Grace

Tequila teases in Tweezer, Guelah, and YEM. Cocaine jam in YEM, and Cocaine lyrics sung in YEM vocal jam. Last Slave, 10/24/91 Prescott, AZ [240 shows].

This place is a nice open-air venue within the Zoo—you could leave, check out the animals, and be let back in. On stage, Mike added a small rearview mirror to his stand so he could see the Minkin backdrop behind him. The pinnacle of the show came in the second set with YEM > Cocaine > YEM > Halley's > Slave > Cracklin' Rosie. Most were stunned upon exiting this show. —Nathaniel Peirce

Slave had been soundchecked down in Florida earlier in the week, so rumors of its imminent return at the Cincy Zoo ("See the city, see the zoo...") ran rampant. But no one could have predicted the mesmerizing way it would emerge out of the ending Halley's jam, much less the YEM > Cocaine > YEM madness that came first! —Tricia Holmes

One of the groundbreaking 1993 SOAMelts served as a very hot opener. —Al Hunt

8/7/93 [ACCESSIBILITY: ••••] [ATTEND. 5,387; CAP. 16,000] [TIX $16-$18.50]
Darien Lake Performing Arts Center, Darien Center, NY
I: Llama, Bouncing, Poor Heart > Stash > Makisupa, Reba > Maze, Forbin's > Mockingbird, Cavern
II: Also Sprach > Mike's > Sparks > Kung > Mike's > TMWSIY > Avenu > Sloth, Sparkle, My Friend > McGrupp > Purple Rain > HYHU, Antelope
E: Carolina, La Grange

Fishman on vacuum for Purple Rain.

The August 1993 insanity continued in Darien with a segue-filled show. Stash > Makisupa and Reba > Maze in the first set are where it's at. Set II travels even farther afield with a Mike's Song complete with Kung and Sparks, a wild Avenu > Sloth pairing (no return to TMWSIY), and La Grange for an encore. —Pat Stanley

If you listen carefully to this tape during Purple Rain, you can hear a loud POP! followed by Fishman saying, "Whoa!" This is the result of someone throwing an M-80 firecracker that landed between my friend's legs. He jumped up and it exploded, raising a response from Fish. This show took place at an amusement park, which triggers an interesting dialogue in Forbin's about riding the roller coaster of the mind. This very good show should be on everyone's list of tapes. —Dave O'Connor

8/8/93 [ACCESSIBILITY: ••]
Nautica Stage, Cleveland, OH
I: BBFCM, Foam, Loving Cup, Runaway Jim, Horse > Silent, PYITE, FEFY, Paul and Silas, I Didn't Know, Bowie
II: Also Sprach > Rift, Harry Hood, Wilson, It's Ice, Fluffhead, Possum, BBJ, HYHU > Love You > HYHU, Daniel, GTBT
E: MSO, Freebird

Fishman on Madonna washboard for I Didn't Know and vacuum for Love You. Tequila tease in Daniel. Last Loving Cup, 3/30/93 Eugene, OR [50 shows].

8/9/93 [ACCESSIBILITY: ••] [ATTEND. 1,494; CAP. 1,500] [TIX $19.50]
Concert Hall, Toronto, ON
I: Chalkdust, Mound, Fee > Melt, Glide, Nellie Cane > Divided Sky, Memories, Squirming Coil
II: Dinner and a Movie > Tweezer > Tela > My Friend, My Mind's, YEM > Contact, Crimes of the Mind
E: Rocky Top

Who Knows jam (with lyrics) in Chalkdust. Smoke on the Water jam and Speed Racer lyrics in YEM. Psycho Killer and Contact music sung in YEM vocal jam. Dude of Life on vocal for Crimes of the Mind. Venue was changed to the Concert Hall from the Molson Place Harbourfront Pavilion a week before the show.

8/11/93 [ACCESSIBILITY: ••]
Club Eastbrook, Grand Rapids, MI
I: Buried Alive > Runaway Jim, Weigh, It's Ice, Ginseng Sullivan, My Friend, Mango, Stash, Sparkle, Cavern
II: Mike's > Great Gig > Weekapaug, Esther, All Things, Bouncing, Rift, Jesus Left Chicago, MSO, Antelope
E: Adeline, Bold as Love

Ginseng Sullivan performed acoustic with Trey on acoustic guitar, Mike on upright bass, Fish on Madonna washboard and Page on piano. Fishman on vacuum for Great Gig. Concert debut: Ginseng Sullivan.

This comes from somebody who was lucky enough to be at this show. I think the Great Gig speaks for the whole night—I actually thought the vacuum was gonna take Fishman's lips off. Weekapaug goes off—Trey was in his own zone and took it to the next level. Antelope was a great closer. In the first set, the quick drop-out transition from All Things into Bouncing is choice. The energy during Bouncing is just as strong on the tape as it was that night (minus the goose bumps). —Mark Daniel

8/12/93 [ACCESSIBILITY: ••••] [ATTEND. 2,426; CAP. 7,514] [TIX $16.75-$19.75]
Meadow Brook Music Festival, Rochester, MI
I: AC/DC Bag, Reba, Chalkdust, Guelah, Nellie Cane, Melt, Horse > Silent, Poor Heart, Squirming Coil
II: Also Sprach > Landlady > Tweezer > Reggae Jam > Landlady > Tweezer, Lizards, Sloth, Maze, Lawn Boy, BBJ, Golgi, Possum
E: Fire, Freebird

Tweezer jam in Possum.

"Get back" is a musical signal Phish sometimes uses in the midst of crazy jams to jump back into the previous song they were jamming on, like in the 3/13/92 Antelope > BBFCM > Antelope. The second set at Meadowbrook contains another prime example of this technique—Trey sends the band reeling between the slowing Tweezer jam and a faster jam, then back to the set-opening Landlady before finally returning to Tweezer. Outrageously groovy. —Andre Holton

8/13/93 [ACCESSIBILITY: ••••] [ATTEND. 1,711; CAP. 1,979] [TIX $17.50]
Murat Theater, Indianapolis, IN
I: Lengthwise > Llama, Makisupa > Foam, Stash, Ginseng Sullivan, Fluffhead, My Mind's, Horn, Bowie
II: Buried Alive > Rift, Bathtub Gin > Ya Mar, Mike's > Lifeboy, Oh Kee > Suzie, Amazing Grace
E: Highway to Hell

Fishman on Madonna washboard for Ginseng Sullivan. Ya Mar, Mango and Magilla jams in Bowie. Weekapaug tease in Bathtub Gin.

I was in a terrible mood for this show, I mean terrible. I was quite miserable when I climbed into the ornate third balcony at the Murat Theater. But as the band had done a few nights earlier in Grand Rapids, they reminded me exactly why I was there, and floated me away from my little state of anger and disappointment. An extra-long first set was highlighted by a Makisupa, a tingly Bowie, and a solid Fluffhead. Second set, during an unfucking-real Mike's, Trey emerged from the dry ice and started chopping with his guitar like it was an axe, with only his upper body exposed through the smoke. Then they slipped into Lifeboy. Now for all you folks who bust out your lighters for Lifeboy because you think it's a touching melody, or for all you folks who can't stand Lifeboy for that very reason, try hearing the Murat version. Trippy and explosive. Yeah, Murat was so good, even Lifeboy made me cringe. —Andy Bernstein

The "Murat Gin" is, of course, one of the great musical moments in Phish history. The jam segment just departs for another planet, completely leaving behind any semblance of a normal Bathtub Gin—the hose is pumping full pressure! Eventually, the jam segues into Ya Mar, and then into Mike's Song, which is just as unbelievably amazing as the Gin jam. This half-hour of Phish intensity is unmatched. (Don't miss the long, trippy Bowie that closes the first set, complete with a cool Ya Mar jam with Fishman on woodblocks that segues into the Mango Song ending, then to a jazz jam that samples Magilla.) —Jos Conti

8/14/93 [ACCESSIBILITY: ••] [ATTEND. 5,643; CAP. 25,000] [TIX $17.50]
World Music Theater, Tinley Park, IL
I: Chalkdust, Guelah, Divided Sky, Horse > Silent, It's Ice, Sparkle, Melt, Esther, Poor Heart, Cavern
II: Also Sprach > Antelope > Sparks > Walk Away > Have Mercy > Antelope, Mound, Squirming Coil, Daniel, YEM, Purple Rain > HYHU, Golgi
E: La Grange

Fishman on vacuum for Purple Rain.

There's nothing as thrilling as seeing the band get "stuck in a jam," veering so far off the original tune that it seems they can't find their way back—and don't want to. This may be a bit more common today, but back in 1993 it still was relatively rare. So watching Phish get so far away from Antelope that they find themselves in Sparks and Walk Away—and then somehow finding their way back to Antelope—was worth the price of admission by itself. —Andy Bernstein

This particular show is a favorite of mine. Though the first set is pretty much unremarkable with the exception of Divided Sky, the second set smokes. Antelope is a slice of heaven, with Sparks and Walk Away jammed in the middle. I always like Purple Rain and here Fishman doesn't disappoint. A must-have for any true Phish phan. —Tony Krupka

8/15/93 [ACCESSIBILITY: ••] [ATTEND. 1,071; CAP. 1,430] [TIX $17.50-$18.50]
Macauley Theater, Louisville, KY
I: Sample, All Things, Runaway Jim, Fee, Paul and Silas, Stash, Forbin's > Mockingbird, Chalkdust
II: Rift > Tweezer, Lizards, Landlady, Bouncing, Maze, Glide, Adeline, Ginseng Sullivan, Nellie Cane, Freebird
E: Harry Hood

Ginseng Sullivan and Nellie Cane performed acoustic with Trey on acoustic guitar, Mike on upright bass, Fishman on Madonna washboard and Page on piano.

For the tape collector, the biggest problem one faces dealing with August 1993 isn't deciding which tapes to seek out—it's deciding which tapes not to acquire! The classics

Saturday, August 14, 1993

WORLD MUSIC THEATER, Tinley Park, IL

During the summer of 1993 it was possible to trade anything you owned for a Phish ticket. This period of time was known as the"Wonder Years" because if you had a half a brain and no cash you could still easily experience what I consider the most enjoyable three hours of your life, practically every night. And when Phish took a day off you were able to earn enough money from the lot scene to enjoy such places as Disney World or a water park with an all-Scandinavian female staff (Grand Rapids, check it out).

To celebrate my last show of the tour, I decided to put five doses on my tongue—what better way to end an incredible summer? I grabbed a pack full of my Phamily Phun T-shirts figuring I'd trade one for a ticket, and then move the rest inside between sets. Now, normally I'm pretty careful when selling shirts, but while I was just trying to trade one for a ticket, which is legal, I wasn't really thinking about the cops.

That was pretty dopey. The cops sure as hell didn't know or care that at that moment, as I paraded around the grounds with a backpack and a T-shirt flapping in the wind, that I was trading and not selling. Within minutes, the Tinley Park Police apprehended me for vending. One of the officers that had me in custody was a rookie cop undergoing training, and of course I was lucky enough to be the first person he ever frisked and handcuffed.

He was instructed by his superior to check my groin area for a hard object. I explained offhandedly that I wasn't that easy. The rookie cop seemed to become upset with the fact that I was cooperating with sarcasm, and the only way he was able to vent his frustration was with idiocy. That's when he proceeded to warn me not to touch his gear in the back-seat of the vehicle. Now I, of course, wasn't about to touch his gear, but I was having a good time looking at it. Just as the car sped away, I was starting to get off on the five hits that I had forgotten since the start of this ordeal.

The police had a station on the premises, which moved things along relatively quickly. Even though I was in the station, I could hear the ending of Chalkdust—it even prompted me to bust a couple of moves in the fingerprint room. As the room was spinning, I smiled for my mug shot which probably outdid my yearbook picture. Divided Sky began to echo through the halls. It took me five minutes of pre-peak rhetoric to convince the authorities that I did not pose a threat to their society and that I should be permitted into the show.

I ran in at full speed and caught the end of Divided Sky. After a solid first set including a brilliantly dampened Split Open and Melt, I was mentally and physically prepared for the second set. Immediately following the 2001 Theme, which opened so many second sets in summer 1993, Antelope began its usual subtle grooves. The jam was slowly working its way up when it found its way to a repeated series of standard block rock-n-roll chords. As they brought it to a pinnacle, each member was emphasizing different rhythmic sections of the chord progression. They brilliantly combined simplicity with a very jagged finish. A few minutes later Trey composed a majestic sounding tune appropriate for a trumpeter at a Buckingham Palace royal gathering. What made it special was that each note was trilled with its half note neighbor and it was all done in a minor key that gave it a distinct Phish flavor. The Antelope lasted at least twenty-five minutes and included segues into and out of Walk Away, Sparks, and Have Mercy. Don't forget, I was tripping my balls off and was convinced that Phish was able to manipulate the echoes generated in the spacious amphitheater. But the show fizzled out after a solid YEM.

Exiting the show, we spotted a shady-looking character who stole one hundred dollars from some friends of ours who made the mistake of picking him up on the highway and giving him a ride to the show. After an hour of interrogation, this guy—who went by the name of "Free" and apparently thought everything was—admitted to the crime. He then punched me in the head. I had to spend the next eight hours of my trip with a throbbing bruise on my forehead. Believe me, I was actually able to feel the tumors forming.

Thank God for that smokin' Antelope.

—Charlie Lazarus

(8/2, 8/13, and 8/20) are automatic. The other heavy-hitters (8/6, 8/7, and 8/14) appear on a lot of tapelists, too. From there, things get a bit trickier. 8/28 certainly has its fans, as do 8/11, 8/12, 8/16, 8/25, and 8/26—see, almost all of them. But one show I often don't see on people's tapelists is 8/15/93 Louisville, KY, and let me tell you, it's not because of the music. Though this show lacks the stellar setlists of some of those listed above, the jams in Stash and Tweezer are as hot as anything Phish played that month. —Josh Albini

8/16/93 [ACCESSIBILITY: ••] [ATTEND. 1,700; CAP. 1,700] [TIX $15.50-$17]
American Theater, St. Louis, MO
I: Axilla, Possum >Horn, Reba, Sparkle, Foam, I Didn't Know, Melt, Squirming Coil
II: Mike's > Faht > Weekapaug, Mound, It's Ice > My Friend, Poor Heart, BBJ, A-Train, GTBT
E: Amazing Grace, Rocky Top
Fishman on Madonna washboard for I Didn't Know. Black Magic Woman jam in Weekapaug.

This show sticks out for one reason: the second set Mike's Song > Faht > Weekapaug Groove. Mike's is played pretty basic, nothing fancy but still great. After Mike's, Trey came forward to play the acoustic guitar commonly used at the beginning of The Horse. Then the forest animal noises of Faht came over the P.A. system. Trey threw his hands in the air like something was wrong as the forest noises continued into what becomes an amazing Weekapaug. Mike's bass holds this version down nicely, as it usually does. Another added bonus to this set was a very good rendition of Take the A-Train. —Mike Noll

8/17/93 [ACCESSIBILITY: ••] [ATTEND. 1,993; CAP. 3,253] [TIX $10.50]
Memorial Hall, Kansas City, KS
I: Wilson, Llama, Guelah, Divided Sky, Weigh, Maze, Fluffhead, FEFY, Daniel
II: Also Sprach > Bowie, Horse > Silent, Rift, Suzie, YEM, Purple Rain > HYHU, MSO, Cavern
E: Memories, Fire
Fishman on vacuum for Purple Rain.

8/20/93 [ACCESSIBILITY: •••••] [ATTEND. 8,047; CAP. 9,250] [TIX $19.25-$20.35]
Red Rocks Amphitheatre, Morrison, CO
I: Divided Sky, Harpua, Poor Heart, Maze, Bouncing, It's Ice > Wedge, Ginseng Sullivan, Rift, Antelope
II: Also Sprach > Slave, Melt, Squirming Coil, My Friend, Chalkdust, YEM > Purple Rain, Cavern
E: Mango, Freebird
Ginseng Sullivan performed acoustic with Trey on acoustic guitar, Mike on bass, Fishman on Madonna washboard, and Page on piano. Mimi Fishman and Fishman on vacuum for Purple Rain.

This was the first Phish show at Red Rocks, and I anticipated many great things. But when I arrived, it was raining and I was seriously bummed. I went into the show wondering when it would stop, and like an act of God, it cleared five minutes before the show. What better way to start the show but with a Divided Sky, followed by a great Harpua? Red Rocks brings out the best in performers. —Jeff Salvatore

Phish's ability to somehow top everyone's already high expectations is a key to the band's magic. For their first Red Rocks show, everyone expected the world, so the band delivered a universe. The show benefits from inspired choices like the Divided Sky opener, the summer's only Wedge (the last one until 1995) and the Mango Song encore, but it's the music that really makes this show fly. Antelope and Split Open, in particular, are two of the very best performances of these songs. —Melissa Wolcott

I think the Split Open and Melt on this night is a true testament to the band's amazing musical skill. Page's dexterity on the piano during this song makes me long to tickle the ivories with half his talent. —Amanda Litton

When the rain stopped, the guys played Divided Sky and the clouds literally parted and the sun came out. I laughed, cried, and danced at the same time. This is the concert where I fell in love with the making of music. —Jake Hunter

8/21/93 [ACCESSIBILITY: ••••]
SaltAir, Salt Lake City, UT

"Rock Band"

8/20/93 Red Rocks Amphitheater, Morrison, CO

When Phish announced their 1993 summer tour itinerary, many fans drew bright red circles around two August dates—the tour-closer at Berkeley's Greek Theater, and a night about a week before that at Red Rocks Amphitheater in Morrison, CO. Both were storied venues, home to historic shows throughout rock history. U2, it was said, made a name for itself as a band with a famous 1983 Red Rocks gig (later made available on video) in which Bono uttered the immortal line, "This is Red Rocks! This is the Edge!"

Trey had mocked that very line way back when, at a Nectar's show on 7/25/88 that ended up making it onto Junta as a bonus live track. Now, five years later, Phish was to play on that storied stage, nestled among the red rocks of the Colorado backcountry, with a sweeping vista that looked down over hills and the city of Denver in the distance. Of course, everyone within shouting distance of Denver wanted to be there. Happily, ticket availability wasn't a problem: 9,500 tickets were an awful lot for Phish to sell in 1993, and in fact the Red Rocks gig did not sell out. (Three years later, that situation would be drastically altered, as even four shows at the Rocks couldn't satisfy the desire for tickets).

On the day of the show, however, rain clouds blotted out the sun. Everyone who had expected to bake on a hot Colorado afternoon instead reached for their rain ponchos and prayed. The venue opened its doors, and fans rushed up front, huddling under umbrellas while rumors swirled that the show might have to be canceled.

But as the 7:30 starting time drew near, somehow the rain let up. The Phish crew scurried onto the stage, pulling back the tarps that had protected the equipment, and within minutes the crowd was on its feet, cheering the band as they came out on stage. "Cool!" Trey said, and then started up Divided Sky. As its notes floated up the red amphitheater walls and into the sky, the unbelievable happened—a moment of true magic: the sky divided. For the first time all day, the sun peeked through the clouds. One song later, in Harpua, Trey's declaration, "Look, the storm's gone!" brought huge cheers.

Blessed by Mother Nature, the band proceeded to play what still ranks as one of their best shows ever. Incredible jams in Antelope and Split Open and Melt rank among fans' favorite versions of these songs. For many, though, the highlight came when the subtle opening of Slave to the Traffic Light (dusted off after two years of retirement two weeks earlier in Cincinnati) emerged out of 2001. Welcome to Eden.

I: Buried Alive > Poor Heart, Foam, Guelah, Rift, Stash, Sparkle, Landlady, I Didn't Know, Runaway Jim
II: Possum, Horn, Uncle Pen, Fee, Llama, Lawn Boy, Bowie, HYHU > Brain > HYHU, Harry Hood, Daniel
E: Amazing Grace, Nellie Cane

Bela Fleck and the Flecktones opened. Fishman on Madonna washboard for I Didn't Know. Bela Fleck on banjo, and Flecktones Victor Wooten on bass and Future Man on synth-axe drumitar joined Phish for the second set starting with Fee. Bela also sat in on Nellie Cane. Fishman on vacuum for Brain.

8/24/93 [ACCESSIBILITY: ••]
Commodore Ballroom, Vancouver, BC
I: Chalkdust, All Things, Bouncing, It's Ice, Nellie Cane, Melt, Horse > Silent, Uncle Pen, Maze, Golgi
II: Llama, Horn, Ya Mar, Mike's > Ginseng Sullivan > Weekapaug, Wilson > Rift, HYHU > Cracklin' Rosie > HYHU, Antelope
E: Halley's > Poor Heart, Adeline

Baby Gramps opened. I Feel the Earth Move jam in It's Ice.

8/25/93 [ACCESSIBILITY: ••] [ATTEND. 1,783; CAP. 2,979] [TIX $15.50-$17.50]
Paramount Theater, Seattle, WA
I: AC/DC Bag, Daniel, Sample, Sparkle, Foam, Ginseng Sullivan, Nellie Cane, Amazing Grace, Stash, Glide, Cavern
II: Buried Alive, Possum, Mound, My Friend, Paul and Silas, YEM > Bats and Mice, Squirming Coil, GTBT
E: Bold as Love, Rocky Top

Baby Gramps opened. Ginseng Sullivan and Nellie Cane performed acoustic/no amplification with Trey on acoustic guitar, Mike on upright bass, Fishman on Madonna washboard, and Page on piano. Baby Gramps on YEM vocal jam and Bats and Mice. Concert debut: Bats and Mice.

In the midst of an amazing Foam, Trey took the groove way down—down so far, in fact, that he wasn't actually playing at all, though he kept miming his hands as though he was (the "silent jam" reappeared during the 12/9/95 Albany YEM and the 12/30/96 FleetCenter Funky Bitch, among others). The crowd in the small theater stayed silent throughout, and Trey looked up in amazement. After finishing Foam, the band pulled out their acoustic instruments for a special "unplugged" set as a special treat for the very attentive crowd. This became commonplace in 1994, but it was special then. —Lock Steele

8/26/93 [ACCESSIBILITY: •••] [ATTEND. 1,938; CAP. 2,776] [TIX $15.50-$17.50]
Arlene Schnitzer Concert Hall, Portland, OR
I: Runaway Jim, Guelah, Reba, Fee, Melt, Esther, It's Ice, Harry Hood, Golgi
II: Also Sprach > Bowie, Lifeboy, Rift, Jesus Left Chicago, Lizards, HYHU > Bats and Mice > HYHU, Chalkdust
E: Freebird

Baby Gramps opened. Baby Gramps on Bats and Mice; Fishman on vacuum.

A very well-played Jim to open up—the jam between verses was unusually extended. Also look for Split and Ice as stellar versions. The first-set Hood is unexpected and blistering. Bowie gets absolutely insane (as it always does now)—I would go as far as to say chaotic at points. The early version of Lifeboy is nice, but Jesus Left Chicago is played exquisitely with Page and Trey taking their respective solos. —Bob Talatzko

One great thing about Phish shows is the ability of music you think you know so well to surprise you. After an incredible 2001 > Bowie, during which the band showed us some new corners of this amazing song, I thought Lifeboy would give me a moment to catch my breath. But the song built and built to an incredibly moving closing jam that perfectly complemented the raging Bowie before it. —Lock Steele

8/28/93 [ACCESSIBILITY: ••••] [ATTEND. 6,801; CAP. 7,500] [TIX $19.50-$21]
Greek Theater, University of California at Berkeley, Berkeley, CA
I: Llama, Bouncing, Foam, Ginseng Sullivan, Maze > Fluffhead, Stash, Squirming Coil, Crimes of the Mind
II: Also Sprach > Rift, Antelope, Horse > Silent, Sparkle, It's Ice > BBJ, Purple Rain > HYHU, YEM > Contact, Chalkdust
E: Daniel, Amazing Grace

J.J. Cale opened. The Dude of Life on vocals for Crimes of the Mind. Fishman on vacuum for Purple Rain. Brady Bunch jams in Antelope. Oye Como Va in YEM. Trey acknowledges the crew in Daniel.

[10-11/93] American Recording Co., Woodland Hills, CA
Recording and mixing *Hoist*.

1993 Holiday Tour

12/28/93 [ACCESSIBILITY: ••••] [ATTEND. 5,200; CAP. 5,200] [TIX $20]
Bender Arena, American University, Washington, DC
I: Peaches, Poor Heart > Melt, Esther, Oh Kee > Suzie > Ya Mar, It's Ice, Fee, Possum
II: Sample, YEM, My Friend, Lizards, Sloth, FEFY, Uncle Pen, Harry Hood, Highway to Hell
E: Memories, Golgi

Auld Lang Syne tease in Ya Mar. Kashmir jam in Possum. Last Peaches, 6/23/89 Boston, MA [502 shows]. The show was also the debut of the aquarium stage set used for this entire New Year's Run.

12/29/93 [ACCESSIBILITY: ••••] [ATTEND. 10,574; CAP. 10,574] [TIX $18.50]
Veterans Memorial Coliseum, New Haven, CT
I: Runaway Jim, Peaches, Foam, Glide, Divided Sky, Wilson, Sparkle, Stash, Squirming Coil
II: Maze, Bouncing, Fluffhead, Antelope, Contact, BBFCM > Walk Away > BBJ, HYHU > Brain > HYHU, Adeline, Chalkdust
E: Nellie Cane, Cavern

Fishman on vacuum for Brain.

The entire show lacks energy. The only time the band seems to really get into the groove is during a segment of the second set that makes this tape worth listening to: Fluffhead, Antelope, Contact, BBFCM > Walk Away > Big Ball Jam. —Aaron Grossberg

Thursday, December 30, 1993

CUMBERLAND COUNTY CIVIC CENTER, Portland, ME

There's just something special about the New Year's Run—a sense of shared camaraderie among the thousands of people who trek to all four shows, and a real feeling of communal joy when Phish makes the trip worthwhile. Of course, bonus points are added for snowstorms, ice storms and other natural disasters that have to be overcome along the way. If the idea of a winter road trip doesn't fill you with excitement, then the New Year's Run probably isn't for you.

The '93 run sure had its share of bad weather, which makes it that much more fun to remember. On our way to Bender Arena, icy road conditions made the going treacherous—we slowed to 20 mph driving Washington D.C.'s beltway, then finally made it to the show to find a line that stretched around the building. Hundreds of people braving the cold to get up close—that's dedication.

The next night in New Haven, we emerged hot and happy from the Coliseum to find about four inches of snow on the ground and more coming down. Anyone who could afford to spend the night in New Haven did; we were lucky to have friends nearby, so we crashed there, with visions of icy roads dancing in our heads.

We made it to Portland the next day safely, though the snow drifts were deeper in Maine than they had been in Connecticut. We emerged from our car in freezing wind to find a full-scale lot scene underway near the Civic Center, which is right in downtown Portland, across from a Hood Milk factory. People selling T-shirts in the middle of winter—we had to laugh!

Joining the lengthy line outside the Civic Center, we were comforted while we waited by a brief snippet of the Peaches En Regalia soundcheck going on inside. The venue staff was late getting the doors open, but no one really seemed angry about it even though we were jogging in place to keep our blood circulating. Everyone just took it as part of the challenge. (Trey did apologize for keeping us waiting in the cold at the beginning of Forbin's Rap, though).

When the doors finally opened and we made it in, we found the Civic Center a general-admission joy: lots of space for everyone. It's a cute little arena that feels homey, exactly the kind of place you'd expect to find in Maine. It was perfect.

And then there was the music. David Bowie, complete with a prominent Dream On tease, broke the show open from the start. The Curtain, a personal favorite, segued into the still-new Sample, and from there we got a Forbin's > Mockingbird and an outstanding Bathtub Gin. To close the set Phish pulled out the only first set a cappella Freebird they'd ever done. The energy level in the arena zoomed sky-high.

But the best was yet to come. We figured a Mike's Song might be on tap, but we didn't expect a mesmerizing version to slam out of Also Sprach Zarathustra. Mike's wound into something I labeled on my setlist as "Insane Jam!!!" (It became clear six months later that we'd heard the first Simple Jam.) That moved brilliantly into The Horse, with Trey swinging his electric guitar behind his back and strumming the opening to the Horse on his acoustic guitar. Horse/Silent calmed the place down for a minute before Trey started strumming the opening notes to PYITE. Oh, my. High above courtside, we danced our hearts out. Then, another shocker: McGrupp! I hadn't heard it live in two years, and it was a blissful delight, stretching on before a familiar Gordon bass line ambushed it . . . they were moving into Weekapaug. What a run of songs!

The great thing was that everyone knew it. The folks who made the trek to Portland that Holiday Tour were mostly old-school fans; it wasn't the kind of place to see your first Phish show, unlike, say, New Haven. As the band pulled out one surprise after another, the excitement kept mounting. Delirium had almost set in. Purple Rain followed Weekapaug, then for the first time in the set, there was silence from the stage.

Trey conferred with Mike as a group in front of the stage continued their "Slave! Slave! Slave!" chants. And so it was to be — as the opening notes of the first East Coast Slave to the Traffic Light in years soared out and above the crowd, I threw my head back in exultation.

It was a long, cold drive to Worcester, but no one seemed to mind.

—Lock Steele

➤ The highlight of this show was the Fluffhead-Antelope combo. The Fluffhead "Arrival" section contains a jam that abandons any rhythmic structure, producing crazy ambiguity that finally resolves to the G chord. Then they do it again, even more intensely. The Antelope jam begins with a quiet guitar from Trey. At one point, the guitar gains an unbelievable sound and power to finish off the jam in uncanny fashion. —Brendan Neagle

12/30/93 [ACCESSIBILITY: •••••] [ATTEND. 9,150; CAP. 9,150] [TIX $17.50]
Cumberland County Civic Center, Portland, ME
I: Bowie, Weigh, Curtain > Sample, Paul and Silas, Forbin's > Mockingbird, Rift, Bathtub Gin, Freebird
II: Also Sprach > Mike's > Horse > Silent > PYITE > McGrupp > Weekapaug > Purple Rain > HYHU, Slave
E: Rocky Top, GTBT

Dream On jam in Bowie. Simple jam in Mike's. Fishman on vacuum for Purple Rain.

➤ Sometimes, Phish just rewards us all. After thousands of people made it through a blizzard to get to Portland, Phish wasted no time in making the night special. Leading off with Bowie, getting to Curtain, following a Col. Forbin > Mockingbird with a great Gin and the only first set Freebird—it was just one of those nights that Phish wanted to hammer it home that everyone was in for a treat. And that was just the beginning. Set II included not only amazing songs, but splendid playing and segues as well as the first surfacing of the Simple Jam. When it seemed like there couldn't be any more, they busted out Slave, the first since Red Rocks the summer before. Just a splendid, splendid night. —Andy Bernstein

➤ This show happened to fall on my 19th birthday and is one of the most celebrated in Phishtory. There was an unbelievable amount of energy in the arena—somehow I knew this show would be special. I remember thinking after the show that I had just seen musical history. In fact, I had! —Joshua Howley

12/31/93 [ACCESSIBILITY: •••••] [ATTEND. 14,232; CAP. 14,232] [TIX $22.50]
The Centrum, Worcester, MA
I: Llama, Guelah, Stash, Ginseng, Reba, Peaches, I Didn't Know, Antelope
II: Tweezer, Halley's > Poor Heart > It's Ice > Fee > Possum, Lawn Boy, YEM
III: "Into the Phishtank" > New Year's Countdown > Auld Lang Syne > Down with Disease jam, Melt, Lizards, Sparkle, Suzie, HYHU > Cracklin' Rosie > HYHU, Harry Hood, Tweezer Reprise
E: Golgi, Amazing Grace

Fishman on Madonna washboard for Ginseng Sullivan. Roundabout tease before Ginseng Sullivan. Tom Marshall on "Rye, rye, rocco, Marco Esquandolis" vocals in Antelope. Peaches teases in It's Ice, Possum and Suzie. Banana Splits theme jam in Tweezer. Band members donned wetsuits during YEM vocal jam. At about 10 minutes to midnight, band members (or stand-ins?) were lowered from the rafters onto the stage, where they climbed into a giant clam and disappeared. The clam counted down to midnight as the band returned for Auld Lang Syne and giant white balloons dropped from above. Auld Lang Syne tease in Hood. Concert debut: DWD jam. FM broadcast on WBCN-Boston on 1/1/94.

➤ Here's a New Year's Eve show that exceeds Phish's standards. While the setlist may not bowl anyone over, there are some amazing moments. One must note the YEM vocal jam—just wild. Also amazing are Split Open and Harry Hood—two of my favorite versions. What I love best, though, is the Auld Lang Syne > DWD jam, which blows my mind every time I hear it. —Jonathan Banco

➤ Amazing show. Peaches En Regalia teases throughout the entire show, the Harry Hood rocked, and Fishman's Cracklin' Rosie was hilarious. We rung in the New Year with the band descending from the ceiling in scuba suits, then returning to play Auld Lang Syne as huge balloons fell from above. Great time!! —Emily Brown

➤ If you like jams, this is a show to get. Possum is insane—it just goes on and on—and YEM is great. The third set just takes the cake, though. I think that Phish should have put this Harry Hood on *A Live One* instead of the one that's on it. —David Eckers

"New Year's '93"

12/31/93 The Centrum, Worcester, MA

Phish fans from around the country piled into a raging lot scene across the street from the Centrum. This was not just a night of Phish—it was an enormous New Year's celebration where 15,000 partied to pay tribute to ten years of a special band and its ultra-loyal following. For the first time in the band's history, scalpers had no problems moving tickets for $80 to $150 a pop.

For many fans, it took the first half of the first set to squeeze through the tight, unprepared door security. This dilemma was even acknowledged by Trey who asked the audience if everybody had made it in. When the crowd finally settled into Phish's groove, the atmosphere escalated into a cross between a concert and a playoff game as the crowd cheered relentlessly during recognized opening licks and piercing jams. At the end of set I, Phish lyricist Tom Marshall emerged to vocalized his lyrical contribution to Run Like an Antelope for the first time on stage.

Set II created a much darker atmosphere as fans were haunted several times by the Frank Zappa lick from Peaches en Regalia, resurrected three days earlier to pay tribute to his recent death. And when the smoke cleared during the YEM jam, all were confused to find the band members, dressed in scuba gear, leaving the stage for the second set break.

All eyes stayed focused on the stage, which had been designed just for the New Year's Run to look like the inside of a Phish tank. This was by far the most elaborate stage setting of the band's ten-year history. And to the amazement of all, Phish (or perhaps look-alikes) were lowered into the tank from the rafters of the Centrum sporting the scuba gear. But within the moments theatrical enormity, Phish brought things down to earth with light and humorous dialogue, including a mention of Fish's butt cheeks by Trey. The band members landed on stage, climbed into a giant clam shell at the back of the stage, and disappeared. The clam then rose up, counting down to New Year's, then sprayed confetti into the crowd at midnight while giant white balloons dropped from the rafters into the crowd. The band raced back on stage, in their normal clothes, and broke into Auld Lang Syne.

During Auld Lang Syne, a camera crew appeared to film concert material for Phish's first MTV video-to-be. Fans danced to an unfamiliar jam, which was later known to all as Down with Disease.

It was clear to all that the Phish Phenomenon had reached a new level. Phish fans old and new gathered to the hugest and most energetic event of its time. For most, it clinched New Year's plans for years to come.

1994 SPRING Take Another Step

Spring Tour 1994 would see the band push songs from *Hoist*—it's a virtual certainty that any show from this tour contains Julius, Down with Disease, or Sample, if not all three—but not much more than they had played the new songs off *Rift* a year earlier. The band's first video (directed by Mike Gordon), for Down with Disease, received MTV play mostly in the wee hours of the night but never became a hit. Just a week into the tour, Trey tore ligaments in his leg at the Buffalo gig, an injury that he valiantly played through but that may have sapped some of the band's energy early in the tour. By the first week of May, though, the band would reach new heights on a quiet night in Dallas, the famous Tweezerfest, before heading once again for a rendezvous with the Pacific.

4/4/94 [ACCESSIBILITY: ••••] **[ATTEND. 1,323; CAP. 1,323] [TIX $19.50]**
Flynn Theater, Burlington, VT
I: Divided Sky, Sample, Scent of a Mule, Maze, Fee, Reba, Horn, It's Ice, Possum
II: Down with Disease > If I Could, Buried Alive, Landlady, Julius, Magilla, Melt, Wolfman's > I Wanna Be Like You, Oh Kee > Suzie
E: Harry Hood, Cavern

1994

124 Total Show Dates
- **1** one-set show
- **121** two-set shows
- **2** three-set shows

Phan Picks 1994

SHOW	THE SKINNY
1) 10/31/94 Glens Falls, NY	The *White Album* on Halloween.
2) 05/07/94 Dallas, TX	70-minute Tweezerfest.
3) 07/16/94 Fayston, VT	Incredible second set!
4) 06/26/94 Charleston, WV	Gamehendge and *Hoist*.
5) 07/13/94 Patterson, NY	Wild and wacky second set.
6) 06/11/94 Morrison, CO	Red Rocks radio broadcast.
7) 12/31/94 Boston, MA	Flying hot dog rings in 1995.
8) 12/29/94 Providence, RI	Incredible half-hour Bowie.
9) 07/08/94 Mansfield, MA	Gamehendge and a great set II.
10) 12/30/94 New York, NY	Phish's first show at MSG.

MUSICAL RECAP: The Dallas Tweezerfest in May turned a new corner for Phish, and throughout the year they built on their ability to allow one massive jam to carry a set. The fall tour would see several such nights, including the Bangor Tweezer included on *A Live One*.

REPRESENTATIVE JAMS: Tweezer (et al.), 5/7/94; Mike's > Simple, 11/16/94; Weekapaug, 12/28/94; Funky Bitch > Jam > Yerushalayim, 11/22/94.

ORIGINAL SONG DEBUTS: Axilla II (4/16/94), Demand (4/9/94), Dog Faced Boy (4/14/94), Down with Disease (4/4/94), Guyute (10/7/94), If I Could (4/4/94), Julius (4/4/94), N20 (6/25/94), Scent of a Mule (4/4/94), Simple (5/27/94), Wolfman's Brother (4/4/94).

COVER SONG DEBUTS: Bluegrass Breakdown* (11/16/94), Beaumont Rag (10/14/94), Butter Them Biscuits (11/18/94), Dooley (11/20/94), Fixin' to Die (11/17/94), Foreplay (10/7/94), Hi-Hell Sneakers* (4/23/93), I Wanna Be Like You (4/4/94), I'm Blue I'm Lonesome (11/16/94), Long Journey Home (11/16/94), Long Time (10/7/94), Old Home Place (6/26/94), Roll in My Sweet Baby's Arms (11/18/94), Who by Fire* (4/23/94), plus all of The *White Album* (10/31/94).
(*only ever played once)

Dark Horses

SHOW	THE SKINNY
1) 06/17/94 Milwaukee, WI	The O.J. show!
2) 11/30/94 Olympia, WA	Antelope anchors wild 2nd set.
3) 11/16/94 Ann Arbor, MI	30-minute jam out of Simple.
4) 04/29/94 Clearwater, FL	Great setlist, very well played.
5) 04/15/94 New York, NY	The horns do Broadway.

Most-Played Originals:

1) Sample in a Jar	70	56%
2) Julius	65	52%
3) Down with Disease	55	44%
4) Rift	47	38%
5) Bouncing	46	37%
5) Poor Heart	46	37%
7) Sparkle	45	36%
8) Maze	44	35%
8) Scent of a Mule	44	35%
8) Stash	44	35%

Most-Played Covers:

1) Amazing Grace	31	25%
2) Also Sprach	30	24%
3) Nellie Cane	26	21%
4) Ginseng Sullivan	20	16%
5) Good Times Bad Times	17	14%
6) Rocky Top	16	13%
6) Uncle Pen	16	13%
8) Peaches En Regalia	15	12%
9) Old Home Place	13	10%
10) Fire	11	9%
10) Purple Rain	11	9%

First-Set Openers:

1) Runaway Jim	20
2) Llama	14
3) Chalkdust Torture	9
3) Wilson	9
5) My Friend My Friend	7

Second-Set Openers:

1) Also Sprach	24
2) Suzie Greenberg	9
3) The Curtain	6
3) Maze	6
5) Wilson	5
5) Bowie	5
5) Sample	5

Top Henrietta Songs:

1) Purple Rain	11
2) I Wanna Be Like You	9
2) Cracklin' Rosie	6
4) Love You	6
5) Bike	5

A Cappella Songs:

1) Amazing Grace	31
2) Sweet Adeline	25
3) Carolina	5
4) Freebird	5
5) Memories	1

Benefit show to raise money to renovate the Flynn Theater. "My Hometown" line sung before Divided Sky. Second set, starting with Buried Alive and excluding Oh Kee, featured the six-piece Giant Country Horns: Carl Gerhard, trumpet; Dave Grippo, alto sax; Chris Peterman, tenor sax; Mike Hewitt, baritone sax; Don Glasgow, trombone; Joseph Somerville Jr., trumpet. Fishman on vacuum for I Wanna Be Like You. Dave Grippo on congas for Landlady and I Wanna Be Like You. Carl Gerhard on trumpet (solo) for Cavern. Original verse sung in Cavern. Last Magilla, 3/25/93 Santa Cruz, CA [73 shows]. Concert debuts: Scent of a Mule, Down with Disease, If I Could, Julius, Wolfman's, and I Wanna Be Like You.

The Flynn show was a "secret" in the sense that it wasn't announced along with the other spring '94 shows—instead, tickets went on sale one morning, and anyone able to make it to the Flynn Box Office before the line grew too long found themselves in luck. The show was clearly a tough ticket, so most ticketless phans stayed away, though some were drawn by increasingly believable rumors that a horns section would show up. Inside the tiny theater, Phish paid tribute to Burlington with a "Back in my hometown" line to open the show, and then brought out the horns for most of the second set. Like most opening nights, everyone was a little rusty, but seeing the GCH back together, along with a few new friends, made for a special evening. —Lock Steele

A perfect place to see a show. The first set is, as it appears, rather standard. But the debuts of Hoist songs in the second set are fantastic. At the time, I could not get over how good Disease is live (the band knew it, too). The Country Horns are fun but it limits how far the show can go as far as the song selection. Before the first encore, Trey announces an update of the Duke-Arkansas NCAA Championship Game score to a mixed crowd reaction. After Harry, he announces the final score. A funny change in one of the verses of Cavern: instead of "the foggy cavern's musty grime appeared within my palm," Trey exclaims, "the brothel wife then grabbed the knife and slashed me on the tongue." —Matthew Napoli

4/5/94 [ACCESSIBILITY: ••] [ATTEND. 2,042; CAP. 2,042] [TIX $19.50]
Metropolis, Montreal, QC
I: Runaway Jim, Foam, Fluffhead, Glide, Julius, Bouncing, Rift, AC/DC Bag
II: Peaches, Ya Mar, Tweezer, If I Could, YEM > I Wanna Be Like You, Chalkdust, Amazing Grace
E: Nellie Cane, Golgi

Fishman on vacuum for I Wanna Be Like You.

4/6/94 [ACCESSIBILITY: ••] [ATTEND. 1,729; CAP. 1,729] [TIX $17.50]
Concert Hall, Toronto, ON
I: Llama, Guelah, Poor Heart, Stash, Lizards, Sample, Scent of a Mule, Fee > Antelope
II: Curtain > Down with Disease, Wolfman's, Sparkle, Mike's > Lifeboy > Weekapaug, Squirming Coil, Cavern
E: Ginseng Sullivan, Nellie Cane, Adeline

Ginseng Sullivan and Nellie Cane performed acoustic/no amplification, with Trey on acoustic guitar, Fishman on Madonna washboard, Mike on upright bass, and Page on mouth piano. Venue changed from the Palladium in Toronto on day of show.

4/8/94 [ACCESSIBILITY: ••] [ATTEND. 5,231; CAP. 5,318] [TIX $16.75]
Recreation Hall, Penn State University, University Park, PA
I: Maze, Glide > Foam, I Didn't Know, PYITE, Horse > Silent > Down with Disease > If I Could, Lawn Boy, Llama
II: Melt > McGrupp, It's Ice > Sparkle, Harry Hood, Bouncing > BBJ, Bowie, Suzie
E: Contact > BBFCM

Mimi Fishman danced onstage throughout most of the show, played cymbals for I Didn't Know, and counted out "1-2-3-4" for BBFCM. Fishman on cymbals for I Didn't Know. "Owner of a Lonely Heart" tease in Suzie.

The Maze in the first set of this show ranks as one of my favorites. In usual Maze fashion the suspense builds and builds then releases. But this Maze does not want to relent. The band keeps it going until you think there is no possible way to continue—but this is no ordinary band—it's Phish, where anything is possible. I Didn't Know had Mimi Fishman on cymbals, and the Split Open and Melt that opens the second set is unrelenting, especially the jam toward the end. There is no letting up the entire show. —David George

An interesting show, highlighted by, of all things, It's Ice! Definitely one of the more

Saturday, April 9, 1994

BROOME COUNTY ARENA, Binghamton, NY

"You've Never Been to a Phish Show?!" Dave yelled. "Then you don't really like them." I stood there with *Hoist* in my hand and I'd just told him that yeah, I liked Phish. But no, said Dave. Never having seen Phish live, I was not qualified to judge, he said. No, no, I argued, I had listened to *Rift* at least thirty times. I was definitely a fan. Then, fatefully, our friend Pete, a dedicated if circumspect Phishhead, announced, "They're playing Binghamton on Saturday." This was obviously celestial intervention.

Who were we to flout the will of the Almighty? Pete and I became the A-Team of Phish Tour, focused like laser beams on our goal. Binghamton was five hours away, it was a sold-out show, and we had no car or money. But details would not stop us. "Jon must come!" I proclaimed, beginning the juggernaut. Jon was a friend of ours who had heard perhaps one Phish song ever and had not expressed much enthusiasm. Pete inquired as to why Jon was an essential member of the Team. Jon had a car. He was definitely essential. Jon, however, would only go if the tickets were free. The team moved onto its next goal: obtaining tickets. At no cost.

This was a little tricky, but soon the obvious solution of impersonating journalists and scamming free tickets from the record company presented itself. I called Elektra and spoke to a very bitter woman named Sharon, who said she needed a faxed request on the publication's letterhead. And we could only have two tickets. And no photo passes. But something was better than nothing, so I wrote myself a letter of introduction, pasted a newspaper headline on top, and faxed it to Sharon. We didn't hear back for a day, and since it was now Friday, we were a little tense.

But Phish's record company is full of middle-level managers, for they not only employ Sharon to take press-pass requests, but Bill to send out the press passes. And apparently Bill and Sharon are not close. Because Friday, Bill called my roommate Alison, another Team member, and tried to verify the address for the tickets. He posed no match for Alison. "Those were four tickets, right?" she demanded. "Umm, no," said Bill. But Bill crumbled like a stale cookie. Alison convinced him to FedEx four tickets to us. He did.

On Saturday, after an extremely long drive, we arrived in Binghamton. We wandered inside and were directed to seats by Pete, then goggled at the crowd. The show started—the first set was very bouncy and happy. I was thrilled when they played Rift, because at the time I thought it was the absolute apogee of songwriting talent. I also knew all the words to Julius, because as I mentioned, I had just obtained *Hoist*. After Julius they played what I referred to as The Weasel Song, otherwise known as Fee. Then they went into Stash, which I hadn't heard before, but I got very into it.

The set closed with Squirming Coil, which featured an amazing Page solo. I was so surprised that someone was playing the piano at a rock concert, and how few opportunities to become rock stars there are for piano players, that I almost forgot to listen, which would have been a shame because this was, and still is, one of the prettiest things I have ever heard.

The second set did not feature many songs with words in them, so I was a little miffed. They started with Sample in a Jar, which was good because I knew all the words, but then they gave up on singing and just played. They played this game with beach balls bouncing around the crowd—every time one bounced back on stage, a different band member would play. Unfortunately, I was not clued into this at the time, so I was a little bored. Things picked up near the end when they played Cavern—I didn't know the words, but at least there were some.

So my first impression of Phish was that they were a band with a good piano player and not enough words in their songs. My perspective has changed since then—I now get upset if they don't jam enough, I no longer hold *Rift* up as the ultimate example of musical perfection, and I can pick up on a lot of the games the band plays. And I now know that Binghamton was a really great show, empirically speaking. And I was there, even if I didn't appreciate it as much as I should have, or as I would now. And in the end that's all that counts, isn't it? That I was there?

—Monique O'Connell

out-there Ices, plus good jamming throughout most of the second set, makes this show a real sleeper. —Ed Smith

4/9/94 [ACCESSIBILITY: ••••] [ATTEND. 7,200; CAP. 7,200] [TIX $18.50]
Broome County Arena, Binghamton, NY
I: Magilla, Wilson, Rift, Bathtub Gin, Nellie Cane, Julius, Fee, All Things, Stash, Squirming Coil
II: Sample, Reba, Peaches > BBJ, Demand > Mike's > Hydrogen > Weekapaug, Tela > Slave, Cavern
E: Amazing Grace, Highway to Hell

"Little Drummer Boy" jam in BBJ and Weekapaug. "Divided Sky" tease in Weekapaug. Concert debut: Demand.

A fascinating show; the second set is essential in any collection. The first set is nice, as Magilla and Bathtub are pleasant surprises, and the smoke-filled stage during Stash was fun to see, especially considering it doesn't happen anymore. Set II offers the greatest Reba ever (everyone should hear it) and maybe the most obnoxious version of Mike's Song—it's not for the casual fan. Snippets of Divided Sky and Little Drummer Boy decorate a fabulous Weekapaug. Back then Weekapaug had more power and energy than the longer, more articulate versions of the song you hear now. A perfect spot for Tela, and, well, Slave is Slave. —Matthew Napoli

I think of this as the Déjà Vu show because it had so much in common with the Portland show from the previous New Year's run. The venue, the setlist and the quality were just so similar. The Portland show is better known, but this one really holds its own as an absolute classic. —Andy Bernstein

Highway to Hell was a funny response by Phish to the "AC/DC" [Bag] chants by some fans in front of the stage. I'm sure I wasn't the only person to finally "get it"after this show. —Charlie Murphy

4/10/94 [ACCESSIBILITY: ••] [ATTEND. 6,323; CAP. 7,000] [TIX $10.50–$18.50]
Alumni Arena, State University of New York Buffalo, Amherst, NY
I: Runaway Jim, It's Ice, Sparkle, Melt, Esther, Chalkdust, I Didn't Know, Scent of a Mule, Down with Disease
II: My Friend, Ya Mar, Antelope, Fluffhead, Ginseng Sullivan, HYHU > I Wanna Be Like You > HYHU, Harry Hood
E: Bouncing, Golgi

Trey strained his ankle a few hours before this show, an injury that would hamper him for the next month. Fishman on vacuum for I Didn't Know and I Wanna Be Like You.

The show started 45 minutes late due to Trey's pre-show accident that put him on crutches, but that didn't damper the fun. Page took over immediately with brilliant performances on Ice and an amazing piano jam in Scent. Down with Disease shows that it will be a live tune to be reckoned with for years to come—great jam. The highlight, however, is the insanely funny Fish as King Louie (with an injured Trey on drums!) —Tim Foisser

Trey hobbled to center stage with a cast on his leg. Somehow, he maintained a marvelous energy and spirit throughout—he even sat in on drums as Fishman honored us with not one but two vacuum solos in I Didn't Know and I Wanna Be Like You. The boys appeared to have some quality communication with each other this night, particularly noticeable during a syrupy Split Open and Melt and a show-closing, whirling Hood. Bouillabaisse indeed. —Anthony Buchla

Trey played with something to prove during Harry Hood. A truly emotional version. —Bob Talatzko

4/11/94 [ACCESSIBILITY: ••] [ATTEND. 4,500; CAP. 4,500] [TIX $18.50]
Snively Arena, University of New Hampshire, Durham, NH
I: Caravan, Poor Heart, Foam, FEFY, Magilla, Julius, Glide, Divided Sky, Cavern
II: Also Sprach > Maze, Forbin's > Mockingbird, Uncle Pen, Sample > BBJ, YEM, Amazing Grace, Oh Kee > Suzie
E: Possum

YEM featured Brad Sands on trampoline, substituting for the injured Trey. During the trampoline sequence, Trey sat and read a newspaper onstage. "Sunshine of Your Love" teases in YEM.

[4/13/94] [ACCESSIBILITY: ••]
WNEW Studios, New York, NY
Sample, Down with Disease, Julius [version from *Hoist*], Rift.

Live radio broadcast in the afternoon, prior to the Beacon Theater show.

4/13/94 [ACCESSIBILITY: ••] [ATTEND. 3,022; CAP. 3,022] [TIX $20]
Beacon Theater, New York, NY
I: Buried Alive > Poor Heart, Stash, Lizards, Julius, Ginseng Sullivan, Divided Sky, Golgi
II: Faht, Curtain > Sample, Reba, BBJ, Fee, A-Train, Bowie, Purple Rain > HYHU, AC/DC Bag
E: Adeline, GTBT

Ginseng Sullivan performed acoustic/no amplification with same setup as 4/6/94. "A-Train," "Reba" and "Sunshine of Your Love" teases in Bowie. Fishman on vacuum for Purple Rain.

Phish finally hit the Beacon Theater, a place Trey told us the band had always wanted to play. Though the show was sold out, tickets for the Wednesday night show were plentiful—we scored tenth-row seats for $30 each outside the venue. The second set was notable for the last A-Train the band has performed, a solid Bowie and a very good Bag, during which a very drunk fan ran across the stage, cracking up the band. —Lock Steele

4/14/94 [ACCESSIBILITY: •••] [ATTEND. 3,022; CAP. 3,022] [TIX $20]
Beacon Theater, New York, NY
I: Runaway Jim, Foam, Sparkle, Down with Disease, Glide, Rift, Demand > Melt, Squirming Coil
II: Also Sprach > Antelope, Horse > Silent, Scent of a Mule, YEM, Nellie Cane, Dog Faced Boy, Slave
E: Rocky Top

YEM featured an audience member on trampoline, substituting for Trey. Nellie Cane and Dog Faced Boy performed acoustic/no amplification with same setup as 4/6/94. Concert debut: Dog Faced Boy.

This run of shows was the best for me. I had killer seats all three nights and the shows were tremendous. This night, I remember how quiet the crowd got during Dog Faced Boy until someone yelled BABABOOHEY from Howard Stern and even Trey cracked up. I enjoyed the "If I Were a Rich Man" jam during Scent of a Mule—a real crowd-pleaser. —Rob Riner

Everyone had high expectations for the Beacon run. After all, here was Phish playing a three-night stand on Broadway in a small theater they said they'd always wanted to play. Well, maybe it was the lingering results of Trey's injury earlier in the week, but the shows (with the exception of Friday night's appearance of the horns) didn't meet our expectations. Still, sometimes all it takes is one song to make the night worthwhile, and on this night, there was Slave. Ahhhhh. —Lee Johnston

4/15/94 [ACCESSIBILITY: ••••] [ATTEND. 3,022; CAP. 3,022] [TIX $20]
Beacon Theater, New York, NY
I: Llama, Guelah, Paul and Silas, Harry Hood, Wilson > Chalkdust, Bouncing, It's Ice, Down with Disease
II: Maze, If I Could, Oh Kee > Suzie > Landlady, Julius, Wolfman's > Alumni > I Wanna Be Like You > HYHU, Cavern
E: Magilla, Amazing Grace

Second set starting with Suzie, and the Magilla encore, included the six-piece Giant Country Horns with the same lineup as 4/4/94. Carl Gerhard on trumpet for Cavern. Dave Grippo on congas for Landlady and I Wanna Be Like You. Alumni was first verse only. Fishman on vacuum for I Wanna Be Like You. Last Alumni, 10/10/91 Eugene, OR [279 shows].

I believe this was the best of the three at the Beacon. The Giant Country Horns added a jazz sound that enhanced the music—the combination was so tight. Fishman's Jungle Book solo was fun, Magilla is always a treat, and Alumni Blues was a surprise that is always accepted with joy. I wish Phish would play 10 shows here like the Allman Brothers do. I would attend as many as possible. —Rob Riner

I got stuck with standing-room tickets—boy, was it hot and stuffy in the balcony, jammed to the rafters with phans. It shook and swayed. When the Giant Country Horns came out, the balcony rumbled. I had incredible expectations for this show. Unfortunately, I left somewhat disappointed. I suppose every night can't be magical. That's why we go to so many shows—to catch the perfect one. —Dan Kurtz

As best I can remember, this show marked the first time the entire audience chanted the opening to "Wilson." Now it's an accepted part of the Phish experience, but back then it caught me off-guard. Even more surprising was the one verse of Alumni Blues thrown into the mix in the second set. When Trey started singing, "Woke up this morning," it seemed the whole crowd was singing along to that, too. —Lock Steele

4/16/94 [ACCESSIBILITY: ••••] [ATTEND. 10,367; CAP. 10,367] [TIX $18.50]
Mullins Center, University of Massachusetts, Amherst, MA
I: Runaway Jim, Fee, Axilla II, Rift, Stash, Fluffhead, Nellie Cane, Antelope
II: Sample, Poor Heart, Tweezer > Lizards, Julius, Bouncing, YEM, Squirming Coil, Tweezer Reprise
E: Fire

"Vibration of Life" in YEM. "Thank You" teases in YEM. YEM also featured Brad Sands on trampoline, substituting for the injured Trey. Concert debut: Axilla II.

4/17/94 [ACCESSIBILITY: ••] [ATTEND. 4,936; CAP. 7,487] [TIX $20]
Patriot Center, George Mason University, Fairfax, VA
I: Loving Cup, Foam, I Didn't Know, Divided Sky, Mound, Down with Disease > If I Could, MSO, Cavern
II: Bowie, Wolfman's > Uncle Pen, Sloth, Reba, BBJ > Maze, Contact, Golgi
E: Cracklin' Rosie, Bold as Love
Fishman on vacuum for I Didn't Know.

4/18/94 [ACCESSIBILITY: ••] [ATTEND. 4,624; CAP. 4,624] [TIX $18.50]
Bob Carpenter Center, University of Delaware, Newark, DE
I: Chalkdust, Glide > Poor Heart, Julius, My Friend, Rift, Melt, Dog Faced Boy, Oh Kee > AC/DC Bag
II: Also Sprach, Sample, Sparkle > Bathtub Gin > BBJ, Ya Mar, Mike's > TMWSIY > Avenu > TMWSIY > Down with Disease > HYHU > I Wanna Be Like You > HYHU, Cavern
E: GTBT
Mike's featured Big Phil on trampoline, substituting for Trey. Fishman on vacuum for I Wanna be Like You.

4/20/94 [ACCESSIBILITY: ••••] [ATTEND. 6,014; CAP. 6,014] [TIX $16–$18]
Virginia Horse Center, Lexington, VA
I: Runaway Jim, It's Ice, Julius, Bouncing, Axilla II, Stash, Suzie
II: Poor Heart, Antelope, Magilla, Paul and Silas, Sample, BBJ > Harry Hood, Fee, YEM > Somewhere over the Rainbow
E: Highway to Hell
The Dave Matthews Band opened. Dave Matthews performed trampoline routine for Trey during YEM. Somewhere over the Rainbow featured the entire DMB. Last Somewhere Over The Rainbow, 8/17/92 San Juan Capistrano, CA [159 shows].

This was a nice show at a venue that no one knew anything about until we got there. Plus, it was 4/20, which made for a nice day of pre-show festivities. The Over the Rainbow jam with DMB was very sweet, as was Dave Matthews replacing the injured Trey on trampoline during YEM. —M.N.J. Adams

So you'd think that with a date like this, this show would be good. Well, it pooh-poohed. It was hot and loud and dirty (the Horse Center had a dirt floor). The only highlight was the YEM with Dave Matthews. —Terry Watts

4/21/94 [ACCESSIBILITY: ••••] [ATTEND. 5,169; CAP. 5,500] [TIX $18.50]
Lawrence Joel Veterans Memorial Coliseum, Winston-Salem, NC
I: Chalkdust, Sparkle, Foam, Glide, Melt, Lizards, Down with Disease > If I Could, Cavern
II: Also Sprach > Maze, Fluffhead, Mike's > Hydrogen > Weekapaug, Scent of a Mule, BBJ > Possum, Amazing Grace
E: Drums > Jam > All along the Watchtower
The Dave Matthews Band opened. "If I Were a Rich Man" tease in Scent of a Mule. Mike's featured Dave Matthews on trampoline, substituting for Trey. Drum jam in encore featured DMB's Carter Beauford and Fishman. Entire DMB joined on jam out of drums and on Watchtower, with Dave Matthews on lead vocals. Concert debut: All along the Watchtower.

For several years, phans from the South had loudly sung the praises of the Dave Matthews Band to anyone within earshot. The group had built a strong local following by gigging regularly at places like Trax in Charlottesville, and it was clear they were ready to take the next step (though few thought they'd get so big, so fast). Phish knew it, too, because they asked DMB to open for them for two nights on their spring tour, and had the band sit in with them during both shows. This night in Winston-Salem proved the more satisfying of the two, with Fishman and Carter Beauford kicking off the encore with a long drum duo that led into a jam with all the musicians and finally into the DMB's trademark rendition of Watchtower, this time with a Phishy flavor. Jamming collaboration at its finest. —Ernie Greene

4/22/94 [ACCESSIBILITY: ••] [ATTEND. 2,983; CAP. 2,983] [TIX $16.50]
Township Auditorium, Columbia, SC
I: Llama, Horn, Uncle Pen, PYITE, Sample, All Things, Nellie Cane, Divided Sky, Horse > Silent, Bowie
II: Suzie, Julius, Reba, Tweezer, Lifeboy, Runaway Jim, HYHU > I Wanna Be Like You > HYHU, Squirming Coil
E: Father/Son Boogie, Bill Bailey
Fishman on vacuum for I Wanna Be Like You. Jack McConnell, Page's father, on keyboards and vocals for Father/Son Boogie and Bill Bailey.

4/23/94 [ACCESSIBILITY: ••••] [ATTEND. 4,571; CAP. 4,678] [TIX $18]
Fox Theater, Atlanta, GA
I: Funky Bitch, Rift, Fee > Peaches, Poor Heart, Stash, Esther, Down with Disease, Caravan, Hi-Heel Sneakers
II: Wilson > Antelope, Mound, Sample, Sparkle, Harry Hood, Ginseng Sullivan, YEM > Who by Fire, Golgi
E: Freebird
Merle Saunders on keyboard for Caravan and Hi-Heel Sneakers. "Rock and Roll Hoochie Koo" jam in YEM. Jam out of YEM featured Col. Bruce Hampton and all the members of Phish on keyboards. Ginseng Sullivan performed acoustic/no amplification with same setup as 4/6/94. Concert debut: Who by Fire.

"Phinally the Phabulous Fox" the T-shirts said, and they were right! This gorgeous theater provided the backdrop for one of the most underrated shows of the year. Besides a Funky Bitch opener, a very strong early Down with Disease and YEM with Col. Bruce Hampton and the boys banging away on keyboards, this night also has the first guest appearance by longtime Jerry Garcia collaborator Merl Saunders. He sounds right at home with the boys. —Marcia Collins

Excitement ran high for this show, but it was dulled by the fact that the enormous "Freaknick" party had taken over Atlanta for the weekend, turning the town into a total madhouse and backing up traffic for miles. In the midst of it all was the Phish scene, and somehow the boys managed to pull out a great show. —Rich Mazer

Besides being one of the better jammed shows of the spring '94 tour, the Fox is also the only show to feature Phish's rendering of Leonard Cohen's beautiful Who by Fire. The band apparently had a tape of Cohen songs they listened to all the time on the tour bus, and so out of the YEM vocal jam, they paid their respects. It's gorgeous. —Ed Smith

4/24/94 [ACCESSIBILITY: •••] [ATTEND. 2,765; CAP. 2,765] [TIX $16.50]
Grady Cole Center, Charlotte, NC
I: My Friend, Ya Mar, Axilla II, Maze, Bathtub Gin > Jump Monk > Bathtub Gin, Dog Faced Boy, Paul and Silas, It's Ice, Slave
II: Demand > Bowie, Mango, Julius, Forbin's > Mockingbird, Chalkdust, Contact, GTBT
E: Adeline
Last Jump Monk, 3/12/88 Burlington, VT [600 shows].

4/25/94 [ACCESSIBILITY: ••] [ATTEND. 2,134; CAP. 2,400] [TIX $17.50]
Knoxville Civic Auditorium, Knoxville, TN
I: Landlady > Runaway Jim, Fee, Foam, Down with Disease, Ginseng Sullivan, Dog Faced Boy, Tela, Poor Heart, Melt
II: Curtain > Sample, My Mind's > Antelope > Mound, Squirming Coil > Divided Sky, Bouncing, BBJ, BBFCM
E: Amazing Grace, Bold as Love
Ginseng Sullivan and Dog Faced Boy performed acoustic/no amplification with same setup as 4/6/94.

[4/26/94] [ACCESSIBILITY: •••]
Purple Dragon Studios, Atlanta, GA
Sample, Bouncing, Maze, Down with Disease, Fluffhead, Carefree
Live radio broadcast. Carefree is a Sun Ra song.

4/28/94 [ACCESSIBILITY: ••]
SunFest, West Palm Beach, FL
Runaway Jim, Foam, Sample, Rift, Down with Disease, Bouncing, It's Ice, Antelope, Squirming Coil, Julius, GTBT
E: Golgi
Outdoor music festival, with Blues Traveler and others. Phish played one set.

4/29/94 [ACCESSIBILITY: •••]
Boatyard Village Pavilion, Clearwater, FL
I: Halley's, YEM > FEFY, Scent of a Mule, Sloth, Divided Sky, I Didn't Know, Dog Faced Boy, Melt > Sanity, My Mind's, Llama
II: Suzie, Maze, If I Could, Reba, Fee, Uncle Pen, Mike's > Hydrogen > Weekapaug, I Wanna Be Like You > HYHU, Cavern
E: Fire
Fishman on washboard for I Didn't Know and vacuum for Be Like You. Last Sanity, 5/17/92 [200 shows].

The Boatyard was a freaky little place—what a great breeze across the pavilion, a lot of young people walking around on a cement floor, and a small island of eight or nine tapers in the midst. The first set was hot, the sound was sweet, pure and kind. Plenty of room to dance in the rear. The second set is where it was at. Opener Suzie, and the strobes and smoke. Trey kept popping out of the fog in various places. (Word had it that right after the first set, the band jumped on a boat for their setbreak. They went for a boat ride, came back and played the second set.) —Dave Parker

One way I judge a great show is by the amount of random screaming from the band. By that standard (and many others), this show is an absolute home run, probably the best show of April '93—if not the entire first leg of the tour. YEM explores some interesting places, then moves (ignoring the vocal jam) seamlessly into FEFY, a beautiful combination. There's also a warped Split Open that has everyone screaming, into the first Sanity in two years. A torrid Llama closes an incredible first set. —Pat Stanley

4/30/94 [ACCESSIBILITY: •••] [ATTEND. 1,600; CAP. 1,600] [TIX $15–$17]
The Edge, Orlando, FL
I: Chalkdust, Mound, Stash, Poor Heart, Sample, PYITE, Rift, Ginseng Sullivan, Adeline
II: Wilson, Bowie, Wolfman's, Peaches, Harry Hood, Axilla II, McGrupp, Possum, Purple Rain > HYHU, BBFCM
E: Sleeping Monkey, Highway to Hell

Ginseng performed acoustic/no amplification with same setup as 4/6/94. "Wimoweh" jam in Bowie intro and throughout the second set. "Tease medley" in Possum included teases of the songs played previously in the set (in order, Wilson, Bowie, Wolfman's, Peaches, Harry, Axilla II, McGrupp.) Fishman on vacuum for Purple Rain.

Great set II of this show, featuring a nice combination of songs, old and new. They tease "The Lion Sleeps Tonight" throughout the set—pretty funny! Listen to the Possum on this tape for several more teases. It turns out to be one of the best versions of this song, a drawn-out version with lots of jamming. The two encores also help this show stand out from others. Phish was really on fire this night. —Tim Herrman

"Tweezerfest"

5/7/94 The Bomb Factory, Dallas, TX

It used to be the stuff of dreams. "What if," a phan would say, "Phish just jammed for an entire set? You know, what if they started a song and it just didn't end?" The dream was possible because everyone believed Phish capable of it—heck, some of their soundcheck jams stretched for forty five minutes, and Mike Gordon had said before they hoped the informal, relaxed nature of their soundchecks could some day translate to a concert.

So most everyone thought it could happen—but no one expected it, much less at a tiny venue in a state Phish had only played a handful of times. But it was at the Bomb Factory in Dallas, TX, that Phish took their next giant leap forward as a band, taking Tweezer so far afield that it—along with segues and jams into several other songs—ran nearly seventy minutes in length.

The first set of the show gave little indication of what was to follow in the second set, and the first two songs of the second set didn't hint at it either. That's because Phish themselves didn't know what was going to happen. As Trey told Michael Snyder of the *San Francisco Chronicle* a few weeks after the Bomb Factory show, "We try to let the spontaneity take over. We just played Dallas the other night, and the last sixty five minutes of the show were completely improvised. It wasn't planned, but it happened, and we just took off."

Did they ever. Quickly leaving behind the Tweezer theme, Phish took their jam into bluesy jamming, a darker space Trey later said was played in tribute to the hard-rock band Gwar playing next door on the same night, pronounced "Sweet Emotion" (Aerosmith) and "Cannonball" (The Breeders) sections, and full versions of longtime staples Sparks, Makisupa Policeman, Walk Away and Purple Rain, all strung together in one nonstop piece of music. The set closed with an extended Hold Your Head Up jam that turned over into Tweezer Reprise, topping off the set.

At the time, the Bomb Factory seemed like a once-in-a-lifetime show, but by the fall tour, jams of this sort would pop up regularly. "If it wasn't for nights like that," Trey said, "I wouldn't be doing this. I'm not traveling eight months out of the year just to sit in hotel rooms."

5/2/94 [ACCESSIBILITY: ••] [ATTEND. 999; CAP. 999] [TIX $12.50]
Five Points South Music Hall, Birmingham, AL
I: Great Gig, Melt, Bouncing, Down with Disease, It's Ice, Glide, Divided Sky, Suzie, Foam, Sample
II: Runaway Jim, Mound, Reba, Golgi, Lizards, Julius, Lawn Boy, Mike's
E: Cavern

Fishman on vacuum for Great Gig. Oteil Burbridge on guitar and Stacey Starkweather on electric bass for Mike's. Note: Oteil played electric bass and Stacy played acoustic upright bass … Oteil substituted for Trey on tramps.

5/3/94 [ACCESSIBILITY: •••] [ATTEND. 2,149; CAP. 3,000 (VERANDA STAGE)] [TIX $20]
Starwood Amphitheater, Antioch, TN
I: Rift, Guelah, Maze, Sparkle, Stash, Squirming Coil, Scent of a Mule, Sample, Adeline
II: Bowie, If I Could, Fluffhead, Down with Disease, Harpua, Chalkdust, HYHU > I Wanna Be Like You > HYHU, Slave
E: Nellie Cane, Fire

If I Could featured Alison Krauss on vocals. "Sunshine of Your Love" and "Sunshine of My Life" teases in Bowie and Harpua. "Black and White" jam in Bowie intro. Show moved to the main stage at Starwood (from smaller Veranda stage) because of rain.

5/4/94 [ACCESSIBILITY: ••••] [ATTEND. 1,461; CAP. 3,194] [TIX $13.75]
State Palace Theater, New Orleans, LA
I: Runaway Jim, Foam, Sample, It's Ice, Sparkle, Axilla II, Tweezer, Lifeboy, Rift > Tweezer Reprise
II: Antelope, Bouncing, YEM, Landlady, Buried Alive, Julius, Wolfman's, Magilla, Suzie
E: Caravan

Second set starting with YEM and including encore featured the six-piece "Cosmic Country Horns": Carl Gerhard, trumpet; Michael Ray, trumpet; Tony Tate, tenor sax; Dave Grippo, alto sax; Jerome Theriot, baritone sax; and Rick Trolsen, trombone.

The show has high energy throughout, and very enjoyable versions of Tweezer and Tweezer Reprise. But what makes the show is the Antelope, when Trey dedicates the jam to his friend's newborn baby, saying, "I hope you live your life like that last jam." It's very cool to hear. —Jamis Curran

The Horns played on a lot of songs they normally don't. This is the best I've ever heard such a large number of horns play at one time. They were at their best. —David Jones

5/6/94 [ACCESSIBILITY: ••] [ATTEND. 719; CAP. 1,065] [TIX $12.50–$16]
Tower Theater, Houston, TX
I: Down with Disease, Oh Kee > AC/DC Bag, Poor Heart, My Friend, Ya Mar, Stash, Esther, Chalkdust
II: Maze, Golgi, Uncle Pen, Sample, Reba, Axilla II, Julius, HYHU > Bike > HYHU, Bowie
E: Ginseng Sullivan, Freebird

Fishman on vacuum for Bike. Ginseng Sullivan performed acoustic/no amplification with same setup as 4/6/94. Show moved from Bayou City Theater about a week before the show.

5/7/94 [ACCESSIBILITY: •••••] [ATTEND. 1,400; CAP. 2,500] [TIX $13.50–$15]
The Bomb Factory, Dallas, TX
I: Llama, Horn > Divided Sky, Mound, FEFY, Scent of a Mule, Melt, If I Could, Suzie
II: Loving Cup, Sparkle, Tweezer > Sparks > Makisupa > Jam > Sweet Emotion Jam > Walk Away > Jam > Cannonball Jam > Purple Rain > HYHU > Jam > Tweezer Reprise
E: Amazing Grace, Sample

Fishman on vacuum for Purple Rain.

This show is a perfect example of how Phish can push the very boundaries of their songs. Three songs into the second set, Phish breaks into Tweezer, but this is no ordinary Tweezer. No, this is SuperTweezer! The band drifts and floats as they jam for what seems forever. They go for nearly 70 minutes as they go in and out of songs and teases and Tweezer. They even play the Breeders' Cannonball, which goes into Purple Rain with an awesome vacuum solo. The whole thing ends with a Tweezer Reprise. This show is a must-own! —Chad Ashcraft

The Tweezerfest. Folks in Texas had a lot to hoot and holler about: set two had to be the coolest set of jammin' in years. Loving Cup is great and the Tweezer rips—it's got a whole bunch of songs and teases added to it. Check out Trey yelling "suck it!" while Fishman takes a vac solo on Purple Rain. —Michael Rambo

When I first heard this show, I was mesmerized and considered it one of Phish's most epic, ground-breaking performances ever. I still do. My personal favorite part of Tweezerfest is the blues jam that the band howls to. All 67 minutes of this mind-blowing piece of music are held in my mind as true improvisation at its very best. —Chip Croteau

Truth be told, I don't really, really enjoy listening to this tape. It's interesting, sure, but it doesn't hold together as a Tweezer the way the ones from Bangor (11/2/94) or Bozeman (11/28/94) do. Still, the show bears listening for the band's willingness to throw the setlist completely out the window and devote the set to one major song. There are great digital soundboards of this set around that shouldn't be hard to find. —Katie Silver

This show was smaller than some of the parties some of you have been to, but much bigger in a way. —Dave Parker

5/8/94 [ACCESSIBILITY: ••] [ATTEND. 1,585; CAP. 3,900] [TIX $14]
The Backyard Bee Cave, Austin, TX
I: Runaway Jim, Foam, Axilla II, Rift, Down with Disease, Bouncing, Stash, Squirming Coil
II: Also Sprach > Antelope > It's Ice > Fee > Julius > Cavern, YEM > Halley's > GTBT
E: Adeline, Golgi

5/10/94 [ACCESSIBILITY: ••] [ATTEND. 1,695; CAP. 3,000] [TIX $15–$16]
Paolo Soleri Amphitheatre, Santa Fe, NM
I: Buried Alive > Poor Heart, Sample, Divided Sky, Axilla II, It's Ice, Melt, If I Could, Cavern
II: Maze, Wilson, Julius, Reba, Scent of a Mule, Harry Hood, Ginseng Sullivan, Dog Faced Boy, Nellie Cane, Bowie
E: Squirming Coil
Ginseng Sullivan, Dog Faced Boy, and Nellie performed acoustic/no amplification with same setup as 4/6/94.

5/12/94 [ACCESSIBILITY: ••] [ATTEND. 1,121; CAP. 1,121] [TIX $15–$17]
Buena Vista Theater, Tucson, AZ
I: Catapult > Rift, Down with Disease, Fee, Maze, Axilla II, Foam, Bathtub Gin, Lizards, Sample
II: Also Sprach > Antelope, Horse > Silent, Uncle Pen, Fluffhead, Lifeboy, Possum, HYHU > Love You > HYHU, Contact, BBFCM
E: Amazing Grace, Rocky Top
Catapult started with Mike alone onstage, singing. Fishman on vacuum for Love You. Last Catapult, 2/10/93 Geneva, NY [133 shows].

5/13/94 [ACCESSIBILITY: •••] [ATTEND. 1,501; CAP. 1,501] [TIX $16–$18]
Hayden Square, Tempe, AZ
I: Runaway Jim, It's Ice, Julius, Mound, Stash, If I Could, My Friend, Slave, Suzie
II: Chalkdust, Bouncing, Melt, McGrupp, Peaches, Scent of a Mule, YEM, Purple Rain, GTBT
E: Freebird
"Layla" tease in Suzie.

Here's one of those shows that isn't seen on every list, but that you should seek out nonetheless. The first set is solid, with a freaky It's Ice, a rare Mound and a Suzie with a "Layla" tease, courtesy of Page. The second set starts off with an excellent Chalkdust. Split Open and Melt screams from start to finish. For you Zappa fans out there, there's a fine Peaches out of McGrupp, then a phat funky bass solo from Mike in YEM. —Ryan Harsch

5/14/94 [ACCESSIBILITY: ••] [ATTEND. 1,100; CAP. 1,100] [TIX $13–$15.50]
Montezuma Hall, San Diego State University, San Diego, CA
I: Llama, Wilson > Down with Disease > Fee, Reba, Sample, MSO, Ginseng Sullivan, Bowie
II: Curtain > Mike's > Hydrogen > Weekapaug > TMWSIY > Avenu > TMWSIY > PYITE, FEFY, Lizards, Cavern
E: Bold as Love
Ginseng Sullivan performed acoustic/no amplification with same setup as 4/6/94.

5/16/94 [ACCESSIBILITY: ••] [ATTEND. 2,200; CAP. 2,200] [TIX $17.50]
Wiltern Theater, Los Angeles, CA
I: Buried Alive > Poor Heart, Sample > Divided Sky, Axilla II, Rift, Down with Disease > Bouncing, Stash, Adeline
II: Also Sprach > Antelope, Sparkle, It's Ice, Julius > YEM, BBFCM > Amazing Grace > BBFCM
E: Fee, Rocky Top
"BBFCM" jam in Antelope. "Louie Louie" jam in YEM.

5/17/94 [ACCESSIBILITY: ••] [ATTEND. 1,876; CAP. 1,876] [TIX $16.50]
Arlington Theater, Santa Barbara, CA
I: Suzie, Maze, Mound, If I Could, Scent of a Mule, Ginseng Sullivan, Dog Faced Boy, Melt, Squirming Coil
II: Runaway Jim, Glide, Tweezer > Lifeboy, Uncle Pen, BBJ, Sample, HYHU > Love You > HYHU, Slave
E: Highway to Hell
Ginseng Sullivan and Dog Faced Boy performed acoustic/no amplification. Cake delivered to Page to celebrate his birthday during his Squirming Coil piano solo. Fishman on vacuum for Love You.

5/19/94 [ACCESSIBILITY: ••••] [ATTEND. 2,359; CAP. 2,504] [TIX $17.50]
Hult Center, Eugene, OR
I: Halley's > Llama, My Friend, Poor Heart > Stash, Horse > Silent, Down with Disease, Mango, Cavern
II: Sample, Sparkle, Mike's > Hydrogen > Weekapaug, Lizards, Julius, BBJ, Harry Hood, Golgi
E: Ginseng Sullivan, Nellie Cane, Adeline, Fire
Ginseng Sullivan and Nellie Cane performed acoustic/no amplification with same setup as 4/6/94.

Stellar Halley's Comet opener, right into Llama. This show took place in a pretty small room, so they used non-amplification a couple of times for some acoustic numbers. Then the second set got really out of control. Mike's Groove had a very sinister feel—it almost felt as if they were ready to jump into Simple, but that wouldn't come for a couple more weeks. —Bob Talatzko

This is simply a very well-played, well-jammed show. Stash in the first set just goes there—this is probably the hottest version of this song I've ever heard. There's a real feeling of intimacy at the Pacific Northwest shows from this era, and I think the music benefits from it. —Melissa Wolcott

5/20/94 [ACCESSIBILITY: ••] [ATTEND. 2,541; CAP. 3,500] [TIX $17–$19]
Campus Recreation Center, Evergreen College, Olympia, WA
I: Fee, Maze, If I Could, It's Ice, Bathtub Gin, FEFY, Scent of a Mule, Dog Faced Boy, Carolina, AC/DC Bag
II: Also Sprach > Antelope, Weigh, Axilla II, Wolfman's, Rift, YEM
E: Chalkdust
"Wimoweh" tease in Bathtub Gin. Dog Faced Boy performed acoustic/no amplification.

Think the band doesn't know what's going on in the crowd? We were all surprised at the extremely short second set—it was well under an hour. Word later circulated that Trey cut the show short because he felt like the crowd wasn't really into it. Well, the crowd was into it in a way—a chant of "Fee" from the folks up front convinced the boys to open up with that song—but yeah, this was a typical newbie show with no one really digging the jams. Things got a whole lot better in Seattle and Vancouver. —Tyler Harris

5/21/94 [ACCESSIBILITY: ••] [ATTEND. 1,385; CAP. 1,419] [TIX $18.50]
Moore Theater, Seattle, WA
I: Runaway Jim, Foam, Guelah, Down with Disease, Mound, Stash, Squirming Coil, Tela, Llama
II: Dinner and a Movie > Sample, Bowie, Contact, BBJ, Julius, HYHU > Bike > HYHU, Harry Hood, Amazing Grace
E: Bold as Love
Fishman on vacuum for Bike. Last Dinner and a Movie, 8/9/93 Toronto, ON [54 shows]. Last Carolina, 8/7/93 Darien Lake, NY [55 shows].

5/22/94 [ACCESSIBILITY: •••] [ATTEND. 989; CAP. 989] [TIX $23]
Vogue Theater, Vancouver, BC
I: Demand > Sloth, Divided Sky, Glide, Melt, Fluffhead, MSO, Ginseng Sullivan, Dog Faced Boy, Axilla II
II: Down with Disease, Bouncing, It's Ice, McGrupp > Tweezer > Lifeboy, Rift, Slave, Tweezer Reprise
E: Sleeping Monkey
MSO, Ginseng Sullivan, and Dog Faced Boy performed acoustic/no amplification with same setup as 4/6/94.

5/23/94 [ACCESSIBILITY: •••] [ATTEND. 2,474; CAP. 3,042] [TIX $17]
Civic Auditorium, Portland, OR

I: Chalkdust, Sample, Foam, Fee > Maze, Horse > Silent, Julius, Reba, Cavern
II: Wilson, Antelope, If I Could, Sparkle, PYITE, YEM, Possum
E: Ginseng Sullivan, Amazing Grace, Highway to Hell
Ginseng Sullivan performed acoustic/no amplification with same setup as 4/6/94.

5/25/94 [ACCESSIBILITY: ••] [ATTEND. 2,250; CAP. 2,250] [TIX $19.50]
Warfield Theater, San Francisco, CA
I: Curtain > Sample, Uncle Pen, Stash, Forbin's > Mockingbird, Axilla II, Scent of a Mule, MSO, Adeline, Chalkdust
II: Rift, Tweezer, Lifeboy, Maze, Contact > BBJ, Julius, HYHU > Purple Rain > HYHU, Squirming Coil
E: Sleeping Monkey, Tweezer Reprise
MSO performed acoustic/no amplification with same setup as 4/6/94. Fishmen on vacuum for Purple Rain.

5/26/94 [ACCESSIBILITY: ••] [ATTEND. 2,250; CAP. 2,250] [TIX $19.50]
Warfield Theater, San Francisco, CA
I: Buried Alive > Poor Heart, Cavern, Demand > Melt, Sparkle, It's Ice > Catapult, Divided Sky, Sample
II: Also Sprach > Antelope, Fluffhead, Down with Disease > Mound, Ginseng Sullivan, Dog Faced Boy, YEM, Amazing Grace
E: GTBT
Ginseng and Dog Faced Boy performed acoustic/no amplification with same setup as 4/6/94.

Like the April Beacon run, not every night at the Warfield could claim to be an above-average show. Though the setlist for this night looks solid, the band just wasn't into it at all—the high point of the show came in the first set with cool Demand > SOAM and Ice > Catapult combos. Trey was later quoted as saying that this version of Antelope was the low point of the tour for him. I didn't think it was that bad, but it's clear that the boys just weren't clicking. They turned that around completely the next night, though. —Pat Stanley

5/27/94 [ACCESSIBILITY: ••••] [ATTEND. 2,250; CAP. 2,250] [TIX $19.50]
Warfield Theater, San Francisco, CA
I: Wilson, Runaway Jim, Foam, Bouncing, Bowie, If I Could, PYITE > Harry Hood, Golgi
II: Suzie > Peaches, My Friend, Reba, Lizards, Julius, Nellie Cane, My Mind's, Mike's > Simple > Mike's > O Mio Bambino Caro > Jam > Possum
E: Fire
Nellie Cane and My Mind's performed acoustic/no amplification with the same setup as 4/6/94, plus Morgan Fichter on fiddle. Andrea Baker of the San Francisco Opera Company on vocals for O Mio Bambino Caro. After her solo, band and crew distributed macaroni and cheese boxes to audience members, who played along on Possum and Fire. "Flintstones" tease in Possum Concert debut: Simple.

A very good show that everyone has or should have. An energetic PYITE jams straight into the Hooded one. The first set is very good (except for Bouncin'). The second set offers a psychedelic Reba (above and beyond), and the debut of Simple—it isn't one of my favorites, but this is a damn wild version. Andrea Baker comes out to sing at the end—what a voice. They also really worked up the intro into Possum. —Sean Miller

The best cover that Phish does is Zappa's Peaches. This version is one of the best, with great keyboard work by Page. And to hear it appear out of a Suzie jam is a nice treat, a great transition. Mike's begins with great promise, and instead of forming Hydrogen and Weekapaug it jams into the concert debut of Simple. This version is raw and riotous as band members trade verses, and even Fish goes solo a few times on vocals. This crazy version goes into a stop-and-go Possum with Flintstones teases. —Tim Foisset

The opera singer, the Flintstones licks, how cool. This is another rock n' show from beginning to end. —Chad Gamerke

As Trey took the Mike's Song jam out of the Simple debut, and pushed the groove lower and lower, I thought the band had Slave on their minds. Instead, the groove dropped out to almost nothing, and Trey and Mike crouched down with their instruments as a woman emerged from the back of the stage and walked to the front, where she sang an aria with one of the most beautiful voices I'd ever heard. The crowd fell totally silent for her performance, then exploded in cheers when she finished. She was obviously surprised by the reception, which made the moment even more special. Then the band emerged from the wings with dozens of crates of Kraft Macaroni and Cheese (decorated with Flintstones characters in support of the Flintstones movie then in theaters) and passed them out to the audience. With everyone shaking their boxes—and a few folks spraying pasta around the room, of course—Page started the Possum intro, and the place went crazy. "Shake your macaroni!" Fish bellowed. We all did! —Lock Steele

5/28/94 [ACCESSIBILITY: ••] [ATTEND. 8,571; CAP. 12,000] [TIX $29.50]
Laguna Seca Raceway, Monterey, CA
I: Rift, Sample, Foam, Bouncing, Stash, Horse > Silent, Sloth, Maze, Cavern
II: Axilla II, It's Ice, Tweezer, Lifeboy, Reba, Fee, Llama, YEM, Bass Jam
E: Poor Heart
Laguna Seca Daze festival, with a number of bands. Les Claypool on bass for YEM and Bass Jam. Fishman on vacuum in YEM. "Popeye" jam in YEM.

5/29/94 [ACCESSIBILITY: ••] [ATTEND. 8,571; CAP. 12,000] [TIX $29.50]
Laguna Seca Raceway, Monterey, CA
I: Divided Sky, Guelah, Halley's > Down with Disease, Sparkle, Julius, I Didn't Know, Bowie
II: Nellie Cane, Split Open and Phil, Esther, Chalkdust, McGrupp, Oh Kee > Suzie, Antelope, Freebird
E: Wilson, Golgi, Rocky Top
E2: Harry Hood, GTBT
Laguna Seca Daze festival, with a number of bands. "Guitar Player Is Taking a Leak" jam (so named by Fish) before Harry Hood.

This show is Phish at their humble best, playing at an outdoor festival show in sunny California (a state Phish should play in a little more often, I think!) The first set begins with a beautiful Divided Sky. The rare Halley's Comet, showcasing the vocal talents of the band, gives way to a ripping Down with Disease. But the real high point of this show is one of my favorite Phish songs, Split Open and Melt. This one's nice and long, complete with some vocal weirdness in the end jam, false stops and plenty more sonic oddities. Phans are treated to TWO encores, the second one being Harry Hood, which just takes off and makes you feel good! —Ryan Harsch

1994 SUMMER Tunes Exhumed

Starting a new practice, the band took a short break before resuming their tour in Salt Lake City. As the tour headed east, the setlists became more creative than they had been for most of the spring tour—witness the returns from hibernation of NICU and Mango, as well as continued experimentation with Simple. The use of acoustic instruments onstage, a central part of spring tour, would also continue, albeit to a slightly lesser extent in the bigger outdoor venues.

Tapes from this tour, like the spring tour, are generally high in quality, although the burgeoning size of the tapers' section in 1994 meant that some folks with $39 Walkmans were taping shows and producing tapes of predictably poor sound quality.

6/9/94 [ACCESSIBILITY: •••] [ATTEND. 2,304; CAP. 3,000] [TIX $27.50]
Triad Amphitheatre, Salt Lake City, UT
I: Llama, Guelah, Rift, Down with Disease, It's Ice, If I Could, Maze, Fee, Suzie
II: Melt, Glide, Julius, Halley's > Scent of a Mule, Ginseng Sullivan, Mike's > Hydrogen > Weekapaug, Golgi
E: Highway to Hell
Ginseng Sullivan performed acoustic/no amplification with same setup as 4/6/94.

6/10/94 [ACCESSIBILITY: •••] [ATTEND. 14,349 (BOTH SHOWS); CAP. 9,450] [TIX $20.35]
Red Rocks Amphitheatre, Morrison, CO
I: Runaway Jim, Foam, Sample, Nellie Cane, Demand > Bowie, Lizards, Cavern, Julius
II: Axilla II, Curtain > Tweezer > Lifeboy, Sparkle, Possum, HYHU > I Wanna Be Like You > HYHU, Harry Hood, Tweezer Reprise
E: Sleeping Monkey > Rocky Top
Fishman on vacuum for I Wanna Be Like You. "Tela" tease before Lizards.

6/11/94 [ACCESSIBILITY: •••••] [ATTEND. 14,349 (BOTH SHOWS); CAP. 9,450] [TIX $20.35]
Red Rocks Amphitheatre, Morrison, CO
I: Wilson, Chalkdust, YEM > Rift, Down with Disease, It's Ice, Tela, Stash
II: Also Sprach > Antelope, Fluffhead, Scent of a Mule, Melt, Squirming Coil, Maze, Contact > Frankenstein
E: Suzie
Live FM broadcast. Last Frankenstein, 7/26/91 Athens, GA [329 shows].

This was the second of a two-show run here, on a beautiful day with the sun falling behind the towering red icons of musical energy. Being a hotter show than the first, Trey was not going to let us down. A smokin' 2001 led into Run Like an Antelope, then a fun Fluffhead got everyone bouncing. The second set ended with a Frankenstein that melted everybody, the first one in three years. —Jeff Salvatore

Anyone tuning their FM dial to this show must have been blown away during the first 45 minutes. The boys did not let up until Ice, but not before roaring out five rockers in a row, including a segue between the YEM vocal jam and Rift (perfection!) and a DWD that showed everyone that this newbie was destined for greatness. FM crispies make this one a keeper for driving without the roof. —Paul Sheets

Although all four members of Phish always shine bright on stage, Mike Gordon played some really incredible bass throughout this show. He is master of playing that one right note instead of the ten fast notes, and this show is the perfect example of this. The highlight is in set II—the intro into the Antelope jam is just perfect. Mike weaves through Trey's licks so well! —Michelle Hirsch

6/13/94 [ACCESSIBILITY: •••] [ATTEND. 2,952; CAP. 2,952] [TIX $15]
Memorial Hall, Kansas City, KS
I: Buried Alive > Poor Heart, Sample, Divided Sky, Wolfman's > Dinner and a Movie, Stash, Ginseng Sullivan, Julius
II: Mike's > Hydrogen > Weekapaug, Esther, Cavern, Reba, Jesus Left Chicago, Scent of a Mule, BBJ, HYHU > Terrapin > HYHU, Slave
E: Golgi

Ginseng Sullivan performed acoustic/no amplification with same setup as 4/6/94. Fishman on vacuum for Terrapin. Last Jesus Left Chicago, 8/26/93 Portland, OR [53 shows]. Last Terrapin, 4/29/93 Montreal, Quebec [95 shows].

"The OJ Show"

6/17/94 Eagles Auditorium, Milwaukee, WI

When referring to Phish shows, most people rely on the venue and year, and maybe the night of the stand, like "Red Rocks '96, third night" or "Dayton '95." Holiday shows are worthy of their own names: "Halloween '94" or "New Year's '95," and then there are the rare cases where Phish furnishes event names: "Amy's Farm" or "The Great Went."

Rarest of all, perhaps, are the shows that create a name for themselves: "The O.J. Show," so named because Phish just happened to be on tour the night O.J. Simpson took off down the highway in his white Ford Bronco.

The band members have always been astute pop culture observers—just listening to Harpua over the years gives a sense of that, as the band samples on songs as wide-ranging as "Crossroads," "Black or White" and "Smells Like Teen Spirit." Then there's Trey's penchant for reporting sports scores from the stage, whether for the NFL (8/14/93 Tinley), the NBA (6/22/94 Columbus) or NCAA Basketball (4/4/94 Flynn). But only once has the band directly referred to a cultural event in its show, and that event was the Simpson Bronco chase.

Coming out on stage for the second set, the band had obviously been watching the Bronco chase backstage. As Also Sprach Zarathustra starts up, Trey intones, "Run, O.J.," as Fish chants, "What do you say, O.J.?" Trey keeps repeating "O.J." as the jam progresses; at its peak, "O.J!" is yelled in sync with the music. The O.J. themes continue in Poor Heart and Mike's Song—the prelude to the funniest Phish tribute ever. Yes, Simple makes clear that "We've got O.J. in the band!," poses that timeless question, "What is a band without O.J.?" and concludes, "O.J. is grand!" before the jam dissolves back into Mike's Song.

This show would not be so widely remembered if it hadn't been musically successful. But O.J. antics aside, the second set absolutely rocks. Mike's Groove is powerful—simple, still developing since its debut at the Warfield on May 27—is its second performance ever. Its lyrics and theme even magically surface at the beginning of I Am Hydrogen. Then there's Harpua, complete with samples of Hendrix (Voodoo Child) and even Phish (Simple!).

6/14/94 [ACCESSIBILITY: ••••] [ATTEND. 2,058; CAP. 2,500] [TIX $17.50]
Des Moines Civic Center, Des Moines, IA
I: Llama, Guelah > Adeline > Guelah, Rift, Down with Disease, Fee, My Friend, Uncle Pen, I Didn't Know > MSO > I Didn't Know, Melt
II: Frankenstein, Demand > Bowie, If I Could, It's Ice, Sparkle, YEM, HYHU > Bike > HYHU, Possum
E: Sample

Guelah was split between Asse Festival and The Fly. Fishman on Madonna washboard for I Didn't Know and vacuum for Bike. MSO performed acoustic/no amplification with same setup as 4/6/94. "On Broadway" jam in YEM and Possum.

6/16/94 [ACCESSIBILITY: ••••] [ATTEND. 2,083; CAP. 2,083] [TIX $17.50]
State Theater, Minneapolis, MN
I: Bouncing, Rift, Julius, Fee > Maze, Gumbo, Curtain > Dog Faced Boy, Stash, Squirming Coil
II: Suzie, Antelope, Forbin's > Kung > Mockingbird, BBJ, Down with Disease > Contact, BBFCM > Purple Rain > HYHU, Golgi
E: Ginseng Sullivan, Amazing Grace, GTBT

Fishman on vacuum for Purple Rain. Ginseng Sullivan performed acoustic/no amplification with same setup as 4/6/94. "Heartbreaker" tease in GTBT. Last Gumbo, 4/21/93 Columbus, OH [103 shows].

Talk about filling the hey hole! After four Phishy pop tunes, this Maze is just stunning! Also in set I, a Stash of epic proportions and a Coil closer. After an energetic, exploratory Antelope in set II, there's a trip to Gamehendge complete with Kung chant. An inspirational DWD segues nicely into Contact > BBFCM, then Fishman says (as Prince), "Hello, Minneapolis, it's good to be home!" An all-around excellent show. —Bob Colby

The Bouncing that opens up the first set is beautiful; it floats you gently through the air and sets you down when the band jumps into Rift. Gumbo is a welcome addition to this show, and they play it better than the last time they played it (at the Newport Music Hall on 4/21/93). The Forbin > Kung > Mockingbird trio in the second set is phabulous. Kung in particular stands out. A classic Phish setlist with a few twists. —David George

It was clear from very early on that Down with Disease was going to be a hot, jamming song, but the way Phish takes the jam far out there during set two and then slides into Contact without returning to the lyrical refrain is a sign of things to come. —Ed Smith

6/17/94 [ACCESSIBILITY: ••••]
Eagles Auditorium, Milwaukee, WI
I: Runaway Jim, Foam, Glide, Melt, If I Could, PYITE, Bathtub Gin, Scent of a Mule, Cavern
II: Also Sprach > Sample > Poor Heart, Mike's > Simple > Mike's > Hydrogen > Weekapaug, Harpua > Kung > Harpua, Sparkle > BBJ > Julius, Frankenstein
E: Sleeping Monkey, Rocky Top

"Voodoo Chile" jam in Harpua. "Mission Impossible" jam in Mike's. "Simple" is teased/sung in "Hydrogen" and teased again in "Harpua."

Do you remember where you were on this night? Phish were onstage and most people in America were watching the famous white Bronco going down a California highway. The band also saw this and let everyone know it. 2001 > "What do you say OJ?" was the theme. The boys had a good time with this one, including a "Mission Impossible" jam in Mike's. This tape is a lot of fun. —Michael Rambo

Second set was what made this show special—the famous OJ show. I had no idea what they were talking about, shouting "OJ!" and "Run, OJ, run!" in the middle of 2001. The theme recurred randomly throughout the set. The ballroom was roasting (really, really hot), so we were all grateful for Harpua—not just because it's always fun, but because Trey had us dreaming of cool breezes—aah. There was a girl throwing ice cubes down from the balcony that I thought was an angel. The winding down at the ending of this show was a little disappointing but Sleeping Monkey–Rocky Top always makes me laugh, at least. —Libby Barrow

Whenever you hear about this show, it's always dubbed as the "OJ Show." That was cool, but how about listening to the music? Nice 2001 opener and the Mike's Groove is really strong, one of the best from the tour. I love Harpua where Trey tells how the old man hears the Gamehendge kids singing Simple and how it pisses him off. —Nick Soricelli

I was there, and I haven't yet read a review of this show that gives the venue justice. It was hot! And I don't just mean the music—it had to be at least 115 degrees inside. Fans were set up to cool off the band, and there were some sisters throwing ice off the balcony/bar onto the ballroom floor. Highlights included the entire second set, with the OJ chants. Many lost minds were wandering around downtown Milwaukee that night. Nothing has topped this show since. —Bob Talatzko

6/18/94 [ACCESSIBILITY: ••••] [ATTEND. 8,239; CAP. 8,239] [TIX $18.50]
UIC Pavilion, University of Illinois, Chicago, IL
I: Wilson > Rift, AC/DC Bag, Maze, Mango > Down with Disease, It's Ice, Dog Faced Boy > Divided Sky, Sample
II: Peaches > Bowie > Mind Left Body Jam > Bowie, Horn, McGrupp, Tweezer > Lifeboy, YEM, Chalkdust
E: Bouncing > Tweezer Reprise

"Mind Left Body" jam interspersed in the Bowie intro. "Three Blind Mice," "Voodoo Chile" and "Purple Haze" teases in Bowie. "Immigrant Song" tease in YEM. "Follow the Yellow Brick Road" and "Spam" themes in YEM vocal jam.

The music quality of this show is awesome! They had tons of energy and it definitely came through to the crowd. First set highlights: an intense and haunting Maze and a funky Ice jam, and (of course) we all love Divided Sky. It's the second set that really blew me away, though. They busted out with Peaches (one of my favorites, even though I'm partial to Zappa's version) and then bowled me over with probably the best Bowie I've ever heard! Just look at the rest of the set, it speaks for itself (except Bouncin'). Couldn't ask for much more. This show is guaranteed to make you glow. —Libby Barrow

One of the best-jammed shows of the year, and also one that can be found pretty easily on soundboard. The band plays a very pronounced "Mind Left Body" jam (an old favorite of the Dead's) after starting the Bowie intro, and they do it great justice. From there, they jam into an otherworldly Bowie and later toss in great versions of YEM and Tweezer. This set blows me away. —Ernie Greene

6/19/94 [ACCESSIBILITY: ••] [ATTEND. 1,563; CAP. 1,563] [TIX $18.50]
State Theater, Kalamazoo, MI
I: Suzie, Julius, Lizards, Axilla II, Curtain > FEFY, Scent of a Mule, Stash, Golgi
II: Faht, Antelope, If I Could, Reba, Makisupa, Squirming Coil, MSO, Highway to Hell
E: Freebird

MSO performed acoustic/no amplification with same setup as 4/6/94.

6/21/94 [ACCESSIBILITY: ••] [ATTEND. 3,367; CAP. 3,367] [TIX $18.50]
Cincinnati Music Hall, Cincinnati, OH
I: Runaway Jim, Mound > Sample, It's Ice > Horse
II: Fire, Poor Heart, Down with Disease, My Friend, Melt, Esther, Chalkdust, BBFCM, Ginseng Sullivan, BBFCM, Dog Faced Boy, Adeline, Julius, Sparkle, Harry Hood, Suzie
E: Amazing Grace

First set cut short during Horse after venue fire alarm went off. Ginseng Sullivan, BBFCM (after Ginseng) and Dog Faced Boy performed acoustic/no amplification with same setup as 4/6/94. "Who Knows" tease at end of My Friend.

This show was an interesting one to attend. Smoking was prohibited at the Music Hall, like that would stop anyone. But the alarms in the air ducts went off and Trey, in the middle of Horse, calmly came over the PA and announced that everybody had to leave the building. After what seemed like two hours (only 45 minutes), we were allowed back in. In reverence to the drill, Phish played Fire upon returning. —Sean Miller

Hilarious. We knew something was going to come of the fire alarm. When Trey says, "No smoking," that made the set. No smoking, what else do you need? And then into Fire—hahaha. Classic. —Aaron Mandelman

Fire was the obvious choice to get the crowd back up to speed and set the tempo for the 15-song superset that followed. Several high-energy tunes gave way to a nice acoustic break because everyone had to catch their breath. Then Julius got things going again and Suzie closed the set. Harry Hood was a high point. I long for those no amplification treats that we no longer get. —Justin Weiss

6/22/94 [ACCESSIBILITY: ••••] [ATTEND. 2,294; CAP. 3,750] [TIX $17.50]
Veterans Memorial Auditorium, Columbus, OH
I: Llama, Guelah, Rift, Gumbo, Maze, If I Could, Scent of a Mule, Stash, Golgi
II: Also Sprach > Mike's > Simple > Catapult > Mike's > Simple > Icculus, Simple > Hydrogen > Weekapaug > TMWSIY > Avenu > TMWSIY > Fluffhead, MSO > BBJ, Jesus Left Chicago, Sample
E: Carolina, Cavern

MSO performed acoustic/no amplification. "Midnight Rider" jams in Mike's/Catapult/Mike's. Digital Delay Loop jam between TMWSIY and Fluffhead. Last Icculus, 3/25/93 Santa Cruz, CA [127 shows].

If you like to hear Phish break down their jams into total looseness, then this is your kind of show. The whole second set is transitional, effortlessly moving from one jam to the next. 2001 kicks off the insanity, followed by a Mike's Groove filled to the gills with improvisation. Simple > Icculus > Simple is a great treat. After wrapping it all up with Weekapaug Groove, the band settles things down with a TMWSIY > Avenu > TMWSIY. Refusing to let things go down, Fluffhead follows, and there's also a Jesus Left Chicago, which to my ears is Page's best cover. —Adam Davidoff

The second set is one of my favorites. 2001 > Mike's > Simple > Catapult and more Simple. The wait for Weekapaug is long, but fulfilling with Icculus and Simple (again!) to keep you guessing. The Groove is finally completed and brought down to a beautiful TMWSIY—a breath of fresh air after all the chaos of a killer Mike's. Avenu Malkenu rocks, more TMWSIY and then Fluffhead, absolute perfection! My Sweet One keeps you hanging on and Jesus Left Chicago provides a much-needed break, preparing you for a tight encore to top off a killer set. —Carri A. Johnson

Arguably the best set of the year, the second set in Columbus is led by Mike's Groove—one of the craziest versions ever, with themes from Catapult, Simple and Icculus magically interwoven to create a true masterpiece. After jamming out, Mike's Song drops into Simple's chords, but they don't immediately head to the lyrics—instead, there's a very cool jam for a few minutes on the Midnight Rider theme, then Catapult is sung to the tune of the jam. Catapult jumps back into Mike's Song for a minute (again, a particularly melodious Midnight Rider jam), then they start repeating "I catapult downtown" over and over. Low and behold, the Simple chords re-emerged, this time with lyrics. Out of Simple comes Icculus, including an outrageous "Read the fucking book!" sermon from Trey and "Save your life!" chants. Then they start singing Simple again! —Rich Mazer

6/23/94 [ACCESSIBILITY: ••] [ATTEND. 4,044; CAP. 4,044] [TIX $17.50–$20]
Phoenix Plaza Amphitheater, Pontiac, MI
I: Buried Alive > Poor Heart, Melt, NICU, Foam, Bouncing, Down with Disease, Horse > Silent, PYITE, Julius
II: Frankenstein, Bowie, Mango, Axilla II, Uncle Pen, Tweezer, Lifeboy, Slave
E: Sparkle, Tweezer Reprise

"Sunshine of Your Love" jam in Tweezer. Last NICU, 5/1/92 Milwaukee, WI [248 shows].

6/24/94 [ACCESSIBILITY: •••] [ATTEND. 1,854; CAP. 1,901] [TIX $18.50]
Murat Theater, Indianapolis, IN
I: Divided Sky, Wilson, It's Ice, Fee > Sloth, All Things, Paul and Silas > Horn, Reba, Adeline, Sample
II: Demand > Antelope, Halley's, Curtain > McGrupp > Simple > Sanity, Llama, Dog Faced Boy, Poor Heart, Cavern, Carolina, Down with Disease
E: Rocky Top

Dog Faced Boy, Poor Heart, and Cavern performed acoustic/no amplification with same setup as 4/6/94.

6/25/94 [ACCESSIBILITY: ••] [ATTEND. 4,026; CAP. 4,206] [TIX $18.50]
Nautica Stage, Cleveland, OH
I: N2O, Rift, Julius, NICU, Stash, Mango, Sample, Scent of a Mule, Tela, Chalkdust
II: Suzie, Maze, Sparkle, Bathtub Gin, Axilla II, YEM, HYHU > Cracklin' Rosie > HYHU, Harry Hood, Golgi
E: Highway to Hell

Fishman on vacuum for N2O. Concert debut: N2O.

6/26/94 [ACCESSIBILITY: ••••] [ATTEND. 1,386; CAP. 3,350] [TIX $17.50]
Charleston Municipal Auditorium, Charleston, WV
I: Kung > Llama > Lizards > Tela > Wilson > AC/DC Bag > Forbin's > Mockingbird > Sloth > McGrupp > Divided Sky
II: Julius, Down with Disease, If I Could, Axilla II, Lifeboy, Sample, Wolfman's, Scent of a Mule, Dog Faced Boy, Demand > Melt Jam > Yerushalayim
E: Old Home Place, Amazing Grace, Tube, Fire

Old Home Place performed acoustic/no amplification. First set contained complete Gamehendge narration by Trey—fourth ever live Gamehendge. Second set contained the songs from Hoist*, played in order and almost exactly as on the album—first live performance of the slow ending for Axilla II; Melt Jam and Yerushalayim ending for Demand. Last complete Gamehendge, 3/22/93 Sacramento, CA [133 shows]. Last Tube, 4/12/93 Iowa City, IA [119 shows]. Concert debut: Old Home Place. Last year Yerushalayim, 7/24/93 Mansfield, MA [88 shows].*

What better place to break out a live Gamehendge, narration and all, than their first show in the state nicknamed "Almost Heaven". West Virginia is one of the most beautiful places east of the ol' Miss, and Gamehendge just seems appropriate here. From the opening Kung chant to

Thursday, June 23, 1994

PHOENIX PLAZA, Pontiac, MI

I got to the show about 2:30 or 3:00 in the afternoon, way early, and I saw this beautiful girl run into this elevator, so I went to talk to her. Next thing you know, the elevator opened up, and there we were on top of a parking garage, right where the show was going to be, four stories up. A guard recognized her, and must have just figured I was with her, so we just walked out.

Suddenly, I realized the stage was right in front of me! So I sat down, and as it turns out, this beautiful girl—I mean, a real ten—is a local stripper. The same guy running all of the concession stands at the venue—cappuccino stands and stuff—also ran a bunch of local strip clubs. Then it hits me: all these girls in here, waiting for their assignments, are strippers. And they're all just beautiful! So we're hanging out, and I'm talking to this girl next to me who had seen Phish once, but nobody else there even knew the band. All of a sudden, Phish comes out on stage. I'm thinking, "Oh my God, Phish is here, they're about to soundcheck, I know I'm not allowed to be in here, and it's only a matter of time before I get thrown out." This guy is assigning people positions, and he keeps looking at me and not really saying anything, and Phish starts playing.

I think they started doing The Wedge, and all the girls got up and started doing their dances. They're all gyrating with each other, and taking off their shirts, and they've got spandex on. I'm thinking, "I'm watching Phish play with nobody here, and a bunch of beautiful girls stripping for me. This is too good to be real!"

Meanwhile, Page kept looking at me and grinning, and I started laughing—it seemed to me that Page knew that I wasn't supposed to be in there.

Then I heard Trey start doing NICU, which they hadn't played since '92 at this point. I'm thinking, "Holy shit, NICU!" They all go into it, and they're playing through it, and they get to the verse, "I try to convey what you strive to condone," and Trey fumbles it. But he doesn't just fumble it and fix it, he looks over at Page, and he says, "What's that line?" And I'm thinking, "I try to convey what you strive to condone, I try to convey what you strive to condone!" But Page says, "I don't know." So Trey looks over at Mike and shrugs, and Trey goes back to singing the verse again, just trying to get through it, and I was like, here I've got this rare opportunity to tell Phish the line that they don't know themselves in their own song that they're playing, a song that maybe they're getting ready to bust out after two and a half years of not playing it.

But then I'd probably get thrown out. Or else I could just stay quiet.

They ended up figuring it out, and playing it four times during that soundcheck, getting it down before they broke it out during that show. By the time that happened, I was like, "Oh, NICU, this tune, this is old, this is my fifth time hearing it today."

—Mike Graff

capping it all off with Divided Sky, Phish just beautifully set the mood on this night. —Peter Bukley

Even with their warped minds, Phish must have had to dig pretty deep to come up with the GameHoist idea. Not content with a first-set Gamehendge (the first in well over a year, and a beautiful version at that), the band came out for the second set and played all of *Hoist*, in order, pretty much true to the album. This wacky show is a key part of any good Phish collection. —Tyler Harris

The first-set Gamehendge is great, but a lot of people seemed turned off by the second set, in which Phish plays *Hoist* in order. If you miss the second set, though, you're missing some great music, including a very well-jammed DWD, Axilla II with the slow "don't shine that thing in my face, man" ending played for the first time, and Demand including the Split Open and Melt jam and the Yerushalayim ending. —Melissa Collins

6/29/94 [ACCESSIBILITY: ••] [ATTEND. 5,004; CAP. 19,158] [TIX $13–$17.50]
Walnut Creek Amphitheatre, Raleigh, NC

I: Curtain > Sample, Reba, Mound, Julius, Horse > Silent, Catapult > Bowie, I Didn't Know, Golgi
II: Landlady, Poor Heart, Tweezer, It's Ice, Lifeboy, Divided Sky, Suzie, Cavern
E: Ya Mar, Tweezer Reprise

Fishman on bass drum pedal hitting his leg (amplified by Trey's megaphone and Mike's mic) for I Didn't Know.

6/30/94 [ACCESSIBILITY: ••••] [ATTEND. 6,278; CAP. 10,000] [TIX $16.75–$20]
Classic Amphitheatre, Richmond, VA

I: Down with Disease, Gumbo, Rift, Guelah, Melt, Glide, Scent of a Mule, Bouncing, Frankenstein
II: Wilson, Maze, YEM > Yerushalayim > YEM, Sparkle, Axilla II, Harpua, Antelope, HYHU > Love You > HYHU, Chalkdust
E: Sleeping Monkey, Poor Heart

"Honky Tonk Woman" jam in Harpua, sung by an audience member who was brought onstage. Harpua tease in Antelope intro. Fishman on vacuum for Love You.

It rained very hard before the show but that didn't dampen our fun. Harpua was a great time, with Trey calling up a guy onstage to sing karaoke for Jimmy. Everyone got a real laugh out of that. This was a solid show, nothing extraordinary, but very fun nonetheless. A good time, as always. —M.N.J. Adams

The first set is just a warm-up with smoking versions of Rift and Scent, plus Frank for a great closer. But the real treat came in the second set. Trey fiddles with his wah-pedal all set, leading the boys through a brilliant YEM > City of Gold > YEM. Harpua with a guest appearance from the audience for a Honky Tonk Woman tease (get the tape to find out why we needed a guest!) and a spoken Kung. And with Harpua in mind, Trey prances into Antelope. This Antelope is when it all clicked for me. —Terry Watts

7/1/94 [ACCESSIBILITY: ••] [ATTEND. 12,718; CAP. 12,718] [TIX $15.50–$18.50]
Mann Music Center, Philadelphia, PA

I: Runaway Jim, Foam, Sample, NICU, Stash, Mango, It's Ice, Tela, Julius, Suzie
II: Bowie, If I Could, Fluffhead, Down with Disease, TMWSIY > Avenu > TMWSIY, Possum, HYHU > Terrapin > HYHU, Harry Hood, Cavern
E: Rocky Top

Fishman on vacuum for Terrapin.

7/2/94 [ACCESSIBILITY: ••••] [ATTEND. 10,663; CAP. 10,663] [TIX $20]
Garden State Arts Center, Holmdel, NJ

I: Golgi, Divided Sky, Guelah, FEFY, Scent of a Mule, Tweezer, Lifeboy, Sparkle, Tweezer Reprise
II: Also Sprach, Mike's > Simple > Mike's > Yerushalayim > Hydrogen > Weekapaug, McGrupp, Maze, Sample, Slave, Highway to Hell
E: Rift

"Antelope" and "Also Sprach" teases in Weekapaug.

The second set of this show left the audience delirious. I didn't know that I was that far gone. Mike's > Simple > Mike's needs absolutely no explanation, but Simple was anything but Simple, as it ascends to its complex peak and then quickly yet meticulously blends into Mike's and then Yerushalayim. Hydrogen flows through the crowd like a warm breeze and lulls everyone into a dream which is abruptly but joyfully interrupted by a welcomed Weekapaug with 2001 teases. —Matthew Ashenfelder

This was the first time I really saw Phish—we met a bunch of friends and headed for the amphitheater. As we awaited admittance, a thunderstorm rolled by and the sky filled with large, amazing lightning bolts that we watched from the lawn once inside. The quick storm passed, followed by a raging show complete with strobe lights in Simple, tramps in Mike's and Trey and Mike lying on their backs during Hydrogen. I was hooked! —Beth Castrol

7/3/94 [ACCESSIBILITY: •••] [ATTEND. 8,096; CAP. 12,500] [TIX $19]
The Ballpark (SeaPAC), Old Orchard Beach, ME

I: My Friend, Poor Heart, Down with Disease, Fee, NICU, Horn, Old Home Place, Reba, Axilla II > Bowie
II: Melt, Lizards, Bouncing, It's Ice, Horse > Silent, Julius, Squirming Coil, Antelope, Suzie
E: Fire

Old Home Place performed acoustic, with same setup as 4/6/94. "Over the Rainbow" jam in Reba, and tease in Bowie. "3rd Stone from the Sun" jam in Melt. Fireworks jam in Antelope, leading into Suzie.

"GameHoist"

6/26/94 Municipal Auditorium, Charleston, WV

Phish tends to diss their albums. They seem to make it through the first round of press interviews okay, but usually by the time the album has been out for a few months, the band members distance themselves from it. *A Picture of Nectar* "tried to meld too many styles." *Rift* "got too caught up in its concept" and "tried too hard."

So by the middle of the summer tour in 1994, it was safe to say that Phish was probably sick of *Hoist*, too. The album had been released in March to general derision from longtime fans of the band—the tunes were too radio-friendly, and there wasn't enough jamming. Of course, critics quieted after Phish broke out the songs in concert, adding long jams to Down with Disease and the "duel" segment to Scent of a Mule.

Once the songs had established their live rhythm, Phish had a bunch of new toys to play with, and by the time the summer tour steamed through the midwest in June, the band was hitting on all cylinders. Show after show saw innovative ideas and incredible jams. As the band headed to the verdant hills of West Virginia for its first show ever in that state, many midwest tourheads had dropped off tour, and many East Coasters planned to come on board starting on June 29 in Raleigh, NC.

So the band snuck into a tiny theater in Charleston, WV, and proceeded to play a show so unusual, so totally without precedent, that it led Trey to dub this the "You Snooze, You Lose" tour, given the band's penchant of playing outstanding shows in out-of-the-way venues during the month of June (and, as it turned out, July).

Opening with Kung—the first time ever—Trey started a Gamehendge narration that ran the entire first set. The first live Gamehendge in over a year, the fourth ever, was certainly a well-earned treat. Where things got really weird, though, was in the second set. The boys offered up Julius...and DwD...and If I Could...and suddenly, people realized they were playing *Hoist*. In order. And in the style of the album—well, sort of. They played the slow Axilla II ending live for the first time (this would surface in many later performances, too), and added a Split Open and Melt jam to the end of Demand. But they also jammed out on Julius and DwD, and dueled in Scent, demonstrating what *Hoist* could have sounded like if Phish ran the record company.

Not necessarily at the level of some of Phish's other holiday performances, but this pre–Independence Day gig ranks as an altogether fun show with some real highlights. A beautiful sunset descended upon this minor league baseball park as the show began, with Trey repeatedly shielding his eyes to peer out at the brilliant colors of the sunset bouncing off the clouds. By the time night fell (and they'd played their first East Coast NICU in ages), they brought the house down with a fireworks jam during Antelope, which carried into a raucous Suzie. During the appropriate Fire encore, a giant Phish logo made of sparklers was ignited to the left of the stage. —Andy Bernstein

A very underrated show. Ask anyone who was actually there and they'll say it was one of their top five. The first set was basic except for a Somewhere over the Rainbow jam during Reba and Axilla II meandering into Bowie. Everyone thought they might do some fireworks because they didn't have a show the next day, but no one knew when. The guys came out for the second set and Trey put a life-size cardboard cutout of the Simpson family on the front of the stage. At the end of the set, when Antelope emerged, so did the fireworks. —Mike D'Amico

7/5/94 [ACCESSIBILITY: ••] [ATTEND. 795; CAP. 3,250] [TIX $20]
The Congress Center, Ottawa, ON
I: Rift, Sample, Curtain > Letter to Jimmy Page > If I Could, Uncle Pen, Stash, Esther, Down with Disease, Adeline
II: Also Sprach, PYITE > Sparkle, Bathtub Gin > Lifeboy, Cities > YEM > Great Gig, Ginseng Sullivan, MSO, Amazing Grace, Golgi
E: GTBT

"Nutcracker" tease in beginning of Esther. Fishman on vacuum for Great Gig. Ginseng Sullivan and MSO performed acoustic/no amplification with same setup as 4/6/94. Last Letter to Jimmy Page, 12/7/89 Baltimore, MD [530 shows]. Last Cities, 9/8/88 Burlington, VT [627 shows].

What got into Phish during their two days in Canada? The tour had already seen the breakouts of Gumbo and NICU, but apparently not content with that, the band exhumed Letter to Jimmy Page (which would appear again at Jones Beach, then move back into retirement) and Cities (which wouldn't make another appearance until 1997) for their first show in Canada's capital. Besides the surprises, Stash rocked out, as did most of the second set. This show lacks incredible jamming, but sure pleases. —Tyler Harris

7/6/94 [ACCESSIBILITY: •••] [ATTEND. 957; CAP. 2,100] [TIX $24.57]
Theater St-Denis, Montreal, QC
I: Llama, Fluffhead, Julius, Bouncing, Reba, Axilla II, My Mind's, Carolina, Bowie
II: Landlady, Poor Heart, Tweezer > Lawn Boy, Chalkdust > BBFCM > Sample > BBFCM, Harry Hood, Tweezer Reprise
E: Old Home Place, Nellie Cane, Memories, Funky Bitch

"Free Ride" tease before Llama. "HYHU" and "Also Sprach" jams in Tweezer. Old Home Place and Nellie Cane performed acoustic/no amplification with same setup as 4/6/94. "Munsters" jams in Llama and Bowie. Last Memories, 12/28/93 Washington, DC [69 shows].

This show is rock-solid from start to end. I'd say there were about 600 phans in attendance in a theater that could hold about 1,800 people. In set I, Llama contains a five-second snippet of the Munsters theme and the jam during Julius goes some interesting places. Then, prior to the beginning of Bowie, Trey dedicates this song to the man himself before the Munster's theme rears its head once again during the intro. And what a smoking Bowie it is. That's just set I. Set II opens with a great Landlady that finds Trey sustaining one note for a minute and 15 seconds. It moves on to one of the best Tweezers ever and a four-song encore taboot! —Brian Gressler

7/8/94 [ACCESSIBILITY: ••••] [ATTEND. 31,567 (BOTH SHOWS); CAP. 19,900] [TIX $19.50–$21.50]
Great Woods Center for the Performing Arts, Mansfield, MA
I: Llama > N20 > Lizards > Tela > Wilson > AC/DC Bag > Forbin's > Mockingbird > Sloth > McGrupp > Divided Sky
II: Rift, Sample, Reba > Yerushalayim, It's Ice, Stash, YEM > Frankenstein > YEM, Julius, Golgi
E: Nellie Cane, Cavern

First set contained a complete Gamehendge narration by Trey—fifth ever live Gamehendge. Fishman on vacuum for N20. "Manteca" tease in Reba. Stash from this show appears on A Live One.

Rainy and foggy, a purple sky, and lightning? Then it happened: out came Gamehendge, and we all felt it. The craziest Phish show ever. I'll contest it with anyone! —Langston Knipler

Because of this show, there are about 20,000 extra Phishheads who can claim to have seen a Gamehendge. A thrill beyond almost all thrills. One thing I really enjoyed is how they used the bass line from McGrupp during the narration between songs. On the actual Man Who Stepped into Yesterday tape, it's a portion of Esther which serves this purpose. Having the McGrupp also played in its entirety was an additional treat. —Andy Bernstein

Of course the first set is Gamehendge. Wow. But the second set deserves as much recognition as the first: a powerful Rift to start, the best Stash ever in my opinion (it's on A Live One), and an awesome YEM that sucks its way beautifully into Frankenstein. A must-own show. —Chip Croteau

7/9/94 [ACCESSIBILITY: ••••] [ATTEND. 31,567 (BOTH SHOWS); CAP. 19,900] [TIX $19.50–$21.50]
Great Woods Center for the Performing Arts, Mansfield, MA
I: Runaway Jim, Foam, Gumbo, Maze, Guelah, Scent of a Mule, Down with Disease, Horse > Silent, Antelope
II: Also Sprach > Melt, Fluffhead, Poor Heart, Tweezer > Lifeboy, Sparkle > BBJ, Harry Hood, Suzie
E: Sleeping Monkey > Tweezer Reprise

7/10/94 [ACCESSIBILITY: •••] [ATTEND. 14,774; CAP. 25,105] [TIX $16–$18.50]
Saratoga Performing Arts Center, Saratoga Springs, NY
I: Chalkdust, Horn, Peaches, Rift, Stash, If I Could, My Friend, Julius, Cavern
II: Sample, Bowie, Glide, Ya Mar, Mike's > Hydrogen > Weekapaug, Bouncing, Squirming Coil, Crimes of the Mind
E: Golgi, Rocky Top

Trey yells, "Who is she?" during Ya Mar. "Low Rider" jam in Mike's. The Dude of Life on vocals for Crimes of the Mind.

SARATOGA PERFORMING ARTS CENTER, Saratoga Springs, NY

Sunday, July 10, 1994

So I lose my keys at Great Woods. Not the first time I've lost a set of keys and won't be the last. A real bitch though. I looked around my car but they were nowhere to be found. I'd been selling shirts all day and also taken a long walk through the woods. I figured I lost them then.

The next day at Saratoga I had kind of forgotten about it, intentionally. I really wasn't looking forward to making that plaintive call to my landlord, who couldn't stand me anyway. Shirt sales are going okay, and then this one dude says, "I saw you selling those shirts back in the woods yesterday."

"I lost my keys in those woods," I lament, just making small talk. It was the first time I'd mentioned it all day.

"What kind of keys?" he asks. "Was it a Volkswagon key, on a blue key chain?"

"YES!"

Turns out I didn't even lose them in the woods. He found them near his car. And he just happened to have picked them up and brought them to the next show.

One in a fuckin' million.

—Andy Bernstein

7/13/94 [ACCESSIBILITY: ••••] [ATTEND. 4,975; CAP. 6,000] [TIX $10.50–$20.50]
Big Birch Concert Pavilion, Patterson, NY
I: Buried Alive > Poor Heart, Sample, Foam, Mango, Down with Disease, Fee, It's Ice, FEFY, I Didn't Know, Melt
II: Possum, Cavern/Wilson/Cavern > NICU > Tweezer > Julius > Tweezer > BBFCM > Tweezer > Mound, Slave, Suzie
E: MSO, Tweezer Reprise

Fishman on trombone for I Didn't Know. Aborted ending on Possum led to elongated "blues jam." Cavern started, then Wilson sung, then returned to Cavern closing chorus. "Woody Woodpecker" tease in Tweezer prior to segue into Julius; "Rock and Roll Is Here to Stay" tease in Tweezer after return from Julius. BBFCM is played loosely to the tune of Scent of a Mule. "Slave" jams in Suzie.

This show is the ultimate expression of Phish's transitional grooving. In the second set, there is simply nothing they can't pull off. Following Possum to open the set, the Cavern jam kicks in strong, but wait, it sounds a bit like Wilson too! Suddenly Trey busts out Wilson and afterwards they go right back into the end of Cavern. This winds right into NICU with a great swing into Tweezer. Just when you're getting lost in the Tweezer jam, Julius emerges. There is an oldies jam in the middle, then back to Tweezer, which soon finds its way to BBFCM which has a bluegrassy, Scent of a Mule tinge to it. Relentlessly, Tweezer again emerges, but morphs into Mound. Slave follows, which is excellent, then Suzie, with reoccurring Slave samples in it. —Adam Davidoff

Let's talk about the second set. The madness begins at the end of Possum with an extra-long ending. Then they play the music to Cavern, but when it comes time for the first verse, Trey sings the words to Wilson! "Can you still have fun" > "Give the director a serpent deflector" ends Cavern! Tweezer features a Woody Woodpecker tease from Trey and then there's Julius, out of nowhere. Wow! Great show. —Mike Garofalow

7/14/94 [ACCESSIBILITY: ••] [ATTEND. 7,561; CAP. 12,727] [TIX $10–$19.50]
Finger Lakes Performing Arts Center, Canandaigua, NY
I: Runaway Jim, Bouncing > PYITE > Stash >TMWSIY > Avenu > TMWSIY, Scent of a Mule, Fluffhead, Horse > Silent, Antelope
II: Also Sprach > Sample, Maze, If I Could, Uncle Pen, YEM, Sparkle > BBJ, Harry Hood, Highway to Hell
E: Chalkdust

7/15/94 [ACCESSIBILITY: •••] [ATTEND. 11,019; CAP. 11,019] [TIX $20]
Jones Beach Music Theater, Wantagh, NY
I: Rift, Sample, Divided Sky, Gumbo, Foam, Fee, Melt, Golgi
II: Letter to Jimmy Page > Bowie, Bouncing, Reba > It's Ice > Yerushalayim, Dog Faced Boy, Julius, HYHU > Setting Sail > HYHU, Runaway Jim
E: Sleeping Monkey, Rocky Top

First solar-powered Phish concert, administered by Greenpeace. "Jessica" jam in Bowie. "Brazil" tease in Reba. Fishman on vacuum for Setting Sail, with audience sing-along. Last Setting Sail, 4/20/91 Rochester, NY [383 shows].

7/16/94 [ACCESSIBILITY: ••••] [ATTEND. 11,445; CAP. 15,000] [TIX $20]
SummerStage, Sugarbush North, Fayston, VT
I: Golgi, Down with Disease > N20 > Stash, Lizards, Cavern, Horse > Silent, Maze, Sparkle, Sample
II: Antelope > Catapult > Antelope, Harpua > Also Sprach > Harpua > AC/DC Bag, Scent of a Mule, Harry Hood, Contact, Chalkdust
E: Suzie

Fishman on vacuum for N20.

A legendary show, and I'm so glad I was there! The dentist scenario in N20 was hilarious and even had me feeling dizzy, and then they came in with the drill, metaphorically, in the second set with Antelope/Catapult/Antelope. This Catapult was particularly memorable because it was right before Trey's wedding and after he sung the lines, "There ain't gonna be no wedding," Fish came in with, "You wish!" It was also the night the Shoemaker-Levy comet slammed into Jupiter, and during Trey's narration in Harpua he reminded us of that fact. An absolute 10, wonderful, incredible, cosmic show! The only bad thing about the whole event was the bus situation. The majority of the parking area was away from the mountain, and they bused virtually the entire audience to the concert grounds with only about 10 or 20 buses. It was not unlike herding cattle into pasture—moo! —Lara Wittels

A real mental show, especially the second set. Antelope contains evil shrills and laughter throughout, not to mention Catapult and a Simpsons signal before the final jam! I think a lot of people went out of their minds. Next came Harpua, with praise for Vermont and the story of an old mountain man who wandered around during soundcheck. They see the comet crash into Jupiter, which leads to 2001, then back to the end of Harpua. —Matthew Ashenfelder

What would be better than hanging out on a mountain all day and seeing your favorite band that night? You know the setlist, but did you know Mike and Fish hung out in the parking lot for a good part of the day? Or that Trey was running around onstage with a megaphone like a crazy person during Antelope? —Mike D'Amico

1994 FALL Trick or Trout

Continuing their heavy touring year, Phish returned to the road in early October after just a couple of months off (months which, among other things, saw Trey and Sue get married). The first show marked the debut of Guyute, a song some viewed as the next Phish epic. But the tour's biggest highlight may have been an impromptu week-long tour with bluegrass pal the Reverend Jeff Mosier across the Midwest. And, of course, there were the amazing Halloween and New Year's shows, too.

10/7/94 [ACCESSIBILITY: •••] [ATTEND. 6,177; CAP. 6,177] [TIX $18.50]
Stabler Arena, Lehigh University, Bethlehem, PA
I: My Friend, Julius, Glide, Poor Heart, Divided Sky, Guelah, Stash, Guyute, Golgi
II: Maze, Horse > Silent, Reba, Wilson, Scent of a Mule, Tweezer, Lifeboy, MSO, Tweezer Reprise
E: Foreplay > Long Time, Cavern

Foreplay/Long Time featured Trey on acoustic guitar, Mike on banjo, Fishman on Madonna washboard, and Page on stand-up bass. Concert debuts: Guyute, Foreplay, Long Time.

The first show of the tour included the first Guyute ever, and also marked the debut of the spinning lights that go in circles during Tweeprise—I almost fell over when Chris turned them on. The best part of the show was the crowd, which was very aware of when to be quiet and when to participate. After this show there was one of the biggest and best drum circles I have ever seen. —Joshua Howley

The highlight of this show for me had to be the acoustic version of Boston's Long Time. We had just listened to two great sets and were hoping for a Suzie closer. Instead the boys came out with a banjo, stand-up bass, guitar and Fishman on a brass-plated washboard. A hush fell over the audience. For the first few moments, no one knew what they were playing. When we realized what it was, we practically fell down laughing. —Beth Castrol

10/8/94 [ACCESSIBILITY: ••••] [ATTEND. 10,356; CAP. 10,356] [TIX $18.50]
Patriot Center, George Mason University, Fairfax, VA
I: Chalkdust, Horn, Sparkle, Down with Disease, Guyute, Fee, It's Ice, Lawn Boy > Antelope

We arrived late, and ended up in this backwoods corner of the south lot, then busted out the hits before heading to the bus. I was going to pop two, but they were folded over and I accidentally chomped three. Zack, therefore, had to do the same.

By the time we made it over to the bus it was kicking in. And by the time we got off (the bus), it was pretty damn clear that we were going to trip harder than we'd ever tripped before.

Made it into the venue after about three songs, and at this point, we were starting to enter that scared phase where communication is challenged and any sort of obstacle requires exacting care to traverse. After getting through the gates, we faced this mass of fucking people on a steep goddamn mountain. There's no way in hell we could handle the crowd, but there didn't seem to be a way around them either. That left no choice but to charge on through, heading straight for the back.

Scariest thing I've ever seen, all those faces rushing by, so fast they would have meshed together even if we hadn't been tripping bugoongas.

Bugoongas I tell you.

We made it to the way back, away from the crowds, a good two hundred yards from the stage. Once you're away from people and a safe distance from the stage, everything's supposed to be okay. But it just wasn't. We were cold, and haggard. If felt like we had just gotten the shit kicked out of us. Zack said it was the climb, that we weren't used to running that high that fast. He was partially right. But most of the cause was those little pieces of paper. They were digging in hard, so hard that the amazing visual spectacle from that mountain, the stage dancing in front of a shimmering pond, flanked by a panorama which stretched thirty miles across the valley, that view was just too much. I had to remind myself that gravity only worked in one direction—that I couldn't fall *in* to the valley.

Everything was so loud. Not just the music. The breeze blowing against my arms, a sensation which in other trips I found to give a glorious sense of self-affirmation, was nails against a chalkboard. The sight of trees shaking with that same breeze: the sound of a locomotive.

Call it sensory overload.

I tried to shake everything out, to eliminate every bit of stimulus by staring into the solid blue sky which thankfully lacked even a cloud. But my mind found disturbance where there was none, as the blank sky instantly became patterned with geometric visuals, snowflakes of unwanted sensations. Then a very real horsefly buzzed through my view, and became three or four fucking horseflies, and left a wake, a wave of thick air behind it.

By the time the set break rolled around, we were still cold, still scared, and as far as we could tell, still not coming down.

It conjured memories of Arctic adventurers on National Geographic Specials sharing tales of sure doom only reversed by their experience and positive thinking. In this area, I was long on experience but short of positive thinking. As I shivered like a wet puppy whose mother had just been run over by a bus, a supple tune rang out from down the slope. I hadn't even realized that the band had taken the stage, but the staggered first notes of Antelope instantly transformed the scene.

"Phish saves the day," Zack quipped.

Now, the Antelope to start the second set at Sugarbush was not your everyday Antelope. We're talking about dueling, atonal, arrhythmic stops and starts; we're talking underwater effects; we're talking Catapult right in the fucking middle. And Trey was screaming. Fucking screaming. And I'm supposed to be coming back to reality.

As this splendid, unparalleled Antelope continued to build, sucking in the entire crowd, I felt repelled. Turning away from the stage, I began climbing away, searching for shelter from the overwhelming tidal mass which was the music.

Adding to the peril was the fact that the sound on that mountain was as crystal clear as any I'd ever experienced. It must have been the mountain air or some weird acoustic phenomenon, but a good fifth of a mile from the stage, the music was so refined, so pure, and mercilessly loud.

As Trey repeatedly, unendingly begged for some spike through the climax, I continued to pace upwards, lumbering past the last approving spectators as the song's final declaration was made. With the last chords pounding away, I felt a break ensuing. An Antelope like that could only be followed by a junkie short tune which would give the band and everyone else a chance to catch their collective breath. Still climbing and looking away, I heard words so clear it was as if Trey was whispering in my ear.

"Oom Pa Pa, Oom Pa Pa, Omm Pa Paaa."

Anger, at myself, took over. I was telling myself that it was the greatest Phish show of all time, and I couldn't enjoy it because I went and took so much acid. But that feeling was soon overpowered by complete fright. The first verses of Harpua, distinctly recognized for that enticing melody I loved in every other state, retained its well-structured charm, and that, more than anything, sent me fleeing upward with greater intensity.

The sound was so good, it hurt.

I was climbing up the mountain to escape the splendor of the music.

Clearly, I had completely lost it. Zack, a true friend, took the climb with me. I looked at him and saw waves of colors unpeeling themselves from the ground

"Zack, we've never tripped this hard," I managed to say. "Oh, no," he agreed, shaking his head with assuredness.

As the band whipped in to Also Sprach inside Harpua and then explained that Poster Nutbag had been hit by a comet, the pain wouldn't let up. My best Colonel Forbin imitation continued until we were well past the spectator area, and at least two thousand feet from the stage. Miraculously, the voice of the band only became clearer, and the bizarre, nimble pluckings of AC/DC Bag resonated with the same crushing elegance as the songs which preceded them.

Barely clinging to my wits, and still at the height of discomfort and approaching the reaches of terror, I remembered a conversation with an older friend who, long past her acid days, told me, "If you ever have a bad trip, you will never forget it and you will never trip again."

I wasn't there yet, but I could feel the precipice approaching—sense the spiraling, uncontrolled agony which awaited if I lost grasp of whatever grounding endured. Searching for any sobering, comforting thought, it became clear that I had hit the end of the road with acid. There were no regrets. I'd gotten a hell of a lot out of it, and always wondered just how far I could go; my perch upon the mountain offered a clear, concrete answer.

There was a limit, and a point at which tripping would only force me away from the things I enjoyed the most. I shared this logic with Zack. Although I don't think he really believed me, he acknowledged that it was "the end of an era." Then, still requiring comfort, I announced that it was time to tell my parents that I used LSD. This one, Zack was slower to accept: "You're joking."

But it made perfect sense. Acid was such a part of everything I was. The most productive decisions I ever made came to me while tripping. My sense of humor, in so many ways, developed around the thought patterns and experiences of taking the acid plunge. Everyone who knew me knew how I felt. Knew that half my stories began with, "So I was tripping my balls off with Zack..." And yet, to have the people who gave birth to me not know that, was nothing but a complete lie—it was like living with strangers.

And seeing as how I wasn't going to do it again, coming clean made perfect sense. This resolve somehow brought me back to this planet. Maybe not the surface but at least the breathable atmosphere. My straight-ahead climb became more of a zig-zag, and then just a broad, back-and-forth pace.

I was squeezed between competitive forces; on one side, the blanket of optimism which told me that if I was just honest, and avoided future incursions, everything would be all right. Then, from beneath, came that still menacing force which thundered its bursting magnificence with unrelenting exactitude. The Harry Hood, chimed by four minuscule figures from four football fields below, was so *big*.

continued

Sugarbush North continued

A skyscraper of a Harry Hood. A colossus. Chalkdust then jabbed at me like shattered windowpanes with each of its advancing, layered guitar licks. My pacing continued into the encore. The Suzie proved my suspicion that Phish was, in fact, busting out one of the greatest shows of all time.

Continually I had the need to find and articulate every reason why my parents would be informed of my indiscretions, and I wondered how long after the show it would take before finally my peak was achieved and I could begin a safe rest from the goblins which clawed from the sides.

Pacing, during Suzie, speaking loudly and seriously about what I had to do to improve my life and achieve salvation, I interrupted myself. "Excuse me," I pronounced, and then momentarily turned my authoritative stomp in to a whirling, pirouetting dance to Suzie, right on the beat, until I faced my original direction and continued pontificating.

Zack cracked up. A few seconds later, I did too. It was the first time during this glorious show that my mind allowed myself unadulterated pleasure from the music. I knew I was going to be all right.

And no, I never told my parents.

—David Porter

II: Also Sprach > Sample, Rift, Mike's > Simple > Mike's > Hydrogen > Weekapaug > Fluffhead, HYHU > Purple Rain > HYHU, Harry Hood > Suzie
E: Foreplay > Long Time, Rocky Top

A dozen members of a girls' soccer team did a " We Are the Muppets" cheer between Mike's and Simple. Fishman on vacuum for Purple Rain. Foreplay/Long Time performed acoustic with setup of 10/7/94.

This is my pick for the most underrated show of all time, one which I feel deserves classic status. The first set highlight was the second-ever performance of Guyute, which was so satisfying because it was still ringing in my head from the night before. It also included a wonderfully pure DwD—the jam didn't veer off very much from the dominant chords and melody, but it had so much energy, proving just how great those chords and melody are. But this show really makes its mark in set II, an unrelenting hour and a half of music with a girls soccer team doing a cheer in Mike's and an amazing segue into Simple (where Simple works best, when you're already in psychedelic la-la land!). —Andy Bernstein

10/9/94 [ACCESSIBILITY: ••] [ATTEND. 3,983; CAP. 3,983] [TIX $18.50]
A.J. Palumbo Center, Pittsburgh, PA
I: Runaway Jim, Foam, FEFY, Curtain > Dog Faced Boy, Melt, Squirming Coil
II: Bowie, Bouncing, Scent of a Mule, YEM, Amazing Grace, Julius, Contact, Possum
E: Sleeping Monkey, Poor Heart

Squirming Coil from this show appears on A Live One.

10/10/94 [ACCESSIBILITY: ••] [ATTEND. 2,821; CAP. 2,821] [TIX $18.50]
Palace Theater, Louisville, KY
I: Sample, Divided Sky, Horse > Silent, Sparkle, Stash, Guyute, Old Home Place, Ginseng Sullivan, Nellie Cane, Chalkdust
II: Golgi, Maze, Esther, Tweezer, Fee > Rift, Down with Disease, HYHU > Love You > HYHU, Slave
E: Foreplay > Long Time, Tweezer Reprise

Steve Cooley on banjo for Old Home Place, Ginseng, Sullivan and Nellie Cane, with Trey on acoustic guitar, Mike on banjo, Fishman on Madonna washboard, and Page on mouth piano. Fishman on vacuum for Love You. Foreplay/Long Time performed acoustic with setup of 10/7/94.

10/12/94 [ACCESSIBILITY: ••] [ATTEND. 2,313; CAP. 2,313] [TIX $16.50]
Orpheum Theater, Memphis, TN
I: My Friend, Reba, Sloth, Poor Heart, Melt, Lizards, Guelah, Julius, Adeline
II: Peaches, Bowie, Bouncing, Scent of a Mule, YEM, Nellie Cane, Foreplay > Long Time, Harry Hood, Sample
E: GTBT

Nellie Cane performed acoustic with Trey on acoustic guitar, Mike on banjo, Fishman on mandolin and Page on stand-up bass. Foreplay/Long Time performed acoustic with setup of 10/7/94.

10/13/94 [ACCESSIBILITY: ••] [ATTEND. 2,340; CAP. 3,000] [TIX $10–$16]
Grove Arena, University of Mississippi, Oxford, MS
I: Llama, Gumbo, All Things, Down with Disease, I Didn't Know, Foam, FEFY, Sparkle, Stash
II: Old Home Place, Antelope, If I Could, It's Ice, Amazing Grace, Mike's > Simple > Mike's > Yerushalayim > Weekapaug, Foreplay > Long Time, Cavern
E: Fire

Fishman on Madonna washboard for I Didn't Know. Foreplay/Long Time performed acoustic with setup of 10/7/94.

The outdoor atmosphere at this show was perfect. Everyone was just chillin'; when the music started it was like an explosion of excitement with the upbeat Llama. There wasn't much deep, intense jamming in the first set, but the band still added some kicks. I must say that I Didn't Know was a five-star performance. Then came an incredible Antelope, chock full of teases, seemingly never-ending. It almost made my heart stop with the anticipation of the retreat of the magical guitar trickery. —Chad Mars

10/14/94 [ACCESSIBILITY: •••] [ATTEND. 1,888; CAP. 1,888] [TIX $15–$17.50]
McAlister Auditorium, Tulane University, New Orleans, LA
I: Buried Alive > Sample, Divided Sky, Horse > Silent, PYITE, Bathtub Gin, Adeline, Rift, Forbin's > Mockingbird, Julius
II: Curtain > Tweezer > Lifeboy, Guyute, Chalkdust, Nellie Cane, Beaumont Rag, Foreplay > Long Time, Squirming Coil, Tweezer Reprise
E: Ya Mar, Cavern

Nellie Cane and Bow Mountain Rag performed acoustic with Trey on acoustic guitar, Mike on banjo, Fishman on mandolin, and Page on stand-up bass. Foreplay/Long Time performed acoustic with setup of 10/7/94. Carl Gerhard on trumpet and Michael Ray on trumpet and shaker for Ya Mar and Cavern. Concert debut: Beaumont Rag (also known incorrectly as "Bow Mountain Rag").

Buried Alive is perhaps the best opener they can do, and this one is no joke. PYITE is always good, and they do a weird story in Col. Forbin's about leaving your body that was pretty cool. Second set began with The Curtain. Guyute is always a treat; this is one of the early ones. They played some little acoustic numbers, including a first-timer, before Michael Ray and Carl Gerhard played the hell out of Ya Mar and Cavern. In New Orleans, you need jazz, and the boys didn't fail to meet my expectations. —Christopher Mills

10/15/94 [ACCESSIBILITY: ••••] [ATTEND. 9,979; CAP. 9,979] [TIX $13–$16]
Oak Mountain Amphitheatre, Pelham, AL
I: Wilson, Sparkle, Simple > Maze, Glide, Reba, Down with Disease, Golgi
II: Also Sprach > Runaway Jim, Halley's > Scent of a Mule, YEM > Catapult > YEM, Amazing Grace, Foreplay > Long Time, Bouncing, Suzie
E: Drums > Jam > The Maker

The Dave Matthews Band opened. Foreplay/Long Time performed acoustic with setup of 10/7/94. DMB joined Phish for the encores, which started with Fishman and Carter Beaufort drumming; Dave Matthews sang lead on The Maker. "Moby Dick" jam in Jam before The Maker. Concert debut: The Maker.

10/16/94 [ACCESSIBILITY: ••] [ATTEND. 3,139; CAP. 3,600] [TIX $18.50]
Chattanooga Memorial Auditorium, Chattanooga, TN
I: Rift, Horn, Foam, Fee, Melt, TMWSIY > Avenu > TMWSIY, Axilla, Possum
II: Landlady, Poor Heart, Julius, Fluffhead, BBJ, Antelope, Dog Faced Boy, Adeline, Sample
E: Highway to Hell
E2: Harpua

Dog Faced Boy performed acoustic with Trey on acoustic guitar, Mike on banjo, Fishman on balloon and Page on mouth piano. "Flashlight" jam in Harpua. Last Axilla (part I), 8/16/93 St. Louis, MO [93 shows].

10/18/94 [ACCESSIBILITY: •••] [ATTEND. 1,562; CAP. 4,112] [TIX $8–$14]
Memorial Gym, Vanderbilt University, Nashville, TN
I: Simple, My Friend, I Didn't Know, Poor Heart, Stash, Tela, It's Ice, Guyute, Divided Sky, Amazing Grace
II: Bowie, Horse > Silent, Reba, Scent of a Mule, Lifeboy, Old Home Place, Beaumont Rag, Nellie Cane, Llama
E: MSO

Fishman on vacuum for I Didn't Know. Bela Fleck on banjo for second set (starting with Scent) and encore. Old Home Place, Beaumont Rag, Nellie Cane, and Llama performed acoustic with Trey on acoustic guitar, Mike on stand-up bass, Fishman on Madonna washboard, and Page on mouth piano. Llama started acoustic and finished electric as the members of Phish switched back to their normal instruments in the middle of the song.

During set two, Phish introduced the maestro of modern jazz/rock banjo, Bela Fleck. He hopped on stage for Scent, and after hearing the song with banjo, I felt like all the previous Scents lacked something special. The fivesome then played a series of classic bluegrass tunes that emitted a laid-back, comfortable and content feeling. The most notable, however, was Llama in a bluegrass context which led to a full-blown electric finish, during which Phish and Fleck communicated as only true musicians can. —John Foley

My God, have you heard the Llama at this show? It's amazing! Trey starts strumming the chords on his acoustic guitar, and the crowd roars in recognition when he sings the first line. After the opening acoustic segment, Bela takes a gorgeous banjo solo as the members of Phish one by one migrate back to their electric instruments. They re-enter the jam, then Trey trades licks with Bela as the song wanders for awhile, the jam growing quieter and quieter. Trey thanks the crowd before roaring the song to its finish. —Ed Smith

10/20/94 [ACCESSIBILITY: ••] [ATTEND. 1,905; CAP. 1,905] [TIX $19.50]
Mahaffey Theatre, St. Petersburg, FL
I: Runaway Jim, Golden Lady, Poor Heart, Guelah, Melt > Kung > Melt, Esther, Julius, Guyute, Golgi
II: Lengthwise > Maze, McGrupp, Rift, Harry Hood, Nellie Cane, Foreplay > Long Time, Chalkdust
E: Sample

Nellie Cane and Foreplay/Long Time performed acoustic. Last Lengthwise, 8/13/93 Indianapolis, IN [98 shows]. Concert debut: Golden Lady.

I thought Phish would opt for a Florida version of Harry Hood for inclusion on A Live One, because anyone who's heard this performance will tell you that it hasn't been matched since. And the band did go south for their pick, but they opted for the Gainesville version from a few nights later. Maybe they screwed up their notes—this Hood traverses many interesting places, rising to a glorious peak that makes you want to stand up on your heels and embrace the music. —Melissa Wolcott

10/21/94 [ACCESSIBILITY: ••••] [ATTEND. 3,460; CAP. 3,550] [TIX $16.75–$18.75]
Sunrise Musical Theatre, Sunrise, FL
I: Fee, Down with Disease > Foam, Mango, Old Home Place, Stash, Lizards, Dog Faced Boy, Antelope
II: Also Sprach > Mike's > Simple > Mike's > Hydrogen > Weekapaug, Sleeping Monkey, Curtain > FEFY, Scent of a Mule, Slave
E: Adeline, Foreplay > Long Time, Cavern

"Can't You Hear Me Knocking" jam at end of Weekapaug. Foreplay/Long Time performed acoustic with setup of 10/7/94.

10/22/94 [ACCESSIBILITY: ••] [ATTEND. 1,459; CAP. 6,000] [TIX $17.50–$20]
The Edge Concert Field, Orlando, FL
I: Suzie, Divided Sky, Gumbo, Axilla II, Rift, Melt, Fluffhead, Julius
II: Peaches, Bowie, Horse > Silent, Dinner and a Movie, Tweezer > Wilson, Reba, Amazing Grace, AC/DC Bag, Highway to Hell
E: Uncle Pen, Tweezer Reprise

Fireworks from a Disney World event nearby could be seen during Fluffhead and Julius.

10/23/94 [ACCESSIBILITY: •••••]
Band Shell, University of Florida, Gainesville, FL
I: Chalkdust > My Friend, Sparkle, Simple, Poor Heart, Stash > Catapult > Stash, Tela > Maze, Sample
II: Runaway Jim, Bouncing > Halley's > YEM, Down with Disease > Purple Rain > HYHU, Harry Hood, Fee, GTBT
E: Squirming Coil

Free outdoor concert. Soundcheck: Ginseng Sullivan, Funky Bitch, Golden Lady. "Gypsy Queen" jam in Runaway Jim. "Vibration of Life" during YEM. "Another One Bites the Dust" and "Mission Impossible" teases in YEM, and "Astronomy Domine" themes in YEM vocal jam. Fishman on vacuum for Purple Rain. Harry Hood from this show appears on A Live One.

My favorite part were the trampolines during YEM. Maybe Trey's ankle was a little weak, but he literally fell jumping off. Mike starts up with Another One Bites the Dust, and Trey answers back by playing the *Mission Impossible* theme song. The Purple Rain actually made me cry, like no other Rain since. —Tony Hume

This was a great show for several reasons. First, it was free, and the Band Shell is a great place to see a concert. Second, I got to meet Trey between sets. He was hilarious as he teased some guy who was apparently upset because his girlfriend was madly in love with Trey. Trey told the guy to bring his girlfriend over and he would act like an asshole so she wouldn't like him anymore. Finally, this was a first show for many of my friends who are now loyal phans. I love when I introduce someone to the band and they have positive reactions to it. —Chris Haines

[10/25/94] *Crimes of the Mind* released on Elektra.

10/25/94 [ACCESSIBILITY: ••] [ATTEND. 4,503; CAP. 4,503] [TIX $19.50]
Atlanta Civic Center, Atlanta, GA
I: Fee, Llama, Horn, Julius, Horse > Silent, Melt, Lizards, Sample
II: Mike's > Simple > Mango > Weekapaug > Yerushalayim, Glide, Axilla II > Jesus Left Chicago > BBJ, HYHU > Brain > HYHU, Possum
E: Foreplay > Long Time, Golgi

Fishman on vacuum for Brain. "Magilla" tease in Possum. Foreplay/Long Time performed acoustic with setup of 10/7/94. Last Brain, 12/29/93 New Haven, CT [90 shows].

10/26/94 [ACCESSIBILITY: ••] [ATTEND. 3,500; CAP. 3,500] [TIX $12–$18]
Varsity Gym, Appalachian State University, Boone, NC
I: Simple, It's Ice, NICU, Antelope, Guyute, Dog Faced Boy, Scent of a Mule, Oh Kee > Suzie, Runaway Jim
II: Rift, Bouncing, Reba, Axilla II, YEM > Catapult, HYHU > Cracklin' Rosie > HYHU, Bowie
E: Nellie Cane, Foreplay > Long Time, Amazing Grace

"Vibration of Life" in YEM. Nellie Cane and Foreplay/Long Time performed acoustic with setup of 10/7/94.

I love to hear Trey talk to the audience. I look forward to hearing him speak, whether it be a Harpua Rap or a simple "Thanks for coming out tonight." Well, imagine my pleasure upon hearing the encore of this show. When they retake the stage, Trey comments on how much they've enjoyed their stay in the mountain-surrounded town of Boone, and even compares it to Burlington. This was ultracool for me because I lived there a while. Phish goes on to play some mountain music, followed by bluegrass Boston, then closes it up with Amazing Grace. Man, I dig Phish's diversity. —Amanda Litton

10/27/94 [ACCESSIBILITY: ••] [ATTEND. 6,059; CAP. 6,059] [TIX $16.50–$18.50]
University Hall, University of Virginia, Charlottesville, VA
I: Wilson, Sparkle, Maze, Forbin's > Mockingbird, Divided Sky, Horse > Silent, Poor Heart, Cavern
II: Julius, Ya Mar, Tweezer, Contact, BBFCM, Down with Disease, Adeline
E: Slave > Icculus, Tweezer Reprise

"Vibration of Life" in Forbin's.

You know it's a strange show when Phish jams out the Tweezer Reprise more than the Tweezer. No, seriously, this show does have a unique Tweezer Rep. that goes on for at least a few minutes more than normal. If you like Tweezer Reprise, you'll love this show. Otherwise, keep moving... nothing much to hear here. —Lee Johnston

10/28/94 [ACCESSIBILITY: ••] [ATTEND. 2,713; CAP. 2,713] [TIX $17.50]
Galliard Auditorium, Charleston, SC
I: I Didn't Know, Llama, Guelah, Scent of a Mule, Stash, Glide, Axilla II, All Things, Sample, Carolina
II: Also Sprach > Bowie > Manteca > Bowie, Lizards, Rift, Lifeboy, Chalkdust, Old Home Place, Nellie Cane, Foreplay > Long Time
E: Fee, Highway to Hell

Fishman on vacuum for I Didn't Know. Old Home Place and Nellie performed acoustic with Trey on acoustic guitar, Mike on banjo, Fishman on mandolin, and Page on stand-up bass. Foreplay/Long Time performed acoustic with setup of 10/7/94. Last Manteca, 5/5/93 Albany, NY [133 shows].

10/29/94 [ACCESSIBILITY: ••••] [ATTEND. 3,266; CAP. 3,266] [TIX $18.50]
Spartanburg Memorial Auditorium, Spartanburg, SC
I: My Friend, Sparkle, Simple, Runaway Jim, Foam, Lawn Boy, Melt > Buffalo Bill > Makisupa > Rift
II: Down with Disease > TMWSIY > Avenu > TMWSIY > Sparks > Uncle Pen, YEM, HYHU > Bike > HYHU, Antelope > Sleeping Monkey > Antelope
E: Harry Hood

Fishman on vacuum for Bike. Last Buffalo Bill, 11/21/92 Stony Brook, NY [224 shows]. Last Sparks, 5/7/94 Dallas, TX [65 shows].

Lost in the shadow of Glens Falls is Spartanburg, a groovy gig for the thinking phan. A raging, near-chaotic Split Open and Melt jam in the first set develops a reggae beat, and before you can say "Makisupa Policeman," the boys are playing Buffalo Bill! This song, considered lost forever since its debut in November '92, has an incredible bassline that leads to another reggae jam and then, naturally, to Makisupa. Out of Makisupa, they RAGE into a jam that finally leads to... Rift. Set II is also full of interesting transitions, like TMWISY > Sparks and Antelope with Sleeping Monkey dropped in the middle. —Rich Mazer

10/31/94 [ACCESSIBILITY: •••••] [ATTEND. 7,715; CAP. 7,715] [TIX $18.50]
Glens Falls Civic Center, Glens Falls, NY
I: Frankenstein, Sparkle, Simple, Divided Sky, Harpua, Julius, Horse > Silent, Reba, Golgi
II: Speak to Me tease > "Ed Sullivan Introduction" > Back in the USSR,

Monday, October 31, 1994

GLENS FALLS CIVIC CENTER, Glens Falls, NY

I was on tour during fall '94 and had missed only a few shows when Halloween rolled around.

On our way to Glens Falls, we made a pit stop in Ithaca, NY, where my friends were going to school. I really didn't have much money or time but I really waned to make a good costume. I came up with the idea to go as a "Mounds" candy bar. The only problem was how to make it, but I figured it out in a couple of hours and became convinced it would be a killer costume.

The next day showtime rolled around, and on went the most constrictive, backbreaking costume I saw that night. As I walked to the door someone handed me a little paper "treat." Subsequently, this was the last time I had a "treat." Nonetheless, there I was, a huge tripping candy bar. As I walked through the entrance somebody handed me a piece of paper saying I had qualified to be judged for the costume contest. After the first judging, about seven or eight people were eliminated, leaving myself, a Harry Hood, a Lawnboy, a Bathtub Gin, a Tela, and a Lizard. Oops, forgot about the AC/DC Bag. We were all ushered backstage—the final judging would soon take place on stage.

During the encore, they brought us onto the stage and the audience voted by applause. After an initial round I was left on stage with the Lawnboy. A couple more applause votes later I found myself with a trophy in my left hand, looking out at thousands of people cheering. This was the most intense rush I have ever felt.

A strange postscript: the very next show I was standing by the tour bus when Trey appeared. We spoke a little and I asked if there was any room on the guest list for a wayward candybar. He said, "You got it, man." Amazing, miracled by Trey.

—Shawn "Skip" McFarland

Dear Prudence, Glass Onion, Ob-La-Di Ob-La-Da, Wild Honey Pie, Continuing Story of Bungalow Bill, Guitar Gently Weeps, Happiness Is a Warm Gun, Martha My Dear, I'm So Tired, Blackbird, Piggies, Rocky Raccoon, Don't Pass Me By, Why Don't We Do It in the Road, I Will, Julia, Birthday Jam, Yer Blues, Mother Nature's Son, Everybody's Got Something to Hide Except for Me and My Monkey, Sexy Sadie, Helter Skelter, Long Long Long, Revolution 1, Honey Pie, Savoy Truffle, Cry Baby Cry, Revolution 9, Good Night
III: Bowie, Bouncing, Slave, Rift, Sleeping Monkey, Poor Heart, Antelope
E: Amazing Grace, "Costume Contest," Squirming Coil

Second set was the Beatles' White Album. *All songs from the album were concert debuts. Cake presented to crew member Brad Sands during Birthday. "HYHU" tease before Why Don't We Do It. Speak to Me and Good Night were prerecorded versions played over the PA system. "Vibration of Life," "Vibration of Death," and "War Pigs" jams in Harpua. "Custard Pie" tease before Bowie. "Stash" tease in Antelope.*

Just an all-out Phishfest, with *The White Album* sandwiched between two huge sets! The best Simple you'll ever hear and one of my favorite Harpuas ever. *The White Album* was so good, coming as the effect of thinking they were about to play Dark Side of the Moon wore off. Page out of control on Antelope, a great Bowie, plus a bedtime serenade by Page at 3:30 a.m. What a show! —Casey Grant

The first Halloween Phish show I saw. Musically, everyone knows the second set, but personally the first set is still one of my favorites ever. Still, the concert paled in comparison to the scene outside—I mean, the Disco Bus in the parking lot of Burger King, a guy who said he was the mayor of Glens Falls doing nitrous with us, all the costumes—what a scene! Yum! And just a heck of a concert. —Beth Castrol

Sandwiched between two great sets was the Beatles' *White Album.* "Here's another hint for you all, the walrus was Paul!"—Trey pointed and smiled as he sang this line. Weeks later, I realize he was pointing to the walrus, Paul Languedoc, at the soundboard. Trey also inserts "Guyute the pig" into this song. A great album was performed with the utmost quality. Congrats to Skippy who won the costume contest, making Ithaca College proud. I still watch this show over and over on my VCR. —Ric Hannah

Everyone knows that Phish played with people's minds by playing a "Speak to Me" tease at the beginning of the second set to trick the crowd into thinking the cover album was going to be Pink Floyd. But it's interesting that at the beginning of set III, before David Bowie, they give a tease to another great album that people thought they might play that night. The little guitar tease is the beginning of Led Zeppelin's Custard Pie, the first song off the double album *Physical Graffiti.* —Brian Levine

How much stranger is seeing Fish naked? I thought this was an awesome effort. Note for note, the Green Mountain lads delivered the goods like they were from Liverpool. Was it a steady diet of stouts, porters and ESBs that had me imagining it was the Beatles? A sensational show, and a seminal event in Phishtory. —Dan Kurtz

11/2/94 [ACCESSIBILITY: ••••] [ATTEND. 5,440; CAP. 5,440] [TIX $18]
Bangor Auditorium, Bangor, ME
I: Suzie, Foam, If I Could, Maze, Guyute, Stash, Scent of a Mule, Guitar Gently Weeps
II: Halley's > Tweezer, Mango, Axilla II, Possum, Lizards, Sample
E: Old Home Place, Foreplay > Long Time, Tweezer Reprise

Old Home Place and Foreplay/Long Time performed acoustic with setup of 10/7/94. Tweezer from this show appears on A Live One.

Pouring rain outside, 4,000 people inside in a really small place with wooden bleachers, even. Everyone's liquid! Trey wears the coolest shirt I've ever seen him wear. You know the setlist: TWEEZER! People were losing it. We climbed under the bleachers and ran all over the place. One of the best times of my life. —Langston Knipler

The biggest fault of *A Live One* is not including the Possum from this show along with the Tweezer. Trey jams on a very similar theme in both, making Possum almost a continuation of Tweezer. The picture in the liner notes for *A Live One* of the boys playing acoustic comes from this show because the flowers were thrown onstage by a girl in the audience. By the way, check out the first set. Each song has a great jam. —Brendan Neagle

11/3/94 [ACCESSIBILITY: ••••] [ATTEND. 10,420; CAP. 10,420] [TIX $18.50]
Mullins Center, University of Massachusetts, Amherst, MA
I: Fee, Divided Sky, Wilson > Peaches, Glide, Melt, Dog Faced Boy, Sparkle, Down with Disease
II: Also Sprach > Simple, Poor Heart, Julius, YEM > BBFCM, Harry Hood, Cavern
E: MSO, Nellie Cane, Amazing Grace, Highway to Hell

"Vibration of Life" in YEM. MSO and Nellie Cane performed acoustic with Trey on acoustic guitar, Mike on banjo, Fishman on mandolin, and Page on stand-up bass.

11/4/94 [ACCESSIBILITY: ••••] [ATTEND. 7,799; CAP. 7,799] [TIX $18.50]
Onondaga County War Memorial, Syracuse, NY
I: Sample, It's Ice, Bouncing, Bowie, Forbin's > Mockingbird, Scent of a Mule, Suzie > Chalkdust
II: Curtain > Mike's > Simple > Mike's > Tela > Weekapaug, Ya Mar, Golgi, Slave
E: Loving Cup, Rocky Top

Vibration of Life in Forbin's. Can't You Hear Me Knocking jam at the end of Weekapaug. Last Loving Cup, 5/7/94 Dallas, TX [69 shows].

A very standard setlist. However, the energy level was way greater than normal, maybe because the Vibration of Life took us to Gamehendge. It was the only time that I actually felt I was there. As my friend Gugs put it afterwards, "A stellar show." We saw Ya Mar and no vacuum. Enough said. —Ric Hannah

I was front row and had some 3-D glasses on when, at the end of Mockingbird, Trey asked for them. He wore them throughout Mule, dancing around during the duel, basically buggin' out. Everything looked so cool with those glasses on—he must have been psyched. He then passed them to Gordo for Suzie, and Mike popped and slapped throughout. Second set was old school, with no songs written in the 1990s with the exception of Simple. —Joshua Howley

11/12/94 [ACCESSIBILITY: ••••] [ATTEND. 5,884; CAP. 5,884] [TIX $15–$18]
Mac Center, Kent State University, Kent, OH
I: Runaway Jim, Foam, If I Could, Guyute, Maze, Stash, Esther, Chalkdust
II: Julius, Fluffhead, Down with Disease > Have Mercy > Down with Disease > Lifeboy, Rift, Old Home Place, Nellie Cane, Foreplay > Long Time, Harry Hood, Golgi
E: Sample

Old Home Place and Nellie Cane performed acoustic with Trey on acoustic guitar, Mike on banjo, Fishman on mandolin, and Page on stand-up bass. Foreplay/Long Time performed acoustic with setup of 10/7/94. Last Have Mercy, 8/14/93 Tinley Park, IL [110 shows].

10/31/94 Glens Falls Civic Center, Glens Falls, NY

"The White Album"

By 1966, the Beatles had grown tired of the road. At 9:27 P.M. on August 29, 1966, the Beatles took the stage in Candlestick Park in San Francisco. At 10:00 P.M., after finishing the show with Long Tall Sally, they left the stage forever.

While the group continued to write some of the greatest songs and record some of the greatest albums ever, fans would never get a chance to see them performed live. *Sgt. Pepper's, Abbey Road, The White Album*—these brilliant musical feats would only be performed in front of mirrors, hairbrush in place of microphone, imagination creating the scene. At least until Halloween 1994.

On that night, in Glens Falls, NY, Phish opened their second set with Back in the USSR, the first song from *The White Album*, and the Beatles were magically on stage again.

People often argue over Phish shows. "It was great!" or "Just average." Opinions go on and on, and it can be fruitless to argue, as well as silly—just because you loved a show doesn't mean everyone else should. However, it's true that some shows are simply musically superior to others. That's part of why most phans don't go to just one show a year—it wouldn't be as much fun if the band were four robots and every song was always technically perfect, or every jam was played in perfect sync.

Then there are the historic moments when, regardless of the music, the show is considered a classic. When the band combines both in one night, it's perfection. Glens Falls 10/31/94 was just that.

It would have been enough simply to make a good effort at covering *The White Album*, but to nail it the way they did made it extra special. While My Guitar Gently Weeps was truly memorable, as Trey was challenged to match the great lead performed by Eric Clapton, invited into the studio for the track by close friend George Harrison. Trey proved himself up to the task, so much so that the band went on to perform the song fifteen more times through the end of 1995. And of course there was Phish lunacy—Fishman pulling off his dress during Revolution 9, showing the 8,000-person crowd just what he was made of.

While Phish's musical costume—voted on by postcard by 400 fans, with about 10 percent of the votes cast for *The White Album*—was enough to make it a classic night, the first and third sets of pure Phish may have been even better. The third set in particular—highlighted by all-time great versions of Bowie, Slave and Antelope—was about as good as it gets, played to a delirious audience between 2 and 3 A.M. The encore, a perfectly placed Squirming Coil with the traditional Page piano solo, wound down just after 3:20 A.M.

The show also proved seminal for the scene that developed outside the arena. For the first time, several thousand more fans than there were tickets arrived at the venue. The chaos that engulfed Glens Falls later led Phish manager John Paluska to write a thirty-page manual for venue staffs on how to interact with Phish concert crowds. Inside, the venue security staff just gave up, and before the band took the stage, it became a general-admission affair that will never be forgotten by those lucky enough to be in attendance. The show is rightly remembered as one of Phish's most potent nights ever, and the show is the most heavily-circulated set of Phish tapes in existence.

The first few times I saw DwD live, I was amazed at the strength of the jam. Trey managed to play off the same basic riff for about ten minutes, just building it and building until they finished with "Na, Na, Na Na Na" refrain. But by the time I made it to Kent, the band had already discovered that DwD was a toy with more than one gadget. During the second set, they went into a rendition which began with a pretty basic jam following the lyrics, but it just kept morphing and morphing, to a point where you couldn't begin to figure out how they'd find their way back. They didn't—at least not right away. Instead they went into Have Mercy, a song which only seems to sneak into the greatest shows and the greatest jams. Then, seamlessly, they headed back into DwD and finished it off. At the time, DwD was thought of by many as the radio song, the video song, but that night it became one of my absolute favorite tunes to see live. Of course, I had no idea just what heights that song would reach. —Andy Bernstein

11/13/94 [ACCESSIBILITY: ••] [ATTEND. 2,378; CAP. 2,378] [TIX $18.25]
Erie Warner Theatre, Erie, PA
I: Wilson > Sparkle, Simple > Reba, Axilla II, It's Ice, Horse > Silent, Antelope
II: Suzie, Divided Sky, Lizards, Tweezer > Mango > BBFCM, Amazing Grace, Squirming Coil
E: Funky Bitch, Tweezer Reprise

The venue was tiny, one of the most beautiful theaters I've ever set foot in. We drove eight hours just for this one show so we were expecting a lot. The boys did not let us down. Antelope blew my mind, not to mention the roof, right off the place—definitely the hardest I have ever seen Trey jam, and there was a small voice jam before Marco Esquandolis. Everyone should check this one out—no doubt the best one ever! Second set was great, but I could have walked out satisfied after Antelope. Amazing how far you drive and how short it takes Phish to satisfy. —Joshua Howley

I think the word for this show is phun. It was a great place for Phish to play. The energy was full. The most memorable part was Trey running around the stage with megaphone in hand during BBFCM as the strobe lights went nuts. The encore, Funky Bitch, was a request from someone in the front. —Kevin Word

11/14/94 [ACCESSIBILITY: ••] [ATTEND. 2,364; CAP. 2,364] [TIX $19.50]
Devos Hall, Grand Rapids, MI
I: My Friend, Scent of a Mule, Guelah, Melt, Bouncing, Landlady, Maze, Lawn Boy, Cavern
II: Peaches, Bowie, Yerushalayim, Slave, Poor Heart, Julius, Old Home Place, Nellie Cane, Adeline, YEM
E: Golgi

Cavern had usual lyrics but final refrain was played to the music of Lawn Boy. Old Home Place and Nellie performed acoustic with Trey on acoustic guitar, Mike on banjo, Fishman on mandolin, and Page on stand-up bass.

This is one of my favorite tapes in my collection for three reasons: (1) Cavern's chorus is the music of Lawn Boy; (2) an insane Bowie > Yerushalayim; and (3) Fishman on mandolin! It's not as if these were the only good points of the show, either. It was just perfectly played music all night. —Josh Halman

Another solid show. The most memorable moment of this was the Bowie! Dang, this one got trippy, almost to the point of stopping in the middle, but they took us through a full range of emotions. Trey really got intricate in his pathways of music. This is my favorite David Bowie. There was also a great Peaches opener to set the mood and a very stellar YEM. This was a great show that gets little hype. You should check it out. —Michelle Hirsch

11/16/94 [ACCESSIBILITY: •••] [ATTEND. 4,009; CAP. 4,009] [TIX $17.50–$19.50]
Hill Auditorium, University of Michigan, Ann Arbor, MI
I: Sample, Foam, FEFY, Reba, Axilla II, Lizards, Stash, Pig in a Pen, Tennessee Waltz, Bluegrass Breakdown, Swing Low Sweet Chariot
II: Mike's > Simple, I'm Blue I'm Lonesome, Long Journey Home, Chalkdust, Fee, Antelope
E: Amazing Grace, Suzie

Rev. Jeff Mosier on banjo for Bluegrass Breakdown, and banjo and vocals for Pig in a Pen, Tennessee Waltz, and Swing Low Sweet Chariot. I'm Blue I'm Lonesome and Long Journey Home performed acoustic with Trey on acoustic guitar, Mike on banjo, Fishman on mandolin, and Page on stand-up bass. Last Pig in a Pen, 2/21/93 Atlanta, GA [194 shows]. Last Tennessee Waltz, 5/6/93 Albany, NY [141 shows]. Last Swing Low Sweet Chariot, 10/20/89 Burlington, VT [683 shows]. Concert debuts: Bluegrass Breakdown, I'm Blue I'm Lonesome, and Long Journey Home. Chalkdust from this show appears on A Live One.

God bless the Reverend! Jeff Mosier helped make November '94 one of the hottest months of Phish ever, infusing almost every set with a bluegrass sensibility that can be heard in Phish's music to this day. This was his first night jamming onstage with the boys, and they looked damn excited to have him there. Like Dick Solberg in Albany on 5/6/93, it didn't take long for Mosier to get comfortable (perhaps because he'd played with Phish once before, on 2/21/93). In Pig in a Pen, he introduced us to "the world's premiere bluegrass drummer… Fish!" Swing Low Sweet Chariot, with Mosier on lead vocals for the first Phish rendition since the 1980s, is another major highlight. —Ernie Greene

Still recovering from the hot first set (Stash sizzled, Mosier cooked), I almost hit the roof as Trey started up Mike's Song to kick open the second set. Mike's > Simple was still a frequent occurrence back then, so the Simple chords came as no surprise out of the Mike's jam. It wasn't even that incredible when the band jammed out on Simple, with Trey

drawing out a quietly melodious theme not unlike that of the Halloween show a few weeks earlier. But the jam kept moving—and evolving—and slowing—and then rocking, and before we knew it, we were 35 minutes into the set and still in Simple. Only after hearing the incredible Simples of Fall '96 am I willing to label the start of this set "Mike's > Simple" instead of "Mike's > Simple > Jam!" Add to this set an acoustic interlude, a killer Chalkdust (*A Live One* version), Fee > Antelope, and you'll understand why people were still cheering outside the venue when it was all over. —Rich Mazer

11/17/94 [ACCESSIBILITY: ••••] [ATTEND. 5,786; CAP. 5,786] [TIX $18.50–$20]
Hara Arena, Dayton, OH
I: Helter Skelter, Scent of a Mule, Maze, Bouncing, Wilson, Divided Sky, Dog Faced Boy, Forbin's > Mockingbird, Down with Disease
II: Also Sprach > Bowie, Sleeping Monkey, Sparkle, YEM > HYHU > Love You > HYHU, Slave, Golgi
E: I'm Blue I'm Lonesome, Nellie Cane, Long Journey Home, Fixin' to Die

"Vibration of Life" in Forbin's. "HYHU" was sung, not played, emerging from the YEM vocal jam. Fishman on vacuum for Love You. I'm Blue I'm Lonesome, Nellie Cane, and Long Journey Home performed acoustic with Trey on acoustic guitar, Mike on banjo, Fishman on mandolin, and Page on stand-up bass. Rev. Jeff Mosier on spoons for Long Journey Home and on banjo (electric) and vocals for Fixin' to Die. Concert debut: Fixin' to Die.

The best part is the acoustic, Dixieland-style encore. The boys sound like the mid-'60s Dead (for lack of a better comparison). Trey's got soul in his vocals and the crowd loves it! The vibes definitely come through on tape; you feel like drinkin' cheap whiskey, taking your shoes off, and stomping your feet! Long Journey and Fixin' rock. Also, the grating Fish vocals on Monkey and the venue erupting with the vocals on YEM need to be heard. —Tim Foisser

11/18/94 [ACCESSIBILITY: •••] [ATTEND. 3,717; CAP. 3,717] [TIX $18.50–$20]
MSU Auditorium, Michigan State University, East Lansing, MI
I: Rift, AC/DC Bag, Julius, Horse > Silent, It's Ice, Tela, Melt, Butter Them Biscuits, Old Home Place, Long Journey Home
II: Llama, Bathtub Gin > Lifeboy, Poor Heart, Tweezer > Contact, Possum
E: Roll in My Sweet Baby's Arms, Runaway Jim

Butter Them Biscuits, Old Home Place, and Long Journey Home performed acoustic with Trey on fiddle (for Butter Them Biscuits, his debut performance on fiddle) and acoustic guitar (for Old Home Place and Long Journey Home), Mike on banjo, Fishman on mandolin, and Page on stand-up bass. Rev. Jeff Mosier on banjo (acoustic) for Butter Them Biscuits, Old Home Place, and Long Journey Home, and banjo (electric) for Roll in My Sweet Baby's Arms and Runaway Jim. "Bathtub Gin" teases in Possum. Concert debuts: Butter Them Biscuits, Roll in My Sweet Baby's Arms.

"How about a big hand for Trey—that's the first time he's ever played the fiddle," Fish says at the end of the bluegrass instrumental Butter Them Biscuits. Three days into the Mosier Bluegrass Tour, the band sounds damn good during the three-song bluegrass series that ends the first set, even Trey on his fiddle. The Reverend also spices up the encores, including an electric Runaway Jim. Besides bluegrass, this show shines with an evil version of The Horse that cracks me up, a Bathtub Gin > Lifeboy pairing that fits wonderfully, and a great Possum with Gin jams from Trey. —Tyler Harris

11/19/94 [ACCESSIBILITY: •••] [ATTEND. 2,472; CAP. 2,472] [TIX $19.50]
University of Indiana Auditorium, Bloomington, IN
I: Golgi, Down with Disease, Guyute, Axilla II, Paul and Silas, TMWSIY > Avenu > Antelope, I'm Blue I'm Lonesome, Butter Them Biscuits, Long Journey Home
II: Suzie, Sparkle, YEM, HYHU > Cracklin' Rosie > HYHU, Harry Hood, Amazing Grace, GTBT
E: Squirming Coil

I'm Blue I'm Lonesome, Butter Them Biscuits, and Long Journey Home performed acoustic with Trey on acoustic guitar (for I'm Blue I'm Lonesome and Long Journey Home) and fiddle (for Butter Them Biscuits), Mike on banjo, Fishman on mandolin, and Page on stand-up bass. Reverend Jeff Mosier on banjo for Butter Them Biscuits, and banjo and vocals for I'm Blue I'm Lonesome and Long Journey Home. "Vibration of Life" in YEM. "Spooky" jam in YEM. "Can't You Hear Me Knocking" tease in YEM.

[11/19/94] [ACCESSIBILITY: ••••]
University of Indiana Auditorium Parking Lot, Bloomington, IN
Cripple Creek, Tennessee Waltz, Old Home Place, Dooley, Mountain Dew, Pig in a Pen, Roll in My Sweet Baby's Arms, Long Journey Home, Butter Them Biscuits, I'm Blue I'm Lonesome, Midnight Moonlight, Will the Circle Be Unbroken

Informal parking lot performance after the Indiana Auditorium show, with Mike (banjo and electric bass), Page (bass), Trey (fiddle and guitar), Fishman (mandolin), Rev. Jeff Mosier (banjo), Eric Merrill (fiddle and guitar), and Jeremy (banjo and jaw harp).

This is a must for all phans! It's Phish and friends performing bluegrass music in a parking lot with fiddles and banjoes. Some highlights are Mountain Dew, Cripple Creek, Tennessee Waltz and Dooley. Guest appearances by Rev. Jeff Mosier and Eric Merrill. Phish sounds like a true Kentucky bluegrass band. —Ryan Satz

Great bluegrass—it makes me wonder why the band doesn't do acoustic sets. In front of a small crowd, the down-home music just rolls. Tennessee Waltz, Two Dollar Bill, Blue and Lonesome and Midnight Moonlight are my favorites of this unexpected jam. Makes me wish I was there. —Kyle Niday

11/20/94 [ACCESSIBILITY: ••••] [ATTEND. 7,724; CAP. 7,724] [TIX $18.50]
Dane County Expo Center Coliseum, Madison, WI
I: Chalkdust, Fee, Scent of a Mule, Stash, If I Could, Butter Them Biscuits, Long Journey Home, Dooley, Divided Sky, Sample
II: Also Sprach > Bowie, Glide, Axilla II, Reba > Simple, Rift, HYHU > Terrapin > HYHU, Julius, Cavern
E: Icculus
E2: Fire

Rev. Jeff Mosier on banjo (electric) for If I Could. Butter Them Biscuits, Long Journey Home and Dooley performed acoustic with Trey on fiddle (for Butter Them Biscuits) and acoustic guitar (for Long Journey Home and Dooley), Mike on banjo, Fishman on mandolin, and Page on stand-up bass. Mosier on banjo (acoustic) for Butter Them Biscuits, and on banjo (acoustic) and vocals for Long Journey Home and Dooley. Fishman on vacuum for Terrapin. Concert debut: Dooley.

11/22/94 [ACCESSIBILITY: •••] [ATTEND. 1,796; CAP. 1,796] [TIX $15.50–$17.50]
Jesse Auditorium, University of Missouri, Columbia, MO
I: Buried Alive > Poor Heart, Horn, Foam, Guyute, I Didn't Know, Bouncing, Down with Disease, Adeline
II: Funky Bitch > Jam > Yerushalayim, Cry Baby Cry, Curtain, Blackbird, Runaway Jim > BBFCM, I'm Blue I'm Lonesome, Butter Them Biscuits, Long Journey Home, Harry Hood, Highway to Hell
E: Lizards

End of BBFCM, I'm Blue I'm Lonesome, Butter Them Biscuits and Long Journey Home performed acoustic with Trey on acoustic guitar, Mike on banjo, Fishman on mandolin and Page on stand-up bass.

Great second set! The jam in between Funky Bitch and Yerushalayim shows the band's willingness to go WAY out there. Blackbird is played perfectly, too. My highlight is when Trey asks what the band should play next. He says, "Hell, ask that guy." The guy in the crowd shouts Harry Hood. They respond with a version that is out of this world! Made that guy's night. —Dan Charland

This show was the closest we ever came to returning to *The White Album* because Cry Baby Cry and Blackbird both made it in. —Shawn Miller

This show is a favorite of mine in my collection. Funky Bitch starts off a second set that's unique and different. An ode to the Beatles with Cry Baby Cry and Blackbird, and Phish does these songs justice. BBFCM is awful but the bluegrass mini-set makes up for it. Then Trey lets a fan pick the following song and they do Harry Hood. What, no Destiny Unbound or Prep School Hippie? —Tony Krupka

This is one of those nights where trying to understand the show by looking at the setlist just won't cut it. Funky Bitch > Yerushalayim sounds like a fun little pairing, but let me warn you now, it's oh so much more than that—this very experiMENTAL jam should be heard by all phans of the Golden Hose. —Rich Mazer

11/23/94 [ACCESSIBILITY: ••] [ATTEND. 4,201; CAP. 4,201] [TIX $18.50]
Fabulous Fox Theatre, St. Louis, MO
I: Wilson > Sparkle > Simple > It's Ice, If I Could, Oh Kee > Suzie, Divided Sky, Amazing Grace
II: Maze, Fee, Scent of a Mule, Tweezer, Lifeboy, YEM, Tweezer Reprise
E: Sample

"Vibration of Life" in YEM. "Frankenstein" jam in YEM.

A must-hear second set for YEM fans. Though it's not the longest version, it's probably the spaciest. Very experimental! —Scott Sifton

11/25/94 [ACCESSIBILITY: ••••] [ATTEND. 9,334; CAP. 9,334] [TIX $19.50]
UIC Pavilion, University of Illinois, Chicago, IL
I: Llama, Guelah, Reba, Bouncing, Melt, Esther, Julius, Golgi
II: Also Sprach > Mike's > Simple > Harpua > Weekapaug > Mango > Purple Rain > HYHU, Antelope
E: GTBT

Fishman on vacuum for Purple Rain.

11/26/94 [ACCESSIBILITY: ••] [ATTEND. 2,537; CAP. 2,537] [TIX $17.50]
Orpheum Theatre, Minneapolis, MN

I: My Friend, Possum, Guyute, If I Could, Foam, Horse > Silent, Poor Heart, Cavern
II: Halley's > Bowie, Adeline, Lizards, Sample > Slave
E: Rocky Top

Possum with alternate lyrics ("Someone hit an ostrich..."). Guyute was without second verse. Bowie jam featured, at various times, Fishman on vacuum and mandolin, Trey using a megaphone to create feedback noises, and Mike on single-string bass. Slave from this show appears on A Live One.

A month before the Providence Bowie we all know and love, there was the Minneapolis edition. For all of you who are sure that the 12/29 Bowie served as the groundbreaker, you should have been in the theater on this night. Almost 40 minutes of madness including Fishman on vacuum, Trey using his megaphone to create feedback effects and lots of jamming ranging from exploratory to energizing to apathetic, depending on the moment. You see, it's one of THOSE jams, and everyone in the Orpheum knew it. —Lee Johnston

There were waves of energy visibly emanating from the band during the opening My Friend My Friend into Possum. But set two was where it was at. Halley's Comet > David Bowie was the longest (37 minutes), spaciest, wildest version that I know of! The length says it all. A nice Lizards punctuated the middle of the set, and the "ultra-clean" Slave to the Traffic Light (A Live One version) ends this wonderfully energized show in the beautiful venue that is the Orpheum in Minneapolis! (I've never seen a soundboard of this show, and I've been looking for it since 11/27/94). —Chris Mrachek

11/28/94 [ACCESSIBILITY: ••] [ATTEND. 3,000; CAP. 3,000] [TIX $17.50–$19.50]
Shroyer Gym, Montana State University, Bozeman, MT
I: Chalkdust, Also Sprach, Scent of a Mule, Stash, Guyute, Sparkle, Simple, Divided Sky, Adeline
II: Suzie, NICU, Tweezer, Sleeping Monkey, Julius
E: Fee, Tweezer Reprise

Ten-year-old Cameron McKenney on saxophone for Simple. Snippet from this Tweezer became Montana on A Live One.

In the lexicon of Phish fans, Bozeman means one thing: Tweezer. Phish's first appearance in the Big Sky state saw them show the locals what a great night in Gamehendge is all about as they took Tweezer out for a short spin and then never returned the car. Forty-five minutes of strong improv! —Pat Stanley

If Phish is to release any show "from the vault," it should be Bozeman. In what was clearly a night of ground-breaking music, Tweezer stretched out to 45 minutes, a version which is arguably the most interesting they've ever done. A snippet from this jam comprises the "Montana" track on *A Live One*, but it's hard to enjoy the full Tweezer because no tapers that night nailed a perfect copy of it. Come on, Kevin, kick this one down! —Ernie Greene

11/30/94 [ACCESSIBILITY: ••••] [ATTEND. 3,146; CAP. 3,358] [TIX $19]
Campus Recreation Center, Evergreen College, Olympia, WA
I: Frankenstein, Poor Heart, My Friend, Reba, Forbin's > Mockingbird, Down with Disease, Bouncing, I'm Blue I'm Lonesome, Long Journey Home
II: Halley's > Antelope > MSO > Antelope > Fixin' to Die > Ya Mar > Mike's > Catapult > McGrupp, Cavern
E: Horse > Silent, Amazing Grace

"Vibration of Life" in Forbin's. I'm Blue I'm Lonesome and Long Journey Home performed acoustic with Trey on acoustic guitar, Mike on banjo, Fishman on mandolin, and Page on stand-up bass. Long delay at end of MSO with Trey snoring. Antelope unfinished (no lyric segment); segment before lyric segment had Trey using a megaphone to create feedback noises and Mike on one-string bass.

Phish has often used Tweezer as a song around which to build a set, and on certain nights, DwD, Bowie and Mike's Groove have performed a similar feat. In Olympia, that honor fell to a well-deserving recipient: Antelope! The Antelope jam leads into MSO, complete with Trey snoring at the end, then back into an Antelope chaos jam that found Trey on megaphone. Instead of closing Antelope with the lyrics, the band headed into Fixin' to Die, the last time they've performed this song. Though Antelope "ends" at that point, the strange segues don't: Ya Mar > Mike's > Catapult > McGrupp > Cavern is a wild ride! —Nancy Eddies

This show is worthy of classic status not just because of the other-worldly second set but because it's backed up by a great, great first set. The Down with Disease jam alone is enough reason to get this tape, but add a Frankenstein opener, Reba and Forbin's > Mockingbird and you've got a great start to a great night of music. —Marcia Collins

12/1/94 [ACCESSIBILITY: ••••] [ATTEND. 3,400; CAP. 3,400] [TIX $17.50–$19]
Salem Armory, Salem, OR
I: Sample, Uncle Pen, FEFY, Maze, Guyute, I Didn't Know, Melt, Adeline
II: Peaches, Mound, Tweezer > BBFCM > Makisupa > NICU > Tweezer > Jesus Left Chicago > Harry Hood, Golgi
E: Sleeping Monkey > Tweezer Reprise

Fishman on vacuum for I Didn't Know. "Norwegian Wood" jam in Tweezer.

Well, the boys really had it goin' on toward the end of this tour. Tweezer being absolutely incredible, Makisupa like you've never heard it before, Fishman adding some classic side comments and such a nice segue into Jesus—an impressive jam session that proves how great 1994 was in Phishland. —Alex Banks

My favorite kind of Phish set is the kind where every song is incorporated into one massive jam. There's the more-jam-than-song variety, like the 5/7/94 Tweezerfest, and there's the more-song-than-jam sort, like this show, 12/14/95 Binghamton and the night before this show in Eugene. Salem is my favorite of this select group. The Tweezer jam is mostly Page on synth at first, then becomes a start/stop jam that spaces out before a severe Norwegian Wood jam develops that lasts several minutes and segues into BBFCM. After the usual Creature nonsense, a brief vocal jam leads into Makisupa, which itself turns into a reggae jam that Trey brings ever-so-carefully around into NICU in a perfectly-executed segue. Yes! Trey's doing his thing at the end of NICU, too, playing a pronounced closing jam that's gorgeous, then another jam that returns the band briefly to the Tweezer theme and finally to the opening notes of Jesus Left Chicago. —Tyler Harris

This show may be on my top ten list. The first set included a trippy Maze followed by Guyute (a rare one). Once again, the second set is better. Phish started it all off with Peaches and shortly went to an award-winning Tweezer which sandwiched many versions of Phish favorites. The instrumental section after the final words in Tweezer displayed Phish communicating extremely well: so well, it reminds me of a studio version. This is one of my favorite jams. —John Foley

12/2/94 [ACCESSIBILITY: ••] [ATTEND. 3,541; CAP. 5,732] [TIX $10.50–$16.50]
Recreation Hall at UC Davis, Davis, CA
I: Poor Heart, Also Sprach, Sparkle, Simple > It's Ice, Lizards, Stash, Squirming Coil
II: Chalkdust, Bowie, Buried Alive, Julius, Landlady, Gumbo, Caravan, Suzie
E: Cavern

Second set and encore, starting near the end of Bowie, featured the five-piece Giant Country Horns: Dave Grippo, alto saxophone; Carl Gerhard, trumpet; Michael Ray, trumpet; Peter Apfelbaum, baritone and tenor saxophone; and James Harvey, trombone. Gumbo from this show appears on A Live One.

12/3/94 [ACCESSIBILITY: ••••] [ATTEND. 4,724; CAP. 6,500] [TIX $19.50–$21]
Event Center, San Jose State University, San Jose, CA
I: Wilson, Divided Sky, Guelah, Scent of a Mule, Antelope, Guyute, Sample
II: Frankenstein, Suzie, Buried Alive, Gumbo, Slave, Touch Me, "Horn Introductions," Julius, Cavern
E: Golgi

The Dave Matthews Band opened. Second set (but not encore) featured the Giant Country Horns with the same lineup as 12/2/94. Jam during the horn introductions was based on "Alumni Blues." Last Touch Me, 7/27/91 Atlanta, GA [394 shows].

The first set at SJSU left a little something to be desired, but the second set salvaged the show. Jamming with the Giant Country Horns, Phish produced a set that prevented anyone from catching their breath. The horns on Slave become slightly obnoxious at times, but redeem themselves in the Alumni Jam and Julius. Touch Me was also revived here for the first time since the horn tour in summer '91. —Matthew Ashenfelder

The horns sound a little sloppy, but add a lot to songs like Suzie, Gumbo, Landlady, Julius and Cavern. The horns are especially interesting on the Alumni Blues jam which is already cool just because, well, it's an Alumni Blues jam! Horns do not sound good on Slave, though, which is a shame because otherwise it's a really good version. —Seth Weinglass

12/4/94 [ACCESSIBILITY: ••] [ATTEND. 2,335; CAP. 2,335] [TIX $15–$18.50]
Acker Gym, Chico State University, Chico, CA
I: Runaway Jim, Foam, If I Could, Rift, Tweezer, Fee, Mound, Adeline, Possum
II: Maze, Bouncing, Reba, Axilla II > YEM, HYHU > Purple Rain > HYHU, GTBT
E: Sleeping Monkey > Rocky Top

Fishman on vacuum for Purple Rain.

12/6/94 [ACCESSIBILITY: ••] [ATTEND. 2,500; CAP. 2,900] [TIX $16.50–$20]
Event Center, University of California at Santa Barbara, Santa Barbara, CA

I: Llama, Mound, Down with Disease, Fluffhead, Jesus Left Chicago, Sparkle, Stash, Golgi
II: Curtain > Sample, Also Sprach, Poor Heart, Mike's > Simple > Mango > Weekapaug, HYHU > Bike > HYHU, I'm Blue I'm Lonesome, Foreplay > Long Time, Antelope
E: Back in the USSR

Fishman on vacuum for Bike. I'm Blue I'm Lonesome performed acoustic with Trey on acoustic guitar, Mike on banjo, Fishman on mandolin, and Page on stand-up bass. Foreplay/Long Time performed acoustic with setup of 10/7/94.

This show represents everything that was great about Phish in '94. Jams were tight, energetic, flawless and pushed to the limit without being self-indulgent. The highlight came midway through the second set, when the Burlington boys broke out the big guns. The flow of Mike's > Simple > Mango > Weekapaug worked so well, I would be surprised if it's never repeated. Weekapaug featured an extra jam that took things to yet another level. With this 44 minutes of perfection in the vault, Fishman broke out the vacuum for a rollicking version of Bike. Then the banjo and washboard came out for Blue and Lonesome, with Page nailing the high solo "suitcase" line both times. I crossed my fingers and got my wish: Foreplay > Long Time, which made my night, as I must confess this was one of my favorite albums in junior high (along with Quadrophenia). A tight Antelope closed things out. For the encore, we got the only Back in the USSR played after Glens Falls. The freshman in the row in front of us made the best comment of the night: "If I had stayed back in the dorm studying and missed this, I would have killed myself." —Mike Indgin

12/7/94 [ACCESSIBILITY: ••] [ATTEND. 1,343; CAP. 1,343] [TIX $18.50–$20]
Spreckels Theatre, San Diego, CA
I: Peaches > Runaway Jim, Sloth, Ya Mar, Melt, Guyute, Lifeboy, Chalkdust
II: Rift, Frankenstein, Divided Sky, Fee > Julius, I'm Blue I'm Lonesome, Long Journey Home, Amazing Grace, YEM
E: Cavern

"Gypsy Queen" jam in Runaway Jim. I'm Blue I'm Lonesome and Long Journey Home performed acoustic/no amplification with Trey on acoustic guitar, Mike on banjo, Fishman on mandolin, and Page on upright bass. YEM from this show appears on A Live One.

12/8/94 [ACCESSIBILITY: ••••] [ATTEND. 1,343; CAP. 1,343] [TIX $18.50–$20]
Spreckels Theatre, San Diego, CA
I: Makisupa > Maze, AC/DC Bag, Scent of a Mule, PYITE, Simple > Catapult > Simple, Lizards, Guitar Gently Weeps
II: Possum, My Mind's, Axilla II, Reba, Nellie Cane, Adeline, Bowie, Golgi
E: Horse > Silent, Rocky Top

Nellie Cane performed acoustic/no amplification with Trey on acoustic guitar, Mike on banjo, Fishman on mandolin, and Page on upright bass. Last My Mind, 7/6/94 Montreal, Quebec [57 shows].

This show began the Makisupa opener tradition on nights when phans have tangled with police outside the venue (see also 6/10/95 and 8/6/96)—"Policeman came to my house" indeed! Makisupa > Maze is stunning, and from there the first set is off and running, not one down moment. Tons of energy in AC/DC Bag and PYITE, and a gorgeous Simple jam after they sneak Catapult in. Yummy. —Melissa Wolcott

12/9/94 [ACCESSIBILITY: •••] [ATTEND. 4,200; CAP. 4,200] [TIX $16.50–$17.50]
Mesa Amphitheatre, Mesa, AZ
I: Llama, Foam, Guyute, Sparkle > I Didn't Know, It's Ice > If I Could > Antelope
II: Wilson, Poor Heart > Tweezer > McGrupp, Julius > BBJ, HYHU > Cracklin' Rosie > HYHU, YEM, Suzie
E: I'm Blue I'm Lonesome, Foreplay > Long Time, Tweezer Reprise

"Slave" jam in Tweezer. I'm Blue I'm Lonesome performed acoustic with Trey on acoustic guitar, Mike on banjo, Fishman on mandolin, and Page on upright bass. Foreplay/Long Time performed acoustic with setup of 10/7/94.

12/10/94 [ACCESSIBILITY: ••] [ATTEND. 4,250; CAP. 4,250] [TIX $20]
Santa Monica Civic Auditorium, Santa Monica, CA
I: Fee, Rift, Stash, Lizards, Sample, Divided Sky, Lawn Boy, Chalkdust
II: Simple, Maze, Guyute, Also Sprach, Mike's > Hydrogen > Weekapaug > HYHU > Do It in the Road > HYHU, Poor Heart, Slave, Cavern
E: "Crew Acknowledgment," GTBT

The Dave Matthews Band opened. Fishman on vacuum for Do It in the Road. Jam during crew acknowledgment was based on Chalkdust. Simple from this show appears on A Live One.

1994 HOLIDAY TOUR

12/28/94 [ACCESSIBILITY: ••••] [ATTEND. 10,000; CAP. 10,000] [TIX $19.50]
Philadelphia Civic Center, Philadelphia, PA
I: Mound, Simple, Julius, Bathtub Gin, Bouncing, Axilla II, Reba, Dog Faced Boy, It's Ice, Antelope
II: Suzie > NICU > Mike's > Mango > Weekapaug, Contact, Llama, HYHU > Love You > HYHU, Squirming Coil
E: Bold as Love

"Little Drummer Boy" jam in Weekapaug. Fishman on vacuum for Love You. Last Bold as Love, 5/21/94 Seatle, WA [83 shows].

This was a wonderful old-school Phish show, the perfect start to the '94 Holiday run. Phish treated us to a well above-average first set, complete with Gin and an unexpected Antelope closer, then took things up a notch for the second set. Suzie > NICU > Mike's > Mango proved to be an incredible series, played with just tons of energy. Then came the highlight: an incredibly well-jammed Weekapaug, complete with a long "Little Drummer Boy" jam to set the holiday mood. Strong song selection and inspired playing made this night a special one. —Rich Mazer

Best Weekapaug jam ever, I must say. Like 4/9/94 Binghamton, it jams on Little Drummer Boy, but here it's even more intense. —Amy Duncan

Whenever I take a friend to a Phish show for the first time, one of the first things they often comment on is the light show. No wonder: Chris Kuroda & Co. work magic on the raised platform in the middle of the madness. This night, I staked out space to the right of the soundboard that put me handshake distance from the lighting crew. During Antelope, I noticed that the assistant working a new spiral light didn't have a clue—30 seconds before Trey was to begin the "Rye, rye, rocco" line, he threw a spotlight on Trey. Chris, obvious angered, turned it back down, but the guy botched his cue again, and as the set ended, Chris threw his headset off, yelled at the guy and stormed off. But long before the start of the second set, Chris was back up there, working with the guy to make the second set go seamlessly. He did his job well—the intense Weekapaug seemed even crazier with lights going every which way. —Ed Smith

12/29/94 [ACCESSIBILITY: ••••] [ATTEND. 13,976; CAP. 13,976] [TIX $19.50]
Providence Civic Center, Providence, RI
I: Runaway Jim > Foam, If I Could, Melt, Horse > Silent, Uncle Pen, I Didn't Know, Possum
II: Guyute, Bowie, Halley's > Lizards, HYHU > Cracklin' Rosie > HYHU, GTBT
E: Long Journey Home, Sleeping Monkey

"Dueling Banjos" and "L.A. Woman" teases in Possum. Digital Delay Loop jam in Bowie intro. "Lassie" vocal jam in Bowie. "Heartbreaker" tease in GTBT. Long Journey Home performed acoustic with Trey on acoustic guitar, Mike on banjo, Fishman on mandolin, and Page on upright bass.

This was the culmination of the tour in which, I believe, Phish first truly discovered that there was absolutely no limit to how far they could stretch out a jam. Most of that fall's experimentation occurred during half-hour versions of Tweezer, but in Providence, it all came together during the now-famous Bowie. After a tech'd-out beginning which sounded a lot like The Who's Eminence Front, the jam eventually found its way into a captivating and highly melodic lead by Trey, surely strong enough to be turned into its own song someday. It also had a hint of a Slave variation, before delving into a silly monologue of "Lassie, come home" chants. Not only was this the high point of Phish's 1994 super-jams, but I really think it opened the door for Phish realizing they could compose new tunes on the spot during jams, something that would eventually become commonplace in Down with Disease and frequent in Mike's Groove. —Andy Bernstein

This was just your average Phish show until the second song of the second set. This was not your average Bowie. On a 90-minute tape this takes up almost all of side A and part of side B! The jam never lets down, either—it's the type of jam you can listen to all the way through, rewind, and hear again! —Matt Richardson

The best show of the New Year's Run in '94. The ovation after Bowie was tremendous, as the band uncharacteristically took a bow. Halley's Comet reminded the fans that they attended a special show. —Matthew Napoli

A tape everyone should have in their possession. The second set provided the mother of all Bowies. It jammed for over 30 minutes and touched on every aspect and emotion that music can produce, from the flowing peacefulness of Trey's soft touch to his mad striking of chords that send chills down my spine. —Matthew Ashenfelder

Sweetest segue from Jim into one of the best Foams I have ever heard. —Alex Banks

[12/30/94] [ACCESSIBILITY: •••]
Late Show with David Letterman, Ed Sullivan Theater, New York, NY
Chalkdust

Poor Phish—they looked so nervous, and boy did it show. Definitely the worst Chalkdust ever, played at the request of Sir Dave, no less. —Tyler Harris

12/30/94 [ACCESSIBILITY: ••••] [ATTEND. 19,165; CAP. 19,165] [TIX $22.50]
Madison Square Garden, New York, NY

I: Wilson > Rift, AC/DC Bag, Sparkle, Simple, Stash, Fee > Scent of a Mule, Cavern

II: Sample, Poor Heart > Tweezer, I'm Blue I'm Lonesome, YEM, Purple Rain > HYHU, Harry Hood, Tweezer Reprise

E: Frankenstein

I'm Blue I'm Lonesome performed acoustic with Trey on acoustic guitar, Mike on banjo, Fishman on mandolin, and Page on upright bass. Fishman on vacuum for Purple Rain. Wilson from this show appears on A Live One.

Trey acknowledged having nerves upon taking the stage at Madison Square Garden for the first time, and it shows in the band's tame performance. Despite a heavy-duty second set that includes three of the big guns (Tweezer, YEM and Harry) all well-played and a high-octane, sold-out arena, this show was clearly the weakest of the '94 New Year's run. Still, the strength of the '94 New Year's run is evidenced by the fact that each show has supporters who claim it was "the best of the four"; I have a few friends who swear this show changed their lives. —Tyler Harris

Having played Letterman before the show, the guys had to be on top of the world. To start their first show at MSG, Phish chose Wilson to get the entire audience chanting. They're very tight—AC/DC is stellar, and Cavern is also so tight and hard. Set II has a Tweezer that kicks. The YEM is one of my favorites with lots of tempo and melody changes. Purple Rain with an excellent vacuum solo and the best Harry I've heard from that time. It just keeps going. —Connor Bergman

This lackluster show still has some kicks, though not in the Sample second set opener or Poor Heart. Look to the second set, where Tweezer shines. Blue and Lonesome doesn't really take off, YEM as always is good to hear with the vocal breakdown jam in the middle. Also, Purple Rain kicks ass into Harry Hood > Tweezer Reprise. —Aaron Benton

12/31/94 [ACCESSIBILITY: ••••] [ATTEND. 15,135; CAP. 15,135] [TIX $23.50]
Boston Garden, Boston, MA

I: Golgi, NICU, Antelope, Glide, Mound, Peaches, Divided Sky, Funky Bitch

II: Old Home Place, Maze, Bouncing, Mike's > Buffalo Bill > Mike's > Yerushalayim > Weekapaug, Amazing Grace

III: "Hot Dog Vocals" > MSO, Also Sprach > James Bond Theme > New Year's Countdown > Auld Lang Syne > Tropical Hot Dog Night > Chalkdust > Horse > Silent, Suzie > Slave

E: Simple

Rock and Roll Part 2 played on PA while band took the stage; Trey jammed on it, then the band started Golgi. Tom Marshall on vocals for Antelope. Digital Delay Loop jam in Maze intro. Hot Dog Vocals had the band, offstage, talking about ordering a hot dog and french fries. MSO cut short in the middle by voice over PA system announcing the delivery of "your hot dog"—beginning of the New Year's celebration as band boards giant hot dog and flies over crowd. Bond Theme/Hot Dog Night played over PA (prerecorded). Mike's grandmother walked across the stage waving a shoe during Chalkdust. Extended jam on Suzie. Auld Lang Syne jam at the end of Simple. Bouncing from this show appears on A Live One. Auld Lang Syne jam in Weekapaug.

This show has some sloppy playing, sure—Fishman rushes through the end of Antelope, and there's a bunch more miscues sprinkled throughout the night. But what this show lacks in technical prowess it makes up for in emotion. The second set includes the hottest version of Maze they've ever done, complete with a digital delay loop intro. In the third set, after all the midnight madness had passed, the band took Suzie around one more time. We watched in awe as Trey steered the jam into the quiet depths of the old, rotten Boston Garden and emerged with the opening chords of one of the most glorious Slave to the Traffic Lights ever. Everyone glowed. —Marcia Collins

My first New Year's show; it's still one of my favorite shows of all time. The energy at the start that built up into Golgi was incredible. I never knew Mike sang Phunky Bitch until he stepped up! Appropriate Old Home Place opener for the second set that also had a crazy Maze. Set III had the flying hot dog and a smoking Chalkdust to kick in the New Year that really made up for the short, cut, almost fake Chalkdust on Letterman the night before. The Simple encore was sweet with an Auld Lang Syne tease. I'm glad I saw the last Phish show ever at the old Garden. —Bill Patrick

This show has the best Silent in the Morning: if you listen to the tape, right after the "I think that this exact thing happened to me just last year" line, all you hear is the cheering and screaming of the crowd. The energy that flows out of the tape is great. It makes you want to start yelling for New Year's. Then the Simple encore serves as the perfect end to a wonderful show. The place exploded with joy. Not only did Trey laugh, he let himself go and enjoy the music. —Gina D'Amico

Everyone knows the story of this show, but I have one of my own. Before this show I was hanging out, wanting some coffee, but shit, no wallet. I really needed some java so I dug out my lucky half dollar I had carried for about five years and reluctantly used it for a cup of shitty coffee. Then I turned around and spilled it on the bro behind me. He was wearing a brand new coat and now it was soaked and stained. I felt horrible and just apologized and left. While outside in the cold Boston air the coffee-soiled stranger approached me. He handed me my lucky half dollar AND a full cup of java. My whole attitude changed, and the show that night was the perfect way to exit a great year. I've seen the stranger many times since—it's nice to know there are brothers like him out there. —Justin Weiss

12/31/94 Boston Garden, Boston, MA

"New Year's '94"

The Hot Dog Show, as it later became known, was Phish's first and last solo performance at the old Boston Garden. The culmination of Phish's five years of New Year's Eve shows in and around Boston, New Year's Eve '94 found Phish taking the stage like sports stars to the beat of "Rock and Roll No. 2," which Trey joined before the band dropped into Golgi. The night was off and running.

It would be a night during which Phish pulled out their most elaborate prank to date, the giant hot dog. Prior to the third set—which followed an incredible second set that featured one of the best versions of Maze ever, plus Mike's Song with the rare Buffalo Bill wedged in the middle—the band came over the PA system, and Fishman talked about his desire to order "a giant hot dog." The punch line came in the middle of My Sweet One, when a voice came over the PA system and informed the band, "Your order's ready." As the band started up Also Sprach Zarathustra, a giant hot dog, cola and fries (emblazoned with the Phish logo) dropped from the rafters. What at first seemed like a giant prop turned into something more spectacular when the band—assisted by men wearing "Rocket Scientist" jackets—boarded the hot dog and flew it down to the other end of the venue, playing their instruments and throwing custom-labeled Ping-Pong balls into the crowd. (The band later said the hot dog was kosher, blessed by a rabbi backstage).

Even funnier, perhaps, was the butcher job *Rolling Stone* editors did on Paul Robicheau's review of the show. Among the things that *did not* happen on this night: the band did not wear wet suits, the band did not use the aquarium set (both of those were New Year's '93 props), and the band did not cover the Beatles' *White Album*.

But the band *did* finish the year with an emotional Slave and a Simple encore that returned to Auld Lang Syne, a fitting close to 1994.

1995 SUMMER Stir It Up

Although this tour really began in Idaho in early June, Phish snuck in a mid-May gig which gave them the opportunity to debut a slew of new tunes in front of a small crowd in Lowell, MA—tunes which would make for dramatically different setlists on this tour. Gone were the frequent Golgis, Caverns, Samples, and Juliuses. Instead, the band showed a willingness to mix up their song selection more, even if some of the new setlist combinations did start to look alike a few weeks into the tour. The only problem? The tour's length. For those looking for true improvisation from Vermont's Phinest, this tour didn't offer it to the extent longer tours of the past—or future—would. But this was supposed to be a nice quick tour so Phish could enjoy some personal time off later in the summer before launching into a huge fall tour.

5/16/95 [ACCESSIBILITY: ••••]
Lowell Memorial Auditorium, Lowell, MA

Don't You Wanna Go, Ha Ha Ha > Spock's Brain, Strange Design, Reba, Theme, HYHU > Lonesome Cowboy Bill > HYHU, Free, Glide II > YEM, Adeline, Sample

E: I'll Come Running > Gloria

Voters For Choice benefit concert. Phish headlined bill which included Jen Trynin and the Emergency Broadcast Network, and played one set. A group of fans sang "Happy Birthday" to Page before Adeline. Concert debuts: Don't You Wanna Go, Ha Ha Ha, Spock's Brain, Strange Design, Theme, Lonesome Cowboy Bill, Free, Glide II, I'll Come Running, and Gloria.

1995

81 Total Show Dates
- **1** one-set show
- **78** two-set shows
- **2** three-set shows

Phan Picks 1995

SHOW	THE SKINNY
1) 12/31/95 New York, NY	Most popular show of all time.
2) 10/31/95 Chicago, IL	*Quadrophenia* on Halloween.
3) 12/30/95 New York, NY	Fun show, outstanding Hood.
4) 12/29/95 Worcester, MA	"The Real Gin" in set II.
5) 12/11/95 Portland, ME	Dog Log redux, plus Warren.
6) 11/30/95 Dayton, OH	Insanely well jammed 2nd set.
7) 06/26/95 Saratoga, NY	DwD > Free runs 30+ minutes.
8) 05/16/95 Lowell, MA	Tons of new song debuts.
9) 06/14/95 Memphis, TN	45-minute Tweezer in 2nd set.
10) 11/11/95 Atlanta, GA	Last of three nights at the Fox.

MUSICAL RECAP: 1994's logical extreme—adding epic-length jams to every show—was virtually realized in 1995. Phish's jamming continued to mature, too, reaching a peak in December that arguably marked the extreme of how far Phish could push themselves with that style.

REPRESENTATIVE JAMS: Drowned > Lizards, 12/31/95; Weekapaug > Sea and Sand, 12/31/95; Bathtub Gin > Real Me > Bathtub Gin, 12/29/95.

ORIGINAL SONG DEBUTS: Acoustic Army (6/7/95), Billy Breathes (9/27/95), Cars Trucks Buses (9/27/95), The Fog That Surrounds (9/27/95), Free (5/16/95), Glide II* (5/16/95), Ha Ha Ha (5/16/95), Keyboard Kavalry (9/27/95), Prince Caspian (6/8/95), Spock's Brain (5/16/95), Taste (6/7/95), Theme from the Bottom (5/16/95).

COVER SONG DEBUTS: A Day in the Life (6/10/95), Come Together* (12/8/95), Cryin'* (9/29/95), Don't You Wanna Go (5/16/95), Gloria* (5/16/95), I'll Come Running* (5/16/95), Johnny B. Goode (6/17/95), Hello My Baby (9/27/91), Life on Mars (10/13/95), Lonesome Cowboy Bill (5/16/95), My Generation* (10/31/95), Suspicious Minds (9/30/95), plus all of *Quadrophenia* (10/31/95). (*only ever played once)

Dark Horses

SHOW	THE SKINNY
1) 12/09/95 Albany, NY	Incredible YEM w/silent jam.
2) 11/14/94 Orlando, FL	Half-hour Stash in second set.
3) 12/14/95 Binghamton, NY	Second set is one giant segue.
4) 12/07/95 Niagara Falls, NY	Amazing jams in Melt, Mike's.
5) 10/22/95 Champaign, IL	Gorgeous Tweezer.

Most-Played Originals:		
1) Free	31	56%
2) Sample in a Jar	30	52%
3) Strange Design	28	44%
4) Acoustic Army	27	38%
5) Poor Heart	26	37%
5) Theme	26	37%
7) David Bowie	25	35%
7) Maze	25	35%
7) Antelope	25	35%
7) Stash	25	35%
7) Sparkle	25	35%

Most-Played Covers:		
1) A Day in the Life	23	25%
2) Sweet Adeline	20	21%
3) Ya Mar	18	16%
4) Also Sprach	16	14%
4) Amazing Grace	16	14%
4) Uncle Pen	16	13%
7) Hello My Baby	15	13%
8) Timber Ho	12	12%
8) Guitar Gently Weeps	12	10%
10) Fire	9	9%
10) Frankenstein	9	9%

First-Set Openers:	
1) My Friend My Friend	10
2) AC/DC Bag	7
3) Ya Mar	6
4) Cars Trucks Buses	5
4) Sample in a Jar	5

Second-Set Openers:	
1) Also Sprach	10
2) Timber Ho	8
3) Maze	4
3) Runaway Jim	4
3) Wilson	4

Top Henrietta Songs:	
1) Suspicious Minds	8
2) Cracklin' Rosie	3
2) Lonesome Cowboy Bill	3
4) Bike	1
4) Brain	1
4) Cryin'	1
4) Do It in the Road	1
4) Love You	1
4) Purple Rain	1
4) Terrapin	1

A Cappella Songs:	
1) Sweet Adeline	20
2) Amazing Grace	16
3) Hello My Baby	15
4) Carolina	3

No one had any idea Phish planned to use the Voters For Choice benefit show as a testing ground for an entire set's worth of new material, but Gloria Steinem tipped the crowd off to that in her introduction. All of the then-new songs are now well-known, with the exception of Spock's Brain (which died after summer '95) and Glide II. Too bad—I think Glide II (a.k.a. "Flip") has promise. It starts with a groove reminiscent of Hydrogen, then Trey comes in with a guitar line that's simple but sweet and seems to complement Free's melody. He slowly sings, "Gliiiide, flip flip flip flip...," ending each verse with the refrain, "It's time." That's repeated for about five minutes, then the song suddenly ends. It's a mesmerisingly beautiful idea that's clearly a work in progress. —Lee Johnston

The coolest thing about this tape is the beginning where Gloria Steinem talks about the charity show and how special the atmosphere is. However, when she goes on and on for a few minutes the anxious crowd starts to let her know how they feel. The roar of the crowd is phenomenal when she mentions any name from the band and says Phish alone. —Shannon C. Lancaster

The highlight of the show for me was Spock's Brain, a slow funk that features excellent vocal interplay between all four members. I can't understand why they dropped it after only five performances. Reba was also excellent. The jam included a light playful section, a spacey bass section, a heavy section and the climax! —Brendan Neagle

What makes this tape essential in any collection is hearing Theme and Free as they were originally written. Both have become such free-form songs live and the Billy Breathes version of Free is so different, that only this tape offers a true representation of the well thought-out foundations for each tune. It also marks the night that Phish proved they still could write great songs. *Hoist* had made a few of us wonder. —Andy Bernstein

6/7/95 **[ACCESSIBILITY: •••] [ATTEND. 3,964; CAP. 12,428] [TIX $17–$20]**
Boise State University Pavilion, Boise, ID
I: Possum, Weigh, Taste, Strange Design, Stash, If I Could, Scent of a Mule, Wedge, Funky Bitch, Slave
II: Ha Ha Ha > Maze, Spock's Brain, Theme, Lonesome Cowboy Bill, Acoustic Army, Sample, Harry Hood, Suzie
E: Guitar Gently Weeps

Last Wedge, 8/20/93 Morrison, CO [134 shows]. Last Weigh, 5/20/94 Olympia, WA [89 shows]. Concert debuts: Taste, Acoustic Army.

There couldn't have been much more anticipation for this show, the summer tour opener. In response, Phish spent well over a minute working the crowd into a frenzy, lingering on the Possum intro, getting louder, softer, louder again, softer, and then exploding into the song we know and love. When Trey chooses Weigh, at least you know he's thinking about making interesting choices. A debut therefore seems to fall into that category, as does the second performance of Strange Design. Stash was the centerpiece jam of the set. In the second, the return of the Wedge was exciting but didn't compare (in my opinion) to those 1993 versions with the extended intros. To compensate, Phish gave us Funky Bitch and Slave to close the set. The second set had much new material and was not as coherently unified but it was still far from an average Phish set. The first While My Guitar Gently Weeps encore marked the end of a particularly creative night for Trey and friends. —Greg Schwartz

6/8/95 **[ACCESSIBILITY: •••] [ATTEND. 5,923; CAP. 12,000] [TIX $17–$20]**
Delta Center, Salt Lake City, UT
I: Don't You Wanna Go, Ha Ha Ha, Runaway Jim, Guelah, Mound, FEFY, Reba > Caspian, Chalkdust
II: Simple, Rift, Free, Bouncing, Tweezer > Lifeboy, Poor Heart, Julius
E: GTBT

Show moved from Wolf Mountain Amphitheatre in Park City, UT, because of inclement weather. Concert debut: Caspian.

When we were informed that the Yanni concert was moved from Wolf Mountain to the Delta Center, we were sure they'd move the Phish show there too (disappointing—Wolf Mountain seemed like a perfect place for Phish to do their thing). The only good part, besides the music, about the Delta Center show came when I went to the box office to exchange my tickets and ended up with fifth row seats. Delta Center security was so tight that they were confiscating balloons. This led to a chant for Big Ball Jam, but I guess the band didn't want their beach balls treated as contraband so they skipped it. They did debut Prince Caspian. —Justin Weiss

6/9/95 **[ACCESSIBILITY: ••••] [ATTEND. 9,216; CAP. 9,216] [TIX $17–$20]**
Red Rocks Amphitheatre, Morrison, CO
I: My Friend, Divided Sky, Strange Design, Oh Kee > AC/DC Bag, Theme, Taste, Sparkle, Antelope
II: Melt, Wedge, Scent of a Mule, Cavern, Bowie, Acoustic Army, Adeline, Slave
E: Squirming Coil

LOWELL MEMORIAL AUDITORIUM, Lowell, MA

Tuesday, May 16, 1995

I saw a blurb for this show deep in the *Boston Globe* a few days before tickets went on sale—"Bands to play benefit concert for Pro-Choice group." So this wasn't a secret gig, per se, although you had to be relatively in-the-know to snag tickets.

I got through to Ticketmaster twenty minutes after tickets went on sale, certain that they would have sold out. But they had seats, and weeks later, I found I snagged fifth row tickets on the floor—this show took almost a day to sell out despite a venue capacity of just under 3,000. About five days before the show, the folks from Voters for Choice sent a mailer to my P.O. box thanking me for buying tickets and offering full instructions on how to claim them at the door. I don't know if they were afraid of anti-abortionist violence—the three older men holding "Abortion Kills Babies" signs outside the venue didn't seem much of a threat, at least in the physical sense— or ticket scalping, but buying tickets to this show was much easier than picking up the tickets on hold at will-call. Show ID, show Ticketmaster number, show ID again—you had to pity the ticketless wandering in front of the venue this night.

We made it inside during Jen Trynin's set. Her band closed up shop, and a nice woman from Massachusetts Voters for Choice came out to give a lengthy intro for Gloria Steinem, at which point my friend and I turned to each other in disbelief. Steinem, the famous feminist, the former president of the National Organization for Women, was not only in the house but had the task of introducing Phish. Well, at least she tried. Most of the crowd couldn't wait for Steinem to finish. But Gloria did manage to tip the band's hand in her intro: "There'll be more new songs that you've never heard before!"

Driving to the show, I had expected one, maybe two new songs, but this night just kept coming. A gospely opener (Don't You Wanna Go), then Ha Ha Ha, into Spock's Brain, then a new (and at that point untitled) ballad sung by Page. Whew—four new ones in a row. Immediately following was one of the best Rebas ever, trailed by more rollouts: Theme from the Bottom—the best of the new batch, I thought at the time—and a cover of the Velvet Underground's Lonesome Cowboy Bill sung by Fish.

The Henrietta interlude also saw a vote for the name of the song that became Spock's Brain. Trey offered the crowd four choices: The Plane, The First Single, Israel, and Spock's Brain; as the crowd saw it, it was no contest. More new songs followed—I recall really liking Free and not comprehending what I gather is now called Glide II.

A few people off to my right sang a brief Happy Birthday to Page during the a cappella part. After it was over, I couldn't say that it had felt like a Phish show. It wasn't bad, it was just something different.

But that this show happened at all deserves special note. When the Brookline Clinic shootings shocked the nation in January '95, it impacted the band—John Paluska lived next door to one of the targeted clinics and worked to arrange this gig.

A good show for a good cause.

—Chris De Gieson

Holy Red Rocks! First night had such lax security and a really laid-back crowd. They treated us to an assortment of new and old. The Divided Sky seemed like a treat, then we listened objectively to new songs thereafter. Strange Design drew a lukewarm response but Theme, Taste and Acoustic Army were hits. I've never seen a crowd be so quiet as the Red Rocks crowd during Acoustic Army. Solid versions of SOAM, Bowie, Slave and a rare Wedge carried us through the second set, then Page squared things away with a beautiful Coil encore. —Trevor Norris

As always, Red Rocks is an experience in and of itself. It always seems like the fans are crazier and the music sounds better. Divided Sky may have been the best I'd ever heard. Overall, a nice performance. —Lindsey Bates

Tickets were harder to get this year but it seemed that everyone who went to the park got one. —Julie Hunter

The encore, a Page solo Squirming Coil on his baby grand, sounded so sweet. The second it ended, a huge lightning bolt struck behind the stage and the wind picked up! —Emily Brown

6/10/95 [ACCESSIBILITY: ••••] [ATTEND. 9,216; CAP. 9,216] [TIX $17–$20]
Red Rocks Amphitheatre, Morrison, CO
I: Makisupa > Llama, Caspian, It's Ice, Free, Rift, YEM > HYHU > Lonesome Cowboy Bill > HYHU, Suzie
II: Maze, Fee, Uncle Pen, Mike's > Hydrogen > Weekapaug, Amazing Grace, Sample
E: Day in the Life

Fishman on vacuum for Lonesome Cowboy Bill. Concert debut: Day in the Life.

Phish has this strange habit of giving me exactly what I want to hear when I want to hear it. For example, a Makisupa opener with Trey's 4:20 wake-up call. Or a YEM that ends in a vocal HYHU which introduces the last-ever (to the relief of many) Lonesome Cowboy Bill, with the only Lonesome Cowboy Bill vacuum solo. Suzie is a great closer. Similarly, Maze is always a killer opener. And Mike's > Hydrogen > Groove is the ideal centerpiece. Second set was definitely too short but the highlight of the show was the A Day in the Life encore. I instantly recognized the intro chords and immediately picked up on the band's excitement. That huge chord that marks the end of Sgt. Pepper (you know the one) also marked the end of the Red Rocks run, and the band left the stage triumphantly. —Greg Schwartz

As rain fell, the boys treated us to a massive, from-the-pages-of-history Mike's > I Am Hydrogen > Weekapaug. Thirty minutes of intensely inspirational jamming. —Amy Duncan

Apparently, the boys decided on the day of the first Red Rocks show that it would be cool to learn A Day in the Life to play the next day. Word got around the scene quickly that Phish had a big musical surprise in store for us on the second night, and I could not have been more blown away when they nailed the debut performance. —Tyler Harris

6/13/95 [ACCESSIBILITY: •••] [ATTEND. 8,268; CAP. 19,949] [TIX $17.50–$20]
Riverport Amphitheatre, Maryland Heights, MO
I: Runaway Jim, Foam, Bouncing, Stash, Strange Design, Taste, Reba, HYHU > Terrapin > HYHU, Sparkle, Chalkdust
II: Bowie, Lizards, Axilla II, Theme, Acoustic Army, Harry Hood, Golgi
E: Adeline, Julius

Fishman on vacuum for Terrapin. "Dave's Energy Guide" tease in Chalkdust.

This was definitely the worst show of the '95 summer tour. The classical Phish atmosphere was not there. Making the trip from Red Rocks was almost a waste of time. Even on tape, there is no mood. Stay away from this one. —Sean Miller

6/14/95 [ACCESSIBILITY: ••••] [ATTEND. 5,234; CAP. 5,234] [TIX $20]
Mud Island Amphitheatre, Memphis, TN
I: Don't You Wanna Go, Gumbo, NICU, Mound, Cavern, Possum, All Things, Amazing Grace, Horse > Silent, Spock's Brain, Melt
II: Also Sprach > Poor Heart, Tweezer, Acoustic Army, Guitar Gently Weeps
E: Simple > Rocky Top > Tweezer Reprise

It was an outdoor show on the Mississippi River—beautiful. First set was great; Don't You Wanna Go, Gumbo and NICU were great choices played well. But in the second set, the show seemed to go downhill. The Tweezer was unbearable, at least 30 minutes long. It felt never-ending—Phish is the only band that can play a song for 30 minutes without actually playing the song. But the encore made up for the Tweezer. It was three songs long: Simple, Rocky Top and Tweezer Reprise. This was a good show but definitely not one of their best. —Melanie and Melita Terrell

Some Phish jams aren't for the faint of heart. The Mud Island Tweezer, another in the series of experimental Tweezers begun at Bangor on 11/2/94 and continued in Bozeman on 11/28/94—and to continue later this tour at Finger Lakes—is probably the least musically satisfying of the batch, but for those interested in hearing Phish push the boundaries of improvisational rock, potholes and all, Mud Island is worth checking out. —Ed Smith

6/15/95 [ACCESSIBILITY: •••] [ATTEND. 13,571; CAP. 18,920] [TIX $18–$22]
Lakewood Amphitheatre, Atlanta, GA
I: My Friend, Sparkle, AC/DC Bag, Old Home Place, Taste, Wedge, Stash > I Didn't Know, Fluffhead, Antelope
II: MSC, Ha Ha Ha > Bowie, Strange Design, Theme, Scent of a Mule, Acoustic Army, Slave
E: Bouncing, Frankenstein

Fishman on trombone, Trey on megaphone, and Mike on electric drill for I Didn't Know.

I thought this crowd was a real letdown. We had seats in the pavilion and our section

"Voters For Choice"

5/16/95 Lowell Memorial Auditorium, Lowell, MA

One of Phish's longest-standing band policies was not playing benefit shows for politically charged issues. Besides a NORML benefit played for a few hundred people in the fall of 1988, Phish elected to steer clear of causes on the theory that they didn't want to infuse political messages into their music.

That all changed in January 1995, when a series of shootings at an abortion clinic in the Boston area rocked the nation. Phish's longtime manager, John Paluska, lived next door to one of the targeted clinics, and helped arrange a Voters for Choice benefit show as a way of both raising money for pro-choice causes and thanking the clinic volunteers. For one night, Phish would put aside their unofficial no-cause policy to do what felt right, and in the process, they'd raise $30,000.

The venue was a small 2,900 seat theater in the industrial Massachusetts town of Lowell, and in the crowd that night were workers and volunteers from the clinic, the guests of the bands. Also in attendance was NOW president Gloria Steinem, who served as emcee for Phish's set and later returned to the stage to hug Trey during Phish's impromptu take on "Gloria."

But Phish fans remember Lowell not so much for the cause as for the music. It was a night that saw the breakout of a next generation of Phish music, songs like Free and Theme from the Bottom that would become key components of many sets thereafter.

In the end, though, the band wondered about the costs of playing for a political cause, especially one as charged as the abortion debate. "I am supporting the right for people to make a choice, and I don't like the us-versus-them mentality," Fishman later told *Relix*. But the nature of the event meant that, for better and for worse, Phish had chosen sides. They haven't played an event like Voters For Choice since.

was empty. When we moved to a different, more crowded section, everyone was sitting down. Despite the less-than-enthusiastic response, the band played well—I was pleased with the sets and psyched to have a two-song encore. I loved Fluffhead followed by Antelope and I thought Slave was unbelievable. —Chris Haines

6/16/95 [ACCESSIBILITY: ••••] [ATTEND. 12,956; CAP. 19,903] [TIX $17.50–$20]
Walnut Creek Amphitheatre, Raleigh, NC
I: Halley's > Down with Disease, Esther, Ya Mar, Cry Baby Cry, It's Ice, My Mind's, Dog Faced Boy, Catapult, Melt
II: Runaway Jim > Free, Carolina, YEM, Squirming Coil
E: Bold as Love

"Melt" teases before Dog Faced Boy. YEM featured Boyd Tinsley on fiddle. "Oye Como Va" jam in YEM.

This beautiful day started off with a Three Little Birds soundcheck, then the show itself offered the first-ever experimental Jim into Free. —Waylon Bayard

Halley's > DwD opener, are you kidding? A prelude to an incredible first set. A precious Esther leads to Ya Mar. Cry Baby Cry was another treat. Fish kept teasing the SOAM opening, just trying to get this thing going. Dog Faced Boy and Catapult chilled us out before an insane SOAM finally came. The second set was one of those where you had to be there. Experimental Jim > Free was too intense. YEM with Boyd Tinsley was exciting, and Mike's bass solo at the end of YEM is sick. Nice Coil and an always-welcome Bold as Love encore. Great show at a great venue. —Trevor Norris

Boyd Tinsley of the Dave Matthews Band makes YEM shine at this show, but this version of Free is a definite must-listen. Wow. —Dave Swank

They really screwed up the Cry Baby Cry; it hasn't been played since. —Joshua Howley

6/17/95 [ACCESSIBILITY: ••••] [ATTEND. 16,253; CAP. 23,000] [TIX $18–$22]
Nissan Pavilion at Stone Ridge, Gainesville, VA
I: Divided Sky, Suzie, Taste, Fee, Uncle Pen, Julius, Lawn Boy, Curtain > Stash
II: Wilson, Maze, Mound, Tweezer > Johnny B. Goode > Tweezer > McGrupp, Acoustic Army, Adeline, Harry Hood, Sample
E: Three Little Birds

Dave Matthews on guitar and vocals and Leroi Moore on saxophone for Three Little Birds. Concert debuts: Johnny B. Goode, Three Little Birds.

The first set opener, Divided Sky, proved to be an omen for a good show. In set one, a great version of Julius showed up, as well as an incredibly good Curtain > Stash—very trippy. The second set featured Tweezer > Johnny B. Goode > Tweezer that rocked hard. JBG was totally unexpected and rocked way harder than Chuck Berry. The encore, Three Little Birds with Dave Matthews and Leroi Moore, was a cool surprise. —Jay Green

The band soundchecked Johnny B. Goode before the show, but no one really thought they'd play it during one of their sets. Chris Kuroda, joking around with the tapers before the first set, said, "I was wondering what they were going to break into next—Around and Around?" But then, in the midst of a very interesting Tweezer jam, out it came. The band charged through it, just ripping it up, then brought the jam back out the other side into a spacey realm similar to the portion of the Bozeman Tweezer christened "Montana" on *A Live One*. —Lock Steele

6/19/95 [ACCESSIBILITY: ••••] [ATTEND. 19,964; CAP. 19,964] [TIX $18.50–$20]
Deer Creek Amphitheatre, Noblesville, IN
I: Theme > Poor Heart, AC/DC Bag, Tela, PYITE, Reba, Strange Design, Rift, Cavern, Antelope
II: Simple > Bowie, Mango, Loving Cup, Sparkle, YEM, Acoustic Army, Possum
E: Day in the Life

Possum played heavy-metal style, missing final verse.

This was the first time Phish ever played Deer Creek and it was a sold-out show. Deer Creek is the best place to hear any band—the sound is crystal clear and the scene is so peaceful. Loving Cup was the highlight for my show, though every song was played with exactness and clarity. Solid show from start to finish; they certainly made a mark for themselves at Deer Creek. —Rob Koeller

The first 45 minutes of this show, to my ears, is the tightest Phish has ever played. Theme from the Bottom is just so on, with Trey playing some very beautiful and soulful grooves throughout. Everything is played so well but I have to single out the PYITE and Reba. The latter in particular is flawless—guaranteed to be one of your favorite versions. There's also the worst lyric flub I've ever heard on a Phish tape. It comes during Rift and is so flubbed that Trey is obviously quite amused. —Russell Lane

6/20/95 [ACCESSIBILITY: ••••] [ATTEND. 10,685; CAP. 18,781] [TIX $20]
Blossom Music Center, Cuyohoga Falls, OH
I: Llama, Spock's Brain, Ginseng Sullivan, Foam, Bathtub Gin, If I Could, Taste, I Didn't Know, Melt
II: Halley's, Chalkdust, Caspian, Uncle Pen, Mike's > Contact, Weekapaug > HYHU > Cracklin' Rosie > HYHU, Highway to Hell
E: Slave, Amazing Grace

Fishman on vacuum for I Didn't Know. Last Ginseng Sullivan, 10/10/94 Louisville, KY [58 shows].

The best show in the midwest in summer '95. Spock's Brain was very harmonious. Mike didn't miss a beat in Ginseng Sullivan. Damn fine rendition of I Didn't Know. Uncle Pen is always a show-stopper and this one was a beauty. The show ended with the pent-up energy enclosed in the little ditty known as Slave to the Traffic Light. —Sean Miller

In the second set they jam a theme in between Mike's Song and Contact that will always stand out in my mind. It was like a journey into the world of the unknown, bringing me so far out of reality, carrying me around, then dropping me down into a slow-starting Contact. My friends often thank me for playing this tape during a camping trip we went on, because they hadn't realized the full power of Phish live until they heard this. —Dan Charron

6/22/95 [ACCESSIBILITY: •••] [ATTEND. 13,204; CAP. 13,204] [TIX $20]
Finger Lakes Performing Arts Center, Canandaigua, NY
I: Sample, Scent of a Mule, Ha Ha Ha, Divided Sky, Guelah, It's Ice, Strange Design, Maze, Cavern, Adeline
II: Theme > Tweezer > Tweezer Reprise
E: Acoustic Army, Guitar Gently Weeps

"My Generation" jam in Tweezer.

First set was great: new tunes, and I always love something a cappella. But the second set, ugh! Don't get me wrong, Tweezer is one of my faves, but halfway through I was just standing there scratching my head. The worst show I ever saw. —John Cunningham

Canandaigua is my favorite place to see a show. Every time Phish plays there, the weather is clear and warm and the atmosphere is groovy. First set was good, but the second set on the other hand... Tweezer > Tweezer Reprise, they played well but it was intolerable for me. Luckily, they kicked ass for While My Guitar Gently Weeps. —David White

This second set deserves a second glance. It may not have been the best Tweezer in history, but it was the last of the great Tweezerfests of '94–'95. Theme was at that point the most intense of the new tunes, and this version is still my favorite. It never really ended, and Tweezer never really started. It never really sounded like a normal Tweezer either, though it was ferocious through and through. Trey was losing it to the point of it breaking down to just heavy noise—I had seen Trey run around screaming with the bullhorn before, but never with so much evil in him. Somewhere in the midst of this jam was a crazy My Generation jam with the strange bluegrass harmony we would hear again on Halloween. But no other recognizable themes popped up until Tweezer Reprise surfaced 45 minutes later. Out of that hell, however, came the most beautiful moment in Phish musical history. After all the screaming and aural assaults, Trey crouched down and hid under the piano, Mike crouched behind the drums, and Fish ducked to make himself disappear. They didn't stop playing, they just hid to put Page in the limelight. This is the moment that the basic melody for Keyboard Kavalry was born. Page began a simple, beautiful melody that built from nothing into sheer energy during the next few minutes. It climbed higher until the others reappeared and eventually exploded into Tweezer Reprise. The tape is worth having for these five minutes of music alone. —Davey Inkrea

6/23/95 [ACCESSIBILITY: ••••] [ATTEND. 16,643; CAP. 16,643] [TIX $22.50–$25]
Waterloo Village Music Center, Stanhope, NJ
I: Simple, Chalkdust, Caspian, Reba, Ginseng Sullivan, Free, Taste, YEM
II: Runaway Jim, Lizards, Wedge, Antelope, Harpua > Waterloo Jam > Llama, GTBT
E: Day in the Life

Waterloo Jam, Llama, and GTBT featured John Popper on harmonica. Harpua unfinished. Concert debut: Waterloo Jam.

After you see a guy on a body board with a big blood spot, it's hard to have a good time. The scene was chaotic. No one had a clue, not the cops or the staff. I walked three miles and missed almost the whole first set. The encore, A Day in the Life, as well as Popper's cameo during Waterloo, were surreal. The bus ride on the way back to the auxiliary lots was also an experience, driving on two wheels going around hairpin turns. The bus driver was a heavy metal maiden from hell! —Dan Kurtz

Thousands of fans got to the show late; fortunately, I wasn't one of them because this show kicked ass from the get-go. The boys were on fire throughout the first set which featured lots of classics and soon-to-be classics. The second set, however, was by far dominant. After the rocking Antelope, Harpua was an unexpected treat but what followed was even more tasty: John Popper came out to lead the boys out of Waterloo and into Llama. —Eric Acquafredda

In light of the tragedy and the mayhem at this show, it's easy to forget that it was a superb performance with everything from a YEM to close the first set, a very strong Runaway Jim, and a simply terrific Wedge, a song the band sometimes struggles performing live but one that hit on all cylinders that night. —Scott Sifton

6/24/95 [ACCESSIBILITY: •••] [ATTEND. 13,700; CAP. 13,700] [TIX $18.50–$20]
Mann Music Center, Philadelphia, PA
I: Fee, Rift, Spock's Brain, Julius, Glide, Mound, Stash, Horse > Silent, Squirming Coil
II: Also Sprach > Halley's > Bowie, Lifeboy, Suzie, Harry Hood, Acoustic Army, Adeline, Golgi
E: Bold as Love

I thought I'd mention this show merely for the second set Bowie, but then I realized there's more to this show than one would think. It starts off with a real good Fee > Rift combo and follows with Julius which had a DwD flavor to it. The rest of the first is average.... So on to set 2, with one of my all time favorite pieces: 2001 > Halley's > Bowie. The Bowie is hands-down my favorite of all time. The jam goes off into dark space, then slowly comes back and rolls like a freight train out of control. A must have! Hood is really beautiful as is the Acoustic Army where Trey thanks the crowd for being so quiet and attentive. If only all crowds would be like this. —Brian Watkins

When they played Spock's Brain as the third song of the night, we obviously had no idea the song was headed for the closet. Through fall '97, the band hasn't played it since. I hope Phish dusts off this forgotten gem and shines it up some time soon. Besides being a rare song with writing credited to the entire group (like Tweezer and Theme), Spock's would fit amazingly well with Phish's current funk jamming style. —Scott Sifton

The best Bowie I have ever seen. Even when the guys at the soundboard thought it was over (they killed the lights), Phish kept going. Also during this set, Mike and Trey chased each other around onstage. They were running around Page and behind Fishman several times. It was hilarious! —Tim Herrman

6/25/95 [ACCESSIBILITY: ••••] [ATTEND. 13,700; CAP. 13,700] [TIX $18.50–$20]
Mann Music Center, Philadelphia, PA
I: Ya Mar > AC/DC Bag, Taste, Theme, If I Could > Sparkle, Divided Sky, I Didn't Know, Melt
II: Maze, Sample, Scent of a Mule, Mike's > Do It in the Road > HYHU > Weekapaug, Amazing Grace, Cavern
E: Bouncing > Slave

Fishman on vacuum for I Didn't Know.

The opening combo of Ya Mar > AC/DC Bag is perhaps the greatest way to open a show. My friend Jay swears he heard Page playing that classical masterpiece Rhapsody in Blue during Divided Sky. Seeing Fishman's hip thrusting motions during Why Don't We Do It in the Road has left a memorable, yet scary, impression on my mind. —Ric Hannah

In many ways, this should have been a great show: a solid first set with a strong opening duo and lots of jamming room in Theme, Divided Sky and SOAM, and a second set built around the suite of Mike's > Do It in the Road > Weekapaug, all capped off by a please-everyone Bouncin' > Slave encore. But something just didn't click on this night; though some of the jams are on, this show lacks the apparent unity of purpose that makes a show like the following night in Saratoga so special. —Rich Mazer

6/26/95 [ACCESSIBILITY: ••••] [ATTEND. 18,662; CAP. 20,296] [TIX $17–$20]
Saratoga Performing Arts Center, Saratoga Springs, NY
I: My Friend, Don't You Wanna Go, Bathtub Gin, NICU > Sloth, My Mind's, It's Ice, Dog Faced Boy, Tela, Possum
II: Down with Disease > Free > Poor Heart > YEM, Strange Design, Antelope
E: Sleeping Monkey > Rocky Top

"Heartbreaker" jam in Possum.

WATERLOO CONCERT FIELD, Stanhope, NJ

Friday, June 23, 1995

A Phish fan named Daniel Malone died after falling from a car while on the way to this show at the Waterloo Village Concert Field.

Police told the media that he and many others chose not to wait for a bus, but if you were there, you know there were no buses available and hundreds of cars did not even make it to parking lots because highway exits were needlessly blocked off.

I have never experienced a concert-going nightmare that even compares to the hell that broke loose at Waterloo that summer. Thousands of fans jammed the highway, the off-ramps, and the "satellite" parking lots, and the system broke down.

With local police refusing to provide instructions or assistance, Malone and many of us were faced with the difficult choice of walking an unknown distance and missing at least half the show (as thousands did—I arrived at the end of the first set despite hitting the off-ramp to the venue a full hour before the scheduled start of the show), or jumping on the back of a car. While Daniel's decision to do just that was a tragic mistake, it was one made by many that night, and the police made no attempt to stop people or offer an alternative even after the show when they knew of the accident.

By not providing enough buses or adequate instructions, and interfering with cars' ability to get to assigned parking areas—parking spots were still open well after showtime, although some people were routed to lots more than three miles from the venue including a "Wild West Village" which, according to Waterloo officials, had never been used as a parking lot at one of their concerts before— authorities showed a complete and total contempt for Phish fans which led to disaster.

As far as I'm concerned, Waterloo, the Mt. Olive Police, and Delsener-Slater productions were directly responsible for the death of Daniel Malone. After hundreds of wonderful nights, there was one which everyone would like to forget, but no one should.

Rest in peace, Daniel.

—Andy Bernstein

"Come From Top the Mountain"

7/2&3/95 Sugarbush North, Fayston, VT

The legend of Sugarbush made its way around Phish circles rapidly after the band's unforgettable performance there in July 1994. A tour closer which featured an Antelope, Harpua and Harry Hood in one set, the show was even more notable for the venue—a stage perched on the side of a mountain, with a backdrop of miles of sky.

Needless to say, when Phish announced a two-day tour finale at Sugarbush for 1995, just about every fan in the Northeast marked it on their calendar. The fact that it came during the July 4 weekend, and that on-site, on-mountain camping adjacent to the concert site would be available, only further increased the anticipation.

By 11 A.M. on July 2, the day of the first show, a seemingly never-ending line of cars sloped its way up the mountain. The venue had warned that only cars with ticket-holders would be allowed in. And although the shows had only sold out days before, hordes of ticketless caravans arrived—and all somehow seemed to find their way in.

By showtime it was clear that thousands upon thousands of ticketless fans had made their way to Sugarbush, to the parking lot, and up the ski hill which formed the makeshift amphitheater. In fact, fans were pouring over the flimsy barriers which flanked the viewing area. A few guards tried to stop the first fence-hoppers, but when a sea of people oozed in from every side, venue security just gave up.

It was a free show. On a beautiful night, on a mountain, in Vermont. Nothing could have been more perfect.

A local DJ kicked off the festivities by welcoming everyone, including the gate crashers. The only request was that no one light campfires (it had been a dry summer in Vermont) and that everyone be patient with the bus system which imported and exported fans to satellite parking lots. The crowd was just a wee bit larger then they'd expected—the police estimated over 7,000 fence hoppers, plus 12,500 paid.

When Phish finally took the stage, anticipation and energy surged from the bottom of the ski hill to the very top. Thousands of bug-eyed fans squished their way up close, but an equal number fanned out up the slope, even past the downed barrier which marked the end of the viewing zone.

Rumors, accurate ones, that the best sound was actually far away from the stage in the mountain air, led many to watch from afar. The uninterrupted view of the Mad River Valley also attracted some intrepid climbers, a few of whom even made it all the way up to the top of Sugarbush North, about 4,000 feet above sea level and an equal distance from the stage.

And ah yes, there was a show. An unforgettable show. The first set featured the somewhat rare Gumbo and Curtain, and the impeccably rare Camel Walk, the first since 2/24/89—one of the longest stretches Phish had ever gone without playing a song before busting it back.

But what made the show stand out was performance more than setlists. It wasn't just that they played Camel Walk, it was that they ripped Camel Walk, played it different then ever before, with an eerie mix of restrain and abandon. That sort of tension marked the entire show. It wasn't a night of insane, down-the-neck hanging notes, it was a night of eerie precision.

The second set opened with a splendid Runaway Jim (it was this tour that the band first truly started opening up that song for extended improvisation) which segued into a slow but thundering Makisupa. Those perched high up on the ski hill were treated to a view of a far-off lightning storm which at one point actually appeared to fire to the beat of Mike's bass notes. The night went on to feature a captivating Tweezer, which morphed into Ha Ha Ha. Before it was all done there was a Slave and a Halley's Comet.

But even as the show ended, the night had just begun. On-mountain camping beckoned many, and an extended tent city stretched up a ski trail parallel to the stage area. It was Phish summer camp. The realization of a dream.

Night two was, by many opinions, not as strong as night one, but featured the breakout of Timber Ho after over 250 shows. But the weekend was about more than just music. It was about hordes of Phish fans coming together in the promised land, and realizing for the first time just how many of us there are.

This show contains, among other things, the first really huge Down with Disease, a song Phish had been avoiding most of the summer. Set I was incredible, with a Bathtub Gin in which Trey screams unintelligibly during the jam. Tela > Possum is, of course, an awesome dip into Gamehendge to close the set. The second set had a tough act to follow, so how does the band respond? Four huge jams, clearly highlighted by the new wide-open DwD which flowed surprisingly cleanly into Free. Can't complain about YEM or Antelope which more than make up for Poor Heart and Strange Design. —Greg Schwartz

This was one night where Phish was at their absolute best for an entire show. The crowd was so into the music: during Don't You Wanna Go, everyone was grooving in the same direction. The best Possum ever closed the first set, and the second set was unlike any other ever. The jamming was so tight, Fishman tore everything up. Poor Heart was different, and the YEM bass solo was too much. Smoke (I swear to God) started coming off Mike's bass. Sleeping Monkey was played as the encore for the only time that summer, capping off the best show that I have ever seen. —Joshua Howley

Sometimes Phish's jamming becomes so infectious that even normally tame songs fall under the sway. After the wonderful DwD (one of the most together jams the band has ever performed in that song) the jam led not to the DwD refrain but instead into a beautiful Free. The surprise came in Poor Heart—Trey became fixated on a downbeat noise and signaled Fish throughout the song to make a heavy beat effect. —Tyler Harris

Best Possum ever. The jam had to be at least 15 to 20 minutes and in the middle of it they started to play Heartbreaker by Zeppelin. It was very vague at first but then the crowd noticed this and went insane. —David Eckers

[6/27/95] *A Live One* released on Elektra.

6/28/95 [ACCESSIBILITY: ••••] [ATTEND. 11,055; CAP. 11,055] [TIX $22.50]
Jones Beach Music Theater, Wantagh, NY
I: Axilla II > Foam, FEFY, Reba, PYITE, Stash, Fluffhead, Chalkdust
II: Sample, Poor Heart, Tweezer > Gumbo, Sparkle, Suzie, Harry Hood, Tweezer Reprise
E: Adeline, Guitar Gently Weeps

"Ha Ha Ha" tease before Axilla. "Cannonball" and "Dave's Energy Guide" jams in Tweezer.

What is it about Tweezer jams that provoke such strong love/hate emotions? I know people who thought this show sucked, but for me the Tweezer—complete with a full Cannonball jam and a pronounced Dave's Energy Guide—hinted at the next evolution in Phish's jamming to follow during fall tour. Instead of taking Tweezer everywhere in the course of one set, like Bozeman, Mud Island and FLPAC, they explored a more focused series of ideas. Needless to say, I thought it rocked. —Pat Stanley

6/29/95 [ACCESSIBILITY: ••••] [ATTEND. 11,055; CAP. 11,055] [TIX $22.50]
Jones Beach Music Theater, Wantagh, NY
I: Runaway Jim, Taste, Horse > Silent, Divided Sky, Cavern, Rift, Simple, Melt, Carolina
II: Free > Bowie, Strange Design, YEM, Acoustic Army, Day in the Life
E: Theme

"Cannonball" jam in Runaway Jim.

6/30/95 [ACCESSIBILITY: ••••] [ATTEND. 19,400; CAP. 19,400] [TIX $17.50–$20.50]
Great Woods Center for the Performing Arts, Mansfield, MA
I: AC/DC Bag, Scent of a Mule, Horn, Taste, Wedge, Lizards, Mound, Fee, Antelope
II: Also Sprach > Possum > Ha Ha Ha, TMWSIY > Avenu > Mike's > Contact > Weekapaug, Amazing Grace, Squirming Coil
E: HYHU > Cracklin' Rosie > HYHU, Golgi

I have to wonder about the traffic planners who okay 19,400 person venues with a single lane of access from the highway. A huge overflow crowd for Phish on this night (and the next night, too) backed traffic up for miles. With memories of Waterloo several weeks before in our minds, a group of us decided to leave the car and walk down the shoulder of the highway. Along the way, we enjoyed a flourishing roadside lot scene; in the end, most cars made it to the lot before the band came onstage. Whew—they would have missed a very good show, capped by one of the stronger Mike's Grooves I've ever heard. —Melissa Wolcott

It was a hot and humid summer day. Shirts were off, liquid was pouring and the smoke was green. This is an awesome background to a killer show. (It's ten times better than the next night's; this show should have been broadcast on WBCN.) A young Taste, rare Wedge, Ha Ha Ha, and a nice Mike's > Contact > Groove arrangement. —Greg Marceau

An interesting first set. Aside from the Wedge, the songs were standard fillers, save for a wonderful Antelope, their best first set closer, which salvaged the set. A super second set is highlighted by a great Possum and Weekapaug. The set slows down after that point. However, being at Great Woods, arguably the best place to see Phish on the East Coast, fans knew they had the next night to look forward to. —Matthew Napoli

7/1/95 [ACCESSIBILITY: ••••] [ATTEND. 19,400; CAP. 19,400] [TIX $17.50–$20.50]
Great Woods Center for the Performing Arts, Mansfield, MA
I: Ya Mar, Llama, If I Could, All Things, It's Ice, Caspian, Melt, Bouncing, Chalkdust
II: Wilson, Maze, Theme, Uncle Pen, Stash, Strange Design, Acoustic Army, Harry Hood, Suzie
E: Funky Bitch

Live FM broadcast on WBCN in Boston. Long instrumental intro to If I Could. Fishman on vacuum and Mike on electric drill for jam in the middle of It's Ice. "Sunshine of Your Love" tease in Suzie.

This show came just after the release of A Live One and was the first post-release show to be radio broadcast in the Boston area. In response, Phish decided not to jam, which is particularly noticeable in the second set. The show, of course, includes a handful of tunes from the album: Bouncin', Chalkdust, Wilson, Stash, Hood. Highlights are limited, including the Suzie (with Sunshine of Your Love reference) and a Funky Bitch encore dedicated to the tourheads. The mid-second set Stash was intense, but not to the level of performance a year earlier at Great Woods (which appears on the album), and was framed by songs one hopes never to see in the core of the second set: Uncle Pen, Strange Design and Acoustic Army. Basically, 7/1/95 lacked the intensity of other shows at the good Woods, probably due to the radio influence. —Greg Schwartz

When Phish jams, we all know we're listening to something special. But when they decide to show their softer side, be prepared to be amazed. This ballad-laden show is beautiful, particularly Strange Design. —Dave Swank

For a somewhat maligned performance, this show does have two musical moments that stand out. After a rocking Llama, the band went into a beautiful, melodic jam that turned into If I Could. (It's been said that this is the long instrumental beginning of this song that the band axed from Hoist after recording it.) Then, in the second set, the band put all the pressure on Harry Hood to deliver the goods—and it did. This is one of the most profoundly moving Hoods the band has ever played. —Amy Manning

7/2/95 [ACCESSIBILITY: •••••] [ATTEND. 13,500; CAP. 13,500] [TIX $22.50]
SummerStage at Sugarbush North, Fayston, VT
I: Sample, Divided Sky, Gumbo, Curtain > Julius, Camel Walk, Reba, I Didn't Know, Rift, Guitar Gently Weeps
II: Runaway Jim > Makisupa > Scent of a Mule, Tweezer > Ha Ha Ha, Sleeping Monkey, Acoustic Army, Slave
E: Halley's, Tweezer Reprise

Last Camel Walk, 2/24/89 Burlington, VT [691 shows].

What a way to end the tour, high (in more ways than one) on a mountaintop. Everything about these Sugarbush shows was beautiful—the location, the music and the people. On the first night, set I proved solid with the one-time return of Camel Walk serving as the added treat. A mind-bending, 20-minute version of Runaway Jim set a trippy pace for set II. The rest of set II was smooth, jamming and flowing, leaving us asking for more in the crisp, clear Vermont night. —Jason Deziel

The band brought back to life the funky Camel Walk, which they hadn't played since 1989. Sugarbush is just a great venue to see Phish. The mountains serve as a beautiful backdrop and the mountain on which we danced made us feel as if we were about to fall off—it's steep! Many people say that the acoustics at Sugarbush are somehow mystical in that the higher you climbed up the mountain, the better you could hear. This is just not true. I will say, though, once again, "moo." (see 7/16/94) —Lara Wittels

In the middle of the second set, people stopped watching the band and looked to the sky. Two young men climbed a ski lift tower and were swaying to the excellent music while showing off their Independence Day party favors. For a moment, it looked like the band was more interested in the young men's show than their own! —Beth Castrol

Don't overlook this show musically. The first set is nice with the first Camel Walk in over 600 shows, but the second set is incredible. The Runaway Jim goes into some kind of crazy jam which leads unexpectedly to a phat Makisupa with some Bob Marley riffs and a few pot references (4:20, dank), into Scent of a Mule and all followed by a super-funky Tweezer. One of my favorite shows. —Bryan McCraner

7/3/95 [ACCESSIBILITY: ••••] [ATTEND. 13,500; CAP. 13,500] [TIX $22.50]
SummerStage at Sugarbush North, Fayston, VT
I: My Friend, Poor Heart, Antelope, Loving Cup, Sparkle, It's Ice, If I Could, Maze, Strange Design, Free, Cavern
II: Timber Ho > Bowie > Johnny B. Goode > Bowie, AC/DC Bag, Lizards > BBFCM, Day in the Life, Possum, Squirming Coil
E: Simple, Amazing Grace

Monday, July 3, 1995

SUGARBUSH NORTH, Fayston, VT

I never talk that much about Sugarbush because *everyone* I talk to was *there*. This is one of the best concerts I've ever been to—the music was fantastic and the boys were on. However, what made this show were the thousands and thousands of Phishheads—not newbies but honest-to-God Phishheads, which definitely helped the show.

I got there real early, taking my 1963 Dodge Dart 270 with the Vermont PHISH license plates. A large crowd of people followed behind us taking pictures, and one girl said, "Oh my God, me and my friends were just talking about who in Vermont has the PHISH plates when you drove by!" Once we'd parked, we climbed up the hill to secure space close to the stage. As showtime approached, people kept squeezing in, making us all feel nervous about being crushed.

As soon as the music started, though, the crowd thinned out—I could hold my arms out and twirl about without hitting anyone. I was about thirty feet from the stage all night, in ecstasy.

In the first set, this guy next to me blew up this large inflatable moose and tossed it. It bounced around the crowd for a while with its feet sticking straight up. Finally someone whipped the moose at the stage and it sat down right by Page during Antelope. Nobody on stage noticed it until the break when Page looked to his right and saw it. He yelled to Trey and pointed, and as they left the stage Page put it under his arm and lugged it off. Very cool.

In set II, during BBFCM, it got wild. Trey threw everything off the stage—picks, water cups, whatever he could get his hands on. Then the unbelievable happened: someone threw a four-foot tall George Jetson doll on stage, Trey grabbed it and stuffed it between himself and the guitar and made it look like George was playing. Then he unstrapped and held his custom-made Paul Languedoc guitar at arm's length, straight out, and *dropped it*! Crazy!

This show also gets the best encore award, with the best version of Simple I've ever heard. They nailed it. At the end of the show, they all walked out to the edge of the stage and individually thanked the crowd for giving *them* a great tour, while still tossing things to the crowd. Trey played with a hackysack and threw it to the crowd, then they all grabbed Jon and made like they were going to throw him off the stage.

After the show, I waited for an hour to get on a bus to go back to Sugarbush South where we had parked, and finally said screw it and walked. Walking around some slow-pokes, I ran out of the way of a bus and fell on the side of the road, badly twisting my ankle. It was very dark and there was nothing around so I had to limp the six miles up to South. I was never so happy to see my car.

The next morning I couldn't even step on my ankle. I called my boss and told him I couldn't make it to work and why, and he didn't believe me. I limped around work in pain for a week.

Was the show worth it? Yes, OH GOD YES!

—David A. Clement

"Timber Ho" teases in Bowie intro. "Bathtub Gin" teases in Bowie and Possum. Lizards abandoned after Trey makes lyrics mistake. Last Timber Ho, 12/30/92 Springfield, MA [257 shows].

What can I say about the second set of the second night? It was absolutely intense; they never let up. A Day in the Life normally serves as a breather for the band; we could tell that the energy was just biding its time and waiting to resurface. And it did! Just look at the second set—look at it! —Lara Wittels

A great show turned into a hilarious one during Lizards. Trey completely blanks out on some lyrics. The music keeps playing, then an eerie silence falls on the stage. The music stops and Fish says from behind his drums, "I think you need a teleprompter there, Trey." Then they break into an unbelievable BBFCM. It was really funny. —Chris Regan

My sixth consecutive show of the impressive summer tour ended on the mountain. The first set was plain as day for the band was noticeably waiting for the sun to go down. The second set started with the breakout of Timber Ho, as surprising as it was rockin'. Beautiful segue into Bowie, hanging on to Timber a little. Strong jam with Johnny rocking in the middle. Trey forgot the words of Lizards as Fishman mumbled about the need for a teleprompter. This was extremely hilarious, as was Trey and Mike kicking the hackysack thrown up on stage before Amazing Grace. Ah, Phish at home! —Alex Banks

After camping on the mountain after the first night's show, we had the entire second day to explore the mountain before the evening's show. Steep ski trails led us to gorgeous alpine fields of wildflowers and verdant pastures. Near the top, we met one group of fans who told us they'd hiked for three days over the ridges and mountains, with their final stop being the Phish shows. In my mind, this event served as the first large-scale gathering of the tribe, an annual event that would swell considerably by the time of the Clifford Ball the next summer. —Melissa Collins

[7/13/95]
Late Show With David Letterman, Ed Sullivan Theater, New York, NY
Julius (with horns)

1995 FALL Checkmate

For most fans, the '95 summer tour had been satisfying, but with less than a month's worth of shows, Phish did not have the opportunity to dig as far into its bag of musical tricks as it had in the past. But the vast fall tour would satiate even the most rabid of fans as the band held nothing to be sacred except the breaking of new musical ground. Songs that had been played as often as every other night only a year before seldom surfaced—Golgi, for example, was played live only three times, and Glide only twice. Other older songs received re-examination, as can be seen in the slow-shuffle version of Poor Heart that saw a November debut. And some songs seldom seen in recent years, such as Tube, returned from hibernation.

The band also experimented with setlist structure, opening the October 21 show in Lincoln, Nebraska, with Tweezer Reprise, and then closing the first set with another Tweezer Reprise, despite the fact the "real" Tweezer wasn't played that night. Notably, this sort of experimentation was undertaken in front of large crowds—for the first time, the band would play arena and amphitheater-sized venues from coast to coast, starting the tour in the 14,000-seat Cal Expo Amphitheatre and finishing the year with two sold-out nights at 20,000-seat Madison Square Garden. All of this came on a stage flanked by a giant chess board, as the band challenged the audience to two games of chess in the first-ever band-versus-audience chess match.

Offstage, the Phish Tickets-by-Mail system continued to evolve, functioning with remarkable efficiency and winning praise from virtually all customers. The system proved so popular that about half of those who mail-ordered for New Year's Eve tickets were rejected.

9/27/95 [ACCESSIBILITY: ••••] [ATTEND. 5,336; CAP. 14,500] [TIX $18$25]
Cal Expo Amphitheatre, Sacramento, CA
I: Wolfman's, Rift, Free, It's Ice, I Didn't Know, Fog That Surrounds, Strange Design, Chalkdust, Squirming Coil
II: CTB, AC/DC Bag, Bowie, Billy Breathes, Keyboard Kavalry, Harry Hood, Hello My Baby, Day in the Life
E: Possum

"Johnny B. Goode" tease in Possum. Fishman on trombone for I Didn't Know. Harry Hood unfinished. Last Wolfman's, 6/26/94 Charleston, WV [88 shows]. Concert debuts: Fog That Surrounds, CTB, Billy Breathes, Keyboard Kavalry, Hello My Baby.

9/28/95 [ACCESSIBILITY: ••] [ATTEND. 5,200; CAP. 5,200] [TIX $18.50$20]
Summer Pops, Embarcadero Center, San Diego, CA
I: CTB, Runaway Jim, Billy Breathes, Scent of a Mule, Stash, Fee, Fog That Surrounds, Acoustic Army, Slave
II: Theme, Poor Heart, Don't You Wanna Go, Tweezer, Keyboard Kavalry, Amazing Grace, Sample, Antelope
E: Fire

East Coasters, eat your heart out. Imagine an uncrowded Phish show in a wide-open outdoor venue with the sun setting over the water on one side and a sparkling skyline on the other. Highlights came in the second set, including Tweezer—not too long like the Mud Island and Finger Lakes versions—they explored it nicely before the three non-keyboardists zombie-walked their way over to Page's area where they did a four-part keyboard jam. (I think this shtick should be called "Too Much Time on the Tour Bus" because I think that's how this brainstorm came about.) Then, after Amazing Grace and Sample, IT happened. For me, the entire show can be summed up in one word: Antelope. How many climaxes can one song have? Get the tape and find out. —Mike Indgin

9/29/95 [ACCESSIBILITY: •••] [ATTEND. 6,162; CAP. 6,162] [TIX $22.50]
Greek Theater, Los Angeles, CA
I: AC/DC Bag, Sparkle, Divided Sky, Strange Design, CTB, YEM, Adeline, Suzie
II: Also Sprach > Maze, Free, Ya Mar, Melt, Billy Breathes, HYHU > Cryin' > HYHU, Day in the Life
E: Chalkdust

Fishman on vacuum for Cryin'. Concert debut: Cryin'.

Probably the funniest show I have on tape. The second set is decent but one song tops it off: Fishman took center stage and with lyrics in hand sang Cryin' by Aerosmith. This was the only time it was done and I can understand why—it's probably the worst display of vocals I've ever heard from such a talented musician. But I laugh my ass off every time I listen to it. —Chuck Adams

Outside, thousands of ticketless miracle seekers swam through the crowd frantically searching for that elusive extra, in sharp contrast to the scene at San Diego where the venue wasn't even sold out until showtime. Trey was ON the entire night. At one point he was flailing around so much his glasses went flying off. That kind of unbridled intensity is why I love this band. The second set began with the 2001 theme which discoed into the highlight of the show (besides Fishman's surprise): an absolutely amazing Maze. It's hard to describe what these boys are able to pull off when they're on like this, so I won't even try. After a Split Open and Melt featuring the most spaced-out jamming of the night, Fishman made his way to center stage with his vacuum in one hand and lyric sheets in the other. "I don't really know the words to this song... but that isn't the point," he said. What followed had every single person at the Greek laughing hysterically: his murderous rendition of Aerosmith's Cryin'. He botched the second half, throwing his crib notes in the air, but this just added to the hilarity of it all. In the parking lot, my friends all echoed the same sentiment: "Now I see why you like this band." —Mike Indgin

9/30/95 [ACCESSIBILITY: ••••] [ATTEND. 14,299; CAP. 20,000] [TIX $17.50]
Shoreline Amphitheatre, Mountain View, CA
I: My Friend, CTB, Chess Game Jam, Reba, Uncle Pen, Horn, Antelope, I'm Blue I'm Lonesome, Sample
II: Runaway Jim, Fog That Surrounds, If I Could, Scent of a Mule, Mike's > Keyboard Kavalry > Weekapaug, HYHU > Suspicious Minds > HYHU, Cavern
E: Amazing Grace, GTBT

Chess Game Jam (played to tune of "White Rabbit") marked the start of the first band-versus-audience chess match. "Antelope" tease before Horn. I'm Blue I'm Lonesome performed acoustic with Trey on acoustic guitar, Mike on banjo, Fishman on mandolin, and Page on upright bass, dedicated to Jerry Garcia. Concert debuts: Chess Game Jam (and the chess game), Suspicious Minds.

This show features two solid sets, on Trey's birthday. It is also notable for the introduction of the band-versus-audience chess game. Reba is probably the fastest one I've ever heard; Antelope is smokin'; and Blue and Lonesome is touching, as Trey dedicates it to the late Jerry Garcia. The second set is highlighted by an awesome Fog and a wicked duel in Scent, yet the real centerpiece is Mike's Song and its smooth segue from a trippy, spacey jam into Keyboard Kavalry and then onto Weekapaug that put us all on a funk rollercoaster. Fishman emerges for a hilarious cover of Elvis Presley's Suspicious Minds as well. What a show! —Ryan Harsch

Phish's first appearance at the Dead's "home," A.D. J.G., provided an interesting atmosphere. I interpreted odd feelings among the crowd and the security personnel. Phish played well, but lacked the presence of energy that a venue of this size demands of all performers. Fishman donned an Elvis cape for a hilarious rendition of Suspicious Minds that drew the loudest response of the night. —Anthony Buchla

Fall Tour '95 meant chess, as the band challenged the audience to the ultimate battle of the brains. Each side made one move a night, the band at the start of the show and the audience—after setbreak consultation at the Greenpeace table—at the beginning of the second set. As a Fall '95 *Schvice* noted, "The band's convoluted strategy has kept the audience guessing. Victory is inevitable for one of the teams...." Things looked good for the audience when a northern California chess master showed up at the Greenpeace table and lent his expertise on the game's debut night at Shoreline. The audience dropped the first game, then rebounded to win the second. —Marcia Collins

10/2/95 [ACCESSIBILITY: ••] [ATTEND. 5,000; CAP. 5,000]* [TIX $20]
Seattle Center Arena, Seattle, WA
I: Poor Heart, Wolfman's, Rift, Chess Game Jam, Stash, Acoustic Army, Fog That Surrounds, Theme, Tela, Bowie
II: Wilson, CTB, Bathtub Gin, Llama, Simple, Keyboard Kavalry, Slave, Hello My Baby, Lizards, Antelope
E: Day in the Life

Baby Gramps opened. "Night Moves" played as Chess Game Jam. Fishman on vacuum in Slave.

10/3/95 [ACCESSIBILITY: •••] [ATTEND. 5,000; CAP. 5,000]* [TIX $20]
Seattle Center Arena, Seattle, WA
I: Maze, Guelah, Foam, FEFY, I'm Blue I'm Lonesome, Free, TMWSIY > Avenu > TMWSIY, Sample, YEM
II: Timber Ho, It's Ice, Sparkle, Harry Hood, Billy Breathes, Faht, Adeline, Melt, Squirming Coil
E: Rocky Top

Baby Gramps opened. I'm Blue I'm Lonesome performed acoustic. Last Faht, 6/19/94 Kalamazoo, MI [99 shows].

10/5/95 [ACCESSIBILITY: ••] [ATTEND. 6,873; CAP. 9,040] [TIX $20]
Memorial Coliseum, Portland, OR
I: Chalkdust, Ha Ha Ha, Fog That Surrounds, Horse > Silent, CTB, Strange Design, Divided Sky, Acoustic Army, Julius, Suzie
II: Also Sprach > Runaway Jim, Forbin's > Mockingbird, Scent of a Mule, Cavern, Bowie, Lifeboy, Amazing Grace **E:** Guitar Gently Weeps

10/6/95 [ACCESSIBILITY: ••] [ATTEND. 2,539; CAP. 2,539] [TIX $26.50]
Orpheum Theatre, Vancouver, BC
I: Ya Mar, Stash, Billy Breathes, Reba, I'm Blue I'm Lonesome, Rift, Free, Lizards, Sample
II: Poor Heart, Maze, Theme, NICU, Tweezer, Keyboard Kavalry, Suspicious Minds, Slave
E: Hello My Baby, Day in the Life

I'm Blue I'm Lonesome performed acoustic/no amplification.

10/7/95 [ACCESSIBILITY: ••••] [ATTEND. 2,594; CAP. 2,594] [TIX $20]
Spokane Opera House, Spokane, WA
I: Julius, Gumbo, Fog That Surrounds, Mound, Possum, Mango, Acoustic Army, Wilson, Antelope
II: Makisupa, CTB, Melt, Strange Design, It's Ice, Contact, Frankenstein, Harry Hood, Adeline
E: Fire

Harry Hood unfinished.

The Northwest shows offered the chance to see Phish in the best venues of the fall '95 tour. Each place was a small, plush, classy theater or opera house. Spokane rocked! Gumbo, Mound, Possum, Antelope all in the first set. The Acoustic Army is jammin'. Makisupa to open the second set, plus a great Frankenstein followed by a huge Harry. Fire to encore, can't ask for much more. —Sean Smith

Every tour needs a good controversy, and during the opening leg of the fall '95 tour, everyone was talking about why Phish wasn't finishing Harry Hood. This would be the last time during the fall that they wouldn't sing the final "You can feel good about Hood" refrain, but it didn't matter—Phish devoted all their energy to the jam, unquestionably one of the best Hood jams ever. You really owe it to yourself to hear it. —Scott Sifton

10/8/95 [ACCESSIBILITY: •••] [ATTEND. 6,534; CAP. 6,534] [TIX $19.50]
Adams Fieldhouse, University of Montana, Missoula, MT
I: AC/DC Bag, Demand > Sparkle, Wolfman's, Reba, I'm Blue I'm Lonesome, Caspian, Uncle Pen, Free
II: Keyboard Kavalry, CTB, Timber Ho, Ya Mar, Sample, YEM, Suspicious Minds, Dog Faced Boy, Bowie, Keyboard Kavalry Reprise
E: Bouncing, Rocky Top

I'm Blue I'm Lonesome performed acoustic. Last Demand, 6/26/94 Charleston, WV [97 shows].

10/11/95 [ACCESSIBILITY: ••••] [ATTEND. 8,157; CAP. 10,000] [TIX $18–$20]
Compton Terrace Amphitheater, Tempe, AZ
I: Stash, Old Home Place, Cavern, Divided Sky, If I Could, Fog That Surrounds, Acoustic Army, Julius, Sample
II: Possum, Bathtub Gin, Mound, Mike's > McGrupp > Weekapaug, Llama, Suzie > Crossroads, Hello My Baby, Day in the Life
E: Chalkdust

"Buried Alive" tease in Julius. "Crossroads" and "Sunshine of Your Love" teases in Suzie. Last Crossroads, 5/8/93 Durham, NH [196 shows].

10/13/95 [ACCESSIBILITY: ••••] [ATTEND. 2,781; CAP. 2,781] [TIX $18.50]
Will Rogers Auditorium, Fort Worth, TX
I: Ya Mar, Also Sprach > Maze, Billy Breathes, I'm Blue I'm Lonesome, Caspian, Melt, Fluffhead, Life on Mars
II: Tube, Uncle Pen, Theme, Wilson, Antelope, Keyboard Kavalry, Lizards, Guitar Gently Weeps, Adeline, Squirming Coil
E: Bold as Love

I'm Blue I'm Lonesome performed acoustic/no amplification. Last Tube, 6/26/94 Charleston, WV [99 shows]. Concert debut: Life on Mars.

This was an awesome show. Trey explained to us that this was the town in which he was born. Maybe that served as an energizer, because the show is quite pumping and fast. Wilson is particularly intense, and I was impressed with the sound of WMGGW—Trey makes his guitar cry during the solo. —Jeffrey Ellenbogen

When a set opens with a song like Tube, you know you're in for a crazy night. (It was the first Tube we heard since June '94.) Still, the great Tube was later outdone by a Theme > Wilson > Antelope combination. Great show; the boys were on. —Mark Daniel

10/14/95 [ACCESSIBILITY: ••••] [ATTEND. 2,652; CAP. 2,652] [TIX $17.50]
Austin Music Hall, Austin, TX
I: AC/DC Bag, CTB, Kung > Free, Sparkle, Stash > Catapult, Acoustic Army, It's Ice, Tela, Runaway Jim
II: Reba, Rift, YEM, Hello My Baby, Scent of a Mule, Cavern
E: Day in the Life

"Baracuda" tease before Reba. John Medeski on keyboards, Billy Martin on drums, Chris Wood on upright bass, and Dominick Fallo on trumpet for YEM.

Relaxing with friends before a show is fun, but when you're at home, it's great fun! I was ready for a good show after the previous night's magic, and the band didn't let me down. The first set contained a great long Stash followed by Tela a couple of songs later. The second set again felt magic with Medeski Martin and Wood and Dominick Fallo joining in on a ripping YEM, then a unique and fun Scent of a Mule. —William Thurston

Page is joined by John Medeski on keyboard, Fish plays vacuum and trombone, Billy Martin plays drums, Chris Wood on bass, Trey on his drum kit, Mike on bass and horn, plus a little trumpet. Chaos, sweet chaos. —Dave Swank

This night's MMW jam, unlike the one on 10/17, really works. Yum! —Rich Mazer

10/15/95 [ACCESSIBILITY: ••••] [ATTEND. 2,652; CAP. 2,652] [TIX $17.50]
Austin Music Hall, Austin, TX
I: Buried Alive > Poor Heart, Slave, I Didn't Know, Demand > Llama, Foam, Strange Design, I'm Blue I'm Lonesome, Bowie
II: Julius, Simple, Tweezer, Lizards, Sample, Suspicious Minds, Harry Hood, Tweezer Reprise
E: Funky Bitch

Even though neither set clicked enough to make this a great night, the boys were having fun and enjoying themselves enough to kick out several great versions of tunes. I was all smiles when the third song turned out to be Slave, and I love a first set Bowie closer. The fun they were having on this night didn't end even though the first set did. They came back out on fire for the second set. I love a Tweezer night and I especially love a Lizards and a Harry before the Reprise comes. The Lizards played on this night sounded so different then the one of two nights before, proving how special a song it is. —Eric Segovia

The show was great, although more chill than the previous two. A mellow first set was followed by a surprising second set, including a groovy Suspicious Minds into a truly beautiful Harry Hood. —William Thurston

10/17/95 [ACCESSIBILITY: ••••] [ATTEND. 3,286; CAP. 3,286] [TIX $20]
State Palace Theatre, New Orleans, LA
I: Sample, Stash, Uncle Pen, AC/DC Bag > Maze, Glide, Sparkle, Free, Strange Design, Amazing Grace
II: Mound > Caspian, Fog That Surrounds, Suzie > Keyboard Kavalry > Jam
E: Long Journey Home, I'm Blue I'm Lonesome

Medeski Martin & Wood opened. Nathan, a Gospel singer in the audience, sang Amazing Grace after the band performed it to close the first set. The singer later joined in on the jam at end of set two, which also featured John Medeski on keyboards, Billy Martin on drums and Chris Wood on upright bass. Fishman on vacuum and trombone during the jam. Nathan on vocals during the jam. Long Journey Home and I'm Blue I'm Lonesome performed acoustic.

The second set to this show features a fabulous jam with Medeski Martin and Wood (clocking in at 25-plus minutes). Starting off slow and spacey, this jam really heats up by the end. After a slow start, things get going when each member trades licks with each other, getting faster and faster and then slowing down as Fishman brings out his vacuum, then switches to trombone. Things slowly speed up again as Fishman trades trombone licks with everybody, then as Trey switches to his percussion kit a guy named Nathan joins in on vocals, mostly using the Doo note; you'll have to hear this one because this is the best part of the jam. Everybody is into the jam playing great, as Nathan grunts and groans, "Gotta get down doo doo doo doo," then things abruptly slow down and Trey thanks the crowd on behalf of MMW. Definitely a set worth looking for if you like Surrender to the Air, but I wish it was more groovy than spacey. —Mike Noll

10/19/95 [ACCESSIBILITY: ••••] [ATTEND. 7,753; CAP. 8,408] [TIX $20]
Municipal Auditorium, Kansas City, MO
I: CTB, Runaway Jim, Horn, PYITE, Esther, Chalkdust, Theme, Acoustic Army, Melt, Billy Breathes, Cavern
II: Frankenstein, Poor Heart, Mike's > Hydrogen > Weekapaug > Lawn Boy, BBFCM > Kung, HYHU > Suspicious Minds > HYHU, Possum
E: Day in the Life

Recording of Trey's daughter Eliza crying was played over the PA system during Billy Breathes.

This night was the beginning of the Great Midwestern Tear from KC to Cedar Rapids and Lincoln in fall '95. This show's highlights included PYITE, Billy Breathes with a Trey narration of his newborn daughter crying on a playback machine, Frankenstein and the entire second set. BBFCM was a very insane jam. —Sean Miller

Although the setlist really isn't that bad, this show is really weak. It doesn't flow well, and never really gets going. The Mike's Groove in the second set hints at a high-energy conclusion to the show, but it's followed by four rather weak songs. Good Possum and a good encore, but it's too little, too late. —Ben Ross

10/20/95 [ACCESSIBILITY: ••••] [ATTEND. 7,686; CAP. 7,686] [TIX $18.50–$20]
Five Seasons Arena, Cedar Rapids, IA
I: My Friend, Ya Mar, Ha Ha Ha, Divided Sky, Fee, Rift, Free, Hello My Baby, Amazing Grace, Amazing Grace Jam
II: Timber Ho, Scent of a Mule, Simple, Maze, Gumbo, Guitar Gently Weeps, Long Journey Home, I'm Blue I'm Lonesome, Bouncing, Antelope
E: Sleeping Monkey, Rocky Top

Guest performer on bagpipes for Amazing Grace Jam. Long Journey Home and I'm Blue I'm Lonesome performed acoustic. Last Amazing Grace Jam, 5/8/93 Durham, NH [202 shows].

Great town with good vibes and anal but harmless cops (one questioned me on my incense use), and a very small arena reminiscent of the '92–'93 tours. The show started slowly in the first set, including Trey, who with megaphone to mouth forgot the lyrics to Fee. But then things heated up: the bagpipe jam was a pleasant surprise. The second set started off with five really strong tunes that rocked! Then a sweet Antelope tease before Bouncin' got my mouth watering. It came, of course, to close the show. This was a small-time Phish party in Iowa. —Alex Banks

The first set Amazing Grace was mind-blowing—an electric jam followed by a guest on bagpipes that just brought the house down! —Jamis Curran

10/21/95 [ACCESSIBILITY: ••••] [ATTEND. 7,500; CAP. 7,500] [TIX $17.50]
Pershing Auditorium, Lincoln, NE
I: Tweezer Reprise, Chalkdust, Guelah, Reba, Wilson, CTB, Kung, Lizards, Strange Design, Acoustic Army, GTBT > Tweezer Reprise
II: Also Sprach > Bowie, Lifeboy, Sparkle, YEM, Purple Rain > HYHU, Harry Hood, Suzie **E:** Highway to Hell

"Black or White" tease before GTBT. "Thriller" teases before and during Harry Hood. "Beat It" teased throughout first set and in Harry Hood and Suzie. Fishman on vacuum for Purple Rain.

This is probably our favorite live Phish experience. The show was full of fun stuff—they opened up and closed the first set with Tweezer Reprise. They teased Michael Jackson's "Beat It" during Harry Hood and Suzie because Halloween was coming up and everyone thought they were going to do Thriller, so Phish played along. During the YEM vocal jam they started snoring. It was great. The encore was Highway to Hell, and during it all the hippies started headbanging. —Melanie and Melita Terrell

From the first phat bass note this show kicked ass! There were two high-school age girls with staff shirts on directly in front of Mike and Trey, and from the look on their faces they had no clue what Phish was about. When Mike dropped that first Boooooommmm, at the beginning of Tweezer Reprise, the girl in front of him (and me) just beamed a huge grin and mouthed, "Wow!" Needless to say, she had her back to the audience most of the night. Trey later treated the girls to some classic Gene Simmons-esque tongue lashing during the Highway to Hell encore. —Russell Lane

Tweezer Reprise for an opener? Why, that's unheard of! Well, there's a first time for everything. Reba is phenomenal—it carries the show on its back, and it's my personal favorite jam of any song in my tape collection. Purple Rain had no lyrics besides "Purple Rain"—the band just hummed the whole song. —Chad Mars

10/22/95 [ACCESSIBILITY: ••••] [ATTEND. 12,788; CAP. 12,788] [TIX $18–$20]
Assembly Hall, Champaign, IL
I: AC/DC Bag, My Mind's, Sloth, Runaway Jim, Weigh > NICU, FEFY, It's Ice, Poor Heart > Sample, I'm Blue I'm Lonesome, Stash
II: Golgi, Possum > Catapult > Curtain > Tweezer > Makisupa > BBFCM, Life on Mars, Uncle Pen, Slave > Cavern
E: Adeline, Squirming Coil

Bonus lyrics in Makisupa.

After a dud of a first set, as the boys always do, they saved us. The great jamming starts in Possum and, after a vocal Catapult, continues. Makisupa is a total crowd-pleaser. A jamming Uncle Pen brings back life. This is also a crazy Adeline. Pick up set II! —Charlie Gubman

The Many Incredible Tweezers of Fall '95 got their start on this night with a version that might be the best of the batch and perhaps the best ever. I guess it depends how you like your Tweezers. Phish's style this fall was not to slip segues and teases into the Tweezer jams but instead to just rock out. I hear the melodious jamming in this version when I dream of what heaven might be like. —Tyler Harris

10/24/95 [ACCESSIBILITY: •••] [ATTEND. 10,114; CAP. 10,114] [TIX $19]
Dane County Coliseum, Madison, WI
I: My Friend, Paul and Silas, Fog That Surrounds, Fee > Llama, Horse > Silent, Demand > Maze, Wolfman's, Acoustic Army, Caspian, Melt
II: Julius, Theme, Bouncing, YEM > Sleeping Monkey, Antelope, Contact, Cavern
E: Day in the Life

Concert debut of the reworked version of Fog That Surrounds. Last Paul and Silas, 11/19/94 Indianapolis, IN [63 shows].

The beginning of this show was definitely scary. Me and my friends had secured places right down in front but with the combination of excitement, lack of air, and being smashed in the surging crowd, we all fainted! As I was getting up, I realized we weren't the only ones—people seemed to be dropping like flies. I escaped to the lobby for some air, giving up the prime floor spot and missing My Friend and most of Paul and Silas, but at least I could breathe. Then the reworked Fog That Surrounds made its debut and I knew I was still in for quite an evening. The Demand > Maze combo had me questioning my perception of time and Split Open at the end of the set reminded me of melting into the floor at the beginning. Set II was trippy! I swam with Phish underwater in Theme From the Bottom and then laughed at Lucifer in the weirdest YEM jam I've ever heard. A pre-Halloween trick (I only had to wait a few more days for the real treat!) —Libby Barrow

A better-than-average show with great jams. One of the craziest vocal jams at the end of YEM, and the best performance of Antelope that I have witnessed. —Matt Bussman

The jamming in set II is absolutely out of control! This is just an absolute must-have set, a real classic of Phish's musicianship on a night where most everything soared. Things rock from the start with a Julius that's guaranteed to change the way you think of this song if you're a Julius doubter, or enlighten you further if you're a Julius believer. YEM's jam segment is also amazing, including a sung-skat segment from Trey and a series of very cohesive jams that approaches the famous 12/9/95 Albany YEM. But they save the best for last with the most exploratory, exuberant Antelope ever. Ever! —Scott Sifton

10/25/95 [ACCESSIBILITY: ••] [ATTEND. 8,198; CAP. 10,000] [TIX $19.50]
St. Paul Civic Center Arena, St. Paul, MN
I: Ya Mar, Sample, Divided Sky, Wedge, Scent of a Mule, Free, Strange Design, Long Journey Home, I'm Blue I'm Lonesome, Chalkdust
II: Reba, Life on Mars, CTB, Mike's, Sparkle > Weekapaug, Suzie > Crossroads
E: Fire

Long Journey Home and I'm Blue I'm Lonesome performed acoustic. "Breathe" jam in Mike's.

Most of the show was standard fall '95 fare which, while fun, doesn't really stand out as a sweet tape. The second set does show sparks, however, with solid jamming in Reba and a spacey Mike's Groove. Life on Mars is my highlight. What a perfect cover! —Jamis Curran

The first set was pretty average, and I thought the second set opener Reba was a disappointment, but not for long. The jam was incredibly upbeat and they soared with energy. Proceeding into Mike's Song, they broke into a Floyd tune during the jam. The controversial issue was, did they play Breathe or the beginning of Shine On You Crazy Diamond? It was odd to hear Sparkle before finishing with Weekapaug. —Erin Ferris

10/27/95 [ACCESSIBILITY: ••••] [ATTEND. 7,875; CAP. 7,875] [TIX $20]
Wings Stadium, Kalamazoo, MI
I: Runaway Jim, Fluffhead, Fog That Surrounds, Horn, I Didn't Know, Rift, Stash, Fee > Suspicious Minds
II: Also Sprach > Bowie, Dog Faced Boy, Poor Heart, Simple, McGrupp, Keyboard Kavalry, Bouncing, Possum
E: Life on Mars

Fishman on vacuum for I Didn't Know.

The arena was tiny to begin with so everybody knew it was gonna be an intimate jam session. Rockin' Fluffhead had everybody singing. The second set was boomin' with the greatest Poor Heart of all time—Trey just explodes with bluegrass guitar. Possum features signals including fall down, but hardly anyone knew what was going on. —Alex Banks

This was the first chance I had to hear the boys after coming back from a stint with the Peace Corps. We entered the stadium after they had already begun the first set, and looking down the length of the rink to see them already pouring it on was as big a high as living on Kilimanjaro or on the edge of the Serengeti. —Eric Shaw

10/28/95 [ACCESSIBILITY: •••••] [ATTEND. 12,968; CAP. 12,968] [TIX $20]
The Palace, Auburn Hills, MI
I: AC/DC Bag, Mound, Timber Ho, Uncle Pen, Sample, Lizards, Billy Breathes, Acoustic Army, Caspian, Antelope
II: Maze, Theme > Scent of a Mule, YEM, Strange Design, Frankenstein, Chalkdust
E: Guitar Gently Weeps

Hello Antelope. This was a very fun show, especially for people who came into the show thinking about how bad a venue the Palace is. Well, the show was great, with a nice Timber Ho and Lizards in set I, which concluded with an amazing Antelope! It started very delicately and exponentially acquired energy until we were running out of control (in a good way). They used their frequent tension and release method in getting everyone's soul waiting for that climax note. Oh, it felt nice when they hit it. —Michelle Hirsch

My brother and I took our parents to this show. What an event it was for them to experience the lot. They never imagined anything like it. Our Dad only liked it when they played cover tunes, but our Mom got connected with the energy and enjoyed all of it. She couldn't believe how friendly people were, just offering joints to her (she never has smoked). Little did they know my brother and I were huffin' some dank right next to them. What a great time! —Bryan McCraner

10/29/95 [ACCESSIBILITY: ••••] [ATTEND. 6,712; CAP. 6,712] [TIX $20]
Louisville Gardens, Louisville, KY
I: Buried Alive > Poor Heart, Julius, PYITE, CTB, Horse > Silent, Melt, NICU, Gumbo, Slave, Adeline
II: Makisupa > Bowie, Mango, It's Ice > Kung > It's Ice, Shaggy Dog, Possum, Lifeboy, Amazing Grace **E:** Funky Bitch

"Beat It" tease before Buried Alive and in Possum. Last Shaggy Dog, 11/3/88 Boston, MA [727 shows].

This is a great unheard-of show. Set I proves itself with Buried Alive, PYITE, NICU, Gumbo and Slave. Then set II makes me smile with Makisupa > Bowie, Mango Song, the first Shaggy Dog in the '90s > Possum, and a favorite Funky Bitch encore. —J.J. Southard

Definitely one of the best shows I've ever seen! A smoking Buried Alive > Poor Heart opener, then near the end of the first set they really cover some ground: Split Open, followed by NICU > Gumbo > Slave! Could it get any better? Obviously, I didn't realize what they had planned for the second set. It starts with a funky Makisupa, moving into a powerful Bowie. After an It's Ice with a nicely placed Kung in the middle, they brought out the first Shaggy Dog since 1988, seguing that into a phenomenal Possum, complete with "Beat It" tease. A truly unstoppable show. —Otis

10/31/95 [ACCESSIBILITY: •••••] [ATTEND. 18,311; CAP. 18,311] [TIX $22.50]
Rosemont Horizon, Chicago, IL
I: Icculus, Divided Sky, Wilson, Ya Mar, Sparkle, Free, Guyute, Antelope, Harpua
II: Thriller Tease > I Am the Sea, The Real Me, Quadrophenia, Cut My Hair, The Punk Meets the Godfather, I'm One, The Dirty Jobs, Helpless Dancer, Is It in My Head, I've Had Enough, 5:15, Sea and Sand, Drowned, Bell Boy, Doctor Jimmy, The Rock, Love Reign O'er Me
III: YEM, Jesus Left Chicago, Day in the Life, Suzie
E: My Generation

"Beat It" tease in Harpua, which also included a Mike Gordon–narrated dream sequence. Second set was the Who's Quadrophenia; all songs from the album were concert debuts. The second set featured a horn section: Dave Grippo, alto saxophone; Don Glasgo, trombone; Joe Somerville Jr., trumpet; and Alan Parshley, French horn. Bell Boy featured Phish crew member Leigh Fordham in costume and on vocals. Jesus Left Chicago featured Grippo, and Suzie featured Grippo, Glasgo, and Somerville. My Generation (performed acoustic, concert debut) ended with Trey intentionally triggering a backstage explosion after the band destroyed their instruments. Last Guyute, 12/29/94 Providence, RI [50 shows]. Last Icculus, 11/20/94 Madison, WI [64 shows]. Last Jesus Left Chicago, 12.6.94 Santa Barbara, CA [56 shows].

The best show I've ever seen of any kind. The anticipation of the second set was like an hour of butterflies in my stomach. When the house lights went down and the sound of waves crashing onto the Cliffs of Dover was heard, it all became clear—Quadrophenia. Only Phish could pull off Quadrophenia better than the Who! Then, an amazing YEM, complete with trippy-huge light show and mind vocalizations that made the stage appear to melt more than normal. —Daniel Grilfand

In my opinion this is the best of Phish's three 'Ween tenures. It kicks off appropriately with a hilarious Icculus in which the book battles the Halloween spirits. Trey exclaims, "The book is getting its ass kicked!" The set ends with Guyute, a crazy Antelope and a Harpua hinting at a Thriller second set. Quadrophenia was a better choice for a cover album even than the White Album. Phish did much more to liven up this album. The third set is killer too. The YEM is so long, people wondered if it would be the whole set—42 minutes, to be exact. My Generation encore was weak—they didn't jam it out as much as Pete Townshend would have, although the destruction of the instruments on stage added to the ambiance. —Ben Ross

For me, this is a must-have show. Not only am I a lifetime Who fan, but Quadrophenia is my favorite album. Page was right on during Sea and Sand, mimicking Roger to a T. This is yet another excellent example of Phish's incredible versatility. They had everything covered—even the BBC voice-overs. I was floored! —Dan Kurtz

This was hands-down the most intense Phish show I ever saw—sorry to anyone who couldn't be there to be a part of the cycle of energy. Anyhow, it is of course an amazing YEM—hard to believe they could weave through it so intensely for 40 minutes. Guyute was long-awaited but the changes were worth the wait—the tension up to Page's chords is so strong and the release from those chords makes me want to hug the person next to me. —Michelle Hirsch

I can sum up this show in three letters: YEM. Absolutely brilliant and original, you can tell the Who influence by listening to the tape. The horns at the end of the third set are a nice treat. During Suzie, Trey sings the same verse three times. Before the final chorus, Fish says, "What the fuck?" and Trey says, "Oh, I sang that verse three times." —Pete Morse

11/9/95 [ACCESSIBILITY: ••••] [ATTEND. 4,515; CAP. 4,515] [TIX $22.50]
Fox Theatre, Atlanta, GA
I: Tweezer Reprise, Divided Sky, Caspian, PYITE, Simple, Reba, Tela, Sample
II: Theme > Julius, Lizards, Bathtub Gin > TMWSIY > Avenu > TMWSIY > Life on Mars, Hello My Baby, Squirming Coil
E: Loving Cup

"We Are the Champions" tease before Theme. "Rift" jam in Bathtub Gin.

10/31/95 Rosemont Horizon, Chicago, IL

"Quadrophenia"

With Phish's almost untarnished track record of outdoing themselves, anticipation ran high for their second annual musical costume on Halloween in 1995. Since the show was more centrally located, Phish folk flocked from around the country to squeeze in to the Rosemont Horizon, as the show became the first true national Phish event.

While Phish claimed only a small midwest following just two years before, this date would arguably become the most eagerly sought after ticket in Phish history. It sold out in a matter of hours and ticket brokers easily gouged their way to anywhere from $75 to $150 for a sacred spot inside. Of course, ticket scarcity and multitudes of counterfeits left many disappointed under the wet skies of Chicago.

As planes made their way overhead to and from O'Hare Airport, another buzz was heard in the lot prior to the show. It was that of attempting to guess what musical costume Phish would don for the second set. Many fans believed that the band would play *Thiller* by Michael Jackson, speculation fueled by "Beat It" teases from shows leading up to Rosemont. Some grew even more convinced when Trey snuck a little "Beat It" into Harpua during a startlingly good first set, one which featured the return of Guyute after nearly a year on hiatus, an Icculus show opener, and one of the best early versions of Free.

During the "Beat It" jam, they actually went as far as to announce that Jimmy was listening to "the album Phish was going to play tonight." Some thought they had spilled the beans, missing the past tense of the reference. But most remained cynical. After all, why would they make it so obvious?

Other rumors persisted, such as Frank Zappa's *Joe's Garage*, The Grateful Dead's *Europe '72*, and an assortment of Zeppelin and Rolling Stones titles.

Quadrophenia was lightly rumored before the show but only one mention among many possibilities. As the rolling ocean sounds filled the dark arena at the start of the second set, most were silent with the exception of hardcore Who fans, who didn't need to think twice. And when the band exploded into the first notes of The Real Me, the portion of the audience with working knowledge of classic rock knew exactly where Phish was going.

Quadrophenia, it turns out, actually came in second in fan voting behind *Joe's Garage*, but they cashed in their executive privilege and chose The Who's rock opera about a boy named, of all things, Jimmy, who has four personalities (corresponding to each member of The Who) and who embarks on a drug and fight-filled journey to Brighton in search of his true identity.

Phish played the album masterfully and one can argue they even outdid Pete Townshend and crew, who performed *Quadrophenia* months later with the help of sheet music and about a dozen backup musicians. Phish played it by heart with a relatively bare-bones setup which did include Dave Grippo and Joe Somerville of the reformed Giant Country Horns, along with Don Glasgo on trombones and Alan Parshley on French Horn. But Page masterfully handled most of *Quadrophenia*'s orchestration with his synthesizer, and Trey zealously took to Townshend's guitar parts, windmills and all.

With much of the audience lacking familiarity with *Quadrophenia*, it became a sit-down affair for many in the crowd. But the band lifted everyone to their feet with an uplifting performance of 5:15, one of many musical highlights in the set.

In subsequent interviews, Trey said he had never been a big *Quadrophenia* fan before, but learned that night what great arena rock it made. For the most part, the performance was fairly true to the album version—a simply remarkable feat—but they did mix things up a little, especially on The Dirty Jobs, during which Page plays the piano part too fast for Trey to keep up. Fishman handled vocal duties on the show's finale, the emotionally-charged Love Reign O'er Me.

Set III arguably didn't match up to the last set of the previous year's marathon but contained what was probably the longest YEM ever (including the unmistakable phrase "I want to fuck you in the ass" slipped in by one of the band members during the vocal jam) and a vicious sax solo by Dave Grippo on a great Jesus Left Chicago.

And as Phish always manages to do, they made light of the grand performance by encoring with My Generation, played bluegrass-style on old, beat-up instruments. Then, they destroyed them with a Who-esque explosion. This show was not without its critics, but by most accounts, it ranks as one of the most special nights in Phish's rich concert history.

11/10/95 [ACCESSIBILITY: ••••] [ATTEND. 4,515; CAP. 4,515] [TIX $22.50]
Fox Theatre, Atlanta, GA
I: Bouncing, Runaway Jim, Fog That Surrounds, Old Home Place, It's Ice, Dog Faced Boy, Maze, Guyute, Cavern
II: Free, Scent of a Mule, YEM > Crossroads > YEM, Strange Design, Sparkle, AC/DC Bag, Adeline
E: Harry Hood

The Fox Theater is a great place to see a show. Inside, there are many small rooms and large velvet chairs—it resembles a castle. It is such a small venue that tickets were in high demand for this three-night stop. Outside in the streets, there seemed to be as many people searching for tickets as there were tickets. Two songs that stick out in my mind from this night are Guyute and Harry Hood. Guyute is truly one of Phish's best songs and should be included in their rotation more frequently. Harry Hood, a real crowd-pleaser, was a great treat for an encore and perfect close to the evening. —Chris Haines

A friend of ours from Athens sold us fourth-row seats for below face value! Too bad the setlist didn't suit my taste. Bouncin' opener? Blah! But then Page went off on Maze. Guyute was great, the first time I'd ever heard it. It gives me hope for more huge jams in the future. The second set was saved by YEM, though I wasn't crazy about the Crossroads in the middle. (Brickhouse a week later in Charleston was much better.) Hood encore was a treat as usual. —Trevor Norris

11/11/95 [ACCESSIBILITY: ••••] [ATTEND. 4,515; CAP. 4,515] [TIX $22.50]
Fox Theatre, Atlanta, GA
I: CTB, Mike's > Day in the Life, Poor Heart, Weekapaug, Horse > Silent, Ya Mar, Stash, Amazing Grace, Fee, Chalkdust
II: Also Sprach > Bowie, Suzie, Uncle Pen, Fluffhead, Sleeping Monkey, Frankenstein > Suspicious Minds > HYHU, Antelope
E: Acoustic Army, GTBT

For the last of three shows at the Fox Theater, lucky fans were treated to a tremendous show. First set Mike's Song, one of the best I've heard, caught everyone off guard. After a smoking Stash and Amazing Grace, the first set seemed to be over as band members began to exit the stage. But Page encouraged the rest to come back and they closed with not only Fee but Chalkdust as well. I thought the roof would come off during Suzie and Fluffhead. This Fox show is essential in any collection. —Matthew Napoli

The setlist of this show is amazing. Each song seems a perfect compliment to the one before and after it. A combination which I had never heard before, Mike's > Day in the Life, blew me away. These are two songs which have no obvious musical link but the smooth, lengthy transition is perfect. The second set features two of the rockingest covers: Frankenstein and Good Times Bad Times. —Mike Jett

An incredibly well-played show, easily one of the best of the year. The boys break out Mike's Groove in the first set for the first time since 12/1/92 Denison, a feat that wouldn't happen again until Amsterdam in summer '97. It's a Mike's with second-set intensity, really a strong version. The musical highlight of a great second set is the powerful Antelope closer. —Lee Johnston

11/12/95 [ACCESSIBILITY: •••] [ATTEND. 5,321; CAP. 10,654] [TIX $20]
Stephen C. O'Connell Center, Gainesville, FL
I: My Friend, Llama, Bouncing, Guelah, Reba, I Didn't Know, Fog That Surrounds, If I Could, Melt, Hello My Baby

II: Curtain > Tweezer, Keyboard Kavalry, Sample, Slave, HYHU > Cracklin' Rosie > HYHU, Possum, Tweezer Reprise
E: Fire

Fishman on vacuum for I Didn't Know.

The O'Connell Center is one of the worst places you can go to see a live show. The place is like a high school gymnasium and security seems to get a kick out of shining a flashlight in your face whenever possible. The setlist wasn't anything spectacular, but one of the lighter moments of the show occurred during Fishman's rendition of Cracklin' Rosie. About halfway through the song he screwed up the lyrics, stopped and said, "Oh shit! I screwed that up. Can we do it again?" The band said no and picked up from where they left off. —Chris Haines

11/14/95 [ACCESSIBILITY: ••••] [ATTEND. 3,301; CAP. 5,240] [TIX $20]
University of Central Florida Arena, Orlando, FL
I: Chalkdust, Foam, Billy Breathes, Divided Sky, Esther, Free, Julius, I'm Blue I'm Lonesome, Cavern
II: Maze, Gumbo, Stash > Manteca > Stash > Dog Faced Boy > Stash, Strange Design, YEM
E: Wedge, Rocky Top

Vocals only on Dog Faced Boy. "25 or 6 to 4" tease in Stash. "Immigrant Song" jam in YEM. Last Manteca 10/28/94 Charleston, SC [85 shows].

Probably the best jam of the tour, if not the year, came during the band's Florida swing. A rare second-set Stash flows for over 30 minutes, wandering through Manteca and the Dog Faced Boy lyrics while also developing a number of very memorable, melodic themes of its own. For die-hard fans of Phish's improv, this set is just a rare, wondrous treat. —Ernie Greene

Best version of Stash I've ever heard. It was about half an hour long and featured a Manteca jam. —Tim Herrman

The taper section was on the side of the stage due to a smaller-than-normal floor area. First set: of course Chalkdust opens a University show; also check out the crazy Trey playing/screaming in between verses in Cavern. Second set: You see the list, you can imagine how insane Stash was. An a cappella Dog Faced Boy still haunts my dreams and nightmares. Be sure to listen to Trey singing the Immigrant Song intro in the middle of YEM. And don't forget the Wedge encore. —Tony Hume

The first set of this show contains a beautiful Esther which flows perfectly into Free. But what a great second set. An unbelievable Stash > Manteca > Stash > Dog Faced Boy > Stash. Page does an incredible job on Strange Design. Listen closely to YEM and you will hear some Zeppelin thrown in just to make it a little sweeter. —John E. Campion

11/15/95 [ACCESSIBILITY: ••] [ATTEND. 4,314; CAP. 7,365] [TIX $19.50]
Sundome, Tampa, FL
I: Poor Heart, AC/DC Bag, FEFY, Rift, Caspian, Sparkle, Melt, Adeline, Squirming Coil
II: Wilson, Theme, Scent of a Mule, Mike's > Life on Mars > Weekapaug, Fee, Guitar Gently Weeps
E: Suzie

The band wins the first band-versus-audience chess game, taking a 1-0 lead over the audience in the match.

11/16/95 [ACCESSIBILITY: ••••] [ATTEND. 5,078; CAP. 6,300] [TIX $21]
West Palm Beach Auditorium, West Palm Beach, FL
I: CTB, Runaway Jim, Chess Game Jam, Horn, Mound, Ya Mar, Simple, Timber Ho, Guyute, Funky Bitch
II: Day in the Life, Bowie, Lifeboy, Uncle Pen, Ha Ha Ha, Harry Hood, HYHU > Brain > HYHU, Amazing Grace, Possum
E: Brown Eyed Girl

Second band-versus-audience chess game begins during Chess Game Jam. Fishman on vacuum for Brain. Butch Trucks on drums for Possum, which also included Fishman on trombone and a "One Way Out" jam. Jimmy Buffet on vocals for Brown Eyed Girl. Concert debut: Brown Eyed Girl. Last Brain, 10/25/94 Atlanta, GA [90 shows].

The second set had some great tunes: ADITL, Uncle Pen and Ha Ha Ha. But the best part came at the end—first there was Possum with Butch Trucks, then even better was the Brown Eyed Girl encore with Jimmy Buffet. It was cool to hear a classic like that with Buffet. —Chuck Adams

When Possum started up, Butch Trucks from the Allman Brothers Band took over on drums and Fish played trombone, which sounded just great. I love Brown Eyed Girl, so when Jimmy Buffet is in tow I'm in a state of ecstasy. Butch and Buffet—this was a great show. —Billy O'Malley

11/18/95 [ACCESSIBILITY: ••••] [ATTEND. 9,115; CAP. 9,858] [TIX $20]
North Charleston Coliseum, North Charleston, SC
I: Dinner and a Movie, Bouncing, Reba, Lawn Boy, PYITE, Slave, I'm Blue I'm Lonesome, Sample
II: AC/DC Bag, Sparkle, Free, I'm So Tired, YEM, Contact, BBFCM > Acoustic Army > BBFCM, Cavern
E: Bill Bailey

I'm Blue I'm Lonesome performed acoustic. "Brickhouse" jam in YEM. Page's Father, Dr. Jack McConnell, on keyboard and vocals for Bill Bailey. Last Dinner and a Movie, 10/22/94 Orlando, FL [93 shows]. Last I'm So Tired, 10/31/94 Glens Falls, NY [88 shows]. Last Bill Bailey, 4/22/94 Columbia, SC [163 shows].

A sweet Dinner opener led to Fishman completely flubbing the beginning of Bouncin'. Reba, PYITE and Slave were nice first set treats. Second set had a Bag opener and the only I'm So Tired besides Halloween '94 (a cool song which was probably appropriate considering how long this tour was). YEM > Brickhouse > YEM was the bomb! The Bill Bailey encore with Dr. Jack McConnell doing the old soft-shoe was a good way to close a good show in my hometown. —Trevor Norris

Sometimes when you see a notation like "Brickhouse tease" on a setlist, you figure Trey maybe hit a few bars of the song somewhere in a long jam. But "Brickhouse" is ALL OVER this incredible YEM, one of the most rocking jam segments I've ever heard in this song. Trey and Mike are both on fire! —Rich Mazer

Our seats were in the family section, and this was a benefit for Dr. McConnell's clinic. We met all of the friends and family of the McConnells. Then we won backstage passes from the Greenpeace brothers. So off it was to the aftershow room with a fridge full of Bass Ale. There we waited for the boys to come in. Being a guitarist, I was most excited talking to Trey. We talked about Surrender to the Air and the previous and past year's Florida shows. As it was getting near to time for us to leave, I told Trey we were driving back to Orlando because my band had to play. He told me, "It's good to see you have your priorities in order." When I told him we did some of his songs, he jokingly replied, "Oh yeah? Try Foam!" —Tony Hume

11/19/95 [ACCESSIBILITY: ••] [ATTEND. 9,295; CAP. 9,796] [TIX $20]
Charlotte Coliseum, Charlotte, NC
I: Makisupa > Maze, Poor Heart, Rift > Stash, Strange Design, It's Ice, Hello My Baby, Julius, Squirming Coil
II: Theme > Also Sprach, Curtain > Tweezer > Billy Breathes, Scent of a Mule, Harry Hood, Suzie
E: Life on Mars, Tweezer Reprise

Slow version of Poor Heart (concert debut). "James Bond Theme" teases in Stash. "Tweezer" teases in Suzie.

11/21/95 [ACCESSIBILITY: ••••] [ATTEND. 7,879; CAP. 8,361] [TIX $20]
Lawrence Joel Veterans Memorial Coliseum, Winston-Salem, NC
I: Fee, Chalkdust, Caspian, Divided Sky, Long Journey Home, I'm Blue I'm Lonesome, Guyute, My Friend, Dog Faced Boy, Runaway Jim
II: Simple, Bowie > Take Me to the River > Bowie, Glide, Ya Mar, Mike's > Keyboard Kavalry > Suspicious Minds > HYHU, Carolina, Day in the Life
E: GTBT

I'm Blue I'm Lonesome and Long Journey Home performed acoustic. Concert debut: Take Me to the River.

Perhaps my favorite of the shows I saw this fall, this show had it all—old favorites, acoustic numbers, Keyboard Kavalry, Fishman going crazy in a light-up cape singing Suspicious Minds, a cappella, Beatles, Talking Heads, Zeppelin. This show was a true carnival! Trey was killing it all night. —Terry Watts

A unique situation at the Lawrence Joel Coliseum: no ushers for the floor seating. I didn't have floor seats but with no one checking we walked right down and sat ten rows back, center, and no one gave us any problems. Unbelievable second set. David Bowie kicked ass. The Keyboard Kavalry sounded very cool, and Fish dressed like Elvis got a laugh. An action-packed solid show. —Eric Higel

Absolutely the most spacey show I've ever seen. Most songs seemed to morph, like the band really had no expectations for the evening. Very groovy from start to finish though the second set takes the cake with a unique Bowie > Take Me to the River > Bowie. —Waylon Baynard

11/22/95 [ACCESSIBILITY: ••••] [ATTEND. 14,830; CAP. 18,000] [TIX $22.50]
USAir Arena, Landover, MD

I: CTB, Wilson, Antelope, Fluffhead, Uncle Pen, Cavern, Fog That Surrounds, Lizards, Sample, Adeline
II: Rift, Free > Llama, Bouncing, YEM, Strange Design
E: Poor Heart, Frankenstein

Slow version of Poor Heart. Rift abandoned after Fishman mistake.

This show had the famed half-hour Free. I didn't like it. It just doesn't do anything. Its only redeeming quality is the musical debate at the end: Fish wants to segue into Bouncin'. Trey is very reluctant and ultimately chooses Llama. The transition is a tad sloppy but novel nonetheless. —Scott Kushner

A memorable moment came when the second set opened with Rift: about half a minute into the song the band comes to a stop (Fish couldn't keep a beat). Trey jokingly says, "I'd like to credit that last one to our drummer, Mr. Jon Fishman." Then they burst into the most amazing Free I've ever witnessed. This Free went on for about a half hour, then they drifted beautifully into Llama in a segue highlighted by Trey's drum kit. A decent Llama followed, and a good YEM with a great vocal jam topped off the night. —John Foley

A 30-minute Free, but bigger isn't necessarily better. The improv gets a bit forced—nice try, but no cigar. Slow Poor Heart is a nice change for an encore, then Frankenstein. First set is pretty standard, with strong versions of Antelope and Sample as highlights. —Bob Colby

The Free jam is very interesting and different from the ones in 1996. You should hear it. At points, it's reminiscent of Runaway Jim. —Libby Barrow

11/24/95 [ACCESSIBILITY: ••] [ATTEND. 10,669; CAP. 18,742] [TIX $20]
Pittsburgh Civic Arena, Pittsburgh, PA
I: Oh Kee > AC/DC Bag, Curtain, Sparkle, Stash, Tela, I'm Blue I'm Lonesome, Maze, Suzie
II: Chalkdust, Theme, Reba, Catapult, Scent of a Mule, Bathtub Gin, Acoustic Army, HYHU > Bike > HYHU, Fee, Julius
E: Life on Mars, Rocky Top

I'm Blue I'm Lonesome performed acoustic. Fishman on vacuum for Bike. Last Oh Kee, 6/9/95 Morrison, CO [56 shows]. Last bike, 12.6.94 Santa Barbara, CA [68 shows].

11/25/95 [ACCESSIBILITY: ••••] [ATTEND. 12,903; CAP. 12,903] [TIX $20–$22.50]
Hampton Coliseum, Hampton, VA
I: Poor Heart, Day in the Life > Bowie, Billy Breathes, Fog That Surrounds, Bouncing, Rift, Wolfman's, Runaway Jim
II: Timber Ho > Kung > Mike's > Rotation Jam > Mike's, Long Journey Home, I'm Blue I'm Lonesome, Strange Design > Weekapaug, Harry Hood, Hello My Baby, Poor Heart
E: Fire

Standard version of Poor Heart opened the show, then the slow version of Poor Heart closed second set. "Poor Heart" teases (slow and fast) before Fire. Long Journey Home and I'm Blue I'm Lonesome performed acoustic. Concert debut: Rotation Jam (band members rotated instruments).

The first set was weak—the only songs I enjoyed were Bowie and Rift. The second set, filled with variety, made up for the first. Mike's Song showed up but segued into a weird jam. Everybody switched instruments (each taking a turn on all three other roles) allowing Fishman to make his glorious debut on electric guitar. Trey should start his own band—he sounded great on bass, drums and piano. Mike's Song came back out of this but there was no Weekapaug. It finally came after two acoustic songs and Strange Design. Poor Heart closed the set and was slowed down to counter the standard version that opened the show. —Jay Green

After a rather textbook first set, they came back and threw us a curveball (isn't that the reason we keep coming back?), complete with a screaming Kung and a Harry Hood that was so inspired I lost total consciousness and felt like I was flying over breaking waves with the warm sun on my face—all this while completely sober. —Colm Connell

If 5/7/94 is Tweezerfest, then I guess 11/25/95 must be PoorHeartfest. The show was bookended by Poor Hearts: set one opened with the regular, upbeat Poor Heart, and set two closed with the slow-shuffle version they started playing the week before this show. When the band came out for the encore, they teased both versions, then Trey asked the crowd, "Get it?" Ah, high-concept Phish humor—what a treat. —Marcia Collins

11/28/95 [ACCESSIBILITY: ••] [ATTEND. 4,323; CAP. 6,000] [TIX $18–$25]
Civic Coliseum, Knoxville, TN
I: Stash, Dinner and a Movie > Bouncing, Foam, I Didn't Know, Divided Sky, Guyute, Hello My Baby, Sample
II: Also Sprach > Maze, Suzie, Uncle Pen, Free, HYHU > Wind beneath My Wings > HYHU, Antelope, Contact, BBFCM, Funky Bitch
E: Squirming Coil

"25 or 6 to 4" tease in Suzie. Fishman on vacuum for I Didn't Know. Wind beneath My Wings was dedicated to Col. Bruce Hampton, who sat in a chair onstage reading a newspaper while Fishman sang. Concert debut: Wind beneath My Wings.

This is a perfect picture of a basically good, solid, pleasing Phish show. There weren't any standouts during set one—everything was satisfying but standard. Suzie and Uncle Pen broke up the great jams in both Maze and Free. To see Col. Bruce on stage was a thrill. —Jason Deziel

This was my first show; I hate the fact that I am a latecomer, so to speak, but I can guarantee I heard nothing until I heard live Phish. I will never forget the image of Trey going off when they opened up with Stash and the beams of red light shined down. It was then I knew I loved this band! As far as first shows go, the music rocked, but the setlist in retrospect was weak. Regardless, it was incredible, and how could I forget Fishman serenading Col. Bruce with that all-time favorite Wind beneath My Wings? —Amanda Litton

11/29/95 [ACCESSIBILITY: ••••] [ATTEND. 5,958; CAP. 7,000] [TIX $20]
Nashville Municipal Auditorium, Nashville, TN
I: AC/DC Bag, Ya Mar, Reba, If I Could, It's Ice, Theme, Acoustic Army, Fee, Melt
II: Timber Ho, Sparkle, Simple, Possum, YEM, Fog That Surrounds, Poor Heart, I'm Blue I'm Lonesome, Long Journey Home, Slave
E: Day in the Life

Bela Fleck on banjo for the second set, starting with Fog That Surrounds. "Heart and Soul" jam played to introduce Bela before Fog That Surrounds.

After a fairly mediocre first set, the second set just blows my mind. A great Timber Ho kicks things off, and then comes the real fun. Halfway through the set, out comes Bela Fleck! They play some good bluegrass tunes and then the best Slave my ears have ever experienced. A banjo has never sounded so sweet as it did during this fine tune. —Josh Harman

Whenever Bela is involved, it's gonna be gooood, especially if it's for half a set! Check out that setlist! Also nice to hear how talented they all can be by playing acoustic guitars on Acoustic Army. —Mark Selby

11/30/95 [ACCESSIBILITY: ••••] [ATTEND. 9,961; CAP. 11,000] [TIX $20–$22]
Ervin J. Nutter Center, Dayton, OH
I: Sample, Curtain, Ha Ha Ha, Julius, NICU, Bathtub Gin, Rift, FEFY, Lizards, Fire
II: CTB, Tweezer > Makisupa > Antelope, Scent of a Mule, Free, Strange Design, Amazing Grace
E: Harry Hood

Many Phish shows have second sets better than the first, but seldom is the imbalance as severe as it is here. The second set is absolutely one of the must-have sets of the fall tour, featuring a wonderful Tweezer > Makisupa > Antelope trio that has to be heard to be appreciated. That's because this is no normal Tweezer—like its kindred spirit on 12/2, it explores beautiful melodious realms before seguing into Makisupa, which itself has a crazy segue into an unbelievable, unreal, thrilling Antelope (Trey starts Antelope, then returns to play around with Makisupa before churning back into Antelope). —Scott Sifton

This show features one of my favorite combinations of Phish songs. It has a nicely jammed Tweezer which segues into Makisupa's reggae vibe. Then comes the part I'm fond of: Makisupa Policemantelope. There's a nice combination of the two between Makisupa and Antelope—it's a wonderful combo. —Jeffrey Ellenbogen

My first live Phish experience, and not a bad start. The Sample opener excited me as it was something that sounded familiar. I was overwhelmed by the energy and danced like crazy until the boys slowed it down with a disappointing FEFY. Lizards kept the FEFY-heads happy but Fire brought us all back around. Second set was pretty tight; Antelope blew me away! All was well until they slowed back down, or so I thought until I listened to the lyrics to Strange Design, which inspired the first of many free hugs! Needless to say, I was hooked! —Carri A. Johnson

12/1/95 [ACCESSIBILITY: ••••] [ATTEND. 8,588; CAP. 8,588] [TIX $20]
Hersheypark Arena, Hershey, PA
I: Buried Alive > Down with Disease, Theme, Poor Heart, Wolfman's, Chalkdust, Forbin's > Mockingbird, Stash, Cavern
II: Halley's > Mike's > Weekapaug, Mango, Wilson, HYHU > Suspicious Minds > HYHU, Bowie > Catapult > Bowie
E: Suzie

"Chocolate" chants by Trey during Forbin's and Bowie.

I left school early to make it to this show with my friends and it was well worth the trip. First off, the parking lot was buzzing and all of the trees inside the lot were decorated with Christmas lights, which made it extra welcoming. The Arena was a good size and security was minimal. The highlight of this show is Trey's narration after Col. Forbin in which he gives the biggest clue as to where to find the Rhombus, mentioning "King of Prussia, Pennsylvania" over and over again and telling us it would be the best clue we'd get.... As well, a great chocolate story is mixed in with it. The Mike's > Weekapaug was also stellar. —David George

One of the best Phish shows I've been to. Hersheypark was decorated for the holidays. Christmas lights and music abound, along with the smell of "Mmmm, chocolate," as Trey, doing his Homer Simpson impression, fantasized. Buried Alive rocked the stadium as an opener. Awesome rhombus narration during Forbin's/Mockingbird (I think everybody, the following day, made way to King of Prussia, PA, in search of the elusive rhombus). Fishman's Elvis impression was mind-blowing in Suspicious Minds, especially when the lights dimmed and his Elvis cape lit the stage—beautiful! —Lara Wittels

The start of one of the sickest months of music in Phish history! What was it about December '95 that pushed them to another level? Well, in a month of incredible jams, seemingly every show has a major highlight that just HAS to be heard. Hershey's contribution? The first-ever Mike's directly into Weekapaug which is much more than the setlist indicates. Get this one and the Niagara 12/7 version (the other Mike's right into Weekapaug)—they're both awesome. —Ernie Greene

12/2/95 [ACCESSIBILITY: ••••] [ATTEND. 10,558; CAP. 10,558] [TIX $18–$22]
Veterans Memorial Coliseum, New Haven, CT
I: Caspian, Runaway Jim, Mound, Guelah, Reba, MSO, Free, Fog That Surrounds, Bouncing, Possum
II: Also Sprach > Maze, Simple, Faht, Tweezer, Day in the Life, Golgi, Squirming Coil, Tweezer Reprise
E: Bold as Love
Last MSO, 6/15/95 Atlanta, GA [58 shows].

After having to travel to the past 30 or so shows, I expected a great time in my home state of Connecticut. Wrong! It was like a high school punk madhouse. The crowd seemed overtaken by troublemakers, not tourheads; some 17-year-old Pearl Jam/Nirvana wannabe pushed a girl I was with to the ground. Why? Because she asked his barely conscious friend if he was okay. Set I was basic, a few nice jams but no real standouts. The first half of set II picked up the pace, spacey but tight, and who would have expected Fishman to bust out Faht? The show lost all momentum when the set ended with selections of A Day in the Life, Golgi, and then the dreaded, slow, energy-draining piano exit Squirming Coil. Without question, this was the worst Phish show I've ever attended. —Jason Deziel

First show! After taking Metro North two hours from New York we were greeted by nothing. New Haven was basically closed with the exception of a Burger King that should've been for lack of cleanliness. The Coliseum was a '50s-style minor league hockey arena erected between two highways. After braving three checkpoints by the police and inhaling the smoke that filled the arena, we were greeted with the magic that is Phish. After Reba, I was converted, and the band and Chris's light magic on Tweezer made me a devotee. Life would never be the same. —Lee Schiller

A better show to hear on tape than in person, because you can fast-forward directly to Tweezer. Chris Kuroda later cited this Tweezer as a tour highlight, but it's much more than that—it's an absolute must-hear, as Phish develops several gorgeous jams in a version of the song that isn't overly long but damn sure is overly powerful! Add it to the short list of classic Phish jams, no question. —Al Hunt

12/4/95 [ACCESSIBILITY: •••] [ATTEND. 10,509; CAP. 10,509] [TIX $20]
Mullins Center, University of Massachusetts, Amherst, MA
I: Julius, Gumbo, Divided Sky, PYITE, Stash, My Mind's, Axilla II, Horse > Silent, Hello My Baby, Guitar Gently Weeps
II: Timber Ho, Sparkle, Ya Mar, Antelope, Billy Breathes, CTB, YEM, Sample, Frankenstein
E: Bouncing, Rocky Top

12/5/95 [ACCESSIBILITY: ••••] [ATTEND. 10,509; CAP. 10,509] [TIX $20]
Mullins Center, University of Massachusetts, Amherst, MA
I: Horn, Chalkdust, Fog That Surrounds, Lizards, Free, Esther, Bowie, I'm Blue I'm Lonesome
II: Poor Heart, Bathtub Gin > Keyboard Kavalry, Scent of a Mule > Lifeboy, Harry Hood, Cavern
E: Theme, Adeline
I'm Blue I'm Lonesome performed acoustic.

At one point Trey dedicates Lizards to Dick Vitale, the sports broadcaster, whom he had just met backstage. Dick Vitale at a Phish show? What's next, Captain Lou Albano playin' the drums with Fishman? —Josh Letourneau

I have friends who disagree, but I don't think Phish has ever played a great show at the Mullins Center. The place is so cavernous that the music just sort of gets lost on its way to the audience. This show might be the exception—there's a lot of meat in the first set (Free, Esther, Bowie), and an amazing Bathtub Gin in the second set that clocks in at over 25 minutes before the boys march westward for Keyboard Kavalry. The Lifeboy, Harry Hood pairing also taps an emotional reservoir, but if you're going to pick up this show, it'll be for the Gin. —Pat Stanley

12/7/95 [ACCESSIBILITY: ••••] [ATTEND. 8,767; CAP. 9,000] [TIX $20]
Niagara Falls Convention Center, Niagara Falls, NY
I: Old Home Place, Curtain > AC/DC Bag, Demand > Rift, Slave, Guyute, Bouncing, Possum, Hello My Baby
II: Melt, Strange Design, Fog That Surrounds, Reba, Julius, Sleeping Monkey, Sparkle, Mike's > Weekapaug, Amazing Grace
E: Uncle Pen
"In-a-Gadda-Da-Vida" jam in Melt. "Itsy Bitsy Spider" jam in Reba.

One of the most underrated shows, in my opinion. An excellent Slave in the first set, then, to open off the second set is an amazing SOAMelt. They tease In-a-Gadda-Da-Vida and just jam the hell out of it. Then later in the set they pull out a phat Mike's > Weekapaug. Not as good as Hershey, but still an unbelievable version. —Kevin Weiss

In a strange attempt to alternate incredible jams with more plebian crowd-favorites, the second set of this show is truly unique. It starts with a raging Split Open and Melt that is just amazing, worthy of "best version" consideration without a doubt. As if to counter this amazing achievement with a no-improv song, the band follows with Strange Design. The opposite happens later in the set when a basic Sparkle precedes what might be the best Mike's Groove ever. The jamming that carries the band from Mike's across the great divide into Weekapaug is glorious, but then the band jams out the other side of Weekapaug, creating a Mike's > Weekapaug > Jam that is unlike any version of this song I've ever heard. —Josh Albini

Quite a sick tease of "Itsy Bitsy Spider" during Trey's solo in Reba. But what stole the show was Page on keys—incredible organ work during Julius. You gotta love any set that opens with good bluegrass such as My Old Home Place. I almost forgot Fishman's voice not working too well during Sleeping Monkey—at least he gave us a chuckle. —Mark Selby

Is this the only show where both sets end in a cappella tunes? —Charlie Murphy

12/8/95 [ACCESSIBILITY: ••••] [ATTEND. 10,656; CAP. 10,656] [TIX $20–$22]
Convocation Center, Cleveland State University, Cleveland, OH
I: Sample, Poor Heart, Simple > Runaway Jim > Fluffhead, It's Ice, Acoustic Army, Caspian, GTBT
II: Also Sprach > Tweezer > Kung > Tweezer > Love You, Squirming Coil, Tweezer Reprise, Antelope
E: Come Together, Day in the Life
"Brady Bunch Theme" tease in Antelope. Concert debut: Come Together, in memory of John Lennon, who died 12/8/80. Last Love You, 12/28/94 Philadelphia, PA [73 shows].

A few segues grab my attention. Maybe because I've only been listening for two years, but the Simple > Jim > Fluffhead is unbelievable. If I'm not mistaken you can hear the Jim teases in Simple a good minute before they kick into it. I love it. The encore of this show is amazing: back-to-back Beatles, dedicated to John Lennon on the anniversary of his death. —Jeff Bernier

This was a cold and snowy night, and also the anniversary of the day John Lennon got shot. The venue was right down the street from the Rock and Roll Hall of Fame, so I don't think anyone knew what to expect. Both sets were good, not the best, but the encores were great. Their tribute to John probably made him cry from above. —Kevin Word

12/9/95 [ACCESSIBILITY: ••••] [ATTEND. 16,363; CAP. 16,363] [TIX $18–$22]
Knickerbocker Arena, Albany, NY
I: Maze, Theme, NICU, Sloth, Rift, Bouncing, Free, Billy Breathes, Dog Faced Boy, Chalkdust
II: Timber Ho, Wilson, Gumbo, YEM, Lawn Boy, Slave, Crossroads, Adeline
E: Loving Cup
Trey triggered Beavis and Butt-head sound effects in Wilson. Silent Jam in YEM. "Shaft" line sung in YEM.

The band lifted our spirits with a most memorable YEM. It was aggressive and kept the Knick grooving, including a silent jam and a stinky vocal jam. Trey sure can pull those windmills! Phish succeeded at slapping a smile on all faces that had to bear the blizzard to get to the show. Anyone else get involved in the I-90 pile-up? —Mark Selby

The band played a great silent jam that you had to see to really appreciate. About halfway through YEM, they faded the music to silence and built it back up again—but without any sound! It lasted about half a minute, and on tape all you hear is the phans' reaction. Every move was an exact replica of what it would take to play the jam with audible music! —Melissa Mixer

A simply incredible, melodic, heavily improvised YEM. Phish at their very, very, best. It's the level of performance you wait 20 to 30 shows to hear, and you damn well better appreciate it. —Andy Bernstein

Phish opened up the second set with an insane Timber which displayed Phish communication at its best. Out of all my tapes, I probably listen to this one song the most. Trey tried to get the crowd psyched up for Wilson by using his Beavis and Butt-head keychain, but unfortunately the crowd just stood there and laughed. This followed with Gumbo and its saloon-style Page conclusion. Another notable was a beautiful YEM with an intense improv section. —John Foley

12/11/95 [ACCESSIBILITY: ••••] **[ATTEND. 8,958; CAP. 8,958] [TIX $20]**
Cumberland County Civic Center, Portland, ME
I: My Friend, Ha Ha Ha, Stash, Caspian, Reba, Dog Log, Llama, Dog Log, Tube, McGrupp, Julius, Cavern
II: Curtain > Bowie, Mango, Fog That Surrounds, Scent of a Mule, Harry Hood, HYHU > Suspicious Minds > HYHU, Funky Bitch
E: Guitar Gently Weeps

Trey cued audience sound effects (booing) during first Dog Log. Second Dog Log performed lounge-lizard style with more cued sound effects (screaming). Warren Haynes on guitar for Funky Bitch and Guitar Gently Weeps. Last Dog Log, 8/2/93 Ybor City, FL [217 shows].

North-country boys that they are, Phish knew their fans deserved something special for making the trek north in the middle of December. Early in the first set, Trey revealed a secret he said he'd been keeping all tour. Noting that the band performs Dog Log during soundchecks before a lot of shows, Trey said they've been recording them for inclusion on an all–Dog Log album. And this night, Trey told us we were going to play a role in the creation of the album-to-be. The band would play Dog Log but we had to be really quiet at the beginning, mimicking the empty-room soundcheck conditions. Then, on signal, we were supposed to boo and scream at Phish as though they were the worst band in history. A minute into Dog Log, Trey lifted his arm and the Civic Center began to shake under attack from thunderous screaming and yelling. Dog Log ended there—Trey flashed one of those giddy smiles and said, "That was awesome! That's going on the album!" Then, following a great Llama, Trey decided that Dog Log was so much fun, he wanted to do another one. This time, we were told to shriek as loudly and obnoxiously as we could on his signal. Again, the effect was fantastic. As a thank you for our help, we received the tour's second Tube. —Russell Kahn

What a great venue—tiny for an arena. This was a goof of a show. I had a great time during Dog Log, and obviously I wasn't alone as everyone there seemed to be on that groove. My friends and I were also in town for the Gov't Mule show the following night, so Warren Haynes's presence didn't surprise us. Funky Bitch was a tasty treat. Suspicious Minds was played on the anniversary of a scheduled Elvis show in Portland that was canceled because of the King's death. The tapes don't do this gem justice. —Dan Kurtz

12/12/95 [ACCESSIBILITY: •••] **[ATTEND. 10,430; CAP. 13,500] [TIX $18–$22]**
Providence Civic Center, Providence, RI
I: Ya Mar, Sample, Divided Sky, Lifeboy, PYITE, Horse > Silent, Antelope, I'm Blue I'm Lonesome, Squirming Coil
II: Free, Sparkle, Down with Disease > Lizards, Simple, Runaway Jim
E: Fire

I'm Blue I'm Lonesome performed acoustic.

Bad vibes in Providence—weird after the glorious 12/29/94 show in the same room—bummed everyone out and decreased our enjoyment of what otherwise would have been a good show. A massive fight broke out on the floor during setbreak, with one guy led away in handcuffs (he tried to grab the tapers' microphone stands as the police led him past the tapers' section, which was pretty funny). A long Down with Disease in the second set didn't work most of the time; a tighter Runaway Jim, on the other hand, did. —Tyler Harris

The highlight of the show was Down with Disease. Many people say '96 was the year of the DwD, but I believe DwD started to take off at this show. It clocked in at about 35 minutes. —Jon Bahr

This is the unknown sleeper of fall/winter '95; no one I trade with has it and no one talks about it, but it smokes! The Ya Mar opener was more funky than usual and sets a great pace. They blew up everything during set I—top-notch versions of Divided Sky and Antelope. The assholes fighting by the SBD during setbreak bummed a lot of people out, along with the large presence of drunken frat boy types. The great version of Free couldn't stand anything to the best version of Down With Disease ever—words can't describe it. There was also a terrific version of Runaway Jim to end set II (they should really use this in more places than the usual set-opening location it often gets). —Jason Deziel

12/14/95 [ACCESSIBILITY: ••••] **[ATTEND. 7,160; CAP. 7,160] [TIX $18–$25]**
Broome County Arena, Binghamton, NY
I: Suzie, Llama, Horn, Foam, Makisupa, Melt, Tela, Fog That Surrounds, MSO, Frankenstein
II: Curtain > Tweezer > Timber Ho > Tweezer, Keyboard Kavalry, Halley's > NICU > Slave
E: Bold as Love

Bonus lyrics in Makisupa. Silent Jam in Melt. Page solo between NICU and Slave.

The most underrated tape in my collection. Second set rocks with an outstanding Tweezer > Timber > Tweezer. Page lays on the synthesizers during the jam, while Fish and Mike provide the noise. Beautiful chaos! Timber is a perfect version, as is the set-opener Curtain—the vocal harmonies are dead-on. A nice Halley's into NICU jam is all Trey. Add a brilliant Axis encore and you have yourself a great tape. —Tim Foisser

Well, I will admit to my bias to begin. This show took place in my town and to say I was excited as all hell to go is an understatement. Opening with Suzie and Llama was energizing; I also loved SOAMelt, and Makisupa had the cool Khadafi-joint narration. I got my first Frankenstein—man, what a great closer! The second set was a giant segue. Curtain was sweet, the following Tweezer was fun. Perhaps the best was Keyboard Kavalry, which was new to me, a very pretty, simple, yet powerful little tune. A final word: Halley's Comet was grrrrreat! —Daniel Paden

The second set of this show has one of the most powerful arrangements of songs ever. Explanation won't do it justice, so I'll just spell it out for you: Curtain > Tweezer > Timber Ho > Tweezer > Keyboard Kavalry, Halley's Comet > NICU > Slave! The encore? Bold as Love! You must hear this to comprehend it! —Otis

12/15/95 [ACCESSIBILITY: ••••] **[ATTEND. 18,645; CAP. 18,645] [TIX $22.50]**
CoreStates Spectrum, Philadelphia, PA
I: Chalkdust > Harry Hood > Wilson, Maze > Ha Ha Ha > Suspicious Minds, CTB, Bouncing, Free > Possum
II: Tweezer Reprise, Runaway Jim, It's Ice > Bathtub Gin > Rotation Jam > Also Sprach > Bowie, Adeline
E: GTBT > Tweezer Reprise

Band members rotated instruments after Fishman vacuum solo in Bathtub Gin.

There are not enough good things that I can say about this show, except that it is awesome! The setlist is all that I could ever want and the band plays every song so well. Chalkdust opener is hot and segues perfectly into a Hood that would knock your fridge over. The Spectrum is where Trey saw his first concert (Jethro Tull), he tells the crowd before a smoking Ha Ha Ha that is shorter than other versions but is the tightest one I've heard. David Bowie as usual has an awesome jam included with it. I can't keep this tape out of my deck! —David George

They finished the Tweezer from the night before (then did it again!?). I remember Trey respectfully dedicating Good Times Bad Times to Mike Tyson, who was going to be there the next night. —Colm Connell

Very schtick-oriented show, highlighted by the rotation jam. If you're at a show to see them jam and they end up just doing a lot of schtick, you'd better hope you're in the mood for it. I wasn't. —Lisa Paddock

12/16/95 [ACCESSIBILITY: ••] **[ATTEND. 8,500; CAP. 8,500] [TIX $18–$22]**
Olympic Center, Lake Placid, NY
I: Buried Alive > AC/DC Bag, Fog that Surrounds, Ya Mar, Sloth, Divided Sky, Dog Faced Boy, Julius, Suzie
II: Sample, Reba, Scent of a Mule, Cavern, Mike's > Simple > Weekapaug, Squirming Coil
E: Fire

12/17/95 [ACCESSIBILITY: ••••] **[ATTEND. 8,500; CAP. 8,500] [TIX $18–$22]**
Olympic Center, Lake Placid, NY
I: My Friend, Poor Heart, Day in the Life, Antelope, Mango, Tube, Stash, Lizards, Chalkdust
II: Bouncing, Maze, Free, Also Sprach > Harry Hood, Sparkle, Tweezer > Tweezer Reprise
E: Hello My Baby, Runaway Jim

Page solo between Tweezer and Tweezer Reprise.

I'd love it if every town welcomed us with the hospitality Lake Placid does. The local

restaurants even incorporated Phish songs into their menus! While the setlist seems like nothing special, the music was finely crafted. I found myself constantly thinking, this is how this song is meant to be played! A perfect show to send us home with after such a phenomenal tour. —Colm Connell

It's nice when the tour-ender falls on your birthday, especially when you know the show will be better than last night. Nothing too unusual in the first set (although Antelope through Stash was a standout portion). Chalkdust provided the tour thank-yous. The second set was interesting, not because of the song choices but the way they were ordered and combined. Bouncin' is better as an opener, because that way it doesn't destroy an amazing set. Free extends past its usual ending (to the extent that I wrote "Jam" on my setlist) before landing in 2001 land, a creative choice for mid-second set. Hood (out of 2001!) goes the same way: they play through the "You can feel good!" and eventually land in Sparkle. Tweezer develops into a Page solo, which seemed likely to end the show, but the band returned for the Reprise. Jim is a strange tour-ender, as one usually thinks of it as an opener, but on this night it seemed to fit. —Greg Schwartz

1995 HOLIDAY TOUR
Temporal Rift

New Year's Eve '93 at the Centrum in Worcester, MA, was, at the time, far and away the largest indoor venue Phish had ever played on its own. But as '95 drew to a close, the two-night stand at Worcester served as just a warm-up for Phish's most ambitious and high-profile gigs to date: a pair of shows at Madison Square Garden to close out the year.

Through the entire, no-repeats run, the band seemed to be building up to the final show, with many fans agreeing that each night was noticeably better than the one which preceded it—except perhaps for the great 12/29 show topping 12/30—and that the New Year's show took a giant step ahead of any show in memory. The midnight prank was not quite as grand as 1994's flying hot dog, with the band instead fiddling in the Gamehendge Time Laboratory at the rear of the stage and turning Fish—who had gotten a shave onstage between sets I and II—into the baby New Year as he emerged from a flying crate. The first Sanity in a year and a half captured more attention.

12/28/95 [ACCESSIBILITY: ••••] [ATTEND. 14,462; CAP. 14,462] [TIX $23.50]
The Centrum, Worcester, MA
I: Melt, Gumbo, Curtain > Julius, Guyute, Horn, Rift, FEFY, Possum
II: Timber Ho, Theme, Wilson, Buried Alive, Tweezer, I Didn't Know, Uncle Pen, Slave
E: Fee, Tweezer Reprise

The venue sound system cut out during Rift and the band continued to play through its monitors until the sound system came back on right before the final "and silence contagious..." line. "Johnny B. Goode" tease in Wilson. Fishman on vacuum for I Didn't Know.

In my opinion (and I realize this may draw slack), this was the best show of the '95 holiday tour. Why? I think it was because it was the first holiday show and they played a lot of great tunes that you don't hear all the time. Guyute, Horn, Rift was an amazing stretch, and then the PA went out during Rift and the band kept going, realizing and smiling at what was going on as they kept playing. La Grange was great the following night, but I enjoyed this show more. —Jeff Bernier

The first of the four shows on the New Year's Run was a true indication of how great these shows would be. Although we had the worst seats possible, behind the band, it didn't stop everyone in our section from dancing and enjoying ourselves. The highlight of the night occurred during Rift. The speakers went out and there was no sound for a good part of the song. The band continued to play and the crowd kept dancing. When the sound finally kicked back on (right before the "and silence contagious in moments like these" line), the crowd let out an enormous cheer. However, there was nothing else out of the ordinary or too spectacular at this show. —Chris Haines

12/29/95 [ACCESSIBILITY: ••••] [ATTEND. 14,462; CAP. 14,462] [TIX $23.50]
The Centrum, Worcester, MA
I: My Friend, Poor Heart, Down with Disease, Fog That Surrounds, NICU, Stash, Fluffhead, Llama, Adeline
II: Makisupa, CTB, Bathtub Gin > The Real Me > Bathtub Gin > McGrupp, BBFCM > Bass Jam > La Grange, Bouncing, Fire
E: Golgi

Jim Stinnette (Mike's bass instructor) on bass and Mike on bass for Bass Jam. Last La Grange, 8/14/93 Tinley Park, IL [215 shows].

A decent first set, but once again Phish unleashes during the second. Notables in the second set were an upbeat Cars Trucks Buses followed by Bathtub Gin > The Real Me > Bathtub Gin, the best sandwich sequence I have ever witnessed. Even better than any Mike's > I Am > Weekapaug I've ever heard—truly vintage Phish. They didn't stop there—McGrupp with a particularly spooky piano section was followed by a bass duet with Gordon and his instructor, Jim Stinnette. Remember, those are just the highlights of a perfect-10 show. This was the best show I've ever been to. —John Foley

Somewhere in the middle of Bathtub > Real Me > Bathtub, a.k.a. "The Real Gin," I discovered the meaning of life. Simply incredible. —Melissa Wolcott

While the first set seemed predictable at the time, nothing could have prepared me for the second set. Whatever was happening anywhere else in the universe did not matter. If sunlight could have made sound, it would've been Trey's guitar during the greatest Makisupa ever. From then on I didn't stop spinning. I couldn't. The set was an absolute masterpiece. Everyone was gleaming. If I could have only one live recording, this would be it. If you don't have this tape, get it! —Colm Connell

The second set is perfect for those of you looking to turn on potential phans. It contains reggae, jazz, blues, rock, punk, a bunch of covers and the best damn segue I've ever heard (Bathtub > Real Me). It even has Bouncin', so the phan-to-be will know at least one original. For those who already know, this show will please still since it flows soooo well. What do you expect? It's the New Year's Run! —Paul Sheets

12/30/95 [ACCESSIBILITY: •••••] [ATTEND. 18,252; CAP. 18,252] [TIX $25]
Madison Square Garden, New York, NY
I: Caspian, Also Sprach > Suzie, Bowie, Simple, It's Ice > Kung > It's Ice, TMWSIY > Avenu > TMWSIY, Divided Sky, Sample
II: Ya Mar, Free, Harry Hood, AC/DC Bag, Lifeboy, Scent of a Mule, Cavern, Antelope
E: Day in the Life

"Auld Lang Syne" tease in Ya Mar.

There was one thing about this show that still has a big impact on me—the Hood in the second set. I think it's the best thing Phish has ever produced in concert. Yeah, their rotation jams are cool, but this song, this version is musical perfection to my ears. Whenever it is a nice day, I like to throw on my sunglasses, put on my walkman and go to class with this song ringing through my body. From the part of "Thank you Mr. Miner, thank you Mr. Hood" on, it is like jumping off a ledge and floating down slowly in a state of ecstasy. From the lows to the highs, this song is what defines Phish, and it is the most amazing thing to listen to. The crowd, obviously, felt the same way. —Brett Pessin

The setlist could not have been better for my ear. Avenu Malkenu blew my hat off. I was singing the Hebrew words and this dude next to me couldn't believe it. I told him we sang this in Temple and it blew his mind! —Rob Rimer

A good upbeat setlist, but most of the songs were pretty mainstream. I would have hoped for a little more creativity during a holiday show. —Kate O'Neil

12/31/95 [ACCESSIBILITY: •••••] [ATTEND. 18,252; CAP. 18,252] [TIX $30]
Madison Square Garden, New York, NY
I: PYITE, Sloth, Reba, Squirming Coil, Maze, Forbin's > Mockingbird, Sparkle, Chalkdust
II: Drowned > Lizards, Axilla II, Runaway Jim, Strange Design, Hello My Baby, Mike's
III: "Mad Science Experiment" > New Year's Countdown > Auld Lang Syne > Weekapaug > Sea and Sand, YEM, Sanity, Frankenstein
E: Johnny B. Goode

"Shine" jam in Forbin's, with Tom Marshall on vocals. Lyrics in Runaway Jim included "Runaway Dave" and "Runaway Daubs," referencing Trey's friends in attendance. Digital Delay Loop jam at the end of Mike's. During the mad science experiment, Page, Trey, and Mike worked at a huge machine at the rear of the stage while Fishman ascended to become the New Year's baby. "Auld Lang Syne" teases in Weekapaug. Audience won the second band-versus-audience chessgame as band resigned, tying the match at 1-1. The king from the chess board was thrown into crowd and caught by Rob Fasman of Springfield, NJ. Between the first and second sets, Fishman has his beard shaved off onstage. Last Sanity, 6/24/94 Indianapolis, IN [147 shows]. Last Johnny B. Goode, 7/3/95 Fayston, VT [58 shows].

I tried to find the black cloud in the silver lining, but it wasn't happening. One of the best shows by anyone, ever. Our seats, first level about 20 feet from the stage; the fans, mellow and friendly; the music, even more astonishing; the security, what security? You could've brought in a grenade launcher. But who wanted to? Throw in an amazing interpretation of the Who's Drowned, a scintillating Mike's Song, the choreography of the Mad Scientists and

Baby Fishman, and a rare Sanity, and you've got a show for the ages. The black cloud did come: our train trip back to Philly took five hours. —Lee Schiller

The band was so on this night! The best show I've ever been to. The second set started with a kick-ass version of Drowned, which some claim contains a "Fire on the Mountain" tease. Personally, I don't hear it. The jams on all the songs were unbelievable in the second set, especially Lizards, Runaway Jim and Mike's Song. The jam in Mike's closes the set nicely with a digital delay loop effects jam by Trey. —Seth Weinglass

All three sets of this show are incredible. A PYITE opener is a great start and I love the Reba—a great jam without whistling. Forbin/Mockingbird is cool, with Trey explaining how while not on tour, the band members make time in the Gamehendge time lab. Great Drowned > Lizards opener for set II and an excellent Runaway Jim. The Mike's into weirdness jam is nice too. Set III's Weekapaug > Sea and Sand is phat, followed by a scary YEM. Sanity is a great surprise and the encore is rippin'. Great way to ring in '96. —Nick Soriecelli

It was just amazing. I was in the audience, just thinking, "This is one of the greatest moments of my life and Phish history." I heard the Who play Drowned live in 1996, but Phish just jammed it. They made everyone say, Yeah, this is music. It was a great way to ring in the New Year. —Billy O'Malley

Another year has gone by, and another hell of a New Year's. During Col. Forbin's, Trey got to talking about time and how the band controls time when they are off tour by making time run in Gamehendge. He then continues to say what if we were stuck in 1994, and we woke up to hearing the same song over and over. Tom Marshall then appeared on stage and sang part of Shine. —Ryan Danyew

Auld Lang Syne! I was fortunate to be in a suite for this show—drinking champagne and spraying it onto my fellow phans was a complete and joyous experience. —Rob Rimer

If I have to pick one sequence of songs that showcases Phish at their very, very best, it would be the Auld Lang Syne > Weekapaug > Sea and Sand run from the third set of their MSG New Year's masterpiece. Moving from Auld Lang Syne into Weekapaug, the band's energy is incredible. They develop a jam in Weekapaug that is so powerful, so gorgeous, that I am overcome with emotion every time I hear it. Eventually, it drops into a piano solo, and Page starts singing the wonderfully moving Sea and Sand. —Scott Sifton

1996 SPRING Jazz/Joyous

The winter of 1996 saw Phish disappoint its fans by calling off a tour which had been tentatively slated for the spring. Instead, they headed into the studio to record *Billy Breathes*. Phish's only scheduled performance as a band came at the New Orleans Jazz & Heritage Festival on April 26, a one-set quickie which was more remarkable for the number of Phish fans who made a pilgrimage to Louisiana than for its musical content. Later that spring, after visiting the Joyous Lake Club in Woodstock, NY, while recording *Billy Breathes* nearby, Phish decided to put on a secret show. Several hundred fans lucky enough to be tipped off showed up early to secure their entrance to the 200-person club, which was filled well beyond legal limit by the time the band took the stage around 11 P.M. The surprise show—which many expected to someday grace the stage at Nectar's—had finally happened.

[2/96–4/96] Bearsville Studios, Bearsville, NY
Recording for *Billy Breathes*.

4/26/96 [ACCESSIBILITY: ••••]
The Fairgrounds, New Orleans, LA
Ya Mar, AC/DC Bag, Sparkle, Stash, CTB, YEM > Wolfman's, Scent of a Mule, Also Sprach > Harry Hood, Sample, Day in the Life, Bowie
E: Hello My Baby, Cavern

New Orleans Jazz & Heritage Festival. Phish played one set on the main concert stage, preceding the Meters. "When the Saints Come Marching In" tease in Ya Mar. Michael Ray on trumpet for CTB. A cappella start to Wolfman's.

All the heads at Jazzfest created a great atmosphere—everyone seemed really proud of the boys for being invited to play. But the long layoff showed as Trey was especially sloppy. Most songs were short versions that remained true to form. Michael Ray on CTB

"New Year's '95"

Madison Square Garden, New York, NY

The greatest show of all time. That's how readers of *The Pharmer's Almanac* rate New Year's Eve, 1995. To many, this show represents the absolute culmination of Phish's journey to greatness.

MSG. New York City. About 30,000 fans showed up and for the first time, Phish had center stage to the world—for no one can top New Year's Eve at the Garden.

But the band wasn't content just ruling three dimensions.

Trey set up their annual prank by letting fans know about Phish's "time production lab" during the Col. Forbin's narration in set one, which also found Phish lyricist Tom Marshall emerging onto the stage to sing a couple of lines from Collective Soul's 1994 hit "Shine," which allowed everyone a stroll down memory lane.

Between sets, Fishman got a shave onstage, as fans milled about in aisles so crowded it became clear that many had either sneaked in or breezed through with counterfeits—a genuine fire hazard.

But the true explosion came on stage in the second set. It opened with The Who's Drowned, which they debuted exactly two months earlier in *Quadrophenia*. But unlike Halloween, Phish took Drowned for a long spin—one of the major musical highlights of the show.

It's tough to talk of highlights when practically every song in the second and third sets would stand way out at other shows. Fans tend to throw around superlatives about many songs from many nights spent with Phish, but when people discuss this show, phrases like "monumental" have completely different meanings.

Ask a knowledgeable fan to rate the ten best single-song performances in Phish history. It would not be insane if that fan picked at least four from this show. Drowned, Runaway Jim, Mike's Song and Weekapaug were all miniature shows in themselves, with wonderful improvised licks and incredible melodies made up on the spot. The audience was absolutely captivated.

The middle stanza saw the breathtaking performances of Runaway Jim and Mike's, which finished with Trey alone on stage, creating a digital delay loop effect which rang out over the P.A. even after he had left the stage, reminding the crowd that, yes, there was more to come.

As the third set got underway at about five minutes to midnight, Phish unveiled the Gamehendge time laboratory, and the crowd roared in amusement when Trey, Page and Mike worked at a huge machine at the back of the stage to produce a diapered Fishman baby New Year at the stroke of midnight, hanging from the lights in what looked like a coffin. It was definitely a grand experiment, but in all its electricity, it didn't hold water to the musical brilliance of the evening.

They rang in the New Year with a Weekapaug that saw Phish jam as melodiously and powerfully as they'd ever jammed before. When the jam led to a Page piano solo, an emotional highlight of the show followed with his performance of another *Quadrophenia* remnant, "Sea and Sand," the only time the song has resurfaced since Halloween '95. An unquestionably strong YEM, and Sanity (that hadn't been heard since June '94) followed, then Phish charged up the crowd for '96 by just tearing through Frankenstein and the surprise encore, Johnny B. Goode.

For some, the highlight was just to be inside, on a night when the lack of security guards gave the show a general-admission feel and Phish gave everyone a night to remember.

If Phish never achieves this sort of musical height again, they should not be ashamed. For many, a show better than 12/31/95 only exists in the imagination.

1996

70 Total Show Dates
- **14** one-set shows
- **51** two-set shows
- **5** three-set shows

Phan Picks 1996

SHOW	THE SKINNY
1) 08/16/96 Plattsburgh, NY	First night of the Clifford Ball.
2) 12/06/96 Las Vegas, NV	Primus and Elvii join encore.
3) 10/31/96 Atlanta, GA	*Remain in Light* on Halloween.
4) 08/17/96 Plattsburgh, NY	Ben and Jerry at the Ball.
5) 12/31/96 Boston, MA	Gospel choir for Bohemian.
6) 08/13/96 Noblesville, IN	Great from start to finish.
7) 06/06/96 Woodstock, NY	The surprise club show.
8) 04/25/96 New Orleans, LA	Jazzfest, with Michael Ray.
9) 10/23/96 Hartford, CT	Bob Gullotti joins for 2nd set.
10) 11/15/96 St. Louis, MO	The "M" set, with Popper.

MUSICAL RECAP: In a transitional stage of sorts between 1995's Trey-led jamming and 1997's funk, the band played around with a bunch of different ideas. Some jams, like those played with Karl Perazzo on his minitour around Halloween, gave a hint of things to come. Others, like the Bathtub Gin from 11/7/96, showed the band's willingness to try many different themes and ideas all in the course of the same jam.

REPRESENTATIVE JAMS: Bathtub Gin, 11/7/96; Crosseyed and Painless, 11/2/96; Down with Disease, 8/16/96; Mike's Groove, 12/6/96.

ORIGINAL SONG DEBUTS: Character Zero (6/6/96), Mid-Highway Blues* (11/23/96), Swept Away > Steep (10/16/96), Talk (8/5/96), Train Song (7/21/96), Waste (6/6/96).

COVER SONG DEBUTS: Bohemian Rhapsody* (12/31/96), Mean Mr. Mustard* (11/15/96), Sixteen Candles* (12/29/96), The Star Spangled Banner (10/17/96), We're an American Band* (11/16/96), and all of *Remain in Light* (10/31/96). (*only ever played once)

Dark Horses

SHOW	THE SKINNY
1) 11/02/96 West Palm, FL	C&P > Antelope is just nuts.
2) 11/30/96 Sacramento, CA	Horn and banjo join Phish.
3) 11/27/96 Seattle, WA	Tweezer > DWD Reprise.
4) 08/06/96 Morrison, CO	Electricity at Red Rocks.
5) 10/29/96 Tallahassee, FL	Perazzo's first night.

Most-Played Originals:		
1) Taste	28	40%
2) Sample in a Jar	26	37%
3) You Enjoy Myself	23	33%
4) Chalkdust Torture	22	31%
5) Character Zero	21	30%
5) Poor Heart	21	30%
5) Sparkle	21	30%
8) Down with Disease	20	29%
8) Runaway Jim	20	29%
8) Stash	20	29%
8)Theme	20	29%

Most-Played Covers:		
1) Ya Mar	19	27%
2) Hello My Baby	17	24%
3) Also Sprach	16	23%
4) A Day in the Life	15	21%
5) Funky Bitch	14	20%
6) Life on Mars	10	14%
7) Fire	9	13%
7) Sweet Adeline	9	13%
7) Timber Ho	9	13%
10) Star Spangled Banner	8	11%

First-Set Openers:	
1) Chalkdust Torture	8
1) Runaway Jim	8
3) Ya Mar	6
4) My Friend My Friend	5
4) Wilson	5

Second-Set Openers:	
1) Also Sprach Zarathustra	7
2) AC/DC Bag	4
2) Down with Disease	4
2) Timber Ho	4
5) Bowie	3
5) Curtain	3
5) Jim	3

Top Henrietta Songs:	
1) Purple Rain	3
2) Bike	2
2) Suspicious Minds	2
4) Cracklin' Rosie	1
4) Terrapin	1

A Cappella Songs:	
1) Hello My Baby	17
2) Sweet Adeline	9
3) Star Spangled Banner	8
4) Amazing Grace	6
5) Carolina	1

and the YEM > a cappella Wolfman's opening were highlights. Bourbon Street was a madhouse. Best time I've ever had in New Orleans. —Trevor Norris

This CTB is not to be missed. Michael Ray comes out and tears the whole place apart. Ya Mar is also great with a Saints Go Marching In tease. —Michael Rotkowitz

Upon listening to the Jazzfest tape, I was severely disappointed by the band's completely flat performance. Phish seemed to play the songs like it was their job, not their love. A particular lowpoint is the end of Harry Hood—what is usually a superb buildup falls flat. The only redeeming feature of this show is Michael Ray's performance on CTB. —Pete Morse

During David Bowie, Trey licks in a little "Birdland" just for the festival! Then, whoever introduces the band at the end of the encore goes through their names correctly, but when he gets to Fishman, "on drums, Fishman Jon" is what he says. —Eric Shaw

The rain at the end of Cavern was awesome! —Erin Ferris

[5/96–6/96] Bearsville Studios, Bearsville, NY
Recording and mixing of *Billy Breathes*.

6/6/96 [ACCESSIBILITY: •••••]
Joyous Lake, Woodstock, NY
I: Melt, Poor Heart, Runaway Jim, Funky Bitch, Theme from the Bottom, BBFCM, Scent of a Mule, Highway to Hell
II: AC/DC Bag, YEM, Chalkdust, Sparkle, Stash, Waste, Character Zero, Bowie, Fee > Sample
E: Ya Mar, Fire

Unannounced show; Phish played under the name "Third Ball." Juan Hung Low opened. Soundcheck: Funky Bitch, Taste, Waste. "Wilson" tease in Runaway Jim. Trey used a beer bottle as a slide in BBFCM. "Cocaine" tease in Scent of a Mule, with Trey on keyboard for part of the jam. Waste cut short because it didn't have an ending yet. Concert debuts: Waste, Character Zero.

Having attended this show, it will remain a part of my personal Phishtory forever. The sound pretty much sucked, as did all the wannabe fans. But we hung out with Page for 45 minutes during Juan Hung Low's set and no one recognized him. Just being there was the greatest highlight. —Ric Hannah

The surprise gig. Only a precious few got to enjoy this one, but boy do I wish I was one of them—just like the old days, up close and personal. And you can hear it in the music: AC/DC Bag and YEM in the second set are perfect, then comes the debut of Waste, which Fishman dubs "no ending" because Trey tells the crowd the song doesn't have an ending yet. During the Character Zero debut, Fishman again chimes in with, "This is better than Machine Gun," which was requested by an audience member. Truly another page in the Phishtory book. —Peter Bukley

This is the best show I own. You can tell it was played in a bar from the crispness of the vocals, music and audience. —Brent Baker

1996 SUMMER Europe

The first time Phish toured Europe, it was summer '92, and the band played several weeks of shows, most as opening act for the Violent Femmes. To say the match wasn't made in heaven would be an understatement—at the Phish/Femmes show in Paris, one Femme fan stood with his back toward Phish and his middle index finger raised in the air through Phish's entire set. The band later wondered why they'd been in such a rush to get over there.

Summer 1996 offered Phish the chance to go back to Europe, again to serve primarily as an opening act. But their tour partner this time was old friend Carlos Santana, promising a friendlier reception. Phish actually considered not including the European tour information in the newsletter or on the hotline, in the interest of building new audiences. But that, it was decided, would have really sucked.

The tour didn't see as much onstage collaboration between the two bands as there had been in '92, though Phish did sit in with Santana, and vice versa.

For Phish, the tour served as a chance to promote a newly released European CD, *Stash*, a greatest-hits kind of disc with tracks drawn from previous Phish albums. As a result, most of their sets opening for Santana saw certain songs appear over and over again. Phish managed to break free of that regimen by playing five solo shows, including their first gig in Amsterdam. That show, at the legendary 950-person capacity Melkweg Club, was by some accounts the toughest ticket in Phish history. The previous night's solo show at the

Shepherd's Bush Empire in London, England, proved to be an easier ticket, and drew almost 1,000 local fans by some estimates. Phish had started catching on overseas.

[7/2/96]
Speedway Stadium, Lonigo, Italy
Opened for Santana. Phish's set was rained out, but Phish sat in with Santana during part of his set.

7/3/96 [ACCESSIBILITY: ••]
Stadia Brtamasco, Trento, Italy
Runaway Jim, Stash, Sparkle, Taste, Llama
Opened for Santana. Taste and Llama featured Carlos Santana and Karl Perazzo. Last Taste, 6/30/95 Mansfield, MA [64 shows].

7/5/96 [ACCESSIBILITY: ••]
Stadio Olimpico, Rome, Italy
Funky Bitch, Chalkdust, AC/DC Bag, YEM, Scent of a Mule, Bowie
E: Adeline
Opened for Santana. Phish was soundchecking Funky Bitch when the venue doors opened, so they kept playing.

My friends and I had been standing outside looking at the wares of the only hemp jewelry vendor when suddenly a familiar chord hit me like thunder. "Jesus, that's Funky Bitch!" I grabbed my bag and raced to the entrance. Once I got past the guards I realized there were only about 200 yards between the entrance to the stadium and the source of that sweet sound, and I fucking took off. I raced up the stairs and arrived at the floor where an enormous black stage was set up, with huge stacks of speakers on each side. And there they were—Page, Trey, Mike! There were maybe 25 fans in front of the stage with about 10,000 seats, bare, blue and without backs. The next thing I knew Chalkdust was hitting my face. I had been worried about a letdown because everyone said the Udine show was "short," but Phish never fails to amaze me. This night was just that good. —Russell Kahn

7/6/96 [ACCESSIBILITY: •••]
Duomo Square, Pistoia, Italy
Also Sprach > Reba, Poor Heart, Day in the Life, Maze, Harry Hood
Opened for Santana.

7/7/96 [ACCESSIBILITY: ••]
Parco Acquatico, Milan, Italy
Sample, Divided Sky, Bouncing, Curtain > Tweezer, Adeline, Uncle Pen, Cavern, Antelope > Suzie
Opened for Santana.

7/9/96 [ACCESSIBILITY: ••]
Centre Internationale de Deauville, Deauville, France
Theme, Poor Heart, Taste, CTB, Mike's, Bouncing, Character Zero
Opened for Santana.

7/10/96 [ACCESSIBILITY: ••]
Le Zenith, Paris, France
Chalkdust, Ya Mar, Melt, Waste, Bowie, Hello My Baby, GTBT
Opened for Santana.

When I sat down near the front of the stage, a young French boy with shoulder-length blond hair under a Phish cap sat down near me, smiled, and said "Bonjour." As it turned out, his name was Julian, his favorite band was Phish, and he had driven 330 kilometers (with his Dad) to see the show. I dubbed him the first French Phishhead! The kid was so pumped, getting high-fives from all around—and he was only sixteen! He had seen his first show the year before in New Jersey, and he owned one tape, which I identified as Sacramento 3/22/93. A friend of mine promised to send him more free of charge. When I imagine Julian playing Phish songs for his friends in the middle of France and another European friend dubbing the OJ show for his friends in Rome, I see the European network beginning. —Russell Kahn

Mike sang a verse of Ya Mar in French. His accent was so bad that several locals, when asked for a translation, said they couldn't make out a word he was saying. —Shep Williams

7/11/96 [ACCESSIBILITY: ••••]
Shepherd's Bush Empire, London, England
I: Runaway Jim, Cavern, Reba, I Didn't Know, Sparkle, Stash, Scent of a Mule, Sample
II: Harry Hood, Bouncing, Also Sprach > Maze, Lizards, HYHU > Terrapin > HYHU, YEM, Hello My Baby
E: Day in the Life
Fishman on vacuum for I Didn't Know and Terrapin. Last Terrapin, 6/13/95 St. Louis, MO [84 shows].

The second set starts with a good Harry Hood. Page's piano in the beginning reggae part is very funky. The band plays nice transitions throughout the rest of Hood, going rapidly into Bouncing after the "You can feel good about Hood" refrain. A nice Also Sprach Zarathustra segues into a slowish Maze that's not as hectic as others. Fishman blows the vacuum on Terrapin, then a fairly basic YEM leads to a nice bass solo from Mike. Ragtime Gal closes out the set. The encore, A Day in the Life, gets a nice response in the home of the Beatles. —Mike Noll

The London show was a letdown. A Beatles encore was fitting in the heart of London, and the crowd exploded while I silently shook my head. You'd think after all the 45-minute sets they'd been playing, they'd be ready to go crazy. —Russell Kahn

7/12/96 [ACCESSIBILITY: ••••]
Melkweg, Amsterdam, Netherlands
I: Wilson > Divided Sky, Horn, Melt, Ya Mar > Funky Bitch, Taste, Theme, Tweezer > Llama
II: It's Ice, Caspian > Mike's > Antelope, Purple Rain, Ska Groove Jam > NICU, Slave, Suzie
III: Bowie, Free, Hello My Baby
E: Bathtub Gin, Johnny B. Goode
Antelope unfinished. "Ska Groove" Jam before NICU based on chords yelled out by audience members. Fishman on vacuum for Purple Rain. Last Purple Rain, 10/21/95 Lincoln, NE [50 shows].

On paper, this show looks unbelievable, but actually, it's not that great. Something was definitely going on this night—the band sounds like they're practicing on their own, doing whatever they feel like. No song in the second set comes close to finishing. About a half of Slave is played and the encores are about the same length. Worth listening to as it's probably like no other show you've heard. —Matthew Napoli

Although the band is not at their best musically, the smooth segues and crowd interaction make up for it. The band meanders through many of their best songs and even tries to make up a new one before going into NICU. Highlights are Ya Mar > Funky Bitch and the entire third set, as the boys rip it up. —Jamis Curran

Friday, July 12, 1996

MELK WEG, Amsterdam, Netherlands

Before the Phish show at the Melk Weg on Friday, my friend Joe and I sat outside at the Bullfrog and had a drink and a smoke with two of his friends. The girl at the table was holding the joint when the waiter came over and said, "I'm sorry, you'll have to finish that somewhere else." She apologized, took another drag and passed it to me. I hesitated and then said, "I thought he asked us not to smoke here." Everyone laughed. The waiter had been referring to her McDonald's milkshake.

Girl drinks shake and smokes joint at restaurant. Waiter asks girl to put shake away. Welcome to Amsterdam! This entire place reeks of bud. Every time you turn the corner the strong smell floats past your nose. The coffee shops are insane. I knew they would be, but I still can't get over it.

The show let in at about 10:00. The streets were filled with heads and hippies, most waving their fingers in the air. I knew that with a 950-person capacity, people were going to be shut out, so I kept checking my ticket to convince myself I was in. Phish in Amsterdam. The thought gave me chills.

My guess going into the show was that, while it would be a great deal of fun, it would not be Phish at their musical best—they'd be too fucked-up. Listen to the tape and you'll find that to be exactly true. The entire second set was chaos.

They played their first ska song . . . . It's Ice morphed into Prince Caspian which melted into Mike's which found its way to Antelope. None of the songs was ever completed.

"Yell out a chord!" screamed Trey after "Purple Rain." He let the audience dominate the next song, "Ska Groove," whose only lyrics were, "Okay, we need some now"; and then stopped to plug in his cord—an action which Fish dubbed "the Trey-is-plugging-his-cord-in Jam." They were as random and fucked-up as I've ever seen them. The show ended at nearly 3:00 A.M., and I stumbled home at 4:00, seeing for the first time the beauty of Amsterdam.

—Russell Kahn

The best thing about this show on tape is that you can tell this is a really small place. It sounds like the old days. —Jonathan Banco

7/13/96 [ACCESSIBILITY: ••]
The Dour Festival, Dour, Belgium
Sample, Runaway Jim, Cavern, Reba, Poor Heart, Melt, Fire, Funky Bitch, Chalkdust, YEM
Music festival featuring numerous bands, but not Santana. Phish played one set.

This show (you can tell from the tapes) was a special one for the band. They do a little more chatting than normal on stage, emitting a friendly vibe. As far as the setlist goes, the band treated the foreigners to decent versions of Reba, SOAM and YEM (of course, these songs are always great). The ambiance of the whole European tour, which I was lucky enough to see, was similar to this show. —John Foley

7/15/96 [ACCESSIBILITY: •••]
Lido La Marna, Sesto Calende, Italy
I: My Friend, PYITE, FEFY, Guyute, Possum, I Didn't Know, Harry Hood, Cavern
II: Down with Disease > Maze, Loving Cup, Makisupa > It's Ice > Julius, Purple Rain, Uncle Pen, Antelope
E: Golgi
Fishman on vacuum for Purple Rain.

I wasn't lucky enough to have been at the show, but a tape definitely does the job. The first set is filled with excellent songs including several surprises for the first set like Harry and Possum. But the second set proves they continued rocking with spacy jams and an always audience-pleasing Purple Rain. If that still wasn't enough, how about closing the second set with a full-jammed, energetic Antelope? —Adam Rizzuti

7/17/96 [ACCESSIBILITY: ••]
Theatre Antique, Vienne, France
Divided Sky, Sample, Bowie, Ya Mar, Funky Bitch
Opened for Santana.

7/18/96 [ACCESSIBILITY: ••]
Nice Jazz Festival, Nice, France
Julius, CTB, Bouncing, Stash, Hello My Baby, It's Ice, YEM
Opened for Santana.

7/19/96 [ACCESSIBILITY: ••]
Les Arenes, Arles, France
Runaway Jim, Foam, Adeline, Waste, Squirming Coil
Opened for Santana. Phish sat in with Santana for part of Santana's set.

Inside the coliseum in Arles, France.
Photo courtesy of Christine Holbrook.

Photo courtesy of Christine Holbrook.

7/21/96 [ACCESSIBILITY: ••]
The Forum, Nuremburg, Germany
I: Golgi, Guelah, Rift, Tweezer, If I Could, My Mind's, Melt, Horse > Silent, Taste, Train Song, Fee > Timber Ho > Johnny B. Goode
II: Llama, Theme, Reba, Life on Mars, Free, Antelope, Simple, Caspian, Suzie
E: Harry Hood
Concert debut: Train Song.

Touring with Phish in Europe was a very intimate experience, reminiscent of the days when the band could be found hanging out around the venue before and after the show. Those of us traveling from one country to the next formed a small community, and plenty of friendships were made that continue to stand the test of time. The band paid tribute to that spirit on this night, when they dedicated the first-ever live performance of Train Song to those of us on tour. —Amy Duncan

7/22/96 [ACCESSIBILITY: ••]
Tanzbrunnen, Cologne, Germany
Sample, Poor Heart, Cavern, Maze, Bouncing, Stash, Day in the Life, YEM
Opened for Santana.

7/23/96 [ACCESSIBILITY: •••] [ATTEND. 713; CAP. 1,000]* [TIX $18]
Markthalle, Hamburg, Germany
I: AC/DC Bag, Foam, Theme, Gumbo, Scent of a Mule > Down with Disease > McGrupp > Stash, Hello My Baby
II: Also Sprach > Runaway Jim, Loving Cup, Sparkle, Mike's > Hydrogen > Weekapaug, HYHU > Bike > HYHU, Slave
E: Rocky Top
A cappella solo by Trey in Scent of a Mule. Fishman on vacuum for Bike. Last Hydrogen, 10/19/95 Kansas City, MO [61 shows].

I heard the Markthalle held about 1,000 people, but in my estimate it couldn't have been more than six or seven hundred. It was a great venue with a low, close stage and a dance floor where everyone could see the band. There were elevated sides for great viewing, too. For the last solo show of the European tour, it had to be special. The first set was really, really good. I've never heard a Scent of a Mule so fierce. It was my third on the tour, and I was tired of the Fiddler on the Roof routine, but this time it really took off. Page and Trey had great communication and were the best I'd seen them in Europe. 2001 and Runaway Jim set the tone for the second set and led into Loving Cup, the song that had caused me to regret missing the Sesto Calende show—I never thought they'd play it again. Phish did not disappoint. Backstage after the show, Page and I talked about the show and the tour. He said Hamburg was his favorite. —Russell Kahn

A promo poster in Hamburg included the words "Explosiv," "Virtuos" and "Cult" under the over-used Phish outdoors in the forest promotional photo. During the show, Trey looked at Page, Mike and Fish and shouted, "Explosiv! Virtuos! Cult!" —Amy Duncan

7/24/96 [ACCESSIBILITY: ••]
Music Hall, Hannover, Germany
Chalkdust, Ya Mar, Julius, YEM, Golgi
Opened for Santana.

7/25/96 [ACCESSIBILITY: ••] [Attend. 4,000; CAP. 4,000]* [TIX $35]
Stadtpark, Hamburg, Germany
Poor Heart, PYITE, Sample, It's Ice > Antelope, Life on Mars, Harry Hood, Cavern
Opened for Santana.

1996 SUMMER U.S. Tour

Returning from their month in Europe, Phish was rumored to be playing a surprise show for the Olympians in Atlanta before the start of their U.S. summer tour (no such show ever materialized). Instead, the band rested up for a week before embarking on their shortest summer tour ever—a slate of eleven gigs, starting only as far west as Utah and finishing with what promised to be an event like no other in Plattsburgh, NY.

The venues, familiar and unfamiliar, found Phish playing to crowds as small as 10,000 people at Wolf Mountain and upwards of 35,000 at Alpine Valley. Alpine Valley marked the band's biggest show ever, until the next weekend when the Clifford Ball drew 75,000 people each day to northern New York State.

8/4-7/96 Red Rocks Amphitheater, Morrison, CO

"On The Rocks"

It was the best of times, it was the worst of times. When Phish announced their U.S. summer tour schedule, fans were shocked to find that the band planned only eleven North American dates. Four of those eleven, however, were scheduled for Red Rocks, a venue with a very special rock history and Phish history. Since the band's inaugural show on the Rocks in August '93, the band had twice returned for two-night stands. Now, they planned to do four in a row, and fans from all over the country—somehow sensing that seeing Phish in a beautiful state park with only 9,500 other phriends might be too good to last forever—booked their plane tickets and gassed up their vans.

Those who feared Phish had already outgrown Red Rocks cited the previous year's growing pains, when police unleashed tear gas on an unruly crowd outside the venue. To counteract ticketless fans swarming the tiered parking lots of the venue and attempting to climb their way in, promoter Barry Fey closed Red Rocks Park to all non-concert goers.

Ticketless fans lined the highway to the venue, but once in the lots, it appeared the policy of keeping out the ticketless had been, for the most part, successful. A wonderfully relaxed parking lot scene developed, and most sensed that they were sharing the occasion with fans who'd gone Phishing more than a few times before. License plates from Maine, Florida and Alaska were spotted.

The first two nights came off without a hitch—Phish played well, and the scenery was as grand as everyone remembered. But while fans danced to a great Mike's Groove on night two, hundreds (some say thousands) of ticketless fans unable to gain access to the park massed two miles away in Morrison, CO, population 450. The situation clearly was already a little tense when a twenty-one-year-old woman was hit by a pickup truck on Morrison's main drag around 8:30 p.m.

What happened next remains a source of controversy. According to the Denver media, when EMTs and police arrived at the scene to help the girl, their efforts were blocked by fans who planned to heal her holistically, or "purify the body," as one cop later told the *Rocky Mountain News*. The injured girl was eventually taken to an area hospital and treated for minor injuries, but the police seized on the incident and attempted to clear fans out of Morrison. Then things turned ugly. "Hell no, we won't go," the crowd chanted, some throwing bottles at police officers in the fight that followed.

The media went to town with the story. "Rock Fans Battle Police: 12 Arrested, Morrison Shut Down After Phish Crowd Refuses to Leave," blared the *News* in a front-page banner headline. The "disturbance," as the *News* referred to it, easily caught the attention of the Denver media who showed up at Red Rocks on Monday night to put together predictable articles on "hippies invading Red Rocks."

Of course, the 9,500 fans at the show knew nothing of the riot until they picked up newspapers the next morning. Phish took the stage on Tuesday night all smiles, despite the media blitz, and opened with Makisupa Policeman. Whether Phish meant the song as a statement about the Morrison incident was intentionally left vague, but later in the first set Trey did reference the melée. The *News* article about the Morrison incident quoted an individual identified as "21-year-old Marcus Esquandolis" shouting "You are slime!" at police officers during the standoff. During the Antelope lyric segment, Trey changed the "Marco Esquandolis" line to "21-year-old Phish fan Marcus Esquandolis," cracking up himself and the audience.

That night's show soared. As storm clouds moved in near the end of the first set, mist whipped around the venue during Lizards, engulfing the band in a fog not of their own making. This awe-inspiring sight was topped in set two when the skies opened during an electric BBFCM and Phish, charged up on their own energy and that of Mother Nature, tore into the song as rain and wind swept the amphitheater. Purple Rain and an emotional Harry Hood made the show one for the ages.

By the next day, Red Rocks promoter Barry Fey was on the front page of the *Post* stating the obvious: Phish had outgrown Red Rocks. So all the fans headed for the final night's gig knew they were probably going to witness Phish's last-ever show at Red Rocks. The atmosphere in the lot was playful but reflective, which seemed to be the band's mood, too. During Ya Mar in the first set, Trey remarked, "I want to tell you guys what an incredible time we had the last four nights. I will never forget it, and I hope you feel the same way." As the crowd cheered, he added, "This place is beautiful—I hope we can come back."

The band's final show at Red Rocks might not have achieved the heights of some of their previous engagements there, but when Trey referenced the giant iguana during a Forbin's rap in the second set, it was a nod to the band's own history—the famous Harpua of '93.

The biggest irony of the whole stand might have been that the Morrison incident may not have really happened the way most of the news media said it did. Reporter Michael Roberts of the weekly *Denver Westword* paper visited Morrison several weeks after the incident and interviewed the townsfolk. In response to the so-called "purifying the body" of the injured woman, one Red Rocks Grille staffer told Roberts, "I don't know where they got that from. I was right there, and that never happened." Another Grille staffer added, "Based on what I saw, everything in the papers was fiction."

The staffers related a very different view of the events to Roberts. After the woman was knocked down by the pickup truck, people—including an EMT and a doctor—rushed to the girl's side. A crowd gathered to watch and, when asked to take a step back, all complied, with the exception of two angry fans who jumped into the pickup truck and started jumping up and down. When police tried to haul the kids out of the truck, someone threw a bottle at the cops. "It was an isolated incident," a staffer told Roberts. But police used the incident to shut down the street, and things grew worse from there. Roberts concluded, "Reporters did their best to turn the incident into a skankier version of Riot on Sunset Strip." Phish and their fans paid the price.

At three stops on the tour—Red Rocks, Deer Creek and the Clifford Ball—Phish treated audiences to acoustic mini-sets featuring material recorded during the *Billy Breathes* sessions, plus old friend Strange Design.

Another old friend, Red Rocks, hosted Phish's first four-night run at the same venue in this decade. When a riot involving several hundred ticketless fans in the nearby town of Morrison, CO, made front-page news in Denver, however, the last two nights of the Red Rocks run turned into a farewell party to one of the most beautiful places to hear live music in the country. Happily, the bad vibes disappeared by the time of the Clifford Ball, which drew thousands of people from all over the country—fitting, for the largest concert event in North America in 1996.

8/2/96 [ACCESSIBILITY: ••••] [ATTEND. 10,707; CAP. 12,250] [TIX $22.50–$25]
Wolf Mountain, Park City, UT
I: Ya Mar, Down with Disease, Guelah, Poor Heart, Foam, Theme, Golgi, Tweezer, Hello My Baby, Possum
II: Runaway Jim, Simple, Taste, Free, Fluffhead, Caspian, Horse > Silent, Antelope
E: PYITE

Page on theremin for a "Somewhere over the Rainbow" jam before Ya Mar.

Minutes prior to Phish's entrance, a double rainbow appeared on the horizon behind the stage. When they came out, Page wove a few notes of "Somewhere over the Rainbow" on theremin. Down with Disease jammed long and solid as a prelude to its fall development. The tunes complemented each other well, and Mike's bass work was dominant from start to finish. Runaway Jim included a Dog Log tease (I think) and Antelope had a "Star Wars" tease from Trey. —Anthony Buchla

Somewhere over the Rainbow—a great opener after viewing two full rainbows over the stage. Ya Mar was very upbeat, filled with Mike's howls and yells, but the Foam was different, almost on a slower beat. This show also features the first Prince Caspian they played with the new beginning heard on Billy Breathes. PYITE was an odd but exhilarating encore. —Erin Ferris

Wolf Mountain is a great place to see a show. Tucked into the base of a small ski hill, the amphitheater looks out over a ski lodge behind the stage to the valley beyond. It's an intimate venue, almost quaint in comparison to some of the fortresses Phish would play later in the tour. The ultimate Phish sunny-skies opener, Ya Mar, brought cheers from the lawn as the band got the groove going. From there, the set progressed like the first set of most tour openers: the band committed lots of little musical miscues, the song selection didn't bowl anyone over, and yet we were thrilled to be hearing Phish live again. The second set saw the American debuts of the reworked Taste and Prince Caspian, and there was Fluffhead: as its opening notes rang out, we found ourselves swamped in a wave of joyous screaming, people delighted and thrilled to be up on the mountain. —Lock Steele

8/4/96 [ACCESSIBILITY: ••••] [ATTEND. 9,240; CAP. 9,240] [TIX $25]
Red Rocks Amphitheatre, Morrison, CO
I: Chalkdust, Funky Bitch, Guyute, Fee, Melt, Mango, Sloth, Maze, Loving Cup
II: AC/DC Bag > Reba > Scent of a Mule, Sample, Bowie, Adeline, Slave
E: Rocky Top

Page on theremin for a "Star Trek Theme" jam before Rocky Top.

Ahhh! Back at the good ole Red Rocks of Colorado. I'm so glad I made it back for Phish's last stand here, and what a fat show they pulled out to kick off the four-day stand. With a Chalkdust opener through the most intense Maze I've ever heard, I was again shocked by the musical prowess the band displayed. The first set closer, Loving Cup, really torqued on my alternate reality helmet. I'm truly sad Phish won't be back here—a beautiful venue plus a smokin' show equaled a perfect time. —William Thurston

The first-night setlist was filled with random song choices probably meant to throw us off. Trey wore a Grinch t-shirt (from Dr. Seuss) which was funny. A good show to open up for four nights at Red Rocks, which is a beautiful place for a show. The atmosphere was great. —Melanie and Melita Terrell

My first show at the Rocks. Extreme energy raged between the band and the crowd, and the setlist was stellar: Funky Bitch and Guyute in the first three songs proves that. Overall, from the time I hit the line at 4:20 to get in, to the marshmallow fights, Red Rocks will always be my favorite arena, and these shows one of the best experiences of my life. —Geoff Lynch

8/5/96 [ACCESSIBILITY: ••••] [ATTEND. 9,240; CAP. 9,240] [TIX $25]
Red Rocks Amphitheatre, Morrison, CO
I: Wilson, Poor Heart, Guelah, Divided Sky, Wolfman's, Foam, If I Could, Julius, Squirming Coil
II: Also Sprach, Down with Disease > It's Ice, Halley's, Waste, Talk, Train Song, Strange Design, Amazing Grace, Mike's > Hydrogen > Weekapaug
E: Cavern

Page on theremin for a "Somewhere over the Rainbow" jam at the end of Halley's. Acoustic mini-stage featured Trey on acoustic guitar, Mike on acoustic bass, Fishman on a smaller drum set, and Page on a smaller piano for Waste, Talk, Train Song, and Strange Design. Concert debut: Talk, and the mini-stage.

Of course every Red Rocks show is great in its own way. The setlist of this one is one of my favorites, including Halley's Comet into Somewhere over the Rainbow, with Page on the very odd-sounding theremin, and Waste. What's unique about this show is the four acoustic songs: Waste, Talk, Train Song and Strange Design, performed on a mini stage with acoustic instruments. Page even left the baby grand and was banging keys on an upright. There's also a cool solo jam by Page and a great Mike's, which makes every show! —Ryan Satz

In the middle of Divided Sky, Trey stopped playing and everyone sat down and took a rest, an idea suggested by the "crowd participation flyers" circulated around by Phish.Net fans. —Melanie and Melita Terrell

I have always wanted to hear Phish play If I Could in concert, but I never thought I would. That song means so much to me, so when I heard them play it, I was in heaven. It was the most amazing song I have ever heard Phish play. —Melissa Keller

After an excellent second set start of 2001 > DwD > Ice > Halley's, Page moved to theremin while the rest of the band, joined by crew hands, pushed back Trey and Mike's cabinets to slide forward something that had been hidden under a tarp. When the lights came up, there stood two stools, a mini–drum kit and a standup piano. Trey relieved our curiosity: "We're taking this opportunity to play you guys some songs off the album we just recorded." After this sweet acoustic interlude—the first time they ever used the acoustic mini-stage—I was surprised and pleased when the boys cranked up Mike's Song. Like the DwD earlier in the set, the Mike's jam rose then flattened several times. The jamming, straight ahead as Mike's Songs go, was nevertheless spirited and forceful. The Weekapaug jam was similarly standard at first until Trey got a neat riff going, fast and sweet. Fish joined in, his drumming setting a relentless pace. The jam didn't wander for long before returning to the Weekapaug theme, then the band left the stage to tremendous applause. This was my favorite set of the '96 Red Rocks stand. —Lock Steele

8/6/96 [ACCESSIBILITY: ••••] [ATTEND. 9,240; CAP. 9,240] [TIX $25]
Red Rocks Amphitheatre, Morrison, CO
I: Makisupa, Rift, Suzie, Simple, Theme, Lizards, Dinner and a Movie, Horn, Antelope
II: Curtain > Tweezer, Caspian, Day in the Life, BBFCM, Purple Rain, Harry Hood > Tweezer Reprise
E: Johnny B. Goode

"Simple" tease in Suzie. "21-year-old Phish fan Marcus Esquandolis" lyrics in Antelope. "Norwegian Wood" jam in Tweezer. Crowd-participation flyers got the crowd to shout "Hood!" after each "Harry" the band sang.

The debate as to which Red Rocks show was the best will go on forever, but this is my choice, hands-down. A wonderful first set with some real crowd pleasers, but the real action took place in set II, when ominous thunderclouds approached the theater, and Phish seemed to feed off the energy created by the lightning behind them. Curtain was followed by an utterly blistering Tweezer, without a doubt one of the best ever, one which accomplished that level without veering away from the basics of the song all that much. They just rocked it. When the thunder turned into a downpour during BBCFM, Phish caught the cue and went into Purple Rain, with Chris shining purple lights into the sheets of water. Then came an unforgettable, emotionally charged Harry Hood. On some tapes you can hear the rain hitting umbrellas, and it's not a distraction, it's perfection. —Andy Bernstein

They rocked the mountain with an amazing Hood—this was the first show where all the crowd screamed "Hood" after "Harry," and Trey gave us thumbs-up for that. We all felt like there was no other place in the world we would rather be. —Michelle Hirsch

Makisupa opener was in context after the police fucked with everyone in Morrison. The complete focus of this show was the second set. In a couple of words, it was totally insane. During BBFCM, Trey ran around the stage (I mean, he did laps). A thunderstorm came in and the band played Purple Rain. Harry Hood with "Hood" chants proved the crowd participation flyers worked. Lightning flashes caused everyone to cheer. —Morgan Laster

The marshmallow fight before the show was a trip. —Joe Galbraith

8/7/96 [ACCESSIBILITY: •••] [ATTEND. 9,240; CAP. 9,240] [TIX $25]
Red Rocks Amphitheatre, Morrison, CO
I: PYITE, Sparkle, Stash, Ya Mar, Gumbo, Taste, Lawn Boy, 99 Years, Ode to a Dream, Doin' My Time
II: Runaway Jim, Free, Forbin's > Mockingbird, Possum, Life on Mars, YEM, Hello My Baby
E: Bouncing, Golgi

Tim O'Brien on mandolin and vocals for 99 Years and acoustic guitar and vocals for Ode to a Dream and Doin' My Time. "Gypsy Queen" jam in Runaway Jim.

For the last show, anticipation ran high. According to news reports, this would be Phish's last performance here. The music was good but not anything crazy. Mandolin player Tim O'Brien served up some hot bluegrass in the first set, while the second set featured a nice Runaway Jim opener and Forbin > Mockingbird. Possum was fun to hear, but the encore was not because I hate Bouncing and Golgi. I guess they were waiting for Clifford Ball with the goods. —Morgan Laster

Probably tired by now, the band staggered over this one. PYITE and Ya Mar get things rolling, and it was nice to hear Gumbo. First set ends with bluegrass legend Tim O'Brien on mandolin. In the second set, Runaway Jim is stellar, and Trey reminds us of the Red Rocks iguana in Col. Forbin's. After nice jamming in Possum, the rest of the set kind of drags along. —Charlie Gubman

Forbin's > giant iguana > Mockingbird rekindled sentimental memories for those of us at the 1993 Red Rocks show. —Jake Hunter

When everyone was in the parking lot before the show, a group passed out sparklers to everyone for when Phish played Sparkle. When the band pulled it out for the second song of the night, I would say over half of those at Red Rocks lit up their sparklers. It was pretty cool. —Melissa Keller

8/10/96 [ACCESSIBILITY: ••••] [ATTEND. 34,639; CAP. 34,639] [TIX $19.50–$23]
Alpine Valley, East Troy, WI
I: My Friend, Poor Heart, AC/DC Bag, Fee, Reba, I Didn't Know, Horse > Silent, Rift, Bathtub Gin, Cavern
II: Wilson, Down with Disease, Scent of a Mule, Free, Fluffhead, HYHU > Whipping Post > HYHU, Harry Hood, Day in the Life
E: Contact, Fire

Fishman on vacuum for I Didn't Know. "Gypsy Queen" jam in Bathtub Gin.

The sound where my seats were located (eighth row in front of Mike) was horrible—bad venue acoustics in general along with plenty of feedback. The band seemed pretty beat at Alpine, not really enthused about playing. It was the most local crowd of the summer, more of a beerfest to most; the only song most of them were interested in during set one was Silent. The only real show highlight was the revival of Whipping Post. (There was also a 14- or 15-year-old kid a few seats down from me holding a micro-cassette recorder in the air, telling people to be quiet around his tape deck.) —Jason Deziel

The whole second set was smoking. I'll single out the comic relief portion of the show when Fishman took center stage and Trey (on drums) led the band through Hold Your Head Up. As they finished, Fishman bowed and Trey started HYHU again. Fishman looked at Trey and said, "All right, thank you," and "Thank you so much," then Trey started HYHU again. It was most humorous. When Fish finally got to sing, he chose Whipping Post, a version that rivals the shrieking rendition from 12/5/92 Chicago. —Russell Lane

Alpine Valley floored me by its sheer size. The sea of fans on the lawn by showtime looked incredible—35,000 phans in the middle of dairy country! The early part of the second set had hints of brilliance—the DwD jam, and a vocal jam by Trey in lieu of the guitar duel in Scent—but it wasn't until the Fishman song that things got crazy. After a long HYHU interval, Fishman started Whipping Post, the first in ages and a real treat. After the song, Trey pointed to Fish and said, "Ladies and gentlemen, the Dork!" That referenced a bootleg t-shirt Trey was wearing which had a photo of Fishman on the front and "The Dork" printed on the back. "Best T-shirt I've seen in 13 years," Trey told us, adding, "Sorry, Amy." Before the encore, the sea of lighters that floated above the lawn in tribute seemed, like the Harry Hood moments before, impossibly large. —Lock Steele

8/12/96 [ACCESSIBILITY: •••] [ATTEND. 21,079; CAP. 21,079] [TIX $19.50-$22.50]
Deer Creek Amphitheatre, Noblesville, IN
I: Ya Mar, Melt, Esther, Chalkdust, Weigh, It's Ice, Dog Faced Boy, Taste, Oh Kee > Suzie
II: Timber Ho, Sparkle, Simple, Caspian > McGrupp, Antelope, Hello My Baby, Golgi, Possum
E: Sample

"Voodoo Child" tease in Possum intro.

The beautiful two-day stand started with Ya Mar into a worthy Split Open. Then Esther, which just tickled my body and soul. Weigh into It's Ice fit just right. The Suzie set closer also was great—I danced out of my shoes and found myself screaming. High points in the second set for me were McGrupp, Antelope and Possum. —Brian Hart

The opener, Ya Mar, was fun, but the rarely-played Esther and Weigh were set highlights—the selection seemed so unpredictable but so perfect. Timber Ho to kick off set II was unforgettable, but McGrupp and Antelope topped it off. Before Possum, Trey used Phish's secret on-stage language to produce a Simpsons theme into a "D'oh!" and a scene where the band drops limp over their instruments, then revives and resumes Possum's introduction. —Brian Boehm

We had never been to Deer Creek, so that's where we drove to instead of Noblesville. We were late but caught the second set and a good laugh. —David Okimoto

8/13/96 [ACCESSIBILITY: ••••] [ATTEND. 21,079; CAP. 21,079] [TIX $19.50–$22.50]
Deer Creek Amphitheatre, Noblesville, IN
I: Divided Sky, Tube, Tela, Maze, FEFY, Old Home Place, PYITE, Llama, Glide, Slave
II: AC/DC Bag, Lizards, Mike's > Lifeboy > Weekapaug, Waste, Train Song, Strange Design, Adeline, Bowie
E: Sleeping Monkey, Rocky Top

Short jam before AC/DC Bag. Page on theremin for a "Somewhere over the Rainbow" jam out of Weekapaug. Acoustic mini-stage featured Trey on acoustic guitar, Mike on acoustic bass, Fishman on a smaller drum set, and Page on a smaller piano for Waste, Train Song, and Strange Design. Last Glide, 11/21/95 Winston-Salem, NC [51 shows].

There is nothing like gettin' down in the middle of a cornfield somewhere in Indiana. I had a soul-cleansing show that I can't wait to tell my grandchildren about. Even my pet peeve, Sleeping Monkey, was enhanced by the singing of a beautiful voice coming from a nearby girl. I never even saw her face—I didn't have to. —Colm Connell

If you were at this show, you really got your money's worth. Not only was it totally jammed out, but it was nice and long. The Slave was an absolute epic! The changes were flawless with Trey just wailing and Page answering with a delicate piano roll—back and forth until I thought Trey's guitar would just melt. —Russell Lane

The second set was the raw essence of the "take it to the top, drop it off and reel it back up" theory. From beginning to end, it is truly explosive, tight and absolutely unpredictable. —Waylon Baynard

I can easily say this is in the top five Phish shows I have heard or attended. But being detoured out of the parking lot and through a drug checkpoint after the show really snapped my head back into reality after narrowly getting through. People were getting searched for no reason except for the way they looked. —Jason Deziel

This first set is something dreams are made of. —Josh Harman

8/14/96 [ACCESSIBILITY: ••••] [ATTEND. 25,100; CAP. 25,100] [TIX $25]
Hersheypark Stadium, Hershey, PA
I: Wilson > Down with Disease, Fee > Poor Heart, Reba, Mango, Gumbo, Stash, Hello My Baby
II: Runaway Jim> YEM, Horse > Silent, CTB, Tweezer, Theme, HYHU > Cracklin' Rosie > HYHU, Sample > Tweezer Reprise
E: Julius

This show just screams average—pitifully low on improv, the signature of any great show. The only real jams I felt myself melting for were the opening Wilson > Down with Disease segue that whipped the crowd into a frenzy, and the jam in Tweezer. The rest of the show seemed to be just up-tempo versions of album songs, rushed in one after another. —Aaron Grossberg

This is one of very few shows that I just don't care for. It's unfortunate to hear such an average show at such a great venue. —Josh Halman

The Wilson opener wasn't completely finished—instead, Phish went into a weird jam that had everyone confused. It's definitely worth getting a copy of this show to hear it. Reba is another highlight: Trey mimicked a little baby that was sitting on the mother's shoulders in the audience. Everyone got a good laugh out of it as the band continued a solid and tight performance of this song. —Tim Herrman

Not the most pleasant show to attend, given the fact that horrible traffic jams snarled the roads leading to the venue. But on tape, this show is the hidden gem of the '96 summer tour. Excellent jamming in Down with Disease, Reba and especially Tweezer make this a show worth acquiring. —Ernie Greene

[8/15/96]
Soundcheck, Clifford Ball, Plattsburgh Air Force Base, Plattsburgh, NY
Page and Trey noodle as they enter the stage area. Long blues jam > long funk jam, HYHU > slow Tweezer Reprise > HYHU, Old Home Place, slow Little Drummer Boy (LDB) jam, LDB jam 2 > LDB/Frankenstein jam (Mike

introduced Frankenstein theme on bass) > LDB/Frankenstein jam 2 > LDB/Frankenstein jam 3 > Frank/Spock's Brain jam > Frankenstein/Spock's jam 2 > vocal: "Deep in the Heart of Texas!", Clifford Ball jam (as named by Trey in the jam), Clifford Ball/slow Peaches En Regalia jam > Tweezer Reprise (Page introduced Rep on piano)

Soundcheck ran from about 9:00 P.M. to about 9:55 P.M.

The single most significant event for me at the Clifford Ball, musically, was the soundcheck Thursday night. Tapers were scarcely to be found, but it drew most of the campsite dwellers to the fence to hear a one-set practice session. As I recall, after they played Old Home Place, the audience cheered so loudly that the band could hear it from the half-mile (or so) away that they were. During the Little Drummer Boy jam that followed, Paul turned the PA up and Chris started doing the huge lights over the wall towards the crowd, acknowledging that they had a HUGE, FULLY ATTENTIVE audience a HALF MILE away. My friend Michael Sauda and I began discussing and scribbling the list as soon as we realized they were soundchecking. The setlist above is what we came up with from start to finish. The titles are somewhat arbitrary—we define the jams as we hear popular Phish themes occurring and overlapping in the jam. —Dave Schall

8/16/96 [ACCESSIBILITY: •••••] [ATTEND. 135,627 (BOTH DAYS)] [TIX $20–$30]
The Clifford Ball, Plattsburgh Air Force Base, Plattsburgh, NY
I: Chalkdust, Bathtub Gin, Ya Mar, AC/DC Bag, Esther, Divided Sky, Halley's, Bowie
II: Melt, Sparkle, Free, Squirming Coil, Waste, Talk, Train Song, Strange Design, Hello My Baby, Mike's > Simple > Contact > Weekapaug
III: Makisupa, Also Sprach > Down with Disease > NICU, Life on Mars, Harry Hood > Fireworks Jam
E: Amazing Grace

Acoustic mini-stage featured Trey on acoustic guitar, Mike on acoustic bass, Fishman on a smaller drum set, and Page on a smaller piano for Waste, Talk, Train Song, and Strange Design. Fireworks during Harry Hood and into Fireworks jam.

The best weekend of my life, hanging out with old friends, new friends, seeing Phish outside while the sun was setting, battling to keep your spot in front of the stage was just an awesome experience. Six full sets, with festivities! It was controlled chaos. The best Phish experience to date. —Eric Higel

Is this Phishstock? What is going on here? Over 70,000 fans, and possibly one of the best shows ever. —David Eckers

Could anyone have realized that a small, jamming band from Vermont with no media attention could attract 75,000 fans for the largest concert in North America in 1996? I don't think even the band conceived of that. They certainly didn't provide enough camping space, and water was miles away (thank god for mist tents!), but for the largest Phish concert in history the band offered fired-up versions of Disease, Hood and Weekapaug that will go down in the annals of history as some of their best. Me? My friends and I sat on top of the hill by Ball Square, taking all of this in. Information overload! —Lee Schiller

As 70,000 people packed in, Phish kicked off the two-day festival with a kick-ass first set featuring a hot AC/DC jam, then an extended silent jam during Divided played to an incredible sunset (Fish faked the cymbal, then they finally kicked into the jam). They later played a long and amazing second set, treating us to some of their new songs acoustic, a quick a cappella and then a phatty Mike's > Simple > Contact > Weekapaug. The third set kept right up with a crazy 2001 > DwD plus a fireworks display after Hood. —Ryan Danyew

In the third set, I experienced Phishtacy—every note clicked with my psyche and the fireworks sent me into outer space. Amazing Grace brought us back to earth to get us ready for the post-show partying. Too bad it took me an hour to find my tent! —Ian Rufe

Harry Hood at the Clifford Ball changed my feelings about this song. Phish played it like it was the last song they were ever going to play. Of course, the fireworks were the icing on the cake. Everyone was in awe. Even now, listening to the tape, it makes me feel like I'm hearing the song for the first time all over again. —Gina D'Amico

Until this day, I hadn't heard live Phish for a long time. The entire summer I dreamed about being in Plattsburgh. As the clouds turned orange and purple, and all the people around me smiled and joked, I realized I was in heaven. When that sweet twang of Chalkdust opened this show, it gave me that feeling of freedom and happiness that I had been longing for. —John McMeecking

[8/17/96]
Flatbed Jam, Clifford Ball, Plattsburgh Air Force Base, Plattsburgh, NY

In the predawn hours following the August 16 show, Phish played a 45-minute set of mellow jazz on a flatbed truck that toured the Clifford Ball campground.

It's about 3 a.m. I had just cracked the night's last brew when I noticed some lights glowing in the distance. Not too alert to what was happening, I decided to walk over and see what it was. I could not believe my eyes when I saw Phish playing softly, just barely audible. It reminded me of some dreamy Floyd, but that description does this treat no justice. One of the coolest "sets" ever. —Casey Grant

This was very personal, very Phishlike. The music blurred as the band moved so I didn't get to listen to everything they played, but I found it very soothing. I was really excited to tell everyone in the morning what they missed while they were passed out! —Jen Verdon

8/17/96 [ACCESSIBILITY: •••••] [ATTEND. 135,627 (BOTH DAYS)] [TIX $20–$30]
The Clifford Ball, Plattsburgh Air Force Base, Plattsburgh, NY
I: Old Home Place, PYITE, Reba, CTB, Lizards, Sample, Taste, Fee, Maze, Suzie
II: Curtain, Runaway Jim, It's Ice, Brother, Fluffhead, Antelope, Golgi, Slave
III: Wilson, Frankenstein, Scent of a Mule, Tweezer, Day in the Life, Possum, Tweezer Reprise
E: Harpua

Ben Cohen and Jerry Greenfield on vocals for Brother. A female acrobat performed on ropes above the stage during Antelope, and trampolinists jumped during Tweezer. "Heartbreaker" jam in Wilson. Page/Fishman duel in Scent of a Mule instead of Page/Trey. Harpua was unfinished after a stunt plane missed its cue and the band cut the song short, leaving the stage with feedback noise ringing out.

The day began with the tiny patter of raindrops coming from a small shower from the Adirondacks to cool off me and the olfactory-challenged 50,000 that shared my ground. But that didn't last as by noon the clouds disappeared, chased by the hot August sun. This set the stage for eight hours of music by Phish and their classically-minded friends. Highlight? How about everything, well, everything except for an unfinished Harpua and a foolish fan who ran onto the stage. But even before these events unfolded, I realized as I warmed my hands on a bonfire in Ball Square (to counteract the cool Adirondack winds) that nothing could mar the moment. And nothing did. —Lee Schiller

The Clifford Ball became an instant classic, and those who were there know why. The first set of the second day was fair, basically a warm-up for the night's second and third sets. The second set was perhaps the greatest single set I've seen. From a deep Runaway Jim to a surprise Brother, this set had everything. After a powerful Fluffhead and Antelope, I felt fortunate that the set would include one more—Golgi. Then the first chords of Slave started. —Matthew Napoli

An endless sea of fans put the band on a pedestal from which they played intense, beautiful music. —Jeff Lozier

Day two of the gathering at the Clifford Ball. The afternoon set was typical, but the last two were extraordinary. Curtain, Runaway Jim, It's Ice got it off to an excellent start, but then they pulled Brother from its grave (last played 8/2/93) and had guest appearances by Ben & Jerry. A memorable Antelope with an acrobat swinging over the stage followed. The set ended with the best Slave I'd ever heard. Third set with a Tweezer with trampolinists. Wild! Harpua encore had Jimmy flying over the Ball (and a stunt plane)—cut short. —Ryan Danyew

Set 2 of this show is all you need to know, especially after the way-phunky jam in It's Ice. The song selection isn't what this set is about—it's about the intensity. I never felt so much intensity from the band before, though this did cause Golgi and Slave to suffer a bit from acceleration. But the intensity! Usually everyone goes nuts afterwards, but following this set, folks couldn't utter a peep. —Charlie Murphy

Phish sounded crystal-clear as they put their hearts out into the whole venue. They deserved this. They work harder than any band around. —Langston Knipler

A great weekend. The weather was great, the shows will live in history, and Phish put together one of the best weekends eternity will ever know. But the highlight for me was meeting Trey in Oakledge Park a couple of days later while he was rollerblading. I told him it was the best fuckin' show I'd ever been to. He said, "Thanks. I had the best fuckin' time playing it." Let's do this every year! —Beth Castrol

When it was all over, I felt like I just got off roller skates. —Joel Zeigler

1996 FALL Billy raves

Phish hit the road in fall '96 just as *Billy Breathes* hit stores. For the band, it was a time of renewed media interest—following the great success of the Clifford Ball, suddenly it seemed that every magazine wanted a piece of them. Articles surfaced in *Entertainment Weekly* and, by the winter of '96–'97, *GQ* and *Rolling Stone*, among others. *Rolling Stone*, in fact, awarded *Billy Breathes* a coveted four-star rating, with music critic Richard Gehr (a good friend of the band)

"The Clifford Ball"

8/16&17/96 Plattsburgh Air Force Base, Plattsburgh, NY

Since the very beginning, Phish was never content playing traditional music venues. At the first chance they'd get, the band would invite friends and fans to outdoor gatherings which offered more than just a concert.

Perhaps the idea first blossomed with the Ian's Farm shows in the 1980s, followed by the series of Townshend Family Park shows and, of course, Amy's Farm in 1991. But in the days when Phish played from the back of a flatbed truck, they probably never imagined something of the scale of the Clifford Ball.

For one weekend in August 1996, over 70,000 Phish fans lived as family in upstate New York. A decommissioned Air Force base was transformed into a Phish theme park, a fantasy land centered by six sets of Phish and countless surprises.

Phish derived the name Clifford Ball after an Air Mail aviation pioneer of the same name. They had spotted a plaque in a Pittsburgh airport dedicated to the semi-obscure pilot, who was referred to as "a beacon of light in the world of flight." For some reason, it tickled Phish's fancy, and they tried to convince organizers of what would be the H.O.R.D.E. in 1992 to name the tour The Clifford Ball. When that failed, they wrote in the liner notes of A Live One that it was recorded "live at Clifford Ball."

When the real Clifford Ball kicked off after months of preparation, the first fans began arriving a full two days before the first set of music. By the time the sun came up on Friday, August 16, a tent city covered much of the base, as fans set up shop in areas called "Camping Kirk" and "Camping Picard." A licensed 24-hour radio station was "Balling all the time," playing rare Phish bootlegs and grabbing hold of band members from time to time for pointed commentary.

Planes hired by the band circled the event, dragging banners with such cryptic Phishy statements as "A Dime From Here Would Penetrate" and "Evan Dando." The aviation theme even extended to the main entrance, where all concert goers drove under a huge banner telling them to "Prepare for Flight."

Sprinkled around the campsites were several giant plywood cut-outs of Clifford Ball himself, and inside the concert ground, a thirty-five-foot tall statue of Cliff towered over Ball Square—a land of crafts and make-believe with miniature houses. The village grounds would later play host to an actual wedding, as Michael Rehberg and Toodle Lee of Macon, GA, became the first couple to ever tie the knot at a Phish show. And the event was even graced by Clifford Ball's grandson, whom the band flew up from his home in Florida for the event.

By the time the band finally took the stage at dusk on Friday night, most attendees had already shouted, "I'm having such a great time" repeatedly. For many, it was almost hard to fully digest the show with so much other excitement.

But those who kept their attention on the stage were treated to a show which easily lived up to the occasion, including one of the most melodic and heavily-improvised Bathtub Gins ever in the first set; a sublime segue between Mike's and Simple in the second that led to a "Mike's Suite" of songs—Contact and Weekapaug; and an equally brilliant Down with Disease in the third. Friday night's third set ended with fireworks going off behind the stage during Harry Hood.

Not only was Phish at their best on stage, but many fans commented on the prowess of those offstage. The sound—often impossible to perfect in large outdoor venues—was crystal clear throughout the spacious viewing area, even to fans who were stuck several football fields away from the stage. (Large video screens provided some relief, too.)

Every facet of the Ball seemed to run smoothly. Plenty of food; plenty of drink. Few lines; fewer hassles. Well past midnight on Friday night, when most exhausted fans were asleep, Phish made an appearance on the back of the same sort of flatbed truck which once served as a permanent stage in their outdoor extravaganzas. This one also had a generator, which powered Phish's instruments as they plucked their way through a mellow, rolling jam as the truck inched its way through the camping area. Hundreds of fans followed on bike or foot.

Saturday saw Phish kick off the festivities around 4 P.M., playing an afternoon set before giving the stage over to "The Clifford Ball Orchestra," a full symphony which played several of Trey's favorite classical pieces including Stravinsky's The Firebird, during which a glider flew through the air and seemed to dance to the music.

The two Phish sets that followed were a virtual buffet of fan favorites as Phish packed virtually every epic tune left in the arsenal into one evening. Fluffhead, Run Like an Antelope and Slave to the Traffic Light all surfaced in set II, along with Brother, the first since August of 1993. During that song, famous Vermont ice cream makers Ben and Jerry lent guest vocals. The shenanigans continued in the third set when trampoline artists joined the band on stage, bouncing up and down during Tweezer.

The encore offered the most confusing and debated moment of The Ball. Phish sent the crowd into a frenzy with the first notes of Harpua, soon after which a fan jumped on stage and lunged for Trey, only to be apprehended by security. The band seemed genuinely thrown off, and wound up abandoning the song half way through, leaving only ringing feedback from the amplifiers as they left the stage.

Many fans felt that the fan who jumped on stage had interrupted the band's concentration. In September, Trey addressed the confusion by going online and sharing that the band had expected to see an airplane flying overhead but couldn't (in fact, it was there, but behind the stage at an angle the band could not see, or so Trey said). That led them to cut the Harpua short.

But another theory speculates that after giving fans so much, Phish just had to leave something over for next time.

hailing the album as "a breath of fresh air." The album's single, Free, even drew significant radio play, the first Phish single to perform well on the charts.

In the concert environment, however, little changed. The band kept alternating setlists like they had always done, and in fact it was getting harder and harder to hear some songs live, what with the ever-increasing breadth of Phish's playlist. Fans who just needed to hear a particular song had to plan on attending a long string of concerts to satiate their desire.

For those who didn't really care what the band played, so long as they played it well, the fall tour offered both satisfaction and concern. There were a bunch of real musical highlights, including the Halloween show in Atlanta, which saw Phish tackle the Talking Heads with aplomb, and the band's first-ever Las Vegas gig, which many immediately tagged as the best show of the year. There were super-long jams, too, like the 30-minute Bathtub Gin in Louisville and the 27-minute Crosseyed and Painless in West Palm Beach. But unlike on previous tours, there didn't seem to be much played this fall that the band hadn't done before. Had Phish peaked? fans nervously wondered. Phish's answer came the next February in Europe.

[10/15/96] *Billy Breathes* released on Elektra.

10/16/96 [ACCESSIBILITY: •••] [ATTEND. 8,391; CAP. 8,391] [TIX $23.50]
Olympic Center, Lake Placid, NY
I: CTB, Down with Disease, Wilson, Buried Alive, Poor Heart, Billy Breathes, Mound, Sample, It's Ice, Horse > Silent, Character Zero
II: Wolfman's, Taste, Train Song, Simple, Swept Away > Steep, Caspian, Antelope, Squirming Coil, Johnny B. Goode
E: Waste

Concert debuts: Swept Away, Steep.

This show was sour—the band just didn't seem into it at all. Songs like Ice and Antelope proved this by their lack of jamming and intensity. Lake Placid wasn't the fun spot it was the year before and I think this was because of the music. But since it was the first show of the tour, we knew that it was just going to get better from here. —Geoff Lynch

Phish played two totally different sets. The first set was a tad flat (rusty!), and Trey seemed pissed at Fishman. Lots of subtle (and not-so-subtle) mistakes. Set II was another story as the band came out and raged. Wolfman's opener had me asking "What horns?" and Antelope had more tension and release than any version I've heard. Johnny B. Goode has been changed to Johnny B. Rockin'! —Charlie Murphy

10/17/96 [ACCESSIBILITY: ••] [ATTEND. 13,758; CAP. 13,758] [TIX $23.50–$25.50]
Bryce Jordan Center, Penn State University, State College, PA
I: Also Sprach > Funky Bitch, Sparkle > Tweezer > Theme, Talk, PYITE, Character Zero, Day in the Life, Tweezer Reprise
II: Ya Mar, Chalkdust, Bathtub Gin, Scent of a Mule, Free, Lizards, Star Spangled Banner, Bowie
E: Golgi

Trey on acoustic guitar for Talk. Concert debut: Star Spangled Banner.

The first 2001 show opener (of a two-set show) set the pace. Phish was "on" for this whole show. Tweezer flows seamlessly into Theme. Trey's vocal jam in Scent is pretty phat. I'm trying to be objective, but was this the most phar-out Lizards ever? First-ever a cappella Star Spangled Banner, sung in preparation for their singing it at a L.A. Lakers game in December, followed by none other than Mr. Bowie to close set II. —Charlie Murphy

A spacey 2001 which Phish played completely in the dark except for red lights behind them was an unexpected first-set opener. Then, even more unexpectedly, Funky Bitch—Mike held "Every time I see her" for what felt like minutes. When Trey switched to acoustic for Talk I hoped he'd stay on it longer, but the sound of Punch You made me forget about it. "Hook it up, Trey!" —Mark Garofalow

I talked to numerous people who were disappointed by this show. What were they listening to? Very cool Funky Bitch as Mike was really getting into it. Punch just raged! Chalkdust had a nice extended jam. Then Bathtub was taken to levels I've never seen or heard before. And the debut of the Star Spangled Banner, with one big bright spotlight shining on the U.S. flag, honestly gave me goosebumps. —Ric Hannah

10/18/96 [ACCESSIBILITY: •••] [ATTEND. 15,268; CAP. 15,268] [TIX $21–$23]
Pittsburgh Civic Arena, Pittsburgh, PA
I: Runaway Jim, Guelah, Old Home Place, CTB, Stash, Strange Design, Divided Sky, Billy Breathes, Taste, Sample
II: Suzie, Maze, YEM, Reba, Waste, Harry Hood
E: Julius

"Do You Feel Like I Do?" tease in YEM.

This was one of your basic Phish shows, featuring a lot of songs off Billy Breathes. The first set was hot—Cars Trucks Buses was key. The second set was all right but nothing to write home about. I remember it was just a rainy day. —Kevin Word

Pittsburgh is the cleanest city I've ever seen. By the time we got to the arena it was pouring rain, but that didn't stop me from breaking out the drums and enjoying it. Someone I met complained about this show's setlist: "I've seen better." Haven't we all? I can't stand negative people at shows. Besides, I did hear a phenomenal Taste and a YEM that made me think I was gettin' down in some disco in the '70s. I didn't hear it at the show, but in the YEM jam there's a "Do You Feel Like I Do?" Frampton tease. —Colm Connell

10/19/96 [ACCESSIBILITY: •••] [ATTEND. 17,567; CAP. 17,567] [TIX $22.50–$24.50]
Marine Midland Arena, Buffalo, NY
I: My Friend, Rift, Free, Esther, Llama, Gumbo, Down with Disease, Caspian, Frankenstein
II: AC/DC Bag, Sparkle, Slave, Bouncing, Melt, Fluffhead, Swept Away > Steep > Antelope, Hello My Baby
E: Fee, Rocky Top

"Wish You Were Here" tease before AC/DC Bag.

We had stopped at RIT to pick up a friend on the way to the show when we got in an accident. A girl we went to school with was driving and she handled the whole thing so well—she pushed on to the show, and we were rewarded with My Friend as an opener. My buddy loved it! I got off on the Split Open and Melt as always, and the AC/ DC Bag was rocking (the "Wish You Were Here" tease right before the Bag caught us by surprise). All in all, a great show—one that proved to us that you're lucky just to make it to any show! —Daniel Paden

To say one word for this show, I would say "exhausted." We drove over 300 miles to Buffalo—about as long as I had ever spent in a car, and arrived to terrible weather but a fun lot scene. We were tired but so excited for the show. A packed second set was incredible, but the Fee encore just doesn't do it for me, not to mention Trey flubbed the lyrics at least twice. —John McMeecking

This was my first show since the Clifford Ball. After the band abruptly walked off stage during Harpua there, I wondered if this show's atmosphere would be any different. Definitely not. —Adam Rizzuti

This show has no amazing parts or songs, but is still, for some odd reason, a phenomenal show. —Dave O'Connor

10/21/96 [ACCESSIBILITY: ••••] [ATTEND. 17,102; CAP. 17,102] [TIX $25–$27]
Madison Square Garden, New York, NY
I: Star Spangled Banner, Sample, CTB, Sloth, Divided Sky, Character Zero, Ginseng Sullivan, Stash, Waste, Possum
II: Wilson, Chalkdust, Wolfman's, Reba, Train Song, Maze, Life on Mars, Simple, Horse > Silent, Bowie
E: Funky Bitch

Last Ginseng Sullivan, 6/23/95 Stanhope, NJ [103 shows].

The boys opted to open with the Star Spangled Banner. The first set was all right—an electric Waste was nice but I like the acoustic version better. In the second set, a killer Simple with the nice segue into Horse led to the finale, David Bowie, a good one at that. It seemed that they held back on the jamming this night. The second set seemed like another first set, but I can't really complain with the killer Garden sound. —Christopher Mills

Before the second set, someone threw a t-shirt up onto the stage and it landed right at Trey's feet. He picks it up, unrolls it, takes a look and nods his head like he really likes it. I found out later it was thrown by one of my friends who had 10th row seats, and it was one of the shirts we made for our trip to Hersheypark on summer tour. Besides that, this was basically a solid show. They definitely rocked the house. —Peter Bukley

The Yankees had a World Series game in the Bronx on this night, so it seemed appropriate to open with the Star Spangled Banner. The highlight of the first set was Stash, which took forever to come back into a recognizable form. I almost lost control before Trey brought me back—"Control for smilers can't be bought." The extra-long Simple was a much-needed addition to the second set, and the Funky Bitch encore left me heading for the exit with a big smile on my face. —Mike Garofalow

Though the tour was less than a week old at this point, it was already becoming clear that the boys wanted to make Simple one of their centerpiece songs for the fall. Their increased attention to Maze was also obvious, as Simple and Maze held down the middle of the second set. Simple on this night was long and cool, but not as gorgeous as some versions later in the tour would be. They were still getting warmed up. —Rich Mazer

10/22/96 [ACCESSIBILITY: ••••] [ATTEND. 17,102; CAP. 17,102] [TIX $25–$27]
Madison Square Garden, New York, NY
I: Curtain > Runaway Jim, Bouncing, It's Ice, Talk, Melt, Sparkle > Free, YEM
II: Also Sprach > Down with Disease, Taste, Mango, Lawn Boy, Scent of a Mule, Mike's > Swept Away > Steep > Weekapaug
E: All along the Watchtower

Trey on acoustic guitar for Talk. A dance/circus troupe (including Mimi Fishman) joined Phish onstage during Weekapaug and All along the Watchtower. Buddy Miles on drums and vocals, and Merl Saunders on keyboard for All along the Watchtower (Fishman played Trey's mini–drum kit.) Last Watchtower, 4/21/94 Winston-Salem, NC [226 shows].

With two years of holiday tour performances at MSG under their belt, the band felt confident enough to book themselves for two nights in New York in the middle of the week, in the middle of October. Their big challenge would be recreating some of the energy and magic that flows like water around New Year's Eve. On the first night, they played a solid show, but one which seemed underwhelming given the fact that this was, after all, MSG, and Phish merchandising had printed up special "What is a band without skyscrapers?" t-shirts just for these two shows. But on the second night, from the Curtain opener to the amazing YEM set-closer (one of the year's best) in the first set, to the 2001 > DwD opener and Mike's Groove (with circus dancers!) in the second, the band proved they were capable of rockin' MSG on any occasion. Yeeha! —Tyler Harris

The energy level in the Garden was already fever-pitched during Weekapaug, thanks to some inspired jamming and the fact that word had spread among the crowd that the Yankees, playing in the World Series against the Braves, had scored an amazing come-from-behind win in game three. But MSG got even louder when a dance/circus troupe emerged from backstage to cavort on stage during Weekapaug. With about 30 freaks gyrating among the bandmembers, climbing on top of Page's piano, spinning around Trey and just gettin' down with Phish, the arena just exploded. The band built Weekapaug up to an incredible climax, then took it around one more time, without lyrics, topping off an incredible performance with an amazing finish. —Lee Johnston

As the second set ended, I was screaming with so much pleasure. THIS is where I want to be, THIS is what I love. My sister, Caroline, wondered how the encore would ever top that Weekapaug. But then Trey welcomed out two new friends of his, Buddy Miles and Merl Saunders—maybe they could top that Weekapaug! The lovable Buddy Miles announced that he would play the drums for a Bob Dylan song, All along the Watchtower. It was a beautiful version of the rock classic. The circus dancers reappeared and the crowd was going nuts. At the end of the song, one of the circus dancers, the Viking with the clubs, threw her clubs into the crowd. It flew by me, over my head. Then I felt something hit my ankle. THE CLUB! I stood on my chair and waved it around. Later, as I walked out onto the crowded New York street, fans hugged me and took my picture because I caught the club. As I looked around, I knew it had been, undisputedly, the greatest night of my life. —Mike Palmer

Great second set, but the encore was only enjoyable if you wanted some comic relief. "Let's hear it for Phish!" Buddy Miles screams throughout Watchtower. —Rich Mazer

10/23/96 [ACCESSIBILITY: ••••] [ATTEND. 15,587; CAP. 15,587] [TIX $22.50]
Hartford Civic Center, Hartford, CT
I: PYITE, Poor Heart, AC/DC Bag, Foam, Hello My Baby, Character Zero, Rift, Theme, Antelope
II: Brother, Ya Mar, Tweezer, Lizards, Llama, Suzie, Slave, Julius
E: Chalkdust

Bob Gullotti on a second drum set for the second set and encore.

A fairly plain, but good, first set laid the foundation for a killer set II. Bob Gullotti (on a second drum kit) was a fantastic addition for the entire second set. Brother opened the set—only the second one since 1993! The best Ya Mar ever in my opinion (check out this drum solo!) and a great Slave are thrown in, making this show a must have. The best show I've ever attended—just an amazing vibe. —Jon Bahr

Bob Gullotti came out to his drum set, warmed up the skins with a few taps and I knew what we were in for. Fish kicked the opening beats for Brother and Bob jumped right in on the snare to accentuate the rhythm. The whole set, Fish and Bob played off each other. There was a drum solo during Ya Mar in which Fish and Bob just rocked out. During Tweezer, Trey got on his drum kit, and with Page on the Moog they created such a groove. The whole set amazed all. The Llama was so powerful that I almost fell down. —Brendan Neagle

10/25/96 [ACCESSIBILITY: ••••] [ATTEND. 13,702; CAP. 13,702] [TIX $22.50]
Hampton Coliseum, Hampton, VA
I: Ha Ha Ha, Taste, Makisupa, Maze, Billy Breathes, Mound, Guelah, I Didn't Know, Stash, Squirming Coil
II: Tube, Caspian, Timber Ho, TMWSIY > Avenu > TMWSIY, NICU, Free, Strange Design, Harry Hood, Cavern, Star Spangled Banner
E: Johnny B. Goode

Fishman on vacuum for I Didn't Know. Trey debuted a new Languedoc guitar.

This show was a GREAT time—highlights include Stash, Squirming Coil, Tube and NICU. When Trey told us from the stage that Hampton was his favorite venue to play, we unanimously agreed. Many people I've talked to share the opinion that this was the best time they've ever had at a Phish show. —M.N.J. Adams

Saturday, October 26, 1996

CHARLOTTE COLISEUM, Charlotte, NC

I couldn't wait to go to this concert because I hoped to meet the band for a second time. I kind of know the band because Jon Fishman is my second cousin. Last year at the Charlotte concert I got to meet everyone, except for Mike, briefly. This year we had passes to soundcheck, dinner and the aftershow.

My dad, my brother, my friend and I arrived at Charlotte Coliseum at about 3:15 P.M. We went to get our passes and they told us they didn't have them. We found a guard and he led us down to the parking lot where the buses were parked. He left us with yet another guard. This one didn't want to let us go in, but after about fifteen minutes of persuading him, we got backstage. We found someone back there and asked if there were passes under our name. He called back to Jon and they gave us passes! I was so happy!! We were sitting backstage waiting for the band to start soundcheck when Trey walked out. We said hi to him and I asked him if he remembered us. I think he did! My friend and I gave him a poster that we had made and he said something like, "Cool, show that to the rest of the band and we'll hang it up in the bus or something."

Then Jon went out to test his new electric drums. We followed him out and sat in the front row while he played. Then out came Page, Mike and finally Trey. They messed around for a while and then played Dog Log, Old Home Place and Funky Bitch. Trey showed me his new Languedoc guitar. This would be only his second night playing it. While we were sitting there, Brad came out and handed us four tickets. They were about 100 times better than the seats we already had. We thanked him and later thanked Jon for the seats.

When they were finished we went backstage for dinner. The only band member that was there was Page. His parents were also there and they were as nice as he is! We ate and then got ready for the show.

The first set was fiery and had an awesome Reba in it. During intermission, I went backstage and talked to Jon and Page for a while. Mike rode his bike around backstage and strangely stared at us. My friend asked him for a pick and he threw one to him. Then came out Trey! I told him that they played a great first set. Then he said, "Aren't you Jason Roberts?" And I said, "Yeah!" He knew my name because I had recently won a Jimi Hendrix guitar competition and I got to play at Madison Square Garden in April. Jon had given him the newspaper article that I was in. We talked about the competition for a while and he wished me luck at Madison Square Garden and I thanked him and asked him for a pick. He pulled one out of his pocket and gave it to me. I ran out to see the second set.

They played a great second set with You Enjoy Myself! After they finished playing Waste, Trey stopped and said that this next song was for Fish's cousin! That's me! I couldn't believe it. He told the audience about the competition and wished me luck again. Then they started playing Run Like an Antelope! I still can't believe that they dedicated my absolute favorite song to me!! At the end of the set, I ran backstage and quickly thanked them for the wonderful night. They came back out and played an encore of Fire by Hendrix! I was so happy. One of my biggest dreams came true.

—Jason Roberts

I'm sure someone remembers the naked guy escorted out at intermission, screaming while standing up and falling down. I recall an awesome Stash in the first set; Tube and Timber Ho in the second ripped. Hampton is such a nice place to see a show. Hotels are close by and security lets you enjoy yourself. —Phil Valle

10/26/96 [ACCESSIBILITY: ••] [ATTEND. 17,580; CAP. 17,580] [TIX $20–$24.50]
Charlotte Coliseum, Charlotte, NC
I: Julius, CTB, Wolfman's, Reba, Train Song, Character Zero, It's Ice, Theme, Sample
II: Down with Disease, YEM, Sparkle, Simple, McGrupp, Waste, Antelope
E: Fire

I met Mike on his bike ride in the parking lot and talked with him for about five or ten minutes before a crowd formed—what a nice guy and what a way to start the evening. With the exception of Julius (not a favorite of mine), set I was outstanding. The extraordinary Reba was trippy and fast-paced, whipping the crowd into a frenzy for the rest of the evening. The second set saw one jam after another with superb versions of Down with Disease and YEM. A splendid jam out of Simple really topped off the night before it even made it to McGrupp. —Jason Deziel

Maybe the band had some pre-Halloween nerves, but they didn't take any of the shows in the week leading up to 10/31 that far out there. The setlist for this show is strong, including a second set packed with DwD, YEM, Simple and Antelope, but a truly insane jamfest this show was not. —Ernie Greene

10/27/96 [ACCESSIBILITY: ••] [ATTEND. 7,868; CAP. 10,842] [TIX $20–$22]
North Charleston Coliseum, North Charleston, SC
I: Runaway Jim, PYITE, AC/DC Bag, Fee, Scent of a Mule > Catapult > Scent of a Mule, Melt, Talk, Taste, Suzie
II: Chalkdust, Bathtub Gin, Rift, Caspian, Ya Mar, Tweezer, Fluffhead, Life on Mars, Tweezer Reprise
E: Possum, Carolina

Page on theremin for Catapult. Trey on acoustic guitar for Talk. "In-a-Gadda-Da-Vida" jam in Melt. "Norwegian Wood" jam in Taste. Last Catapult, 12/1/95 Hershey, PA [57 shows]. Last Carolina, 11/21/95 Winston Salem, NC [64 shows].

Another wonderful switched-up, mixed-up setlist. I love when Phish plays shows like this. A bunch of Scent and Tweezer. Possum for an encore—that's splendid. Fluffhead and Catapult jam at this show—I'm lucky to own it, and to have seen it! —Dary Whitcraft

I love it when the band throws me for a loop in a song like Scent where I think I know what to expect. During Trey's duel segment in Scent of a Mule, Mike came out to the front of the stage with only a microphone and crooned his little ditty Catapult. When he was finished, we noticed Page had migrated to the theremin, where he teased out the Catapult tune almost perfectly. After that, they returned to their instruments and finished off Scent. Cool. —Marcia Collins

10/29/96 [ACCESSIBILITY: •••] [ATTEND. 4,760; CAP. 13,200] [TIX $20–$22]
Tallahassee–Leon County Civic Center, Tallahassee, FL
I: Chalkdust, Guelah, CTB, Taste, Bouncing, Stash, Train Song, Billy Breathes, Poor Heart, Bowie
II: Rift, Mike's > Hydrogen > Horse > Silent, Weekapaug, Wedge, Character Zero, Suspicious Minds, Slave, Hello My Baby
E: GTBT

Karl Perazzo on drums and percussion for the entire show. Rift intro played by percussion instead of guitar. "Houses in Motion" jam in Mike's. Last Wedge, 11/14/95 Orlando, FL [70 shows].

Front-row mail-order seats for the debut of Phish as a five-piece—this was the first of several shows with Karl Perazzo sitting in on drums and percussion. Karl even pointed at me several times with his drumsticks. Just before the second set, some guy next to me handed Page a cantaloupe that said "Welcome back to Tallahassee" and "Roll like a cantaloupe." During Mike's, the band was lagging and Trey (still in mid-jam) yells, "Come on!" and the song raised another level. Check out the Rift with a percussion intro instead of a Trey intro, and Perazzo's eggshaking beat on Hello My Baby. —Tony Hume

Although this show did not sell out, the energy inside the Civic Center was incredible. Perazzo's playing raised the music to a whole new level, as evidenced in the amazing second set. It featured one of the best Mike's Songs I've ever heard. Fishman's performance of Suspicious Minds was his first song of the fall tour. Unfortunately, a few people ruined a perfect evening by vandalizing a police car outside the Civic Center. —Chris Haines

10/31/96 [ACCESSIBILITY: ••••] [ATTEND. 16,495; CAP. 16,495] [TIX $26]
The Omni, Atlanta, GA
I: Sanity, Highway to Hell, Down with Disease > YEM > Caspian, Reba, Forbin's > Mockingbird, Character Zero, Star Spangled Banner

The Omni, which was demolished a year after the Halloween show.

II: Born under Punches (The Heat Goes On), Crosseyed and Painless, Great Curve, Once in a Lifetime, Houses in Motion, Seen and Not Seen, Listening Wind, Overload
III: Brother, Also Sprach > Maze, Simple > Swept Away > Steep, Jesus Left Chicago, Suzie
E: Frankenstein

Second set was the Talking Heads' Remain in Light (all songs concert debut). Remain in Light featured David Grippo on saxophone, Gary Gazaway on trumpet, and Karl Perazzo on drums and percussion. Armchair brought to center stage for Houses—Mike sat in the chair to sing, with Trey on bass. Industrial madness broke loose onstage at the end of the second set—four television sets were brought onstage, Fishman played vacuum, and the others onstage used various tools to create weird sounds. Entire third set and encore also featured Perazzo. Jesus Left Chicago, Suzie, and Frankenstein also featured Grippo and Gazaway. Last Jesus Left Chicago, 10/31/95 Chicago, IL [76 shows].

It doesn't say enough that this show opens with Sanity. It's Halloween and I definitely had no intentions of it coming my way on this night. Every song in the first set was a highlight: DWD, Highway to Hell, YEM, Col. Forbin's. Is this some sort of sick joke? They knocked me on my ass. —Brett Pessin

I was never a big fan of the Talking Heads so I wasn't sure if I would like set II, but it is a musical masterpiece. Phish took Remain in Light, tweaked it, and made it their own. Crosseyed and Painless, Houses in Motion and Overload were spectacular. A lot of good audience tapes are out there—get one and turn it up! —Michael Rambo

Remain in Light? Talking Heads? Who would have thunk it? Most at the show agreed this was a very fresh and interesting choice for the boys. Born under Punches was totally awesome as was Once in a Lifetime, a favorite of mine since I was younger. Lots were taken aback when the boys first started, but once the show heated up so did the crowd. Good choice, guys! —M.N.J. Adams

All I have to say is, if Trey thinks he was shaking after this show, he should have seen us. I was a little unsure as to how I would perceive the Talking Heads set, but upon hearing set II my mind and body were sent to different realms. Crosseyed and Painless left me just that. The Great Curve and Houses in Motion traverse sequences of chords that I didn't know could be played. The conclusion of Listening Wind and Overload was perfect for Halloween and so was Phish's performance. —Matthew Ashenfelder

Remain in Light was beautiful—David Byrne would have swooned. One of the unique things about this show was the Phishbill given out as you entered the Omni. Like the Playbills of Broadway shows, it featured ads for Gordeaux fine liquors and Scent of a Fool cologne, as well as bios on all the players and info on Remain in Light. —Emily Binard

Without a doubt, the absolute highlight of the show musically is percussionist Karl Perazzo. His work in Brother and Also Sprach in particular is killer. Overall, this is musically speaking the best show I've ever heard. Jesus Left Chicago with Grippo on sax is always a plus, and the story about the evil Mockingbird is pretty cool too. —Mike Jett

WHO'S WHO IN THE CAST

JON FISHMAN studied drumming under the guise of Paul Gartsky at Goddard College (an accredited institution!). He forefronted the head-up/head-down method of drumming and in 1987 he had the honor of teaching this percussion protocol to the Queen of England. He also wrote all the words and music to *Remain in Light* and designed the typeface in which this text appears. Jon wore his "I'm not a transvestite" dress to other pop album performances, including a rendition of *Quadrophenia* by The Who. That performance was enough to inspire The Who to return to the same city exactly one year later and perform it themselves.

TREY "LEADERSHIP QUALITIES" ANASTASIO directed the ensemble, telling them to sing better and play better because, quote, you're not really singing it right. To get acquainted with Talking Heads music, he lived with David Byrne for over three years, sharing a toothbrush and breakfast cereals. He's been in movies using the stage name "Chuck Norris" and directed a rendition of the Beatles' White Album in 1994.

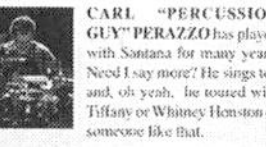
CARL "PERCUSSION GUY" PERAZZO has played with Santana for many years. Need I say more? He sings too and, oh yeah, he toured with Tiffany or Whitney Houston or someone like that.

DAVID "THE TRUTH" GRIPPO is a saxophone player. He played with the Giant Country Horns a few years ago, and by the way, if there's one thing about a horn section, it's that there's nothing quite like it. Another thing about the Giant Country Horns is that this *is* a giant country, namely the biggest country in the world. It's also the country with the most people in it. These are facts that "The Truth" shared with me while on tour. Next paragraph -- Truth has played with over 1800 local bands. Truth told me his birthday was February 30, same as Tina Weymouth's.

MIKE "GAKTOIDLER" GORDON graduated from UVM (University of Ver Mont) in 1987. He played a Talking Heads song once in his high school band and hopes that that makes him qualified for this "thing." He never had heard this album before, but played "Psycho Killer" for thirty-eight minutes once. He decided to help write these little blurbs, including this very sentence, which he was the writer of.

PAGE "CHAIRMAN OF THE BOARDS" ARTHUR CONAN DOYLE MCCONNELL tickled the ivories and plastics, if you will, tonight. He studied at Goddard University (not to be confused with Goddard College, which is the same thing). He also received an Honorary Doctorate in Music from Oxford immediately after singing a Beach Boys medley for the Queen of England. Page had to pre-program many "synthesizer patches" for this performance, a skill well suited to a man who invented the first computer decades ago.

GARY "EL BUHO" GAZAWAY is fabulous. At least that's what Louis Armstrong said in the '30's about him. Armstrong thinks this guy is deluxe. And he is. Listen to the timbre. He not only played on the original *Remain In Light*, he wrote all horn parts on all albums. He left his trumpet at home, though, so he'll be playing tonight on, you guessed it, his trumpet, which he didn't really leave at home.

A page from the "Phishbill" handed out at the show.

Incredible, incredible show, packed to the breaking point with hot song after hot song. The first set rivaled that of 10/31/94 in its song selection (DwD, YEM, Forbin's) and song selection humor (Sanity > Hell opener). If set three of this show had been a little stronger, this might have been the greatest Phish show of all time. Still, we were more than happy to settle for Brother, plus Maze and Simple (the two unsung stars of fall tour '96) and the now-traditional Jesus Left Chicago with horns. —Lee Johnston

11/2/96 [ACCESSIBILITY: ••••] [ATTEND. 10,795; CAP. 20,025] [TIX $20–$24.75]
Coral Sky Amphitheater, West Palm Beach, FL
I: Ya Mar, Julius, Fee, Cavern, Taste, Stash, Free, Johnny B. Goode
II: Crosseyed and Painless, Antelope, Waste, Harry Hood, Day in the Life, Adeline
E: Funky Bitch

Karl Perazzo on drums and percussion for the entire show. Butch Trucks on drums for Funky Bitch, with Fishman on Trey's mini–drum kit. Trey says "Norton Charleton Heston" instead of "Marco Esquandolis" in Antelope lyrics. Segments of the second set were broadcast on a syndicated nationwide FM radio program in March 1997.

A great show in a beautiful place, the only open-air venue of the tour—the skies were blue and the sun was shining. Crosseyed and Painless was the most intense Phish song I ever heard. It lasted for 27 minutes, and jammed the whole entire time. I never danced so long in my life. I was ready to take a seat when they segued right into Antelope. Let me tell you—it was the sickest Antelope I'd ever heard, too. Trey summed it up after Antelope when he walked up to his mic and simply said, "Whooaa." Thank God they played Waste next, because I had to sit down and catch my breath. I found myself up again upon hearing the opening of Hood, which proved to be one of the best of the tour. When they came out for the encore, I noticed an extra person with them. It turned out to be Butch Trucks again (he joined them at West Palm in '95). He jammed with them on a ripping version of Funky Bitch to end the show. It was the hottest second set I've heard in a while. —Tom Pinnick

Ya Mar to open is a sign of good things to come, but the second set is what this show is all about. Crosseyed and Painless goes for about 25 minutes, followed by Antelope. At this point you can rewind the tape and do it all over again. A nice Hood was played, too. I highly recommend this show. —Michael Rambo

In spring '97, Phish got to choose a portion of one of their fall shows for national radio broadcast. They chose part of West Palm Beach II, including the Crosseyed and Painless into Antelope, which runs about 40 minutes and is probably their best jam of the year. Mike later posted part of his journal from November 2 to www.phish.com. He wrote, "Playing with Karl takes away the problems of 'rushing' the rhythms. . . . The Talking Heads song and the jam that followed were great. The whole set was great. . . . Had a 'bit of a musical experience' in West Palm." So did everyone there! —Ed Smith

11/3/96 [ACCESSIBILITY: ••] [ATTEND. 7,187; CAP. 11,000] [TIX $20–$22]
Stephen C. O'Connell Center, Gainesville, FL
I: My Friend, Runaway Jim, Billy Breathes, Sloth, NICU, Sample, Theme, Bouncing, Character Zero
II: Timber Ho, Divided Sky, Wolfman's, Sparkle, Tweezer, Life on Mars, Possum, Tweezer Reprise
E: Fire

Karl Perazzo on drums and percussion for the entire show.

This is one of the poorer Phish shows I've ever been to. We did get to hear a near-30 minute Funky Bitch soundcheck, but the crowd seemed more buzzed than into the music and believe it or not, got more excited over Sparkle than anything else. The music was actually good, but lacked the passion of most other shows. This was the last Karl Perazzo show—that man is a monster! —Tony Hume

A medium-to-high-grade Phish show. There are a couple of jewels like the Tweezer jam and Possum, and the smooth My Friend opener. —Daryl Whitcraft

"Remain in Light"

10/31/96 The Omni, Atlanta, GA

During the days leading up to 1995's Halloween extravaganza in Chicago, Phish littered their sets with Michael Jackson musical references, screwing with phans' minds before breaking out *Quadrophenia*. In 1996, the band took the opposite tact, all but telling fans in the weeks leading up to Halloween that they'd be covering a Talking Heads album.

"It's going to be by an American band, an American album, an '80s album," Fishman told the *Atlanta Journal-Constitution* a week before the show. "There's one song that everyone has heard, but it's not as high-profile as *The White Album*. But then again, what is?"

The band had been longtime admirers of the Talking Heads, covering Cities throughout the 1980s. But no one knew for sure whether the band was really going to play "an '80s American album," or whether it was just another Phishy mind game. In any case, the decision was Phish's to make, because for the first time the band elected to choose their cover album instead of having the fans vote on it.

On the day of the show, the traditional party atmosphere surrounded the Omni. Tickets were tough—the show was, of course, an immediate sellout—but not impossible; extras changed hands in front of the venue in the $40 to $80 range. For the first time at a Phish show, MTV news cameras were on the scene, interviewing fans for *The Week in Rock*, which later included some concert footage.

Phans entering the arena received a "PHISHBILL," designed as a spoof on *Playbill* that listed "Phish in Talking Heads' *Remain in Light*," and named the band along with several guests. Inside the Phishbill was a two-page essay written by *Rolling Stone* journalist Parke Puterbaugh (who later wrote the *Rolling Stone* Phish article in winter '97) that discussed the influence *Remain in Light* had on the members of Phish. If it was all a prank, it was a pretty elaborate one.

The show started with the first Sanity since New Year's '95, a fitting opener that slammed right into Highway to Hell—another nice touch. From there, the first set soared with epics, including yet another great '96 Down with Disease and a long YEM. As the set passed the one-hour point, the band was still rocking, ripping into Col. Forbin's Ascent, where Trey spun a trippy tale of Col. Forbin climbing the mountain and the face of Icculus becoming that of Talking Heads frontman David Byrne. The "evil Halloween mockingbird" failed to return the Helping Friendly Book to the people of Gamehendge "because it's Halloween," then the band rocked out Character Zero.

As a second drum set was constructed during the setbreak, it became obvious that the Phishbill wasn't a joke. Longtime Santana band percussionist Karl Perazzo had played with Phish at their previous gig in Florida and would sit in for the musical costume. Also joining the band for set II would be GCH member Dave Grippo and trumpet player Gary Gazaway, who played on the original *Remain in Light* and wrote the horn parts to the album. The die was cast.

Instead of the drama associated with *The White Album* or *Quadrophenia*, Phish thrived on the musicality of *Remain in Light*. Whereas the band had focused in previous years on replicating the original albums, they turned *Remain in Light* into a jam showcase, taking the songs further out there than David Byrne could probably have ever imagined. Perazzo's driving percussion provided a platform for the rest of the band—as Fishman pointed out in Puterbaugh's Phishbill article, "It's almost like all the instruments are drums . . . Even the background vocals are like drum parts."

According to Phishbill, it was Trey who urged Phish to cover *Remain in Light*. "I practically learned how to play guitar by listening to [it]," he told Puterbaugh. Both Page and Mike covered Talking Heads songs in pre-Phishy days, too, so the album represented a homecoming of sorts for the band.

Near the end of the set, things got weird during Overload as four television sets were brought onto stage and white noise poured from the PA system. Phans watched, transfixed, as the band and friends freaked out for a few minutes—walking strangely around the stage, using jackhammers, screaming unintelligibly—then left the stage.

On a night of treats, it was the ultimate trick.

11/6/96 [ACCESSIBILITY: ••] [ATTEND. 5,501; CAP. 6,000] [TIX $20.50]
Knoxville Civic Coliseum, Knoxville, TN
I: Melt, CTB, FEFY, Taste, Train Song, Poor Heart, PYITE, Billy Breathes, Bowie
II: Wilson, Curtain > Mike's > Swept Away > Steep > Weekapaug, Scent of a Mule, Sample, Funky Bitch
E: Rocky Top

On the way up from Gainesville, we took the wrong highway. Needless to say, it took a while to get to Knoxville, but when we got there we went to a bar and there were Trey and Gordo. I had a nice conversation with Trey in which he kept talking about my shirt. The show was nice with a great Punch. The second set Wilson > Curtain > Mike's Groove is solid. Trey said hello to all the people he met in Knoxville—that was me!—then finished things off with an appropriate Rocky Top encore. —Will Lehnert

11/7/96 [ACCESSIBILITY: ••••] [ATTEND. 10,110; CAP. 12,000] [TIX $20]
Rupp Arena, Lexington, KY
I: Chalkdust, Weigh > Rift > Guelah, Stash, Waste, Guyute, Free > Tela, Character Zero
II: Suzie > Bathtub Gin, HYHU > Bike > HYHU, YEM
E: Frankenstein
Fishman on vacuum for Bike.

This was a fantastic show. Chalkdust opens, then comes the only Weigh of the tour (the show also had the only Tela of the fall, as well as the tour's first Guyute). Second set featured an amazing Bathtub Gin with the Chairman of the Boards taking control. Also, in my humble opinion, the best YEM since 6/11/94 Red Rocks. —Will Lehnert

The second set: four songs?! The Suzie > Bathtub Gin opener has to be one of the craziest performances I have ever seen from Phish. Trey was totally going off on his guitar during Bathtub. The YEM closer topped it all off. I don't think I've ever had a more wonderful night of music than this. —Dan Charron

The second set epitomizes what Phish was all about during the Fall '96 tour—two huge jams (Gin and YEM) that traverse a lot of places and spaces. Bathtub Gin, very arguably the best version ever, is certainly the longest—over 25 minutes. The jam segment is normal Gin-style wandering at first, but when Trey moves over to his mini–drum kit and Page steps up to his clavinet, the jam takes a U-turn. Page just dominates, absolutely rocking out while Trey, Mike and Fish provide a firm foundation for his jamming. When Trey moves back to his guitar, a wonderfully directed jam develops that rages, peaks, and heads into an entirely different jam segment, which itself transforms into a funky bass-and-drums affair that segues right into HYHU! Instead of playing six songs to showcase their different styles, Phish now does it in just one song! —Josh Albini

Before the second set, Trey says to the crowd, "Fish hasn't sung this tour yet, has he? He lost his privilege." (Apparently Trey forgot Suspicious Minds on 10/29). When the crowd cheers, Trey says, "You're going to have to do better than that," and the crowd goes absolutely wild. After the monstrous Suzie > Bathtub, Fishman heads for center stage with the Electrolux, declaring, "Well, by gum, you've brought me out of the penalty box. It's good to be back!" A hilarious Bike ensues. —Lee Johnston

11/8/96 [ACCESSIBILITY: •••] [ATTEND. 16,535; CAP. 16,535] [TIX $18–$20]
Assembly Hall, Champaign, IL
I: Runaway Jim > Axilla, All Things, Mound, Down with Disease, Caspian, Reba, Golgi, Antelope
II: Also Sprach > Maze, Bouncing, Simple, Loving Cup, Mike's, Star Spangled Banner, Weekapaug
E: Theme
Last Axilla, 10/16/94 Chattanooga, TN [170 shows]. Last All Things, 7/1/95 Mansfield, MA [108 shows].

Before this show, I considered Simple just another good song played between the big guns (jam songs). But once again, Phish took a step up, playing an intricate and jammed-out Simple. Clearly the best I've ever heard! Not even Trey's breaking amp (which he kicked harder than usual) stopped the intense groove. The jam included Cecilia teases, amazing Page chords and creative Mike lines. And how nice it was to follow this jam with Loving Cup—this show was a beautiful buzz! —Michelle Hirsch

This show was average at best. Runaway Jim was a very predictable opener, then the show became slow and methodical until Down with Disease took flight. Antelope was a nice highlight to a rather mediocre set. 2001 and the rest of the second set were subtle and a little cautious. —Andy Kahn

As Phish goes into Axilla, Trey has guitar problems and gives his amp a kick, causing a roar from the crowd. Trey does this again during Simple. Then at the beginning of Weekapaug Groove, Mike's bass makes this horrible rattling noise, ruining my enjoyment of this song. To solve a night of equipment problems and to get something out of the evening, Phish encored with a nice Theme, building up slowly then climaxing at the end. —Mike Noll

11/9/96 [ACCESSIBILITY: •••] [ATTEND. 18,359; CAP. 18,359] [TIX $22.50]
The Palace, Auburn Hills, MI
I: Buried Alive > Poor Heart, Sloth, Divided Sky, Horn, Tube, Talk, Melt, Lizards, Character Zero
II: Bowie, Day in the Life, YEM, Taste > Swept Away > Steep > Harry Hood
E: Julius
Trey on acoustic guitar for Talk.

This was a solid show. For such a large venue, Phish rocked the whole boat! And what a second set—Bowie opener was tight and great. They grasped the energy they want to obtain and held it solid throughout the song. I prefer the hard/intense Bowies, so those who agree should check this one out. The YEM was just as tight—some great bass weaving throughout. Just as I thought they would throw out a Cavern ending, they whipped out a ripping Hood with a nice transition from Steep. Thanks Page! —Michelle Hirsch

Phish played a great first set which yielded Sloth and a great Tube. Lizards went well, plus a good Character Zero. The second set, however, sucked. It had a decent Hood to keep it afloat, but Bowie? Day in the Life > YEM just didn't cut it, either. Julius is the worst song to end a show, but here that's what they chose. —Chris Regan

11/11/96 [ACCESSIBILITY: ••••] [ATTEND. 8,211; CAP. 9,500] [TIX $22.50–$24.50]
Van Andel Arena, Grand Rapids, MI
I: Chalkdust, Guelah, CTB, AC/DC Bag, Sparkle, Brother, Theme, Axilla, Runaway Jim

Saturday, November 9, 1996

THE PALACE, Auburn Hills, MI

From the time my brother Mike received mail-order seats for the second row, I knew the show at The Palace in Auburn Hills would be special to me. I flew to Michigan to see my brother, but it was more to see the show. I got there the night before and seeing my seat location on the seating chart, I made the decision to make a sign for a song that hopefully the band would play. I decided on Tube, a nice little rarity that rages.

We got to the Palace and met my brother's friends Jeremy, Goldie and Christina. They had come down from Buffalo and would also be sitting with my Bro's friend from school, Dave. They had awful seats so we stubbed all four of them down to our wonderful spots and the show began. I had my Buried Alive shirt on and my sign in hand as the band came out. I held my sign high. I'm sure Trey saw it as they opened with Buried Alive (coincidence, maybe) that segued into a Poor Heart. Both good show openers. Next came Sloth, which was rockin' as usual, followed by Divided Sky. After a stellar version of Divided there was a couple second pause and I held my sign high—I'm sure Mike and Trey and Fish all saw it.

But they busted into Horn, my first and a decent version of it as well. After Horn there was another pause and I held up my sign once again. Trey began strumming and I knew it from the brief little strumming it was Tube! . . . and a kick-ass version at that.

I danced my ass off with a smile the size of Utah. After Tube, Trey went over and got his acoustic guitar, then stepped up to the mic and said hello to the crowd. He then said, "That last song was for my friend down here with a sign so he doesn't have to hold it up all night long." At that moment I almost lost my shit.

With the band's dedication to me followed by a second set featuring Bowie, YEM and Hood, it was enough to make me smile the rest of my life.

—Butch Weiss

II: Timber Ho, Divided Sky, Gumbo, Curtain > Sample, Tweezer, Swept Away > Steep > Maze, Contact, Slave
E: Waste, Cavern

This was my last show of the fall tour, and I was pleased to see a good show to end (with a great view thanks to general admission). The light show pleased my senses, but my favorite part of the show had to be Page's ragtime solo at the end of Gumbo. Once finished, he cast a menacing glare on the crowd as Trey yelled in delight. —Josh Halman

Mother nature wasn't kind to Phish and the fans during our November trek from Michigan down across the midwest to the Pacific Northwest. Rain, sleet, ice and snow attempted to keep us away from the shows, starting in Grand Rapids, but most of us slogged through the mess and were rewarded for it. This was another solid show, nothing outrageous but nothing to gripe about either. —Melissa Wolcott

At first it was shocking when they broke out into Divided Sky in the second set, mostly because they played it the show before at the Palace. Thanks to G.A., I was able to ask Trey with my eyes "Why?" He looked at me with a disappointed look which reminded me of one of the most beautiful sunsets Michigan had that night. The sky was on fire with shades of red, orange and pink one can only imagine in dreams of ideal sunsets. I closed my eyes during this Divided Sky and saw those magical colors once again. —Michelle Hirsch

[11/12/96]
Target Center, Minneapolis, MN
Star Spangled Banner
Phish sang a cappella before the Timberwolves-Lakers NBA game.

11/13/96 [ACCESSIBILITY: •••] [ATTEND. 10,093; CAP. 12,919] [TIX $19–$21]
Target Center, Minneapolis, MN
I: Down with Disease, Bouncing, It's Ice, Ya Mar, Taste, Train Song, Reba, Character Zero, Adeline
II: Also Sprach > Suzie, Caspian > YEM, Theme, Golgi
E: GTBT
Extended jam out of Suzie.

It was my 21st birthday and all I wanted was to see Character Zero. They kicked down one of the fattest Zeros all tour. The Ya Mar was also huge, and Suzie Greenberg had an amazing reprise. —Sean Smith

When we arrived at the Target Center, it was freezing cold, so we boiled up some hot chocolate. There was all this talk before the show of it being a special show, that the band told the tapers to bring extra tapes because they were gonna play three sets and so on. This got me really pumped up and curious to discover what the band had in store for us. The Target Center was a nice place, just like a regular-sized arena but new. Set I proved very standard with an average DWD opener into Bouncin'. Set II opened with a funky 2001 into a incredible Suzie Greenberg. Next was Caspian which led into a phat You Enjoy Myself, including a sick vocal jam and even a very cool polka jam. I enjoyed this show, even though it ended up being nothing spectacular. —Dom DeLuca

It's not often the band uses Suzie as an excuse to jam. There's the brief Suzie reprise on 12/31/94 that slides into Slave, and there's the JAM that emerges from Suzie at this show. For a solid ten minutes or so, the band leaves Suzie behind, working their way through a jam that eventually arrives at Caspian. If you're willing to call this a "Suzie Jam," then this is certainly the most jammed Suzie Greenberg ever. —Ernie Greene

11/14/96 [ACCESSIBILITY: •••] [ATTEND. 6,847; CAP. 10,000] [TIX $23]
Hilton Coliseum, Ames, IA
I: AC/DC Bag, Uncle Pen, Wolfman's, CTB, Free, All Things, Bathtub Gin, Talk, Julius
II: Llama, Sample, Taste, Swept Away > Steep, Scent of a Mule, Life on Mars, Demand > Antelope, Day in the Life
E: Stash, Hello My Baby
"James Bond Theme" tease in Stash. Last Demand, 12/7/95 Niagara Falls, NY [64 shows].

Very good show with good songs. AC/DC Bag gets it all started, then a short version of Free carries into a jammy Bathtub Gin and the sweet melody of Talk. The second set was good but lacked some real jams. Trey "Demand"s us to Run Like an Antelope, before telling us about A Day in the Life. ADITL popped up in such a sweet slot, after Antelope, that you're almost forced to like it even if you don't. To make up for it all, a Stash encore was well-received and helped us all leave feeling pretty happy. —Christopher Mills

This show was relatively short, but sweet. Set-opener AC/DC Bag really jams out into a speedy Uncle Pen. Bathtub Gin seems like it's played in slow motion for a while. In the second set, Scent of a Mule into the Russian jam is awesome—they do a little vocal jamming in the middle of it. —Shannon C. Lancaster

The band appeared to cut their performance short, probably because of the ice storm raging outside. Rumors circulated that the next day's show was going to be canceled. After it was over—including a very long and well-jammed Stash encore which shocked me because I had never heard a Stash encore before—we hopped in the car and began to drive. The weather was exceptionally bad; we saw over 10 accidents, mostly tractor-trailers that slid off the road. —Dom DeLuca

11/15/96 [ACCESSIBILITY: ••••] [ATTEND. 14,492; CAP. 18,000] [TIX $20–$22]
Keil Center, St. Louis, MO
I: Wilson, Divided Sky, Bouncing, Character Zero, PYITE, Caspian, Ginseng Sullivan, Train Song, Chalkdust, Taste, Cavern
II: Makisupa, Maze, McGrupp, Melt, TMWSIY > Avenu >TMWSIY, My Mind's, Mike's > Sleeping Monkey > Mean Mr. Mustard > Weekapaug
E: Funky Bitch
Mean Mr. Mustard, Weekapaug, and Funky Bitch featured John Popper on harmonica. Trey said the second set was "brought to you by the letter 'M' and the number '420.'" (All songs except Weekapaug included a word that started with the letter M). Concert debut: Mean Mr. Mustard.

"The second set is brought to you by the letter M and the number 420." Trey's line surmises the whole second set which contains great segues, a Beatles tune and John Popper. Some people dog this set because they say it lacks extended jamming, notably on Mike's, but if your view of a great show isn't based on how few words there are, you'll love it. —Paul Sheets

Set II is the famous "M" set—all of the songs have "M" as the main word in the title: Makisupa, Maze, McGrupp. . . . The performance of the Beatles' Mean Mr. Mustard is fun

Wednesday, November 13, 1996

TARGET CENTER, Minneapolis, MN

This was the show that made me a true believer. Until this fateful evening at Minneapolis's second largest (and worst sounding) venue, I still held on to the last of the stereotyped visions The Man had sold me about what a "Deadhead" (and subsequently, a "Phishhead") was. I caught a show here and there but I was unwilling to go that final step into drop-everything-and-hit-the-road mode, and I was still suspicious of those who did. Then Phish took the stage for the second set after an entertaining first round and spoke directly to me like missionaries on a quest to convert the last doubter.

I compiled a wish list before my partners and I left Eau Claire, WI, for a Minneapolis, Ames, St. Louis jaunt. This list hung around my neck on a laminated card I named the Phish Locator. It was four songs long. Before the show I had commented to my friends Eric and Kara how it would be cool to link Theme from the Bottom and YEM somehow, since they both have a cappella vocal jams in them. Wish list song number one came with Taste in the first set.

Then Phish cranked out the second set, including wish list song number two—YEM, with intense lights and the vocal jam ending, which glided into, ohmygodcoulditbe?! Theme from the Bottom, wish list song number three. I was in tears. But as they say in the Veg-o-Matic commercials, "Wait . . . there's more!" Theme carried me to a new Phish height—it was Hulk Hogan, the Macho Man Savage, Rick Flair and George "The Animal" Steele (that'd be Fishman) on stage lifting me above their heads for the body slam: Golgi Apparatus, my fourth and final wish list song.

The lights went up and I had that classic glued-to-my-seat-cause-I-don't-know-what-to-do immobility. Had that just happened?. I consulted the wish list. Yep, there were the four songs. I stood apart, in silence, just staring at the deconstruction of the stage and wondering if I was truly, somehow intrinsically connected with the band. Had they known and played that show for me alone? Had we connected through some mysterious ESP-like higher consciousness? It's easier to say, "No, of course not—it's coincidence," but Phish gave me that feeling of a higher power, and I knew then I could never see them enough.

—Jason Hendrington

and Trey has a good time with it. The highlight of the show is John Popper's guest appearance, which doesn't shock me because Popper seems to show up everywhere these days, with Phish, Dave Matthews and even Pearl Jam. —Craig Rothenberg

The debut of Mean Mr. Mustard set the stage for the mean old man himself, John Popper (it also led to the only non-M song, Weekapaug). This was "WeekaPopper Groove" at its phinest, as it has mainly a Popper jam—so much so that some lyrics are left out. —Jon Bahr

The encore was a predictable Phunky Bitch, which held some confusion for the band. Trey wanted to break it down and let John go off, but the guys thought he was shutting it down and ended the song. John Popper was surprised but Fishman jumped on a phunky beat and saved it. As the guys left the stage, Trey seemed unsatisfied. I, however, was very satisfied. Do yourself a favor and get this tape. —Justin Weiss

The Maze was truly one of the best I've ever heard. —Russell Lane

11/16/96 [ACCESSIBILITY: •••] [ATTEND. 10,960; CAP. 10,960] [TIX $20–$22]
Omaha Civic Auditorium, Omaha, NE
I: Poor Heart, Down with Disease, Guyute, Gumbo, Rift, Free, Old Home Place, Bowie, Lawn Boy, Sparkle, Frankenstein
II: La Grange, Runaway Jim > Kung > Catapult > Axilla > Harry Hood, Suzie, Amazing Grace
E: We're an American Band

Trey on cowbell and Mike dancing with scarf during Kung. "Vibration of Life" in Kung. "Leigh Fordham" sung in Axilla and in Harry Hood. "La Grange" tease in Harry Hood. "La Grange" and "Axilla" teases in Suzie. Concert debut: We're an American Band. Last Kung, 12/30/95 New York, NY [55 shows].

One of the more controversial shows of the tour with the "Vibration of Life" with Trey saying, "This was written by God." For those people who have problems with this, I say, chill out. He's just having fun. Anyways, Guyute was ripping. Is it ever not? The second set offered a lot with a La Grange > Runaway. I was standing up against the front boards, and I have never seen such a huge smile on Trey's face as he had during Hood. Hood started off weird when, during the "Harry, where do you go when the lights go out?" they yelled someone else's name. I'm not sure what they were saying, but the song put a bigger smile on my face than Trey's. The American Band encore was sick—"I left my woman in Omaha"—the place erupted. Good music, good friends, good times. —Brett Pessin

This was an excellent show in a small venue, which made it even better. It was snowing like crazy outside but it didn't stop the kids from coming out—the streets of Omaha were packed, and the setlist was fat. In the second set there was a Vibration of Life > Kung chant > Catapult during which Mike came out front and did a dance shaking his hips and waving a sash around. He actually danced on his own without Trey, who was grooving nearby on his drum kit. —Melanie and Melita Terrell

11/18/96 [ACCESSIBILITY: ••] [ATTEND. 7,432; CAP. 10,000] [TIX $22.50–$24.50]
Mid-South Coliseum, Memphis, TN
I: CTB, Timber Ho, Poor Heart, Taste, Billy Breathes, Chalkdust, Guelah, Ginseng Sullivan, Reba, Character Zero
II: Also Sprach > Simple > Swept Away > Steep, Scent of a Mule, Tweezer, Hello My Baby, Tweezer Reprise, Llama
E: Waste, Johnny B. Goode

Gary Gazaway on trumpet for Tweezer, Hello My Baby, Tweezer Reprise, Llama, and Johnny B. Goode.

I am a bit partial to this show because it took place on my 21st birthday. To me the band really pushed Billy Breathes material on this night. Cars Trucks Buses really rocked—it's slowly becoming my favorite "new tune." Ginseng Sullivan was a rare treat and Reba was phenomenal. Also Sprach had traces of Pink Floyd in it and the 10-plus-minute Scent had me dehydrated from dancing. —Tony Krupka

A great show, thanks in large part to the trumpet stylings of Gary "El Buho" Gazaway, who played with Phish for Remain in Light, too (he wrote the horn parts for the album originally). This is a solid second set, both in song selection and in performance quality. Tweezer with Gary is particularly interesting, and his additions to Hello My Baby make this one a cappella song worth hearing. —Ed Smith

Set II opened with a nice funked-up 2001 that led into a tight Simple. I'm not a huge Simple fan, but all the Simples I saw on this tour were great—it's really developing as a jam song. Simple led into Swept Away > Steep. Out of Steep came Scent of a Mule with a nice vocal jam which they did in Mule for much of the tour. A phenomenal Tweezer followed with Gary Gazaway on trumpet—definitely my favorite version of the fall. When the boys stepped up for an a cappella Ragtime Gal, Gary took a nice solo. He stayed out there for the smokin' Reprise and then an amazing version of Llama. —Dom DeLuca

11/19/96 [ACCESSIBILITY: ••] [ATTEND. 6,134; CAP. 9,000] [TIX $20]
Municipal Auditorium Arena, Kansas City, MO
I: Ya Mar, AC/DC Bag, Foam, Theme, Mound, Stash, Fee, Taste, Loving Cup
II: Bowie, Day in the Life, Bathtub Gin, YEM, Star Spangled Banner, Fire
E: Squirming Coil

"Vibration of Life" between Bathtub Gin and YEM. "Groove Is in the Heart" jam in YEM.

This setting for this show was perfect—the art-deco architecture fit nicely with Chris Kuroda's lights. AC/DC Bag was a favorite out on the dance floor. Mound made me feel like I was flying. The second set was highlighted by a You Enjoy Myself that contained a "Groove Is in the Heart" tease. I'm not real sure how long this YEM is, but let's put it this way: it's worth owning. —Chad Ashcraft

For the band's last show in the midwest, they treated us to a great second set reminiscent of Lexington several weeks earlier—a long (though not as long as 11/7 Lexington) Bathtub Gin and a long (even longer than 11/7) YEM, with a verse of Dee-Lite's "Groove Is in the Heart" dropped right in the middle. Phish sets used to average about 10 songs each, but as their jam style continues to stretch songs waaaaay out, the number of second sets with only four to six songs continues to grow. That's a trend I can live with! —Dave Sharpe

11/22/96 [ACCESSIBILITY: ••] [ATTEND. 4,509; CAP. 7,500] [TIX $22.50]
Spokane Arena, Spokane, WA
I: It's Ice, Runaway Jim, Wolfman's, Taste, Ginseng Sullivan, Sample, FEFY, Train Song, Stash, Cavern
II: Down with Disease, Caspian, Maze, Billy Breathes, Swept Away > Steep, Character Zero, Theme, Slave, Hello My Baby
E: Julius

"Cocaine" (sung as "Spokane") jam before Julius.

Treacherous road conditions and rain led to a well-put It's Ice opener (with the band completely blowing the segue back into the song after the long Page jam). Wolfman's Brother was an interesting choice, highlighting this set of mellow jamming and new material. Down with Disease was an intense opener to a set that went downhill after the next hour and a half with lots of Billy Breathes material and a Julius encore. This show seemed to be a tease for the next night to come. —Brian Boehm

Perhaps the foul, stormy weather dampened the feeling of joy one feels seeing Phish, or maybe this was an off night. The timely It's Ice/Jim intro had me thinking "classic show," but on this night, naught. After a quality Taste, the first set just played itself out. The second set brought much promise with DwD and Maze being quite intense. But once again the brakes were applied and instead of grooving, I felt like snoozing (exception: Character Zero). Even the usually lively Julius seemed a bit slow and stale. —Greg Kelly

11/23/96 [ACCESSIBILITY: •••] [ATTEND. 4,902; CAP. 8,000] [TIX $29.50–$31.50]
Pacific Coliseum, Vancouver, BC
I: Chalkdust, Guelah, CTB, Divided Sky, PYITE, Mid-Highway Blues, Melt, Rift, Funky Bitch
II: Curtain, Mike's > Simple > Makisupa > Axilla > Weekapaug > Catapult > Waste, Amazing Grace, Harry Hood
E: GTBT

Concert debut: Mid-Highway Blues (a.k.a. Late Night on the Highway).

Classic opener Chalkdust Torture foreshadows an intense set to come. After Divided Sky and Punch was the first time they stopped this set. Midnight on the Highway, a first-ever, made the experience much more intimate before closing with the favorite Funky Bitch. Curtain > Mike's couldn't have pleased the crowd more—then came the opening notes of Makisupa. "Woke up in the morning, border guard in my bunk, turned the fucking dog on the bus, and found my dank," Trey remarked on the day's adventure. Harry Hood closes this monumental show, perfectly capping this very kind evening. —Brian Boehm

The setlist from this show, especially the second set, is obviously insane. The band had a lot of energy, too, with the downside being somewhat sloppy—that is, unfocused—jamming. This was a really fun show, with the boys debuting the bluegrass tune they learned while waiting at the border after their drug bust and again referencing the incident in Makisupa, but if you pick up this show expecting to be blown away by the band's musical prowess you're barking up the wrong tape. Still, the bonus Hood after Amazing Grace sure made us happy. —Melissa Wolcott

11/24/96 [ACCESSIBILITY: ••] [ATTEND. 7,876; CAP. 8,500] [TIX $22.50]
Memorial Coliseum, Portland, OR
I: Poor Heart, AC/DC Bag, All Things, Bouncing, Reba, Character Zero, Strange Design, Taste, I Didn't Know, Sample, Antelope

II: Also Sprach > Sparkle, Bowie, Day in the Life > YEM > Loving Cup > Suzie

E: Ginseng Sullivan, Cavern

Fishman on vacuum for I Didn't Know. Trey says "Norton Charleton Heston" instead of "Marco Esquandolis" in Antelope lyrics.

The evolution of Henrietta's nickname continues! After Zero Man, Moses Brown, Tubbs and Greasy Fizeek (among many others) came his fall '96 name, Norton Charleton Heston. In Portland, Trey introduces Norton for a vacuum solo in I Didn't Know, then substitutes "Norton Charleton Heston" for "Marco Esquandolis" in Antelope, a change made several times this month. As for the Portland show, the general feeling can be summed up by the 2001 > Sparkle combo—in other words, not one of the band's hotter nights. —Dave Sharpe

11/27/96 [ACCESSIBILITY: ••••] [ATTEND. 7,924; CAP. 7,924] [TIX $22.50]

Key Arena, Seattle, WA

I: Julius > My Friend > Ya Mar, Chalkdust, Sloth, Uncle Pen, Free > Theme, Bold as Love

II: Down with Disease > Jesus Left Chicago, Scent of a Mule, Tweezer > Down with Disease, Star Spangled Banner, Fire

E: Waste, Tweezer Reprise

"Brady Bunch Theme" skatted and played by Trey in Scent of a Mule, which also included Fishman on vacuum. "Sweet Emotion" jam in Tweezer. Down with Disease reprise out of Tweezer was instrumental, no lyrics, with a "Can't You Hear Me Knocking" jam at the end. Last Bold as Love, 12/14/95 Binghamton, NY [67 shows].

A sardined-packed Key Arena crowd tried to find their footing during another up-and-down first set. Even the usually forceful Sloth wilted under these cramped quarters. Axis turned my thoughts to Jimi and what could have been, much like the first set. In set II, a bombastic DwD faded into a soulful Jesus Left Chicago (sweet!). During Trey's solo/vocal part in Scent, he offered the crowd the Brady Bunch theme. Tweezer was the set's centerpiece, starting slow then growing, eventually leading to a Sweet Emotion sing-a-long which led back into the DwD jam. Fantastic! —Greg Kelly

Listening to set II of this show on tape puts me in one of the best moods. Everything about it is excellent; you can't appreciate the setlist unless you hear this tape. I had never been a big Down with Disease fan but I love all 25 minutes of it. The guitar following the Mule duel in Scent is probably the coolest I have heard. But Tweezer is what really does it for me: nice jamming—a Sweet Emotion tease and chorus—and then the song somehow morphs back into DWD. This set is a DWD/Tweezerfest and it kicks ass. The feeling of hearing this tape is like the ultimate back massage. —Adam Rizzuti

In the depths of a dense Tweezer jam, the band started singing the "Sweet Emotion" refrain. As that died out, Trey got a sweet melody going that ever so slowly drifted into the Down with Disease theme. It took about 30 seconds until it was clear he was definitely playing DwD, at which time Fishman realized it, too, and immediately accelerated his slower drum beat to the fast DwD rhythm, more or less ruining the delicacy of the segue Trey constructed. But the jam in the DwD Reprise is cool—they don't sing the refrain, instead jamming out for a few minutes before ending with the Stones jam "Can't You Hear Me Knockin'." Great set! —Tyler Harris

11/29/96 [ACCESSIBILITY: ••] [ATTEND. 12,640; CAP. 12,640] [TIX $25]

Cow Palace, Daly City, CA

I: Frankenstein, NICU, CTB, Character Zero, Divided Sky, Bathtub Gin, Life on Mars, Maze, Suzie

II: Wilson > Simple > Sparks, Sparkle, Taste, Swept Away > Steep, YEM, Waste, Harry Hood

E: Sample

Last Sparks, 10/29/94 Spartanburg, SC [173 shows].

Playing at the Cow Palace on the outskirts of San Francisco, the boys didn't play a particularly bad show, but then again, they didn't play a particularly good one either. Like many of the gigs during this tour, Phish oscillated between solid jamming (including a cool Simple > Jam > Sparks and a very good Taste) and dullsville. At the Cow Palace, I found it to be more of the latter. —Dave Sharpe

I had front row seats, smack dab in between Trey and Mike. Near the end of the first set, during Maze, I was crushed into the rail. I looked back and to my surprise there was a tweaked-out hippie looking at me. He had particles of vomit dangling from his long beard and dreads. He then threw up all over the guy right next to me, as everyone pushed him around. Lots of people tried to ask him questions, but all that would come out of his mouth was a big "AAAAAAH!" All of us found him to be more entertaining than Phish. Finally the security guards let him over the rail, and walked behind him as he was jumping up and down, screaming at Trey and Page. But of course guys like that always make it back to the front. Sure enough, we looked over to our left later in the set and there he was, bothering someone else as he yelped, "AAAAAH!" So when Phish came back for the second set, we all started yelling like the guy did, pointing at Phish. Trey and Page looked at us as if we were nuts, and just laughed. The next night in Sacramento, I saw the guys I watched the show with the night before. We greeted each other, and they told me that "AAAAAAH!" was in the house. We all had a big laugh. It was a demented, memorable Phish experience! —Mike Hood

11/30/96 [ACCESSIBILITY: ••••] [ATTEND. 7,800; CAP. 7,800] [TIX $22.50]

Arco Arena, Sacramento, CA

I: Runaway Jim, PYITE, All Things, Bouncing, Stash, Fluffhead, Old Home Place, Uncle Pen, Caspian, Chalkdust

II: La Grange, It's Ice, Glide, Brother, Contact, Also Sprach > Timber Ho, Taste, Funky Bitch, Amazing Grace, Amazing Grace Jam

E: Possum

John McEuen on banjo for Old Home Place and Uncle Pen. Peter Apfelbaum on tenor saxophone for Timber Ho, Taste, and Funky Bitch. McEuen on lap slide guitar and Apfelbaum on tenor saxophone for Amazing Grace Jam and Possum. "Do That Stuff" teases in Also Sprach. Last Amazing Grace Jam, 10/20/95 Cedar Rapids, IA [103 shows].

This show featured two awesome guests which definitely affected Phish's sound. In the first set, John McEuen came out for Old Home Place and Uncle Pen. Both of these songs benefited from his banjo. Then during the second set, Peter Apfelbaum came out for Timber Ho, Taste and Funky Bitch. Taste with saxophone is so different—there's a spacey jazz feel to the jam. Later, McEuen returns with slide guitar and they jam on the Amazing Grace theme following Phish's a cappella version. —Jeffrey Ellenbogen

My favorite non-Vegas west coast '96 show had almost all highs, with some being eight miles or so up. The opening six songs had me thinking '92–'93, not only by the titles but in style, too. Funky, intense, groovy all tweaked together, with Fluff growing to amazing status. Then John McEuen of the N.G.D.B. joined the band for two traditionals. The audience, myself included, pondered what the second set would be: no one guessed right. After opening the second set with five songs not repeated out west (in the U.S., anyway), a sax player guested on an incredible 2001 > Timber Ho. The rest of the set featured all the guests making great music and spirit. This is a must-have. —Greg Kelly

Everyone I talked to loved this show, but I found it enjoyable only to the extent that the special guests infused the second set with a very different sound. (Listen to Apfelbaum's contribution to the opening of Taste for the most pleasing example of this.) The guests left Phish mostly unable to jam out, so they responded with an unusual setlist (La Grange, Glide, Brother). —Dave Sharpe

12/1/96 [ACCESSIBILITY: •••] [ATTEND. 8,402; CAP. 9,000] [TIX $25–$27]

Pauley Pavilion, University of California at Los Angeles, Los Angeles, CA

I: Peaches, Poor Heart, Cavern, CTB, Character Zero, Curtain > Down with Disease, Train Song, Horse > Silent, Sample, Antelope

II: Tweezer > Sparkle, Simple > Day in the Life, Reba, Swept Away > Steep > Tweezer Reprise > Johnny B. Goode, Slave

E: Highway to Hell

Trey sings "Norton Charleton Heston" instead of "Marco Esquandolis" in Antelope. Last Peaches, 12/31/94 Boston, MA [144 shows].

The revival (after almost two years) of Peaches En Regalia ("Written by a hometown boy, Frank Zappa," Trey announced) set the tone for a great evening of music in the intimate Pauley Pavilion. Both seats featured good jams that didn't stretch on for too long—DwD in the first, Tweezer and Reba in the second—and both sets appeared to close at least once before the band decided to tack on one extra song (or, in the case of the second set, two. The bonus Slave was another major highlight). —Rich Mazer

It's the second set after a decent first set where we saw the first Peaches since 12/31/94. My friend Dave and I were kicking back during the setbreak when a rather large guy in the front row, wearing a Hideo Nomo jersey, went to get an ice cream sandwich. (Nomo is a pitcher for the Dodgers who is from Japan and has a wild windup.) Through Tweezer and Sparkle, this guy was jumping up and down right in front of Trey. Trey kept on looking down at him and laughing. During Simple this guy is going nuts and it looks like he's going to throw his ice cream right onto Trey. After the saxophone verse, Trey screams, "Hey Nomo!!!" It's pretty easy to hear on the tapes. No one who was at the show seems to remember it until I play the tapes for them—I don't even know if "Nomo" knew that Trey was screaming at him. He was just having such a good time (and looking funny as hell doing it). —Marc Olson

12/2/96 [ACCESSIBILITY: ••] [ATTEND. 5,818; CAP. 10,000] [TIX $22–$24.50]
America West Arena, Phoenix, AZ
I: Rocky Top > AC/DC Bag, Bouncing, YEM > I Didn't Know, Theme, Gumbo, Julius
II: Ya Mar, Divided Sky, Wolfman's, Taste, Free, Scent of a Mule > Harry Hood, Adeline **E:** Fire

Fishman on vacuum for I Didn't Know.

Sunny Arizona! The weather was hot and the scene was awesome. I would never have called Rocky Top to open the show, but it was fun. A little later in the set, they pulled out YEM, the definite highlight. In set II, a nice Wolfman's flowed right into Taste, then the boys did Scent of a Mule. But before the Russian jam segment, they broke right into Harry—it really came out of nowhere. What a Harry it was, very long and the definite highlight of the show for me. It wasn't a crazy show, but I just had a wonderful time. —Dom DeLuca

[12/3/96]
Great Western Forum, Inglewood, CA
Star Spangled Banner

Phish sang a cappella before the Lakers-Supersonics NBA game.

At first I didn't recognize the band (it's the first time I've ever seen Fishman in men's clothes). But once I spotted the four sharply dressed fluffheads at courtside, I grabbed my pal Frank and we ran over to meet them. We wished them all good luck and I shook Trey's hand, telling him they were going to kick ass. And kick ass they did. Clocking in at just over a minute, the boys did us proud with perfect pitch and soaring harmonies. They trotted off

Friday, December 6, 1996

ALADDIN THEATER, Las Vegas, NV

Wow. Las Vegas. We arrived to this show the day before and pulled right into the parking lot at the Aladdin. We were standing next to the car when this elderly couple came up to us and greeted us: "You guys must be Phish fans." We chatted with them, then they said "You must know our daughter Amy," referring to Amy Skelton. Of course!

We walked into the Aladdin and scored a cheap room for only $25 that night. The night of the show it jumped to $80, but we got a few people in on it and figured what the heck? It was the last show of the tour—let's go out in style, plus the show was downstairs!

Still not having a ticket, I thought I would never get into the show. It was a very small theater and the last show of the tour—who would want to give their ticket up? I waited in the lobby of the hotel, asking everyone who came in if they had an extra. After only an hour of doing this, I found a guy who sold me his extra for $20! I couldn't have been more thrilled—I ran upstairs and hid my golden ticket.

My friend also scored a $20 ticket from a kind guy staying across the hall from us. We put our stuff in the hotel room, settled in, then hit the streets of Las Vegas for some evening fun.

The morning of the show, I woke up excited for the last show of the tour. The will call window was right inside the Aladdin, and the heads were pouring in. The tourists had no clue what was going on. I heard Aladdin staffers whispering to people, "These guys are just like the Grateful Dead people, very nice." There was also a rodeo convention going on at the same time in the hotel so sparks flew between the cowboys and the hippies. Pretty funny stuff to watch! Vegas Ticketmaster released more tickets to the sold out show that afternoon, so most folks grabbed tickets. By 7 P.M. I saw more than twenty people selling their extras for face value (though I did see one poor guy snatch a ticket for $150.)

I headed into the show about 7:15, incredibly excited. The theater was beautiful. I couldn't believe they were going to play there, in one of the best theaters I have seen them in. I chose my spot on Page's side right above the first section, where I had an amazing view and tons of room. The lights went down and they broke into a sweet Wilson. Peaches followed—the best version of '96, in my opinion (even though there weren't too many). The set kept rocking with an incredible 2001, the longest and funkiest version I'd ever heard; a groovy You Enjoy Myself followed by a hilarious vocal jam about donuts; and a spacey, long Down with Disease that led into Frankenstein to rock the first set out.

It was such an amazing set that I didn't know what to expect for set two. I didn't want to get my hopes up too much because I'd been to a lot of tour enders and they hadn't all been great. I was just hoping for some good songs.

After two months on the road, it had come down to only one set. The band took the stage and kicked into a smokin' Julius to start. They kept the speed up with an average, upbeat Sparkle, then dropped the bomb—an intense Mike's Song with a wicked fat jam that took off and eventually led straight into Simple. There wasn't much of a Simple tease—I could tell immediately which direction they were heading. Simple was long and great, with a cool jam afterwards, and when it ended, I thought it was time for Weekapaug.

But the boys thought differently, and before I knew it, Fish rolled out the drumbeat for Harry. I couldn't have been happier—I wanted to hear one more Harry before tour ended and I got it. Harry was beautiful—Trey's solos were amazing and Page's key work was breathtaking. After "You can feel good about Hood," they went into the jam they do after the verse and then Mike kicked into Weekapaug. Things couldn't have been going better. This Weekapaug was amazing. Almost ten minutes into it they had a groove going where they would stop and then start back up, then stop again. Each time I thought it was over, but no, they'd kick back into it. Finally, gloriously, it finished.

After Phish took the stage for one last a cappella, Sweet Adeline, they ended the set with an amazing Good Times Bad Times that really summed up my feelings about the tour.

Now it was time for the encore, I was just waiting for a Slave or Suzie encore, nothing special, but the lights went down and they took the stage. I noticed a few others with them, and my friend whispered to me it was Les Claypool. I had no clue what to expect. They broke into a song and I couldn't believe my ears—it was Harpua, and what a weird version it was. They totally slowed down the song. The story section arrived and Les Claypool told a little story about weed, then Trey talked about Las Vegas and camping while more special guests came out and started yodelling.

The whole place was just in shock. Everyone stared at the stage, sharing this incredible moment. The yodelling ended and Trey went back to the story, saying Jimmy was on his way to Las Vegas but was stopped at the border by four Elvises who told him couldn't come to Vegas unless he sang an Elvis song better than them.

That's when they started to play Suspicious Minds. I was freaking out. I stopped dancing for a few seconds and looked at the stage, where I saw four Elvis impersonators and Fishman, who was pretending to fight them. Then he took the mic and sang the song.

After the song, Jimmy had won and the Poster/Harpua fight materialized. I was really hoping for an ending, but I didn't know what to expect especially after this unique version and what happened when they played Harpua at the Clifford Ball. But they finished it with the wonderful ending I love, making this the best Harpua I'd ever heard and, at half an hour long, the longest encore I'd ever seen them do.

But it wasn't over. They broke into a really hot Suzie Greenberg featuring Les and most of the rest of Primus, plus everyone else (even the Elvises) just having a blast, dancing around. At the end of Suzie, an Elvis took the mic and led the band into a hilarious Suzie Q jam. Suzie/Suzie ended and they thanked us all for a great tour.

What a show! I think it may have been the best show I've ever seen, definitely top three at least. Afterward we headed back to the hotel for the post-show festivities—it was the end of the tour and we wanted to "party down" with the family we made in the months we spent on the road. Those months of my life taught me a lot, showed me a lot and will never be forgotten. Never had such a good time—thank you, Phish!

—Dom DeLuca

court to hearty applause. Then we ambushed them again, shaking their hands and engaging them in witty banter as they passed by. It wasn't much of a conversation, but at least we didn't ask them to play Destiny Unbound. —Mike Indgin

12/4/96 [ACCESSIBILITY: •••] [ATTEND. 5,779; CAP. 9,500] [TIX $22.50–$24.50]
San Diego Sports Arena, San Diego, CA
I: My Friend, Chalkdust, Horn, Uncle Pen, Timber Ho, Sample, Train Song, Guyute, Character Zero, Lizards, Bowie
II: Ha Ha Ha, Mike's > Caspian > Sparkle > PYITE, Life on Mars, Reba, Lawn Boy, Weekapaug
E: Jesus Left Chicago

Lawn Boy dedicated to the tour's caterers, who were brought up onstage to dance during the song.

Back in California once again, the weather was beautiful. We hung out on the beach all day in San Diego, enjoying the water and the weather, then headed over to the parking lot where we heard everyone groveling for Vegas tickets. Inside, a really sweet first set included a crazy Guyute which just rocked me, a sweet Timber Ho and a ripping Bowie to end it. Set II opened with Ha Ha Ha into a Mike's Song with a phat, funky jam that led into Caspian. Later in the set, Page took the microphone for Lawn Boy and Trey invited the tour's caterers on stage and danced with two of them. A hot Weekapaug rocked this set out and closed it. Such a fun, well-played set! The encore, Jesus Left Chicago, was unusual but also fun to hear (great solos). So this was it—Las Vegas was next, the last and final stop we all so anticipated. —Dom DeLuca

It was a shock when they broke out Mike's Groove during the second set in Vegas because they'd played such a strong version of it (Weekapaug especially) the show before in San Diego. The entire second set of this show is really worth hearing, for the powerful Weekapaug and gorgeous Reba. —Melissa Wolcott

12/6/96 [ACCESSIBILITY: ••••] [ATTEND. 6,487; CAP. 6,487] [TIX $22.50]
Aladdin Theater for the Performing Arts, Las Vegas, NV
I: Wilson, Peaches, Poor Heart, Also Sprach > Llama, YEM, CTB, Down with Disease > Frankenstein
II: Julius, Sparkle, Mike's > Simple > Harry Hood > Weekapaug, Adeline, GTBT
E: Harpua > Les Claypool Rap > Harpua > Yodeling > Harpua > Suspicious Minds > Harpua > Suzie

"Blister in the Sun" tease in Simple. Les Claypool on bass and Larry LaLonde (both of Primus) on guitar for encore. John McEuen and Anamiekl and Heather August yodeled. Four Elvis impersonators joined Phish onstage for Suspicious Minds, with Fishman taking over on lyrics. Suzie featured everyone already onstage, plus Brian Mantia (of Primus) on drums. "Suzie Q" jam (sung by one of the Elvis impersonators) at the end of Suzie.

I must write of this show; it was like no other. 2001 > Llama, YEM was superb, really reaching. Sweet Adeline kinda sucked because they didn't use mics—the Aladdin isn't that small, guys. Otherwise, a magical night. How about the set-long Harpua madness as an encore! I've had dreams (nightmares?) about the four Elvii singing around Fish. The band dug Vegas! —Dave Matson

YEM featured one of Mike's finest bass jams. Mike's > Simple > Jam is one of the best ever. Harry soared high and hard into a tantalizing Weekapaug where Trey delivers a great blues solo. A truly rocking Good Times Bad Times ends it well. Did I mention the 30-minute encore with Les and Larry from Primus featuring four Elvii and yodelers during Harpua and Suzie? The best show ever! —Chip Croteau

This was the last show of the fall tour. The whole second set was incredible, and the encore was just all-out amazing. It started out with Harpua, then two guys from Primus came out to sing Wildwood Weed and then yodelers came out for Cowboy's Sweetheart. It then went back into Harpua then Fish and a bunch of Elvis impersonators sang Suspicious Minds (by Elvis), back into Harpua, then everything just went crazy during Suzie Greenberg. —Matt Fitone

A great first set, including four instrumentals, was topped by an even greater second set. Check out the "Blister in the Sun" teases in Simple, and the encore, which needs its own tape! Basically, it's Harpua > Suzie, but there is much more: half of Primus, yodelers, and four Elvis impersonators (and Tubbs as the fifth). This is the funniest Harpua ever (always bet on 17!), then a great Suzie with something like 14 people onstage! Even the Elvii took turns singing during Suzie. —Jon Bahr

One of the best shows of 1996. It includes the first 2001 > Llama ever and a crazy Down with Disease in the first set. The second set Mike's > Simple > Harry > Weekapaug is awesome—the best Weekapaug I've ever heard. Then a crazy jammed out Good Times Bad Times closes the set. Harpua as the encore is a slightly moderated version (they sing the chorus slower). The Elvis impersonators are great—just hilarious! —Kevin Weiss

The 30-minute encore is by far my favorite Harpua ever. In the story, Jimmy and Poster are walking through the desert when they begin to hear Suspicious Minds (this is when the Elvis impersonators came out on stage), then they ended up in a casino where Poster saw Harpua and they fought. Phish and their guests jammed into various songs such as "I Wish I Was a Cowboy's Sweetheart" and "Wildwood Weed," along with yodelers. It ended with Suzie G > Suzie Q. —Chuck Adams

Woohoo! Elvis impersonators, Primus, 45-minute Harpua encore, a how long Mike's Groove—the list goes on! A must have show—not a poor moment for four hours! A hairy, groovin' time, fer sure! —Paul Sheets

After a 12-hour drive from Boulder, CO, my friends and I were hurting. Driving all through the night in a snowstorm had the team morale down, but we knew what was in store: Phish's last show of the tour, and their first time in Las Vegas. After a power nap, we felt it was our duty to go check out the town before the show. As the four of us walked out of Caesar's Palace, we saw the band's bus. I knocked on the bus door but there was no one there. After a hearty meal, me and my friend Pete walked back up to the bus and gave another knock. The bus driver nodded "no," but all of a sudden, Trey

12/6/96 Aladdin Theater, Las Vegas, NV

"Las Vega$"

The city of sin seemed like an incongruous place for a Phish concert, but the fair city of Las Vegas, NV, was nevertheless tapped as the site for Phish's tour-finishing show. Though the band had played the west coast for years, they had somehow always missed Vegas. The fall *Schvice* made it clear that the band was excited for the gig—Phish's first "casino show" since their July 18, 1991, gig with the Giant Country Horns at Hampton Beach Casino on the coast of New Hampshire.

Besides playing a town they'd never hit before, the Vegas gig also offered the only theater show of the tour—the 9,000-seat Aladdin would play host to the band. As phans started pouring into town the day before the show, a scene developed which many likened to the earlier days—the band's bus was parked out front, and a number of fans chatted it up with Trey, Page, Mike and Fish during their weekend in Vegas. Though the show was sold out, plenty of extras floated around, burning those who paid big bucks for a ticket in advance of the evening's performance.

The show—considered the best of the year by many—got off to a fast start with Wilson and Peaches en Regalia, which had been revived earlier in the week in Los Angeles for the first time since New Year's '94. Building on their early momentum, the band dove into a long Also Sprach Zarathustra (the longest-ever, at least until New Year's Eve) and an incredible You Enjoy Myself (complete with a "donut" vocal jam). And the band kept packing it in—Down with Disease, Cars Trucks Buses and a Frankenstein closer took everyone to setbreak.

When the second set opened with Julius, it seemed a fitting tribute to the nearby Caesar's Palace. But when Phish kept jamming—and jamming—on the tune, it turned into something even more powerful. After a quick Sparkle, the band erupted into Mike's Song even though they'd played it two nights earlier in San Diego. Creating a sequence that some phans thought they'd only dream of, the band took Mike's into a very long, gorgeous Simple and then rattled out the start of Harry Hood. When Weekapaug sandwiched this foursome, the Aladdin erupted. The rockingest GTBT ever—at least until 12/30/96—closed the set.

The encore, of course, is the stuff of which legends are made. Les Claypool joined Phish onstage for the first time since Laguna Seca Daze 5/28/94, and this time hauled his fellow Primus bandmates along with him. And that was only the start of the cavalcade of guest stars, from John McEuen and yodeling friends to four Elvis impersonators who squared off with Fish at the front of the stage. The first Harpua since Plattsburgh was, joyously, completed, then the band took it around into Suzie Greenberg, complete with a little "Suzie Q" action from the Elvii at the end.

The tour complete, a long night of partying on the strip lay ahead.

came out to talk to us. "Are you psyched to play tonight Trey?" "I am so fucking psyched, man." Talking to him and Mike for awhile got us totally pumped up for the show: Trey is not only psyched to play, he is fucking psyched. Then my friend Pete says, "So, Mike, you gonna drop some bombs on us tonight?" Mike looked at Pete and said, "What?" Catching up with my two other friends later on, I told them what happened and their jaws hit the ground. "Yeah, we were hanging with Phish in Vegas." Not bad, considering it was my birthday. The Aladdin is a cozy venue that seats about 7,000. Wilson, Peaches really got things started off right and there were no signs of slowing down. They played the best 2001 I have ever heard with Page stealing the show early. YEM, Down with Disease > Frankenstein were all sweet and it was apparent the second set was going to rip. The Julius opener was a revival version for me, blowing the lid off the song. Mike's > Simple > Hood > Weekapaug was sick. Over an hour of music right there. Weekapaug was real good, with the band breaking in between the song and jumping right back in like it was a joke. Good Times closer summed up everything, with Page belting out his lines. I am not even going to get into the huge encore. Primus and Phish, any questions? —Brett Pessin

Old school scene. Kids hanging out in the city of cheese. What a trip. —Langston Knipler

1996 HOLIDAY TOUR

After the 1995 Holiday run, during which the band played three of their most popular concerts ever, fans embarked on the '96 run with soaring expectations. Perhaps it was inevitable that the band wouldn't rise to the incredible heights they achieved the year before, but they still gave it a hell of a shot. As had become tradition, no songs were repeated in the course of the run—something that seemed to hamper the New Year's Eve show, considering the mass of jam songs played in Philadelphia, especially during the second set on 12/29. That night's Spectrum show was named by most as the best of the lot musically, with the New Year's Eve show offering plenty of fun (a Tweezer Reprise first set closer, a massive balloon drop, and an appearance by the Boston Community Choir) but not as much pure jamming as some hoped to hear. Still, it was New Year's, it was Boston, and it was a whole lot of fun.

12/28/96 [ACCESSIBILITY: ••••] [ATTEND. 18,324; CAP. 18,324] [TIX $24–$27]
CoreStates Spectrum, Philadelphia, PA

I: Runaway Jim, NICU, Wolfman's, It's Ice, Billy Breathes, Ginseng Sullivan, Melt, Mango, Frankenstein

II: Makisupa > Maze, Bouncing > TMWSIY > Avenu, Mike's > Strange Design > Weekapaug, Star Spangled Banner

E: Johnny B. Goode

Trey spoke about his fondness for the Flyers (John LeClair in particular) and thanked someone for throwing him a Tickle-Me-Elmo doll. (The Elmo Doll was thrown by phan Hillary Schupf.) The band also dedicated the Star Spangled Banner to Kate Smith, the singer who sang God Bless America before Flyers games.

First show of the New Year's run and I just couldn't wait to get in. The Runaway Jim, NICU opener got my hopes up as we were expecting this to be an anything-goes first show of the run. Although the rest of the setlist seems pretty average, these guys were just on all night. The band came out of TMWSIY > Avenu Malkenu right into Mike's Song, which really got us going. Strange Design brought things down a little—thank God for Mike's opening notes going into Weekapaug. The closing of this show kind of killed the flow. Oh well. —Peter Bukley

A solid first set with its fair share of treats—Jim opener, Split, Frankenstein closer. The second set was full of pleasant surprises. Maze was an early tour surprise as the band stretched it to the limits and further! But MWS > Avenu > Mike's! was an even bigger treat. —Eric Acquafredda

Monday, December 30, 1996

FLEETCENTER, Boston, MA

During set one I was in a horrible, horrible place, physically as well as mentally. The group of boys next to the aisle where I was attempting to dance (not an inch of space for that) sang every word to Sloth in my ear and a posse of seven sixteen-year-old girls wearing big old vests, little backpacks and perfume crowded my moving space. I was set to move but I could barely make it up the steps it was so packed.

I started thinking some horrible thoughts. The fact that I was even thinking in the first place is pretty telling—my mind was definitely not on the show. Anyway, all of a sudden I understood what all those former Phish fans have been saying—it's just not the same —but they say it based on the sound and I think it based on the crowd. Then I realized how closely tied together these two are.

Just as the crowd affects the music, the music affects the crowd. People clap to the beat whenever there is a familiar song or rhythm, people scream during a cappella, people talk during mellow jams. In Philadelphia, Page was going off during YEM and as soon as an obvious rhythm came along, masses of people started clapping to it. It seemed like he had to change his jam. Point is, if people desire to clap, they want a "normal" beat, and a normal beat is the opposite of a crazy jam. Therefore, the masses do not want a crazy jam. And the masses have power. I believe that because they are driving me nuts.

I ended up in the hallway leading into the section to the side/rear of the stage, though even there security dudes kept coming through and telling people to leave. I perfected the ability to shut them out, to keep on twirling as they walked through all of us. Eventually they made all the twirlers go outside of the stage area by the neon nacho stands—out where it's impossible to hear the music and they pull down this big black curtain so we couldn't see in.

What do we do? I talked to lots of people who were weirded out by that stuff too—all the people exiled to the hall with me. But the band can't really say, "Please don't clap to our music."

And who am I to designate an "us" and a "them"? It can't be measured by the number of shows—Phish shows are the thing to do; everybody and their grandma went to Plattsburgh. Dancing is no measure—some of the most intense phans don't move a muscle during a whole show.

But that is precisely the good stuff—the membership, the community, the family. I've felt the family thing big time since Vegas and it has grown greater and greater.

The bond seems to grow out of necessity, as a means of survival. As the crowd grows bigger, the family grows tighter. I love the feeling of dancing around strangers, of stopping to catch my breath after Phish has led us on some phenomenal musical journey and smiling at the guy next to me who shares the same glow. And I have met some wonderful people and for the most part, except for the set in hell, I've found great people with whom to enjoy the show. And this fact, that there is still a family, that the smile of a stranger shared during AC/DC Bag can counter and bury all the negative feelings I experienced earlier, is what it's all about.

I know that I can get there still, that no matter what, I love these guys and will never stop going. But it has become a big challenge—of overcoming the crowd, of accepting that we are nearing the end of the decade, that Phish is huge, that MSG is an unusual venue, that tickets are not a given, that Vegas was an exception, that even Great Woods is impossible, that the whole deal is new, that this change is natural and what is inevitable is liberating.

To allow myself to grove with this, to surrender to the flow so to speak and just be comfortable with this happening as it will, of course feels better than being bitter. I still admire attempts to awaken the masses, the flyers spread out which actually have to explain that it is important to be quiet at the beginning of Foam or in Divided Sky, the built-up frustration eventually manifested by a "SHUT UP!" to the babblers and screamers during Sweet Adeline.

And I can only hope more and more people will get the bug, will feel it, and Phish won't just be a "thing" but more like a "way." All I can say right now is that I still have one more night to go and that's all that really matters.

—Julie Beck

🐟 The first set contained an insane It's Ice bringing on a mid-set Ginseng, then closing with a kick-ass Frankenstein. A pretty decent first set beholds a killer second set! Opened with Makisupa (Trey said "stink stank stunk") into a long, drawn-out Maze. Tearing up the rest of the set was TMWSIY > a crazy Avenu which powerfully went into a fatty Mike's and then a subtle Strange Design, and, yup, Weekapaug. What a way to ring in the Holiday Tour! —Adam Brilhante

12/29/96 [ACCESSIBILITY: ••••] [ATTEND. 18,324; CAP. 18,324] [TIX $24–$27]
CoreStates Spectrum, Philadelphia, PA
I: Poor Heart, Caravan, Cavern, Taste, Guelah, Train Song, Rift, Free, Squirming Coil, La Grange
II: Bowie, Day in the Life, Bathtub Gin, Lizards, YEM > Rotation Jam > Sixteen Candles > YEM, Harpua
E: Rocky Top

Sixteen Candles performed by Mike on piano, after he rotated there during the Rotation Jam and after he repeatedly yelled "Sex!" "Champagne Supernova" jam in Harpua, with Tom Marshall on vocals. Last Caravan, 12/2/94 Davis, CA [160 shows]. Last Rotation Jam, 12/15/95 Philadelphia [74 shows]. Concert debut: Sixteen Candles.

🐟 The second set started off with an absolutely sick Bowie. After listening to the tape, at 17+ minutes, I declared it my personal favorite Bowie since 12/29/94 Providence. In Bathtub Gin, Page absolutely destroyed his keyboard, going insane in the opening solo. After a quality Lizards, it began. The enchanting opening notes of YEM filled the Spectrum. I watched Fishman walk around the back of the stage after Trey jumped on the sticks. I expected a nice Fishman tune, but wait—rotation jam. Later, Fishman takes the bass from Page and starts slappin' away. During this, Mike is going off on the keys and Page picks up the guitar and jams. And let me tell you, Page rocks. They jammed hard, into Mike's beautiful cover of Sixteen Candles. What followed? "Oom pa pa, oom pa pa," the sounds of Harpua. —Chip Croteau

🐟 The second set of this show was the best of the '96 holiday run. Through trademark Phishiness (Mike's take on Sixteen Candles) to superb musicanship (David Bowie) to special guests (Tom Marshall doing his best Liam Gallagher) to awe-inspiring theatrics and light work (YEM), this set defined the experience that is Phish. Throw a Harpua into the broth and you've got quite a meal. —Lee Schiller

🐟 During Harpua, Trey tells of Harpua and Poster Nutbag's trip to Hell. There they meet the Uber-Demon—Tom Marshall dressed as Liam Gallagher of Oasis. This all happens as "Champagne Supernova" plays on "Jimmy's radio." It was so funny watching all of the teeny-boppers freak out thinking it was really one of the Gallagher brothers. What a great way to build up to New Year's! —Peter Bukley

12/30/96 [ACCESSIBILITY: ••••] [ATTEND. 18,484; CAP. 18,484]* [TIX $25]
FleetCenter, Boston, MA
I: Ya Mar, Sloth, Llama, Gumbo, Reba, Talk, Funky Bitch, Theme, GTBT
II: Timber Ho, Uncle Pen, AC/DC Bag, Guyute, Tweezer > Lifeboy, Scent of a Mule, Slave
E: Possum

Trey on acoustic guitar for Talk. PA cut out during Funky Bitch, leading to a "silent jam" for about three and a half minutes before system became operational again and Funky Bitch continued. Steven Wright on bell for Scent of a Mule, which had a Page/Mike duel.

🐟 Perhaps NYE fell flat because they played so hard the night before. Set one was a Page-fest: four organ solo songs to open the set, including a very grooving Ya Mar opener. We all know that the sound went out during Funky Bitch. Too bad: Trey was taking the finest, bluesiest solo he'd ever taken—nothing spacey, nothing experimental. Just raw power. Couldn't the sound have gone out during Talk when we were all sitting down? —Scott Kushner

🐟 A very good show musically and a very different set list. A few phans around me commented on the set list being "songs plays less often but not often enough for NYE." One fan was very upset, saying, "They're playing all throw-backs." Personally, I found the show very enjoyable. The night was almost like waiting not to hear songs because that meant they would play them on NYE. The highlight, without a doubt, was Possum. —Jeff Bernier

Tuesday, December 31, 1996

FLEETCENTER, Boston, MA

My pomposity about the previous night has lessened. New Year's Eve was totally phenomenal: great show, great crowd, great New Year's dig, thousands of balloons and a choir.

My night was just wonderful. I had a great feeling the whole show—I met a guy who is moving to New Mexico, ran into people I haven't seen since college and even high school, and found a broom.

We left our stuff under a platform, and a champagne bottle broke right there—glass everywhere. I decided to wander around the area a little bit and went over to the hallway where I had been the night before. Not surprisingly, there was this funky guy I had met last night, one of those people it was fun to just share a show experience with even though I didn't know him at all. But the amazing thing was he happened to have a broom and was sweeping the aisle. I borrowed the broom to bring to my section and swept up the glass. It felt really good to be doing that; it was totally bizarre yet natural.

The whole night was like this, even the song choices. Everything was natural in its obscurity (or obscure as its nature, I'm not sure). Axilla I and Tweezer Reprise. The simultaneous intensity and simplicity of the balloons, the professionalism yet unexpectedness of the choir and Bohemian Rhapsody.

The night was entirely magical in a very real, tangible way. I feel like I was able to break out of my rut, to dive beyond the annoyances and just fully be there and flow with everything. I had a great spot to dance in. Behind Page's side, rear stage, is definitely the place for me now. Those times that I actually opened my eyes, I found I had an amazing view. It was really cool to see the faces of the people in the front rows. The balloons were so amazing that I could barely close my eyes during Down with Disease and this experience of having my eyes open was completely new and invigorating for me.

I've met some great people these past couple of days. But the greatest individuals I encountered during these shows were a group of four guys from a high school in Boston's surrounding suburban vortex. These guys were sophomores and juniors, younger than the kids I've led on summer programs, yet I totally connected with them. They were right on, intense, funny individuals. I met them on the T into the first Boston Garden show. We talked the whole ride there, and I remember this blanket-clad guy Nick telling me about his school, show experiences, and his life's experiences.

He had some really great things to say; they all did. I ran into them again on the T on the way home after New Year's. It felt like a reunion. These guys were inspiring. Knowing that there are high school kids out there with such intense thoughts and powers of expression was redeeming after encountering the whining, drunk high school kids at the show because Phish has become the thing to do New Year's Eve. These guys were my last Phish interaction of these shows and it was with them that I said good-bye to another New Year's run. I couldn't imagine a better sense of closure.

This interaction with these guys just epitomizes my whole experience over these days. It's like this perpetual mingling of anonymity and intense belonging. Who knows if I'll ever see these kids again. I am not sure if I ever told them my name, but in our few interactions, we developed a bond, a familiarity, an appreciation of each other which I will not forget. There is just something amazing about going to shows alone, unattached to any specific individuals, any plans.

I thrived on the anonymity. I felt I was just another girl dancing, another person there for the experience that was there for all to indulge in. All the while, I know that everyone around me is equally as anonymous and this is something we all share, something that brings us together, something which allows us to belong to one another.

It is this union which I am left with, and this union which I carry with me from show to show and which carries me through the times between. And as always, as a Phish chapter closes, I am overwhelmed with mixed feelings of loss, emptiness, inspiration and rejuvenation.

And I know that no matter what, no matter how big this thing gets, no matter how overwhelmed I feel by the crowd, as long as the band still plays, the unions will inevitably exist, and I will continue to go to the shows.

—Julie Beck

My passion for Phish is outlined in the cycle of energy that flows through both the band members and all the phans at the show. How nice it is to use the Funky Bitch from set one as a clear example. Yes, the sound blew out and yes, many people were reminded of the Rift the year before at Worcester 12/28/95. But no, the energy did not stop flowing. Phish played on. We couldn't hear Trey play with his teeth, or Page play with his toes, but we still felt the energy flow—the energy that perhaps is my only healthy addiction. —Michelle Hirsch

12/31/96 [ACCESSIBILITY: ••••] [ATTEND. 18,484; CAP. 18,484]* [TIX $30]
FleetCenter, Boston, MA
I: Axilla, Peaches, PYITE, CTB, Stash, Horse > Silent, Divided Sky, Sample, Tweezer Reprise
II: Chalkdust, Wilson, Sparkle, Simple > Swept Away > Steep > Harry Hood > Caspian, Character Zero
III: Also Sprach > New Year's Countdown > Auld Lang Syne > Down with Disease, Suzie, Antelope, Bohemian Rhapsody, Julius
E: Amazing Grace

Remote-controlled miniature hot air balloon floated around the venue between the second and third sets. Arena clock counted down to midnight, starting after the end of the second set at 11:10 P.M. Giant balloon drop (reportedly a world record) from arena ceiling flooded the stage and floor during Auld Lang Syne and Down with Disease. Boston Community Choir on vocals for Bohemian Rhapsody, Julius, and Amazing Grace. FM broadcast on WBCN-Boston on 1/1/97. Concert debut: Bohemian Rhapsody.

New Year's Eve!! How lucky we were to get tickets for this show. Colder on this night—the drum circle moved inside; police tried but couldn't break it up. First set was solid, second set was solid, third set was phenomenal. 2001 > ALS > DWD with the balloons set the gear shift for the high gear of my soul. I have to say I wasn't thrilled with the encore but the post-show glow lasts throughout the year. —Ian Rufe

Ten minutes before midnight Phish took the stage with a slow-to-start 2001 that made me wish it was 2001 instead of 1997. Then, this is the shit: Auld Lang Syne > Down with Disease with a long end and middle jam that gave way to Suzie, new and full of life. Antelope was long and hot. Then the real magic came: the Boston Community Choir took the stage with their red robes and Phish began Bohemian Rhapsody. Next was Julius, and I've never seen a better version of this song. A sweet and mellow encore of Amazing Grace—the choir added so much. Get this tape. —Aaron Benton

WOW! Amazing! This show proves Phish is only going to get better and we'd better not miss it. The first of three sets set a nice tone for a fascinating night. Horse > Silent proves to be as beautiful as ever. The new songs in set II offer a taste of an ever-expanding future. The first songs of the third set are so wide open and generally free. Queen is back with Bohemian Rhapsody and the choir only made it better. —Andy Kahn

Yeah, I know NYE shows are always favorites. This one was different, though: no theme, just music (which is okay by me!). Very solid sets I and II, great buildup to climax with 2001 > Auld Lang Syne > DWD at 12:00. Then Bohemian Rhapsody with the Boston Community Choir. Where'd they get that idea for that? Only Phish could pull something like that off. —Mike D'Amico

This was the most disappointing Phish experience I'd ever had. My feeling has always been that the New Year's Eve show ought to be a celebration of improvisational rock (i.e., MSG '95 and Boston '94). This concert was not. Set one fell flat. Tweezer Reprise was the most energetic tune and it was half-assed. Set two was better, and the Character Zero was admittedly rocking, but it didn't make up for the show's shortcomings. I also felt very cheated that DWD was the New Year's Song instead of Brother. —Scott Kushner

The band's placement of Down with Disease as the "New Year's Song," where it also appeared (as a jam, anyway) in 1993, cemented it as the song of the year. After playing it only four times in 1995, DwD was lavished with attention by the boys, raising it to the ranks of their greatest jam songs. Hurrah! —Ernie Greene

The FleetCenter is large, sterile and boring. It was up to Phish to transform it into an intimate, friendly venue. Once again, they worked their magic and we all shared in the groove. Peace, love, and Happy New Year! —Amy Manning

12/31/96 FleetCenter, Boston, MA

"New Year's '96"

New Year's Eve, Phish, and Boston (or at least Worcester) are linked so closely that it was only a matter of time until Phish returned to Beantown for its year-end fete. After taking off for the Big Apple for New Year's '95, Phish returned home in 1996. The final days of the year found the band at the FleetCenter for a pair of gigs *Boston Globe* writer Steve Morse termed "the toughest tickets in a long time."

Indeed, the word on the scene for New Year's at the FleetCenter was "rejected," as Phish Tickets-by-Mail was forced to turn away more fans than ever. The ticketless partied in subzero weather, hoping against hope they would make it inside for the toasty atmosphere of New Year's Phish.

Those who were lucky enough to get in witnessed history yet again. Though the new FleetCenter lacked the character of the old Boston Garden, Phish tried to make up for it with T-shirts that labeled the venue the "new Boston Garden," and of course with their music.

A generally solid first set ended on a crazy note with a Tweezer Reprise that brought closure to the previous night's Tweezer, and a solid second set included long jams in Simple and Hood. Then, between the second and third sets, the crowd watched as a remote-controlled hot air balloon motored around the venue while scoreboards counted down to midnight starting at 11:10 P.M.

Sometime within about ten minutes of midnight, the band re-emerged and broke into Also Sprach Zarathustra. The crowd gave a huge cheer when the countdown clock hit 4:20 and an even louder roar as midnight arrived and thousands of balloons poured from the FleetCenter rafters while Phish kicked into Down with Disease. The set ended with a surprise visit by the Boston Community Choir, who backed up Phish during their first attempt at Queen's Bohemian Rhapsody. The singers stuck around for a go at Julius and Amazing Grace. Though microphone problems muted the choir in the arena, they came through loud and clear on the next day's FM-radio broadcast.

1997 WINTER Club Crawl

In February, the band headed back across the Atlantic to Europe, hoping to build on its audiences of the previous summer with three weeks of solo shows.

Musically, the tour became Phish's latest version of "let's show the doubters what we're made of." Grumblings that 1996 hadn't been the band's best year were forgotten as Phish played a string of extremely interesting, improvisational shows, utilizing a bunch of strange new tunes like Carini and Walfredo penned especially for the smaller venues of the European tour. Most notably, the tour saw the evolution of a funkier jamming style that continued to de-emphasize Trey's guitar leads that so defined Phish's style for much of the 1990s. Recognizing this musical evolution as a breakthrough for the band, Phish later mined the tour's penultimate show, in Hamburg, Germany, for the live album *Slip Stitch and Pass*.

2/13/97 [ACCESSIBILITY: •••]
Shepherds Bush Empire, London, England
I: Chalkdust, Wolfman's, Also Sprach > Stash, Walfredo, Taste, Waste, Poor Heart, Character Zero, Peaches, Love Me, Bowie
II: Julius, CTB, My Soul, PYITE > Jam > Slave, When the Circus Comes, Maze > Rocka William, Harry Hood, Frankenstein
E: Caspian, Johnny B. Goode

Maze unfinished. Concert debuts: Walfredo, Love Me (also known incorrectly as "Treat Me Like a Fool"), My Soul, When the Circus Comes, and Rocka William.

First show of the European tour! A very American crowd a couple thousand people strong packed into the Empire to see the boys break out a bunch of new songs, including two that feature the band members rotating instruments. For Walfredo, a little ditty about the band's experiences opening for Santana in summer '92, everyone moved one instrument to the right—Trey on piano and vocals, Mike on guitar, Fish on bass and Page on drums ("Fish played the vacuum and ruined your set" is one line I recall). Rocka William found Trey and Fish trading places, and Mike and Page swapping, with Fish belting out the pretty dark lyrics. A fun show got the tour started right. —James Daly

In a radio interview broadcast in London several days before the Shepherds Bush Empire gig, Mike and Fish revealed that Trey made it all the way to Newark airport before realizing he'd forgotten his passport. I guess even rock stars aren't exempt from international laws, because he missed his flight. —Scott Sifton

2/14/97 [ACCESSIBILITY: ••]
Le Botanique, Brussels, Belgium
I: Runaway Jim, NICU, YEM, Adeline, Axilla, It's Ice, Billy Breathes, Uncle Pen, Antelope
II: AC/DC Bag, Ya Mar, Down with Disease, Funky Bitch, Reba, Walfredo, Rocka William, Scent of a Mule > Day in the Life
E: Character Zero

Scent of a Mule unfinished.

Seeing Phish in Europe was amazing—the worst view in most of these clubs would be only about 20 rows back in an American venue, so it really didn't matter to us what they played. The room in Brussels was relatively clean and small, and the band responded with an incredible opening threesome: Jim, NICU, YEM! The second set drew its strength from a very good Down with Disease, plus back-to-back rotation songs Walfredo and Rocka William. Then the band came out into the bar after the show and hung out with the phans for awhile. —James Daly

2/16/97 [ACCESSIBILITY: ••••]
Wartesaal, Cologne, Germany
I: Beauty of My Dreams, Melt, Bouncing, Crosseyed and Painless, Guelah, Ginseng Sullivan, Tweezer, Waste, Cavern, Chalkdust
II: Sample, CTB, Free, Sparkle, Simple > When the Circus Comes, Swept Away > Steep > Bowie, Loving Cup, Tweezer Reprise
E: Theme, Johnny B. Goode

Show was later broadcast on "Rockplast," a German television show. Concert debut: Beauty of My Dreams.

This show was in the old waiting room of the Cologne train station. The band was separated from the fans by about 10 feet, a space occupied by at least six television cameras. Throughout the show, the cameras were all over the stage, getting cool angles on the

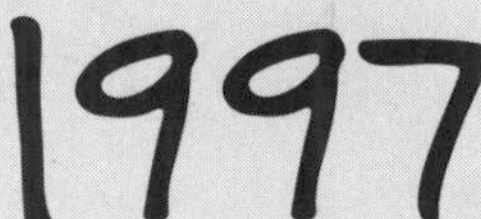

78 Total Show Dates
- **6** one-set show
- **69** two-set shows
- **3** three-set shows

STATS AND TABLES ARE GOOD FOR YOU

There are certain things that we're probably better off not knowing too much about (like the stuff that holds dredlocks together, what's goin' on there?). Happily, Phish setlist patterns do not fall into this category. It's like the age-old paradox of those strands of lint your sweaters leave behind in your belly button: the more you learn about them, the more mysterious and enchanting they become. So without apology, *The Pharmer's Almanac* attempts to break down 1997 in every which way possible, from the most popular shows to songs about dogs. (Compiled by Andy Shirey)

Phan Picks 1997

SHOW	THE SKINNY
1) 08/16/97 Limestone, ME	Three incredible, unique sets.
2) 11/22/97 Hampton, VA	Mike's Groove opener, segue 2nd set.
3) 08/17/97 Limestone, ME	Second set stands out.
4) 12/30/97 New York, NY	Harpua w/T.M. and wild encore.
5) 11/30/97 Worcester, MA	58-minute Runaway JAM.
6) 12/07/97 Dayton, OH	Psycho Killer & Boogie On?!
7) 07/31/97 Mountain View, CA	Shoreline, w/Garcia tribute.
8) 03/01/97 Hamburg, Germany	Immortalized on *Slip Stitch*.
9) 08/09/97 East Troy, WI	Alpine delivers the goods, and Gods.
10) 12/31/97 New York, NY	Another NYE at MSG!

ORIGINAL SONG DEBUTS: Black Eyed Katy (11/13/97), Bye Bye Foot (6/14/97), Carini (2/17/97), Dirt (6/14/97), Dogs Stole Things (6/13/97), Farmhouse (11/7/97 on Conan O'Brian; 11/16/97), Fooled By Images* (6/14/97), Ghost (6/13/97), I Don't Care (6/16/97), I Saw It Again (6/14/97), Limb By Limb (6/13/97), Oblivious Fool (6/13/97), Piper (6/14/97), Rocka William (2/13/97), Time (6/25/97), Twist Around (6/14/97), Vultures (6/13/97), Wading in the Velvet Sea (6/13/97), Walfredo (2/13/97), Water in the Sky (6/13/97).

COVER SONG DEBUTS: Beauty of My Dreams (2/16/97), Cecilia* (6/25/97), Cinammon Girl (3/18/97), Emotional Rescue (11/21/97), Funny as it Seems (6/20/97), Got My Mojo Workin'* (2/25/97), Izabella (6/13/97), Little Red Rooster* (2/25/97), Love Me (2/13/97), Love Me Like a Man* (3/18/97), My Soul (2/13/97), One Meatball* (2/25/97), Psycho Killer* (12/7/97), Reconsider Baby* (3/18/97), Roses Are Free (12/11/97), Soul Shakedown Party (2/17/97), Stand* (6/13/97), Them Changes* (11/30/97), When the Circus Comes (2/13/97).
(*only played once)

Dark Horses

SHOW	THE SKINNY
1) 06/25/97 Lille, France	Wild second set; DWD > Piper > DWD.
2) 07/09/97 Lyon, France	Bela & Flecktones sit in for set II.
3) 02/26/97 Stuttgart, Germany	Camel Walk, Dog Log, and tons more.
4) 11/17/97 Denver, CO	Not many songs, but tons of jams.
5) 11/21/97 Hampton, VA	21-min. Emotional Rescue opener.

1997: RAW TALLIES, REVIVALS and EPITAPHS

The Elite of '97: *Billy*'s livelier side continues to Breathe, My Soul busts loose with some good ol' blues, and funk madness resonates through Ghost and Black-Eyed Katy. Here's a look at the songs heard most in 1997:

Most-Played Originals		
1) Character Zero	32	41%
2) Taste	30	38%
3) Ghost	28	36%
4) Theme	27	35%
5) Chalkdust	26	33%
6) Harry Hood	23	29%
7) Limb by Limb	22	28%
7) Prince Caspian	22	28%
7) Stash	22	28%
10) Dogs Stole Things	20	26%
10) Dirt	20	26%

Most-Played Covers		
1) My Soul	30	38%
2) Beauty of My Dreams	21	27%
3) Loving Cup	16	21%
4) Ginseng Sullivan	15	19%
4) Rocky Top	15	19%
4) When the Circus Comes	15	19%
7) Also Sprach	14	18%
7) Funky Bitch	14	18%
9) Ya Mar	13	17%
10) Frankenstein	10	13%
10) Hello My Baby	10	13%
10) Johnny B. Goode	10	13%

Stats, Stats, and More STATS

Most-Played Originals by Tour

SPRING '97 (EUROPE)		SUMMER '97 (EUROPE)	
1) My Soul	9	1) Ghost	10
1) Char Zero	9	1) Dogs	10
3) Waste	8	1) Taste	10
4) Taste	7	4) Limb	9
4) Chalkdust	7	4) Theme	9

SUMMER '97 (US)		FALL '97 (US)	
1) Ghost	10	1) My Soul	9
2) Dirt	9	2) B.E. Katy	8
2) Water	9	2) Ghost	8
4) Limb	8	2) Char Zero	8

TOTALS FOR ALL OF 1997			
1) Char Zero	32	4) Ghost	28
2) My Soul	30	5) Theme	27
2) Taste	30		

STREAKIN' in '97

The Phellas usually do a pretty good job restraining themselves from playing even their most espoused new tunes at consecutive shows, but every so often they get a little carried away and before you know it, some song's showing up in stretches of back-to-back setlists.

Songs Played in Three or More Shows in a Row:

1) Limb by Limb	6	6/14	to	6/22
2) Dogs Stole Things	4	6/13	to	6/19
3) My Soul	3	2/25	to	2/28
3) Carini	3	2/26	to	3/1
3) My Soul (again)	3	11/23	to	11/28

Phish DOGma: No, not an analysis of the moral underpinnings of Gamehendge—I'm talking about the band's apparent fetish for tunes about pooches (no doubt a tribute to their largest non-human tour following).

		TIMES PLAYED	
Epic Tales of Doghood:	DEBUT	TOTAL	IN '97
Runaway Jim	03-28-90	257	16
McGrupp	05-03-85	72	5
Harpua	08-09-87	44	2*
Shaggy Dog	10-15-86	8	0
Hearty Dose of Dog:			
Dogs Stole Things	06-13-97	20	20
Dog Faced Boy	04-14-94	34	1
Dog Log	10-30-85	13	1
No Dogs Allowed	07-23-88	3	0
Make (Some) Reference to Dogs:			
Rocky Top	09-12-87	151	15
Cavern	01-30-88	295	11
Golgi Apparatus	10-15-86	303	4
My Sweet One	09-09-89	186	1
Demand	04-09-94	14	0

* Actually, '97 only featured one "entire" Harpua

I don't want a goldfish: Alas it's true. In every episode of Harpua, Jimmy's cat Poster Nutbag dies, but worry not my dear phriends, for Phish's extensive repertoire of animal songs can remedy all of your defunct-feline sorrows. Together with the doggy-ditties above, the animal tunes listed here comprise more than 5% of all the songs Phish has ever performed.

		TIMES PLAYED	
	DEBUT	TOTAL	IN '97
Wolfman's Brother	04-04-94	43	18
Run Like an Antelope	10-17-85	264	16
Guyute (pig)	10-07-94	43	11
Vultures	06-13-97	10	10
TimberHo (mule)	04-29-87	45	9
Possum	10-30-85	291	7
Llama	10-30-90	248	7
Scent of a Mule	04-04-94	91	7
The Horse	03-07-92	116	5
Lizards	01-27-88	223	4
Sleeping Monkey	03-06-92	52	4
Fee (weasel)	08-21-87	218	3
Camel Walk	10-17-85	16	3
BBFCM	08-21-87	92	1
Famous Mockingbird	02-08-88	97	0
Freebird	07-15-93	20	0
Pig in a Pen	02-21-93	2	0
Blackbird	10-31-94	2	0

band. Phish responded to this interesting scenario by playing most of the catchy songs (Bouncing, etc.). They also broke out tunes like Circus Comes to Town, which seemed to be enjoyed by the largely American audience. —Jeffrey Ellenbogen

This show demonstrates Phish's tendency to react (in my opinion, negatively) to the concept of their show being broadcast. Numerous cameras stared at the band the whole show, contributing to the energy. The focus of the show was definitely new material: five tracks from Billy Breathes, including Theme, which is a great encore. There were also two new covers and the second post-Halloween appearance of Crosseyed and Painless. Add to the mix the favorite crowd pleasers (Bouncin', Cavern, Sparkle, Sample) and you have the makings of a pretty lame, made-for-TV show. However, even the TV audience needs a sick jam, and this show has three (Crosseyed, Tweezer and Bowie), but even those didn't get very far out there. Oh well. —Greg Schwartz

2/17/97 [ACCESSIBILITY: ••••]
Paradiso, Amsterdam, Holland
I: Soul Shakedown Party > Divided Sky, Wilson, My Soul, Guyute, Timber Ho, Billy Breathes, Llama, Bathtub Gin > Golgi
II: Squirming Coil > Down with Disease > Carini > Jam > Taste > Down with Disease, Suzie, Caspian
E: Sleeping Monkey, Rocky Top

DwD reprise out of Taste included lyrical refrain. Concert debut: Soul Shakedown Party, Carini.

We arrived early to find a sparse scene of kids. We walked around back and heard what sounded like Marley playing inside. After a few moments, we realized it was Phish, soundchecking Soul Shakedown Party. Wow! Inside the renovated church was an amazing show waiting to develop. Highlights: during Wilson, the stain glass windows behind the stage lit up to the call of "Wilson . . . Wilson." Second set Squirming Coil segued into space, suddenly Mike stepped forward and started DwD. Mike goes sick! DwD actually becomes Lucy (or something), and there's a real segue into Taste. This was an epic jam! —Jeffrey Ellenbogen

Obviously, the band had a tough task to follow summer '96's curfew-free Melkweg show. I heard the soundcheck, so the Soul Shakedown opener wasn't the surprise it should have been. Yet it was another excuse to partake of the diggity, in a place where you don't need excuses. Our visit to Gamehendge was cut short by fairly uncreative 12-bar blues. Thank heavens for Guyute! I've never heard Billy Breathes so jammed and in such beautiful fashion. The whole set was gorgeous, if not long enough, with Trey promising more to come. It was obvious upon returning that at least Trey had watched his setbreak go up in smoke. Sometimes you can just tell that he's itching to jam. During the usual ending Coil solo by Page, Trey never really stopped playing. Instead he helped control the jam, turning it into the spacey intro that precedes Mike's huge bass intro to Down with Disease. The tempo was so fast, it was obvious that the band wanted to get right into the jam. And so they did, completely losing any semblance of the original song. After about ten minutes, a song/rap emerges (it could be described as Golden Earring meets Megadeth at a poetry workshop but I wouldn't), and is gone like a hallucination, quickly returning to the jam. Trey pulls everyone almost seamlessly into Taste, which once again slides into jam. As Trey solos, I began to recognize a familiar melody and before I could catch my breath, they're back in DwD, more than half an hour later. Second set was also too short, but seriously sweet. —Greg Schwartz

The second set has an absolute must-hear, 45-minute jamfest starting and ending with Down with Disease. Starting DwD out of Coil, the band drifts into a long jam which eventually segues into the concert debut of Carini Had a Lumpy Head. The jam out of Carini is just amazing, really experimental, and finally landing in Taste. The Taste jam also takes off, with Trey bringing it back around into a full DwD reprise, with the closing lyrics. So tasty! —Josh Albini

2/18/97 [ACCESSIBILITY: ••]
Bataclan, Paris, France
I: Beauty of My Dreams, Cavern, PYITE, Runaway Jim, NICU, Stash, Waste, Walfredo, Character Zero, Slave
II: Peaches, Also Sprach > My Soul, Maze, Wolfman's, Reba, Train Song, Harry Hood > Frankenstein
E: Bold as Love

It's pretty hard to be in any kind of bad mood after a Phish show, especially one like Paris, a "greatest hits" show which included a Slave dedicated to "a friend of ours [who] got hit by a car today." But after the show, my spirits were down a bit. Maybe it was because I knew the next Phish show I'd see wouldn't be for about six months. Maybe it was the remnants of rain in the air. Maybe it was the flashing neon sign right outside our hostel window. Then again, there were the three assholes I caught videotaping the show

On the Fringe: Openers, Closers, and Encores: Despite the band's abandonment of pre-scripted setlists, you can still count on Runaway Jim openers, Antelope closers, and Rocky Top encores. The first table below lists the songs which appeared most frequently in their respective positions in '97, while the second table reveals those songs which aren't necessarily played very often but which tend to show up in certain spots when they do appear.

Most-Played Openers, Closers & Encores

CHAMPIONS BY RAW TALLY

#1 Opener	Runaway Jim	**9**
#1 Closer	Character Zero	**18**
#1 Encore	Rocky Top/My Soul	**7**
#1 Closer or Encore	Character Zero	**23**

FIRST-SET OPENERS		SECOND-SET	
1) **Runaway Jim**	5	1) **DWD**	7
2) Ghost	4	2) Timber Ho	6
2) NICU	4	3) Wolfman's	5
2) Julius	4	4) Runaway Jim	4
5) Chalkdust	3	4) Stash	4
5) PYITE	3		

CLOSERS		ENCORE	
1) **Character Zero**	18	1) **My Soul**	7
2) Antelope	9	1) Rocky Top	7
3) Slave	7	3) When the Circus Comes	6
3) YEM	7	4) Character Zero	5
3) Harry Hood	7	5) four tied at	4

CHAMPIONS BY PERCENTAGE

	Times Played in Spot	Total	% in Spot
Opener (either set)			
1) **Buried Alive**	2	2	100%
2) The Curtain	2	3	67%
3) Runaway Jim	9	16	56%
4) NICU	6	15	40%
Opener (set II)			
1) **Timber**	7	9	78%
2) Down with Disease	7	18	39%
Closer			
1) **Run Like an Antelope**	11	16	69%
2) Weekapaug Broove	5	11	45%
3) Cavern	5	11	45%
Closer or Encore			
1) **Tweezer Reprise**	10	10	100%
1) Bold as Love	5	5	100%
2) Good Times Bad Times	4	5	80%
3) Character Zero	24	32	75%
4) Rocky Top	11	15	73%
5) Possum	5	7	71%
Utility Player (Opener, Closer, or Encore)			
1) **The Squirming Coil**	7	8	88%
2) Julius	13	15	87%
3) Carini	5	6	83%
4) Chalkdust Torture	12	26	46%
5) Guyute	5	11	45%

Stats, Stats, and More STATS

because the only security in the whole place were the coat-checkers who made everyone check in every coat and every bag before entering the show. This not only made a lot of people late getting in, but it also created an hour-or-better wait after the show to get our shit. Phish seemed a little tired, too, which, despite a pretty good show, summed up the evening—tired. —Jason Hedrington

2/20/97 [ACCESSIBILITY: •••]
Teatro Smeraldo, Milan, Italy
I: Curtain > Tweezer, Soul Shakedown Party > Chalkdust, Love Me, Taste, Gumbo, When the Circus Comes > Bowie, Tweezer Reprise
II: Sample, CTB, Character Zero, Uncle Pen, Stash, Bouncing, Free, Swept Away > Steep > Day in the Life, Runaway Jim, Adeline
E: Julius

Look at the setlist for this show and tell me the sets shouldn't be reversed. Anyways, if you're getting the tapes, get the first set! It's really hot, starting with a Curtain > Tweezer opener that rocks. Follow that up with Soul Shakedown Party (glad to see they didn't limit it to just Amsterdam), strong versions of the Elvis classic Love Me, Taste and Gumbo, plus David Bowie, then Tweeprise to close? Damn fine set. —Lee Johnston

2/21/97 [ACCESSIBILITY: •••]
Tenax, Florence, Italy
I: My Soul, Foam, Down with Disease, Lizards, Crosseyed and Painless, YEM
II: Ya Mar, Antelope > Wilson, Oh Kee > AC/DC Bag, Billy Breathes, Reba, Waste, Caspian
E: Character Zero

Antelope unfinished. Wilson played heavy-metal style. Last Oh Kee, 8/12/96 Noblesville, IN [50 shows].

The American scene continued in Firenze, where anticipation ran high for the first-ever solo Phish show in the city of the Uffizi. The first set was a very pleasant affair, climaxing

Stats, Stats, and More STATS

The fast turnover rate of SLOW TUNES: What seemed to start off as a parody (you know, "it isn't nearly fast enough for you") has spawned quite a cozy little genre of mellow, ballad-like songs. However, not unlike the more mainstream radio-ready tunes these songs cannot help but resemble, their longevity would appear to be rather limited and the band seems to tire of them quickly.

Turnover Rate of Slow Tunes

***PRE-BILLY BREATHES* BALLADS**

	peak year	# played at peak	in '97
Fast Enough For You	'93	17	1
The Horse > Silent in the Morning	'93	39	5
If I Could	'94	34	0
Lifeboy	'94	24	1
Strange Design	'95	28	3

BALLADS FROM *BILLY BREATHES* AND BEYOND

	Fall 96	Spring 97	Summer 97 (Europe)	Summer 97 (US)	Fall 97
Waste	28 (11)	53 (8)	14 (3)	05 (1)	04 (1)
Talk	15 (06)	07 (1)	10 (2)	00 (0)	00 (0)
Train Song	28 (11)	13 (2)	05 (1)	11 (2)	24 (6)
Billy Breathes	23 (09)	33 (5)	14 (3)	21 (4)	08 (2)
Swept > Steep	33 (13)	27 (4)	05 (1)	11 (2)	08 (2)
Dirt	—	—	24 (5)	47 (9)	24 (5)
Wading in a Velvet Sea	—	—	33 (7)	16 (3)	00 (0)

TID BIT TABLE

	# Times in '97	Details (the nitty-gritty)
Repriseless Tweezers	1 of 10	muy malo
Tweezerless Reprises	1 of 10	these can be pretty confusing
Vacuum solos	3	2 in I Didn't Know
Hydrogenated Mike's Grooves	5 of 12	42% (up from 20%? in '96)
Weekapaug-free Mike's Songs	1 of 12	el peor
Buried Hearts (Buried Alive > Poor Heart)	1 of 2	well, they *used* to do it a lot
Mockingbirdless Forbin's	1 of 1	not so famous
Silent Horses (The Horse > Silent in the Morning)	all	well woopty-do
TMWSInto Avenus (TMWSIY > Avenu Malkenu)	all	well woopty-do
Swept Steeps (Swept > Steep)	all	well woopty-do
Totally Aborted songs	2	My Friend, Guelah Papyrus

Top Henrietta Songs:	
Cecilia	1
Do it in The Road	1
Love You	1

A Cappella Songs:	
Hello My Baby	10
Sweet Adeline	6
Carolina	1
Star Spangled	1

Top Bluegrass Songs:	
1) Ginseng Sullivan	15
1) Rocky Top	15
3) Poor Heart	10
5) Uncle Pen	7
5) Scent of a Mule	7
7) My Old Home Place	2
9) Paul and Silas	1

Stats, Stats, and More STATS

Stepping into Yesterday: 1997 witnessed the revival of a handful of slumbering songs, a couple of them hailing from the Goddard days.

	# PLAYED IN '97	NOT PLAYED SINCE
1) Sneaking Sally Through the Alley	1	'88
2) Daniel	1	'93
3) Magilla	3	'94
4) Buffalo Bill	1	'94
5) Cities	9	'94
6) Boogie On, Reggae Woman	1	'95

On the way upward: In addition to the revived tunes above, a cluster of reasonably active songs from '96 went on to achieve (significantly) greater setlist-stuffing status in '97.

	TIMES PLAYED IN '96	IN '97	% INCREASE
1) Bold as Love	1	5	400%
2) NICU	6	15	150%
3) Rocky Top	7	15	114%
4) Loving Cup	6	12	100%
4) Jesus Left Chicago	3	6	100%
6) Ginseng Sullivan	6	11	83%
6) Guyute	6	11	83%
8) Wolfman's Brother	10	18	80%
9) Billy Breathes	8	14	75%

Sink a boulder in the water: This group of songs enjoyed consistent playing time in '96, only to sink deep into reserve status in '97.

	TIMES PLAYED IN '96	IN '97	% DECREASE
1) Rift	11	1	91%
2) Life on Mars?	10	1	90%
3) It's Ice	14	2	85%
4) Fee	10	2	80%
5) Suzie Greenberg	17	4	76%
6) Divided Sky	16	4	75%
7) Guelah Papyrus	11	3	73%
8) A Day in the Life	15	5	67%
9) Golgi Apparatus	10	4	60%
9) Lizards	10	4	60%
11) AC/DC Bag	17	7	59%
11) Scent of a Mule	17	7	59%
13) Reba	19	9	53%
14) Sparkle	21	10	48%

Hanging by a thread. . . These dried-up Goliaths have seen healthier days, but they aren't ready for burial just yet.

	PEAK YEAR	TIMES PLAYED AT PEAK	IN '97
My Sweet One	'91	69	1
Oh Kee Pa	'91	41	2
Fee	'94	40	2
My Friend My Friend	'93	39	2
All Things Reconsidered	'92	39	1
Glide	'92	34	1
I Didn't Know	'93	33	2
Dinner and a Movie	'91	31	1
Strange Design	'95	28	2
Buried Alive	'93	23	2
Lifeboy	'94	24	1
Dog Faced Boy	'94	23	1
Paul and Silas	'91	23	1
BBFCM	'91	19	1
Contact	'90	18	2

A tranquil and motionless sleep? This lot of one-time heavyweights stepped into or remained in the freezer in '97.

	PEAK YEAR	TIMES PLAYED AT PEAK	LAST PLAYED
Amazing Grace	'93	54	12-31-96
If I Could	'94	34	03-05-96
Mound	'93	34	10-25-96
Nellie Cane	'94	26	12-08-94
Acoustic Army	'95	27	12-08-95
Cracklin' Rosie	'92	25	08-14-96
Brother	'91	25	11-30-96
Esther	'90	17	10-19-96
Famous Mockingbird	'93	16	10-31-96

with the song we all expected, YEM. After singing the first "Wash Uffizi, drive me to Firenze" refrain, Trey shouted, "This one's for you!" But the real highlight came in the second set, when the Antelope jam veered away from the "rye, rye rocco" closing and took on a heavy-metal feel. In the midst of a driving beat, Trey started yelling the lyrics to Wilson. He "sang" (if you could call it that) all of Wilson with this totally wild industrial beat, then finally segued into Oh Kee Pa, of all things. —James Daly

2/22/97 [ACCESSIBILITY: ••]
Teatro Olimpico, Rome, Italy

I: Walfredo, Also Sprach > Funky Bitch, Theme, NICU, When the Circus Comes, Talk, Melt, I Didn't Know, Character Zero

II: Chalkdust, Bathtub Gin > Sparkle, Simple > Jesus Left Chicago, Harry Hood, Free, Hello My Baby

E: Johnny B. Goode

Fishman on vacuum for I Didn't Know. "Bowie" teases in Chalkdust. Simple featured a Page piano solo.

Definitely not the pick of the Europe '97 lot, Rome was the worst of the four straight amazing Italy gigs. Can't fault the boys for that; after all, the 2/21 and 2/23 shows were practically instant classics. But the second set in Roma did have some nice touches, including Jesus Left Chicago and of course Harry Hood. —Scott Sifton

2/23/97 [ACCESSIBILITY: ••••]
Fillmore, Cortemaggiore, Italy

I: Carini, Axilla, All Things, Sloth, Love Me, Rift, Fluffhead, Frankenstein, Bowie

II: Daniel, Suzie, Maze, Horse > Silent, Peaches, Mike's > Do It in the Road > HYHU, GTBT

E: Billy Breathes, Rocky Top

Photo courtesy of George Lyons.

To open the show, prerecorded version of Carini played over PA; Phish joined in as they took the stage. Fishman on vacuum for Do It in the Road. "Tweezer Reprise" jam in GTBT. Last Daniel, 8/28/93 Berkeley, CA [287 shows]. Last Do It in the Road, 6/25/95 Philadelphia, PA [144 shows].

After Europe tour ended, everyone I talked to declared Stuttgart and Hamburg the best of the bunch, but my vote goes to Cortemaggiore. Playing the Fillmore, a cozy little hall with a garish venue logo for the backdrop behind the band, Phish just ripped it up. The first set opened with the first real Carini or Lucy or whatever it's called (the one in Amsterdam was kind of lost in the middle of a long jam), and ending with an amazing Fluffhead/Frankenstein/Bowie run. They opened the second set with the first Daniel since summer '93, went to town on Maze, then gave us the tour's first Mike's Song, which jammed way out before "the rebirth of Henrietta" (as Trey puts it) brought Fishman forward for Do It in the Road. A steaming GTBT—with a Tweezer Reprise jam!—finishes off this already-legendary set. —James Daly

Weird that the boys would bring back Daniel for a one-time performance, but with different lyrics and a different tempo. It's gotten a little more biblical. Besides that revival, check out Mike's jam in this set. It never segues into Simple, but after a raging Mike's jam, they enter the outro jam and just mellow out, much like a Simple jam. There's a really gorgeous passage of quiet jamming before the music just fades to nothing for a second, then Do It in the Road cranks up. —Rich Mazer

Stats, Stats, and More STATS

. . . AND I KNEW MY TIME HAD COME

Has Gamehendge reached the end of its road? 1997 setlists were not kind to Prussia's cast of characters, but a handful of quirks have kept the scene bizarre and unpredictable as usual. Colonel Forbin's Ascent veered off course and wound up in the clutches of Ken Kesey's band of Merry Pranksters; traditional powers Divided Sky and Llama have been relegated to a rather stubendous "rare token appearance" status; and still not a peep out of the Famous Mockingbird since the descent of its evil twin on Halloween '96.

	DEBUT	TOTAL TIMES PLAYED	PEAK YEAR	#PLAYED IN '97
Lizards	01-30-88	215	'91	4
Tela	03-12-88	60	'91	1
Wilson	10-15-86	138	'94	7
AC/DC Bag	04-1-86	162	'89	8
Colonel Forbin's Ascent	03-12-88	88	'93	1
Famous Mockingbird	02-08-88	88	'93	0
The Sloth	08-21-87	114	'91	3
Possum	10-30-85	255	'91	7
McGrupp	05-03-85	72	'89	5
Punch You in the Eye	08-17-89	75	'93	17
TMWSIY	03-11-87	58	'91	1
Divided Sky	08-09-87	252	'91	4
Icculus	04-01-80	14	'92,'94	0
Llama	10-30-90	241	'91	7

2/25/97 [ACCESSIBILITY: ••]
Incognito, Munich, Germany
I: Runaway Jim, My Soul, One Meatball, Little Red Rooster, Got My Mojo Workin', Stash, Waste, Taste, Loving Cup
II: Beauty of My Dreams, Sample > PYITE > Free, Fee, My Friend, Down with Disease, Caspian, La Grange, Adeline
E: Chalkdust

Sydney Ellis on vocals for One Meatball, Little Red Rooster, Got My Mojo Workin', My Friend aborted after about a minute because of Trey mess-up. Concert debuts: One Meatball, Little Red Rooster, Got My Mojo Workin'.

Super-small venue hinted at how it must've been back at Nectar's. A special guest, Sydney Ellis, did a fabulous job on several songs in the first set. We saw another Taste, a My Friend My Friend cut short by Trey, and Mike taking over on Down with Disease. Sweet Adeline with no mics was more than awesome. —Matt Bussman

[2/26/97]
Badeu-Badeu Studios, Stuttgart, Germany
Interview, Train Song, Walfredo, "Goodbye Jam"

In-studio accoustic set, broadcast live on Stuttgart radio station.

2/26/97 [ACCESSIBILITY: ••••]
Longhorn, Stuttgart, Germany
I: Camel Walk, Llama, My Friend, Harry Hood, My Soul, Tube, Carini, Rocka William, Dog Log, Guitar Gently Weeps
II: Buried Alive > Poor Heart, Ha Ha Ha > Jam > YEM > Kung > Theme, Scent of a Mule > Magilla > Scent of a Mule, Slave
E: Highway to Hell

Magilla played as Page's duel in Scent. Last Magilla, 5/4/94 New Orleans, LA [260 shows]. Last Dog Log, 12/11/95 Portland, ME [90 shows]. Last Guitar Gently Weeps, 12/11/95 Portland, ME [90 shows]. Last Camel Walk, 7/2/95 Fayston, VT [140 shows].

What a cool European setting for a great selection of tunes: Camel Walk opener, Dog Log, Tube and other lesser-played gems. The second set included a reaching jazz jam. Rocka William was a switch-up of the boys (Trey on drums, Mike on keys, Page on bass and Fish on lead) which is pretty special. Overall, one of the better European shows during this tour. —Dave Matson

One glance at the setlist makes it clear that Phish had it going on in Stuttgart! Not just Camel Walk, but Camel Walk as an opener to a set that includes rarities (Dog Log), jamming (Harry) and trademark Phish wackiness (Rocka William, Carini). The first set is so obviously phenomenal that you might be inclined to overlook the second set, but it's also a winner, built around an incredible YEM that follows a jamming (yes, really) Ha Ha Ha. Scent of a Mule has Page and Trey scatting, just wild stuff, then Slave as a finishing touch. Amazing, amazing show—if they played something like this in the states, people would lose their shit! —Rich Mazer

2/28/97 [ACCESSIBILITY: •••]
Huxley's Neue Welt, Berlin, Germany
I: Carini, Paul and Silas, My Soul, CTB, Peaches, Stash, Swept Away > Steep > Ya Mar, Character Zero
II: Taste, Drowned > Caspian > Frankenstein, Bowie, Love Me, Axilla > Waste, Julius
E: Day in the Life

"Oh Kee" teases in Ya Mar. Page piano solo in Caspian. Last Paul and Silas, 10/24/95 Madison, WI [120 shows]. Last Drowned, 12/31/95 New York, NY [82 shows].

Tucked between two of the hottest Phish shows in recent memory, Berlin is easy to overlook. Despite its paltry length (the entire show is less than two hours long), there are some sweet moments. The second set includes the first Drowned since New Year's Eve '95, and although it's not as strong a version as 12/31/95, it's good to see it back in the band's current repertoire. Caspian, which follows Drowned, includes a Page solo that eventually leads the band into a rocking Frankenstein. Trey later recalled this show as a special, softer night in front of a very attentive audience. —Scott Sifton

After the first-set opener, Trey remarks, "'Carini Had a Lumpy Head' is the official title of that song," ending the week-long debate about whether the tune—first played in Amsterdam—was called Lucy, Song for Carini, or something else entirely. —James Daly

3/1/97 [ACCESSIBILITY: ••••]
Markthalle, Hamburg, Germany
I: Cities, Oh Kee, Down with Disease, Weigh, Beauty of My Dreams, Wolfman's > Jesus Left Chicago, Reba, Hello My Baby, Possum
II: Carini, Dinner and a Movie, Mike's > Lawn Boy > Weekapaug, Mango, Billy Breathes, Theme
E: Taste, Adeline

"Can't You Hear Me Knocking" jams in Down with Disease and at end of Weekapaug. "The End" and "Careful with the Axe, Eugene" jams in Mike's Song. Last Cities, 7/5/94 Ottawa, ON [222 shows]. Last Dinner and a Movie, 8/6/96 Morrison, CO [59 shows]. Show was delay-broadcast on German radio. Portions of this show comprise the live Phish album Slip Stitch and Pass.

It's not always safe to declare a show "classic" before the band has even left the stage, but the Hamburg show has already gained fame among fans that resembles that of 12/30/93 or 10/31/94. Though only time will tell if this show remains among the all-time favorites, it sure is a great one. Right from the opener—the first Cities in almost three years—it's clear the band is going to mix things up, then Trey tells the crowd that he's psyched to be back in the cool room that's the Markthalle. An amazing first set includes a very good Down with Disease and the first experimental Wolfman's Brother, a version that foreshadowed Phish's summer '97 versions. Though the jam never came all the way back around to the Wolfman's theme, the band followed a cool little groove into Jesus Left Chicago, then topped off the set with a great Reba and a wild "heavy-metal" Possum (hear it to understand). The second set is crazier—Mike's Song jams into "The End," and a bunch of other lyric strangeness erupts in Weekapaug. —Ernie Greene

3/2/97 [ACCESSIBILITY: ••]
Pumpehuset, Copenhagen, Denmark
I: Johnny B. Goode, Uncle Pen, Sample, Guyute, My Soul, Runaway Jim, Antelope > Catapult > Life on Mars, Chalkdust, Hello My Baby
II: Also Sprach > Maze, Swept Away > Steep > PYITE, Waste, Character Zero, Slave, Tweezer Reprise
E: YEM

Antelope unfinished. "Gypsy Queen" jam in Runaway Jim.

A big letdown for the European tour closer. A few nice ones in the first set, but only half of Antelope and another My Soul. 2001 > Maze was a good start for set two, but more new songs dropped the ball. Punch You is always good, but the YEM encore seemed to lack much effort and had a weak vocal jam. —Matt Bussman

HAMBURG, Germany

Our last stop on a week-long tour across Europe was Hamburg, the northern port city where the Beatles did some of their first gigging thirty-five years ago. We got there pretty early in the day and killed the afternoon in the famed Red Light district, which turned out to be totally lame. I was expecting something really out there, but it was nothing more than a touristy Times Square. And of course each of us was competing to show who was less interested in the skin houses, so of course we didn't do anything, just walked around without really going in anywhere.

We still got to the show really early and lined up with about a dozen heads. When the doors were opened, we found ourselves in a simply awesome venue—it was tiny, but had a stepped floor where you could see the stage from any corner. I'm so used to clubs in New York where you have to be right in front of the stage or you can't see anything.

It was pretty crowded on the floor by the time the show started, but we had a good spot, maybe five feet from the stage and right in the middle. As in Stuttgart a few days earlier, Phish made their intentions clear with a breakout for the first song, Cities. Although they'd take it to further heights during that summer, it was a great version, and the excitement could literally be felt in the tiny hall, as waves of heat descended upon the audience. It must have been one hundred degrees by the time Cities was over, and it got significantly hotter on the floor as the set went on. An early-show Down with Disease made it clear that Phish had lofty goals for the night. Then they really began hitting the zone a few songs later during Wolfman's Brother.

Trey has a ball in Hamburg.

Photo courtesy of George Lyons.

I had probably only seen Wolfman's about half a dozen times. I'd really enjoyed it, too, seeing it as a rocking tune which was actually much better without the horns. But Wolfman's took on a whole different life that night in Hamburg. The funky, wah-wah-drenched take on the song was followed by a simply incredible jam, the kind you can really get lost in and almost forget what song started it all.

And you could see the band getting excited. They knew they were on to something and everyone in that hot little club sensed it.

By Reba, two songs later, I had inched my way closer to the stage and was looking right up at Trey.

His face exuded such intensity as the song went from section to section. Here was a song he'd played about 250 times, and yet it seemed that every single note meant so much to him. Every movement in his fingers seemed to flow from his face—buckled and bent in every direction—as his torso hovered in close to the neck of the instrument. You almost felt like you were intruding on an intimate moment between man and guitar, like you should ask if they wanted to be alone together.

The set powered on and on, closing with a Possum that threatened to wipe out half the crowd with heat stroke.

Luckily the venue staff opened some windows or got some fans going during set break, or they might have had a problem on their hands. We moved back a little, but were still closer to Trey than Page was to Fishman.

The second set led off with Carini, which we'd seen nearly every night but sure as hell weren't sick of. Then Dinner and a Movie led into Mike's Song.

There are Mikes, and then there are Mikes. And there's little doubt that it's because of this Mike's that Phish later decided to make Hamburg, out of a thousand shows to choose from, their first-ever single-show live album.

The vocal section was followed by this straight-ahead, funked-out jam that really seemed to know exactly where it was headed. Kuroda immediately caught the mood with these sort of silver metallic lights. It wasn't a very long Mike's. It didn't need to be, because every progression made a point and didn't leave anything over. Page was all over his synthesizer, laying down these throaty, psychedelic grooves while Trey just went nuts. And we're watching this splendid convergence from spitting distance.

This entire cramped room was just on fire. Dead silence from the crowd erupted into wild applause as Trey fired the crescendo notes. And then, in this Mike's that was so perfect everything almost seemed preplanned, they went not into Hydrogen but into these Arabic-sounding notes, a familiar set of notes, something that said jungle, that said head popping from the water as the credits roll to *Apocalypse Now*. "The End."

I'd always wanted Phish to play "The End." I saw it as a potential Fishman tune, a joke of sorts. But here we were at the edge of sanity and, yeah, it did sort of feel like a joke as Trey sang the first lyrics, but it also felt like the most tripped-out mindphuck I'd ever experienced.

A scream came, before Mike played with an effect he'd been fiddling with all tour. Trey then hit a pedal and it was all over. He began this quick rhythmic strum and Mike followed with a couple of bass notes.

The weirdest thing—it wasn't working. It just went nowhere. I was trying to follow it with my ears, waiting for it to be satisfying, believing it would be satisfying. But after a few seconds, Trey realized he'd backed himself into a dead end, and whispered over to Page, before turning to the others to make sure they all knew what was next: Lawn Boy.

Talk about contrast. Just to remind us of that, Fishman sang, "And he walked on down the hall," over the loungy lead-in notes.

Seconds later, they were back in Weekapaug, with Mike slapping away and Trey still singing "And he walked on down the hall . . ."

This of course leads into the Oedipal section (if you don't know it, please see the damn movie). Fish took the lead vocal: "I want to kill you." He then looked over at Trey with this nervous sort of "should I?" look. "Mother . . ." he sang. And then Trey let Fish off the hook. "I want to cook you breakfast," a voice came from the center of the stage. "I want to borrow the car."

It's amazing how, even in the height of inspiration, Phish always manage to be themselves, to say the things and play the notes that make them who they are.

"Tryin' to make a woman that you move . . ."

The rest of Weekapaug was short, but size doesn't always matter. My favorite part came when Trey stepped off a peddle, backed up and did this happy little dance and flashed the grin of a toddler as he peered up at the lights, still jamming away. Jesus Christ, it was downright precious. And as if I hadn't already seen enough to make my head spin, that little moment sent me on symbolic journey number 547, under the category of "Why everyone loves Phish."

It's not just the music. It's that they're so damn likeable. People forget that. You just look up at these people, so blessed, so extraordinarily talented, and in the back of your mind you're thinking, "It couldn't have happened to a better bunch of guys."

—Andy Bernstein

1997 SPRING Time Out

Forsaking a U.S. spring tour for the third consecutive year, the band spent the spring practicing and writing as well as making several cameo appearances. The band used the release of Ben & Jerry's Phish Food ice cream as a good excuse to play their first Flynn Theater show since April '94, an affair spiced up by horn players Dave Grippo and James Harvey and the gospel stylings of Tammy Fletcher.

Besides the Flynn show, Phish made another appearance on Letterman, and individually, all of the band members also remained active. Page sat in with the Allman Brothers for the second year in a row during their March stand at the Beacon Theater in New York City, while Fishman joined Phish cover band Stash for several songs during a May gig of theirs in his hometown of Syracuse. Trey and Mike, meanwhile, teamed up with several members of Burlington band the Pants and James Harvey to form "New York," which played a May gig at Club Toast in Burlington and featured the debut of several songs that would join the Phish catalog in June, including I Saw It Again and Dirt. And Mike and Fish appeared on the syndicated radio program House of Blues, treating the audience to a recorded live version of My Soul. Then, before their trip abroad in June, Phish snuck in a set at Phish crew member Brad Sands's house, playing all their new material for the small crowd. What a barbecue that must have been!

[3/5/97]
Late Show with David Letterman, Ed Sullivan Theater, New York, NY
Character Zero

3/18/97 [ACCESSIBILITY: ••••]
Flynn Theater, Burlington, VT
I: Cinnamon Girl, NICU > Sample > PYITE > My Soul, Beauty of My Dreams, Harry Hood > CTB, Suzie, Character Zero
II: Taste, Drowned > Caspian, Bowie, Love Me, Reconsider Baby, Love Me Like a Man, Waste > Chalkdust, Slave
E: Hello My Baby, Funky Bitch

Benefit concert for cleanup of Lake Champlain, co-sponsored by Ben & Jerry's. Dave Grippo on alto saxophone and James Harvey on trombone for CTB, Suzie, Character Zero, and Funky Bitch. Tammy Fletcher on vocals for Reconsider Baby and Love Me Like a Man. Concert debuts: Cinnamon Girl, Reconsider Baby, and Love Me Like a Man. Live FM broadcast on WIZN-Burlington.

The Flynn! What can I say in such a small space to do it justice. It was everything I've ever dreamed of (literally—I had a real psychic dream about this one that came true) for a Phish show. Cinnamon Girl! The Horns on CTB, Suzie and Character Zero! Awesome Bowie! Tammy was very entertaining. You could even see little Eliza on the side of the stage. Slave, and then an awesome encore, left me just beaming. It was beautiful! People just staggered across the street to the park afterwards, stunned. I'll never forget it. By far my favorite show ever. —Libby Barrow

Phish gets iced at the Spectrum.

Good ol' Phish—they'll never forget where they're from. Another Phish dream come true—I was one of the very lucky folks who actually got a voucher (instead of tickets, to prevent scalping). Inside the lobby of the Flynn, we were handed Phish Food in little cups. Ben and Jerry came out and introduced the band, and they weren't the first special guests—at the beginning of CTB, two mics were brought out in front of Fish, then out walked James Harvey and Dave Grippo! They raged on CTB and went off even more on Suzie. Best first set ever? Definitely in the top three I've seen. In set II, after a climactic Bowie and Treat Me Like a Fool, Trey walked to the front of the stage and introduced Tammy Fletcher (of Tammy Fletcher and the Disciples, a local blues/gospel group) for two tunes. She has such a wonderful voice—I was amazed. After Funky Bitch, again with Harvey and Grippo, I woke up . . . and it was the strangest thing—all my friends had the same dream. —Mike D'Amico

I didn't get a ticket for this show because I wasn't meant to—this show was strictly for phriends of old and a few lucky Burlingtonians. Thankfully, it was radio broadcast in the area, and we decided to go to Burlington to find a spot and listen in. What a tight show! You could just tell how much fun they were having. I'm sure I wasn't the only one caught off-guard by the Cinnamon Girl opener, but Trey's guitar tone sounded great on that one. CTB, Suzie and Character Zero with Grippo and Harvey created some of the hottest musical fire I've ever heard. Just so pure. —Casey Grant

[5/18/97]
CoreStates Spectrum, Philadelphia, PA
Star Spangled Banner

Phish performed a cappella before the Flyers-Rangers NHL playoff game.

1997 SUMMER New World

In several interviews from 1996, Trey spoke of a latent desire to "rewrite the live Phish catalog." Few took him seriously, though, until the band kicked off the summer of 1997 in a small room in Dublin, Ireland, and played virtually half a show's worth of new material. That was something pretty special—akin, perhaps, to the Lowell show of May 1995 that saw the debuts of Free, Theme, and Strange Design, among others. But it was something else again when the same thing happened the next night in Dublin, with another new group of songs. The Phish concert landscape was shifting.

Souvenir! Phans pull down Phish posters in Amsterdam, July 1997.

Photo courtesy of Anthony Buchla.

Within the week, Phish had debuted well over a dozen new originals, plus a handful of new covers. And phans on tour across Europe, as the band again played small halls and occasionally larger music festivals, debated rumors that Phish had retired twenty-five older songs. What made the reports especially chilling were the names of the songs supposedly put away—Mike's Groove and YEM apparently among them. Though the rumor proved to be generally unfounded, the band did wait a few weeks before reviving Mike's and YEM, and instead focused on new material that continued the shift toward funk-oriented jamming begun on the Europe tour in February. That trend would later continue on the other side of the Atlantic during the American summer tour.

DUBLIN, Ireland

Friday, June 13, 1997,

I didn't plan on seeing a show in Europe until the 16th in London. I had just flown into Heathrow on the 11th and met my friend Paul up near Manchester that night. The next day we found ourselves in Wales and couldn't resist the temptation to hop the ferry to Dublin to catch the kick-off of the summer tour. It was a fitting omen that the opening night was Friday the 13th of June.

We had trouble securing a room in Dublin, which was overcrowded and pretty much booked up for the weekend. The only rooms we could get were in a hostel about fifteen minutes south of Dublin in the neighboring town of Dun Laughorie, and unfortunately circumstances arose which made it necessary to check into the hostel before going to the show. At noon on the 13th we arrived at the Holyhead ferry station and realized that the earliest ferry we could get on didn't leave until 4:00 and had an arrival time at 7:00 in Dublin.

Paul and I jumped on the ship and met up with about seven other kids heading to the shows. It was a blast as we warmed up for the show by listening to the "house band," a two piece Irish band of a keyboards and guitar, as they played everything from Oasis to Janis while singing in a thick Irish accent. But, alas, the fun came to an end as we deboarded at 7:00. Next we encountered the seemingly endless wait for baggage pick-up and were finally ready to roll at 7:30. Outside the boat it was impossible to catch a taxi so we started the two mile hike out of the docking area. Halfway through the first mile we caught a ride from an overly friendly trucker who was eager to rap about Irish politics as he took us south toward our hostel. He was only able to take us halfway there and dropped us off at a bus stop.

Photo courtesy of Anthony Buchla.

Time: 8:15. We waited at the bus stop for about fifteen minutes and the bus showed no signs of arriving soon. A mutually frustrated woman who was waiting with us started to hail a taxi and, since we said we were going in the same direction, offered to pay for our fare.

Time: 9:00. We finally arrived at the hostel, checked in, and got the last two beds in the entire place. By the time we dropped off all of our baggage and got a cab to head down to the SFX Center it was already 9:25. At this point we were praying that shows started later in Dublin than they do in the States. It was here that we realized that the SFX Center was still rarely used for concerts. So rarely used, that the cab driver had no idea where it was. We drove in circles for what seemed to be an eternity when finally we made a turn down a dark side street and came a small, discrete building where we could hear the beginnings of Maze blaring from within.

Photo courtesy of Anthony Buchla.

Time: 10:00. We finally made it and ran up to the door to try to buy tickets to get in. A bouncer gruffly told us that the ticket window was closed and that we should come back tomorrow. After withstanding about a minute of our slightly pathetic pleading, he gave us an exasperated look and escorted us both inside the venue for free. It's hard to even begin to describe the feelings of relief and excitement after the day we had had. It was an incredible flashback to some of the older days of Phish in a tiny hall with perhaps five hundred people there. Right away we both knew that our trip was well worth the struggles and frustration of the entire day.

The second set was filled with debuts including Vultures, Water in the Sky, Oblivious Fool, and Ghost, which turned out to be the song of the year. The music was also very different from Phish shows in the past. I remember telling my friend, "Hey, Trey's playing with his soul instead of his hands!" The new phunktafied Phish was born. Even familiar songs such as Chalkdust took on new, funkier tones. I remember what seemed to be a flawless transition of Chalkdust > Ghost > Oblivous Fool where I was left shaking my head in disbelief. However, the highlight for me came in the encore as we witnessed the debut of Sly and the Family Stone's "Stand" and Hendrix's "Izabella," both of which were also segued nicely together. The encore confirmed what I had felt all set. The new era of Phish was upon us and we were all knee-deep in the phunk.

—Todd Hagle

6/13/97 [ACCESSIBILITY: ••]
S.F.X. Centre, Dublin, Ireland
I: Theme, Dogs Stole Things, Beauty of My Dreams, Billy Breathes, Limb by Limb, Wolfman's > Wading in the Velvet Sea, Taste
II: Stash, Maze, Water in the Sky, Vultures, Slave, Chalkdust > Ghost > Oblivious Fool, Character Zero
E: Stand > Izabella

"La Bamba" and "Tequila" jams before Stash. Concert debuts: Dogs Stole Things, Limb by Limb, Wading in the Velvet Sea, Water in the Sky, Vultures, Ghost, Oblivious Fool, Stand, Izabella.

What a crazy place to start the summer—two nights in Dublin! Before the show in this cozy little hall (we could practically touch the stage), rumors circulated that Phish had retired something like twenty-five of their old songs, and when they packed the show with mostly new songs, even the biggest doubters got a little nervous. But the new songs sounded great! I especially enjoyed the debut of Limb by Limb and Vultures, two songs marked by lyrical complexity and an intriguing new musical turn.
—Jerry Guthrie

The new songs sounded good, but what really grabbed me about the tour opener was the excellent Stand > Izabella double encore. This turned out to be the only performance of Stand for the rest of the year. Go figure. —James Daly

6/14/97 [ACCESSIBILITY: ••]
S.F.X. Centre, Dublin, Ireland
I: Down with Disease, NICU, Dirt, Talk, My Soul, CTB, Limb by Limb, Bye Bye Foot, Free, Caspian
II: Twist Around, Piper, I Saw It Again, Fooled by Images, Dogs Stole Things, Waste, Bowie, Cavern
E: When the Circus Comes, Rocky Top

Concert debuts: Dirt, Bye Bye Foot, Twist Around, Piper, I Saw It Again, Fooled by Images.

Great show! Though not many people have bothered to acquire the Dublin tapes, this is really a good one to pick up. Lots more song debuts make for a very different second set, but one that will introduce you in a hurry to Phish's 1997 catalog.
—Melissa Wolcott

The energy at the SFX Centre was raging on the second night. The room held about a thousand people, I'd say, and though the incredible amount of new tunes limited the crowd's reaction, there was a neat moment in David Bowie when a clap-along led Trey to sling his guitar over his back and kick up his heels in a brief Russian folk dance before ripping into the jam. —Jerry Guthrie

6/16/97 [ACCESSIBILITY: ••]
Royal Albert Hall, London, England
I: Squirming Coil > Dogs Stole Things, Taste, Water in the Sky, Sample, Beauty of My Dreams, Theme, Chalkdust, Wolfman's, Oblivious Fool
II: Limb by Limb, Ghost, I Don't Care > Reba, Wading in the Velvet Sea, Dirt, Harry Hood
E: Cities, Poor Heart
Concert debut: I Don't Care (provisional title).

High expectations for this show—in one of the world's most storied venues—proved hard to live up to, as the tour-heads and band were both still struggling with the new material. Squirming Coil opener was a curveball, and from there the show seemed to get even mellower. Maybe that was because the gorgeous Royal Albert Hall was only about halffull, or maybe the band was simply intimidated. The only real musical highpoint came in the encore: "Think of London . . ." Trey sang in Cities, and we all cheered like crazy. —Jerry Guthrie

Both the outside and the inside of the Hall were gorgeous and reaked of elegance. The Fox in St. Louis, a gorgeous theater in its own right, looks like a dump compared to this place. Before the show started all heads were just turned upward in amazement at the architecture and beauty of the building. The one highlight that sticks out from the first set was my first taste of the new and improved Wolfman's. The second set included Reba and Hood, which as usual were completely satisfying. They closed with Poor Heart, which gave the British folks a taste of good ol' American bluegrass rock. —Todd Hagle

6/19/97 [ACCESSIBILITY: ••]
Arena, Vienna, Austria
I: Limb by Limb, Dogs Stole Things, Theme > PYITE, Water in the Sky, Maze, Waste, Vultures, Runaway Jim
II: Stash > Ghost > I Saw It Again, Wading in the Velvet Sea, Piper, Jesus Left Chicago, Caspian
E: Beauty of My Dreams, Character Zero, Hello My Baby

Pretty straightforward show in a cool little room, highlighted by developing jams in some of the new songs, notably Ghost. The Piper/Jesus Left Chicago/Caspian run to close the second set was neat, though, and frankly, in rooms this size, it's much easier to digest new material because you can watch the band creating it right before your eyes. —James Daly

Man, guitar, and famous T-shirt, 6/19/97.

Photo courtesy of George Lyons.

6/20/97 [ACCESSIBILITY: ••]
Archa Theatre, Prague, Czech Republic
I: Taste, Cities > Horn > Funny as It Seems > Limb by Limb > I Don't Care > Antelope
II: Bowie, Ghost, Bye Bye Foot, Ginseng Sullivan, Cavern, Twist Around, Bouncing, Julius
E: When the Circus Comes, Rocky Top
Concert debut: Funny as It Seems.

The thought of a Phish show in Prague seemed too perfect, so we had to make the trip. Having not yet seen a show on the tour, we were surprised with the amount of new material, but it all sounded pretty good to my ears. The whole first set was fun, from a good Taste opener into Cities, and then some new songs leading into an Antelope closer. Set II wasn't quite as strong but still had some kicks, and when it was all over, we were happy to find ourselves in one of the coolest cities on the tour. We decided to hang around for a couple of days, skipping the upcoming festival shows, a move made by a lot of the heads on this tour. —Melissa Wolcott

6/21/97 [ACCESSIBILITY: ••]
Hurricane Festival, Eichenring, Scheessel, Germany
Sample, Also Sprach > Poor Heart, Taste, Dirt, Theme, Swept Away > Steep, Limb by Limb, Dogs Stole Things, Harry Hood, Chalkdust, Jam > Twist Around, Cavern
E: My Soul
Music festival; Phish played one set.

Not many of the people that we had been seeing along the tour made it to this show (due to the distance and the price of the ticket); I only recognized about twenty or so people. Phish was set up under a big tent that was open all the way around—they weren't popular enough to play on the main stage. The majority of the audience were German locals and one got the feeling that they had never heard much if anything at all about "this Phish group" when the band opened with Sample. The set progressed, and when the band got us floating with Theme from the Bottom, the whole crowd began to catch on. Theme drifted into Swept Away which the crowd seemed to really dig, especially after the Theme jam. Steep got everyone rocking again and then came a very sweet Limb by Limb with the debut of the Fishman drum-solo ending. I thought he was just jamming out and Trey, Mike, and Page were boppin' their heads and laughing, then Trey encouraged Fish to "try it again"; after Fish's second attempt Trey explained that he had written this beat on a drum machine and thought it humanly impossible to play—then he gave it to Fish to learn and "he's almost got it." —Scott Shannon

6/22/97 [ACCESSIBILITY: •••]
WDR/Loreley Festival, Lorely, St. Goarschausem, Koblenz, Germany
Taste, Water in the Sky, Stash, Dirt, Uncle Pen, Character Zero, Theme, Hello My Baby, Ghost
E: Limb by Limb
Music festival; Phish played one set. Delayed broadcast on German TV show "Rockplast."

Look for a video of this one going around out there, courtesy of the same German TV show that also broadcast Phish's Cologne show from 2/16/97. Though this is a festival set and therefore too short for my liking, it's fun to watch the band's intensity in some of the new jams, especially Ghost and Limb by Limb. —Ed Smith

Crooning in Koblenz.

Photo courtesy of Jason Gleason.

6/24/97 [ACCESSIBILITY: •••]
La Laiterie, Strasbourg, France
I: Melt, Beauty of My Dreams, Dogs Stole Things, Vultures, Guelah, Runaway Jim, Talk, Free, Caspian, Rocky Top
II: Wolfman's > Reba, NICU, Twist Around, Piper, Wading in the Velvet Sea, Ghost
E: Loving Cup
Guelah abandoned. "Gypsy Queen" jam in Runaway Jim. Live FM broadcast in Strasbourg.

After skipping several shows because Phish was only going to be playing one set each, we arrived in Strasbourg for another two-set affair in another venue so small that it literally took our breath away. I love seeing Phish in Europe! More new songs dominated the show (they really gave them a workout over here), and the Loving Cup encore seemed like a big thank-you for letting the band indulge on the new stuff. —Melissa Wolcott

From the opening Split Open it was apparent that things were strange. The band seemed to be a little disjointed and off the beat. The sloppiness culminated in a botched and abandoned Guelah, which prompted Trey to quip that he was just happy they could get to the line in the song about Paris. Miraculously they all of a sudden pulled everything together and unleashed an excellent Runaway Jim with a stellar "Gypsy Queen" jam. One of the highlights was a funky/spacey Wolfman's Brother. Loving Cup then capped things off in grand fashion. —Todd Hagle

6/25/97 [ACCESSIBILITY: ••••]
L'Aeronef, Lille, France
I: Oblivious Fool, Dogs Stole Things, Taste, Billy Breathes, AC/DC Bag, Old Home Place, Theme, Wading in the Velvet Sea, I Saw It Again, Limb by Limb, My Soul
II: Down with Disease > Piper > Down with Disease > Time > McGrupp > Makisupa > Cecilia > HYHU > Rocka William > Antelope
E: Guyute

"Can't You Hear Me Knocking" jam in Down with Disease. McGrupp performed reggae-style. Fishman on towel for Cecilia. Concert debuts: Time (provisional title), Cecilia.

As I walked through the doors, the stage appeared in front of me and an enormous shiver ran down my spine. This was hands-down the smallest crowd I'd ever seen for a Phish show—and words couldn't do justice to what those three hundred fans and myself experienced during the second set. It began with DWD that sent the venue into a frenzy. When they returned to DWD after a nice jam and a detour through the new song Piper, everyone was excited, but it wasn't until the unfamiliar sounds of McGrupp that it became clear that this wasn't exactly going to be a standard set. This McGrupp started off sounding so strange that it took me a minute to realize what they were playing, and it continued in reggae-style, unlike any version I'd ever heard before. When they hit the opening chords to Guyute for the encore, the crowd went into complete hysteria —Marco Burgio

This show ended up being the smallest of the first half of the tour. The venue was situated on the side of this gigantic bus and subway terminal/office complex. As we climbed the five flights of fire escape–like stairs on the side of this building we passed Mike Gordon strolling by in the rain checking out the not-so-much-of-a scene and perhaps doing a little shopping. Inside, the room had a large curtain dividing it in half—there couldn't have been more than three hundred people at this show and the band treated us to the best show of the tour thus far. It's the second set that makes it so great. Down with Disease to open expanded into a great, funky jam segueing into new favorite Piper, then back into DWD, but they didn't stop there—the jam continued into a concert debut of an interestingly funky, albeit strange tune Time, which worked its way into the best version of McGrupp ever; it was balls-out reggae, with Trey more speaking the lines than singing and the band and crowd yelling, "He looks too much like Dave!" probably ten times over. After Makisupa, Trey set up a chair at center stage and took the sticks out of Fish's hands while maintaining the same beat. Fish sat on the chair, put a towel over his knee, and as the rest of the band faded out we heard Fish pounding on the towel as he began to sing Simon & Garfunkel's classic Cecilia. He only knew a few lines of the song but kept singing and singing. I was doubled over with laughter. —Scott Shannon

6/27/97 [ACCESSIBILITY: ••]
Glastonbury Festival, Worthy Farm, Pilton, Somerset, England
Wilson, Chalkdust, Stash, Dogs Stole Things, Poor Heart, Taste, Bouncing, Character Zero

Music festival; Phish played one set.

Another music festival; not much to say about this one—probably the most boring set I've ever seen from Phish, as only Stash allowed ample room to jam and it wasn't that hot. The locals seemed to enjoy it, though, so at least someone got their money's worth. —James Daly

6/29/97 [ACCESSIBILITY: ••]
Roskilde Festival, Roskilde, Denmark
YEM, Taste, Bouncing, Beauty of My Dreams, Chalkdust, Theme, Character Zero
E: My Soul

Music festival; Phish played one set.

The first notes of this show were a joyous relief and release—YEM. Rumors had swirled for two weeks that it had been "retired" along with about twenty-five other Phish classics, and though we could hardly believe that the boys would put away this masterpiece, the nagging fear had traveled with us for most of the tour. How nice it was to have it back, though the rest of this festival set seemed immediately forgettable. —James Daly

7/1/97 [ACCESSIBILITY: ••••]
Paradiso, Amsterdam, The Netherlands
I: Ghost, Horn, Ya Mar, Limb by Limb > Funny as It Seems, I Saw It Again, Dirt, Reba, Dogs Stole Things
II: Jam > Timber Ho, Bathtub Gin > Cities > Jam, Loving Cup, Slave
E: When the Circus Comes

"Back of the worm" vocals in Ghost, Ya Mar, and Cities. Fishman on piano for jam at beginning of second set. "When the Saints Go Marching In" tease in jam out of Cities.

The Paradiso is a beautiful venue with a churchlike feel to it. Behind the stage are two large stained-glass windows, and in the rear of the building is a large balcony that wraps around the sides. The only downside to the Paradiso is the terrible heat that smothers the audience. The second set, with only five songs played, plus the encore, was clearly 100 percent jamming. Bathtub Gin > Cities > Loving Cup was nuts, with serious jamming everywhere. Cities literally came out of nowhere, and, because of the time, I was sure Loving Cup would close the second set. When Trey began the opening licks to Slave, the whole crowd erupted. Slave was beautiful as usual, and when the show was finally over, at least half the crowd hung around instead of leaving. —Marco Burgio

Amsterdam does strange things to the Vermont boys—the normal rules are forgotten, replaced with a reckless abandon that makes every Phish show in this town a memorable event. The first set of the first-night Paradiso show laid a nice foundation for a very memorable set II. Like the February Paradiso show, the songs morphed into the next, starting with Fishman taking the stage on keyboards for a strange jam that developed into Timber Ho. The Bathtub > Cities sequence that follows is absolutely must-hear. —Jerry Guthrie

What the . . .? Fishman wears a suit and plays keyboards to start Set II in Amsterdam.

Photo courtesy of George Lyons.

7/2/97 [ACCESSIBILITY: ••••]
Paradiso, Amsterdam, The Netherlands
I: Mike's > Simple > Maze, Strange Design, Ginseng Sullivan, Vultures, Water in the Sky, Weekapaug
II: Jam > Stash > Jam > Llama > "Wormtown" > Wading in the Velvet Sea
E: Free
E2: Bowie

"Wormtown" was Steve Miller's "Swingtown" reworked with "back of the worm" vocals and a worm rap by Trey.

I strolled into the Paradiso the next night, and everyone felt that after last night's show—which was not at all disappointing—the band would nevertheless try to top themselves tonight. As the band stepped onto the stage, Trey began the opening chords to Mike's Song, and I thought, "Thank you, now this is more like it." When they went into Simple, the night just kept getting better. Throughout the set, Chris Kuroda played with the lights on the stained-glass windows which they'd rigged up to the lightboard. Simply awesome. The set was a short but sweet sixty minutes in length. The second set had a ridiculous three songs in it, but what was more ridiculous was that it lasted about an hour and a half. The stretched-out set included some of the most incredible, spacey jamming I'd ever heard. Trey kept mentioning worms, referring to Amsterdam as "Wormtown." The next night, in Nuremburg, he explained it to me. The story went like this: one day in

Photo courtesy of Anthony Buchla.

The beauty of my dreams: Cernobbio, Italy.

Photo courtesy of Marco Burgio.

Amsterdam, Trey was using one of the toilets that openly line the streets in Amsterdam and he was completely fucked up at the time. He said while he was pissing, he actually felt like he was riding on a worm. He was completely overcome by the feeling—thus the saying, "I'm on the back of a worm!" —Marco Burgio

In Ghost, Trey vocalized and enlightened us about the set of worm allusions. He said that while going to the bathroom in a Port-a-Potty, he was sucked into the toilet and had to spend the night riding on the back of one of the giant worms that live in the canals of Amsterdam. The Wormtown jam segued nicely into Wading in the Velvet Sea. —Todd Hagle

Mike's Song opener, the first since 1990, speaks for itself. Trey flashed a shit-eating grin as he cranked out the first notes, acknowledging the uniqueness of the moment. But again, it was the second set—with jamming that swam around the traditional bounds of songs—that blew our minds. Stash ran nearly thirty minutes, eventually finding its way into Llama and then Trey's Wormtown rap. The double encore, Free then Bowie, echoed the previous summer's third set in this magical town. —Jerry Guthrie

7/3/97 [ACCESSIBILITY: •••]
Serenadenhof, Nuremberg, Germany
I: Piper, My Soul, Divided Sky, Beauty of My Dreams, Taste, Train Song, Theme, Rocky Top
II: Ghost, CTB, Billy Breathes, Sparkle, Harry Hood, Cavern
E: Character Zero

I went into the venue and purchased my ticket, and discovered that the concert area was surrounded by a 30-foot wall covered with plants. As the band came on, Trey immediately commented on the venue, "Look at this place, it's like one giant plant." At this point it was rather pleasant outside, but I could see the clouds rolling in. As if on cue, as soon as Divided Sky began, the rain started. I was right in the front row and the only part of the venue not covered by a tent was the first three rows. But everyone in the front, including myself, decided to keep standing in the rain instead of pushing back. The showers lasted through Beauty of My Dreams, which made for a great experience. In set II, we were treated to a 30-minute version of Ghost, easily the longest of the European tour. —Marco Burgio

7/5/97 [ACCESSIBILITY: ••]
Piazza Risorgimento, Cernobbio (near Como), Italy
Julius, Bouncing, Uncle Pen, Sample, Theme, Caspian, Twist Around, Piper, Harry Hood > Love You > HYHU, Poor Heart, Character Zero, GTBT
E: Squirming Coil

Free outdoor show; Phish played one set. Soundcheck: Funky Bitch, Ginseng. "Groove Is in the Heart" and "Fluffhead" teases in Twist Around. Fishman on vacuum for Love You. "Walk This Way" tease in GTBT. Trey asked Chris Kuroda to turn the lights off during Harry Hood jam. Last Love You, 12/8/95 Cleveland, OH [111 shows].

With the lake and the Alps behind and villas scattered throughout the mountains, this venue was easily the most beautiful place Phish played thus far on the tour. There were approximately five hundred people at the concert, many of whom were there just out of curiosity. Rumor was that the band would be playing one long set instead of two. This ended up being the case, and since it was a free show, no one really complained. The highlight of the show was Harry Hood. Yes, they played it the previous show, but this was not your standard Hood. As they reached the point where Trey begins the long jam right after Mr. Miner, he said, "Chris, shut the lights off so we can see the mountains." As the jam began to build, Trey slowly turned around, just staring up at the mountains. It was the most emotional Hood I have ever experienced. —Marco Burgio

7/6/97 [ACCESSIBILITY: •••]
Spiaggia di Rivoltana, Desenzano/Genova, Italy
I: Runaway Jim, Old Home Place, Dogs Stole Things, Stash, Horse > Silent, CTB, Scent of a Mule, Chalkdust
II: Free, YEM, Waste, Rocky Top, Funky Bitch
E: My Soul

Soundcheck was open to the public and included audience karaoke and limbo contest. Soundcheck setlist: Blow Wind Blow, Jam, Oblivious Fool, Beauty of My Dreams, "Hell's Bells" jam, Shook Me All Night Long (Fishman on lead vocals), Oom Bop (Fishman on vocals as "James Brown performing Hanson's M-M-M Bop"), Karaoke Contest (all sung by audience members, except Day-O, sung by the band, with limboing by audience): Another One Bites the Dust, And It Stoned Me, Only Shallow, Day-O.

Though Paul apparently asked the tapers not to record the surprise soundcheck, it was a temptation that some folks just couldn't pass up. Their indiscretion is our reward, because this is obviously a great moment in Phishtory. I wish I could have been there to see audience members take the microphone and sing great versions of Another One Bites the Dust (actually sung as "Another One Rides the Bus"), Stoned Me, and Only Shallow, or Phish taking over for Day-O to finish the limbo contest, but at least we can be there now from the tapes. Get it! —Ed Smith

The show on this night obviously paled in comparison to the special soundcheck earlier in the day. Besides the loose, informal atmosphere and the hilarious band-audience interaction, check out the "debut" of the instrumental tune Blow Wind Blow, later played on the second night at the Gorge in early August. —Lee Johnston

7/9/97 [ACCESSIBILITY: ••••]
Le Transbordeur, Lyon/Villeurbanne, France
I: PYITE > Caspian, Ginseng Sullivan, Melt, Dirt, Taste, Adeline, Harry Hood
II: Down with Disease > My Soul > CTB > YEM, Ghost, Poor Heart
E: Hello My Baby

Bela Fleck on banjo, Victor Wooten on bass, and Future Man on synth-axe drumitar for YEM, Ghost, and Poor Heart.

There was a pretty solid rumor that Bela Fleck and the Flecktones would join Phish in Lyon. Someone said that on Bela Fleck's Web page it said "jamming with Phish" under their tour dates for 7/9/97. During You Enjoy Myself, our wishes were granted as Bela Fleck and the Flecktones came out and took their positions. The rest of the show was absolutely rocking. Highlights for me were when Flecktone bassist Victor Wooten and Mike were simultaneously playing the same bass, and when Bela and Trey faced off two feet apart from each other, exchanging licks. If you haven't heard this on tape yet, I highly recommend doing whatever it takes to get this show. —Marco Burgio

Tape traders have gone batty for the Lille show from earlier in this tour, but the sec-

GENOVA, Italy

Sunday, July 6, 1997

After taking the train with a group of other fans to Desenzano, we ended up waiting an hour and a half for a bus that dropped us off right in front of the beach where the show would be. Not many people know about this place, but believe me when I say it is breathtaking. The town sports the biggest lake in Italy and the water was fresh and clear. As we stepped onto the rocky beach, we saw the crew setting up the stage. I never thought any venue could beat that of the day before in Como, but sure enough, this place was equally if not more beautiful.

View from the stage.

Photo courtesy of Marco Burgio.

Around four P.M. I went swimming in the lake and as I was treading water I noticed Mike Gordon taking his clothes off. He had his fluorescent green bathing suit on and he dove into the water.

A bit later, Trey strolled down the beach and they all climbed onstage for the soundcheck. The soundcheck proved to be amazing, to say the least. I was lucky to be in the front row, pressed against the gates, where I snapped some great photos. And I wasn't the only one—the crazy soundcheck witnessed by about ninety people began with the band taking pictures of each other. I found it amusing to see the simplicity of their cameras.

After the boys finished enjoying the moment, they picked up their instruments and began an open jam. About one minute in, Trey looked Mike's way and said, "You're the bassist, right?" Mike acknowledged the remark and kept playing. My take on it was that Trey must have felt that Mike wasn't playing hard enough, and I witnessed a quick change in sound after the comment. After jamming for a few minutes, they went into Oblivious Fool (unplayed since the remarkable show in Lille a few weeks earlier) followed by Beauty of My Dreams.

At the conclusion of Beauty of My Dreams, the band paused and church bells could be heard ringing from a bell tower located next to the beach. Trey found this amusing and began to play "Hell's Bells." They then went into a full cover of "Shook Me All Night Long."

The highlight of the soundcheck (as if everything they'd already done wasn't enough) was when Mike suggested to Trey that they get a limbo contest going. They set up Mike's microphone as the limbo pole and then asked the crowd if someone wanted to sing. An eager male obliged and jumped up onstage. Trey then summoned for a few people to come up onstage to participate in the limbo contest.

At first, I hesitated, but when I saw other people jumping the fence to the stage, I couldn't resist.

The limbo contest began with the tune "Another One Bites the Dust" sung by that guy from the crowd. He altered the lyrics a bit and sang, "Another one rides the bus!" which I hadn't even noticed until hearing the tapes. I stood on the stage awaiting my turn, exhilarated as I took in where I was and what I was doing. I made it through one round, but got bounced after practically falling in the second round accompanied by the boos of the crowd. I quickly stepped off the stage and left the limboing to people that had a clue.

By this point, another guy from the crowd came onstage and took over vocals. He offered to sing "Stoned Me" and was very impressive. After this song was over, the limbo contest was reduced to three people, all of whom were female. After a very impressive stand by all the finalists, the winner was crowned and the soundcheck came to a close.

After the soundcheck, I returned to the hotel to call my roommate back in the States to inform him of the spectacle that I both witnessed and participated in. There was no answer, so I left a detailed message on his answering machine, knowing full well that he would never understand the experience I had just been a part of. Then I walked across the street to get some food and wine to prepare me for the show that was about two hours away.

Overall, the show wasn't that impressive. The soundcheck was easily the highlight, and the scenery was obviously another added bonus.

—Marco Burgio

Trey taking a picture of Page during the soundcheck.

Photo courtesy of Marco Burgio.

ond set of this show is where the real European action is, in my opinion. Béla Fleck, making his first appearance onstage with Phish since November 1995, brings his sublime banjo stylings to a great YEM jam, Ghost, and Poor Heart—not to mention the deep groove that fellow Flecktones Victor Wooten and Future Man help create. Simply marvelous! —Lee Johnston

7/10/97 [ACCESSIBILITY: •••]

Espace Julien, Marseille, France

I: Dogs Stole Things, Limb by Limb, Ginseng Sullivan, Bathtub Gin, Llama > Wading in the Velvet Sea, Lizards, Oblivious Fool

II: Also Sprach > Julius, Magilla > Ya Mar, Ghost > Take Me to the River

E: Funky Bitch

"Magilla" tease in Ya Mar, which also featured a number of duets between the band members. Members of Son Seals Band joined for Funky Bitch: Dan Rabinovitz, trumpet; Justin Smith, rhythm guitar; Johnny B. Gayden, bass; and David Russell, drums. Last Take Me to the River, 11/21/95 Winston-Salem, NC [126 shows].

Before the show, I watched three guys walk up to the stage and then I saw Fishman come out. Fishman looked really happy to see them, but I had no idea who they were. As Fishman was talking to one of them, I walked up to one of the guys and said, "I don't mean to be rude, but who are you guys?" He replied, "We're the Son Seals Band out of Chicago." Much later, as the crowd yelled for an encore, out came Phish and, low and behold, the members of the Son Seals Band. They jammed out on a Funky Bitch like none other. —Marco Burgio

For the last two-set Phish show of the European tour, this was a rocking affair. Besides the Funky Bitch encore with special friends, we were thrilled by the Ghost > Take Me to the River pairing that closed the second set. I was surprised that few people recognized TMTTR as the classic Talking Heads song, previously played by Phish in the middle of David Bowie from 11/21/95 (tour rumors also credited both Bruce Springsteen and Joni Mitchell as the song's author). —Jerry Guthrie

7/11/97 [ACCESSIBILITY: ••]

Doctor Music Festival, Pyrenees, Spain

Chalkdust, Bouncing, Stash, Beauty of My Dreams, Wolfman's, Johnny B. Goode, YEM

E: Character Zero

Music festival; Phish played one set. The band following Phish at the festival was soundchecking on a nearby stage while Phish played.

🐟 Another fairly straightforward festival set was enhanced by the beautiful scenery high in the mountains of Spain. Plenty of Phish friends, like Blues Traveler and Primus, were also at this festival, but no guest appearances materialized. Instead, the band left us with a beautiful YEM and a rocking Zero encore, and plenty of smiles. This was a great tour. —Jerry Guthrie

1997 SUMMER
"Find Yourself a City"

Phish offered a more generous summer tour to U.S. fans than they had in summer 1996, but with only nineteen shows, some fans (especially those in the Northeast) still felt a little slighted. What the tour lacked in length, however, it made up for in execution, as Phish returned from the smaller venues of Europe ready to show off their funk awakening to the much larger amphitheater crowds.

The tour garnered rave reviews from virtually all corners of Phish phandom, with people applauding Phish's increasingly funk-oriented jam style and the continued transformation it brought to songs as wide-ranging as Gumbo, Also Sprach Zarathustra, and You Enjoy Myself (which had its ending reworked differently during each performance, and the vocal jam all but eliminated). The centerpiece songs of the tour were named by many as Wolfman's Brother and Cities—two songs that really allowed the band to bring in the funk. Ghost and Loving Cup also served as defining songs. With all of the new, there was of course sadness about the passing of the old. Gamehendge songs surfaced in lesser numbers than ever, and old favorites like Divided Sky and Tweezer became rarities. But there was still plenty of magic to be had, from Trey's Jerry Garcia tribute at Shoreline to Ken Kesey's appearance at Darien Lake to the giant Great Went, which drew over 60,000 fans a day to a remote upper corner of Maine.

7/21/97 **[Accessibility: •••] [Attend. 20,074; Cap. 20,074] [TIX $25]**
Virginia Beach Amphitheater, Virginia Beach, VA
I: Ghost, Dogs Stole Things, Piper, Dirt, Ginseng Sullivan, Bathtub Gin, Character Zero
II: Wolfman's > Magilla, Bowie, Wading in the Velvet Sea, Theme > Multi-instrument Jam > Funky Bitch, Slave
E: Loving Cup

"Drowned" jam in Bathtub Gin. "Birdland" jam in Bowie intro. Leroi Moore on saxophone for jam out of Theme, Multi-instrument Jam, and Funky Bitch. During the "multi-instrument jam," all five people onstage played two or three instruments (Trey on three guitars, Mike on two basses, etc.).

🐟 The tapers' section buzzed with word that the band would treat us to an entire first set's worth of new material, and from the get-go, it seemed like they just might. Four great new songs got a solid reception (except from a girl behind me, who griped, "Why are they playing this stuff?"), and in Bathtub Gin, Trey welcomed us to the tour and announced the names of the new tunes. Set II was a jam-fest, including a Trey-led, very improvised Magilla jam, a very nice Bowie with elongated "Birdland" jam in the intro, and a wild multi-instrument jam out of Theme with DMB's Leroi Moore. —Scott Sifton

🐟 A rainbow over the stage after a torrid preshow shower reminded us of the summer tour opener the previous year in Utah, and the great Ghost opener introduced many of us to this new gem of the Phish catalog. But it was the wild jam with Leroi Moore in set II that made this show something really special. After Leroi took a few solos, he strapped on another sax and proceeded to play both at once. Not to be outdone, Trey took on another guitar, Mike added another bass, and Page used his feet to play his organ, piano, and keyboard all at the same time. While the crowd went nuts, Trey signaled Funky Bitch, and before we knew it, we were off and running. After Leroi left the stage to huge cheers, the Slave closer was pure gravy. —Rick Clancy

7/22/97 **[Accessibility: •••] [Attend. 19,910; Cap. 19,910] [TIX $27]**
Walnut Creek Amphitheater, Raleigh, NC
I: Runaway Jim > My Soul, Water in the Sky, Stash, Bouncing, Vultures, Bye Bye Foot, Taste
II: Down with Disease > Mike's > Simple > Hydrogen > Weekapaug, Hello My Baby
E: When the Circus Comes, Harry Hood

"Hydrogen" teases in Weekapaug.

🐟 The lot scene at Walnut Creek is one of the most pleasant to be found on the East Coast amphitheater circuit. Cars filled the grassy fields and fans lounged in the sun and under the trees while the strains of the Water in the Sky soundcheck floated out from the venue. By the time we headed in, about an hour before showtime, ominous clouds were on the horizon, and during the new Fishman ballad Bye Bye Foot, the rain started. That led Phish into an energized Taste, and as thunder roared overhead, the band capped off the Taste jam in fine fashion, then cut the set short. Throughout setbreak, wind and rain swept the amphitheater—we huddled for cover and still got soaked to the skin. But the wait was worth it for the second set, which opened with DWD and intricately segued into Mike's Song, to everyone's delight. The rest of the set is what legends are made of. —Sue Trafton

🐟 Both sets are short but hot, hot, hot (and wet, wet, wet). Runaway Jim > My Soul is a perfect segue, and as Trey creeps from DWD into Mike's, you can hear the crowd's excitement at the turn of events. Up on the lawn, we were delirious! The entire DWD > Mike's Groove sequence runs almost an hour and is probably the best Mike's Groove of the summer, complete with a great Simple and the always-bewitching Hydrogen (which Trey teased us with again in Weekapaug). Add a bonus Harry Hood encore and you have a great night in hurricane country. Next time I'm bringing my rain poncho. —Josh Albini

7/23/97 **[Accessibility: •••] [Attend. 19,028; Cap. 19,028] [TIX $25]**
Lakewood Amphitheater, Atlanta, GA
I: Julius, Dirt, NICU, Dogs Stole Things, Ginseng Sullivan, Water in the Sky, Limb by Limb, Melt, Billy Breathes, Possum
II: PYITE, Ghost > Sample, YEM > Rocky Mountain Way > Chalkdust
E: Frankenstein

Klezmer-type jam (similar to middle segment of Scent of a Mule) out of YEM into Rocky Mountain Way. Concert debut: Rocky Mountain Way.

🐟 A solid first set, featuring the best Julius I have ever heard, going over fifteen minutes, was followed by the best and most energetic set I have ever witnessed. After an excellent PYITE opener, they went into a perfectly jammed Ghost. The Sample that followed was definitely a crowd-pleaser as it got everybody up and going. This must have pumped the band up and they decided to get nasty. Trey threw the Russian/Scent jam into YEM, going absolutely crazy in the vocal jam. Rocky Mountain Way was a suprise, to say the least. They then proceeded to completely tear Chalkdust apart, with Trey pulling away from the mic early at the end of every verse, so he could get a jump start on the jamming. At the close, I just stood there, awestruck, as Trey and Fish payed tribute to Trey's guitar, "Pepe-Le-Pew." —Mike Jett

🐟 Like the first set of many summer tour shows, Lakewood's first set had some cool moments—a fun Julius opener and groovy Possum closer—but lacked cohesion. The second set was a totally different story, as the band perfectly balanced extended jams with crowd-pleasing favorities. Ghost is easily the best version of the summer, twenty-seven minutes of very interesting improvisation (some tour-heads would later grumble that Ghost peaked on this night, and slowly declined for the rest of the tour), then a rocking Sample revived those unfamiliar with the previous number. Similarly, the YEM > Rocky Mountain Way combo mixed a wild Klezmer-type jam out of YEM into a classic rock favorite before Chalkdust, with Trey whispering the verses and ripping back into the chords, provided the exclamation point. —Josh Albini

7/25/97 **[Accessibility: ••] [Attend. 9,515; Cap. 20,111] [TIX $25]**
Starplex Amphitheater, Dallas, TX
I: Beauty of My Dreams, Wolfman's > Maze, Water in the Sky, Bathtub Gin > Makisupa > AC/DC Bag
II: Chalkdust > Taste > Ya Mar > Drums Jam > Ghost > Character Zero
E: Theme

Entire second set with Bob Gullotti on a second drum set. Drums Jam featured Fishman and Gullotti.

🐟 The Dallas show marked one of the rare occasions in which a first set outshined the second, as the Bathtub Gin > Makisupa > AC/DC Bag segment to close the set was a series which would have been a highlight at any show. In set II, Bob Gullotti joined the band onstage for some double-barrel drumming action. His appearance at the two Texas shows had been announced ahead of time, and he seemed to know Phish's music far better than during his first appearance with the band in Hartford on the 1996 fall tour. He and Fishman shared the spotlight for a drum jam during Ya Mar, before the band joined back in for Ghost. Dallas marked the only time on the tour that Ghost comprised the meat of the second set alone, an idea which received a mixed reception, at best. —Andy Bernstein

7/26/97 [ACCESSIBILITY: •••] [ATTEND. 11,477; CAP. 15,000] [TIX $25–$27]

South Park Meadows, Austin, TX

I: Limb by Limb, Dogs Stole Things, Poor Heart, Stash, Billy Breathes, CTB, Dirt, YEM > Izabella

II: Timber Ho > Bowie, Harry Hood > Blister in the Sun > Harry Hood > Free, Waste > Johnny B. Goode

E: Bouncing, Cavern

Bob Gullotti on a second drum set for the entire show. Blister in the Sun was one verse only; concert debut. Harry Hood unfinished.

Unlike Dallas, we were treated to the sounds of two drummers from start to finish, and the show never let up. A solid first set included the hot new song Limb by Limb as an opener and a fierce YEM > Izabella sequence to close. Then set II didn't have a single dull moment, leading off with a jammed-out Timber Ho which some later termed a tour highlight. A fine Bowie was then followed by an unfinished Harry Hood—though we were never told to feel good about Hood, the boys treated us to a verse of Blister in the Sun by old European tour buddies the Violent Femmes. Following the show, many Phish-heads sampled the famed Austin nightlife—which was in full swing on its own as phans were still in the clear minority in the many downtown bars. —Andy Bernstein

7/29/97 [ACCESSIBILITY: ••] [ATTEND. 10,147; CAP. 20,246] [TIX $25–$27]

Desert Sky Pavilion, Phoenix, AZ

I: Theme, Beauty of My Dreams, Gumbo, Dirt, Sparkle, Ghost, Swept Away > Steep > Loving Cup

II: Oblivious Fool, Antelope, Wading in the Velvet Sea, Twist Around, Taste, Sample, Rocky Top, Squirming Coil

E: Possum

We were psyched for Phish's first show at Desert Sky, and though the place was nowhere near sold out, there was still a palpable energy in the air at showtime. Unfortunately the show didn't live up to our expectations. The new funked-out version of Gumbo was a treat, but the rest of the show seemed too overwhelmed with new material to ever really soar. —Sue Trafton

Lots of the seldom-played new songs highlighted a very different second set. Oblivious Fool, debuted in Europe in June, was the only version played on the U.S. tour, and Wading in the Velvet Sea and Twist Around also made only infrequent appearances. After Taste, however, the set pretty much flattened out, before the Possum encore bopped us up the highway to Ventura. —Dave Sharpe

7/30/97 [ACCESSIBILITY: •••] [ATTEND. 13,205; CAP. 13,205] [TIX $25]

Ventura County Fairgrounds, Ventura, CA

I: NICU, Wolfman's > Chalkdust, Water in the Sky, Stash, Weigh, Piper, CTB, Character Zero

II: PYITE, Free, Bowie > Cities > Bowie, Bouncing, Uncle Pen, Caspian, Fire

E: My Soul

I wasn't expecting much from this show because the venue is pretty schwag—it's basically just a dirty racetrack. But this show raged! The phunky new direction of Wolfman's Brother was a pleasant surprise and sign of Phish's current musical evolution which I think is just great. In set II, a Simpsons cue led into one of the top musical highlights of the year—David Bowie > Cities > David Bowie. The Bowie jam had started to ramble, but suddenly took a really funky direction. I didn't know where they were going, but I just started grooving. I looked around and saw everyone else doing the same. It was a great moment—none of us knew where we were heading, but we were all sharing in a groove. And then they busted out Cities! —Greg Schwartz

The new Free jam arrangement is spectacular, and this show offers the best version of this song out there. Following Free, they go into Bowie, which does not always excite me, but as the jam started getting all funky, I was thinking this had to be the best Bowie ever. Then Cities emerged and I freaked. Pure musical magic! —Mike Jett

7/31/97 [ACCESSIBILITY: ••••] [ATTEND. 19,621; CAP. 19,621] [TIX $25]

Shoreline Amphitheater, Mountain View, CA

I: Ghost, Ya Mar, Dogs Stole Things, Limb by Limb, Dirt, Maze, Glide, I Saw It Again, YEM

II: Runaway Jim > When the Circus Comes, Vultures, McGrupp, Mike's > Hydrogen > Weekapaug

E: Cinnamon Girl

"Sweet Home Alabama" tease before Runaway Jim. "Happy Birthday" tease in Weekapaug, with Trey paying tribute to Jerry Garcia.

From the moment they hit the stage with the Ghost opener, I felt that the band was totally invoking the cosmic Bay Area/GD vibe. I couldn't help but feel like I Saw It Again was symbolic of Phish being the next generation of the Grateful Dead musical thing. Maybe that's just me, but it seemed even more significant in light of the fact that this was the only place they played it on the U.S. tour. And then, completely out of left field—YEM! All of us in those first few rows felt especially blessed to see a YEM like that up close to close the first set. The Runaway Jim that opened the second set could well have been called Runaway Jimi—Trey was getting downright cosmic in the open-ended exploration of the tune. Later, in Weekapaug, they were locked into such a tight groove, sounding so crisp—it was oh so sweet. When Trey started playing Happy Birthday, I knew more special vibes were heading our way. When he actually verbalized it by saying that he wanted to wish Jerry a happy birthday and vowed that "We're gonna try and keep his spirit alive in music for the next decade," all my theories were confirmed. I knew that it was no coincidence that this tour had Phish at Shoreline on the eve of Jerry's birthday and had us waking up in San Francisco on the day of his birthday, August 1. —Greg Schwartz

Trey remarked on Fish's sleek black outfit following a very funky Limb by Limb in the first set, telling the crowd that he tried to master the song's drumbeat in his frock but couldn't get it down right until he switched to his black summer suit. Limb By Limb, like the rest of this show, just raged—I think it topped all the other West Coast shows (including the Gorge), and might have been better than all the pre-Went shows on this tour. —Dave Sharpe

After the short but powerful Mike's Groove, complete with the Jerry Garcia tribute at the Dead's old home, the band left the stage to huge applause. Backstage, word was that the band used a tape deck to relearn Cinnamon Girl (debuted at the Flynn show in March) for the encore. Another nice touch, near Neil Young's home. If you seek out these tapes, you won't be disappointed. —Ed Smith

8/2/97 [ACCESSIBILITY: ••••] [ATTEND. 20,000; CAP. 20,000] [TIX $20.95]

The Gorge, George, WA

I: Theme, Ginseng Sullivan, Ghost, Dogs Stole Things, Divided Sky, Wolfman's, Water in the Sky, Melt

II: Down with Disease > Tweezer > Down with Disease > Johnny B. Goode, Sparkle, Wading in the Velvet Sea, Loving Cup, Tweezer Reprise

E: Harry Hood

Trey asked Chris Kuroda to turn the lights off during the Harry Hood jam.

Sickness, total sickness. The venue, breathtaking; the scene, more relaxed than news reports would have you believe; and the music, wondrous. The Tweezer jam is just so pure, so perfect, that you have to rejoice. I hope Phish makes the Gorge an annual stop—how about three sets next time, guys? —Amy Duncan

We were almost as excited for the Gorge this summer as we were for Red Rocks in previous years. Though the place is bigger than Red Rocks, its physical surroundings are perhaps even more dramatic. The stage towers over part of the Columbia River valley, offering amazing views behind the band. The Saturday night show was sold out, and rocked from the start with a textural Theme opener, the only Divided Sky of the U.S. tour (a little rusty), and a great Wolfman's in the style of Hamburg. But it was in set II that the metaphoric fireworks came out, with a DWD > Tweezer that wandered into an amazingly gorgeous jam before coming around into a brief DWD Reprise reminiscent of the Seattle show from November '96. Harry Hood is also a particularly notable version, finishing the evening in beautiful fashion. —Rick Clancy

Photo courtesy of Jay Archibald.

8/3/97 [ACCESSIBILITY: •••] **[ATTEND. 17,871; CAP. 20,000] [TIX $20.95]**
The Gorge, George, WA
I: Bathtub Gin > Foam > Blow Wind Blow, Dirt, Vultures, My Mind's, Twist Around > Jesus Left Chicago, Limb by Limb, Character Zero
II: Julius, Simple, Fluffhead, Lifeboy, Taste, Hello My Baby, Frankenstein
E: Bouncing, Slave

Last My Mind's, 11/15/96 St. Louis, MO [61 shows].

The scene seemed fairly mellow after the previous night's show, so we hadn't partied too hard. That left us really primed for this one. We staked out a place in line and scored the best of both worlds—a spot on the floor way close up, and a great chill spot on the ledges. I watched the first set on the ledges, thinking that was the place to take it all in. Limb by Limb made a huge impression on me, then came a raging Character Zero set closer. I enjoyed the set very much, but by the end, I knew I had to go down front for the second set. Before I went down, though, I noticed that the Big Dipper was positioned directly above the band—it looked like it was pouring the cosmic ooze right onto the stage! Very cool. The second set was amazing. I feel that they were at the top of their game, just playing so well. Simple was absolutely "eargasmic." Trey went off on Fluffhead, which really pleased all the phans who feared it was one of the rumored "shelved" songs. But the real fireworks came during Taste. I felt like a bit of that cosmic ooze slipped into the jam at one point, and Trey just channeled it for all it was worth. The scene after the show was one of the all-time greats. Everyone was so happy, partying all night long. —Greg Schwartz

A bit of a downer to close the West Coast tour. I had hoped for another funkfest like Saturday's, but instead the band played what I'd call a Sunday show—relaxed, mellow, and not too ambitious. Trey later called this his favorite show in the first half of the tour, with Jesus Left Chicago and Foam his personal highlights, but I was disappointed by the second set, because it never really went *there*. Still, the Gorge was a damn fine time. —Dave Sharpe

8/6/97 [ACCESSIBILITY: ••] **[ATTEND. 15,121; CAP. 21,000] [TIX $25–$27]**
Riverport Amphitheater, Maryland Heights, MO
I: NICU, Stash, Beauty of My Dreams, Twist Around > Also Sprach > AC/DC Bag, Ya Mar, YEM
II: Runaway Jim > My Soul, Ghost, Caspian, CTB, Sample, Antelope > Makisupa Jam > Antelope
E: Julius

Page on theremin and Mike on minidrum kit for Makisupa Jam.

I wasn't expecting a whole lot from this show, because I don't care for the vibe here. I'd seen both Phish and the Dead here in '95, and the lot scene sucks—they have security going around all day busting people for selling jewelry, sodas, grilled cheese, or whatever. But inside, the venue is nice, much like Deer Creek, and the show was kind. This was the no-letdown tour. The long-awaited appearance of 2001 made my day, and getting another YEM to close the first set proved another pleasant surprise. The highlight of the second set was definitely the Antelope > Makisupa jam > Antelope. Combined with the Julius encore, it felt like the band was aware of the lot scene and making a clear statement to phans—have fun on tour, but watch it. Once again, Phish showed how tuned in they are to what's going on around them, one of the things that continues to make them special in a way that most bands aren't. —Greg Schwartz

8/8/97 [ACCESSIBILITY: ••] **[ATTEND. 22,493; CAP. 25,000] [TIX $25–$27]**
New World Music Theatre, Tinley Park, IL
I: CTB, Gumbo > Lizards, Dirt, It's Ice, Water in the Sky, Character Zero
II: Wolfman's > Free, Limb by Limb, Loving Cup, Caspian, Chalkdust
E: Hoochie Coochie Man, Messing with the Kid

Sugar Blue on harmonica for encores. Last Hoochie Coochie Man, 4/10/93 Chicago, IL [381 shows]. Concert debut: Messing with the Kid. Show broadcast live over the Internet (video and audio) on JamTV.

Sometimes, highlights come in strange packages. When I told friends who weren't there that Gumbo was the best song of the night, they thought I was dissing the show. Well, maybe it would have been nice to have a few epics blow me out of my seat, but hearing an endless Gumbo with just an amazing series of grooves made this night really special, unique, and I definitely walked out of the gargantuan World Music Theatre with a huge grin. Character Zero also raged (by summer's end I was getting sick of it, and starting to recategorize it in my mind as one of the "this again?" tunes, but at that point I couldn't get enough), and Wolfman's was another jamathon. Hey, this may not have been the best show of the tour, but if you want to hear what summer 1997 was all about—great jams in strange places—get this tape. — Lynne Golden

Great show! First set had the best Gumbo Phish has ever played, about twenty-five minutes long—gotta love that funk! Not to mention one of the phattest Zeros of the summer, and a mind-blowing Wolfman's > Free. We also got kicked a long, jammed out Loving Cup and a matching Chalkdust. What could be a better encore than bringing out a hometown harmonica man, Sugar Blue? Hoochie Coochie Man is jammin', but Messin' with the Kid is the superfunk! —R. J. Bee

Saw this one from my computer, broadcast across the Internet on JamTV, with decent audio and jerky video. Plenty of long, funky jamming in the funk vehicles Gumbo and Wolfman's, plus a great encore with Sugar Blue. If more Phish shows are broadcast over the Net, I fear becoming the ultimate couch potato! —Adam Brinton

8/9/97 [ACCESSIBILITY: ••••] **[ATTEND. 34,642; CAP. 34,642] [TIX $25–$27]**
Alpine Valley Music Theater, East Troy, WI
I: Theme, PYITE, Ghost > Taste, Dogs Stole Things, Reba, Lawn Boy, Crossroads
II: Wilson > Foam, Mike's > Funny as It Seems > Simple > Swept Away > Steep > Scent of a Mule > Slave > Weekapaug
E: When the Circus Comes, Rocky Top

Last Crossroads, 12/9/95 Albany, NY [125 shows].

This show absolutely ruled—from start to finish, probably the most rip-rocking show of the tour, if you judge it just on pure musical intensity. The entire first set was awesome—Theme/PYITE/Ghost/Taste had this show energized from the get-go, and Reba was reminiscent of the brilliant 12/31/95 version. The second set raged all the way through, but it was the Scent of a > Slave to the > Groove segment that was truly mind-blowing. Scent was extra incredible because of the high strangeness that took place during the Mule Duel. I swear Trey was stalking around the stage like he was a mind-controlled android. And then he and Mike lay on their backs and pedaled their legs as on a bicycle. Then they'd get up, jam a few chords, and get back down and do it again. They must have done this five times. I know there's precedent for doing weird stuff during the Mule Duel, but I'd never seen anything this bizarre. This show is an all-time keeper. —Greg Schwartz

Ever since Phish discovered da funk, they seem to be enjoying playing PYITE a lot more. The opening segment goes perfectly with their new sound, and was particularly stretched out (or was it just that my mind was being stretched by it?) at this show. —Randy Moon

8/10/97 [ACCESSIBILITY: •••] **[ATTEND. 20,891; CAP. 20,891] [TIX $25–$27]**
Deer Creek Music Center, Noblesville, IN
I: Bathtub Gin > Sparkle, Down with Disease, Dirt, CTB, Billy Breathes, Melt, Bye Bye Foot, Ginseng Sullivan, Harry Hood
II: Cities > GTBT > Rotation Jam > HYHU > Rocka William, Bowie
E: Cavern

Page on theremin during the jam preceding Rotation Jam. Last Rotation Jam, 12/29/96 Philadelphia, PA [50 shows].

The Deer Creek adventure should be experienced by all at one time or another. After we found our campground (someone's backyard) near the venue, we set up camp and made our way on the path to the amphitheater. First-set highlights included the Bathtub Gin opener, a solid midset DWD, and of course the Hood closer. The moon was rising in the night sky and a slight breeze swept the lawn as the lights went down for set II. Trey teased us with his Languedoc—Punch? AC/DC Bag? Ghost? The seconds seemed like hours, then Trey dropped us the treat we'd been waiting to see—the crowd cheered in unison as Trey sang, "Think of London. . . ." This was a Cities like no other, its relentless funk getting funkier and into deeper and deeper grooves. Twenty-two minutes later, the jam grinded to an abrupt halt. As Trey dropped to the floor of the stage we heard the first notes of Good Times Bad Times ring out. They settled on a jam out of Good Times and from out of nowhere came the theremin, everyone's favorite summer toy of Page's. All the while Mike, Trey, and Fish moved about on the stage, trading places for a rotation jam that brought us to the new Fishman song Rocka William. Dressed in his pimplike purple and black outfit, Fish took Trey's place as guitarist and the crowd responded loudly to the "children of the corn" lyric. The jam out of Rocka had the corn around us swaying and eventually led into a creepy, set-closing David Bowie. The band encored short and to the point with Cavern, perfectly closing the first night of Deer Creek. —Keith McRary

A local newspaper scribe trashed this show to bits—who cares, though? Part of the Deer Creek experience is forgetting about society, or making our own. — Lynne Golden

8/11/97 [ACCESSIBILITY: •••] **[ATTEND. 20,891; CAP. 20,891] [TIX $25–$27]**
Deer Creek Music Center, Noblesville, IN
I: Makisupa > Maze, Water in the Sky, Guyute, Guelah, Limb by Limb, Horn, Antelope
II: Timber Ho, Piper, Vultures, My Soul, YEM, Character Zero
E: Squirming Coil

Over the years I've learned that there is only one surefire way to predict a great show—Makisupa. If it's there, then you know it's going to be a hot night. The band won't toy with it otherwise. Now when Makisupa *leads off* the first set . . . three songs later my suspicions were confirmed by Guyute, which drew an utter roar of ecstacy from the crowd. Limb by Limb was great as always, and Horn really worked too, a nice contrast to the complex and multitextural Limb by Limb. The Antelope which followed was downright sinister, and set the tone for a fantastic set II. Gottal love Vultures, another ominous sort of tune. Great work by Kuroda too. —Randy Moon

This would prove to be one of the most memorable nights of my life. I scored a fourth-row ticket only to find that the fourth row was double-booked by mail order and Ticketmaster. They made all the people with mail orders stand at the far right of the venue, trying to figure out where to stick us, when the boys came onstage and started Makisupa. Trey throwing in "schwag" could not have summed my feelings up better at that point. However, the yellow shirts decided to "make" us stand in the space between the first row and the security wall! It was unbelievable. Guyute was one of the better I've heard. By the time they ended the set with Antelope, I felt like I had won the lottery. In set II, getting to see YEM from the front row was really something special. —Mike Jett

Definitely not one of my favorite shows. Everything was tripped out to the max, and I didn't feel that they were playing that well. I have to tip my hat to Guyute and Antelope in the first set, both amazing as usual. The Squirming Coil encore was great, beautiful solo by Page, but besides that, there was nothing special. Let me rephrase this: Bad show. Good Guyute. —R. J. Bee

8/13/97 [ACCESSIBILITY: ••] [ATTEND. 23,335; CAP. 23,335] [TIX $25–$27]

Star Lake Amphitheater, Burgettstown, PA

I: Amoreena, Poor Heart, Water in the Sky, Gumbo, Horse > Silent, Beauty of My Dreams, Crosseyed and Painless, Wilson, Adeline

II: Runaway Jim, Ghost > Izabella, Sleeping Monkey, McGrupp, Sample, Also Sprach, Golgi, Frankenstein

E: Theme

"Little Drummer Boy" jam at the end of Wilson. Concert debut: Amoreena.

For whatever reason, the Star Lake show was a mix of some solid highlights and notable gaffes. Was Mike singing off-key for the start of Poor Heart? Sure sounded like it. But the first set—which opened strangely with the debut of Elton John's Amoreena with Page on vocals—did improve, highlighted by a long Gumbo and a fantastic Crosseyed and Painless. A fun Wilson with a severe "Little Drummer Boy" jam cranked everyone up for the second set. But set II featured more ups and downs. When Trey goofed during the opening Runaway Jim, he announced the flub to the crowd with a "whoops." Things heated up midway through the set with a funky, long 2001, which served as the show's centerpiece jam. After an apparent Golgi set closer, the upbeat Frankenstein emerged and closed the set with high energy. —Brian Celentano

The buzz was already in the air for the upcoming Great Went when we pulled into Star Lake on Wednesday. From the opener (Elton John's Amoreena, sung ably by Page) to the tour's only Crosseyed and Painless (play it more!) to a jammed-out Wilson with a "Little Drummer Boy" tease, the first set was mixed-up mayhem! Two thumbs up! Set II fell back into the summer 1998 groove, which wasn't a bad thing by any means. Trey did screw up the Jim opener, but a tasty Ghost > Izabella more than made up for it. —Josh Albini

This show reminds me of the Hersheypark show that preceded the Clifford Ball in summer 1996—a few solid musical highlights like CE&P, Ghost, and 2001 wedged in between a bunch of overplayed crowd favorites. There's no real flow to the songs at this show—perhaps the band had their mind on other things to come. —Sue Trafton

8/14/97 [ACCESSIBILITY: ••••] [ATTEND. 21,738; CAP. 21,738] [TIX $25]

Darien Lake Performing Arts Center, Darien Center, NY

I: Ya Mar, Funky Bitch, Fluffhead, Limb by Limb, Free, CTB, Tela, Train Song, Billy Breathes, Antelope

II: Chalkdust, Love Me, Sparkle, Harry Hood > Forbin's > Pranksters Jam > Camel Walk, Taste

E: Bouncing, Rocky Top

Pranksters jam with Ken Kesey, Ken Babbs, and the Merry Pranksters. "Frankenstein" jam during part of the Bozos narration. Last Forbin's, 10/31/96 Atlanta, GA [78 shows]. Last Tela, 11/7/96 Lexington, KY [74 shows].

There was a feeling in the air, that special feeling that only manifests itself once or twice a tour, if the planets are in alignment and the spells are cast. The music was good, especially the opening Ya Mar/Funky Bitch/Fluffhead trio in set one, but the magic of place and people proved more powerful as Ken Kesey and his gang of Pranksters—the catalysts of the 1960s Acid Tests featuring the Dead as house band—emerged onto the stage during Trey's rap in Col. Forbin's Ascent. This passing of the torch, so to speak, was something truly special, something I would not trade any song played on this tour to have missed. —Tyler Harris

I was skeptical about this show, because I had heard many negative reports about the Hershey show that had preceded the Clifford Ball in summer '96. But this was to be another historic moment in Phishtory. Inside, I encountered a phellow who informed me that Ken Kesey and the Merry Pranksters were here, and would be "coming onstage to tell stories with Phish." "No way!" I exclaimed. He then showed me his Kesey-autographed ticket stub. Sweet! As the show got underway, my anticipation ran high. I was stoked for Tela in the first set, which infused a welcome Gamehendge energy into the show. The Antelope that ended the first set was a pleasant surprise, but couldn't compare to the one from Deer Creek. The second set would turn out to be an all-time keeper. The long-awaited appearance of Col. Forbin really sent things to another level. I love Trey's stories that always accompany this song, and I fully expected this to be the moment for the Pranksters. So it was. To me, it was another unmistakable acknowledgment of the link/transference of the cosmic "scene" between the Dead and Phish, and Kesey alluded to this himself. It was a surreal scene indeed, as Kesey and the band were joined onstage by the *Wizard of Oz* characters and several others Kesey referred to as the "Bozos." After Kesey's rap, Trey was in fine form as the Pranksters left the stage, remarking, "That's what happens thirty years later when you take too much acid." Then Trey provided another classic Phish moment when he said, "We're supposed to go into Famous Mockingbird here, but the funk's too deep." The crowd roared with approval as they continued the phunk jam and then busted out Camel Walk! The crowd was way stoked after this one, and the mood ran high as the Great Went beckoned at last. —Greg Schwartz

8/16/97 [ACCESSIBILITY: ••••] [ATTEND. 61,588 FOR BOTH SHOWS] [TIX $70 FOR BOTH SHOWS AND CAMPING]

The Great Went, Loring Air Force Base, Limestone, ME

I: Makisupa > Harpua, Chalkdust, Theme, PYITE, Ghost, Ginseng Sullivan, YEM, Train Song, Character Zero, Squirming Coil

II: Wolfman's > Simple > My Soul, Jam > Slave, Rocky Top, Julius

III: Halley's > Cities > Llama > Lawn Boy, Limb by Limb, Funky Bitch

E: Contact, Loving Cup

Harpua was second-half only, starting where the song ended at the Clifford Ball. "Odd Couple Theme" in jam out of Simple. Vocal reprise of Halley's chorus in jam out of Halley's. Fireworks during Funky Bitch. Last Harpua, 12/29/96 Philadelphia, PA [54 shows]. Last Halley's Comet, 8/16/96 Plattsburgh, NY [92 shows]. Last Contact, 11/30/96 Sacramento, CA [60 shows].

The traffic jam stretched forever, but the local residents welcomed us with open arms, so the good vibes were flowing before we even made it to the Went campgrounds. That was just the beginning to another amazing Phish fantasy, the Great Went. Just as well run as the Clifford Ball, and the music was even better—exploratory, improvisational jamming at its finest, this time with a side of funk for breakfast! Nothing could be finer. —Sarah Barrow

Phish in the most remote corner of the most remote state in the Northeast? Sounds great! We knew we couldn't miss it, and I'm glad we didn't. So much Went on in the campgrounds that it was almost hard to remember to make it inside the concert campground for the shows, but they raged! Night one highlights included an overlong first set, then two sets of jamming intensity to follow, including Wolfman's > Simple > My Soul in set II and, what I thought to be the musical highlight of the weekend, Halley's > Jam > Cities > Llama in set III. Pick up the tapes from the FM radio broadcast; they do this great show justice. —Rick Clancy

Two musical highlights really stand out from night one: the Simple into the Odd Couple Theme was just sublime. I remember hearing it played again on Went radio Monday morning and everyone around me just stopped and took a break from tearing down their tents. A line of grins must have been stretched out for two miles. Then there was the Halley's. It was unlike any I'd heard before—slow, funky, and *jammed*, the perfect prelude to a Cities of similar ilk. —Amy Furci

O.K. So what was up with the laundry? There were these huge laundry lines with oversized pieces of clothing hanging from them on both sides of the stage. There are children starving in China and Phish is spending their money on making clothing big enough for King Kong. Just kidding. I wish every suffering person in the world could experience the unique joy that was the Went. —Gabe Levy

If you weren't at the Went, you've probably heard a million people talk about how far away it was from civilization. But you really can't pound that in enough. I mean, we're driving through the woods up north and there aren't even any towns. It was like the desert or the tundra, only it was rich, beautiful timberland. And, oh, thousands of other Phishheads on the road. Never have I felt so much a part of something, something awesome. A literal movement. When we finally hit the exit off 95, there was civilization again. I looked on the map and saw that Aroostook County actually had a few people living in it, despite its isolation. Driving through the actual town of Limestone I saw the strangest sight—about fifty local kids were lined up behind a sign that said "Show us your tits. $1." I don't know what their problem was but from what I heard, everyone else in the area was happy to have us. Thank you, residents of Limestone, ME! —Connie Allen

The previous night we had been listening to the last set of the Clifford Ball, with the aborted Harpua encore. I remarked to my friend, "I'll bet they finish that Harpua at the Went." He replied with great conviction, "No way will they do that." So it's about four o'clock, and we figure we better get into the show. We're still a good distance from the gates when the band hits the stage at 4:20 with Makisupa! D'oh! We should have foreseen such a move. My consternation only increases when they segue into the completion of last year's Harpua. We finally get in right as they go into Chalkdust. Oh well, lesson learned. The first day's show was stellar all the way through, with the third set a big winner, finely jammed throughout. Halley's Comet > Cities and the Funky Bitch that closed the show with accompanying spectacular fireworks display! The vibe was high as they totally jammed it out, surely one of the highlights of the summer. —Greg Schwartz

All three sets of this show stand on their own as miniature masterpieces. The first set, played during the waning hours of daylight, has a more laid-back feel as the music stretches on for almost two hours. The second and third sets are tighter, funkier, and a little darker, but even more outrageous. They did a great job integrating the old, the new, and the weird (listen for an "Odd Couple" jam in Simple) like only Phish can. —Scott Sifton

I thought Halley's to open the third set was a treat, but the jam out of the lyrics broke new ground. After jamming along for a while, Trey starts back up part of the lyrical refrain, "I'm going down, to the central part of town," and the jam twists onward, eventually arriving at Cities. Wow! —Pat Stanley

For the second and third sets, we walked around the grounds amazed. The music sounded so great and provided the perfect ambiance for exploring the square. We saw the Gordon Stone Trio, dressed as beatniks, playing between sets. In the village, Went Central, we bought coffee from a temperamental coffeeman that made us think of the Soup Nazi. While in line, we heard a fine drum solo by Fish and the a capella Limb by Limb closing. I had to dance when I heard Funky Bitch—like all of the long jams this night, they were really rocking out. The lights were really cool and I danced, or tried to (it's hard to dance to Phish with a radio strapped around your neck and a steaming cup of coffee in your hand). I laughed and danced as the fireworks started. That made me laugh hard because the fireworks were cooler than Portland's Fourth of July show. It was terrific. —The Reverend

The Went had a much different feel to it than the Clifford Ball. Limestone is literally in the middle of nowhere and its distance weeded out the weak and unadventurous. In order to avoid the terrible option of setting up camp one to two miles away from the venue many showed up Friday afternoon. And those like me who showed up after midnight were treated to a two-hour wait to get in and a 40-degree rainstorm, which pelted the tents and exposed the unprepared to an element of misery. When daylight broke, incredible Shakedown downs blossomed into action offering hot coffee and the best French toast money could buy. We knew the drive was worth every mile. —Charlie Lazurus

Just about the only thing that didn't happen at the Went was that the Rolling Stones didn't show up. They had been practicing for their upcoming tour in Canada and were rumored to be flying in, but it didn't happen. But who needs the Stones when you've got Phish, and a Loving Cup encore to close one of the greatest shows I've ever seen? —James Daly

[8/16/97]

Disco Set, Great Went, Loring Air Force Base, Limestone, ME

In the pre-dawn hours following the August 16 show, Phish deejayed a set of disco/rave music from a miniature portable stage near the entrance to the concert grounds.

Long after the first night's show, we were chilling out at a phan-produced disco party at someone's van. "Phish's playing!" a guy yelled from down the runway, and after we sprinted about a quarter of a mile, we saw the glow of bright white lights from the back of another flatbed truck. But a mellow jam this was not—the band was deejaying a techno affair of wild electronic music under a spinning disco ball! Nothing recognizably Phishy could be heard, which probably disappointed the handful of tapers who set up their gear about twenty feet from the makeshift stage. "Keep the disco beat alive!" Trey told us as they left the stage, magically disappearing back into the night. —Scott Sifton

Disco was the theme of this weekend! "Don't forget to check out the disco!" Trey told us at the end of the second set that night, and we figured his words were a tip-off to some more late-night fun. We were right! Right near the concert gates, they set up a mini-stage at about 2:30 A.M. and created electronic music for about five hundred mostly befuddled fans. Watching M.C. Neon Cell Gap (as they called Page) banging away on a keyboard, looking very serious under the harsh glow of the white lighting, is my funniest memory of the weekend. —Sue Trafton

Saturday and Sunday, August 16-17, 1997

"Great Went"

In the months after the Clifford Ball, people couldn't talk enough about what a great time they'd had coming together with over 75,000 other Phish fans at a decommissioned Air Force Base in Plattsburgh, NY (just a stone's throw from Burlington, VT, the band's home base). The event had run so smoothly, with so few hassles, that everyone just assumed the Base would host another such party the next summer.

But that was before the Plattsburgh City Council had its word. Concerned about the death of one concert goer (apparently as the result of a pre-existing condition), the council voted near the end of 1996 to ban all future rock concerts from the base. Clifford Ball II had been unceremoniously canceled.

While worried fans fretted on the Internet, Phish and Dionysian Productions—in a classic case of "When life gives you lemons, make lemonade"—looked at other options. What they found seemed so perfect, so made-to-be, that much later, you couldn't help but think that maybe it was for the best that Plattsburgh had said no to round two.

Instead of upstate New York, the summer-tour ending shows would take place in the far remote corner of northern Maine at Loring Air Force Base in the tiny hamlet of Limestone—a town so far from mainstream society that driving there requires traveling through towns that have no names to speak of, just letters and numbers. "An easy drive from anywhere," Phish joked in the *Schvice*, though the band themselves opted to fly in through Canada, the border for which was only miles away from the Base.

A new location also called for a new event name. Jettisoning Clifford Ball, the band turned to David Lynch, director of the classic television series *Twin Peaks* and its spin-off movie, *Fire Walk With Me*. In that movie, the character Jacques Renault says at one point, "I am the Great Went." Like the plaque in the Pittsburgh airport, it caught Phish's fancy, and they had their event name.

Fans started rolling into Aroostik County, home to the Went, two days before the first note of music would be sounded. By Friday the 15th, campers almost totally filled a two-mile long stretch of campground, with tents staked so closely together that everyone got to know their neighbors before even stepping outside. That night, a cold and ferocious rainstorm drenched the tent city, leaving many freezing and exhausted as the sun rose over the endless sea of canvas.

But early arrivals were also treated to two "From the Archive" shows over 88.9 FM, WENT radio, hosted by Phish tape vault archivist Kevin Shapiro, and lots more weirdness, like a poetry reading from Vermont's own Bruce Burgess and Trey singing the praises of "goo balls."

Perhaps Trey had already been to the campground, where a mile-long

continued

"Great Went" cont.

stretch of vendors created a market the likes of which Northern Maine had probably never seen before. Vending was unofficially permitted throughout the weekend, adding another dimension to the experience.

Indeed, fans camped along the runways had to walk through the vending stretch on Saturday afternoon on the way to the concert grounds at the far end of the base. Though the first set was supposed to start at 4 P.M. Phish appropriately waited until 4:20 before emerging to the strains of Makisupa Policeman (including another "goo balls" reference by Trey). Then they wasted no time in ripping into the second half of Harpua, picking up where they had left off at the Clifford Ball, reminding the crowd that this was a gathering of familiar friends.

That little musical wink from the band to the audience set the stage for two days of sharing and artistic exchange between Phish and the devotees who made it all possible. Trey followed Chalkdust with greetings and the confession that the first three songs were a soundcheck of sorts, as there had been no time for a pre-show warmup. The marathon set-clocking in at close to two hours, by far the longest of the weekend, continued on with a cornucopia of crowd favorites, mostly newer songs but also YEM and The Squirming Coil.

Set two led off with Wolfman's Brother, which had already been hailed as the song of the tour by many. To those who had not yet been exposed to Wolfman's funky alter-ego, it was an enticing treat, especially on the Went's larger-than-life, crystal-clear sound system. That was followed by what some felt was the Went's best musical moment—a Simple jam that morphed into the familiar Odd Couple theme, into My Soul, then an improvised jam,and finally Slave. Capping off the set with Rocky Top and Julius, Trey announced "in rock-n-roll tradition" that the Great Went was now the largest city in Maine. "We're bigger than Portland," he bragged. "And a whole lot cooler than Portland, too."

More memorable moments came in set three, kicking off with a slower, crisper, downright funkier take on Halley's Comet, including an unprecedented ending jam that led the band back into a lyrical reprise and then, Cities. Before the night was done, the band had knocked the crowd over with Llama, the great new tune, Limb By Limb, a Funky Bitch backed by fireworks, and a great Contact > Loving Cup encore.

But it wasn't quite done. At the end of set two, Trey had told fans to be sure and check out a mysterious "disco." Savvy phans knew to expect some sort of late-night appearance from the band, like at the Clifford Ball, and this year's surprise came in the form of a stationary disco/rave in which each band member took to keyboards and sampling devices to play electronic music to a crowd of between 500 and 1,000 confused but excited onlookers.

Sunday afforded everyone the chance to explore the vastness of the tent city at Loring. Several bands set up stages in the parking lots, and a little before noon, over 1,000 people took their clothes off for a world-record setting group nude photo. Inside the venue, fans who made it in early for the 4 P.M. afternoon set had time to explore the Alice-in-Wonderland-like playground of randomness. A maze of maize was planted in the grass for fans to navigate. A circle of outhouses surrounded a pile of working bathtubs ("the Port-O-Let Piazza"). A crafts fair, a make-believe village, and a tent for activist groups and other bands to perform could also be found, as well as a towering wooden sculpture to the far right of the stage which fans were invited to help build with original pieces of art.

Musically, the second day of the Great Went kicked off with the breakout of The Wedge, the first since the fall of 1996 and only the second since 1995. The band seemed to struggle with it, however, and reserved the next portion of the set for several new tunes, before getting back into familiar territory with a torrid Maze and a long but somewhat lackluster Tweezer. The afternoon setbreak featured members of the Bangor Symphony Orchestra performing Stravinsky's "Histoire du Soldat," a favorite piece of Trey's from his childhood. After the hour-long narrated piece came to an end, the BSO finished their set with Debussy's "Claire de Lune,' while a white glider silently floated overhead, trailing colored smoke across the glorious sunset. A giant laundry-line of giant clothing, strung from the stage, swung quietly in the breeze.

As night fell, Phish returned for a set that would provide the most memorable, seminal moments of the Went. It began in grand musical fashion, with a long Down with Disease morphing into a splendid Bathtub Gin, a performance that to some represented the musical highlight of the Went, if not of the year. But the calling-card of the weekend came during a long 2001. Throughout the set, the band had taken turns painting odd shapes on pieces of wood set up on easels on the sides of the stage. Now it was time to act.

Trey took to the microphone and directed phans' attention to the giant sculpture to the right of the stage. To those not in the know, he explained how phans had built the edifice throughout the weekend. It was part of something Phish had conceived of a year before, an embodiment of the band and phans creating art together. Then, the giant puzzle pieces the band had painted on stage were lifted into the audience, and the crowd passed the Phish contributions towards the sculpture. As workers began tacking Phish's pieces on, the band kicked into Harry Hood.

Photo courtesy of Jessica Fausty.

During the jam portion of Hood, Trey asked Chris to turn off the stage lights, allowing the band and audience to jam under only the light of the full moon. As the jam picked up steam, fans near the stage began hurling light sticks and neon necklaces into the air. The band's goal of creating art with the audience was realized in an unexpected form: the fans had made a light show of their own. The spectacle clearly touched Trey: "Go get more of those, they look cool," he told the crowd, sounding almost choked up. 63,000 people and four very special musicians were creating beauty together in the middle of nowhere.

Rather than raging, set three seemed to let everyone back down a bit, even after it started in promising fashion with the first Buffalo Bill since New Year's Eve 1994, and segued into a rarities' suite including Weigh and Guyute. But the expected Mike's Groove never came, as the band instead closed the set with an improvisational Scent of a Mule and Prince Caspian. The final sendoff occurred during the Tweezer Reprise encore—a giant match was ignited and lowered onto the art sculpture, setting it ablaze. As the crowd filed out of the concert compound, the art tower collapsed into embers.

The band and the audiences' collaboration would be left in Limestone forever, but the memories would not.

🐟 As we headed back to our campsite we came upon the second stage near the gate. There was really good techno coming from the stage, and a huge crowd of kids dancing in front of it. After sitting and watching for a few minutes, we realized that the DJ were Phish. I wish I could have gotten close enough to see better, but there was no way. It got to be pretty intense and we retreated back to watch from a hill. Watching the minirave from such a distance, listening to the beautiful, strange *new* sounds coming to us gently distorted by the wind, seemed like, well, prayer. I sat there and thought about all the good things in our life, and Phish techno seemed to be the only appropriate music to be playing. It was great. —The Reverend

8/17/97 [ACCESSIBILITY: ••••] [ATTEND. 61,588 FOR BOTH SHOWS] [TIX $70 FOR BOTH SHOWS AND CAMPING]

The Great Went, Loring Air Force Base, Limestone, ME

I: Wedge, Beauty of My Dreams, Dogs Stole Things > Vultures, Water in the Sky, Maze, Bouncing > Tweezer > Taste, Carolina

II: Down with Disease > Bathtub Gin > Uncle Pen, Also Sprach > Art Jam > Harry Hood

III: Buffalo Bill > NICU > Weigh > Guyute > Dirt, Scent of a Mule > Caspian

E: When the Circus Comes, Tweezer Reprise

"Cities" jam in Tweezer. During the "art jam," the members of Phish passed paintings done onstage earlier in the set out over the heads of the crowd to the art tower located to the right of the stage. Trey asked Chris Kuroda to turn the lights off during the Harry Hood jam, and the crowd created a glowstick array near the stage. The art tower was set aflame during Tweezer Reprise. Last Buffalo Bill, 12/31/94 Boston, MA [204 shows]. Last Carolina, 10/27/96 North Charleston, SC [82 shows].

🐟 If the Clifford Ball served as many people's introduction to Phish, the Great Went helped everyone take the next step. This was a true Phish phan crowd! You had to be, to make the unreal drive "way up north," as the fliers put it. But those who made it will never forget it—two days of inspired music, old friends, and good times. Can't wait for next year! —Rick Clancy

🐟 The mile-long Shakedown was a big aspect of what made this event so unique and special. Anything and everything you could imagine for sale, all night long. Throughout the weekend, I couldn't help but have a great feeling about the sense of community. Here we were, bigger than Portland, the largest city in Maine! "And a whole lot cooler than Portland too," as Trey remarked at Saturday's show. It felt like a glimpse of both past and future combined—a self-reliant gypsy-type bazaar out of the past, that was also like a near-utopian glimpse of our harmonious future. The rest of the world ceased to exist. Everything we needed was right here, and nothing else mattered except "sharing in a groove." —Greg Schwartz

🐟 After Saturday night's mind-melt, I wasn't sure my body could process any more music on Sunday, but the opening strains of the Wedge refreshed me, and I was set to boogie for another six hours. The afternoon set was highlighted by a hot Maze, but set II was where the real action was: DWD > Jam > Bathtub Gin > Jam > Uncle Pen was so solid, so amazing, that I practically fainted. When they followed it with the longest 2001 ever, plus Harry Hood with the glowsticks, I had a whole new definition of nirvana. —Amy Duncan

🐟 Set II of this show is my favorite set of live Phish ever. Just listen to the jams out of DWD and Bathtub Gin and you'll have an idea why, but there's also the band-crowd connection during the Art Jam, when the band passed its painted puzzle pieces over the crowd for hoisting onto the art tower far to the right of the stage, and then in Harry Hood, when fans near the stage created a mural of lights after Kuroda turned out the lights. —Pat Stanley

🐟 Some people dog the third set of this show as not offering enough jamming, but jeez, after a weekend like no other, it sounded like the perfect capper to me. I'm especially fond of the Buffalo Bill > NICU > Weigh > Guyute > Dirt sequence, as it runs the gamut of Phish's music from funk and reggae to rock and wackiness. The Caspian closer is also profoundly moving. —Ed Smith

🐟 If your parents pictured the Great Went as a bunch of freaks running around naked, they were right! I was one of the just over a thousand people lucky enough to get in on the world record–setting nude photo. A few hundred more people were turned away. It took close to an hour for the whole thing to go down. First we signed release forms, then moved to some bike racks and took all our clothes off. What a beautiful sight! Then we moved over to a cement area and all lay down for two poses. You weren't even allowed to wear socks or jewelry. We were all in the buff (or should I say buph). Then about two months later I got a poster tube in the mail with Phish as the return address. It was a glossy black-and-white poster of a thousand naked people. —James Ellis

🐟 Sorry to all who weren't, but to fully appreciate the magic of the band and audience art, you just had to be there. When the band members took turns painting on giant pieces of wood during the second set, we wondered what the hell was up, but then Trey told us that the band always aspires to create art with the audience and had found a tangible way to make that happen. Even more amazing was the way they torched the sculpture during Tweezer Reprise, a smoking end to a smokin' weekend. —Sue Trafton

🐟 Dear Phish Fans: I realize none of you would have any idea who I am, but I felt that someone should write and tell you just how our area felt about your converging on our community. You all have a right to know. When I found a copy of your "Pharmer's Almanac Tour Extra," I thought perhaps this was a good way to notify you.

I was a member of the Safety Team stationed at west gate one. I had the good fortune to speak to many of you before, during, and after the shows. I cannot tell you how very pleased I was to discover just how friendly, polite, and receptive you all were. Your kindness has not gone unnoticed. You made the effort to speak of how nice you found our community and area residents. As you have guessed, this is a small area where many have never had the opportunity to see so many people at one time. To many it was indeed a culture shock, but a pleasant one.

History has taught us (incorrectly, I might add) to judge an entire generation by a few. You have corrected that misconception totally and the nation should most definitely be aware of this fact. You were certainly aptly representative of the country, since you seemed to hail from all fifty states. The dignity and respect you displayed was overwhelming. The kindness you showed to each other and to our area citizens will not be forgotten. Our memories of you are more fond than you could know. You must realize that as the convoy of thousands of cars literally swarmed our quiet roads, we had no idea what to expect. You have proven a credit to your generation(s).

It has been rumored that Phish has expressed interest in returning and making this a yearly summer tour ending. Rest assured that this is our hope as well. Believe me, we understand the drive for most of you was incredibly long, but be assured, the welcome mat is out for all of you, should you ever decide to return. And we hope to see you again and again. . . .

I was fortunate enough to also be among the few Safety members who were involved in the final sweep after the finale. It was quite a wonderful surprise to see dozens of phans picking up around the concert grounds. No one had told or asked you to, which makes it all that much more impressive. You are obviously a group who has more respect for the land than any group I have seen. It is terribly important that you are aware of exactly how you are spoken of now that the show and the exodus are over.

The area television station (WAGM in Presque Isle) aired a tribute to the phans. It was an edited combination of videos they filmed as well as what they acquired from a local air crew who filmed as they passed overhead. The background music was Louie Armstrong's "What a Wonderful World" and I cannot tell you how beautiful it turned out. The woman responsible for putting this piece together was WAGM's news anchor, Sue Bernard. It brought tears to the eyes of many of us who watched it. It was a wonderful and very moving tribute and, as mentioned, it was for and about the phans.

Our community is normally very quiet and laid back. We are so far north that we tend to be forgotten and/or ignored by the rest of the country. When 63,000–66,000 of you converged on this area, you made us the largest "city" in our state of Maine. The things you said to and about us made us extremely proud. You treated us with respect, understanding, and patience. We thank you for that. You have also been able to show many people just how wonderful young people can be.

For the way our community treated you, I am enormously proud. I have heard *no* ill remarks or complaints. Enjoy the rest of your years knowing that you have made a small, fairly closeknit community very happy and honored to have had you as our guests. We truly hope to see you again. Thank you from the bottom of our hearts. —Becky Hafford

Phunky Phall

Among the most notable developments of the fall tour was Phish's tendency to morph between songs like never before, often not taking a breather for even a second during an entire set. This practice led to some controversy among setlist scribes, debating what in fact constitutes a segue and what is just one song quickly being followed by another.

Well, we have a totally different take on segues. Not only are we attempting to be liberal in classifying them, amply throwing around the (>) symbol, we've come up with a visual device to graphically illustrate the strange paths Phish was taking us all on throughout the fall. At times it seemed they were "snaking" through sets, slithering their way from song to song. Therefore we present the "jam snake" where appropriate, for quick indication of where Phish found the unrelenting groove in each show. With these setlists we also present show ratings in five categories. These ratings, although determined by a panel of seven knowledgeble fans, are entirely subjective and should be considered a springboard for debate and not an authoritive stamp. If you are one of those fans who gets visibly upset when you hear opinions about shows which differ from your own (you know who you are), then you better strap on your seatbelt, because we've got five different categories ready to rub you every which way.

[11/7/97]
Late Night with Conan O'Brien, NBC Studios, New York, NY
Farmhouse

11/13/97
Thomas and Mack Center, Las Vegas, NV [ATTEND. 10,634; CAP. 12,000] [TIX $23.75]

I: Chalkdust, Black Eyed Katy, Theme, Train Song, Melt, Beauty of My Dreams, My Soul, YEM, Character Zero
II: Stash, PYITE, Caspian, Bouncing, Mike's > Hydrogen > Weekapaug
E: Loving Cup

Setlist Scenario 4
Lean on the Scene 5
Funk-factor 3
Musical Mastery 4
Segue Satiation 2

"Green River" tease at start of Hydrogen. Concert debut: Black Eyed Katy.

Following a historic show at Las Vegas's Alladin Theater in 1996—featuring a half-hour encore that brought yodelers, banjo players, Primus, and four Elvis impersonators to the stage—Phish returned to is desert oasis to kick off their 1997 fall tour, this time at the much larger Thomas and Mack Center. But once inside the spacious arena, fans realized that they were in for a more intimate show than expected as a giant curtain blocked off about half of the seats, and the boys seemed as excited as the crowd to be back in the Phish bowl. Highlights included the debut of new funk instrumental Black Eyed Katy and an always-welcome first-set YEM.

Set II started strong with Stash/PYITE, then later soared with Mike's Groove. The Mike's Song jam didn't crash into Hydrogen like most pre-1997 versions; instead, the band wandered through funkier realms, eventually arriving at the Hydrogen theme without a crescendo. It was no common Hydrogen, either, as Trey failed to find the right notes and instead opted to intentionally butcher the song, flashing a big smile to Mike and Fish along the way. He made up for it in Weekapaug, however, as a solid jam suddenly took off in double time, and the band roared through to the closing chorus at a mind-numbing rate. The boys were back.

11/14/97
West Valley Center, West Valley, UT [ATTEND. 8,325; CAP. 8,400] [TIX $21.50–$23]

I: Runaway Jim, Gumbo, Maze, FEFY, Also Sprach > Funky Bitch, Guyute, Antelope
II: Wolfman's > Piper > Twist Around, Jam > Slave
E: Bold as Love

Setlist Scenario 4
Lean on the Scene 2
Funk-factor 4
Musical Mastery 4
Segue Satiation 4

Maze unfinished. "Marco Esquandolis" whistled instead of spoken in Antelope. Last FEFY, 11/22/96 Spokane, WA [68 shows]. Last Bold as Love, 2/18/97 Paris, France [50 shows].

Subfreezing temperatures greeted the tour's second stop, reminding everyone that fall tour was—of course—going to be cold, cold, cold.

A jam-packed first set, probably one of the best of the tour, simply overflowed with inspiration. After a short but sweet Jim opener and a dip into Gumbo's funk, the band cut Maze short and drifted into the only FEFY of the year. But the first half of the set was only a warm-up for what followed: a 2001/Guyute/Antelope triad. After Guyute, Trey dedicated the song to Paul Languedoc because Paul had told Trey that "any song with whistling is a good song." To extend that theory to Antelope, Trey whistled the "Rye, rye, rocco, Marco Esquandolis" lines before running out of control into setbreak.

The second set would give the tour's first indication that the boys had again rewritten the rules of live Phish, as four- and five-song second sets would stretch out into abandon, becoming the rule, not the exception. Wolfman's, having lost no lustre from the attention lavished on it during summer tour, opened up, and eventually found its way into a new space jam that heralded the coming of the reworked Piper. The Twist Around > Slave pairing that followed saw the often-overlooked Twist mellow out into a "space jam" (the highlight of the show for some), which then dissolved magically into a Slave that soared through the new hockey arena.

11/16/97
McNichols Sports Arena, Denver, CO [ATTEND. (TWO-SHOW TOTAL) 25,887; CAP. 17,650] [TIX $25–$27.50]

I: NICU, My Soul, Black Eyed Katy, Farmhouse, Old Home Place, Billy Breathes, CTB, Scent of a Mule, Poor Heart, Taste, Hello My Baby
II: Timber Ho > Simple, Wilson > Harry Hood > Izabella
E: Bowie

Setlist Scenario 3
Lean on the Scene 2
Funk-factor 3
Musical Mastery 3
Segue Satiation 3

Pete Wernick on banjo for Scent of a Mule and Poor Heart. Concert debut: Farmhouse.

It had been well over a year since Phish last played a show in Colorado (the four-night Red Rocks stand in summer 1996) when the band rolled into town for two nights at McNichols Arena.

The first night's first set seemed a warm-up of sorts, as Phish chose mostly shorter songs, including the first concert appearance of Farmhouse, debuted two weeks earlier on Conan O Brian's show. Toward the end of the set, bluegrass legend Pete Wernick emerged to play banjo on Scent of a Mule and Poor Heart. He dueled briefly with Page and Trey in Scent, and soloed to perfection in Poor Heart, but the band didn't capitalize on the energy he created, as the set finished quickly with an unexceptional Taste. The long-deprived Colorado fans were left literally begging for more.

The second set, only five songs, provided more jam space. Simple and Harry Hood had moments of delicate joy, and the crowd chanted with vigor in Wilson. The rocking set-closing Izabella—the Hendrix tune played sparingly on summer tour—and a surprise Bowie encore (the first on American soil since February 1989), left everyone excited for the next night's show as the crowd filtered back out into the bitter cold of a Denver November.

Surprisingly, the show was not sold out—a far cry from when thousands of ticketless fans surrounded the Red Rocks region the summer before.

11/17/97
McNichols Sports Arena, Denver, CO [ATTEND. (TWO-SHOW TOTAL) 25,887; CAP. 17,650] [TIX $25–$27.50]

I: Tweezer, Reba, Train Song, Ghost, Fire
II: Down with Disease > Oblivious Fool > Johnny B. Goode > Jesus Left Chicago, When the Circus Comes, YEM
E: Character Zero

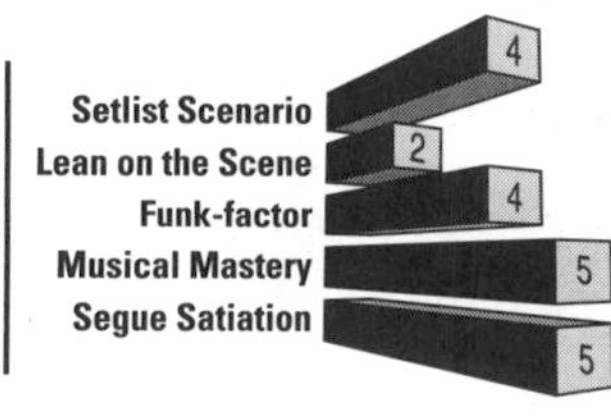

The 1997 fall tour was the first with a high percentage of multiple-night stands. As early as 1994, Trey told interviewer Steve Silberman in *Dupree's Diamond News*, "I really like doing two-nighters, because [we can] hang out with people. . . . I felt that I knew who was in the audience, and what they were going through."

The second Denver show seemed to prove the wisdom of Trey's theory. A five-song first set offered a sharp contrast to the tamer first set of the night before, including a Tweezer opener, the now-rare Reba, and a 20-plus-minute Ghost.

The second set also got off to a fast, rocking start with Down with Disease. But like much of this tour, the setlist doesn't exactly help explain where things went from there. Johnny B. Goode, following the rare new song Oblivious Fool, is usually a rip-roaring number, but on this night it carried the band into another space jam (or "atmosphere jam," as some phans prefer calling it) similar in feel to the Twist Around space jam from Utah. Though the set also included Jesus Left Chicago and a YEM closer, it was that Johnny B. Goode jam that made this night a special one.

11/19/97
Assembly Hall, Champaign, IL [ATTEND. 16,420; CAP. 16,420] [TIX $20.50–$24.50]

I: Julius, Bathtub Gin > Llama, Dirt, Limb by Limb, Funky Bitch, Theme, Ginseng Sullivan, Fee > Time > Antelope
II: Also Sprach > Wolfman's > Makisupa > Taste
E: Possum

"Crosseyed and Painless" teases in jam out of Wolfman's. "Walk Away" tease in spacey jam out of Makisupa.

By the tour's fifth show, several new musical trends had already emerged: second sets were routinely less than six songs long and included healthy doses of the funk-style jamming that evolved over the course of the year, along with thematic space jams that often earned their own labels on some phan's setlists.

The band's stop at Assembly Hall, now a familiar Phish venue, saw further refinements of these exciting musical developments. The first set was nothing to sneer at—with the tour's first Bathtub Gin and Limb by Limb, plus an Antelope closer—but once again it was the segue-filled second set that demanded greater attention.

Opening with 2001, now routinely stretched out past fifteen minutes, Phish moved into a near 30-minute Wolfman's. Initially, the jam took on the funky tones heard in most versions of the song in 1997, but Trey took a left turn and led the band into a hard-rock realm. As the tempo increased, Walk Away (forgotten by the band since the Dallas Tweezerfest on 5/7/94) seemed poised to reemerge, but instead the bottom dropped out of the jam, and the subtle strains of Makisupa were heard. Jamming versions of Taste and the encore Possum capped off another adventurous night.

11/21/97
Hampton Coliseum, Hampton, VA [Attend. 13,656; Cap. 13,656] [TIX $22.50]

I: Emotional Rescue > Melt, Beauty of My Dreams, Dogs Stole Things, PYITE, Lawn Boy, Chalkdust, Caspian
II: Ghost > AC/DC Bag, Slave, Loving Cup
E: Guyute

Digital delay loop jam at the end of Caspian. Teases in Ghost included "Sparks," "Guyute," and "Spooky." Concert debut: Emotional Rescue.

The first night at the ever-popular Hampton Coliseum started on a wild note when the band broke out the Rolling Stones' Emotional Rescue for the first time, and stretched it out for over twenty minutes. They followed it with a strong Split Open and Melt—two songs into the show, Phish was already at peak intensity. Later in the set, that intensity would again be felt in an unconventional Chalkdust jam that echoed the jam out of Emotional Rescue earlier in the set. And like all good Phish sets, there was a touch of comic relief, too, as Fishman took an "anti–drum solo" in place of Mike's usual bass solo in Lawn Boy, drumming methodically along to the song's rhythm while the crowd cheered.

Set II saw more great jamming, first in a Ghost opener that offered a touch of space, and then in an amazing AC/DC Bag jam that broke the normal bounds of the song, as Phish did with so many songs on the tour. It was one of those jam sequences that offer something for everyone, as the band alternated intensity with spaciness for over a quarter of an hour. From the depths of a space jam, Slave emerged and soared, in a version that some named as the tour's best. A rocking Loving Cup closed the set, and a surprise Guyute encore left the crowd wondering what the band could possibly do to top themselves the next night.

11/22/97
Hampton Coliseum, Hampton, VA [Attend. 13,656; Cap. 13,656] [TIX $22.50]

I: Mike's > Hydrogen > Weekapaug, Harry Hood, Train Song, Billy Breathes, Frankenstein, Izabella
II: Halley's > Tweezer > Black Eyed Katy > Piper, Antelope
E: Bouncing, Tweezer Reprise

Setlist Scenario 5
Lean on the Scene 5
Funk-factor 5
Musical Mastery 5
Segue Satiation 5

"Destiny Unbound" lyric chant by crowd at start of second set inspired "human sacrifice" dialogue with Trey. "Mike-o Esquandolis" sung in Antelope.

On night two in Hampton, the crowd reached playoff intensity immediately, doing the wave before Phish had even taken the stage. Once they emerged, they tuned up for a minute, then Trey cranked up Mike's Song.

The place went absolutely nuts. Throughout the first few minutes of the first Mike's Song show opener in the States since 1990, waves of cheering swept through the crowd. About forty minutes later, after the band drifted through Hydrogen and Weekapaug (including a false-start ending), the crowd cheered and cheered. Conferring about what to play next, the boys selected Harry Hood, and suddenly it was a show for the ages.

To start set II, the general admission crowd near the stage attempted a Destiny Unbound lyric chant. "That sounds like a horrible cannibalistic chant for people who want blood," Trey remarked. "Is that the human sacrifice part of the show?" Mike Gordon then stepped up to his mic, but Destiny wasn't to be—instead, it was Halley's Comet.

Only the most jaded phan could be disappointed. Halley's stretched way out (finally dipping into Tweezer after about twenty-five minutes), starting a series of segues that wouldn't stop until the band closed things out with Antelope well over an hour later.

11/23/97
Lawrence Joel Veterans Memorial Coliseum, Winston-Salem, NC [Attend. 14,153; Cap. 14,153] [TIX $22.50–$25]

I: My Soul, Theme, Black Eyed Katy, Sparkle, Twist Around, Stash > NICU, Fluffhead, Character Zero
II: Bathtub Gin, Down with Disease > Low Rider Jam > Down with Disease, Bold as Love
E: Julius

"Izabella" tease in Down with Disease before "Low Rider" jam. "Don't Stop till You Get Enough" tease in Down with Disease jam after "Low Rider" jam. Last pronounced "Low Rider" jam, 7/10/94 Saratoga Springs, NY [266 shows].

Many expected the band to be worn out from the two nights at Hampton, and figured the Sunday night Winston-Salem show might be a good one to skip. Well, on a tour that offered virtually no letdowns, they were of course mistaken, and some even said the boys took it up a notch.

The audience packed in to the super-sold-out venue for a straight-ahead first set, from the My Soul opener to another Black Eyed Katy, which the band was clearly enjoying playing. Stash provided the jamming highlights, and though there were some miscues sprinkled into Fluffhead, it drew its usual warm reception from the crowd.

But set II would again offer a plethora of improvisational insanity, especially in the Bathtub Gin opener that just raged. Instead of funking or spacing it out, Phish turned the jam up a notch, pure intensity. DWD, which followed, saw the expected mellowing of the jam sequence. Trey latched onto the Low Rider theme, and the rest of the band followed him, with both Fishman and Trey singing a few verses. Then, like the Vegas Weekapaug from the tour opener, the band upshifted the tempo and circled back around to the DWD theme at double time, tossing in a brief jam on Michael Jackson's "Don't Stop till You Get Enough," just to top things off in style.

Really, it was just a three-song second set, showing just how far Phish can take their jams these days.

11/26/97
Hartford Civic Center, Hartford, CT [Attend. 16,500; Cap. 16,500] [TIX $27.50]

I: Tweezer > Sparkle, Gumbo, My Soul, McGrupp, Dirt, Melt, Horse > Silent, Taste
II: Character Zero > Also Sprach > Cities > Ya Mar > PYITE > Caspian, Poor Heart, Tweezer Reprise
E: Cavern

Original verse sung in Cavern.

After being virtually ignored for shows in the summer 1996 and summer 1997 tours, and having only one New England show on fall tour 1996, Northeastern phans gasped in delight when the fall 1997 schedule was released—Hartford, three in Worcester, and two each in Philadelphia and Albany!

The tour's second Tweezer opener seemed an omen of good things to come in the Civic Center, but from there the mostly disjointed first set struggled to find unity of purpose.

Set II did not have the same problem. After several minutes of spacey jamming that had people thinking 2001 or Bowie, the band cut into Character Zero—an unconventional opener choice. But the jam took off into the most incredible Character Zero yet, stretching out for almost twenty minutes before the band found itself in 2001. Out of a chilling, multiclimactic Zarathustra would come the only Cities of the tour, faster than the Went's version and just as impressive. A segue into Ya Mar, and then PYITE, had the crowd ecstatic.

Not much of note happened toward the end of the set, though in the "random events" department, there is a Poor Heart that starts out as Rocky Top, and the first performance of the missing verse to Cavern since the Flynn Theater, 4/4/94.

11/28/97

Worcester Centrum, Worcester, MA [ATTEND. 14,189; CAP. 14,189] [TIX $25]

I: Curtain, YEM > I Didn't Know, Maze, Farmhouse, Black Eyed Katy, Theme, Rocky Top
II: Timber Ho, Limb by Limb, Slave, Ghost, Johnny B. Goode
E: My Soul

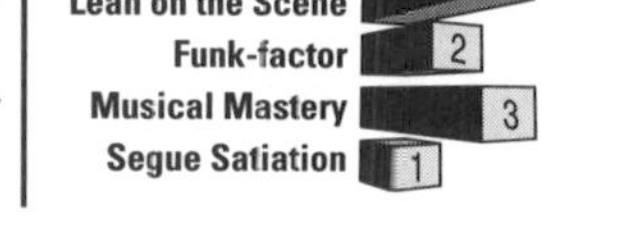

Fishman on vacuum for I Didn't Know. Last Curtain, 2/20/97 Milan, Italy [57 shows]. Last I Didn't Know, 2/22/97 Rome, Italy [55 shows].

Three nights at the Worcester Centrum—home to Phish's New Year's show in 1993 and the famous Bathtub Gin > Real Me > Bathtub Gin on the holiday tour in 1995—seemed too good to be true. All three shows sold out in a hurry, though tickets wouldn't be tough to find in the lots; these may have been the three most miracled Phish shows ever.

The band wasted no time in blowing some minds, opening with Curtain, a song not seen since Europe the winter before. It slammed into, of all things, You Enjoy Myself, and just two songs into the show, most felt they'd gotten their money's worth. Indeed, the opening pairing was probably the musical highlight of the evening, and definitely of the first set, though some vacuum action from Henrietta in I Didn't Know was a treat, and both Maze and Black Eyed Katy brought some thrills.

The second set was primarily anchored around two of the most popular new songs from summer 1997, Limb by Limb and Ghost. Though some complained that the set was too short, it seemed very well paced, as the band followed the melodious Limb by Limb with an enchanting Slave, then the deep funk of Ghost, and finally the straight-ahead rock of Johnny B. Goode. The My Soul encore (played for the third show in a row) drew groans from fans on tour, but no one could be too grumpy with two more nights still to come.

11/29/97

Worcester Centrum, Worcester, MA [ATTEND. 14,189; CAP. 14,189] [TIX $25]

I: Wedge, Foam, Simple, TMWSIY > Avenu > TMWSIY, Sloth, Ginseng Sullivan, I Saw It Again, Horn, Water in the Sky, Bowie
II: Runaway Jim > Strange Design > Harry Hood, Caspian, Suzie
E: Buffalo Bill > Moby Dick Jam > Fire

Setlist Scenario 3
Lean on the Scene 4
Funk-factor 4
Musical Mastery 5
Segue Satiation 4

Harry Hood and Weekapaug jams in Runaway Jim. Drum solo in "Moby Dick" jam. Last TMWSIY > Avenu > TMWSIY, 12/28/96 Philadelphia, PA [67 shows]. Last Sloth, 2/23/97 Cortemaggiore, Italy [55 shows]. Last pronounced "Moby Dick" jam, 2/19/93 Atlanta, GA [434 shows].

The Wedge opener was the most notable moment of a very songwriterly first set that featured eleven tunes, including a bunch not seen in a while like TMWSIY/Avenu, Sloth, and Horn.

What followed in the second set was later termed the musical highlight of the Worcester stand, and perhaps the entire tour. The opening Runaway Jim weighed in at a mind-altering fifty-eight minutes, with snippets of Harry Hood and an all-out, unmistakable Weekapaug jam to finish things off. Although not for beginners, it was Phish at their most ambitious, and it thrilled most of the audience.

Strange Design offered a moment for everyone to catch their breath before the Harry Hood that had teased the crowd in Jim finally emerged in its real clothes. A relentless Caspian locked poised to close the set until Trey signaled for the only Suzie Greenberg on the summer of fall tour. The band botched the version badly (Fishman explained by shouting, "I thought you said Golgi!"), but it was still fun. And the encore, led off by "Fishman's favorite song," as Trey put it, brought the rarity Buffalo Bill, followed by a wild drum solo and then several minutes of Moby Dick jamming, before a shot of Fire capped off an epic night.

11/30/97

Worcester Centrum, Worcester, MA [ATTEND. 14,189; CAP. 14,189] [TIX $25]

I: Guyute, Funky Bitch, Wolfman's, Love Me, Squirming Coil, Loving Cup
II: NICU, Stash, Free > Piper, When the Circus Comes, Antelope
E: Them Changes

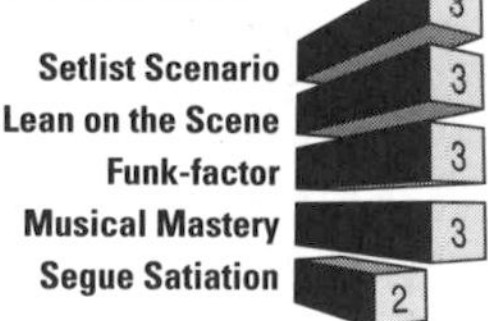

Jam out of Wolfman's had a heavy-metal theme and included some portions of Sanity and Esther lyrics shouted/sung by Trey, then band jammed in total darkness for about five minutes after Trey asked Chris Kuroda to turn off the lights. Stash unfinished. Concert debut: Them Changes.

Still delirious from the Runaway jam the night before, the Sunday night Centrum crowd was treated to a Guyute opener that immediately locked everyone back in the groove. The first half of the first set would provide some of the evening's highest points, as the second song, Funky Bitch, offered a jam clocked in at over fifteen minutes. With raw power pouring off the stage, the band took the crowd to the limits.

Then they did it again. Wolfman's served as the excuse this time, spinning out into the funk as Trey overpowered the limits of the jam. Though Wolfman's has lately offered a funk overflow, this jam eventually moved in a heavy-metal direction, growing louder and more ominous with each passing note. In the midst of this noise, Trey stepped up to his mic and started *shouting* some of the Sanity lyrics, then repeated "Esther tried in vain" several times, before moving into a heavy-metal riff similar in feel to a more basic Split Open and Melt. That continued for almost ten minutes as Kuroda killed the lights; Trey and Mike hid behind their amps, still repeating the power chords.

The second set was maybe the most uneven of the weekend. The Stash jam was interesting but not mind-blowing, and one of the few Frees of the fall was a real treat. When its thematic jam swirled into the spacey new opening to Piper, the crowd stood awestruck. A surprise one-timer, Buddy Miles's Them Changes (also done by Hendrix/Band of Gypsies) offered redemption during the encore, and closed out the Centrum stand in style.

[12/1/97]

CoreStates Spectrum, Philadelphia, PA

Star Spangled Banner

Phish sang a cappella before the Flyers-Sabres NHL game.

12/2/97

CoreStates Spectrum, Philadelphia, PA [ATTEND. (TWO-SHOW TOTAL) 29,640; CAP. 16,090] [TIX $25–$27.50]

I: Buried Alive > Down with Disease > Makisupa, Chalkdust, Ghost, Divided Sky, Dirt > Taste, Star Spangled Banner
II: Mike's > Simple > Dog Faced Boy > Ya Mar > Weekapaug, Bouncing, Character Zero
E: Ginseng Sullivan, Sample

Setlist Scenario 4
Lean on the Scene 2
Funk-factor 3
Musical Mastery 4
Segue Satiation 4

Down with Disease jam in Weekapaug. Last Buried Alive, 2/26/97 Stuttgart, Germany [55 shows]. Last Dog Faced Boy, 8/12/96 Noblesville, IN [109 shows]. Last Star Spangled Banner, 12/28/96 Philadelphia, PA [69 shows].

Phish rolled into Philly a day early to sing the Star Spangled Banner at a Flyers game (Trey was the between-periods interview on the TV broadcast). On show day, the scene at the Spectrum was a little more chaotic, as a "younger crowd" had clearly caught onto Phish in the Philadelphia area and wanted in on the fun. Though the setlist looks amazing—including the revivals of several old favorites, like the rocking Buried Alive to kick off the show—the first set was not considered to be the band at their best.

But they turned it around handsomely in the second—Mike's Song rolled into Simple and then the rare Dog Faced Boy—last seen at Deer Creek in summer 1996. During Ya Mar, Trey bid hello to his grandfather, who was on hand to see the boys presented with a gold record backstage. Before the jamming stopped, they found their way back into a superb and unrelenting Weekapaug, the clear highlight of the show. The jam took on a slower feel than most before accelerating near the end and coming back around to the Weekapaug theme. Things got a little basic from there, as the Bouncing/Character Zero closing duo seemed best suited for many of the first-timers in attendance, as did a Sample encore.

12/3/97

CoreStates Spectrum, Philadelphia, PA [ATTEND. (TWO-SHOW TOTAL) 29,640; CAP. 16,090] [TIX $25–$27.50]

I: PYITE, My Soul, Drowned, Old Home Place, Gumbo > Also Sprach > YEM
II: Bowie > Possum > Jam > Caspian > Frankenstein > Harry Hood
E: Crossroads

Setlist Scenario 4
Lean on the Scene 2
Funk-factor 5
Musical Mastery 4
Segue Satiation 5

"Couldn't Stand the Weather" (a Stevie Ray Vaughn tune) during Drowned. "Take Me Out to the Ballgame" tease in Bowie intro. "Jam" was similar to segment heard during "Ghost" at Worcester 11/28. Bowie unfinished. Last Drowned, 3/18/97 Burlington, VT [52 shows].

Back in the Spectrum, Phish led off with PYITE, always a popular choice as an opener to get the joint jumping. And jump it did—as at the previous night's show, Phish didn't slouch in song selection. The first set was packed with favorites, including cover song rarity Drowned (and a fantastic funk jam which followed), along with a great Gumbo > 2001 > YEM combo to close the set, jammed with appropriate intensity.

The second set was another nonstop. Starting things off with the telltale beats of Bowie, Phish raged the jam and then moved into Possum without ever returning to the closing Bowie coda. Possum wasn't an all-time great version, but it still had the crowd pumped up, and it led into a funk jam that sounded suspiciously like Black Eyed Katy, but was actually its unnamed alter-ego, the same jam that would later find a home in Tube. (Confusion over which funk jams were Black Eyed Katy pervaded the tour.)

A moving Caspian, a rocking Frankenstein, and then a bonus Harry Hood capped off the set, and though the Hood wasn't as gorgeous as some, it finished a segue sequence that saw nothing but jamming for well over an hour. A surprise Crossroads encore was a final treat before the band left Philadelphia for a return trip to the Midwest.

12/5/97

CSU Convocation Center, Cleveland State University, Cleveland, OH [ATTEND. 13,238; CAP. 13,238] [TIX $22.50–$25]

I: Ghost > Wilson, Funky Bitch > Black Eyed Katy, Sparkle, Runaway Jim > My Friend, Ginseng Sullivan, Limb by Limb, Character Zero
II: Stash, Bouncing, Julius > Slave, Lizards, Loving Cup, Chalkdust
E: Bold as Love

JULIUS > JAM > SL

Last My Friend, 2/26/97 Stuttgart, Germany [57 shows].

Perhaps the band was finally getting a little fatigued, now three weeks into the tour, as they hit the CSU Convocation Center.

Like virtually all Phish shows, though, it had its moments. The tour's only Ghost opener didn't stretch on as long as some versions of this song, but it got the crowd funked up, a vibe that later continued in Funky Bitch and Black Eyed Katy. Runaway Jim didn't match Worcester's insanity, but provided some nice, exploratory jamming before it segued into the first My Friend since the winter Europe tour. As it was the first My Friend since Fishman's September wedding, Trey shot him a look during the "My friend, my friend, he's got a wife" line, and got a big smile in return.

Set II was also a fairly basic affair, with a little spice thrown in. Though the Stash opener kindled hopes of a 30- or 60-minute epic, the jam petered out after only about fifteen minutes, and led to a rather uninspired Bouncing/Julius sequence. In the depths of the Julius jam, though, things started to get a little more interesting, and the band managed a nice segue into a Slave that had a darker, heavier feel than most. The too-rare Lizards and nice versions of Loving Cup and Chalkdust filled the rest of the set. Though fun, they didn't sparkle with the jamming excitement seen at so many other shows this tour.

12/6/97

The Palace, Auburn Hills, MI [ATTEND. 17,666; CAP. 17,666] [TIX $23.50–$25]

I: Golgi, Antelope, Train Song, Bathtub Gin > Foam, Sample, Fee, Maze, Cavern
II: Tweezer > Izabella > Twist Around > Piper > Sleeping Monkey > Tweezer Reprise
E: Rocky Top

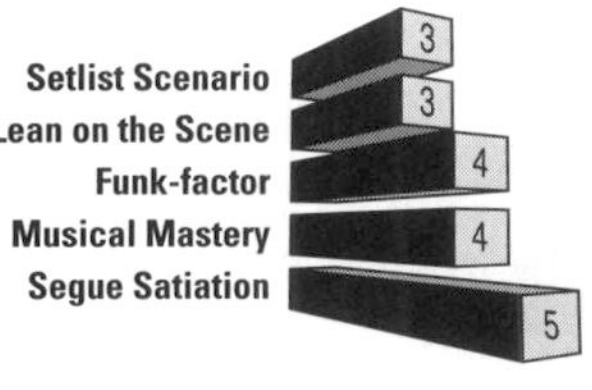

Though phans lament the Palace as one of the most annoying venues in the country, Phish continues to make it a frequent stop on almost all cold-weather swings through the Midwest. Again, the first set was marked by inconsistency, but when Antelope popped up as the second song of the show, it was hard to complain about anything that followed.

Like they did so many times on this tour, Phish left a fairly basic first set behind and turned the second set into an all-out jamfest. Though a Tweezer opener is always welcome, things really heated up when Trey cranked up the jam and led the band into Izabella and then into new song Twist Around. The next half hour or so provided the highlight of the night, as a good Twist Around jam turned over into Piper. After Piper had risen to its heights, the crowd and band deliriously soaring together, it dipped down into a different rocking jam that would be hard to rival in terms of pure intensity. If this is the future of Piper jams, then the future sure is bright. A fun Sleeping Monkey followed, and the craziness of Tweezer Reprise roared this short but raging set to its close.

12/7/97

Ervin J. Nutter Center, Wright State University, Dayton, OH [ATTEND. 11,447; CAP. 11,447] [TIX $22.50–$25]

I: AC/DC Bag > Psycho Killer > Jesus Left Chicago, My Mind's, It's Ice > Swept Away > Steep > It's Ice, Theme, Tube, Jam > Slave
II: Timber Ho > Wolfman's > Boogie On, Reggae Woman > Reba, Guyute, Possum
E: Day in the Life

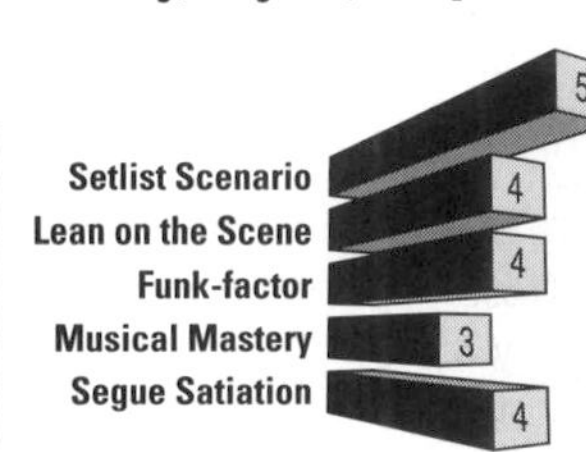

Whistled second verse to Guyute. Concert debut: Psycho Killer (complete version; Psycho Killer lyrics were sung in YEM vocal jam 8/9/93 Toronto, ON). Last Boogie On, Reggae Woman, 3/21/88 Burlington, VT [925 shows]. Last Day in the Life, 2/28/97 Berlin, Germany [58 shows]. Last Tube, 2/26/97 Stuttgart, Germany [59 shows].

As anyone who saw a number of shows on the 1997 fall tour can attest, virtually every show had memorable moments that were joyous to experience and unquestionably worth tracking down on tape. But it's only a select few nights that will be long remembered from start to finish. Dayton was among that select group.

What jumps out immediately from this setlist are the rarities: Psycho Killer out of AC/DC Bag, and Stevie Wonder's Boogie On, Reggae Woman, a Phish concert staple back in the Nectar's days that languished, forgotten, until this night. But really, across the board, this night sparkles with inspired song choices (check out the wild It's Ice > Swept Away > Steep > It's Ice sandwich in set I) and great jamming, like the funk jam in Tube.

Though the improvisation wasn't as gorgeous as that seen in some of November's second sets, the music from Timber Ho to Wolfman's to Boogie On in set II is something special. Top that off with three more jamming songs—Reba, Guyute, and Possum—and a John Lennon tribute as the encore a day before the seventeenth anniversary of his death, and you can expect that people will still be talking about Dayton's legendary show for a long time to come.

12/9/97

Bryce Jordan Center, Penn State University, State College, PA
[ATTEND. 11,090; CAP. 12,000] [TIX $22.50–$25]

I: Mike's > Chalkdust > My Soul > Stash > Hydrogen > Weekapaug, Dogs Stole Things, Beauty of My Dreams, Horn, Loving Cup
II: Julius, Simple > Timber Ho, Contact, Axilla, Harry Hood
E: Fire

Setlist Scenario	4
Lean on the Scene	4
Funk-factor	4
Musical Mastery	4
Segue Satiation	4

Bowie teases in Timber Ho. Brief return to Axilla jam in Harry Hood intro. Last Axilla, 2/28/97 Berlin, Germany [59 shows].

When Mike's Song opened up the second night Hampton show, it seemed like an impossible dream realized. When it opened up State College show several weeks later, it seemed like par for the course for Phish at this point in time. On a tour which saw the band abandon the use of preplanned setlists, virtually all the rules were out the window, so why not throw a couple more first-set Mike's Grooves out there for public consumption?

Clearly, it was a choice that met with the crowd's approval, though instead of offering the traditional Mike's > Hydrogen > Groove trio, Phish dove from the Mike's jam into the Chalkdust riff, then the often-played My Soul. It was a novel sequence to be sure, as was the Stash > Hydrogen > Weekapaug that followed.

Set II had trouble matching the first set's intensity. The Julius opener was more rocking than usual, though, and the Simple jam moved into such a spacey realm that some wondered if they'd ever come back. Eventually, Fishman's rhythms led them to Timber Ho and a funky middle jam, before the crashing chords of Axilla I turned the vibe on its head. A Harry Hood set closer, complete with a brief Axilla jam, left everyone with smiles.

12/11/97

War Memorial, Rochester, NY [ATTEND. 9,000; CAP. 9,000] [TIX $27.50]

I: PYITE > Down with Disease > Maze, Dirt, Limb by Limb, Loving Cup, Rocky Top
II: Drowned > Roses Are Free > BBFCM > Ghost > Down with Disease > Johnny B. Goode
E: Waste

Setlist Scenario	4
Lean on the Scene	4
Funk-factor	5
Musical Mastery	4
Segue Satiation	4

Down with Disease reprise was instrumental only, no vocals. Concert debut: Roses Are Free. Last BBFCM, 8/6/96 Morrison, CO [118 shows].

As the band headed back into New York State for the tour's final three shows, the weather turned cold and wet. Inside, the band dried off the dancers with a hot PYITE > DWD > Maze opening group, and also showed some fire with Limb by Limb and yet another Loving Cup (but who's complaining?). The second set, though, would see things really get steamy.

Opening with Drowned—the first Drowned set opener since the legendary 12/31/95 MSG show—Phish set their sights high, then slowed things down and wound their way into a new cover song, Roses Are Free by Ween, seen several weeks later on New Year's Eve. Its ending jam wound up into BBFCM, the first since Red Rocks '96, and a lot of fun for Trey as he stormed around the stage, inciting mayhem. Ghost followed, and led to a brief DWD reprise (no lyrics) and then, like the Gorge, into Johnny B. Goode. The show closed out on a slower, more thoughtful note with Waste, but left some grumbling that—in spite of a completely segued second set—there hadn't been enough jamming. By this point, fans were getting a little spoiled.

12/12/97

Pepsi Arena, Albany, NY [ATTEND. 17,000; CAP. 17,000] [TIX $25]

I: Funky Bitch > Also Sprach > Camel Walk, Taste, Bouncing, Tweezer, Train Song, Character Zero
II: I Saw It Again > Piper, Swept Away > Steep, Caspian > Izabella, Tweezer Reprise
E: Guyute, Antelope

Setlist Scenario	4
Lean on the Scene	3
Funk-factor	3
Musical Mastery	3
Segue Satiation	2

"Llama" teases in jam out of I Saw It Again. "Buried Alive" teases in Antelope.

The first night at Albany was unique in that its best moments came at the beginning and end. When the band opened the two-show run with the rare Funky Bitch followed by 2001 and then the even rarer Camel Walk, it seemed as though the band might have a historic night on the way. But the rest of the first set and all of the second had fewer surprises. Tweezer was of course welcomed by the audience, but was not among the better versions of the song.

Set II then led off with an extended version of I Saw It Again, which led many to predict a better future for that new and seldom-played song. The Piper which followed was also pleasing to many in the audience hearing it for only the first or second time. Where this show lagged, however, was in the "meat" portion of set II, where Phish usually find their most climactic moments. Swept Away > Steep, and then a closing Caspian > Izabella were not enough for the band to earn their way into Tweezer Reprise, and many in the crowd were somewhat disappointed.

But alas, the boys were just trying to confuse us a bit. The encore of Guyute, and then Antelope (with a playful Buried Alive tease) sent 17,000 people onto the streets of Albany with huge grins, ready for one more night of fun in a city which has played host to many a fine Phish performance.

12/13/97

Pepsi Arena, Albany, NY [ATTEND. 17,000; CAP. 17,000] [TIX $25]

I: Ya Mar, Axilla, Theme, Ginseng Sullivan, Strange Design, Sample, Vultures, Tube, GTBT
II: NICU, PYITE > Ghost > Mike's > Llama > When the Circus Comes, Weekapaug > Catapult > Weekapaug, Harry Hood
E: My Soul, Squirming Coil

Setlist Scenario	4
Lean on the Scene	3
Funk-factor	4
Musical Mastery	4
Segue Satiation	4

J. Willis Pratt opened. "Dude of Life" and "Bring the Dude!" chants in Mike's jam. Band jammed in darkness during Harry Hood while audience members tossed glowsticks around. Last Catapult, 3/2/97 Copenhagen, Denmark [60 shows].

Anticipation always runs high for the last show of the tour, and Albany proved no exception. Those who made it in early were treated to a set from Fishman-friend J. Willis Pratt before Phish ambled out for their last fall tour show.

The first set seemed an amalgam of the last month, from the long jam out of Ya Mar, to the textural jam of Theme from the Bottom, to the overplayed (though still appreciated) Ginseng Sullivan, and then the funky new middle jam of Tube. Second set highlights included another good (if not great) Ghost jam, and a wild Mike's Song jam that heard the band beckoning the Dude of Life to the stage (he didn't make it) with miniature solos designed to "bring the Dude!"

After the fast jam sped into Llama, they detoured into When the Circus Comes before finding their way back into Weekapaug, complete with a Catapult recitation from Mike. The Harry Hood closer marked one of the tour's most memorable moments, and turned an event into a tradition with a repeat of the Great Went's lights-out glowstick war. It may have even surpassed the Went's in intensity and duration. A neon glow covered the stage as the fall tour faded to black.

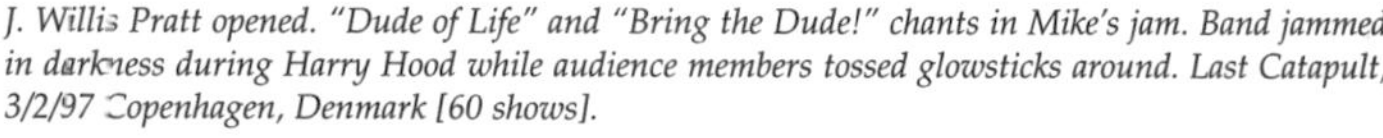

1997 Holiday Tour

12/28/97

USAir Arena, Landover, MD [ATTEND. 18,000; CAP. 18,000] [TIX $25]

I: Julius, Cities > Curtain > Sample, Old Home Place, Runaway Jim > Farmhouse, Funky Bitch, Melt, Bouncing, Character Zero
II: Axilla, Simple, Ghost > Drowned, Scent of a Mule, Halley's > Slave, Rocky Top, Cavern
E: Bold as Love

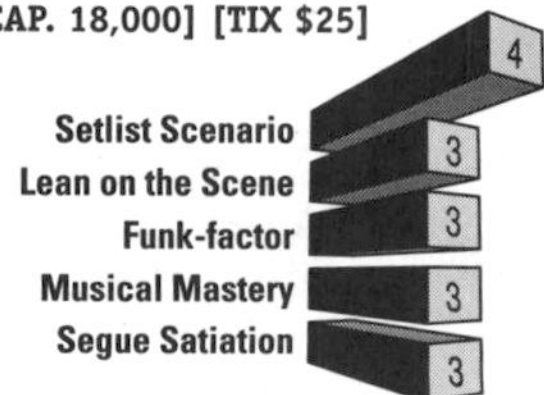

Slow jam in Scent of a Mule in place of duel.

As the host of 1997's first holiday tour show, the new USAir Arena seemed the odd man out—with three shows to follow at MSG, even stalwarts who usually took in all four holiday shows opted out of making the drive to D.C. But as they so often do, Phish rewarded those who ventured south with an interesting setlist and some solid jamming.

A rocking Julius opener set the mood right away, and then the band pulled out the tour's first surprise, an early-set Cities that funked right into Curtain. Other first-set surprises included new tune Farmhouse, forgotten since Worcester, and nice jams in Funky Bitch and Split Open and Melt. Axilla I opened the second set, with the Axilla II ending tacked on, as at Albany. A nice Simple jam was to cause problems, though, as feedback rang out, causing Trey to remark on "ghosts in the machine" that need to be cleared up before they could move on. Appropriately, Ghost followed, and then another treat, Drowned. Scent of a Mule featured a slower jam in lieu of the duel, and a stunning Halley's > Slave sequence reminded everyone that yes, this was the first holiday tour show and Phish was going to make each one special.

12/29/97

Madison Square Garden, New York, NY [ATTEND. 18,923; CAP. 18,923] [TIX $25.50–$33]

I: NICU, Golgi, Crossroads, CTB, Train Song, Theme, Fluffhead, Dirt, Antelope

II: Down with Disease > Bowie > Possum, Tube > Jam > Tube, YEM

E: GTBT

Setlist Scenario	4
Lean on the Scene	2
Funk-factor	4
Musical Mastery	4
Segue Satiation	3

Down with Disease and Bowie unfinished. "I Can't Turn You Loose" jams in Possum. "Jam" in Tube was similar to Ghost jam from 11/28/97 and jam after Possum on 12/3/97.

The three Madison Square Garden shows were naturally fast sellouts, but tickets on this night (in sharp contrast to the next two) were available at below face value as desperate phans tried to unload their extras for even ten dollars. Anyone who got in at that price got the bargain of a lifetime, as Phish served up a raging show that would, incredibly, be topped the next night.

After a well-received NICU opener and the now-rare Golgi came a miniature transportation suite, with Crossroads, CTB, and Train Song filling the middle of the set. But it was the Fluffhead toward the end that got the crowd cheering louder, and the surprise Antelope closer that got the audience going ballistic. Was Tom Marshall in the wings? No, that would wait for another night.

The no-nonsense second set was to be a playground of jamming. DWD's jam didn't do anything too spectacular (indeed, the song seems to have peaked momentarily after so many great 1996 versions), but the Bowie > Possum pairing that followed was simply magic. Partway through the outro coda on Bowie, the band slammed into Possum, a version of the song that included several dips into the Blues Brothers favorite "I Can't Turn You Loose," with spotlights on Trey and Page. Another pleasant surprise, a "Funk jam on Tube" sandwich, shook MSG and then, oh yes, there was YEM, capping off the amazing set.

12/30/97

Madison Square Garden, New York, NY [ATTEND. 18,923; CAP. 18,923] [TIX $25.50–$33]

I: Sneaking Sally > Taste, Water in the Sky, PYITE, Stash, Chalkdust, Day in the Life

II: AC/DC Bag, McGrupp, Harpua > Izabella > Harry Hood > My Soul, Sleeping Monkey, Guyute

E: Carini > Black Eyed Katy > Sneaking Sally Jam > Frankenstein

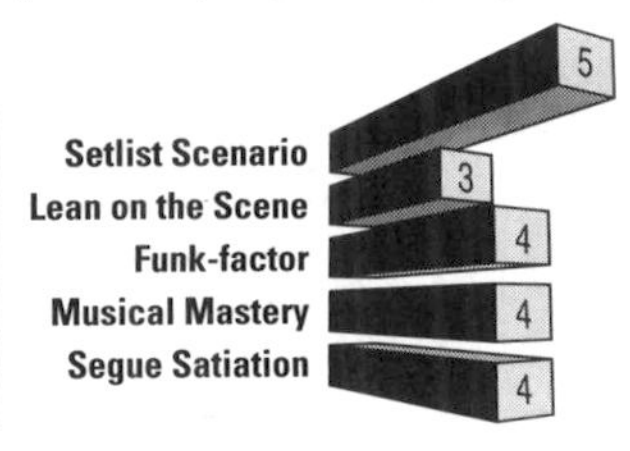

Tom Marshall on vocals for "I'm Gonna Be (500 Miles)" jam in Harpua. Harry Hood unfinished; band jammed in darkness while audience members tossed glowsticks around (glowstick jam reprised during Frankenstein). Fishman on vacuum in Frankenstein. Last Sneaking Sally, 5/28/89 Hebron, NY [861 shows]. Last Carini, 3/1/97 Hamburg, Germany [64 shows].

Amidst all the anticipation for the New Year's show, December 30 emerged as the clear highlight of the holiday tour. The best word to describe this performance would be "unrelenting." It seemed to be on its way to a close when the band capped off a crazy Harpua with the Jimi Hendrix cover Izabella well after 11:00 P.M., but the band couldn't resist heading into Harry Hood. During the jam Trey eked out "topher," a signal to Chris Kuroda to kill the stage lights, and the inevitable glowstick war followed, with fans pelting Trey with neon-colored necklaces. That Harry Hood never quite found its way to the end, as the band unleashed an upbeat My Soul, which most expected would finally bring the set to a close. But wait. Trey then announced that due to time constraints, they would forgo an encore and do just one more song—Guyute.

Of course, there was an encore, or as some excitedly called it, a third set. Upon taking the stage again, Trey announced that the band was supposed to have been done by 11:00, but it now was only twelve minutes to midnight, so why not keep going until New Year's Eve?

In fact, they jammed their way well past 12:00, piecing together a four-song blitz of Carini Had a Lumpy Head (the first time they played it since the Winter Europe tour), Black Eyed Katy, Sneaking Sally through the Alley reprise (broken out during the first set after not being played since 5/28/89), and a superextended version of Frankenstein—complete with a Fishman vacuum cleaner solo. By the time it was all over, it was 12:25. Rumor is that Phish was fined $11,000 for going past 11:30, and once they'd realized they were already paying for an additional hour, they thought they might as well use it! And yes, they did actually play longer on the 30th than the 31st.

12/31/97

Madison Square Garden, New York, NY [ATTEND. 18,923; CAP. 18,923] [TIX $25.50–$33]

I: Emotional Rescue, Ya Mar, MSO, Beauty of My Dreams, Wolfman's, Limb by Limb, Horse > Silent, Sloth, Fire

II: Timber Ho, Mike's > Piper > When the Circus Comes > Roses Are Free > Weekapaug

III: Also Sprach > New Year's Countdown > Auld Lang Syne > Tweezer > Maze > Caspian > Loving Cup

E: New York New York > Tweezer Reprise

Setlist Scenario	4
Lean on the Scene	5
Funk-factor	3
Musical Mastery	4
Segue Satiation	5

A giant white sphere hung from the arena scoreboard, on which images were projected at various times throughout the show, including images during Also Sprach (eggs, udder balls, olives) that referenced the Harpua narration from the night before. The ball opened at midnight and balloons dropped into the crowd. "Auld Lang Syne" tease in Ya Mar. "Birdland" tease in Maze. Concert debut: New York New York. Last MSO, 12/14/95 Binghamton, NY [155 shows].

One could argue that the New Year's show really began with the Dec. 30 appearance of Harpua. Trey ignored the usual story of Poster Nutbag, instead sharing a personal tale of how he got his own television in the fourth grade and the cartoon "Lost in Space" began to speak to him, commanding him to store food from the family kitchen and go off to a mysterious field. Once there he found a pentagonal star and began to lay the food down on each point of the star—an olive, some fried eggs, steak, even a little beef jerky. Somehow a rubber ball with udders was also involved. Then, images of Trey's future appeared—or so the story went—and he saw Page and Mike and Fish, not knowing who they were, and the grown up Tom Marshall. At that point, the very real Tom Marshall appeared and began singing the Proclaimers' ditty "500 Miles."

Well, the egg, the olive, and the steak along with several other random images surfaced again on New Year's Eve.

Hanging from the rafters at Madison Square Garden that night was a giant, inverted dome which served as a projection screen. Four large video projectors were set up in each corner of the arena, and flashed a light show onto the dome complete with dancing steaks and olives, along with the rubber udder ball. Other images, too nonsensical to describe, also boogied on the screen. This light show went on and off throughout the night.

Musically, it was a New Year's show which may not have ranked with some of the great performances of New Years past, but was still a solid three sets' worth of Phish which kept 20,000 people smiling. As one fan said, "It was the worst ten orgasms I ever had."

Photo courtesy of Jay Archibald.

The band had basically stacked the deck against themselves. Vowing two years before not to repeat songs during a holiday tour, they had already cashed in almost all their most valuable chips. The epics—Slave, Antelope, YEM, Fluffhead, Harry Hood, and Harpua—were already on the table, as were jamathons like Down with Disease, Simple, and Cities.

But, of course, Phish never quite runs out of surprises.

The show kicked off with Mike on lead vocals for Phish's weird version of the Rolling Stones' Emotional Rescue, played once before in Hampton. Although this set never quite caught fire, an extended Wolfman's Brother—similar to many of the summer performances which often ranked as show highlights—featured some quirky repeated grooves, and then Limb by Limb made a welcome appearance after having surfaced only sporadically during the fall tour. The Sloth and then Fire closed the set, previewing a high-energy middle stanza which led off with the ever-popular Timber Ho! The rest of the set was what one might call a "1997 Special," a series of songs strung together through brilliant segues and intricate jamming. An upbeat Mike's Song led to the mind-altering Piper (which was featured in some very key points of shows throughout the year) into the cover songs When the Circus Comes and Roses Are Free, and finally into a long and precise Weekapaug to close the set. Phish then took the stage about fifteen minutes before midnight for a 2001 jam, similar to how they rang in the New Year in Boston as 1996 came to a close.

The light show continued on the inverted dome, and with ten seconds to go, a clock appeared which counted it down. As the New Year rang, the dome opened and hundreds of oversized balloons showered down onto the audience. Each was painted like one of the random images which had been on the screen all night.

Phish meanwhile busted into Tweezer, as the band struggled against the large balloons which were being hurled onto the stage and knocking over microphones. One of their stagehands actually stood at front with a needle, popping the balloons as they approached the band.

The set found its way into Maze and then Prince Caspian (which, like Piper, had been occupying some high-rent real estate in shows throughout the year) before heading into a memorable Loving Cup.

For the encore, Page crooned the Big Apple audience with a loungy "New York, New York," followed by Tweezer Reprise.

And that was it for Phish in 1997. The New Year's show may not have quite lived up to expectations following the splendid performances which marked the year. But if New Year's is about fun and celebration, then the band was clearly up to the task.

1998 SPRING The Island Tour

"We were bored," was Trey's explanation of the surprise mini-tour. Spring had just sprung and what better way to kick off the season than Phish's first spring run in the U.S. in four years? The *Doniac Schvice* played no role in promoting these shows, which sold out via power of word of mouth and the Internet.

It seemed that this was the perfect opportunity for the boys to limber up a bit before diving into the studio for their next album project. It also allowed them to explore "Birds of a Feather" and "Roget" which were both debuted on opening night. The run was cleverly refered to as "The Island Tour," which Dry Goods saw as a merchandising opportunity to produce "Island Tour" T-shirts, allowing fans to take home a souvenier commemorating a terrific Long Island/Rhode Island adventure.

4/2/98
Nassau Colliseum, Uniondale, NY
I: Tube, My Mind's Got a Mind of Its Own, Sloth, NICU, Stash* > Horn, Waste, Chalkdust Torture

II: Punch You In the Eye, Simple, Birds of a Feather, Wolfman's Brother > Sneaking Sally Through the Alley > Roget > Twist Around, Sleeping Monkey, Rocky Top
E: Guyute

Concert Debut: Birds of a Feather and Roget

The lot scene was over-saturated with extra tickets; it was clear that the six-ticket maximum offered by Ticketmaster caused a massive overbuy which made it difficult for some to even give 'em away. Phish kicked off their first ever Nassau Colliseum set in funky form with Tube. This set proved to be the weakest of the tour hands-down, with the only interesting glitch being an unfinished Stash which somehow segued into Horn.

Phish brought back a funky groove and its undercurrents were felt for most of the set. Things warmed up with PYITE and Simple which came to an end with a rolling jam giving bounce to the crowd. Birds of a Feather was then debuted. This new tune seems to be influenced by Talking Heads material from *Remain in Light*, especially in the chorus where a repeated Melody is underwoven by a driving rhythm and texture. After a rich Wolfman's Brother came Sneakin' Sally Through the Alley, bringing back wonderful memories of 12/30/97 when it was both resurrected and reprised in that classic show. Fans were then treated to another new tune titled "Roget," which is multi-sectional featuring some dark/frightening lyrics with somber musical arranging to back it up. The darkness continued in the "Twist Around Jam" with some spooked-out music coupled with Karoda's lighting mastery. And when it looked as if they closed the door with Sleeping Monkey and Rocky Top, they reached back and belted out a mind-blowing Guyute encore.

4/3/98
Nassau Colliseum, Uniondale, NY
I: Mike's Song > My Old Place > Weekapaug Groove, Trainsong, Billy Breathes, Beauty of My Dreams, Dog Stole Things, Reba, My Soul
II: Roses Are Free > Piper > Loving Cup, Antelope
E: Carini, Halley's Comet, Tweezer Reprise

Crosseyed and Painless Tease in Weekapaug. Pete Carini chases fan off stage during Loving Cup and "Carini's gonna getchya" is sung during first section of Antelope.

The sign that this show would be an all-time keeper came at the very beginning with a Mike's opener. Energy levels were brought down a peg when they sandwiched in My Own Homeplace, only to be up-lifted by a Weekapaug which teased the haunting chorus melody from Crosseyed and Painless.

Set 2 was Phish at their absolute best where they added extensions onto the Roses are Free opener and Funkified the Piper Jam, which was longer than normal and absolutely mouth-watering. During Loving Cup, a fan jumped on stage and quickly dived back into the crowd narrowly escaping Pete Carini who was sprinting to send him flying off the stage with a bit of propulsion. At the end of the song Fishman joked, "If you're going to run on stage, don't let Carini get you." Fishman's comment continued in the form of falsetto harmonies at the cadences of the opening section of Antelope. Phish repeated the improvised "Carini's gonna getchya" throughout the section which added Phish-style comedy to an already stellar show. The fierce Antelope also featured a steamy reggae version of the Marco Esquandolas section. And appropriately enough, "Carini" opened the encore followed by a Halley's Comet and Tweezer Reprise. An epic encore for a most epic show.

4/4/98
Providence Civic Center, Providence, RI
I: Tweezer > Taste, Bouncin, Funky Bitch, Ginseng Sullivan, Limb by Limb, Lawn Boy, Character Zero
II: Birds of a Feather > Also Sprach > Brother, Ghost > Lizards, David Bowie
E: Harry Hood

After the ending of Brother, Trey said they were going to play it again and they proceeded for a few measures and stopped. "Can't Turn You Loose" tease in Ghost

The ticketless had a lot of trouble in an extremely sold out situation at the Civic Center. Like the night before, Phish opened with a show-stoppin' jam song—Tweezer, which segued into a fierce Taste. This quality set 1 was highlighted by a solid performance of Limb by Limb and closed with tremendous energy with an outpouring of Character Zero.

Set 2 started with Birds of a Feather, in which they seemed to have settled down into a much tighter groove than its debut two nights earlier. 2001 was very much of the funk variety but also featured some very David Bowie-like guitar soloing, giving it a much different psychedelic flavor. Then came the opening riff to Brother which was the first performance since 11/30/96. Unlike most performances of Brother, Phish stretched it out by playing variations of Brother's rhythmic and melodic motives. When they finally finished, Trey announced that they will play it again. After they played a couple of bars Trey joked that it was "the single-edit radio-friendly version." Ghost was nicely embellished with "The Blues Brother Theme" and then trickled into a magnifcent performance of Lizards. After the Bowie closer, Phish continued the Island Tour tradition by playing a gem for an encore—Harry Hood.

4/5/98
Providence Civic Center, Providence, RI
I: Oh Kee Pa Ceremony > You Enjoy Myself, Theme From the Bottom, McGrupp, Bathtub Gin > Cities, Sparkle, Split Open and Melt
II: Down with Disease > Ya Mar > Jam > Prince Caspian, Maze > Oblivious Fool > Possum > Jam > Cavern
E: Axis: Bold as Love

During funk jam in Possum, Trey says, "This is for all those that came down wanting to dance."

For the second time in Phishtory, Oh Kee Pa segued into YEM. The last time was 7/31/92 and for the fourth straight night, the show opened in unorthodox fashion. The "Island Tour" was coming to a bittersweet end, but not before the boys rustled up some rare gems like McGrupp, played only four times the year before. A tightly wound Bathtub Gin found its way into Cities which later seemed to foreshadow a dose of funk that came later on, marked by one juicy segue after another. Trey changed up the lyric in Ya Mar by singing "my grandpa" instead of "no good pa." Possum deviated from its normal bluesy sound to intense funk and that's where Trey said that those people that want to leave can do so but "this is for all those that came down wanting to dance." He then said, "We're gonna funk it out," which Phish proceeded to do. A few minutes into the funky jam the chords sounded for Cavern, and they sat on those chords for a while and played the downright funkiest version of the song ever. A complete stylistic overhaul.

LIFETIME STATS

It's a testament to Phish's ever-changing concert setlists that statistics can offer some insight into the Phish experience. Though it's never certain which patterns will continue and which will wither away, these listings provide at least a partial glimpse into the mind of the band.

Set I Openers (of a two-set show)		Set II Openers	
1) Runaway Jim	63	1) Also Sprach	63
2) Chalkdust	46	2) Runaway Jim	29
3) Buried Alive	45	2) Suzie Greenberg	29
4) Llama	42	4) Wilson	28
5) Golgi	37	5) Chalkdust	27
6) Suzie Greenberg	34	6) The Curtain	26
7) The Landlady	33	7) Mike's Song	25
8) Wilson	28	8) Golgi Apparatus	23
9) My Friend	22	9) Llama	21
10) AC/DC Bag	21	10) Timber Ho	19
11) Rift	15	11) The Landlady	17
11) The Curtain	15	11) Axilla I	17
13) Divided Sky	14	13) AC/DC Bag	16
13) Ya Mar	14	14) Buried Alive	15
15) Oh Kee Pa	12	14) Down with Disease	15
15) Possum	12	16) Dinner and a Movie	14
17) Sample in a Jar	10	16) Maze	14
18) Maze	9	18) Possum	13
18) Fee	9		
18) I Didn't Know	9		

Encores

1) Rocky Top	92	11) Highway to Hell	29
2) Amazing Grace	59	12) Cavern	25
2) Sweet Adeline	59	13) Bold as Love	24
4) GTBT	55	13) Carolina	24
5) Fire	54	15) Lawn Boy	22
6) Tweezer Reprise	50	16) Squirming Coil	21
7) Contact	44	16) Possum	21
8) Sleeping Monkey	38	18) Suzie	20
9) Golgi	37	19) Memories	19
10) BBFCM	33	20) Freebird	16

Common Segues

Hydrogen > Weekapaug	220	Forbin > Mockingbird	78
Mike's > Hydrogen	211	Dinner > Bouncing	36
Mike's > H2 > Week	209	Oh Kee Pa > AC/DC Bag	32
Horse > Silent	113	Buried > Poor Heart	31
Oh Kee Pa > Suzie	101	Swept Away > Steep	22

Other Frequent Play Patterns

Runaway Jim, Foam	46	Divided Sky, Guelah	18
Sparkle, Stash	31	Llama, Guelah	20
Stash, Squirming Coil	30	Split Open, Bouncing	20
Stash, Lizards	26	Landlady, Runaway Jim	18
Poor Heart, Stash	23	Llama, Foam	18
Runaway Jim, It's Ice	22	Poor Heart, Tweezer	18
Foam, Sparkle	21	Rift, Guelah	17
Contact, BBFCM	20	Landlady, Bouncing	17
It's Ice, Sparkle	20	Fee, Maze	17
Rift, Stash	20	Guelah, Rift	17
Chalkdust, Bouncing	18		

Played on New Year's Eve

1) Auld Lang Syne	9	4) Divided Sky	6
2) Antelope	7	5) Sparkle	5
2) Mike's Groove	7	5) Stash	5

Song Play Statistics

Phish's huge stable of original songs have grown at a hapharzard rate, with sometimes only a handful of new tunes joining the repertoire in any given year, while sometimes—like in 1997—it's an avalanche. And there are even more cover songs to condend with than originals! How do the numbers boil down?

- Total Number of Original Songs played in the 1990s: **158**
- Number of Original Songs from 1980s not yet played in 1990s: **10**
- Total Number of Cover Songs played in the 1990s*: **187**
- Number of Cover Songs from 1980s not yet played in 1990s: **33**

Songs Played Per Year

1990: 59 originals, 35 covers, 3 Dude of Life songs = 97 songs played
1991: 69 originals, 29 covers, 5 Dude of Life songs = 103 songs played
1992: 78 originals, 31 covers, 1 Dude of Life song = 110 songs played
1993: 85 originals, 58 covers, 1 Dude of Life song = 144 songs played
1994: 98 originals, 68 covers*, 1 Dude of Life song = 167 songs played
1995: 105 originals, 58 covers* = 163 songs played
1996: 103 originals, 45 covers* = 148 songs played
1997: 120 originals, 61 covers = 181 songs played

* Tally does not include Halloween cover songs played only at the Halloween show; if those are added to the tally, 1994 has 23 additional covers for a total of 91 covers and 190 songs played overall; 1995 has 14 additional covers for a total of 72 covers and 177 songs played overall; 1996 has 7 additional covers for a total of 52 covers and 155 songs played overall. Also, the Total Cover Song tally rises from 187 to 231.

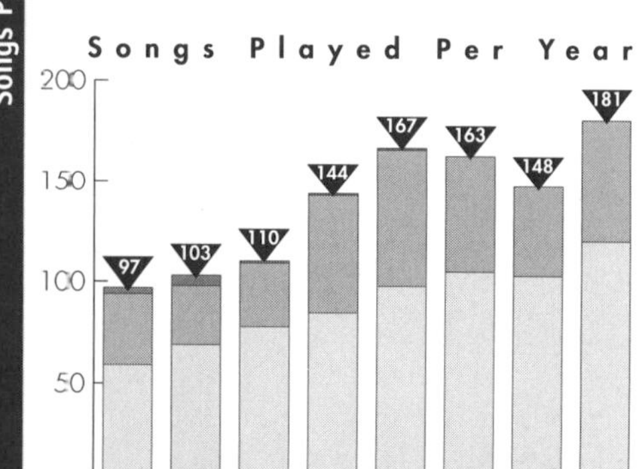

Original Song Debuts Per Year

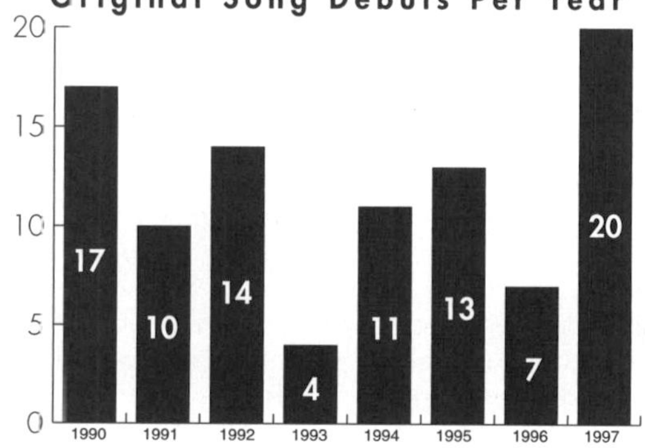

1990: 17
1991: 10
1992: 14
1993: 4
1994: 11
1995: 13
1996: 7
1997: 20

Set-ting Sail

Breakdown of twelve big song appearances by set, starting in 1990. Note that second set tallies also include third set appearances of the song.

Antelope: 117 first set; 101 second set; 2 encores
David Bowie: 114 first set; 112 second set; 2 encores
Divided Sky: 192 first set; 31 second set; 1 encore
Down with Disease: 59 first set; 39 second set; 0 encores
Harpua: 4 first set; 25 second set; 5 encores
Harry Hood: 22 first set; 131 second set; 13 encores
Mike's Groove: 51 first set; 199 second set; 0 encores
Possum: 112 first set; 100 second set; 19 encores
Reba: 161 first set; 89 second set; 0 encores
Stash: 223 first set; 55 second set; 2 encores
Tweezer: 43 first set; 169 second set; 0 encores
YEM: 109 first set; 195 second set; 3 encores

"I love a good pie chart as much as anyone."

—Mike Gordon, December 1997

Jazz Standards

Once an integral part of the Phish repertoire, the inclusion of jazz covers has dwindled to virtually nothing in recent years. The band has said this is a result of larger venue sizes, which they generally do not find a good atmosphere for jazz standards (one exception to this rule: 12/29/96 Caravan). Here are jazz covers played by Phish, with most recent performance dates:

Take the A-Train	78 times, last on 4/13/94 at the Beacon Theater, New York, NY
Caravan	37 times, last on 12/29/96 at CoreStates Spectrum, Philadelphia, PA
Donna Lee	20 times, last on 7/12/91 at Colonial Theater, Keene, NH
Satin Doll	12 times, last on 5/8/93 at UNH Field House, Durham, NH
Manteca	9 times, last on 11/14/95 at UCF Arena, Orlando,FL
How High The Moon	3 times, last on 3/8/93 at Sweeny Center, SantaFe, NM
Jump Monk	2 times, last on 4/24/94 at Grady Cole Center, Charlotte, NC

Most-Played Fishman Songs

1) Love You	75
2) Terrapin	48
3) Cracklin' Rosie	46
4) Brain	30
4) Purple Rain	30

Most-Played Bluegrass Songs, all-time

1) Uncle Pen	176
2) Rocky Top	151
3) Paul and Silas	72
4) Ginseng Sullivan	51
5) Nellie Cane	41

Henrietta Helpings/Fishman Songs per Year

Back in the early 1990s, Fishman songs started surfacing practically every night, and in 1992 and 1993, you could expect that the middle-to-end of every second set would feature a vacuum (or perhaps trombone) interlude. But Fishman has grown more shy in recent years. A look:

1990: 29 songs—at 28% of shows. (Brain, 8; Love You, 8; Terrapin, 5; others, 8).

1991: 51 songs—at 40% of shows. (Love You, 21; Terrapin, 13; Touch Me, 9; others, 8).

1992: 75 songs—at 62% of shows (or 79%, excepting sets opening for Santana). (Cracklin' Rosie, 25; Love You, 20; Terrapin, 12; Lengthwise, 6; others, 12).

1993: 98 songs—at 89% of shows. (Love You, 17; Purple Rain, 15; Lengthwise, 15; Terrapin, 11; Cracklin' Rosie, 11; Brain, 8; Bike, 7; others, 5).

1994: 47 songs—at 38% of shows. (Purple Rain, 11; Be Like You, 9; Cracklin' Rosie, 6; Love You, 6; Bike, 5; others, 10).

1995: 22 songs—at 27% of shows (Suspicious Minds, 8; others, 14).

1996: 11 songs—at 16% of shows (Purple Rain, 3; others, 8).

1997: 3 songs—at 4% of shows (others, 3).

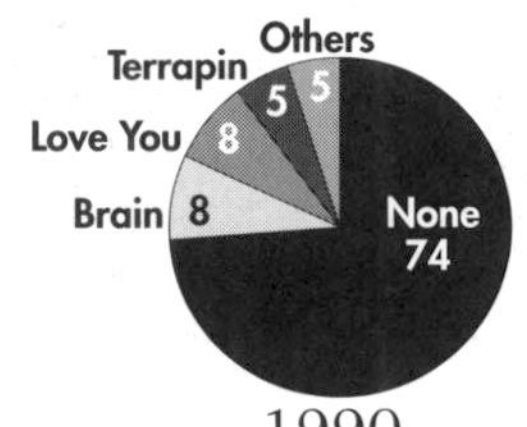

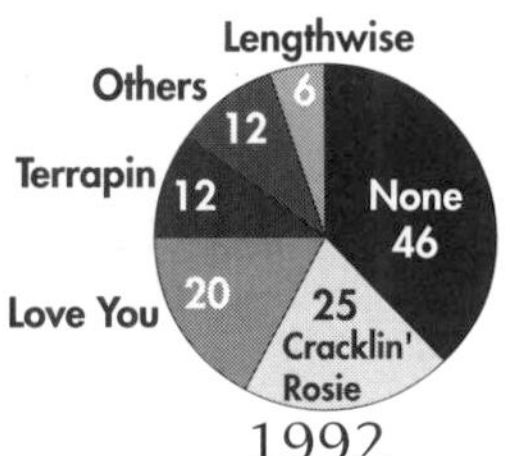

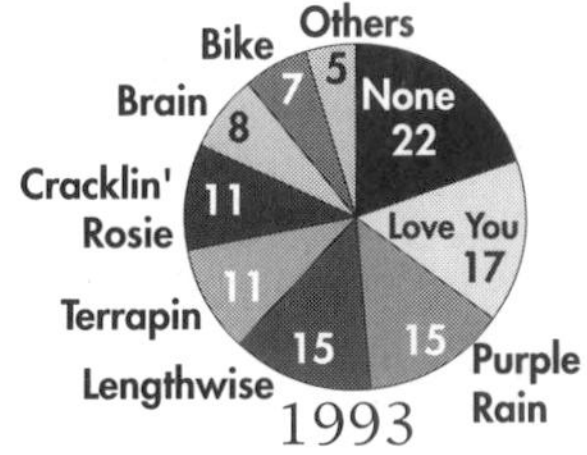

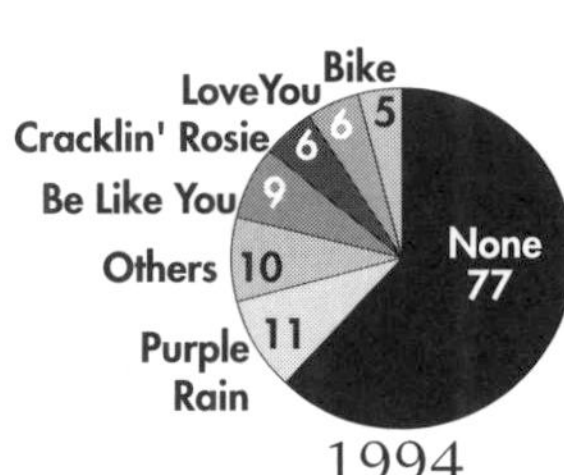

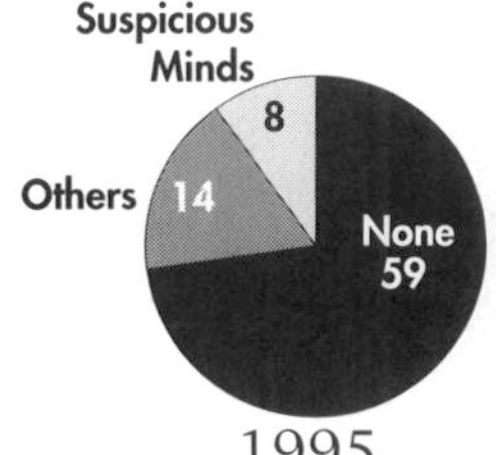

Photo courtesy of George Lyons.

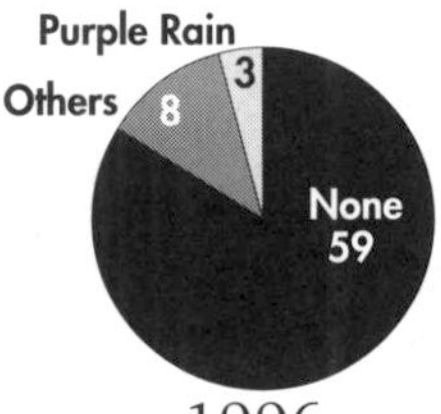

All the Songs

6

Photo courtesy of George Lyons.

Cracking the Code . . .

Song title as it appears in the setlist section.

Number of concerts played prior to the song debut (bracketed number at top of column).

Total number of times played (asterisk indicates more info appears in the Stories sidebar).

Number of concerts since the song was last played (all numbers in 2nd column below the bracket).

Actual song title and authors. The [bracketed] title is the abbreviation used in the before/after columns in this section.

Date of concert (first column).

Set (1 is first set, 2 is second set, 3 is third set, E is encore, E2 is separate second encore, and 1a is the first set of a single-set show.)

Songs played immediately before (left column) and immediately after (right column) on that date.

Axilla [33]*[Axilla]
By Anastasio/Marshall

11/19/92	[480]	1	Esther	Horse
11/20/92	1	1	*OP1	All Things
11/22/92	2	2	*OP2	My Friend
11/27/92	3	2	*OP2	PoorHeart
12/01/92	3	2	*OP2	Curtain
12/07/92	6	1	*OP1	PoorHeart
12/11/92	3	2	Esther	Bouncing

All the Songs is an ultimate chronicle of every time Phish has played every original song, as documented in the *Almanac*'s setlists section through December 31, 1997.

There's a wealth of information here if you know how to access it. This reference section is designed to allow easy determination of the number of times and the dates on which Phish has played every original song. The section can also be used to help identify undated setlists, as the song performed immediately before and after the profiled song is noted in the list.

Listed under the title, author, and total number of times played is every documented show at which Phish has played the song, followed by the number of shows since the band last played it, the set in which it was played, and the song played immediately before and after.

The bold-faced number following the list (e.g., >> **12/31/97 633**) is the song's lapse through 12/31/97.

Show components listed within quotation marks in the setlists, such as "Crew Acknowledgment," are not considered songs so are omitted.

Similarly, setlists not considered to be concert performances, as noted by brackets surrounding the date in the setlist section (e.g., [7/15/95]) are also omitted.

The SONGWRITERS

Writing credit for the majority of Phish songs goes to the songwriting team of Tom Marshall and Trey Anastasio, who have collaborated since their grade-school days. Tom writes the lyrics and Trey the music, with Tom often offering lots of poems and other writings to Trey, who then sifts through them and sets them to music. Trey has also written both the words and the music to many songs, including most of the Gamehendge saga—his senior thesis at Goddard College—and epics such as You Enjoy Myself, Reba, and David Bowie. The Dude of Life has also contributed lyrics and melodies to some of Trey's compositions, as have some other friends of the band.

Mike Gordon has written his fair share of songs, too, from Mound and Simple to Scent of a Mule and Contact. Fishman added lyrics to many earlier Phish songs but limits his songwriting hand to "deeper" songs such as Lengthwise and Ha Ha Ha nowadays (plus his new ballad, Bye Bye Foot). Page, a contributor to several songs, has written two songs performed by Phish—Magilla and Cars Trucks Buses.

• All the Songs Phish Has Performed •

and the Stories Behind Them

AC/DC BAG

Inspiration: Written as part of the Gamehendge saga, AC/DC Bag is sung from Wilson's perspective. The AC/DC Bag is the electronic hangman that carries out Wilson's sentence of death on his accountant, Mr. Palmer.

Musical Evolution and History: Since its debut in the late 1980s, AC/DC Bag has been one of the band's most popular songs. Up through 1990, the band considered it one of their showpiece songs, offering a lively structure with room to jam. For most of the 1990s, the song kept its original structure, including a fade-out ending jam, though it was often delivered at a faster pace than most 1980s performances. In 1996 and 1997, the band began taking a more free-form approach to the jam out of the lyrical section, sometimes abandoning the fade-out ending to jam out, like they did at Dayton, OH, on 12/7/97, when the outro jam led them into an impromptu performance of Talking Heads' "Psycho Killer." Other notable versions include the slowed-down, Trey-centric performance at Sugarbush on 7/16/94, and the often-overlooked performance at nearby Lake Placid the following year, on 12/16/95.

Rotation History: One of Phish's most-played songs from the 1980s through 1991, it became a relative rarity from late 1991 through 1993, appearing only once between 11/1/91 and 2/19/93, with gaps of 74 and 84 performances. It moved back it into heavy rotation beginning in 1995, when it often served as a show opener. By 1997, the song had become a relative rarity once again, appearing only eight times over the course of 78 shows.

Discography: Has not yet appeared on a Phish album, though it does appear on the "White Album."

AC/DC Bag [182] [ACDCBag]

By Anastasio

04/01/86	[4]	2	Slipknot	McGrupp
04/15/86	1	1a	*OP1	Reagan
10/31/86	2	2	*OP2	SwingLow
12/06/86	1	1a	Katy	Bowie
04/24/87	4	1a	Golgi	Possum
08/10/87	4	1	Fire	Possum
08/29/87	6	2	Timber Ho	Divided
09/12/87	2	1	Golgi	Possum
10/14/87	2	2	Bowie	Divided
01/30/88	3	1	Mustang	Possum
02/07/88	1	1a	Bowie	Timber Ho
03/11/88	2	2	Harpua	Alumni
03/12/88	1	1a	Wilson	Forbin's
03/21/88	1	1a	Fire	Possum
03/31/88	1	1	Fee	Possum
05/15/88	3	1a	WhipPost	Possum
06/15/88	3	2	Lizards	Sloth
06/20/88	2	1	Fluffhead	Lizards
06/21/88	1	2	IDK	Flat Fee
07/12/88	2	1	Slave	Antelope
07/23/88	1	1	OYWD	Possum
08/06/88	4	2	Golgi	Satin Doll
09/08/88	2	1	Wild Child	Forbin's
09/24/88	2	3	Curtain	*CL3
10/12/88	1	2	Sloth	Possum
10/29/88	1	3	Possum	Foam
11/05/88	2	2	Lizards	Fee
02/07/89	7	1	Dinner	Lizards
02/17/89	1	1a	*OP1	YEM
02/24/89	2	2	*OP2	YEM
03/03/89	1	1	Foam	Curtain
03/30/89	3	3	Foam	BBFCM
04/20/89	9	1	*OP1	Fluffhead
05/06/89	9	1	Bold	Forbin's
05/13/89	6	1	*OP1	Alumni
05/20/89	4	1	*OP1	Alumni
05/21/89	1	1	Ya Mar	Divided
05/26/89	1	1	Bold	Mike's
05/27/89	1	1	*OP1	Mike's
06/23/89	6	1	*OP1	YEM
06/30/89	2	2	WalkAway	Curtain
08/12/89	3	1a	Suzie	Ya Mar
08/17/89	1	2	WalkAway	Mango
08/19/89	2	1	TMWSIY	PYITE
08/23/89	1	2	YEM	Foam
08/26/89	1	2	Slave	Donna Lee
09/09/89	4	1	Divided	McGrupp
10/01/89	1	2	*OP2	MSO
10/07/89	2	2	Lizards	Bowie
10/14/89	3	1	*OP1	Divided
10/20/89	1	2	IDK	Donna
10/21/89	1	1	Foam	Lizards
10/22/89	1	2	McGrupp	MSO
10/26/89	1	2	Clod	Reba
10/31/89	2	1	Suzie	Divided
11/02/89	1	2	Who Do	MSO
11/09/89	3	2	Oh Kee	McGrupp
11/10/89	1	1	Divided	MSO
11/11/89	1	1a	Bathtub	MSO
11/16/89	1	2	Sloth	Tela
11/30/89	2	1	Oh Kee	Foam
12/07/89	4	1	A-Train	Fee
12/08/89	1	1	Who Do	MSO
12/16/89	3	1	Curtain	Lawn Boy
12/29/89	1	1	Oh Kee	Lizards
12/31/89	2	1	Oh Kee	Antelope
01/27/90	4	1	Oh Kee	MSO
02/09/90	8	1	Bouncing	Sqirm Coil
02/10/90	1	2	Esther	Rocky Top
02/24/90	6	2	Sloth	Fee
03/03/90	4	1	Oh Kee	Reba
03/07/90	1	2	Oh Kee	Sqirm Coil
03/08/90	1	2	MSO	Caravan
03/09/90	1	1	Oh Kee	*CL1
03/11/90	1	2	Slave	Bowie
03/17/90	1	2	Oh Kee	Foam
04/05/90	3	2	Jesus	Donna
04/07/90	2	1	Suzie	Sqirm Coil
04/13/90	5	1	Oh Kee	Reba
04/20/90	3	2	Oh Kee	Jesus
05/10/90	10	2	Oh Kee	Lizards
05/11/90	1	2	Oh Kee	Lizards
05/13/90	2	1	Oh Kee	Dinner
05/24/90	4	1	Oh Kee	Golgi
06/16/90	7	1	*OP1	Divided
09/13/90	1	2	Oh Kee	Bur Alive
09/15/90	2	1	Oh Kee	Asse Fest
09/28/90	5	2	*OP2	Esther
10/01/90	1	2	Lawn Boy	*CL2
10/30/90	8	3	Contact	*CL3
11/04/90	4	1	Carolina	Curtain
12/08/90	11	1	Foam	Divided
12/29/90	2	E	Donna	*CL E
02/07/91	5	E	*OP E	*CL E
02/08/91	1	1	*OP 1	Reba
02/15/91	3	2	Oh Kee	Harry
02/26/91	8	1	Oh Kee	Golgi
03/15/91	10	1	Oh Kee	Lizards
03/23/91	5	2	Oh Kee	MSO
04/16/91	13	1	Oh Kee	Tela
04/21/91	4	1	Oh Kee	Tela
05/03/91	5	2	*OP2	Curtain
05/12/91	3	2	Oh Kee	Antelope
05/25/91	4	1a	Oh Kee	Fee
07/12/91	2	1	Donna	Rocky Top
07/14/91	2	3	*OP3	Landlady
07/21/91	5	2	Esther	Contact
07/25/91	3	1	Flat Fee	Adeline
10/06/91	13	1	Oh Kee	Brother
10/13/91	4	1	Tela	Sloth
11/01/91	12	1	*OP1	Sparkle
05/16/92	74	2	Oh Kee	Rosie
02/19/93	84	E	*OPE	*CLE
03/12/93	14	2	*OP2	My Friend
03/22/93	8	2	Wilson	Forbin's
03/31/93	7	E	*OPE	Adeline
04/14/93	9	2	*OP2	MSO
04/22/93	6	E	*OPE	AmGrace
05/03/93	9	2	*OP2	Curtain
05/08/93	4	E	*OPE	*CLE
07/31/93	16	E	*OPE	Freebird
08/12/93	8	1	*OP1	Reba
08/25/93	9	1	*OP1	Daniel
04/05/94	8	1	Rift	*CL1
04/13/94	6	2	PurplRain	*CL2
04/18/94	5	1	Oh Kee	*CL1
05/06/94	13	1	Oh Kee	PoorHeart
05/20/94	10	1	Carolina	*CL1
06/18/94	16	1	Rift	Maze
06/26/94	7	1	Wilson	Forbin's
07/08/94	8	1	Wilson	Forbin's
07/16/94	6	2	Harpua	Scent
10/22/94	13	2	AmGrace	HwayHell
11/18/94	16	1	Rift	Julius
12/08/94	15	1	Maze	Scent
12/30/94	5	1	Rift	Sparkle
06/09/95	5	1	Oh Kee	Theme
06/15/95	4	1	Sparkle	Old Home
06/19/95	3	1	PoorHeart	Tela
06/25/95	5	1	Ya Mar	Taste
06/30/95	4	1	*OP1	Scent
07/03/95	3	2	Bowie	Lizards
09/27/95	1	1	CTB	Bowie
09/29/95	2	1	*OP1	Sparkle
10/08/95	7	1	*OP1	Demand
10/14/95	3	1	*OP1	CTB
10/17/95	2	1	Uncle Pen	Maze
10/22/95	4	1	*OP1	My Mind
10/28/95	4	1	*OP1	Mound
11/10/95	4	2	Sparkle	Adeline
11/15/95	4	1	PoorHeart	FEFY
11/18/95	2	2	*OP2	Sparkle
11/24/95	4	1	Oh Kee	Curtain
11/29/95	3	1	*OP1	Ya Mar
12/07/95	6	1	Curtain	Demand
12/16/95	7	1	BurAlive	Fog
12/30/95	4	2	Harry	Life Boy
04/26/96	2	1a	Ya Mar	Sparkle
06/06/96	1	2	*OP2	YEM
07/05/96	2	1a	Chalkdust	YEM
07/23/96	14	1	*OP1	Foam
08/04/96	4	2	*OP2	Reba
08/10/96	4	1	PoorHeart	Free
08/13/96	2	2	*OP2	Lizards
08/16/96	2	1	Ya Mar	Esther
10/19/96	5	1	*OP2	Sparkle
10/23/96	3	1	PoorHeart	Foam
10/27/96	3	1	PYITE	Fee
11/11/96	9	1	CTB	Sparkle
11/14/96	2	1	*OP1	Uncle Pen
11/19/96	4	1	Ya Mar	Foam
11/24/96	3	1	PoorHeart	All Things
12/02/96	5	1	Rocky Top	Bouncing
12/30/96	5	2	Uncle Pen	Guyute
02/14/97	3	2	*OP2	Ya Mar
02/21/97	5	2	Oh Kee	Billy
06/25/97	17	1	Billy	Old Home
07/25/97	14	1	Makisupa	*CL1
08/06/97	7	1	Also Sprac	Ya Mar
11/21/97	14	2	Ghost	Slave
12/07/97	11	1	*OP1	Psycho Killer
12/30/97	7	2	*OP2	McGrupp
>> 12/31/97	**1**			

ACOUSTIC ARMY

Inspiration: Seemingly born of the well-known desire of the band members to show off their prowess on a range of instruments, Acoustic Army served as an excuse for them each to don acoustic guitars and sit on barstools at the front of the stage, where they would strum this Trey-written instrumental (complete with false ending).

Musical Evolution and History: With all four guitar parts clearly composed, versions of this song differ little from performance to performance. Trey, not surprisingly, plays the lead role in the song, while the others hold down the groove.

Rotation History: This served as a defining song of summer tour 1995 when it was played at almost every show, to the delight of crowds who loved to see the band pull out another innovative trick. It was played less frequently on fall tour 1995, then dropped out of rotation completely and hasn't been heard from since.

Discography: Has not yet appeared on a Phish album.

Acoustic Army [27] [AArmy]

By Anastasio

06/07/95	[740]	2	LCBill	Sample
06/09/95	2	2	Bowie	Adeline
06/13/95	2	2	Theme	Harry
06/14/95	1	2	Tweezer	Guitar
06/15/95	1	2	Scent	Slave
06/17/95	2	2	McGrupp	Adeline
06/19/95	1	2	YEM	Possum
06/22/95	2	E	*OPE	Guitar
06/24/95	2	2	Harry	Adeline
06/29/95	4	2	YEM	DayinLife
07/01/95	2	2	Str Design	Harry
07/02/95	1	2	Sl Monkey	Slave
09/28/95	3	1	Fog	Slave
10/02/95	3	1	Stash	Fog
10/05/95	2	1	Divided	Julius
10/07/95	2	1	Mango	Wilson
10/11/95	2	1	Fog	Julius
10/14/95	2	1	Catapult	It's Ice
10/19/95	3	1	Theme	Split&Melt
10/21/95	2	1	Str Design	GTBT
10/24/95	2	1	Wolfman's	Caspian
10/28/95	3	1	Billy	Caspian
11/11/95	5	E	*OPE	GTBT
11/18/95	5	2	BBFCM	BBFCM
11/24/95	4	2	Bathtub	Bike
11/29/95	3	1	Theme	Fee
12/08/95	7	1	It's Ice	Caspian
>> 12/31/97	**207**			

ALL THINGS RECONSIDERED

Inspiration: While Trey was composing this short instrumental piece, he recognized its similarity to the theme song for National Public Radio's popular news and information show "All Things Considered." Rather than struggle to differentiate his new composition from the NPR show's theme, he instead altered the piece to make it an even closer variation to the "All Things Considered" theme, then affixed the punny "All Things Reconsidered" title to it.

Musical Evolution and History: Although this song was introduced on the first show of the fall tour in 1991, the band only played it that once because they found it so technically demanding to play. On the first show of the 1992 spring tour, in Portsmouth, NH, on 3/6/92, the band brought the song back in perfected form, and has played it the same way (when they can get the complex compositional structure right) since. Band members claim they botched this song horribly when they performed it on NPR's "MountainStage Live" radio show later that month, on 3/22/92.

Rotation History: Heavily played in 1992 and 1993, All Things has languished since then, including a 108-show lapse from 7/1/95 in Mansfield, MA, to 11/8/96 in Champaign, IL. In 1997, the song only surfaced once in concert, at Cortemaggiore, Italy, on 2/23/97.

Discography: Appeared on *Rift* (1993), as that disc's only purely instrumental track.

All Things Reconsidered [77] [All Things]

By Anastasio

09/25/91	[336]	E	*OPE	BBFCM
03/06/92	49	1	Reba	Bowie
03/11/92	2	2	BabyLem	Harry
03/19/92	5	1	Mockbird	Bowie
03/21/92	2	2	PoorHeart	Bowie
03/25/92	2	2	Reba	Sqirm Coil
03/26/92	1	1	RunJim	Foam
03/30/92	3	1	IDK	Sloth
04/01/92	2	1	Brother	Sparkle
04/03/92	1	1	Fluffhead	Split&Melt
04/05/92	2	2	Split&Melt	YEM
04/07/92	2	2	PoorHeart	Tweezer
04/13/92	3	1	Fee	Foam
04/15/92	1	1	IDK	RunJim
04/18/92	3	1	Sparkle	Antelope
04/22/92	3	1	Stash	Suzie
04/25/92	3	2	Silent	Dinner
05/01/92	3	2	Wilson	MSO
05/03/92	2	1	Fee	Split&Melt
05/05/92	1	2	Bouncing	Foam
05/06/92	1	2	YEM	Bouncing
05/08/92	2	1	Mound	Bouncing
05/12/92	3	1	Reba	Sloth
05/14/92	1	1	Suzie	Sloth
05/17/92	3	2	Sqirm Coil	Brother
06/27/92	6	1a	Maze	Chalkdust
07/14/92	8	2	Fee	Reba
07/15/92	1	2	McGrupp	Harry
07/21/92	5	1a	*OP1	Possum
07/27/92	5	1a	Golgi	Bowie
07/30/92	2	1a	It's Ice	Maze
08/17/92	7	1	Wilson	Foam
08/24/92	4	1a	PoorHeart	Tweezer
11/20/92	8	1	Axilla	Suzie
11/22/92	2	1	Horn	Bathtub
11/28/92	4	1	FEFY	Mike's
12/01/92	2	2	My Friend	Uncle Pen
12/03/92	2	1	Fee	Split&Melt
12/10/92	6	1	IDK	Reba
12/12/92	2	1	PoorHeart	Bouncing
12/29/92	3	2	FEFY	Mike's
02/04/93	4	1	FEFY	Stash
02/06/93	2	2	Adeline	Mike's
02/12/93	5	2	My Friend	Reba
02/17/93	3	1	Weigh	Sloth
02/20/93	3	1	Weigh	Divided
02/23/93	3	2	PYITE	Mike's
03/02/93	4	1	Fee	Chalkdust
03/13/93	7	1	Fee	Split&Melt
03/21/93	6	1	Esther	Split&Melt
03/26/93	4	1	PYITE	Split&Melt
03/30/93	3	1	PoorHeart	Golgi
04/03/93	4	2	Mound	Sloth
04/09/93	2	2	Suzie	Llama
04/17/93	6	1	My Friend	Golgi
04/22/93	4	2	Bouncing	Tweezer
04/27/93	4	2	My Friend	Maze
04/30/93	2	1	Lawn Boy	Possum
05/06/93	5	1	Silent	Llama
07/16/93	6	1	FEFY	Nellie
07/28/93	9	1	*OP1	RunJim
08/02/93	4	1	Suzie	Bathtub
08/11/93	6	2	Esther	Bouncing
08/15/93	4	1	Sample	RunJim
08/24/93	5	1	Chalkdust	Bouncing
04/09/94	12	1	Fee	Stash
04/22/94	11	1	Sample	Nellie
06/24/94	41	1	Sloth	Paul&Silas
10/13/94	22	1	Gumbo	DWD
10/28/94	12	1	Axilla 2	Sample
06/14/95	39	1	Possum	AmGrace
07/01/95	14	1	If I Could	It's Ice
11/08/96	108	1	Axilla	Mound
11/14/96	4	1	Free	Bathtub
11/24/96	7	1	ACDCBag	Bouncing
11/30/96	3	1	PYITE	Bouncing
02/23/97	17	1	Axilla	Sloth
>> 12/31/97		**69**		

ALUMNI BLUES

Inspiration: Written in the late 1980s, around the time the members of Phish were graduating from college, the likely inspiration for this song is not hard to see. Featuring the catchy refrain, "I'm all right 'cause I got a degree," and a great jam segment, this song became one of Phish's earliest trademark pieces, appearing at virtually every show in the 1980s.

Musical Evolution and History: Though the music for Alumni has remained relatively unchanged, the band has experimented with a second verse of lyrics which appears in most post-1989 versions of the song. Most versions of the song from the 1980s feature the instrumental piece Letter to Jimmy Page wedged in the middle immediately following the first verse, leading to numerous setlists labeled "Alumni > Letter to Jimmy Page > Alumni."

Rotation History: Once heavily played, this song has languished in recent years because Fishman apparently dislikes it. Prior to its one-verse-only appearance at the Beacon Theater in New York City on 4/15/94 (with the Giant Country Horns), it hadn't been played at all since fall '91. Trey has said that it will probably only surface if Phish tours again with a horn section, and the band did tease the crowd with it on 12/3/94 in San Jose, CA, at another horns show, but didn't sing any of the lyrics at that time. Since then, it hasn't been heard from at all.

Discography: For reasons unknown, the band chose to leave Alumni Blues off of *Junta* (1989), even though they had a studio recording of the song already in the bag. As a result, it has not yet appeared on a Phish album, though it did appear on the "White Album."

Alumni Blues [63] [Alumni]

By Anastasio

10/17/85	[4]	1a	Jam	Mike's
10/30/85	1	1a	Reviv	PrepHipp
04/01/86	2	2	McGrupp	Reagan
04/15/86	1	1a	CamlWalk	*CL1
10/31/86	2	2	Icculus	*CL2
03/23/87	4	1	Mike's	YEM
04/24/87	1	1a	Dave's	I am H2
04/29/87	1	1	Katy	Golgi
08/10/87	3	1	Peaches	Golgi
08/29/87	3	1	*OP1	Curtis
09/12/87	2	2	Suzie	GTBT
11/19/87	4	2	Corrina	Suzie
01/30/88	1	1	Sally	A-Train
02/07/88	1	1a	Golgi	Peaches
03/11/88	2	2	ACDCBag	Antelope
03/31/88	3	2	*OP2	Lizards
05/14/88	2	2	Fluffhead	A-Train
05/15/88	1	1a	*OP1	Golgi
05/25/88	2	1	FunkBitch	Peaches
06/15/88	1	1	Suzie	YEM
06/18/88	1	2	*OP2	BBFCM
06/21/88	2	2	Flat Fee	Jesus
07/11/88	1	1	Golgi	*CL1
07/23/88	2	2	La Grange	Peaches
07/24/88	1	2	Lizards	OYWD
09/24/88	7	1	OYWD	YEM
10/12/88	1	2	*OP2	YEM
10/29/88	1	2	Fee	WalkAway
11/03/88	1	1	Fee	GTBT
11/05/88	1	1	Fluffhead	Bowie
12/02/88	2	2	GTBT	Lizards
01/26/89	1	1a	Golgi	YEM
02/07/89	4	2	Contact	Fee
02/17/89	1	1a	A-Train	Antelope
03/03/89	3	1	Divided	GTBT
04/15/89	10	1	OYWD	IDK
05/05/89	10	1	Fluffhead	Jam
05/13/89	7	1	ACDCBag	YEM
05/20/89	4	1	ACDCBag	YEM
08/17/89	16	3	Halley's	Contact
09/09/89	6	2	YEM	Split&Melt
10/01/89	1	1	*OP1	McGrupp
10/06/89	1	1a	Dinner	Harry
10/07/89	1	1	Makisupa	GTBT
10/14/89	3	1	Fee	YEM
10/31/89	6	2	Mockbird	Lizards
12/07/89	13	1	Weekpaug	Divided
12/09/89	2	2	Esther	Fee
02/09/90	17	2	A-Train	Foam
02/23/90	6	1	*OP1	YEM
04/06/90	14	2	IDK	GTBT
04/13/90	6	2	Foam	YEM
04/20/90	3	1	Divided	Ya Mar
05/19/90	15	1	Ya Mar	Adeline
10/05/90	20	2	Ya Mar	Uncle Pen
12/07/90	20	E	*OPE	*CLE
02/14/91	11	1	Esther	Bouncing
04/06/91	22	1	Jesus	*CL1
04/20/91	8	E	Horn	*CLE
07/13/91	19	1	Suzie	TMWSIY
07/15/91	2	E	Contact	*CLE
10/10/91	21	1	Golgi	Lizards
04/15/94	279	2	Wolfman's	BeLikeYou
>> 12/31/97		**342**		

ANARCHY

Inspiration: More comic relief than song, this mid-1980s creation features the band chanting "Anarchy!"

Original Songs

PLAYED BY YEAR

The number of times and the percentage of shows in which a song was played during a given year.

AC/DC Bag

1990	27	26%
1991	18	14%
1992	1	1%
1993	11	10%
1994	13	10%
1995	21	26%
1996	17	24%
1997	8	10%

Acoustic Army

1995	27	33%
1996	0	0%
1997	0	0%

All Things Reconsidered

1991	1	1%
1992	40	33%
1993	24	22%
1994	5	4%
1995	2	2%
1996	4	6%
1997	1	1%

Alumni Blues

1990	8	8%
1991	6	5%
1992	0	0%
1993	0	0%
1994	1	1%
1995	0	0%
1996	0	0%
1997	0	0%

Asse Festival

1990	16	16%
1991	1	1%

Axilla

1992	8	7%
1993	15	14%
1994	1	1%
1995	0	0%
1996	5	7%
1997	6	8%

Axilla II

1994	35	28%
1995	4	5%
1996	0	0%
1997	0	0%

Bathtub Gin

1990	18	17%
1991	22	17%
1992	9	7%
1993	7	6%
1994	11	9%
1995	10	12%
1996	10	14%
1997	12	15%

as they jam in punk-rock style for about ten seconds, as a humorous send-up.

Musical Evolution and History: With only a few moments' worth of jam, there wasn't really anywhere for this song to go. Watch for pairings with its sister song, Revolution, as on 10/17/95 at Hunt's in Burlington, VT.

Rotation History: Appears on a handful of setlists from 1985, 1986, and 1987, but none since.

Discography: Has not appeared on a Phish album.

Anarchy [6] [Anarchy]

By Anastasio (?)

03/04/85	[1]	1a	*OP1	CamlWalk
05/03/85	1	E	*OPE	*CLE
10/17/85	1	1a	Revol	CamlWalk
04/15/86	4	1a	YEM	CamlWalk
04/29/87	8	3	GTBT	Makisupa
08/10/87	3	2	WhipPost	Tush
>> 12/31/97	947			

THE ASSE FESTIVAL

Inspiration: Trey dedicated the song to his composition teacher, Ernie Stires, whose inspiration can be heard in the song's fugue structure.

Musical Evolution and History: Initially performed as a stand-alone instrumental composition. The Asse Festival has been performed as the middle section of Guelah Papyrus since February 1991, though it did surface once on its own after the debut of Guelah, on 4/27/91 in Port Chester, NY. Other than placement, though, the song has remained unchanged since its debut as part of the giant batch of new songs at the Wetlands Preserve in New York City on 9/13/90.

Rotation History: Heavily played on its debut tour, fall 1990, it appeared as part of Guelah starting in February 1991 with that song's debut. It can still be heard there today.

Discography: As part of Guelah Papyrus on *A Picture of Nectar* (1992).

The Asse Festival [17] [Asse Fest]

By Anastasio

Now played as the middle section in Guelah Papyrus.

09/13/90	[222]	1	Tube	Antelope
09/14/90	1	2	*OP2	Sqirm Coil
09/15/90	1	1	ACDCBag	Bowie
09/22/90	4	E	*OPE	Golgi
09/28/90	1	1	Lizards	Antelope
10/05/90	3	1	Stash	Bouncing
10/07/90	2	1	Mockbird	Sqirm Coil
10/30/90	4	1	Donna	Suzie
10/31/90	1	1	YEM	MSO
11/02/90	1	1	Cavern	Possum
11/04/90	2	1	FunkBitch	MSO
11/08/90	1	1	Sqirm Coil	IDK
11/10/90	1	2	YEM	Fee
11/30/90	5	2	*OP2	Sqirm Coil
12/07/90	3	1	YEM	RunJim
12/08/90	1	2	Llama	Dinner
04/27/91	55	1	Adeline	RunJim
>> 12/31/97	658 (as a stand-alone song)			

AXILLA/AXILLA (PART II)

Musical Inspiration: A two-part suite about a character getting his "loins dissolved." The original Axilla featured particularly Tom Marshall-esque lyrics; the band decided not to include it on *Rift* because it didn't fit with the album's theme. A year later, when they chose to include the song on *Hoist*, they opted to revise the lyrics because they feared they would stand out in their absurdity. So, keeping the musical structure and pounding "Axilla!" refrain, Marshall wrote new lyrics to the song. Supposedly, part II continues the story begun in part I, in which a witch dissolved the loins of the song's narrator. In part II, the narrator laments this unfortunate turn of events. Both Axillas are said to be set in the later years of Gamehendge, but the Gamehendge connection is unclear. Some note that Axilla means "armpit" (actually spelled ascella) in Italian, a fact that doesn't clarify much.

Musical Evolution and History: Besides the lyrics switch noted above, the other change to this song is the addition of the slow ending heard on *Hoist* (the part where Trey's slowed-down voice can be heard saying, "Don't shine that thing in my face, man"). That ending made its concert debut on 6/26/94 in Charleston, WV (the GameHoist show), then appeared in concert regularly thereafter. Interestingly, since the revival of the original Axilla in fall 1996, the band has often tacked the slow Axilla II ending onto Axilla.

Rotation History: Axilla (unofficially called Axilla I) debuted on fall tour 1992, Trey terming it "my favorite of the new songs" on 11/19/92 in Colchester, VT. It appeared less frequently starting with summer tour 1993, and by spring tour 1994, it was supplanted by Axilla II and the release of *Hoist*. Axilla II was played frequently in 1994 (with one rogue appearance by Axilla I, on 10/16/94 in Chattanooga, TN), but only a couple of times in 1995 before it disappeared completely from setlists after its appearance on 12/31/95. In the fall of 1996, the band revised Axilla I, which was played a bunch of times in late 1996 and 1997. The two Axillas have never been played together at a show.

Discography: Axilla has not yet appeared on a Phish album. Axilla (Part II) appears on *Hoist* (1994).

Axilla [35] [Axilla]

By Anastasio/Marshall

11/19/92	[480]	1	Esther	Horse
11/20/92	1	1	*OP1	All Things
11/22/92	2	2	*OP2	My Friend
11/27/92	3	2	*OP2	PoorHeart
12/01/92	3	2	*OP2	Curtain
12/07/92	6	1	*OP1	PoorHeart
12/11/92	3	2	Esther	Bouncing
12/30/92	5	2	*OP2	Rift
02/04/93	3	1	*OP1	Foam
02/17/93	10	2	*OP2	Landlady
02/21/93	4	2	*OP2	Curtain
02/23/93	2	2	*OP2	MSO
03/03/93	5	2	*OP2	Curtain
03/09/93	4	2	*OP2	Rift
03/12/93	1	2	My Friend	Sparkle
03/17/93	4	2	*OP2	Glide
03/25/93	6	2	*OP2	Curtain
04/01/93	6	2	*OP2	Curtain
04/05/93	3	2	*OP2	PoorHeart
04/16/93	6	2	*OP2	Curtain
05/02/93	13	1	*OP1	Sparkle
07/28/93	18	2	Also Sprac	MSO
08/16/93	15	1	*OP1	Possum
10/16/94	93	1	TMWSIY	Possum
11/08/96	170	1	RunJim	All Things
11/11/96	2	1	Theme	RunJim
11/16/96	4	2	Catapult	Harry
11/23/96	4	2	Makisupa	Weekpaug
12/31/96	12	1	*OP1	Peaches
02/14/97	2	1	Adeline	It's Ice
02/23/97	7	1	Carini	All Things
02/28/97	3	2	Love Me	Waste
12/09/97	59	2	Contact	Harry
12/13/97	3	1	Ya Mar	Theme
12/28/97	1	2	*OP2	Simple
>> 12/31/97	3			

Axilla II [37] [Axilla 2]

By Anastasio/Marshall

04/16/94	[626]	1	Fee	Rift
04/20/94	3	1	Bouncing	Suzie
04/24/94	4	1	Ya Mar	Maze
04/30/94	4	2	Harry	McGrupp
05/04/94	3	1	Sparkle	Tweezer
05/06/94	1	2	Reba	Julius
05/08/94	2	1	Foam	Rift
05/10/94	1	1	Divided	It's Ice
05/12/94	1	1	Maze	Foam
05/16/94	3	1	Divided	Rift
05/22/94	5	1	Dog Faced	*CL1
05/25/94	2	1	Mockbird	Scent
05/28/94	3	2	*OP2	It's Ice
06/10/94	3	2	*OP2	Curtain
06/19/94	7	1	Lizards	Curtain
06/23/94	3	2	Mango	Uncle Pen
06/25/94	2	2	Bathtub	YEM
06/26/94	1	2	If I Could	Life Boy
06/30/94	2	2	Sparkle	Harpua
07/03/94	3	1	Reba	Bowie
07/06/94	2	1	Reba	My Mind
10/22/94	20	1	Gumbo	Rift
10/25/94	2	2	Glide	Jesus
10/26/94	1	2	Reba	YEM
10/28/94	2	1	Glide	All Things
11/02/94	3	2	Mango	Possum
11/13/94	4	1	Reba	It's Ice
11/16/94	2	1	Reba	Lizards
11/19/94	3	1	Guyute	Paul&Silas
11/20/94	1	2	Glide	Reba
12/04/94	10	2	Reba	YEM
12/08/94	3	2	My Mind	Reba
12/28/94	3	1	Bouncing	Dog Faced
06/13/95	9	2	Lizards	Theme
06/28/95	12	1	*OP1	Foam
12/04/95	49	1	My Mind	Horse
12/31/95	14	2	Lizards	RunJim
>> 12/31/97	148			

BATHTUB GIN

Inspiration: Friend-of-the-band Suzannah Goodman penned the catchy lyrics to this tune, with music supplied by Trey.

Musical Evolution and History: From the start, it was clear that the band liked Bathtub Gin, but the musical heights which this song would reach were not obvious for quite a while. Debuted on stage in spring 1989 and recorded shortly thereafter at Archer Studios for inclusion in *Lawn Boy*, the studio version includes the sounds of Fishman smashing bottles wrapped in towels.

For most of Bathtub's early career, the song featured a jam segment following the lyrics that would eventually come back around to the Bathtub Gin theme before finishing. That still happens during some performances of the song (like the enchanting version from the Clifford Ball, 8/16/96). But the ones that fans sometimes enjoy more see the jam take off in a wild, other direction without ever returning to the Gin theme. The granddaddy of these Gins is the famed Murat Gin from 8/13/93 in Indianapolis, IN, when the Gin jam suddenly takes on a Weekapaug-like intensity and soars for about ten minutes before eventually arriving at Ya Mar. Other top-notch Gins include 12/29/95's version at Worcester, MA, which includes the Who's "Real Me" in the middle, in one of the most perfectly constructed segues in Phishtory; 11/7/96 Lexington, KY, a 25-minute version that travels to many spaces and places; and 8/17/97 Great Went, which although not as long as Lexington's version, might be the most intense Bathtub Gin jam yet performed. Also of note: 12/30/93 Portland, ME, short but hot; 4/24/94 Charlotte, NC, with jazz standard Jump Monk in the middle; 5/20/94 Olympia, WA, another not overlong but scorching version; 12/5/95 Amherst, MA, long and beautiful; 7/1/97 Amsterdam, Gin > Jam > Cities; and 7/21/97 Virginia Beach, VA, gorgeous Drowned-like jam and a tour welcome from Trey.

Rotation History: Never overplayed or underplayed, Bathtub Gin has surfaced at a fairly reliable rate in concert since its debut in the spring of 1989 (although it did take a 52-show break during 1992).

The song often appeared in the first set in its early days, but many of the most celebrated performances have come in the second set.

Discography: Appears on *Lawn Boy* (1990).

Bathtub Gin [117] [Bathtub]

By Anastasio/Goodman

05/26/89	[102]	2	Split&Melt	Antelope
05/27/89	1	1	Fluffhead	GTBT
05/28/89	1	2	Weekpaug	Sanity
06/30/89	7	2	Slave	Mike's
08/19/89	7	2	Divided	*CL2
09/09/89	6	1	Makisupa	PYITE
10/26/89	10	2	WalkAway	Sloth
10/31/89	2	1	WalkAway	Possum
11/02/89	1	1	*OP1	Foam
11/03/89	1	1	Mockbird	MSO
11/09/89	3	1	MSO	YEM
11/10/89	2	1	Harry	Mike's
11/11/89	1	1a	Golgi	ACDCBag
11/16/89	1	1	Weekpaug	Foam
11/30/89	2	1	*OP1	Divided
12/08/89	5	1	MSO	Antelope
12/09/89	1	1	Lawn Boy	Golgi
12/31/89	5	1	Antelope	Lizards
01/27/90	4	1	Carolina	Ya Mar
01/28/90	1	2	YEM	Mike's
02/10/90	8	1	YEM	Bouncing
02/15/90	1	1	Caravan	Mike's
02/17/90	2	1a	Caravan	Mike's
02/23/90	2	2	Reba	Jesus
02/24/90	1	2	La Grange	Lawn Boy
03/07/90	5	2	Sqirm Coil	Split&Melt
03/08/90	1	2	Divided	MSO
04/07/90	8	1	*OP1	Possum
04/26/90	8	2	Esther	Oh Kee
05/04/90	4	2	Tweezer	Oh Kee
05/10/90	2	1	MSO	Possum
05/13/90	3	1	*OP1	Oh Kee
06/08/90	9	1	MSO	Tweezer
06/16/90	2	2	MSO	YEM
09/15/90	3	2	MSO	Foam
12/03/90	27	1	*OP1	FunkBitch
02/15/91	13	2	Bowie	Ya Mar
03/07/91	14	E	*OPE	*CLE
03/16/91	5	1	Landlady	Curtain
03/23/91	4	2	Chalkdust	Oh Kee
04/06/91	8	1	YEM	Icculus
04/22/91	10	2	Chalkdust	Uncle Pen
05/10/91	8	1	Landlady	BurAlive
05/12/91	2	2	Bowie	PoorHeart
07/12/91	6	1	Landlady	Donna
07/14/91	2	3	Chalkdust	Mike's
07/20/91	4	1	Landlady	MSO
07/24/91	3	1	Split&Melt	Landlady
10/13/91	18	2	Llama	Sqirm Coil
10/19/91	4	2	Llama	Sparkle
10/28/91	5	2	Paul&Silas	YEM
10/31/91	2	1	Foam	Paul&Silas
11/13/91	9	2	Golgi	Sqirm Coil
11/15/91	2	2	Llama	PoorHeart
11/16/91	1	2	MSO	Brother
11/20/91	2	1	Paul&Silas	Sqirm Coil
11/22/91	2	2	Landlady	Antelope
12/05/91	5	1	Llama	It's Ice
03/11/92	6	2	Lizards	My Mind
03/27/92	11	2	Rift	Dinner
04/06/92	8	2	Dinner	Paul&Silas
04/18/92	8	2	Manteca	Manteca
04/25/92	6	2	Maze	YEM
05/12/92	12	2	Landlady	YEM
11/22/92	52	1	All Things	Adeline
12/06/92	11	2	BBJ	YEM
12/30/92	9	2	Rift	YEM
02/21/93	17	2	Lizards	Rosie
03/16/93	15	2	Tweezer	Esther
03/28/93	10	2	Mound	YEM
04/24/93	19	2	Foam	Dinner
08/02/93	28	1	All Things	Makisupa
08/13/93	8	2	Rift	Ya Mar
12/30/93	13	1	Rift	Freebird
04/09/94	6	1	Rift	Nellie
04/18/94	8	2	Sparkle	BBJ
04/24/94	5	1	Maze	Dog Faced
05/12/94	12	1	Foam	Lizards
05/20/94	6	1	It's Ice	FEFY
06/17/94	15	1	PYITE	Scent
06/25/94	7	2	Sparkle	Axilla 2
07/05/94	7	2	Sparkle	Life Boy
10/14/94	15	1	PYITE	Adeline
11/18/94	22	2	Llama	Life Boy
12/28/94	18	1	Julius	Bouncing
06/20/95	15	1	Foam	If I Could
06/26/95	5	1	Wanna Go	NICU
10/02/95	11	2	CTB	Llama
10/11/95	6	2	Possum	Mound
11/09/95	15	2	Lizards	TMWSIY
11/24/95	11	2	Scent	AArmy
11/30/95	4	1	NICU	Rift
12/05/95	4	2	PoorHeart	Keyboard
12/15/95	7	2	It's Ice	Rotation
12/29/95	4	2	CTB	McGrupp
07/12/96	12	E	*OPE	Johnny B.
08/10/96	16	1	Rift	Cavern
08/16/96	4	1	Chalkdust	Ya Mar
10/17/96	3	2	Chalkdust	Scent
10/27/96	8	2	Chalkdust	Rift
11/07/96	6	2	Suzie	Bike
11/14/96	5	1	All Things	Talk
11/19/96	4	2	DayinLife	YEM
11/29/96	5	1	Divided	Life Mars
12/29/96	7	2	DayinLife	Lizards
02/17/97	6	1	Llama	Golgi
02/22/97	4	2	Chalkdust	Sparkle
07/01/97	19	2	Timber Ho	Cities
07/10/97	6	1	Ginseng	Llama
07/21/97	2	1	Ginseng	CharZero
07/25/97	3	1	Water	Makisupa
08/03/97	6	1	*OP1	Foam
08/10/97	4	1	*OP1	Sparkle
08/17/97	5	2	DWD	Uncle Pen
11/19/97	5	1	Julius	Llama
11/23/97	3	2	*OP2	DWD
12/06/97	8	1	Train Song	Foam
>> 12/31/97	**9**			

BIG BALL JAM

Inspiration: The "music" for this song depends on how the crowd interacts with three oversized beachballs thrown into the audience which "control" Page, Trey, and Mike. As audience members hit the balls, the musicians play a note; should a fan hold on to a ball, the band member keeps jamming until the ball is released back into the air. Although other bands have thrown balls into the audience for fans to play with, Phish is apparently the first band to try this participatory element.

Musical Evolution and History: The idea for the Big Ball Jam—which was officially introduced to the crowd on 11/19/92 in Colchester, VT—seemed to come from several experiences the band had on the 1992 spring tour. First, at the Flynn Theater show in Burlington, VT, on 3/12/92, audience members were batting a beachball around up front, and Trey got the idea to play along to the bouncing ball. A similar thing happened in Eugene, OR, on 4/22/92, and the seed was planted. Though most Big Ball Jams are a cacophonous musical nightmare, sometimes Trey attempted to string a musical theme through the jam, as he does with "Little Drummer Boy" on 4/9/94 at Binghamton, NY. Most versions of BBJ end with Trey, Mike, and Brad Sands forming a ring at the center of the stage for the audience to shoot the balls through. Giant cheers erupt when the audience scores.

Rotation History: This band-audience game could be counted on for frequent second-set comic relief in fall 1992 and throughout 1993 and 1994 (appearing in 23 straight shows in spring 1993), but the band has stopped Big Balling since the end of the 1994 fall tour, perhaps because of swelling venue sizes.

Discography: Has not yet appeared on a Phish album.

Big Ball Jam [99] [BBJ]

By Phish

11/19/92	[480]	2	Tweezer	PoorHeart
11/22/92	3	2	Tweezer	Tweezer
11/23/92	1	2	Weekpaug	Weekpaug
11/28/92	3	2	Tweezer	TMWSIY
12/02/92	3	2	Tweezer	Tela
12/03/92	1	2	BBJ	Rosie
12/06/92	3	2	Paul&Silas	Bathtub
12/08/92	2	2	MSO	Sl Monkey
12/10/92	1	2	MSO	Maze
12/11/92	1	2	Paul&Silas	Sqirm Coil
12/13/92	2	2	MSO	Rosie
12/29/92	2	2	MSO	FEFY
12/30/92	1	2	Possum	Love You
12/31/92	1	2	MSO	Stash
02/03/93	1	2	Terrapin	Possum
02/04/93	1	2	Uncle Pen	Lngthwise
02/06/93	2	2	Uncle Pen	Lngthwise
02/07/93	1	2	Bouncing	Glide
02/09/93	1	2	Sample	Stash
02/11/93	2	2	Mound	Bouncing
02/12/93	1	2	PoorHeart	FEFY
02/13/93	1	2	YEM	Lngthwise
02/15/93	1	2	PoorHeart	Bike
02/17/93	1	2	MSO	Horn
02/19/93	2	2	Ya Mar	Lawn Boy
02/20/93	1	2	FEFY	Terrapin
02/25/93	4	2	Uncle Pen	FEFY
02/26/93	1	2	Mound	YEM
02/27/93	1	2	Sample	Ya Mar
03/05/93	3	2	MSO	Love You
03/06/93	1	2	Paul&Silas	FEFY
03/08/93	1	2	Stash	My Friend
03/09/93	1	2	Silent	Love You
03/12/93	1	2	Mound	Chalkdust
03/13/93	1	2	Uncle Pen	Mike's
03/14/93	1	2	Rift	Great Gig
03/18/93	3	2	Uncle Pen	Brain
03/21/93	2	2	MSO	Rosie
03/24/93	2	2	Mound	FEFY
03/25/93	1	E	MSO	Adeline
03/26/93	1	2	YEM	Oh Kee
03/28/93	2	2	Paul&Silas	Love You
03/30/93	1	2	Life Boy	Weigh
03/31/93	1	2	Harry	It's Ice
04/01/93	1	2	PoorHeart	Terrapin
04/02/93	1	2	Lizards	Bike
04/10/93	4	2	Glide	Mike's
04/12/93	1	2	It's Ice	YEM
04/13/93	1	2	FEFY	Mike's
04/14/93	1	2	Mound	YEM
04/16/93	1	2	Uncle Pen	Bike
04/17/93	1	2	Suzie	Sqirm Coil
04/18/93	1	2	Mound	Mike's
04/20/93	1	2	Sample	TMWSIY
04/21/93	1	2	Silent	Mike's
04/22/93	1	2	Lizards	YEM
04/23/93	1	2	Paul&Silas	Mike's
04/24/93	1	2	Mound	YEM
04/25/93	1	2	Uncle Pen	Mike's
04/27/93	1	2	Lizards	YEM
04/29/93	1	2	Mound	Reba
04/30/93	1	2	Mound	Harry
05/01/93	1	2	Sqirm Coil	Halley's
05/02/93	1	2	Lizards	Uncle Pen
05/03/93	1	2	RunJim	Love You
05/05/93	1	2	Weigh	Ya Mar
05/06/93	1	2	Uncle Pen	Sqirm Coil
05/07/93	1	2	Fee	YEM
05/08/93	1	2	Jam	Mike's
05/29/93	1	1a	Cavern	YEM
07/17/93	4	2	Sparkle	Mike's
07/21/93	2	1a	RunJim	PurplRain
07/23/93	2	2	Uncle Pen	YEM
08/08/93	12	2	Possum	Love You
08/12/93	3	2	Lawn Boy	Golgi
08/16/93	4	2	PoorHeart	A-Train
08/28/93	7	2	It's Ice	PurplRain
12/29/93	2	2	WalkAway	Brain

Original Songs Played by Year
(continued)

Big Ball Jam

1992	14	12%
1993	64	58%
1994	22	18%
1995	0	0%
1996	0	0%
1997	0	0%

BBFCM

1990	11	11%
1991	20	16%
1992	9	7%
1993	11	10%
1994	14	11%
1995	6	7%
1996	2	3%
1997	1	1%

Billy Breathes

1995	13	16%
1996	8	11%
1997	14	18%

Black Eyed Katy

1997	7	9%

Bouncing

1990	58	56%
1991	64	50%
1992	55	45%
1993	46	42%
1994	40	32%
1995	22	27%
1996	17	24%
1997	19	24%

Brother

1991	26	20%
1992	13	11%
1993	1	1%
1994	0	0%
1995	0	0%
1996	5	7%
1997	0	0%

Buffalo Bill

1992	1	1%
1993	0	0%
1994	2	2%
1995	0	0%
1996	0	0%
1997	2	3%

Buried Alive

1990	16	16%
1991	30	24%
1992	18	15%
1993	26	24%
1994	13	10%
1995	5	6%
1996	2	3%
1997	2	3%

Bye Bye Foot

1997	4	5%

04/08/94	6	2	Bouncing	Bowie
04/09/94	1	2	Peaches	Demand
04/11/94	2	2	Sample	YEM
04/13/94	1	2	Reba	Fee
04/17/94	4	2	Reba	Maze
04/18/94	1	2	Bathtub	Ya Mar
04/21/94	2	2	Scent	Possum
04/25/94	4	2	Bouncing	BBFCM
05/17/94	15	2	Uncle Pen	Sample
05/19/94	1	2	Julius	Harry
05/21/94	2	2	Contact	Julius
05/25/94	3	2	Contact	Julius
06/13/94	8	2	Scent	Love You
06/16/94	2	2	Mockbird	DWD
06/17/94	1	2	Sparkle	Julius
06/22/94	4	2	MSO	Jesus
07/09/94	13	2	Sparkle	Harry
07/14/94	3	2	Sparkle	Harry
10/16/94	11	2	Fluffhead	Antelope
10/25/94	6	2	Jesus	Brain
12/09/94	30	2	Julius	Rosie
>> 12/31/97		**234**		

BIG BLACK FURRY CREATURE FROM MARS

Inspiration: Whatever inspired Mike to write this manic, crazed piece is not known, but suffice it to say it's probably better that way. One of the most loved and hated songs in the Phish catalog, Big Black Furry Creature from Mars is very different from anything else the band has to offer.

Musical Evolution and History: The musical structure of the song has remained fairly consistent over the years, though the Mike Gordon–supplied lyrics are often ad-libbed with hilarious results. Also hilarious are the onstage antics of the band during this song. In 1991, 1992, and 1993, Trey and Mike often used BBFCM as an excuse to climb onto their amps or to lie dead at the front of the stage. Since then, Trey has often grabbed his megaphone, racing around the stage and revving up the crowd during the frenetic jam. This sort of inspired madness is why a lot of fans love the song. A good example is the "Guacamole!" version from Gunnison, CO, 4/6/92.

Rotation History: Played often through the mid-1990s, the song has become a relative rarity in recent years, appearing only twice in 1996 and once in 1997.

Discography: Has not yet appeared on a Phish album.

Big Black Furry Creature from Mars [92] [BBFCM]

By Gordon

08/21/87	[19]	3	*OP3	McGrupp
08/29/87	2	1	Makisupa	Flat Fee
09/12/87	2	1	Curtain	*CL1
11/19/87	2	2	Divided	*CL2
01/30/88	1	3	Bike	CamlWalk
05/14/88	8	2	Lizards	Jesus
05/25/88	3	3	IKALittle	Corrina
06/18/88	2	2	Alumni	SwingLow
07/25/88	7	3	Harpua	Sanity
08/06/88	2	2	Sanity	Slave
10/29/88	6	3	Terrapin	Timber Ho
11/03/88	1	2	IDK	Harpua
01/26/89	4	1a	Contact	Fire
02/05/89	2	1a	Harry	Curtis
02/06/89	1	2	Harry	Curtis
03/30/89	8	3	ACDCBag	Satin Doll
10/06/89	54	1a	HwayHell	*CL1
12/09/89	25	2	Contact	*CL2
01/28/90	10	E	Lawn Boy	*CLE
02/25/90	15	2	Fluffhead	*CL2
03/09/90	6	2	Contact	*CL2
04/22/90	17	2	Esther	Harry
04/28/90	3	E	*OPE	*CLE
05/11/90	6	E	*OPE	*CLE
05/15/90	3	1	Caravan	*CL1
06/07/90	7	E	Lawn Boy	*CLE
10/31/90	21	E	Uncle Pen	*CLE
11/08/90	4	2	YEM	*CL2
11/24/90	4	2	GTBT	*CL2
02/03/91	12	E	Jesus	*CLE
02/15/91	5	E	Caravan	*CLE
03/13/91	17	E	A-Train	*CLE
03/23/91	6	E	A-Train	*CLE
04/04/91	6	2	Love You	Magilla
04/12/91	4	E	Contact	Sqirm Coil
04/19/91	5	E	Paul&Silas	*CLE
05/03/91	8	E	A-Train	*CLE
05/11/91	4	E	*OPE	*CLE
05/17/91	3	2	Bike	*CLE
07/11/91	3	E	Contact	*CLE
07/14/91	3	E	Contact	*CLE
07/19/91	3	2	Mango	*CL2
07/24/91	4	E	Contact	*CLE
09/25/91	5	E	All Things	*CLE
09/28/91	3	E	Contact	*CLE
10/11/91	8	E	Adeline	*CLE
11/02/91	15	E	Contact	*CLE
11/12/91	6	E	Ya Mar	Split&Melt
11/23/91	9	E	Jesus	*CLE
03/13/92	12	1	Antelope	Antelope
03/30/92	11	2	YEM	Sqirm Coil
04/06/92	6	E	*OPE	*CLE
04/18/92	8	E	Contact	*CLE
04/24/92	5	E	Contact	*CLE
05/02/92	5	E	Sl Monkey	*CLE
05/08/92	5	E	*OPE	*CLE
06/23/92	11	1a	Uncle Pen	Brain
11/21/92	43	E	BuffaloBill	*CLE
02/07/93	27	E	Contact	*CLE
02/21/93	11	2	Sqirm Coil	*CL2
02/25/93	3	2	Golgi	*CL2
03/06/93	6	2	Rosie	*CL2
03/13/93	4	E	AmGrace	*CLE
03/28/93	12	E	Contact	*CLE
04/17/93	13	E	Adeline	*CLE
05/02/93	12	2	Rosie	*CL2
07/23/93	14	2	YEM	Chalkdust
08/08/93	12	1	*OP1	Foam
12/29/93	16	2	Contact	WalkAway
04/08/94	6	E	Contact	*CLE
04/25/94	15	2	BBJ	*CL2
04/30/94	3	2	PurplRain	*CL2
05/12/94	8	2	Contact	*CL2
05/16/94	3	2	YEM	*CL2
06/16/94	17	2	Contact	PurplRain
06/21/94	4	2	Chalkdust	Dog Faced
07/06/94	12	2	Chalkdust	Harry
07/13/94	4	2	Tweezer	Tweezer
10/27/94	20	2	Contact	DWD
11/03/94	5	2	YEM	Harry
11/13/94	3	2	Mango	AmGrace
11/22/94	7	2	RunJim	I'm Blue
12/01/94	6	2	Tweezer	Makisupa
07/03/95	35	2	Lizards	DayinLife
10/19/95	16	2	Lawn Boy	Kung
10/22/95	3	2	Makisupa	Life Mars
11/18/95	14	2	AArmy	Cavern
11/28/95	6	2	Contact	FunkBitch
12/29/95	17	2	McGrupp	Jam
06/06/96	4	1	Theme	Scent
08/06/96	22	2	DayinLife	PurplRain
12/11/97	118	2	Roses	Ghost
>> 12/31/97		**6**		

BILLY BREATHES

Inspiration: Named for Eliza, Trey and Sue's first daughter, born in the summer of 1995, on whom Trey bestowed the nickname "Billy." This slow ballad almost has the feel of a lullabye, especially its soothing refrain, "Softly sing sweet songs."

Musical Evolution and History: Billy Breathes has remained relatively unchanged since its debut on the 1995 fall tour, even surviving the *Billy Breathes* sessions without any major structural changes. One notable in-concert version on 10/19/95 in Kansas City, MO, features a tape of Eliza crying playing over the PA system during this song.

Rotation History: Though Phish often tends to overplay their new songs, Billy Breathes has not faced that problem, appearing only about a dozen times in 1995 and 1997, and even less than that in 1996.

Discography: Title song on *Billy Breathes* (1996).

Billy Breathes [35] [Billy]

By Anastasio

09/27/95	[761]	2	Bowie	Keyboard
09/28/95	1	1	RunJim	Scent
09/29/95	1	2	Split&Melt	Cryin'
10/03/95	3	2	Harry	Faht
10/06/95	2	1	Stash	Reba
10/13/95	4	1	Maze	I'm Blue
10/19/95	4	1	Split&Melt	Cavern
10/28/95	7	1	Lizards	AArmy
11/14/95	7	1	Foam	Divided
11/19/95	4	2	Tweezer	Scent
11/25/95	4	1	Bowie	Fog
12/04/95	6	2	Antelope	CTB
12/09/95	4	1	Free	Dog Faced
10/16/96	42	1	PoorHeart	Mound
10/18/96	2	1	Divided	Taste
10/25/96	5	1	Maze	Mound
10/29/96	3	1	Train Song	PoorHeart
11/03/96	3	1	RunJim	Sloth
11/18/96	10	1	Taste	Chalkdust
11/22/96	2	2	Maze	SweptAwy
12/28/96	10	1	It's Ice	Ginseng
02/14/97	5	1	It's Ice	Uncle Pen
02/17/97	2	1	Timber Ho	Llama
02/21/97	3	2	ACDCBag	Reba
02/23/97	2	E	*OPE	Rocky Top
03/01/97	4	2	Mango	Theme
06/13/97	3	1	Beauty	Limb
06/25/97	8	1	Taste	ACDCBag
07/03/97	5	2	CTB	Sparkle
07/23/97	8	1	Split&Melt	Possum
07/26/97	2	1	Stash	CTB
08/10/97	9	1	CTB	Split&Melt
08/14/97	4	1	Train Song	Antelope
11/16/97	5	1	Old Home	CTB
11/22/97	4	1	Train Song	Frankstein
>> 12/31/97		**18**		

BLACK EYED KATY

Inspiration: With their funk jamming style becoming more pronounced through the spring and summer of 1997, Phish apparently decided that they wanted a funk instrumental to add to their repertoire. Thus came Black Eyed Katy, which debuted on the 1997 fall tour.

Musical Evolution and History: Though Black Eyed Katy, as it appeared in concert the first few times, has an obvious structure (including a series of starts and stops), some fans on the 1997 fall tour had a tough time telling it apart from other (nameless) seemingly precomposed funk jams which often popped up. Therefore, "Black Eyed Katy" listings in setlists should be considered a bit dubious, at least until setlist scribes become better at recognizing its signature riffs.

Rotation History: New on fall tour 1997.

Discography: Written since the release of Phish's last album, so it has not yet appeared on a Phish album as of this printing.

Black Eyed Katy [6] [BE Katy]

By Anastasio/Phish?

11/13/97	[942]	1	Chalkdust	Theme
11/16/97	2	1	My Soul	Farmhouse
11/22/97	4	2	Tweezer	Piper
11/23/97	1	1	Theme	Sparkle
11/28/97	2	1	Farmhouse	Theme
12/05/97	5	1	FunkBitch	Sparkle
>> 12/31/97		**10**		

BOUNCING AROUND THE ROOM

Inspiration: Trey has said that this was one of the easiest songs he ever wrote. After receiving Tom Marshall's dream-inspired lyrics in the mail, he sat down, and within about an hour had come up with this short, catchy tune that remains one of the best-known and most popular (or unpopular; see Readers' Survey results) songs in the Phish catalog.

Musical Evolution and History: The song has changed little since its debut in 1990, with the exception of a minor lyric change from the quick-recorded *Lawn Boy* version. Because all live versions of this song are virtually carbon copies of each other, some fans scorn the song as uninteresting, but for many fans attending their first Phish show, catching Bouncing is a real treat.

Rotation History: Heavily played since its debut in 1990 to the present, the song used to appear at least once every two shows but now appears roughly once every four shows.

Discography: Appears on *Lawn Boy* (1990) and on *A Live One* (1995) as a live track taken from 12/31/94 Boston, MA, that was released as the first single for the album.

Bouncing Around the Room [321] [Bouncing]

By Anastasio/Marshall

01/20/90	[157]	1a	Suzie	Reba
01/27/90	3	1	MSO	Wilson
01/28/90	1	2	Antelope	Caravan
02/09/90	7	1	WalkAway	ACDCBag
02/10/90	1	1	Bathtub	Possum
02/17/90	3	1a	Split&Melt	Foam

02/23/90	2	1	WalkAway	Antelope
02/25/90	2	1	Sqirm Coil	Bowie
03/09/90	6	1	Ya Mar	Forbin's
03/11/90	1	2	MSO	Dinner
04/13/90	11	1	Dinner	Fluffhead
04/20/90	3	1	Dinner	Forbin
04/22/90	2	2	Dinner	YEM
04/25/90	1	2	Dinner	Mike's
04/26/90	1	1	Dinner	IDK
04/28/90	1	1	Dinner	Possum
04/29/90	1	1a	Dinner	Uncle Pen
05/04/90	2	1	TMWSIY	Possum
05/06/90	1	1	Possum	Uncle Pen
05/10/90	1	1	Uncle Pen	Divided
05/11/90	1	1	Uncle Pen	Possum
05/13/90	2	1	Dinner	RunJim
05/19/90	2	2	Dinner	Rift
05/23/90	1	1	Uncle Pen	Possum
05/24/90	1	1	Sloth	Tweezer
05/31/90	1	1a	Dinner	Caravan
06/01/90	1	1a	*OP1	YEM
06/05/90	1	2	Dinner	MSO
06/07/90	1	1	Dinner	Tweezer
06/08/90	1	1	Foam	YEM
06/09/90	1	1	Dinner	Tweezer
06/16/90	1	1	Uncle Pen	Timber Ho
09/13/90	1	1	Paul&Silas	Possum
09/14/90	1	1	Suzie	Landlady
09/16/90	2	1a	Dinner	Sloth
09/22/90	3	2	Uncle Pen	Stash
09/28/90	1	1	Landlady	Oh Kee
10/01/90	1	1	Dinner	Tweezer
10/05/90	2	1	Asse Fest	Antelope
10/06/90	1	1a	Dinner	Foam
10/07/90	1	2	BurAlive	Tweezer
10/08/90	1	1	Landlady	Foam
10/12/90	1	1	Dinner	Uncle Pen
10/30/90	2	1	Landlady	Donna
10/31/90	1	1	Stash	YEM
11/02/90	1	1	Landlady	Divided
11/03/90	1	1	Dinner	Llama
11/04/90	1	1	Curtain	Tube
11/08/90	1	2	Dinner	YEM
11/10/90	1	1	Landlady	RunJim
11/17/90	2	1	RunJim	YEM
11/24/90	1	1	Llama	Stash
11/30/90	2	1	Dinner	Tweezer
12/07/90	3	1	Stash	Landlady
12/08/90	1	2	Dinner	Antelope
12/28/90	1	E	*OPE	HwayHell
12/29/90	1	2	Dinner	Destiny
12/31/90	1	1	Landlady	MSO
02/01/91	1	1	Split&Melt	Bowie
02/03/91	2	2	Split&Melt	Oh Kee
02/07/91	1	1	Split&Melt	Sqirm Coil
02/08/91	1	2	Horn	Lizards
02/09/91	1	2	Landlady	Harry
02/14/91	1	2	Alumni	IDK
02/16/91	2	1	Landlady	Llama
02/21/91	3	2	Landlady	Stash
02/26/91	4	2	Stash	Landlady
02/27/91	1	1	Split&Melt	Fire
02/28/91	1	1	Landlady	Foam
03/01/91	1	1	Dinner	BurAlive
03/06/91	2	1	MSO	Bowie
03/13/91	4	2	Split&Melt	MSO
03/15/91	1	1	Dinner	Oh Kee
03/17/91	2	1	Carolina	Landlady
03/22/91	2	1	Destiny	Split&Melt
03/28/91	2	1a	Landlady	YEM
04/05/91	6	1	Landlady	Divided
04/11/91	2	1	Dinner	Foam
04/19/91	6	1	Dinner	Divided
04/20/91	1	1	Chalkdust	YEM
04/26/91	4	2	Split&Melt	MSO
04/27/91	1	E	*OPE	GTBT
05/02/91	1	1	Foam	Landlady
05/03/91	1	1	*OP1	Foam
05/12/91	3	1	Chalkdust	Dinner
05/16/91	1	2	Dinner	Landlady
05/25/91	3	1	Chalkdust	YEM
07/12/91	2	1	Dinner	BurAlive
07/13/91	1	1	Split&Melt	Frankstein
07/14/91	1	2	Dinner	Split&Melt
07/15/91	1	1a	Stash	Mike's
07/19/91	2	1	Landlady	Bowie
07/21/91	2	1	Landlady	Mike's
07/23/91	1	1	Flat Fee	Mike's
07/24/91	1	2	MSO	FunkBitch
07/26/91	2	1	BurAlive	Landlady
08/03/91	2	2	Chalkdust	Tweezer
09/26/91	2	1	Llama	Divided
09/28/91	1	1	Landlady	Chalkdust
10/02/91	2	1	Brother	Chalkdust
10/03/91	1	1	It's Ice	Llama

10/04/91	1	2	Brother	Foam
10/06/91	2	1	Divided	PoorHeart
10/10/91	1	1	Split&Melt	Landlady
10/11/91	1	1	Llama	RunJim
10/13/91	2	2	Jesus	Love You
10/15/91	1	2	Brother	RunJim
10/17/91	1	1	Landlady	Divided
10/19/91	2	1	Chalkdust	MSO
10/24/91	2	2	Dinner	TweezRep
10/27/91	2	1	Brother	Harry
11/02/91	4	1	Foam	Forbin's
11/07/91	2	2	Brother	MSO
11/12/91	4	1	Brother	Tube
11/14/91	2	E	*OPE	GTBT
11/15/91	1	2	Love You	Possum
11/21/91	4	1	Chalkdust	PoorHeart
11/23/91	2	1	Brother	Golgi
11/30/91	2	2	It's Ice	MSO
12/04/91	1	1	Dinner	Bowie
12/05/91	1	1	It's Ice	Possum
12/31/91	3	2	Brother	BurAlive
03/06/92	1	2	Llama	NICU
03/12/92	3	2	It's Ice	Sqirm Coil
03/14/92	2	2	Split&Melt	Oh Kee
03/17/92	1	1	Rift	Antelope
03/21/92	3	E	*OPE	Rocky Top
03/27/92	4	1	Glide	Antelope
03/28/92	1	1	Rift	Landlady
03/30/92	1	2	Rosie	TweezRep
04/01/92	2	1	Foam	Brother
04/04/92	2	1	Chalkdust	It's Ice
04/07/92	3	1	Split&Melt	Rift
04/12/92	2	2	Split&Melt	Rift
04/16/92	3	1	It's Ice	Split&Melt
04/17/92	1	1	Maze	Landlady
04/21/92	3	1	NICU	Bowie
04/23/92	2	1	Llama	It's Ice
04/25/92	2	1	Chalkdust	Rift
04/29/92	1	1	Rift	A-Train
05/02/92	3	1	Maze	Stash
05/03/92	1	2	Dinner	Oh Kee
05/05/92	1	2	Chalkdust	All Things
05/06/92	1	2	All Things	Uncle Pen
05/08/92	2	1	All Things	Bowie
05/12/92	3	1	Dinner	BurAlive
05/14/92	1	1	My Friend	Antelope
05/15/92	1	1a	Stash	Love You
05/16/92	1	1	Split&Melt	MSO
05/18/92	2	1	Maze	Divided
06/20/92	2	1a	BurAlive	Foam
06/27/92	3	1a	Chalkdust	Uncle Pen
07/10/92	5	1a	*OP1	Llama
07/12/92	2	1a	Chalkdust	Divided
07/16/92	3	1	Dinner	Maze
07/17/92	1	1a	Maze	RunJim
07/22/92	4	1a	PoorHeart	Maze
07/28/92	5	1a	Chalkdust	Uncle Pen
07/31/92	2	1a	Chalkdust	Oh Kee
08/17/92	6	2	My Friend	Bowie
08/27/92	6	1a	Chalkdust	Landlady
08/29/92	2	1a	Rift	Maze
10/30/92	2	1a	Maze	Rift
11/19/92	1	2	Weekpaug	It's Ice
11/21/92	2	1	It's Ice	Maze
11/23/92	2	1	Mound	Memories
11/28/92	3	2	TMWSIY	Sqirm Coil
11/30/92	1	1	Foam	PoorHeart
12/01/92	1	1	Split&Melt	Rift
12/03/92	2	1	Split&Melt	Uncle Pen
12/05/92	2	1	Chalkdust	Rift
12/07/92	2	1	Split&Melt	YEM
12/11/92	3	2	Esther	Axilla
12/12/92	1	1	All Things	Antelope
12/13/92	1	2	Mound	Llama
12/28/92	1	1	It's Ice	Rift
12/31/92	3	1	Maze	Rift
02/04/93	2	1	Foam	Maze
02/06/93	2	1	Wedge	Antelope
02/09/93	2	1	Bowie	PoorHeart
02/11/93	2	2	BBJ	Love You
02/13/93	2	1	Bowie	PoorHeart
02/17/93	2	1	It's Ice	Fluffhead
02/21/93	4	1	Dinner	Antelope
02/23/93	2	1	Rift	Split&Melt
02/25/93	1	1	Stash	IDK
02/27/93	2	1	Maze	It's Ice
03/03/93	2	1	Foam	Maze
03/06/93	2	1	PYITE	Maze
03/09/93	2	1	Foam	Maze
03/13/93	2	1	FunkBitch	Maze
03/17/93	3	1	Foam	Stash
03/19/93	2	1	Foam	Rift
03/22/93	2	1	Stash	Rift
03/25/93	2	1	Possum	Stash
03/27/93	2	2	It's Ice	Chalkdust

03/31/93	3	2	Maze	Uncle Pen
04/02/93	2	1	Foam	Divided
04/10/93	4	2	Maze	Rift
04/12/93	1	1	Tube	PoorHeart
04/14/93	2	1	Maze	It's Ice
04/17/93	2	1	Foam	Stash
04/20/93	2	1	Stash	It's Ice
04/22/93	2	2	Llama	All Things
04/25/93	3	1	Possum	It's Ice
04/27/93	1	1	Foam	Rift
04/30/93	2	1	Maze	PoorHeart
05/02/93	2	2	Uncle Pen	Antelope
05/05/93	2	1	Stash	It's Ice
05/07/93	2	2	Rift	Maze
05/29/93	2	1a	Chalkdust	Rift
07/16/93	3	2	Maze	YEM
07/21/93	3	1a	Rift	RunJim
07/24/93	3	1	Mango	Sqirm Coil
07/29/93	4	2	Maze	It's Ice
08/03/93	4	2	Maze	It's Ice
08/07/93	2	1	Llama	PoorHeart
08/11/93	3	2	All Things	Rift
08/15/93	4	2	Landlady	Maze
08/20/93	3	1	Maze	It's Ice
08/24/93	2	1	All Things	It's Ice
08/28/93	3	1	Llama	Foam
12/29/93	2	2	Maze	Fluffhead
04/05/94	4	1	Julius	Rift
04/08/94	2	2	Harry	BBJ
04/10/94	2	E	*OPE	Golgi
04/15/94	4	1	Chalkdust	It's Ice
04/16/94	1	2	Julius	YEM
04/20/94	3	1	Julius	Axilla 2
04/25/94	5	2	Divided	BBJ
04/28/94	1	1a	DWD	It's Ice
05/02/94	3	1	Split&Melt	DWD
05/04/94	2	2	Antelope	YEM
05/08/94	3	1	DWD	Stash
05/13/94	3	2	Chalkdust	Split&Melt
05/16/94	2	1	DWD	Stash
05/22/94	5	2	DWD	It's Ice
05/27/94	4	1	Foam	Bowie
05/28/94	1	1	Foam	Stash
06/16/94	7	1	*OP1	Rift
06/18/94	2	E	*OPE	TweezRep
06/23/94	4	1	Foam	DWD
06/30/94	5	1	Scent	Frankstein
07/03/94	3	2	Lizards	It's Ice
07/06/94	2	1	Julius	Reba
07/10/94	3	2	Weekpaug	Sqirm Coil
07/14/94	2	1	RunJim	PYITE
07/15/94	1	2	Bowie	Reba
10/09/94	4	2	Bowie	Scent
10/12/94	2	2	Bowie	Scent
10/15/94	3	2	Long Time	Suzie
10/23/94	6	2	RunJim	Halley's
10/26/94	2	2	Rift	Reba
10/31/94	4	3	Bowie	Slave
11/04/94	3	1	It's Ice	Bowie
11/14/94	3	1	Split&Melt	Landlady
11/17/94	2	1	Maze	Wilson
11/22/94	4	1	IDK	DWD
11/25/94	2	1	Reba	Split&Melt
11/30/94	3	1	DWD	I'm Blue
12/04/94	4	2	Maze	Reba
12/28/94	6	1	Bathtub	Axilla 2
12/31/94	3	2	Maze	Mike's
06/08/95	3	2	Free	Tweezer
06/13/95	3	1	Foam	Stash
06/15/95	2	E	*OPE	Frankstein
06/25/95	8	E	*OPE	Slave
07/01/95	5	1	Split&Melt	Chalkdust
10/03/95	12	E	*OPE	Rocky Top
10/20/95	7	2	I'm Blue	Antelope
10/24/95	3	2	Theme	YEM
10/27/95	2	2	Keyboard	Possum
11/10/95	5	1	*OP1	RunJim
11/12/95	2	1	Llama	Guelah
11/18/95	4	1	Dinner	Reba
11/22/95	3	2	Llama	YEM
11/25/95	2	1	Fog	Rift
11/28/95	1	1	Dinner	Foam
12/02/95	4	1	Fog	Possum
12/04/95	1	E	*OPE	Rocky Top
12/07/95	2	1	Guyute	Possum
12/09/95	2	1	Rift	Free
12/15/95	4	1	CTB	Free
12/17/95	2	2	*OP2	Maze
12/29/95	2	2	La Grange	Fire
07/07/96	8	1a	Divided	Curtain
07/09/96	1	1a	Mike's	CharZero
07/11/96	2	1a	Harry	ASZ
07/18/96	5	1a	CTB	Stash
07/22/96	3	1a	Maze	Stash
08/07/96	8	E	*OPE	Golgi

Original Songs Played by Year *(continued)*

Camel Walk

1990	0	0%
1991	0	0%
1992	0	0%
1993	0	0%
1994	0	0%
1995	1	1%
1996	0	0%
1997	3	4%

Carini

1997	6	8%

CTB

1995	21	26%
1996	19	27%
1997	17	22%

Catapult

1992	2	2%
1993	1	1%
1994	9	7%
1995	5	6%
1996	3	4%
1997	2	3%

Cavern

1990	19	18%
1991	73	57%
1992	58	48%
1993	51	46%
1994	43	35%
1995	23	28%
1996	17	24%
1997	11	14%

Chalkdust

1991	62	49%
1992	45	37%
1993	52	47%
1994	38	31%
1995	24	30%
1996	22	31%
1997	26	33%

Character Zero

1996	21	30%
1997	32	41%

Chess Jam

1995	3	4%
1996	0	0%
1997	0	0%

Col. Forbin's

1990	9	9%
1991	16	13%
1992	14	12%
1993	16	15%
1994	11	9%
1995	3	4%
1996	2	3%
1997	1	1%

10/19/96	10	2	Slave	Split&Melt
10/22/96	2	1	RunJim	It's Ice
10/29/96	5	1	Taste	Stash
11/03/96	3	1	Theme	CharZero
11/08/96	3	2	Maze	Simple
11/13/96	3	1	DWD	It's Ice
11/15/96	2	1	Divided	CharZero
11/24/96	6	1	All Things	Reba
11/30/96	4	1	All Things	Stash
12/02/96	2	1	ACDCBag	YEM
12/28/96	3	2	Maze	TMWSIY
02/16/97	6	1	Split&Melt	Crosseyed
02/20/97	3	2	Stash	Free
06/20/97	14	2	Twist	Julius
06/27/97	5	1a	Taste	CharZero
06/29/97	1	1a	Taste	Beauty
07/05/97	4	1a	Julius	Uncle Pen
07/11/97	4	1a	Chalkdust	Stash
07/22/97	2	1	Stash	Vultures
07/26/97	3	E	*OPE	Cavern
07/30/97	2	2	Bowie	Uncle Pen
08/03/97	3	E	*OPE	Slave
08/14/87	7	E	*OPE	Rocky Top
08/17/97	2	1	Maze	Tweezer
11/13/97	1	2	Caspian	Mike's
11/22/97	6	E	*OPE	TweezRep
12/02/97	6	2	Weekpaug	CharZero
12/05/97	2	2	Stash	Julius
12/12/97	5	1	Taste	Tweezer
12/28/97	2	1	Split&Melt	CharZero
>> 12/31/97		**5**		

BROTHER

Inspiration: A lyrically nonsensical song about somebody jumping in the tub with your brother, Brother follows in the best Phish tradition of attaching wacky lyrics to a cool musical structure.

Musical Evolution and History: With room for crazy, wide-open jamming, Brother has changed subtly with each performance. Though no versions stand out for extreme length, some of the more interesting Brothers include 3/20/92 Binghamton, NY, "jumping in the alligator pit!"; 4/17/92 San Francisco, CA, when a bathtub was wheeled on stage at the Warfield and a parade of people walked across the stage and jumped in it; 8/17/96 Clifford Ball, with Ben and Jerry taking a frisky vocal turn; 10/23/96 Hartford, CT, with Bob Gullotti on a second drum set; and 10/31/96 Atlanta, GA, with Karl Perazzo adding percussion.

Rotation History: Heavily played during its debut tour in fall 1991 and then in spring 1992, Brother was heard from again only once in 1993, at the great Tampa, FL, show on 8/2/93. Then, after not playing it in 1994 and 1995, the band answered the requests of many when the song reappeared at the Clifford Ball on 8/17/96, featuring ice cream kings Ben and Jerry on vocals. It was played four times on the 1996 fall tour, but didn't come up for air in 1997.

Discography: Has not yet appeared on a Phish album.

Brother [45] [Brother]

By Anastasio/Marshall

09/25/91	[335]	1	*OP1	PoorHeart
09/26/91	1	2	Sqirm Coil	Sparkle
09/28/91	2	1	Foam	Golgi
10/02/91	2	1	Reba	Bouncing
10/04/91	2	2	MSO	Bouncing
10/06/91	2	1	ACDCBag	Terrapin
10/10/91	1	2	*OP2	Reba
10/12/91	2	1	Dinner	Brain
10/15/91	2	2	*OP2	Bouncing
10/18/91	2	2	*OP2	Uncle Pen
10/27/91	5	1	Fluffhead	Bouncing
10/31/91	3	1	Memories	Ya Mar
11/07/91	4	2	*OP2	Bouncing
11/08/91	1	1	Mango	Eliza
11/09/91	1	1	Horn	Adeline
11/12/91	2	1	Uncle Pen	Bouncing
11/14/91	2	1	Sparkle	Mango
11/16/91	2	2	Bathtub	YEM
11/19/91	1	1	Sparkle	Horn
11/20/91	1	E	Magilla	*CLE
11/22/91	2	1	Sparkle	Fee
11/23/91	1	1	Uncle Pen	Bouncing
11/30/91	2	1	Sqirm Coil	Paul&Silas
12/04/91	1	1	PoorHeart	Sqirm Coil
12/07/91	3	2	Sparkle	Lizards
12/31/91	1	2	*OP2	Bouncing
03/07/92	2	1	*OP1	My Mind
03/11/92	1	2	My Mind	BabyLem
03/13/92	2	2	Wilson	Horse
03/20/92	4	1	Reba	Glide
03/24/92	2	2	Mango	Uncle Pen
03/26/92	2	2	PoorHeart	TMWSIY
04/01/92	5	1	Bouncing	All Things
04/06/92	4	1	Reba	Esther
04/17/92	7	2	*OP2	YEM
04/25/92	7	1	Reba	Tela
05/06/92	7	1	Tela	Forbin's
05/17/92	9	2	All Things	Sanity
07/14/92	14	1	Horn	IDK
08/02/93	143	1	PoorHeart	Oh Kee
08/17/96	257	2	It's Ice	Fluffhead
10/23/96	7	2	*OP2	Ya Mar
10/31/96	5	3	*OP3	Also Sprac
11/11/96	7	1	Sparkle	Theme
11/30/96	12	2	Glide	Contact
>> 12/31/97		**86**		

BUFFALO BILL

Inspiration: As described by Trey in an issue of the *Doniac Schvice*, Buffalo Bill chronicles one of Fishman's backcountry adventures when he was "tied to a log, bent over, and Buffalo Bill'd."

Musical Evolution and History: This short, reggae-ish song with an overpowering bass line has appeared only five times in Phish history, sounding pretty much the same each time. Special note must be made of Mike Gordon's ferocious bass licks on this song at the Boston Garden on 12/31/94.

Rotation History: Buffalo Bill has a unique concert history. The band played it as the encore of their 11/21/92 show at Stony Brook, NY, then put it away, leaving most fans to assume that it had been a one-time treat. But in the midst of a crazy Split Open and Melt jam in Spartanburg, SC, on 10/29/94, Buffalo Bill came thundering back out, as it did two months later on New Year's Eve in the midst of a Mike's Song jam. Then it went back into hibernation before it opened the third set of the Great Went show on 8/17/97, and served as the first encore at Worcester, MA, on 11/29/97, at which point Trey described it as "Fishman's favorite song."

Discography: Has not yet appeared on a Phish album, though the Riker's Mailbox track on *Hoist* (1994) is taken from a version of Buffalo Bill—played backwards—which was an outtake for the album.

Buffalo Bill [5] [BuffaloBill]

By Anastasio/Marshall

11/21/92	[482]	E	*OPE	BBFCM
10/29/94	224	1	Split&Melt	Makisupa
12/31/94	31	2	Mike's	Mike's
08/17/97	204	3	*OP3	NICU
11/29/97	11	E	*OPE	Moby Dick
>> 12/31/97		**14**		

BUNDLE OF JOY

Inspiration: Offering a sense of relentless optimism about life, this little ditty has the phrase "la la la la la la, life is just a bundle of joy," repeated over and over again.

Musical Evolution and History: Played occasionally as a stand-alone song in the 1980s, Trey later integrated it into Fluff's Travels, where it can still be heard in concert today. Not every Fluff's contains the Bundle of Joy lyrics, though the music is always present; listen carefully after the Clod segment, as sometimes a band member mutters the words very quietly.

Rotation History: Played as part of Fluffhead/Fluff's Travels since the late 1980s.

Discography: Appears on *Junta* (1989) as part of Fluff's Travels (Part 5: Bundle of Joy).

Bundle of Joy [5] [BundleJoy]

By Anastasio

Now played as part of Fluff's Travels.

08/21/87	[19]	2	Harpua	Harpua
08/29/87	1	3	Harpua	Harpua
09/12/88	25	1a	Avenu	CamlWalk
10/20/89	43	1	Harpua	Forbin's
11/03/89	7	1	Clod	YEM
>> 12/31/97		**828 (as a stand-alone song)**		

BURIED ALIVE

Inspiration: The link between this frenzied instrumental and its ominous title is not known, but the music does create a panicked feeling. At the time of its debut performance at the Wetlands Preserve on 9/13/90, Trey told the crowd it resulted from "a very strange dream." Hmmm.

Musical Evolution and History: As a short, composed piece, Buried Alive has been performed in a similar manner through its history.

Rotation History: Frequently appeared in setlists in the early 1990s, but less so in recent years (only twice in 1996 and twice in 1997). It's often a show-opener, and for much of 1992, 1993, and 1994 it led into Poor Heart, a sequence that most recently appeared on 2/26/97 in Stuttgart, Germany. It also served as a platform for the Giant Country Horns, who contributed to this song on the horns tour in summer 1991 and at sporadic performances since then, including 4/4/94, 4/15/94, 5/4/94, 12/2/94, and 12/3/94.

Discography: Has not yet appeared on a Phish album.

Buried Alive [113] [BurAlive]

By Anastasio

09/13/90	[222]	1	Minute	Paul&Silas
09/14/90	1	2	Sqirm Coil	Tweezer
09/15/90	1	1	*OP1	Divided
09/22/90	4	1	*OP1	Horn
10/07/90	6	2	*OP2	Bouncing
10/30/90	4	2	Terrapin	Bowie
10/31/90	1	1	*OP1	Possum
11/02/90	1	1	Possum	Possum
11/10/90	4	1	MSO	Lizards
11/16/90	1	1	Suzie	Foam
11/17/90	1	2	*OP2	Fluffhead
11/24/90	1	1	*OP1	Possum
11/26/90	1	1	Reba	YEM
12/08/90	5	1	*OP1	RunJim
12/29/90	2	2	*OP2	RunJim
12/31/90	1	1	Auld	Possum
02/08/91	5	1	Reba	Forbin's
02/09/91	1	2	Golgi	Fluffhead
02/14/91	1	1	McGrupp	Reba
02/15/91	1	1	Fee	Mango
02/16/91	1	2	Reba	RunJim
02/26/91	7	2	*OP2	RunJim
02/27/91	1	2	Suzie	Cavern
03/01/91	2	1	Bouncing	Mike's
03/15/91	7	2	*OP2	Possum
03/16/91	1	2	Magilla	Sqirm Coil
03/22/91	3	2	Sqirm Coil	Cavern
04/12/91	11	2	Tela	Reba
04/16/91	3	2	Magilla	Uncle Pen
05/02/91	9	2	IDK	Possum
05/04/91	2	2	Mockbird	Harry
05/10/91	2	1	Bathtub	Lizards
05/16/91	3	1	*OP1	Golgi
05/18/91	2	1	*OP1	Golgi
07/12/91	3	1	Bouncing	Flat Fee
07/20/91	6	2	*OP2	Reba
07/24/91	3	1	Sqirm Coil	Split&Melt
07/26/91	2	1	TMWSIY	Bouncing
08/03/91	2	3	Lizards	Possum
09/27/91	3	1	Reba	Esther
10/03/91	4	2	Destiny	Sqirm Coil
10/27/91	15	1	Mango	Guelah
11/12/91	11	1	*OP1	Golgi
11/20/91	6	1	*OP1	Possum
12/07/91	9	2	*OP2	Reba
12/31/91	1	2	Bouncing	Auld
03/12/92	4	1	Reba	Rift
03/17/92	3	1	*OP1	Possum
03/21/92	3	2	*OP2	Oh Kee
03/26/92	3	2	*OP2	Oh Kee
04/07/92	10	1	*OP1	Possum
04/16/92	5	1	*OP1	Possum
04/19/92	3	1	*OP1	NICU
05/01/92	8	2	Sanity	Wilson

05/07/92	5	1	PoorHeart	My Friend
05/12/92	4	1	Bouncing	Uncle Pen
06/20/92	7	1a	*OP1	Bouncing
08/17/92	31	1	*OP1	PoorHeart
08/24/92	4	1a	*OP1	PoorHeart
11/22/92	10	1	*OP1	Oh Kee
11/25/92	2	1	*OP1	PoorHeart
11/30/92	3	2	*OP2	RunJim
12/13/92	12	1	*OP1	Wilson
12/31/92	4	1	*OP1	PoorHeart
02/06/93	4	2	Lengthwise	Possum
02/07/93	1	1	Suzie	PoorHeart
02/11/93	3	1	Suzie	PoorHeart
02/17/93	4	1	*OP1	Possum
02/21/93	4	1	Suzie	PYITE
02/25/93	3	1	*OP1	PoorHeart
03/02/93	3	1	*OP1	PoorHeart
03/05/93	2	1	*OP1	PoorHeart
03/12/93	4	1	*OP1	PoorHeart
03/16/93	3	1	Adeline	PoorHeart
03/27/93	9	2	*OP2	Halley's
03/30/93	2	1	*OP1	PoorHeart
04/02/93	3	1	*OP1	PoorHeart
04/09/93	3	2	*OP2	Suzie
04/14/93	4	1	*OP1	PoorHeart
04/21/93	5	1	*OP1	PoorHeart
04/27/93	5	1	*OP1	PoorHeart
05/03/93	5	1	*OP1	Rift
05/07/93	3	1	*OP1	PoorHeart
07/16/93	5	1	Ya Mar	FEFY
07/18/93	2	1	*OP1	Rift
07/23/93	3	1	*OP1	Rift
08/06/93	10	2	*OP2	Tweezer
08/11/93	14	1	*OP1	RunJim
08/13/93	2	2	*OP2	Rift
08/21/93	6	1	*OP1	PoorHeart
08/25/93	2	2	*OP2	Possum
04/04/94	7	2	If I Could	Landlady
04/13/94	7	1	*OP1	PoorHeart
05/04/94	17	2	Landlady	Julius
05/10/94	4	1	*OP1	PoorHeart
05/16/94	4	1	*OP1	PoorHeart
05/26/94	8	1	*OP1	PoorHeart
06/13/94	7	1	*OP1	PoorHeart
06/23/94	8	1	*OP1	PoorHeart
07/13/94	14	1	*OP1	PoorHeart
10/14/94	10	1	*OP1	Sample
11/22/94	25	1	*OP1	PoorHeart
12/02/94	7	2	Bowie	Julius
12/03/94	1	2	Suzie	Gumbo
10/15/95	47	1	*OP1	PoorHeart
10/29/95	10	1	*OP1	PoorHeart
12/01/95	18	1	*OP1	DWD
12/16/95	11	1	*OP1	ACDCBag
12/28/95	2	2	Wilson	Tweezer
10/16/96	36	1	Wilson	PoorHeart
11/09/96	17	1	*OP1	PoorHeart
02/26/97	32	2	*OP2	PoorHeart
12/02/97	55	1	*OP1	DWD
>> 12/31/97		**12**		

BYE BYE FOOT

Inspiration: A slow, soft ballad, Bye Bye Foot marks the first more serious tune penned by Fishman. The partial lyrics to this love song of sorts were published in a summer 1997 edition of the *Schvice*.

Musical Evolution and History: Too new to have evolved much.

Rotation History: Debuted on summer tour 1997, when it appeared four times; it was forgotten by the band during the fall tour.

Discography: Has not yet appeared on a Phish album.

Bye Bye Foot [4] [Bye Bye]

By Fishman

06/14/97	[905]	1	Limb	Free
06/20/97	3	2	Ghost	Ginseng
07/22/97	16	1	Vultures	Taste
08/10/97	12	1	Split&Melt	Ginseng
>> 12/31/97	**32**			

CAMEL WALK

Inspiration: One of the last remnants of original rhythm guitar player Jeff Holdsworth, Camel Walk is still performed by Phish in his absence. This funky, wacked-out tune has become a fan favorite since its revival at Sugarbush in summer 1995.

Musical Evolution and History: Early versions of this song from 1985 and 1986 feature Jeff singing lead, and his guitar adds another dimension to the song. The band's performances for the rest of the 1980s without Jeff are a little more spartan. When Camel Walk returned from retirement in summer 1995, Phish seemed to have a better sense of the song, nailing the performance at Sugarbush on 7/2/95 with a mix of funk, disco, and rock. The 1997 performances of the song have been equally well received.

Rotation History: Played throughout the 1980s, then not again until 1995, when it walked out once on 7/2/95. In 1997, the band played it three times, first as a surprise opener in Stuttgart, Germany, on 2/26/97; next, out of Col. Forbin's Ascent/ Pranksters Jam in Darien Lake, NY, on 8/14/97 (Trey: "We're supposed to go into Famous Mockingbird here, but the funk's too deep"); and in Albany, NY, on 12/12/97.

Discography: Has not yet appeared on a Phish album.

Camel Walk [16] [CamlWalk]

By Holdsworth

03/04/85	[1]	1a	Anarchy	Ganja
10/17/85	2	1a	Anarchy	Antelope
04/15/86	4	1a	Anarchy	Alumni
10/15/86	1	1a	SwingLow	Shaggy
10/31/86	1	1	Sally	Golgi
03/23/87	4	1	WDYLM	Golgi
08/21/87	3	1	Wilson	*CL1
11/19/87	8	3	A-Train	La Grange
01/30/88	1	3	BBFCM	Harry
07/25/88	20	3	Icculus	*CL3
09/12/88	5	1a	BundleJoy	Harry
02/24/89	15	2	YEM	*CL2
07/02/95	691	1	Julius	Reba
02/26/97	140	1	*OP1	Llama
08/14/97	40	2	Jam	Taste
12/12/97	22	1	Also Sprac	Taste
>> 12/31/97		**5**		

CARINI HAD A LUMPY HEAD

Inspiration: This wacky song, written specifically for the smaller venues of the 1997 winter Europe tour, apparently takes its name from the band's drum tech, Pete Carini, who may or may not actually have a lumpy head, as the song's lyrics state. Pete appeared on stage briefly when the band performed the song at Madison Square Garden on 12/30/97. While Carini is known as one of the nicest guys in the Phish family, there are rumors that this song is also a stab at an unknown villain in the music world. It contains one of the few instances of profanity in a Phish lyric ("The thesis that you're writing is a piece of shit / I'm glad you finally finished it"). This song is also known among fans as "Lucy" or "Lucy Had a Lumpy Head," though Trey clarifies the song's correct title on 2/28/97 in Berlin.

Musical Evolution and History: The first version of this song—which became an instant fan favorite—emerged out of an incredible Down with Disease jam in Amsterdam on 2/17/97. A week later, Phish opened their 2/23/97 show in Cortemaggiore, Italy, with a recorded (soundcheck) version of it, then came on stage and took over.

Rotation History: Played five times on that Europe tour (including a stretch of three straight shows), Carini wasn't heard from again until it surfaced as the surprise first encore at MSG on 12/30/97.

Discography: Has not yet appeared on a Phish album.

Carini Had a Lumpy Head [6] [Carini]

By Phish

02/17/97	[892]	2	DWD	Jam
02/23/97	5	1	*OP1	Axilla
02/26/97	2	1	Tube	RockaW
02/28/97	1	1	*OP1	Paul&Silas
03/01/97	1	2	*OP2	Dinner
12/30/97	64	E	*OPE	BE Katy
>> 12/31/97		**1**		

CARS TRUCKS BUSES

Inspiration: Page wrote this song, which he says was partially inspired by the style of jazz trio Medeski, Martin & Wood, for a movie soundtrack he composed for a friend. Trey listened to a tape of the songs while driving down a highway in New Jersey, and this piece stood out for him. At the time, he was passing under a "Cars, Trucks, Buses" sign on the highway, and that stuck as the name.

Musical Evolution and History: As a composed instrumental, CTB has been mostly unchanged since its debut on fall tour 1995, although some versions stretch out a bit longer than others. But one notable

Original Songs Played by Year *(continued)*

Contact

1990	20	19%
1991	15	12%
1992	8	7%
1993	14	13%
1994	13	10%
1995	6	7%
1996	4	6%
1997	2	3%

Curtain

1990	4	4%
1991	20	16%
1992	15	12%
1993	13	12%
1994	17	14%
1995	11	14%
1996	8	11%
1997	3	4%

David Bowie

1990	24	23%
1991	36	28%
1992	37	31%
1993	33	30%
1994	38	31%
1995	25	31%
1996	19	27%
1997	17	22%

Demand

1994	9	7%
1995	4	5%
1996	1	1%
1997	0	0%

Destiny Unbound

1990	5	5%
1991	18	14%
1992	0	0%
1993	0	0%
1994	0	0%
1995	0	0%
1996	0	0%
1997	0	0%

Dinner

1990	35	34%
1991	33	26%
1992	15	12%
1993	4	4%
1994	3	2%
1995	2	2%
1996	1	1%
1997	1	1%

Dirt

1997	20	26%

Divided Sky

1990	42	41%
1991	45	35%
1992	28	23%
1993	31	28%
1994	39	31%
1995	20	25%
1996	16	23%
1997	4	5%

version came the next spring, when Michael Ray added his trumpet to the song at the Jazz & Heritage Festival in New Orleans on 4/26/96.
Rotation History: Played regularly since fall tour 1995.
Discography: Appears on *Billy Breathes* (1996).

Cars Trucks Buses [56] [CTB]
By McConnell

09/27/95	[761]	2	*OP2	ACDCBag
09/28/95	1	1	*OP1	RunJim
09/29/95	1	1	Str Design	YEM
09/30/95	1	1	My Friend	Chess
10/02/95	1	2	Wilson	Bathtub
10/05/95	2	1	Silent	Str Design
10/07/95	2	1	Makisupa	Split&Melt
10/08/95	1	1	Keyboard	Timber Ho
10/14/95	3	1	ACDCBag	Kung
10/19/95	3	1	*OP1	RunJim
10/21/95	2	1	Wilson	Kung
10/25/95	3	2	Life Mars	Mike's
10/29/95	3	1	PYITE	Horse
11/11/95	4	1	*OP1	Mike's
11/16/95	4	1	*OP1	RunJim
11/22/95	4	1	*OP1	Wilson
11/30/95	5	2	*OP2	Tweezer
12/04/95	3	2	Billy	YEM
12/15/95	8	1	Suspicious	Bouncing
12/29/95	4	1	Makisupa	Bathtub
04/26/96	3	1a	Stash	YEM
07/09/96	6	1a	Taste	Mike's
07/18/96	7	1a	Julius	Bouncing
08/14/96	15	2	Silent	Tweezer
08/17/96	2	1	Reba	Lizards
10/16/96	1	1	*OP1	DWD
10/18/96	2	1	Old Home	Stash
10/21/96	2	1	Sample	Sloth
10/26/96	4	1	Julius	Wolfman's
10/29/96	2	1	Guelah	Taste
11/06/96	4	1	Split&Melt	FEFY
11/11/96	4	1	Guelah	ACDCBag
11/14/96	2	1	Wolfman's	Free
11/18/96	3	1	*OP1	Timber Ho
11/23/96	3	1	Guelah	Divided
11/29/96	3	1	NICU	CharZero
12/01/96	2	1	Cavern	CharZero
12/06/96	3	1	YEM	DWD
12/31/96	4	1	PYITE	Stash
02/13/97	1	2	Julius	My Soul
02/16/97	2	2	Sample	Free
02/20/97	3	2	Sample	CharZero
02/28/97	6	1	My Soul	Peaches
03/18/97	3	1	Harry	Suzie
06/14/97	2	1	My Soul	Limb
07/03/97	12	2	Ghost	Billy
07/06/97	2	1	Silent	Scent
07/09/97	1	2	My Soul	YEM
07/26/97	1	7	Billy	Dirt
07/30/97	2	1	Piper	CharZero
08/06/97	4	2	Caspian	Sample
08/08/97	1	1	*OP1	Gumbo
08/10/97	2	1	Dirt	Billy
08/14/97	3	1	Free	Tela
11/16/97	5	1	Billy	Scent
12/29/97	20	1	Crossroads	Train Song
>> 12/31/97		**2**		

CATAPULT

Inspiration: A Mike Gordon spoken-word piece, Catapult's inspiration seems to spring from somewhere in the deep recesses of Mike's mind.
Musical Evolution and History: Recorded for inclusion on *A Picture of Nectar* (including the "Dr. Davis, telephone please" line from a sound effects CD) in 1991, it wasn't clear if Catapult would ever surface in concert. But then it popped up as part of David Bowie on 4/17/92 in San Francisco, CA, minus the "Dr. Davis" line. In general, Catapult has made some of its best (and wackiest) appearances as parts of other songs. On 6/22/94, it served as the bridge between a glorious Mike's and Simple, but was sung to an entirely different tune. It surfaced again during the insane Antelope at Sugarbush on 7/16/94, and when Trey crooned the line "There ain't gonna be no wedding," Fish shouted back, "You wish!" a reference to the fact that Trey and Sue were set to be married weeks later. Fish, apparently not wanting to create any tension, immediately said, "I take that back!"
Rotation History: Sporadically played since its debut, many fans consider catching a Catapult as a welcome surprise treat at a show, perhaps comparable to seeing Kung.
Discography: Appears on *A Picture of Nectar* (1992).

Catapult [22] [Catapult]
By Gordon

04/17/92	[413]	1	Bowie	Bowie
04/21/92	3	2	Weigh	Lively Up
02/10/93	96	1	IDK	Antelope
05/12/94	133	1	*OP1	Rift
05/26/94	11	1	It's Ice	Divided
06/29/94	19	1	Silent	Bowie
07/16/94	13	2	Antelope	Antelope
10/15/94	8	2	YEM	YEM
10/23/94	6	1	Stash	Stash
10/26/94	2	2	YEM	Rosie
11/30/94	21	2	Mike's	McGrupp
12/08/94	7	1	Simple	Simple
06/16/95	15	1	Dog Faced	Split&Melt
10/14/95	27	1	Stash	AArmy
10/22/95	6	1	Possum	Curtain
11/24/95	18	2	Reba	Scent
12/01/95	5	2	Bowie	Bowie
10/27/96	57	1	Scent	Scent
11/16/96	13	2	Kung	Axilla
11/23/96	4	2	Weekpaug	Waste
03/02/97	26	1	Antelope	Life Mars
12/13/97	60	2	Weekpaug	Weekpaug
>> 12/31/97		**4**		

CAVERN

Inspiration: This song's lyrics came about as a result of a series of e-mail exchanges between Tom Marshall and Scott Herman, who each added a line at a time. Trey then set their bizarre exchange to music.
Musical Evolution and History: Musically, Cavern is much the same since its debut, though the lyrics have undergone slight revision. The original version of this song performed in 1990 included the line "a penile erector" in place of the current "a picture of nectar." The band changed it when Page said he felt silly singing the first version and they realized the change could honor Nectar Rorris, who booked Phish at his Burlington restaurant/bar Nectar's in the band's formative years. The original Cavern also had an extra verse, performed most recently on 4/4/94 in Burlington, VT, and on 11/26/97 in Hartford, CT—"The brothel wife then grabbed a knife / And slashed me on the tongue / I turned the blade back on the bitch / And dropped her in the dung." Its somewhat mysogynistic lyrics seem to mandate its rare status. The band performed one acoustic version of this song, on 6/24/94 in Indianapolis, IN, and a few fantastic takes with the Giant Country Horns. While Cavern does not have any "jam" sections, several sections do lend themselves to quick improvisations, which make versions of the song vary subtly. On some nights, Trey will follow up each verse with a heavy-metalish, ringing guitar twang, while he tends to be more melodic on others. General cadence and the prominence of Page also vary, evidenced most clearly in the slowed-down performance at the 4/11/91 Carleton College show.
Rotation History: For much of the early 1990s, Cavern was one of the band's most heavily played songs, but in recent years it has slipped a bit. Still, it's rare to see the band go more than half a dozen shows without playing it.
Discography: Appears on *A Picture of Nectar* (1992).

Cavern [295] [Cavern]
By Anastasio/Marshall/Herman

03/28/90	[185]	2	Rift	HwayHell
04/05/90	2	2	Fee	Mike's
04/06/90	1	1	*OP1	YEM
04/12/90	5	1	A-Train	Jesus
04/20/90	4	1	Ya Mar	Dinner
04/22/90	2	1	IDK	MSO
04/26/90	2	2	Suzie	Adeline
04/28/90	1	2	*OP2	Harry
09/14/90	19	2	Magilla	Lizards
10/08/90	12	1	Foam	Reba
10/12/90	1	1	Uncle Pen	Esther
10/30/90	2	1	Uncle Pen	Sqirm Coil
10/31/90	1	1	MSO	Antelope
11/02/90	1	1	Esther	Asse Fest
11/10/90	4	1	RunJim	MSO
11/17/90	2	1	YEM	Eliza
12/01/90	4	1	*OP1	Landlady
12/08/90	3	1	Divided	Landlady
12/29/90	2	2	Lizards	Stash
02/03/91	4	2	Landlady	Mango
02/07/91	1	2	Uncle Pen	Love You
02/08/91	1	2	Mango	Lawn Boy
02/09/91	1	2	Harry	Love You
02/14/91	1	1	Destiny	Mango
02/16/91	2	1	Divided	A-Train
02/21/91	3	2	Golgi	Landlady
02/27/91	5	2	BurAlive	Sqirm Coil
02/28/91	1	1	Weekpaug	TMWSIY
03/01/91	1	1	Divided	Sqirm Coil
03/06/91	2	1	Possum	Divided
03/13/91	4	1	YEM	Divided
03/15/91	1	2	Paul&Silas	Destiny
03/16/91	1	2	Sqirm Coil	YEM
03/22/91	3	1	BurAlive	Reba
03/23/91	1	2	Uncle Pen	Bowie
03/28/91	1	1a	Divided	Landlady
04/05/91	6	1	Divided	Magilla
04/11/91	2	1	RunJim	Paul&Silas
04/12/91	1	2	Fluffhead	Tela
04/16/91	3	1	Paul&Silas	Mango
04/19/91	2	1	Divided	Lizards
04/20/91	1	2	Paul&Silas	TMWSIY
04/21/91	1	2	Harry	IDK
04/27/91	4	1	RunJim	Landlady
05/02/91	1	1	Sqirm Coil	Bowie
05/04/91	2	1	Suzie	Reba
05/10/91	1	1	Bowie	Ya Mar
05/16/91	2	1	Foam	Divided
05/17/91	1	2	Magilla	Bike
05/18/91	1	1	Divided	Possum
05/25/91	1	1a	YEM	Sqirm Coil
07/11/91	1	2	Dinner	TMWSIY
07/12/91	1	1	Rocky Top	Bowie
07/14/91	2	2	Magilla	Antelope
07/15/91	1	1a	Lizards	Sqirm Coil
07/18/91	1	1	A-Train	Mike's
07/19/91	1	1	Fee	Sqirm Coil
07/21/91	2	1	*OP1	Divided
07/23/91	1	2	Reba	Lizards
07/24/91	1	1	Landlady	Tela
07/25/91	1	1	Adeline	Antelope
07/26/91	1	1	Suzie	TMWSIY
07/27/91	1	1a	Suzie	PoorHeart
08/03/91	1	2	Esther	IDK
09/25/91	1	2	Sparkle	Jesus
09/27/91	2	1	RunJim	Reba
09/28/91	1	2	Sparkle	Antelope
09/29/91	1	1a	*OP1	Divided
10/02/91	2	1	PoorHeart	Reba
10/03/91	1	1	Divided	Possum
10/04/91	1	1	PoorHeart	Divided
10/06/91	2	2	IDK	Sqirm Coil
10/10/91	1	2	PoorHeart	Antelope
10/11/91	1	2	Curtain	Foam
10/17/91	4	1	Divided	PoorHeart
10/18/91	1	2	MSO	*CL2
10/28/91	6	1	RunJim	Reba
11/01/91	3	2	Tela	PoorHeart
11/07/91	3	1	Sparkle	It's Ice
11/12/91	4	2	Magilla	Love You
11/13/91	1	1	Esther	Divided
11/15/91	2	1	Sparkle	Curtain
11/16/91	1	1	Ya Mar	*CL1
11/19/91	1	2	Dinner	Bowie
11/20/91	1	2	Bike	*CL2
11/22/91	2	1	Possum	Sparkle
11/24/91	2	2	Divided	Mango
11/30/91	1	1	Divided	Sqirm Coil
12/04/91	1	1	RunJim	PoorHeart
12/05/91	1	E	Glide	*CLE
12/07/91	2	1	Curtain	Mango
12/31/91	1	2	Reba	MSO
03/06/92	1	1	Rift	Sparkle
03/11/92	2	1	Divided	*CL1
03/12/92	1	2	MSO	*CL2
03/14/92	2	1	RunJim	Reba
03/17/92	1	1	Possum	Sparkle
03/20/92	2	2	Mango	Uncle Pen
03/24/92	2	2	Harry	*CL2
03/26/92	2	2	Lizards	Rosie
03/28/92	2	1	Glide	*CL1
03/30/92	1	1	RunJim	*CL1
03/31/92	1	2	Lizards	Dinner
04/04/92	3	2	Harpua	*CL2
04/06/92	2	2	Uncle Pen	*CL2
04/09/92	2	2	Terrapin	*CL2
04/12/92	1	2	Harry	*CL2
04/15/92	2	1	Uncle Pen	IDK
04/17/92	2	1	IDK	Reba
04/19/92	2	1	My Friend	Maze
04/21/92	1	E	Adeline	*CLE
04/23/92	2	1	*OP1	Curtain
04/24/92	1	2	Bowie	Ya Mar
04/30/92	3	E	Carolina	*CLE
05/02/92	2	2	Rosie	*CL2
05/05/92	2	2	Sqirm Coil	*CL2
05/06/92	1	1	Sparkle	*CL1
05/08/92	2	1	Curtain	Reba
05/10/92	2	1a	Uncle Pen	Reba
05/12/92	1	2	Llama	RunJim
05/14/92	1	2	Glide	Rift
05/15/92	1	1a	Foam	Sparkle
05/16/92	1	1	Lizards	Bowie
05/17/92	1	2	Harry	*CL2
05/18/92	1	2	Rift	Love You
06/19/92	1	1a	Sparkle	YEM
06/24/92	3	1a	Sparkle	Rocky Top
07/01/92	3	1a	Curtain	Rift

07/10/92	3	1a	Lizards	Antelope
07/11/92	1	1a	Sqirm Coil	YEM
07/14/92	2	1	PoorHeart	*CL1
07/22/92	7	1a	Rift	Bowie
08/02/92	9	1a	Bowie	Rocky Top
08/17/92	4	2	A-Train	*CL2
08/23/92	3	1a	Sparkle	Foam
10/30/92	7	1a	Rift	Sqirm Coil
11/19/92	1	2	Lngthwise	*CL2
11/23/92	4	2	Lngthwise	*CL2
11/25/92	1	1	Adeline	Antelope
11/27/92	1	2	A-Train	*CL2
11/30/92	2	2	Terrapin	*CL2
12/01/92	1	1	Rift	Fluffhead
12/03/92	2	2	A-Train	*CL2
12/04/92	1	1	Mockbird	*CL1
12/06/92	2	2	Carolina	*CL2
12/10/92	3	2	Adeline	*CL1
12/12/92	2	1	Sparkle	Reba
12/13/92	1	2	Harry	*CL2
12/28/92	1	2	Harry	*CL2
12/31/92	3	1	Divided	Foam
02/04/93	2	2	Harry	*CL2
02/09/93	4	E	*OPE	Rocky Top
02/11/93	2	2	Lizards	*CL2
02/13/93	2	2	Sqirm Coil	*CL2
02/18/93	3	1	Sparkle	Reba
02/20/93	2	1	Fluffhead	*CL1
02/22/93	2	1	Foam	IDK
02/25/93	2	1	PoorHeart	Maze
02/26/93	1	1	IDK	*CL1
03/03/93	3	1	Lawn Boy	*CL1
03/05/93	1	1	PoorHeart	Foam
03/08/93	2	2	PoorHeart	Uncle Pen
03/12/93	2	1	PoorHeart	Possum
03/16/93	3	1	McGrupp	*CL1
03/18/93	2	2	Sqirm Coil	*CL2
03/19/93	1	1	Fluffhead	Antelope
03/21/93	1	2	Harry	*CL2
03/24/93	2	1	AmGrace	*CL1
03/26/93	2	1	Divided	*CL1
03/30/93	3	1	Divided	*CL1
04/01/93	2	2	Terrapin	*CL2
04/03/93	2	2	Love You	*CL2
04/09/93	2	1	Divided	*CL1
04/10/93	1	2	Hoochie	*CL2
04/13/93	2	1	Caravan	*CL1
04/16/93	2	1	Harry	*CL1
04/18/93	2	1	IDK	*CL1
04/21/93	2	E	Adeline	*CLE
04/24/93	3	2	Harry	*CL2
04/27/93	2	2	Love You	*CL2
04/30/93	2	1	Divided	Lawn Boy
05/01/93	1	2	Weekpaug	*CL2
05/03/93	2	1	Lawn Boy	*CL1
05/05/93	1	E	AmGrace	*CLE
05/08/93	3	1	Satin Doll	*CL1
05/29/93	1	1a	Sparkle	BBJ
07/16/93	3	2	Harry	*CL2
07/18/93	2	1	Uncle Pen	*CL1
07/23/93	3	1	Lawn Boy	*CL1
07/25/93	2	E	*OPE	*CLE
07/28/93	2	1	PoorHeart	*CL1
07/30/93	2	1	Reba	*CL1
07/31/93	1	1	Divided	*CL1
08/03/93	2	1	Llama	*CL1
08/07/93	2	1	Mockbird	*CL1
08/11/93	3	1	Sparkle	*CL1
08/14/93	3	1	PoorHeart	*CL1
08/17/93	3	2	MSO	*CL2
08/20/93	1	2	PurplRain	*CL2
08/25/93	3	1	Glide	*CL1
12/29/93	4	E	Nellie	*CLE
04/04/94	3	E	Harry	*CLE
04/06/94	2	2	Sqirm Coil	*CL2
04/09/94	2	2	Slave	*CL2
04/11/94	2	1	Divided	*CL1
04/15/94	3	2	BeLikeYou	*CL2
04/17/94	2	1	MSO	*CL1
04/18/94	1	2	BeLikeYou	*CL2
04/21/94	2	1	If I Could	*CL1
04/29/94	6	2	BeLikeYou	*CL2
05/02/94	2	E	*OPE	*CLE
05/08/94	5	2	Julius	YEM
05/10/94	1	1	If I Could	*CL1
05/14/94	3	2	Lizards	*CL2
05/19/94	3	1	Mango	*CL1
05/23/94	4	1	Reba	*CL1
05/26/94	2	1	PoorHeart	Demand
05/28/94	2	1	Maze	*CL1
06/10/94	3	1	Lizards	Julius
06/13/94	2	2	Esther	Reba
06/17/94	3	1	Scent	*CL1
06/22/94	4	E	Carolina	*CLE
06/24/94	2	2	PoorHeart	Carolina
06/29/94	3	2	Suzie	*CL2
07/01/94	2	2	Harry	*CL2
07/08/94	5	E	Nellie	*CLE
07/10/94	2	1	Julius	*CL1
07/13/94	1	2	Possum	NICU
07/16/94	3	1	Lizards	Horse
10/07/94	1	E	Long Time	*CLE
10/13/94	5	2	Long Time	*CL2
10/14/94	1	E	Ya Mar	*CLE
10/21/94	5	E	Long Time	*CLE
10/27/94	5	1	PoorHeart	*CL1
11/03/94	5	2	Harry	*CL2
11/14/94	4	1	Lawn Boy	*CL1
11/20/94	5	2	Julius	*CL2
11/26/94	4	1	PoorHeart	*CL1
11/30/94	2	2	McGrupp	*CL2
12/02/94	2	E	*OPE	*CLE
12/03/94	1	2	Julius	*CL2
12/07/94	3	E	*OPE	*CLE
12/10/94	3	2	Slave	*CL2
12/30/94	3	1	Scent	*CL1
06/09/95	5	2	Scent	Bowie
06/14/95	3	1	Mound	Possum
06/19/95	4	1	Rift	Antelope
06/22/95	2	1	Maze	Adeline
06/25/95	3	2	AmGrace	*CL2
06/29/95	3	1	Divided	Rift
07/03/95	4	1	Free	*CL1
09/30/95	4	2	Suspicious	*CL2
10/05/95	3	2	Scent	Bowie
10/11/95	4	1	Old Home	Divided
10/14/95	2	2	Scent	*CL2
10/19/95	3	1	Billy	*CL1
10/22/95	3	2	Slave	*CL2
10/24/95	1	2	Contact	*CL2
11/10/95	7	1	Guyute	*CL1
11/14/95	3	1	I'm Blue	*CL1
11/18/95	3	2	BBFCM	*CL2
11/22/95	3	1	Uncle Pen	Fog
12/01/95	6	1	Stash	*CL1
12/05/95	3	2	Harry	*CL2
12/11/95	4	1	Julius	*CL1
12/16/95	4	2	Scent	Mike's
12/30/95	4	2	Scent	Antelope
04/26/96	2	E	HelloBaby	*CLE
07/07/96	4	1a	Uncle Pen	Antelope
07/11/96	3	1	RunJim	Reba
07/13/96	2	1a	RunJim	Reba
07/15/96	1	1	Harry	*CL1
07/22/96	5	1a	PoorHeart	Maze
07/25/96	3	1a	Harry	*CL1
08/05/96	3	E	*OPE	*CLE
08/10/96	3	1	Bathtub	*CL1
10/25/96	13	2	Harry	SSB
11/02/96	5	1	Fee	Taste
11/11/96	6	E	Waste	*CLE
11/15/96	3	1	Taste	*CL1
11/22/96	4	1	Stash	*CL1
11/24/96	2	E	Ginseng	*CLE
12/01/96	2	1	PoorHeart	CTB
12/29/96	5	1	Caravan	Taste
02/16/97	5	1	Waste	Chalkdust
02/18/97	2	1	Beauty	PYITE
06/14/97	12	2	Bowie	*CL2
06/20/97	3	2	Ginseng	Twist
06/21/97	1	1a	Twist	*CL1
07/03/97	8	2	Harry	*CL2
07/26/97	10	E	Bouncing	*CLE
08/10/97	9	E	*OPE	*CLE
11/26/97	14	E	*OPE	*CLE
12/06/97	7	1	Maze	*CL1
12/28/97	6	2	Rocky Top	*CL2
>> 12/31/97	3			

CHALKDUST TORTURE

Inspiration: Another product of Tom Marshall's mind, this sort-of anthem to childhood apparently reminisces about a classroom ("I sat in the chair and my synapses burned"), then pleads, "Can't I live while I'm young?" Like all Tom Marshall lyrics, though, this one is open to wide interpretation.

Musical Evolution and History: Trey lifted a guitar riff he'd contributed to the Dude of Life's song "Self" in 1990 for what would become Chalkdust. The earliest versions of this song, performed in winter/spring 1991, show the basic structure for the song worked out, but Phish wouldn't nail the jam immediately. It took a couple of years for them to make this into one of their best pure rock songs. The album version on *A Picture of Nectar* has Trey's voice electronically altered, making him sound less like himself and more like a generic sixties rock 'n' roll singer. Released as the only single off *Nectar* in 1992, this was the first Phish song to receive any radio airplay to speak of outside Vermont. Two years later, appearing for the first time on *The Late Show with David Letterman* in December 1994, the band performed the single worst version of this song ever at the request of Dave, who had heard it on New York radio. Always a crowd favorite, Chalkdust can be an occasional showstopper and varies in length tremendously. Among the more popular versions is Sugarbush 7/16/94.

Rotation History: One of the band's most heavily played songs since its debut, it was played one in every three shows in 1997, often as a set opener or closer.

Discography: Appears on *A Picture of Nectar* (1992) and *A Live One* (1995) as a live track taken from 11/16/94 Ann Arbor, MI.

Chalkdust Torture [269] [Chalkdust]

By Anastasio/Marshall

02/02/91	[258]	1	YEM	*CL1
02/03/91	1	1	Reba	Foam
02/07/91	1	2	*OP2	TMWSIY
02/09/91	2	1	Reba	*CL1
02/15/91	2	2	Terrapin	*CL2
02/16/91	1	2	*OP2	Reba
03/15/91	17	2	Harry	*CL2
03/17/91	2	1	Slave	*CL1
03/23/91	3	2	*OP2	Bathtub
03/28/91	1	1a	Magilla	*CL1
04/05/91	6	1	Reba	Foam
04/11/91	2	1	Sqirm Coil	*CL1
04/15/91	3	1	Fee	Forbin's
04/16/91	1	2	Reba	Magilla
04/20/91	3	1	Esther	Bouncing
04/22/91	2	2	*OP2	Bathtub
04/26/91	1	1	*OP1	Sqirm Coil
05/02/91	2	2	*OP2	PoorHeart
05/03/91	1	1	Foam	TMWSIY
05/10/91	2	2	McGrupp	Love You
05/11/91	1	2	*OP2	YEM
05/12/91	1	1	*OP1	Bouncing
05/16/91	1	1	Mockbird	YEM
05/17/91	1	1	*OP1	Drums
05/18/91	1	1	Golgi	YEM
05/25/91	1	1	Landlady	Bouncing
07/13/91	3	2	*OP2	Guelah
07/14/91	1	3	Esther	Bathtub
07/18/91	2	1	*OP1	Foam
07/20/91	2	1	*OP1	Foam

Original Songs Played by Year *(continued)*

Dog Faced Boy

1994	23	19%
1995	9	11%
1996	1	1%
1997	1	1%

Dog Log

1990	1	1%
1991	1	1%
1992	0	0%
1993	1	1%
1994	0	0%
1995	2	2%
1996	0	0%
1997	1	1%

Dogs Stole Things

1997	20	26%

Don't Get Me Wrong

1990	3	3%
1991	0	0%
1992	0	0%
1993	0	0%
1994	0	0%
1995	0	0%
1996	0	0%
1997	0	0%

Down with Disease

1994	55	44%
1995	5	6%
1996	20	29%
1997	17	22%

Eliza

1990	3	3%
1991	6	5%
1992	6	5%
1993	0	0%
1994	0	0%
1995	0	0%
1996	0	0%
1997	0	0%

Esther

1990	22	21%
1991	16	13%
1992	12	10%
1993	17	15%
1994	11	9%
1995	4	5%
1996	3	4%
1997	0	0%

Faht

1992	4	3%
1993	4	4%
1994	2	2%
1995	2	2%
1996	0	0%
1997	0	0%

07/23/91	2	1	*OP1	Foam
07/24/91	1	1	Golgi	Sqirm Coil
07/26/91	2	1	*OP1	Reba
08/03/91	2	2	Reba	Bouncing
09/25/91	1	2	YEM	*CL2
09/26/91	1	2	Lawn Boy	*CL2
09/28/91	2	1	Bouncing	Sqirm Coil
10/02/91	2	1	Bouncing	Golgi
10/03/91	1	1	*OP1	Foam
10/04/91	1	1	Memories	Reba
10/10/91	3	1	*OP1	Foam
10/11/91	1	1	Guelah	YEM
10/12/91	1	1	Fluffhead	A-Train
10/15/91	2	1	*OP1	Foam
10/17/91	1	1	Esther	Golgi
10/19/91	2	1	Foam	Bouncing
10/27/91	4	1	MSO	Mango
10/31/91	3	1	Sloth	Sparkle
11/01/91	1	2	It's Ice	Eliza
11/07/91	3	1	Memories	Foam
11/09/91	2	2	*OP2	Fluffhead
11/12/91	2	2	Guelah	Magilla
11/13/91	1	1	Sparkle	Esther
11/15/91	2	1	*OP1	Sparkle
11/16/91	1	2	Horn	Terrapin
11/19/91	1	1	Horn	Love You
11/21/91	2	1	*OP1	Bouncing
11/23/91	2	1	Sparkle	Uncle Pen
11/24/91	1	2	Mango	A-Train
11/30/91	1	2	*OP2	Uncle Pen
12/04/91	1	2	Lizards	Love You
12/07/91	3	2	Reba	Sparkle
03/07/92	3	2	Weigh	Horn
03/14/92	4	1	Fee	A-Train
03/19/92	2	2	Glide	NICU
03/25/92	4	2	MSO	Rosie
03/26/92	1	E	Sl Monkey	Harpua
03/30/92	3	2	Weigh	Rosie
04/01/92	2	2	Horn	Rosie
04/04/92	2	1	Uncle Pen	Bouncing
04/06/92	2	1	Esther	Guelah
04/09/92	2	2	Silent	Terrapin
04/15/92	3	2	*OP2	YEM
04/19/92	4	1	Fee	IDK
04/25/92	5	1	Tela	Bouncing
04/30/92	2	2	Silent	Rosie
05/02/92	2	2	YEM	Rosie
05/05/92	2	2	*OP2	Bouncing
05/06/92	1	2	Uncle Pen	Terrapin
05/08/92	2	2	Silent	Terrapin
05/12/92	3	2	Guelah	Terrapin
05/15/92	2	1a	Love You	YEM
05/17/92	2	1	PoorHeart	*CL1
06/23/92	4	1a	*OP1	Reba
06/27/92	2	1a	All Things	Bouncing
07/12/92	7	1a	Adeline	Bouncing
07/15/92	2	1	Silent	Lizards
07/17/92	2	1a	*OP1	Sparkle
07/26/92	7	1a	*OP1	It's Ice
07/28/92	2	1a	*OP1	Bouncing
07/31/92	2	1a	Suzie	Bouncing
08/02/92	2	1a	*OP1	Guelah
08/13/92	1	1a	*OP1	Foam
08/19/92	4	1a	*OP1	Landlady
08/23/92	2	1a	*OP1	Maze
08/27/92	3	1a	*OP1	Bouncing
08/29/92	2	1a	*OP1	Rift
11/20/92	4	2	*OP2	Fluffhead
11/25/92	4	2	*OP2	Foam
11/28/92	2	1	Esther	Sparkle
12/01/92	2	2	Curtain	My Friend
12/03/92	2	1	Uncle Pen	Horse
12/05/92	2	1	Landlady	Bouncing
12/07/92	2	2	*OP2	Reba
12/11/92	3	1	Lizards	Guelah
12/13/92	2	2	Fluffhead	TMWSIY
12/30/92	3	1	Esther	Fluffhead
02/04/93	3	2	*OP2	Wedge
02/06/93	2	2	*OP2	Mound
02/09/93	2	1	Wedge	Esther
02/12/93	3	1	Wedge	IDK
02/15/93	2	1	Esther	Mound
02/18/93	2	1	*OP1	Guelah
02/21/93	3	1	Horn	Esther
02/23/93	2	1	Lawn Boy	Wedge
02/26/93	2	2	Glide	Mound
03/02/93	2	1	All Things	Horse
03/05/93	2	2	Landlady	Guelah
03/08/93	2	E	Terrapin	*CLE
03/12/93	2	2	BBJ	Lngthwise
03/16/93	3	2	Esther	YEM
03/18/93	2	1	*OP1	Guelah
03/19/93	1	E	AmGrace	*CLE
03/22/93	2	1	*OP1	Guelah
03/25/93	2	1	*OP1	Guelah
03/27/93	2	2	Bouncing	TMWSIY
03/31/93	3	2	Harpua	*CL2
04/02/93	2	2	Bike	*CL2
04/09/93	3	1	*OP1	Sparkle
04/10/93	1	1	Uncle Pen	Lawn Boy
04/13/93	2	1	Mockbird	Guelah
04/16/93	2	1	*OP1	Guelah
04/20/93	3	2	*OP2	Fluffhead
04/22/93	2	1	Reba	Esther
04/23/93	1	1	Lawn Boy	*CL1
04/24/93	1	1	*OP1	Guelah
04/29/93	3	2	*OP2	It's Ice
05/01/93	2	2	*OP2	Fluffhead
05/03/93	2	1	Weigh	Esther
05/06/93	2	1	*OP1	Mound
05/08/93	2	1	*OP1	Guelah
05/29/93	1	1a	*OP1	Bouncing
07/15/93	2	E	*OPE	Freebird
07/17/93	2	1	Reba	Horse
07/21/93	2	E	*OPE	*CLE
07/23/93	2	2	BBFCM	HwayHell
07/28/93	4	2	Great Gig	*CL2
07/30/93	2	1	Esther	IDK
08/02/93	2	1	*OP1	Guelah
08/06/93	2	1	Nellie	Suzie
08/09/93	3	1	*OP1	Mound
08/12/93	2	1	Reba	Guelah
08/14/93	2	1	*OP1	Guelah
08/15/93	1	1	Mockbird	*CL1
08/20/93	3	2	My Friend	YEM
08/24/93	2	1	*OP1	All Things
08/26/93	2	2	Bats&Mice	*CL2
08/28/93	1	2	Contact	*CL2
12/29/93	2	2	Adeline	*CL2
04/05/94	4	2	BeLikeYou	AmGrace
04/10/94	4	1	Esther	IDK
04/15/94	4	1	Wilson	Bouncing
04/18/94	3	1	*OP1	Glide
04/21/94	2	1	*OP1	Sparkle
04/24/94	3	2	Mockbird	Contact
04/30/94	4	1	*OP1	Mound
05/03/94	2	2	Harpua	BeLikeYou
05/06/94	2	1	Esther	*CL1
05/13/94	5	2	*OP2	Bouncing
05/20/94	5	E	*OPE	*CLE
05/23/94	3	1	*OP1	Sample
05/25/94	1	1	Adeline	*CL1
05/29/94	4	2	Esther	McGrupp
06/11/94	3	1	Wilson	YEM
06/18/94	5	2	YEM	*CL2
06/21/94	2	2	Esther	BBFCM
06/25/94	4	1	Tela	*CL1
06/30/94	3	2	Love You	*CL2
07/06/94	5	2	Lawn Boy	BBFCM
07/10/94	3	1	*OP1	Horn
07/14/94	2	E	*OPE	*CLE
07/16/94	2	2	Contact	*CL2
10/08/94	2	1	*OP1	Horn
10/10/94	2	1	Nellie	*CL1
10/14/94	3	2	Guyute	Nellie
10/20/94	4	2	Long Time	*CL2
10/23/94	3	1	*OP1	My Friend
10/28/94	4	2	Life Boy	Old Home
11/04/94	5	1	Suzie	*CL1
11/12/94	1	1	Esther	*CL1
11/16/94	3	2	LongJourn	Fee
11/20/94	4	1	*OP1	Fee
11/28/94	5	1	*OP1	Also Sprac
12/02/94	3	2	*OP2	Bowie
12/07/94	4	1	Life Boy	*CL1
12/10/94	3	1	Lawn Boy	*CL1
12/31/94	4	3	Auld	Horse
06/08/95	3	1	Caspian	*CL1
06/13/95	3	1	Sparkle	*CL1
06/20/95	6	2	Halley's	Caspian
06/23/95	2	1	Simple	Caspian
06/28/95	4	1	Fluffhead	*CL1
07/01/95	3	1	Bouncing	*CL1
09/27/95	3	1	Str Design	Sqirm Coil
09/29/95	2	E	*OPE	*CLE
10/05/95	4	1	*OP1	Ha Ha Ha
10/11/95	4	E	*OPE	*CLE
10/19/95	5	1	Esther	Theme
10/21/95	2	1	TweezRep	Guelah
10/25/95	3	1	I'm Blue	*CL1
10/28/95	2	2	Frankstein	*CL2
11/11/95	5	1	Fee	*CL1
11/14/95	2	1	*OP1	Foam
11/21/95	5	1	Fee	Caspian
11/24/95	2	2	*OP2	Theme
12/01/95	5	1	Wolfman's	Forbin's
12/05/95	3	1	Horn	Fog
12/09/95	3	1	Dog Faced	*CL1
12/15/95	4	1	*OP1	Harry
12/17/95	2	1	Lizards	*CL1
12/31/95	4	1	Sparkle	*CL1
06/06/96	2	2	YEM	Sparkle
07/05/96	2	1a	FunkBitch	ACDCBag
07/10/96	4	1a	*OP1	Ya Mar
07/13/96	3	1a	FunkBitch	YEM
07/24/96	8	1a	*OP1	Ya Mar
08/04/96	3	1	*OP1	FunkBitch
08/12/96	5	1	Esther	Weigh
08/16/96	3	1	*OP1	Bathtub
10/17/96	3	2	Ya Mar	Bathtub
10/21/96	3	2	Wilson	Wolfman's
10/23/96	2	E	*OPE	*CLE
10/27/96	3	2	*OP2	Bathtub
10/29/96	1	1	*OP1	Guelah
11/07/96	5	1	*OP1	Weigh
11/11/96	3	1	*OP1	Guelah
11/15/96	2	1	Train Song	Taste
11/18/96	2	1	Billy	Guelah
11/23/96	3	1	*OP1	Guelah
11/27/96	2	1	Ya Mar	Sloth
11/30/96	2	1	Caspian	*CL1
12/04/96	3	1	My Friend	Horn
12/31/96	5	2	*OP2	Wilson
02/13/97	1	1	*OP1	Wolfman's
02/16/97	2	1	Cavern	*CL1
02/20/97	3	1	SSP	Love Me
02/22/97	2	2	*OP2	Bathtub
02/25/97	2	E	*OPE	*CLE
03/02/97	4	1	Life Mars	HelloBaby
03/18/97	1	2	Waste	Slave
06/13/97	1	2	Slave	Ghost
06/16/97	2	1	Theme	Wolfman's
06/21/97	3	1a	Harry	Jam
06/27/97	4	1a	Wilson	Stash
06/29/97	1	1a	Beauty	Theme
07/06/97	5	1	Scent	*CL1
07/11/97	3	1	*OP1	Bouncing
07/23/97	3	2	RMWay	*CL2
07/25/97	1	2	*OP2	Taste
07/30/97	3	1	Wolfman's	Water
08/08/97	5	2	Caspian	*CL2
08/14/97	5	2	*OP2	Love Me
08/16/97	1	1	Harpua	Theme
11/13/97	2	1	*OP1	BE Katy
11/21/97	5	1	Lawn Boy	Caspian
12/02/97	7	1	Makisupa	Ghost
12/05/97	2	2	Lovin Cup	*CL2
12/09/97	3	1	Mike's	My Soul
12/30/97	6	1	Stash	DayinLife
>> 12/31/97	**1**			

CHARACTER ZERO

Inspiration: Murky, but one rumor is that "the man Mulcahey" is what the band sometimes called producer Steve Lillywhite during the *Billy Breathes* sessions, but that may have followed from the song lyric, not the other way around.

Musical Evolution and History: One of a handful of songs recorded for inclusion on *Billy Breathes* before ever being performed live, Character Zero has, over the past few years, become one of the band's rockingest numbers. Though many versions stand out for their infectious energy, the second-set opener from Hartford, CT, on 11/26/97 is among the longest to date, with a great 15-minute jam that segues into Also Sprach without returning to the closing vocals.

Rotation History: After its debut at the unannounced Joyous Lake show on 6/6/96 and one performance in Europe, Character Zero was not taken out for a spin again during the U.S. summer tour that followed. But after the release of *Billy Breathes* in the fall it appeared frequently, particularly setting the crowd on fire on both Halloween and New Year's. It then became the most-played Phish song of 1997, often serving as a first-set closer.

Discography: Appears on *Billy Breathes* (1996).

Character Zero [53] [CharZero]

By Anastasio/Marshall

06/06/96	[820]	2	Waste	Bowie
07/09/96	5	1a	Bouncing	*CL1
10/16/96	25	1	Silent	*CL1
10/17/96	1	1	PYITE	DayinLife
10/21/96	3	1	Divided	Ginseng
10/23/96	2	1	HelloBaby	Rift
10/26/96	2	1	Train Song	It's Ice
10/29/96	2	2	Wedge	Suspicious
10/31/96	1	1	Mockbird	SSB
11/03/96	2	1	Bouncing	*CL1
11/07/96	2	1	Tela	*CL1
11/09/96	2	1	Lizards	*CL1
11/13/96	2	1	Reba	Adeline
11/15/96	2	1	Bouncing	PYITE
11/18/96	2	1	Reba	*CL1
11/22/96	2	2	Steep	Theme
11/24/96	2	1	Reba	Str Design
11/29/96	2	1	CTB	Divided
12/01/96	2	1	CTB	Curtain
12/04/96	2	1	Guyute	Lizards
12/31/96	5	2	Caspian	*CL2
02/13/97	1	1	PoorHeart	Peaches
02/14/97	1	E	*OPE	*CLE
02/18/97	3	1	Walfredo	Slave
02/20/97	1	2	CTB	Uncle Pen
02/21/97	1	E	*OPE	*CLE
02/22/97	1	1	IDK	*CL1
02/28/97	4	1	Ya Mar	*CL1
03/02/97	2	2	Waste	Slave
03/18/97	1	1	Suzie	*CL1
06/13/97	1	2	Oblivious	*CL2
06/19/97	3	E	Beauty	HelloBaby
06/22/97	3	1a	Uncle Pen	Theme
06/27/97	3	1a	Bouncing	*CL1
06/29/97	1	1a	Theme	*CL1
07/03/97	3	E	*OPE	*CLE
07/05/97	1	1a	PoorHeart	GTBT
07/11/97	4	E	*OPE	*CLE
07/21/97	1	1	Bathtub	*CL1
07/25/97	3	2	Ghost	*CL2
07/30/97	3	1	CTB	*CL1
08/03/97	3	1	Limb	*CL1
08/08/97	2	1	Water	*CL1
08/11/97	3	2	YEM	*CL2
08/16/97	3	1	Train Song	Sqirm Coil
11/13/97	2	1	YEM	*CL1
11/17/97	3	E	*OPE	*CLE
11/23/97	4	1	Fluffhead	*CL1
11/26/97	1	2	*OP2	Also Sprac
12/02/97	4	2	Bouncing	*CL2
12/05/97	2	1	Limb	*CL1
12/12/97	5	1	Train Song	*CL1
12/28/97	2	1	Bouncing	*CL1
>> 12/31/97	**3**			

Chess Game Jam [3] [Chess]

By Phish

09/30/95	[765]	1	CTB	Reba
10/02/95	1	1	Rift	Stash
11/16/95	27	1	RunJim	Horn
>> 12/31/97	**174**			

CLOD

Inspiration: The desire to string a bunch of crazy words together and call it a song (boozy, groggy, etc.).

Musical Evolution and History: Frequently played on its own in the

1980s, Clod was integrated into Fluff's Travels, where it can still be heard today in pretty much the same musical form, minus its original first word, "swift."

Rotation History: Played as part of Fluffhead/Fluff's Travels since the late 1980s.

Discography: Appears on *Junta* (1989) as part of Fluff's Travels (Part 4: Clod).

Clod [8] [Clod]

By Anastasio

Now played as part of Fluff's Travels.

12/06/86	[10]	1a	Bowie	Bowie
05/11/87	6	1a	Sally	Peaches
08/21/87	3	1	Harry	Curtain
08/29/87	2	2	*OP2	Slave
09/12/87	2	1	TMWSIY	Slave
10/14/87	2	2	McGrupp	Makisupa
10/26/89	109	2	Dinner	ACDCBag
11/03/89	4	1	Split&Melt	BundleJoy
>> 12/31/97	**828 (as a stand-alone song)**			

COLONEL FORBIN'S ASCENT

Inspiration: A Gamehendge song that chronicles Colonel Forbin's trek up the highest mountain in Gamehendge in search of the prophet Icculus, who is said to live atop it. It is followed in the Gamehendge narrative by Famous Mockingbird or, on special occasions, Icculus.

Musical Evolution and History: The music to Forbin's is pretty much the same now as it was in the 1980s, but the big change came on spring tour 1992 when Trey started adding complex narratives (known as the "Forbin's rap") to all performances of this song, between Forbin's and Famous Mockingbird. Along with Harpua, Forbin's is the other place to expect a trippy tale from Trey, who has taken numerous audiences on trips to Gamehendge or beyond. Virtually every Forbin's rap since 1992 is worth hearing.

Rotation History: Once a fairly common treat back in 1992, 1993, and 1994, Forbin's has become a real rarity from 1995 on, with only six total performances over the past three years. That has led some fans to consider any show with Forbin's as a special one, and Trey has responded with some particularly timely narratives, like the David Byrne Icculus on 10/31/96 and the appearance of the Merry Pranksters on 8/14/97.

Discography: Has not yet appeared on a Phish album, and likely never will, as Trey has avowed to keep Gamehendge songs out of all commercial projects for eternity.

Colonel Forbin's Ascent [96] [Forbin's]

By Anastasio

03/12/88	[32]	1a	ACDCBag	Mockbird
03/21/88	1	1a	IDK	Mockbird
03/31/88	1	2	Lizards	Mockbird
06/21/88	11	1	Lizards	Mockbird
07/11/88	1	1	Bold	Mockbird
07/23/88	2	1	Jam	Mockbird
07/24/88	1	1	FunkBitch	Mockbird
09/08/88	5	1	ACDCBag	Mockbird
10/12/88	3	1	Wilson	Mockbird
11/11/88	4	1	Possum	Mockbird
01/26/89	2	1a	Icculus	Mockbird
02/05/89	2	1	Curtis	Mockbird
02/18/89	4	1	*OP1	Mockbird
02/24/89	1	1	Foam	Mockbird
03/03/89	1	2	WalkAway	Mockbird
05/06/89	21	1	ACDCBag	Mockbird
05/28/89	14	1	Antelope	Mockbird
08/23/89	15	2	Antelope	Mockbird
08/26/89	1	1	Fluffhead	Mockbird
10/20/89	11	1	BundleJoy	Mockbird
10/22/89	2	1	La Grange	Mockbird
10/31/89	3	2	Reba	Mockbird
11/03/89	2	1	*OP1	Mockbird
11/30/89	7	2	Possum	Mockbird
01/28/90	22	1	Carolina	Mockbird
02/25/90	15	1	MSO	Mockbird
03/09/90	6	1	Bouncing	Mockbird
04/07/90	7	2	Golgi	Mockbird
04/20/90	8	1	Bouncing	Mockbird
10/07/90	37	1	Destiny	Mockbird
11/02/90	6	2	Suzie	Mockbird
11/26/90	8	2	Uncle Pen	Mockbird
12/28/90	5	1	Llama	Mockbird
02/08/91	7	1	BurAlive	Mockbird
03/16/91	22	1	Rocky Top	Mockbird
03/23/91	4	1	Possum	Mockbird
04/04/91	6	1	Llama	Mockbird
04/15/91	6	1	Chalkdust	Mockbird
04/21/91	5	2	Landlady	Mockbird
05/02/91	5	1	Landlady	Mockbird
05/04/91	2	2	Llama	Mockbird
05/16/91	5	1	Divided	Mockbird
07/14/91	7	1	MSO	Mockbird
10/13/91	25	1	Landlady	Mockbird
10/27/91	8	2	Llama	Mockbird
11/02/91	5	1	Bouncing	Mockbird
11/13/91	7	2	Bowie	Mockbird
11/20/91	5	1	Possum	Mockbird
12/07/91	9	1	Foam	Mockbird
03/19/92	9	1	Dinner	Mockbird
03/24/92	3	1	Llama	Mockbird
03/31/92	6	1	Llama	Mockbird
04/16/92	11	1	Maze	Icculus
04/21/92	4	2	Dinner	Mockbird
04/24/92	3	1	RunJim	Icculus
05/02/92	5	1	RunJim	Icculus
05/06/92	3	1	Brother	Mockbird
05/17/92	9	1	Llama	Mockbird
11/21/92	47	1	Maze	Mockbird
11/27/92	4	1	Divided	Mockbird
12/04/92	6	1	Maze	Mockbird
12/08/92	4	1	Llama	Mockbird
12/31/92	8	2	Sparkle	Mockbird
02/07/93	5	1	Sparkle	Mockbird
02/19/93	9	1	Maze	Mockbird
02/25/93	5	1	Maze	Mockbird
03/08/93	7	1	Llama	How High
03/18/93	7	1	Maze	Mockbird
03/22/93	3	2	ACDCBag	Mockbird
03/25/93	2	2	Uncle Pen	Icculus
04/05/93	9	1	Stash	Mockbird
04/13/93	4	1	Possum	Mockbird
04/21/93	6	1	Maze	Mockbird
04/25/93	4	1	RunJim	Mockbird
05/03/93	6	1	Split&Melt	Mockbird
07/29/93	18	1	My Mind	Mockbird
08/07/93	6	1	Maze	Mockbird
08/15/93	7	1	Stash	Mockbird
12/30/93	11	1	Paul&Silas	Mockbird
04/11/94	8	2	Maze	Mockbird
04/24/94	11	2	Julius	Mockbird
05/25/94	22	1	Stash	Mockbird
06/16/94	10	2	Antelope	Kung
06/26/94	9	1	ACDCBag	Mockbird
07/08/94	8	1	ACDCBag	Mockbird
10/14/94	13	1	Rift	Mockbird
10/27/94	10	1	Maze	Mockbird
11/04/94	6	1	Bowie	Mockbird
11/17/94	5	1	Dog Faced	Mockbird
11/30/94	9	1	Reba	Mockbird
10/05/95	43	2	RunJim	Mockbird
12/01/95	35	1	Chalkdust	Mockbird
12/31/95	16	1	Maze	Mockbird
08/07/96	25	2	Free	Mockbird
10/31/96	18	1	Reba	Mockbird
08/14/97	78	2	Harry	Jam
>> 12/31/97		**27**		

CONTACT

Inspiration: A rare Mike Gordon love song, Contact fuses memorable lyrics ("The tires are the thing on your car that makes contact with the road") with heartfelt sentiment. An unusually high number of fans seem to recall Contact as one of their first positive Phish experiences. Along with Chalkdust Torture, it is the first Phish song to receive any sort of national radio airplay, as it occasionally popped up on the syndicated novelty music show "Dr. Demento."

Musical Evolution and History: Not much to speak of, as the song varies little from performance to performance. On 7/30/93, the band led off the show by playing Contact from backstage and strolling out slowly. In recent years, the band has sometimes led the audience in a side-to-side arm waving during the final chorus, a memorable sight, to be sure.

Rotation History: A frequent favorite turned rarity, Contact took its first break from rotation with a 62-show gap in 1992, and later surfaced only once every ten to fifteen shows through 1994 and 1995. After appearing just four times in 1996, it was performed only twice in 1997.

Discography: Appears on *Junta* (1989).

Contact [108] [Contact]

By Gordon

06/15/88	[40]	2	Sloth	Dinner
06/21/88	3	2	GTBT	Peaches
07/23/88	3	3	YEM	Harry
10/12/88	9	2	YEM	Sloth
10/29/88	1	1	La Grange	Harry
11/03/88	1	2	WhipPost	Bold
12/02/88	3	1	Divided	YEM
01/26/89	1	1a	Possum	BBFCM
02/07/89	4	2	Timber Ho	Alumni
02/18/89	2	1a	La Grange	Bowie
03/04/89	3	2	Antelope	*CL2
05/06/89	20	2	Suzie	Fire
05/13/89	6	2	Brain	*CL2
05/20/89	4	2	Foam	A-Train
05/21/89	1	1	Foam	Mike's
05/28/89	3	2	Possum	Jam
06/23/89	5	E	*OPE	GTBT
08/17/89	7	3	Alumni	Antelope
08/26/89	4	E	*OPE	Lizards
10/01/89	5	2	Brain	Split&Melt
10/07/89	2	2	Bowie	HwayHell
10/31/89	9	E	*OPE	Antelope
11/30/89	9	2	Suzie	Bowie
12/09/89	6	2	Weekpaug	BBFCM
12/15/89	1	1a	Jesus	Bowie
12/31/89	4	E	*OPE	*CLE

Original Songs Played by Year
(continued)

Famous Mockingbird

1990	9	9%
1991	16	13%
1992	14	12%
1993	16	15%
1994	11	9%
1995	3	4%
1996	2	3%
1997	0	0%

Farmhouse

1997	3	4%

Fast Enough for You

1992	9	7%
1993	17	15%
1994	13	10%
1995	8	10%
1996	4	6%
1997	1	1%

Fee

1990	22	21%
1991	31	24%
1992	25	21%
1993	33	30%
1994	39	31%
1995	14	17%
1996	10	14%
1997	3	4%

Flat Fee

1990	0	0%
1991	8	6%
1992	0	0%
1993	0	0%
1994	0	0%
1995	0	0%
1996	0	0%
1997	0	0%

Fluffhead

1990	9	9%
1991	19	15%
1992	18	15%
1993	20	18%
1994	19	15%
1995	8	10%
1996	6	9%
1997	5	6%

Foam

1990	36	35%
1991	61	48%
1992	53	44%
1993	39	35%
1994	36	29%
1995	8	10%
1996	6	9%
1997	5	6%

Fog That Surrounds

1995	22	27%
1996	0	0%
1997	0	0%

02/10/90	13	1	Carolina	Bowie
02/23/90	5	E	*OPE	IDK
02/24/90	1	2	Lawn Boy	*CL2
03/08/90	6	E	*OPE	GTBT
03/09/90	1	2	La Grange	BBFCM
03/28/90	3	1	Split&Melt	La Grange
04/04/90	1	E	*OPE	HwayHell
04/05/90	1	2	Brain	Golgi
04/25/90	13	E	*OPE	*CLE
05/04/90	5	E	*OPE	*CLE
05/19/90	7	E	*OPE	*CLE
05/24/90	2	2	HwayHell	*CL2
06/09/90	6	E	Landlady	*CLE
09/16/90	5	E	*OPE	*CLE
10/07/90	9	E	*OPE	*CLE
10/30/90	4	3	GTBT	ACDCBag
11/04/90	4	E	*OPE	HwayHell
11/16/90	3	E	*OPE	Fire
11/26/90	3	E	Fire	HwayHell
12/08/90	5	E	*OPE	HwayHell
02/09/91	9	E2	*OPE2	Rocky Top
02/15/91	2	E2	*OPE2	Golgi
03/23/91	23	2	Bowie	*CL2
04/04/91	6	E	*OPE	Uncle Pen
04/12/91	4	E	*OPE	BBFCM
07/11/91	23	E	*OPE	BBFCM
07/14/91	3	E	*OPE	BBFCM
07/15/91	1	E	Caravan	Alumni
07/21/91	4	2	ACDCBag	TweezRep
07/24/91	2	E	*OPE	BBFCM
07/27/91	3	E	Touch Me	*CLE
09/28/91	5	E	*OPE	BBFCM
10/12/91	9	1	Rocky Top	Golgi
11/02/91	14	E	*OPE	BBFCM
11/30/91	17	E	*OPE	Rocky Top
03/13/92	10	E	*OPE	Fire
04/01/92	13	2	TweezRep	Rocky Top
04/07/92	5	E	*OPE	TweezRep
04/18/92	7	E	*OPE	BBFCM
04/24/92	5	E	*OPE	BBFCM
05/05/92	7	E	*OPE	Rocky Top
11/28/92	62	E	*OPE	TweezRep
12/11/92	11	E	*OPE	GTBT
02/07/93	11	E	AmGrace	BBFCM
02/15/93	6	E	*OPE	Fire
03/13/93	18	1	Split&Melt	Llama
03/28/93	12	E	*OPE	BBFCM
04/14/93	11	E	Lngthwise	TweezRep
04/25/93	9	2	Tweezer	Uncle Pen
05/03/93	6	2	Tweezer	It's Ice
05/06/93	2	E	Adeline	TweezRep
05/30/93	4	1a	Split&Melt	Llama
07/22/93	6	2	It's Ice	Possum
07/30/93	7	1	*OP1	Llama
08/09/93	7	2	YEM	Crimes
08/28/93	13	2	YEM	Chalkdust
12/29/93	2	2	Antelope	BBFCM
04/08/94	6	E	*OPE	BBFCM
04/17/94	8	2	Maze	Golgi
04/24/94	6	2	Chalkdust	GTBT
05/12/94	12	2	Love You	BBFCM
05/21/94	7	2	Bowie	BBJ
05/25/94	3	2	Maze	BBJ
06/11/94	7	2	Maze	Frankstein
06/16/94	3	2	DWD	BBFCM
07/16/94	23	2	Harry	Chalkdust
10/09/94	3	2	Julius	Possum
10/27/94	14	2	Tweezer	BBFCM
11/18/94	12	2	Tweezer	Possum
12/28/94	18	2	Weekpaug	Llama
06/20/95	15	2	Mike's	Weekpaug
06/30/95	8	2	Mike's	Weekpaug
10/07/95	12	2	It's Ice	Frankstein
10/24/95	11	2	Antelope	Cavern
11/18/95	13	2	YEM	BBFCM
11/28/95	6	2	Antelope	BBFCM
08/10/96	45	E	*OPE	Fire
08/16/96	4	2	Simple	Weekpaug
11/11/96	20	2	Maze	Slave
11/30/96	12	2	Brother	Also Sprac
08/16/97	60	E	*OPE	Lovin Cup
12/09/97	19	2	Timber Ho	Axilla
>> 12/31/97	7			

THE CURTAIN

Inspiration: The Curtain is the only Phish song for which Marc Daubert—a friend of Trey's and occasional Phish percussionist in the early years—shares songwriting credit. Trey has commented that he considers it to be very different-sounding than most Phish tunes for this reason. At Ian's Farm on 8/21/87, Trey explained that the fall of televangelist Jimmy Swaggart inspired the lyrics to this song, but whether that's actually the case is unknown. The lyric "Chanting words from a psalm" (not "song," as is often thought) lends some credence to this.

Musical Evolution and History: In the mid to late 1980s, The Curtain continued with a slow instrumental ending Trey sometimes termed "The Curtain With." The band stopped playing it in The Curtain by 1989, and then in 1992, Trey transferred that ending instrumental section into the middle section of Rift, speeding it up for the new version of the song. But The Curtain, for its part, hasn't really changed since 1989. Though additional original lyrics for The Curtain apparently exist, they are not documented on any tapes.

Rotation History: Long a popular choice as a show or set opener, The Curtain is another song that has been neglected in recent years after receiving considerable attention in the early 1990s.

Discography: Has not yet appeared on a Phish album.

The Curtain [109] [Curtain]

By Anastasio/Daubert

08/10/87	[18]	1	Fee	*CL1
08/21/87	1	1	Clod	Light Up
08/29/87	2	2	SwingLow	McGrupp
09/12/87	2	1	YEM	BBFCM
05/15/88	14	1a	A-Train	Flat Fee
05/25/88	2	1	*OP1	Rocky Top
06/18/88	2	1	*OP1	FunkBitch
06/21/88	2	1	Suzie	Lizards
07/11/88	1	1	Suzie	FunkBitch
07/23/88	2	2	Fire	Terrapin
09/24/88	8	3	Fluffhead	ACDCBag
02/06/89	10	1	Suzie	Wilson
02/24/89	4	1	TMWSIY	Foam
03/03/89	1	1	ACDCBag	Antelope
06/30/89	42	2	ACDCBag	Slave
11/02/89	26	1	Fee	Reba
11/09/89	3	1	Ya Mar	MSO
12/16/89	13	1a	*OP1	ACDCBag
03/09/90	29	2	*OP2	Dog Log
04/18/90	13	1	Uncle Pen	Foam
10/05/90	37	2	Golgi	Ya Mar
11/04/90	10	1	ACDCBag	Bouncing
02/15/91	22	1	*OP1	Wilson
03/16/91	19	1	Bathtub	Rocky Top
03/23/91	4	1	IDK	Possum
04/04/91	6	2	*OP2	RunJim
04/19/91	9	2	Harry	Golgi
04/22/91	3	1	*OP1	RunJim
04/27/91	3	2	*OP2	Possum
05/03/91	2	2	ACDCBag	Sloth
05/12/91	5	2	PoorHeart	Golgi
05/18/91	3	2	Suzie	Stash
07/13/91	4	1	*OP1	RunJim
08/03/91	12	2	*OP2	Reba
10/11/91	12	2	*OP2	Cavern
10/17/91	4	2	*OP2	Oh Kee
10/28/91	7	1	*OP1	RunJim
11/02/91	4	1	Suzie	Llama
11/09/91	4	1	*OP1	RunJim
11/15/91	5	1	Cavern	Split&Melt
11/23/91	6	2	*OP2	Mike's
12/07/91	6	1	Stash	Cavern
03/13/92	6	1	*OP1	Split&Melt
03/24/92	6	2	*OP2	Mike's
04/03/92	8	2	*OP2	Sloth
04/19/92	12	2	*OP2	Mike's
04/23/92	3	1	Cavern	Split&Melt
04/30/92	4	1	*OP1	Split&Melt
05/05/92	4	1	Golgi	Sparkle
05/08/92	3	1	*OP1	Cavern
05/17/92	7	2	*OP2	Possum
07/01/92	8	1a	*OP1	Cavern
11/21/92	39	2	Carolina	Mike's
12/01/92	7	2	Axilla	Chalkdust
12/06/92	5	2	Suzie	Stash
12/12/92	5	2	Glide	Tweezer
12/29/92	3	2	*OP2	Tweezer
02/05/93	5	2	*OP2	Tweezer
02/21/93	13	2	Axilla	Stash
02/27/93	5	2	*OP2	Stash
03/03/93	2	2	Axilla	Split&Melt
03/06/93	2	1	Horn	Split&Melt
03/16/93	6	2	My Friend	Tweezer
03/25/93	7	2	Axilla	Sample
04/01/93	6	2	Axilla	Possum
04/16/93	9	2	Axilla	Maze
04/25/93	8	2	Wilson	Tweezer
05/03/93	6	2	ACDCBag	Tweezer
08/06/93	23	1	PoorHeart	Sample
12/30/93	19	1	Weigh	Sample
04/06/94	4	2	*OP2	DWD
04/13/94	5	2	Faht	Sample
04/25/94	11	2	*OP2	Sample
05/14/94	13	2	*OP2	Mike's
05/25/94	8	1	*OP1	Sample
06/10/94	6	2	Axilla 2	Tweezer
06/16/94	4	1	Gumbo	Dog Faced
06/19/94	3	1	Axilla2	FEFY
06/24/94	4	2	Halley's	McGrupp
06/29/94	3	1	*OP1	Sample
07/05/94	5	1	Sample	LTJP
10/09/94	11	1	FEFY	Dog Faced
10/14/94	4	2	*OP2	Tweezer
10/21/94	5	2	Sl Monkey	FEFY
11/04/94	11	2	*OP2	Mike's
11/22/94	9	2	Cry Baby	Blackbird
12/06/94	10	2	*OP2	Sample
06/17/95	18	1	Dog Faced	Stash
07/02/95	12	1	Gumbo	Julius
10/22/95	20	2	Catapult	Tweezer
11/12/95	10	2	*OP2	Tweezer
11/19/95	5	2	Also Sprac	Tweezer
11/24/95	3	1	ACDCBag	Sparkle
11/30/95	4	1	Sample	Ha Ha Ha
12/07/95	5	1	Old Home	ACDCBag
12/11/95	3	2	*OP2	Bowie
12/14/95	2	2	*OP2	Tweezer
12/28/95	4	1	Gumbo	Julius
07/07/96	9	1a	Bouncing	Tweezer
08/06/96	18	2	*OP2	Tweezer
08/17/96	7	2	*OP2	RunJim
10/22/96	6	1	*OP1	RunJim
11/06/96	9	2	Wilson	Mike's
11/11/96	4	2	Gumbo	Sample
11/23/96	8	2	*OP2	Mike's
12/01/96	5	1	CharZero	DWD
02/20/97	13	1	*OP1	Tweezer
11/28/97	57	1	*OP1	YEM
12/28/97	12	1	Cities	Sample
>> 12/31/97	3			

DAVE'S ENERGY GUIDE

Inspiration: Cowritten by Trey and his friend Dave Abrahams, Dave's Energy Guide is a short instrumental that shares many musical similarities with King Crimson's "Discipline."

Musical Evolution and History: Appears pretty much in its original form throughout the 1980s.

Rotation History: Not fully played in the 1990s, DEG has reputedly been played by Phish several times in the last couple of years. The confusion on the matter started mainly because of discussions on the Phish.Net in early 1995 about the crazy, spacey David Bowie played in Providence, RI, on 12/29/94. Some listeners swore they heard Dave's Energy Guide—or something that sounded a lot like it—woven in. Other songs believed by some to contain DEG include the Tweezer at Jones Beach on 6/29/95—probably the closest they've come in this decade to pulling out a real DEG—and Trey's solo at the end of the Mike's Song at Madison Square Garden on 12/31/95. But the music produced by Trey in each of these instances is part of his (relatively new) digital feedback loop, used in many jams since fall tour 1994. Although these do sound like DEG at times, these performances do not match with the song as it appears on tapes from the 1980s.

Discography: Has not yet appeared on a Phish album.

Dave's Energy Guide [6] [Dave's]

By Anastasio/Abrahams

10/17/85	[3]	1a	Mike's	Revol
11/23/85	2	1a	Antelope	*CL1
10/31/86	4	1	Melt Guns	Sally
04/24/87	5	1a	YEM	Alumni
04/29/87	1	2	Melt Guns	A-Train
08/06/88	35	1	Cities	Cities
>> 12/31/97	916			

DAVID BOWIE

Inspiration: A good excuse to jam, its only lyrics are "David Bowie" and "UB40," though there's no known connection between David Bowie (the performer) and Phish, though Phish did start covering his "Life on Mars?" in 1995.

Musical Evolution and History: The basic intro/jam/coda structure has been intact since its composition in the mid-1980s, but Bowie falls into that elite class of jam songs where every version is different, and the good ones are really something special. For much of the 1980s and early 1990s, Bowie jams were fiery and not too long, often making the song a good first-set closer. But on the 1994 fall tour, things began to stretch out. On 11/26/94 in Minneapolis, MN, Bowie ran for over a half hour of insanity, a version that was topped a month later on 12/29/94 in Providence, RI—a performance many think is still the best Bowie the band has

ever done. It led off with a long digital feedback loop intro (reminiscent of the Who song "Eminence Front") and the lyric section then followed with an epic musical foray into the unknown, which found its way to variations on Slave to the Traffic Light and a subtler lick stolen from McGrupp, as well as a strange "Lassie, come home" chant. This performance easily represents one of the best examples of Phish improvisation and onstage composition, and prompted the band to take a rear midset bow when all was said and done. It ranks as a must-listen for all Phish fans, and fitting as it does on one side of a tape with set-opener Guyute, many fans say it is among the Phish tapes they play most. Other fantastic Bowies include 2/19/93 Atlanta, GA, happy birthday to Fish and Moby Dick jams; 5/8/93 Durham, NH, with "Jessica" intro and "Have Mercy" in the middle; 8/13/93 Indianapolis, IN, with Ya Mar, Mango, and Magilla segments; 8/26/93 Portland, OR, for its overall intensity; 12/30/93 Portland, ME, show opener with "Dream On" teases; 6/18/94 Chicago, IL, with "Mind Left Body Jam" intro; 7/15/94 Wantagh, NY, with Jimmy Page intro, more "Jessica," and a raging jam; 10/31/94 Glens Falls, NY, intense jamming; and 11/21/95 Winston-Salem, NC, with "Take Me to the River" in the middle; and 7/30/97 Ventura, CA, with Cities.

Rotation History: Heavily played since its debut in 1986, and one of the few songs which seem to work anywhere in either set. It still, however, often serves as a first-set closer, as it has since its debut.

Discography: Appears on *Junta* (1989).

David Bowie [267] [Bowie]

By Anastasio

10/31/86	[9]	2	Peaches	Mercy
12/06/86	1	1a	ACDCBag	Flufhead
04/24/87	4	1a	I am H2	Reagan
08/09/87	3	2	*OP2	YEM
08/10/87	1	2	Icculus	Jesus
08/21/87	1	3	Makisupa	Jam
09/27/87	5	1	*OP1	FunkBitch
10/14/87	1	2	*OP2	ACDCBag
02/07/88	4	1a	IDK	ACDCBag
03/11/88	2	1	Lizards	*CL1
06/20/88	9	2	Curtis	*CL2
07/24/88	5	2	Cities	*CL2
09/24/88	7	2	*OP2	Lizards
10/12/88	1	1	Golgi	Lizards
11/03/88	2	2	Harpua	*CL2
11/05/88	1	1	Alum	*CL1
11/11/88	1	1	Mockbird	*CL1
02/05/89	4	1	Corrina	La Grange
02/06/89	1	E	*OPE	*CLE
02/18/89	3	1a	Contact	*CL1
03/03/89	2	2	A-Train	*CL2
04/15/89	10	1	Foam	*CL1
04/20/89	2	1	Foam	*CL1
05/06/89	9	1	Mockbird	*CL1
05/13/89	6	2	*OP2	Suzie
05/20/89	4	2	A-Train	Golgi
05/26/89	2	2	*OP2	Mango
06/23/89	7	2	Possum	*CL2
08/19/89	9	2	Curtis	Undone
08/26/89	2	2	Foam	*CL2
09/09/89	4	2	MSO	*CL1
10/07/89	3	1	ACDCBag	Contact
10/21/89	5	2	Dog Log	*CL1
10/26/89	2	2	No Dogs	*CL2
10/31/89	2	2	YEM	Wilson
11/16/89	7	2	Tela	*CL2
11/30/89	2	2	Contact	*CL2
12/09/89	6	1	Rocky Top	Lawn Boy
12/15/89	1	1a	Contact	*CL1
02/09/90	16	2	Curtis	*CL2
02/10/90	1	1	Contact	*CL1
02/25/90	7	1	Bouncing	Satin Doll
03/07/90	4	1	Lizards	*CL1
03/11/90	3	2	ACDCBag	*CL2
04/05/90	4	1	Ya Mar	Carolina
04/07/90	2	1	Weekpaug	MSO
04/18/90	6	2	Jaeger	*CL2
04/25/90	5	1	MSO	*CL1
05/06/90	6	2	Esther	Terrapin
05/13/90	6	1	Divided	*CL1
06/05/90	7	1	A-Train	Lawn Boy
09/15/90	7	1	Asse Fest	Golgi
09/22/90	4	1	IDK	*CL1
10/04/90	3	1	Uncle Pen	*CL1
10/06/90	2	1a	Brain	Carolina
10/30/90	5	2	BurAlive	*CL2
11/02/90	2	2	IDK	*CL2
11/04/90	2	1	MSO	*CL1
11/17/90	4	1	Suzie	*CL1
11/24/90	1	1	Suzie	*CL1
11/26/90	1	1	Donna	Divided
12/07/90	3	2	No Good	*CL2
12/29/90	3	1	Esther	Lawn Boy
02/01/91	2	1	Bouncing	*CL1
02/03/91	2	2	*OP2	Sqirm Coil
02/08/91	2	1	Guelah	*CL1
02/15/91	3	2	*OP2	Bathtub
02/21/91	4	2	Uncle Pen	*CL2
02/27/91	5	2	Sqirm Coil	Lawn Boy
03/01/91	2	2	Love You	*CL2
03/06/91	2	1	Bouncing	*CL1
03/13/91	4	1	Sqirm Coil	*CL1
03/17/91	3	1	Lizards	*CL2
03/23/91	3	2	Cavern	Contact
03/28/91	1	1a	MSO	Sqirm Coil
04/04/91	5	2	Guelah	Lawn Boy
04/16/91	7	1	Tela	*CL1
04/21/91	4	2	IDK	*CL2
05/02/91	5	1	Cavern	Adeline
05/10/91	4	1	*OP1	Cavern
05/12/91	2	2	*OP2	Bathtub
05/18/91	3	2	Guelah	Terrapin
07/12/91	3	1	Cavern	*CL1
07/19/91	5	1	Bouncing	Fee
07/20/91	1	1	MSO	*CL2
07/24/91	3	2	Guelah	Jesus
09/26/91	6	1	Foam	*CL1
10/04/91	6	1	Magilla	*CL1
10/11/91	4	2	Foam	Mango
10/13/91	2	2	Love You	*CL2
10/17/91	2	2	Suzie	Lawn Boy
10/24/91	4	1	TMWSIY	*CL1
10/28/91	3	1	Fee	Carolina
10/31/91	2	2	MSO	Horn
11/07/91	4	2	Horn	A-Train
11/13/91	5	2	*OP2	Forbin's
11/19/91	4	2	Cavern	*CL2
11/24/91	5	1	IDK	*CL1
12/04/91	2	1	Bouncing	*CL1
03/06/92	5	1	All Things	*CL1
03/12/92	3	2	Uncle Pen	Rosie
03/19/92	4	1	All Things	*CL1
03/21/92	2	2	All Things	Weigh
03/24/92	1	1	Landlady	*CL1
03/26/92	2	1	NICU	*CL1
03/28/92	2	1	Landlady	Glide
04/01/92	3	1	Landlady	Carolina
04/05/92	3	2	Landlady	Love You
04/09/92	3	2	Suzie	TMWSIY
04/13/92	2	1	A-Train	*CL2
04/17/92	3	1	Catapult	*CL1
04/21/92	3	1	Bouncing	*CL1
04/24/92	3	2	*OP2	Cavern
04/29/92	2	1	A-Train	*CL1
05/02/92	3	2	Glide	Tela
05/08/92	5	1	Bouncing	Memories
05/12/92	3	1	Horn	*CL1
05/16/92	3	1	Cavern	*CL1
06/27/92	7	1a	Uncle Pen	*CL1
07/09/92	4	1a	Guelah	Glide
07/16/92	6	1	Rift	*CL1
07/19/92	3	1a	RunJim	Adeline
07/22/92	2	1a	Cavern	*CL1
07/27/92	4	1a	All Things	Horn
08/02/92	5	1a	Suzie	Cavern
08/17/92	4	1	Bouncing	*CL1
08/20/92	2	1a	Sqirm Coil	Adeline
11/20/92	10	1	Walk Line	*CL1
11/23/92	3	1	Memories	*CL1
11/27/92	2	2	Walk Line	Horse
12/01/92	3	2	Dinner	*CL2
12/04/92	3	2	Suzie	Esther
12/07/92	3	2	Fee	Love You
12/11/92	3	1	Memories	*CL1
12/13/92	2	1	IDK	*CL1
12/30/92	3	1	Timber Ho	*CL1
02/03/93	2	1	Guelah	*CL1
02/05/93	2	1	Reba	*CL1
02/09/93	3	1	*OP1	Bouncing
02/11/93	2	1	Lawn Boy	*CL1
02/13/93	2	1	*OP1	Bouncing
02/17/93	2	2	Landlady	Glide
02/19/93	2	1	PoorHeart	*CL1
02/22/93	3	1	IDK	*CL1
02/25/93	2	1	IDK	*CL1
03/02/93	3	1	IDK	*CL1
03/08/93	4	1	Glide	*CL1
03/12/93	2	1	Silent	*CL1
03/14/93	2	2	Halley's	Curtis
03/18/93	3	1	IDK	*CL1
03/22/93	3	1	Sparkle	*CL1
03/27/93	4	1	IDK	*CL1
03/31/93	3	1	IDK	*CL1
04/05/93	4	1	Mockbird	*CL1
04/10/93	2	1	Lawn Boy	*CL1
04/20/93	7	1	Lawn Boy	*CL1
04/27/93	6	1	Sparkle	*CL1
05/01/93	3	1	Glide	*CL1
05/08/93	6	2	*OP2	Mercy
07/15/93	3	2	*OP2	Horse
07/17/93	2	1	Oh Kee	*CL1
07/25/93	6	1	IDK	*CL1
07/30/93	4	2	Sqirm Coil	*CL2
08/08/93	6	1	IDK	*CL1
08/13/93	4	1	Horn	*CL1
08/17/93	4	2	Also Sprac	Horse
08/21/93	2	2	Lawn Boy	Brain
08/26/93	3	2	Also Sprac	Life Boy
12/30/93	4	1	*OP1	Weigh
04/08/94	5	2	BBJ	Suzie
04/13/94	4	2	A-Train	PurplRain
04/17/94	4	2	*OP2	Wolfman's
04/22/94	4	1	Silent	*CL1
04/24/94	2	2	Demand	Mango
04/30/94	4	2	Wilson	Wolfman's
05/03/94	2	2	*OP2	If I Could
05/06/94	2	2	Bike	*CL2
05/10/94	3	2	Nellie	*CL2
05/14/94	3	1	Ginseng	*CL1
05/21/94	5	2	Sample	Contact
05/27/94	5	1	Bouncing	If I Could
05/29/94	2	1	IDK	*CL1
06/10/94	2	1	Demand	Lizards
06/14/94	3	2	Demand	If I Could
06/18/94	3	2	Peaches	Horn
06/23/94	4	2	Frankstein	Mango
06/29/94	4	1	Catapult	IDK
07/01/94	2	2	*OP2	If I Could
07/03/94	2	1	Axilla 2	*CL1
07/06/94	2	1	Carolina	*CL1
07/10/94	3	2	Sample	Glide
07/15/94	3	2	LTJP	Bouncing
10/09/94	4	2	*OP2	Bouncing
10/12/94	2	2	Peaches	Bouncing
10/18/94	5	2	*OP2	Horse
10/22/94	3	2	Peaches	Horse
10/26/94	3	2	Rosie	*CL2
10/28/94	2	2	Also Sprac	Lizards
10/31/94	2	3	*OP3	Bouncing
11/04/94	3	1	Bouncing	Forbin's
11/14/94	3	2	Peaches	YSZahov
11/17/94	2	2	Also Sprac	Manteca
11/20/94	3	2	Also Sprac	Glide
11/26/94	4	2	Halley's	Adeline
12/02/94	4	2	Chalkdust	BurAlive
12/08/94	5	2	Adeline	Golgi
12/29/94	4	2	Guyute	Halley's
06/09/95	6	2	Cavern	AArmy
06/13/95	2	2	*OP2	Lizards

Original Songs Played by Year *(continued)*

Fooled by Images

1997	1	1%

Free

1995	31	38%
1996	17	24%
1997	13	17%

Ghost

1997	28	36%

Glide

1991	10	8%
1992	34	28%
1993	30	27%
1994	20	16%
1995	3	4%
1996	2	3%
1997	1	1%

Glide II

1995	1	1%
1996	0	0%
1997	0	0%

Golgi

1990	28	27%
1991	63	50%
1992	41	34%
1993	47	43%
1994	42	34%
1995	6	7%
1996	10	14%
1997	4	5%

Guelah

1991	44	35%
1992	42	35%
1993	41	37%
1994	18	15%
1995	6	7%
1996	11	16%
1997	3	4%

Gumbo

1990	2	2%
1991	6	5%
1992	0	0%
1993	2	2%
1994	9	7%
1995	10	12%
1996	8	11%
1997	7	9%

Guyute

1994	19	15%
1995	8	10%
1996	6	9%
1997	11	14%

Ha Ha Ha

1995	13	16%
1996	2	3%
1997	1	1%

06/15/95	2	2	Ha Ha Ha	Str Design
06/19/95	3	2	Simple	Mango
06/24/95	4	2	Halley's	Life Boy
06/29/95	4	2	Free	Str Design
07/03/95	4	2	Timber Ho	ACDCBag
09/27/95	1	2	ACDCBag	Billy
10/02/95	4	1	Tela	*CL1
10/05/95	2	2	Cavern	Life Boy
10/08/95	3	2	Dog Faced	Keyboard
10/15/95	4	1	I'm Blue	*CL1
10/21/95	4	2	Also Sprac	Life Boy
10/27/95	4	2	Also Sprac	Dog Faced
10/29/95	2	2	Makisupa	Mango
11/11/95	4	2	Also Sprac	Suzie
11/16/95	4	2	DayinLife	Life Boy
11/21/95	3	2	Simple	Glide
11/25/95	3	1	DayinLife	Billy
12/01/95	4	2	Suspicious	*CL2
12/05/95	3	1	Esther	I'm Blue
12/11/95	4	2	Curtain	Mango
12/15/95	3	2	Also Sprac	Adeline
12/30/95	5	1	Suzie	Simple
04/26/96	2	1a	DayinLife	*CL1
06/06/96	1	2	CharZero	Fee
07/05/96	2	1a	Scent	*CL1
07/10/96	4	1a	Waste	HelloBaby
07/12/96	2	3	*OP3	Free
07/17/96	3	1a	Sample	Ya Mar
08/04/96	9	2	Sample	Adeline
08/13/96	6	2	Adeline	*CL2
08/16/96	2	1	Halley's	*CL1
10/17/96	3	2	SSB	*CL2
10/21/96	3	2	Silent	*CL2
10/29/96	6	1	PoorHeart	*CL1
11/06/96	5	1	Billy	*CL1
11/09/96	3	2	*OP2	DayinLife
11/16/96	5	1	Old Home	Lawn Boy
11/19/96	2	2	*OP2	DayinLife
11/24/96	3	2	Sparkle	DayinLife
12/04/96	6	1	Lizards	*CL1
12/29/96	3	2	*OP2	DayinLife
02/13/97	3	1	Love Me	*CL1
02/16/97	2	2	Steep	Lovin Cup
02/20/97	3	1	Circus	TweezRep
02/23/97	3	1	Frankstein	*CL1
02/28/97	3	2	Frankstein	Love Me
03/18/97	3	2	Caspian	Love Me
06/14/97	2	2	Waste	Cavern
06/20/97	3	2	*OP2	Ghost
07/02/97	8	E2	*OPE2	*CLE2
07/21/97	7	2	Magilla	Wading
07/26/97	4	2	Timber Ho	Harry
07/30/97	2	2	Free	Bouncing
08/10/97	7	2	RockaW	*CL2
11/16/97	8	E	*OPE	*CLE
11/29/97	8	1	Water	*CL1
12/03/97	3	2	*OP2	Possum
12/29/97	9	2	DWD	Possum
>> 12/31/97		**2**		

DEAR MRS. REAGAN

Inspiration: Like Nancy Reagan—the song's topic and target—this one is a relic of the 1980s. Performed as sort of a Dylan parody in the mid-1980s, it contains what are clearly the most political Phish lyrics ever to reach the audience's ears, and questions Madam Nancy for her stance on drugs.

Musical Evolution and History: None to speak of, as the song was more lyric-based than music-oriented.

Rotation History: Played in the mid-1980s, gone by 1988. Should Phish ever return it to the stage, it would represent the ultimate breakout.

Discography: Has yet to appear on a Phish album.

Dear Mrs. Reagan [7] [Reagan]

By Anastasio

04/01/86	[6]	2	Alumni	*CL2
04/15/86	1	1a	ACDCBag	PrepHipp
04/24/87	7	1a	Bowie	Slave
08/10/87	4	2	Tush	*CL2
09/12/87	5	1	Wilson	Golgi
02/07/88	6	1a	Peaches	IDK
06/15/88	12	2	WhipPost	*CL2
>> 12/31/97	**926**			

DEMAND

Inspiration: Unclear.

Musical Evolution and History: The album version of this song as it appears on *Hoist* is actually an amalgam of three different songs: Demand, Split Open and Melt (the *Hoist* version includes a live recording of Split Open from 4/21/93 in Columbus, OH, which kicks in after the first car sound effects), and Yerushalayim Schel Zahav, the Hebrew prayer which appears at the very end of *Hoist*. In concert, the song ends where the car sound effects begin on the album, except for the version played at the GameHoist show on 6/26/94, which includes the Melt and Yerushalayim jams. In interviews, band members have called it *Hoist*'s avant-garde song, and it has also been likened to Broadway show tunes.

Rotation History: Played only nine times in its debut year of 1994 (including twice into Split Open and Melt itself, on 4/14/94 and 5/26/94) it's appeared even less since then. After making a brief cameo appearance in 1996 on 11/14/96 in Ames, IA, it hasn't appeared since.

Discography: Appears on *Hoist* (1994).

Demand [14] [Demand]

By Anastasio/Marshall

04/09/94	[619]	2	BBJ	Mike's
04/14/94	4	1	Rift	Split&Melt
04/24/94	9	2	*OP2	Bowie
05/22/94	20	1	*OP1	Sloth
05/26/94	3	1	Cavern	Split&Melt
06/10/94	5	1	Nellie	Bowie
06/14/94	3	2	Frankstein	Bowie
06/24/94	8	1	*OP2	Antelope
06/26/94	2	2	Dog Faced	S&M Jam
10/08/95	97	1	ACDCBag	Sparkle
10/15/95	4	1	IDK	Llama
10/24/95	6	1	Silent	Maze
12/07/95	26	1	ACDCBag	Rift
11/14/96	64	2	Life Mars	Antelope
>> 12/31/97	**96**			

DESTINY UNBOUND

Inspiration: Another Mike Gordon song that tells a story, this one's sort of a love story about a fictional couple named Highway Jill and Highway Bill.

Musical Evolution and History: Debuted in September 1990, the song was reworked several times until it settled into a sharp, solid groove in fall 1991. Unfortunately, at that point, the band decided to retire it, reportedly because they feared it sounded too much like a Dead song, or because they just didn't like it. On its final twelve appearances, it followed Landlady.

Rotation History: Last played on 11/15/91. The band apparently promised to bring it back if the audience all yelled the song's first line in unison, but despite an incredible attempt to coordinate this effort at Red Rocks in August 1996—and again on the 1997 fall tour in Hampton, VA, and Worcester, MA—the band hasn't yet obliged (though the attempt on 11/22/97 at Hampton did spark a funny human sacrifice dialogue with Trey). It seems as though the band just doesn't want to play this song, or is having fun at fans' expense. Trey apparently told fans in Europe during summer 1996 that Destiny Unbound wouldn't be played again "for a long time."

Discography: Has not yet appeared on a Phish album.

Destiny Unbound [23] [Destiny]

By Gordon

09/14/90	[223]	2	Lizards	Fire
09/22/90	5	2	Tweezer	Fee
10/04/90	3	1	Lizards	Sloth
10/07/90	3	1	Landlady	Forbin's
12/29/90	21	2	Bouncing	Antelope
02/02/91	3	1	Stash	YEM
02/03/91	1	1	Esther	Reba
02/07/91	1	2	Sloth	YEM
02/14/91	3	1	Reba	Cavern
02/26/91	9	2	Landlady	Possum
03/15/91	10	2	Cavern	IDK
03/22/91	4	1	Landlady	Bouncing
04/11/91	10	2	Landlady	Mike's
04/19/91	6	2	Landlady	MSO
04/22/91	3	2	Landlady	Sqirm Coil
05/12/91	10	1	Landlady	Llama
09/26/91	21	2	Landlady	Mike's
10/03/91	5	2	Landlady	BurAlive
10/06/91	3	2	Landlady	Harry
10/15/91	5	1	Landlady	YEM
10/27/91	7	1	Landlady	A-Train
11/01/91	4	1	Landlady	Sqirm Coil
11/15/91	10	2	Landlady	Harry
>> 12/31/97	**596**			

DINNER AND A MOVIE

Inspiration: The Dude of Life penned this lyrically repetitive song, which simply says, "Let's go out to dinner and see a movie," over and over again. Despite the song's simple structure, Trey has recently said that he feels it is one of the few songs they got right on *Junta*.

Musical Evolution and History: The earliest versions of this song start with lyrics, but by 1989, Trey added the musical introduction that is still heard today.

Rotation History: A very common choice in 1990 and 1991 (when it was often paired with Bouncing around the Room, a combination that still surfaces now and then), Dinner and a Movie has appeared much less often in recent years—only once in 1996 and once in 1997.

Discography: Appears on *Junta* (1989).

Dinner and a Movie [108] [Dinner]

By Anastasio/Dude of Life

11/19/87	[27]	3	*OP3	Curtis
03/11/88	4	2	Fluffhead	Harry
03/21/88	2	1a	Possum	IDK
06/15/88	7	2	Contact	A-Train
07/23/88	6	3	Harry	Slave
08/06/88	4	1	FunkBitch	Fire
02/07/89	15	1	Makisupa	ACDCBag
08/26/89	55	3	Suzie	Antelope
10/01/89	5	2	Reba	Fluffhead
10/06/89	1	1a	Bold	Alumni
10/07/89	1	2	*OP2	Possum
10/20/89	4	2	WalkAway	IDK
10/26/89	3	2	*OP2	Clod
12/09/89	17	1	*OP1	La Grange
02/09/90	17	2	*OP2	Ya Mar
02/10/90	1	1	*OP1	Oh Kee
02/15/90	1	1	Divided	Caravan
02/17/90	2	1a	Suzie	Caravan
02/23/90	2	1	Rocky Top	Ya Mar
03/03/90	5	2	*OP2	Caravan
03/08/90	2	1	*OP1	YEM
03/11/90	2	2	Bouncing	A-Train
04/06/90	5	1	Ya Mar	Oh Kee
04/13/90	6	1	FunkBitch	Bouncing
04/20/90	3	1	Cavern	Bouncing
04/22/90	2	2	*OP2	Bouncing
04/25/90	1	2	La Grange	Bouncing
04/26/90	1	1	Uncle Pen	Bouncing
04/28/90	1	1	Uncle Pen	Bouncing
04/29/90	1	1	YEM	Bouncing
05/13/90	7	1	ACDCBag	Bouncing
05/19/90	2	2	Fee	Bouncing
05/24/90	2	2	Foam	Possum
05/31/90	1	1a	YEM	Bouncing
06/01/90	1	1a	Suzie	Fee
06/05/90	1	2	Caravan	Bouncing
06/07/90	1	2	MSO	Bouncing
06/09/90	2	1	Reba	Bouncing
09/14/90	3	1	Stash	IDK
09/16/90	2	1a	*OP1	Bouncing
09/28/90	2	2	Gumbo	YEM
10/01/90	1	1	Magilla	Bouncing
10/06/90	3	1a	Sqirm Coil	Bouncing
10/12/90	3	1	YEM	Bouncing
11/03/90	5	1	*OP1	Bouncing
11/08/90	2	2	Oh Kee	Bouncing
11/30/90	6	1	Esther	Bouncing
12/08/90	3	2	Asse Fest	Bouncing
12/29/90	2	2	Jesus	Bouncing
02/02/91	3	1	Guelah	Esther
02/15/91	6	1	Sloth	Magilla
02/21/91	4	1	Reba	Split&Melt
02/26/91	4	2	RunJim	Stash
03/01/91	3	1	Tweezer	Bouncing
03/15/91	7	1	Stash	Bouncing
04/05/91	12	2	Sloth	Harry
04/11/91	2	1	Magilla	Bouncing
04/19/91	6	1	FunkBitch	Bouncing
05/10/91	11	1	Ya Mar	Sloth
05/12/91	2	1	Bouncing	Stash
05/16/91	1	2	RunJim	Bouncing
05/18/91	2	E	*OPE	RunJim
05/25/91	1	1a	Reba	Sloth
07/11/91	1	2	*OP2	Cavern
07/12/91	1	1	*OP1	Bouncing
07/14/91	2	2	Gumbo	Bouncing
07/15/91	1	1a	Landlady	Stash
07/20/91	3	2	Caravan	Flat Fee
07/23/91	2	2	Adeline	Gumbo
07/26/91	3	2	Stash	YEM
09/27/91	5	2	Mango	Oh Kee
10/12/91	10	1	A-Train	Brother
10/18/91	4	2	Guelah	Mike's
10/24/91	3	2	Slave	Bouncing
10/28/91	3	2	Wilson	Stash

10/31/91	2	2	Horn	Tube
11/08/91	5	1	Landlady	Stash
11/12/91	3	2	*OP2	Stash
11/14/91	2	2	*OP2	Antelope
11/19/91	3	2	Reba	Cavern
11/22/91	3	1	Lawn Boy	Stash
12/04/91	4	1	Sqirm Coil	Bouncing
03/13/92	9	1	Maze	Divided
03/19/92	3	1	Silent	Forbin's
03/21/92	2	1	Silent	Sqirm Coil
03/27/92	4	2	Bathtub	Magilla
03/31/92	3	2	Cavern	My Friend
04/06/92	5	2	*OP2	Bathtub
04/18/92	8	2	TMWSIY	Harry
04/21/92	2	2	*OP2	Forbin's
04/25/92	4	2	All Things	Harry
05/03/92	5	2	Rosie	Bouncing
05/12/92	7	1	It's Ice	Bouncing
07/16/92	20	1	Wilson	Bouncing
11/20/92	30	2	FEFY	Harry
12/01/92	8	2	Love You	Bowie
12/11/92	9	2	*OP2	Mike's
02/21/93	22	1	Esther	Bouncing
04/12/93	34	2	*OP2	Tweezer
04/24/93	10	2	Bathtub	Mound
08/09/93	33	2	*OP2	Tweezer
05/21/94	54	2	*OP2	Sample
06/13/94	11	1	Wolfman's	Stash
10/22/94	38	2	Silent	Tweezer
11/18/95	93	1	*OP1	Bouncing
11/28/95	6	1	Stash	Bouncing
08/06/96	43	1	Lizards	Horn
03/01/97	59	2	Carini	Mike's
>> 12/31/97	**65**			

DIRT

Inspiration: One of the new class of Tom Marshall lyrics that express an urge to live outside of mainstream society, Dirt expresses a desire to "live beneath the dirt . . . where I'll be free of push and shove / like all those swarming up above."

Musical Evolution and History: New on summer tour 1997, this upbeat ballad with a memorable guitar line has gained strength with each performance as the band works out the jam. But as a composed piece, individual performances haven't varied much from one to the next.

Rotation History: Played frequently on summer and fall tours in 1997.

Discography: Has not yet appeared on a Phish album.

Dirt [20] [Dirt]

By Anastasio/Marshall

06/14/97	[905]	1	NICU	Talk
06/16/97	1	2	Wading	Harry
06/21/97	3	1a	Taste	Theme
06/22/97	1	1a	Stash	Uncle Pen
07/01/97	5	1	Saw It	Reba
07/09/97	5	1	Split&Melt	Taste
07/21/97	3	1	Piper	Ginseng
07/23/97	2	1	Julius	NICU
07/26/97	2	1	CTB	YEM
07/29/97	1	1	Gumbo	Sparkle
07/31/97	2	1	Limb	Maze
08/03/97	2	1	Blow	Vultures
08/08/97	2	1	Lizards	It's Ice
08/10/97	2	1	DWD	CTB
08/17/97	5	3	Guyute	Scent
11/19/97	5	1	Llama	Limb
11/26/97	4	1	McGrupp	Split&Melt
12/02/97	4	1	Divided	Taste
12/11/97	6	1	Maze	Limb
12/29/97	4	1	Fluffhead	Antelope
>> 12/31/97	**2**			

DIVIDED SKY

Inspiration: A Gamehendge song which is not part of The Man Who Stepped into Yesterday recording but, as described in the liner notes to *Junta*, is part of an ancient Gamehendge ritual of the Lizard people, in which three chosen individuals climb the rhombus in the middle of a vast field to pay homage to Icculus by way of song. That's a wink to Trey's own childhood, when he and his Princeton, NJ, friends would climb a rhombus to write music. He has said he doesn't like the version on *Junta*.

Musical Evolution and History: Trey lifted the song's melody from an Anastasio family musical, "Gus the Christmas Dog," but the song is much more than that. Like Phish's best songs, Divided Sky offers the band a platform of structure from which to improvise—most of the first few minutes, through "the note" (when Trey pauses, staring up at the ceiling), are composed, as is the end jam, with the middle section improvised around preset themes. Early versions of Divided Sky had an ending like the song's opening, but that was changed by the late 1980s to the form the song has today. The strength of the song's jam varies by performance; some of the most outstanding ones through Phishtory include 7/21/91 Parksville, NY, with the Giant Country Horns; 11/19/92 Colchester, VT, with "Those Were the Days" teases; and 10/31/94 Glens Falls, NY, pure emotional power.

Rotation History: For most of the 1990s, Divided Sky could be counted on to appear at least every several shows, but in 1997 that changed. Reportedly including Divided Sky in the group of "25 retired songs" for summer tour 1997, the band only played it once, on 8/2/97 at the Gorge, a slightly rusty version. Similarly, the fall tour only contained one Sky, on 12/2/97 in Philadelphia, PA.

Discography: Appears on *Junta* (1989), a partially acoustic version, and also on their "White Album."

The Divided Sky [268] [Divided]

By Anastasio

08/09/87	[17]	2	Ya Mar	Fluffhead
08/10/87	1	1	Quinn	GTBT
08/21/87	1	1	Peaches	FunkBitch
08/29/87	2	2	ACDCBag	Harpua
09/12/87	2	2	Fee	Dog Log
10/14/87	2	2	ACDCBag	McGrupp
11/19/87	2	2	Possum	BBFCM
01/30/88	1	2	Fluffhead	Curtis
02/08/88	2	2	Peaches	Lizards
03/21/88	3	1a	Sally	Boogie On
07/23/88	13	1	No Dogs	No Dogs
09/24/88	8	1	A-Train	Bold
10/29/88	2	2	WalkAway	Curtis
11/05/88	2	2	Sparks	*CL2
11/11/88	1	1	*OP1	YEM
12/02/88	1	1	A-Train	Contact
01/26/89	1	1a	A-Train	Fee
02/06/89	3	1	Golgi	OYWD
02/17/89	2	1a	Fee	Split&Melt
03/03/89	3	1	IDK	Alumni
03/30/89	3	1	McGrupp	Price
04/15/89	7	2	Mango	Split&Melt
04/20/89	2	2	*OP2	WalkAway
04/30/89	5	1	Lizards	Wilson
05/06/89	4	2	Slave	Antelope
05/09/89	4	1	Possum	*CL1
05/20/89	7	1	Wilson	IDK
05/21/89	1	1	ACDCBag	*CL1
05/28/89	3	1	*OP1	Antelope
08/19/89	14	2	A-Train	Bathtub
08/26/89	2	1	Split&Melt	YEM
09/09/89	4	1	Suzie	ACDCBag
10/14/89	6	1	ACDCBag	IDK
10/20/89	1	1	Reba	Golgi
10/22/89	2	1	Tela	IDK
10/26/89	1	1	Fee	IDK
10/31/89	2	1	ACDCBag	Fee
11/02/89	1	2	Kung	McGrupp
11/10/89	4	1	Fee	ACDCBag
11/30/89	4	1	Bathtub	Ya Mar
12/07/89	4	1	Alumni	*CL1
12/15/89	3	1a	Possum	Antelope
12/29/89	2	1	*OP1	Ya Mar
12/31/89	2	2	Split&Melt	Fee
01/27/90	4	2	Terrapin	*CL2
02/15/90	10	1	Suzie	Dinner
02/24/90	2	1	Golgi	Esther
03/01/90	2	1	Ya Mar	IDK
03/03/90	2	2	Carolina	*CL2
03/08/90	2	2	*OP2	Bathtub
04/06/90	5	1	Uncle Pen	Ya Mar
04/08/90	2	1	*OP1	FunkBitch
04/09/90	1	2	Jesus	Love You
04/12/90	2	1	Jesus	GTBT
04/20/90	4	1	A-Train	Alumni
04/22/90	2	1	*OP1	Uncle Pen
04/25/90	1	1	Brain	MSO
04/29/90	3	1a	Uncle Pen	Fluffhead
05/10/90	4	1	Bouncing	Tweezer
05/13/90	3	1	Uncle Pen	Bowie
05/23/90	3	1	*OP1	Ya Mar
05/31/90	2	1a	Uncle Pen	Oh Kee
06/01/90	1	1a	YEM	Slave
06/05/90	1	2	Adeline	Caravan
06/07/90	1	2	Uncle Pen	Love You
06/08/90	1	1	YEM	*CL1
06/16/90	2	1	ACDCBag	Wilson
09/13/90	1	1	Landlady	Foam
09/15/90	2	1	BurAlive	Paul&Silas
09/22/90	4	1	MSO	Tela
09/28/90	1	2	YEM	*CL2
10/07/90	5	1	*OP1	Uncle Pen
10/12/90	2	2	Terrapin	Paul&Silas
11/02/90	4	1	Bouncing	Sloth
11/08/90	3	2	Suzie	Tweezer
11/10/90	1	2	Llama	Bike
11/16/90	1	1	Llama	Golgi
11/24/90	2	E	Lawn Boy	*CLE
11/26/90	1	1	Bowie	Makisupa
11/30/90	1	2	Gumbo	IDK
12/01/90	1	1	Llama	Foam
12/03/90	1	1	Reba	MSO
12/08/90	2	1	ACDCBag	Cavern
12/28/90	1	2	MSO	No Good
12/31/90	2	1	Suzie	IDK
02/15/91	8	1	Wilson	Spilt
02/16/91	1	1	MSO	Cavern
02/27/91	8	1	Golgi	IDK
02/28/91	1	2	Guelah	*CL2
03/01/91	1	1	Foam	Cavern
03/06/91	2	1	Cavern	Love You
03/13/91	4	1	Cavern	Esther
03/16/91	2	2	Llama	Guelah
03/23/91	4	1	Sloth	Fee
03/28/91	1	1a	Golgi	Cavern
04/04/91	5	2	MSO	Love You
04/05/91	1	1	Bouncing	Cavern
04/12/91	3	1	Uncle Pen	Guelah
04/19/91	5	1	Bouncing	Cavern
04/21/91	2	1	Wilson	Foam
05/02/91	5	2	PoorHeart	Fee
05/03/91	1	1	TMWSIY	Fee
05/16/91	6	1	Cavern	Forbin's
05/18/91	2	1	Foam	Cavern
05/25/91	1	1a	*OP1	Landlady
07/11/91	1	1	Suzie	Flat Fee

Original Songs Played by Year *(continued)*

Halley's

1990	0	0%
1991	0	0%
1992	0	0%
1993	7	6%
1994	12	10%
1995	6	7%
1996	2	3%
1997	3	4%

Harpua

1990	3	3%
1991	4	3%
1992	6	5%
1993	6	5%
1994	7	6%
1995	2	2%
1996	3	4%
1997	2	3%

Harry Hood

1990	13	13%
1991	22	17%
1992	18	15%
1993	19	17%
1994	31	25%
1995	22	27%
1996	19	27%
1997	23	29%

Horn

1990	5	5%
1991	17	13%
1992	25	21%
1993	19	17%
1994	12	10%
1995	9	11%
1996	4	6%
1997	5	6%

Horse > Silent

1992	26	21%
1993	39	35%
1994	28	23%
1995	9	11%
1996	9	13%
1997	5	6%

I Am Hydrogen

1990	53	51%
1991	49	39%
1992	35	29%
1993	25	23%
1994	14	11%
1995	2	2%
1996	3	4%
1997	5	6%

I Didn't Know

1990	24	23%
1991	36	28%
1992	26	21%
1993	33	30%
1994	15	12%
1995	10	12%
1996	6	9%
1997	2	3%

07/13/91	2	2	Guelah	Flat Fee
07/14/91	1	2	Caravan	Gumbo
07/19/91	3	2	Suzie	IDK
07/21/91	2	1	Cavern	Guelah
07/25/91	3	1	Suzie	Flat Fee
08/03/91	3	1	Sloth	Golgi
09/26/91	2	1	Bouncing	Fee
09/29/91	3	1a	Cavern	IDK
10/03/91	2	1	Fee	Cavern
10/04/91	1	1	Cavern	Guelah
10/06/91	2	1	Foam	Bouncing
10/17/91	6	1	Bouncing	Cavern
10/24/91	4	1	Ya Mar	IDK
10/28/91	3	2	*OP2	Wilson
11/01/91	3	1	Tube	Adeline
11/08/91	4	1	PoorHeart	Mango
11/13/91	4	1	Cavern	IDK
11/15/91	2	1	MSO	Lawn Boy
11/19/91	2	1	Wilson	*CL1
11/22/91	3	1	Foam	Lawn Boy
11/24/91	2	2	Tube	Cavern
11/30/91	1	1	Sparkle	Cavern
12/06/91	3	2	Horn	Tela
12/31/91	2	1	Guelah	Esther
03/06/92	1	1	Oh Kee	Guelah
03/11/92	2	1	Mound	Cavern
03/13/92	2	1	Dinner	Mound
03/17/92	2	1	IDK	Guelah
03/27/92	7	1	Sloth	Guelah
03/31/92	3	1	Wilson	Glide
04/05/92	4	1	Guelah	Wilson
04/07/92	2	1	Fee	Horse
04/12/92	2	1	Guelah	Horse
04/18/92	5	1	Wilson	Guelah
04/22/92	3	1	Guelah	Mound
05/01/92	6	1	Sloth	Guelah
05/05/92	3	1	Guelah	IDK
05/09/92	4	2	Suzie	Tela
05/18/92	7	1	Bouncing	Guelah
06/30/92	6	1a	Golgi	Guelah
07/12/92	6	1a	Bouncing	Fluffhead
07/15/92	2	2	Sloth	Esther
07/26/92	9	1a	It's Ice	Weigh
11/19/92	21	1	Mound	Esther
11/23/92	4	1	Guelah	Mound
11/27/92	2	1	Wilson	Forbin's
12/02/92	4	1	Foam	FEFY
12/05/92	3	1	Mound	Adeline
12/08/92	3	1	Guelah	Mound
12/13/92	4	1	Wilson	It's Ice
12/29/92	2	1	My Friend	Wilson
12/31/92	2	1	Wilson	Cavern
02/03/93	1	1	Wedge	IDK
02/06/93	3	1	Horn	Lawn Boy
02/10/93	3	1	Sloth	Tela
02/15/93	4	1	Guelah	Esther
02/20/93	4	1	All Things	Horse
02/26/93	5	1	Horn	IDK
03/09/93	7	1	Esther	Glide
03/16/93	4	1	IDK	McGrupp
03/21/93	4	1	Sloth	Esther
03/26/93	4	1	Fluffhead	Cavern
03/30/93	3	1	Glide	Cavern
04/02/93	3	1	Bouncing	IDK
04/09/93	3	1	It's Ice	Cavern
04/14/93	4	1	Silent	IDK
04/18/93	3	1	Sparkle	Fee
04/23/93	4	1	My Friend	Guelah
04/30/93	5	1	Silent	Cavern
05/02/93	2	1	Sparkle	Mound
05/07/93	4	1	Horn	IDK
07/15/93	4	1	Sample	Mound
07/18/93	3	1	Esther	Uncle Pen
07/22/93	2	1	Sample	Mound
07/24/93	2	1	Nellie	Guelah
07/29/93	4	1	FunkBitch	Weigh
07/31/93	2	1	Nellie	Cavern
08/06/93	3	1	Horn	Nellie
08/09/93	3	1	Nellie	Memories
08/14/93	4	1	Guelah	Horse
08/17/93	3	1	Guelah	Horse
08/20/93	1	1	*OP1	Harpua
12/29/93	7	1	Glide	Wilson
04/04/94	3	1	*OP1	Sample
04/11/94	6	1	Glide	Cavern
04/13/94	1	1	Ginseng	Golgi
04/17/94	4	1	IDK	Mound
04/22/94	4	1	Nellie	Horse
04/25/94	3	2	Sqirm Coil	Bouncing
04/29/94	2	1	Sloth	IDK
05/02/94	2	1	Glide	Suzie
05/07/94	4	1	Horn	Mound
05/10/94	2	1	Sample	Axilla 2
05/16/94	4	1	Sample	Axilla 2
05/22/94	5	1	Sloth	Glide
05/26/94	3	1	Catapult	Sample
05/29/94	3	1	*OP1	Guelah
06/13/94	4	1	Sample	Wolfman's
06/18/94	4	1	Dog Faced	Sample
06/24/94	5	1	*OP2	Wilson
06/26/94	2	1	McGrupp	*CL1
06/29/94	1	2	Life Boy	Suzie
07/02/94	3	1	Golgi	Guelah
07/08/94	4	1	McGrupp	*CL1
07/15/94	5	1	Sample	Gumbo
10/07/94	2	1	PoorHeart	Guelah
10/10/94	3	1	Sample	Horse
10/14/94	3	1	Sample	Horse
10/18/94	3	1	Guyute	AmGrace
10/22/94	3	1	Suzie	Gumbo
10/27/94	4	1	Mockbird	Horse
10/31/94	3	1	Simple	Harpua
11/03/94	2	1	Fee	Wilson
11/13/94	3	2	Suzie	Lizards
11/17/94	3	1	Wilson	Dog Faced
11/20/94	3	1	Dooley	Sample
11/23/94	2	1	Suzie	AmGrace
11/28/94	3	1	Simple	Adeline
12/03/94	4	1	Wilson	Guelah
12/07/94	3	2	Frankstein	Fee
12/10/94	3	1	Sample	Lawn Boy
12/31/94	4	1	Peaches	FunkBitch
06/09/95	4	1	My Friend	Str Design
06/17/95	6	1	*OP1	Suzie
06/22/95	3	1	Ha Ha Ha	Guelah
06/25/95	3	1	Sparkle	IDK
06/29/95	3	1	Silent	Cavern
07/02/95	3	1	Sample	Gumbo
09/29/95	4	1	Sparkle	Str Design
10/05/95	4	1	Str Design	AArmy
10/11/95	4	1	Cavern	If I Could
10/20/95	6	1	Ha Ha Ha	Fee
10/25/95	4	1	Sample	Wedge
10/31/95	4	1	Icculus	Wilson
11/09/95	1	1	TweezRep	Caspian
11/14/95	4	1	Billy	Esther
11/21/95	5	1	Caspian	LongJourn
11/28/95	4	1	IDK	Guyute
12/04/95	5	1	Gumbo	PYITE
12/12/95	6	1	Sample	Life Boy
12/16/95	3	1	Sloth	Dog Faced
12/30/95	4	1	TMWSIY	Sample
07/07/96	7	1a	Sample	Bouncing
07/12/96	4	1	Wilson	Horn
07/17/96	3	1a	*OP1	Sample
08/05/96	10	1	Guelah	Wolfman's
08/13/96	5	1	*OP1	Tube
08/16/96	2	1	Esther	Halley's
10/18/96	4	1	Str Design	Billy
10/21/96	2	1	Sloth	CharZero
11/03/96	9	2	Timber Ho	Wolfman's
11/09/96	4	1	Sloth	Horn
11/11/96	1	2	Timber Ho	Gumbo
11/15/96	3	1	Wilson	Bouncing
11/23/96	5	1	CTB	PYITE
11/29/96	3	1	CharZero	Bathtub
12/02/96	3	2	Ya Mar	Wolfman's
12/31/96	6	1	Silent	Sample
02/17/97	4	1	SSP	Wilson
07/03/97	25	1	My Soul	Beauty
08/02/97	14	1	DogsStole	Wolfman's
12/02/97	23	1	Ghost	Dirt
>> 12/31/97	**12**			

DOG FACED BOY

Inspiration: A song about remorse for lost love, this short song fit *Hoist*'s theme of having more meaningful lyrics. Of course, that didn't stop *Newsweek* magazine from mocking the line "I won't lend another hand to the worm girl of Hanoi."

Musical Evolution and History: None to speak of, as the band recorded it for *Hoist* before ever playing it in concert. However, the band did play several acoustic versions of this song in 1994, including the song's debut at the Beacon Theater in New York, NY, on 4/14/94. That version, along with several others from 1994, featured rare "emotion solos" from Fishman.

Rotation History: Played often in its debut year of 1994, and sporadically through 1995 and 1996, before taking a 109-show break and resurfacing on 12/2/97.

Discography: Appears on *Hoist* (1994).

Dog Faced Boy [34] [Dog Faced]

By Fishman/Anastasio/Gordon/Marshall

04/14/94	[623]	2	Nellie	Slave
04/18/94	4	1	Split&Melt	Oh Kee
04/24/94	5	1	Bathtub	Paul&Silas
04/25/94	1	1	Ginseng	Tela
04/29/94	2	1	IDK	Split&Melt
05/10/94	8	2	Ginseng	Nellie
05/17/94	5	1	Ginseng	Split&Melt
05/20/94	2	1	Scent	Carolina
05/22/94	2	1	Ginseng	Axilla 2
05/26/94	3	2	Ginseng	YEM
06/16/94	9	1	Curtain	Stash
06/18/94	2	1	It's Ice	Divided
06/21/94	2	2	BBFCM	Adeline
06/24/94	3	2	Llama	PoorHeart
06/26/94	2	2	Scent	Demand
07/15/94	13	2	YSZahov	Julius
10/09/94	4	1	Curtain	Split&Melt
10/16/94	6	2	Antelope	Adeline
10/21/94	3	1	Lizards	Antelope
10/26/94	4	1	Guyute	Scent
11/03/94	6	1	Split&Melt	Sparkle
11/17/94	6	1	Divided	Forbin
12/28/94	19	1	Reba	It's Ice
06/16/95	12	1	My Mind	Catapult
06/26/95	8	1	It's Ice	Possum
10/08/95	16	2	Suspicious	Bowie
10/27/95	12	2	Bowie	PoorHeart
11/10/95	5	1	It's Ice	Maze
11/14/95	3	2	Stash	Stash
11/21/95	5	1	My Friend	RunJim
12/09/95	13	1	Billy	Chalkdust
12/16/95	5	1	Divided	Julius
08/12/96	40	1	It's Ice	Taste
12/02/97	109	2	Simple	Ya Mar
>> 12/31/97	**12**			

DOG LOG

Inspiration: One of a crop of Phish dog-related songs from the 1980s, based on Trey's dog, Marley. It is, quite splendidly, a ditty about stepping in dog poop. It is the favorite Phish tune of Phish soundman Paul Languedoc, and is played often during soundchecks.

Musical Evolution and History: The song has remained pretty much unchanged since its debut in the mid-1980s, though different versions can take on different tones as the band sees fit, as several soundcheck versions in circulation among tapers indicate. It took on another life on 12/11/95 in Portland, ME, when Trey announced that they were recording an all Dog Log album. He asked that the audience be very quiet, mimicking soundcheck conditions, but then boo and hiss on cue. Later in the show, the band played a very different version of Dog Log, this time asking the audience to cheer wildly.

Rotation History: Played sporadically in 1990 and once in 1991 (on 5/4/91 in Somerville, MA), Dog Log has only been played at four shows since then, most recently in the first set of the great Stuttgart, Germany, show on 2/26/97.

Discography: Has not yet appeared on a Phish album.

Dog Log [13] [Dog Log]

By Anastasio

10/30/85	[4]	1a	Harry	Possum
04/15/86	3	1a	Mercy	Possum
12/06/86	3	1a	YEM	Tush
04/29/87	5	2	Lushngton	Melt Guns
08/21/87	4	1	*OP1	Peaches
09/12/87	4	2	Divided	Curtis
10/21/89	109	1	Lizards	Bowie
03/09/90	50	2	Curtain	Slave
05/04/91	129	2	*OP2	Llama
08/02/93	281	1	My Mind	La Grange
12/11/95	217	1	Reba	Llama
12/11/95	0	1	Llama	Tube
02/26/97	90	1	RockaW	Guitar
>> 12/31/97	**67**			

DOGS STOLE THINGS

Inspiration: As Trey described to the crowd at Virginia Beach, VA, on 7/21/97, the song is about people's pets (dogs and cats) stealing their owners' souls while the humans sleep.

Musical Evolution and History: One of the funky new crop of summer 1997 tunes, Dogs Stole Things has a brief jam segment but otherwise is pretty much unchanged from performance to performance.

Rotation History: Played frequently on summer tour 1997, but less often that fall.

Discography: Has not yet appeared on a Phish album.

Dogs Stole Things [20] [Dogs Stole]

By Anastasio/Marshall

06/13/97	[904]	1	Theme	Beauty
06/14/97	1	2	Fooled	Waste
06/16/97	1	1	Sqirm Coil	Taste
06/19/97	1	1	Limb	Theme
06/21/97	2	1a	Limb	Harry
06/24/97	2	1	Beauty	Vultures
06/25/97	1	1	Oblivious	Taste
06/27/97	1	1a	Stash	PoorHeart
07/01/97	2	1	Reba	*CL1
07/06/97	4	1	Old Home	Stash
07/10/97	2	1	*OP1	Limb
07/21/97	2	1	Ghost	Piper
07/23/97	2	1	NICU	Ginseng
07/26/97	2	1	Limb	PoorHeart
07/31/97	3	1	Ya Mar	Limb
08/02/97	1	1	Ghost	Divided
08/09/97	4	1	Taste	Reba
08/17/97	6	1	Beauty	Vultures
11/21/97	6	1	Beauty	PYITE
12/09/97	12	2	Weekpaug	Beauty
>> 12/31/97	**7**			

DON'T GET ME WRONG

Inspiration: Trey cowrote this song with Blues Traveler frontman John Popper in 1990, with Trey supplying the music and Popper the lyrics.

Musical Evolution and History: The music for this song was extracted from the original version of Reba, as it was performed in fall 1989. In those old Rebas, that instrumental section followed the lyrics, but was removed by Trey by early 1990.

Rotation History: Played three times on fall tour 1990 with Popper and Phish, but not since.

Discography: Has not yet appeared on a Phish album.

Don't Get Me Wrong [3] [Don't Get]

By Anastasio/Popper

10/06/90	[233]	E	*OPE	*CLE
10/08/90	2	1	*OP1	Landlady
12/28/90	18	2	No Good	FunkBitch
>> 12/31/97	**712**			

DOWN WITH DISEASE

Inspiration: During a two-week bout with mononucleosis, Tom Marshall wrote the lyrics to this song.

Musical Evolution and History: One of the group of songs recorded for *Hoist* before ever appearing in concert, DWD appeared briefly as the postmidnight jam in Worcester, MA, on 12/31/93 before receiving its formal concert debut on the first show of the 1994 spring tour, 4/4/94 in Burlington, VT. During that month, the song adhered more closely to its *Hoist* version, though a middle much longer than the album version was evident from the debut. It was also the first single from *Hoist*, but was not a radio hit. In short time, the band had dropped the cheesy "na na na na" refrain leading back into the final chorus when performing it live, and by that summer, the true jam potential of the song had started to shine through.

Early standout versions of the song include 4/6/94 Toronto, ON, early signs of greatness; 11/12/94 Kent, OH, with Have Mercy in the middle; and 11/30/94 Olympia, WA, a great jam. Standouts in 1995 included 6/26/95 Saratoga Springs, NY, a 20-minute jam into Free; and 12/12/95 Providence, RI, the longest Disease ever, at nearly 35 minutes. Many regarded DWD as the song of the year for 1996, as the band played many great versions, including 8/16/96 Clifford Ball, an amazing melodious jam; and 12/31/96 Boston, MA, as the New Year's jam, as balloons falling from the ceiling filled the stage. In 1997, high points included 2/17/97 Amsterdam, a wild jam with Carini and Taste in the middle; and 8/2/97 George, WA, with Tweezer and then a DWD reprise. Unfortunately, DWD can be one of the band's more inconsistent songs, as non-jammed-out versions occasionally disappoint the crowd (12/2/97 is a good example).

Rotation History: Played virtually every other show in 1994, the band seemed to have forgotten DWD by 1995, playing it only five times. But in 1996, they rediscovered the song, lavishing it with attention that continued throughout 1997.

Discography: Appears on *Hoist* (1994), with backing vocals by Rose Stone and Jean McClean.

Down with Disease [97] [DWD]

By Anastasio/Marshall

04/04/94	[615]	2	*OP2	If I Could
04/06/94	2	2	Curtain	Wolfman's
04/08/94	1	1	Silent	If I Could
04/10/94	2	1	Scent	*CL1
04/14/94	3	1	Sparkle	Glide
04/15/94	1	1	It's Ice	*CL1
04/17/94	2	1	Mound	If I Could
04/18/94	1	2	TMWSIY	BeLikeYou
04/21/94	2	1	Lizards	If I Could
04/23/94	2	1	Esther	Caravan
04/25/94	2	2	Foam	Ginseng
04/28/94	1	1a	Rift	Bouncing
05/02/94	3	1	Bouncing	It's Ice
05/03/94	1	2	Fluffhead	Harpua
05/06/94	2	1	*OP1	Oh Kee
05/08/94	2	1	Rift	Bouncing
05/12/94	2	2	Also Sprac	Horse
05/14/94	2	1	Wilson	Fee
05/16/94	1	1	Rift	Bouncing
05/19/94	2	1	Silent	Mango
05/21/94	2	1	Guelah	Mound
05/22/94	1	2	*OP2	Bouncing
05/26/94	3	2	Fluffhead	Mound
05/29/94	3	1	Halley's	Sparkle
06/09/94	1	1	Rift	It's Ice
06/11/94	2	1	Rift	It's Ice
06/14/94	2	1	Rift	Fee
06/16/94	1	2	BBJ	Contact
06/18/94	2	1	Mango	It's Ice
06/21/94	2	2	PoorHeart	My Friend
06/23/94	2	1	Bouncing	Horse
06/24/94	1	2	Carolina	*CL2
06/26/94	2	2	Julius	If I Could
06/30/94	2	1	*OP1	Gumbo
07/01/94	1	2	Fluffhead	TMWSIY
07/03/94	2	1	PoorHeart	Fee
07/05/94	1	1	Esther	Adeline
07/09/94	3	1	Scent	Horse
07/13/94	2	1	Mango	Fee
07/16/94	3	1	Golgi	N20
10/08/94	2	1	Sparkle	Guyute
10/10/94	2	2	Rift	Love You
10/13/94	2	1	All Things	IDK
10/15/94	2	1	Reba	Golgi
10/21/94	4	1	Fee	Foam
10/23/94	2	2	YEM	PurplRain
10/27/94	3	2	BBFCM	Adeline
10/29/94	2	2	*OP2	TMWSIY
11/03/94	3	1	Sparkle	*CL1
11/12/94	2	2	Fluffhead	Life Boy
11/17/94	4	1	Mockbird	*CL1
11/19/94	2	1	Golgi	Guyute
11/22/94	2	1	Bouncing	Adeline
11/30/94	5	1	Mockbird	Bouncing
12/06/94	5	1	Mound	Fluffhead
06/16/95	17	1	Halley's	Esther
06/26/95	8	2	*OP2	Free
12/01/95	48	1	BurAlive	Theme
12/12/95	8	2	Sparkle	Lizards
12/29/95	6	1	PoorHeart	Fog
07/15/96	14	2	*OP2	Maze
07/23/96	6	1	Scent	McGrupp
08/02/96	3	1	Ya Mar	Guelah
08/05/96	2	2	ASZ	It's Ice
08/10/96	3	2	Wilson	Scent
08/14/96	3	1	Wilson	Fee
08/16/96	1	3	ASZ	NICU
10/16/96	2	1	CTB	Wilson
10/19/96	3	1	Gumbo	Caspian
10/22/96	2	2	Also Sprac	Taste
10/26/96	3	2	*OP2	YEM
10/31/96	3	1	HwayHell	YEM
11/08/96	5	1	Mound	Caspian
11/13/96	3	1	*OP1	Bouncing
11/16/96	3	1	PoorHeart	Guyute
11/22/96	3	2	*OP2	Caspian
11/27/96	3	2	*OP2	Jesus
12/01/96	3	1	Curtain	Train Song
12/06/96	3	1	CTB	Frankstein
12/31/96	4	3	Auld	Suzie
02/14/97	2	2	Ya Mar	FunkBitch
02/17/97	2	2	Sqirm Coil	Carini
02/21/97	3	1	Foam	Lizards
02/25/97	3	2	My Friend	Caspian
03/01/97	3	1	Oh Kee	Weigh
06/14/97	4	1	*OP1	NICU
06/25/97	7	2	*OP2	Time
07/09/97	8	2	*OP2	My Soul
07/22/97	4	2	*OP2	Mike's
08/02/97	7	2	*OP2	Tweezer
08/10/97	5	1	Sparkle	Dirt
08/17/97	5	2	*OP2	Bathtub
11/17/97	4	2	*OP2	Oblivious
11/23/97	4	2	Bathtub	Bold
12/02/97	5	1	BurAlive	Makisupa
12/11/97	6	1	PYITE	Maze
12/29/97	4	2	*OP2	Bowie
>> 12/31/97	**2**			

ELIZA

Inspiration: An instrumental dedicated by Trey to his then-girlfriend, now-wife, Sue, whose middle name is Eliza. Trey wrote the drum part to this song by sitting at Fish's drum set and basing the arrangement on how his drums were positioned.

Musical Evolution and History: None to speak of, as the song was always performed as composed.

Rotation History: Played sporadically in 1990, 1991, and 1992, but not since 5/14/92 Port Chester, NY.

Discography: Appears on *A Picture of Nectar* (1992).

Eliza [15] [Eliza]

By Anastasio

09/15/90	[224]	2	Split&Melt	MSO
11/17/90	22	1	Cavern	Oh Kee
11/24/90	1	2	Stash	Landlady
10/13/91	97	E	*OPE	Uncle Pen
11/01/91	12	2	Chalkdust	Mike's
11/08/91	4	1	Brother	Golgi
11/15/91	6	2	Weekpaug	Tube
11/23/91	6	2	Tweezer	Landlady
12/06/91	5	2	It's Ice	Sparkle
03/12/92	6	2	Tweezer	It's Ice
03/24/92	7	1	Foam	Rift
04/07/92	12	2	Tweezer	YEM
04/21/92	9	1	It's Ice	NICU
05/08/92	13	1	It's Ice	Llama
05/14/92	4	2	Fluffhead	Mike's
>> 12/31/97	**534**			

ESTHER

Inspiration: In this case, the story really is the song. One of Trey's most

Original Songs Played by Year *(continued)*

I Don't Care

1997	2	3%

I Saw It Again

1997	7	9%

Icculus

1990	0	0%
1991	1	1%
1992	3	2%
1993	1	1%
1994	3	2%
1995	1	1%
1996	0	0%
1997	0	0%

If I Could

1994	34	27%
1995	9	11%
1996	2	3%
1997	0	0%

It's Ice

1991	21	17%
1992	40	33%
1993	55	50%
1994	40	32%
1995	18	22%
1996	14	20%
1997	3	4%

Julius

1994	65	52%
1995	21	26%
1996	16	23%
1997	15	19%

Keyboard Kavalry

1995	12	15%
1996	0	0%
1997	0	0%

Kung

1990	0	0%
1991	0	0%
1992	1	1%
1993	6	5%
1994	4	3%
1995	7	9%
1996	1	1%
1997	1	1%

Landlady

1990	31	30%
1991	81	64%
1992	41	34%
1993	15	14%
1994	9	7%
1995	0	0%
1996	0	0%
1997	0	0%

unique compositions, he sounded out interesting phrases then morphed them into verses and set it to music. It tells the story of the young girl Esther and an Armenian man who offers her a doll.

Musical Evolution and History: Though the music to Esther has remained pretty much unchanged, an early version of the song from 9/12/88 features an entire set of alternate lyrics. A computer-animated video for Esther, produced by Rhode Island video firm CoSA, was shown between sets at the Somerville Theater on 7/19/91. Other noteworthy events include the 7/18/93 show in Pittsburgh, when a freight train rolled by behind the stage and "chugga-chugged" to the exact beat of the Esther intro being played by the band. Three years later, on night one of the Clifford Ball, a fan-made Esther doll thrown on stage reportedly prompted the band to play the song.

Rotation History: Played with some frequency in the early 1990s, Esther has grown more rare in recent years, and wasn't performed at all in 1997.

Discography: Appears on *Junta* (1989).

Esther [96] [Esther]

By Anastasio

09/12/88	[53]	1a	Harry	*CL1
02/07/89	12	1	*OP1	McGrupp
04/14/89	13	2	Weekpaug	*CL2
04/15/89	1	1	Weekpaug	YEM
04/20/89	2	1	Fire	Suzie
05/05/89	8	E	*OPE	*CLE
05/06/89	1	1	Weekpaug	Sloth
05/09/89	3	2	Slave	Antelope
05/28/89	11	1	Slave	Suzie
11/02/89	33	1	Split&Melt	GTBT
12/09/89	14	2	Fluffhead	Alumni
01/20/90	6	1a	Lawn Boy	Mike's
02/10/90	12	2	La Grange	ACDCBag
02/24/90	6	1	Divided	Possum
03/03/90	4	2	Fluffhead	FunkBitch
03/07/90	1	1	Possum	A-Train
04/06/90	8	2	La Grange	Sloth
04/09/90	3	2	FunkBitch	Uncle Pen
04/13/90	3	1	Fluffhead	La Grange
04/22/90	5	2	How High	BBFCM
04/25/90	1	2	YEM	La Grange
04/26/90	1	2	How High	Bathtub
05/06/90	5	2	Harry	Bowie
05/31/90	9	1a	Caravan	Tweezer
06/16/90	6	2	Golgi	Tweezer
09/28/90	8	2	ACDCBag	Gumbo
10/04/90	2	1	Landlady	Possum
10/06/90	2	1a	Suzie	Possum
10/12/90	3	1	Cavern	Tweezer
11/02/90	4	1	Weekpaug	Cavern
11/17/90	6	2	Weekpaug	Love You
11/30/90	3	1	Weekpaug	Dinner
12/29/90	5	1	YEM	Bowie
02/02/91	3	1	Dinner	Stash
02/03/91	1	1	Tweezer	Destiny
02/14/91	4	2	RunJim	Alumni
02/28/91	11	1	Foam	Mike's
03/13/91	7	1	Divided	Llama
03/17/91	3	2	RunJim	MSO
04/20/91	19	1	Landlady	Chalkdust
07/14/91	20	3	Landlady	Chalkdust
07/21/91	5	2	Sloth	ACDCBag
08/03/91	6	2	Tweezer	Cavern
09/27/91	3	1	BurAlive	Tweezer
10/03/91	4	2	Weekpaug	Landlady
10/17/91	9	1	Stash	Chalkdust
11/13/91	18	1	Chalkdust	Cavern
11/21/91	6	1	Split&Melt	Mike's
12/31/91	9	1	Divided	Llama
03/17/92	7	2	Tweezer	Mike's
04/06/92	15	1	Brother	Chalkdust
04/18/92	8	1	Split&Melt	Possum
04/30/92	8	1	Rift	Antelope
05/07/92	6	1	RunJim	Split&Melt
07/15/92	23	2	Divided	MSO
08/17/92	19	2	Tweezer	Mike's
11/19/92	11	1	Divided	Axilla
11/28/92	7	1	Stash	Chalkdust
12/04/92	5	2	Bowie	Possum
12/11/92	6	2	Weekpaug	Axilla
12/30/92	5	1	Split&Melt	Chalkdust
02/09/93	7	1	Chalkdust	Maze
02/12/93	3	1	Split&Melt	Wedge
02/15/93	2	1	Divided	Chalkdust
02/21/93	5	1	Chalkdust	Dinner
03/09/93	11	1	Maze	Divided
03/16/93	4	2	Bathtub	Chalkdust
03/21/93	4	1	Divided	All Things
03/30/93	7	1	Llama	Stash
04/16/93	11	1	Split&Melt	Llama
04/22/93	5	1	Chalkdust	Stash
05/03/93	9	1	Chalkdust	Split&Melt
07/18/93	10	1	Maze	Divided
07/30/93	9	1	Stash	Chalkdust
08/11/93	8	2	Weekpaug	All Things
08/14/93	3	1	Split&Melt	PoorHeart
08/26/93	8	1	Split&Melt	It's Ice
12/28/93	2	1	Split&Melt	Oh Kee
04/10/94	9	1	Split&Melt	Chalkdust
04/23/94	11	1	Stash	DWD
05/06/94	9	1	Stash	Chalkdust
05/29/94	18	2	Split&Melt	Chalkdust
06/13/94	4	2	Weekpaug	Cavern
06/21/94	6	2	Split&Melt	Chalkdust
07/05/94	11	1	Stash	DWD
10/10/94	12	2	Maze	Tweezer
10/20/94	7	1	Split&Melt	Julius
11/12/94	13	1	Stash	Chalkdust
11/25/94	10	1	Split&Melt	Julius
06/16/95	25	1	DWD	Ya Mar
10/19/95	30	1	PYITE	Chalkdust
11/14/95	14	1	Divided	Free
12/05/95	15	1	Free	Bowie
08/12/96	40	1	Split&Melt	Chalkdust
08/16/96	3	1	ACDCBag	Divided
10/19/96	5	1	Free	Llama
>> 12/31/97	113			

FAHT

Inspiration: A simple guitar line, played by Fishman, combined with nature and city sound effects, this parody of new age music is one of Fish's funniest creations. The band originally wanted to name the song "Windham Hell" for inclusion on *A Picture of Nectar*, but fear of action from well-known new age music and sound effects label Windham Hill Records prompted Phish to come up with another name. Reportedly, when the band got this news, Fishman was away on vacation and in his absence the band decided to rename the song Faht. Why? The late fall 1991 Phish Update contained a Fish's Forum in which the word "raht" was misspelled "faht." The typo, at a crucial point in the essay, angered Fishman because it made the piece unintelligible. The other band members thought it would be funny to tell Fish that Elektra had misspelled "Windham Hell" as "Faht."

Musical Evolution and History: As on *Nectar*, live versions of Faht feature prerecorded sound effects played over the PA system while Fishman plays the guitar line, usually sitting on a stool at the center of the stage.

Rotation History: Played only a dozen times in its history, Faht is a true rarity. After surprising the New Haven, CT, crowd with it on 12/2/95, Fish hasn't Fahted since.

Discography: Appears on *A Picture of Nectar* (1992).

Faht [12] [Faht]

By Fishman

11/22/92	[483]	2	YEM	Golgi
11/27/92	3	2	Silent	A-Train
12/04/92	6	2	Harry	YEM
12/11/92	6	2	Sqirm Coil	Possum
07/15/93	80	2	Possum	Lizards
07/17/93	2	2	Weekpaug	Rift
07/23/93	4	2	Antelope	My Friend
08/16/93	19	2	Mike's	Weekpaug
04/13/94	19	2	*OP2	Curtain
06/19/94	45	2	*OP2	Antelope
10/03/95	99	2	Billy	Adeline
12/02/95	37	2	Simple	Tweezer
>> 12/31/97	163			

FAMOUS MOCKINGBIRD

Inspiration: A Gamehendge song, usually preceded by a "Forbin's rap" narrative by Trey and, prior to that, Colonel Forbin's Ascent. Famous Mockingbird chronicles Icculus's summoning of the Mockingbird to retrieve the Helping Friendly Book from the highest turret of Wilson's castle.

Musical Evolution and History: Musically, the song has remained unchanged. The biggest switch to the Forbin's > Mockingbird duo came in spring 1992 when Trey started adding longer narratives between the two songs.

Rotation History: Like Forbin's, this once-frequent occurrence has dwindled, and the Mockingbird didn't soar at all in 1997. The one chance, in Darien Lake on 8/14/97, was cut short because "the funk is too deep," as Trey put it, and for the first time in ages, finished a Forbin's with a song other than Mockingbird (in that case, Camel Walk).

Discography: Has not yet appeared on a Phish album and, as a Gamehendge song, Trey has pledged, to never incorporate it into any commercial project.

Fly Famous Mockingbird [97] [Mockbird]

By Anastasio

02/08/88	[30]	2	Harry	TMWSIY
03/12/88	2	1a	Forbin's	Sloth
03/21/88	1	1a	Forbin's	*CL1
03/31/88	1	2	Forbin's	A-Train
06/21/88	9	1	Forbin's	Fire
07/11/88	1	1	Forbin's	Golgi
07/23/88	2	1	Forbin's	Mike's
07/24/88	1	1	Forbin's	Sally
09/08/88	5	1	Forbin's	Bold
10/12/88	3	1	Forbin's	*CL1
11/11/88	4	1	Forbin's	Bowie
01/26/89	2	1	Forbin's	Sloth
02/05/89	2	1a	Forbin's	WhipPost
02/18/89	4	1a	Forbin's	Lizards
02/24/89	1	1	Forbin's	Antelope
03/03/89	1	2	Forbin's	Lizards
05/06/89	21	1	Forbin's	Bowie
05/28/89	14	1	Forbin's	Fee
08/23/89	15	2	Forbin's	Ya Mar
08/26/89	1	1	Forbin's	Harry
10/20/89	11	1	Forbin's	YEM
10/22/89	2	1	Forbin's	YEM
10/31/89	3	2	Forbin's	Alumni
11/03/89	2	1	Forbin's	Bathtub
11/30/89	7	2	Forbin's	Undone
01/28/90	16	1	Forbin's	Commun
02/25/90	15	1	Forbin's	FunkBitch
03/09/90	6	1	Forbin's	Sloth
04/07/90	7	2	Forbin's	FunkBitch
04/20/90	8	1	Forbin's	Possum
06/01/90	19	1a	Forbin's	*CL1
10/07/90	18	1	Forbin's	Asse Fest
11/02/90	6	2	Forbin's	MSO
11/26/90	8	2	Forbin's	Wilson
12/28/90	6	1	Forbin's	Mike's
02/08/91	7	1	Forbin's	MSO
03/16/91	22	1	Forbin's	Oh Kee
03/23/91	4	1	Forbin's	Rocky Top
04/04/91	6	1	Forbin's	Possum
04/15/91	6	1	Forbin's	Llama
04/21/91	5	1	Forbin's	LLama
05/02/91	5	1	Forbin's	Llama
05/04/91	2	2	Forbin's	BurAlive
05/16/91	5	1	Forbin's	Chalkdust
07/14/91	7	1	Forbin's	Sloth
10/13/91	25	1	Forbin's	Tela
10/27/91	8	2	Forbin's	Sparkle
11/02/91	5	1	Forbin's	Possum
11/13/91	7	2	Forbin's	Golgi
11/20/91	5	1	Forbin's	Sparkle
12/07/91	9	1	Forbin's	MSO
03/19/92	9	1	Forbin's	All Things
03/24/92	3	1	Forbin's	Landlady
03/31/92	6	1	Forbin's	Antelope
04/16/92	11	1	Icculus	Antelope
04/21/92	4	2	Forbin's	Tweezer
04/24/92	3	1	Icculus	Uncle Pen
05/02/92	5	1	Icculus	Sparkle
05/06/92	3	1	Forbin's	Sparkle
05/17/92	9	1	Forbin's	MSO
11/21/92	47	1	Forbin's	Possum
11/27/92	4	1	Forbin's	Split&Melt
12/04/92	6	1	Forbin's	Cavern
12/08/92	4	1	Forbin's	Uncle Pen
12/31/92	8	1	Forbin's	MSO
02/07/93	5	1	Forbin's	Rift
02/19/93	9	1	Forbin's	Sparkle
02/25/93	5	1	Forbin's	Rift
03/08/93	7	1	How High	Sparkle
03/18/93	7	1	Forbin's	Sparkle
03/22/93	3	2	Forbin's	Sloth
03/25/93	2	2	Kung	Wedge
04/05/93	9	1	Forbin's	Bowie
04/13/93	4	1	Forbin's	Chalkdust
04/21/93	6	1	Forbin's	Rift
04/25/93	4	1	Forbin's	Maze
05/03/93	6	1	Forbin's	Possum
07/29/93	18	1	Forbin's	Possum
08/07/93	6	1	Forbin's	Cavern
08/15/93	7	1	Forbin's	Chalkdust
12/30/93	11	1	Forbin's	Rift
04/11/94	8	2	Forbin's	Uncle Pen
04/24/94	11	2	Forbin's	Chalkdust
05/25/94	22	1	Forbin's	Axilla 2
06/16/94	10	2	Forbin's	BBJ
06/26/94	9	1	Forbin's	Sloth
07/08/94	8	1	Forbin's	Sloth
10/14/94	13	1	Forbin's	Julius
10/27/94	10	1	Forbin's	Divided
11/04/94	6	1	Forbin's	Scent
11/17/94	5	1	Forbin's	DWD
11/30/94	9	1	Forbin's	DWD
10/05/95	43	2	Forbin's	Scent
12/01/95	35	1	Forbin's	Stash
12/31/95	16	1	Forbin's	Sparkle

08/07/96	25	2	Forbin's	Possum
10/31/96	18	1	Forbin's	CharZero
>> 12/31/97		105		

FARMHOUSE

Inspiration: Reportedly, Trey and Tom Marshall recently rented an old farmhouse for a weekend to go write songs. When they arrived, they found a note from the owner warning them that there were clusterflies in the farmhouse, and they incorporated the note into the lyrics of this song.

Musical Evolution and History: None to speak of, as the song debuted so recently.

Rotation History: A new song on fall tour 1997, Farmhouse gained immediate fame when the band played it for the first time ever on Conan O'Brien's "Late Night" show, on 11/7/97, prior to ever playing it in concert.

Discography: Has not yet appeared on a Phish album.

Farmhouse [2] [Farmhouse]

By Anastasio/Marshall

11/16/97	[944]	1	BE Katy	Old Home
11/28/97	7	1	Maze	BE Katy
12/28/97	11	1	RunJim	Funky Bitch
>> 12/31/97		3		

FAST ENOUGH FOR YOU

Inspiration: A song literally about love and life. Tom Marshall wrote the lyrics about how his girlfriend wanted to get married while he wanted to wait awhile, and how that wasn't "fast enough" for her. But Trey has said that the words had a resonance with the rest of the band, all of whom faced the challenge of staying close to loved ones while spending the majority of each year on the road. The song became the thematic centerpiece of the *Rift* album concept. It also was the single for *Rift*, and received airplay on, of all things, adult-oriented stations (which in radio doesn't mean pornography, it means more like Barry Manilow and Muzak). This prompted frustration from many fans and did bring a few confused older fans to concerts in 1993. In response to a letter which criticized the song, Mike defended FEFY in a Phish newsletter, saying that hearing Phish express such a level of emotion in a tune brought tears to his eyes.

Musical Evolution and History: Appears in concert much as on *Rift*, though the album version does feature Gordon Stone on pedal steel guitar (a role he reprised for the song's debut in Colchester, VT, on 11/19/92) and the closing Trey guitar jam is much longer on stage than on the album version.

Rotation History: Lightly played from 1992 through 1994, it's surfaced only about a dozen times since 1995, including its one 1997 appearance on 11/14/97 in West Valley, UT.

Discography: Appears on *Rift* (1993).

Fast Enough for You [51] [FEFY]

By Anastasio/Marshall

11/19/92	[480]	2	PoorHeart	Llama
11/20/92	1	2	YEM	Dinner
11/25/92	4	2	Foam	YEM
11/28/92	2	1	Sparkle	All Things
12/02/92	3	1	Divided	PoorHeart
12/04/92	2	1	Sparkle	Maze
12/07/92	3	1	Foam	Split&Melt
12/13/92	5	1	Rift	IDK
12/29/92	2	2	BBJ	All Things
02/04/93	4	1	Maze	All Things
02/07/93	3	2	Llama	My Mind
02/12/93	4	2	BBJ	YEM
02/15/93	2	2	Rift	Reba
02/20/93	4	2	Weekpaug	BBJ
02/25/93	4	2	BBJ	Brain
03/03/93	4	2	MSO	Terrapin
03/06/93	2	2	BBJ	YEM
03/13/93	4	2	Weekpaug	Love You
03/24/93	8	2	BBJ	YEM
04/13/93	14	2	Uncle Pen	BBJ
07/16/93	24	1	BurAlive	All Things
07/18/93	2	2	Mound	Oh Kee
07/29/93	8	1	Landlady	My Mind
08/08/93	7	1	PYITE	Paul&Silas
08/17/93	8	1	Fluffhead	Daniel
12/28/93	7	2	Sloth	Uncle Pen
04/11/94	10	1	Foam	Magilla
04/29/94	14	1	YEM	Scent
05/07/94	8	1	Mound	Scent
05/14/94	5	2	PYITE	Lizards
05/20/94	4	1	Bathtub	Scent
06/19/94	17	1	Curtain	Scent
07/02/94	10	1	Guelah	Scent
07/13/94	7	1	It's Ice	IDK
10/09/94	6	1	Foam	Curtain
10/13/94	3	1	Foam	Sparkle
10/21/94	6	2	Curtain	Scent
11/16/94	15	1	Foam	Reba
12/01/94	11	1	Uncle Pen	Maze
06/08/95	15	1	Mound	Reba
06/28/95	15	1	Foam	Reba
10/03/95	11	1	Foam	I'm Blue
10/22/95	13	1	NICU	It's Ice
11/15/95	12	1	ACDCBag	Rift
11/30/95	10	1	Rift	Lizards
12/28/95	14	1	Rift	Possum
07/15/96	15	1	PYITE	Guyute
08/13/96	16	1	Maze	Old Home
11/06/96	18	1	CTB	Train Song
11/22/96	11	1	Sample	Train Song
11/14/97	68	1	Maze	Also Sprac
>> 12/31/97		23		

FEE

Inspiration: Trey wrote this story about the weasel named Fee, his love, Milly, and his rival, Floyd. As story-songs go, it's one of Phish's catchiest and best, and many fans say (or, more aptly, admit) that it was their first favorite Phish song.

Musical Evolution and History: The song entered the band's repertoire in 1987, but when they recorded it for inclusion on *Junta*, engineer Gordon Hookailo created a vocal effect by recording Trey's voice by holding a microphone up to a pair of headphones as Trey's voice sounded through. Trey often recreates this effect in concert by speaking the verses through a megaphone, then singing the choruses without the megaphone.

Rotation History: Another song that has drawn a lot of fans to Phish, Fee is getting harder to find in concert these days, with only three performances in 1997.

Discography: Appears on *Junta* (1989) and on Absolute A-Go-Go's release of *Lawn Boy* (1990), but was cut from Elektra's 1992 *Lawn Boy* reissue.

Fee [219] [Fee]

By Anastasio

08/09/87	[17]	1	*OP1	Harry
08/10/87	1	1	Fluffhead	Curtain
08/21/87	1	2	Flat Fee	Skin It
09/12/87	2	2	Sally	Divided
09/27/87	1	2	Fire	*CL2
11/19/87	3	2	IDK	Corrina
01/30/88	1	3	*OP3	Suzie
03/31/88	3	1	Golgi	ACDCBag
05/25/88	2	3	La Grange	IKALittle
06/15/88	1	1	La Grange	Timber Ho
06/20/88	2	2	Tela	Golgi
09/12/88	10	1a	A-Train	Bold
09/24/88	1	2	Possum	Sparks
10/12/88	1	1	Foam	Mike's
10/29/88	1	2	WhipPost	Alumni
11/03/88	1	1	Possum	Alumni
11/05/88	1	2	ACDCBag	Mike's
11/11/88	1	2	Jazz	Bold
01/26/89	2	1a	Divided	GTBT
02/06/89	3	1	Peaches	La Grange
02/07/89	1	2	Alumni	Antelope
02/17/89	1	1a	YEM	Divided
03/04/89	1	1	Weekpaug	Golgi
05/05/89	19	1	Jam	*CL1
05/27/89	14	1	FunkBitch	YEM
05/28/89	1	1	Mockbird	Slave
06/23/89	5	1	Donna	Mike's
08/17/89	7	2	Mango	YEM
10/07/89	9	1	Suzie	La Grange
10/14/89	3	1	Split&Melt	Alumni
10/21/89	2	1	*OP1	Ya Mar
10/22/89	1	2	MSO	Possum
10/26/89	1	1	YEM	Divided
10/31/89	2	1	Divided	WalkAway
11/02/89	1	1	Weekpaug	Curtain
11/10/89	4	1	Suzie	Divided
11/30/89	4	2	Undone	Split&Melt
12/07/89	4	1	ACDCBag	Mike's
12/09/89	2	2	Alumni	Mike's
12/31/89	5	2	Divided	*CL2
02/10/90	13	2	Donna	Mike's
02/24/90	6	2	ACDCBag	Sqirm Coil
03/28/90	10	1	Ya Mar	WalkAway
04/05/90	2	2	Tweezer	Cavern
04/07/90	2	2	Bold	RunJim
04/08/90	1	2	Weekpaug	MSO
04/18/90	5	2	La Grange	Sloth
04/20/90	2	1	La Grange	Oh Kee
05/06/90	9	2	*OP2	Harry
05/19/90	6	2	Suzie	Dinner
05/24/90	2	2	Horn	WalkAway
06/01/90	2	1a	Dinner	Foam
06/07/90	2	1	Possum	Reba
06/09/90	1	2	La Grange	Foam
06/16/90	1	E	Suzie	Rocky Top
09/15/90	3	1	Landlady	Tube
09/22/90	4	2	Destiny	Uncle Pen

Original Songs Played by Year *(continued)*

Lawn Boy

1990	18	17%
1991	27	21%
1992	12	10%
1993	24	22%
1994	7	6%
1995	4	5%
1996	4	6%
1997	4	5%

Lengthwise

1992	6	5%
1993	15	14%
1994	1	1%
1995	0	0%
1996	0	0%
1997	0	0%

Leprechaun

1993	3	3%
1994	0	0%
1995	0	0%
1996	0	0%
1997	0	0%

Letter to Jimmy Page

1990	0	0%
1991	0	0%
1992	0	0%
1993	0	0%
1994	2	2%
1995	0	0%
1996	0	0%
1997	0	0%

Lifeboy

1993	9	8%
1994	24	19%
1995	10	12%
1996	2	3%
1997	1	1%

Limb by Limb

1997	22	28%

Lizards

1990	35	34%
1991	38	30%
1992	24	20%
1993	28	25%
1994	28	23%
1995	17	21%
1996	9	13%
1997	4	5%

Llama

1990	15	15%
1991	67	53%
1992	63	52%
1993	46	42%
1994	36	29%
1995	13	16%
1996	10	14%
1997	7	9%

10/05/90	4	2	Split&Melt	Possum
10/12/90	4	2	Possum	Landlady
10/31/90	3	2	Tweezer	Oh Kee
11/03/90	2	2	Stash	Uncle Pen
11/10/90	3	2	Asse Fest	Llama
02/15/91	20	1	Spilt	BurAlive
02/21/91	4	1	Split&Melt	Llama
02/27/91	5	1	YEM	MSO
03/17/91	11	2	Tweezer	Slave
03/23/91	3	1	Divided	Llama
04/05/91	7	E	*OPE	Oh Kee
04/11/91	2	E	*OPE	Possum
04/15/91	3	1	Split&Melt	Chalkdust
04/21/91	5	2	Possum	Landlady
05/02/91	5	2	Divided	Split&Melt
05/03/91	1	1	Divided	Paul&Silas
05/12/91	5	1	Llama	Foam
05/25/91	4	1a	ACDCBag	Foam
07/12/91	1	E	Frankstein	Tweezer
07/19/91	2	1	Bowie	Cavern
07/21/91	1	E2	*OPE2	Suzie
08/03/91	2	1	Llama	Sqirm Coil
09/26/91	2	1	Divided	It's Ice
10/03/91	5	1	Llama	Divided
10/06/91	3	2	Stash	Landlady
10/10/91	1	2	Suzie	Mike's
10/18/91	6	2	IDK	Split&Melt
10/28/91	6	1	Foam	Bowie
10/31/91	2	2	Llama	MSO
11/07/91	4	E	*OPE	Rocky Top
11/08/91	1	E	*OPE	Suzie
11/12/91	3	1	Harry	Foam
11/14/91	2	2	Antelope	Paul&Silas
11/19/91	3	1	RunJim	Sparkle
11/22/91	3	1	Brother	Foam
11/23/91	1	2	Landlady	Love You
12/05/91	4	2	Weekpaug	Sloth
03/11/92	6	1	Maze	Split&Melt
03/14/92	3	1	Stash	Chalkdust
03/25/92	6	1	Rift	Maze
03/31/92	5	2	Weekpaug	Stash
04/07/92	6	1	It's Ice	Divided
04/13/92	3	1	NICU	All Things
04/16/92	2	1	Rift	Maze
04/19/92	3	1	Maze	Chalkdust
04/23/92	3	2	Tweezer	Maze
04/30/92	4	1	Split&Melt	Maze
05/03/92	3	1	Uncle Pen	All Things
05/07/92	3	2	Weekpaug	Bike
05/09/92	2	1	Rift	Maze
05/18/92	7	2	Weekpaug	Bike
07/14/92	13	2	Tweezer	All Things
11/19/92	31	1	Maze	Foam
11/22/92	3	1	Suzie	Maze
11/25/92	2	1	Landlady	Maze
11/30/92	3	E	*OPE	Fire
12/03/92	3	1	Maze	All Things
12/04/92	1	E	*OPE	Rocky Top
12/06/92	2	1	Foam	My Friend
12/07/92	1	2	It's Ice	Bowie
12/10/92	2	1	Foam	PoorHeart
12/13/92	3	1	It's Ice	Uncle Pen
02/03/93	5	1	Rift	Llama
02/07/93	4	1	Split&Melt	RunJim
02/11/93	3	1	Stash	Rift
02/15/93	3	2	Bike	Llama
02/19/93	3	1	Split&Melt	Maze
02/22/93	3	1	Maze	Sparkle
02/26/93	3	1	Foam	Split&Melt
02/27/93	1	2	Terrapin	Llama
03/02/93	1	1	It's Ice	All Things
03/13/93	7	1	Maze	All Things
03/16/93	2	1	It's Ice	Maze
03/18/93	2	1	Rift	Maze
03/24/93	4	1	Foam	PoorHeart
03/26/93	2	1	Foam	PYITE
03/28/93	2	1	Maze	It's Ice
04/01/93	3	2	Possum	Ya Mar
04/05/93	3	1	It's Ice	Maze
04/12/93	3	2	Tweezer	Paul&Silas
04/18/93	5	1	Divided	Maze
04/22/93	3	1	Stash	Rift
04/25/93	3	2	Weekpaug	TweezRep
04/29/93	2	1	Rift	Oh Kee
05/01/93	2	1	Split&Melt	Sample
05/07/93	5	2	Maze	BBJ
07/18/93	7	2	Oh Kee	YEM
07/25/93	5	1	Stash	Rift
08/03/93	7	1	Foam	Rift
08/09/93	4	1	Mound	Split&Melt
08/15/93	5	1	RunJim	Paul&Silas
08/21/93	4	2	Uncle Pen	Llama
08/26/93	3	1	Reba	Split&Melt
12/28/93	2	1	It's Ice	Possum
12/31/93	3	2	It's Ice	Possum
04/04/94	1	1	Maze	Reba
04/06/94	2	1	Scent	Antelope
04/09/94	2	1	Julius	All Things
04/13/94	3	2	BBJ	A-Train
04/16/94	3	1	Julius	All Things
04/20/94	3	2	Harry	YEM
04/23/94	3	1	Rift	Peaches
04/25/94	2	1	RunJim	Foam
04/29/94	2	2	Reba	Uncle Pen
05/07/94	6	1	Mound	Scent
05/08/94	1	2	It's Ice	Julius
05/12/94	2	1	DWD	Maze
05/14/94	2	1	DWD	Reba
05/16/94	1	E	*OPE	Rocky Top
05/20/94	3	1	*OP1	Maze
05/23/94	3	1	Foam	Maze
05/28/94	4	2	Reba	Llama
06/09/94	2	1	Maze	Suzie
06/14/94	4	1	DWD	My Friend
06/16/94	1	1	Julius	Maze
06/24/94	7	1	It's Ice	Sloth
07/03/94	7	1	DWD	NICU
07/13/94	6	1	DWD	It's Ice
07/15/94	2	1	Foam	Split&Melt
10/08/94	3	1	Guyute	It's Ice
10/10/94	2	2	Tweezer	Rift
10/16/94	5	1	Foam	Split&Melt
10/21/94	3	1	*OP1	DWD
10/23/94	2	2	Harry	GTBT
10/25/94	1	1	*OP1	Llama
10/28/94	3	E	*OPE	HwayHell
11/03/94	4	1	*OP1	Divided
11/16/94	5	2	Chalkdust	Antelope
11/20/94	4	1	Chalkdust	Scent
11/23/94	2	2	Maze	Scent
11/28/94	3	E	*OPE	Tweezer
12/04/94	5	1	Tweezer	Mound
12/07/94	2	2	Divided	Julius
12/10/94	3	1	*OP1	Rift
12/30/94	3	1	Stash	Scent
06/10/95	6	2	Maze	Uncle Pen
06/17/95	5	1	Taste	Uncle Pen
06/24/95	5	1	*OP1	Rift
06/30/95	5	1	Mound	Antelope
09/28/95	5	1	Stash	Fog
10/20/95	15	1	Divided	Rift
10/24/95	3	1	Fog	Llama
10/27/95	2	1	Stash	Suspicious
11/11/95	6	1	AmGrace	Chalkdust
11/15/95	3	2	Weekpaug	Guitar
11/21/95	4	1	*OP1	Chalkdust
11/24/95	2	2	*OP2	Julius
11/29/95	3	1	AArmy	Split&Melt
12/28/95	15	E	*OPE	Tweezer
06/06/96	5	2	Bowie	Sample
07/21/96	14	1	Train Song	Timber Ho
08/04/96	6	1	Guyute	Split&Melt
08/10/96	4	1	ACDCBag	Reba
08/14/96	3	1	DWD	PoorHeart
08/17/96	2	1	Taste	Maze
10/19/96	4	E	*OPE	Rocky Top
10/27/96	6	1	ACDCBag	Scent
11/02/96	3	1	Julius	Cavern
11/19/96	12	1	Stash	Taste
02/25/97	24	2	Free	My Friend
11/19/97	48	1	Ginseng	Time
12/06/97	11	1	Sample	Maze
>> 12/31/97	**9**			

FLAT FEE

Inspiration: Trey wrote this big band-style instrumental as an assignment for his composition teacher Ernie Stires, who complimented the song as one of Trey's best early efforts.

Musical Evolution and History: The mid-1980s versions of the song, without a horn section, sound less evolved than the 1991 horn versions, but compositionally, the song is unchanged.

Rotation History: Because Flat Fee was written to be performed with a horn section, Phish dropped the song after playing it a few times in the mid-1980s. But when they toured with the Giant Country Horns in July 1991, they returned the song to their repertoire as it was meant to be heard. Since then, it hasn't been played.

Discography: Has not yet appeared on a Phish album.

Flat Fee [14] [Flat Fee]

By Anastasio

03/11/87	[12]	1a	Antelope	YEM
08/21/87	7	2	Sparks	Fee
08/29/87	2	1	BBFCM	Lushngton
03/11/88	10	1	Slave	Corrina
05/15/88	6	1a	Curtain	WhipPost
06/21/88	6	2	ACDCBag	Alumni
07/11/91	277	1	Divided	MSO
07/12/91	1	1	BurAlive	Reba
07/13/91	1	2	Divided	Paul&Silas
07/15/91	2	1a	Weekpaug	Lizards
07/20/91	3	2	Dinner	Golgi
07/23/91	2	1	Stash	Bouncing
07/25/91	2	1	Divided	ACDCBag
07/26/91	1	2	YEM	FunkBitch
>> 12/31/97	**634**			

FLUFFHEAD

Inspiration: The first lyrical segment, about Fluffhead (a man with a horrible disease), sprang from the Dude of Life's mind and was put together with a bunch of other musical pieces to create the monstrous Fluffhead > Fluff's Travels suite.

Musical Evolution and History: The song had come together in its current form by the time it was recorded for *Junta* in 1988. The band labeled it in two parts, Fluffhead (the part for which the Dude of Life wrote the lyrics) and Fluff's Travels; some tapers still label it as two songs though the two are always played together. Fluff's Travels includes six distinct parts: Fluff's Travels, The Chase, Who Do? We Do!, Clod, Bundle of Joy, and The Arrival. Several of these parts (Clod, The Chase, Bundle of Joy) were played individually at times in the 1980s, and part of the song Lushington was also incorporated into what became Fluff's Travels. Despite its daunting complexity, however, versions of Fluffhead differ little from performance to performance. The version from 7/30/93 begins and ends with Trey on acoustic guitar.

Rotation History: Never overplayed, Fluffhead surfaced more often in the early 1990s than it does now. In 1997, it appeared five times in concert, down from a peak of twenty in 1993.

Discography: Appears on *Junta* (1989); Fluff's Travels also appears on their "White Album."

Fluffhead [152] [Fluffhead]

(includes Fluff's Travels, by Anastasio)

By Anastasio/Dude of Life

12/01/84	[0]	1a	Skip	*CL1
10/15/86	8	1a	Mustang	Sally
10/31/86	1	1	Shaggy	*CL1
03/23/87	4	1	Sparks	Peaches
04/24/87	1	1a	Possum	YEM
04/29/87	1	3	Peaches	GTBT
08/09/87	2	2	Divided	McGrupp
08/10/87	1	1	Possum	Fee
09/12/87	4	2	La Grange	*CL2
09/27/87	1	2	Fire	*CL2
10/14/87	1	1	Chase	Possum
11/19/87	2	1	Timber Ho	IDK
01/30/88	1	2	Fire	Divided
02/08/88	2	2	*OP2	Wilson
03/11/88	1	2	*OP2	Dinner
03/31/88	3	1	Possum	*CL1
05/14/88	2	2	Jesus	Alumni
05/15/88	1	1a	GTBT	Shaggy
05/25/88	2	2	Jesus	WhipPost
06/15/88	1	1	McGrupp	Golgi
06/20/88	2	1	YEM	ACDCBag
06/21/88	1	1	*OP1	Rocky Top
07/12/88	2	1	Timber Ho	Jesus
07/24/88	2	2	Light Up	La Grange
07/25/88	1	2	Light Up	*CL2
08/03/88	1	2	I am H2	Harry
08/27/88	2	1	WalkAway	Mike's
09/24/88	3	3	GTBT	Curtain
10/29/88	2	3	*OP3	GTBT
11/03/88	1	1	Golgi	Possum
11/05/88	1	1	WalkAway	Alumni
01/26/89	3	1a	Wilson	Icculus
02/07/89	4	3	Sanity	Suzie
02/17/89	1	1a	Antelope	*CL1
03/04/89	4	2	Possum	Lizards
03/30/89	2	1	Ya Mar	Antelope
04/15/89	7	2	Suzie	*CL2
04/20/89	2	1	ACDCBag	Shook
04/30/89	5	1a	Terrapin	*CL1
05/05/89	3	1	Ya Mar	Alumni
05/13/89	7	1	La Grange	Possum
05/27/89	7	1	A-Train	Bathtub
06/23/89	6	2	Sloth	Harry
06/30/89	2	1	Donna	Antelope
08/26/89	9	1	*OP1	Forbin's
10/01/89	5	2	Dinner	Possum
10/21/89	7	1	McGrupp	Foam
12/09/89	19	2	A-Train	Esther
01/28/90	10	1	Tela	La Grange
02/25/90	15	2	Lizards	BBFCM
03/03/90	3	2	Caravan	Esther
04/13/90	15	1	Bouncing	Esther
04/22/90	5	2	YEM	How High
04/29/90	4	1a	Divided	WalkAway
10/30/90	35	2	Curtis	Terrapin
11/03/90	3	E	*OPE	Fire
11/17/90	5	2	BurAlive	Mike's
02/09/91	16	2	BurAlive	Landlady
02/16/91	3	2	Guelah	Rocky Top
03/13/91	16	1	*OP1	Landlady
03/17/91	3	1	Foam	Uncle Pen
04/12/91	13	2	YEM	Cavern
04/20/91	6	1	Llama	MSO
04/26/91	4	1	Possum	PoorHeart
04/27/91	1	2	Weekpaug	Tweezer
05/04/91	3	2	Guelah	Mike's
05/17/91	6	2	Landlady	Magilla
08/03/91	17	3	Ya Mar	Lawn Boy
10/12/91	13	1	Uncle Pen	Chalkdust
10/17/91	3	2	Lawn Boy	YEM
10/27/91	6	1	Guelah	Brother
11/01/91	4	1	Split&Melt	Uncle Pen
11/09/91	5	2	Chalkdust	PoorHeart
11/16/91	6	1	Sparkle	Foam
11/24/91	6	1	Landlady	Sparkle
12/05/91	3	1	Ya Mar	Llama
03/13/92	8	1	Mound	Antelope
03/20/92	4	1	Rift	Maze
03/26/92	4	1	Stash	Uncle Pen
04/03/92	6	1	Maze	All Things
04/13/92	7	2	Llama	Sparkle
04/17/92	3	2	YEM	Sqirm Coil
04/24/92	6	1	Landlady	Sparkle
05/03/92	6	2	Silent	Guelah
05/07/92	3	2	Tweezer	Golgi
05/14/92	5	2	Rift	Eliza
07/12/92	16	1a	Divided	Uncle Pen
07/16/92	3	2	Landlady	TMWSIY
11/20/92	30	2	Chalkdust	Tube
12/01/92	8	1	Cavern	Maze
12/03/92	2	2	Guelah	Mike's
12/06/92	3	1	Llama	Antelope
12/13/92	6	2	Llama	Chalkdust
12/30/92	3	1	Chalkdust	Paul&Silas
02/11/93	9	1	Rift	Llama

02/17/93 4 1 Bouncing Golgi
02/20/93 3 1 Silent Cavern
02/26/93 5 1 Split&Melt Llama
03/12/93 8 1 Stash Horse
03/19/93 6 1 Stash Cavern
03/26/93 5 1 Split&Melt Divided
04/01/93 5 1 Paul&Silas Lawn Boy
04/05/93 3 1 Maze Paul&Silas
04/20/93 9 2 Chalkdust Sample
04/23/93 3 1 Split&Melt My Friend
05/01/93 6 2 Chalkdust My Friend
05/06/93 4 1 Llama Possum
07/24/93 12 2 Split&Melt Maze
07/30/93 5 2 PoorHeart My Friend
08/08/93 6 2 It's Ice Possum
08/13/93 4 1 Ginseng My Mind
08/17/93 4 1 Maze FEFY
08/28/93 6 1 Maze Stash
12/29/93 2 2 Bouncing Antelope
04/05/94 4 1 Foam Glide
04/10/94 4 2 Antelope Ginseng
04/16/94 5 1 Stash Nellie
04/21/94 4 2 Maze Mike's
05/03/94 9 2 If I Could DWD
05/12/94 6 2 Uncle Pen Life Boy
05/22/94 8 1 Split&Melt MSO
05/26/94 3 2 Antelope DWD
06/11/94 6 2 Antelope Scent
06/22/94 8 2 TMWSIY MSO
07/01/94 7 2 If I Could DWD
07/06/94 4 1 Llama Julius
07/09/94 2 2 Split&Melt PoorHeart
07/14/94 3 1 Scent Horse
10/08/94 4 2 Weekpaug PurplRain
10/16/94 7 2 Julius BBJ
10/22/94 4 1 Split&Melt Julius
11/12/94 11 2 Julius DWD
12/06/94 18 1 DWD Jesus
06/15/95 16 1 IDK Antelope
06/28/95 10 1 Stash Chalkdust
10/13/95 17 1 Split&Melt Life Mars
10/27/95 10 1 RunJim Fog
11/11/95 6 1 Uncle Pen Sl Monkey
11/22/95 8 1 Antelope Uncle Pen
12/08/95 11 1 RunJim It's Ice
12/29/95 9 1 Stash Llama
08/02/96 23 2 Free Caspian
08/10/96 5 2 Free WhipPost
08/17/96 5 2 Brother Antelope
10/19/96 4 2 Split&Melt SweptAwy
10/27/96 6 2 Tweezer Life Mars
11/30/96 21 1 Stash Old Home
02/23/97 17 1 Rift Frankstein
08/03/97 35 2 Simple Lifeboy
08/14/97 7 1 FunkBitch Limb
11/23/97 10 1 NICU CharZero
12/29/97 15 1 Theme Dirt
>> 12/31/97 2

FOAM

Inspiration: Unclear, though theories abound, including the one that says this song is about the path of a male sperm.

Musical Evolution and History: Considered by the band to be one of the most difficult songs they play, and among their favorites, versions have been speeded up and slowed down over the years. The jam in the middle of the song offers some room for improvisation, and Trey has sometimes used this as an excuse for a near-silent jam or silent jam, as in Seattle, WA, on 8/25/93.

Rotation History: Played all the time until 1994, Foam often surfaced as the second song of the first set, often following Runaway Jim (a pairing some referred to as Runaway Foam). Though Foam's appearances have been more sporadic in recent years, Phish tipped its cap to the past in Worcester, MA, on 11/29/97 when Foam followed The Wedge as, yes, the second song of the first set.

Discography: Appears on *Junta* (1989).

Foam [267] [Foam]

By Anastasio

10/12/88 [55] 1 Lizards Fee
10/29/88 1 3 ACDCBag Terrapin
11/03/88 1 1 Shaggy *CL1
11/11/88 2 1 Slave Possum
02/07/89 6 1 McGrupp Sloth
02/24/89 3 1 Curtain Forbin's
03/03/89 1 1 YEM ACDCBag
03/30/89 3 3 Peaches ACDCBag
04/15/89 7 1 McGrupp Bowie
04/20/89 1 1 McGrupp Bowie
05/13/89 15 1 Possum WalkAway
05/20/89 4 2 Weekpaug Contact
05/21/89 1 1 Harry Contact
08/23/89 18 2 ACDCBag GTBT
08/26/89 1 2 FunkBitch Bowie
09/09/89 4 1 *OP1 Oh Kee
10/01/89 1 1 Wilson Ya Mar
10/21/89 7 1 Fluffhead ACDCBag
10/22/89 1 1 Ya Mar Rocky Top
11/02/89 4 1 Bathtub Mike's
11/16/89 6 1 Bathtub Oh Kee
11/30/89 2 1 ACDCBag Lizards
12/09/89 6 1 Lizards In a Hole
02/09/90 17 2 Alumni Curtis
02/17/90 4 1a Bouncing HwayHell
02/23/90 2 1 Possum Carolina
02/25/90 2 1 *OP1 MSO
03/01/90 1 2 GTBT Mike's
03/08/90 3 1 Ya Mar Carolina
03/17/90 3 2 ACDCBag YEM
04/04/90 2 1 Possum Divided
04/07/90 3 2 RunJim YEM
04/09/90 2 2 La Grange Harry
04/13/90 3 2 Antelope Alumni
04/18/90 1 1 Curtain YEM
04/25/90 5 2 *OP2 Adeline
04/26/90 1 1 Possum YEM
04/28/90 1 1 Rift Antelope
05/13/90 8 2 Weekpaug Donna
05/24/90 4 2 *OP2 Dinner
06/01/90 2 1a Fee Forbin's
06/08/90 3 1 Weekpaug Bouncing
06/09/90 1 2 Fee Oh Kee
06/16/90 1 3 Ya Mar Oh Kee
09/13/90 1 1 Divided Tube
09/15/90 2 2 Bathtub Minute
10/06/90 9 1a Bouncing YEM
10/08/90 2 1 Bouncing Cavern
10/30/90 3 2 Magilla Reba
10/31/90 1 2 RunJim Tweezer
11/02/90 1 2 MSO YEM
11/03/90 1 1 Magilla RunJim
11/08/90 2 1 Lizards Uncle Pen
11/16/90 2 1 BurAlive YEM
11/24/90 2 1 Possum Mike's
12/01/90 3 1 Divided Tweezer
12/07/90 2 1 RunJim Llama
12/08/90 1 1 RunJim ACDCBag
12/28/90 1 1 RunJim Horn
02/01/91 3 1 MSO Tweezer
02/03/91 2 1 Chalkdust Golgi
02/07/91 1 1 RunJim MSO
02/09/91 2 1 RunJim Guelah
02/14/91 1 2 Weekpaug Sqirm Coil
02/26/91 9 1 *OP1 Sqirm Coil
02/28/91 2 1 Bouncing Esther
03/01/91 1 1 Wilson Divided
03/15/91 7 1 Llama MSO
03/17/91 2 1 Weekpaug Fluffhead
03/22/91 2 2 Antelope Paul&Silas
04/05/91 8 1 Chalkdust Mike's
04/11/91 2 1 Bouncing Carolina
04/15/91 3 1 Ya Mar RunJim
04/21/91 5 1 Divided Magilla
04/26/91 3 1 PoorHeart YEM
05/02/91 4 1 Drums Bouncing
05/03/91 1 1 Bouncing Chalkdust
05/10/91 3 2 PoorHeart McGrupp
05/12/91 2 1 Fee RunJim
05/16/91 1 1 Golgi Cavern
05/18/91 2 1 Paul&Silas Divided
05/25/91 1 1a Fee Reba
07/13/91 3 1 RunJim Llama
07/18/91 4 1 Chalkdust RunJim
07/20/91 1 1 Chalkdust Sqirm Coil
07/23/91 2 1 Chalkdust Sqirm Coil
07/25/91 2 1 Sloth Suzie
07/26/91 1 1 MSO Suzie
07/27/91 1 1a Llama Oh Kee
08/03/91 1 1 Wilson Oh Kee
09/25/91 1 1 PoorHeart Llama
09/26/91 1 1 Lizards Bowie
09/28/91 2 1 Stash Brother
10/02/91 2 1 Llama Sqirm Coil
10/03/91 1 1 Chalkdust Uncle Pen
10/04/91 1 2 Bouncing RunJim
10/06/91 2 1 Suzie Divided
10/10/91 1 1 Chalkdust Paul&Silas
10/11/91 1 2 Cavern Bowie
10/15/91 3 1 Chalkdust Sqirm Coil
10/18/91 2 1 RunJim Paul&Silas
10/19/91 1 1 RunJim Chalkdust
10/24/91 2 1 Suzie PoorHeart
10/28/91 3 1 Oh Kee Fee
10/31/91 2 1 Sparkle Bathtub
11/02/91 2 1 Paul&Silas Bouncing
11/07/91 2 1 Chalkdust Sparkle
11/09/91 2 1 RunJim Sparkle
11/12/91 2 1 Fee Llama
11/14/91 2 1 Reba Tube
11/16/91 2 1 Fluffhead Stash
11/19/91 1 1 Uncle Pen RunJim
11/21/91 2 1 Reba Horn
11/22/91 1 1 Fee Divided
11/23/91 1 1 Reba RunJim
11/30/91 2 1 Llama Sparkle
12/05/91 2 2 Tube Mike's
12/06/91 1 1 Memories Reba
12/07/91 1 1 RunJim Forbin's
12/31/91 1 1 Possum Sparkle
03/07/92 2 1 My Mind RunJim
03/12/92 2 1 RunJim Sparkle
03/14/92 2 1 Sparkle Rift
03/21/92 4 1 RunJim Sparkle
03/24/92 1 1 PoorHeart Eliza
03/26/92 2 1 All Things Sparkle
03/28/92 2 1 RunJim Sparkle
03/30/92 1 1 Llama Guelah
04/01/92 2 1 Golgi Bouncing
04/04/92 2 1 RunJim Reba
04/06/92 2 1 Suzie Sparkle
04/09/92 2 1 Sparkle Guelah
04/13/92 2 1 All Things A-Train
04/15/92 1 1 Suzie Guelah
04/17/92 2 1 RunJim Sparkle
04/22/92 4 1 Llama Reba
04/24/92 2 2 Ya Mar Mike's
04/29/92 2 1 Suzie Sparkle
05/02/92 3 2 Tela YEM
05/05/92 2 2 All Things Mike's
05/06/92 1 1 Llama Reba
05/07/92 1 1 My Friend RunJim
05/09/92 2 1 RunJim Sparkle
05/15/92 4 1a Golgi Cavern
05/16/92 1 1 Maze Glide
05/18/92 2 1 Guelah PoorHeart
06/20/92 2 1a Bouncing RunJim
06/27/92 3 1a RunJim Sparkle
07/11/92 6 1a RunJim Sparkle
07/15/92 3 1 Suzie My Friend
07/18/92 3 1a Suzie Llama
07/24/92 4 1a MSO Tweezer
07/25/92 1 1a RunJim Sparkle
08/01/92 6 1a Golgi PoorHeart
08/13/92 2 1a Chalkdust YEM
08/17/92 3 1 All Things My Friend
08/20/92 2 1a Golgi Stash
08/23/92 1 1a Cavern RunJim
08/28/92 4 1a PoorHeart Stash
11/19/92 4 1 Fee Glide
11/21/92 2 1 RunJim Glide
11/23/92 2 1 RunJim Glide
11/25/92 1 2 Chalkdust FEFY
11/28/92 2 1 MSO Stash
11/30/92 1 1 Llama Bouncing
12/02/92 2 1 Suzie Divided
12/04/92 2 1 Llama PoorHeart
12/06/92 2 1 RunJim Fee
12/07/92 1 1 Sparkle FEFY
12/10/92 2 1 Llama Fee
12/12/92 2 1 Llama Sparkle
12/28/92 2 1 Sparkle Glide
12/31/92 3 1 Cavern IDK
02/04/93 2 1 Axilla Bouncing
02/06/93 2 1 Golgi Wilson
02/10/93 3 1 Lovin Cup Guelah

Original Songs Played by Year *(continued)*

Magilla

1990	11	11%
1991	25	20%
1992	5	4%
1993	1	1%
1994	6	5%
1995	0	0%
1996	0	0%
1997	3	4%

Makisupa

1990	2	2%
1991	0	0%
1992	0	0%
1993	4	3%
1994	5	4%
1995	9	11%
1996	7	10%
1997	7	9%

TMWSIY

1990	3	3%
1991	17	13%
1992	9	7%
1993	5	4%
1994	8	6%
1995	4	5%
1996	3	4%
1997	1	1%

Mango Song

1990	0	0%
1991	20	16%
1992	8	7%
1993	3	3%
1994	14	11%
1995	6	7%
1996	4	6%
1997	1	1%

Maze

1992	55	45%
1993	54	49%
1994	44	35%
1995	25	31%
1996	17	24%
1997	16	21%

McGrupp

1990	2	2%
1991	5	4%
1992	3	2%
1993	5	5%
1994	13	10%
1995	5	6%
1996	4	6%
1997	5	6%

Mid-Highway Blues

1996	1	1%
1997	0	0%

02/18/93	6	1	Tweezer	Sparkle
02/20/93	2	1	Golgi	Sloth
02/22/93	2	1	Sparkle	Cavern
02/26/93	3	1	RunJim	Fee
03/03/93	3	1	Rift	Bouncing
03/05/93	1	1	Cavern	Sloth
03/09/93	3	1	RunJim	Bouncing
03/14/93	3	1	Lovin Cup	Guelah
03/17/93	2	1	RunJim	Bouncing
03/19/93	2	1	Llama	Bouncing
03/24/93	3	1	Llama	Fee
03/26/93	2	1	Sparkle	Fee
03/31/93	4	1	RunJim	Sparkle
04/02/93	2	1	PoorHeart	Bouncing
04/13/93	6	1	Suzie	Sparkle
04/17/93	3	1	Llama	Bouncing
04/21/93	3	1	PoorHeart	Guelah
04/24/93	3	2	Llama	Bathtub
04/27/93	2	1	PoorHeart	Bouncing
05/01/93	3	1	RunJim	Guelah
05/05/93	3	1	Guelah	Sparkle
05/30/93	5	1a	PoorHeart	Ya Mar
07/15/93	1	1	Stash	IDK
07/18/93	3	1	Rift	Guelah
07/22/93	2	1	Llama	Horn
07/25/93	3	1	Wilson	Mound
07/28/93	2	1	Sample	Nellie
07/31/93	3	1	Mound	Nellie
08/03/93	2	1	Nellie	Fee
08/08/93	3	1	BBFCM	Lovin Cup
08/13/93	4	1	Makisupa	Stash
08/16/93	3	1	Sparkle	IDK
08/21/93	3	1	PoorHeart	Guelah
08/25/93	2	1	Sparkle	Ginseng
08/28/93	2	1	Bouncing	Ginseng
12/29/93	2	1	Peaches	Glide
04/05/94	4	1	RunJim	Fluffhead
04/08/94	2	1	Glide	IDK
04/11/94	3	1	PoorHeart	FEFY
04/14/94	2	1	RunJim	Sparkle
04/17/94	3	1	Lovin Cup	IDK
04/21/94	3	1	Sparkle	Glide
04/25/94	4	1	Fee	DWD
04/28/94	1	1a	RunJim	Sample
05/02/94	3	1	Suzie	Sample
05/04/94	2	1	RunJim	Sample
05/08/94	3	1	RunJim	Axilla 2
05/12/94	2	1	Axilla 2	Bathtub
05/21/94	7	1	RunJim	Guelah
05/23/94	2	1	Sample	Fee
05/27/94	3	2	RunJim	Bouncing
05/28/94	1	1	Sample	Bouncing
06/10/94	3	1	RunJim	Sample
06/17/94	5	1	RunJim	Glide
06/23/94	5	1	NICU	Bouncing
07/01/94	6	1	RunJim	Foam
07/09/94	6	1	RunJim	Gumbo
07/13/94	2	1	Sample	Mango
07/15/94	2	1	Gumbo	Fee
10/09/94	4	1	RunJim	FEFY
10/13/94	3	1	IDK	FEFY
10/16/94	3	1	Horn	Fee
10/21/94	3	1	DWD	Mango
10/29/94	7	1	RunJim	Lawn Boy
11/02/94	2	1	Suzie	If I Could
11/12/94	3	1	RunJim	If I Could
11/16/94	3	1	Sample	FEFY
11/22/94	5	1	Horn	Guyute
11/26/94	3	1	If I Could	Horse
12/04/94	6	1	RunJim	If I Could
12/09/94	4	1	Llama	Guyute
12/29/94	3	1	RunJim	If I Could
06/13/95	8	1	RunJim	Bouncing
06/20/95	6	1	Ginseng	Bathtub
06/28/95	6	1	Axilla 2	FEFY
10/03/95	11	1	Guelah	FEFY
10/15/95	8	1	Llama	Str Design
11/14/95	16	1	Chalkdust	Billy
11/28/95	9	1	Bouncing	IDK
12/14/95	12	1	Horn	Makisupa
07/19/96	22	1a	RunJim	Adeline
07/23/96	3	1	ACDCBag	Theme
08/02/96	3	1	PoorHeart	Theme
08/05/96	2	1	Wolfman's	If I Could
10/23/96	15	1	ACDCBag	HelloBaby
11/19/96	18	1	ACDCBag	Theme
02/21/97	21	1	My Soul	DWD
08/03/97	35	1	Bathtub	Blow
08/09/97	3	2	Wilson	Mike's
11/29/97	17	1	Wedge	Simple
12/06/97	5	1	Bathtub	Sample
>> 12/31/97		**9**		

THE FOG THAT SURROUNDS

Inspiration: A reworking of Taste featuring similar music but different lyrics.

Musical Evolution and History: For the first part of fall tour 1995 (when Fog debuted), Fishman—who did not sing on the original version of Taste—sang new verses and Trey and Page joined for a chorus kept from Taste. But the version of the song played during November and December 1995 had Fishman singing some verses and Trey singing verses lifted from Taste. Most notable about Fog was that the instrumental portion featured Trey picking out a progressing melody on lead guitar (which in the current version of Taste is instead expressed through chord changes). Unlike in the original version of Taste, the band did not return to vocals after the instrumental section of the song. Colloquial names used by fans for the reworked version of this song include "Another Taste" and "Taste the Fog." But in recording sessions for *Billy Breathes* the band decided to rework the song yet again and call it Taste, so "The Fog That Surrounds" name appears dead.

Rotation History: Only seen on fall tour 1995.

Discography: Has not yet appeared on a Phish album.

The Fog That Surrounds [22] [Fog]

By Anastasio/Marshall

09/27/95	[761]	1	IDK	Str Design
09/28/95	1	1	Fee	AArmy
09/30/95	2	2	RunJim	If I Could
10/02/95	1	1	AArmy	Theme
10/05/95	2	1	Ha Ha Ha	Horse
10/07/95	2	1	Gumbo	Mound
10/11/95	2	1	If I Could	AArmy
10/17/95	4	2	Caspian	Suzie
10/24/95	5	1	Paul&Silas	Fee
10/27/95	2	1	Fluffhead	Horn
11/10/95	5	1	RunJim	Old Home
11/12/95	2	1	IDK	If I Could
11/22/95	7	1	Cavern	Lizards
11/25/95	2	1	Billy	Bouncing
11/29/95	2	2	YEM	PoorHeart
12/02/95	3	1	Free	Bouncing
12/05/95	2	1	Chalkdust	Lizards
12/07/95	1	2	Str Design	Reba
12/11/95	3	2	Mango	Scent
12/14/95	2	1	Tela	MSO
12/16/95	2	1	ACDCBag	Ya Mar
12/29/95	3	1	DWD	NICU
>> 12/31/97		**150**		

FOOLED BY IMAGES

Inspiration: Part of the new group of songs written for summer 1997.

Musical Evolution and History: None to speak of, as the song has only been played once.

Rotation History: If you want to hear this one, you'll have to track down a particular show—6/14/97 in Dublin, Ireland.

Discography: Has not yet appeared on a Phish album.

Fooled by Images [1] [Fooled]

By Anastasio/Marshall

06/14/97	[905]	2	Saw It	Dogs Stole
>> 12/31/97		**61**		

FREE

Inspiration: One of the crop of debuts at the Lowell, MA, show on 5/16/95, Free gave the band a new jam vehicle complete with cool lyrics. There is various speculation about the meaning of the song's lyrics, including one theory that it is about childbirth. One darker rumor is that it stems from a cruise Tom Marshall took with his wife, and his fantasy to throw her overboard ("In a minute I'll be free / You'll be splashing in the sea / Hear the tiny cry as the ship goes sliding by").

Musical Evolution and History: The earliest versions of the song featured a fairly direct and structured—but still hypnotic—jam which brought the song back to its opening lyrics. The song then quickly evolved to include a very textural middle jam sequence that often featured Trey fading back on his mini drum kit. That summer, several notable versions emerged from long jams, like the one out of Runaway Jim on 6/16/95 and the one out of DWD on 6/26/95. That fall, Free continued to emerge as a jam vehicle, and on 11/22/95 in Landover, MD, it stretched out to over thirty minutes, the longest Free yet (though not all fans thought it was a particularly great version). When the band recorded this for inclusion on *Billy Breathes*, they reworked the feel of the song, deemphasizing the pronounced guitar line that seemed to define the song, and adding a different jam to the middle. Phish played around with this new version live in Europe in July 1996, but returned to the original Free for the rest of 1996. However, for the summer tour in 1997, with Trey's drum kit gone from the stage, the band remade the song's jam segment to more closely adhere to the *Billy Breathes* version. Also, when the band recorded Free for the album, they made one slight lyrics change: "As we go sliding by" was changed to "As the ship goes sliding by." Free received some radio airplay, and actually made *Billboard*'s alternative rock singles chart, but did not even crack the top 100 on the pop charts.

Rotation History: One of the most-played songs during its debut year of 1995, Free has moved into moderate rotation over 1996 and 1997.

Discography: Appears on *Billy Breathes* (1996), for which it was released as the first single.

Free [61] [Free]

By Anastasio/Marshall

05/16/95	[738]	1a	LCBill	Flip
06/08/95	2	2	Rift	Bouncing
06/10/95	2	1	It's Ice	Rift
06/16/95	4	2	RunJim	Carolina
06/23/95	5	1	Ginseng	Taste
06/26/95	3	2	DWD	PoorHeart
06/29/95	2	2	*OP2	Bowie
07/03/95	4	1	Str Design	Cavern
09/27/95	1	1	Rift	It's Ice
09/29/95	2	2	Maze	Ya Mar
10/03/95	3	1	I'm Blue	TMWSIY
10/06/95	2	1	Rift	Lizards
10/08/95	2	1	Uncle Pen	*CL1
10/14/95	3	1	Kung	Sparkle
10/17/95	2	1	Sparkle	Str Design
10/20/95	2	1	Rift	HelloBaby
10/25/95	4	1	Scent	Str Design
10/31/95	4	1	Sparkle	Guyute
11/10/95	2	2	*OP2	Scent
11/14/95	3	1	Esther	Julius
11/18/95	3	2	Sparkle	I'm Tired
11/22/95	3	2	Rift	Llama
11/28/95	3	2	Uncle Pen	Wind
11/30/95	2	2	Scent	Str Design
12/02/95	2	1	MSO	Fog
12/05/95	2	1	Lizards	Esther
12/09/95	3	1	Bouncing	Billy
12/12/95	2	2	*OP2	Sparkle
12/15/95	2	1	Bouncing	Possum
12/17/95	2	2	Maze	Also Sprac
12/30/95	3	2	Ya Mar	Harry
07/12/96	11	3	Bowie	HelloBaby
07/21/96	6	2	Life Mars	Antelope
08/02/96	5	2	Taste	Fluffhead
08/07/96	4	2	RunJim	Forbin's
08/10/96	1	2	Scent	Fluffhead
08/16/96	4	2	Sparkle	Sqirm Coil
10/17/96	3	2	Scent	Lizards
10/19/96	2	1	Rift	Esther
10/22/96	2	1	Sparkle	YEM
10/25/96	2	2	NICU	Str Design
11/02/96	5	1	Stash	Johnny B.
11/07/96	3	1	Guyute	Tela
11/14/96	5	1	CTB	All Things
11/16/96	2	1	Rift	Old Home
11/27/96	6	1	Uncle Pen	Theme
12/02/96	4	2	Taste	Scent
12/29/96	4	1	Rift	Sqirm Coil
02/16/97	5	2	CTB	Sparkle
02/20/97	3	2	Bouncing	SweptAwy
02/22/97	2	2	Harry	HelloBaby
02/25/97	2	2	PYITE	Fee
06/14/97	7	1	Bye Bye	Caspian
06/24/97	6	1	Talk	Caspian
07/02/97	5	E	*OPE	*CLE
07/06/97	3	2	*OP2	YEM
07/26/97	8	2	Harry	Waste
07/30/97	2	2	PYITE	Bowie
08/08/97	5	2	Wolfman's	Limb
08/14/97	5	1	Limb	CTB
11/30/97	14	2	Stash	Piper
>> 12/31/97		**13**		

FUCK YOUR FACE

Inspiration: More of a spoken piece than a song, it tells the story of someone buying a new guitar, plugging it in and playing it to prove that "This gonna fuck your face."

Musical Evolution and History: Only played in its original form.
Rotation History: Only played once.
Discography: Appears on the "white tape."

Fuck Your Face [1] [Fuck]

By Gordon

04/29/87	[15]	1	Cities	*CL1
>> 12/31/97	**951**			

GHOST

Inspiration: Supposedly, Tom Marshall's lyrics refer to an imaginary childhood friend he called "the ghost."
Musical Evolution and History: Perhaps the most funked-out tune debuted in summer 1997, the band immediately made Ghost a showcase for their new jam style. With a long segment following the opening lyrical segment, the song became an immediate fan favorite, though by the end of the year, some complained that the jams tended to be more boring than exploratory. But on at least several occasions, Phish played Ghosts to be reckoned with: check out the 30-plus-minute version on 7/3/97 in Nuremburg, Germany, and the 27-minute gem from Atlanta, GA, on 7/23/97.
Rotation History: One of the most commonly played songs on the summer and fall 1997 tours.
Discography: Has not yet appeared on a Phish album.

Ghost [28] [Ghost]

By Anastasio/Marshall

06/13/97	[904]	2	Chalkdust	Oblivious
06/16/97	2	2	Limb	Don't Care
06/19/97	1	2	Stash	Saw It
06/20/97	1	2	Bowie	Bye Bye
06/22/97	2	1a	HelloBaby	*CL1
06/24/97	1	2	Wading	*CL2
07/01/97	4	1	*OP1	Horn
07/03/97	2	2	*OP2	CTB
07/09/97	3	2	YEM	PoorHeart
07/10/97	1	2	Ya Mar	River
07/21/97	2	1	*OP1	Dogs Stole
07/23/97	2	2	PYITE	Sample
07/25/97	1	2	Drums	CharZero
07/29/97	2	1	Sparkle	SweptAwy
07/31/97	2	1	*OP1	Ya Mar
08/02/97	1	1	Ginseng	Dogs Stole
08/06/97	2	2	My Soul	Caspian
08/09/97	2	1	PYITE	Taste
08/13/97	3	2	RunJim	Isabella
08/16/97	2	1	PYITE	Ginseng
11/17/97	5	1	Train Song	Fire
11/21/97	2	2	*OP2	ACDCBag
11/28/97	4	2	Slave	Johnny B.
12/02/97	3	1	Chalkdust	Divided
12/05/97	2	1	*OP1	Wilson
12/11/97	4	2	BBFCM	DWD
12/13/97	2	2	PYITE	Mike's
12/28/97	1	2	Simple	Drowned
>> 12/31/97	**3**			

GLIDE

Inspiration: Trey, Tom, and Dave Abrahams cooked this one up in high school back in 1982, and during recording sessions for *A Picture of Nectar* in summer 1991, Phish dusted it off and rearranged it.
Musical Evolution and History: Since its debut on 9/27/91 in Rochester, NY, Glide has changed little, except for the length of the pause before the final "Gliiiiide," which can stretch on forever. The *Nectar* version of the song features Page on harmonica, but he hasn't yet translated that skill to concert, apparently because it's not easy to play harmonica and piano at the same time. During 1993, Mike and Trey would slide back and forth on a slipper gliding board during the performance of this song and It's Ice.
Rotation History: Another one that got a lot of attention from 1991 to 1994, but little since; lucky concertgoers at Shoreline Amphitheater on 7/31/97 received 1997's only rendition.
Discography: Appears on *A Picture of Nectar* (1992).

Glide [100] [Glide]

By Phish (after Anastasio/Marshall/Abrahams)

09/27/91	[337]	E	*OPE	Rocky Top
10/27/91	19	E	*OPE	Possum
10/31/91	3	E	*OPE	Possum
11/09/91	6	E	*OPE	Possum
11/14/91	4	2	It's Ice	Tweezer
11/16/91	2	E	*OPE	Rocky Top
11/19/91	1	E	*OPE	Rocky Top
11/22/91	3	E	*OPE	Suzie
11/30/91	3	1	*OP1	Llama
12/05/91	2	E	*OPE	Cavern
03/17/92	10	2	RunJim	Sloth
03/19/92	1	2	*OP2	Chalkdust
03/20/92	1	1	Brother	Rift
03/25/92	3	1	Maze	RunJim
03/27/92	2	1	Maze	Bouncing
03/28/92	1	1	Bowie	Cavern
03/31/92	2	1	Divided	Split&Melt
04/04/92	3	2	Weekpaug	MSO
04/12/92	5	2	*OP2	Split&Melt
04/18/92	5	2	*OP2	Oh Kee
04/22/92	3	2	*OP2	Antelope
04/24/92	2	2	Love You	Llama
04/30/92	3	2	*OP2	Tweezer
05/02/92	2	2	*OP2	Bowie
05/05/92	2	1	It's Ice	Antelope
05/07/92	2	2	Fluffhead	Mike's
05/14/92	5	2	*OP2	Cavern
05/16/92	2	1	Foam	Split&Melt
05/18/92	2	2	*OP1	Llama
07/09/92	9	1a	*OP1	Oh Kee
07/12/92	3	1a	Maze	Possum
07/15/92	2	1	*OP1	Oh Kee
07/16/92	1	2	Llama	Faul&Silas
11/19/92	29	1	Foam	Split&Melt
11/21/92	2	1	Foam	PoorHeart
11/23/92	2	1	Foam	Split&Melt
11/27/92	2	2	Possum	It's Ice
11/30/92	2	2	Maze	Uncle Pen
12/02/92	2	2	Llama	Lngthwise
12/04/92	2	1	Stash	Sparkle
12/07/92	3	1	Maze	Sparkle
12/12/92	4	2	Maze	Curtain
12/28/92	2	1	Foam	It's Ice
12/31/92	3	2	Stash	GTBT
02/04/93	2	1	Sample	Antelope
02/07/93	3	2	BBJ	YEM
02/13/93	5	1	It's Ice	Rift
02/17/93	2	2	Bowie	My Friend
02/20/93	3	2	Tweezer	Mike's
02/22/93	2	2	Tweezer	YEM
02/26/93	3	2	Tweezer	Chalkdust
03/03/93	3	2	Weekpaug	MSO
03/08/93	3	1	It's Ice	Bowie
03/09/93	1	1	Divided	PYITE
03/13/93	2	2	It's Ice	Uncle Pen
03/17/93	3	2	Axilla	Reba
03/25/93	6	1	Stash	Rift
03/30/93	4	1	Stash	Divided
04/05/93	5	2	Tweezer	YEM
04/10/93	2	2	Rift	BBJ
04/17/93	5	1	It's Ice	My Friend
04/20/93	2	1	It's Ice	Uncle Pen
04/25/93	5	1	It's Ice	RunJim
04/29/93	2	1	Llama	Rift
05/01/93	2	1	It's Ice	Bowie
05/05/93	3	1	It's Ice	Maze
05/08/93	3	1	Stash	My Friend
07/16/93	4	2	Split&Melt	Maze
07/21/93	3	1a	Maze	Rift
07/24/93	3	2	Maze	Sparkle
08/09/93	12	1	Split&Melt	Nellie
08/15/93	5	2	Maze	Adeline
08/25/93	6	1	Stash	Cavern
12/29/93	4	1	Foam	Divided
04/05/94	4	1	Fluffhead	Julius
04/08/94	2	1	Maze	Foam
04/11/94	3	1	Julius	Divided
04/14/94	2	1	DWD	Rift
04/18/94	4	1	Chalkdust	PoorHeart
04/21/94	2	1	Foam	Split&Melt
05/02/94	8	1	It's Ice	Divided
05/17/94	11	2	RunJim	Tweezer
05/22/94	4	1	Divided	Split&Melt
06/09/94	7	2	Split&Melt	Julius
06/17/94	6	1	Foam	Split&Melt
06/30/94	10	1	Split&Melt	Scent
07/10/94	8	2	Bowie	Ya Mar
10/07/94	5	1	Julius	PoorHeart
10/15/94	7	1	Maze	Reba
10/25/94	7	2	YSZahov	Axilla 2
10/28/94	3	1	Stash	Axilla 2
11/03/94	4	1	Peaches	Split&Melt
11/20/94	9	2	Bowie	Axilla 2
12/31/94	19	1	Antelope	Mound
06/24/95	15	1	Julius	Mound
10/17/95	23	1	Maze	Sparkle
11/21/95	20	1	Bowie	Ya Mar
08/13/96	51	1	Llama	Slave
11/30/96	34	2	It's Ice	Brother
07/31/97	50	1	Maze	Saw It
>> 12/31/97	**36**			

GLIDE II

Inspiration: Apparently a sequel of sorts to Glide, this song shares little of the whimsy of Glide. Instead, it features the band members repeating the word "flip" over and over again (which led many to believe the song's title was Flip), then Trey pronounces, "It's time."
Musical Evolution and History: None to speak of, because the song has been played live only once. However, during the recording sessions for *Billy Breathes*, the band recorded an instrumental version of the song, but decided not to include it on the album. That version can be found on a bootleg tape of *Billy* outtakes making the rounds among tapers. Part of the middle section of this song is taken almost exactly from part of Guyute, which may explain the song's retirement.
Rotation History: Played only once, at the Lowell, MA, show on 5/16/95.
Discography: Has not yet appeared on a Phish album, though it was

Original Songs Played by Year *(continued)*

Mike's Song		
1990	54	52%
1991	49	39%
1992	36	30%
1993	41	37%
1994	27	22%
1995	16	20%
1996	15	21%
1997	12	15%

Mound		
1992	20	17%
1993	34	31%
1994	18	15%
1995	12	15%
1996	4	6%
1997	0	0%

My Friend My Friend		
1992	20	17%
1993	39	35%
1994	19	15%
1995	12	15%
1996	6	9%
1997	3	4%

My Sweet One		
1990	34	33%
1991	72	57%
1992	32	26%
1993	19	17%
1994	14	11%
1995	3	4%
1996	0	0%
1997	1	1%

N20		
1995	3	4%
1996	0	0%
1997	0	0%

NICU		
1992	12	10%
1993	0	0%
1994	10	8%
1995	9	11%
1996	6	9%
1997	15	19%

Oblivious Fool		
1997	5	6%

Oh Kee Pa		
1990	53	51%
1991	44	35%
1992	20	17%
1993	11	10%
1994	8	6%
1995	2	2%
1996	1	1%
1997	2	3%

Piper		
1997	15	19%

recorded for possible inclusion on *Billy Breathes*.

Glide II [1] [Glide 2]

By Anastasio/Marshall

05/16/95	[738]	1a	Free	YEM
>> 12/31/97	**228**			

GOLGI APPARATUS

Inspiration: Perhaps the original Phish song, the lyrics were written by Trey and Tom and their grade-school friends, then reworked many years later for use by Phish. One of its authors, Aaron Woolfe, was at a party in California years later and was not aware at the time that Trey was in a successful band. He heard the song played on the homeowner's stereo and, needless to say, was slightly tweaked. But no one at the party believed he had helped write the song.

Musical Evolution and History: Not much, as Golgi has rocked out pretty much from the start. Like many Phish songs, it's performed at a faster pace in the 1990s than in the 1980s.

Rotation History: Overplayed to the point of absurdity in the early 1990s, fans back then could expect Golgi at least every other night, often as an opener, closer, or even encore. But since 1995 Phish has limited its performances of Golgi, making the song more of a treat.

Discography: Appears on *Junta* (1989).

Golgi Apparatus [301] [Golgi]

By Anastasio/Marshall/Woolfe/Szuter

10/15/86	[8]	1a	Peaches	SwingLow
10/31/86	1	1	CamlWalk	Slave
03/06/87	2	1	Corrina	Quinn
03/11/87	1	1a	Corrina	Quinn
03/23/87	1	2	CamlWalk	SwingLow
04/24/87	1	1	Alumni	SwingLow
04/29/87	1	1	Alumni	SwingLow
05/11/87	1	1a	*OP1	Corrina
08/10/87	2	1	Alumni	Wilson
08/21/87	1	2	Harpua	Sparks
09/12/87	2	1	Reagan	ACDCBag
09/27/87	1	1	FunkBitch	Peaches
10/14/87	1	1	YEM	Slave
01/30/88	3	3	Lizards	Bike
03/11/88	2	1	Wilson	Slave
03/21/88	2	1a	Suzie	McGrupp
03/31/88	1	1	IDK	Fee
05/15/88	3	1a	LTJP	YEM
05/23/88	1	1a	A-Train	YEM
05/25/88	1	1	Peaches	Sally
06/15/88	1	1	Fluffhead	La Grange
06/18/88	1	1	Possum	La Grange
06/20/88	1	2	Fee	Satin Doll
06/21/88	1	2	Peaches	*CL2
07/11/88	1	1	Mockbird	Alumni
07/24/88	3	1	WalkAway	FunkBitch
08/06/88	3	2	*OP2	ACDCBag
08/27/88	1	1a	A-Train	Tela
09/24/88	3	1	*OP1	OYWD
10/12/88	1	1	IDK	Bowie
10/29/88	1	1	Time Loves	Bold
11/03/88	1	1	Fire	Fluffhead
11/05/88	1	1	A-Train	WalkAway
12/02/88	2	1	Sloth	Bold
01/26/89	1	1	IDK	Alumni
02/06/89	2	1	A-Train	Divided
02/07/89	1	1	Weekpaug	*CL1
02/17/89	1	1a	Split&Melt	A-Train
02/18/89	1	1a	GTBT	Wilson
03/04/89	3	1	Fee	GTBT
03/30/89	2	2	La Grange	*CL2
04/15/89	7	2	FunkBitch	Slave
05/05/89	10	1	*OP1	YEM
05/06/89	1	2	Harry	Slave
05/13/89	6	1	YEM	La Grange
05/20/89	4	2	Bowie	*CL2
05/26/89	2	2	Antelope	*CL2
10/01/89	23	1	Jam	Harry
10/06/89	1	1a	Sloth	Bold
10/07/89	1	1	*OP1	Ya Mar
10/14/89	3	1	IDK	Ya Mar
10/20/89	1	1	Divided	Antelope
10/22/89	2	1	Reba	In a Hole
10/26/89	1	1	Oh Kee	YEM
11/02/89	3	2	Oh Kee	YEM
11/03/89	1	1	Reba	*CL1
11/09/89	2	1	IDK	Ya Mar
11/11/89	2	1a	Oh Kee	Bathtub
12/07/89	7	E	*OPE	*CLE
12/09/89	2	1	Bathtub	*CL1
12/16/89	2	1a	In a Hole	*CL1
02/09/90	15	1	*OP1	Oh Kee
02/23/90	6	2	*OP2	Reba
02/24/90	1	1	YEM	Divided
03/01/90	2	1	*OP1	Ya Mar
03/08/90	3	2	Curtis	*CL2
04/04/90	5	1	*OP1	YEM
04/05/90	1	2	Contact	*CL2
04/07/90	2	2	*OP2	Forbin's
04/08/90	1	2	*OP2	WalkAway
04/12/90	3	1	*OP1	Ya Mar
04/22/90	6	E	Lawn Boy	*CLE
05/19/90	13	1	*OP1	Ya Mar
05/24/90	2	1	ACDCBag	*CL1
06/05/90	3	E	WhipPost	*CLE
06/16/90	4	2	*OP2	Esther
09/15/90	3	1	Bowie	Stash
09/22/90	4	E	Asse Fest	*CLE
10/04/90	3	1	*OP1	Landlady
10/05/90	1	2	*OP2	Curtain
10/07/90	2	2	GTBT	*CL2
10/12/90	2	1	Tweezer	*CL1
11/02/90	4	1	*OP1	Landlady
11/04/90	2	2	*OP2	Rocky Top
11/16/90	3	1	Divided	*CL1
12/07/90	7	1	*OP1	Stash
12/08/90	1	2	Tela	No Good
12/28/90	1	1	Weekpaug	*CL1
12/31/90	2	2	*OP2	Stash
02/03/91	3	1	Foam	*CL1
02/07/91	1	1	Sqirm Coil	*CL1
02/09/91	2	2	*OP2	BurAlive
02/14/91	1	1	Oh Kee	*CL1
02/15/91	1	E2	Contact	*CLE2
02/16/91	1	2	Love You	*CL2
02/21/91	3	2	*OP2	Cavern
02/26/91	4	1	ACDCBag	La Grange
02/27/91	1	1	*OP1	Divided
02/28/91	1	1	MSO	*CL1
03/01/91	1	2	*OP2	Landlady
03/06/91	2	1	*OP1	YEM
03/13/91	6	2	Oh Kee	*CL2
03/16/91	2	1	TMWSIY	Reba
03/22/91	3	E	Magilla	*CLE
03/28/91	2	1a	*OP1	Divided
04/04/91	5	1	Carolina	*CL1
04/12/91	4	1	Rocky Top	*CL1
04/16/91	3	1	*OP1	YEM
04/19/91	2	2	Curtain	Landlady
04/21/91	2	1	*OP1	Rocky Top
04/27/91	4	1	Stash	*CL1
05/04/91	3	E	RunJim	*CLE
05/12/91	4	2	Curtain	Magilla
05/16/91	1	1	BurAlive	Foam
05/17/91	1	E	Lawn Boy	*CLE
05/18/91	1	1	BurAlive	Chalkdust
07/12/91	3	2	*OP2	Sqirm Coil
07/14/91	2	1	Sqirm Coil	Guelah
07/19/91	3	1	*OP1	Landlady
07/20/91	1	2	Flat Fee	Stash
07/23/91	2	E	Caravan	*CLE
07/24/91	1	1	*OP1	Chalkdust
07/25/91	1	2	Landlady	Sqirm Coil
07/26/91	1	1	Landlady	*CL1
08/03/91	2	1	Divided	*CL1
09/26/91	2	2	*OP2	Sqirm Coil
09/28/91	2	1	Brother	Memories
10/02/91	2	1	Chalkdust	*CL1
10/04/91	2	E	Adeline	Rocky Top
10/06/91	2	1	Terrapin	*CL1
10/10/91	1	1	Llama	Alumni
10/12/91	2	1	Contact	*CL1
10/15/91	2	2	Ya Mar	*CL2
10/17/91	1	1	Chalkdust	*CL1
10/19/91	2	1	Stash	*CL1
10/27/91	4	1	Harry	*CL1
11/02/91	5	2	*OP2	Antelope
11/08/91	3	1	Eliza	*CL1
11/12/91	3	1	BurAlive	Uncle Pen
11/13/91	1	2	Mockbird	Bathtub
11/14/91	1	1	Mango	RunJim
11/15/91	1	1	Lawn Boy	*CL1
11/20/91	3	2	*OP2	It's ice
11/21/91	1	E	Adeline	*CLE
11/23/91	2	1	Bouncing	*CL1
11/24/91	1	2	YEM	*CL2
11/30/91	1	2	Antelope	*CL2
12/04/91	1	2	Love You	*CL2
12/05/91	1	1	*OP1	Paul&Silas
12/07/91	2	E	Adeline	*CLE
12/31/91	1	1	Llama	*CL1
03/07/92	2	E	Adeline	*CLE
03/12/92	2	2	*OP2	Tweezer
03/14/92	2	2	*OP2	Llama
03/19/92	2	1	Sparkle	Horse
03/21/92	2	1	Stash	*CL1
03/24/92	1	1	Rift	Horse
03/25/92	1	2	Rosie	*CL2
03/27/92	2	2	Love You	*CL2
03/30/92	2	2	*OP2	Uncle Pen
04/01/92	2	1	*OP1	Foam
04/03/92	1	1	Split&Melt	*CL1
04/07/92	4	2	My Mind	*CL2
04/09/92	1	1	Sqirm Coil	*CL1
04/13/92	2	1	*OP1	Uncle Pen
04/15/92	1	2	MSO	*CL2
04/17/92	2	E	*OPE	*CLE
04/19/92	2	1	IDK	*CL1
04/23/92	3	2	Rosie	*CL2
04/24/92	1	1	Sqirm Coil	*CL1
04/29/92	2	1	Love You	*CL2
05/01/92	2	2	Terrapin	*CL2
05/05/92	3	1	*OP1	Curtain
05/06/92	1	2	A-Train	*CL2
05/08/92	2	2	Harry	*CL2
05/09/92	1	2	Rosie	*CL2
05/15/92	4	1a	*OP1	Foam
05/16/92	1	1	Horn	Lizards
06/23/92	5	1a	Brain	*CL1
06/30/92	3	1a	*OP1	Divided
07/10/92	4	1a	Maze	Lizards
07/15/92	4	2	Harry	*CL2
07/27/92	10	1a	*OP1	All Things
08/01/92	4	1a	*OP1	Foam
08/20/92	7	1	*OP1	Foam
11/22/92	12	2	Faht	*CL2
11/28/92	4	2	Harpua	*CL2
12/02/92	3	E	*OPE	Rocky Top
12/05/92	3	1	Uncle Pen	*CL1
12/10/92	4	1	*OP1	Llama
12/12/92	2	2	Sqirm Coil	*CL2
12/28/92	2	1	Rift	Adeline
02/06/93	7	1	*OP1	Foam
02/09/93	2	1	Maze	*CL1
02/12/93	3	1	*OP1	Maze
02/13/93	1	1	Maze	*CL1
02/17/93	2	1	Maze	*CL1
02/20/93	3	1	*OP1	Foam
02/23/93	3	1	*OP1	My Friend
02/25/93	1	2	Brain	BBFCM
02/27/93	2	1	*OP1	Rift
03/02/93	1	E	*OPE	TweezRep
03/06/93	3	1	Maze	RunJim
03/08/93	1	1	*OP1	Rift
03/12/93	2	2	Harry	*CL2
03/14/93	2	E	Adeline	*CLE
03/17/93	2	2	Great Gig	*CL2
03/19/93	2	2	Love You	*CL2
03/22/93	2	2	*OP2	It's Ice
03/25/93	2	2	Weekpaug	*CL2
03/27/93	2	2	PoorHeart	*CL2
03/30/93	2	1	All Things	My Friend
04/02/93	3	1	Maze	*CL1
04/09/93	3	E	Adeline	*CLE
04/12/93	2	1	*OP1	Tube
04/14/93	2	1	IDK	*CL1
04/17/93	2	1	All Things	Antelope
04/20/93	2	2	WhipPost	*CL2
04/22/93	2	1	Rift	*CL1
04/23/93	1	2	*OP2	Maze
04/25/93	2	1	IDK	*CL1
04/27/93	1	2	*OP2	My Friend
04/30/93	2	2	YEM	*CL2
05/02/93	2	1	IDK	*CL1
05/05/93	2	1	Maze	*CL1
05/07/93	2	E	AmGrace	*CLE
05/30/93	3	1a	Llama	*CL1
07/16/93	2	1	Daniel	My Friend
07/18/93	2	2	PurplRain	*CL2
07/22/93	2	1	Stash	*CL1
07/24/93	2	E	*OPE	Freebird
07/30/93	5	2	My Friend	Sqirm Coil
08/03/93	3	2	PurplRain	*CL2
08/12/93	6	2	BBJ	Possum
08/14/93	2	2	PurplRain	*CL2
08/24/93	6	1	Maze	*CL1
08/26/93	2	1	Harry	*CL1
12/28/93	2	E	Memories	*CLE
12/31/93	3	E	*OPE	AmGrace
04/05/94	2	E	Nellie	*CLE
04/10/94	4	E	Bouncing	*CLE
04/13/94	2	1	Divided	*CL1
04/17/94	4	2	Contact	*CL2
04/23/94	5	2	Who By Fire	*CL2
04/28/94	3	E	*OPE	*CLE
05/02/94	3	2	Reba	Lizards
05/06/94	3	2	Maze	Golgi
05/08/94	2	E	Adeline	*CLE
05/19/94	7	2	Harry	*CL2
05/27/94	7	1	Harry	*CL1
05/29/94	2	E	Wilson	Rocky Top
06/09/94	1	2	Weekpaug	*CL2
06/13/94	3	E	*OPE	*CLE
06/16/94	2	2	PurplRain	*CL2
06/19/94	3	1	Stash	*CL1
06/22/94	2	1	Stash	*CL1
06/25/94	3	2	Harry	*CL2
06/29/94	2	1	IDK	*CL1
07/02/94	3	1	*OP1	Divided
07/05/94	2	2	AmGrace	*CL2
07/08/94	2	2	Julius	*CL2
07/10/94	2	E	*OPE	Rocky Top
07/15/94	3	1	Split&Melt	*CL1
07/16/94	1	1	*OP1	DWD
10/07/94	1	1	Guyute	*CL1
10/10/94	3	2	*OP2	Maze
10/15/94	4	1	DWD	*CL1
10/20/94	3	2	Guyute	*CL1
10/25/94	4	E	Long Time	*CLE
10/31/94	5	1	Reba	*CL1
11/04/94	3	2	Ya Mar	Slave
11/12/94	1	2	Harry	*CL2
11/14/94	2	E	*OPE	*CLE
11/17/94	2	2	Slave	*CL2
11/19/94	2	1	*OP1	DWD
11/25/94	4	1	Julius	*CL1
12/01/94	4	2	Harry	*CL2
12/03/94	2	E	*OPE	*CLE
12/06/94	2	1	Stash	*CL1
12/08/94	2	2	Bowie	*CL2
12/31/94	6	1	*OP1	NICU
06/13/95	6	2	Harry	*CL2
06/24/95	9	2	Adeline	*CL2
06/30/95	5	E	Rosie	*CLE
10/22/95	22	2	*OP2	Possum
12/02/95	24	2	DayinLife	Sqirm Coil
12/29/95	13	E	*OPE	*CLE
07/15/96	14	E	*OPE	*CLE
07/21/96	4	1	*OP1	Guelah
07/24/96	3	1a	YEM	*CL1
08/02/96	2	1	Theme	Tweezer
08/07/96	4	E	Bouncing	*CLE
08/12/96	2	2	HelloBaby	Possum
08/17/96	4	2	Antelope	Slave
10/17/96	2	E	*OPE	*CLE
11/08/96	15	1	Reba	Antelope
11/13/96	3	2	Theme	*CL2
02/17/97	23	1	Bathtub	*CL1
08/13/97	46	2	Also Sprac	Frankstein
12/06/97	19	1	*OP1	Antelope
12/29/97	7	1	NICU	Crossroads
>> 12/31/97	**2**			

GUELAH PAPYRUS

Inspiration: A section of the lyrics

refers nostalgically to Dave Abrahams's mother, Guelah, who would intrude into Dave's bedroom and spoil the childhood fun of Trey, Tom, and Dave.

Musical Evolution and History: Guelah is made up of three parts: Guelah Papyrus, The Asse Festival, and Guelah (The Fly), which have never been performed apart since the song's debut on 2/1/91 in Providence, RI (except for one last solo shot of The Asse Festival on 4/27/91). Despite this, some tapers still label the song "Guelah Papyrus > Asse Festival > Guelah Papyrus." Performances of it differ little from show to show, and feature a strange dance by Trey and Mike.

Rotation History: Back in the *Nectar* days, Guelah got plenty of play, but its glory started to fade in 1994. In 1997, it surfaced live only three times.

Discography: Appears on *A Picture of Nectar* (1992).

Guelah Papyrus [165] [Guelah]

By Anastasio/Marshall

02/01/91	[257]	1	Magilla	RunJim
02/02/91	1	1	Suzie	Dinner
02/03/91	1	1	RunJim	MSO
02/07/91	2	2	TweezRep	Uncle Pen
02/08/91	1	1	RunJim	Bowie
02/09/91	1	1	Foam	MSO
02/15/91	2	2	Ya Mar	MSO
02/16/91	1	2	RunJim	Fluffhead
02/21/91	3	2	Stash	Uncle Pen
02/26/91	4	1	Llama	MSO
02/28/91	2	2	Llama	Divided
03/01/91	1	2	Llama	Sloth
03/07/91	3	2	Weekpaug	MSO
03/13/91	3	2	MSO	RunJim
03/16/91	2	2	Divided	MSO
03/22/91	3	2	RunJim	Terrapin
03/28/91	2	1a	YEM	MSO
04/04/91	5	2	RunJim	Bowie
04/12/91	4	1	Divided	Oh Kee
04/22/91	8	1	Llama	Oh Kee
04/26/91	2	2	MSO	Landlady
05/04/91	4	1	Split&Melt	Fluffhead
05/17/91	6	2	Possum	Rocky Top
05/18/91	1	2	MSO	Bowie
07/13/91	4	2	Chalkdust	Divided
07/14/91	1	1	Golgi	MSO
07/18/91	3	1	RunJim	Suzie
07/21/91	2	1	Divided	PoorHeart
07/24/91	2	2	Possum	Bowie
08/03/91	4	1	RunJim	Llama
09/26/91	2	1	MSO	Lizards
09/28/91	2	2	Llama	Sparkle
10/02/91	2	2	MSO	RunJim
10/04/91	2	1	Divided	Sparkle
10/11/91	4	1	MSO	Chalkdust
10/18/91	5	2	Uncle Pen	Dinner
10/27/91	5	1	BurAlive	Fluffhead
11/02/91	5	2	Sparkle	WalkAway
11/12/91	6	2	Weekpaug	Chalkdust
11/21/91	7	1	PoorHeart	Reba
11/23/91	2	1	RunJim	Sparkle
11/30/91	2	1	Paul&Silas	YEM
12/06/91	3	1	Landlady	IDK
12/31/91	2	1	Lizards	Divided
03/06/92	1	1	Divided	Maze
03/13/92	4	1	PoorHeart	Maze
03/17/92	2	1	Divided	Rift
03/24/92	4	2	Weekpaug	Mango
03/27/92	3	1	Divided	Maze
03/30/92	2	1	Foam	Sparkle
04/03/92	3	1	Rift	Sparkle
04/05/92	2	1	Llama	Divided
04/06/92	1	1	Chalkdust	Sqirm Coil
04/09/92	2	1	Foam	Llama
04/12/92	1	1	PoorHeart	Divided
04/15/92	2	1	Foam	Sparkle
04/18/92	3	1	Divided	PoorHeart
04/21/92	2	1	Rift	Possum
04/22/92	1	1	Sparkle	Divided
04/23/92	1	1	Uncle Pen	Sqirm Coil
04/29/92	3	1	RunJim	Rift
05/01/92	2	1	Divided	It's Ice
05/03/92	2	2	Fluffhead	Mike's
05/05/92	1	1	Rift	Divided
05/07/92	2	1	Rift	Possum
05/09/92	2	1	Split&Melt	Rift
05/12/92	2	2	YEM	Chalkdust
05/17/92	4	2	Possum	Sqirm Coil
05/18/92	1	1	Divided	Foam
06/24/92	4	1a	Uncle Pen	IDK
06/30/92	2	1a	Divided	Possum
07/09/92	3	1a	RunJim	Bowie
07/14/92	4	1	Rift	Maze
07/16/92	2	1	Maze	Rift
08/02/92	14	1a	Chalkdust	Rift
08/15/92	3	1a	Sparkle	Maze
08/19/92	2	1a	RunJim	YEM
11/21/92	12	2	Uncle Pen	Sqirm Coil
11/23/92	2	1	Rift	Divided
11/30/92	4	2	RunJim	Maze
12/03/92	3	2	Rift	Fluffhead
12/05/92	2	1	Rift	Split&Melt
12/08/92	3	1	Uncle Pen	Divided
12/11/92	2	1	Chalkdust	Sparkle
12/12/92	1	2	Rift	YEM
12/29/92	3	1	RunJim	Llama
02/03/93	3	1	PoorHeart	Bowie
02/05/93	2	1	Llama	Rift
02/10/93	4	1	Foam	Reba
02/12/93	2	1	Maze	Sparkle
02/15/93	2	1	Sparkle	Divided
02/18/93	2	1	Chalkdust	PoorHeart
02/22/93	4	1	Rift	PoorHeart
02/27/93	4	1	Rift	Maze
03/03/93	2	1	Maze	Paul&Silas
03/05/93	1	2	Chalkdust	Uncle Pen
03/08/93	2	1	Rift	Oh Kee
03/12/93	2	1	Possum	Rift
03/14/93	2	1	Foam	Sparkle
03/18/93	3	1	Chalkdust	Rift
03/22/93	3	1	Chalkdust	Uncle Pen
03/25/93	2	1	Chalkdust	It's Ice
03/27/93	2	1	Llama	Rift
04/01/93	4	1	Llama	Rift
04/03/93	2	1	Rift	Sparkle
04/09/93	2	1	Sparkle	Stash
04/13/93	3	1	Chalkdust	Caravan
04/16/93	2	1	Chalkdust	Sparkle
04/18/93	2	1	Rift	Split&Melt
04/21/93	2	1	Foam	Maze
04/23/93	2	1	Divided	Lawn Boy
04/24/93	1	1	Chalkdust	PoorHeart
04/27/93	2	1	Stash	It's Ice
05/01/93	3	1	Foam	Split&Melt
05/05/93	3	1	Rift	Foam
05/08/93	3	1	Chalkdust	Rift
05/30/93	2	1a	Maze	PoorHeart
07/18/93	4	1	Foam	Maze
07/24/93	4	1	Divided	Rift
08/02/93	7	1	Chalkdust	PoorHeart
08/06/93	2	2	Tweezer	Sqirm Coil
08/12/93	5	1	Chalkdust	Nellie
08/14/93	2	1	Chalkdust	Divided
08/17/93	3	1	Llama	Divided
08/21/93	2	1	Foam	Rift
08/26/93	3	1	RunJim	Reba
12/31/93	5	1	Llama	Stash
04/06/94	3	1	Llama	PoorHeart
04/15/94	7	1	Llama	Paul&Silas
05/03/94	14	1	Rift	Maze
05/21/94	13	1	Foam	DWD
05/29/94	7	1	Divided	Halley's
06/09/94	1	1	Llama	Rift
06/14/94	4	1	Llama	Rift
06/22/94	6	1	Llama	Rift
06/30/94	6	1	Rift	Split&Melt
07/02/94	2	1	Divided	FEFY
07/09/94	5	1	Maze	Scent
10/07/94	6	1	Divided	Stash
10/12/94	4	1	Lizards	Julius
10/20/94	6	1	PoorHeart	Split&Melt
10/28/94	7	1	Llama	Scent
11/14/94	8	1	Scent	Split&Melt
11/25/94	8	1	Llama	Reba
12/03/94	6	1	Divided	Scent
06/08/95	13	1	RunJim	Mound
06/22/95	10	1	Divided	It's Ice
10/03/95	16	1	Maze	Foam
10/21/95	12	1	Chalkdust	Reba
11/12/95	11	1	Bouncing	Reba
12/02/95	14	1	Mound	Reba
07/21/96	31	1	Golgi	Rift
08/02/96	5	1	DWD	PoorHeart
08/05/96	2	1	PoorHeart	Divided
10/18/96	11	1	RunJim	Old Home
10/25/96	5	1	Mound	IDK
10/29/96	3	1	Chalkdust	CTB
11/07/96	5	1	Rift	Stash
11/11/96	3	1	Chalkdust	CTB
11/18/96	5	1	Chalkdust	Ginseng
11/23/96	3	1	Chalkdust	CTB
12/29/96	10	1	Taste	Train Song
02/16/97	5	1	Crosseyed	Ginseng
06/24/97	20	1	Vultures	RunJim
08/11/97	26	1	Guyute	Limb
>> 12/31/97	**30**			

GUMBO

Inspiration: With lyrics by Fishman and music by Trey, Gumbo joined a select crop of Fish/Trey songs (like Harpua) when it was debuted in fall 1990.

Musical Evolution and History: In its early years, Gumbo seemed like a song tailor-made for the Giant Country Horns (many fans especially love the 7/21/91 Arrowhead Ranch encore version, with special guest Steve-O on washboard). Indeed, after the summer 1991 horns tour, Phish didn't even give Gumbo another shot until 1993. By 1995, however, the band felt more confident with the song, and in 1997, Gumbo joined the group of songs that received a major funk makeover. Instead of a brief jam section, the band suddenly stretched the song out to fifteen minutes or more on a regular basis; some of the best of this new crop of Gumbos include 8/8/97 Tinley Park, IL, and 11/14/97 West Valley, UT.

Rotation History: Never played more than ten times in a year, Gumbo has always been a special concert treat. It was out of rotation completely from summer 1991 through 4/16/93, then again from 4/21/93 through 6/16/94, after which it started surfacing more regularly.

Discography: Appears on *A Live One* (1995), as a live track taken from 12/2/94 Davis, CA, with the Giant Country Horns.

Gumbo [44] [Gumbo]

By Anastasio/Fishman

09/28/90	[229]	2	Esther	Dinner
11/30/90	20	2	Lizards	Divided
07/12/91	72	1	MSO	Mike's
07/14/91	2	2	Divided	Dinner
07/19/91	3	1	YEM	Touch Me
07/21/91	2	E	*OPE	Touch Me
07/23/91	1	2	Dinner	Touch Me
07/25/91	2	2	Lizards	Touch Me

Original Songs Played by Year *(continued)*

Poor Heart

1991	33	26%
1992	47	39%
1993	57	52%
1994	46	37%
1995	26	32%
1996	21	30%
1997	11	14%

Possum

1990	58	56%
1991	49	39%
1992	35	29%
1993	31	28%
1994	20	16%
1995	21	26%
1996	10	14%
1997	7	9%

Prince Caspian

1995	17	21%
1996	17	24%
1997	22	28%

PYITE

1990	0	0%
1991	0	0%
1992	0	0%
1993	18	16%
1994	12	10%
1995	9	11%
1996	16	23%
1997	18	23%

Reba

1990	36	35%
1991	52	41%
1992	45	37%
1993	29	26%
1994	36	29%
1995	23	28%
1996	19	27%
1997	10	13%

Rift

1990	5	5%
1991	0	0%
1992	54	45%
1993	68	62%
1994	47	38%
1995	20	25%
1996	11	16%
1997	1	1%

Rocka William

1997	5	6%

Rotation Jam

1995	2	2%
1996	1	1%
1997	1	1%

04/16/93	226	E	*OPE	AmGrace
04/21/93	4	2	Weekpaug	*CL2
06/16/94	103	1	Maze	Curtain
06/22/94	5	1	Rift	Maze
06/30/94	6	1	DWD	Rift
07/09/94	7	1	Foam	Maze
07/15/94	4	1	Divided	Foam
10/13/94	7	1	Divided	Axilla 2
10/22/94	7	1	Divided	Rift
12/02/94	26	2	Landlady	Caravan
12/03/94	1	2	BurAlive	Slave
06/14/95	17	1	Wanna Go	NICU
06/28/95	11	2	Tweezer	Sparkle
07/02/95	4	1	Divided	Curtain
10/07/95	10	1	Julius	Fog
10/20/95	8	2	Maze	Guitar
10/29/95	7	1	NICU	Slave
11/14/95	6	2	Maze	Stash
12/04/95	14	1	Julius	Divided
12/09/95	4	2	Wilson	YEM
12/28/95	7	1	Split&Melt	Curtain
07/23/96	21	1	Theme	Scent
08/07/96	7	1	Ya Mar	Taste
08/14/96	4	1	Mango	Stash
10/19/96	6	1	Llama	DWD
11/11/96	15	2	Divided	Curtain
11/16/96	4	1	Guyute	Rift
12/02/96	10	1	Theme	Julius
12/30/96	5	1	Llama	Reba
02/20/97	7	1	Taste	Circus
07/29/97	34	1	Beauty	Dirt
08/08/97	6	1	CTB	Lizards
08/13/97	4	1	Water	Horse
11/14/97	5	1	RunJim	Maze
11/26/97	7	1	Sparkle	My Soul
12/03/97	5	1	Old Home	Also Sprac
>> 12/31/97	**11**			

GUYUTE

Inspiration: The story of an ugly pig named Guyute, this song excited fans after its debut in fall 1994, as many hoped it heralded Trey's return to writing longer-form epics. It has since grown to become one of the most popular Phish songs among fans.

Musical Evolution and History: The band took Guyute out of rotation after the fall tour in 1994, supposedly to rework it, but when it reappeared at Halloween '95, the only change was the whistling segment following the first verse. Since then, it has been played pretty much the same way each night, although many versions in 1997 were slightly botched. Also of note: Trey makes a Guyute reference during the band's version of The Beatles' song "Glass Onion" during the 10/31/94 performance of *The White Album*.

Rotation History: Unplayed from 12/29/94 until 10/31/95, when it returned to light rotation. The band started playing it more often in 1997, to the delight of nearly everyone.

Discography: Has not yet appeared on a Phish album.

Guyute [43] [Guyute]

By Anastasio/Marshall

10/07/94	[688]	1	Stash	Golgi
10/08/94	1	1	DWD	Fee
10/10/94	2	1	Stash	Old Home
10/14/94	3	2	Life Boy	Chalkdust
10/18/94	3	1	It's Ice	Divided
10/20/94	1	1	Julius	Golgi
10/26/94	5	1	Antelope	Dog Faced
11/02/94	5	1	Maze	Stash

11/12/94	3	1	If I Could	Maze
11/19/94	6	1	DWD	Axilla 2
11/22/94	2	1	Foam	IDK
11/26/94	3	1	Possum	If I Could
11/28/94	1	1	Stash	Sparkle
12/01/94	2	1	Maze	IDK
12/03/94	2	1	Antelope	Sample
12/07/94	3	1	Split&Melt	Life Boy
12/09/94	2	1	Foam	Sparkle
12/10/94	1	2	Maze	Also Sprac
12/29/94	2	2	*OP2	Bowie
10/31/95	50	1	Free	Antelope
11/10/95	2	1	Maze	Cavern
11/16/95	5	1	Timber Ho	FunkBitch
11/21/95	3	1	I'm Blue	My Friend
11/28/95	4	1	Divided	HelloBaby
12/07/95	7	1	Slave	Bouncing
12/28/95	9	1	Julius	Horn
07/15/96	15	1	FEFY	Possum
08/04/96	10	1	FunkBitch	Fee
11/07/96	25	1	Waste	Free
11/16/96	7	1	DWD	Gumbo
12/04/96	11	1	Train Song	CharZero
12/30/96	4	2	ACDCBag	Tweezer
02/17/97	5	1	My Soul	Timber Ho
03/02/97	10	1	Sample	My Soul
06/25/97	10	E	*OPE	*CLE
08/11/97	25	1	Water	Guelah
08/17/97	5	3	Weigh	Dirt
11/14/97	2	1	FunkBitch	Antelope
11/21/97	4	E	*OPE	*CLE
11/30/97	6	1	*OP1	FunkBitch
12/07/97	5	2	Reba	Possum
12/12/97	3	E	*OPE	Antelope
12/30/97	4	2	Sl Monkey	*CL2
>> 12/31/97	**1**			

HA HA HA

Inspiration: Fishman, who apparently thought it would be cool to write a song with only the words "Ha Ha Ha" as lyrics.

Musical Evolution and History: This short, composed piece has varied little since its debut, though on occasion the band has gotten a little frisky with it, like in Stuttgart, Germany, on 2/26/97. It's also helped complete some cool segues; check out Tweezer > Ha Ha Ha from Sugarbush on 7/2/95.

Rotation History: Played thirteen times in its debut year of 1995, it's become an absolute rarity since then, appearing just twice in 1996 and once in 1997 (at the above-mentioned Stuttgart show).

Discography: Has yet to appear on a Phish album.

Ha Ha Ha [16] [Ha Ha Ha]

By Fishman

05/16/95	[738]	1a	Wanna Go	Spock's
06/07/95	1	2	*OP2	Maze
06/08/95	1	1	Wanna Go	RunJim
06/15/95	5	2	MSO	Bowie
06/22/95	5	1	Scent	Divided
06/30/95	7	2	Possum	TMWSIY
07/02/95	2	2	Tweezer	Sl Monkey
10/05/95	8	1	Chalkdust	Fog
10/20/95	10	1	Ya Mar	Divided
11/16/95	15	2	Uncle Pen	Harry
11/30/95	9	1	Curtain	Julius
12/11/95	8	1	My Friend	Stash
12/15/95	3	1	Maze	Suspicious
10/25/96	45	1	*OP1	Taste
12/04/96	26	2	*OP2	Mike's
02/26/97	16	2	PoorHeart	YEM
>> 12/31/97	**67**			

HALLEY'S COMET

Inspiration: The band's old friend and Goddard classmate Nancy Taube wrote the lyrics to this one, and often joined Phish on stage in the 1980s to lend his vocal prowess to this song. The bebop beat and funky lyrics make this one a favorite of many fans.

Musical Evolution and History: Most versions of Halley's in the 1980s and following its return in 1993 never really departed from the song's fairly precise structure. Yes, the jam at the end occasionally took a cool little turn, like when it segued into Page's theremin solo at Red Rocks on 8/5/96. But when Halley's appeared for the first time in 1997 at the Great Went on 8/16/97, the band had a real treat in store—instead of dropping quickly into another song after a brief jam, they opted to jam out on Halley's, returning briefly to the chorus before eventually seguing into "Cities." Another great Halley's jam followed in fall 1997 on 11/22/97 at Hampton, VA, when Halley's opened the second set and then Phish funked out for nearly twenty minutes before starting up Tweezer. There is one Halley's jam which preceded the 1997 incarnations—an 8/17/89 performance at the Front in Burlington. Nancy Taube appeared on stage with the boys for a sloppy ten-minute performance in which Fish constantly shouted, "I hate this song! This song sucks!" One version of Halley's not to be missed is the one which led into the breakout of Slave on 8/6/93 at the Cincinnati Zoo. On the lyric "Your body is reeling," Page sings in a falsetto, which really adds a subtle but splendid peak to the tune. Trey also screams "Hey!" after some of the verses.

Rotation History: Played throughout the 1980s, the band swore (from the stage—check out the tape!) on 8/17/89 that they would never play Halley's Comet again. That promise went by the wayside on 3/14/93 in Gunnison, CO, when Phish opened the second set with the first Halley's of the 1990s. Since then, Halley's has remained a rare treat, and took a year off from appearances between the Clifford Ball and the Great Went, but generally surfaces at least a few times a year.

Discography: Has not yet appeared on a Phish album.

Halley's Comet [37] [Halley's]

By Phish/Nancy Taube

10/31/86	[9]	1	Sally	CrJam
04/29/87	6	2	A-Train	Quinn
05/14/88	21	2	IDK	Light Up
06/20/88	6	1	Lizards	Wilson
10/29/88	14	2	*OP2	WhipPost
05/26/89	47	1	Sanity	Sloth
08/17/89	14	3	Possum	Alumni
03/14/93	418	2	*OP2	Bowie
03/27/93	10	2	BurAlive	It's Ice
04/17/93	14	2	Landlady	YEM
05/01/93	11	2	BBJ	Paul&Silas
08/06/93	25	2	YEM	Slave
08/24/93	13	E	*OPE	PoorHeart
12/31/93	7	2	Tweezer	PoorHeart
04/29/94	21	1	*OP1	YEM
05/08/94	7	2	YEM	GTBT
05/19/94	7	1	*OP1	Llama
05/29/94	9	1	Guelah	DWD
06/09/94	1	2	Julius	Scent
06/24/94	12	2	Antelope	Curtain
10/15/94	24	2	RunJim	Scent
10/23/94	6	2	Bouncing	YEM
11/02/94	7	2	*OP2	Tweezer
11/26/94	14	2	*OP2	Bowie
11/30/94	2	2	*OP2	Antelope
12/29/94	11	2	Bowie	Lizards
06/16/95	11	1	*OP1	DWD
06/20/95	3	2	*OP2	Chalkdust
06/24/95	3	2	Also Sprac	Bowie
07/02/95	7	E	*OPE	TweezRep
12/01/95	43	2	*OP2	Mike's
12/14/95	9	2	Keyboard	NICU
08/05/96	30	2	It's Ice	Waste
08/16/96	7	1	Divided	Bowie
08/16/97	92	3	*OP3	Cities
11/22/97	8	2	*OP2	Tweezer
12/28/97	15	2	Scent	Slave
>> 12/31/97	**3**			

HARPUA

Inspiration: The song chronicles the misadventures of Harpua, a mangy mutt, which are recounted by Trey during a hilarious "Harpua rap" in the middle of each version. The rap usually features tales of little Jimmy and his cat, Poster Nutbag, plus whatever other weirdness Trey decides to cook up.

Musical Evolution and History: The oldest versions of the song, from the mid-1980s, lack the complexity and narration which are the hallmarks of most post-1989 versions of Harpua. By that point, the basic story line had already been established, and Trey would tell the crowd about Jimmy and Poster, including the exchange between "father" (Mike) and "son" (Page). Around this time it became standard practice to sample songs by other artists in the middle of the narration as Jimmy "listens to his radio," or some other such device. These jams have ranged from Nirvana's "Smells Like Teen Spirit" (5/9/92) to Spin Doctors' "Jimmy Olsen's Blues" (11/28/92) to Abba's "Waterloo" (6/23/95, with John Popper) to Michael Jackson's "Beat It" (10/31/95). Other recent versions have featured plenty of Elvis Presley (the insane 30-minute encore in Las Vegas on 12/6/96), and appearances by Tom Marshall singing Oasis's "Champagne Supernova" (12/29/96), and the Proclaimers', "I

Wanna Be (500 Miles)" (12/20/97). Often Harpua's humor comes from its deviations from its basic structure. Although Harpua is supposed to kill Poster Nutbag in each episode, on 7/16/94, for instance, Poster was hit by a comet. On 10/31/95, Mike handles parts of the narration, telling a story of his "raccoon dream." Although the Harpua rap sometimes features references to Gamehendge (like on 6/17/94 or 10/31/94), Harpua is not per se a Gamehendge song.

Rotation History: Sporadically played, much to the disappointment of fans who worship this song and consider its appearance a sign of a truly great show. Perhaps because fans enjoy Harpua so much, the song has sparked controversies several times in the Phish phan community. A severely shortened performance of Harpua at the Clifford Ball on 8/17/96 concerned fans, who wondered why the band walked off the stage with the song only half finished. In response, Trey posted a letter on the Web several weeks later saying that a plane that was supposed to appear overhead for a special effect in the middle of the song was hidden behind the stage where the band couldn't see it, so they cut it short. Fittingly, a year later at the Great Went on 8/16/97, Phish played the second half of Harpua, ending the version they'd left unfinished a year earlier. Another incomplete Harpua can be heard on 6/30/94. They played the only complete Harpua of 1997 the night before New Year's Eve in New York City.

Discography: Has yet to appear on a Phish album.

Harpua [48] [Harpua]

By Anastasio/Fishman

08/09/87	[17]	1	Harry	Suzie
08/21/87	2	2	Mike's	Golgi
08/29/87	2	2	Divided	*CL2
03/11/88	10	2	Curtis	ACDCBag
05/15/88	6	1a	Sloth	*CL1
05/25/88	2	3	Corrina	Antelope
06/21/88	4	2	*OP2	IDK
07/25/88	5	3	Skin It	BBFCM
11/03/88	9	2	BBFCM	Bowie
04/20/89	24	2	Love You	*CL2
05/09/89	12	2	Bold	WhipPost
10/14/89	37	2	Possum	*CL2
10/20/89	1	1	*OP1	BundleJoy
11/10/89	10	2	Possum	HwayHell
03/11/90	42	2	Split&Melt	Slave
04/07/90	6	2	Bike	*CL2
06/09/90	31	2	Terrapin	*CL2
04/18/91	81	E	*OPE	*CLE
04/26/91	6	2	Harry	*CL2
05/03/91	3	2	YEM	TweezRep
10/28/91	45	2	WhipPost	HwayHell
12/07/91	25	2	Terrapin	*CL2
03/26/92	14	E	Chalkdust	*CLE
04/04/92	7	2	My Friend	Cavern
04/22/92	13	2	Rosie	RunJim
05/09/92	13	2	Tweezer	Llama
11/28/92	58	2	Love You	Golgi
12/31/92	17	3	Weekpaug	Sqirm Coil
02/12/93	9	2	Harry	*CL2
03/31/93	34	2	YEM	Chalkdust
04/14/93	9	2	YEM	RunJim
05/07/93	18	2	Harry	HwayHell
07/25/93	12	2	PurplRain	TweezRep
08/20/93	19	1	Divided	PoorHeart
05/03/94	33	2	DWD	Chalkdust
06/17/94	27	2	Weekpaug	Sparkle
06/30/94	10	2	Axilla 2	Antelope
07/16/94	12	2	Antelope	ACDCBag
10/16/94	9	E2	*OPE2	*CLE2
10/31/94	11	1	Divided	Julius
11/25/94	14	2	Simple	Weekpaug
06/23/95	30	2	Antelope	Wloo Jam
10/31/95	34	1	Antelope	*CL1
08/17/96	64	E	*OPE	*CLE
12/06/96	35	E	*OPE	Suzie
12/29/96	2	2	YEM	*CL2
08/16/97	54	1	Makisupa	Chalkdust
12/30/97	25	2	McGrupp	Izabella
>> 12/31/97		**1**		

HARRY HOOD

Inspiration: A very popular song among longtime fans, the source of this song's lyrics is much debated. According to the most believable rumors, several band members rented an apartment on 155 King Street in Burlington around 1985 which faced a Hood Milk billboard featuring the Hood Dairy slogan "You can feel good about Hood" and the Hood cartoon mascot Harry Hood. (H. P. Hood Dairy is a large New England dairy founded in 1846 and still going strong.) The lights going out on the billboard late at night inspired the "Harry, Harry, where do you go when the lights go out?" line. Mail received at the same address referred to a "Mr. Miner" who leased the apartment previously; one letter closed with the line, "Thank You, Mr. Miner." (*Almanac* research has documented a "Floyd Miner" at the King Street address in 1982.) Some of the lyrics came from the band's roommate and first fan Brian Long. Several times in concert, Trey has introduced Harry Hood by telling the audience, "This is a song about milk."

Musical Evolution and History: Another product of Trey and Fish's Europe trip in the summer of 1985, Trey penned the music to Harry Hood there along with YEM. The band soon added it to their concert repertoire, and it remains a mainstay to this day, in pretty much the same structure as it was originally composed. The song has three parts: the introduction leading up to the "Harry, Harry" verse; the passage between "Harry" and "Thank You, Mr. Miner"; and the third, heavily improvisational section before the final "You can feel good about Hood" refrain. Back at Goddard College 11/23/85, Mike Gordon had an intensely spiritual moment while playing Hood, and he says it's a peak he's never achieved again.

Fans still marvel at the ability of Harry Hood to stay fresh and different performance after performance while still staying true to the structure of the song. Some favorite Hoods include two clean 1990 Colorado versions, 4/22/90 and 11/4/90; 11/30/91 Port Chester, NY; 4/18/92 Palo Alto, CA, with "Linus and Lucy" jam; 12/31/93 Worcester, MA, an emotional, postmidnight version with "Auld Lang Syne" jam; 10/20/94 St. Petersburg, FL; 11/12/94 Kent, OH, the all-time favorite of some fans; 7/1/95 Mansfield, MA, another emotional powerhouse; 10/7/95 Spokane, WA, unfinished but amazing; 12/30/95 New York, NY; and more recently, 8/2/97 George, WA, encore with the starry sky. Also notable is the phan contribution to this song: at Red Rocks on 8/6/96, crowd participation flyers passed out by Phish.Net fans encouraged fans to shout "Hood!" after each "Harry" sung by the band. That chant has caught on and can now be heard at most Phish shows. And Trey's penchant for having Chris Kuroda turn out the lights during the jam part of the song was seen often in 1997, including 7/5/97, 8/2/97, 8/17/97, 12/13/97, and 12/30/97. Beginning with the Hood on 10/7/95, Phish showed a willingness to leave Hood unfinished, something which has become more common in recent years. Examples from 1997 include 7/26 and 12/30.

Rotation History: Played often throughout the 1980s and 1990s, Hood is one of the rare older songs whose concert appearances have increased in recent years. Phish played it twenty-three times in 1997, the highest percentage of show of any year in the 1990s.

Discography: Appears on *A Live One* (1995) as a live version taken from the 10/23/94 show in Gainesville, FL.

Harry Hood [199] [Harry]

By Anastasio/Phish/Brian Long

10/30/85	[4]	1a	*OP1	Dog Log
04/01/86	2	1	Mercy	Pendulum
10/15/86	2	1a	Mercy	Peaches
10/31/86	1	2	Mercy	Sanity
03/06/87	2	2	Freebird	TMSG
08/09/87	6	1	Fee	Harpua
08/21/87	2	1	FunkBitch	Clod
08/29/87	2	2	Possum	Timber Ho
11/19/87	6	1	Sally	Fire
01/30/88	1	3	CamlWalk	*CL3
02/08/88	2	2	Antelope	Mockbird
03/11/88	1	2	Dinner	Curtis
07/23/88	15	3	Contact	Dinner
08/03/88	3	2	Fluffhead	Satin Doll

Original Songs Played by Year
(continued)

Run Like an Antelope

1990	27	26%
1991	21	17%
1992	33	27%
1993	38	35%
1994	42	34%
1995	25	31%
1996	19	27%
1997	16	21%

Runaway Jim

1990	20	19%
1991	55	43%
1992	54	45%
1993	41	37%
1994	34	27%
1995	24	30%
1996	20	29%
1997	16	21%

Sample

1993	24	22%
1994	70	56%
1995	30	37%
1996	26	37%
1997	16	21%

Sanity

1990	0	0%
1991	0	0%
1992	6	5%
1993	0	0%
1994	2	2%
1995	1	1%
1996	1	1%
1997	0	0%

Scent of a Mule

1994	44	35%
1995	23	28%
1996	17	24%
1997	7	9%

Setting Sail

1991	1	1%
1992	0	0%
1993	0	0%
1994	1	1%
1995	0	0%
1996	0	0%
1997	0	0%

Silent in the Morning
[See Horse]

Simple

1994	30	24%
1995	20	25%
1996	16	23%
1997	12	15%

Slave

1990	6	6%
1991	2	2%
1992	0	0%
1993	3	3%
1994	22	18%
1995	19	23%
1996	12	17%
1997	17	22%

09/12/88	4	1a	CamlWalk	Esther
10/29/88	3	1	Contact	*CL1
02/05/89	7	1	WalkAway	BBFCM
02/06/89	1	2	WalkAway	BBFCM
05/06/89	26	2	Fire	Golgi
05/13/89	6	2	Lizards	Brain
05/21/89	5	1	*OP1	Foam
05/28/89	5	3	Mango	*CL3
06/23/89	5	2	Fluffhead	Ya Mar
08/17/89	7	1	Rocky Top	Mike's
08/19/89	2	2	YEM	*CL2
08/26/89	2	1	Mockbird	Split&Melt
09/09/89	4	2	Split&Melt	WalkAway
10/01/89	1	1	Golgi	Wilson
10/06/89	1	1a	LTJP	Possum
10/20/89	5	2	Split&Melt	SwingLow
10/22/89	2	2	*OP2	Reba
11/10/89	8	1	La Grange	Bathtub
12/08/89	9	2	*OP2	Tela
01/20/90	7	1a	Weekpaug	Carolina
04/06/90	31	2	Sloth	Caravan
04/09/90	3	2	Foam	Jesus
04/13/90	3	2	Sloth	Caravan
04/22/90	5	2	BBFCM	Fire
04/28/90	3	2	Cavern	Caravan
05/06/90	4	2	Fee	Esther
05/10/90	1	2	RunJim	Caravan
05/15/90	4	1	Suzie	Bike
05/24/90	3	2	WalkAway	HwayHell
06/09/90	6	2	GTBT	TMWSIY
09/15/90	4	2	Minute	Possum
11/04/90	18	1	Tube	FunkBitch
02/09/91	20	2	Bouncing	Cavern
02/15/91	2	2	ACDCBag	Terrapin
03/15/91	18	2	IDK	Chalkdust
04/05/91	12	2	Dinner	IDK
04/19/91	8	2	*OP2	Curtain
04/21/91	2	2	Uncle Pen	Cavern
04/26/91	3	2	IDK	Harpua
05/02/91	2	E	*OPE	*CLE
05/04/91	2	2	BurAlive	Horn
05/10/91	2	2	*OP2	Wilson
07/14/91	10	3	Touch Me	*CL3
08/03/91	11	E2	*OPE2	*CLE2
10/06/91	10	2	Destiny	IDK
10/12/91	3	1	Brain	TweezRep
10/15/91	2	E	Memories	*CLE
10/19/91	3	2	Terrapin	*CL2
10/27/91	4	1	Bouncing	Golgi
10/31/91	3	2	IDK	*CL2
11/12/91	8	1	Sloth	Fee
11/15/91	3	2	Destiny	Love You
11/21/91	4	2	Wilson	It's Ice
11/30/91	4	2	Uncle Pen	It's Ice
03/11/92	8	2	All Things	Rocky Top
03/14/92	3	2	Suzie	Rosie
03/20/92	3	2	Uncle Pen	Terrapin
03/24/92	2	2	Suzie	Cavern
03/27/92	3	2	Magilla	Love You
04/03/92	5	2	Llama	Suzie
04/12/92	6	2	Rosie	Cavern
04/18/92	5	2	Dinner	Love You
04/25/92	6	2	Dinner	Weigh
04/30/92	2	2	Rosie	TweezRep
05/08/92	7	2	Terrapin	Golgi
05/17/92	7	2	Sparkle	Cavern
07/15/92	15	2	All Things	Golgi
11/20/92	31	2	Dinner	Terrapin
11/25/92	4	E	*OPE	Carolina
12/04/92	7	2	Carolina	Faht
12/13/92	8	2	Rosie	Cavern
12/28/92	1	2	Bike	Cavern
02/04/93	5	2	Lngthwise	Cavern
02/12/93	7	2	Terrapin	Harpua
02/20/93	6	2	Terrapin	TweezRep
03/02/93	7	2	Choochoo	AmGrace
03/12/93	6	2	Lngthwise	Golgi
03/21/93	7	2	Rosie	Cavern
03/31/93	8	2	Uncle Pen	BBJ
04/16/93	10	1	Rift	Cavern
04/24/93	7	2	Bike	Cavern
04/30/93	4	2	BBJ	Brain
05/07/93	6	2	Great Gig	Harpua
07/16/93	5	2	PurplRain	Cavern
07/28/93	9	2	My Friend	Great Gig
08/08/93	8	2	Rift	Wilson
08/15/93	6	E	*OPE	*CLE
08/21/93	4	2	Brain	Daniel
08/26/93	3	1	It's Ice	Golgi
12/28/93	2	2	Uncle Pen	HwayHell
12/31/93	3	3	Rosie	TweezRep
04/04/94	1	E	*OPE	Cavern
04/08/94	3	2	Sparkle	Bouncing
04/10/94	2	2	BeLikeYou	*CL2
04/15/94	4	1	Paul&Silas	Wilson
04/20/94	4	2	BBJ	Fee
04/23/94	3	2	Ginseng	YEM
04/30/94	5	2	Peaches	Axilla 2
05/10/94	7	2	Scent	Ginseng
05/19/94	6	2	BBJ	Golgi
05/21/94	2	2	Bike	AmGrace
05/27/94	5	1	PYITE	Golgi
05/29/94	2	E2	*OPE2	GTBT
06/10/94	2	2	BeLikeYou	TweezRep
06/21/94	8	2	Sparkle	Suzie
06/25/94	4	2	Rosie	Golgi
07/01/94	4	2	Terrapin	Cavern
07/06/94	4	2	BBFCM	TweezRep
07/09/94	2	2	BBJ	Suzie
07/14/94	3	2	BBJ	HwayHell
07/16/94	2	2	Scent	Contact
10/08/94	2	2	PurplRain	Suzie
10/12/94	3	2	Long Time	Sample
10/20/94	6	2	Rift	Nellie
10/23/94	3	2	PurplRain	Fee
10/29/94	5	E	*OPE	*CLE
11/03/94	3	2	BBFCM	Cavern
11/12/94	2	2	Long Time	Golgi
11/19/94	6	2	Rosie	AmGrace
11/22/94	2	2	LongJourn	HwayHell
12/01/94	6	2	Jesus	Golgi
12/30/94	11	2	PurplRain	TweezRep
06/07/95	3	2	Sample	Suzie
06/13/95	4	2	AArmy	Golgi
06/17/95	4	2	Adeline	Sample
06/24/95	5	2	Suzie	AArmy
06/28/95	3	2	Suzie	TweezRep
07/01/95	3	2	AArmy	Suzie
09/27/95	3	2	AArmy	HelloBaby
10/03/95	5	2	Sparkle	Billy
10/07/95	3	2	Frankstein	Adeline
10/15/95	5	2	Suspicious	TweezRep
10/21/95	4	2	PurplRain	Suzie
11/10/95	9	E	*OPE	*CLE
11/16/95	5	2	Ha Ha Ha	Brain
11/19/95	2	2	Scent	Suzie
11/25/95	4	2	Weekpaug	HelloBaby
11/30/95	3	E	*OPE	*CLE
12/05/95	4	2	Life Boy	Cavern
12/11/95	4	2	Scent	Suspicious
12/15/95	3	1	Chalkdust	Wilson
12/17/95	2	2	Also Sprac	Sparkle
12/30/95	3	2	Free	ACDCBag
04/26/96	2	1a	ASZ	Sample
07/06/96	4	1a	Maze	*CL1
07/11/96	4	2	*OP2	Bouncing
07/15/96	3	1	IDK	Cavern
07/21/96	4	E	*OPE	*CLE
07/25/96	4	1a	Life Mars	Cavern
08/06/96	4	2	PurplRain	TweezRep
08/10/96	2	2	WhipPost	DayinLife
08/16/96	4	2	Life Mars	Jam
10/18/96	4	2	Waste	*CL2
10/25/96	5	2	Str Design	Cavern
11/02/96	5	2	Waste	DayinLife
11/09/96	5	2	Steep	*CL2
11/16/96	5	2	Axilla	Suzie
11/23/96	4	2	AmGrace	*CL2
11/29/96	3	2	Waste	*CL2
12/02/96	3	2	Scent	Adeline
12/06/96	2	2	Simple	Weekpaug
12/31/96	4	2	Steep	Caspian
02/13/97	1	2	RockaW	Frankstein
02/18/97	4	2	Train Song	Frankstein
02/22/97	3	2	Jesus	Free
02/26/97	3	1	My Friend	My Soul
03/18/97	4	1	Beauty	CTB
06/16/97	3	2	Dirt	*CL2
06/21/97	3	1a	Dogs Stole	Chalkdust
07/03/97	8	2	Sparkle	Cavern
07/05/97	1	1a	Piper	Love You
07/09/97	2	1	Adeline	*CL1
07/22/97	4	E	Circus	*CLE
07/26/97	3	2	Bowie	Free
08/02/97	4	E	*OPE	*CLE
08/10/97	5	1	Ginseng	*CL1
08/14/97	3	2	Sparkle	Forbin's
08/17/97	2	2	Jam	*CL2
11/16/97	3	2	Wilson	Izabella
11/22/97	4	1	Weekpaug	Train Song
11/29/97	4	2	Str Design	Caspian
12/03/97	3	2	Frankstein	*CL2
12/09/97	4	2	Axilla	*CL2
12/13/97	3	2	Weekpaug	*CL2
12/30/97	3	2	Izabella	My Soul
>> 12/31/97	**1**			

HORN

Inspiration: Tom Marshall wrote the lyrics apparently in reference to the growing bitterness the band felt in 1990 about being pursued by record companies to sign a recording contract.

Musical Evolution and History: Although Horn is not complex musically, Trey said he considered it a landmark in his songwriting career when he composed it in 1990 because of its ability to communicate emotion in a simple fashion. Once, during the early nineties, he remarked that he'd like to play the song more often but felt it didn't work well as a frequently played tune. It has not changed from its original compositional form.

Rotation History: Not played very often in recent years, but the band has never completely forgotten it, either. Its peak year came in 1992 when it appeared twenty-five times; in 1997, it was down to five.

Discography: Appears on *Rift* (1993).

Horn [95] [Horn]

By Anastasio/Marshall

05/24/90	[214]	2	MSO	Fee
06/16/90	7	1	Reba	Uncle Pen
09/22/90	7	1	BurAlive	MSO
12/28/90	26	1	Foam	Reba
12/29/90	1	1	Rocky Top	Oh Kee
02/08/91	6	2	Weekpaug	Bouncing
03/15/91	21	2	Possum	Paul&Silas
04/15/91	17	2	Weekpaug	MSO
04/18/91	2	2	Paul&Silas	Suzie
04/20/91	2	E	*OPE	Alumni
05/04/91	8	2	Harry	Rocky Top
10/19/91	41	2	Tweezer	PoorHeart
10/28/91	5	E	*OPE	Rocky Top
10/31/91	2	2	Bowie	Dinner
11/07/91	4	2	Tube	Bowie
11/09/91	2	1	YEM	Brother
11/13/91	3	E	*OPE	MSO
11/16/91	3	2	YEM	Chalkdust
11/19/91	1	1	Brother	Chalkdust
11/21/91	2	1	Foam	Split&Melt
11/23/91	2	2	Weekpaug	PoorHeart
11/30/91	2	2	MSO	IDK
12/06/91	3	2	YEM	Divided
03/07/92	4	2	Chalkdust	Mike's
03/25/92	10	2	YEM	MSO
04/01/92	6	2	Tweezer	Chalkdust
04/05/92	3	1	Rift	It's Ice
04/16/92	7	2	Weekpaug	PoorHeart
04/23/92	6	2	NICU	Tweezer
04/24/92	1	2	Mango	Love You
04/29/92	2	E	*OPE	Rocky Top
05/01/92	2	1	It's Ice	IDK
05/03/92	2	1	Rift	RunJim
05/12/92	7	1	Uncle Pen	Bowie
05/14/92	1	1	Maze	Reba
05/16/92	2	1	MSO	Golgi
05/18/92	2	1	PoorHeart	Sparkle
06/20/92	2	1a	It's Ice	Love You
07/01/92	5	1a	Rift	Split&Melt
07/14/92	6	1	RunJim	Brother
07/27/92	11	1a	Bowie	Suzie
07/30/92	2	1a	Rift	Sparkle
08/01/92	2	1a	Sqirm Coil	Llama
08/17/92	5	2	Weekpaug	Terrapin
08/27/92	6	1a	Landlady	Sparkle
11/22/92	8	1	Sparkle	All Things
12/02/92	7	1	Sparkle	YEM
12/07/92	5	2	Llama	MSO
02/06/93	13	1	Maze	Divided
02/17/93	8	2	BBJ	YEM
02/21/93	4	1	Uncle Pen	Chalkdust
02/26/93	4	1	Llama	Divided
03/06/93	5	1	Llama	Curtain
03/18/93	8	1	Sparkle	IDK
03/25/93	5	1	Rift	Magilla
04/03/93	8	1	Reba	Antelope
04/18/93	9	1	Maze	IDK
04/29/93	8	1	RunJim	Llama
05/07/93	7	1	Lizards	Divided
07/16/93	5	1	Nellie	Antelope
07/22/93	4	1	Foam	My Mind
07/24/93	2	1	Llama	Nellie
08/06/93	9	1	Rift	Divided
08/13/93	6	1	My Mind	Bowie
08/16/93	3	1	Possum	Reba
08/21/93	3	2	Possum	Uncle Pen
08/24/93	1	2	Llama	Ya Mar
04/04/94	8	1	Reba	It's Ice
04/22/94	15	1	Llama	Uncle Pen
05/07/94	11	1	Llama	Divided
06/18/94	25	2	Bowie	McGrupp
06/24/94	5	1	Paul&Silas	Reba
07/03/94	7	1	NICU	Old Home
07/10/94	5	1	Chalkdust	Peaches
10/08/94	6	1	Chalkdust	Sparkle
10/16/94	7	1	Rift	Foam
10/25/94	6	1	Llama	Julius
11/22/94	17	1	PoorHeart	Foam
06/30/95	38	1	Scent	Taste
09/30/95	7	1	Uncle Pen	Antelope
10/19/95	12	1	RunJim	PYITE
10/27/95	6	1	Fog	IDK
11/16/95	10	1	Chess	Mound
12/05/95	13	1	*OP1	Chalkdust
12/14/95	6	1	Llama	Foam
12/28/95	4	1	Guyute	Rift
07/12/96	13	1	Divided	Split&Melt
08/06/96	14	1	Dinner	Antelope
11/09/96	25	1	Divided	Tube
12/04/96	16	1	Chalkdust	Uncle Pen
06/20/97	25	1	Cities	Funny
07/01/97	7	1	Ghost	Ya Mar
08/11/97	22	1	Limb	Antelope
11/29/97	15	1	Saw It	Water
12/09/97	7	1	Beauty	Lovin Cup
>> 12/31/97	**7**			

THE HORSE

Inspiration: Unclear, as the song was thought by fans to be the first part of Silent in the Morning until the release of *Rift* in early 1993 indicated otherwise. Many pre-1993 setlists label the Horse > Silent in the Morning suite simply as Silent in the Morning.

Musical Evolution and History: Not much to speak of, though throughout 1993, Trey played acoustic guitar on this song, then switched to electric guitar for Silent in the Morning. That sometimes led to improvisational introductions to The Horse, which made the song almost twice as long as its current very short form.

Rotation History: The Horse > Silent duo was played a lot in 1992, 1993, and 1994, but not nearly as much since. The Horse has never intentionally been played without being followed by Silent. However, when a fire alarm went off at the Cincinnati Music Hall on 6/21/94, Phish abandoned The Horse in progress, leaving it as the only Horse without Silent.

Discography: Appears on *Rift* (1993).

The Horse/Silent in the Morning [116/116] [Horse] [Silent]

By Anastasio/Marshall

03/07/92	[385]	1	RunJim	Maze
03/13/92	3	2	Brother	Landlady
03/19/92	3	1	Golgi	Dinner
03/21/92	2	1	Split&Melt	Dinner
03/24/92	1	1	Golgi	Llama
03/27/92	3	2	Weekpaug	MSO
04/01/92	4	2	YEM	Uncle Pen
04/05/92	3	2	YEM	Maze
04/07/92	2	1	Divided	Split&Melt
04/09/92	1	2	Weekpaug	Chalkdust
04/12/92	1	1	Divided	It's Ice
04/19/92	6	2	Weekpaug	MSO
04/22/92	2	2	Antelope	Rift
04/25/92	3	2	YEM	All Things
04/30/92	2	2	YEM	Chalkdust
05/03/92	3	2	Tweezer	Fluffhead
05/05/92	1	2	Weekpaug	PoorHeart
05/08/92	3	2	YEM	Chalkdust
05/16/92	6	2	YEM	Oh Kee
07/15/92	16	1	Split&Melt	Chalkdust
11/19/92	30	1	Axilla	Antelope
11/21/92	2	2	Weekpaug	Uncle Pen
11/27/92	4	2	Bowie	Faht
12/03/92	5	1	Chalkdust	Reba
12/08/92	5	2	Weekpaug	It's Ice
12/29/92	6	2	Tweezer	MSO
02/03/93	3	2	Tweezer	Sparkle
02/05/93	2	2	Tweezer	Paul&Silas
02/10/93	4	2	YEM	Rosie
02/20/93	8	1	Divided	Fluffhead
03/02/93	7	1	Chalkdust	IDK
03/09/93	5	2	Weekpaug	BBJ
03/12/93	1	1	Fluffhead	Bowie
03/17/93	4	2	Weekpaug	Great Gig
03/24/93	5	2	YEM	Terrapin
03/26/93	2	2	Tweezer	YEM
03/30/93	3	2	Weekpaug	Brain
04/02/93	3	2	Llama	Mike's
04/09/93	3	1	Stash	Maze
04/12/93	2	1	Stash	Reba
04/14/93	2	1	Kung	Divided
04/16/93	1	2	Weekpaug	Uncle Pen
04/18/93	2	2	Tweezer	Possum
04/21/93	2	2	Sqirm Coil	BBJ
04/24/93	3	1	Stash	Rift
04/27/93	2	2	YEM	Love You
04/30/93	2	1	Stash	Divided
05/02/93	2	1	Stash	PoorHeart
05/06/93	3	1	Split&Melt	All Things
05/08/93	2	2	Bowie	It's Ice
05/30/93*	2	1a	Ya Mar	Antelope
07/15/93	1	2	Bowie	Sparkle
07/17/93	2	1	Chalkdust	Oh Kee
07/23/93	4	1	Maze	PYITE
07/25/93	2	2	Tweezer	Maze
07/28/93	2	1	Split&Melt	PoorHeart
07/30/93	2	2	Tweezer	PoorHeart
08/03/93	3	1	Stash	Ya Mar
08/08/93	3	1	RunJim	PYITE
08/12/93	3	1	Split&Melt	PoorHeart
08/14/93	2	1	Divided	It's Ice
08/17/93	3	2	Bowie	Rift
08/24/93	3	1	Split&Melt	Uncle Pen
08/28/93	3	2	Antelope	Sparkle
12/30/93	3	2	Mike's	PYITE
04/08/94	5	1	PYITE	DWD
04/14/94	5	2	Antelope	Scent
04/22/94	7	1	Divided	Bowie
05/12/94	14	2	Antelope	Uncle Pen
05/19/94	5	1	Stash	DWD
05/23/94	4	1	Maze	Julius
05/28/94	4	1	Stash	Sloth
06/21/94*	11	1	It's Ice	*CL1
06/23/94	2	1	DWD	PYITE
06/29/94	4	1	Julius	Catapult
07/03/94	4	2	It's Ice	Julius
07/09/94	4	1	DWD	Antelope
07/14/94	3	1	Fluffhead	Antelope
07/16/94	2	1	Cavern	Maze
10/07/94	1	2	Maze	Reba
10/10/94	3	1	Divided	Sparkle
10/14/94	3	1	Divided	PYITE
10/18/94	3	2	Bowie	Reba
10/22/94	3	2	Bowie	Dinner
10/25/94	2	1	Julius	Split&Melt
10/27/94	2	1	Divided	PoorHeart
10/31/94	3	1	Julius	Reba
11/13/94	5	1	It's Ice	Antelope
11/18/94	4	1	Julius	It's Ice
11/26/94	6	1	Foam	PoorHeart
11/30/94	2	E	*OPE	AmGrace
12/08/94	7	E	*OPE	Rocky Top
12/29/94	4	1	Split&Melt	Uncle Pen
12/31/94	2	3	Chalkdust	Suzie
06/14/95	7	1	AmGrace	Spock's
06/24/95	8	1	Stash	Sqirm Coil
06/29/95	4	1	Taste	Divided
10/05/95	11	1	Fog	CTB
10/24/95	13	1	Llama	Demand
10/29/95	4	1	CTB	Split&Melt
11/11/95	4	1	Weekpaug	Ya Mar
12/04/95	16	1	Axilla 2	HelloBaby
12/12/95	6	1	PYITE	Antelope
07/21/96	24	1	Split&Melt	Taste
08/02/96	5	2	Caspian	Antelope
08/10/96	5	1	IDK	Rift
08/14/96	3	2	YEM	CTB
10/16/96	3	1	It's Ice	CharZero
10/21/96	4	2	Simple	Bowie
10/29/96	6	2	I am H2	Weekpaug
12/01/96	21	1	Train Song	Sample
12/31/96	7	1	Stash	Divided
02/23/97	9	2	Maze	Peaches
07/06/97	22	1	Stash	CTB
08/13/97	19	1	Gumbo	Beauty
11/26/97	12	1	Split&Melt	Taste
12/31/97	15	1	Limb	Sloth
>> 12/31/97		1		

Note: 05/30/93 is Silent only; 06/21/94 is Horse only.

I AM HYDROGEN

Inspiration: A short instrumental piece written by Trey, Hydrogen is the only part of the classic Mike's Groove trio (Mike's Song > I Am Hydrogen > Weekapaug Groove) for which Mike does not carry songwriting credit.

Musical Evolution and History: A simple, short piece, Hydrogen has changed little since the 1980s, though occasionally Trey will screw with the tempo or tone just to liven things up a bit (he's also totally butchered it a few times—for a recent example, listen to 11/13/97 Las Vegas, NV).

Rotation History: Though it first surfaced on its own in 1987, by 1988 Phish had integrated Hydrogen into the middle of Mike's Groove, where it stayed without moving until it was displaced by "Auld Lang Syne" on 12/31/92 in Boston, MA. From that point forward, Mike's Groove could be either Hydrogenated or non-Hydrogenated. From 5/8/93 Durham, NH, until 4/9/94 Binghamton, NY, Hydrogen was in complete regression, and it only appeared twice in 1995. But by 1997, good ol' Hydrogen was popping up in roughly half of all Mike's Grooves. Since 1988, there hasn't been a single performance of I Am Hydrogen not immediately followed by Weekapaug.

Discography: Has yet to appear on a Phish album.

I Am Hydrogen [226] [I am H2]

By Anastasio

04/24/87	[14]	1a	Alumni	Bowie
04/29/87	1	3	LTGTR	*CL3
07/23/88	31	1	Mike's	Weekapaug
07/24/88	1	1	Mike's	Weekapaug
07/25/88	1	2	Mike's	Weekapaug
08/03/88	1	2	Mike's	Fluffhead
10/12/88	4	1	Mike's	Weekapaug
11/05/88	4	2	Mike's	Weekapaug
11/11/88	1	2	Mike's	Weekapaug
02/07/89	5	1	Mike's	Weekapaug
03/03/89	4	2	Mike's	Weekapaug
03/04/89	1	1	Mike's	Weekapaug
03/30/89	2	2	Mike's	Weekapaug
04/14/89	6	2	Mike's	Weekapaug
04/15/89	1	1	Mike's	Weekapaug
04/20/89	2	2	Mike's	Weekapaug
05/06/89	9	1	Mike's	Weekapaug
05/09/89	3	1	Mike's	Weekapaug
05/20/89	7	2	Mike's	Weekapaug
05/21/89	1	1	Mike's	Weekapaug
05/26/89	1	1	Mike's	Weekapaug
05/27/89	1	1	Mike's	Weekapaug
05/28/89	1	2	Mike's	Weekapaug
06/23/89	5	1	Mike's	Weekapaug
06/30/89	2	2	Mike's	Weekapaug
08/17/89	1	1	Mike's	Weekapaug
08/19/89	2	1	Mike's	Weekapaug
10/06/89	8	1	Mike's	Weekapaug
10/07/89	1	1	Mike's	Weekapaug
10/21/89	5	2	Mike's	Weekapaug
10/26/89	2	1	Mike's	Weekapaug
11/02/89	3	1	Mike's	Weekapaug
11/09/89	3	2	Mike's	Weekapaug
11/10/89	1	1	Mike's	Weekapaug
11/16/89	2	1	Mike's	Weekapaug
12/07/89	6	1	Mike's	Weekapaug
12/09/89	2	2	Mike's	Weekapaug
12/16/89	2	1a	Mike's	Weekapaug
12/29/89	1	1	Mike's	Weekapaug
12/31/89	2	2	Mike's	Weekapaug
01/20/90	1	1a	Mike's	Weekapaug
01/27/90	3	1	Mike's	Weekapaug
01/28/90	1	2	Mike's	Weekapaug
02/09/90	7	1	Mike's	Weekapaug
02/10/90	1	1	Mike's	Weekapaug
02/15/90	1	1	Mike's	Weekapaug
02/17/90	2	1a	Mike's	Weekapaug
02/23/90	2	2	Mike's	Weekapaug
03/01/90	3	2	Mike's	Weekapaug
03/03/90	2	1	Mike's	Weekapaug
03/07/90	1	2	Mike's	Weekapaug
03/08/90	1	2	Mike's	Weekapaug
03/28/90	4	2	Mike's	Weekapaug
04/04/90	1	2	Mike's	Weekapaug
04/05/90	1	2	Mike's	Weekapaug
04/07/90	2	1	Mike's	Weekapaug
04/08/90	1	2	Mike's	Weekapaug
04/18/90	5	1	Mike's	Weekapaug
04/20/90	2	2	Mike's	Weekapaug
04/22/90	2	1	Mike's	Weekapaug
04/25/90	1	2	Mike's	Weekapaug
04/26/90	1	2	Mike's	Weekapaug
04/28/90	1	2	Mike's	Weekapaug
05/04/90	3	2	Mike's	Weekapaug
05/06/90	1	1	Mike's	Weekapaug
05/11/90	2	1	Mike's	Weekapaug
05/13/90	2	2	Mike's	Weekapaug
05/23/90	3	2	Mike's	Weekapaug
06/05/90	4	1	Mike's	Weekapaug
06/07/90	1	2	Mike's	Weekapaug
06/09/90	1	1	Mike's	Weekapaug
06/16/90	1	3	Mike's	Weekapaug
09/13/90	1	2	Mike's	Weekapaug
09/16/90	2	1a	Mike's	Weekapaug
10/05/90	7	1	Mike's	Weekapaug
10/07/90	2	1	Mike's	Weekapaug
10/12/90	2	2	Mike's	Weekapaug
10/30/90	2	2	Mike's	Weekapaug
10/31/90	1	2	Mike's	Weekapaug
11/02/90	1	1	Mike's	Weekapaug
11/03/90	1	2	Mike's	Weekapaug
11/04/90	1	2	Mike's	Weekapaug
11/08/90	1	1	Mike's	Weekapaug
11/10/90	1	1	Mike's	Weekapaug
11/16/90	1	2	Mike's	Weekapaug
11/17/90	1	2	Mike's	Weekapaug
11/24/90	1	1	Mike's	Weekapaug
11/26/90	1	2	Mike's	Weekapaug
11/30/90	1	1	Mike's	Weekapaug
12/07/90	3	2	Mike's	Weekapaug
12/08/90	1	1	Mike's	Weekapaug
12/28/90	1	1	Mike's	Weekapaug
12/31/90	2	1	Mike's	Weekapaug
02/08/91	5	2	Mike's	Weekapaug
02/14/91	2	2	Mike's	Weekapaug

Original Songs Played by Year *(continued)*

Sleeping Monkey

1992	18	15%
1993	5	5%
1994	17	14%
1995	6	7%
1996	2	3%
1997	4	5%

Sloth

1990	14	14%
1991	30	24%
1992	16	13%
1993	14	13%
1994	9	7%
1995	5	6%
1996	6	9%
1997	3	4%

Sparkle

1991	32	25%
1992	64	53%
1993	58	53%
1994	45	36%
1995	25	31%
1996	21	30%
1997	10	13%

Split Open and Melt

1990	7	7%
1991	32	25%
1992	34	28%
1993	42	38%
1994	42	34%
1995	20	25%
1996	16	23%
1997	11	14%

Spock's Brain

1995	5	6%
1996	0	0%
1997	0	0%

Squirming Coil

1990	29	28%
1991	63	50%
1992	52	43%
1993	42	38%
1994	26	21%
1995	18	22%
1996	7	10%
1997	8	10%

Stash

1990	14	14%
1991	45	35%
1992	54	45%
1993	56	51%
1994	44	35%
1995	25	31%
1996	20	29%
1997	22	28%

Strange Design

1995	28	35%
1996	7	10%
1997	3	4%

02/16/91	2	1	Mike's	Weekapaug
02/21/91	3	1	Mike's	Weekapaug
02/26/91	4	2	Mike's	Weekapaug
02/28/91	2	1	Mike's	Weekapaug
03/01/91	1	1	Mike's	Weekapaug
03/07/91	3	2	Mike's	Weekapaug
03/15/91	4	1	Mike's	Weekapaug
03/17/91	2	1	Mike's	Weekapaug
03/22/91	2	2	Mike's	Weekapaug
04/05/91	8	1	Mike's	Weekapaug
04/11/91	2	2	Mike's	Weekapaug
04/15/91	3	2	Mike's	Weekapaug
04/19/91	3	1	Mike's	Weekapaug
04/21/91	2	1	Mike's	Weekapaug
04/27/91	4	2	Mike's	Weekapaug
05/04/91	3	1	Mike's	Weekapaug
05/10/91	2	2	Mike's	Weekapaug
05/12/91	2	2	Mike's	Weekapaug
05/17/91	2	1	Mike's	Weekapaug
07/11/91	3	2	Mike's	Weekapaug
07/12/91	1	2	Mike's	Weekapaug
07/14/91	2	3	Mike's	Weekapaug
07/15/91	1	1a	Mike's	Weekapaug
07/18/91	1	1	Mike's	Weekapaug
07/21/91	3	1	Mike's	Weekapaug
07/23/91	1	1	Mike's	Weekapaug
07/25/91	2	2	Mike's	Weekapaug
07/27/91	2	1a	Mike's	Weekapaug
09/26/91	3	2	Mike's	Weekapaug
09/28/91	2	2	Mike's	Weekapaug
10/03/91	3	2	Mike's	Weekapaug
10/04/91	1	2	Mike's	Weekapaug
10/10/91	3	2	Mike's	Weekapaug
10/13/91	3	1	Mike's	Weekapaug
10/18/91	3	2	Mike's	Weekapaug
10/24/91	3	2	Mike's	Weekapaug
10/27/91	2	2	Mike's	Weekapaug
11/01/91	4	2	Mike's	Weekapaug
11/08/91	4	2	Mike's	Weekapaug
11/12/91	3	2	Mike's	Weekapaug
11/15/91	3	2	Mike's	Weekapaug
11/19/91	2	2	Mike's	Weekapaug
11/21/91	2	1	Mike's	Weekapaug
11/23/91	2	2	Mike's	Weekapaug
12/04/91	3	2	Mike's	Weekapaug
12/05/91	1	2	Mike's	Weekapaug
12/31/91	3	3	Mike's	Weekapaug
03/07/92	2	2	Mike's	Weekapaug
03/14/92	4	1	Mike's	Weekapaug
03/17/92	1	2	Mike's	Weekapaug
03/20/92	2	2	Mike's	Weekapaug
03/24/92	2	2	Mike's	Weekapaug
03/27/92	3	2	Mike's	Weekapaug
03/31/92	3	2	Mike's	Weekapaug
04/04/92	3	2	Mike's	Weekapaug
04/06/92	2	2	Mike's	Weekapaug
04/09/92	2	2	Mike's	Weekapaug
04/13/92	2	2	Mike's	Weekapaug
04/16/92	2	2	Mike's	Weekapaug
04/19/92	3	2	Mike's	Weekapaug
04/21/92	1	2	Mike's	Weekapaug
04/23/92	2	2	Mike's	Weekapaug
04/24/92	1	2	Mike's	Weekapaug
04/29/92	2	2	Mike's	Weekapaug
05/01/92	2	2	Mike's	Weekapaug
05/03/92	2	2	Mike's	Weekapaug
05/05/92	1	2	Mike's	Weekapaug
05/07/92	2	2	Mike's	Weekapaug
05/14/92	5	2	Mike's	Weekapaug
05/18/92	4	2	Mike's	Weekapaug
07/16/92	15	2	Mike's	Weekapaug
08/17/92	18	2	Mike's	Weekapaug
11/19/92	11	2	Mike's	Weekapaug
11/21/92	2	2	Mike's	Weekapaug
11/23/92	2	2	Mike's	Weekapaug
11/28/92	3	1	Mike's	Weekapaug
12/01/92	2	1	Mike's	Weekapaug
12/03/92	2	2	Mike's	Weekapaug
12/05/92	2	2	Mike's	Weekapaug
12/08/92	3	2	Mike's	Weekapaug
12/11/92	2	2	Mike's	Weekapaug
12/29/92	4	2	Mike's	Weekapaug
02/06/93	6	2	Mike's	Weekapaug
02/09/93	2	2	Mike's	Weekapaug
02/11/93	2	2	Mike's	Weekapaug
02/15/93	3	2	Mike's	Weekapaug
02/18/93	2	2	Mike's	Weekapaug
02/20/93	2	2	Kung	Weekapaug
02/23/93	3	2	Mike's	Weekapaug
02/27/93	3	2	Mike's	Weekapaug
03/03/93	2	2	Mike's	Weekapaug
03/05/93	1	2	Mike's	Weekapaug
03/09/93	3	2	Mike's	Weekapaug
03/13/93	2	2	Mike's	Weekapaug
03/17/93	3	2	Mike's	Weekapaug
03/19/93	2	2	Mike's	Weekapaug
03/22/93	2	2	Mike's	Weekapaug
03/25/93	2	2	Mike's	Weekapaug
03/27/93	2	2	Mike's	Weekapaug
03/30/93	2	2	Mike's	Weekapaug
04/02/93	3	2	Mike's	Weekapaug
04/13/93	6	2	Mike's	Weekapaug
04/16/93	2	2	Mike's	Weekapaug
04/23/93	6	2	Mike's	Weekapaug
04/25/93	2	2	Mike's	Weekapaug
04/29/93	2	2	Mike's	Weekapaug
05/08/93	8	2	Mike's	Weekapaug
04/09/94	44	2	Mike's	Weekapaug
04/21/94	10	2	Mike's	Weekapaug
04/29/94	6	2	Mike's	Weekapaug
05/14/94	11	2	Mike's	Weekapaug
05/19/94	3	2	Mike's	Weekapaug
06/09/94	10	2	Mike's	Weekapaug
06/13/94	3	2	Mike's	Weekapaug
06/17/94	3	2	Mike's	Weekapaug
06/22/94	4	2	Simple	Weekapaug
07/02/94	8	2	YSZahov	Weekapaug
07/10/94	6	2	Mike's	Weekapaug
10/08/94	6	2	Mike's	Weekapaug
10/21/94	10	2	Mike's	Weekapaug
12/10/94	34	2	Mike's	Weekapaug
06/10/95	9	2	Mike's	Weekapaug
10/19/95	34	2	Mike's	Weekapaug
07/23/96	61	2	Mike's	Weekapaug
08/05/96	5	2	Mike's	Weekapaug
10/29/96	19	2	Mike's	Horse
07/22/97	64	2	Simple	Weekapaug
07/31/97	6	2	Mike's	Weekapaug
11/13/97	12	2	Mike's	Weekapaug
11/22/97	6	1	Mike's	Weekapaug
12/09/97	11	1	Stash	Weekapaug
>> 12/31/97	**7**			

I DIDN'T KNOW

Inspiration: Another Nancy Taube creation, I Didn't Know features vocals from Trey, Mike, and Page and an interlude in the middle where Fishman shows off his prowess on one of his many strange instruments. It's basically an a cappella tune with some bass thrown in, but is always performed with microphones.

Musical Evolution and History: None to speak of, besides the ever-changing vacuum, trombone, plastic, Madonna washboard (complete with cone-shaped breasts), and whatever-else solos from Fishman.

Rotation History: Heavily played until 1993, I Didn't Know has been in decline in recent years. 1997 saw but two performances.

Discography: Has yet to appear on a Phish album.

I Didn't Know [188] [IDK]

By Phish/Nancy Taube

09/27/87	[24]	2	Wilson	Fluffhead
11/19/87	3	2	Fluffhead	Fee
02/07/88	2	1a	Reagan	Bowie
03/21/88	4	1a	Dinner	Forbin's
03/31/88	1	1	*OP1	Golgi
05/14/88	2	2	Fire	Halley's
05/15/88	1	1a	Peaches	Sloth
05/23/88	1	1a	Light Up	Peaches
05/25/88	1	3	Sloth	Ya Mar
06/15/88	1	1	Timber Ho	*CL1
06/21/88	3	2	Harpua	ACDCBag
10/12/88	12	1	*OP1	Golgi
10/29/88	1	3	Antelope	Wilson
11/03/88	1	2	Suzie	BBFCM
11/05/88	1	2	Weekapaug	GTBT
12/02/88	2	2	*OP2	GTBT
01/26/89	1	1a	*OP1	Golgi
02/06/89	2	1	OYWD	*CL1
03/03/89	5	1	Antelope	Divided
03/04/89	1	1	A-Train	Mike's
04/15/89	9	1	Alumni	McGrupp
04/30/89	7	1	*OP1	YEM
05/05/89	3	2	Antelope	A-Train
05/06/89	1	1	YEM	Mike's
05/09/89	3	2	Antelope	Lizards
05/20/89	7	1	Divided	Possum
08/12/89	14	1a	Swing	YEM
10/14/89	16	1	Divided	Golgi
10/20/89	1	2	Dinner	ACDCBag
10/22/89	2	1	Divided	GTBT
10/26/89	1	1	Divided	Wilson
11/09/89	6	1	*OP1	Golgi
12/07/89	9	1	*OP1	YEM
12/08/89	1	2	Slave	YEM
12/15/89	2	1a	*OP1	Possum
12/31/89	4	1	*OP1	YEM
02/09/90	12	E	*OPE	*CLE
02/10/90	1	E	*OPE	HwayHell
02/23/90	5	E	Contact	GTBT
02/24/90	1	1	Possum	A-Train
03/01/90	2	1	Divided	YEM
03/08/90	4	2	Caravan	Lizards
04/04/90	5	2	Sloth	GTBT
04/06/90	2	2	Reba	Alumni
04/22/90	11	1	Possum	Cavern
04/26/90	2	1	Bouncing	Antelope
04/28/90	1	2	Caravan	Reba
05/24/90	12	2	Possum	MSO
05/31/90	1	1a	Tweezer	Uncle Pen
06/08/90	4	1	Tweezer	Mike's
09/14/90	4	1	Dinner	*CL1
09/22/90	5	1	Landlady	Bowie
10/05/90	4	1	*OP1	Mike's
10/07/90	2	2	MSO	Lizards
11/02/90	6	2	Lizards	Bowie
11/08/90	3	1	Asse Fest	Mike's
11/16/90	2	2	RunJim	Possum
11/30/90	4	2	Divided	Sloth
12/29/90	6	1	*OP1	Llama
12/31/90	1	1	Divided	Landlady
02/14/91	7	2	Bouncing	Landlady
02/27/91	10	1	Divided	Landlady
03/07/91	5	2	Possum	Mike's
03/15/91	4	2	Destiny	Harry
03/23/91	5	1	Llama	Curtain
04/05/91	7	2	Harry	MSO
04/19/91	8	1	Stash	Rocky Top
04/21/91	2	2	Cavern	Bowie
04/26/91	3	2	Landlady	Harry
05/02/91	2	1	MSO	BurAlive
05/17/91	8	1	Stash	Mike's
05/25/91	2	2	*OP2	Golgi
07/14/91	4	1	Sloth	Possum
07/18/91	2	2	Landlady	Possum
07/19/91	1	2	Divided	MSO
07/21/91	2	2	Tweezer	RunJim
07/24/91	2	2	FunkBitch	Frankstein
07/27/91	3	1a	Possum	Landlady
08/03/91	1	2	Cavern	YEM
09/27/91	3	1	It's Ice	*CL1
09/29/91	2	1a	Divided	It's Ice
10/02/91	1	E	Possum	Rocky Top
10/06/91	4	2	Harry	Cavern
10/10/91	1	2	Antelope	Sparkle
10/18/91	6	2	Weekapaug	Fee
10/24/91	3	1	Divided	TMWSIY
10/28/91	3	1	Reba	Tube
10/31/91	2	2	Tube	Harry
11/07/91	4	1	RunJim	Llama
11/08/91	1	2	Sqirm Coil	Mike's
11/13/91	4	1	Divided	Terrapin
11/22/91	7	2	Sqirm Coil	Llama
11/24/91	2	1	It's Ice	Bowie
11/30/91	1	2	Horn	Antelope
12/05/91	2	2	Sqirm Coil	MSO
12/06/91	1	1	Guelah	*CL1
03/12/92	6	1	Stash	Reba
03/17/92	3	1	It's Ice	Divided
03/24/92	4	2	Uncle Pen	Oh Kee
03/28/92	4	2	Carolina	Adeline
03/30/92	1	1	Maze	All Things
04/01/92	2	1	RunJim	Landlady
04/04/92	2	1	Lizards	Antelope
04/15/92	7	1	Cavern	All Things
04/17/92	2	1	Stash	Cavern
04/19/92	2	1	Chalkdust	Golgi
04/23/92	3	1	It's Ice	Possum
05/01/92	5	1	Horn	Possum
05/03/92	2	1	Split&Melt	Rift
05/05/92	1	1	Divided	It's Ice
05/09/92	4	1	Sqirm Coil	Antelope
05/10/92	1	1a	Reba	YEM
05/17/92	5	1	Reba	Stash
06/24/92	5	1a	Guelah	Sparkle
06/27/92	1	E	*OPE	GTBT
07/14/92	8	1	Brother	PoorHeart
07/30/92	13	1a	Maze	Possum
11/30/92	26	1	It's Ice	Reba
12/10/92	9	1	Split&Melt	All Things
12/13/92	3	1	FEFY	Bowie
12/30/92	3	1	Reba	Timber Ho
12/31/92	1	1	Foam	Antelope
02/03/93	1	1	Divided	My Friend
02/05/93	2	1	PYITE	PoorHeart
02/07/93	2	1	Rift	Split&Melt
02/10/93	2	1	Tela	Catapult
02/12/93	2	1	Chalkdust	A-Train
02/15/93	2	1	Guelah	Antelope
02/22/93	6	1	Cavern	Bowie
02/25/93	2	1	Bouncing	Bowie
02/26/93	1	1	Divided	Cavern
03/02/93	2	1	Silent	Bowie
03/05/93	2	1	It's Ice	Possum
03/09/93	3	1	PYITE	Antelope
03/16/93	4	1	Maze	Divided
03/18/93	2	1	Horn	Bowie
03/24/93	4	1	Maze	Sample
03/27/93	3	1	Sample	Bowie
03/31/93	3	1	Reba	Bowie
04/02/93	2	1	Divided	Sparkle
04/09/93	3	1	Maze	It's Ice
04/14/93	4	1	Divided	Golgi
04/18/93	3	1	Horn	Cavern
04/21/93	2	1	PYITE	Antelope
04/25/93	4	1	Maze	Golgi
05/02/93	5	1	Maze	Golgi
05/07/93	4	1	Divided	Antelope
05/30/93	3	1a	Antelope	Split&Melt
07/15/93	1	1	Foam	My Mind
07/25/93	8	1	My Mind	Bowie
07/30/93	4	1	Chalkdust	Reba
08/08/93	6	1	Paul&Silas	Bowie
08/16/93	7	1	Foam	Split&Melt
08/21/93	3	1	Landlady	RunJim
12/31/93	8	1	Peaches	Antelope
04/08/94	4	1	Foam	PYITE
04/10/94	2	1	Chalkdust	Scent
04/17/94	6	1	Foam	Divided
04/29/94	9	1	Divided	Dog Faced
05/29/94	23	1	Julius	Bowie
06/14/94	5	1	Uncle Pen	MSO
06/29/94	11	1	Bowie	Golgi
07/13/94	10	1	FEFY	Split&Melt
10/13/94	9	1	DWD	Foam
10/18/94	4	1	My Friend	PoorHeart
10/28/94	8	1	*OP1	Llama
11/22/94	14	1	Guyute	Bouncing
12/01/94	6	1	Guyute	Split&Melt
12/09/94	7	1	Sparkle	It's Ice
12/29/94	3	1	Uncle Pen	Possum
06/15/95	10	1	Stash	Fluffhead
06/20/95	4	1	Taste	Split&Melt
06/25/95	4	1	Divided	Split&Melt
07/02/95	6	1	Reba	Rift
09/27/95	2	1	It's Ice	Fog
10/15/95	13	1	Slave	Demand
10/27/95	8	1	Horn	Rift
11/12/95	7	1	Reba	Fog
11/28/95	10	1	Foam	Divided
12/28/95	16	2	Tweezer	Uncle Pen
07/11/96	12	1	Reba	Sparkle
07/15/96	3	1	Possum	Harry
08/10/96	15	1	Reba	Horse
10/25/96	13	1	Guelah	Stash
11/24/96	20	1	Taste	Sample
12/02/96	5	1	YEM	Theme
02/22/97	15	1	Split&Melt	CharZero
11/28/97	55	1	YEM	Maze
>> 12/31/97	**15**			

I DON'T CARE

Inspiration: Apparently, the band and fans have taken a cue from the song's title, as little is known about it.

Musical Evolution and History: Got off to a glorious beginning, segued into Reba at a Royal Albert Hall show. But after setting up Antelope four nights later, it never appeared again.

Rotation History: Played only twice.
Discography: Has not yet appeared on a Phish album.

I Don't Care [2] [Don't Care]
Author Unknown

06/16/97	[906]	2	Ghost	Reba
06/20/97	2	1	Limb	Antelope
>> 12/31/97	**58**			

I SAW IT AGAIN
Inspiration: Perhaps wanting to add another hard rock–style tune to their repertoire, Phish debuted this short, loud number in the summer of 1997.
Musical Evolution and History: The cacophonous yells of "I Saw It Again!" don't go on for too long, so there's little evolution to speak of. However, the version of this song that opened the second set in Albany on 12/12/97 gave hope that it may eventually become something more than just a bad joke, as a great jam stretched out of I Saw It Again and eventually segued into Piper.
Rotation History: Played seven times in 1997, its debut year.
Discography: Has yet to appear on a Phish album.

I Saw It Again [7] [Saw It]
By Anastasio/Marshall

06/14/97	[905]	2	Piper	Fooled
06/19/97	2	2	Ghost	Wading
06/25/97	5	1	Wading	Limb
07/01/97	3	1	Funny	Dirt
07/31/97	15	1	Glide	YEM
11/29/97	22	1	Ginseng	Horn
12/12/97	8	2	*OP2	Piper
>> 12/31/97	**5**			

ICCULUS
Inspiration: A Gamehendge song, named for the prophet/god of the land who wrote the Helping Friendly Book.
Musical Evolution and History: The song is more of a send-up of rock culture than a real tune, as Trey often narrates for as long as five minutes before launching into the song's 20-*second* jam. Several 1988 versions, like the 7/25/88 one immortalized on the *Junta* re-release, are particularly funny, as are most versions from spring 1992 onward, especially the NBA Finals dialogue on 6/22/94 Columbus, OH ("Read the fucking book! Save your life!" Trey repeats, or the Halloween Icculus on 10/31/95 in Chicago, IL, when Trey proclaims, "The book is getting its ass kicked!") Though the song sometimes appeared in the "Forbin's rap" between Forbin's and Mockingbird (notably in spring 1992), it can pop up anywhere.
Rotation History: Very rarely played, as it has appeared under ten times in the 1990s. Since its last appearance, on 10/31/95, fans have been waiting for its return, but to no avail. The jam that closes the song has never been extended, but easily could be if Phish were ever so inspired.
Discography: Appears on the Elektra re-release of *Junta* as a live bonus track, misdated 5/3/88 (it's actually 7/25/88).

Icculus [18] [Icculus]
By Anastasio/Marshall

04/01/86	[6]	1	Jam	YEM
10/31/86	3	2	Skin It	Alumni
12/06/86	1	1a	Jam	McGrupp
08/10/87	7	2	La Grange	Bowie
05/15/88	19	1a	Possum	McGrupp
07/25/88	13	3	Sanity	CamlWalk
01/26/89	13	1a	Fluffhead	Forbin's
02/06/89	3	2	Curtis	WhipPost
08/12/89	50	1a	Possum	Antelope
04/06/91	181	1	Bathtub	Antelope
04/16/92	116	1	Forbin's	Mockbird
04/24/92	7	1	Forbin's	Mockbird
05/02/92	5	1	Forbin's	Mockbird
03/25/93	119	2	Forbin's	Kung
06/22/94	127	2	Simple	Simple
10/27/94	35	E	Slave	TweezRep
11/20/94	14	E	*OPE	Fire
10/31/95	67	1	*OP1	Divided
>> 12/31/97	**181**			

IF I COULD
Inspiration: Born of the desire to write more meaningful songs for *Hoist*, Trey penned this song of longing and wrote the music for it.
Musical and Evolution History: One of the group of songs tested in the studio before being performed live, If I Could had a long instrumental intro that was later cut from *Hoist* (what appears to be the intro appears in concert on 7/1/95 in Mansfield, MA). Perhaps looking for the sort of adult-oriented radio play which Fast Enough for You off *Rift* received, Elektra included If I Could on the list of highlighted songs on *Hoist*'s shrink wrap (Sample in a Jar also got top billing). Bluegrass legend-in-the-making Alison Krauss joined Trey for a duet on the song in the studio (and in concert on 5/3/94), with Page assuming her vocal duties (in a rearranged fashion) in other instances. The song has the potential for a beautiful outro jam, sort of like Lifeboy, but to date Phish has played it pretty tame with If I Could.
Rotation History: Heavily played in its debut year of 1994, If I Could has fallen off the map since then. It hasn't been played since 8/5/96 at Red Rocks.
Discography: Appears on *Hoist* (1994), with Alison Krauss on guest vocals and the Richard Green Fourteen on strings.

If I Could [45] [If I Could]
By Anastasio

04/04/94	[615]	2	DWD	BurAlive
04/05/94	1	2	Tweezer	YEM
04/08/94	2	1	DWD	Lawn Boy
04/15/94	6	2	Maze	Oh Kee
04/17/94	2	1	DWD	MSO
04/21/94	3	1	DWD	Cavern
04/29/94	6	2	Maze	Reba
05/03/94	3	2	Bowie	Fluffhead
05/07/94	3	1	Split&Melt	Suzie
05/10/94	2	1	Melt	Cavern
05/13/94	2	1	Stash	My Friend
05/17/94	3	1	Mound	Scent
05/20/94	2	1	Maze	It's Ice
05/23/94	3	2	Antelope	Sparkle
05/27/94	3	1	Bowie	PYITE
06/09/94	3	1	It's Ice	Maze
06/14/94	4	2	Bowie	It's Ice
06/17/94	2	1	Split&Melt	PYITE
06/19/94	2	2	Antelope	Reba
06/22/94	2	1	Maze	Scent
06/26/94	4	2	DWD	Axilla 2
07/01/94	3	2	Bowie	Fluffhead
07/05/94	3	1	LTJP	Uncle Pen
07/10/94	4	1	Stash	My Friend
07/14/94	2	2	Maze	Uncle Pen
10/13/94	8	2	Antelope	It's Ice
11/02/94	15	1	Foam	Maze
11/12/94	3	1	Foam	Guyute
11/20/94	7	1	Stash	Butter
11/23/94	2	1	It's Ice	Oh Kee
11/26/94	2	1	Guyute	Foam
12/04/94	6	1	Foam	Rift
12/09/94	4	1	It's Ice	Antelope
12/29/94	3	1	Foam	Split&Melt
06/07/95	4	1	Stash	Scent
06/20/95	10	1	Bathtub	Taste
06/25/95	4	1	Theme	Sparkle
07/01/95	5	1	Llama	All Things
07/03/95	2	1	It's Ice	Maze
09/30/95	4	2	Fog	Scent
10/11/95	7	1	Divided	Fog
11/12/95	18	1	Fog	Split&Melt
11/29/95	11	1	Reba	It's Ice
07/21/96	34	1	Tweezer	My Mind
08/05/96	7	1	Foam	Julius
>> 12/31/96	**125**			

IN A HOLE
Inspiration: Unclear, but this weird little song wasn't around very long, anyway.
Musical Evolution and History: Unveiled in the fall of 1989, In a Hole (also known as "I Fell in a Hole" or just "Hole") has an upbeat rhythm that didn't vary between its few performances.
Rotation History: Played six times between October and December 1989, but not since. Its last appearance was 12/16/89.
Discography: Has yet to appear on a Phish album.

In a Hole [6] [In a Hole]
By Phish

10/20/89	[131]	2	Swing	*CL2
10/21/89	1	1	Ya Mar	McGrupp
10/22/89	1	2	Golgi	McGrupp
10/26/89	1	2	PYITE	No Dogs

Original Songs Played by Year
(continued)

Suzie Greenberg

1990	48	47%
1991	49	39%
1992	45	37%
1993	22	20%
1994	42	34%
1995	22	27%
1996	17	24%
1997	4	5%

Swept Away/Steep

1996	13	19%
1997	9	12%

Talk

1996	8	11%
1997	3	4%

Taste

1995	10	12%
1996	28	40%
1997	30	38%

Tela

1990	9	9%
1991	14	11%
1992	9	7%
1993	5	5%
1994	12	10%
1995	7	9%
1996	2	3%
1997	1	1%

Theme from the Bottom

1995	26	32%
1996	20	29%
1997	27	35%

Time

1997	2	3%

Train Song

1996	14	20%
1997	10	13%

Tube

1990	5	5%
1991	15	12%
1992	2	1%
1993	1	1%
1994	1	1%
1995	3	4%
1996	3	4%
1997	3	4%

Tweezer

1990	29	28%
1991	33	26%
1992	30	25%
1993	37	34%
1994	31	25%
1995	18	22%
1996	16	23%
1997	10	13%

12/09/89	17	1	Foam	Rocky Top
12/16/89	2	1	Lizards	Golgi
>> 12/31/97	**813**			

IT'S ICE

Inspiration: A close listen to the lyrics gives a sense of what this song's about: a reflected image in the ice battling for control of the "real" person skating above. Trey has called these some of Tom Marshall's most amazing lyrics, and he can often be seen mouthing the words on stage while Page handles the actual vocals.

Musical Evolution and History: The opening and closing lyric segments of this song are as written in 1991, but the middle jam section has undergone a number of changes. Starting in the summer of 1993, the band began to really experiment with the song, adding piano solos (like the "I Feel the Earth Move" jam on 8/24/93), cool jams (like the "Peaches"-infused 12/31/93 version), or even Kung (10/29/95 and 12/30/95). Fall 1997 even saw a crazy It's Ice > Swept Away > Steep > It's Ice package on 12/7/97 in Dayton, OH.

In the antics department, Trey and Mike often slid on their gliders during this song in 1993. Plus, there's bonus karma from when It's Ice served as the gateway to Gamehendge on 3/22/93 Sacramento, CA.

Rotation History: Played often in 1991–1992 and 1994–1995, and one out of every two shows in 1993, Ice has fallen from those heights, as it was played only three times total in 1997.

Discography: Appears on *Rift* (1993).

It's Ice [191] [It's Ice]

By Anastasio/Marshall

09/25/91	[335]	1	MSO	Landlady
09/26/91	1	1	Fee	MSO
09/27/91	1	1	Paul&Silas	IDK
09/29/91	2	1a	IDK	PoorHeart
10/03/91	2	1	Uncle Pen	Bouncing
10/10/91	4	1	RunJim	Llama
10/13/91	3	2	Sqirm Coil	MSO
10/19/91	4	1	Suzie	RunJim
10/27/91	4	2	Sparkle	Mike's
11/01/91	4	2	MSO	Chalkdust
11/07/91	3	1	Cavern	YEM
11/09/91	2	2	PoorHeart	Tweezer
11/13/91	3	1	RunJim	Sparkle
11/14/91	1	2	Paul&Silas	Glide
11/16/91	2	1	RunJim	Sparkle
11/20/91	2	2	Golgi	MSO
11/21/91	1	2	Harry	Mango
11/24/91	3	1	Sparkle	IDK
11/30/91	1	2	Harry	Bouncing
12/05/91	2	1	Bathtub	Bouncing
12/06/91	1	2	*OP2	Eliza
03/06/92	3	1	Sparkle	Oh Kee
03/12/92	3	2	Eliza	Bouncing
03/17/92	3	1	Sparkle	IDK
03/25/92	5	1	RunJim	Antelope
04/04/92	8	1	Bouncing	Sparkle
04/05/92	1	1	Horn	Possum
04/07/92	2	1	Possum	Fee
04/12/92	2	1	Silent	Sparkle
04/16/92	3	1	Possum	Bouncing
04/18/92	2	1	Possum	Sparkle
04/21/92	2	1	Possum	Eliza
04/23/92	2	1	Bouncing	IDK
04/29/92	3	1	Sparkle	RunJim
05/01/92	2	1	Guelah	Horn
05/03/92	2	1	Possum	Uncle Pen
05/05/92	1	1	IDK	Glide
05/08/92	3	1	Uncle Pen	Eliza
05/12/92	3	1	Possum	Dinner
05/16/92	3	2	RunJim	Paul
06/20/92	4	1a	RunJim	Horn
07/14/92	11	1	Sparkle	RunJim
07/16/92	2	1	PoorHeart	Sparkle
07/21/92	4	1a	Possum	Sparkle
07/26/92	4	1a	Chalkdust	Divided
07/30/92	3	1a	Sparkle	All Things
08/17/92	7	2	Suzie	Tweezer
08/25/92	5	1a	RunJim	Sparkle
11/19/92	6	2	Bouncing	Walk Line
11/21/92	2	1	PoorHeart	Bouncing
11/25/92	3	1	Sparkle	Sqirm Coil
11/27/92	1	2	Glide	McGrupp
11/30/92	2	1	Sparkle	IDK
12/03/92	3	2	Lawn Boy	MSO
12/04/92	1	2	Possum	Sqirm Coil
12/07/92	3	2	MSO	Fee
12/08/92	1	2	Silent	Lizards
12/11/92	2	1	RunJim	Uncle Pen
12/13/92	2	1	Divided	Fee
12/28/92	1	1	Glide	Bouncing
12/31/92	3	2	RunJim	Sparkle
02/03/93	1	2	RunJim	Tweezer
02/05/93	2	2	Paul&Silas	YEM
02/07/93	2	1	PoorHeart	Sparkle
02/10/93	2	2	RunJim	Sqirm Coil
02/13/93	3	1	PoorHeart	Glide
02/17/93	2	1	RunJim	Bouncing
02/19/93	2	2	RunJim	Paul&Silas
02/22/93	3	2	RunJim	Uncle Pen
02/25/93	2	2	Suzie	Sparkle
02/27/93	2	1	Bouncing	Sparkle
03/02/93	1	1	Sparkle	Fee
03/05/93	2	1	Sparkle	IDK
03/08/93	2	1	Sparkle	Glide
03/13/93	3	2	Lizards	Glide
03/16/93	2	1	PoorHeart	Fee
03/17/93	1	1	Paul&Silas	Oh Kee
03/19/93	2	2	RunJim	Uncle Pen
03/22/93	2	2	Golgi	Lizards
03/25/93	2	1	Guelah	Possum
03/27/93	2	2	Halley's	Bouncing
03/28/93	1	1	Fee	Lawn Boy
03/31/93	2	2	BBJ	YEM
04/05/93	4	1	Llama	Fee
04/09/93	1	1	IDK	Divided
04/12/93	2	2	Paul&Silas	BBJ
04/14/93	2	1	Bouncing	Stash
04/17/93	2	1	Stash	Glide
04/20/93	2	1	Bouncing	Glide
04/22/93	2	1	Sparkle	Reba
04/23/93	1	2	Curtis	Paul&Silas
04/25/93	2	1	Bouncing	Glide
04/27/93	1	1	Guelah	Sparkle
04/29/93	1	2	Chalkdust	Ya Mar
05/01/93	2	1	Sample	Glide
05/03/93	2	2	Contact	McGrupp
05/05/93	1	1	Bouncing	Glide
05/08/93	3	2	Silent	Sqirm Coil
07/15/93	3	2	Sparkle	Life Boy
07/17/93	2	2	Sqirm Coil	Sparkle
07/22/93	3	2	Sparkle	Contact
07/23/93	1	1	RunJim	Lawn Boy
07/27/93	3	1a	Sparkle	PurplRain
07/29/93	2	2	Bouncing	Life Boy
07/31/93	2	2	RunJim	Maze
08/03/93	2	2	Bouncing	YEM
08/08/93	3	2	Wilson	Fluffhead
08/11/93	2	1	Weigh	Ginseng
08/14/93	3	1	Silent	Sparkle
08/16/93	2	2	Mound	My Friend
08/20/93	2	1	Bouncing	Wedge
08/24/93	2	1	Bouncing	Nellie
08/26/93	2	1	Esther	Harry
08/28/93	1	2	Sparkle	BBJ
12/28/93	1	1	Ya Mar	Fee
12/31/93	3	2	PoorHeart	Fee
04/04/94	1	1	Horn	Possum
04/08/94	3	2	McGrupp	Sparkle
04/10/94	2	1	RunJim	Sparkle
04/15/94	4	1	Bouncing	DWD
04/20/94	4	1	RunJim	Julius
04/24/94	4	1	Paul&Silas	Slave
04/28/94	2	1a	Bouncing	Antelope
05/02/94	3	1	DWD	Glide
05/04/94	2	1	Sample	Sparkle
05/08/94	3	2	Antelope	Fee
05/10/94	1	1	Axilla 2	Split&Melt
05/13/94	2	1	RunJim	Julius
05/16/94	2	2	Sparkle	Julius
05/20/94	3	1	If I Could	Bathtub
05/22/94	2	2	Bouncing	McGrupp
05/26/94	3	1	Sparkle	Catapult
05/28/94	2	2	Axilla 2	Tweezer
06/09/94	2	1	DWD	If I Could
06/11/94	2	1	DWD	Tela
06/14/94	2	2	If I Could	Sparkle
06/18/94	3	1	DWD	Dog Faced
06/21/94	2	1	Sample	Horse
06/24/94	3	1	Wilson	Fee
06/29/94	3	2	Tweezer	Life Boy
07/01/94	2	1	Mango	Tela
07/03/94	2	2	Bouncing	Horse
07/08/94	3	2	YSZahov	Stash
07/13/94	3	1	Fee	FEFy
07/15/94	2	2	Reba	YSZahov
10/08/94	3	1	Fee	Lawn Boy
10/13/94	4	2	If I Could	AmGrace
10/18/94	4	1	Tela	Guyute
10/26/94	6	1	Simple	NICU
11/04/94	7	1	Sample	Bouncing
11/13/94	2	1	Axilla 2	Horse
11/18/94	4	1	Silent	Tela
11/23/94	4	1	Simple	If I Could
12/02/94	6	1	Simple	Lizards
12/09/94	6	1	IDK	If I Could
12/28/94	2	1	Dog Faced	Antelope
06/10/95	8	1	Caspian	Free
06/16/95	4	1	Cry Baby	My Mind
06/22/95	4	1	Guelah	Str Design
06/26/95	4	1	My Mind	Dog Faced
07/01/95	4	1	All Things	Caspian
07/03/95	2	1	Sparkle	If I Could
09/27/95	1	1	Free	IDK
10/03/95	5	2	Timber Ho	Sparkle
10/07/95	3	2	Str Design	Contact
10/14/95	4	1	AArmy	Tela
10/22/95	6	1	FEFY	PoorHeart
10/29/95	5	2	Mango	Shaggy
11/10/95	3	1	Old Home	Dog Faced
11/19/95	7	1	Str Design	HelloBaby
11/29/95	6	1	If I Could	Theme
12/08/95	7	1	Fluffhead	AArmy
12/15/95	5	2	RunJim	Bathtub
12/30/95	5	1	Simple	TMWSIY
07/12/96	11	2	It's Ice	Caspian
07/15/96	2	2	Makisupa	Julius
07/18/96	2	1a	HelloBaby	YEM
07/25/96	6	1a	Sample	Antelope
08/05/96	3	2	DWD	Halley's
08/12/96	4	1	Weigh	Dog Faced
08/17/96	4	2	RunJim	Brother
10/16/96	2	1	Sample	Horse
10/22/96	3	1	Bouncing	Talk
10/26/96	3	1	CharZero	Theme
11/13/96	11	1	Bouncing	Ya Mar
11/22/96	6	1	*OP1	RunJim
11/30/96	5	2	La Grange	Glide
12/28/96	5	1	Wolfman's	Billy
02/14/97	5	1	Axilla	Billy
08/08/97	44	1	Dirt	Water
12/07/97	24	1	My Mind	Theme
>> 12/31/97	**8**			

JULIUS

Inspiration: Author Tom Marshall has said he wrote this song from Julius Caesar's perspective, though some Classics majors have in turn questioned the song's historical veracity.

Musical Evolution and History: Recorded in the studio for *Hoist* before it ever saw the light of Kuroda, Julius was initially thought of as a horn song because the Tower of Power horns are featured on the song on the album. But by playing Julius more than every other night in 1994, they quickly got away from that, and established the song as a solid rocker. Though some fans tired of it after a few listens, great versions do emerge, such as 10/24/95 Madison, WI; 12/6/96 Las Vegas, NV; and 12/31/96 Boston, MA, with the Boston Community Choir on vocals. The band also performed it during their second appearance on "Late Night with David Letterman," with horn help, on 7/15/95.

Rotation History: Has never lacked for attention, especially during its debut year, when it was the second-most-played song of the year. In 1996 and 1997, it appeared in roughly one out of every five shows.

Discography: Appears on *Hoist* (1994), with the Tower of Power horns, the Rickey Grundy Chorale, and Rose Stone and Jean McClain on backing vocals.

Julius [117] [Julius]

By Anastasio/Marshall

04/04/94	[615]	2	Landlady	Magilla
04/05/94	1	1	Glide	Bouncing
04/09/94	3	1	Nellie	Fee
04/11/94	2	1	Magilla	Glide
04/13/94	1	1	Lizards	Ginseng
04/15/94	2	2	Landlady	Wolfman's
04/16/94	1	2	Lizards	Bouncing
04/18/94	2	1	PoorHeart	My Friend
04/20/94	1	1	It's Ice	Bouncing
04/22/94	2	2	Suzie	Reba
04/24/94	2	2	Mango	Forbin's
04/28/94	2	1a	Sqirm Coil	GTBT
05/02/94	3	2	Lizards	Lawn Boy
05/04/94	2	2	BurAlive	Wolfman's
05/06/94	1	2	Axilla 2	Bike
05/08/94	2	2	Fee	Cavern
05/10/94	1	2	Wilson	Reba
05/13/94	2	1	It's Ice	Mound
05/16/94	2	2	It's Ice	YEM
05/19/94	2	2	Lizards	BBJ
05/21/94	2	2	BBJ	Harry
05/23/94	2	1	Silent	Reba
05/25/94	1	2	BBJ	PurplRain
05/27/94	2	2	Lizards	Nellie
05/29/94	2	1	Sparkle	IDK
06/09/94	1	2	Glide	Halley's
06/10/94	1	1	Cavern	*CL1
06/13/94	2	1	Ginseng	*CL1
06/16/94	2	1	Rift	Fee
06/17/94	1	1	BBJ	Frankstein
06/19/94	2	1	Suzie	Lizards
06/21/94	1	2	Adeline	Sparkle
06/23/94	2	1	PYITE	*CL1
06/25/94	2	1	Rift	NICU
06/26/94	1	2	*OP2	DWD
06/29/94	1	1	Mound	Horse
07/01/94	2	1	Tela	Suzie
07/03/94	2	2	Silent	Sqirm Coil
07/06/94	2	1	Fluffhead	Bouncing
07/08/94	1	2	YEM	Golgi
07/10/94	2	1	My Friend	Cavern
07/13/94	1	2	Tweezer	Tweezer
07/15/94	2	2	Dog Faced	SettingSail
10/07/94	2	1	My Friend	Glide
10/09/94	2	2	AmGrace	Contact
10/12/94	2	1	Guelah	Adeline
10/14/94	2	1	Mockbird	*CL1
10/16/94	2	2	PoorHeart	Fluffhead
10/20/94	2	1	Esther	Guyute
10/22/94	2	1	Fluffhead	*CL1
10/25/94	2	1	Horn	Horse
10/27/94	2	2	*OP2	Ya Mar
10/31/94	3	1	Harpua	Horse
11/03/94	2	2	PoorHeart	YEM
11/12/94	2	2	*OP2	Fluffhead
11/14/94	2	2	PoorHeart	Old Home
11/18/94	3	1	ACDCBag	Horse
11/20/94	2	2	Terrapin	Cavern

11/25/94	3	1	Esther	Golgi
11/28/94	2	2	Sl Monkey	*CL2
12/02/94	3	2	BurAlive	Landlady
12/03/94	1	2	Touch Me	Cavern
12/07/94	3	2	Fee	I'm Blue
12/09/94	2	2	McGrupp	BBJ
12/28/94	2	1	Simple	Bathtub
06/08/95	6	2	PoorHeart	*CL2
06/13/95	3	E	Adeline	*CLE
06/17/95	4	1	Uncle Pen	Lawn Boy
06/24/95	5	1	Spock's	Glide
07/02/95	7	1	Curtain	CamlWalk
10/05/95	8	1	AArmy	Suzie
10/07/95	2	1	*OP1	Gumbo
10/11/95	2	1	AArmy	Sample
10/15/95	3	2	*OP2	Simple
10/24/95	6	2	*OP2	Theme
10/29/95	4	1	PoorHeart	PYITE
11/09/95	2	2	Theme	Lizards
11/14/95	4	1	Free	I'm Blue
11/19/95	4	1	HelloBaby	Sqirm Coil
11/24/95	3	2	Fee	*CL2
11/30/95	4	1	Ha Ha Ha	NICU
12/04/95	3	1	*OP1	Gumbo
12/07/95	2	2	Reba	Sl Monkey
12/11/95	3	1	McGrupp	Cavern
12/16/95	4	1	Dog Faced	Suzie
12/28/95	2	1	Curtain	Guyute
07/15/96	15	2	It's Ice	PurplRain
07/18/96	2	1a	*OP1	CTB
07/24/96	5	1a	Ya Mar	YEM
08/05/96	4	1	If I Could	Sqirm Coil
08/14/96	6	E	*OPE	*CLE
10/18/96	5	E	*OPE	*CLE
10/23/96	4	2	Slave	*CL2
10/26/96	2	1	*OP1	CTB
11/02/96	4	1	Ya Mar	Fee
11/09/96	5	E	*OPE	*CLE
11/14/96	3	1	Talk	*CL1
11/22/96	5	E	*OPE	*CLE
11/27/96	3	1	*OP1	My Friend
12/02/96	4	1	Gumbo	*CL1
12/06/96	2	2	*OP2	Sparkle
12/31/96	4	3	Bohemian	*CL3
02/13/97	1	2	*OP2	CTB
02/20/97	5	E	*OPE	*CLE
02/28/97	6	2	Waste	*CL2
06/20/97	8	2	Bouncing	*CL2
07/05/97	10	1a	*OP1	Bouncing
07/10/97	3	2	Also Sprac	Magilla
07/23/97	4	1	*OP1	Dirt
08/03/97	7	2	*OP2	Simple
08/06/97	1	E	*OPE	*CLE
08/16/97	7	2	Rocky Top	*CL2
11/19/97	6	1	*OP1	Bathtub
11/23/97	3	E	*OPE	*CLE
12/05/97	7	2	Bouncing	Slave
12/09/97	3	2	*OP2	Simple
12/28/97	4	1	*OP1	Cities
>> 12/31/97	**3**			

KEYBOARD KAVALRY

Inspiration: Perhaps happy with their guitar efforts in Acoustic Army that summer, the band unveiled a group keyboard jam on the fall tour in 1995. Keyboard Kavalry (also known as Keyboard Army) features Mike, Fish, and Trey robot-walking over to Page, where each plays a different keyboard instrument.

Musical Evolution and History: The melody to this song was apparently born out of part of the long Tweezer jam at FLPAC on 6/22/95. Once the band learned the piece, it varied little from performance to performance.

Rotation History: Appeared thirteen times in fall 1995, but not since.

Discography: Has not yet appeared on a Phish album.

Keyboard Kavalry [13] [Keyboard]

By Phish

09/27/95	[761]	2	Billy	Harry
09/28/95	1	2	Tweezer	AmGrace
09/30/95	2	2	Mike's	Weekapaug
10/02/95	1	2	Simple	Slave
10/06/95	3	2	Tweezer	Suspicious
10/08/95	2	2	*OP2	CTB
10/13/95	2	2	Antelope	Lizards
10/17/95	3	2	Suzie	Jam
10/27/95	7	2	McGrupp	Bouncing
11/12/95	7	2	Tweezer	Sample
11/21/95	6	2	Mike's	Suspicious
12/05/95	10	2	Bathtub	Scent
12/14/95	6	2	Tweezer	Halley's
>> 12/31/97	**155**			

KUNG

Inspiration: More a poem or chant than a song, this Fishman creation is a spoken-word piece akin to Catapult, though perhaps even more creatively weird. Trey usually leads it up, trying his best to sound ominous and larger than life, kind of like when the Wizard of Oz tries to scare Dorothy. It contains lines such as "We can stage a runaway golfcart marathon."

Musical Evolution and History: None to speak of, because there's really no music. The speed with which the poem is recited does vary, though.

Rotation History: Kung appeared a few times in 1989, then was reintroduced as the New Year's chant in Boston on 12/31/92. Since then, Kung has at times served as a gateway to Gamehendge—or simply as a call to stage a runaway golfcart marathon. It's often inserted in the middle of another song. Because it is not a "song" per se, it is occasionally left off fans' setlists.

Discography: Has not yet appeared on a Phish album.

Kung [22] [Kung]

By Fishman

10/31/89	[136]	E	Antelope	Antelope
11/02/89	1	2	YEM	Divided
12/31/92	367	3	Harpua	Harpua
02/20/93	15	2	Mike's	I am H2
03/08/93	11	2	My Friend	YEM
03/25/93	12	2	Icculus	Mockbird
04/14/93	14	1	Stash	Horse
05/08/93	19	1	Stash	Stash
08/07/93	20	2	Sparks	Mike's
06/16/94	69	2	Forbin's	Mockbird
06/17/94	1	2	Harpua	Harpua
06/26/94	8	1	*OP1	Llama
10/20/94	25	1	Split&Melt	Split&Melt
10/14/95	75	1	CTB	Free
10/19/95	3	2	BBFCM	Suspicious
10/21/95	2	1	CTB	Lizards
10/29/95	6	2	It's Ice	It's Ice
11/25/95	14	2	Timber Ho	Mike's
12/08/95	9	2	Tweezer	Tweezer
12/30/95	10	1	It's Ice	It's Ice
11/16/96	55	2	RunJim	Catapult
02/26/97	27	2	YEM	Theme
>> 12/31/97	**67**			

THE LANDLADY

Inspiration: Originally composed as part of Punch You in the Eye, Trey extracted The Landlady and turned it into its own song during the period of PYITE's retirement in the early 1990s.

Musical Evolution and History: As a composed piece, The Landlady varies little from performance to performance, though when the song was performed with the Giant Country Horns (as it often has been), another angle is added. One good example of some non-PYITE Landlady fun came on 8/12/93 in Rochester, MI, when the band used Landlady as a springboard for a wild Tweezer jam, then returned to the Landlady theme. When appearing in PYITE, it is accompanied by a dance from Mike and Trey.

Rotation History: Landlady was played a lot in the early 1990s; in fact, it surfaced in nearly two-thirds of all shows from 1991 alone! When PYITE returned from retirement in 1993, the band still managed fifteen separate Landladys, and nine separate versions (many with the horns) in 1994. But since the boys played it with the horns in Davis, CA, on 12/2/94, Landlady has only been seen in PYITE.

Discography: Appears on *A Picture of Nectar* (1992).

The Landlady [177] [Landlady]

By Anastasio

04/07/90	[189]	1	Lizards	WalkAway
06/09/90	31	E	*OPE	Contact
09/13/90	2	1	*OP1	Divided
09/14/90	1	2	Bouncing	Reba
09/15/90	1	1	Paul&Silas	Fee
09/16/90	1	1a	Sloth	Reba
09/22/90	3	1	Wilson	IDK
09/28/90	1	1	*OP1	Bouncing
10/01/90	1	1	Lizards	Magilla
10/04/90	1	1	Golgi	Esther
10/05/90	1	1	MSO	Tela
10/06/90	1	1a	*OP1	Sqirm Coil
10/07/90	1	1	Stash	Destiny
10/08/90	1	1	Don't Get	Bouncing
10/12/90	1	2	Fee	Terrapin
10/30/90	2	1	*OP1	Bouncing
10/31/90	1	2	*OP2	Reba
11/02/90	1	1	Golgi	Bouncing
11/03/90	1	2	*OP2	Mike's
11/08/90	2	1	*OP1	Possum
11/10/90	1	1	Reba	Bouncing
11/16/90	1	2	*OP2	Mike's
11/17/90	1	1	Sqirm Coil	RunJim
11/24/90	1	2	Eliza	RunJim
11/26/90	1	1	*OP1	RunJim
11/30/90	1	1	*OP1	Mike's
12/01/90	1	1	Cavern	Llama
12/07/90	2	1	Bouncing	YEM
12/08/90	1	1	Cavern	Mike's
12/28/90	1	2	*OP2	Possum
12/31/90	2	1	IDK	Bouncing
02/01/91	1	2	Reba	Mango
02/03/91	2	2	Sqirm Coil	Cavern
02/07/91	1	1	MSO	Mango
02/08/91	1	E	*OPE	La Grange
02/09/91	1	2	Fluffhead	Bouncing
02/14/91	1	2	IDK	Possum
02/16/91	2	1	A-Train	Bouncing

Original Songs Played by Year *(continued)*

Tweezer Reprise

1991	18	14%
1992	23	19%
1993	29	26%
1994	25	20%
1995	16	20%
1996	10	14%
1997	10	13%

Twist Around

1997	8	10%

Vultures

1997	10	14%

Wading in the Velvet Sea

1997	10	14%

Walfredo

1997	4	5%

Waste

1996	17	24%
1997	13	17%

Water in the Sky

1997	16	21%

The Wedge

1993	9	8%
1994	0	0%
1995	7	9%
1996	1	1%
1997	2	3%

Weekapaug

1990	54	52%
1991	49	39%
1992	36	30%
1993	37	34%
1994	22	18%
1995	15	19%
1996	13	19%
1997	11	14%

Weigh

1992	11	9%
1993	14	13%
1994	1	1%
1995	2	2%
1996	2	3%
1997	3	4%

Wilson

1990	6	6%
1991	14	11%
1992	17	14%
1993	17	15%
1994	27	22%
1995	13	16%
1996	12	17%
1997	7	9%

02/21/91	3	2	Cavern	Bouncing
02/26/91	4	2	Bouncing	Destiny
02/27/91	1	1	IDK	YEM
02/28/91	1	1	*OP1	Bouncing
03/01/91	1	2	Golgi	Reba
03/06/91	2	1	YEM	Sqirm Coil
03/07/91	1	2	Oh Kee	Sloth
03/13/91	3	1	Fluffhead	YEM
03/16/91	2	1	Reba	Bathtub
03/17/91	1	1	Bouncing	Mike's
03/22/91	2	1	YEM	Destiny
03/28/91	2	1a	Cavern	Bouncing
04/04/91	5	1	Lawn Boy	MSO
04/05/91	1	1	*OP1	Bouncing
04/11/91	2	2	Lawn Boy	Destiny
04/12/91	1	2	*OP2	RunJim
04/15/91	2	2	MSO	Lizards
04/19/91	3	2	Golgi	Destiny
04/20/91	1	2	MSO	Esther
04/21/91	1	2	Fee	Forbin's
04/22/91	1	2	Uncle Pen	Destiny
04/26/91	1	1	Cavern	MSO
04/27/91	1	1	Cavern	MSO
05/02/91	1	1	Bouncing	Forbin's
05/03/91	1	2	Sloth	RunJim
05/10/91	3	1	Sloth	Bathtub
05/12/91	2	1	Lizards	Destiny
05/16/91	1	2	Bouncing	Sqirm Coil
05/17/91	1	2	Rocky Top	Fluffhead
05/25/91	2	1a	Divided	Chalkdust
07/11/91	1	1	Lizards	*CL1
07/12/91	1	1	Reba	Bathtub
07/13/91	1	E	*OPE	*CLE
07/14/91	1	3	ACDCBag	Esther
07/15/91	1	1a	Suzie	Dinner
07/18/91	1	2	Lizards	IDK
07/19/91	1	1	Golgi	Bouncing
07/20/91	1	1	Suzie	Bathtub
07/21/91	1	1	Lizards	Bouncing
07/23/91	1	2	Lizards	Tweezer
07/24/91	1	1	Bathtub	Cavern
07/25/91	1	2	*OP2	Golgi
07/26/91	1	1	Bouncing	Golgi
07/27/91	1	1a	IDK	Mike's
09/25/91	2	1	It's Ice	Caravan
09/26/91	1	2	Sparkle	Destiny
09/28/91	2	1	*OP1	Bouncing
09/29/91	1	1a	PoorHeart	YEM
10/02/91	2	2	*OP2	YEM
10/03/91	1	2	Esther	Destiny
10/06/91	3	2	Fee	Destiny
10/10/91	1	1	Bouncing	RunJim
10/11/91	1	1	*OP1	MSO
10/13/91	2	1	Reba	Forbin's
10/15/91	1	1	Reba	Destiny
10/17/91	1	1	Memories	Bouncing
10/19/91	2	1	*OP1	Suzie
10/27/91	4	2	Tela	Destiny
10/31/91	3	2	*OP2	Llama
11/01/91	1	1	Sparkle	Destiny
11/02/91	1	1	WalkAway	RunJim
11/07/91	2	1	YEM	RunJim
11/08/91	1	1	Tube	Dinner
11/09/91	1	2	Tela	Terrapin
11/13/91	3	1	*OP1	RunJim
11/15/91	2	2	Tube	Destiny
11/16/91	1	1	*OP1	Uncle Pen
11/20/91	2	2	Tela	Bike
11/22/91	2	2	MSO	Bathtub
11/23/91	1	2	Eliza	Fee
11/24/91	1	1	Stash	Fluffhead
12/04/91	2	1	Reba	RunJim
12/06/91	2	1	Magilla	Guelah
12/31/91	2	2	RunJim	Reba
03/07/92	2	1	Mango	Rift
03/13/92	3	2	Silent	Lizards
03/19/92	3	1	*OP1	Rift
03/21/92	2	1	*OP1	RunJim
03/24/92	1	1	Mockbird	Bowie
03/26/92	2	1	*OP1	RunJim
03/28/92	2	1	Bouncing	Bowie
03/30/92	1	1	*OP1	Llama
04/01/92	2	1	IDK	Bowie
04/03/92	1	1	*OP1	PoorHeart
04/05/92	2	2	Weigh	Bowie
04/09/92	3	1	*OP1	Sparkle
04/13/92	2	1	Lizards	NICU
04/15/92	1	2	Reba	NICU
04/17/92	2	1	Bouncing	Bowie
04/23/92	5	2	*OP2	PoorHeart
04/24/92	1	1	Sloth	Fluffhead
04/29/92	2	2	*OP2	Possum
05/01/92	2	1	PoorHeart	NICU
05/03/92	2	1	*OP1	Possum
05/07/92	3	2	*OP2	Sparkle
05/10/92	3	1a	*OP1	Suzie
05/12/92	1	2	*OP2	Bathtub
05/17/92	4	1	*OP1	Llama
06/19/92	2	1a	*OP1	Suzie
07/09/92	8	1a	Suzie	Sparkle
07/11/92	2	1a	*OP1	RunJim
07/14/92	2	1	*OP1	Rift
07/16/92	2	2	Weigh	Fluffhead
08/15/92	17	1a	*OP1	Sparkle
08/17/92	1	1	PoorHeart	Reba
08/19/92	1	1a	Chalkdust	RunJim
08/24/92	3	1a	Tweezer	Reba
08/27/92	2	1a	Bouncing	Horn
08/30/92	3	1a	Uncle Pen	Reba
11/21/92	4	1	*OP1	RunJim
11/25/92	3	1	PoorHeart	Fee
12/01/92	4	1	*OP1	MSO
12/05/92	4	1	*OP1	Chalkdust
12/12/92	6	1	Reba	Split&Melt
12/30/92	4	1	*OP1	Sparkle
02/11/93	9	2	*OP2	Wilson
02/17/93	4	2	Axilla	Bowie
03/05/93	12	2	*OP2	Chalkdust
03/13/93	5	1	*OP1	FunkBitch
03/17/93	3	1	*OP1	RunJim
03/24/93	5	2	*OP1	Split&Melt
03/28/93	4	1	*OP1	FunkBitch
04/03/93	5	1	*OP1	Rift
04/17/93	8	2	Reba	Halley's
04/25/93	7	1	*OP1	Possum
07/17/93	15	1	*OP1	RunJim
07/29/93	9	1	Rift	FEFY
08/12/93	10	2	Also Sprac	Lizards
08/15/93	3	2	Lizards	Bouncing
08/21/93	4	1	Sparkle	IDK
04/04/94	9	2	BurAlive	Julius
04/15/94	9	2	Suzie	Julius
04/25/94	9	1	*OP1	RunJim
05/04/94	6	2	YEM	Julius
06/29/94	35	2	*OP2	PoorHeart
07/06/94	6	2	*OP2	PoorHeart
10/16/94	16	2	*OP2	PoorHeart
11/14/94	17	1	Bouncing	Maze
12/02/94	13	2	Julius	Gumbo

>> 12/31/97 240 (as a stand-alone song)

LAWN BOY

Inspiration: A sort of ode to nature, night, and suburbia that is Phish at their lounge-lizard best.

Musical Evolution and History: Besides the summer of 1991, when the Giant Country Horns added a jazz element to this song, Lawn Boy has remained pretty much unchanged. In concert, Page usually stands to croon this song in his best lounge-lizard style, and Mike takes a bass solo. However, occasionally Mike gives up his solo to another band member, like 11/21/97 in Hampton, VA, when Fish took an "anti-drum solo" (an intentionally boring solo) in the middle of Lawn Boy. The recorded version on the Elektra re-release of *Lawn Boy* differs from the original album from Absolute A-Go-Go records. Somehow, the Elektra version is speeded up.

Rotation History: Played fairly frequently through 1993, the song has been a picture of stability over the past three years, appearing four times in 1995, 1996, and 1997.

Discography: Appears as the title track on *Lawn Boy* (1990).

Lawn Boy [105] [Lawn Boy]

By Anastasio/Marshall

11/30/89	[145]	1	Antelope	Frankstein
12/08/89	5	2	Possum	Fire
12/09/89	1	1	Bowie	Bathtub
12/16/89	2	1a	ACDCBag	Mike's
12/29/89	1	1	Lizards	Mike's
01/20/90	3	1a	La Grange	Esther
01/28/90	3	E	*OPE	BBFCM
02/24/90	14	2	Bathtub	Contact
04/18/90	20	2	Bold	Jaeger
04/22/90	4	E	*OPE	Golgi
04/26/90	2	1	Antelope	*CL1
06/05/90	14	1	Bowie	Possum
06/07/90	1	E	*OPE	BBFCM
06/09/90	1	1	Possum	Reba
06/16/90	1	1	Timber Ho	Possum
09/22/90	6	1	Lizards	Possum
10/01/90	2	2	*OP2	ACDCBag
11/02/90	10	E	*OPE	La Grange
11/16/90	5	1	Weekapaug	Tube
11/17/90	1	2	Possum	Rocky Top
11/24/90	1	E	*OPE	Divided
12/03/90	4	1	Antelope	Frankstein
12/29/90	4	1	Bowie	Rocky Top
02/02/91	3	2	Antelope	*CL2
02/08/91	3	2	Cavern	Mike's
02/09/91	1	E	*OPE	Suzie
02/14/91	1	1	Stash	Oh Kee
02/16/91	2	E	*OPE	Fire
02/27/91	8	2	Bowie	Oh Kee
03/17/91	11	E	*OPE	La Grange
03/28/91	4	E	*OPE	Fire
04/04/91	5	2	Bowie	Landlady
04/11/91	3	2	Split&Melt	Landlady
04/22/91	9	E	*OPE	Rocky Top
05/17/91	12	E	*OPE	Golgi
07/19/91	9	E	*OPE	RunJim
07/21/91	2	2	RunJim	Sloth
07/26/91	4	E	*OPE	Frankstein
08/03/91	2	3	Fluffhead	MSO
09/26/91	2	2	Weekapaug	Chalkdust
09/28/91	2	2	Antelope	Lizards
10/02/91	2	2	RunJim	Stash
10/04/91	2	2	RunJim	Stash
10/12/91	5	1	TweezRep	Rocky Top
10/17/91	3	2	Bowie	Fluffhead
11/07/91	13	E2	*OPE2	Fire
11/15/91	7	1	Divided	Golgi
11/22/91	5	1	Divided	Dinner
12/06/91	6	E	*OPE	Rocky Top
12/31/91	2	E	*OPE	Rocky Top
03/20/92	9	E	*OPE	Fire
03/24/92	2	E	*OPE	Fire
04/01/92	7	E	*OPE	GTBT
04/05/92	3	E	*OPE	Rocky Top
04/12/92	4	2	YEM	NICU
04/19/92	6	2	Llama	Brain
05/01/92	8	E	*OPE	GTBT
05/17/92	13	E	*OPE	GTBT
11/27/92	51	1	Split&Melt	Reba
12/03/92	5	2	Weekapaug	It's Ice
12/05/92	2	2	Maze	Mike's
12/08/92	3	2	Antelope	Sparkle
02/04/93	10	2	Weekapaug	Uncle Pen
02/06/93	2	1	Divided	Wedge
02/11/93	4	1	Llama	Bowie
02/13/93	2	1	Stash	Maze
02/18/93	3	1	Reba	Antelope
02/19/93	1	2	BBJ	FunkBitch
02/23/93	4	1	Reba	Chalkdust
02/27/93	3	1	PYITE	Antelope
03/03/93	2	1	RunJim	Cavern
03/09/93	4	1	Reba	Mike's
03/16/93	4	2	Bike	Llama
03/21/93	4	1	PYITE	Possum
03/28/93	6	1	It's Ice	Antelope
04/01/93	3	1	Fluffhead	Antelope
04/10/93	5	1	Chalkdust	Bowie
04/20/93	7	1	Uncle Pen	Bowie
04/23/93	3	1	Guelah	Chalkdust
04/30/93	5	1	Cavern	All Things
05/03/93	3	1	Possum	Cavern
05/06/93	2	1	Possum	WYBG
07/23/93	11	1	It's Ice	Cavern
08/12/93	15	2	Maze	BBJ
08/21/93	7	2	Llama	Bowie
12/31/93	8	2	Possum	YEM
04/08/94	4	1	If I Could	Llama
05/02/94	19	2	Julius	Mike's
07/06/94	43	2	Tweezer	Chalkdust
10/08/94	9	1	It's Ice	Antelope
10/29/94	17	1	Foam	Split&Melt
11/14/94	7	1	Maze	Cavern
12/10/94	20	1	Divided	Chalkdust
06/17/95	14	1	Julius	Curtain
10/19/95	29	2	Weekapaug	BBFCM
11/18/95	17	1	Reba	PYITE
12/09/95	15	2	YEM	Slave
08/07/96	35	1	Taste	99 Years
10/22/96	12	2	Mango	Scent
11/16/96	17	1	Bowie	Sparkle
12/04/96	11	2	Reba	Weekapaug
03/01/97	18	2	Mike's	Weekapaug
08/09/97	34	1	Reba	Crossroad
08/16/97	5	3	Llama	Limb
11/21/97	7	1	PYITE	Chalkdust

>> 12/31/97 19

LENGTHWISE

Inspiration: A Fishman creation about relationships, offering some genuine wisdom.

Musical Evolution and History: Recorded in fall 1992 for *Rift*, Lengthwise is a vocal-only piece that has Fish quietly repeating the lyrics over and over again, with snoring in the background. It ends with the ringing of an alarm clock that leads into Maze. In concert, he often performed it in a similarly sparse manner, but on several occasions he spiced things up. During the debut of the song on 11/19/92 in Colchester, VT, he added a reggae flair to it that enlivened the crowd. (And the band also told the audience that they like Lengthwise so much they put it on the new album twice.) That was repeated 2/4/93 in Providence, RI, as he sent up a full reggae version which evolved into a rocking Elvis-like take, complete with crazy lyric improvisations. Another reggae version surfaced on 2/17/93 in Winston-Salem, NC, and several other Lengthwises from that month included audience sing-alongs.

Rotation History: Played on the 1992 fall tour and the 1993 spring and summer tours, Lengthwise has only been heard from once after that: as the second-set opener on 10/20/94 in St. Petersburg, FL. Sadly, it's been dormant since then.

Discography: Appears on *Rift* (1993), twice.

Lengthwise [22] [Lengthwise]

By Fishman

11/19/92	[480]	2	Llama	Cavern
11/20/92	1	2	Terrapin	*CL2
11/23/92	3	2	Weekapaug	Cavern
12/02/92	6	2	Glide	Sqirm Coil
12/06/92	4	2	TMWSIY	Carolina
12/08/92	2	2	Suzie	MSO
02/04/93	10	2	BBJ	Harry
02/06/93	2	2	BBJ	BurAlive
02/13/93	6	2	BBJ	Sqirm Coil
02/17/93	2	2	YEM	Sqirm Coil
02/26/93	8	2	YEM	Sqirm Coil

03/12/93	8	2	Chalkdust	Harry
03/16/93	3	2	Bike	Bike
03/31/93	12	2	*OP2	Maze
04/10/93	6	2	*OP2	Maze
04/14/93	3	E	*OPE	Contact
04/23/93	7	2	Weekapaug	Sqirm Coil
04/30/93	5	1	*OP1	Maze
05/30/93	9	1a	*OP1	Maze
08/03/93	16	2	*OP2	Maze
08/13/93	7	1	*OP1	Llama
10/20/94	98	2	*OP2	Maze
>> 12/31/97	**268**			

LEPRECHAUN

Inspiration: A short instrumental piece written by Trey for the 1993 summer tour. It was similar in sound to several Allman Brothers compositions.

Musical Evolution and History: None to speak of, due to its short lifespan.

Rotation History: When this song debuted at Weedsport, NY, on 7/15/93, it seemed like a nice little treat, and when it popped up in the middle of Mike's Groove on 7/17/93 and 7/31/93, it seemed as though the band might have found a sometimes-replacement for Hydrogen. But then it was never heard from again.

Discography: Has not yet appeared on a Phish album.

Leprechaun [3] [Leprech]

By Anastasio

07/15/93	[578]	1	My Mind	RunJim
07/17/93	2	2	Mike's	Weekapaug
07/31/93	11	2	Mike's	Weekapaug
>> 12/31/97	**375**			

LETTER TO JIMMY PAGE

Inspiration: Trey wrote this instrumental piece, perhaps as a tribute to Jimmy Page (Trey was an absolute Zeppelin freak in high school).

Musical Evolution and History: Played most often in the middle of Alumni Blues, Letter to Jimmy Page has also been heard on its own. As a composed piece, it varies little from performance to performance.

Rotation History: Besides its in-Alumni appearances, it made two surprise appearances on its own in 1994. In Ottawa, ON, on 7/5/94, it emerged out of The Curtain, and then several weeks later at Jones Beach, on 7/15/94, it opened the second set and led the band into Bowie. That's its last appearance to date.

Discography: Appears on their "White Album," but no formal Phish studio albums.

Letter to Jimmy Page [28] [LTJP]

By Anastasio

10/17/85	[3]	1a	Alumni	Alumni
10/30/85	1	1a	Alumni	Alumni
04/01/86	2	2	Alumni	Alumni
04/15/86	1	1a	Alumni	Alumni
10/31/86	2	2	Alumni	Alumni
03/23/87	4	1	Alumni	Alumni
04/24/87	1	1	Alumni	Alumni
04/29/87	1	1	Alumni	Alumni
05/11/87	1	1a	Corrina	YEM
08/10/87	2	1	Alumni	Alumni
08/29/87	3	1	Alumni	Alumni
09/12/87	2	1	Alumni	Alumni
11/19/87	4	2	Alumni	Alumni
02/07/88	2	1a	Alumni	Alumni
03/11/88	2	2	Alumni	Alumni
03/31/88	3	2	Alumni	Alumni
05/14/88	2	2	Alumni	Alumni
05/15/88	1	1a	Alumni	Alumni
12/02/88	23	2	Alumni	Alumni
02/07/89	5	2	Alumni	Alumni
04/15/89	14	2	Alumni	Alumni
05/13/89	17	1	Alumni	Alumni
08/19/89	22	2	Alumni	Alumni
10/06/89	8	1a	Alumni	Alumni
10/14/89	4	1	Alumni	Alumni
12/07/89	19	1	Alumni	Alumni
07/05/94	530	1	Curtain	If I Could
07/15/94	7	2	*OP2	Bowie
>> 12/31/97	**280**			

LIFEBOY

Inspiration: Another in the 1992–1993 series of "more serious" songs from the Marshall/Anastasio songwriting duo, Lifeboy includes some of Phish's only lyrics to comment on religion ("you don't get a refund if you overpray"). A lifeline, mentioned in the song, was a way to save people from sinking ships before the advent of high technology. The song was written in one night over the phone as Trey and Tom traded ideas. Trey has called it one of his best-ever songwriting experiences.

Musical Evolution and History: The lyrics and basic structure of the song have been the same since its debut in Portland, ME, on 2/3/93, but the band has grown more aggressive with the closing jam, often raising it to intense levels. A particularly strong version can be heard from the 8/13/93 Murat Theater show. When the band recorded the song for inclusion on *Hoist* in the fall of 1993, Trey remade the song as a softer ballad, choosing an acoustic guitar, singing the vocals in a more strained fashion, as he thought the narrator of the song might sing them, and adding Bela Fleck's banjo to the mix. Since then, Lifeboy performances have included the vocal variation but have otherwise mostly reverted to the pre-*Hoist* format.

Rotation History: Played most frequently in 1994, when it was released on *Hoist* and often followed Tweezer in concert, Lifeboy came up for air only once in 1997, on 8/3/97 at The Gorge.

Discography: Appears on *Hoist* (1994), with Bela Fleck on banjo and Morgan Fichter on fiddle.

Lifeboy [45] [Life Boy]

By Anastasio/Marshall

02/03/93	[505]	2	YEM	Terrapin
02/06/93	3	2	Weekapaug	Uncle Pen
03/14/93	26	2	YEM	Rift
03/30/93	12	2	Tweezer	BBJ
04/17/93	12	2	YEM	Oh Kee
07/15/93	20	2	It's Ice	Possum
07/29/93	11	2	It's Ice	Sparkle
08/13/93	11	2	Mike's	Oh Kee
08/26/93	9	2	Bowie	Rift
04/06/94	8	2	Mike's	Weekapaug
04/22/94	13	2	Tweezer	RunJim
05/04/94	9	1	Tweezer	Rift
05/12/94	5	2	Fluffhead	Possum
05/17/94	4	2	Tweezer	Uncle Pen
05/22/94	4	2	Tweezer	Rift
05/25/94	2	2	Tweezer	Maze
05/28/94	3	2	Tweezer	Reba
06/10/94	3	2	Tweezer	Sparkle
06/18/94	6	2	Tweezer	YEM
06/23/94	4	2	Tweezer	Slave
06/26/94	3	2	Axilla 2	Sample
06/29/94	1	2	It's Ice	Divided
07/02/94	3	1	Tweezer	Sparkle
07/05/94	2	2	Bathtub	Cities
07/09/94	3	2	Tweezer	Sparkle
10/07/94	6	2	Tweezer	MSO
10/14/94	6	2	Tweezer	Guyute
10/18/94	3	2	Scent	Old Home
10/28/94	8	2	Rift	Chalkdust
11/12/94	6	2	DWD	Rift
11/18/94	5	2	Bathtub	PoorHeart
11/23/94	4	2	Tweezer	YEM
12/07/94	10	1	Guyute	Chalkdust
06/08/95	10	2	Tweezer	PoorHeart
06/24/95	12	2	Bowie	Suzie
10/05/95	15	2	Bowie	AmGrace
10/21/95	11	2	Bowie	Sparkle
10/29/95	6	2	Possum	AmGrace
11/16/95	8	2	Bowie	Uncle Pen
12/05/95	13	2	Scent	Harry
12/12/95	5	1	Divided	PYITE
12/30/95	7	2	ACDCBag	Scent
08/13/96	29	2	Mike's	Weekapaug
12/30/96	41	2	Tweezer	Scent
08/03/97	45	2	Fluffhead	Taste
>> 12/31/97	**34**			

LIMB BY LIMB

Inspiration: This Page/Trey duet was part of the large crop of songs introduced in summer 1997, and earned recognition as one of the best of the batch. It features all four band members serving up various vocal parts, including a Trey/Page tradeoff on lead vocals, and Fishman crooning the title phrase over a drum solo. Its jam segment is often compared to the jam segment in Taste.

Musical Evolution and History: Is just starting to evolve, as the band works on the middle jam segment. The version from the third set of the Great Went, on 8/16/97, is probably the strongest version of Limb by Limb performed in 1997.

Rotation History: A common occurrence following its debut in 1997, especially the summer.

Discography: Has not yet appeared on a Phish album.

Original Songs Played by Year *(continued)*

Wolfman's Brother

1994	9	7%
1995	6	7%
1996	10	14%
1997	18	23%

You Enjoy Myself

1990	57	55%
1991	47	37%
1992	47	39%
1993	53	48%
1994	38	31%
1995	23	28%
1996	23	33%
1997	19	24%

Limb by Limb [22] [Limb]

By Anastasio/Marshall

06/13/97	[904]	1	Billy	Wolfman's
06/14/97	1	1	CTB	Bye Bye
06/16/97	1	2	*OP2	Ghost
06/19/97	1	1	*OP1	Dogs Stole
06/20/97	1	1	Funny	Don't Care
06/21/97	1	1a	Steep	Dogs Stole
06/25/97	3	1	Saw It	My Soul
07/01/97	3	1	Ya Mar	Funny
07/10/97	6	1	Dogs Stole	Ginseng
07/23/97	4	1	Water	Split&Melt
07/26/97	2	1	*OP1	Dogs Stole
07/31/97	3	1	Dogs Stole	Dirt
08/03/97	1	3	Jesus	CharZero
08/08/97	2	2	Free	Lovin Cup
08/11/97	3	1	Guelah	Horn
08/14/97	2	1	Fluffhead	Free
08/16/97	1	3	Lawn Boy	FunkBitch
11/19/97	6	1	Dirt	FunkBitch
11/28/97	5	2	Timber Ho	Slave
12/05/97	5	1	Ginseng	CharZero
12/11/97	4	1	Dirt	Lovin Cup
12/31/97	6	1	Wolfman	Horse
>> 12/31/97	**0**			

LIZARDS

Inspiration: A Gamehendge song sung from the perspective of Colonel Forbin upon his arrival in Gamehendge. The Lizards are the race of native inhabitants of Gamehendge who once lived in peace and harmony (as told in the Helping Friendly Book) before being enslaved by Wilson.The great warrior Rutherford the Brave is a key character in this tune, which is one of those rare Phish songs which is popular with both newer and veteran phans alike.

Musical Evolution and History: Another remnant of past Anastasio family musicals, Lizards was adapted from a piece called "If I Were a

MIKE'S GROOVE

SHARING IN THE GROOVE

What's in the middle of Mike's Groove?

There's nothing more exhilarating than a great Mike's Groove, whether it's a classic Mike's > Hydrogen > Weekapaug or something far more complex. Though the band swore in the early 1990s that Mike's Groove would always adhere to its classical three-piece structure, the band threw those rules out the window in 1993, and since then has treated audiences to all shapes and sizes of musical suits bookended by Mike's Song and Weekapaug Groove. Here's an overview of the magic and mystery that is Mike's.

BASIC STATS since the formation of Mike's Groove on 7/23/88

Total Mike's Song performances: 297
Total Weekapaug performances: 274
Total Hydrogen performances: 226
Total Simple performances: 77

Mike's > Hydrogen > Weekapaug: 209 times
Mike's > Hydrogen > Weekapaug since 1/1/93: 39 times
Mike's > One Other Song > Weekapaug since 1/1/93: 26 times
Mike's > Weekapaug: 2 (12/1/95 in Hershey, PA and 12/7/95 in Niagra Falls, NY.)
Mike's and Weekapaug, but no Hydrogen: 50 times
Mike's, but no Hydrogen and no Weekapaug: 15 times

Mike's Grooves with Simple somewhere within: 19 times
Mike's > Simple > Mike's: 7 times, most recently on 11/4/94 in Syracuse, NY
Mike's > Simple > another song (not Mike's): 10 times, most recently on 12/2/97 in Philadelphia, PA
Mike's > Simple: once (11/16/94 in Ann Arbor, MI.)

THE CLASSIC

Mike's > Hydrogen > Weekapaug
In 1993: 23 times
Since 1994: 16 times (4/9/94; 4/21/94; 4/29/94; 5/14/94; 5/19/94; 6/9/94; 6/13/94; 7/10/94; 12/10/94; 6/10/95; 10/19/95; 7/23/96; 8/5/96; 7/31/97; 11/13/97; 11/22/97).

SIMPLETONS

When a very rough version of Simple emerged in the midst of Mike's Song at the Warfield Theater on 5/27/94, it changed the face of Mike's Groove—the old threesome became a foursome, as Simple appeared in the middle of Mike's Song ten times in 1994, and out of the Mike's jam four additional times that year. Since 1994, Simple hasn't joined Mike's Groove as often, but it still surfaces there on special occassions.

SIMPLE GROOVES

Mike's > Simple > Mike's > O Mio Babbino Caro > Possum, 5/27/94 San Francisco, CA (Simple debut)
Mike's > Simple > Mike's > Hydgrogen > Weekapaug: 6/17/94, 10/8/94, and 10/21/94
Mike's > Simple > Mike's > Yerushalayim > Hydgrogen > Weekapaug: 7/2/94 Holmdel, NJ
Mike's > Simple > Mike's > Yerushalayim > Weekapaug: 10/13/94 Oxford, MS
Mike's > Simple > Mango > Weekapaug: 10/25/94 and 12/6/94
Mike's > Simple > Mike's > Tela > Weekapaug: 11/4/94 Syracuse, NY
Mike's > Simple, 11/16/94 Ann Arbor, MI
Mike's > Simple > Harpua > Weekapaug: 11/25/94 Chicago, IL
Mike's > Simple > Weekapaug: 12/16/95 Lake Placid, NY
Mike's > Simple > Contact > Weekapaug: 8/16/96 Plattsburgh, NY
Mike's > Simple > Makiuspa > Axilla > Weekapaug: 11/23/96 Vancouver, BC

Dog." The song provides little room for improvisation, and has remained pretty much the same since the 1980s.

Rotation History: Played at roughly a third of all shows until things started to lighten up in 1995. In 1997, Lizards was played only four times.

Discography: Has not yet appeared on a Phish album.

Lizards [233] [Lizards]

By Anastasio

01/30/88	[28]	3	Suzie	Golgi
02/08/88	2	2	Divided	Antelope
03/11/88	1	1	Corrina	Bowie
03/12/88	1	1a	McGrupp	Tela
03/21/88	1	1a	Timber Ho	Fire
03/31/88	1	2	Alumni	Forbin's
05/14/88	2	2	YEM	BBFCM
05/15/88	1	1a	Shaggy	Sally
06/15/88	3	2	*OP2	ACDCBag
06/20/88	2	1	ACDCBag	Halley's
06/21/88	1	1	Curtain	Forbin's
07/12/88	2	2	Cities	Sally
07/23/88	1	1	Weekapaug	OYWD
07/24/88	1	2	La Grange	Alumni
09/12/88	6	1a	Satin Doll	TMWSIY
09/24/88	1	2	Bowie	WalkAway
10/12/88	1	1	Bowie	Foam
10/29/88	1	1	Suzie	TimeLoves
11/03/88	1	1	WalkAway	Shaggy
11/05/88	1	2	Bold	ACDCBag
11/11/88	1	2	Timber Ho	WhipPost
12/02/88	1	2	LTJP	*CL2
01/26/89	1	1a	YEM	A-Train
02/07/89	4	1	ACDCBag	*CL1
02/18/89	2	1a	Mockbird	WalkAway
03/03/89	2	2	Mockbird	Split&Melt
03/04/89	1	2	Fluffhead	Antelope
04/14/89	8	1	Bold	Sloth
04/20/89	3	2	Split&Melt	Mike's
04/30/89	5	1	McGrupp	Divided
05/09/89	7	2	IDK	Bold
05/13/89	3	2	Bold	Harry
05/20/89	4	1	YEM	Wilson
06/23/89	9	1	Weekapaug	Antelope
08/17/89	7	2	YEM	*CL2
08/19/89	8	1	Mango	Mike's
08/26/89	2	E	Contact	La Grange
10/01/89	5	2	Split&Melt	*CL2
10/07/89	2	2	Possum	ACDCBag
10/21/89	5	1	ACDCBag	Dog Log
10/26/89	2	1	Wilson	Mike's
10/31/89	2	2	Alumni	HwayHell
11/09/89	4	2	PYITE	Mike's
11/10/89	1	2	Sloth	Brain
11/30/89	4	1	Foam	MSO
12/07/89	4	2	WalkAway	Antelope
12/09/89	2	1	La Grange	Foam
12/16/89	2	1	Weekapaug	In a Hole
12/29/89	1	1	ACDCBag	Lawn Boy
12/31/89	3	1	Bathtub	Satin Doll
02/24/90	18	E	*OPE	Cavern
02/25/90	1	2	Makisupa	Fluffhead
03/01/90	1	2	*OP2	GTBT
03/03/90	2	1	Sqirm Coil	Oh Kee
03/07/90	1	1	A-Train	Bowie
03/08/90	1	2	IDK	Mike's
03/28/90	4	2	Jesus	Split&Melt
04/04/90	1	2	Weekapaug	Uncle Pen
04/05/90	4	1	YEM	Fire
04/07/90	2	1	Sqirm Coil	Landlady
04/08/90	1	2	WalkAway	Slave
04/29/90	13	1a	Love You	Fire
05/04/90	2	1	YEM	*CL1
05/11/90	3	2	ACDCBag	Tweezer
05/19/90	4	1	YEM	HwayHell
05/23/90	1	2	Tweezer	La Grange
06/05/90	4	2	MSO	YEM
06/07/90	1	1	YEM	GTBT
06/16/90	3	2	YEM	Antelope
09/13/90	1	E	*OPE	La Grange
09/14/90	1	2	Cavern	Destiny
09/22/90	4	2	Stash	Lawn Boy
09/28/90	1	1	Sqirm Coil	Asse Fest
10/01/90	1	1	Sqirm Coil	Landlady
10/04/90	1	1	Sqirm Coil	Destiny
10/07/90	3	2	IDK	GTBT
10/30/90	4	3	Paul&Silas	GTBT
10/31/90	1	1	Sqirm Coil	Stash
11/02/90	1	2	YEM	IDK
11/08/90	3	1	Possum	Foam
11/10/90	1	1	BurAlive	Mike's
11/16/90	1	2	Paul&Silas	RunJim
11/24/90	2	1	Sqirm Coil	Oh Kee
11/30/90	2	2	Stash	Gumbo
12/29/90	6	2	RunJim	Cavern
02/07/91	5	2	Love You	Sloth
02/08/91	1	2	Bouncing	Antelope
02/21/91	7	1	Llama	Mike's
02/26/91	4	2	Possum	Mike's
03/15/91	10	1	ACDCBag	Mike's
03/17/91	2	1	Stash	Bowie
03/23/91	3	2	Tweezer	Uncle Pen
04/05/91	7	2	Stash	Sloth
04/11/91	2	2	TMWSIY	Split&Melt
04/15/91	3	2	Landlady	Possum
04/19/91	3	1	Cavern	Stash
04/22/91	3	2	MSO	HwayHell
04/27/91	3	1	Llama	Suzie
05/03/91	2	1	Tweezer	Adeline
05/10/91	3	1	BurAlive	Possum
05/12/91	2	1	Stash	Landlady
05/16/91	1	2	MSO	GTBT
05/18/91	2	2	Terrapin	*CL2
07/11/91	2	1	Stash	Landlady
07/13/91	2	2	Paul&Silas	Stash
07/15/91	2	1a	Flat Fee	Cavern
07/18/91	1	2	Split&Melt	Landlady
07/21/91	3	1	Split&Melt	Landlady
07/23/91	1	2	Cavern	Landlady
07/25/91	2	2	Jesus	Gumbo
07/26/91	1	2	Adeline	TweezRep
08/03/91	2	3	MSO	BurAlive
09/26/91	2	1	Guelah	Foam
09/28/91	2	2	Lawn Boy	PoorHeart
10/10/91	7	1	Alumni	*CL1
10/11/91	1	1	YEM	Llama
10/18/91	5	1	Llama	Adeline
10/24/91	3	2	Weekapaug	Uncle Pen
11/14/91	15	2	Brain	TweezRep
11/22/91	6	2	Llama	YEM
12/04/91	4	2	Sparkle	Chalkdust
12/07/91	3	2	Brother	Terrapin
12/31/91	1	1	Stash	Guelah
03/11/92	3	2	Sloth	Bathtub
03/13/92	2	2	Landlady	My Mind
03/20/92	4	1	Maze	Mound
03/26/92	4	2	My Friend	Cavern
03/31/92	4	2	Stash	Cavern
04/04/92	3	1	Sparkle	IDK
04/07/92	3	2	My Friend	Maze
04/13/92	3	1	Stash	Landlady
04/16/92	2	2	Llama	Mike's
04/18/92	2	2	TweezRep	Mound
04/23/92	4	1	Weekapaug	NICU
04/29/92	3	2	Llama	Mike's
05/01/92	2	2	Mound	Llama
05/16/92	12	1	Golgi	Cavern
07/10/92	12	1a	Golgi	Cavern
07/15/92	4	1	Chalkdust	Antelope
07/26/92	9	1a	Split&Melt	Llama
11/20/92	22	1	Stash	Memories
11/25/92	4	2	YEM	Tweezer
12/02/92	5	1	Stash	Sparkle
12/05/92	3	1	Split&Melt	Mound
12/08/92	3	2	It's Ice	Antelope
12/11/92	2	1	Stash	Chalkdust
12/28/92	3	2	YEM	Bike
02/04/93	5	1	Stash	Sample
02/09/93	4	2	Stash	Bike
02/13/93	4	2	Tweezer	Llama
02/18/93	3	2	Stash	PYITE
02/21/93	3	2	Stash	Bathtub
02/23/93	2	2	Stash	PYITE
03/02/93	4	2	Tweezer	Llama
03/08/93	4	2	YEM	AmGrace
03/13/93	3	2	Tweezer	It's Ice
03/19/93	5	2	Sample	Mike's
03/22/93	2	2	It's Ice	Tela
03/28/93	5	1	Split&Melt	Sloth
04/02/93	4	2	Weekapaug	BBJ
04/16/93	8	2	Maze	Mike's
04/22/93	5	2	Tweezer	BBJ
04/27/93	4	2	Maze	BBJ
05/02/93	4	2	YEM	BBJ
05/07/93	4	1	Caravan	Horn
07/15/93	4	2	Faht	WalkAway
07/25/93	8	2	Maze	PurplRain
07/28/93	2	2	Antelope	Mound
08/03/93	5	2	YEM	Sparkle
08/12/93	6	2	Landlady	Sloth

08/15/93	3	2	Tweezer	Landlady
08/26/93	7	2	Jesus	Bats&Mice
12/28/93	2	2	My Friend	Sloth
12/31/93	3	3	Split&Melt	Sparkle
04/06/94	3	1	Stash	Sample
04/13/94	5	1	Stash	Julius
04/16/94	3	2	Tweezer	Julius
04/21/94	4	1	Split&Melt	DWD
05/02/94	8	2	Golgi	Julius
05/12/94	7	1	Bathtub	Sample
05/14/94	2	2	FEFY	Cavern
05/19/94	3	2	Weekapaug	Julius
05/27/94	7	2	Reba	Julius
06/10/94	4	1	Bowie	Cavern
06/19/94	7	1	Julius	Axilla 2
06/26/94	6	1	Llama	Tela
07/03/94	5	2	Split&Melt	Bouncing
07/08/94	3	1	N20	Tela
07/16/94	6	1	Stash	Cavern
10/12/94	5	1	Split&Melt	Guelah
10/21/94	7	1	Stash	Dog Faced
10/25/94	3	1	Split&Melt	Sample
10/28/94	3	2	Bowie	Rift
11/02/94	3	2	Possum	Sample
11/13/94	4	2	Divided	Tweezer
11/16/94	2	1	Axilla 2	Stash
11/22/94	5	E	*OPE	*CLE
11/26/94	3	2	Adeline	Sample
12/02/94	4	1	It's Ice	Stash
12/08/94	5	1	Simple	Guitar
12/10/94	2	1	Stash	Sample
12/29/94	2	2	Halley's	Rosie
06/13/95	8	2	Bowie	Axilla 2
06/23/95	8	2	RunJim	Wedge
06/30/95	6	1	Wedge	Mound
07/03/95	3	2	ACDCBag	BBFCM
10/02/95	5	2	HelloBaby	Antelope
10/06/95	3	1	Free	Sample
10/13/95	4	2	Keyboard	Guitar
10/15/95	2	2	Tweezer	Sample
10/21/95	4	1	Kung	Str Design
10/28/95	5	1	Sample	Billy
11/09/95	3	2	Julius	Bathtub
11/22/95	10	1	Fog	Sample
11/30/95	5	1	FEFY	Fire
12/05/95	4	1	Fog	Free
12/12/95	5	2	DWD	Simple
12/17/95	4	1	Stash	Chalkdust
12/31/95	4	2	Drowned	Axilla 2
07/11/96	9	2	Maze	Terrapin
08/06/96	15	1	Theme	Dinner
08/13/96	4	2	ACDCBag	Mike's
08/17/96	3	1	CTB	Sample
10/17/96	2	2	Free	SSB
10/23/96	5	2	Tweezer	Llama
11/09/96	11	1	Split&Melt	CharZero
12/04/96	16	1	CharZero	Bowie
12/29/96	3	2	Bathtub	YEM
02/21/97	9	1	DWD	Crosseyed
07/10/97	26	1	Wading	Oblivious
08/08/97	13	1	Gumbo	Dirt
12/05/97	22	2	Slave	Lovin Cup
>> 12/31/97	**10**			

LLAMA

Inspiration: Set in the post-Wilson years of Gamehendge, when avarice and greed have taken over once again, Llama chronicles a scene from a battle. It's considered a Gamehendge tune but is not part of the original Gamehendge story—it's from the later years of the saga, which have not yet been fully chronicled by Trey.

Musical Evolution and History: A short but hot jam song since its debut in 1990, Llama has grown fiercer and more powerful with passing years. Versions of note include 7/25/92 in Stowe, VT, with Carlos Santana, and a very cool performance on 10/18/94 in Nashville, TN, when Bela Fleck sits in for a version that starts acoustic and finishes electric. More recently, the rocking version that emerged from the Halley's > Cities jam on 8/16/97 at the Great Went is also worthy of attention.

Rotation History: Very heavily played in the early 1990s, the band has backed off on Llama a little bit, though it still shows up more than most songs.

Discography: Appears on *A Picture of Nectar* (1992).

Llama [248] [Llama]

By Anastasio/Marshall

10/30/90	[238]	2	Reba	Curtis
11/03/90	3	1	Bouncing	Sqirm Coil
11/04/90	1	2	Rocky Top	Mike's
11/08/90	1	1	Uncle Pen	Sqirm Coil
11/10/90	1	2	Fee	Divided
11/16/90	1	1	Magilla	Divided
11/17/90	1	1	*OP1	Sqirm Coil
11/24/90	1	2	*OP2	Bouncing
11/26/90	1	1	Makisupa	*CL1
11/30/90	1	1	MSO	Possum
12/01/90	1	1	Landlady	Divided
12/07/90	2	1	Foam	*CL1
12/08/90	1	2	*OP2	Asse Fest
12/28/90	1	1	Reba	Forbin's
12/29/90	1	1	IDK	YEM
02/08/91	6	2	*OP2	Mango
02/09/91	1	2	Sqirm Coil	*CL2
02/15/91	2	1	Magilla	*CL1
02/16/91	1	1	Bouncing	Mango
02/21/91	3	1	Fee	Lizards
02/26/91	4	1	Sqirm Coil	Guelah
02/28/91	2	2	Reba	Guelah
03/01/91	1	2	Reba	Guelah
03/13/91	6	1	Esther	Sqirm Coil
03/15/91	1	1	*OP1	Foam
03/16/91	1	2	*OP2	Divided
03/22/91	3	1	*OP1	YEM
03/23/91	1	1	Fee	IDK
04/04/91	6	1	Sqirm Coil	Forbin's
04/06/91	2	1	Magilla	YEM
04/11/91	1	2	Reba	TMWSIY
04/12/91	1	1	*OP1	Uncle Pen
04/15/91	2	1	Mockbird	*CL1
04/18/91	2	2	*OP2	Reba
04/20/91	2	1	Reba	Fluffhead
04/21/91	1	2	Mockbird	Uncle Pen
04/22/91	1	1	PoorHeart	Guelah
04/26/91	2	1	YEM	*CL1
04/27/91	1	1	Reba	Lizards
05/02/91	1	1	Mockbird	Sqirm Coil
05/04/91	2	2	Dog Log	Forbin's
05/12/91	4	1	Destiny	Fee
05/16/91	1	1	Magilla	*CL1
05/25/91	3	1a	Sqirm Coil	Oh Kee
07/13/91	3	1	Foam	Oh Kee
07/14/91	1	1	Reba	Sqirm Coil
07/18/91	2	1	*OP2	Llama
07/20/91	2	1	Sqirm Coil	Oh Kee
07/23/91	2	2	*OP2	Reba
07/25/91	2	2	Sqirm Coil	PoorHeart
07/27/91	2	1a	*OP1	Foam
08/03/91	1	1	Guelah	Fee
09/25/91	1	1	Foam	Tela
09/26/91	1	1	*OP1	Bouncing
09/28/91	2	2	*OP2	Guelah
10/02/91	2	1	*OP1	Foam
10/03/91	1	1	Bouncing	Fee
10/04/91	1	E	Love You	*CLE
10/06/91	2	E	Possum	*CLE
10/10/91	1	1	It's Ice	Golgi
10/11/91	1	1	Lizards	Bouncing
10/13/91	2	2	*OP2	Bathtub
10/15/91	1	2	PoorHeart	Oh Kee
10/18/91	2	1	Wilson	Lizards
10/19/91	1	2	*OP2	Bathtub
10/27/91	4	2	*OP2	Forbin's
10/31/91	3	2	Landlady	Fee
11/02/91	2	1	Curtain	Reba
11/07/91	2	1	IDK	*CL1
11/09/91	2	1	Sparkle	Reba
11/12/91	2	1	Foam	*CL1
11/13/91	1	2	Sqirm Coil	Possum
11/14/91	1	1	Uncle Pen	Reba

MIKE'S GROOVE *continued*

Mike's > Simple > Harry Hood > Weekapaug: 12/6/96 Las Vegas, NV
Mike's > Simple > Maze, Strange Design, Ginseng Sullivan, Vultures, Water in the Sky, Weekapaug: 7/2/97 Amsterdam, Netherlands
Mike's > Simple > Hydrogen > Weekapaug: 7/22/97 Raleigh, NC
Mike's > Funny as it Seems > Simple > Swept Away/Steep > Scent > Weekapaug: 8/9/97 East Troy, WI
Mike's > Simple > Dog Faced Boy > Ya Mar > Weekapaug: 12/2/97 Philadelphia, PA

THREE-PIECE GROOVE

In three-piece Mike's Grooves, various songs have substituted for Hydrogen since Auld Lang Syne first took its place on 12/31/92 in Boston, MA. The most common pairings:

4	Mike's > Great Gig > Weekapaug: 4/10/93, 4/21/93, 5/1/93, and 8/11/93.
2	Mike's > Contact > Weekapaug: 6/20/95 and 6/30/95.
2	Mike's > Leprechaun > Weekapaug: 7/17/93 and 7/31/93.
2	Mike's > Lifeboy > Weekapaug: 4/6/94 and 8/13/96 (and Mike's > Lifeboy only on 8/13/93)
2	Mike's > Swept Away/Steep > Weekapaug, 10/22/96 and 11/6/96.

In chronological order, the fourteen following songs have made one-time appearances in the middle of three-piece Grooves: Auld Lang Syne, 12/31/92; Yerushalyim, 7/24/93; Faht, 8/16/93; Ginseng Sullivan, 8/24/93; Mango, 12/28/94; Do It In the Road, 6/25/95; Keyboard Kavalry, 9/30/95; McGrupp, 10/11/95; Sparkle, 10/25/95; Life on Mars, 11/15/95; Simple, 12/16/95; Star Spangled Banner, 11/8/96; Strange Design, 12/28/96; and Lawn Boy, 3/1/97.

BREAKING UP IS HARD TO DO

Is bigger better? In the case of Mike's Groove, that depends. On six occassions, the band has chosen to add two or three songs (other than Hydrogen or Simple) between Mike's and Weekapaug; sometimes, these pairings sound heaven-made, other times forced.

Mike's > TMWISY > Avenu > TMWISY > Weekapaug: 2/4/93 Providence, RI
Mike's > Day in the Life, Poor Heart, Weekapaug: 11/11/95 Atlanta, GA
Mike's > Rotation Jam > Mike's, Long Journey Home, I'm Blue I'm Lonesome, Strange Design > Weekapaug: 11/25/95 Hampton, VA
Mike's > Sleeping Monkey > Mean Mr. Mustard > Weekapug: 11/15/96 St. Louis, MO
Mike's > Llama > When the Circus Comes, Weekapaug > Catapult > Weekapaug: 12/13/97 Albany, NY
Mike's > Piper > When the Circus Comes > Roses Are Free > Weekapaug: 12/31/97 New York, NY

BIG BREAKUPS

It's rare that Mike's and Weekapaug appear in the same show separated by more than three songs, but it has happened seven times between 1993 and 1997. On 7/2/97 in Amsterdam, Mike's opened the set and Weekapaug closed it, after six songs were played in between. (By the way, only once have Mike's and Weekapaug appeared at the same show, but in different sets—on 12/31/95 in New York City—though they were only separated in a musical sense by Auld Lang Syne.)

Mike's > Sparks > Curtis Lowe, Rift, Squirming Coil > Weekapaug: 8/2/93 Tampa, FL
Mike's > Horse > Silent > PYITE > McGrupp > Weekapaug: 12/30/93 Portland, ME
Mike's > Caspian > Sparkle > PYITE, Life On Mars, Reba, Lawn Boy, Weekapaug: 12/4/96 San Diego, CA
Mike's > Simple > Maze, Strange Design, Ginseng Sullivan, Vultures,

MIKE'S GROOVE *continued*

Water in the Sky, Weekapaug: 7/2/97 Amsterdam, Netherlands
Mike's > Funny as It Seems > Simple > Swept Away/Steep > Scent > Weekapaug: 8/9/97 East Troy, WI
Mike's > Chalkdust > My Soul, Stash > Hydrogen > Weekapaug: 12/9/97 University Park, PA

FUN WITH HYDROGEN
Hydrogen is usually left out of the Mike's Groove fun, appearing only in the middle of classic Mike's > Hydrogen > Weekapaug sequences. But a few times, Hydrogen has popped up in more elaborate settings, including:

Mike's > Simple > Catapult > Mike's > Simple > Icculus > Simple > Hydrogen > Weekapaug, 6/22/94 Columbus, OH
Mike's > Hydrogen > Horse > Silent > Weekapaug, 10/29/96
Mike's > Chalkdust > My Soul, Stash > Hydrogen > Weekapaug, 12/9/97

TOTAL INSANITY
In the best of times, all hell can break loose in the middle of a Mike's Groove. The two most notable occurences include the "Mike's > Everything > Groove" from Atlanta, 2/20/93; and the "Mike's > Everything Else > Groove" from Columbus, OH, 6/22/94.

2/20/93: Mike's > Teases > My Mind's > Mike's > Vibration of Life > Kung > Hydrogen > Weekapaug > Have Mercy > Rock and Roll All Night > Weekapaug
6/22/94: Mike's > Simple > Catapult > Mike's > Simple > Icculus > Simple > Hydrogen > Weekapaug

MIKE ALONE
Mike's Songs with no Weekapaug came on 4/18/93; 5/6/93; 8/7/93; 8/13/93; 4/18/94; 5/2/94; 5/27/94; 11/16/94; 11/30/94; 11/21/95, 7/9/96; 7/12/96; and 2/23/97.

OTHER SANDWICHES
Simple often appeared in the middle of Mike's Song. Several other tunes have had the honor of appearing in the midst of Mike's or Weekapaug, including:

In Mike's Song:
Mike's > Crossroads > Mike's: 5/8/93 Durham, NH
Mike's > Simple > Catapult > Mike's: 6/22/94 Columbus, OH
Mike's > Buffalo Bill > Mike's: 12/31/94 Boston, MA
Mike's > Rotation Jam > Mike's: 11/25/95 Hampton, VA

In Weekapaug
Weekapaug > Have Mercy > Rock and Roll All Night > Weekapaug, 2/20/93 Atlanta, GA
Weekapaug > Nellie Cane > Weekapaug, 2/23/93 Orlando, FL
Weekapaug > Makisupa > Weekapaug, 4/29/93 Montreal, QC
Weekapaug > Catapult > Weekapaug, 12/13/97 Albany, NY

11/15/91	1	2	*OP2	Bathtub
11/16/91	1	2	Terrapin	*CL2
11/20/91	2	1	Sqirm Coil	YEM
11/22/91	2	2	IDK	Lizards
11/23/91	1	1	*OP1	Reba
11/30/91	2	1	Glide	Foam
12/04/91	1	1	*OP1	Reba
12/05/91	1	1	Fluffhead	Bathtub
12/06/91	1	2	Tela	WhipPost
12/31/91	2	1	Esther	Golgi
03/06/92	1	2	Mound	Bouncing
03/11/92	2	2	*OP2	NICU
03/12/92	1	1	Magilla	YEM
03/14/92	2	2	Golgi	Sqirm Coil
03/17/92	1	2	Love You	*CL2
03/24/92	4	1	Silent	Forbin's
03/27/92	3	1	*OP1	Reba
03/30/92	2	1	Landlady	Foam
03/31/92	1	1	Reba	Forbin's
04/01/92	1	2	*OP2	YEM
04/03/92	1	2	Mango	Harry
04/05/92	2	1	*OP1	Guelah
04/06/92	1	2	NICU	Mound
04/09/92	2	1	Guelah	Mound
04/13/92	2	2	*OP2	Fluffhead
04/16/92	2	2	Sanity	Lizards
04/18/92	2	2	Mound	TMWSIY
04/19/92	1	2	Mango	Lawn Boy
04/22/92	2	1	*OP1	Foam
04/23/92	1	1	Sqirm Coil	Bouncing
04/24/92	1	2	Glide	*CL2
04/29/92	2	2	Oh Kee	Lizards
05/01/92	2	2	Lizards	Terrapin
05/02/92	1	1	Sqirm Coil	*CL1
05/05/92	2	2	PoorHeart	Love You
05/06/92	1	1	*OP1	Foam
05/08/92	2	1	Eliza	Mound
05/09/92	1	2	Harpua	Rosie
05/12/92	2	2	PoorHeart	Cavern
05/17/92	4	1	Landlady	Forbin's
05/18/92	1	2	Glide	TMWSIY
06/20/92	2	1a	Love You	*CL1
06/24/92	2	1a	RunJim	Adeline
07/10/92	6	1a	Bouncing	Reba
07/14/92	3	2	Reba	Sqirm Coil
07/16/92	2	2	TMWSIY	Glide
07/18/92	2	1a	Foam	Reba
07/25/92	5	1a	YEM	FunkBitch
07/26/92	1	1a	Lizards	*CL1
07/27/92	1	1a	Suzie	Adeline
08/01/92	4	1a	Horn	*CL1
08/14/92	3	1a	Sqirm Coil	Adeline
08/19/92	3	1a	Uncle Pen	*CL1
08/25/92	3	1a	Sqirm Coil	Adeline
08/27/92	2	1a	YEM	*CL1
08/30/92	3	1a	Reba	Memories
11/19/92	2	2	FEFY	Lngthwise
11/21/92	2	2	A-Train	*CL2
11/23/92	2	2	Walk Line	Weigh
11/27/92	2	1	Reba	Mound
11/30/92	2	1	*OP1	Foam
12/01/92	1	2	Uncle Pen	Love You
12/02/92	1	2	Tela	Glide
12/04/92	2	1	*OP1	Foam
12/06/92	2	1	Sqirm Coil	Fluffhead
12/07/92	1	2	Reba	Horn
12/08/92	1	1	Wilson	Forbin's
12/10/92	1	1	Golgi	Foam
12/12/92	2	1	*OP1	Foam
12/13/92	1	2	Bouncing	Fluffhead
12/29/92	2	1	Guelah	My Friend
12/30/92	1	2	A-Train	*CL2
12/31/92	1	3	DGirl	*CL3
02/03/93	1	1	Fee	Wedge
02/05/93	2	1	*OP1	Guelah
02/07/93	2	2	*OP2	FEFY
02/11/93	3	1	Fluffhead	Lawn Boy
02/13/93	2	2	Lizards	YEM
02/15/93	1	2	Fee	*CL2
02/19/93	3	2	Love You	AmGrace
02/22/93	3	2	Oh Kee	Love You
02/26/93	3	1	Fluffhead	Horn
02/27/93	1	2	Fee	*CL2
03/02/93	1	2	Lizards	YEM
03/06/93	3	1	*OP1	Horn
03/08/93	1	1	Oh Kee	Forbin's
03/13/93	3	1	Contact	Wilson
03/16/93	2	2	Lawn Boy	AmGrace
03/19/93	3	1	Suzie	Foam
03/21/93	1	2	Ya Mar	YEM
03/24/93	2	1	*OP1	Foam
03/27/93	3	1	*OP1	Guelah
03/30/93	2	1	My Friend	Esther
04/01/93	2	1	*OP1	Guelah
04/02/93	1	2	Uncle Pen	Horse
04/05/93	2	1	*OP1	It's Ice
04/09/93	1	2	All Things	Mound
04/12/93	2	1	Reba	Satin Doll
04/16/93	3	1	Esther	Sample
04/17/93	1	1	*OP1	Foam
04/20/93	2	2	My Friend	YEM
04/22/93	2	2	*OP2	Bouncing
04/24/93	2	2	*OP2	Foam
04/29/93	3	1	Horn	Glide
05/02/93	3	2	*OP2	PYITE
05/06/93	3	1	All Things	Fluffhead
05/30/93	4	1a	Contact	Golgi
07/16/93	2	E	*OPE	Freebird
07/22/93	4	1	*OP1	Foam
07/24/93	2	1	*OP1	Horn
07/30/93	5	1	Contact	Uncle Pen
08/03/93	3	1	Ya Mar	Cavern
08/07/93	2	1	*OP1	Bouncing
08/13/93	5	1	Lngthwise	Makisupa
08/17/93	4	1	Wilson	Guelah
08/21/93	2	2	Fee	Lawn Boy
08/24/93	1	2	*OP2	Horn
08/28/93	3	1	*OP1	Bouncing
12/31/93	4	1	*OP1	Guelah
04/06/94	3	1	*OP1	Guelah
04/08/94	1	1	Lawn Boy	*CL1
04/15/94	6	1	*OP1	Guelah
04/22/94	6	1	*OP1	Horn
04/29/94	5	1	My Mind	*CL1
05/07/94	6	1	*OP1	Horn
05/14/94	5	1	*OP1	Wilson
05/19/94	3	1	Halley's	My Friend
05/21/94	2	1	Tela	*CL1
05/28/94	6	2	Fee	YEM
06/09/94	2	1	*OP1	Guelah
06/14/94	4	1	*OP1	Guelah
06/22/94	6	1	*OP1	Guelah
06/24/94	2	2	Sanity	Dog Faced
06/26/94	2	1	Kung	Lizards
07/06/94	7	1	*OP1	Fluffhead
07/08/94	1	1	*OP1	N20
10/13/94	12	1	*OP1	Gumbo
10/18/94	4	2	Nellie	*CL2
10/25/94	5	1	Fee	Horn
10/28/94	3	1	IDK	Guelah
11/18/94	11	1	*OP2	Bathtub
11/25/94	5	1	*OP1	Guelah
12/06/94	8	1	*OP1	Mound
12/09/94	3	1	*OP1	Foam
12/28/94	2	2	Contact	Love You
06/10/95	8	1	Makisupa	Caspian
06/20/95	7	1	*OP1	Spock's
06/23/95	2	2	Jam	GTBT
07/01/95	7	1	Ya Mar	If I Could
10/02/95	7	2	Bathtub	Simple
10/11/95	6	2	Weekapaug	Suzie
10/15/95	3	1	Demand	Foam
10/24/95	6	1	Fee	Horse
11/12/95	9	1	My Friend	Bouncing
11/22/95	7	2	Free	Bouncing
12/11/95	13	1	Dog Log	Dog Log
12/14/95	2	1	Suzie	Horn
12/29/95	5	1	Fluffhead	Adeline
07/03/96	5	1a	Taste	*CL1
07/12/96	7	1	Tweezer	*CL1
07/21/96	6	2	*OP2	Theme
08/13/96	12	1	PYITE	Glide
10/19/96	7	1	Esther	Gumbo
10/23/96	3	2	Lizards	Suzie
11/14/96	14	2	*OP2	Sample
11/18/96	3	2	TweezRep	*CL2
12/06/96	11	1	Also Sprac	YEM
12/30/96	3	1	Sloth	Gumbo
02/17/97	5	1	Billy	Bathtub
02/26/97	7	1	CamlWalk	My Friend
07/02/97	17	2	Jam	Worms
07/10/97	5	1	Bathtub	Wading
08/16/97	19	3	Cities	Lawn Boy
11/19/97	6	1	Bathtub	Dirt
12/13/97	16	2	Mike's	Circus
>> 12/31/97		4		

LUSHINGTON

Inspiration: A strange little ditty that didn't make it past 1987; if you want to hear this one, you'll have to find the tapes.

Musical History and Evolution: Lushington appears in similar form for its three documented 1987 performances, then Trey took a portion of the music and fashioned it into part of the Who Do? We Do! section in Fluff's Travels. It still appears there to this day.

Rotation History: None to speak of since way back when.

Discography: Has not yet appeared on a Phish album, unless you count its appearance in Fluff's Travels on *Junta* (1989).

Lushington [3] [Lushngton]

By Anastasio

03/11/87	[12]	1a	YEM	Possum
04/29/87	3	2	*OP2	Dog Log
08/29/87	6	1	Flat Fee	Suzie
>> 12/31/97	**945**			

MAGILLA

Inspiration: This jazz tune is one of Page's two originals currently performed by Phish, the other being Cars Trucks Buses.

Musical History and Evolution: As a composed piece, Magilla's basic structure has been unchanged since its debut at the Wetlands Preserve on 9/13/90. In both 1991 and 1994, the Giant Country Horns helped spice it up, and at Virginia Beach, VA, on 7/21/97, Trey led a particularly improvisational Magilla jam out of Wolfman's Brother.

Rotation History: Played often in 1990 and 1991, Magilla became a real rarity for a while, surfacing only once in 1993, in Santa Cruz, CA, on 3/25/93. The band rediscovered the song on spring tour 1994, playing it six times between the Flynn Theater show on 4/4/94 and the New Orleans, LA, show on 5/4/94. Both of those shows, and the performance on 4/15/94 in New York City, featured the Giant Country Horns. In retirement since 5/4/94, it reemerged after a 260-show lapse in Stuttgart, Germany, on 2/26/97, and appeared twice more that year.

Discography: Appears on *A Picture of Nectar* (1992).

Magilla [51] [Magilla]

By McConnell

09/13/90	[223]	2	Weekapaug	Stash
09/14/90	1	2	Tweezer	Cavern
09/15/90	1	1	Stash	Sqirm Coil
09/16/90	1	1a	Weekapaug	Antelope
09/22/90	3	1	Suzie	Wilson
10/01/90	2	1	Landlady	Dinner
10/12/90	6	2	Paul&Silas	Mike's
10/30/90	2	2	Weekapaug	Foam
11/03/90	3	1	Suzie	Foam
11/16/90	4	1	YEM	Llama
12/31/90	11	2	RunJim	YEM
02/01/91	1	1	Tweezer	Guelah
02/15/91	7	1	Dinner	Llama
03/16/91	19	2	Split&Melt	BurAlive
03/22/91	3	E	*OPE	Golgi
03/23/91	2	1a	Suzie	Chalkdust
04/04/91	5	2	BBFCM	HwayHell
04/05/91	1	1	Cavern	Reba
04/06/91	1	1	*OP1	Llama
04/11/91	1	1	Tweezer	Dinner
04/15/91	3	2	Possum	Fire
04/16/91	1	2	Chalkdust	BurAlive
04/21/91	4	1	Foam	MSO
05/12/91	11	2	Golgi	Mike's
05/16/91	1	1	YEM	Llama
05/17/91	1	2	Fluffhead	Cavern
07/14/91	6	2	Split&Melt	Cavern
07/19/91	3	2	MSO	Tweezer
07/25/91	5	2	Touch Me	Mike's
08/03/91	3	E	*OPE	Care
10/04/91	8	1	Suzie	Bowie
10/11/91	4	2	PoorHeart	Possum
10/17/91	4	E	*OPE	Rocky Top
11/12/91	17	2	Chalkdust	Cavern
11/20/91	6	E	*OPE	Brother
12/06/91	8	1	Sqirm Coil	Landlady
03/12/92	6	1	Rift	Llama
03/27/92	16	2	Dinner	Harry
04/13/92	12	2	Weekapaug	Ya Mar
04/25/92	10	1	Rift	Antelope
05/08/92	9	2	Stash	Maze
03/25/93	114	1	Horn	Antelope
04/04/94	73	2	Julius	Split&Melt
04/09/94	4	1	*OP1	Wilson
04/11/94	2	1	FEFY	Julius
04/15/94	3	E	*OPE	AmGrace
04/20/94	4	2	Antelope	Paul&Silas
05/04/94	11	2	Wolfman's	Suzie
02/26/97	260	2	Scent	Scent
07/10/97	22	2	Julius	Ya Mar
07/21/97	2	2	Wolfman's	Bowie
>> 12/31/97		**43**		

MAKISUPA POLICEMAN

Inspiration: One of the earliest Phish originals, this simple reggae tune has in recent years served as Trey's way of referencing pot smoking from the stage. "Dank" and "4:20" are sometimes muttered in the opening lyric segments; a strange verse about Khadafi has also surfaced (10/22/95 and 12/14/95). Most recently, Trey has offered an even wider variety of terms in the opening verse, including "schwag" at Deer Creek in summer '97 and "gooballs" at the Great Went. Some fans take this to be Trey's commentary on the drug scene at that particular show.

Musical History and Evolution: More free-form than many Phish songs, Makisupa can morph into any length and use almost any words the band desires. Most versions in recent years contain a reggaelike outro jam that stretches on for about five minutes. Perhaps more than any other Phish tune, Makisupa has improved with the upgrading of Phish's sound system, which now can enunciate the big bass notes better than ever. A great example of this came during the Sugarbush show on 7/2/95, when Mike's bass line thundered through the trees and—legend has it—lightning began to fire to the beat behind the stage.

Rotation History: After appearing regularly at Phish shows through 1990, Makisupa disappeared from sight in 1991 and 1992 before returning to light rotation in 1993. Since then, it has remained an occasional treat, sometimes as a set or show opener. Some fans say it is a sign of a good show, as Makisupa usually only appears when the band is "on."

Discography: Has not yet appeared on a Phish album.

Makisupa Policeman [48] [Makisupa]

By Anastasio

12/01/84	[0]	1a	Slave	SpanFlea
05/03/85	1	1a	McGrupp	Antelope
04/15/86	5	1a	Slave	Mercy
03/11/87	5	1a	TMWSIY	*CL1
04/29/87	3	3	Anarchy	Antelope
05/11/87	1	1a	TMWSIY	Ya Mar
08/29/87	5	1	Sally	BBFCM
09/12/87	2	2	Antelope	Fire
10/14/87	2	2	Clod	*CL2
07/12/88	20	1	Jesus	Slave
02/07/89	20	1	Golgi	Dinner
03/30/89	7	E	*OPE	*CLE
09/09/89	52	1	McGrupp	Bathtub
10/07/89	3	1	La Grange	Alumni
10/14/89	3	1	YEM	GTBT
02/25/90	46	2	McGrupp	Lizards
11/26/90	72	1	Divided	Llama
04/29/93	319	2	Weekapaug	Weekapaug
08/02/93	25	1	Bathtub	My Mind
08/07/93	3	1	Stash	Reba
08/13/93	5	1	Llama	Foam
05/07/94	41	2	Sparks	Jam
06/19/94	26	2	Reba	Sqirm Coil
10/29/94	39	1	BuffaloBill	Rift
12/01/94	19	2	BBFCM	NICU
12/08/94	6	1	*OP1	Maze
06/10/95	11	1	*OP1	Llama
07/02/95	17	2	RunJim	Scent
10/07/95	10	2	*OP2	CTB
10/22/95	10	2	Tweezer	BBFCM
10/29/95	5	2	*OP2	Bowie
11/19/95	10	1	*OP1	Maze
11/30/95	7	2	Tweezer	Antelope
12/14/95	10	1	Foam	Split&Melt
12/29/95	5	2	*OP2	CTB
07/15/96	14	2	Lovin Cup	It's Ice
08/06/96	12	1	*OP1	Rift
08/16/96	6	3	*OP3	ASZ
10/25/96	9	1	Taste	Maze
11/15/96	14	2	*OP2	Maze
11/23/96	5	2	Simple	Axilla
12/28/96	9	2	*OP2	Maze
06/25/97	27	2	McGrupp	Cecilia
07/25/97	14	1	Bathtub	ACDCBag
08/11/97	11	1	*OP1	Maze
08/16/97	3	1	*OP1	Harpua
11/19/97	6	2	Wolfman's	Taste
12/02/97	8	1	DWD	Chalkdust
>> 12/31/97		**12**		

THE MAN WHO STEPPED INTO YESTERDAY

Inspiration: Composed by Trey, this is an instrumental acoustic piece whose title mirrors that of his Goddard College senior thesis, a fantasy tale in music. TMWSIY nonetheless appears in concert separate from the Gamehendge myth (it has never been included in a live Gamehendge performance). Its appearance in concert is always linked with Avenu Malkenu, usually both before and after Avenu.

Musical History and Evolution: A beautifully composed piece, the only evolution in TMWSIY is its pairing with Avenu Malkenu. From the time the two songs started appearing together as TMWSIY > Avenu Malkenu > TMWSIY pairings in 1987, they were always played that way until 1993, when the band started blowing off the return to TMWSIY after Avenu Malkenu on select occasions. These rare TMWSIY > Avenu pairings include 7/22/93, 8/7/93, 11/19/94, and 6/30/95.

Rotation History: Besides a brief surge in 1991, TMWSIY has appeared only sporadically in the 1990s. Its rarest year was 1997, when it only surfaced once, in Worcester, MA, on 11/29/97.

Discography: Has not yet appeared on a Phish album.

The Man Who Stepped Into Yesterday [60] [TMWSIY]

By Anastasio

03/11/87	[12]	1a	Peaches	Makisupa
05/11/87	4	1a	Peaches	Makisupa
08/29/87	5	1	Ya Mar	*CL1
09/12/87	2	1	*OP1	Clod
02/08/88	7	2	Mockbird	*CL2
07/24/88	17	3	*OP3	Peaches
09/12/88	6	1a	Lizards	Avenu
02/24/89	15	1	*OP1	Curtain
08/19/89	50	1	Suzie	ACDCBag
08/26/89	2	3	*OP3	Suzie
03/09/90	62	1	*OP1	Caravan
05/04/90	23	1	Adeline	Bouncing
06/09/90	15	2	Harry	La Grange
02/07/91	40	2	Chalkdust	Tweezer
02/09/91	2	1	Sloth	RunJim
02/28/91	12	1	Cavern	MSO
03/16/91	9	1	*OP1	Golgi
04/11/91	13	2	Llama	Lizards
04/20/91	7	2	Cavern	Tweezer
04/27/91	5	2	Possum	Mike's
05/03/91	2	1	Chalkdust	Divided
05/17/91	7	1	Suzie	Stash
07/11/91	3	2	Cavern	Mike's
07/13/91	2	1	Alumni	Split&Melt
07/20/91	5	2	Stash	YEM
07/26/91	5	1	Cavern	BurAlive
07/27/91	1	1a	Stash	Possum
10/24/91	21	1	IDK	Bowie
11/02/91	7	2	Antelope	Sparkle
11/21/91	13	2	Tweezer	RunJim
03/26/92	22	2	Brother	My Friend
04/09/92	11	2	Bowie	MSO
04/18/92	6	2	Llama	Dinner
05/18/92	23	2	Llama	Mike's
07/16/92	15	2	Fluffhead	Llama
11/28/92	36	2	BBJ	Bouncing
12/06/92	7	2	YEM	Lngthwise
12/13/92	6	2	Chalkdust	MSO
12/30/92	3	2	YEM	Possum
02/04/93	3	2	Mike's	Weekapaug
03/27/93	38	2	Chalkdust	Mike's
04/20/93	16	2	BBJ	My Friend
07/22/93	23	2	Paul&Silas	Avenu
08/07/93	12	2	Mike's	Avenu
04/18/94	32	2	Mike's	DWD
05/14/94	19	2	Weekapaug	PYITE
06/22/94	23	2	Weekapaug	Fluffhead
07/01/94	7	2	DWD	Possum
07/14/94	9	1	Stash	Scent
10/16/94	11	1	Split&Melt	Axilla
10/29/94	10	2	DWD	Sparks
11/19/94	11	1	Paul&Silas	Avenu
06/30/95	40	2	Ha Ha Ha	Avenu
10/03/95	9	1	Free	Sample
11/09/95	20	2	Bathtub	Life Mars
12/30/95	31	1	It's Ice	Divided
10/25/96	40	2	Timber Ho	NICU
11/15/96	14	2	Split&Melt	My Mind
12/28/96	14	2	Bouncing	Mike's
11/29/97	67	1	Simple	Sloth
>> 12/31/97		**14**		

THE MANGO SONG

Inspiration: Trey fashioned the song's refrain from a screenplay idea of his friend Aaron Woolfe that described a child of the Vietnam war whose "hands and feet were mangled" but who grew up to be a genius. After Trey and Tom Marshall started singing a chorus slightly distorting those words (turning "mangled" into "mango"), Trey wrote the verses to describe a moment in the life of a waiter with a drug addiction, as described in the liner notes to *A Picture Of Nectar.*

Musical History and Evolution: Debuted in 1989, the band dropped this one for a while before bringing it back on spring tour 1991 in a slightly reworked form. Since then, the song's basic structure has remained unchanged.

Rotation History: Debuted in 1989, not played in 1990, Mango returned to the forefront in 1991 with twenty appearances. After laying low in 1992 and 1993, 1994 proved another good Mango vintage, with fourteen appearances. After limited playings in 1995 and 1996, all signs pointed to 1997 delivering another bumper Mango crop, but instead the band just played it once, in Hamburg, Germany, on 3/1/97.

Discography: Appears on *A Picture of Nectar* (1992).

The Mango Song [62] [Mango]

By Anastasio

03/30/89	[72]	2	*OP2	Mike's
04/15/89	7	2	Slave	Divided
05/26/89	23	2	Bowie	Split&Melt
05/28/89	2	3	Split&Melt	Harry
08/17/89	12	2	ACDCBag	Fee
08/19/89	2	1	Bold	Lizards
02/01/91	139	2	Landlady	*CL2
02/03/91	2	2	Cavern	Split&Melt
02/07/91	1	1	Landlady	Split&Melt
02/08/91	1	2	Llama	Cavern
02/09/91	1	1	*OP1	Sloth
02/14/91	1	1	Cavern	Stash
02/15/91	1	1	BurAlive	Sloth
02/16/91	1	1	Llama	Mike's
04/16/91	35	1	Cavern	Oh Kee
07/19/91	26	2	Tweezer	BBFCM
09/27/91	11	2	Split&Melt	Dinner
10/11/91	9	2	Bowie	Sloth
10/28/91	10	1	Chalkdust	BurAlive
11/08/91	8	1	Divided	Brother
11/14/91	5	1	Brother	Golgi
11/19/91	3	2	Weekapaug	Sloth
11/21/91	2	2	It's Ice	Uncle Pen
11/24/91	3	2	Cavern	Chalkdust
12/04/91	2	2	Stash	Mike's
12/07/91	3	1	Cavern	Antelope
03/07/92	3	1	Maze	Landlady
03/20/92	7	2	Sloth	Cavern
03/24/92	2	2	Guelah	Brother
04/03/92	8	2	YEM	Llama
04/19/92	12	2	Tube	Llama
04/24/92	4	2	Weekapaug	Horn
05/03/92	6	2	Weekapaug	Rosie
05/17/92	11	1	Stash	PoorHeart
07/24/93	150	1	Stash	Bouncing
08/11/93	13	1	My Friend	Stash
08/20/93	7	E	*OPE	Freebird
04/24/94	27	2	Bowie	Julius
05/19/94	17	1	DWD	Cavern
06/18/94	17	1	Maze	DWD
06/23/94	4	2	Bowie	Axilla 2
06/25/94	2	1	Stash	Sample
07/01/94	4	1	Stash	It's Ice
07/13/94	8	1	Foam	DWD
10/21/94	15	1	Foam	Old Home
10/25/94	3	2	Simple	Weekapaug
11/02/94	6	2	Tweezer	Axilla 2
11/13/94	4	2	Tweezer	BBFCM
11/25/94	9	2	Weekapaug	PurplRain
12/06/94	8	2	Simple	Weekapaug
12/28/94	5	2	Mike's	Weekapaug
06/19/95	14	2	Bowie	Lovin Cup
10/07/95	21	1	Possum	AArmy
10/29/95	15	2	Bowie	It's Ice
12/01/95	18	2	Weekapaug	Wilson
12/11/95	7	2	Bowie	Fog
12/17/95	5	1	Antelope	Tube
08/04/96	26	1	Split&Melt	Sloth
08/14/96	7	1	Reba	Gumbo
10/22/96	8	2	Taste	Lawn Boy
12/28/96	30	1	Split&Melt	Frankstein
03/01/97	16	2	Weekapaug	Billy
>> 12/31/97	**65**			

MAZE

Inspiration: The source for Tom Marshall's lyrics about a poor soul lost in a maze, trying to find his way out, are unclear, but the song has been a hit with fans since its spring 1992 debut.

Musical History and Evolution: As a new song in spring 1992, Maze already had a lot of strength (check out 3/13/92 Providence, RI, and 5/16/92 Boston, MA, among other hot versions from that tour), perhaps surprising considering it was the last of the new group of songs debuted that year that the band learned. The basic structure of the song—lyrics intro, Page jam, Trey jam, and return to lyrics—has been intact since the song's debut, but the improvisational jams have built to sensational heights on some occasions, including 12/31/94 Boston, MA (with digital delay loop intro), and more recently at the Great Went on 8/17/97. After the release of *Rift* in spring 1993, the band toyed with releasing a shortened version of Maze as the second single off the album, but scuttled that idea soon after the redubbed version reached radio stations because they decided not to compromise artistically to court radio play.

Rotation History: A favorite of the band's since its debut, Maze surfaced in virtually every other show in 1992 and 1993, and in 1997 could be found in concert approximately once every five shows.

Discography: Appears on *Rift* (1993).

Maze [211] [Maze]

By Anastasio/Marshall

03/06/92	[385]	1	Guelah	Reba
03/07/92	1	1	Silent	Mango
03/11/92	1	1	Reba	Fee
03/13/92	2	1	Guelah	Dinner
03/20/92	4	1	Fluffhead	Lizards
03/25/92	3	1	Fee	Glide
03/27/92	2	1	Guelah	Glide
03/30/92	2	1	Sparkle	IDK
04/03/92	3	1	Sparkle	Fluffhead
04/05/92	2	2	Silent	Weigh
04/07/92	2	2	Lizards	Bike
04/12/92	2	1	Sparkle	Reba
04/16/92	3	1	Fee	Forbin's
04/17/92	1	1	Reba	Bouncing
04/19/92	2	1	Reba	Fee
04/21/92	1	2	Sanity	Memories
04/23/92	2	2	Fee	Rosie
04/25/92	2	2	*OP2	Bathtub
04/30/92	2	1	Fee	Reba
05/02/92	2	1	Reba	Bouncing
05/06/92	3	1	My Mind	Tela
05/08/92	2	2	Magilla	YEM
05/09/92	1	1	Fee	Sqirm Coil
05/14/92	3	1	Sparkle	Horn
05/16/92	2	1	*OP1	Foam
05/18/92	2	1	Suzie	Bouncing
06/23/92	3	1a	Reba	Adeline
06/27/92	2	1a	Reba	All Things
07/10/92	5	1a	Sparkle	Golgi
07/12/92	2	1a	Uncle Pen	Glide
07/14/92	1	1	Guelah	Sparkle
07/16/92	2	1	Bouncing	Guelah
07/17/92	1	1a	Sqirm Coil	Bouncing
07/19/92	2	1a	PoorHeart	RunJim
07/22/92	2	1a	Bouncing	Rift
07/30/92	6	1a	All Things	IDK
08/15/92	6	1a	Guelah	RunJim
08/23/92	4	1a	Chalkdust	Sparkle
08/29/92	5	1a	Bouncing	YEM
10/30/92	2	1a	RunJim	Bouncing
11/19/92	1	1	*OP1	Fee
11/21/92	2	1	Bouncing	Forbin's
11/22/92	1	1	Fee	Reba
11/25/92	2	1	Fee	Sparkle
11/28/92	2	2	Avenu	TMWSIY
11/30/92	1	2	Guelah	Glide
12/01/92	1	1	Fluffhead	Adeline
12/03/92	2	1	*OP1	Fee
12/04/92	1	1	FEFY	Forbin's
12/05/92	1	2	Sparkle	Lawn Boy
12/07/92	2	1	PoorHeart	Glide
12/10/92	2	2	BBJ	YEM
12/12/92	2	2	*OP2	Glide
12/28/92	2	1	*OP1	Sparkle
12/31/92	3	1	PoorHeart	Bouncing
02/04/93	2	1	Bouncing	FEFY
02/06/93	2	1	My Friend	Horn
02/09/93	2	1	Esther	Golgi
02/12/93	3	1	Golgi	Guelah
02/13/93	1	1	Lawn Boy	Golgi
02/17/93	2	1	Fluffhead	Golgi
02/19/93	2	1	Fee	Forbin's
02/22/93	3	1	PoorHeart	Fee
02/25/93	2	1	Cavern	Forbin's
02/27/93	2	1	Guelah	Bouncing
03/03/93	2	1	Bouncing	Guelah
03/06/93	2	1	Bouncing	Golgi
03/09/93	2	1	Bouncing	Esther
03/13/93	2	1	Bouncing	Fee
03/16/93	2	1	Fee	IDK
03/18/93	2	1	Fee	Forbin's
03/21/93	2	1	*OP1	Sparkle
03/24/93	2	1	PoorHeart	IDK
03/26/93	2	1	*OP1	Sparkle
03/28/93	2	1	Sloth	Fee
03/31/93	2	2	Lngthwise	Bouncing
04/02/93	2	1	Sparkle	Golgi
04/05/93	2	1	Fee	Fluffhead
04/09/93	1	1	Silent	IDK
04/10/93	1	2	Lngthwise	Bouncing
04/14/93	3	1	PoorHeart	Bouncing
04/16/93	1	2	Curtain	Lizards
04/18/93	2	1	Fee	Horn
04/21/93	2	1	Guelah	Forbin's
04/23/93	2	2	Golgi	Curtis
04/25/93	2	1	Mockbird	IDK
04/27/93	1	2	All Things	Lizards
04/30/93	2	1	Lngthwise	Bouncing
05/02/93	2	1	PoorHeart	IDK
05/05/93	2	1	Glide	Golgi
05/07/93	2	2	Bouncing	Fee
05/30/93	3	1a	Lngthwise	Guelah
07/16/93	2	2	Glide	Bouncing
07/18/93	2	1	Guelah	Esther
07/21/93	1	1a	Sqirm Coil	Glide
07/23/93	2	1	Nellie	Horse
07/24/93	1	2	Fluffhead	Glide
07/25/93	1	2	Silent	Lizards
07/29/93	3	2	*OP2	Bouncing
07/31/93	2	2	It's Ice	Sparkle
08/03/93	2	2	Lngthwise	Bouncing
08/07/93	2	1	Reba	Forbin's
08/12/93	4	2	Sloth	Lawn Boy
08/15/93	3	2	Bouncing	Glide
08/17/93	2	1	Weigh	Fluffhead
08/20/93	1	1	PoorHeart	Bouncing
08/24/93	2	1	Uncle Pen	Golgi
08/28/93	3	1	Ginseng	Fluffhead
12/29/93	2	2	*OP2	Bouncing
04/04/94	3	1	Scent	Fee
04/08/94	3	1	*OP1	Glide
04/11/94	3	2	Also Sprac	Forbin's
04/15/94	3	2	*OP2	If I Could
04/17/94	2	2	BBJ	Contact
04/21/94	3	2	Also Sprac	Fluffhead
04/24/94	3	1	Axilla 2	Bathtub
04/29/94	3	2	Suzie	If I Could
05/03/94	3	1	Guelah	Sparkle
05/06/94	2	2	*OP2	Golgi
05/10/94	3	2	*OP2	Wilson
05/12/94	1	1	Fee	Axilla 2
05/17/94	4	1	Suzie	Mound
05/20/94	2	1	Fee	If I Could
05/23/94	3	1	Fee	Horse
05/25/94	1	2	Life Boy	Contact
05/28/94	3	1	Sloth	Cavern
06/09/94	2	1	If I Could	Fee
06/11/94	2	2	Sqirm Coil	Contact
06/16/94	3	1	Fee	Gumbo
06/18/94	2	1	ACDCBag	Mango
06/22/94	3	1	Gumbo	If I Could
06/25/94	3	2	Suzie	Sparkle
06/30/94	3	2	Wilson	YEM
07/02/94	2	2	McGrupp	Sample
07/09/94	5	1	Gumbo	Guelah
07/14/94	3	2	Sample	If I Could
07/16/94	2	1	Silent	Sparkle
10/07/94	1	2	*OP2	Horse
10/10/94	3	2	Golgi	Esther
10/15/94	4	1	Simple	Glide
10/20/94	3	2	Lngthwise	McGrupp
10/23/94	3	1	Tela	Sample
10/27/94	3	1	Sparkle	Forbin's
11/02/94	4	1	If I Could	Guyute
11/12/94	3	1	Guyute	Stash
11/14/94	2	1	Landlady	Lawn Boy
11/17/94	2	1	Scent	Bouncing
11/23/94	5	2	*OP2	Fee
12/01/94	5	1	FEFY	Guyute
12/04/94	3	2	*OP2	Fee
12/08/94	3	1	Makisupa	ACDCBag
12/10/94	2	2	Simple	Guyute
12/31/94	4	2	Old Home	Bouncing
06/07/95	2	2	Ha Ha Ha	Spock's
06/10/95	3	2	*OP2	Fee
06/17/95	5	2	Wilson	Mound
06/22/95	3	1	Str Design	Cavern
06/25/95	3	2	*OP2	Sample
07/01/95	5	2	Wilson	Theme
07/03/95	2	1	If I Could	Str Design
09/29/95	3	2	Also Sprac	Free
10/03/95	3	1	*OP1	Guelah
10/06/95	2	2	PoorHeart	Theme
10/13/95	4	1	Also Sprac	Billy
10/17/95	3	1	ACDCBag	Glide
10/20/95	2	2	Simple	Gumbo
10/24/95	3	1	Demand	Wolfman's
10/28/95	3	2	*OP2	Theme
11/10/95	4	1	Dog Faced	Guyute
11/14/95	3	2	*OP2	Gumbo
11/19/95	4	1	Makisupa	PoorHeart
11/24/95	3	1	I'm Blue	Suzie
11/28/95	3	2	Also Sprac	Suzie
12/02/95	4	2	Also Sprac	Simple
12/09/95	5	1	*OP1	Theme
12/15/95	4	1	Wilson	Ha Ha Ha
12/17/95	2	2	Bouncing	Free
12/31/95	4	1	Sqirm Coil	Forbin's
07/06/96	5	1a	DayinLife	Harry
07/11/96	4	2	ASZ	Lizards
07/15/96	3	2	DWD	Lovin Cup
07/22/96	5	1a	Cavern	Bouncing
08/04/96	5	1	Sloth	Lovin Cup
08/13/96	6	1	Tela	FEFY
08/17/96	3	1	Fee	Suzie
10/18/96	3	2	Suzie	YEM
10/21/96	2	2	Train Song	Life Mars
10/25/96	3	1	Makisupa	Billy
10/31/96	4	3	Also Sprac	Simple
11/08/96	5	2	Also Sprac	Bouncing
11/11/96	2	2	Steep	Contact
11/15/96	3	2	Makisupa	McGrupp

11/22/96	4	2	Caspian	Billy
11/29/96	4	1	Life Mars	Suzie
12/28/96	6	2	Makisupa	Bouncing
02/13/97	4	2	Circus	RockaW
02/18/97	4	2	My Soul	Wolfman's
02/23/97	4	2	Suzie	Horse
03/02/97	5	2	Also Sprac	SweptAwy
06/13/97	2	2	Stash	Water
06/19/97	3	1	Water	Waste
07/02/97	9	1	Simple	Str Design
07/25/97	10	1	Wolfman's	Water
07/31/97	4	1	Dirt	Glide
08/11/97	7	1	Makisupa	Water
08/17/97	4	1	Water	Bouncing
11/14/97	2	1	Gumbo	FEFY
11/28/97	8	1	IDK	Farmhouse
12/06/97	6	1	Fee	Cavern
12/11/97	3	1	DWD	Dirt
12/31/97	6	3	Tweezer	Caspian
>> 12/31/97	**0**			

MCGRUPP AND THE WATCHFUL HOSEMASTERS

Inspiration: Not part of Trey's recording of The Man Who Stepped Into Yesterday, McGrupp is a Gamehendge song told from the perspective of a shepherd who has fled Prussia (the capital city of Gamehendge) after the fall of Wilson and established a rural home on the shores of the Baltic Sea. Tom Marshall originally wrote the song as a poem and sent it to Trey, who posted it on his dorm room door. Soon after, sometime around 1986–87, the conjunction of McGrupp's lyrics with the words to Wilson (written by Tom and Aaron Woolfe) sparked the idea for Gamehendge in Trey's mind as a way to tie them all together. Note that in the Gamehendge myth, Colonel Forbin's dog is named McGrupp, as is directly mentioned in the song's somewhat confused lyrics. Also, Dave Abrahams, referenced in the song ("He looks too much like Dave"), is a childhood friend of Trey and Tom's.

Musical History and Evolution: McGrupp began its career as Tom Marshall originally wrote it—as a poem. By 12/6/86, Trey raided the music to Skippy the Wondermouse and set the lyrics of McGrupp to it, giving the words a tune. By the late 1980s, the outro jam that still appears had been added to the song. Also, though McGrupp did not appear on the original "Man Who Stepped into Yesterday" thesis recording, the band has included it in live Gamehendge performances on 3/22/93, 6/26/94, and 7/8/94. Its distinctive bass line has also been used as background for narrative portions during Gamehendge performances. Individual versions of McGrupp vary somewhat, especially in the strength of the musical explosion out of the aforementioned bass line. Experimental McGrupps also began to surface in 1997, at both the Lille, France, show 6/25 and again in New York City on 12/30.

Rotation History: Lightly played for most of the 1990s, McGrupp was most frequently heard in 1994, when the band played it thirteen times. In 1997, the band played it five times.

Discography: Has not yet appeared on a Phish album.

McGrupp and the Watchful Hosemasters [75] [McGrupp]

By Anastasio/Marshall

05/03/85	[2]	1a	WhipPost	Makisupa
10/17/85	1	1a	Antelope	*CL1
04/01/86	3	2	ACDCBag	Alumni
12/06/86	5	1a	Icculus	GTBT
04/29/87	5	3	Jam	Curtis
08/09/87	2	2	Fluffhead	Corrina
08/21/87	2	3	BBFCM	Makisupa
08/29/87	2	2	Curtain	Possum
10/14/87	4	2	Divided	Clod
11/19/87	2	1	*OP1	Sparks
02/07/88	2	1a	Fire	Shaggy
03/12/88	2	1a	JumpMonk	Lizards
03/21/88	1	1a	Golgi	Sally
05/15/88	4	1a	Icculus	Wilson
06/15/88	3	1	Rocky Top	Fluffhead
06/18/88	1	2	Rocky Top	Jesus
07/24/88	6	3	Jesus	Antelope
02/07/89	18	1	Esther	Foam
03/03/89	4	1	Wilson	YEM
03/30/89	3	1	Bold	Divided
04/15/89	7	1	IDK	Foam
04/20/89	2	1	Possum	Foam
04/30/89	5	1	YEM	Lizards
06/30/89	25	1	YEM	Possum
08/17/89	5	1	Suzie	Sloth
09/09/89	8	1	ACDCBag	Makisupa
10/01/89	1	1	Alumni	Jam
10/21/89	7	1	In a Hole	Fluffhead
10/22/89	1	2	In a Hole	ACDCBag
11/02/89	4	2	Divided	Fluffhead
11/09/89	3	2	ACDCBag	PYITE
11/10/89	1	2	*OP2	Fluffhead
12/08/89	9	1	Reba	ACDCBag
02/25/90	22	2	Reba	Makisupa
05/23/90	37	2	La Grange	A-Train
02/14/91	50	1	MSO	BurAlive
05/10/91	50	2	Foam	Chalkdust
05/25/91	6	1	Sloth	*CL1
10/13/91	29	1	Sloth	Mike's
12/31/91	35	3	Tweezer	Mike's
05/14/92	49	2	Weekapaug	Stash
07/15/92	18	2	Stash	All Things
11/27/92	36	2	It's Ice	Walk Line
03/16/93	49	1	Divided	Cavern
03/22/93	5	2	Sloth	Mike's
05/03/93	31	2	It's Ice	FunJim
08/07/93	24	2	My Friend	FurplRain
12/30/93	18	2	PYITE	Weekapaug
04/08/94	5	2	Split&Melt	It's Ice
04/30/94	18	2	Axilla 2	Possum
05/13/94	9	2	Split&Melt	Peaches
05/22/94	7	2	It's Ice	Tweezer
05/29/94	6	2	Chalkdust	Ch Kee
06/18/94	8	2	Horn	Tweezer
06/24/94	5	2	Curtain	Simple
06/26/94	2	1	Sloth	Divided
07/02/94	4	2	Weekapaug	Maze
07/08/94	4	1	Sloth	Divided
10/20/94	17	2	Maze	Rift
11/30/94	26	2	Catapult	Cavern
12/09/94	8	2	Tweezer	Julius
06/17/95	15	2	Tweezer	AArmy
10/11/95	24	2	Mike's	Weekapaug
10/27/95	11	2	Simple	Keyboard
12/11/95	27	1	Tube	Julius
12/29/95	7	2	Bathtub	BBFCM
07/23/96	20	1	DWD	Stash
08/12/96	9	2	Caspian	Antelope
10/26/96	13	2	Simple	Waste
11/15/96	13	2	Maze	Split&Melt
06/25/97	41	2	Time	Makisupa
07/31/97	18	2	Vultures	Mike's
08/13/97	8	2	Sl Monkey	Sample
11/26/97	12	1	My Soul	Dirt
12/30/97	15	2	ACDCBag	Harpua
>> 12/31/97	**1**			

MID-HIGHWAY BLUES

Inspiration: This bluegrass number, played one time, was written on the U.S./Canada border on 11/23/96 while the band's bus was being searched by the border patrol. During the delay, the band learned the song, then played it at their show that night in Vancouver, BC. The song's title is provisional; it is also sometimes referred to as "Late Night on the Highway."

Musical History and Evolution: None.

Rotation History: Only played once.

Discography: Has not yet appeared on a Phish album.

Mid-Highway Blues [1] [Highway]

By Gordon

11/23/96	[877]	1	PYITE	Split&Melt
>> 12/31/97	**90**			

MIKE'S SONG

Inspiration: As the front end of the very popular "Mike's Groove" suite of songs (which includes Weekapaug Groove as its end piece and I Am Hydrogen as its original and still-frequent bridge), Mike's Song has been around since Mike Gordon composed it in 1984 as a Motown-sounding song on his four-track recorder. A tape from 1985 chronicles Trey announcing the title for Mike's Song as "Microdot," but Mike says it was eventually named after him because at the time, he hadn't contributed any other songs to the group's repertoire. Since the late 1980s, Mike's Song had served, with You Enjoy Myself, as one of the band's trampoline songs, although for the past several years the tramps have only appeared during YEM (trampless Mikes began to surface in 1995). Mike's Song is also one of the two songs during which Chris Kuroda heavily triggers the onstage fog machines (the other is Great Gig in the Sky).

Musical History and Evolution: Early versions of this powerhouse were kind of bluesy before the psychedelic jam was perfected in the late 1980s. Mike's Song has a traditional structure around which the jam operates: after the opening lyrical segment, the jam improvises before returning to a series of peaks; it then wanders again, peaks again, and drops into a series of descending notes which historically paved the way for the segue into Hydrogen. In recent years, the band has not always "finished" Mike's Song by hitting the trademark descending notes, and even on occasion it's gone directly into Weekapaug. By 1997, the band had found additional ways to get to Hydrogen (see 11/22/97 Hampton, VA, for example). Simply put, Mike's Song may be the band's most versatile and brilliant creation.

For fans, picking a best-ever list of Mike's Groove is tough, as everyone has their treasured favorites. The version from 12/31/95 in New York is regarded as one of the best Mike's Songs ever by many, who cite its monster jam and spacey digital delay loop ending. Some other favored versions of the original Mike's > Hydrogen > Groove suite include 5/28/89 Hebron, NY, "Here comes the beer!"; 4/19/92 Santa Cruz, CA; 4/21/92 Eureka, CA, amazing Weekapaug jam; 11/28/92 Port Chester, NY, raging jamming throughout; 12/31/92 Boston, MA, with Auld Lang Syne and New Year's substituting for Hydrogen; 5/8/93 Durham, NH, with Crossroads jam; 12/30/93 Portland, ME, amazing jam out of Mike's Song with Simple themes; 4/9/94 Binghamton, NY, "Little Drummer Boy" jamming in Weekapaug, as on the even-better 12/28/94 Philadelphia, PA, version; 6/27/94 Milwaukee, WI, "Run, OJ, Run"; 6/10/95 Morrison, CO, thirty minutes of madness; and 7/22/97 Raleigh, NC, as rain swept the amphitheater.

As time goes on, versions that dismiss Hydrogen and often split up Mike's and Weekapaug with more than one song have become more frequent. Great versions of these include 11/11/95 Atlanta, GA, rare first set Mike's/Weekapaug; 11/6/96 Knoxville, TN, with Swept Away > Steep; and 12/6/96 Las Vegas, NV, long and grand with Simple and Hood.

Several great versions that do not rely on the raw strength of the jamming include 2/20/93 Atlanta, GA, the famous Mike's > Everything > Groove; 5/6/93 Albany, NY, Mike's into "Ob-La-Di" jam into bluegrass jam; 5/27/94 San Francisco, CA, Simple jam into "O Sole Mio" aria; 6/22/94 Columbus, OH (too many song inserts to mention); and

3/1/97 Hamburg, Germany, with "The End" and "Careful with That Axe, Eugene" sequences, as heard on *Slip Stitch and Pass.*

Rotation History: Mike's Song almost always appears as part of Mike's Groove, which since its formation in 1988 through 12/31/92 was always composed of the three-song combo Mike's Song > I Am Hydrogen > Weekapaug Groove. When Mike's instead led into Auld Lang Syne at that 1992 New Year's show, it ushered in a whole new era of surprises following Mike's, creating Mike's Song > any song(s) > Weekapaug suites or even wilder combinations. And on 4/18/93, the band played a Mike's without eventually following up with a Weekapaug for the first time. And 1993 also marked the first time in which Mike's and Weekapaug surfaced in separate parts of the show, detached not only by other songs but by breaks in playing. For much of 1994, Simple was integrated into the midst of Mike's Song jams, and is still a frequent segue out of Mike's Song. Versions of Mike's Groove on 12/1/95 in Hershey, PA, and 12/7/95 Niagara Falls, NY, are the only two to feature straight Mike's > Weekapaug duos; the Niagara version is particularly spectacular, especially the jam out of Weekapaug. Mike's has appeared without Weekapaug only a smattering of times since 1988: on 4/18/93, 5/6/93, 8/7/93, 5/2/94, 5/27/94, 11/16/94, 11/30/94, 11/21/95, 7/9/96, and 7/12/96; it has been separated by one set from Weekapaug only once, in New York, NY, on 12/31/95. Its play frequency has dropped in recent years from a one-in-five-show average for 1994, 1995, and 1996 to a rarer one-in-seven average in 1997.

Discography: Appears on *Slip Stitch and Pass* (1997).

Mike's Song [297] [Mike's]

By Gordon

10/17/85	[3]	1a	Alumni	Dave's
11/23/85	2	1a	*OP1	WhipPost
10/15/86	3	1a	Quinn	Mercy
12/06/86	2	1a	*OP1	Jam
03/23/87	3	1	FunkBitch	Alumni
08/21/87	6	2	*OP2	Harpua
06/18/88	22	2	IKALittle	Corrina
07/23/88	5	1	Mockbird	I am H2
07/24/88	1	1	Sally	I am H2
07/25/88	1	2	*OP2	I am H2
08/03/88	1	2	Peaches	I am H2
08/27/88	2	1a	Fluffhead	A-Train
10/12/88	4	1	Fee	I am H2
10/29/88	1	2	Curtis	A-Train
11/05/88	2	2	Fee	I am H2
11/11/88	1	2	*OP2	I am H2
02/07/89	6	1	Possum	I am H2
03/03/89	4	2	*OP2	I am H2
03/04/89	1	1	IDK	I am H2
03/30/89	1	2	Mango	I am H2
04/14/89	6	2	Brain	I am H2
04/15/89	1	1	*OP1	I am H2
04/20/89	2	3	Lizards	I am H2
05/06/89	9	1	IDK	I am H2
05/09/89	3	1	Ya Mar	I am H2
05/20/89	7	2	Bold	I am H2
05/21/89	1	1	Contact	I am H2
05/26/89	1	1	ACDCBag	I am H2
05/27/89	1	1	ACDCBag	I am H2
05/28/89	1	2	Fire	I am H2
06/23/89	5	1	Fee	I am H2
06/30/89	2	2	Bathtub	I am H2
08/17/89	5	1	Harry	I am H2
08/19/89	2	1	Lizards	I am H2
10/06/89	8	1a	Timber Ho	I am H2
10/07/89	1	1	Ya Mar	I am H2
10/21/89	1	2	*OP2	I am H2
10/26/89	2	1	Lizards	I am H2
11/02/89	3	1	Foam	I am H2
11/09/89	3	2	Lizards	I am H2
11/10/89	1	1	Bathtub	I am H2
11/16/89	2	1	*OP1	I am H2
12/07/89	6	1	Fee	I am H2
12/09/89	2	2	Fee	I am H2
12/16/89	2	1a	Lawn Boy	I am H2
12/29/89	1	1	Lawn Boy	I am H2
12/31/89	3	2	*OP2	I am H2
01/20/90	1	1a	Esther	I am H2
01/27/90	3	1	Funky	I am H2
01/28/90	1	2	Bathtub	I am H2
02/09/90	7	1	Sqirm Coil	I am H2
02/10/90	1	2	Fee	I am H2
02/15/90	1	1	Bathtub	I am H2
02/17/90	2	1a	Bathtub	I am H2
02/23/90	2	2	Suzie	I am H2
03/01/90	3	2	Foam	I am H2
03/03/90	2	1	*OP1	I am H2
03/07/90	1	2	Tela	I am H2
03/08/90	1	2	Lizards	I am H2
03/28/90	4	2	FunkBitch	I am H2
04/04/90	1	2	*OP2	I am H2
04/05/90	1	2	Cavern	I am H2
04/07/90	2	1	Tweezer	I am H2
04/08/90	1	2	Slave	I am H2
04/18/90	5	1	*OP1	I am H2
04/20/90	2	2	Caravan	I am H2
04/22/90	2	1	Slave	I am H2
04/25/90	1	2	Bouncing	I am H2
04/26/90	1	2	Curtis	I am H2
04/28/90	1	2	MSO	I am H2
05/04/90	3	2	Oh Kee	I am H2
05/06/90	1	1	Tweezer	I am H2
05/11/90	2	1	*OP1	I am H2
05/13/90	2	2	*OP2	I am H2
05/23/90	3	2	Antelope	I am H2
06/05/90	4	1	Uncle Pen	I am H2
06/07/90	1	2	Love You	I am H2
06/08/90	1	1	IDK	I am H2
06/09/90	1	1	Uncle Pen	I am H2
06/16/90	1	3	Brain	I am H2
09/13/90	1	2	*OP2	I am H2
09/16/90	2	1a	Paul&Silas	I am H2
09/28/90	4	2	Paul&Silas	I am H2
10/05/90	7	1	IDK	I am H2
10/07/90	2	1	Sqirm Coil	I am H2
10/12/90	2	2	Magilla	I am H2
10/30/90	2	2	*OP2	I am H2
10/31/90	1	2	Love You	I am H2
11/02/90	1	1	Sloth	I am H2
11/03/90	1	2	Landlady	I am H2
11/04/90	1	2	Llama	I am H2
11/08/90	1	1	IDK	I am H2
11/10/90	1	1	Lizards	I am H2
11/16/90	1	2	Landlady	I am H2
11/17/90	1	2	Fluffhead	I am H2
11/24/90	1	1	Foam	I am H2
11/26/90	1	2	Wilson	I am H2
11/30/90	1	1	Landlady	I am H2
12/07/90	3	2	*OP2	I am H2
12/08/90	1	1	Landlady	I am H2
12/28/90	1	1	Mockbird	I am H2
12/31/90	2	1	MSO	I am H2
02/08/91	5	2	Lawn Boy	I am H2
02/14/91	2	2	*OP2	I am H2
02/16/91	2	1	Mango	I am H2
02/21/91	3	1	Lizards	I am H2
02/26/91	4	1	Lizards	I am H2
02/28/91	6	1	Esther	I am H2
03/01/91	1	1	BurAlive	I am H2
03/07/91	3	2	IDK	I am H2
03/15/91	4	1	Lizards	I am H2
03/17/91	2	1	Landlady	I am H2
03/22/91	2	2	Terrapin	I am H2
04/05/91	8	1	Foam	I am H2
04/11/91	2	2	Destiny	I am H2
04/15/91	3	2	Jam	I am H2
04/19/91	3	1	Rocky Top	I am H2
04/21/91	2	1	Tela	I am H2
04/27/91	4	2	TMWSIY	I am H2
05/04/91	3	1	Fluffhead	I am H2
05/10/91	2	2	Love You	I am H2
05/12/91	2	2	Magilla	I am H2
05/17/91	2	1	IDK	I am H2
07/11/91	3	2	TMWSIY	I am H2
07/12/91	1	2	Gumbo	I am H2
07/14/91	2	3	Bathtub	I am H2
07/15/91	1	1a	Bouncing	I am H2
07/18/91	1	1	Cavern	I am H2
07/21/91	4	1	Bouncing	I am H2
07/23/91	1	1	Bouncing	I am H2
07/25/91	2	2	Magilla	I am H2
07/27/91	2	1a	Landlady	I am H2
09/26/91	3	2	Destiny	I am H2
09/28/91	2	2	PoorHeart	I am H2
10/03/91	3	2	Paul&Silas	I am H2
10/04/91	1	2	Sqirm Coil	I am H2
10/10/91	3	2	Fee	I am H2
10/13/91	3	1	McGrupp	I am H2
10/18/91	3	2	Dinner	I am H2
10/24/91	3	2	*OP2	I am H2
10/27/91	2	2	It's Ice	I am H2
11/01/91	4	2	Eliza	I am H2
11/08/91	4	2	IDK	I am H2
11/12/91	3	2	Paul&Silas	I am H2
11/15/91	3	2	PoorHeart	I am H2
11/19/91	2	2	MSO	I am H2
11/21/91	2	1	Esther	I am H2
11/23/91	2	2	Curtain	I am H2
12/04/91	3	2	Mango	I am H2
12/05/91	1	2	Foam	I am H2
12/31/91	3	3	McGrupp	I am H2
03/07/92	2	2	Horn	I am H2
03/14/92	4	1	A-Train	I am H2
03/17/92	1	2	Esther	I am H2
03/20/92	2	2	*OP2	I am H2
03/24/92	2	2	Curtain	I am H2
03/27/92	3	2	*OP2	I am H2
03/31/92	3	2	*OP2	I am H2
04/04/92	3	2	*OP2	I am H2
04/06/92	2	2	Paul&Silas	I am H2
04/09/92	2	2	MSO	I am H2
04/13/92	2	2	Sparkle	I am H2
04/16/92	2	2	Lizards	I am H2
04/19/92	3	2	Curtain	I am H2
04/21/92	1	2	Tela	I am H2
04/23/92	2	2	PoorHeart	I am H2
04/24/92	1	2	Foam	I am H2
04/29/92	2	2	Lizards	I am H2
05/01/92	2	2	MSO	I am H2
05/03/92	2	2	Guelah	I am H2
05/05/92	1	2	Foam	I am H2
05/07/92	2	2	Glide	I am H2
05/14/92	5	2	Eliza	I am H2
05/18/92	4	2	TMWSIY	I am H2
07/16/92	15	2	Paul&Silas	I am H2
08/17/92	18	2	Esther	I am H2
11/19/92	11	2	*OP2	I am H2
11/21/92	2	2	Curtain	I am H2
11/23/92	2	2	Weigh	I am H2
11/28/92	3	1	All Things	I am H2
12/01/92	2	1	Adeline	I am H2
12/03/92	2	2	Fluffhead	I am H2
12/05/92	2	2	Lawn Boy	I am H2
12/08/92	3	2	*OP2	I am H2
12/11/92	2	2	Dinner	I am H2
12/29/92	4	2	All Things	I am H2
12/31/92	2	3	*OP3	Auld
02/04/93	2	2	Wedge	TMWSIY
02/06/93	2	2	All Things	I am H2
02/09/93	2	2	PYITE	I am H2
02/11/93	2	2	Uncle Pen	I am H2
02/15/93	3	2	Reba	I am H2
02/18/93	2	2	PYITE	I am H2
02/20/93	2	2	Glide	Kung
02/23/93	3	2	All Things	I am H2
02/27/93	3	2	Ya Mar	I am H2
03/03/93	2	2	Mound	I am H2
03/05/93	1	2	Uncle Pen	I am H2
03/09/93	3	2	Lawn Boy	I am H2
03/13/93	2	2	BBJ	I am H2
03/17/93	3	2	Mound	I am H2
03/19/93	2	2	Lizards	I am H2
03/22/93	2	2	McGrupp	I am H2
03/25/93	2	2	Wedge	I am H2
03/27/93	2	2	TMWSIY	I am H2
03/30/93	2	2	Weigh	I am H2
04/02/93	3	2	Silent	I am H2
04/10/93	4	2	BBJ	Great Gig
04/13/93	2	2	BBJ	I am H2
04/16/93	2	2	Lizards	I am H2
04/18/93	2	2	BBJ	Ya Mar
04/21/93	2	2	BBJ	Great Gig
04/23/93	2	2	BBJ	I am H2
04/25/93	2	2	BBJ	I am H2
04/29/93	2	2	Reba	I am H2
05/01/93	2	2	Paul&Silas	Great Gig
05/06/93	2	2	Sqirm Coil	Ob-La Jam
05/08/93	2	2	BBJ	I am H2
07/17/93	5	2	BBJ	Leprech
07/24/93	5	2	Sparkle	YSZahov
07/31/93	6	2	Sparkle	Leprech
08/02/93	1	2	Also Sprac	Sparks
08/07/93	3	2	Also Sprac	Sparks
08/11/93	3	2	*OP2	Great Gig
08/13/93	2	2	Ya Mar	Life Boy
08/16/93	3	2	*OP2	Faht
08/24/93	4	2	Ya Mar	Ginseng
12/30/93	6	2	Also Sprac	Mike's
04/06/94	4	2	Sparkle	Life Boy
04/09/94	2	2	Demand	I am H2
04/18/94	8	2	Ya Mar	TMWSIY
04/21/94	2	2	Fluffhead	I am H2
04/29/94	6	2	Uncle Pen	I am H2
05/02/94	2	2	Lawn Boy	*CL2
05/14/94	9	2	Curtain	I am H2
05/19/94	3	2	Sparkle	I am H2
05/27/94	7	2	My Mind	O Mio
06/09/94	3	2	Ginseng	I am H2
06/13/94	3	2	*OP2	I am H2
06/17/94	3	2	PoorHeart	I am H2
06/22/94	4	2	Also Sprac	Simple
07/02/94	8	2	Also Sprac	YSZahov
07/10/94	6	2	Ya Mar	I am H2
10/08/94	6	2	Rift	I am H2
10/13/94	4	2	AmGrace	YSZahov
10/21/94	6	2	Also Sprac	I am H2
10/25/94	3	2	*OP2	Simple
11/04/94	8	2	Curtain	Tela
11/16/94	4	2	*OP2	Simple
11/25/94	7	2	Also Sprac	Simple
11/30/94	3	2	Ya Mar	Catapult
12/06/94	5	2	PoorHeart	Simple
12/10/94	4	2	Also Sprac	I am H2
12/28/94	1	2	NICU	Mango
12/31/94	3	2	Bouncing	YSZahov
06/10/95	5	2	Uncle Pen	I am H2
06/20/95	7	2	Uncle Pen	Contact
06/25/95	4	2	Scent	DoInRoad
06/30/95	4	2	Avenu	Contact
09/30/95	7	2	Scent	Keyboard
10/11/95	7	2	Mound	McGrupp
10/19/95	5	2	PoorHeart	I am H2
10/25/95	5	2	CTB	Sparkle
11/11/95	7	1	CTB	DayinLife
11/15/95	3	2	Scent	Life Mars
11/21/95	4	2	Ya Mar	Keyboard
11/25/95	3	2	Kung	LongJourn
12/01/95	4	2	Halley's	Weekapaug
12/07/95	4	2	Sparkle	Weekapaug
12/16/95	7	2	Cavern	Simple
12/31/95	5	2	HelloBaby	Jam
07/09/96	7	1a	CTB	Bouncing
07/12/96	3	2	Caspian	Antelope
07/23/96	8	2	Sparkle	I am H2
08/05/96	4	2	AmGrace	I am H2
08/13/96	5	2	Lizards	Life Boy
08/16/96	2	2	HelloBaby	Simple
10/22/96	7	2	Scent	SweptAwy
10/29/96	5	2	Rift	I am H2
11/06/96	4	2	Curtain	SweptAwy
11/08/96	2	2	Lovin Cup	SSB
11/15/96	5	2	My Mind	Sl Monkey
11/23/96	5	2	Curtain	Simple
12/04/96	7	2	Ha Ha Ha	Caspian
12/06/96	1	2	Sparkle	Simple
12/28/96	1	2	Avenu	Str Design
02/23/97	12	2	Peaches	DoInRoad
03/01/97	4	2	Dinner	Lawn Boy
07/02/97	15	1	*OP1	Simple
07/22/97	8	2	DWD	Simple
07/31/97	6	2	McGrupp	I am H2
08/09/97	5	2	Foam	Funny
11/13/97	7	2	Bouncing	I am H2
11/22/97	6	1	*OP1	I am H2
12/02/97	6	2	*OP2	Simple
12/09/97	5	1	*OP1	Chalkdust
12/13/97	3	2	Ghost	Llama
12/31/97	4	2	Timber Ho	Piper
>> 12/31/97	**0**			

MONTANA

Inspiration: This song title appears on *A Live One* but not on any setlists because Montana is actually an excerpt from the 45-minute version of Tweezer performed in Bozeman, MT, on 11/28/94.

Musical History and Evolution: None.

Rotation History: None.

Discography: Appears on *A Live One* (1995).

MOUND

Inspiration: Musical, as Mike came up with the tune and then fashioned words to fit the music.

Musical History and Evolution: Mike wrote many more lyrics for this song than were included in its live performance version; some of these lyrics outtakes are included in the liner notes to *Rift*. Many of Mound's lyrics also evolved as Mike made changes to fit them to the music. During the *Rift* sessions, the band slightly rearranged the song, making it more pleasing to play live, according to Trey. During performances of the song in 1992 and 1993, the band often tried to lead the audience in the clap-along intro, but that has mostly disappeared from concert in recent years. The band has also stressed that the clapping heard on *Rift* was not mechanical but rather the result of their best clapping efforts.

Rotation History: Played most in 1993, the year of *Rift*'s release, Mound was one of the few Phish originals played heavily in the 1990s not to appear at all in 1997. Its last concert appearance, as of New Year's 1997, came on 11/19/96 in Kansas City, MO.

Discography: Appears on *Rift* (1993).

Mound [87] [Mound]

By Gordon

03/06/92	[384]	2	Stash	Llama
03/11/92	2	1	Split&Melt	Divided
03/13/92	2	1	Divided	Fluffhead
03/20/92	4	1	Lizards	Antelope
03/25/92	3	2	Tweezer	Reba
03/30/92	4	2	Tweezer	YEM
04/06/92	6	2	Llama	Stash
04/09/92	2	1	Llama	Reba
04/18/92	6	2	Lizards	Llama
04/22/92	3	1	Divided	Stash
04/29/92	4	2	Possum	Oh Kee
05/01/92	2	2	Weekapaug	Lizards
05/08/92	6	1	Llama	All Things
11/19/92	52	1	Split&Melt	Divided
11/23/92	4	1	Divided	Bouncing
11/27/92	2	1	Llama	Memories
12/02/92	4	2	Possum	Tweezer
12/05/92	3	1	Lizards	Divided
12/08/92	3	1	Divided	Adeline
12/13/92	4	2	Suzie	Bouncing
02/06/93	8	2	Chalkdust	Stash
02/11/93	4	2	Weekapaug	BBJ
02/15/93	3	1	Chalkdust	Stash
02/18/93	2	2	Weekapaug	AmGrace
02/26/93	7	2	Chalkdust	BBJ
03/03/93	3	2	Split&Melt	Mike's
03/06/93	2	1	Split&Melt	PYITE
03/12/93	3	2	YEM	BBJ
03/17/93	4	2	Jesus	Mike's
03/24/93	5	2	Tweezer	BBJ
03/26/93	2	2	Tweezer	Horse
03/28/93	2	2	RunJim	Bathtub
03/31/93	2	1	Split&Melt	PYITE
04/03/93	3	2	Stash	All Things
04/09/93	2	2	Llama	My Friend
04/14/93	4	2	Tweezer	BBJ
04/18/93	3	2	Possum	BBJ
04/21/93	2	2	Possum	Split&Melt
04/24/93	3	2	Dinner	BBJ
04/29/93	3	2	Ya Mar	BBJ
04/30/93	1	2	Tweezer	BBJ
05/02/93	2	1	Divided	Stash
05/06/93	3	1	Chalkdust	Split&Melt
05/08/93	2	1	Rift	Stash
07/15/93	3	1	Divided	Stash
07/18/93	3	2	Antelope	FEFY
07/22/93	2	1	Divided	Ya Mar
07/25/93	3	1	Foam	Stash
07/28/93	2	2	Lizards	My Friend
07/31/93	3	1	Split&Melt	Foam
08/09/93	6	1	Chalkdust	Fee
08/14/93	4	2	Antelope	Sqirm Coil
08/16/93	2	2	Weekapaug	It's Ice
08/25/93	5	2	Possum	My Friend
04/17/94	18	1	Divided	DWD
04/23/94	5	2	Antelope	Sample
04/25/94	2	2	Antelope	Sqirm Coil
04/30/94	3	1	Chalkdust	Stash
05/02/94	1	2	RunJim	Reba
05/07/94	4	1	Divided	FEFY
05/13/94	4	1	Julius	Stash
05/17/94	3	1	Maze	If I Could
05/21/94	3	1	DWD	Stash
05/26/94	4	2	DWD	Ginseng
06/21/94	13	2	DWD	Split&Melt
06/29/94	6	1	Reba	Julius
07/13/94	10	2	Tweezer	Slave
12/01/94	41	2	Peaches	Tweezer
12/04/94	3	1	Fee	Adeline
12/06/94	1	1	Llama	DWD
12/28/94	5	1	*OP1	Simple
12/31/94	3	1	Glide	Peaches
06/08/95	3	1	Guelah	FEFY
06/14/95	4	1	NICU	Cavern
06/17/95	3	2	Maze	Tweezer
06/24/95	5	1	Glide	Stash
06/30/95	5	1	Lizards	Fee
10/07/95	12	1	Fog	Possum
10/11/95	2	2	Bathtub	Mike's
10/17/95	4	2	*OP2	Caspian
10/28/95	8	1	ACDCBag	Timber Ho
11/16/95	9	1	Horn	Ya Mar
12/02/95	11	1	RunJim	Guelah
10/16/96	47	1	Billy	Sample
10/25/96	7	1	Billy	Guelah
11/08/96	9	1	All Things	DWD
11/19/96	8	1	Theme	Stash
>> 12/31/97	92			

MY FRIEND MY FRIEND

Inspiration: Apparently, the idea for the lyrics to this song came to Tom Marshall when a friend of his told him he'd received a set of knives as a wedding present.

Musical History and Evolution: Little has changed with the song's musical structure, although its name has undergone revision. Originally introduced as Knife during its debut performance on 3/6/92 in Portsmouth, NH, the band had redubbed it My Friend My Friend by the time of the *Rift* sessions that fall. During those sessions at Burlington's White Crow Studios, the band went on a local radio station and announced that anyone interested in singing for the next Phish album could come down to the recording studio and join the fun. The group sing-along at the end of this song on the album is the result of that invitation. For most of 1993, Trey performed the intro to this song—until right before the lyrics begin—on acoustic guitar, then switched to electric guitar for the rest of the song. On 2/25/97 in Munich, Germany, Trey flubbed the song, stopped it midstream, and said something like, "I'm not going to pretend I know how to play this song." The band nailed it the next night, but then did not play it again until the fall tour.

Rotation History: Played commonly in 1992 and 1993, and less often in 1994, 1995, and 1996, My Friend was another oldie to become a rarity in 1997, as it was seen only three times. Starting in 1994, Phish often chose it as a show opener.

Discography: Appears on *Rift* (1993).

My Friend, My Friend [99] [My Friend]

By Anastasio/Marshall

03/06/92	[384]	2	*OP2	PoorHeart
03/11/92	2	1	Suzie	Paul&Silas
03/19/92	5	2	Suzie	Sqirm Coil
03/21/92	2	2	A-Train	PoorHeart
03/26/92	3	2	TMWSIY	Lizards
03/31/92	4	2	Dinner	MSO
04/04/92	3	2	Rosie	Harpua
04/07/92	3	2	YEM	Lizards
04/19/92	8	1	Paul&Silas	Reba
04/25/92	5	1	Suzie	Paul&Silas
05/01/92	3	1	Suzie	PoorHeart
05/07/92	5	1	BurAlive	Foam
05/14/92	5	1	PoorHeart	Bouncing
07/15/92	18	1	Foam	Uncle Pen
08/17/92	19	1	Foam	Bouncing
11/22/92	14	2	Axilla	MSO
12/01/92	6	2	Chalkdust	All Things
12/06/92	5	1	Fee	MSO
12/11/92	4	1	Sparkle	Memories
12/29/92	4	1	Llama	Divided
02/03/93	3	1	IDK	PoorHeart
02/06/93	3	1	Wilson	Maze
02/09/93	2	1	PoorHeart	Rift
02/12/93	3	2	*OP2	All Things
02/17/93	3	2	Glide	MSO
02/19/93	2	1	Sparkle	PoorHeart
02/23/93	4	1	Golgi	Rift
03/02/93	4	2	*OP2	Uncle Pen
03/08/93	4	2	BBJ	Kung
03/12/93	2	2	ACDCBag	Axilla
03/16/93	3	2	*OP2	Curtain
03/18/93	2	2	*OP2	PoorHeart
03/21/93	2	2	Lovin Cup	Rift
03/27/93	5	1	Reba	Uncle Pen
03/30/93	2	1	Golgi	Llama
04/01/93	2	1	Sqirm Coil	Paul&Silas
04/03/93	2	1	Sqirm Coil	Reba
04/09/93	2	2	Mound	YEM
04/10/93	1	1	Sqirm Coil	Uncle Pen
04/13/93	2	2	*OP2	Rift
04/17/93	3	1	Glide	All Things
04/20/93	2	2	TMWSIY	Llama
04/23/93	3	1	Fluffhead	Divided
04/27/93	3	2	Golgi	All Things
04/29/93	1	E	*OPE	*CLE
05/01/93	2	2	Fluffhead	Sqirm Coil
05/05/93	3	2	RunJim	Manteca
05/08/93	3	1	Glide	Reba
07/16/93	4	1	Golgi	Ya Mar
07/23/93	5	2	Faht	Uncle Pen
07/28/93	4	2	Mound	Harry
07/30/93	2	2	Fluffhead	Golgi
08/07/93	5	2	Sparkle	McGrupp
08/09/93	2	2	Tela	My Mind
08/11/93	1	1	Ginseng	Mango
08/16/93	5	2	It's Ice	PoorHeart
08/20/93	2	2	Sqirm Coil	Chalkdust
08/25/93	3	2	Mound	Paul&Silas
12/28/93	3	2	YEM	Lizards
04/10/94	9	2	*OP2	Ya Mar
04/18/94	7	1	Julius	Rift
04/24/94	5	1	*OP1	Ya Mar
05/06/94	8	1	PoorHeart	Ya Mar
05/13/94	5	1	If I Could	Slave
05/19/94	4	1	Llama	PoorHeart
05/27/94	7	2	Peaches	Reba
06/14/94	7	1	Fee	Uncle Pen
06/21/94	5	2	DWD	Split&Melt
07/03/94	10	1	*OP1	PoorHeart
07/10/94	5	1	If I Could	Julius
10/07/94	5	1	*OP1	Julius
10/12/94	4	1	*OP1	Reba
10/18/94	5	1	Simple	IDK
10/23/94	4	1	Chalkdust	Sparkle
10/29/94	5	1	*OP1	Sparkle
11/14/94	7	1	*OP1	Scent
11/26/94	9	1	*OP1	Possum
11/30/94	2	1	PoorHeart	Reba
06/09/95	17	1	*OP1	Divided
06/15/95	4	1	*OP1	Sparkle
06/26/95	9	1	*OP1	Wanna Go
07/03/95	6	1	*OP1	PoorHeart
09/30/95	4	1	*OP1	CTB
10/20/95	13	1	*OP1	Ya Mar
10/24/95	3	1	*OP1	Paul&Silas
11/12/95	9	1	*OP1	Llama
11/21/95	6	1	Guyute	Dog Faced
12/11/95	14	1	*OP1	Ha Ha Ha
12/17/95	5	1	*OP1	PoorHeart
12/29/95	2	1	*OP1	PoorHeart
07/15/96	14	1	*OP1	PYITE
08/10/96	14	1	*OP1	PoorHeart
10/19/96	9	1	*OP1	Rift
11/03/96	10	1	*OP1	RunJim
11/27/96	15	1	Julius	Ya Mar
12/04/96	5	1	*OP1	Chalkdust
02/25/97	15	2	Fee	DWD
02/26/97	1	1	Llama	Harry
12/05/97	57	1	RunJim	Ginseng
>> 12/31/97	10			

MY SWEET ONE

Inspiration: Because Fishman wrote this song while at Mike's parents' house, the band sometimes jokes that Fish meant it as a love ballad to Mike's mom.

Musical History and Evolution: Little to speak of, though the band often performed the song with its acoustic lineup in 1994.

Rotation History: Played at more than half of all shows in 1991, MSO surfaced frequently through 1994. But in 1995, it popped up only three times, and after 12/14/95 in Binghamton, NY, not again until the band revived it on New Year's Eve 1997 in New York, NY.

Discography: Appears on *Lawn Boy* (1990).

My Sweet One[186] [MSO]

By Fishman

09/09/89	[124]	1	Wilson	Bowie
10/01/89	1	2	ACDCBag	Reba
10/22/89	8	2	ACDCBag	Fee
11/02/89	4	2	ACDCBag	*CL2
11/03/89	1	1	Bathtub	Split&Melt
11/09/89	2	1	Curtain	Bathtub
11/10/89	1	1	ACDCBag	YEM
11/11/89	1	1a	ACDCBag	YEM
11/16/89	1	1	Suzie	Reba
11/30/89	2	1	Lizards	Antelope
12/08/89	5	1	ACDCBag	Bathtub
01/27/90	10	1	ACDCBag	Bouncing
02/25/90	16	1	Foam	Forbin's

03/03/90	3	1	Weekapaug	Sqirm Coil
03/08/90	2	2	Bathtub	ACDCBag
03/11/90	2	2	Antelope	Bouncing
04/07/90	6	1	Bowie	Suzie
04/08/90	1	2	Fee	Antelope
04/18/90	5	1	YEM	A-Train
04/22/90	4	1	Cavern	Slave
04/25/90	1	1	Divided	Bowie
04/28/90	2	2	Reba	Mike's
05/04/90	3	1	Reba	YEM
05/10/90	2	1	Tweezer	Bathtub
05/13/90	3	2	Tweezer	Reba
05/24/90	4	2	IDK	Horn
06/05/90	3	2	Bouncing	Lizards
06/07/90	1	2	*OP2	Dinner
06/08/90	1	1	Possum	Bathtub
06/16/90	2	2	Tweezer	Bathtub
09/15/90	3	2	Eliza	Bathtub
09/22/90	4	1	Horn	Divided
09/28/90	1	1	Stash	Sqirm Coil
10/05/90	3	1	Weekapaug	Landlady
10/07/90	2	2	Tweezer	IDK
10/08/90	1	1	Reba	YEM
10/31/90	4	1	Asse Fest	Cavern
11/02/90	1	2	Mockbird	Foam
11/04/90	2	1	Asse Fest	Bowie
11/10/90	2	1	Cavern	BurAlive
11/30/90	5	1	Tweezer	Llama
12/01/90	1	1	Tweezer	YEM
12/03/90	1	1	Divided	Antelope
12/28/90	3	2	Oh Kee	Divided
12/31/90	2	1	Bouncing	Mike's
02/01/91	1	1	*OP1	Foam
02/03/91	2	1	Guelah	Tweezer
02/07/91	1	1	Foam	Landlady
02/08/91	1	1	Mockbird	Stash
02/09/91	1	1	Guelah	Tweezer
02/14/91	1	1	*OP1	McGrupp
02/15/91	1	2	Guelah	Oh Kee
02/16/91	1	1	Sloth	Divided
02/26/91	7	1	Guelah	Reba
02/27/91	1	1	Fee	Split&Melt
02/28/91	1	1	TMWSIY	Golgi
03/06/91	3	1	Love You	Bouncing
03/07/91	1	2	Guelah	GTBT
03/13/91	3	2	Bouncing	Guelah
03/15/91	1	1	Foam	Stash
03/16/91	1	2	Guelah	Split&Melt
03/17/91	1	2	Esther	Sqirm Coil
03/23/91	3	2	ACDCBag	Tweezer
03/28/91	1	1a	Guelah	Bowie
04/04/91	5	2	Landlady	Divided
04/05/91	1	2	IDK	GTBT
04/11/91	2	2	*OP2	Reba
04/12/91	1	2	Reba	GTBT
04/15/91	2	2	Horn	Landlady
04/16/91	1	2	*OP2	Reba
04/19/91	2	2	Destiny	Sqirm Coil
04/20/91	1	1	Fluffhead	Landlady
04/21/91	1	1	Magilla	Oh Kee
04/22/91	1	2	Stash	Lizards
04/26/91	2	2	Bouncing	Guelah
04/27/91	1	1	Landlady	Reba
05/02/91	1	2	Tela	IDK
05/04/91	2	1	Reba	Split&Melt
05/16/91	5	2	Tweezer	Lizards
05/18/91	2	2	Stash	Guelah
07/11/91	2	1	Flat Fee	Stash
07/12/91	1	2	Tweezer	Gumbo
07/14/91	2	1	Guelah	Forbin's
07/19/91	3	2	IDK	Magilla
07/20/91	1	1	Bathtub	Bowie
07/23/91	2	1	Sqirm Coil	Oh Kee
07/24/91	1	2	Jesus	Bouncing
07/25/91	1	1	*OP1	Sloth
07/26/91	1	1	Reba	Foam
08/03/91	2	3	Lawn Boy	Lizards
09/25/91	1	1	Tela	It's Ice
09/26/91	1	1	It's Ice	Guelah
09/28/91	2	1	Sqirm Coil	Stash
10/02/91	2	2	YEM	Guelah
10/04/91	2	2	*OP2	Brother
10/06/91	2	2	*OP2	Stash
10/11/91	2	1	Landlady	Guelah
10/13/91	2	2	It's Ice	Jesus
10/18/91	3	2	Split&Melt	Cavern
10/19/91	1	2	Bouncing	Stash
10/27/91	4	1	*OP1	Chalkdust
10/31/91	3	2	Fee	Bowie
11/01/91	1	2	Tweezer	It's Ice
11/07/91	3	2	Bouncing	Reba
11/09/91	2	2	Terrapin	TweezRep
11/13/91	3	E	Horn	Adeline
11/15/91	2	1	Sqirm Coil	Divided
11/16/91	1	2	Tube	Bathtub
11/19/91	1	2	Tube	Mike's
11/20/91	1	2	It's Ice	Antelope
11/22/91	2	2	Tube	Landlady
11/23/91	1	2	Love You	TweezRep
11/30/91	2	2	Bouncing	Horn
12/04/91	1	2	*OP2	Stash
12/05/91	1	2	IDK	TweezRep
12/07/91	2	1	Mockbird	Stash
12/31/91	1	2	Cavern	Antelope
03/07/92	2	2	*OP2	Tweezer
03/12/92	2	2	Rosie	Cavern
03/19/92	4	2	NICU	Stash
03/21/92	2	1	Sqirm Coil	Stash
03/25/92	2	2	Horn	Chalkdust
03/27/92	2	2	Silent	Magilla
03/31/92	3	2	My Friend	Love You
04/04/92	3	2	Glide	Tweezer
04/09/92	4	2	TMWSIY	Mike's
04/15/92	3	2	Rosie	Golgi
04/19/92	4	2	Silent	Tube
05/01/92	8	2	All Things	Mike's
05/06/92	4	2	*OP2	Stash
05/08/92	2	2	Wilson	Stash
05/12/92	3	1	*OP1	Reba
05/16/92	3	1	Bouncing	Horn
05/17/92	1	1	Mockbird	Reba
07/10/92	11	E	*OPE	*CLE
07/15/92	4	2	Esther	Stash
07/24/92	7	1a	*OP1	Foam
11/22/92	26	2	My Friend	Tweezer
11/25/92	2	2	Rosie	TweezRep
11/28/92	2	1	*OP1	Foam
12/01/92	2	1	Landlady	Split&Melt
12/03/92	2	2	It's Ice	BBJ
12/06/92	3	1	My Friend	Sloth
12/07/92	1	2	Horn	It's Ice
12/08/92	1	2	Lngthwise	BBJ
12/10/92	1	2	Tela	BBJ
12/13/92	3	2	TMWSIY	BBJ
12/29/92	2	2	Silent	BBJ
12/31/92	2	2	Mockbird	BBJ
02/09/93	6	2	Weigh	Sample
02/17/93	6	2	My Friend	BBJ
02/19/93	2	2	FunkBitch	Love You
02/23/93	4	2	Axilla	Stash
03/03/93	5	2	Glide	FEFY
03/05/93	1	2	Jesus	BBJ
03/13/93	5	E	*OPE	AmGrace
03/21/93	6	2	YEM	BBJ
03/25/93	3	E	*OPE	BBJ
03/30/93	4	E	*OPE	AmGrace
04/03/93	4	2	Jesus	Love You
04/09/93	2	2	YEM	Love You
04/14/93	4	2	ACDCBag	Tweezer
05/03/93	15	2	Love You	TweezRep
07/28/93	17	2	Axilla	Antelope
08/08/93	8	E	*OPE	Freebird
08/11/93	2	2	Jesus	Antelope
08/17/93	6	2	PurplRain	Cavern
04/17/94	22	1	If I Could	Cavern
05/14/94	20	1	Sample	Ginseng
05/22/94	6	1	Fluffhead	Ginseng
05/25/94	2	1	Scent	Adeline
06/14/94	9	1	IDK	IDK
06/19/94	4	2	Sqirm Coil	HwayHell
06/22/94	2	2	Fluffhead	BBJ
07/05/94	10	2	Ginseng	AmGrace
07/13/94	5	E	*OPE	TweezRep
10/07/94	4	2	Life Boy	TweezRep
10/18/94	9	E	*OPE	*CLE
11/03/94	12	E	*OPE	Nellie
11/30/94	15	2	Antelope	Antelope
12/31/94	13	3	*OP3	Also Sprac
06/15/95	8	2	*OP2	Ha Ha Ha
12/02/95	58	1	Reba	Free
12/14/95	8	1	Fog	Frankstein
12/31/97	155	1	Ya Mar	Beauty
>> 12/31/97	**0**			

George Foremans

Songs that stayed on the shelf longest before making triumphant returns, with dates and the number of shows the band went without playing it .

ORIGINAL Song Name	Period of Retirement	Lapse
1) Camel Walk	02/24/89 to 07/02/95	691
2) Letter to Jimmy Page	12/07/89 to 07/05/94	530
3) Halley's Comet	08/17/89 to 03/14/92	418
4) Setting Sail	04/20/91 to 07/15/94	383
5) Kung	11/02/89 to 12/31/92	367
5) PYITE	11/09/89 to 02/05/93	367
7) Makisupa	11/26/90 to 04/29/93	319
8) Sanity	05/28/89 to 03/11/92	282
9) Dog Log	05/03/91 to 08/02/93	280
10) Alumni Blues	10/10/91 to 04/15/94	279
11) Magilla	05/04/94 to 02/26/97	260
12) Brother	08/02/93 to 08/17/96	257
13) NICU	5/01/92 to 06/23/94	248
14) Slave	10/24/91 to 08/06/93	240
15) Gumbo	07/25/91 to 04/16/93	226

COVER Song Name	Period of Retirement	Lapse
1) Boogie On . . . Woman	03/21/88 to 12/07/97	925
2) Sneaking Sally	05/28/89 to 12/30/97	861
3) Shaggy Dog	11/03/88 to 10/29/95	727
4) Cities	09/08/88 to 07/05/94	627
5) Jump Monk	03/12/88 to 04/24/94	600
6) Have Mercy	10/31/86 to 02/20/93	510
7) Peaches En Regalia	06/23/89 to 12/28/93	502
8) Ride Captain Ride	05/28/89 to 12/12/92	395
9) Touch Me	07/27/91 to 12/03/94	394
10) Satin Doll	02/25/90 to 04/12/93	378
11) Frankenstein	07/26/91 to 06/11/94	329
11) How High the Moon	04/26/90 to 03/08/93	329
13) La Grange	03/17/91 to 12/29/95	307
14) Curtis Lowe	10/30/90 to 03/14/93	296
15) Daniel	08/28/93 to 02/23/97	287

N20

Inspiration: More of an aural fantasy than song, N20 (the chemical name for laughing gas) is created with Fishman on vacuum and the other band members creating appropriate backup noises.

Musical History and Evolution: Though it appeared on Phish's "White Album" circa 1987, N20 didn't make its first concert appearance until 6/25/94 in Cleveland, OH, when the band opened the show with it. It appeared twice more that summer, including 7/8/94 in Mansfield, MA, when it helped serve as the gateway to Gamehendge (with Col. Forbin sitting in a dentist's chair).

Rotation History: Three times on summer tour 1994, but not seen since.

Discography: Has not yet appeared on a Phish album, though it can be found on their "White Album."

N20 [3] [N20]

By Phish

06/25/94	[672]1	*OP1	Rift	
07/08/94	9	1	Llama	Lizards
07/16/94	6	1	DWD	Stash
>> 12/31/97	**279**			

NICU

Originally introduced on 3/6/92 as "In an Intensive Care Unit" (a name which may have been a play on a lyric in the song, "And I see you"), this song is now called NICU (pronounced N-I-C-U). NICU is apparently not meant as an acronym for anything, although fans have pointed out that the initials N.I.C.U. do substitute for "Neonatal Intensive Care Unit" in hospitals. Some, in fact, claim that it is sung from the perspective of a newborn baby, although others say the lyrics of the song seem to have no bearing on hospitals at all.

Musical History and Evolution: NICU went through a number of musical revisions during spring tour 1992—the original version, debuted in March 1992, moved slower than the current one, offering more of a reggae feel; the band accelerated it during April 1992, then gave up on the song altogether for a while. The version reintroduced in summer 1994 omitted the lyrical "da-da-da-da" bridge between the end of the verses and the last section of refrains that had been added in April 1992. Now, NICU features quick, ska-like guitar strumming, while the original picked out the melody with a slow lead.

Rotation History: After its appearance on 5/1/92 in Milwaukee, WI, NICU didn't appear in concert again until 6/23/94 in Pontiac, MI, when the band unexpectedly brought it back. It appeared sporadically in 1995 and 1996, then more often in 1997 as the band fashioned it into a frequent show and set opener.

Discography: Has not yet appeared on a Phish album.

NICU [52] [NICU]

By Anastasio/Marshall

03/06/92	[384]	2	Bouncing	Possum
03/11/92	2	2	Llama	Sloth
03/19/92	5	2	Chalkdust	MSO
03/26/92	5	1	Uncle Pen	Bowie
04/06/92	9	2	Weekapaug	Llama
04/12/92	3	2	Lawn Boy	Rosie
04/13/92	1	1	Landlady	Fee
04/15/92	1	2	Landlady	Rosie
04/19/92	4	1	BurAlive	Stash
04/21/92	1	1	Eliza	Bouncing
04/23/92	2	2	Lizards	Horn
05/01/92	5	1	Landlady	Sloth
06/23/94	248	1	Split&Melt	Foam
06/25/94	2	1	Julius	Stash
07/01/94	4	1	Sample	Stash
07/03/94	2	1	Fee	Horn
07/13/94	6	2	Cavern	Tweezer
10/26/94	19	1	It's Ice	Antelope
11/28/94	20	2	Suzie	Tweezer
12/01/94	2	2	Makisupa	Tweezer
12/28/94	9	2	Suzie	Mike's
12/31/94	3	1	Golgi	Antelope
06/14/95	7	1	Gumbo	Mound
06/26/95	10	1	Bathtub	Sloth
10/06/95	14	2	Theme	Tweezer
10/22/95	11	1	Weigh	FEFY
10/29/95	5	1	Split&Melt	Gumbo
11/30/95	17	1	Julius	Bathtub
12/09/95	7	1	Theme	Sloth
12/14/95	3	2	Halley's	Slave
12/29/95	5	1	Fog	Stash
07/12/96	12	2	PurplRain	Slave
08/16/96	20	3	DWD	Life Mars
10/25/96	9	2	TMWSIY	Free
11/03/96	6	1	Sloth	Sample
11/29/96	16	1	Frankstein	CTB
12/28/96	6	1	RunJim	Wolfman's
02/14/97	5	1	RunJim	YEM
02/18/97	3	1	RunJim	Stash
02/22/97	3	1	Theme	Circus
03/18/97	7	1	CinnGirl	Sample
06/14/97	2	1	DWD	Dirt
06/24/97	6	2	Reba	Twist
07/23/97	14	1	Dirt	Dogs Stole
07/30/97	4	1	*OP1	Wolfman's
08/06/97	4	1	*OP1	Stash
08/17/97	8	3	BuffaloBill	Weigh
11/16/97	3	1	*OP1	My Soul
11/23/97	5	1	Stash	Fluffhead
11/30/97	4	2	*OP2	Stash
12/13/97	9	2	*OP2	PYITE
12/29/97	3	1	*OP1	Golgi
>> 12/31/97	**1**			

NO DOGS ALLOWED

Inspiration: Another Anastasio family creation, No Dogs Allowed is an oldie written by Trey in collaboration with his mother, who penned the lyrics.

Musical History and Evolution: Little to speak of.

Rotation History: Appeared in Phish setlists in 1988 and 1989, but not yet in the 1990s.

Discography: Has not yet appeared on a Phish album.

No Dogs Allowed [3] [No Dogs]

By Anastasio

07/23/88	[46]	1	Bold	*CL1
10/20/89	85	2	*OP2	WalkAway
10/26/89	3	2	In a Hole	Bowie
>> 12/31/97	**832**			

OBLIVIOUS FOOL

Inspiration: Tom Marshall's lyrics apparently reference a person with delusions of herodom.

Musical History and Evolution: Not much yet, as the band played it only five times in 1997. Less funk-jam oriented than many of the new songs, Oblivious Fool fits easily into the rock 'n' roll genre.

Rotation History: After four appearances on the summer tour (far less than many of the new songs got) Oblivious Fool only was played once on the 1997 fall tour, in Denver, CO, on 11/17/97.

Discography: Has not yet appeared on a Phish album.

Oblivious Fool [6] [Oblivious]

By Anastasio/Marshall

06/13/97	[904]	2	Ghost	Char Zero
06/16/97	1	1	Wolfman's	*CL1
06/25/97	6	1	*OP1	Dogs Stole
07/10/97	9	1	Lizards	*CL1
07/29/97	7	2	*OP2	Antelope
11/17/97	17	2	DWD	Johnny B.
>> 12/31/97	**21**			

THE OH KEE PA CEREMONY

Inspiration: A Native American rite of passage takes on a slightly different meaning in the world of Phish. For young men in some Native American tribes, the Oh Kee Pa ritual involved body piercing as a test of willpower to overcome pain. Phish adapted this for the twentieth century by sequestering themselves in a room, usually about once a year in the 1980s, and just jam for hours on end. They termed this "The Oh Kee Pa Ceremony" and affixed the title to a short instrumental piece that may have arisen from one of the sessions; Union Federal, on *Junta*, is a direct recording of a 25-minute segment of a much longer Oh Kee Pa Ceremony from 1988–89.

Musical History and Evolution: As a composed piece, Oh Kee Pa has changed little since its debut.

Rotation History: Heavily played in the early 1990s, when it frequently served as a segue into Suzie Greenberg, AC/DC Bag, and, on several occasions, Llama, Oh Kee Pa has been played far less in recent years (once in 1996, twice in 1997).

Discography: Appears on *Lawn Boy* (1990).

The Oh Kee Pa Ceremony [161] [Oh Kee]

By Anastasio

08/17/89	[116]	1	Ya Mar	McGrupp
08/19/89	2	1	*OP1	Suzie
09/09/89	6	1	Foam	Suzie
10/01/89	1	1	Ya Mar	Suzie
10/20/89	6	1	YEM	Reba
10/22/89	2	1	YEM	Suzie
10/26/89	1	1	*OP1	Golgi
10/31/89	2	1	*OP1	Suzie
11/02/89	1	2	*OP2	Golgi
11/09/89	3	2	*OP2	ACDCBag
11/10/89	1	1	Split&Melt	Suzie
11/11/89	1	1a	*OP1	Golgi
11/16/89	1	1	Foam	Suzie
11/30/89	2	1	Ya Mar	ACDCBag
12/07/89	4	2	*OP2	Suzie
12/08/89	1	1	*OP1	Suzie
12/29/89	4	1	Ya Mar	ACDCBag
12/31/89	2	1	YEM	ACDCBag
01/20/90	1	1a	*OP1	Suzie
01/27/90	3	1	Ya Mar	ACDCBag
02/09/90	8	1	Golgi	Suzie
02/10/90	1	1	Dinner	Suzie
02/15/90	1	1	Carolina	Suzie
02/17/90	2	1a	*OP1	Suzie
02/23/90	2	2	Tela	Suzie
03/03/90	5	1	Lizards	ACDCBag
03/07/90	1	2	*OP2	ACDCBag
03/08/90	1	1	Carolina	Suzie
03/09/90	1	1	Reba	ACDCBag
03/17/89	2	2	Bold	ACDCBag
03/28/90	1	1	Uncle Pen	Suzie
04/05/90	2	1	Carolina	Suzie
04/06/90	1	1	Dinner	Suzie
04/08/90	2	1	Brain	Suzie
04/13/90	4	1	La Grange	ACDCBag
04/18/90	1	2	WalkAway	Bold
04/20/90	2	2	Fee	ACDCBag
04/22/90	2	1	Uncle Pen	Suzie
04/26/90	2	2	Bathtub	Suzie
04/28/90	1	1	Adeline	Suzie
05/04/90	3	2	Bathtub	Mike's
05/10/90	2	2	Reba	ACDCBag
05/11/90	1	2	*OP2	ACDCBag
05/13/90	2	1	Bathtub	ACDCBag
05/15/90	1	1	Tweezer	Suzie
05/19/90	1	2	Reba	Suzie
05/23/90	1	1	Brain	Suzie
05/24/90	1	1	YEM	ACDCBag
05/31/90	1	1a	Divided	Suzie
06/01/90	1	1a	Possum	Suzie
06/05/90	1	1	Ya Mar	Suzie
06/09/90	3	2	Foam	Suzie
06/16/90	1	3	Foam	Suzie
09/13/90	1	2	GDS	ACDCBag
09/15/90	2	1	Tube	ACDCBag
09/22/90	4	1	Tela	Suzie
09/28/90	1	1	Bouncing	Suzie
10/01/90	1	1	Tweezer	Suzie
10/05/90	2	1	Tela	Suzie
10/06/90	2	1a	YEM	Suzie
10/08/90	2	1	YEM	Possum
10/31/90	4	2	Fee	Suzie
11/03/90	2	1	Sqirm Coil	Suzie
11/04/90	1	2	RunJim	Suzie
11/08/90	1	2	Tweezer	Dinner
11/17/90	3	1	Eliza	Suzie
11/24/90	1	1	Lizards	Suzie
11/30/90	2	E	Caravan	Suzie
12/07/90	3	2	Sqirm Coil	Suzie
12/28/90	2	2	Manteca	MSO
12/29/90	1	1	Horn	Suzie
02/02/91	3	1	*OP1	Suzie
02/03/91	1	2	Bouncing	Suzie
02/14/91	4	1	Lawn Boy	Golgi
02/15/91	1	2	MSO	ACDCBag
02/26/91	8	1	Reba	ACDCBag
02/27/91	1	2	Lawn Boy	Sloth
03/01/91	2	E	*OPE	Suzie
03/07/91	3	2	*OP2	Landlady
03/13/91	3	2	Terrapin	Golgi
03/15/91	1	1	Bouncing	ACDCBag
03/16/91	1	1	Mockbird	Suzie
03/22/91	3	2	*OP2	Suzie
03/23/91	1	2	Bathtub	ACDCBag
03/28/91	1	1a	Sqirm Coil	Suzie
04/04/91	5	1	*OP1	Suzie
04/05/91	1	E	Fee	Suzie
04/12/91	3	1	Guelah	Suzie
04/16/91	3	1	Mango	ACDCBag
04/18/91	1	2	Reba	Sloth
04/20/91	2	2	Tweezer	Suzie
04/21/91	1	1	MSO	ACDCBag
04/22/91	1	1	Guelah	Suzie
05/04/91	6	1	*OP1	Suzie
05/11/91	3	2	Reba	Suzie
05/12/91	1	2	Sqirm Coil	ACDCBag
05/17/91	2	1	PoorHeart	Suzie
05/18/91	1	2	*OP2	Suzie
05/25/91	1	1a	Llama	ACDCBag
07/11/91	1	1	*OP1	ACDCBag
07/12/91	1	2	Touch Me	Suzie
07/13/91	1	1	Llama	Suzie
07/15/91	2	1a	*OP1	Suzie
07/20/91	3	1	Llama	Suzie
07/23/91	2	1	MSO	Suzie
07/27/91	4	1a	Foam	Suzie
09/27/91	4	2	Dinner	Suzie
09/29/91	2	1a	YEM	Suzie
10/02/91	1	2	Stash	Suzie
10/06/91	4	1	PoorHeart	ACDCBag
10/10/91	1	2	Sparkle	Suzie
10/15/91	4	2	Llama	Suzie
10/17/91	1	2	Curtain	Suzie
10/19/91	2	2	YEM	Terrapin
10/24/91	2	1	*OP1	Suzie
10/28/91	3	1	Tube	Foam
03/06/92	27	1	It's Ice	Divided
03/14/92	5	2	Bouncing	Suzie
03/19/92	2	2	Stash	Suzie
03/21/92	2	2	BurAlive	Suzie
03/24/92	1	2	IDK	Suzie
03/26/92	2	2	BurAlive	Suzie
03/30/92	3	E	Sl Monkey	Suzie
04/09/92	8	2	*OP2	Suzie
04/15/92	3	1	*OP1	Suzie
04/18/92	3	2	Glide	Suzie
04/29/92	7	2	Mound	Llama
05/03/92	4	2	Bouncing	Suzie
05/16/92	10	2	Silent	ACDCBag
07/09/92	11	1a	Glide	Suzie
07/15/92	5	1	Glide	Suzie
07/31/92	13	1a	Bouncing	Suzie
08/02/92	2	1a	Rift	Suzie
11/22/92	18	1	BurAlive	Suzie
12/10/92	14	2	Love You	Suzie
12/29/92	5	1	Tela	Suzie
02/22/93	19	2	YEM	Llama
03/08/93	9	1	Guelah	Llama
03/17/93	6	1	It's Ice	Suzie
03/26/93	7	2	BBJ	Suzie
04/17/93	15	2	Life Boy	Suzie
04/29/93	9	1	Fee	Antelope
07/17/93	13	1	Silent	Bowie
07/18/93	1	2	FEFY	Fee
08/02/93	11	1	Brother	Suzie
08/13/93	8	2	Life Boy	Suzie
12/28/93	11	1	Esther	Suzie
04/04/94	4	2	BeLikeYou	Suzie
04/11/94	6	2	AmGrace	Suzie
04/15/94	3	2	If I Could	Suzie
04/18/94	3	1	Dog Faced	ACDCBag
05/06/94	13	1	DWD	ACDCBag
05/29/94	18	2	McGrupp	Suzie
10/26/94	45	1	Scent	Suzie
11/23/94	17	1	If I Could	Suzie
06/09/95	21	1	Str Design	ACDCBag
11/24/95	56	1	*OP1	ACDCBag
08/12/96	48	1	Taste	Suzie
02/21/97	50	2	Wilson	ACDCBag
03/01/97	6	1	Cities	DWD
>> 12/31/97	**65**			

PIPER

Inspiration: Tom Marshall's three-line lyrics, repeated over and over again in the song, seem to mesh perfectly with a building jam composed by Trey. Though many initially thought it was called "Words," Trey clarified the correct title in Virginia Beach, VA, on 7/21/97.

Musical History and Evolution: One of the crop of new songs debuted on summer tour 1997, the song has quickly become a band and fan favorite. During the summer tour, a composed intro jam led to a peak and the lyrics, then the jam faded out rather quickly. On fall tour 1997, the band began stretching Piper out further, adding a more spacey introduction before the composed jam, and returning again to the lyrical refrain in the midst of a new outro jam. This song is definitely a work in progress, but it was played at some of the most climactic moments of fall 1997 shows.

Rotation History: Commonly played throughout summer and fall 1997.

Discography: Has not yet appeared on a Phish album.

Piper [15] [Piper]
By Anastasio/Marshall

06/14/97	[905]	2	Twist	Saw It
06/19/97	2	2	Wading	Jesus
06/24/97	4	2	Twist	Wading
06/25/97	1	2	DWD	DWD
07/03/97	5	1	*OP1	My Soul
07/05/97	1	1a	Twist	Harry
07/21/97	5	1	Dogs Stole	Dirt
07/30/97	6	1	Weigh	CTB
08/11/97	8	2	Timber Ho	Vultures
11/14/97	6	2	Wolfman's	Twist
11/22/97	5	2	BE Katy	Antelope
11/30/97	5	2	Free	Circus
12/06/97	4	2	Twist	Sl Monkey
12/12/97	4	2	Saw It	SweptAway
12/31/97	5	2	Mike's	Circus
>> 12/31/97		0		

POOR HEART

Inspiration: Written by Mike in the 1980s after his four-track recording machine that he was using to complete his senior film project was ripped off, the lyrics originally referred to someone stealing "my four-track" instead of "my poor heart." (The line "You won't steal my tape recorder" survived lyrics revisions in the early 1990s). There's a third verse which has never been performed in concert by Phish.

Musical History and Evolution: The original four-track version of Poor Heart was never performed live by Phish; indeed, to make the song concert-worthy, Mike changed the lyrics around for the song's concert debut in spring 1991. Initially, the band seemed to struggle somewhat with the song, unsure how to play it; for parts of 1991, Fishman added a drum-based intro preceding the first guitar line that was later dropped. By 1992, the song had evolved into its current form. However, on fall tour 1995, the band debuted a slower version of Poor Heart that surfaced in concert a handful of times (on 11/19/95, 11/22/95, and 11/25/95 in Hampton, VA, the great "Poor Heartfest," when the original Poor Heart opened the show, the slow Poor Heart closed the second set, and the band teased both versions before the encore).

Rotation History: Played virtually every third show from 1991 through 1996 (and even more often in 1993), the standard version of Poor Heart took a bit of a rest in 1997, appearing only eleven times. The slow version of Poor Heart hasn't appeared since 11/25/95.

Discography: Standard version appears on *A Picture of Nectar* (1992).

Poor Heart [241] [PoorHeart]
By Gordon

04/22/91	[305]	1	Reba	Llama
04/26/91	2	1	Fluffhead	Foam
05/02/91	2	2	Chalkdust	Divided
05/10/91	4	2	Wilson	Foam
05/11/91	1	2	YEM	Reba
05/12/91	1	2	Bathtub	Curtain
05/17/91	2	1	Reba	Oh Kee
07/18/91	8	2	Reba	Split&Melt
07/21/91	3	1	Guelah	Split&Melt
07/25/91	3	2	Llama	Jesus
07/27/91	2	1a	Cavern	Stash
08/03/91	1	1	Sqirm Coil	Sloth
09/25/91	1	1	Brother	Foam
09/26/91	1	E	Memories	Adeline
09/28/91	2	2	Lizards	Mike's
09/29/91	1	1a	It's Ice	Landlady
10/02/91	1	1	Sqirm Coil	Cavern
10/04/91	2	1	Reba	Cavern
10/06/91	2	1	Bouncing	Oh Kee
10/10/91	1	2	Reba	Cavern
10/11/91	1	2	Sloth	Magilla
10/15/91	3	2	RunJim	Llama
10/17/91	1	1	Cavern	Stash
10/19/91	2	2	Horn	YEM
10/24/91	2	1	Foam	Stash
10/28/91	3	1	Cavern	Reba
11/01/91	3	2	Cavern	TweezRep
11/08/91	4	1	Stash	Divided
11/09/91	1	2	Fluffhead	It's Ice
11/15/91	5	2	Bathtub	Mike's
11/21/91	4	1	Bouncing	Guelah
11/23/91	2	2	Horn	Tweezer
12/04/91	3	1	Cavern	Brother
03/06/92	5	2	My Friend	Stash
03/13/92	4	1	Split&Melt	Guelah
03/17/92	2	2	Sloth	Tweezer
03/21/92	3	2	My Friend	All Things
03/24/92	1	1	Stash	Foam
03/26/92	2	2	Suzie	Brother
04/03/92	6	1	Landlady	Stash
04/05/92	2	1	Wilson	Stash
04/07/92	2	2	*OP2	All Things
04/12/92	2	1	Suzie	Guelah
04/16/92	3	2	Horn	Terrapin
04/18/92	2	1	Guelah	Split&Melt
04/22/92	3	2	YEM	Rosie
04/23/92	1	2	Landlady	Mike's
04/25/92	2	E	Terrapin	*CLE
05/01/92	3	1	My Friend	Landlady
05/05/92	3	2	Silent	Llama
05/07/92	2	1	Suzie	BurAlive
05/09/92	2	E	*OPE	TweezRep
05/12/92	2	2	Terrapin	Llama
05/14/92	1	1	Reba	My Friend
05/16/92	2	2	Rosie	TweezRep
05/17/92	1	1	Mango	Chalkdust
05/18/92	1	1	Foam	Horn
07/14/92	13	1	IDK	Cavern
07/16/92	2	1	*OP1	It's Ice
07/19/92	3	1a	*OP1	Maze
07/22/92	2	1a	Reba	Bouncing
08/01/92	8	1a	Foam	Stash
08/14/92	3	1a	*OP1	Stash
08/17/92	2	1	BurAlive	Landlady
08/24/92	4	1a	BurAlive	All Things
08/28/92	3	1a	*OP1	Foam
11/19/92	4	2	BBJ	FEFY
11/21/92	2	1	Glide	It's Ice
11/23/92	2	2	*OP2	Stash
11/25/92	1	1	BurAlive	Landlady
11/27/92	1	2	Axilla	Possum
11/30/92	2	1	Bouncing	Stash
12/02/92	2	1	FEFY	Stash
12/04/92	2	1	Foam	Stash
12/05/92	1	2	*OP2	Tweezer
12/07/92	2	1	Axilla	Maze
12/10/92	2	1	Fee	Split&Melt
12/12/92	2	1	Split&Melt	All Things
12/28/92	2	2	*OP2	Split&Melt
12/31/92	3	1	BurAlive	Maze
02/03/93	1	1	My Friend	Guelah
02/05/93	2	1	IDK	Reba
02/07/93	2	1	BurAlive	It's Ice
02/09/93	1	1	Bouncing	My Friend
02/11/93	2	1	BurAlive	Stash
02/12/93	1	2	Reba	BBJ
02/13/93	1	1	Bouncing	It's Ice
02/15/93	1	2	Wedge	BBJ
02/18/93	2	1	Guelah	Tweezer
02/19/93	1	1	My Friend	Bowie
02/22/93	3	1	Guelah	Maze
02/23/93	1	E	Adeline	*CLE
02/25/93	1	1	BurAlive	Cavern
02/27/93	2	2	Stash	Sample
03/02/93	1	1	BurAlive	Stash
03/05/93	2	1	BurAlive	Cavern
03/06/93	1	E	Adeline	TweezRep
03/08/93	1	2	*OP2	Cavern
03/12/93	2	1	BurAlive	Cavern
03/16/93	3	1	BurAlive	It's Ice
03/18/93	2	2	My Friend	Split&Melt
03/21/93	2	1	Split&Melt	PYITE
03/24/93	2	1	Fee	Maze
03/27/93	3	2	Rosie	Golgi
03/30/93	2	1	BurAlive	All Things
04/01/93	2	2	Tweezer	BBJ
04/02/93	1	1	BurAlive	Foam
04/05/93	2	2	Axilla	Caravan
04/12/93	3	1	Bouncing	Stash
04/14/93	2	1	BurAlive	Maze
04/18/93	3	2	*OP2	Tweezer
04/21/93	2	1	BurAlive	Foam
04/24/93	3	1	Guelah	Stash
04/27/93	2	1	BurAlive	Foam
04/30/93	2	1	Bouncing	Stash
05/02/93	2	1	Silent	Maze
05/05/93	2	2	My Friend	Weigh
05/07/93	2	1	BurAlive	Split&Melt
05/30/93	3	1a	Guelah	Foam
07/16/93	2	2	YEM	PurplRain
07/18/93	2	2	Also Sprac	Antelope
07/22/93	2	1	Ya Mar	Stash
07/23/93	1	2	Also Sprac	Antelope
07/28/93	4	1	Silent	Cavern
07/30/93	2	2	Silent	Fluffhead
08/02/93	2	1	Guelah	Brother
08/03/93	1	E	*OPE	Freebird
08/06/93	1	1	Split&Melt	Curtain
08/07/93	1	1	Bouncing	Stash
08/12/93	4	1	Silent	Sqirm Coil
08/14/93	2	1	Esther	Cavern
08/16/93	2	2	My Friend	BBJ
08/20/93	2	1	Harpua	Maze
08/21/93	1	1	BurAlive	Foam
08/24/93	1	E	Halley's	Adeline
12/28/93	4	1	Peaches	Split&Melt
12/31/93	3	2	Halley's	It's Ice
04/06/94	3	1	Guelah	Stash
04/11/94	4	1	Caravan	Foam
04/13/94	1	1	BurAlive	Stash
04/16/94	3	2	Sample	Tweezer
04/18/94	2	1	Glide	Julius
04/20/94	1	2	*OP2	Antelope
04/23/94	3	1	Peaches	Stash
04/25/94	2	1	Tela	Split&Melt
04/30/94	3	1	Stash	Sample
05/06/94	4	1	ACDCBag	My Friend
05/10/94	3	1	BurAlive	Sample
05/16/94	4	1	BurAlive	Sample
05/19/94	2	1	My Friend	Stash
05/26/94	6	1	BurAlive	Cavern
05/28/94	2	E	*OPE	*CLE
06/13/94	5	1	BurAlive	Sample
06/17/94	3	2	Sample	Mike's
06/21/94	3	2	Fire	DWD
06/23/94	2	1	BurAlive	Split&Melt
06/24/94	1	2	Dog Faced	Cavern
06/29/94	3	2	Landlady	Tweezer
06/30/94	1	E	Sl Monkey	*CLE
07/03/94	3	1	My Friend	DWD
07/06/94	2	2	Landlady	Tweezer
07/09/94	2	2	Fluffhead	Tweezer
07/13/94	2	1	BurAlive	Sample
10/07/94	4	1	Glide	Divided
10/09/94	2	E	Sl Monkey	*CLE
10/12/94	2	1	Sloth	Split&Melt
10/16/94	4	2	Landlady	Julius
10/18/94	1	1	IDK	Stash
10/23/94	4	1	Simple	Stash
10/27/94	3	1	Silent	Cavern
10/31/94	3	3	Sl Monkey	Antelope
11/03/94	2	2	Simple	Julius
11/14/94	4	2	Slave	Julius
11/18/94	3	2	Life Boy	Tweezer
11/22/94	3	1	BurAlive	Horn
11/26/94	3	1	Silent	Cavern
11/30/94	2	1	Frankstein	My Friend
12/02/94	2	1	*OP1	Also Sprac
12/06/94	3	2	Also Sprac	Mike's
12/09/94	3	2	Wilson	Tweezer
12/10/94	1	2	DoInRoad	Slave
12/30/94	3	2	Sample	Tweezer
06/08/95	4	2	Life Boy	Julius
06/14/95	4	2	Also Sprac	Tweezer
06/19/95	4	1	Theme	ACDCBag
06/26/95	6	2	Free	YEM
06/28/95	1	2	Sample	Tweezer
07/03/95	5	1	My Friend	Antelope
09/28/95	2	2	Theme	Wanna Go
10/02/95	3	1	*OP1	Wolfman's
10/06/95	3	2	*OP2	Maze
10/15/95	6	1	BurAlive	Slave
10/19/95	2	2	Frankstein	Mike's
10/22/95	3	1	It's Ice	Sample
10/27/95	3	2	Dog Faced	Simple
10/29/95	2	1	BurAlive	Julius
11/11/95	4	1	DayinLife	Weekapaug
11/15/95	3	1	*OP1	ACDCBag
11/19/95	3	1	Maze	Rift
11/22/95	2	E	*OPE	Frankstein
11/25/95	2	1	*OP1	DayinLife
11/25/95	0	2	HelloBaby	*CL2
11/29/95	2	2	Fog	I'm Blue
12/01/95	2	1	Theme	Wolfman's
12/05/95	3	2	*OP2	Bathtub
12/08/95	2	1	Sample	Simple
12/17/95	7	1	My Friend	DayinLife
12/29/95	2	1	My Friend	DWD
06/06/96	4	1	Split&Melt	RunJim
07/06/96	3	1a	Reba	DayinLife
07/09/96	2	1a	Theme	Taste
07/13/96	4	1a	Reba	Split&Melt
07/22/96	6	1a	Sample	Cavern
07/25/96	3	1a	*OP1	PYITE
08/02/96	1	1	Guelah	Foam
08/05/96	2	1	Wilson	Guelah
08/10/96	3	1	My Friend	ACDCBag
08/14/96	3	1	Fee	Reba
10/16/96	3	1	BurAlive	Billy
10/23/96	6	1	PYITE	ACDCBag
10/29/96	4	1	Billy	Bowie
11/06/96	4	1	Train Song	PYITE
11/09/96	3	1	BurAlive	Sloth
11/16/96	5	1	*OP1	DWD
11/18/96	1	1	Timber Ho	Taste
11/24/96	4	1	*OP1	ACDCBag
12/01/96	4	1	Peaches	Cavern
12/06/96	3	1	Peaches	Also Sprac
12/29/96	2	1	*OP1	Caravan
02/13/97	3	1	Waste	CharZero
02/26/97	10	1	BurAlive	Ha Ha Ha
06/16/97	7	E	Cities	*CLE
06/21/97	3	1a	Also Sprac	Taste
06/27/97	4	1a	Dogs Stole	Taste

07/05/97	5	1a	Love You	CharZero
07/09/97	2	2	Ghost	*CL2
07/26/97	7	1	Dogs Stole	Stash
08/13/97	11	1	Amarina	Water
11/16/97	6	1	Scent	Taste
11/26/97	6	2	Caspian	TweezRep
>> 12/31/97	**16**			

POSSUM

Inspiration: Originally written by Jeff Holdsworth about a truck driver's encounter with a possum, Trey reworked the lyrics in the mid 1980s to turn it into a Gamehendge song. Told from the perspective of Icculus looking down from his mountain perch at a possum on the road, its actual title is apparently "Oh! Possum," but it has fallen out of use among fans.

Musical History and Evolution: In its earliest days, Possum featured Jeff on lead vocals and made use of his rhythm guitar as an integral part of the song's jam. After his departure from Phish, the band reworked the song, with Mike taking over on lead vocals and the jam evolving to fit the band's new lineup. For much of 1992, the song's drumbeat introduction was stretched out with secret language symbols and, on several occasions, secret language lessons from Trey. Some popular versions of this great jam tune include 4/5/92 Boulder, CO, long intro jam; 4/30/92 Madison, WI, a fierce jam; 5/17/92 Schenectady, NY, an incredible version replete with numerous teases; 7/15/92 Charlottesville, VA, 15-minute encore with vacuum freeze; 12/28/93 Washington, D.C., with "Kashmir" jam; 4/30/94 Orlando, FL, with tease medley; 5/27/94 San Francisco, CA, with audience on macaroni; and 6/26/95 Saratoga Springs, NY, with "Heartbreaker" jam.

Rotation History: Very frequently played in the late 1980s and 1990, Possum settled into a roughly every-third-show groove from 1991 through 1993. It's less common than that now, appearing ten times in 1996 and only seven times in 1997.

Discography: Has yet to appear on a Phish album.

Oh Possum [291] [Possum]

By Holdsworth, with lyrics reworked by Anastasio

10/30/85	[4]	1a	Dog Log	Slave
04/15/86	3	1a	Dog Log	YEM
03/06/87	4	2	Tell Me	FWorld
03/11/87	1	1a	Lushngton	Sally
04/24/87	2	1a	ACDCBag	Fluffhead
05/11/87	2	1a	YEM	Slave
08/10/87	2	1	ACDCBag	Fluffhead
08/29/87	3	2	McGrupp	Harry
09/12/87	2	1	ACDCBag	YEM
09/27/87	1	1	A-Train	Phase
10/14/87	1	1	Fluffhead	*CL1
11/19/87	2	2	Suzie	Divided
01/30/88	1	1	ACDCBag	Jesus
03/12/88	4	1a	Sloth	Antelope
03/21/88	1	1a	ACDCBag	Dinner
03/31/88	1	1	ACDCBag	Fluffhead
05/15/88	3	1a	ACDCBag	Icculus
05/23/88	1	1a	Peaches	GTBT
06/18/88	3	1	FunkBitch	Golgi
07/23/88	5	1	ACDCBag	WalkAway
09/08/88	6	2	*OP2	YEM
09/24/88	2	2	WalkAway	Fee
10/12/88	1	2	ACDCBag	GTBT
10/29/88	1	3	YEM	*CL3
11/03/88	1	1	Fluffhead	Fee
11/05/88	1	1	YEM	A-Train
11/11/88	1	1	Foam	Forbin's
01/26/89	2	1a	Sloth	Contact
02/07/89	4	1	Sloth	Mike's
02/18/89	2	1a	WalkAway	GTBT
03/03/89	2	2	Fee	WalkAway
03/04/89	1	2	*OP2	Fluffhead
04/14/89	8	1	Sloth	*CL1
04/20/89	3	1	Sloth	McGrupp
04/30/89	5	E	*OP1	*CL2
05/06/89	4	1	Sloth	Bold
05/09/89	3	1	Sloth	Divided
05/13/89	3	1	Fluffhead	Foam
05/20/89	4	1	IDK	*CL1
05/26/89	2	3	Curtis	Jam
05/28/89	2	2	A-Train	Contact
06/23/89	5	2	Split&Melt	Bowie
06/30/89	2	1	McGrupp	Donna
08/12/89	3	1a	YEM	Icculus
08/17/89	2	3	PYITE	Halley's
08/26/89	4	1	YEM	*CL1
09/09/89	4	2	WalkAway	*CL2
10/01/89	1	2	Fluffhead	YEM
10/06/89	1	1a	Harry	HwayHell
10/07/89	1	2	Dinner	Lizards
10/14/89	3	2	HwayHell	Harpua
10/22/89	3	2	Fee	*CL2
10/26/89	1	2	Fluffhead	PYITE
10/31/89	2	1	Bathtub	*CL1
11/10/89	5	2	Brain	Harpua
11/30/89	4	2	Reba	Forbin's
12/07/89	4	2	Lawn Boy	Undone
12/08/89	1	2	YEM	Lawn Boy
12/15/89	2	1a	IDK	Divided
12/16/89	1	E	*OPE	*CLE
02/10/90	16	1	Bouncing	Carolina
02/23/90	5	1	YEM	Foam
02/24/90	1	1	Esther	IDK
02/25/90	1	1	Rift	*CL1
03/01/90	1	1	YEM	*CL1
03/03/90	2	1	YEM	*CL1
03/07/90	1	1	Reba	Esther
03/08/90	1	1	YEM	Ya Mar
03/09/90	1	1	Sloth	Donna
03/28/90	3	1	*OP1	Ya Mar
04/04/90	1	1	A-Train	Foam
04/05/90	1	1	*OP1	Ya Mar
04/07/90	2	1	Bathtub	Tweezer
04/08/90	1	1	Uncle Pen	*CL1
04/12/90	3	1	Uncle Pen	YEM
04/13/90	1	2	Caravan	HwayHell
04/18/90	1	1	A-Train	*CL1
04/20/90	2	1	Mockbird	*CL1
04/22/90	2	1	Suzie	IDK
04/26/90	2	1	*OP1	Foam
04/28/90	1	1	Bouncing	YEM
04/29/90	1	1a	Carolina	Ya Mar
05/04/90	2	1	Bouncing	Reba
05/06/90	1	1	*OP1	Bouncing
05/10/90	1	1	Suzie	*CL1
05/11/90	1	1	Reba	Bouncing
05/13/90	2	2	Adeline	*CL2
05/15/90	3	1	*OP1	Tela
05/19/90	1	2	*OP2	Reba
05/23/90	1	1	Bouncing	Adeline
05/24/90	1	2	Dinner	IDK
05/31/90	1	1a	*OP1	YEM
06/01/90	1	1a	Slave	Oh Kee
06/05/90	1	1	Lawn Boy	*CL1
06/07/90	1	1	Donna	Fee
06/08/90	1	1	*OP1	MSO
06/09/90	1	1	*OP1	Lawn Boy
06/16/90	1	1	Lawn Boy	*CL1
09/13/90	1	1	Bouncing	*CL1
09/15/90	2	2	Lawn Boy	*CL2
09/22/90	4	2	Lawn Boy	*CL2
10/01/90	2	1	*OP1	Sqirm Coil
10/04/90	1	1	Esther	Sqirm Coil
10/05/90	1	2	Fee	*CL2
10/06/90	1	1a	Esther	Brain
10/08/90	2	1	Oh Kee	*CL1
10/12/90	1	2	*OP2	Fee
10/30/90	2	1	Sqirm Coil	*CL1
10/31/90	1	1	BurAlive	Sqirm Coil
11/02/90	1	1	BurAlive	*CL1
11/03/90	1	2	Reba	Love You
11/08/90	2	1	Landlady	Lizards
11/10/90	1	2	Bike	*CL2
11/16/90	1	2	IDK	*CL2
11/17/90	1	2	Love You	Lawn Boy
11/24/90	1	1	BurAlive	Foam
11/30/90	2	1	Llama	*CL1
12/28/90	5	2	Landlady	Sqirm Coil
12/31/90	2	1	BurAlive	*CL1
02/07/91	4	1	Bouncing	Sqirm Coil
02/14/91	3	2	Landlady	*CL2
02/16/91	2	E2	*OPE2	*CL2
02/26/91	7	2	Destiny	Lizards
02/27/91	1	2	Love You	*CL2
03/01/91	2	2	Sloth	Love You
03/06/91	2	1	Sqirm Coil	Cavern
03/07/91	1	2	Reba	IDK
03/15/91	4	2	BurAlive	Horn
03/16/91	1	E	Manteca	*CLE
03/23/91	4	1	Mockbird	Rocky Top
04/04/91	6	E	Mockbird	Carolina
04/06/91	2	1	Antelope	Jesus
04/11/91	1	E	Fee	*CLE
04/15/91	3	2	Lizards	Magilla
04/18/91	2	2	Sqirm Coil	*CL2
04/21/91	3	2	*OP2	Fee
04/26/91	3	1	Sloth	Fluffhead
04/27/91	1	2	Curtain	TMWSIY
05/02/91	2	2	BurAlive	*CL2
05/04/91	2	2	Rocky Top	*CL2
05/10/91	2	1	Lizards	Stash
05/17/91	4	2	*OP2	Guelah
05/18/91	1	1	Cavern	*CL1
05/25/91	1	E	*OPE	*CLE
07/14/91	4	1	IDK	*CL1
07/18/91	2	2	IDK	*CL2
07/20/91	2	E	*OPE	*CLE
07/24/91	3	2	*OP2	Guelah
07/27/91	3	1a	TMWSIY	IDK
08/03/91	1	3	BurAlive	*CL3
09/25/91	1	1	Reba	*CL1
09/27/91	2	2	*OP2	Tela
10/02/91	3	E	*OPE	IDK
10/03/91	1	1	Cavern	*CL1
10/06/91	3	E	Adeline	Llama
10/11/91	2	2	Magilla	*CL2
10/17/91	4	2	Love You	*CL2
10/24/91	4	2	Terrapin	*CL2
10/27/91	2	E	Glide	*CLE
11/02/91	5	1	Mockbird	*CL1
11/07/91	2	E	Glide	*CLE
11/09/91	2	E	Glide	*CLE
11/13/91	3	2	Llama	*CL2
11/15/91	2	2	Bouncing	*CL2
11/20/91	3	1	BurAlive	Forbin's
11/22/91	2	1	*OP1	Cavern
12/05/91	5	1	Bouncing	*CL1
12/06/91	1	2	WhipPost	*CL2
12/31/91	2	1	*OP1	Foam
03/06/92	1	2	NICU	*CL2
03/13/92	4	2	Love You	*CL2
03/14/92	1	2	Rosie	*CL2
03/17/92	1	1	BurAlive	Cavern
03/20/92	2	2	Terrapin	*CL2
03/26/92	4	2	Rosie	*CL2
03/31/92	4	2	Love You	*CL2
04/03/92	2	2	Sloth	Weigh
04/05/92	2	1	It's Ice	Adeline
04/07/92	2	1	BurAlive	It's Ice
04/13/92	3	2	Love You	*CL2
04/16/92	2	1	BurAlive	It's Ice
04/18/92	2	1	Esther	It's Ice
04/21/92	2	1	Guelah	It's Ice
04/23/92	2	1	IDK	*CL1
04/29/92	3	2	Landlady	Mound
05/01/92	2	1	IDK	*CL1
05/03/92	2	1	Landlady	It's Ice
05/07/92	3	1	Guelah	*CL1
05/10/92	3	1a	YEM	*CL1
05/12/92	1	1	Sloth	It's Ice
05/14/92	1	2	Rosie	*CL2
05/17/92	3	2	Curtain	Guelah
06/30/92	7	1a	Guelah	Adeline
07/12/92	6	1a	Glide	*CL1
07/15/92	2	E	*OPE	*CLE
07/21/92	5	1a	All Things	It's Ice
07/30/92	7	1a	IDK	*CL1
11/21/92	20	1	Mockbird	*CL1
11/27/92	4	2	PoorHeart	Glide
12/02/92	4	2	Wilson	Mound
12/04/92	2	2	Esther	It's Ice
12/06/92	2	E	*OPE	*CLE
12/11/92	4	2	Faht	*CL2
12/30/92	5	2	TMWSIY	BBJ
02/03/93	2	2	BBJ	*CL2
02/06/93	3	2	BurAlive	*CL2
02/10/93	3	2	Rosie	*CL2
02/17/93	5	1	BurAlive	Weigh
02/20/93	3	1	Sloth	Weigh
02/23/93	3	2	Terrapin	*CL2
03/05/93	6	1	IDK	*CL1
03/12/93	4	1	Cavern	Guelah
03/21/93	7	1	Lawn Boy	*CL1
03/25/93	3	1	It's Ice	Bouncing
03/28/93	3	2	Love You	*CL2
04/01/93	3	2	Curtain	Fee
04/09/93	4	2	Love You	*CL2
04/13/93	3	1	Sparkle	Forbin's
04/18/93	4	2	Silent	Mound
04/21/93	2	2	*OP2	Mound
04/25/93	4	1	Landlady	Bouncing
04/30/93	3	1	All Things	*CL1
05/03/93	3	1	Mockbird	Lawn Boy
05/06/93	2	1	Fluffhead	Lawn Boy
05/30/93	4	E	*OPE	*CLE
07/15/93	1	2	Life Boy	Faht
07/22/93	5	2	Contact	Paul&Silas
07/29/93	6	1	Mockbird	*CL1
08/08/93	7	2	Fluffhead	BBJ
08/12/93	3	2	Golgi	*CL2
08/16/93	4	1	Axil	Horn
08/21/93	3	2	*OP2	Horn
08/25/93	2	2	BurAlive	Mound
12/28/93	3	1	Fee	*CL1
12/31/93	3	2	Fee	Lawn Boy
04/04/94	1	1	It's Ice	*CL1
04/11/94	6	E	*OPE	*CLE
04/21/94	8	2	BBJ	AmGrace
04/30/94	7	2	McGrupp	PurplRain
05/12/94	8	2	Life Boy	Love You
05/23/94	9	2	YEM	*CL2
05/27/94	3	2	Mike's	*CL2
06/10/94	4	2	Sparkle	BeLikeYou
06/14/94	3	2	Bike	*CL2
07/01/94	13	2	TMWSIY	Terrapin
07/13/94	8	2	*OP2	Cavern
10/09/94	6	2	Contact	*CL2
10/16/94	6	1	Axil	*CL1
10/25/94	6	2	Brain	*CL2
11/02/94	6	2	Axilla 2	Lizards
11/18/94	8	2	Contact	*CL2
11/26/94	6	1	My Friend	Guyute
12/04/94	6	1	Adeline	*CL1
12/08/94	3	2	*OP2	My Mind
12/29/94	4	1	IDK	*CL1
06/07/95	4	1	*OP1	Weigh
06/14/95	5	1	Cavern	All Things
06/19/95	4	2	AArmy	*CL2
06/26/95	6	1	Tela	*CL1
06/30/95	3	2	Also Sprac	Ha Ha Ha
07/03/95	3	2	DayinLife	Sqirm Coil
09/27/95	1	E	*OPE	*CLE
10/07/95	8	1	Mound	Mango
10/11/95	2	2	*OP2	Bathtub
10/19/95	5	2	Suspicious	*CL2
10/22/95	3	2	Golgi	Catapult
10/27/95	3	2	Bouncing	*CL2
10/29/95	2	2	Shaggy	Life Boy
11/12/95	5	2	Rosie	TweezRep
11/16/95	3	2	AmGrace	*CL2
11/29/95	8	2	Simple	YEM
12/02/95	3	1	Bouncing	*CL1
12/07/95	3	1	Bouncing	HelloBaby
12/15/95	6	1	Free	*CL1
12/28/95	3	1	FEFY	*CL1
07/15/96	15	1	Guyute	IDK
08/02/96	9	1	HelloBaby	*CL1
08/07/96	4	2	Mockbird	Life Mars
08/12/96	2	1	Golgi	*CL1
08/17/96	4	3	DayinLife	TweezRep
10/21/96	5	1	Waste	*CL1
10/27/96	5	E	*OPE	Carolina
11/03/96	4	2	Life Mars	TweezRep
11/30/96	17	E	*OPE	*CLE
12/30/96	7	E	*OPE	*CLE
03/01/97	14	1	HelloBaby	*CL1
07/23/97	24	1	Billy	*CL1
07/29/97	3	E	*OPE	*CLE
11/19/97	18	E	*OPE	*CLE
12/03/97	9	2	Bowie	Jam
12/07/97	3	2	Guyute	*CL2
12/29/97	6	2	Bowie	Tube
>> 12/31/97	**2**			

PREP SCHOOL HIPPIE

Inspiration: Trey's prep school background undoubtedly played into the creation of this song, which mocks the phenomenon of wealthy kids setting off to follow the Grateful Dead around. A favorite find on old tapes, the band retired this one long before it could offend a particular segment of their fanbase.

Musical History and Evolution: Not much to speak of, as the song only appears on a handful of tapes from the mid 1980s.

Rotation History: Not heard of since 1986.

Discography: Has not yet appeared on a Phish album.

Prep School Hippie [3] [PrepHipp]

Author Unknown

10/30/85	[4]	1a	Alumni	Skip
04/15/86	3	1a	Reagan	Quinn
12/06/86	3	1a	Sally	Jam
>> 12/31/97	**956**			

PRINCE CASPIAN

Inspiration: The song is named after the C. S. Lewis character that appears in *The Narnia Chronicles*; Tom Marshall's lyrics reference those Lewis works.

Musical History and Evolution: In its original form in 1995, Caspian was a short, nonjammed song that some fans immediately dismissed as a rare Phish clunker. That version featured only the lyrics segment that now forms just the middle of the song. That's because in spring 1996, in recording sessions for *Billy Breathes*, Trey crafted a new instrumental introduction and closing jam which became part of live performances of the song in summer 1996. In 1997, the band frequently brought more energy and passion to the closing jam of this song, often stretching it out for well over ten minutes in the set-closer spot.

Rotation History: Frequently played since its debut on summer tour 1995.

Discography: Appears on *Billy Breathes* (1996).

Prince Caspian [56] [Caspian]

By Anastasio/Marshall

06/08/95	[740]	1	Reba	Chalkdust
06/10/95	2	1	Llama	It's Ice
06/20/95	7	2	Chalkdust	Uncle Pen
06/23/95	2	1	Chalkdust	Reba
07/01/95	7	1	It's Ice	Split&Melt
10/08/95	12	1	I'm Blue	Uncle Pen
10/13/95	2	1	I'm Blue	Split&Melt
10/17/95	3	2	Mound	Fog
10/24/95	5	1	AArmy	Split&Melt
10/28/95	3	1	AArmy	Antelope
11/09/95	3	1	Divided	PYITE
11/15/95	5	1	Rift	Sparkle
11/21/95	4	1	Chalkdust	Divided
12/02/95	8	1	*OP1	RunJim
12/08/95	4	1	AArmy	GTBT
12/11/95	2	1	Stash	Reba
12/30/95	8	1	*OP1	Also Sprac
07/12/96	11	2	It's Ice	Mike's
07/21/96	6	2	Simple	Suzie
08/02/96	5	2	Fluffhead	Horse
08/06/96	3	2	Tweezer	DayinLife
08/12/96	3	2	Simple	McGrupp
10/16/96	5	2	Steep	Antelope
10/19/96	3	1	DWD	Frankstein
10/25/96	4	2	Tube	Timber Ho
10/27/96	2	2	Rift	Ya Mar
10/31/96	2	1	YEM	Reba
11/08/96	5	1	DWD	Reba
11/13/96	3	2	Suzie	YEM
11/15/96	2	1	PYITE	Ginseng
11/22/96	4	2	DWD	Billy
11/30/96	5	1	Uncle Pen	Chalkdust
12/04/96	3	2	Mike's	Sparkle
12/31/96	5	2	Harry	CharZero
02/13/97	1	E	*OPE	Johnny B.
02/17/97	3	2	Suzie	*CL2
02/21/97	3	2	Waste	*CL2
02/25/97	3	2	DWD	La Grange
02/28/97	2	2	Drowned	Frankstein
03/18/97	3	2	Drowned	Bowie
06/14/97	2	1	Free	*CL1
06/19/97	2	2	Jesus	*CL2
06/24/97	4	1	Free	Rocky Top
07/05/97	7	1a	Theme	Twist
07/09/97	2	1	PYITE	Ginseng
07/30/97	9	2	Uncle Pen	*CL2
08/06/97	4	2	Ghost	CTB
08/08/97	1	2	Lovin Cup	Chalkdust
08/17/97	7	3	Scent	*CL3
11/13/97	1	2	PYITE	Bouncing
11/21/97	5	1	Chalkdust	*CL1
11/26/97	3	2	PYITE	PoorHeart
11/29/97	2	2	Harry	Suzie
12/03/97	3	2	Jam	Frankstein
12/12/97	6	2	Steep	Izabella
12/31/97	5	3	Maze	Lovin Cup
>> 12/31/97	**0**			

PUNCH YOU IN THE EYE

Inspiration: Not a part of The Man Who Stepped into Yesterday and not included in live Gamehendge performances, PYITE is nonetheless a Gamehendge song that chronicles an outsider's visit to Gamehendge and his imprisonment by Wilson.

Musical History and Evolution: The song underwent several major rewrites in the 1980s, and its actual title, according to Trey, is "Punch Me in the Eye," but the words used in the lyrics have caught on among tapers and fans, and even Trey now refers to this song by its phan title. The Landlady, which appears mixed into PYITE, was originally part of this song. As such, the correct way to label it is simply PYITE, not PYITE > Landlady > PYITE. Though the changes into Landlady and back into PYITE often sound improvised, they are actually written out, and most versions of PYITE differed little (except for their energy level and technical prowess) between 1993 and 1996. In the summer of 1997, though, the band started stretching out the intro jam, adding several short, funky jams, to crowds' delight.

Rotation History: Played throughout fall 1989, PYITE disappeared after 11/9/89, seemingly never to be heard from again until the band brought it back, following many fan requests, at the Roseland Ballroom in New York, NY, on 2/5/93. The band has played it regularly since then, and it's actually one of the rare oldies to get more play in 1996 and 1997 than in previous years.

Discography: Has not yet appeared on a Phish album.

Punch You in the Eye [78] [PYITE]

By Anastasio

08/17/89	[116]	3	Bold	Possum
08/19/89	2	1	ACDCBag	Rocky Top
09/09/89	6	1	Bathtub	Wilson
10/26/89	10	2	Possum	In a Hole
11/03/89	4	1	YEM	Reba
11/09/89	2	2	McGrupp	Lizards
02/05/93	367	1	Sparkle	IDK
02/09/93	3	2	*OP2	Mike's
02/18/93	7	2	Stash	Mike's
02/21/93	3	1	BurAlive	Uncle Pen
02/23/93	2	2	Lizards	All Things
02/27/93	3	1	Sparkle	Lawn Boy
03/06/93	4	1	Mound	Bouncing
03/09/93	2	1	Glide	IDK
03/14/93	3	1	Reba	RunJim
03/21/93	5	1	PoorHeart	Lawn Boy
03/26/93	4	1	Fee	All Things
03/31/93	4	1	Mound	Sample
04/05/93	4	2	Caravan	Tweezer
04/21/93	10	1	Rift	IDK
05/02/93	9	2	Llama	YEM
07/23/93	14	1	Silent	RunJim
08/08/93	12	1	Silent	FEFY
12/30/93	17	2	Silent	McGrupp
04/08/94	5	1	IDK	Horse
04/22/94	12	1	Uncle Pen	Sample
04/30/94	6	1	Sample	Rift
05/14/94	10	2	TMWSIY	FEFY
05/23/94	7	2	Sparkle	YEM
05/27/94	3	1	If I Could	Harry
06/17/94	9	1	If I Could	Bathtub
06/23/94	5	1	Silent	Julius
07/05/94	9	2	Also Sprac	Sparkle
07/14/94	6	1	Bouncing	Stash
10/14/94	9	1	Silent	Bathtub
12/08/94	37	1	Scent	Simple
06/19/95	17	1	Tela	Reba
06/28/95	7	1	Reba	Stash
10/19/95	21	1	Horn	Esther
10/29/95	8	1	Julius	CTB
11/09/95	2	1	Caspian	Simple
11/18/95	7	1	Lawn Boy	Slave
12/04/95	11	1	Divided	Stash
12/12/95	6	1	Life Boy	Horse
12/31/95	8	1	*OP1	Sloth
07/15/96	12	1	My Friend	FEFY
07/25/96	8	1a	PoorHeart	Sample
08/02/96	1	E	*OPE	*CLE
08/07/96	4	1	*OP1	Sparkle
08/13/96	3	1	Old Home	Llama
08/17/96	3	1	Old Home	Reba
10/17/96	2	1	Talk	CharZero
10/23/96	5	1	*OP1	PoorHeart
10/27/96	3	1	RunJim	ACDCBag
11/06/96	3	1	PoorHeart	Billy
11/15/96	7	1	CharZero	Caspian
11/23/96	5	1	Divided	Highway
11/30/96	4	1	RunJim	All Things
12/04/96	3	2	Sparkle	Life Mars
12/31/96	5	1	Peaches	CTB
02/13/97	1	2	My Soul	Slave
02/18/97	4	1	Cavern	RunJim
02/25/97	5	1	Sample	Free
03/02/97	4	2	Steep	Waste
03/18/97	1	1	Sample	My Soul
06/19/97	4	1	Theme	Water
07/09/97	13	1	*OP1	Caspian
07/23/97	5	2	*OP2	Ghost
07/30/97	4	2	*OP2	Free
08/09/97	6	1	Theme	Ghost
08/16/97	5	1	Theme	Ghost
11/13/97	2	2	Stash	Caspian
11/21/97	5	1	Dogs Stole	Lawn Boy
11/26/97	3	2	Ya Mar	Caspian
12/03/97	5	1	*OP1	My Soul
12/11/97	5	1	*OP1	DWD
12/13/97	2	2	NICU	Ghost
12/30/97	3	1	Water	Stash
>> 12/31/97	**1**			

REBA

Inspiration: Featuring some of Trey's most complex lyrics, Reba tells the story of a witch brewing an epic soup comprising many unique ingredients. The lyrics serve as a jumping-off point for the composed jam and improvisational jam sections of the song. Trey composed Reba as a sort of experiment: he wanted to create a long, multipart song without any repeating portions.

Musical History and Evolution: Debuted in fall 1989, this song underwent a slight transformation between 1989 and 1990 as Trey removed a composed instrumental portion that immediately followed the verses, and fashioned that music into the song Don't Get Me Wrong (with lyrics by John Popper). By most accounts, Reba benefited from the change, as the lyrics now precede more smoothly into the compositional jam segment, and then to the improvisational jam, which can represent Phish jamming at its best, though it seldom includes teases of other songs or surprisingly long jams. Some favored versions of Reba include 4/17/92 San Francisco, CA; 5/16/95 Lowell, MA; and 12/31/95 New York, NY. A recent trend, started on 11/30/92 and employed more frequently since 1994, has been the omission of the whistle jam at the end during some live performances.

Rotation History: Played very frequently in the early 1990s, and on average about one out of every four shows in the mid 1990s, Reba went into a recession of sorts in 1997, as the band played it only ten times, including only two performances on fall tour 1997. Reba is often played at shows which also feature The Squirming Coil, although they are not played together.

Discography: Appears on *Lawn Boy* (1990).

Reba [261] [Reba]

By Anastasio

10/01/89	[125]	2	MSO	Dinner
10/20/89	6	1	Oh Kee	Divided
10/22/89	2	2	Harry	Golgi
10/26/89	1	2	ACDCBag	WalkAway
10/31/89	2	2	Wilson	Forbin's
11/02/89	1	1	Curtain	Split&Melt
11/03/89	1	1	PYITE	Golgi
11/16/89	5	1	MSO	YEM
11/30/89	2	2	*OP2	Possum

12/08/89	5	1	Ya Mar	McGrupp
01/20/90	7	1a	Bouncing	Tela
01/27/90	3	1	Wilson	FunkBitch
02/09/90	8	2	Ya Mar	Wilson
02/23/90	6	2	Golgi	Bathtub
02/25/90	2	2	Jam	McGrupp
03/03/90	3	1	ACDCBag	Rocky Top
03/07/90	1	1	*OP1	Possum
03/09/90	2	1	Antelope	Oh Kee
04/05/90	3	2	*OP2	Uncle Pen
04/06/90	1	2	Caravan	IDK
04/13/90	6	1	ACDCBag	Fire
04/18/90	1	2	FunkBitch	WalkAway
04/25/90	5	2	Adeline	Ya Mar
04/28/90	2	2	IDK	MSO
05/04/90	3	1	Possum	MSO
05/06/90	1	1	Uncle Pen	Tweezer
05/10/90	1	2	Caravan	Oh Kee
05/11/90	1	1	Possum	HwayHell
05/13/90	2	2	MSO	FunkBitch
05/19/90	2	2	Possum	Oh Kee
05/23/90	1	2	Sqirm Coil	Tweezer
05/24/90	1	1	Donna	YEM
06/07/90	4	1	Fee	YEM
06/09/90	2	1	Lawn Boy	Dinner
06/16/90	1	1	Wilson	Horn
09/13/90	1	2	Sparks	Self
09/14/90	1	1	Landlady	Paul&Silas
09/16/90	2	1a	Landlady	Ya Mar
10/08/90	10	1	Cavern	MSO
10/30/90	3	2	Foam	Llama
10/31/90	1	2	Landlady	RunJim
11/03/90	2	2	Uncle Pen	Possum
11/10/90	3	1	*OP1	Landlady
11/26/90	4	1	Sloth	BurAlive
12/03/90	3	1	Ya Mar	Divided
12/28/90	3	1	Horn	Llama
02/01/91	3	2	*OP2	Landlady
02/03/91	2	1	Destiny	Chalkdust
02/08/91	2	1	ACDCBag	BurAlive
02/09/91	1	1	Tweezer	Chalkdust
02/14/91	1	1	BurAlive	Destiny
02/16/91	2	2	Chalkdust	BurAlive
02/21/91	3	1	*OP1	Dinner
02/26/91	4	1	MSO	Oh Kee
02/28/91	2	2	Sqirm Coil	Llama
03/01/91	1	2	Landlady	Llama
03/07/91	3	2	RunJim	Possum
03/13/91	3	2	Sloth	Tweezer
03/16/91	2	1	Golgi	Landlady
03/22/91	3	1	Cavern	Fire
04/05/91	8	1	Magilla	Chalkdust
04/11/91	2	2	MSO	Llama
04/12/91	1	2	BurAlive	MSO
04/16/91	3	2	MSO	Chalkdust
04/18/91	1	2	Llama	Oh Kee
04/20/91	2	1	RunJim	Llama
04/22/91	2	1	Sloth	PoorHeart
04/27/91	3	1	MSO	Llama
05/04/91	3	1	Cavern	MSO
05/11/91	3	2	PoorHeart	Oh Kee
05/17/91	3	1	Jam	PoorHeart
05/25/91	2	1a	Foam	Dinner
07/12/91	2	1	Flat Fee	Landlady
07/14/91	2	1	*OP1	Llama
07/18/91	2	2	Llama	PoorHeart
07/20/91	2	2	BurAlive	Caravan
07/23/91	2	2	Llama	Cavern
07/26/91	3	1	Chalkdust	MSO
08/03/91	2	1	Curtain	Chalkdust
09/25/91	1	1	Caravan	Possum
09/27/91	2	1	Cavern	BurAlive
10/02/91	3	1	Cavern	Brother
10/04/91	2	1	Chalkdust	PoorHeart
10/10/91	3	2	Brother	PoorHeart
10/13/91	3	1	Wilson	Landlady
10/15/91	1	1	Sparkle	Landlady
10/18/91	2	1	Paul&Silas	Wilson
10/28/91	6	1	PoorHeart	IDK
11/02/91	4	1	Llama	Paul&Silas
11/07/91	2	2	MSO	Tube
11/09/91	2	1	Llama	Tube
11/14/91	4	1	Llama	Foam
11/19/91	3	2	Sloth	Dinner
11/21/91	2	1	Guelah	Foam
11/23/91	2	1	Llama	Foam
12/04/91	3	1	Llama	Landlady
12/06/91	2	1	Foam	Uncle Pen
12/07/91	1	2	BurAlive	Chalkdust
12/31/91	1	2	Landlady	Cavern
03/06/92	1	1	Maze	All Things
03/11/92	2	1	Paul&Silas	Maze
03/12/92	1	1	IDK	BurAlive
03/14/92	2	1	Cavern	Sparkle
03/20/92	3	1	Wilson	Brother
03/25/92	3	2	Mound	All Things
03/27/92	2	1	Llama	Paul&Silas
03/31/92	3	1	Rift	Llama
04/04/92	3	1	Foam	Uncle Pen
04/06/92	2	1	Sparkle	Brother
04/09/92	2	1	Mound	Uncle Pen
04/12/92	1	1	Maze	Antelope
04/15/92	2	2	YEM	Landlady
04/17/92	2	1	Cavern	Maze
04/19/92	2	1	My Friend	Maze
04/22/92	2	1	Foam	Sparkle
04/25/92	3	1	Paul&Silas	Brother
04/30/92	2	1	Maze	Uncle Pen
05/02/92	2	1	Sparkle	Maze
05/06/92	3	1	Foam	My Mind
05/08/92	2	1	Cavern	Uncle Pen
05/10/92	2	1a	Cavern	IDK
05/12/92	1	1	MSO	All Things
05/14/92	1	1	Horn	PoorHeart
05/17/92	3	1	MSO	IDK
06/23/92	4	1a	Chalkdust	Maze
06/27/92	2	1a	Sparkle	Maze
07/10/92	5	1a	Llama	Sparkle
07/14/92	3	2	All Things	Llama
07/18/92	4	1a	Llama	Rift
07/22/92	3	1a	*OP1	PoorHeart
08/17/92	13	1	Landlady	Rift
08/24/92	4	1a	Landlady	YEM
08/30/92	5	1a	Landlady	Llama
11/20/92	3	1	Sloth	Sparkle
11/22/92	2	1	Maze	Sparkle
11/27/92	3	1	Lawn Boy	Llama
11/30/92	2	1	IDK	Antelope
12/03/92	3	1	Silent	Adeline
12/05/92	2	2	Walk Line	Sparkle
12/07/92	2	2	Chalkdust	Llama
12/10/92	2	1	All Things	Adeline
12/12/92	2	1	Cavern	Landlady
12/28/92	2	2	Split&Melt	Sloth
12/30/92	2	1	Paul&Silas	IDK
02/05/93	4	1	PoorHeart	Bowie
02/07/93	2	2	My Mind	Tweezer
02/10/93	2	1	Guelah	Sloth
02/12/93	2	2	All Things	PoorHeart
02/15/93	2	2	FEFY	Mike's
02/18/93	2	1	Cavern	Lawn Boy
02/20/93	2	2	Wilson	Tweezer
02/23/93	3	1	Split&Melt	Lawn Boy
03/02/93	4	1	Stash	Sparkle
03/06/93	3	2	Tweezer	Paul&Silas
03/09/93	2	2	Tweezer	Lawn Boy
03/14/93	3	1	Sample	PYITE
03/17/93	2	2	Glide	Jesus
03/22/93	4	1	Weigh	Sparkle
03/27/93	4	1	Stash	My Friend
03/31/93	3	1	Sample	IDK
04/03/93	3	1	My Friend	Horn
04/12/93	4	1	Silent	Llama
04/17/93	4	2	Wilson	Landlady
04/22/93	4	1	It's Ice	Chalkdust
04/29/93	5	2	BBJ	Mike's
05/08/93	8	1	My Friend	Satin Doll
07/17/93	5	1	Stash	Chalkdust
07/30/93	10	1	IDK	Cavern
08/07/93	5	1	Makisupa	Maze
08/12/93	4	1	ACDCBag	Chalkdust
08/16/93	4	1	Horn	Sparkle
08/26/93	6	1	Guelah	Fee
12/31/93	5	1	Ginseng	Peaches
04/04/94	1	1	Fee	Horn
04/09/94	4	2	Sample	Peaches
04/13/94	3	2	Sample	BBJ
04/17/94	4	2	Sloth	BBJ
04/22/94	4	2	Julius	Tweezer
04/29/94	5	2	If I Could	Fee
05/02/94	2	2	Mound	Golgi
05/06/94	3	2	Sample	Axilla 2
05/10/94	3	2	Julius	Scent
05/14/94	3	1	Fee	Sample
05/23/94	7	1	Julius	Cavern
05/27/94	3	2	My Friend	Lizards
05/28/94	1	2	Life Boy	Fee
06/13/94	5	2	Cavern	Jesus
06/19/94	5	2	If I Could	Makisupa
06/24/94	4	1	Horn	Adeline
06/29/94	3	1	Sample	Mound
07/03/94	4	1	Old Home	Axilla 2
07/06/94	2	1	Bouncing	Axilla 2
07/08/94	1	2	Sample	YSZahov
07/15/94	5	2	Bouncing	It's Ice
10/07/94	2	2	Silent	Wilson
10/12/94	4	1	My Friend	Sloth
10/15/94	3	1	Glide	DWD
10/18/94	2	2	Silent	Scent
10/22/94	3	2	Wilson	AmGrace
10/26/94	3	2	Bouncing	Axilla 2
10/31/94	4	1	Silent	Golgi
11/13/94	5	1	Simple	Axilla 2
11/16/94	2	1	FEFY	Axilla 2
11/20/94	4	2	Axilla 2	Simple
11/25/94	3	1	Guelah	Bouncing
11/30/94	3	1	My Friend	Forbin's
12/04/94	4	2	Bouncing	Axilla 2
12/08/94	3	2	Axilla 2	Nellie
12/28/94	3	1	Axilla 2	Dog Faced
05/16/95	4	1a	Str Design	Theme
06/08/95	2	1	FEFY	Caspian
06/13/95	3	1	Taste	Terrapin
06/19/95	5	1	PYITE	Str Design
06/23/95	3	1	Caspian	Ginseng
06/28/95	4	1	FEFY	PYITE
07/02/95	4	1	CamlWalk	IDK
09/30/95	5	1	Chess	Uncle Pen
10/06/95	4	1	Billy	I'm Blue
10/08/95	2	1	Wolfman's	I'm Blue
10/14/95	3	2	*OP2	Rift
10/21/95	5	1	Guelah	Wilson
10/25/95	3	2	*OP2	Life Mars
11/09/95	5	1	Simple	Tela
11/12/95	3	1	Guelah	IDK
11/18/95	4	1	Bouncing	Lawn Boy
11/24/95	4	2	Theme	Catapult
11/29/95	3	1	Ya Mar	If I Could
12/02/95	3	1	Guelah	MSO
12/07/95	3	2	Fog	Julius
12/11/95	3	1	Caspian	Dog Log
12/16/95	4	2	Sample	Scent
12/31/95	5	1	Sloth	Sqirm Coil
07/06/96	5	1a	ASZ	PoorHeart
07/11/96	4	1	IDK	Cavern
07/13/96	2	1a	Cavern	PoorHeart
07/21/96	5	2	Theme	Life Mars
08/04/96	6	2	ACDCBag	Scent
08/10/96	4	1	Fee	IDK
08/14/96	3	1	PoorHeart	Mango
08/17/96	2	1	PYITE	CTB
10/18/96	3	2	YEM	Waste
10/21/96	2	2	Wolfman's	Train Song
10/26/96	4	1	Wolfman's	Train Song
10/31/96	3	1	Caspian	Forbin's
11/08/96	5	1	Caspian	Golgi
11/13/96	3	1	Train Song	CharZero
11/18/96	4	1	Ginseng	CharZero
11/24/96	4	1	Bouncing	CharZero
12/01/96	4	2	DayinLife	SweptAwy
12/04/96	2	2	Life Mars	Lawn Boy
12/30/96	4	1	Gumbo	Talk
02/14/97	3	2	FunkBitch	Walfredo
02/18/97	3	2	Wolfman's	Train Song
02/21/97	2	2	Billy	Waste
03/01/97	6	1	Jesus	HelloBaby
06/16/97	5	2	Don't Care	Wading
06/24/97	5	2	Wolfman's	NICU
07/01/97	4	1	Dirt	Dogs Stole
08/09/97	20	1	Dogs Stole	Lawn Boy
11/17/97	10	1	Tweezer	Train Song
12/07/97	13	2	Boogie	Guyute
>> 12/31/97		**8**		

REVOLUTION

Inspiration: Anarchy's twin, this short heavy-metal tune was a 1980's send-up of heavy metal rock.

Musical History and Evolution: None

Rotation History: Seen in the mid-1980s, but not since.

Discography: Has not yet appeared on a Phish album.

RIFT

Inspiration: Tom Marshall's lyrics apparently reference a narrator's struggle with a relationship-based decision, and the band used the concept of a "rift" in a relationship as the musical theme of their 1993 album *Rift*.

Musical History and Evolution: Rift has enjoyed two very different lives. The first, in 1990, was as a much slower song than what's heard today, offering no repetition of lyrics and closing with an extra verse ("And so fell the weight I never can lift . . .") that's printed in the liner notes to *Rift*. Trey rewrote the song for the 1992 spring tour because he felt the original did not do justice to Tom's lyrics, and in so doing, he refashioned the post-Curtain jam known as "The Curtain With" (heard on some versions of The Curtain in 1987–1988) into the middle segment of Rift, at a much faster pace than the original post-Curtain jam. Since its re-debut in 1992, Rift has remained basically unchanged, except for the speed of the song, which can vary.

Rotation History: Played only five times in its 1990 incarnation, Rift rested in 1991 before storming back in its new 1992 clothes, appearing sixty-eight times in its peak year of 1993 (following the release of *Rift*). Its numbers have dropped sharply every year since then, bottoming out in 1997 with only one performance, on 2/23/97 in Cortemaggiore, Italy.

Discography: Appears on *Rift* (1993).

Rift [206] [Rift]

By Anastasio/Marshall

02/25/90	[176]	1	Satin Doll	Possum
03/28/90	9	2	La Grange	Cavern
04/20/90	12	2	La Grange	Fee
04/28/90	5	1	YEM	Foam
05/19/90	10	2	Bouncing	Jesus
03/06/92	172	1	*OP1	Cavern
03/07/92	1	1	Landlady	Antelope
03/12/92	2	1	BurAlive	Magilla
03/13/92	1	2	Sloth	Love You
03/14/92	1	1	Foam	Stash
03/17/92	1	1	Guelah	Bouncing
03/19/92	1	1	Landlady	Split&Melt
03/20/92	1	1	Glide	Fluffhead
03/24/92	2	1	Eliza	Golgi
03/25/92	1	1	Split&Melt	Fee
03/27/92	2	2	MSO	Bathtub
03/28/92	1	1	Stash	Bouncing
03/31/92	2	1	Split&Melt	Reba
04/03/92	2	1	Stash	Guelah
04/05/92	2	1	Stash	Horn
04/07/92	2	1	Bouncing	Sloth
04/12/92	2	2	Bouncing	YEM
04/16/92	3	1	Split&Melt	Fee
04/18/92	2	2	Suzie	Manteca
04/21/92	2	1	Split&Melt	Guelah
04/22/92	1	2	Silent	Wilson
04/25/92	3	1	Bouncing	Magilla
04/29/92	1	1	Guelah	Bouncing
04/30/92	1	1	Stash	Esther
05/03/92	3	1	IDK	Horn
05/05/92	1	1	Stash	Guelah
05/07/92	2	1	Split&Melt	Guelah
05/09/92	2	1	Guelah	Fee
05/14/92	3	2	Cavern	Fluffhead
05/18/92	4	2	Fee	Cavern
07/01/92	7	1a	Cavern	Horn
07/14/92	6	1	Landlady	Guelah
07/16/92	2	1	Guelah	Bowie
07/18/92	2	1a	Reba	Antelope
07/22/92	3	1a	Maze	Cavern
07/25/92	2	1a	Stash	YEM
07/30/92	4	1a	*OP1	Horn
08/02/92	3	1a	Guelah	Oh Kee

08/17/92	4	1	Reba	Wilson
08/29/92	8	1a	Chalkdust	Bouncing
10/30/92	2	1a	Bouncing	Cavern
11/20/92	2	1	Suzie	Sloth
11/23/92	3	1	Split&Melt	Guelah
11/27/92	2	1	*OP1	Wilson
12/01/92	3	1	Bouncing	Cavern
12/03/92	2	2	*OP2	Guelah
12/05/92	2	1	Bouncing	Guelah
12/08/92	3	1	*OP1	Wilson
12/10/92	1	2	*OP2	Tweezer
12/12/92	2	2	Tweezer	Guelah
12/13/92	1	1	Stash	FEFY
12/28/92	1	1	Bouncing	Golgi
12/30/92	2	2	Axilla	Bathtub
12/31/92	1	1	Bouncing	Wilson
02/03/93	1	1	Lovin Cup	Fee
02/05/93	2	1	Guelah	Split&Melt
02/07/93	2	1	Mockbird	IDK
02/09/93	1	1	My Friend	Wedge
02/11/93	2	1	Fee	Fluffhead
02/13/93	2	1	Glide	Stash
02/15/93	1	2	*OP2	FEFY
02/18/93	2	2	*OP2	Stash
02/19/93	1	1	Lovin Cup	Split&Melt
02/22/93	3	1	*OP1	Guelah
02/23/93	1	1	My Friend	Bouncing
02/25/93	1	1	Mockbird	Stash
02/27/93	2	1	Golgi	Guelah
03/03/93	2	1	*OP1	Foam
03/05/93	1	1	Sloth	Stash
03/06/93	1	2	*OP2	Tweezer
03/08/93	1	1	Golgi	Guelah
03/09/93	1	2	Axilla	Tweezer
03/12/93	1	1	Guelah	Stash
03/14/93	2	2	Life Boy	BBJ
03/18/93	3	1	Guelah	Fee
03/19/93	1	1	Bouncing	Stash
03/21/93	1	2	My Friend	Tweezer
03/22/93	1	1	Bouncing	Weigh
03/25/93	2	1	Glide	Horn
03/27/93	2	1	Guelah	Stash
03/30/93	2	2	Lovin Cup	Tweezer
04/01/93	2	1	Guelah	Stash
04/03/93	2	1	Landlady	Guelah
04/10/93	3	2	Bouncing	Glide
04/13/93	2	2	My Friend	Sloth
04/16/93	2	1	Sample	Harry
04/18/93	2	1	*OP1	Guelah
04/21/93	2	1	Mockbird	PYITE
04/22/93	1	1	Fee	Golgi
04/24/93	2	1	Silent	Caravan
04/27/93	2	1	Bouncing	Stash
04/29/93	1	1	Glide	Fee
05/01/93	2	1	Fee	Sample
05/03/93	2	1	BurAlive	Weigh
05/05/93	1	1	*OP1	Guelah
05/07/93	2	2	*OP2	Bouncing
05/08/93	1	1	Guelah	Mound
05/29/93	1	1a	Bouncing	Stash
07/15/93	2	1	*OP1	Sample
07/17/93	2	2	Faht	GTBT
07/18/93	1	1	BurAlive	Foam
07/21/93	1	1a	Glide	Bouncing
07/23/93	2	1	BurAlive	Caravan
07/24/93	1	1	Guelah	Stash
07/25/93	1	1	Fee	Sloth
07/27/93	1	1a	Also Sprac	Stash
07/29/93	2	1	Weigh	Landlady
07/31/93	2	1	*OP1	Sample
08/02/93	1	2	Curtis	Sqirm Coil
08/03/93	1	1	Fee	Stash
08/06/93	1	1	Sample	Horn
08/08/93	2	2	Also Sprac	Harry
08/11/93	2	1	Bouncing	Jesus
08/13/93	2	1	BurAlive	Bathtub
08/15/93	2	2	*OP2	Tweezer
08/17/93	2	2	Silent	Suzie
08/20/93	1	1	Ginseng	Antelope
08/21/93	1	1	Guelah	Stash
08/24/93	1	2	Wilson	Rosie
08/26/93	2	2	Life Boy	Jesus
08/28/93	1	2	Also Sprac	Antelope
12/30/93	3	1	Mockbird	Bathtub
04/05/94	3	1	Bouncing	ACDCBag
04/09/94	3	1	Wilson	Bathtub
04/14/94	4	1	Glide	Demand
04/16/94	2	1	Axilla 2	Stash
04/18/94	2	1	My Friend	Split&Melt
04/23/94	4	1	FunkBitch	Fee
04/28/94	3	1a	Sample	DWD
04/30/94	2	1	PYITE	Ginseng
05/03/94	2	1	*OP1	Guelah
05/04/94	1	1	Life Boy	TweezRep
05/08/94	3	1	Axilla 2	DWD
05/12/94	2	1	Catapult	DWD
05/16/94	3	1	Axilla 2	DWD
05/20/94	3	2	Wolfman's	YEM
05/22/94	2	2	Life Boy	Slave
05/25/94	2	2	*OP2	Tweezer
05/28/94	3	1	*OP1	Sample
06/09/94	2	1	Guelah	DWD
06/11/94	2	1	YEM	DWD
06/14/94	2	1	Guelah	DWD
06/16/94	1	1	Bouncing	Julius
06/18/94	2	1	Wilson	ACDCBag
06/22/94	3	1	Guelah	Gumbo
06/25/94	3	1	N20	Julius
06/30/94	3	1	Gumbo	Guelah
07/02/94	2	E	*OPE	*CLE
07/05/94	2	1	*OP1	Sample
07/08/94	2	2	*OP2	Sample
07/10/94	2	1	Peaches	Stash
07/15/94	3	1	*OP1	Sample
10/08/94	3	2	Sample	Mike's
10/10/94	2	2	Fee	DWD
10/14/94	3	1	Adeline	Forbin's
10/16/94	2	1	*OP1	Horn
10/20/94	2	2	McGrupp	Harry
10/22/94	2	1	Axilla 2	Split&Melt
10/26/94	3	2	*OP2	Bouncing
10/28/94	2	2	Lizards	Life Boy
10/29/94	1	1	Makisupa	*CL1
10/31/94	1	3	Slave	Sl Monkey
11/12/94	4	2	Life Boy	Old Home
11/18/94	5	1	*OP1	ACDCBag
11/20/94	2	2	Simple	Terrapin
12/04/94	10	1	If I Could	Tweezer
12/07/94	2	2	*OP2	Frankstein
12/10/94	3	1	Fee	Stash
12/30/94	3	1	Wilson	ACDCBag
06/08/95	4	2	Simple	Free
06/10/95	2	1	Free	YEM
06/19/95	6	1	Str Design	Cavern
06/24/95	4	1	Fee	Spock's
06/29/95	4	1	Cavern	Simple
07/02/95	3	1	IDK	Guitar
09/27/95	2	1	Wolfman's	Free
10/02/95	4	1	Wolfman's	Chess
10/06/95	3	1	I'm Blue	Free
10/14/95	5	2	Reba	YEM
10/20/95	4	1	Fee	Free
10/27/95	5	1	IDK	Stash
11/15/95	9	1	FEFY	Caspian
11/19/95	3	1	PoorHeart	Stash
11/22/95	2	2	*OP2	Free
11/25/95	2	1	Bouncing	Wolfman's
11/30/95	3	1	Bathtub	FEFY
12/07/95	5	1	Demand	Slave
12/09/95	2	1	Sloth	Bouncing
12/28/95	7	1	Horn	FEFY
07/21/96	19	1	Guelah	Tweezer
08/06/96	8	1	Makisupa	Suzie
08/10/96	2	1	Silent	Bathtub
10/19/96	9	1	My Friend	Free
10/23/96	3	1	CharZero	Theme
10/27/96	3	2	Bathtub	Caspian
10/29/96	1	2	*OP2	Mike's
11/07/96	5	1	Weigh	Guelah
11/16/96	7	1	Gumbo	Free
11/23/96	4	1	Split&Melt	FunkBitch
12/29/96	10	1	Train Song	Free
02/23/97	11	1	Love Me	Fluffhead
>> 12/31/97		**69**		

RIKER'S MAILBOX

Inspiration: This "song" grew out of the *Hoist* recording session for Buffalo Bill and consists of a 20-second snippet of Buffalo Bill recorded backward in some recording studio trickery. The song's only intelligible lyric, "Olaffub!" is the word "Buffalo" backward. The song takes its name from the unique cow mailbox of Jonathan Frakes, who played Lieutenant William Riker on "Star Trek: The Next Generation" and who played trombone on this song on *Hoist*.

Musical History and Evolution: None.

Rotation History: Never played live in concert.

Discography: Appears on *Hoist* (1994).

ROCKA WILLIAM

Inspiration: For their tour of smaller European venues in February and March 1997, the band composed two rotation/instrument-switching songs, Rocka William and Walfredo. The lyrics to this one are a little more ominous.

Musical History and Evolution: Counting only five appearances to its name, there's not much, though fans seem to appreciate the song for its wacky lyrics and the chance to see Fishman play guitar and sing the lead vocals.

Rotation History: Though the song originally looked to be a Europe-only original, the band followed a rotation jam on 8/10/97 in Deer Creek with this tune, earning cheers with the "children of the corn" line. It hasn't been played since.

Discography: Has not yet appeared on a Phish album.

Rocka William [5] [RockaW]

By Phish

02/13/97	[889]1	Maze	Harry
02/14/97	1 2	Walfredo	Scent
02/26/97	9 1	Carini	Dog Log
06/25/97	13 2	Cecilia	Antelope
08/10/97	24 2	Rotation	Bowie
>> 12/31/97	**32**		

ROTATION JAM

Inspiration: Born of the band members' desire to play each other's instruments, one at a time, the jam rotates clockwise until each member returns to his original instrument. Though original songs Rocka William and Walfredo feature instrument-switching, these are not considered rotation jams on their own.

Musical History and Evolution: As a free-form jam, each Rotation Jam has its own unique feel, but the band does try to keep the jams cohesive by paying close attention to what each of the other band members is playing. It should be noted that Mike Gordon is actually an amazing keyboard player, but doesn't show off during the rotation jams. He did call attention to himself at the 12/29/96 version however, shouting "Sex . . . teen Candles" into the microphone and going into that song.

Rotation History: Debuted on 11/25/95 in Hampton, VA, in the midst of a Mike's Song jam, the Rotation Jam also surfaced later that fall in Philadelphia, PA, on 12/15/95 in a shorter version that emerged from Bathtub Gin. A year later, back at the Spectrum on 12/29/96, the band followed a Rotation Jam out of YEM with Mike's impromptu performance of "Sixteen Candles." The lone Rotation Jam in 1997 came on 8/10 in Deer Creek, when the band ultimately rotated into position for Rocka William.

Rotation Jam [4] [Rotation]

By Phish

11/25/95	[798]2	Mike's	Mike's
12/15/95	14 2	Bathtub	Also Sprac
12/29/96	74 2	YEM	Candles
08/10/97	50 2	GTBT	RockaW
>> 12/31/97	**32**		

RUN LIKE AN ANTELOPE

Inspiration: The main lyrical refrain of this crowd favorite is a product of the Dude of Life, who, during his senior year at the Taft School in Watertown, CT, in 1982 played in the band Space Antelope with Trey. There, he coined the phrase, "Set the gearshift for the high gear of your soul, you've got to run like a space antelope, out of control!" The words immediatly preceding this line are Tom Marshall's first lyrical contribution to a Phish song. During the "Bivouac Jaun" recording sessions in Trey's basement in the spring of 1984, Trey urged Tom to step up to the microphone and "say something." Tom looked over at friend Marc Daubert and, drawing on his knowledge of colonial Mexican history, termed him "Marco Esquandolis." During the recording of Antelope for *Lawn Boy*, the band recorded themselves jogging in place to mimic the sound of stampeding antelope. As is the case with many Phish jam songs, Trey says he is not happy with the album version.

Musical History and Evolution: First heard as a snippet of the jam in 1985, Antelope solidified into a composed song with an open-ended middle jam section by 1986. In recent years, Antelope has functioned both as a tight-jamming first-set closer and as a more open jam song, often anchoring second sets. In the closing refrain, Trey originally sang "Bid you to have any spleef, man?" before switching exclusively to "Bid you to have any spike, man?" by 1989 (Tom Marshall sang that line with Phish on 12/31/93 and 12/31/94). But he still has fun switching things around, changing "Marco Esquandolis" to such lyrics as "Norton Charleton Heston" (November 1996), "Michael Esquandolis" (while pointing to Mike Gordon, 11/22/97), and "21-year-old Phish fan Marcus Esquandolis," referencing a newspaper article at Red Rocks on 8/6/96. Several great Makisupa-in-Antelope escapes have also occurred, including 8/2/93 Tampa, FL ("Marco-Policeman-Dolas") and more recently on 8/6/97 St. Louis, MO (with Page on theremin and Mike on mini drum kit). Besides those versions, many other great Antelopes capture phans' fancy, including 3/13/92 Providence, RI, "Big Black Furry Antelope"; 5/14/92 Port Chester, NY, Spiderman jam and language lesson; 7/18/93 Pittsburgh, PA, fireworks jam and Brother tease; 8/14/93, twenty-five minutes of segue-inspired madness; 7/16/94 Fayston, VT, incredible version and Catapult in the middle; 10/31/94 Glens Falls, NY, great jam with a gaffe at the end (excusable at three A.M.); 11/30/94 Eugene, OR, Antelope anchors wild second set; 10/24/95 Madison, WI, an experimental Antelope jam; 11/11/95 Atlanta, GA, another out-there version; 11/2/96 West Palm Beach, FL, out of CE&P with Karl Perazzo. On the Europe tour in early 1997, the band neglected to finish most versions of Antelope, the most pleasing result being the segue into a heavy-metal version of Wilson in Florence, Italy, on 2/21/97. Also, Antelope's alter ego, Roll Like a Cantaloupe (featuring the same music and suitably altered lyrics) appeared a handful of times in the 1980s and early 1990s (like 7/12/88 and 3/11/90).

Rotation History: Reliably played throughout the 1990s, never more than about one in every three shows, and about one in five shows in 1997. The song can still sometimes be found as a first-set closer, its traditional position for much of 1992 and 1993.

Discography: Appears on *Lawn Boy* (1990), and on their "White Album."

Run Like an Antelope [264] [Antelope]

By Anastasio/Marshall/Dude of Life

10/17/85	[3]	1a	CamlWalk	McGrupp
11/23/85	2	1a	WhipPost	Dave's
03/11/87	7	1a	Freebird	Flat Fee
04/29/87	3	3	Makisupa	Boogie On
09/12/87	8	2	Curtis	Makisupa
02/08/88	7	2	Lizards	Harry
03/11/88	1	2	Alumni	*CL2
03/12/88	1	1a	Possum	*CL1
05/25/88	7	3	Harpua	*CL3
06/18/88	2	2	SwingLow	IKALittle
07/12/88	4	1	ACDCBag	*CL1
07/23/88	1	2	Terrapin	Satin Doll
07/24/88	1	3	McGrupp	*CL3
10/12/88	8	E	*OPE	*CLE
10/29/88	1	3	Donna	IDK
11/03/88	1	2	A-Train	Suzie
02/07/89	8	2	Fee	*CL2
02/17/89	1	1a	Alumni	Fluffhead
02/24/89	2	1	Mockbird	OYWD
03/03/89	1	1	Curtain	IDK
03/04/89	1	2	Lizards	Contact
03/30/89	2	1	Fluffhead	*CL1
04/30/89	14	1	Peaches	Terrapin
05/05/89	3	2	*OP2	IDK
05/06/89	1	2	Divided	*CL2
05/09/89	3	2	Esther	IDK
05/26/89	9	2	Bathtub	Golgi
05/28/89	2	1	Divided	Forbin's
06/23/89	5	1	Lizards	*CL1
06/30/89	2	1	Fluffhead	*CL1
08/12/89	3	1a	Icculus	*CL1
08/17/89	2	3	Contact	*CL3
08/23/89	3	2	*OP2	Forbin's
08/26/89	1	3	Dinner	*CL3
10/01/89	5	1	Suzie	*CL1
10/20/89	6	1	Golgi	*CL1
10/31/89	5	E	Contact	*CLE
11/10/89	5	2	A-Train	*CL2
11/30/89	4	1	MSO	Lawn Boy
12/07/89	4	2	Lizards	Lawn Boy
12/08/89	1	1	Bathtub	*CL1
12/15/89	2	1a	Divided	FunkBitch
12/31/89	4	1	ACDCBag	Bathtub
01/27/90	4	2	Sqirm Coil	Terrapin
01/28/90	1	2	Wilson	Bouncing
02/23/90	13	1	Bouncing	*CL1
02/24/90	1	1	A-Train	*CL1
03/08/90	6	1	A-Train	*CL1
03/09/90	1	1	Donna	Reba
03/11/90	1	2	Carolina	MSO
04/06/90	5	1	Suzie	*CL1
04/08/90	2	2	MSO	*CL2
04/13/90	4	2	*OP2	Foam
04/26/90	7	1	IDK	Lawn Boy
04/28/90	1	1	Foam	*CL1
05/04/90	3	2	HwayHell	*CL2
05/23/90	8	2	A-Train	Mike's
06/09/90	7	2	Suzie	Terrapin
06/16/90	1	2	Lizards	*CL2
09/13/90	1	1	Asse Fest	Minute
09/16/90	3	1a	Magilla	*CL1
09/28/90	4	1	Asse Fest	*CL1
10/05/90	3	1	Bouncing	*CL1
10/31/90	7	1	Cavern	*CL1
11/03/90	2	2	Love You	*CL2
11/30/90	8	2	Sloth	*CL2
12/03/90	2	1	MSO	Lawn Boy
12/08/90	2	2	Bouncing	Tela
12/29/90	2	2	Destiny	*CL2
12/31/90	1	2	Brain	*CL2
02/02/91	2	2	Sloth	Lawn Boy
02/08/91	3	2	Lizards	*CL2
03/16/91	22	1	Suzie	*CL1
03/22/91	3	2	Suzie	Foam
04/19/91	16	2	A-Train	*CL2
05/12/91	13	E	*OPE	Fire
07/14/91	8	2	Cavern	*CL2
07/25/91	8	1	Cavern	*CL1
09/28/91	7	2	Cavern	Lawn Boy
10/10/91	7	2	Cavern	IDK
10/18/91	6	1	Adeline	*CL1
10/27/91	5	2	A-Train	*CL2
11/02/91	5	2	Golgi	TMWSIY
11/12/91	6	2	Love You	*CL2
11/14/91	2	2	Dinner	Fee
11/20/91	4	2	MSO	Tela
11/22/91	2	2	Bathtub	Sqirm Coil
11/30/91	3	2	IDK	Golgi
12/07/91	4	1	Mango	*CL1
12/31/91	1	2	MSO	*CL2
03/07/92	2	1	Rift	*CL1
03/13/92	3	1	Fluffhead	*CL1
03/17/92	2	1	Bouncing	*CL1
03/20/92	2	1	Mound	*CL1
03/25/92	3	1	It's Ice	*CL1
03/27/92	2	1	Bouncing	*CL1
03/31/92	3	1	Mockbird	*CL1
04/04/92	3	1	IDK	*CL1
04/06/92	2	1	Sqirm Coil	*CL1
04/12/92	3	1	Reba	*CL1
04/16/92	3	1	Mockbird	*CL1
04/18/92	2	1	All Things	*CL1
04/22/92	3	2	Glide	Horse
04/25/92	3	1	Magilla	*CL1
04/30/92	2	1	Esther	*CL1
05/05/92	4	1	Glide	*CL1
05/09/92	4	1	IDK	*CL1
05/14/92	3	1	Bouncing	*CL1
05/18/92	4	1	Sparkle	*CL1
07/10/92	10	1a	Cavern	*CL1
07/15/92	4	1	Lizards	*CL1
07/18/92	3	1a	Rift	*CL1
08/30/92	25	1a	Memories	Adeline
11/19/92	2	1	Silent	*CL1
11/22/92	3	1	Adeline	*CL1
11/25/92	2	1	Cavern	*CL1
11/30/92	3	1	Reba	*CL1
12/03/92	3	1	Adeline	*CL1
12/06/92	3	1	Fluffhead	*CL1
12/08/92	2	2	Lizards	Lawn Boy
12/12/92	3	1	Bouncing	*CL1
12/28/92	2	1	Adeline	*CL1
12/31/92	3	1	IDK	*CL1
02/04/93	2	1	Glide	*CL1
02/06/93	2	1	Bouncing	*CL1
02/10/93	3	1	Catapult	*CL1
02/12/93	2	1	A-Train	*CL1
02/15/93	2	1	IDK	*CL1
02/18/93	2	1	Lawn Boy	*CL1
02/21/93	3	1	Bouncing	*CL1
02/23/93	2	1	Paul&Silas	*CL1
02/27/93	3	1	Lawn Boy	*CL1
03/09/93	6	1	IDK	*CL1
03/13/93	2	1	Wilson	*CL1
03/17/93	3	1	Suzie	*CL1
03/19/93	2	1	Cavern	*CL1
03/25/93	4	1	Magilla	*CL1
03/28/93	3	1	Lawn Boy	*CL1
04/01/93	3	1	Lawn Boy	*CL1
04/03/93	2	1	Horn	*CL1
04/12/93	4	1	Satin Doll	*CL1
04/17/93	4	1	Golgi	*CL1
04/21/93	3	1	IDK	*CL1
04/24/93	3	1	Sparkle	*CL1
04/29/93	3	1	Oh Kee	*CL1
05/02/93	3	2	Bouncing	Rosie
05/07/93	4	1	IDK	*CL1
05/30/93	3	1a	Silent	IDK
07/16/93	2	1	Horn	*CL1
07/18/93	2	2	PoorHeart	Mound
07/23/93	3	2	PoorHeart	Faht
07/28/93	4	2	MSO	Lizards
08/02/93	4	2	Bike	*CL2
08/07/93	3	2	PurplRain	*CL2
08/11/93	3	2	MSO	*CL2
08/14/93	3	2	Also Sprac	Sparks
08/20/93	4	1	Rift	*CL1
08/24/93	2	2	Rosie	*CL2
08/28/93	3	2	Rift	Horse
12/29/93	2	2	Fluffhead	Contact
12/31/93	2	1	IDK	*CL1
04/06/94	3	1	Fee	*CL1
04/10/94	3	2	Ya Mar	Fluffhead
04/14/94	3	2	Also Sprac	Horse
04/16/94	2	1	Nellie	*CL1
04/20/94	3	2	PoorHeart	Magilla
04/23/94	3	2	Wilson	Mound
04/25/94	2	2	My Mind	Mound
04/28/94	1	1a	It's Ice	Sqirm Coil
05/04/94	5	2	*OP2	Bouncing
05/08/94	3	2	Also Sprac	It's Ice
05/12/94	2	2	Also Sprac	Horse
05/16/94	3	2	Also Sprac	Sparkle
05/20/94	3	2	Also Sprac	Weigh
05/23/94	3	2	Wilson	If I Could
05/26/94	2	2	Also Sprac	Fluffhead
05/29/94	3	2	Suzie	Freebird
06/11/94	3	2	Also Sprac	Fluffhead
06/16/94	3	2	Suzie	Forbin's
06/19/94	3	2	Faht	If I Could
06/24/94	4	2	Demand	Halley's
06/30/94	4	2	Harpua	Love You
07/03/94	3	2	Sqirm Coil	Suzie
07/09/94	4	1	Silent	*CL1
07/14/94	3	1	Silent	*CL1
07/16/94	2	2	*OP2	Harpua
10/08/94	2	1	Lawn Boy	*CL1
10/13/94	4	2	Old Home	If I Could
10/16/94	3	2	BBJ	Dog Faced
10/21/94	3	1	Dog Faced	*CL1
10/26/94	4	1	NICU	Guyute
10/29/94	3	2	Bike	*CL2
10/31/94	1	3	PoorHeart	*CL3
11/13/94	5	1	Silent	*CL1
11/16/94	2	2	Fee	*CL2
11/19/94	3	1	Avenu	I'm Blue
11/25/94	4	2	PurplRain	*CL2
11/30/94	3	2	MSO	Fixin' Die
12/03/94	3	1	Scent	Guyute
12/06/94	2	2	Long Time	*CL2
12/09/94	3	1	If I Could	*CL1
12/28/94	2	1	It's Ice	*CL1
12/31/94	3	1	NICU	Glide
06/09/95	4	1	Sparkle	*CL1
06/15/95	4	1	Fluffhead	*CL1
06/19/95	3	1	Cavern	*CL1
06/23/95	3	2	Wedge	Harpua
06/26/95	3	2	Str Design	*CL2
06/30/95	3	1	Fee	*CL1
07/03/95	3	1	PoorHeart	Lovin Cup
09/28/95	2	2	Sample	*CL2
09/30/95	2	1	Horn	I'm Blue
10/02/95	1	2	Lizards	*CL2
10/07/95	4	1	Wilson	*CL1
10/13/95	3	2	Wilson	Keyboard
10/20/95	5	2	Bouncing	*CL2
10/24/95	3	2	Sl Monkey	Contact
10/28/95	3	1	Caspian	*CL1
10/31/95	2	1	Guyute	Harpua
11/11/95	3	2	Suspicious	*CL2
11/22/95	8	1	Wilson	Fluffhead
11/28/95	3	2	Wind	Contact
11/30/95	2	2	Makisupa	Scent
12/04/95	3	2	Ya Mar	Billy
12/08/95	3	2	TweezRep	*CL2
12/12/95	3	1	Silent	I'm Blue
12/17/95	4	1	DayinLife	Mango
12/30/95	3	2	Cavern	*CL2
07/07/96	7	1a	Cavern	Suzie
07/12/96	4	2	Mike's	PurplRain
07/15/96	2	2	Uncle Pen	*CL2
07/21/96	4	2	Free	Simple
07/25/96	4	1a	It's Ice	Life Mars
08/02/96	1	2	Silent	*CL2

Dead and Buried

Original songs that haven't been played in so long they may not ever come back, with dates of the song's last live appearance

Song	Last Played
Fuck Your Face	04/29/87
Anarchy	08/10/87
Lushington	08/29/87
Prep School Hippie	12/06/86
Dave's Energy Guide	08/06/88
Dear Mrs. Reagan	06/15/88
No Dogs Allowed	10/26/89
In a Hole	12/16/89
Don't Get Me Wrong	12/28/90
Flat Fee	07/26/91
Destiny Unbound	11/15/91
Eliza	05/14/92
Leprechaun	07/30/93

08/06/96	3	1	Horn	*CL1
08/12/96	3	2	McGrupp	HelloBaby
08/17/96	4	2	Fluffhead	Golgi
10/16/96	1	2	Caspian	Sqirm Coil
10/19/96	3	2	Steep	HelloBaby
10/23/96	3	1	Theme	*CL1
10/26/96	2	2	Waste	*CL2
11/02/96	4	2	Crosseyed	Waste
11/08/96	4	1	Golgi	*CL1
11/14/96	4	2	Demand	DayinLife
11/24/96	7	1	Sample	*CL1
12/01/96	4	1	Sample	*CL1
12/31/96	7	3	Suzie	Bohemian
02/14/97	2	1	Uncle Pen	*CL1
02/21/97	5	2	Ya Mar	Wilson
03/02/97	7	1	RunJim	Catapult
06/20/97	6	1	I Don't Care	*CL1
06/25/97	4	2	RockaW	*CL2
07/29/97	16	2	Oblivious	Wading
08/06/97	5	2	Sample	*CL2
08/11/97	4	1	Horn	*CL1
08/14/97	2	1	Billy	*CL1
11/14/97	4	1	Guyute	*CL1
11/19/97	3	1	Time	*CL1
11/22/97	2	2	Piper	*CL2
11/30/97	5	2	Circus	*CL2
12/06/97	4	1	Golgi	Train Song
12/12/97	4	E	Guyute	*CLE
12/29/97	3	1	Dirt	*CL1
>> 12/31/97	**2**			

RUNAWAY JIM

Inspiration: Another Trey oldie from his youth that he refashioned for Phish.

Musical History and Evolution: Debuted in spring 1990, Jim originally featured a final verse about Jim's death that has been omitted from all versions since the fall of 1990 ("He ran away again on the night he died 'Cus he know I would miss him from the other side"). Musically, the song's open-ended middle jam (the second of two instrumental interludes in the song) has evolved considerably, making it one of the band's best jam numbers when it hits on all cylinders. The song has frequently served as a show or set opener, and often appeared followed by Foam, though only once (on 12/29/94 Providence, RI) has the band crafted an intricate Jim > Foam segue. In recent years, the band has often let the jam finish or segue into another song without coming back around to the closing refrain of lyrics.

Some favored Jims include 8/21/93 Salt Lake City, UT, the first jam to defy the song's previous boundaries; 6/16/95 Raleigh, NC, the 30-minute experimental Jim into Free; 7/2/95 Fayston, VT, not experimental but very sweet, with segue into Makisupa; 12/31/95 New York, NY, raw power, and maybe the best Jim ever, plus a tip of the cap to "Dave" and "Daubs"; 8/7/96 Morrison, CO, one of several great Jims to feature Gypsy Queen jamming; and 11/29/97 Worcester, MA, incredible 60-minute Jim with Harry Hood and Weekapaug jams, among many other themes.

Rotation History: Played at least about one in every five shows throughout the 1990s, Jim continues to be a favorite of the band's.

Discography: Not yet included on a Phish album, though it was recorded during the *Nectar* sessions.

Runaway Jim [263] [RunJim]

By Anastasio

03/28/90	[185]	1	A-Train	YEM
04/07/90	4	2	Fee	Foam
05/04/90	16	2	*OP2	Sloth
05/10/90	2	2	FunkBitch	Harry
05/13/90	3	1	Bouncing	Uncle Pen
10/31/90	29	2	Reba	Foam
11/03/90	2	1	Foam	YEM
11/04/90	1	2	Manteca	Oh Kee
11/10/90	2	1	Bouncing	Cavern
11/16/90	1	2	Lizards	IDK
11/17/90	1	1	Landlady	Bouncing
11/24/90	1	1	Landlady	YEM
11/26/90	1	1	Landlady	Sloth
11/30/90	1	2	Sqirm Coil	Stash
12/01/90	1	1	YEM	*CL1
12/07/90	2	1	Asse Fest	Foam
12/08/90	1	1	BurAlive	Foam
12/28/90	1	1	*OP1	Foam
12/29/90	1	2	BurAlive	Lizards
12/31/90	1	2	Sqirm Coil	Magilla
02/01/91	1	1	Guelah	Split&Melt
02/03/91	2	1	*OP1	Guelah
02/07/91	1	1	*OP1	Foam
02/08/91	1	1	Sqirm Coil	Guelah
02/09/91	1	1	TMWSIY	Foam
02/14/91	1	2	Sqirm Coil	Esther
02/16/91	2	2	BurAlive	Guelah
02/26/91	7	2	BurAlive	Dinner
03/07/91	6	2	Sloth	Reba
03/13/91	3	2	Guelah	Sloth
03/15/91	1	E	Sqirm Coil	*CLE
03/17/91	2	2	*OP2	Esther
03/22/91	2	2	Stash	Guelah
04/04/91	7	2	Curtain	Guelah
04/11/91	3	1	*OP1	Cavern
04/12/91	1	2	Landlady	YEM
04/15/91	2	1	Foam	Split&Melt
04/16/91	1	2	Tweezer	Carolina
04/20/91	3	1	*OP1	Reba
04/22/91	2	1	Curtain	Sloth
04/27/91	3	1	Asse Fest	Cavern
05/03/91	2	2	Landlady	Tela
05/04/91	1	E	Terrapin	Golgi
05/12/91	3	1	Foam	*CL1
05/16/91	1	2	*OP2	Dinner
05/18/91	2	E	Dinner	*CLE
07/13/91	4	1	Curtain	Foam
07/18/91	3	1	Foam	Guelah
07/19/91	1	E	Lawn Boy	*CLE
07/21/91	2	2	IDK	Lawn Boy
08/03/91	6	1	Foam	Guelah
09/25/91	1	2	Jesus	YEM
09/27/91	2	1	*OP1	Cavern
10/02/91	3	2	Guelah	Lawn Boy
10/04/91	2	2	Foam	Lawn Boy
10/10/91	3	1	Landlady	It's Ice
10/11/91	1	1	Bouncing	*CL1
10/13/91	2	1	*OP1	Wilson
10/15/91	1	2	Bouncing	PoorHeart
10/18/91	2	1	*OP1	Foam
10/19/91	1	1	It's Ice	Foam
10/28/91	5	1	Curtain	Cavern
10/31/91	2	1	YEM	*CL1
11/02/91	2	2	Landlady	YEM
11/07/91	2	1	Landlady	IDK
11/09/91	2	1	Curtain	Foam
11/13/91	3	1	Landlady	It's Ice
11/14/91	1	1	Golgi	*CL1
11/16/91	2	1	Wilson	It's Ice
11/19/91	1	1	Foam	Fee
11/21/91	2	2	TMWSIY	*CL2
11/23/91	2	1	Foam	Guelah
12/04/91	3	1	Landlady	Cavern
12/07/91	3	1	Wilson	Foam
12/31/91	1	2	Auld	Landlady
03/07/92	2	1	Foam	Horse
03/12/92	2	1	*OP1	Foam
03/14/92	2	1	*OP1	Cavern
03/17/92	1	2	*OP2	Glide
03/21/92	3	1	Landlady	Foam
03/25/92	2	1	Glide	It's Ice
03/26/92	1	1	Landlady	All Things
03/28/92	2	1	*OP1	Foam
03/30/92	1	1	Sloth	Cavern
04/01/92	2	1	Sparkle	IDK
04/04/92	2	1	*OP1	Foam
04/05/92	1	2	A-Train	*CL2
04/07/92	2	1	Sloth	*CL1
04/15/92	4	1	All Things	*CL1
04/17/92	2	1	*OP1	Foam
04/19/92	2	2	Brain	*CL2
04/22/92	2	2	Harpua	*CL2
04/24/92	2	1	*OP1	Forbin's
04/29/92	2	1	It's Ice	Guelah
05/02/92	3	1	*OP1	Forbin's
05/03/92	1	1	Horn	*CL1
05/07/92	3	1	Foam	Esther
05/09/92	2	1	*OP1	Foam
05/12/92	2	2	Cavern	*CL2
05/16/92	3	2	*OP2	It's Ice
05/18/92	2	2	Love You	*CL2
06/20/92	2	1a	Foam	It's Ice
06/24/92	2	1a	*OP1	Llama
06/27/92	1	1a	*OP1	Foam
07/09/92	4	1a	Sqirm Coil	Guelah
07/11/92	2	1a	Landlady	Foam
07/14/92	2	1	It's Ice	Horn
07/16/92	2	2	*OP2	Weigh
07/17/92	1	1a	Bouncing	*CL1
07/19/92	2	1a	Maze	Bowie
07/21/92	1	1a	Sqirm Coil	*CL1
07/25/92	3	1a	*OP1	Foam
07/28/92	3	1a	Tweezer	*CL1
08/15/92	7	1a	Maze	*CL1
08/19/92	2	1a	Landlady	Guelah
08/23/92	2	1a	Foam	Stash
08/25/92	2	1a	*OP1	It's Ice
08/28/92	2	1a	Sqirm Coil	Rocky Top
10/30/92	3	1a	*OP1	Maze
11/21/92	3	1	Landlady	Foam
11/23/92	2	1	*OP1	Foam
11/27/92	2	1	Memories	*CL1
11/30/92	2	2	BurAlive	Guelah
12/02/92	2	2	Walk Line	*CL2
12/06/92	4	1	*OP1	Foam
12/07/92	1	E	*OPE	*CLE
12/11/92	3	1	*OP1	It's Ice
12/29/92	4	1	FunkBitch	Guelah
12/31/92	2	2	*OP2	It's Ice
02/03/93	1	2	*OP2	It's Ice
02/07/93	4	1	Fee	*CL1
02/10/93	2	2	*OP2	It's Ice
02/13/93	2	2	*OP2	Wilson
02/17/93	3	1	Sloth	It's Ice
02/19/93	2	2	*OP2	It's Ice
02/22/93	3	2	*OP2	It's Ice
02/26/93	3	1	*OP1	Foam
03/03/93	3	1	Sample	Lawn Boy
03/06/93	2	1	Golgi	*CL1
03/09/93	2	1	*OP1	Foam
03/14/93	3	1	PYITE	*CL1
03/17/93	2	1	Landlady	Foam
03/19/93	2	2	*OP2	It's Ice
03/26/93	5	2	Wilson	Tweezer
03/28/93	2	2	WalkAway	Mound
03/31/93	2	1	*OP1	Foam
04/02/93	2	2	*OP2	Sample
04/10/93	4	1	*OP1	Weigh
04/14/93	3	2	Harpua	*CL2
04/20/93	4	1	*OP1	Weigh
04/23/93	3	1	*OP1	Weigh
04/25/93	2	1	Glide	Forbin's
04/29/93	2	1	Sloth	Horn
05/01/93	2	1	*OP1	Foam
05/03/93	2	2	McGrupp	BBJ
05/05/93	1	2	*OP2	My Friend
05/29/93	4	1a	YEM	AmGrace
07/15/93	2	2	Leprech	*CL1
07/17/93	2	1	Landlady	Sample
07/21/93	2	1a	Bouncing	BBJ
07/23/93	2	1	PYITE	It's Ice
07/28/93	4	1	All Things	Ya Mar
07/31/93	3	2	Wilson	It's Ice
08/03/93	2	1	*OP1	Nellie
08/08/93	3	1	Lovin Cup	Horse
08/11/93	2	1	BurAlive	Weigh
08/15/93	4	1	All Things	RunJim
08/21/93	4	1	IDK	*CL1
08/26/93	3	1	*OP1	Guelah
12/29/93	3	1	*OP1	Peaches
04/05/94	4	1	*OP1	Foam
04/10/94	4	1	*OP1	It's Ice
04/14/94	3	1	*OP1	Foam
04/16/94	2	1	*OP1	Fee
04/20/94	3	1	*OP1	It's Ice
04/22/94	2	2	Life Boy	BeLikeYou
04/25/94	3	1	Landlady	Fee
04/28/94	1	1a	*OP1	Foam
05/02/94	3	2	*OP2	Mound
05/04/94	2	1	*OP1	Foam
05/08/94	3	1	*OP1	Foam
05/13/94	3	1	*OP1	It's Ice
05/17/94	3	2	*OP2	Glide
05/21/94	3	1	*OP1	Foam
05/27/94	5	1	Wilson	Foam
06/10/94	4	1	*OP1	Foam
06/17/94	5	1	*OP1	Foam
06/21/94	3	1	*OP1	Foam
07/01/94	8	1	*OP1	Foam
07/09/94	6	1	*OP1	Foam
07/14/94	3	1	*OP1	Bouncing
07/15/94	1	2	SettingSail	*CL2
10/09/94	4	1	*OP1	Foam
10/15/94	5	2	Also Sprac	Halley's
10/20/94	3	1	*OP1	GoldLady
10/23/94	3	2	*OP2	Bouncing
10/26/94	2	1	Suzie	*CL1
10/29/94	3	1	Simple	Foam
11/12/94	5	1	*OP1	Foam
11/18/94	5	E	Baby Arms	*CLE
11/22/94	3	2	Blackbird	BBFCM
12/04/94	9	1	*OP1	Foam
12/07/94	2	1	Peaches	Sloth
12/29/94	5	1	*OP1	Foam
06/08/95	5	1	Ha Ha Ha	Guelah
06/13/95	3	1	*OP1	Foam
06/16/95	3	2	*OP2	Free
06/23/95	5	2	*OP2	Lizards
06/29/95	5	1	*OP1	Taste
07/02/95	3	2	*OP2	Makisupa
09/28/95	3	1	CTB	Billy
09/30/95	2	2	*OP2	Fog
10/05/95	3	2	Also Sprac	Forbin's
10/14/95	6	1	Tela	*CL1
10/19/95	3	1	CTB	Horn
10/22/95	3	1	Sloth	Weigh
10/27/95	3	1	*OP1	Fluffhead
11/10/95	5	1	Bouncing	Fog
11/16/95	5	1	CTB	Chess
11/21/95	3	1	Dog Faced	*CL1
11/25/95	3	1	Wolfman's	*CL1
12/02/95	5	1	Caspian	Mound
12/08/95	4	1	Simple	Fluffhead
12/12/95	3	2	Simple	*CL2
12/15/95	2	2	TweezRep	It's Ice
12/17/95	2	E	HelloBaby	*CLE
12/31/95	4	2	Str Design	Mike's
06/06/96	2	1	PoorHeart	FunkBitch
07/03/96	1	1a	*OP1	Stash
07/11/96	6	1	*OP1	Cavern
07/13/96	2	1a	Sample	Cavern
07/19/96	4	1a	*OP1	Foam
07/23/96	3	2	ASZ	Lovin Cup
08/02/96	3	2	*OP2	Simple
08/07/96	4	2	*OP2	Free
08/14/96	2	2	*OP2	YEM
08/17/96	4	2	Curtain	It's Ice
10/18/96	3	1	*OP1	Guelah
10/22/96	3	1	Curtain	Bouncing
10/27/96	4	1	*OP1	PYITE
11/03/96	4	1	My Friend	Billy
11/08/96	3	1	*OP1	Axilla
11/11/96	2	1	Axilla	*CL1
11/16/96	4	2	La Grange	Kung
11/22/96	3	1	It's Ice	Wolfman's
11/30/96	5	1	*OP1	PYITE
12/28/96	5	1	*OP1	NICU
02/14/97	5	1	*OP1	NICU
02/18/97	3	1	PYITE	NICU
02/20/97	1	2	DayinLife	Adeline
02/25/97	4	1	*OP1	My Soul
03/02/97	4	1	My Soul	Antelope
06/19/97	5	1	Vultures	*CL1
06/24/97	4	1	Guelah	Talk
07/06/97	8	1	*OP1	Old Home
07/22/97	5	1	*OP1	My Soul
07/31/97	6	2	*OP2	Circus
08/06/97	3	2	*OP2	My Soul
08/13/97	5	2	*OP2	Ghost
11/14/97	13	1	*OP1	Gumbo
11/29/97	9	2	*OP2	Str Design
12/05/97	4	1	Sparkle	My Friend
12/28/97	7	1	Old Home	Farmhouse
>> 12/31/97	**3**			

SAMPLE IN A JAR

Inspiration: Tom Marshall's lyrics reference Dave Abrahams's father, Elihu, and also compare the song's narrator to a "sample in a jar" when he's been seatbelted into his car while "foggy, rather groggy."

Musical History and Evolution: Though Sample doesn't change much from version to version, the band did tinker with it slightly during the *Hoist* sessions in fall 1993. Pre-fall versions did not include Page echoing Trey on the second verse, but all post-fall versions (starting on 12/28/93 Washington, D.C.), do.

Rotation History: Played sparingly in its debut year of 1993 but to death in 1994, Sample has become a less-common but still-frequent song in the repertoire in recent years. It fits as both a set opener and closer.

Discography: Appears on *Hoist* (1994).

Sample in a Jar [166] [Sample]

By Anastasio/Marshall

02/04/93	[506]1		Lizards	Glide
02/09/93	4	2	MSO	BBJ
02/27/93	15	2	PoorHeart	BBJ
03/03/93	2	1	Paul&Silas	RunJim
03/14/93	7	1	Paul&Silas	Reba
03/19/93	4	2	Uncle Pen	Lizards
03/24/93	3	1	IDK	AmGrace
03/25/93	1	2	Curtain	Uncle Pen
03/27/93	2	1	Uncle Pen	IDK
03/31/93	3	1	PYITE	Reba
04/02/93	2	2	RunJim	Uncle Pen
04/16/93	8	1	Llama	Rift
04/20/93	3	2	Fluffhead	BBJ
05/01/93	9	1	Rift	It's Ice
07/15/93	9	1	Rift	Divided
07/17/93	2	1	RunJim	My Mind
07/22/93	3	1	My Mind	Foam
07/28/93	5	1	Ya Mar	Foam
07/31/93	3	1	Rift	Ya Mar
08/06/93	3	1	Curtain	Rift
08/15/93	8	1	*OP1	All Things
08/25/93	6	1	Divided	Sparkle
12/28/93	3	2	*OP1	YEM
12/30/93	2	1	Curtain	Paul&Silas
04/04/94	2	1	Divided	Scent
04/06/94	2	1	Lizards	Scent
04/09/94	2	2	*OP2	Reba
04/11/94	2	2	Uncle Pen	BBJ
04/13/94	1	2	Curtain	Reba
04/16/94	3	2	*OP2	PoorHeart
04/18/94	2	2	Also Sprac	Sparkle
04/20/94	1	2	Paul&Silas	BBJ
04/22/94	2	1	PYITE	All Things
04/23/94	1	2	Mound	Sparkle
04/25/94	2	2	Curtain	My Mind
04/28/94	1	1	Foam	Rift
04/30/94	2	1	PoorHeart	PYITE
05/02/94	1	1	Foam	*CL1
05/03/94	1	1	Scent	Adeline
05/04/94	1	1	Foam	It's Ice
05/06/94	1	2	Uncle Pen	Reba
05/07/94	1	E	AmGrace	*CLE
05/10/94	2	1	PoorHeart	Divided
05/12/94	1	1	Lizards	*CL1
05/14/94	2	1	Reba	MSO
05/16/94	1	1	PoorHeart	Divided
05/17/94	1	2	BBJ	Love You
05/19/94	1	2	*OP2	Sparkle
05/21/94	2	2	Dinner	Bowie
05/23/94	2	1	Chalkdust	Foam
05/25/94	1	1	Curtain	Uncle Pen
05/26/94	1	1	Divided	*CL1
05/28/94	2	1	Rift	Foam
06/10/94	3	1	Foam	Nellie
06/13/94	2	1	PoorHeart	Divided
06/14/94	1	E	*OPE	*CLE
06/17/94	2	2	Also Sprac	PoorHeart
06/18/94	1	1	Divided	*CL1
06/21/94	2	1	Mound	It's Ice
06/22/94	1	2	Jesus	*CL2
06/24/94	2	1	Adeline	*CL1
06/25/94	1	1	Mango	Scent
06/26/94	1	2	Life Boy	Wolfman's
06/29/94	1	1	Curtain	Reba
07/01/94	2	1	Foam	NICU
07/02/94	1	2	Maze	Slave
07/05/94	2	1	Rift	Curtain
07/06/94	1	2	BBFCM	BBFCM
07/08/94	1	2	Rift	Reba
07/10/94	2	2	*OP2	Bowie
07/13/94	1	1	PoorHeart	Foam
07/14/94	1	2	Also Sprac	Maze
07/15/94	1	1	Rift	Divided
07/16/94	1	1	Sparkle	*CL1
10/08/94	2	2	Also Sprac	Rift
10/10/94	2	1	*OP1	Divided
10/12/94	1	2	Harry	*CL2
10/14/94	2	1	BurAlive	Divided
10/16/94	2	2	Adeline	*CL2
10/20/94	2	E	*OPE	*CLE
10/23/94	3	1	Maze	*CL1
10/25/94	1	1	Lizards	*CL1
10/28/94	3	1	All Things	Carolina
11/02/94	3	2	Lizards	*CL2
11/04/94	2	1	*OP1	It's Ice
11/12/94	1	E	*OPE	*CLE
11/16/94	3	1	*OP1	Foam
11/20/94	4	1	Divided	*CL1
11/23/94	2	E	*OPE	*CLE
11/26/94	2	2	Lizards	Slave
12/01/94	3	1	*OP1	Uncle Pen
12/03/94	2	1	Guyute	*CL1
12/06/94	2	2	Curtain	Also Sprac
12/10/94	4	1	Lizards	Divided
12/30/94	3	2	*OP2	PoorHeart
05/16/95	2	1	Adeline	*CL1
06/07/95	1	2	AArmy	Harry
06/10/95	3	2	AmGrace	*CL2
06/17/95	5	2	Harry	*CL2
06/22/95	3	1	*OP1	Scent
06/25/95	3	2	Maze	Scent
06/28/95	2	2	*OP2	PoorHeart
07/02/95	4	1	*OP1	Divided
09/28/95	3	2	AmGrace	Antelope
09/30/95	2	1	I'm Blue	*CL1
10/03/95	2	1	TMWSIY	YEM
10/06/95	2	1	Lizards	*CL1
10/08/95	2	2	Ya Mar	YEM
10/11/95	1	1	Julius	*CL1
10/15/95	3	2	Lizards	Suspicious
10/17/95	1	1	*OP1	Stash
10/22/95	4	1	PoorHeart	I'm Blue
10/25/95	2	1	Ya Mar	Divided
10/28/95	2	1	Uncle Pen	Lizards
11/09/95	3	1	Tela	*CL1
11/12/95	3	2	Keyboard	Slave
11/18/95	4	1	I'm Blue	*CL1
11/22/95	3	1	Lizards	Adeline
11/28/95	3	1	HelloBaby	*CL1
11/30/95	2	1	*OP1	Curtain
12/04/95	3	2	YEM	Frankstein
12/08/95	3	1	*OP1	PoorHeart
12/12/95	3	1	Ya Mar	Divided
12/16/95	3	2	*OP2	Reba
12/30/95	4	1	Divided	*CL1
04/26/96	2	1a	Harry	DayinLife
06/06/96	1	2	Fee	*CL2
07/07/96	4	1a	*OP1	Divided
07/11/96	3	1	Scent	*CL1
07/13/96	2	1a	*OP1	RunJim
07/17/96	2	1a	Divided	Bowie
07/22/96	4	1a	*OP1	PoorHeart
07/25/96	3	1a	PYITE	It's Ice
08/04/96	2	2	Scent	Bowie
08/12/96	5	E	*OPE	*CLE
08/14/96	2	2	Rose	TweezRep
08/17/96	2	1	Lizards	Taste
10/16/96	1	1	Mound	It's Ice
10/18/96	2	1	Taste	*CL1
10/21/96	2	1	SSB	CTB
10/26/96	4	1	Theme	*CL1
11/03/96	5	1	NICU	Theme
11/06/96	1	2	Scent	FunkBitch
11/11/96	4	2	Curtain	Tweezer
11/14/96	2	2	Llama	Taste
11/22/96	5	1	Ginseng	FEFY
11/24/96	2	1	IDK	Antelope
11/29/96	2	E	*OPE	*CLE
12/01/96	2	1	Silent	Antelope
12/04/96	2	1	Timber Ho	Train Song
12/31/96	5	1	Divided	TweezRep
02/16/97	3	2	*OP2	CTB
02/20/97	3	2	*OP2	CTB
02/25/97	4	2	Beauty	PYITE
03/02/97	4	1	Uncle Pen	Guyute
03/18/97	1	1	NICU	PYITE
06/16/97	3	1	Water	Beauty
06/21/97	3	1a	*OP1	Also Sprac
07/05/97	9	1a	Uncle Pen	Theme
07/23/97	7	2	Ghost	YEM
07/29/97	3	2	Taste	Rocky Top
08/06/97	5	2	CTB	Antelope
08/13/97	5	2	McGrupp	Also Sprac
12/02/97	16	E	Ginseng	*CLE
12/06/97	3	1	Foam	Fee
12/13/97	5	1	Str Design	Vultures
12/28/97	1	1	Curtain	Old Home
>> 12/31/97	3			

SANITY

Inspiration: The Dude of Life's inspired lyrics reflect on the (in)sanity of life in an unmatched way.

Musical History and Evolution: Played in the 1980s, the band debuted an accelerated version of the song early in 1989 before it fell out of rotation entirely in late spring/summer of that year. The "slow" (original) version of the song was revived on 3/11/92 in Keene, NH, and rare subsequent versions have slowed the song down even further, like on 12/31/95 in New York, NY.

Rotation History: A true rarity, only ten Sanities have appeared thus far in the 1990s. After appearing in light rotation on spring tour 1992, it dropped out of rotation on 5/17/92, then reappeared in 1994 on 4/29/94 and 6/24/94, before hiding again until 12/31/95. The song's next appearance, as the opener on Halloween '96 in Atlanta, is its last appearance to date.

Discography: Appears on the Elektra rerelease of *Junta* (1992), as one of the bonus live tracks, taken from the performance on 7/25/88 (not 5/3/88 as indicated in the *Junta* liner notes).

Sanity [18] [Sanity]

By Phish/Dude of Life

10/31/86	[9]	2	Harry	Skin It
08/21/87	10	3	Jam	SwingLow
07/25/88	29	3	BBFCM	Icculus
08/06/88	2	2	Satin Doll	BBFCM
02/06/89	14	1	All Blues	A-Train
02/07/89	1	3	*OP3	Fluffhead
05/26/89	37	1	Weekapaug	Halley's
05/28/89	2	2	Bathtub	Ride Capt.
03/11/92	282	E	*OPE	Memories
03/20/92	6	2	Weekapaug	Sloth
04/16/92	19	2	*OP2	Llama
04/21/92	4	2	Lively Up	Maze
05/01/92	7	2	*OP2	BurAlive
05/17/92	13	2	Brother	Love You
04/29/94	200	1	Spilt	My Mind
06/24/94	36	2	Simple	Llama
12/31/95	147	3	YEM	Frankstein
10/31/96	43	1	*OP1	HwayHell
>> 12/31/97	105			

SCENT OF A MULE:

Inspiration: Mike Gordon's wild bluegrass/UFO lyrics tell of an outer-space visit to a Southern belle, who befriends the aliens by showing them her elegant Southern home. The tune for the "here's a place of elegance" line comes from sequencing the chords from another part of the song backwards.

Musical History and Evolution: Recorded for inclusion on *Hoist* before ever appearing live, the song has a basic verse-and-chorus structure and no improvisational jamming. But as soon as the song debuted in concert, on 4/4/94 in Burlington, VT, the band added a middle segment that became known as the "Mule Duel," as Trey and Page squared off and traded jams for a few minutes, then segued the music into a Klezmer dance sequence (also known as the "Fiddler on the Roof" part) before returning to the Scent lyrics. Recently, however, the band has varied the song, leading to a Fish-Page duel (8/17/96) and Trey skatting his duel (often on fall tour '96 and on 2/26/97). And by summer 1997, the duel had all but evaporated, with a jam taking its place at the Great Went on 8/17/97 and during the fall tour.

Rotation History: Played very often in 1994, the year of *Hoist*' s release, Scent surfaced often in 1995 and 1996, too, before ebbing in 1997. It was played only seven times that year.

Discography: Appears on *Hoist* (1994), with Bela Fleck on banjo.

Scent of a Mule [91] [Scent]

By Gordon

04/04/94	[615]1		Sample	Maze
04/06/94	2	1	Sample	Fee
04/10/94	3	1	IDK	DWD
04/14/94	3	2	Silent	YEM
04/21/94	6	2	Weekapaug	BBJ
04/29/94	6	1	FEFY	Sloth
05/03/94	3	1	Sqirm Coil	Sample
05/07/94	3	1	FEFY	Split&Melt
05/10/94	2	2	Reba	Harry
05/13/94	2	2	Peaches	YEM
05/17/94	3	1	If I Could	Ginseng
05/20/94	2	1	FEFY	Dog Faced
05/25/94	4	1	Axilla 2	MSO
06/09/94	5	2	Halley's	Ginseng
06/11/94	2	2	Fluffhead	Split&Melt
06/13/94	1	2	Jesus	Split&Melt
06/17/94	3	2	Bathtub	Cavern
06/19/94	2	1	FEFY	Stash
06/22/94	2	1	If I Could	Stash
06/25/94	3	1	Sample	Tela
06/26/94	1	2	Wolfman's	Dog Faced
06/30/94	2	1	Glide	Bouncing
07/02/94	2	1	FEFY	Tweezer
07/09/94	5	1	Guelah	DWD
07/14/94	3	1	TMWSIY	Fluffhead
07/16/94	2	2	ACDCBag	Harry
10/07/94	1	2	Wilson	Tweezer
10/09/94	2	2	Bouncing	YEM
10/12/94	2	2	Bouncing	YEM
10/15/94	3	2	Halley's	YEM
10/18/94	2	2	Reba	Life Boy
10/21/94	2	2	FEFY	Slave

10/26/94	4	1	Dog Faced	Oh Kee
10/28/94	2	1	Guelah	Stash
11/02/94	3	1	Stash	Guitar
11/04/94	2	1	Mockbird	Suzie
11/14/94	3	1	My Friend	Guelah
11/17/94	2	1	Helter	Maze
11/20/94	3	1	Fee	Stash
11/23/94	2	2	Fee	Tweezer
11/28/94	3	1	Also Sprac	Stash
12/03/94	4	1	Guelah	Antelope
12/08/94	4	1	ACDCBag	PYITE
12/30/94	5	1	Fee	Cavern
06/07/95	3	1	If I Could	Wedge
06/09/95	2	2	Wedge	Cavern
06/15/95	4	2	Theme	AArmy
06/22/95	5	1	Sample	Ha Ha Ha
06/25/95	3	2	Sample	Mike's
06/30/95	4	1	ACDCBag	Horn
07/02/95	2	2	Makisupa	Tweezer
09/28/95	3	1	Billy	Stash
09/30/95	2	2	If I Could	Mike's
10/05/95	3	2	Mockbird	Cavern
10/14/95	6	2	HelloBaby	Cavern
10/20/95	4	2	Timber Ho	Simple
10/25/95	4	1	Wedge	Free
10/28/95	2	2	Theme	YEM
11/10/95	4	2	Free	YEM
11/15/95	4	2	Theme	Mike's
11/19/95	3	2	Billy	Harry
11/24/95	3	2	Catapult	Bathtub
11/30/95	4	2	Antelope	Free
12/05/95	4	2	Keyboard	Life Boy
12/11/95	4	2	Fog	Harry
12/16/95	4	2	Reba	Cavern
12/30/95	4	2	Life Boy	Cavern
04/26/96	2	1a	Wolfman's	Also Sprac
06/06/96	1	1	BBFCM	HwayHell
07/05/96	2	1a	YEM	Bowie
07/11/96	5	1	Stash	Sample
07/23/96	9	1	Gumbo	DWD
08/04/96	4	2	Reba	Sample
08/10/96	4	2	DWD	Free
08/17/96	5	3	Frankstein	Tweezer
10/17/96	2	2	Bathtub	Free
10/22/96	4	2	Lawn Boy	Mike's
10/27/96	4	1	Fee	Split&Melt
11/06/96	5	2	Weekapaug	Sample
11/14/96	6	2	Steep	Life Mars
11/18/96	3	2	Steep	Tweezer
11/27/96	5	2	Jesus	Tweezer
12/02/96	4	2	Free	Harry
12/30/96	5	2	Lifeboy	Slave
02/14/97	3	2	RockaW	DayinLife
02/26/97	9	2	Theme	Slave
07/06/97	20	1	CTB	Chalkdust
08/09/97	16	2	Steep	Slave
08/17/97	6	3	Dirt	Caspian
11/16/97	3	1	CTB	PoorHeart
12/28/97	19	2	Drowned	Halley's
>> 12/31/97		3		

SETTING SAIL

Inspiration: A poem written by Tom Marshall that has never really been turned into a song.

Musical History and Evolution: Only performed twice, once leading out of the YEM vocal jam on 4/20/91 in Rochester, NY, and next as a Fishman recitation/audience sing-along in Jones Beach on 7/15/94.

Rotation History: Once in 1991, once in 1994, none since.

Discography: Has yet to appear on a Phish album.

Setting Sail [2] [SettingSail]

By Marshall

04/20/91	[304]	1	YEM	*CL1
07/15/94	383	2	Julius	RunJim
>> 12/31/97	**280**			

SILENT IN THE MORNING

Inspiration: A sweet Tom Marshall lyrical piece that is more heartfelt than many Phish songs.

Musical History and Evolution: Debuted in 1992 with the opening segment later known as The Horse (which until the *Rift* sessions in fall 1992 included the lyrics "Mathilda in between" in lieu of "I'd meet you in between"), Silent was thought to be just one song, with Trey singing the opening and Page the following verses. The release of *Rift* in early 1993 clarified that it was, in fact, two songs, though on 5/30/93 the band did perform Silent without The Horse. Otherwise, the song(s) have stayed pretty much the same over the years, garnering huge cheers on 12/31/94 in Boston, MA, when in the early hours of the New Year, Page sang the "I think that this exact thing happened to me, just last year" line.

Rotation History: See The Horse.

Discography: Appears on *Rift* (1993).

Silent in the Morning [116]

See The Horse

SIMPLE

Inspiration: The mind of Mike Gordon. One theory holds that the four objects in the song refer to the four band members (cymbals—Fish; saxophones—Page; bebop—Trey; skyscrapers—Mike), but that's totally unverified.

Musical History and Evolution: Originally titled "Skyballs and Saxscrapers," the band recorded this song for inclusion on *Hoist* in the fall of 1993 but decided against including it on the album. The song's themes emerged briefly in the jam out of Mike's Song in Portland, ME, on 12/30/93, but the song itself wasn't heard until 5/27/94 in San Francisco, CA, when the band played a very rough version in the midst of Mike's. They debuted it in a more refined form in Milwaukee, WI, on 6/17/94 ("the OJ show," with "We've got OJ in the band"), and played it for most of that summer tour as a jam in Mike's Groove. Since its debut, the song has undergone a number of subtle musical transformations as the band has worked to establish an ending for the song which satisfies them; fall 1994 saw a short, magical musical passage on 10/31/94, a 30-minute jam on 11/16/94, and a very short end-with-refrain version on the '94 New Year's run. By fall 1996, Simple often stretched out in length to over twenty minutes, indicating that maybe the band had found a form they liked for it—a true jam song. Some favored Simples include 10/31/94 and 11/16/94 mentioned above; 7/3/95 Fayston, VT, another beautiful jam; 11/8/96 Champaign, IL, perhaps the best of the long, cool fall '96 versions; and 8/16/97 Great Went, nifty jam into the "Odd Couple" theme.

Rotation History: In moderate rotation since 1994, Simple can still be found in the midst of Mike's Groove, though less often than in the past.

Discography: Appears on *A Live One* (1994), as a live performance taken from Santa Monica, CA, on 12/10/94.

Simple [77] [Simple]

By Gordon

05/27/94	[656]	2	Mike's	Mike's
06/17/94	9	2	Mike's	Mike's
06/22/94	4	2	Mike's	I am H2
06/24/94	2	2	McGrupp	Sanity
07/02/94	6	2	Mike's	Mike's
10/08/94	12	2	Mike's	Mike's
10/13/94	4	2	Mike's	Mike's
10/15/94	2	1	Sparkle	Maze
10/18/94	2	1	*OP1	My Friend
10/21/94	2	2	Mike's	Mike's
10/23/94	2	1	Sparkle	PoorHeart
10/25/94	1	2	Mike's	Mango
10/26/94	1	1	*OP1	It's Ice
10/29/94	3	1	Sparkle	RunJim
10/31/94	1	1	Sparkle	Divided
11/03/94	2	2	Also Sprac	PoorHeart
11/04/94	1	2	Mike's	Mike's
11/13/94	2	1	Sparkle	Reba
11/16/94	2	2	Mike's	Jam
11/20/94	4	2	Reba	Rift
11/23/94	2	1	Sparkle	It's Ice
11/25/94	1	2	Mike's	Harpua
11/28/94	2	1	Sparkle	Divided
12/02/94	3	1	Sparkle	It's Ice
12/06/94	3	2	Mike's	Mango
12/08/94	2	1	Catapult	Lizards
12/10/94	2	2	*OP2	Maze
12/28/94	1	1	Mound	Julius
12/30/94	2	1	Sparkle	Stash
12/31/94	1	E	*OPE	*CLE
06/08/95	3	2	*OP2	Rift
06/14/95	4	E	*OPE	Rocky Top
06/19/95	4	2	*OP2	Bowie
06/23/95	3	1	*OP1	Chalkdust
06/29/95	5	1	Rift	Split&Melt
07/03/95	4	E	*OPE	AmGrace
10/02/95	5	2	Llama	Keyboard
10/15/95	9	2	Julius	Tweezer
10/20/95	3	2	Scent	Guitar
10/27/95	5	2	PoorHeart	McGrupp
11/09/95	4	1	PYITE	Reba
11/16/95	6	1	Ya Mar	Timber Ho
11/21/95	3	2	*OP2	Bowie
11/29/95	5	2	Sparkle	Possum
12/02/95	3	2	Maze	Faht
12/08/95	4	1	PoorHeart	RunJim
12/12/95	3	2	Lizards	RunJim
12/16/95	3	2	Mike's	Weekapaug
12/30/95	4	1	Bowie	It's Ice
07/21/96	17	2	Antelope	Caspian
08/02/96	5	2	Taste	RunJim
08/06/96	3	1	Suzie	Theme
08/12/96	3	2	Sparkle	Caspian
08/16/96	3	2	Mike's	Contact
10/16/96	2	2	Train Song	SweptAwy
10/21/96	4	2	Life Mars	Horse
10/26/96	4	2	Sparkle	McGrupp
10/31/96	3	3	Maze	SweptAwy
11/08/96	5	2	Bouncing	Lovin Cup
11/18/96	7	2	Also Sprac	SweptAwy
11/23/96	3	2	Mike's	Makisupa
11/29/96	3	2	Wilson	Sparks
12/01/96	2	2	Sparkle	DayinLife
12/06/96	3	2	Mike's	Harry
12/31/96	4	2	Sparkle	SweptAwy
02/16/97	3	2	Sparkle	Circus
02/22/97	5	2	Sparkle	Jesus
07/02/97	20	1	Mike's	Maze
07/22/97	8	2	Mike's	I am H2
08/03/97	8	2	Julius	Fluffhead
08/09/97	3	2	Funny	SweptAwy
08/16/97	5	2	Wolfman's	My Soul
11/16/97	4	2	Timber Ho	Wilson
11/29/97	8	1	Foam	TMWSIY
12/02/97	2	2	Mike's	Dog Faced
12/09/97	5	2	Julius	Timber Ho
12/28/97	4	2	Axilla	Ghost
>> 12/31/97		3		

SKIPPY THE WONDERMOUSE

Inspiration: The Dude of Life, of course.

Musical History and Evolution: Short-lived, as Trey pirated the music from Skippy for McGrupp, where it can still be heard.

Rotation History: Appeared in

Rarities

Original songs debuted before 1/1/97 that surface in concert rarely these days, with total times played since 5/16/95 and the last appearance

Song	Since '95	Last Played
Glide II	1	05/16/95
Icculus	1	10/31/95
Mid-Highway Blues	1	11/23/96
Faht	2	12/02/95
Sanity	2	10/31/96
Brother	3	10/31/96
Dog Log	3	02/26/97
My Sweet One	4	12/31/97
Axilla II	4	12/31/95
Camel Walk	4	12/12/97
Rotation Jam	4	08/10/97
Spock's Brain	5	06/24/95
Harpua	7	12/30/97

1984 and 1985, but not since the musical formation of McGrupp.

Discography: Has not yet appeared on a Phish album.

SLAVE TO THE TRAFFIC LIGHT

Inspiration: Another song in the elite class of few-lyrics-but-great-jam.

Musical History and Evolution: Played at the band's first Nectar's show on 12/1/84, Slave has been around since nearly the beginning. Though in recent years the band has taken the jams to enchanting new heights, the basic song structure has been in place since its debut performance. Since its return from hibernation on summer tour 1993, Slave has been reborn as a fan favorite, especially versions of 8/6/93 Cincinnati, OH, the song's return from retirement at the Cincy Zoo; 8/20/93 Morrison, CO, the only 2001 > Slave; 12/30/93 Portland, ME, the first East Coast Slave in ages; 10/31/94 Glens Falls, NY; 11/26/94 Minneapolis, MN, the powerful version on *A Live One*; 12/31/94 Boston, MA, emotional powerhouse; 8/17/96 Clifford Ball, simply beautiful; and a year later, 8/16/97 Great Went, including a cool yet-unnamed intro jam.

Rotation History: Already uncommon by 1990 (just six performances), Slave surfaced just twice in 1991, once by request in Colorado on 3/17/91, and again that fall on 10/24/91. It wasn't seen again until 8/6/93, when the setting of the Cincinnati Zoo made it too tempting for the band to pass up. It was played twice more that year, and then rejoined regular rotation.

Discography: Appears on *A Live One* (1995), and in shorter version on their "White Album."

Slave to the Traffic Light [113] [Slave]

By Anastasio/Dude of Life

12/01/84	[0]	1a	FOTM	Makisupa
10/30/85	4	1a	Possum	Sally
04/15/86	3	1a	Quinn	Makisupa
10/15/86	1	1a	Wilson	Makisupa
10/31/86	1	1	Golgi	Melt Guns
04/24/87	5	1a	Reagan	*CL1
04/29/87	1	3	Timber Ho	Sparks
05/11/87	1	1a	Possum	Sally
08/29/87	5	2	Clod	SwingLow
09/12/87	2	1	Clod	FunkBitch
10/14/87	2	1	Golgi	Chase
01/30/88	1	2	Wilson	Corrina
03/11/88	3	1	Golgi	Flat Fee
06/20/88	11	1	*OP1	Peaches
07/12/88	3	1	Makisupa	ACDCBag
07/23/88	1	3	Dinner	Curtis
08/06/88	4	2	BBFCM	*CL2
09/08/88	2	1	WalkAway	WildChild
10/29/88	2	3	Timber Ho	Donna
11/05/88	2	1	*OP1	TimeLoves
11/11/88	1	1	YEM	FOam
02/07/89	6	2	Suzie	Bike
04/15/89	14	2	Golgi	Mango
05/06/89	11	2	Golgi	Divided
05/09/89	3	2	IIDBT	Esther
05/26/89	9	3	*OP3	FunkBitch
05/28/89	2	1	Fee	Esther
06/30/89	7	2	Curtain	Bathtub
08/26/89	9	2	Ya Mar	ACDCBag
10/20/89	11	E	La Grange	*CLE
12/08/89	19	2	Timber Ho	IDK
03/01/90	17	E	Carolina	*CLE
03/09/90	5	2	Dog Log	HwayHell
03/11/90	1	2	Harpua	ACDCBag
04/08/90	7	2	Lizards	Mike's
04/22/90	9	1	MSO	Mike's
06/01/90	17	1a	Divided	Possum
03/17/91	68	2	Fee	Chalkdust
10/24/91	70	2	Tube	Dinner
08/06/93	240	2	Halley's	Rosie
08/20/93	11	2	Also Sprac	Split&Melt
12/30/93	8	2	PurplRain	*CL2
04/09/94	6	2	Tela	Cavern
04/14/94	4	2	Dog Faced	*CL2
04/24/94	9	1	It's Ice	*CL1
05/03/94	6	2	BeLikeYou	*CL2
05/13/94	7	1	My Friend	Suzie
05/17/94	3	2	Love You	*CL2
05/22/94	4	2	Rift	TweezRep
06/13/94	10	2	Terrapin	*CL2
06/23/94	8	2	Life Boy	*CL2
07/02/94	7	2	Sample	HwayHell
07/13/94	7	2	Mound	Suzie
10/10/94	7	2	Love You	*CL2
10/21/94	8	2	Scent	*CL2
10/27/94	5	E	*OPE	Icculus
10/31/94	3	3	Bouncing	Rift
11/04/94	3	2	Golgi	*CL2
11/14/94	3	2	YSZahov	PoorHeart
11/17/94	2	2	Love You	Golgi
11/26/94	7	2	Sample	*CL2
12/03/94	5	2	Gumbo	Touch Me
12/10/94	6	2	PoorHeart	Cavern
12/31/94	4	3	Suzie	*CL3
06/07/95	2	1	FunkBitch	*CL1
06/09/95	2	2	Adeline	*CL2
06/15/95	4	2	AArmy	*CL2
06/20/95	4	E	*OPE	AmGrace
06/25/95	4	E	Bouncing	*CLE
07/02/95	6	2	AArmy	*CL2
09/28/95	3	1	AArmy	*CL1
10/02/95	3	2	Keyboard	HelloBaby
10/06/95	3	2	Suspicious	*CL2
10/15/95	6	1	PoorHeart	IDK
10/22/95	5	2	Uncle Pen	Cavern
10/29/95	5	1	Gumbo	Adeline
11/12/95	5	2	Sample	Rosie
11/18/95	4	1	PYITE	I'm Blue
11/29/95	7	2	LongJourn	*CL2
12/07/95	6	1	Rift	Guyute
12/09/95	2	2	Lawn Boy	Crossroad
12/14/95	3	2	NICU	*CL2
12/28/95	4	2	Uncle Pen	*CL2
07/12/96	13	2	NICU	Suzie
07/23/96	8	2	Bike	*CL2
08/04/96	4	2	Adeline	*CL2
08/13/96	6	1	Glide	*CL1
08/17/96	3	2	Golgi	*CL2
10/19/96	4	2	Sparkle	Bouncing
10/23/96	3	2	Suzie	Julius
10/29/96	4	2	Suspicious	HelloBaby
11/11/96	8	2	Contact	*CL2
11/22/96	7	2	Theme	HelloBaby
12/01/96	6	2	JGB	*CL2
12/30/96	6	2	Scent	*CL2
02/13/97	2	2	PYITE	Circus
02/18/97	4	1	CharZero	*CL1
02/26/97	6	2	Scent	*CL2
03/02/97	3	2	CharZero	TweezRep
03/18/97	1	2	Chalkdust	*CL2
06/13/97	1	2	Vultures	Chalkdust
07/01/97	11	2	Lovin Cup	*CL2
07/21/97	8	2	FunkBitch	*CL2
08/03/97	9	E	Bouncing	*CLE
08/09/97	3	2	Scent	Weekapaug
08/16/97	5	2	Jam	Rocky Top
11/14/97	3	2	Jam	*CL2
11/21/97	4	2	ACDCBag	Lovin Cup
11/28/97	4	2	Limb	Ghost
12/05/97	5	2	Julius	Lizards
12/07/97	2	2	Jam	*CL1
12/28/97	5	2	Halley's	Rocky Top
>> 12/31/97		3		

SLEEPING MONKEY

Inspiration: Tom Marshall's lyrics are said by some to be about the tumescence of the male anatomy, but whether that's actually the case is debatable.

Musical History and Evolution: Little, as the song is performed now pretty much as it was debuted in Portsmouth, NH, on 3/6/92. The "Let It Be"-styled closing jam is a part of every performance of this song. The only performance outside the normal realm came with John Popper on harmonica 3/14/92.

Rotation History: Played randomly since its debut, usually as an encore until fall 1994 when the band started mixing it up in the setlist.

Discography: Has not yet appeared on a Phish album.

Sleeping Monkey [52] [Sl Monkey]

By Anastasio/Marshall

03/06/92	[384]	E	*OPE	*CLE
03/11/92	2	E	Carolina	*CLE
03/14/92	3	E	*OPE	GTBT
03/19/92	2	E	*OPE	Rocky Top
03/25/92	4	E	*OPE	TweezRep
03/26/92	1	E	*OPE	Chalkdust
03/30/92	3	E	*OPE	Oh Kee
04/04/92	4	E	*OPE	TweezRep
04/09/92	4	E	*OPE	Rocky Top
04/16/92	4	E	*OPE	*CLE
04/19/92	3	E	*OPE	Cavern
04/23/92	3	E	*OPE	TweezRep
05/02/92	6	E	*OPE	BBFCM
05/07/92	4	E	Adeline	Rocky Top
05/14/92	5	E	*OPE	Rocky Top
07/14/92	17	E	*OPE	*CLE
11/23/92	35	E	*OPE	Rocky Top
12/08/92	12	2	BBJ	*CL2
02/20/93	23	E	*OPE	*CLE
02/27/93	6	E	*OPE	AmGrace
03/21/93	14	E	*OPE	Adeline
05/02/93	31	E	*OPE	AmGrace
08/02/93	22	E	*OPE	AmGrace
04/30/94	44	E	*OPE	HwayHell
05/22/94	16	E	*OPE	*CLE
05/25/94	2	E	*OPE	TweezRep
06/10/94	6	E	*OPE	Rocky Top
06/17/94	5	E	*OPE	Rocky Top
06/30/94	10	E	*OPE	PoorHeart
07/09/94	7	E	*OPE	TweezRep
07/15/94	4	E	*OPE	Rocky Top
10/09/94	4	E	*OPE	PoorHeart
10/21/94	9	2	Weekapaug	Curtain
10/29/94	7	2	Antelope	Antelope
10/31/94	1	3	Rift	PoorHeart
11/17/94	8	2	Bowie	Sparkle
11/28/94	8	2	Tweezer	Julius
12/01/94	2	E	*OPE	TweezRep
12/04/94	3	E	*OPE	Rocky Top
12/29/94	7	E	LongJourn	*CLE
06/26/95	19	E	*OPE	Rocky Top
07/02/95	5	2	Ha Ha Ha	AArmy
10/20/95	18	E	*OPE	Rocky Top
10/24/95	3	2	YEM	Antelope
11/11/95	8	2	Fluffhead	Frankstein
12/07/95	18	2	Julius	Sparkle
08/13/96	40	E	*OPE	Rocky Top
11/15/96	25	2	Mike's	Mustard
02/17/97	21	E	*OPE	Rocky Top
08/13/97	46	2	Isabella	McGrupp
12/06/97	19	2	Piper	TweezRep
12/30/97	8	2	My Soul	Guyute
>> 12/31/97		1		

THE SLOTH

Inspiration: A Gamehendge song. The Sloth is a hitman from the ghetto who is hired by the revolutionaries to kill Wilson.

Musical History and Evolution: Not much, as the driving beat has been a staple of the song since it was written.

Rotation History: An uncommon treat in recent years, including only three performances in 1997.

Discography: Has not yet appeared on a Phish album.

The Sloth [122] [Sloth]

By Anastasio

08/21/87	[19]	2	Creek	*CL2
01/30/88	9	2	YEM	WhipPost
03/12/88	4	1a	Mockbird	Possum
05/15/88	5	1a	IDK	Harpua
05/25/88	2	3	*OP3	IDK
06/15/88	1	2	ACDCBag	Contact
07/23/88	6	2	*OP2	Fire
10/12/88	9	2	Contact	ACDCBag
12/02/88	5	1	*OP1	Golgi
01/26/89	1	1a	Mockbird	Possum
02/07/89	4	1	Foam	Possum
04/14/89	13	1	Lizards	Possum
04/20/89	3	1	Suzie	Possum
05/06/89	9	1	Esther	Possum
05/09/89	3	1	Weekapaug	Possum
05/21/89	8	1	Split&Melt	YEM
05/26/89	1	1	Halley's	YEM
05/28/89	2	3	La Grange	Sally
06/23/89	5	2	*OP2	Fluffhead
08/17/89	7	1	McGrupp	Rocky Top
10/06/89	10	1a	Weekapaug	Golgi
10/26/89	8	2	Bathtub	Fluffhead
11/10/89	7	2	Fluffhead	Lizards
11/16/89	2	2	*OP2	ACDCBag
02/24/90	32	2	*OP2	ACDCBag
03/09/90	7	1	Mockbird	Possum
03/11/90	1	2	A-Train	Ya Mar
04/04/90	3	2	Uncle Pen	IDK
04/06/90	2	2	Esther	Harry
04/13/90	6	2	Curtis	Harry
04/18/90	1	2	Fee	FunkBitch
05/04/90	10	2	RunJim	Uncle Pen
05/24/90	9	1	*OP1	Bouncing
09/16/90	11	1a	Bouncing	Landlady
10/04/90	6	1	Destiny	Uncle Pen
11/02/90	9	1	Divided	Mike's
11/26/90	8	1	RunJim	Reba
11/30/90	1	2	IDK	Antelope
02/02/91	9	2	*OP2	Antelope
02/07/91	2	2	Lizards	Destiny
02/09/91	2	1	Mango	TMWSIY
02/15/91	2	1	Mango	Dinner
02/16/91	1	1	*OP1	MSO
02/27/91	8	2	Oh Kee	Love You
03/01/91	2	2	Guelah	Possum
03/07/91	3	2	Landlady	RunJim
03/13/91	3	2	RunJim	Reba
03/23/91	6	1	*OP1	Divided
04/05/91	7	2	Lizards	Dinner
04/15/91	5	1	*OP1	Ya Mar
04/18/91	2	1	Oh Kee	Paul&Silas
04/20/91	2	2	*OP2	Ya Mar
04/22/91	2	1	RunJim	Reba
04/26/91	2	1	Sqirm Coil	Possum
05/03/91	3	2	Curtain	Landlady
05/10/91	3	1	Dinner	Landlady
05/25/91	6	1a	Dinner	McGrupp
07/14/91	4	1	Mockbird	IDK
07/21/91	5	2	Lawn Boy	Esther
07/25/91	3	1	MSO	Foam
08/03/91	3	1	Wilson	RunJim
10/11/91	12	2	Mango	PoorHeart
10/13/91	2	1	ACDCBag	McGrupp
10/31/91	11	1	Ya Mar	Chalkdust
11/08/91	5	2	*OP2	Sparkle
11/12/91	3	1	Tube	Harry
11/19/91	5	2	Mango	Reba
11/24/91	5	1	*OP1	Paul&Silas
12/05/91	3	2	Fee	Sqirm Coil
03/11/92	6	2	NICU	Lizards
03/13/92	2	2	My Mind	Rift

03/17/92	2	2	Glide	PoorHeart
03/20/92	2	2	Sanity	Mango
03/27/92	5	1	Paul&Silas	Divided
03/30/92	2	1	All Things	RunJim
04/03/92	3	2	Curtain	Possum
04/07/92	4	1	Rift	RunJim
04/24/92	12	1	Uncle Pen	Landlady
05/01/92	4	1	NICU	Divided
05/12/92	9	1	All Things	Possum
05/14/92	1	1	All Things	Sparkle
07/15/92	18	2	*OP2	Divided
11/20/92	31	1	Rift	Reba
12/06/92	13	1	MSO	Sqirm Coil
12/28/92	7	2	Reba	YEM
02/10/93	10	1	Reba	Divided
02/17/93	5	1	All Things	RunJim
02/20/93	3	1	Foam	Possum
03/05/93	9	1	Foam	Rift
03/21/93	11	1	Sparkle	Divided
03/22/93	1	2	Mockbird	McGrupp
03/28/93	5	1	Lizards	Maze
04/03/93	5	2	All Things	YEM
04/13/93	5	2	Rift	Uncle Pen
04/29/93	12	1	Paul&Silas	RunJim
07/25/93	19	1	Rift	My Mind
08/07/93	9	2	Avenu	Sparkle
08/12/93	4	2	Lizards	Maze
12/28/93	12	2	Lizards	FEFY
04/17/94	15	2	Uncle Pen	Reba
04/29/94	9	1	Scent	Divided
05/22/94	17	1	Demand	Divided
05/28/94	5	1	Silent	Maze
06/24/94	14	1	Fee	All Things
06/26/94	2	1	Mockbird	McGrupp
07/08/94	8	1	Mockbird	McGrupp
10/12/94	11	1	Reba	PoorHeart
12/07/94	38	1	RunJim	Ya Mar
06/26/95	24	1	NICU	My Mind
10/22/95	25	1	My Mind	RunJim
12/09/95	29	1	NICU	Rift
12/16/95	5	1	Ya Mar	Divided
12/31/95	5	1	PYITE	Reba
08/04/96	22	1	Mango	Maze
10/21/96	14	1	CTB	Divided
11/03/96	9	1	Billy	NICU
11/09/96	4	1	PoorHeart	Divided
11/27/96	11	1	Chalkdust	Uncle Pen
12/30/96	9	1	Ya Mar	Llama
02/23/97	10	1	All Things	Love Me
11/29/97	55	1	TMWISY	Ginseng
12/31/97	14	1	Silent	Fire
>> 12/31/97	**0**			

SPARKLE

Inspiration: Another song about relationship pressure, penned by Tom Marshall around the time of other *Rift*-era songs in 1991–1992. As a fast, catchy song, it has become one of the most recognized Phish songs, to the dismay of some fans.

Musical History and Evolution: The band has managed to somehow accelerate the frenetic jam, seemingly with every performance, but beyond that, versions of Sparkle differ little from one another. The band did make a very slight lyrics change during the *Rift* sessions in fall 1992, changing the line "the skin that drips down from the tree" to "off the tree."

Rotation History: Incredibly common since its debut on 9/25/91 in Keene, NH, through 1996, Sparkle finally got a bit of a breather in 1997, as it was played only ten times.

Discography: Appears on *Rift* (1993).

Sparkle [254] [Sparkle]

By Anastasio/Marshall

09/25/91	[335]	2	Stash	Cavern
09/26/91	1	2	Brother	Landlady
09/27/91	1	2	Tela	Split&Melt
09/28/91	1	2	Guelah	Cavern
10/04/91	4	1	Guelah	Suzie
10/10/91	3	2	IDK	Oh Kee
10/15/91	4	1	Split&Melt	Reba
10/18/91	6	2	Bathtub	Tweezer
10/27/91	4	2	Mockbird	It's Ice
10/31/91	3	1	Chalkdust	Foam
11/01/91	1	1	ACDCBag	Landlady
11/02/91	1	2	TMWSIY	Guelah
11/07/91	2	1	Foam	Cavern
11/08/91	1	2	Sloth	Split&Melt
11/09/91	1	1	Foam	Llama
11/13/91	3	1	It's Ice	Chalkdust
11/14/91	1	1	Tube	Brother
11/15/91	1	1	Chalkdust	Cavern
11/16/91	1	1	It's Ice	Fluffhead
11/19/91	1	1	Fee	Brother
11/20/91	1	1	Mockbird	Stash
11/22/91	2	1	Cavern	Brother
11/23/91	1	1	Guelah	Chalkdust
11/24/91	1	1	Fluffhead	It's Ice
11/30/91	1	1	Foam	Divided
12/04/91	1	2	Weekapaug	Lizards
12/05/91	1	2	Tweezer	Tube
12/06/91	1	2	Eliza	YEM
12/07/91	1	2	Chalkdust	Brother
12/31/91	1	1	Foam	Stash
03/06/92	1	1	Cavern	It's Ice
03/12/92	3	1	Foam	Stash
03/14/92	2	1	Reba	Foam
03/17/92	1	1	Cavern	It's Ice
03/19/92	1	1	Split&Melt	Golgi
03/21/92	2	1	Foam	Split&Melt
03/25/92	2	1	Wilson	Split&Melt
03/26/92	1	1	Foam	Stash
03/28/92	2	1	Foam	Stash
03/30/92	1	1	Guelah	Maze
04/01/92	2	1	All Things	RunJim
04/03/92	1	1	Guelah	Maze
04/04/92	1	1	It's Ice	Lizards
04/06/92	2	1	Foam	Reba
04/09/92	2	1	Landlady	Foam
04/12/92	1	1	It's Ice	Maze
04/13/92	1	2	Fluffhead	Mike's
04/15/92	1	1	Guelah	Stash
04/17/92	2	1	Foam	Stash
04/18/92	1	1	It's Ice	All Things
04/22/92	3	1	Reba	Guelah
04/24/92	2	1	Fluffhead	Stash
04/29/92	2	1	Foam	It's Ice
05/02/92	3	1	Mockbird	Reba
05/05/92	2	1	Curtain	Stash
05/06/92	1	1	Mockbird	Cavern
05/07/92	1	2	Landlady	Tweezer
05/09/92	2	1	Foam	Split&Melt
05/10/92	1	1a	Suzie	Stash
05/14/92	2	1	Sloth	Maze
05/15/92	1	1a	Cavern	Stash
05/17/92	2	2	Love You	Harry
05/18/92	1	1	Horn	Antelope
06/19/92	1	1a	Sqirm Coil	Cavern
06/24/92	3	1a	IDK	Cavern
06/27/92	1	1a	Foam	Reba
07/09/92	4	1a	Landlady	Stash
07/10/92	1	1a	Reba	Maze
07/11/92	1	1a	Foam	Stash
07/14/92	2	1	Maze	It's Ice
07/16/92	2	1	It's Ice	Wilson
07/17/92	1	1a	Chalkdust	Stash
07/21/92	3	1a	It's Ice	Stash
07/25/92	3	1a	Foam	Stash
07/30/92	4	1a	Horn	It's Ice
08/15/92	6	1a	Landlady	Guelah
08/23/92	4	1a	Maze	Cavern
08/25/92	2	1a	It's Ice	Stash
08/27/92	1	1a	Horn	YEM
11/20/92	6	1	Reba	Stash
11/22/92	2	1	Reba	Horn
11/25/92	2	1	Maze	It's Ice
11/28/92	2	1	Chalkdust	FEFY
11/30/92	1	1	Stash	It's Ice
12/02/92	2	1	Lizards	Horn
12/04/92	2	1	Glide	FEFY
12/05/92	1	2	Reba	Maze
12/07/92	2	1	Glide	Foam
12/08/92	1	2	Lawn Boy	Suzie
12/11/92	2	1	Guelah	My Friend
12/12/92	1	1	Foam	Cavern
12/28/92	2	1	Maze	Foam
12/30/92	2	1	Landlady	Split&Melt
12/31/92	1	1	It's Ice	Forbin's
02/03/93	1	2	Silent	YEM
02/05/93	2	1	Split&Melt	PYITE
02/07/93	2	1	It's Ice	Forbin's
02/10/93	2	2	Walk Line	YEM
02/12/93	2	1	Guelah	Split&Melt
02/15/93	2	1	Suzie	Guelah
02/18/93	2	1	Foam	Cavern
02/19/93	1	1	Mockbird	My Friend
02/22/93	3	1	Fee	Foam
02/25/93	2	2	It's Ice	Wilson
02/27/93	2	1	It's Ice	PYITE
03/02/93	1	1	Reba	It's Ice
03/05/93	2	1	Stash	It's Ice
03/08/93	2	1	Mockbird	It's Ice
03/12/93	2	2	Axilla	YEM
03/14/93	2	1	Guelah	Stash
03/16/93	1	E	*OPE	TweezRep
03/18/93	2	1	Mockbird	Horn
03/21/93	2	1	Maze	Sloth
03/22/93	1	1	Reba	Bowie
03/24/93	1	2	Split&Melt	Tweezer
03/26/93	2	1	Maze	Foam
03/28/93	2	1	FunkBitch	Split&Melt
03/31/93	2	1	Foam	Split&Melt
04/02/93	2	1	IDK	Maze
04/03/93	1	1	Guelah	Split&Melt
04/09/93	2	1	Chalkdust	Guelah
04/10/93	1	1	Weigh	Split&Melt
04/13/93	2	1	Foam	Possum
04/16/93	2	1	Guelah	Split&Melt
04/18/93	2	1	Split&Melt	Divided
04/20/93	1	1	Weigh	Stash
04/22/93	2	1	Suzie	It's Ice
04/23/93	1	1	Weigh	Split&Melt
04/24/93	1	1	SWMB	Antelope
04/27/93	2	1	It's Ice	Bowie
04/30/93	2	2	Wilson	Tweezer
05/02/93	2	1	Axilla	Divided
05/05/93	2	1	Foam	Bouncing
05/07/93	2	1	Split&Melt	Caravan
05/29/93	2	1a	Sqirm Coil	Cavern
07/15/93	2	2	Silent	It's Ice
07/17/93	2	2	It's Ice	BBJ
07/21/93	2	1a	Split&Melt	Sqirm Coil
07/22/93	1	2	WalkAway	It's Ice
07/24/93	2	2	Glide	Mike's
07/27/93	2	1a	Sqirm Coil	It's Ice
07/29/93	2	2	Life Boy	YEM
07/31/93	2	2	Maze	Mike's
08/03/93	2	2	Lizards	PurplRain
08/07/93	2	2	Sloth	My Friend
08/11/93	3	1	Stash	Cavern
08/14/93	3	1	It's Ice	Split&Melt
08/16/93	2	1	Reba	Foam
08/21/93	3	1	Stash	Landlady
08/25/93	2	1	Sample	Foam
08/28/93	2	2	Silent	It's Ice
12/29/93	2	1	Wilson	Stash
12/31/93	2	3	Lizards	Suzie
04/06/94	3	2	Wolfman's	Mike's
04/08/94	1	2	It's Ice	Harry
04/10/94	2	1	It's Ice	Split&Melt
04/14/94	3	1	Foam	DWD
04/18/94	4	2	Sample	Bathtub
04/21/94	2	1	Chalkdust	Foam
04/23/94	2	2	Sample	Harry
05/03/94	7	1	Maze	Stash
05/04/94	1	1	It's Ice	Axilla 2
05/07/94	2	2	Lovin Cup	Tweezer
05/16/94	6	2	Antelope	It's Ice
05/19/94	2	2	Sample	Mike's
05/23/94	4	2	If I Could	PYITE
05/26/94	2	1	Split&Melt	It's Ice
05/29/94	3	1	DWD	Julius
06/10/94	2	2	Life Boy	Possum
06/14/94	3	2	It's Ice	YEM
06/17/94	2	2	Harpua	BBJ
06/21/94	3	2	Julius	Harry
06/23/94	2	E	*OPE	TweezRep
06/25/94	2	2	Maze	Bathtub
06/30/94	3	2	YEM	Axilla 2
07/02/94	2	1	Life Boy	TweezRep
07/05/94	2	2	PYITE	Bathtub
07/09/94	3	2	Life Boy	BBJ
07/14/94	3	2	YEM	BBJ
07/16/94	2	1	Maze	Sample
10/08/94	2	1	Horn	DWD
10/10/94	2	1	Silent	Stash
10/13/94	2	1	FEFY	Stash
10/15/94	2	1	Wilson	Simple
10/23/94	6	1	My Friend	Simple
10/27/94	3	1	Wilson	Maze
10/29/94	2	1	My Friend	Simple
10/31/94	1	1	Frankstein	Simple
11/03/94	2	1	Dog Faced	DWD
11/13/94	3	1	Wilson	Simple
11/17/94	3	2	Sl Monkey	YEM
11/19/94	2	2	Suzie	YEM
11/23/94	3	1	Wilson	Simple
11/28/94	3	1	Guyute	Simple
12/02/94	3	1	Also Sprac	Simple
12/06/94	3	1	Jesus	Stash
12/09/94	3	1	Guyute	IDK
12/30/94	4	1	ACDCBag	Simple
06/09/95	5	1	Taste	Antelope
06/13/95	2	1	Terrapin	Chalkdust
06/15/95	2	1	My Friend	ACDCBag
06/19/95	3	2	Lovin Cup	YEM
06/25/95	5	1	If I Could	Divided
06/28/95	2	2	Gumbo	Suzie
07/03/95	5	1	Lovin Cup	It's Ice
09/29/95	3	1	ACDCBag	Divided
10/03/95	3	2	It's Ice	Harry
10/08/95	4	1	Demand	Wolfman's
10/14/95	3	1	Catapult	AArmy
10/17/95	2	1	Glide	Free
10/21/95	3	2	Life Boy	YEM
10/25/95	3	2	Mike's	Weekapaug
10/31/95	4	1	Ya Mar	Free
11/10/95	2	2	Str Design	ACDCBag
11/15/95	4	1	Caspian	Split&Melt
11/18/95	2	2	ACDCBag	Free
11/24/95	4	1	Curtain	Stash
11/29/95	3	2	Timber Ho	Simple
12/04/95	4	2	Timber Ho	Ya Mar
12/07/95	2	2	Sl Monkey	Mike's
12/12/95	4	2	Free	DWD
12/17/95	4	2	Harry	Tweezer
12/31/95	4	1	Mockbird	Chalkdust
04/26/96	1	1a	ACDCBag	Stash
06/06/96	1	2	Chalkdust	Stash
07/03/96	1	1a	Stash	Taste
07/11/96	6	1	IDK	Stash
07/23/96	8	2	Lovin Cup	Mike's
08/07/96	7	1	PYITE	Stash
08/12/96	2	2	Timber Ho	Simple
08/16/96	3	2	Split&Melt	Free
10/17/96	3	1	FunkBitch	Tweezer
10/19/96	2	2	ACDCBag	Slave
10/22/96	2	1	Split&Melt	Free
10/26/96	3	2	YEM	Simple
11/03/96	5	2	Brother	Tweezer
11/11/96	5	1	ACDCBag	Brother
11/16/96	4	1	Lawn Boy	Frankstein
11/24/96	5	2	Also Sprac	Bowie
11/29/96	2	2	Sparks	Taste
12/01/96	2	2	Tweezer	Simple
12/04/96	2	2	Caspian	PYITE
12/06/96	1	2	Julius	Mike's
12/31/96	4	2	Wilson	Simple
02/16/97	3	2	Free	Simple
02/22/97	5	2	Bathtub	Simple
07/03/97	21	2	Billy	Harry
07/29/97	11	1	Dirt	Ghost
08/02/97	3	2	Johnny B.	Wading
08/10/97	5	1	Bathtub	DWD
08/14/97	3	1	Love Me	Harry
11/23/97	10	1	BE Katy	Twist
11/26/97	1	1	Tweezer	Gumbo
12/05/97	6	1	BE Katy	RunJim
>> 12/31/97	**10**			

SPLIT OPEN AND MELT

Inspiration: Trey has said that he didn't really know what his lyrics meant until he found himself singing them one night onstage and realized they described his life on tour at its most exhausting.

Musical History and Evolution: Though the song's written structure, with room for an improvisational jam built around a set of recurring chords, has been evident since the song's debut in 1989, it took a long time for the band to really nail the song. It shined with the Giant Country Horns in July 1991, as Trey had arranged a horn section for the song on *Lawn Boy* in fall 1989 (also see the double performance from the Front in Burlington, VT, on 10/20/89). The first time they really "got it right" without the horns came on 4/21/93 in Columbus, OH, a version the band later enshrined as the jam out of Demand on *Hoist*. For the next year, the song seemed to just keep going right, including great performances on 8/6/93 Cincinnati, OH, and 8/20/93 Morrison, CO, among others. By 1994, the band was already trying new things with the jam, getting away from the historical structure (check out 11/3/94 Amherst, MA, for a very different version), while still pulling out great versions (6/11/94 Morrison, CO, among others). In recent years, the jam hasn't achieved such heights, though there's always the happy possibility.

Rotation History: Rose from a low of seven performances in 1990 to a peak of forty-two in both 1993 and 1994, then fell off again, down to eleven in 1997.

Discography: Appears on *Lawn Boy* (1990), with horns.

Split Open and Melt [225] [Split & Melt]

By Anastasio

02/17/89	[66]	1a	Divided	Golgi
03/03/89	3	2	Lizards	A-Train
04/15/89	10	2	Divided	Suzie
04/20/89	2	2	YEM	Lizards
05/13/89	15	1	A-Train	*CL1
05/21/89	5	1	Weekapaug	Sloth
05/26/89	1	2	Mango	Bathtub
05/28/89	2	3	Jesus	Mango
06/23/89	5	2	Ya Mar	Possum
08/19/89	9	2	*OP2	A-Train
08/26/89	2	1	Harry	Divided
09/09/89	4	2	Alumni	Harry
10/01/89	1	2	Contact	Lizards
10/14/89	5	1	Ya Mar	Fee
10/20/89	1	2	Donna	Split&Melt
10/22/89	2	1	Rocky Top	Tela
11/02/89	4	1	Reba	Esther
11/03/89	1	1	MSO	Clod
11/10/89	3	1	*OP1	Oh Kee
11/30/89	4	2	Fee	A-Train
12/08/89	5	1	Suzie	Ya Mar
12/31/89	6	2	Ya Mar	Divided
01/28/90	5	1	Suzie	Tela
02/17/90	11	1a	Weekapaug	Bouncing
03/07/90	8	2	Bathtub	Tela
03/11/90	3	2	Ya Mar	Harpua
03/28/90	2	2	Lizards	Contact
09/15/90	39	2	*OP2	Eliza
10/05/90	8	2	Uncle Pen	Fee
02/01/91	25	1	RunJim	Bouncing
02/03/91	2	2	Mango	Bouncing
02/07/91	1	1	Mango	Bouncing
02/15/91	4	1	Divided	Fee
02/21/91	4	1	Dinner	Fee
02/27/91	5	1	MSO	Bouncing
03/13/91	8	2	Suzie	Bouncing
03/16/91	2	2	MSO	Magilla
03/22/91	3	1	Bouncing	Sqirm Coil
04/11/91	10	2	Lizards	Lawn Boy
04/15/91	3	1	RunJim	Fee
04/18/91	3	2	Suzie	Sqirm Coil
04/20/91	1	2	Ya Mar	Sqirm Coil
04/26/91	4	2	Uncle Pen	Bouncing
05/02/91	2	2	Fee	Tela
05/04/91	2	1	MSO	Guelah
07/13/91	11	1	TMWSIY	Bouncing
07/14/91	1	2	Bouncing	Magilla
07/18/91	2	2	PoorHeart	Lizards
07/21/91	3	1	PoorHeart	Lizards
07/24/91	2	1	BurAlive	Bathtub
07/25/91	1	E	*OPE	*CLE
07/26/91	1	E	Frankstein	*CLE
09/27/91	5	2	Sparkle	Mango
10/10/91	8	1	Paul&Silas	Bouncing
10/15/91	4	1	Sqirm Coil	Sparkle
10/18/91	2	2	Fee	MSO
11/01/91	9	1	Sqirm Coil	Fluffhead
11/08/91	4	2	Sparkle	Sqirm Coil
11/12/91	3	E	BBFCM	Memories
11/15/91	3	1	Curtain	Sqirm Coil
11/21/91	4	1	Horn	Esther
12/05/91	6	1	Paul&Silas	Ya Mar
03/11/92	6	1	Fee	Mound
03/13/92	2	1	Curtain	PoorHeart
03/14/92	1	2	Sqirm Coil	Bouncing
03/19/92	2	1	Rift	Sparkle
03/21/92	2	1	Sparkle	Horse
03/25/92	2	1	Sparkle	Rift
03/31/92	5	1	Glide	Rift
04/03/92	2	1	All Things	Golgi
04/05/92	2	2	*OP2	All Things
04/07/92	2	1	Silent	Bouncing
04/12/92	2	2	Glide	Bouncing
04/16/92	3	1	Bouncing	Rift
04/18/92	2	1	PoorHeart	Esther
04/21/92	2	1	Uncle Pen	Rift
04/23/92	2	1	Curtain	Uncle Pen
04/30/92	4	1	Curtain	Fee
05/03/92	3	1	All Things	IDK
05/07/92	3	1	Esther	Rift
05/09/92	2	1	Sparkle	Guelah
05/16/92	5	1	Glide	Bouncing
07/01/92	9	1a	Horn	Adeline
07/15/92	7	1	Uncle Pen	Horse
07/26/92	9	1a	Weigh	Lizards
11/19/92	21	1	Glide	Mound
11/23/92	4	1	Glide	Rift
11/27/92	2	1	Mockbird	Lawn Boy
12/01/92	3	1	MSO	Bouncing
12/03/92	2	1	All Things	Bouncing
12/05/92	2	1	Guelah	Lizards
12/07/92	2	1	FEFY	Bouncing
12/10/92	2	1	PoorHeart	IDK
12/12/92	2	1	Landlady	PoorHeart
12/28/92	2	2	PoorHeart	Reba
12/30/92	2	1	Sparkle	Esther
02/05/93	4	1	Rift	Sparkle
02/07/93	2	1	IDK	Fee
02/12/93	4	1	Sparkle	Esther
02/19/93	5	1	Rift	Fee
02/23/93	4	1	Bouncing	Reba
02/26/93	2	1	Fee	Fluffhead
03/03/93	3	2	Curtain	Mound
03/06/93	2	1	Curtain	Mound
03/13/93	4	1	All Things	Contact
03/18/93	4	2	PoorHeart	Tela
03/21/93	2	1	All Things	PoorHeart
03/24/93	2	2	Landlady	Sparkle
03/26/93	2	1	All Things	Fluffhead
03/28/93	2	1	Sparkle	Lizards
03/31/93	2	1	Sparkle	Mound
04/03/93	3	1	Sparkle	Sqirm Coil
04/10/93	3	1	Sparkle	Sqirm Coil
04/16/93	4	1	Sparkle	Esther
04/18/93	2	1	Guelah	Sparkle
04/21/93	2	2	Mound	Sqirm Coil
04/23/93	2	1	Sparkle	Fluffhead
04/29/93	4	1	*OP1	Paul&Silas
05/01/93	2	1	Guelah	Fee
05/03/93	2	1	Esther	Forbin's
05/06/93	2	1	Mound	Horse
05/07/93	1	1	Mound	Horse
05/30/93	3	1a	IDK	Contact
07/16/93	2	2	Also Sprac	Glide
07/21/93	3	1a	Also Sprac	Sparkle
07/24/93	3	2	Also Sprac	Fluffhead
07/28/93	3	1	Nellie	Horse
07/31/93	3	1	Ya Mar	Mound
08/06/93	3	1	*OP1	PoorHeart
08/09/93	3	1	Fee	Glide
08/12/93	2	1	Nellie	Horse
08/14/93	2	1	Sparkle	Esther
08/16/93	2	1	IDK	Sqirm Coil
08/20/93	2	2	Slave	Sqirm Coil
08/24/93	2	1	Nellie	Horse
08/26/93	2	1	Fee	Esther
12/28/93	2	1	PoorHeart	Esther
12/31/93	3	3	DWD	Lizards
04/04/94	1	2	Magilla	Wolfman's
04/08/94	3	2	*OP2	McGrupp
04/10/94	2	1	Sparkle	Esther
04/14/94	3	1	Demand	Sqirm Coil
04/18/94	4	1	Rift	Dog Faced
04/21/94	2	1	Glide	Lizards
04/25/94	4	1	PoorHeart	*CL1
04/29/94	2	1	Dog Faced	Sanity
05/02/94	2	1	Great Gig	Bouncing
05/07/94	4	1	Scent	If I Could
05/10/94	2	1	It's Ice	If I Could
05/13/94	2	2	Bouncing	McGrupp
05/17/94	3	1	Dog Faced	Sqirm Coil
05/22/94	4	1	Glide	Fluffhead
05/26/94	3	1	Demand	Sparkle
05/29/94	3	2	Nellie	Esther
06/09/94	1	2	*OP2	Glide
06/11/94	2	2	Scent	Sqirm Coil
06/14/94	2	1	IDK	*CL1
06/17/94	2	1	Glide	If I Could
06/21/94	3	2	My Friend	Esther
06/23/94	2	1	PoorHeart	NICU
06/30/94	5	1	Guelah	Glide
07/03/94	3	2	*OP2	Lizards
07/09/94	4	2	Also Sprac	Fluffhead
07/13/94	2	1	IDK	*CL2
07/15/94	2	1	Fee	Golgi
10/09/94	4	1	Dog Faced	Sqirm Coil
10/12/94	2	1	PoorHeart	Lizards
10/16/94	4	1	Fee	TMWSIY
10/20/94	2	1	Kung	Esther
10/22/94	2	1	Rift	Fluffhead
10/25/94	2	1	Silent	Lizards
10/29/94	4	1	Lawn Boy	Bill
11/03/94	3	1	Glide	Dog Faced
11/14/94	4	1	Guelah	Bouncing
11/18/94	3	1	Tela	Butter
11/25/94	5	1	Bouncing	Esther
12/01/94	4	1	IDK	Adeline
12/07/94	5	1	Ya Mar	Guyute
12/29/94	5	1	If I Could	Horse
06/09/95	6	2	*OP2	Wedge
06/14/95	3	1	Spock's	*CL1
06/16/95	2	1	Catapult	*CL1
06/20/95	3	1	IDK	*CL1
06/25/95	4	1	IDK	*CL1
06/29/95	3	1	Simple	Carolina
07/01/95	2	1	Caspian	Bouncing
09/29/95	5	2	Ya Mar	Billy
10/03/95	3	2	Adeline	Sqirm Coil
10/07/95	3	1	CTB	Str Design
10/13/95	3	1	Caspian	Fluffhead
10/19/95	4	1	AArmy	Billy
10/24/95	4	1	Caspian	*CL1
10/29/95	4	1	Silent	NICU
11/12/95	5	1	If I Could	*CL1
11/15/95	2	1	Sparkle	Adeline
11/29/95	9	1	Fee	*CL1
12/07/95	6	2	*OP2	Str Design
12/14/95	5	1	Makisupa	Tela
12/28/95	4	1	*OP1	Gumbo
06/06/96	1	2	Chalkdust	Stash
07/03/96	1	1a	Stash	Taste
07/11/96	6	1	IDK	Stash
07/23/96	8	2	Lovin Cup	Mike's
08/07/96	7	1	PYITE	Stash
08/12/96	2	2	Timber Ho	Simple
08/16/96	3	2	Split&Melt	Fee
10/19/96	5	2	Bouncing	Fluffhead
10/22/96	2	1	Talk	Sparkle
10/27/96	4	1	Scent	Talk
11/06/96	5	1	*OP1	CTB
11/09/96	3	1	Talk	Lizards
11/15/96	4	2	McGrupp	TMWSIY
11/23/96	5	1	Highway	Rift
12/28/96	9	1	Ginseng	Mango
02/16/97	6	1	Beauty	Bouncing
02/22/97	5	1	Talk	IDK
06/24/97	15	1	*OP1	Beauty
07/09/97	9	1	Ginseng	Dirt
07/23/97	5	1	Limb	Billy
08/02/97	6	1	Water	*CL1
08/10/97	5	1	Billy	Bye Bye
11/13/97	6	1	Train Song	Beauty
11/21/97	5	1	Emotional	Beauty
11/26/97	3	1	Dirt	Horse
12/28/97	13	1	FunkBitch	Bouncing
>> 12/31/97		**3**		

SPOCK'S BRAIN

Inspiration: The "Spock's Brain" episode of the original "Star Trek" in which Spock's brain is stolen for use as an energy source on an alien planet.

Musical History and Evolution: Due to its short concert life span, there was little musical change, though the title for this song does have a unique history. At the Lowell, MA, Voters For Choice benefit show on 5/16/95, the audience voted on the title for this song from among four choices given by Trey: "The Plane," "The First Single" (meant as a joke to John Paluska), "Israel," and "Spock's Brain." The vote was overwhelmingly in favor of Spock's Brain after Trey said the song was inspired by that episode of the television show.

Rotation History: Played five times from 5/16/94 through 6/24/95, but not since. Fans have speculated widely on why this promising song has not been played since 6/24/95. The theory that Elektra had asked Phish not to play it live so it could be released as a single off Phish's next studio album evaporated when the song wasn't even included on *Billy Breathes*.

Discography: Has not yet appeared on a Phish album.

Spock's Brain [5] [Spock's]

By Phish

05/16/95	[738]	1a	Ha Ha Ha	Str Design
06/07/95	1	2	Maze	Theme
06/14/95	5	1	Silent	Split&Melt
06/20/95	5	1	Llama	Ginseng
06/24/95	3	1	Rift	Julius
>> 12/31/97	**214**			

THE SQUIRMING COIL

Inspiration: Hinting at non-Phish myths—including that of the Greek legend of Iccarus, who flew too close to the sun, melting his wings made of wax—The Squirming Coil is nevertheless, in the best Phish tradition, not really "about" anything.

Musical History and Evolution: The composed section of the song has remained mostly static since its appearance on *Lawn Boy* in 1990, but Page's solo segment at the end has often been extended to create solo improvisational jams that are a concert favorite. It seems surprising that the band does not more often rejoin Page for a jam out of the Coil solo, as they did in Durham, NH, on 5/8/93.

Rotation History: Played in half of all shows in 1991, Coil has been on the decline since then. It's recently stabilized at about one performance in ten shows.

Discography: Appears on *Lawn Boy* (1990) and on *A Live One* (1994), as a live version taken from 10/9/94 in Pittsburgh, PA.

The Squirming Coil [246] [Sqirm Coil]

By Anastasio/Marshall

01/20/90	[157]	1a	Carolina	Caravan
01/27/90	3	2	YEM	Antelope
01/28/90	1	2	Caravan	YEM
02/09/90	7	1	ACDCBag	Mike's
02/24/90	7	2	Fee	La Grange
02/25/90	1	1	FunkBitch	Bouncing
03/03/90	3	1	MSO	Lizards
03/07/90	1	2	ACDCBag	Bathtub
04/07/90	11	1	ACDCBag	Lizards
05/23/90	24	2	*OP2	Reba
06/05/90	4	1	*OP1	Uncle Pen
09/14/90	6	2	Asse Fest	BurAlive
09/15/90	1	1	Magilla	*CL1
09/22/90	4	2	*OP2	Tweezer
09/28/90	1	1	MSO	Lizards
10/01/90	1	1	Possum	Lizards
10/04/90	1	1	Possum	Lizards
10/06/90	2	1a	Landlady	Dinner
10/07/90	1	1	Asse Fest	Mike's
10/30/90	4	1	Cavern	Possum
10/31/90	1	1	Possum	Lizards
11/03/90	2	1	Llama	Oh Kee
11/08/90	2	1	Llama	Asse Fest
11/17/90	3	1	Llama	Landlady
11/24/90	1	1	Weekapaug	Lizards
11/30/90	2	2	Asse Fest	RunJim
12/07/90	3	2	Tweezer	Oh Kee
12/28/90	2	2	Possum	Tweezer
12/31/90	2	2	Stash	RunJim
02/03/91	3	2	Bowie	Landlady
02/07/91	1	1	Possum	Golgi
02/08/91	1	1	Stash	RunJim
02/09/91	1	2	Love You	Llama
02/14/91	1	2	Foam	RunJim
02/26/91	9	1	Foam	Llama
02/27/91	1	2	Cavern	Bowie
02/28/91	1	2	*OP2	Reba
03/01/91	1	1	Cavern	Tweezer
03/06/91	2	1	Landlady	Possum
03/13/91	4	1	Llama	Bowie
03/15/91	1	E	*OPE	RunJim
03/16/91	1	2	BurAlive	Cavern
03/17/91	1	2	MSO	Tweezer
03/22/91	2	1	Split&Melt	Cavern
03/28/91	2	1a	Bowie	Oh Kee
04/04/91	5	1	YEM	Llama
04/11/91	3	1	YEM	Chalkdust
04/12/91	1	E	BBFCM	*CL1
04/15/91	2	E	*OPE	Rocky Top
04/18/91	2	2	Split&Melt	Possum
04/19/91	1	2	MSO	A-Train
04/20/91	1	2	Split&Melt	Paul&Silas
04/22/91	2	2	Destiny	Stash
04/26/91	2	1	Chalkdust	Sloth
04/27/91	1	2	Tweezer	Wipe Jam
05/02/91	1	1	Llama	Cavern
05/12/91	6	2	Weekapaug	Oh Kee
05/16/91	1	2	Landlady	Tweezer
05/25/91	3	1a	Cavern	Llama
07/12/91	2	2	Golgi	Moose
07/14/91	2	1	Llama	Golgi
07/15/91	1	1a	Cavern	Frankstein
07/19/91	2	1	Cavern	YEM
07/20/91	1	1	Foam	Llama
07/23/91	2	1	Foam	MSO
07/24/91	1	1	Chalkdust	BurAlive
07/25/91	1	2	Golgi	Llama
07/26/91	1	2	FunkBitch	Tweezer
08/03/91	2	1	Fee	PoorHeart
09/25/91	1	2	*OP2	Stash
09/26/91	1	2	Golgi	Brother
09/28/91	2	1	Chalkdust	MSO
10/02/91	2	1	Foam	PoorHeart
10/03/91	1	2	BurAlive	Tweezer
10/04/91	1	2	Stash	Mike's
10/06/91	2	2	Cavern	Rocky Top
10/10/91	1	E	*OPE	Fire
10/13/91	3	2	Bathtub	It's Ice
10/15/91	1	1	Foam	Split&Melt
10/18/91	2	E	WalkAway	*CLE
10/28/91	6	2	YEM	Harpua
11/01/91	3	1	Destiny	Split&Melt
11/08/91	4	2	Split&Melt	IDK
11/12/91	3	2	Stash	Paul&Silas
11/13/91	1	2	Bathtub	Llama
11/15/91	2	1	Split&Melt	MSO
11/20/91	3	1	Bathtub	Llama
11/22/91	2	2	Antelope	IDK
11/30/91	3	1	Cavern	Brother
12/04/91	1	1	Brother	Dinner
12/05/91	1	2	Sloth	IDK
12/06/91	1	1	Uncle Pen	Magilla
12/31/91	2	3	Wilson	Tweezer
03/07/92	2	2	Tweezer	Weigh
03/12/92	2	2	Bouncing	Uncle Pen
03/14/92	2	2	Llama	Split&Melt
03/19/92	2	2	My Friend	Rosie
03/21/92	2	1	Dinner	MSO
03/25/92	2	2	All Things	YEM
03/30/92	4	1	BBFCM	Weigh
04/01/92	2	2	Rosie	TweezRep
04/04/92	2	2	Tweezer	Rosie
04/06/92	2	1	Guelah	Antelope
04/09/92	2	1	Stash	Golgi
04/13/92	2	2	Ya Mar	Love You
04/17/92	3	2	Fluffhead	Tweezer
04/23/92	5	1	Guelah	Llama
04/24/92	1	1	Stash	Golgi
04/30/92	3	2	Tweezer	My Mind
05/02/92	2	1	Stash	Llama
05/05/92	2	2	Love You	Cavern
05/06/92	1	2	Stash	YEM
05/07/92	1	2	Bike	TweezRep
05/09/92	2	1	Maze	IDK
05/16/92	5	2	Tweezer	YEM
05/17/92	1	2	Guelah	All Things
06/19/92	2	1a	Stash	Sparkle
07/09/92	8	1a	Stash	RunJim
07/11/92	2	1a	Stash	Cavern
07/14/92	2	2	Llama	Paul&Silas
07/16/92	2	E	Bayou	*CLE
07/17/92	1	1a	Stash	Maze
07/21/92	3	1a	Stash	RunJim
07/24/92	2	1a	Tweezer	YEM
07/28/92	4	1a	Uncle Pen	Tweezer
08/01/92	3	1a	Stash	Horn
08/14/92	3	1a	Stash	Llama
08/17/92	2	E	*OPE	*CLE
08/20/92	2	1a	Stash	Bowie
08/25/92	3	1a	Stash	Llama
08/28/92	2	1a	Adeline	RunJim
10/30/92	3	1a	Cavern	Stash
11/21/92	3	2	Guelah	Love You
11/23/92	2	2	Stash	Walk Line
11/25/92	1	1	It's Ice	Cavern
11/28/92	2	2	Bouncing	Love You
11/30/92	1	2	YEM	Terrapin
12/02/92	2	2	Lngthwise	Walk Line
12/04/92	2	2	It's Ice	Carolina
12/06/92	2	1	Sloth	Llama
12/07/92	1	2	Love You	Adeline
12/11/92	3	2	BBJ	Faht
12/12/92	1	2	Brain	Golgi
12/29/92	3	2	Terrapin	TweezRep
12/31/92	2	3	Harpua	DGirl
02/05/93	3	2	Love You	TweezRep
02/07/93	2	2	YEM	Brain
02/10/93	2	2	It's Ice	Tweezer
02/13/93	3	2	Lngthwise	Cavern
02/17/93	2	2	Lngthwise	*CL2
02/21/93	4	2	Rosie	BBFCM
02/22/93	1	2	Love You	TweezRep
02/26/93	3	2	Lngthwise	TweezRep
03/03/93	3	2	Terrapin	Adeline
03/05/93	1	2	Love You	AmGrace
03/09/93	3	2	Walk Line	TweezRep
03/14/93	3	2	Great Gig	*CL2
03/18/93	3	2	Brain	Cavern
03/24/93	4	E	Carolina	*CLE
03/27/93	3	E	*OPE	Carolina
04/01/93	4	1	Stash	My Friend
04/03/93	2	1	Split&Melt	My Friend
04/10/93	3	1	Split&Melt	My Friend
04/13/93	2	2	Brain	*CL2
04/17/93	3	2	BBJ	*CL2
04/21/93	3	2	Split&Melt	Horse
04/23/93	2	2	Lngthwise	HwayHell
04/29/93	4	2	Terrapin	*CL2
05/01/93	2	2	My Friend	BBJ
05/06/93	4	2	BBJ	Mike's
05/08/93	2	2	It's Ice	Jam
05/29/93	1	1a	Stash	Sparkle
07/17/93	4	2	Tweezer	It's Ice
07/21/93	2	1a	Sparkle	Maze
07/24/93	3	1	Bouncing	*CL1
07/27/93	2	1a	Stash	Sparkle
07/30/93	3	2	Golgi	Bowie
08/02/93	2	2	Rift	Weekapaug
08/06/93	2	2	Guelah	Uncle Pen
08/09/93	3	1	Memories	*CL1
08/12/93	2	1	PoorHeart	*CL1
08/14/93	2	2	Mound	Daniel
08/16/93	2	1	Split&Melt	*CL1
08/20/93	2	2	Split&Melt	My Friend
08/25/93	3	2	Bats&Mice	GTBT
08/28/93	2	2	Stash	Crimes
12/29/93	2	1	Stash	*CL1
04/06/94	5	2	Weekapaug	Cavern
04/09/94	2	1	Stash	*CL1
04/14/94	4	1	Split&Melt	*CL1
04/16/94	2	2	YEM	TweezRep
04/22/94	5	2	BeLikeYou	*CL2
04/25/94	3	2	Mound	Divided
04/28/94	1	1a	Antelope	Julius
05/03/94	4	1	Stash	Scent
05/08/94	4	1	Stash	*CL1
05/10/94	1	E	*OPE	*CLE
05/17/94	5	1	Split&Melt	*CL1
05/21/94	3	1	Stash	Tela
05/25/94	3	2	PurplRain	*CL2
06/11/94	7	2	Split&Melt	Maze
06/16/94	3	1	Stash	*CL1
06/19/94	3	2	Makisupa	MSO
07/03/94	11	2	Julius	Antelope
07/10/94	5	2	Bouncing	Crimes
10/09/94	7	1	Split&Melt	*CL1
10/14/94	4	2	Long Time	TweezRep
10/23/94	7	E	*OPE	*CLE
10/31/94	6	E	AmGrace	*CLE
11/13/94	5	2	AmGrace	*CL2
11/19/94	5	E	*OPE	*CLE
12/02/94	9	1	Stash	*CL1
12/28/94	8	2	Love You	*CL2
06/09/95	7	E	*OPE	*CLE
06/16/95	5	2	YEM	*CL2
06/24/95	6	1	Silent	*CL1
06/30/95	5	2	AmGrace	*CL2
07/03/95	3	2	Possum	*CL2
09/27/95	1	1	Chalkdust	*CL1
10/03/95	5	2	Split&Melt	*CL2
10/13/95	6	2	Adeline	*CL2
10/22/95	7	E	Adeline	*CLE
11/09/95	7	2	HelloBaby	*CL2
11/15/95	5	1	Adeline	*CL1
11/19/95	3	1	Julius	*CL1
11/28/95	5	E	*OPE	*CLE
12/02/95	4	2	Golgi	TweezRep
12/08/95	4	2	Love You	TweezRep
12/12/95	3	1	I'm Blue	*CL1
12/16/95	3	2	Weekapaug	*CL2
12/31/95	5	1	Reba	Maze
07/19/96	15	1a	Waste	*CL1
08/05/96	8	1	Julius	*CL1
08/16/96	7	2	Free	Waste
10/16/96	2	2	Antelope	Johnny B.
10/25/96	7	1	Stash	*CL1
11/19/96	17	E	*OPE	*CLE
12/29/96	12	1	Free	La Grange
02/17/97	6	2	*OP2	DWD
06/16/97	14	1	*OP1	Dogs Stole
07/05/97	12	E	*OPE	*CLE
07/29/97	10	2	Rocky Top	*CL2
08/11/97	9	E	*OPE	*CLE
08/16/97	3	1	CharZero	*CL1
11/30/97	13	1	Love Me	Lovin Cup
12/13/97	9	E	My Soul	*CLE
>> 12/31/97	**4**			

STASH

Inspiration: The lyrics for this song came from a series of Tom Marshall poems from which Trey excerpted specific phrases and then wrote music around.

Musical History and Evolution: Another song that has had its basic structure since the start but which has achieved great heights as the band has mastered its middle improvisational section. The greatest evolution, perhaps, is the addition of fans' clap-along in place of Fishman's wood-block fills, which was already evident in concert by 1992. Great versions of Stash include 11/20/92 Albany, NY, with Linus and Lucy jam; 7/8/94 Mansfield, MA, included on *A Live One*; 11/14/95 Orlando, FL, the mother of all Stashes with Manteca and Dog Faced Boys jams in the midst of a 30-minute marathon; and 7/2/97 Amsterdam, over thirty minutes with a funky jam, unfinished. On 5/2/92 in Chicago, IL, Trey revised the "Police in the corner, gunning for you" lyric to reference the Rodney King verdict earlier in the week, making it "Police pull you over, beat the shit out of you."

Rotation History: Heavily played throughout the 1990s, including 1997 when many other older songs were seen less often.

Discography: Appears on *A Picture of Nectar* (1992) and on *A Live One* (1995), as a live performance taken from 7/8/94 in Mansfield, MA.

Stash [280] [Stash]

By Anastasio/Marshall

09/13/90	[222]	2	Magilla	GDS
09/14/90	1	1	Paul&Silas	Dinner
09/15/90	1	1	Golgi	Magilla
09/22/90	4	2	Bouncing	Lizards
09/28/90	1	1	Suzie	MSO
10/05/90	3	1	Suzie	Asse Fest
10/07/90	2	1	Uncle Pen	Landlady
10/31/90	5	1	Lizards	Bouncing
11/03/90	2	2	Paul&Silas	Fee
11/24/90	6	2	Bouncing	Eliza
11/30/90	2	2	RunJim	Lizards
12/07/90	3	1	Golgi	Bouncing
12/29/90	3	2	Cavern	Jesus
12/31/90	1	2	Golgi	Sqirm Coil
02/02/91	2	1	Esther	Destiny
02/08/91	3	1	MSO	Sqirm Coil
02/14/91	2	1	Mango	Lawn Boy
02/21/91	5	2	Bouncing	Guelah
02/26/91	4	2	Dinner	Bouncing
03/15/91	10	1	MSO	Dinner
03/17/91	2	1	Uncle Pen	Lizards
03/22/91	2	2	Paul&Silas	RunJim
04/05/91	8	2	Rocky Top	Lizards
04/12/91	3	1	Suzie	Rocky Top
04/19/91	5	1	Lizards	IDK
04/22/91	3	2	Sqirm Coil	MSO
04/27/91	3	1	Suzie	Golgi
05/10/91	5	1	Possum	*CL1
05/12/91	2	1	Dinner	Lizards
05/17/91	2	1	TMWSIY	IDK
05/18/91	1	2	Curtain	MSO
07/11/91	2	1	MSO	Lizards
07/13/91	2	2	Lizards	Brain
07/15/91	2	1a	Dinner	Bouncing
07/18/91	1	1	Suzie	A-Train
07/20/91	2	2	Golgi	TMWSIY
07/23/91	2	1	Suzie	Flat Fee
07/25/91	2	2	Lizards	Touch Me
07/26/91	1	2	*OP2	Dinner
07/27/91	1	1a	PoorHeart	TMWSIY
08/03/91	1	3	*OP3	Ya Mar
09/25/91	1	2	Sqirm Coil	Sparkle
09/28/91	3	1	MSO	Foam
10/02/91	2	2	Lawn Boy	Oh Kee
10/04/91	2	2	Lawn Boy	Sqirm Coil
10/06/91	2	2	MSO	Fee
10/17/91	6	1	PoorHeart	Esther
10/19/91	2	1	MSO	Golgi
10/24/91	2	1	PoorHeart	Ya Mar
10/28/91	3	2	Dinner	Paul&Silas

11/01/91	3	E	Love You	*CLE
11/08/91	4	1	Dinner	PoorHeart
11/12/91	3	2	Dinner	Sqirm Coil
11/16/91	4	1	Foam	Ya Mar
11/20/91	2	1	Sparkle	Paul&Silas
11/22/91	2	1	Dinner	Rocky Top
11/24/91	2	1	Paul&Silas	Landlady
12/04/91	2	2	MSO	Mango
12/07/91	3	1	MSO	Curtain
12/31/91	1	1	Sparkle	Lizards
03/06/92	1	2	PoorHeart	Mound
03/12/92	3	1	Sparkle	IDK
03/14/92	2	1	Rift	Fee
03/19/92	2	2	MSO	Oh Kee
03/21/92	2	1	MSO	Golgi
03/24/92	1	1	*OP1	PoorHeart
03/26/92	2	1	Sparkle	Fluffhead
03/28/92	2	1	Sparkle	Rift
03/31/92	2	2	Fee	Lizards
04/03/92	2	1	PoorHeart	Rift
04/05/92	2	1	PoorHeart	Rift
04/06/92	1	2	Mound	Rosie
04/09/92	2	1	Uncle Pen	Sqirm Coil
04/13/92	2	1	Uncle Pen	Lizards
04/15/92	1	1	Sparkle	Uncle Pen
04/17/92	2	1	Sparkle	IDK
04/19/92	2	1	NICU	Paul&Silas
04/22/92	2	1	Mound	All Things
04/24/92	2	1	Sparkle	Sqirm Coil
04/30/92	3	1	Uncle Pen	Rift
05/02/92	2	1	Bouncing	Sqirm Coil
05/05/92	2	1	Sparkle	Rift
05/06/92	1	2	MSO	Sqirm Coil
05/08/92	2	2	MSO	Magilla
05/10/92	2	1a	Sparkle	Uncle Pen
05/14/92	2	2	McGrupp	Rosie
05/15/92	1	1a	Sparkle	Bouncing
05/17/92	2	1	IDK	Mango
06/19/92	2	1a	Suzie	Sqirm Coil
07/09/92	8	1a	Sparkle	Sqirm Coil
07/11/92	2	1a	Sparkle	Sqirm Coil
07/15/92	3	2	MSO	McGrupp
07/17/92	2	1a	Sparkle	Sqirm Coil
07/21/92	3	1a	Sparkle	Sqirm Coil
07/25/92	3	1a	Sparkle	Rift
08/01/92	6	1a	PoorHeart	Sqirm Coil
08/14/92	3	1a	PoorHeart	Sqirm Coil
08/20/92	4	1a	Foam	Sqirm Coil
08/23/92	1	1a	RunJim	*CL1
08/25/92	2	1a	Sparkle	Sqirm Coil
08/28/92	2	1a	Foam	Adeline
10/30/92	3	1a	Sqirm Coil	Adeline
11/20/92	2	1	Sparkle	Lizards
11/23/92	3	2	PoorHeart	Sqirm Coil
11/28/92	3	1	Foam	Esther
11/30/92	1	1	PoorHeart	Sparkle
12/02/92	2	1	PoorHeart	Lizards
12/04/92	2	1	PoorHeart	Glide
12/06/92	2	2	Curtain	Paul&Silas
12/08/92	2	1	Adeline	*CL1
12/11/92	2	1	Uncle Pen	Lizards
12/13/92	2	1	Uncle Pen	Rift
12/29/92	2	1	Uncle Pen	Tela
12/31/92	2	2	BBJ	Glide
02/04/93	2	1	All Things	Lizards
02/06/93	2	2	Mound	Adeline
02/09/93	2	2	BBJ	Lizards
02/11/93	2	1	PoorHeart	Fee
02/13/93	2	1	Rift	Lawn Boy
02/15/93	1	1	Mound	Guelah
02/18/93	2	2	Rift	Lizards
02/21/93	3	2	Curtain	Lizards
02/23/93	2	2	MSO	Lizards
02/25/93	1	2	It's Ice	Wilson
02/27/93	2	2	Curtain	PoorHeart
03/02/93	1	1	PoorHeart	Reba
03/05/93	2	1	Rift	Sparkle
03/08/93	2	2	Uncle Pen	BBJ
03/12/93	2	1	Rift	Fluffhead
03/14/93	2	1	Sparkle	Paul&Silas
03/17/93	2	1	Bouncing	AmGrace
03/19/93	2	1	Rift	Fluffhead
03/22/93	2	1	Uncle Pen	Bouncing
03/25/93	2	1	Bouncing	Glide
03/27/93	2	1	Rift	Reba
03/30/93	2	1	Esther	Glide
04/01/93	2	1	Rift	Sqirm Coil
04/03/93	2	2	Suzie	Mound
04/05/93	1	1	Paul&Silas	Forbin's
04/09/93	1	1	Guelah	Horse
04/12/93	2	1	PoorHeart	Horse
04/14/93	2	1	It's Ice	Kung
04/17/93	2	1	Bouncing	It's Ice
04/20/93	2	1	Sparkle	Bouncing
04/22/93	2	1	Esther	Fee
04/24/93	2	1	PoorHeart	Horse
04/27/93	2	1	Rift	Guelah
04/30/93	2	1	PoorHeart	Horse
05/02/93	2	1	Mound	Horse
05/05/93	2	1	Sparkle	Bouncing
05/08/93	3	1	Mound	Glide
05/29/93	1	1a	Rift	Sqirm Coil
07/15/93	2	1	Mound	Foam
07/17/93	2	1	My Mind	Reba
07/22/93	3	1	PoorHeart	Golgi
07/24/93	2	1	Rift	Mango
07/25/93	1	1	Mound	Fee
07/27/93	1	1a	Rift	Sqirm Coil
07/30/93	3	1	Uncle Pen	Esther
08/03/93	3	1	Rift	Horse
08/07/93	1	1	PoorHeart	Makisupa
08/11/93	3	1	Mango	Sparkle
08/13/93	2	1	Foam	Ginseng
08/15/93	2	1	Paul&Silas	Forbin's
08/21/93	4	1	Rift	Sparkle
08/25/93	2	1	AmGrace	Glide
08/28/93	2	1	Fluffhead	Sqirm Coil
12/29/93	2	1	Sparkle	Sqirm Coil
12/31/93	2	1	Guelah	Ginseng
04/06/94	3	1	PoorHeart	Lizards
04/09/94	2	1	All Things	Sqirm Coil
04/13/94	3	1	PoorHeart	Lizards
04/16/94	3	1	Rift	Fluffhead
04/20/94	3	1	Axilla 2	Suzie
04/23/94	3	1	PoorHeart	Esther
04/30/94	5	1	Mound	PoorHeart
05/03/94	2	1	Sparkle	Sqirm Coil
05/06/94	2	1	Ya Mar	Esther
05/08/94	2	1	Bouncing	Sqirm Coil
05/13/94	3	1	Mound	If I Could
05/16/94	2	1	Bouncing	Adeline
05/19/94	2	1	PoorHeart	Horse
05/21/94	2	1	Mound	Sqirm Coil
05/25/94	3	1	Uncle Pen	Forbin's
05/28/94	3	1	Bouncing	Horse
06/11/94	4	1	Tela	*CL1
06/13/94	1	1	Dinner	Ginseng
06/16/94	2	1	Dog Faced	Sqirm Coil
06/19/94	3	1	Scent	Golgi
06/22/94	2	1	Scent	Golgi
06/25/94	3	1	NICU	Mango
07/01/94	4	1	NICU	Mango
07/05/94	3	1	Uncle Pen	Esther
07/08/94	2	2	It's Ice	YEM
07/10/94	2	1	Rift	If I Could
07/14/94	2	1	PYITE	TMWSIY
07/16/94	2	1	N20	Lizards
10/07/94	1	1	Guelah	Guyute
10/10/94	3	1	Sparkle	Guyute
10/13/94	2	1	Sparkle	*CL1
10/18/94	4	1	PoorHeart	Tela
10/21/94	2	1	Old Home	Lizards
10/23/94	2	1	PoorHeart	Tela
10/28/94	4	1	Scent	Glide
11/02/94	3	1	Guyute	Scent
11/12/94	3	1	Maze	Esther
11/16/94	3	1	Lizards	Fig in Pen
11/20/94	4	1	Scent	If I Could
11/28/94	5	1	Scent	Guyute
12/02/94	3	1	Lizards	Sqirm Coil
12/06/94	3	1	Sparkle	Golgi
12/10/94	4	1	Rift	Lizards
12/30/94	3	1	Simple	Fee
06/07/95	3	1	Str Design	If I Could
06/13/95	4	1	Bouncing	Str Design
06/15/95	2	1	Wedge	IDK
06/17/95	2	1	Curtain	*CL1
06/24/95	5	1	Mound	Horse
06/28/95	3	1	PYITE	Fluffhead
07/01/95	3	2	Uncle Pen	Str Design
09/28/95	4	1	Scent	Fee
10/02/95	3	1	Chess	AArmy
10/06/95	3	1	Ya Mar	Billy
10/11/95	3	1	*OP1	Old Home
10/14/95	2	1	Free	Catapult
10/17/95	2	1	Sample	Uncle Pen
10/22/95	4	1	I'm Blue	*CL1
10/27/95	3	1	Rift	Fee
11/11/95	6	1	Ya Mar	AmGrace
11/14/95	2	2	Gumbo	Str Design
11/19/95	4	1	Rift	Str Design
11/24/95	3	1	Sparkle	Tela
11/28/95	2	1	*OP1	Dinner
12/01/95	3	1	Mockbird	Cavern
12/04/95	2	1	PYITE	My Mind
12/11/95	5	1	Ha Ha Ha	Caspian
12/17/95	5	1	Tube	Lizards
12/29/95	2	1	NICU	Fluffhead
04/26/96	3	1a	Sparkle	CTB
06/06/96	1	2	Sparkle	Waste
07/03/96	1	1a	RunJim	Sparkle
07/11/96	6	1	Sparkle	Scent
07/18/96	5	1a	Bouncing	HelloBaby
07/22/96	3	1a	Bouncing	DayinLife
07/23/96	1	1	McGrupp	HelloBaby
08/07/96	7	1	Sparkle	Ya Mar
08/14/96	4	1	Gumbo	HelloBaby
10/18/96	5	1	CTB	Str Design
10/21/96	2	1	Ginseng	Waste
10/25/96	3	1	IDK	Sqirm Coil
10/29/96	3	1	Bouncing	Train Song
11/02/96	2	1	Taste	Free
11/07/96	3	1	Guelah	Waste
11/14/96	5	E	*OPE	HelloBaby
11/19/96	4	1	Mound	Fee
11/22/96	1	1	Train Song	Cavern
11/30/96	5	1	Bouncing	Fluffhead
12/31/96	8	1	CTB	Horse
02/13/97	1	1	Also Sprac	Walfredo
02/18/97	4	1	NICU	Waste
02/20/97	1	2	Uncle Pen	Bouncing
02/25/97	4	1	Mojo	Waste
02/28/97	2	1	Peaches	SweptAwy
06/13/97	4	2	*OP2	Maze
06/19/97	3	2	*OP2	Ghost
06/22/97	3	1a	Water	Dirt
06/27/97	3	1a	Chalkdust	Dogs Stole
07/02/97	3	2	Jam	Llama
07/06/97	3	1	Dogs Stole	Horse
07/11/97	3	1a	Bouncing	Beauty
07/22/97	2	1	Water	Bouncing
07/26/97	3	1	PoorHeart	Billy
07/30/97	2	1	Water	Weigh
08/06/97	4	1	NICU	Beauty
11/13/97	9	2	*OP2	PYITE
11/23/97	7	1	Twist	NICU
11/30/97	4	2	NICU	Free
12/05/97	3	2	*OP2	Bouncing
12/09/97	3	1	My Soul	I am H2
12/30/97	6	1	PYITE	Chalkdust
>> 12/31/97	1			

STRANGE DESIGN

Inspiration: This Tom Marshall–penned song about life was created in part to give Page another song to sing lead vocals on.

Musical History and Evolution: In concert, Strange Design has been pretty much the same since the day of its nameless debut on 5/16/95 (the band didn't christen it Strange Design for several more weeks). But during recording sessions for *Billy Breathes* in spring 1996, the band recorded several different versions of Strange Design, including an acoustic version (similar to those performed on the acoustic mini-stage on 8/5/96, 8/13/96, and 8/16/96) and a more Beatles-esque rock version. Though they had originally planned to close the album with the catchier version, they opted to cut it at the last minute because they were never fully pleased with how it sounded, yet feared it could result in a hit single. (They even thought of injecting it with profanity to avoid such a fate). The Beatles-esque version did surface as a bonus track on the "Free" single CD, released in Europe in winter 1997.

Rotation History: Played a lot in its debut year of 1995, it has become stranger since then, appearing only seven times in 1996 and three times in 1997.

Discography: Has not yet appeared on a Phish album, though it was recorded for *Billy Breathes* (1996). That version can be found on the "Free" single CD (Europe, 1997).

Strange Design [38] [Str Design]

By Anastasio/Marshall

05/16/95	[738]	1a	Spock's	Reba
06/07/95	1	1	Taste	Stash
06/09/95	2	1	Divided	Oh Kee
06/13/95	2	1	Stash	Taste
06/15/95	2	2	Bowie	Theme
06/19/95	3	1	Reba	Rift

In THEIR Sleep

Songs played so often, Phish could play them in their sleep. Here are the songs most played by Phish in history. The "most played in a year" ratings show the percentage of shows featuring the song.

MOST PLAYED of all time

1) YEM	382
2) Bouncing	321
3) Golgi	303
4) Mike's	297
5) Cavern	295
6) Possum	291
7) Suzie	286
8) Stash	280
9) Weekapaug	274
10) Divided Sky	269
10) Chalkdust	269
12) Foam	267
12) David Bowie	267
14) Antelope	264
15) Runaway Jim	263

MOST PLAYED in a Year (since 1990 by percentage of shows)

1) Landlady	1991	65%
2) Rift	1993	62%
3) Big Ball Jam	1993	58%
3) Cavern	1991	58%
3) My Sweet One	1991	58%
6) Bouncing	1990	56%
6) Free	1995	56%
6) Possum	1990	56%
6) Sample in a Jar	1994	56%
10) YEM	1990	55%
11) Llama	1991	54%
12) Sparkle	1992	53%
12) Sparkle	1993	53%

06/22/95	2	1	It's Ice	Maze
06/26/95	4	2	YEM	Antelope
06/29/95	2	2	Bowie	YEM
07/01/95	2	2	Stash	AArmy
07/03/95	2	1	Maze	Free
09/27/95	1	1	Fog	Chalkdust
09/29/95	2	1	Divided	CTB
10/05/95	4	1	CTB	Divided
10/07/95	2	2	Split&Melt	It's Ice
10/15/95	5	1	Foam	I'm Blue
10/17/95	1	1	Free	AmGrace
10/21/95	3	1	Lizards	AArmy
10/25/95	3	1	Free	LongJourn
10/28/95	2	2	YEM	Frankstein
11/10/95	4	2	YEM	Sparkle
11/14/95	3	2	Stash	YEM
11/19/95	4	1	Stash	It's Ice
11/22/95	2	2	YEM	*CL2
11/25/95	2	2	I'm Blue	Weekapaug
11/30/95	3	2	Free	AmGrace
12/07/95	5	2	Split&Melt	Fog
12/31/95	12	2	RunJim	HelloBaby
08/05/96	23	2	Train Song	AmGrace
08/13/96	5	2	Train Song	Adeline
08/16/96	2	2	Train Song	HelloBaby
10/18/96	4	1	Stash	Divided
10/25/96	5	2	Free	Harry
11/24/96	20	1	CharZero	Taste
12/28/96	8	2	Mike's	Weekapaug
07/02/97	31	1	Maze	Ginseng
11/29/97	36	2	RunJim	Harry
12/13/97	10	1	Ginseng	Sample
>> 12/31/97	**4**			

SUZIE GREENBERG

Inspiration: Written by the Dude of Life about a real-life Suzie Greenberg whom he dated, the Dude has said the lyrics are "dead-on."

Musical History and Evolution: As a Phish concert staple since its debut way back in the mid 1980s, Suzie has evolved as the band has evolved, never really changing in structure, but accelerating in pace as the band's style has gotten faster. In summer 1991, the Giant Country Horns made this song one of that tour's highlights, and subsequent Suzies have had a hard task to live up to the horn performances. Though most versions of the song are pretty much the same, the speed and energy level varies and the instrumental section does leave room for tight but creative improvisation (an example of this process at its best can be heard on the 8/13/93 Murat Theater show). The band does sometimes play around a bit with the structure, like on 12/31/94 Boston, MA, as the band comes around one more time for a Suzie reprise that segues into Slave, and on 11/13/96 in Minneapolis, MN, when the band performed an extended jam out of Suzie. Horn performances have also changed slightly over the years, as the version from 10/31/96 has horn fills at different portions from versions from 1991.

Rotation History: Played heavily throughout the 1990s until 1997, when the band included it among their group of "retired songs" for that summer's tour. (Word has it that during a performance of Suzie on the winter 1997 European tour, Trey realized he was bored of playing it, and that led to the idea to retire a whole group of songs.) After its appearance at the Flynn Theater on 3/18/97, it came out of retirement only once later in 1997, on 11/29/97 in Worcester, MA, a botched version that has Fishman starting Golgi while the others start Suzie.

Discography: Has yet to appear on a Phish album.

Suzie Greenberg [286] [Suzie]

By Anastasio/Dude of Life

08/09/87	[17]	1	Harpua	*CL1
08/29/87	4	1	Lushngton	Mustang
09/12/87	2	2	*OP2	Alumni
11/19/87	4	2	Alumni	Possum
01/30/88	1	3	Fee	Lizards
03/21/88	5	1a	*OP1	Golgi
05/15/88	4	1a	YEM	GTBT
05/25/88	2	1	Sally	Fire
06/15/88	1	1	*OP1	Alumni
06/18/88	1	1	La Grange	Emma
06/21/88	2	1	Sally	Curtain
07/11/88	1	1	Satin Doll	Curtain
10/29/88	12	1	*OP1	Lizards
11/03/88	1	2	Antelope	IDK
11/05/88	1	E	*OPE	Sparks
02/06/89	6	1	*OP1	Curtain
02/07/89	1	3	Fluffhead	Slave
04/15/89	14	2	Split&Melt	Fluffhead
04/20/89	2	1	Esther	Sloth
05/06/89	9	2	A-Train	Contact
05/13/89	6	2	Bowie	Bold
05/28/89	8	1	Esther	YEM
08/12/89	10	1a	Blue Sky	ACDCBag
08/17/89	2	1	Ya Mar	McGrupp
08/19/89	1	1	Oh Kee	TMWSIY
08/26/89	2	3	TMWSIY	Dinner
09/09/89	4	1	Oh Kee	Divided
10/01/89	1	1	Oh Kee	Antelope
10/07/89	2	1	Weekapaug	Fee
10/22/89	6	1	Oh Kee	Ya Mar
10/31/89	3	1	Oh Kee	ACDCBag
11/10/89	5	1	Oh Kee	Fee
11/16/89	2	1	Oh Kee	MSO
11/30/89	2	2	A-Train	Contact
12/07/89	4	2	Oh Kee	Rocky Top
12/08/89	1	1	Oh Kee	Split&Melt
01/20/90	7	1a	Oh Kee	Bouncing
01/28/90	2	1	*OP1	Suzie
02/09/90	7	1	Oh Kee	YEM
02/10/90	1	1	Oh Kee	YEM
02/15/90	1	1	Oh Kee	Divided
02/17/90	2	1a	Oh Kee	Dinner
02/23/90	2	2	Oh Kee	Mike's
03/03/90	5	E	*OPE	*CLE
03/08/90	2	1	Oh Kee	A-Train
03/28/90	4	1	Oh Kee	A-Train
04/05/90	2	1	Oh Kee	YEM
04/06/90	1	1	Oh Kee	Antelope
04/07/90	1	1	MSO	ACDCBag
04/08/90	1	1	Oh Kee	Uncle Pen
04/22/90	9	1	Oh Kee	Possum
04/26/90	2	2	Oh Kee	Cavern
04/28/90	1	1	Oh Kee	Uncle Pen
05/10/90	5	1	*OP1	Uncle Pen
05/15/90	4	1	Oh Kee	Harry
05/19/90	1	2	Oh Kee	Fee
05/23/90	1	1	Oh Kee	Uncle Pen
05/31/90	2	1a	Oh Kee	*CL1
06/01/90	1	1a	Oh Kee	Dinner
06/05/90	1	1	Oh Kee	A-Train
06/07/90	1	1	*OP1	Donna
06/09/90	2	2	Oh Kee	Antelope
06/16/90	1	3	Oh Kee	Fee
09/14/90	2	1	*OP1	Bouncing
09/22/90	5	1	Oh Kee	Magilla
09/28/90	1	1	Oh Kee	Stash
10/01/90	1	1	Oh Kee	*CL1
10/05/90	2	1	Oh Kee	Stash
10/06/90	1	1a	Oh Kee	Esther
10/12/90	3	1	*OP1	YEM
10/30/90	2	1	Asse Fest	Uncle Pen
10/31/90	1	2	Oh Kee	Love You
11/02/90	1	2	*OP2	Forbin's
11/03/90	1	1	Oh Kee	Magilla
11/04/90	1	2	Oh Kee	Jesus
11/08/90	1	2	*OP2	Divided
11/10/90	1	2	*OP2	YEM
11/16/90	1	1	*OP1	BurAlive
11/17/90	1	1	Oh Kee	Bowie
11/24/90	1	1	Oh Kee	Bowie
11/30/90	2	E	Oh Kee	*CLE
12/07/90	3	2	Oh Kee	No Good
12/29/90	3	1	Oh Kee	*CL1
12/31/90	1	1	*OP1	Divided
02/02/91	2	1	Oh Kee	Guelah
02/03/91	1	2	Oh Kee	*CL2
02/09/91	3	E	Lawn Boy	*CLE
02/21/91	6	E	*OPE	*CLE
02/27/91	5	2	*OP2	BurAlive
03/01/91	2	E	Oh Kee	*CLE
03/13/91	6	2	*OP2	Split&Melt
03/16/91	2	1	Oh Kee	Antelope
03/22/91	3	2	Oh Kee	Antelope
03/28/91	2	1a	Oh Kee	Magilla
04/04/91	5	1	Oh Kee	YEM
04/05/91	1	E	Oh Kee	*CLE
04/12/91	3	1	Oh Kee	Stash
04/18/91	4	2	Horn	Split&Melt
04/20/91	2	2	Oh Kee	Adeline
04/22/91	2	1	Oh Kee	*CL1
04/27/91	3	1	Lizards	Stash
05/04/91	3	1	Oh Kee	Cavern
05/11/91	3	2	Oh Kee	TweezRep
05/17/91	3	1	Oh Kee	TMWSIY
05/18/91	1	2	Oh Kee	Curtain
07/11/91	2	1	Oh Kee	Divided
07/12/91	1	2	Oh Kee	*CL2
07/13/91	1	1	Oh Kee	Alumni
07/14/91	1	2	*OP2	Caravan
07/15/91	1	1a	Oh Kee	Landlady
07/18/91	1	1	Guelah	Stash
07/19/91	1	2	*OP2	Divided
07/20/91	1	1	Oh Kee	Landlady
07/21/91	1	E2	Fee	*CLE2
07/23/91	1	1	Oh Kee	Stash
07/24/91	1	2	Frankstein	*CL2
07/25/91	1	1	Foam	Divided
07/26/91	1	1	Foam	Cavern
07/27/91	1	1a	Oh Kee	Cavern
09/27/91	4	2	Oh Kee	YEM
09/29/91	2	1a	Oh Kee	*CL1
10/02/91	3	2	Oh Kee	*CL2
10/04/91	2	1	Sparkle	Magilla
10/06/91	2	1	*OP1	Foam
10/10/91	1	2	Oh Kee	Fee
10/15/91	4	2	Oh Kee	Love You
10/17/91	1	2	Oh Kee	Bowie
10/19/91	2	1	Landlady	It's Ice
10/24/91	2	1	Oh Kee	Foam
11/02/91	7	1	*OP1	Curtain
11/08/91	3	E	Fee	*CLE
11/15/91	6	E	HwayHell	*CLE
11/22/91	5	E	Glide	*CLE
12/04/91	4	E	Adeline	*CLE
03/11/92	7	1	*OP1	My Friend
03/14/92	3	2	Oh Kee	Harry
03/19/92	2	2	Oh Kee	My Friend
03/21/92	2	2	Oh Kee	A-Train
03/24/92	1	2	Oh Kee	Harry
03/26/92	2	2	Oh Kee	PoorHeart
03/30/92	3	E	Oh Kee	*CLE
04/03/92	3	2	Harry	*CL2
04/06/92	3	1	*OP1	Foam
04/09/92	2	2	Oh Kee	Bowie
04/12/92	1	1	*OP1	PoorHeart
04/15/92	2	1	Oh Kee	Foam
04/16/92	1	2	Adeline	*CL2
04/18/92	2	2	Oh Kee	Rift
04/21/92	2	1	*OP1	Uncle Pen
04/22/92	1	1	All Things	*CL1
04/25/92	3	1	*OP1	My Friend
04/29/92	1	1	*OP1	Foam
05/01/92	2	1	*OP1	My Friend
05/03/92	2	2	Oh Kee	*CL2
05/07/92	3	1	*OP1	PoorHeart
05/09/92	2	2	*OP2	Divided
05/10/92	1	1a	Landlady	Sparkle
05/14/92	2	1	*OP1	All Things
05/16/92	2	E	Adeline	*CLE
05/18/92	2	1	*OP1	Maze
06/19/92	1	1a	Landlady	Stash
07/09/92	8	1a	Oh Kee	Landlady
07/11/92	2	1a	YEM	*CL1
07/15/92	3	1	Oh Kee	Foam
07/18/92	3	1a	*OP1	Foam
07/27/92	7	1a	Horn	Llama
07/31/92	3	1a	*OP1	Chalkdust
08/02/92	2	1a	Oh Kee	Bowie
08/17/92	4	2	*OP2	It's Ice
11/20/92	12	1	All Things	Rift
11/22/92	2	1	Oh Kee	Fee
11/28/92	4	2	*OP2	Paul&Silas
12/02/92	3	1	*OP1	Foam
12/04/92	2	2	*OP2	Bowie
12/06/92	2	2	*OP2	Curtain
12/08/92	2	2	Sparkle	Lngthwise
12/10/92	1	2	Oh Kee	*CL2
12/13/92	3	2	*OP2	Mound
12/29/92	2	1	Oh Kee	*CL1
02/07/93	7	1	*OP1	BurAlive
02/11/93	3	1	*OP1	BurAlive
02/15/93	3	1	AmGrace	Sparkle
02/21/93	5	1	*OP1	BurAlive
02/25/93	3	2	*OP2	It's Ice
03/13/93	10	2	*OP2	Tweezer
03/17/93	3	1	Oh Kee	Antelope
03/19/93	2	1	*OP1	Llama
03/26/93	5	2	Oh Kee	Great Gig
04/03/93	7	2	*OP2	Stash
04/09/93	2	2	BurAlive	All Things
04/13/93	3	1	*OP1	Foam
04/17/93	3	2	Oh Kee	BBJ
04/22/93	4	1	*OP1	Sparkle
05/06/93	11	2	*OP2	Tweezer
07/25/93	13	2	Also Sprac	Tweezer
08/02/93	6	2	Oh Kee	All Things
08/06/93	2	1	Chalkdust	*CL1
08/13/93	6	2	Oh Kee	AmGrace
08/17/93	4	2	Rift	YEM
12/28/93	7	1	Oh Kee	Ya Mar
12/31/93	3	3	Sparkle	Rosie
04/04/94	1	2	Oh Kee	*CL2
04/08/94	3	2	Bowie	*CL2
04/11/94	3	2	Oh Kee	*CL2
04/15/94	3	2	If I Could	Landlady
04/20/94	4	1	Stash	*CL1
04/22/94	2	2	*OP2	Julius
04/29/94	5	2	*OP2	Maze
05/02/94	2	2	Divided	Foam
05/04/94	2	2	Magilla	*CL2
05/07/94	2	1	If I Could	*CL1
05/13/94	4	1	Slave	*CL1
05/17/94	3	1	*OP1	Maze
05/27/94	8	2	*OP2	Peaches
05/29/94	2	2	Oh Kee	Antelope
06/09/94	1	1	Fee	*CL1
06/11/94	2	E	*OPE	*CLE
06/16/94	3	2	*OP2	Antelope
06/19/94	3	1	*OP1	Julius
06/21/94	1	2	Harry	*CL2
06/25/94	4	2	*OP2	Maze
06/29/94	2	2	Divided	Cavern
07/01/94	2	1	Julius	*CL1
07/03/94	2	2	Antelope	*CL2
07/09/94	4	2	Harry	*CL2
07/13/94	2	2	Slave	*CL2
07/16/94	3	E	*OPE	*CLE
10/08/94	2	2	Harry	*CL2
10/15/94	6	2	Bouncing	*CL2
10/22/94	5	1	*OP1	Divided
10/26/94	3	1	Oh Kee	RunJim
11/02/94	5	1	*OP1	Foam
11/04/94	2	1	Scent	Chalkdust
11/13/94	2	2	*OP2	Divided
11/16/94	2	E	AmGrace	*CLE
11/19/94	3	2	*OP2	Sparkle
11/23/94	3	1	Oh Kee	Divided
11/28/94	3	2	*OP2	NICU
12/02/94	3	2	Caravan	*CL2
12/03/94	1	2	Frankstein	BurAlive
12/09/94	5	2	YEM	*CL2
12/28/94	2	2	*OP2	NICU
12/31/94	3	3	Silent	Slave
06/07/95	2	2	Harry	*CL2
06/10/95	3	1	LCBill	*CL1
06/17/95	5	1	Divided	Taste
06/24/95	5	1	Life Boy	Harry
06/28/95	3	1	Sparkle	Harry
07/01/95	3	1	Harry	*CL2
09/29/95	5	1	Adeline	*CL1
10/05/95	4	1	Julius	*CL1
10/11/95	4	1	Llama	Crossroad
10/17/95	4	2	Fog	Keyboard
10/21/95	3	2	Harry	*CL2
10/25/95	3	2	Weekapaug	Crossroad
10/31/95	4	3	DayinLife	*CL3
11/11/95	3	2	Bowie	Uncle Pen
11/15/95	3	E	*OPE	*CLE
11/19/95	3	2	Harry	*CL2
11/24/95	3	1	Maze	*CL1
11/28/95	2	2	Maze	Uncle Pen

12/01/95	3	E	*OPE	*CLE
12/14/95	9	1	*OP1	Llama
12/16/95	2	1	Julius	*CL1
12/30/95	4	1	Also Sprac	Bowie
07/07/96	7	1a	Antelope	*CL1
07/12/96	4	2	Slave	*CL2
07/21/96	6	2	Caspian	*CL2
08/06/96	8	1	Rift	Simple
08/12/96	3	1	Oh Kee	*CL1
08/17/96	3	1	Maze	*CL1
10/18/96	3	2	*OP2	Maze
10/23/96	4	2	Llama	Slave
10/27/96	3	1	Taste	*CL1
10/31/96	2	3	Jesus	*CL3
11/07/96	4	2	*OP2	Bathtub
11/13/96	4	2	Also Sprac	Caspian
11/16/96	3	2	Harry	AmGrace
11/24/96	5	2	Lovin Cup	*CL2
11/29/96	2	1	Maze	*CL1
12/06/96	5	E	Harpua	*CLE
12/31/96	4	3	DWD	Antelope
02/17/97	4	2	DWD	Caspian
02/23/97	5	2	Daniel	Maze
03/18/97	6	1	CTB	CharZero
11/29/97	49	2	Caspian	*CL2
>> 12/31/97	**14**			

SWEPT AWAY/STEEP

Inspiration: The two songs have always been paired together in concert since they were positioned that way on *Billy Breathes*.

Musical History and Evolution: Composed pieces that have varied little since their post–*Billy Breathes* debut on 10/16/96. On *Billy Breathes*, Steep is two portions of the band's "Blob" project stitched together, and live performances attempt to mimic that creation. The Blob was an experiment in which each band member added one single note at a time.

Rotation History: Played sporadically in 1996 and 1997.

Discography: Appears on *Billy Breathes* (1996).

Swept Away/Steep [22] [SweptAwy]/[Steep]

Swept Away
by Anastasio/Marshall

Steep
by Phish

10/16/96	[850]	2	Simple	Caspian
10/19/96	3	2	Fluffhead	Antelope
10/22/96	2	2	Mike's	Weekapaug
10/31/96	6	3	Simple	Jesus
11/06/96	3	2	Mike's	Weekapaug
11/09/96	3	2	Taste	Harry
11/11/96	1	2	Tweezer	Maze
11/14/96	2	2	Taste	Scent
11/18/96	3	2	Simple	Scent
11/22/96	2	2	Billy	CharZero
11/29/96	4	2	Taste	YEM
12/01/96	2	2	Reba	TweezRep
12/31/96	7	3	Simple	Harry
02/16/97	3	2	Circus	Bowie
02/20/97	3	2	Free	DayinLife
02/28/97	6	1	Stash	CharZero
03/02/97	2	2	Maze	PYITE
06/21/97	7	1a	Theme	Limb
07/29/97	19	1	Ghost	Lovin Cup
08/09/97	7	2	Simple	Scent
12/07/97	23	1	It's Ice	It's Ice
12/12/97	3	2	Piper	Caspian
>> 12/31/97	**5**			

TALK

Inspiration: One of several quieter, more reflective songs to emerge from the *Billy Breathes* sessions.

Musical History and Evolution: Not much, though the first two live performances of the song (on summer tour 1996, 8/5/96 and 8/16/96) came on the acoustic mini-stage. Since then, as the band has started performing it electric, Trey used an amplified acoustic guitar.

Rotation History: In rotation for most of 1996, it appeared only three times in 1997, most recently on 6/24/97.

Talk [11] [Talk]
By Anastasio/Marshall

08/05/96	[841]	2	Waste	Train Song
08/16/96	7	2	Waste	Train Song
10/17/96	3	1	Theme	PYITE
10/22/96	4	1	It's Ice	Split&Melt
10/27/96	4	1	Split&Melt	Taste
11/09/96	8	1	Tube	Split&Melt
11/14/96	3	1	Bathtub	Julius
12/30/96	17	1	Reba	FunkBitch
02/22/97	9	1	Circus	Split&Melt
06/14/97	9	1	Dirt	My Soul
06/24/97	6	1	RunJim	Free
>> 12/31/97	**55**			

TASTE

Inspiration: Unclear, though it seems to be about the narrator's love/hate relationship with technology.

Musical History and Evolution: Taste has gone through several distinctly different phases. Debuted on summer tour 1995, the band performed it with Trey on vocals and a middle jam that returned to the lyrics refrain at the end. For fall tour 1995, the band revised the song into The Fog That Surrounds, keeping the basic music and refrain but substituting new Fishman vocals for the lyrics Trey had sung. Partway through that tour, Fog was revised again, adding back in part of Taste, and including a segment where Fish and Trey sang at the same time. Then, in the spring of 1996 during the *Billy Breathes* sessions, Trey rewrote the song yet again, keeping the Fishman verse from The Fog That Surrounds but omitting a guitar solo present in original versions of Taste, and also omitting the return to the lyrics after the jam. That version he redubbed Taste; it's included on *Billy Breathes* under that name. Though initial concert performances of Taste in summer 1996 did not contain imaginative solos, the band started opening the song up more in 1997, including heavily improvisational versions on 3/1/97 Hamburg, Germany (included on *Slip Stitch and Pass*), 7/22/97 Raleigh, NC, and 8/3/97 George, WA, among others.

Rotation History: Performed on summer tour 1995, Taste (at least, the song with that name) disappeared from 6/30/95 until 7/3/96 while the band toyed with Fog That Surrounds.

Discography: Appears on *Billy Breathes* (1996) and *Slip Stitch and Pass* (1997).

Taste [68] [Taste]
By Phish/Marshall

06/07/95	[739]	1	Weigh	Str Design
06/09/95	2	1	Theme	Sparkle
06/13/95	2	1	Str Design	Reba
06/15/95	2	1	Old Home	Wedge
06/17/95	2	1	Suzie	Fee
06/20/95	2	1	If I Could	IDK
06/23/95	2	1	Free	YEM
06/25/95	2	1	ACDCBag	Theme
06/29/95	3	1	RunJim	Horse
06/30/95	1	1	Horn	Wedge
07/03/96	64	1a	Sparkle	Llama
07/09/96	4	1a	PoorHeart	CTB
07/12/96	3	1	FunkBitch	Theme
07/21/96	6	1	Silent	Train Song
08/02/96	5	2	Simple	Free
08/07/96	4	1	Gumbo	Lawn Boy
08/12/96	2	1	Dog Faced	Oh Kee
08/17/96	4	1	Sample	Fee
10/16/96	1	2	Wolfman's	Train Song
10/18/96	2	1	Billy	Sample
10/22/96	3	2	DWD	Mango
10/25/96	2	1	Ha Ha Ha	Makisupa
10/27/96	2	1	Talk	Suzie
10/29/96	1	1	CTB	Bouncing
11/02/96	2	1	Cavern	Stash
11/06/96	2	1	FEFY	Train Song
11/09/96	3	2	YEM	SweptAwy
11/13/96	2	1	Ya Mar	Train Song
11/14/96	1	2	Sample	SweptAwy
11/15/96	1	1	Chalkdust	Cavern
11/18/96	2	1	PoorHeart	Billy
11/19/96	1	1	Fee	Lovin Cup
11/22/96	1	1	Wolfman's	Ginseng
11/24/96	2	1	Str Design	IDK
11/29/96	2	2	Sparkle	SweptAwy
11/30/96	1	2	Timber Ho	FunkBitch
12/02/96	2	2	Wolfman's	Free
12/29/96	4	1	Cavern	Guelah
02/13/97	3	1	Walfredo	Waste
02/17/97	3	2	Jam	DWD
02/20/97	2	1	Love Me	Gumbo
02/25/97	4	1	Waste	Lovin Cup
02/28/97	2	2	*OP2	Drowned
03/01/97	1	E	*OPE	Adeline
03/18/97	2	2	*OP2	Drowned
06/13/97	1	1	Wading	*CL1
06/16/97	2	1	Dogs Stole	Water
06/20/97	2	1	*OP1	Cities
06/21/97	1	1a	PoorHeart	Dirt
06/22/97	1	1a	*OP1	Water
06/25/97	2	1	Dogs Stole	Billy
06/27/97	1	1a	PoorHeart	Bouncing
06/29/97	1	1a	YEM	Bouncing
07/03/97	3	3	Beauty	Train Song
07/09/97	3	1	Dirt	Adeline
07/22/97	4	1	Bye Bye	*CL1
07/25/97	2	2	Chalkdust	Ya Mar
07/29/97	2	2	Twist	Sample
08/03/97	4	2	Lifeboy	HelloBaby
08/09/97	3	1	Ghost	Dogs Stole
08/14/97	4	2	CamlWalk	*CL2
08/17/97	2	1	Tweezer	Carolina
11/16/97	3	1	PoorHeart	HelloBaby
11/19/97	2	2	Makisupa	*CL2
11/26/97	4	1	Silent	*CL1
12/02/97	4	1	Dirt	SSB
12/12/97	7	1	CamlWalk	Bouncing
12/30/97	6	1	Sally	Water
>> 12/31/97	**1**			

TELA

Inspiration: A Gamehendge song, told from the perspective of Colonel Forbin, who falls in love with Tela, a revolutionary.

Musical History and Evolution: The song underwent a number of transformations before the band settled on a version they were happy with in 1991. The current version omits a long, free-form jam performed in 1988, most notably on 8/27/88 Penn State, a version that for many fans represents the peak of Phish in the 1980s.

Rotation History: Never very common, Tela has become a rarity in the past two years, appearing twice in 1996 and once in 1997, on 8/14/97 in Darien Lake, NY.

Discography: Has not yet appeared on a Phish album.

Tela [65] [Tela]
By Anastasio

03/12/88	[32]	1a	Lizards	Wilson
06/20/88	10	2	Sally	Fee
08/27/88	9	1a	Golgi	*CL1
10/22/89	82	1	Split&Melt	Divided
11/16/89	10	2	ACDCBag	Bowie
12/08/89	7	2	Harry	Timber Ho
01/20/90	7	1a	Reba	La Grange
01/28/90	4	1	Split&Melt	Fluffhead
02/23/90	13	2	Jesus	Oh Kee
03/07/90	6	2	Split&Melt	Mike's
03/11/90	3	E	*OPE	*CLE
05/15/90	18	1	Possum	Tweezer
09/22/90	17	1	Divided	Oh Kee
10/05/90	4	1	Landlady	Oh Kee
12/08/90	21	2	Antelope	Golgi
04/12/91	44	2	Cavern	BurAlive
04/16/91	3	1	ACDCBag	Bowie
04/21/91	4	1	ACDCBag	Mike's
05/02/91	5	2	Split&Melt	MSO
05/03/91	1	2	RunJim	YEM
07/24/91	20	1	Cavern	YEM
09/25/91	5	1	Llama	MSO
09/27/91	2	2	Possum	Sparkle
10/13/91	11	1	Mockbird	ACDCBag
10/27/91	8	2	Weekapaug	Landlady
11/01/91	4	2	A-Train	Cavern
11/09/91	5	2	Tweezer	Landlady
11/20/91	8	2	Antelope	Landlady
12/06/91	8	2	Divided	Llama
04/21/92	34	2	Tweezer	Mike's
04/25/92	4	1	Brother	Chalkdust
05/02/92	4	2	Bowie	Foam
05/06/92	3	1	Maze	Brother
05/09/92	3	2	Divided	Tweezer
11/22/92	54	2	Tweezer	YEM
12/02/92	7	2	BBJ	Llama
12/10/92	7	2	Tweezer	MSO
12/29/92	5	1	Tela	Oh Kee
02/10/93	9	1	Divided	IDK
03/18/93	26	2	Split&Melt	YEM
03/22/93	3	2	Lizards	Wilson
05/06/93	33	2	Tweezer	Uncle Pen
08/09/93	24	2	Tweezer	My Friend
04/09/94	22	2	Weekapaug	Slave
04/25/94	14	1	Dog Faced	PoorHeart
05/21/94	18	1	Sqirm Coil	Llama
06/11/94	10	1	It's Ice	Stash
06/25/94	11	1	Scent	Chalkdust
06/26/94	1	1	Lizards	Wilson
07/01/94	3	1	It's Ice	Julius
07/08/94	5	1	Lizards	Wilson
10/18/94	16	1	Stash	It's Ice
10/23/94	4	1	Stash	Maze
11/04/94	9	2	Mike's	Weekapaug
11/18/94	6	1	It's Ice	Split&Melt
06/19/95	32	1	ACDCBag	PYITE
06/26/95	6	1	Dog Faced	Possum
10/02/95	11	1	Theme	Bowie
10/14/95	8	1	It's Ice	RunJim
11/09/95	13	1	Reba	Sample
11/24/95	11	1	Stash	I'm Blue
12/14/95	14	1	Split&Melt	Fog
08/13/96	35	1	Tube	Maze

11/07/96	19	1	Free	CharZero
08/14/97	74	1	CTB	Train Song
>> 12/31/97		**27**		

THEME FROM THE BOTTOM

Inspiration: Part of the batch of songs debuted in May 1995, Theme fit that group's theme of songs with water imagery and room for improvisational jamming.

Musical History and Evolution: The opening and closing lyric segments have been an unchanging part of the song since its debut on 5/16/95, and though the middle jam sequence holds lots of potential, it has not yet been home to any of the truly legendary Phish jams. Still, the textural jams present in this song, especially throughout 1997, are a concert treat.

Rotation History: Holding strong, as it's played roughly one of every three shows.

Discography: Appears on *Billy Breathes* (1996).

Theme from the Bottom [75] [Theme]

By Phish/Marshall

05/16/95	[738]	1a	Reba	LCBill
06/07/95	1	2	Spock's	LCBill
06/09/95	2	1	ACDCBag	Taste
06/13/95	2	2	Axilla 2	AArmy
06/15/95	2	2	Str Design	Scent
06/19/95	3	1	*OP1	PoorHeart
06/22/95	2	2	*OP2	Tweezer
06/25/95	3	1	Taste	If I Could
06/29/95	3	E	*OPE	*CLE
07/01/95	2	2	Maze	Uncle Pen
09/28/95	4	2	*OP2	PoorHeart
10/02/95	3	1	Fog	Tela
10/06/95	3	2	Maze	NICU
10/13/95	4	2	Uncle Pen	Wilson
10/19/95	4	1	Chalkdust	AArmy
10/24/95	4	2	Julius	Bouncing
10/28/95	3	2	Maze	Scent
11/09/95	3	2	*OP2	Julius
11/15/95	5	2	Wilson	Scent
11/19/95	3	2	*OP2	Also Sprac
11/24/95	3	2	Chalkdust	Reba
11/29/95	3	1	It's Ice	AArmy
12/01/95	2	1	DWD	PoorHeart
12/05/95	3	E	*OPE	Adeline
12/09/95	3	1	Maze	NICU
12/28/95	7	2	Timber Ho	Wilson
06/06/96	5	1	FunkBitch	BBFCM
07/09/96	5	1a	*OP1	PoorHeart
07/12/96	3	1	Taste	Tweezer
07/21/96	6	2	Llama	Reba
07/23/96	2	1	Foam	Gumbo
08/02/96	3	1	Foam	Golgi
08/06/96	3	1	Simple	Lizards
08/14/96	5	2	Tweezer	Rosie
10/17/96	4	1	Tweezer	Talk
10/23/96	5	1	Rift	Antelope
10/26/96	2	1	It's Ice	Sample
11/03/96	5	1	Sample	Bouncing
11/08/96	3	E	*OPE	*CLE
11/11/96	2	1	Brother	Axilla
11/13/96	1	2	YEM	Golgi
11/19/96	5	1	Foam	Mound
11/22/96	1	2	CharZero	Slave
11/27/96	3	1	Free	Bold
12/02/96	4	1	IDK	Gumbo
12/30/96	5	1	FunkBitch	GTBT
02/16/97	4	E	*OPE	Johnny B.
02/22/97	5	1	FunkBitch	NICU
02/26/97	3	2	Kung	Scent
03/01/97	2	2	Billy	*CL2
06/13/97	3	1	*OP1	Dogs Stole
06/16/97	2	1	Beauty	Chalkdust
06/19/97	1	1	Dogs Stole	PYITE
06/21/97	2	1a	Dirt	SweptAwy
06/22/97	1	1a	CharZero	HelloBaby
06/25/97	2	1	Old Home	Wading
06/29/97	2	1a	Chalkdust	CharZero
07/03/97	3	1	Train Song	Rocky Top
07/05/97	1	1a	Sample	Caspian
07/21/97	5	2	Wading	Jam
07/25/97	3	E	*OPE	*CLE
07/29/97	2	1	*OP1	Beauty
08/02/97	3	1	*OP1	Ginseng
08/09/97	4	1	*OP1	PYITE
08/13/97	3	E	*OPE	*CLE
08/16/97	2	1	Chalkdust	PYITE
11/13/97	2	1	BE Katy	Train Song
11/19/97	4	1	FunkBitch	Ginseng
11/23/97	3	1	My Soul	BE Katy
11/28/97	2	1	BE Katy	Rocky Top
12/07/97	7	1	It's Ice	Tube
12/13/97	4	1	Axilla	Ginseng
12/29/97	2	1	Train Song	Fluffhead
>> 12/31/97		**2**		

TIME

Inspiration: Unclear.

Musical History and Evolution: This odd, short song surfaced twice in 1997, to the confusion of phans who tried (and failed) to identify it. Indeed, the title given here is provisional, though until the band indicates otherwise, this is how folks refer to it. It was first found in the midst of the great second set at Lille, France, on 6/25/97, then again its muttered lyrics erupted between Fee and Antelope in Champaign, IL, on 11/19/97. It's mostly lyrics-based, with no real jam to speak of.

Rotation History: Two appearances in 1997.

Discography: Has not yet appeared on a Phish album.

Time [2] [Time]

Author Unknown

06/25/97	[912]	2	DWD	McGrupp
11/19/97	34	1	Fee	Antelope
>> 12/31/97		**20**		

TRAIN SONG

Inspiration: Mike Gordon dedicated this song's first performance to fans traveling across Europe with the band in summer 1996, but the song was actually written long before the tour. Still, its train travel theme (and the drinking of a little wine) is evocative of Europe.

Musical History and Evolution: As a composed piece, it is played in concert much as it appears on *Billy Breathes*. It was played acoustic on the mini-stage three times in summer 1996 (8/5/96, 8/13/96, 8/16/96), and electric since then.

Rotation History: Lightly—but not too lightly—played in 1996 and 1997.

Discography: Appears on *Billy Breathes* (1996).

Train Song [25] [Train Song]

By Gordon/J. Linitz

07/21/96	[834]	1	Taste	Fee
08/05/96	7	2	Talk	Str Design
08/13/96	5	2	Waste	Str Design
08/16/96	2	2	Talk	Str Design
10/16/96	2	2	Taste	Simple
10/21/96	4	2	Reba	Maze
10/26/96	4	1	Reba	CharZero
10/29/96	2	1	Stash	Billy
11/06/96	4	1	Taste	PoorHeart
11/13/96	5	1	Taste	Reba
11/15/96	2	1	Ginseng	Chalkdust
11/22/96	4	1	FEFY	Stash
12/01/96	6	1	DWD	Horse
12/04/96	2	1	Sample	Guyute
12/29/96	3	1	Guelah	Rift
02/18/97	7	2	Reba	Harry
07/03/97	24	1	Taste	Theme
08/14/97	22	1	Tela	Billy
08/16/97	1	1	YEM	CharZero
11/13/97	2	1	Theme	Split&Melt
11/17/97	3	1	Reba	Ghost
11/22/97	3	1	Harry	Billy
12/06/97	9	1	Antelope	Bathtub
12/12/97	4	1	Tweezer	CharZero
12/29/97	3	1	CTB	Theme
>> 12/31/97		**2**		

TUBE

Inspiration: Fishman wrote these crazy lyrics, which end with the line that gives the song its name: "It's so stupendous, living in this tube."

Musical History and Evolution: For most of the 1990s, Tube was a short, composed treat, with only a short jam segment in the middle. But in 1997, it got funk-influenced, and the versions on fall tour 1997 (12/7/97 and 12/13/97) featured much longer, funkier jams than any Tubes to come before. The version on the 1997 Holiday Tour, on 12/29/97 in New York, NY, totaled over fifteen minutes long, and included an unnamed funk jam in the middle similar to one performed on 11/28/97 and 12/3/97.

Rotation History: Played every year in the 1990s, but just barely. After being in regular rotation in 1991, Tube appeared only twice in 1992 (4/19/92 and 11/20/92), once in 1993 (4/12/93), once in 1994 (6/26/94), then a handful of times in 1995, 1996, and 1997.

Discography: Has not yet appeared on a Phish album.

Tube [34] [Tube]

By Anastasio/Fishman

09/13/90	[222]	1	Foam	Asse Fest
09/15/90	2	1	Fee	Oh Kee
09/16/90	1	1a	Ya Mar	Tweezer
11/04/90	17	1	Bouncing	Harry
11/16/90	3	2	Lawn Boy	Paul&Silas
10/24/91	109	2	Uncle Pen	Slave
10/28/91	3	1	IDK	Oh Kee
10/31/91	2	2	Dinner	IDK
11/01/91	1	1	Uncle Pen	Divided
11/07/91	3	2	Reba	Horn
11/08/91	1	1	*OP1	Landlady
11/09/91	1	1	Reba	YEM
11/12/91	2	1	Bouncing	Sloth
11/14/91	2	1	Foam	Sparkle
11/15/91	1	2	Eliza	Landlady
11/16/91	1	2	*OP2	MSO
11/19/91	1	2	*OP2	MSO
11/22/91	3	2	*OP2	MSO
11/24/91	2	2	*OP2	Divided
12/05/91	3	2	Sparkle	Foam
04/19/92	34	2	MSO	Mango
11/20/92	67	2	Fluffhead	YEM
04/12/93	73	1	Golgi	Bouncing
06/26/94	119	E	AmGrace	Fire
10/13/95	99	2	*OP2	Uncle Pen
12/11/95	37	1	Dog Log	McGrupp
12/17/95	5	1	Mango	Stash
08/13/96	32	1	Divided	Tela
10/25/96	11	2	*OP2	Caspian
11/09/96	10	1	Horn	Talk
02/26/97	32	1	My Soul	Carini
12/07/97	59	1	Theme	Jam
12/13/97	4	1	Vultures	GTBT
12/29/97	2	2	Possum	YEM
>> 12/31/97		**2**		

TWEEZER

Inspiration: A group jam that grew out of a soundcheck performance, Tweezer is one of the band's most collaborative efforts.

Musical History and Evolution: Apparently the result of the sound-

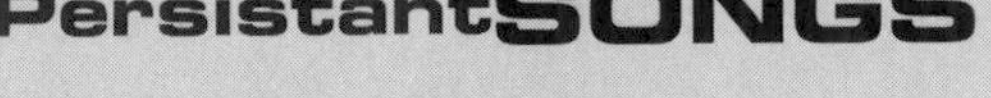

Original songs that have had the shortest lapses between appearances since their debuts (minimum of 50 times played; lapse is the number of shows).

1) Theme	7
2) Maze	10
2) Stash	10
4) YEM	13
5) Bouncing	14
5) Free	14
7) Julius	15
8) Sample in a Jar	16
8) David Bowie	16
8) Poor Heart	16
11) Chalkdust	17
12) Weekapaug	18

check on New Year's Eve 1989, the band toyed with Tweezer in the early spring of 1990, offering a brief tease on 2/25/90, then soundchecking it at the Wetlands on 3/3/90. By the time the band hit the road west at the end of March, they were ready to test the song out in concert, and the folks at Denison University on 3/28/90 were the lucky recipients of what was originally called "Tweezer So Cold." The song's basic structure featured the intro sequence, with lyrics, the improvisational jam, and a fade-out jam at the end; that fade-out jam has been omitted from most performances since 1994 as the band has found numerous other ways to conclude the jam. Though it was clear from 1993 on that Tweezer could get big (see the 20-minute version in Albany, NY, on 5/6/93), it wasn't until spring 1994 that Tweezer got huge. That came in Dallas, TX, on 5/7/94, the famous "Tweezerfest" that stretched on for sixty-seven minutes of jams, teases, and segues into other songs before topping off with an extended Tweezer Reprise. Over the next year, the band pulled out a series of long, experimental Tweezers, including 11/2/94 Bangor, ME, 11/28/94 Bozeman, MT, 6/14/95 Memphis, TN, and 6/22/95 Canandaigua, NY (another virtually whole-set affair); the band opted to include the Bangor version on *A Live One* as a great snapshot of their jamming at that point in time, though some fans find the Bozeman version even superior to Bangor's. Besides those Tweezerfests, there are other varieties of this song, including freak-outs like 11/19/92 Colchester, VT, with fake BBFCM and Burning Ring of Fire vocals; and 2/20/93 Atlanta, GA, extra lyrics and general madness. There are also the melodious versions, like 10/22/95 Champaign, IL, 11/30/95 Dayton, OH, 12/2/95 New Haven, CT (the best of the lot, for many fans); and more recently, good versions on 8/6/96 Morrison, CO (with "Norwegian Wood" jams, like the great one on 12/1/94), 8/14/96 Hershey, PA, and 8/2/97 George, WA.

Rotation History: Reliably played every three or four shows from 1990 through 1996, Tweezer became harder to find in 1997 as the band limited its performances of the song, especially during the summer tour, when it was seen only twice. By the fall tour, however, it was back in more frequent rotation, popping up six times.

Discography: Appears on *A Picture of Nectar* (1992) and on *A Live One* (1995), as a live performance taken from 11/2/94 in Bangor, ME.

Tweezer [203] [Tweezer]

By Phish

03/28/90	[185]	1	WalkAway	Uncle Pen
04/05/90	2	2	Donna	Fee
04/07/90	2	1	Possum	Mike's
04/09/90	2	2	Love You	WhipPost
05/04/90	14	1	Uncle Pen	Bathtub
05/06/90	1	1	Reba	Mike's
05/10/90	1	1	Divided	MSO
05/11/90	1	2	Lizards	Ya Mar
05/13/90	2	2	Donna	MSO
05/15/90	1	1	Tela	Oh Kee
05/23/90	2	2	Reba	Lizards
05/24/90	1	1	Bouncing	Donna
05/31/90	1	1a	Esther	IDK
06/07/90	3	2	Bouncing	Uncle Pen
06/08/90	1	1	Bathtub	IDK
06/09/90	1	1	Bouncing	Uncle Pen
06/16/90	1	2	Esther	MSO
09/14/90	2	2	BurAlive	Magilla
09/16/90	2	1a	Tube	Paul&Silas
09/22/90	3	2	Sqirm Coil	Destiny
10/01/90	2	1	Bouncing	Oh Kee
10/07/90	4	2	Bouncing	MSO
10/12/90	2	1	Esther	Golgi
10/31/90	3	2	Foam	Fee
11/08/90	4	2	Divided	Oh Kee
11/30/90	6	1	Bouncing	MSO
12/01/90	1	1	Foam	MSO
12/07/90	2	2	Caravan	Sqirm Coil
12/28/90	2	2	Sqirm Coil	Oh Kee
02/01/91	3	1	Foam	Magilla
02/03/91	2	1	MSO	Esther
02/07/91	1	2	Stash	Guelah
02/09/91	2	1	MSO	Reba
03/01/91	13	1	Sqirm Coil	Dinner
03/13/91	6	2	Reba	Terrapin
03/17/91	3	2	Sqirm Coil	Fee
03/23/91	3	2	MSO	Lizards
04/11/91	9	1	Paul&Silas	Magilla
04/16/91	4	2	Uncle Pen	RunJim
04/20/91	3	2	TMWSIY	Oh Kee
04/22/91	2	E2	*OPE2	TweezRep
04/27/91	3	2	Fluffhead	Sqirm Coil
05/03/91	2	1	Paul&Silas	Lizards
05/16/91	6	2	Sqirm Coil	MSO
07/12/91	5	2	Moose	MSO
07/19/91	5	2	Magilla	Mango
07/21/91	2	2	*OP2	IDK
07/23/91	1	2	Landlady	Adeline
07/26/91	3	2	Sqirm Coil	Adeline
08/03/91	2	2	Bouncing	Esther
09/27/91	3	1	Esther	Paul&Silas
10/03/91	4	2	Sqirm Coil	Memories
10/12/91	6	1	*OP1	Uncle Pen
10/19/91	5	2	Sparkle	Horn
11/01/91	8	2	*OP2	MSO
11/09/91	5	2	It's Ice	Tela
11/14/91	4	2	Glide	A-Train
11/21/91	5	2	Uncle Pen	TMWSIY
11/23/91	2	2	PoorHeart	Eliza
12/05/91	4	2	*OP2	Sparkle
12/31/91	3	3	Sqirm Coil	McGrupp
03/07/92	2	2	MSO	Sqirm Coil
03/12/92	2	2	Golgi	Eliza
03/17/92	3	2	PoorHeart	Esther
03/25/92	5	2	*OP2	Mound
03/30/92	4	2	Uncle Pen	Mound
04/01/92	2	2	Uncle Pen	Horn
04/04/92	2	2	MSO	Sqirm Coil
04/07/92	3	2	All Things	Eliza
04/17/92	6	2	Sqirm Coil	Uncle Pen
04/21/92	3	2	Mockbird	Tela
04/23/92	2	2	Horn	Fee
04/30/92	4	2	Glide	Sqirm Coil
05/03/92	3	2	*OP2	Horse
05/07/92	3	2	Sparkle	Fluffhead
05/09/92	2	2	Tela	Harpua
05/16/92	5	2	Paul&Silas	Sqirm Coil
07/14/92	15	2	*OP2	Fee
07/24/92	8	1a	Foam	Sqirm Coil
07/28/92	4	1a	Sqirm Coil	RunJim
08/17/92	8	2	It's Ice	Esther
08/24/92	4	1a	All Things	Landlady
11/19/92	7	2	Walk Line	BBJ
11/22/92	3	2	MSO	Tela
11/25/92	2	2	Lizards	Rosie
11/28/92	2	2	Paul&Silas	BBJ
12/02/92	3	2	Mound	BBJ
12/05/92	3	2	PoorHeart	Reba
12/10/92	4	2	Rift	Tela
12/12/92	2	2	Curtain	Rift
12/29/92	3	2	Curtain	Horse
02/03/93	3	2	It's Ice	Horse
02/05/93	2	2	Curtain	Horse
02/07/93	2	2	Reba	BBJ
02/10/93	2	2	Sqirm Coil	Walk Line
02/13/93	3	2	Uncle Pen	Lizards
02/18/93	3	1	PoorHeart	Foam
02/20/93	2	2	Reba	Glide
02/22/93	2	2	Uncle Pen	Glide
02/26/93	3	2	Paul&Silas	Glide
03/02/93	2	2	Uncle Pen	Lizards
03/06/93	3	2	Rift	Reba
03/09/93	2	2	Rift	Reba
03/13/93	2	2	Suzie	Lizards
03/16/93	2	2	Curtain	Bathtub
03/21/93	4	2	Rift	Ya Mar
03/24/93	2	2	Sparkle	Mound
03/26/93	2	2	Curtain	Horse
03/30/93	3	2	Rift	Life Boy
04/01/93	2	2	Ya Mar	PoorHeart
04/05/93	3	2	PYITE	Glide
04/12/93	3	2	Dinner	Fee
04/14/93	2	2	MSO	Mound
04/18/93	3	2	PoorHeart	Horse
04/22/93	3	2	All Things	Lizards
04/25/93	3	2	Curtain	Contact
04/30/93	3	2	Sparkle	Mound
05/03/93	3	2	Curtain	Contact
05/06/93	2	2	Suzie	Tela
07/17/93	7	2	Also Sprac	Sqirm Coil
07/22/93	3	2	Also Sprac	WalkAway
07/25/93	3	2	Suzie	Horse
07/30/93	4	2	Also Sprac	Horse
08/06/93	4	2	Stash	Guelah
08/09/93	3	2	Dinner	Tela
08/12/93	2	2	Landlady	Jam
08/15/93	3	2	Rift	Lizards
12/31/93	12	2	*OP2	Halley's
04/05/94	2	2	Ya Mar	If I Could
04/16/94	9	2	PoorHeart	Lizards
04/22/94	5	2	Reba	Life Boy
05/04/94	9	1	Axilla 2	Life Boy
05/07/94	2	2	Sparkle	TweezRep
05/17/94	7	2	Glide	Life Boy
05/22/94	4	2	McGrupp	Life Boy
05/25/94	2	2	Rift	Life Boy
05/28/94	3	2	It's Ice	Life Boy
06/10/94	3	2	Curtain	Life Boy
06/18/94	6	2	McGrupp	Life Boy
06/23/94	4	2	Uncle Pen	Life Boy
06/29/94	4	2	PoorHeart	It's Ice
07/02/94	3	1	Scent	Life Boy
07/06/94	3	1	PoorHeart	Lawn Boy
07/09/94	2	2	PoorHeart	Life Boy
07/13/94	2	2	NICU	Mound
10/07/94	4	2	Scent	Life Boy
10/10/94	3	2	Esther	Fee
10/14/94	3	2	Curtain	Life Boy
10/22/94	6	2	Dinner	Wilson
10/27/94	4	2	Ya Mar	Contact
11/02/94	4	2	Halley's	Mango
11/13/94	4	2	Lizards	Mango
11/18/94	4	2	PoorHeart	Contact
11/23/94	4	2	Scent	Life Boy
11/28/94	3	2	NICU	Sl Monkey
12/01/94	2	2	Mound	BBFCM
12/04/94	3	1	Rift	Fee
12/09/94	4	2	PoorHeart	McGrupp
12/30/94	4	2	PoorHeart	I'm Blue
06/08/95	4	2	Bouncing	Life Boy
06/14/95	4	2	PoorHeart	AArmy
06/17/95	3	2	Mound	McGrupp
06/22/95	3	2	Theme	TweezRep
06/28/95	5	2	PoorHeart	Gumbo
07/02/95	4	2	Scent	Ha Ha Ha
09/28/95	3	2	Wanna Go	Keyboard
10/06/95	6	2	NICU	Keyboard
10/15/95	6	2	Simple	Lizards
10/22/95	5	2	Curtain	Makisupa
11/12/95	10	2	Curtain	Keyboard
11/19/95	5	2	Curtain	Billy
11/30/95	7	2	CTB	Makisupa
12/02/95	2	2	Faht	DayinLife
12/08/95	4	2	Also Sprac	Love You
12/14/95	4	2	Curtain	Keyboard
12/17/95	3	2	Sparkle	TweezRep
12/28/95	1	2	BurAlive	IDK
07/07/96	9	1a	Curtain	Adeline
07/12/96	4	1	Theme	Llama
07/21/96	6	1	Rift	If I Could
08/02/96	5	1	Golgi	HelloBaby
08/06/96	3	2	Curtain	Caspian
08/14/96	5	2	CTB	Theme
08/17/96	2	3	Scent	DayinLife
10/17/96	2	1	Sparkle	Theme
10/23/96	5	2	Ya Mar	Lizards
10/27/96	3	2	Ya Mar	Fluffhead
11/03/96	4	2	Sparkle	Life Mars
11/11/96	5	2	Sample	SweptAwy
11/18/96	5	2	Scent	HelloBaby
11/27/96	5	2	Scent	DWD
12/01/96	3	2	*OP2	Sparkle
12/30/96	6	2	Guyute	Lifeboy
02/16/97	3	1	Ginseng	Waste
02/20/97	3	1	Curtain	SSP
08/02/97	37	2	DWD	DWD
08/17/97	10	1	Bouncing	Taste
11/17/97	4	1	*OP1	Reba
11/22/97	3	2	Halley's	BE Katy
11/26/97	2	1	*OP1	Sparkle
12/06/97	7	2	*OP2	Izabella
12/12/97	4	1	Bouncing	Train Song
12/31/97	5	3	Auld Lang	Maze
>> 12/31/97		**0**		

TWEEZER REPRISE

Inspiration: Though based on the

Starts AND Stops

Original songs that have had the most lapses of 50 shows or more.

Song	Number of 50+ Lapses	Longest Lapse and When	
1) Dog Log	6	281	2/4/91 to 8/2/93
1) Icculus	6	181	4/6/91 to 4/16/92
1) Tube	6	119	4/12/93 to 6/26/94
4) Kung	4	367	11/2/89 to 12/31/92
4) Wedge	4	134	8/20/93 to 6/7/95
4) Dinner and a Movie	4	93	11/22/94 to 11/18/95
4) Harpua	4	84	6/9/90 to 4/18/91
8) Makisupa Policeman	3	319	11/26/90 to 4/29/93
8) Sanity	3	282	5/28/89 to 3/11/92
8) Magilla	3	260	5/4/94 to 2/26/97
8) Gumbo	3	226	7/25/91 to 4/16/93
8) Tela	3	82	8/27/88 to 10/22/89

Tweezer theme, the reprise is a fully-composed song in its own right.
Musical History and Evolution: Since emerging about a year after Tweezer, on spring tour 1991, Tweezer Reprise has capped off numerous sets and shows with a frenetic, fast-paced jam that often includes some of Chris Kuroda's most mind-blowing light work. Though most performances of this song are the same, there are some jammier occasions, like 10/27/94 Charlottesville, VA, when the band takes it around a few extra times.
Rotation History: For most of 1991 through 1994, Tweezer Reprise followed Tweezer later in the show. But on fall tour 1995, the band started having some Reprise fun without the Tweezer. The first of these, on 10/21/95 Lincoln, NE, saw Tweezer Reprise open the show and close the first set; it also opened the show on 11/9/95 Atlanta, GA, and appeared twice in the second set on 12/15/95 Philadelphia, PA. Its appearances on 12/31/96 and 3/2/97 were also Tweezer-less.
Discography: Appears on *A Picture of Nectar* (1992).

Tweezer Reprise [131] [TweezRep]
By Phish

Date	Gap	Set	Before	After
02/07/91	[260]	2	Tweezer	Guelah
04/16/91	40	2	Carolina	*CL2
04/22/91	5	E2	Tweezer	*CLE
04/27/91	3	2	Jam	*CL2
05/03/91	2	2	Harpua	*CL2
05/11/91	4	2	Suzie	*CL2
07/12/91	7	E	Fee	*CLE
07/21/91	7	2	Contact	*CL2
07/26/91	4	2	Lizards	*CL2
09/27/91	5	2	YEM	*CL2
10/03/91	4	E	Terrapin	*CLE
10/12/91	6	1	Harry	*CL1
11/01/91	13	2	PoorHeart	*CL2
11/09/91	5	2	MSO	*CL2
11/14/91	4	2	Lizards	*CL2
11/23/91	7	2	MSO	*CL2
12/05/91	4	2	MSO	*CL2
12/31/91	3	E	Rocky Top	*CLE
03/07/92	2	2	Rosie	*CL2
03/12/92	2	E	Weigh	*CLE
03/25/92	8	E	Sl Monkey	*CLE
03/30/92	4	2	Bouncing	*CL2
04/01/92	2	2	Sqirm Coil	Rocky Top
04/04/92	2	E	Sl Monkey	*CLE
04/07/92	3	E	Contact	*CLE
04/17/92	6	2	Rosie	*CL2
04/23/92	5	E	Sl Monkey	*CLE
04/30/92	4	2	Harry	*CL2
05/03/92	3	E	Adeline	*CLE
05/07/92	3	2	Sqirm Coil	*CL2
05/09/92	2	E	PoorHeart	*CLE
05/16/92	5	2	PoorHeart	*CL2
07/14/92	15	2	A-Train	*CL2
07/24/92	8	1a	YEM	*CL1
11/22/92	26	E	Carolina	*CLE
11/25/92	2	2	MSO	*CL2
11/28/92	2	E	Contact	*CLE
12/05/92	6	2	WhipPost	*CL2
12/10/92	4	E	Carolina	*CLE
12/12/92	2	2	Ride Capt.	*CLE
12/29/92	3	2	Sqirm Coil	*CL2
02/03/93	3	E	AmGrace	*CLE
02/05/93	2	2	Sqirm Coil	*CL2
02/07/93	2	2	Brain	*CL2
02/10/93	2	E	AmGrace	*CLE
02/13/93	3	E	AmGrace	*CLE
02/20/93	5	2	Harry	*CL2
02/22/93	2	2	Sqirm Coil	*CL2
02/26/93	3	2	Sqirm Coil	*CL2
03/02/93	2	E	Golgi	*CLE
03/06/93	3	E	PoorHeart	*CLE
03/09/93	2	2	Sqirm Coil	*CL2
03/13/93	2	2	Love You	*CL2
03/16/93	2	E	Sparkle	*CLE
03/26/93	8	2	Great Gig	*CL2
03/30/93	3	2	Brain	*CL2
04/01/93	2	E	Carolina	*CLE
04/05/93	3	2	Rosie	*CL2
04/12/93	3	2	Terrapin	*CL2
04/14/93	2	E	Contact	*CLE
04/18/93	3	2	Love You	*CL2
04/22/93	3	2	Love You	*CL2
04/25/93	3	2	Fee	*CL2
04/30/93	3	E	AmGrace	*CLE
05/03/93	3	2	MSO	*CL2
05/06/93	2	E	Contact	*CLE
07/17/93	7	E	Daniel	*CLE
07/25/93	6	2	Harpua	*CL2
08/06/93	8	2	Rosie	*CL2
12/31/93	20	3	Harry	*CL3
04/16/94	11	2	Sqirm Coil	*CL2
05/04/94	14	1	Rift	*CL1
05/07/94	2	2	HYHU	*CL2
05/22/94	11	2	Slave	*CL2
05/25/94	2	E	Sl Monkey	*CLE
06/10/94	6	2	Harry	*CL2
06/18/94	6	E	Bouncing	*CLE
06/23/94	4	E	Sparkle	*CLE
06/29/94	4	E	Ya Mar	*CLE
07/02/94	3	1	Sparkle	*CL1
07/06/94	3	2	Harry	*CL2
07/09/94	2	E	Sl Monkey	*CLE
07/13/94	2	E	MSO	*CLE
10/07/94	4	2	MSO	*CL2
10/10/94	3	E	Long Time	*CLE
10/14/94	3	2	Sqirm Coil	*CL2
10/22/94	6	E	Uncle Pen	*CLE
10/27/94	4	E	Icculus	*CLE
11/02/94	4	E	Long Time	*CLE
11/13/94	4	E	FunkBitch	*CLE
11/23/94	8	2	YEM	*CL2
11/28/94	3	E	Fee	*CLE
12/01/94	2	E	Sl Monkey	*CLE
12/09/94	7	E	Long Time	*CLE
12/30/94	4	2	Harry	*CL2
06/14/95	8	E	Rocky Top	*CLE
06/22/95	6	E	Tweezer	*CL2
06/28/95	5	2	Harry	*CL2
07/02/95	4	E	Halley's	*CLE
10/15/95	15	2	Harry	*CL2
10/21/95	4	1	*OP1	Chalkdust
10/21/95	0	1	GTBT	*CL1
11/09/95	8	1	*OP1	Divided
11/12/95	3	2	Possum	*CL2
11/19/95	5	E	Life Mars	*CLE
12/02/95	9	2	Sqirm Coil	*CL2
12/08/95	4	2	Sqirm Coil	Antelope
12/15/95	5	2	*OP2	RunJim
12/15/95	0	E	GTBT	*CLE
12/17/95	2	2	Tweezer	*CL2
12/28/95	1	E	Fee	*CLE
08/06/96	27	2	Harry	*CL2
08/14/96	5	2	Sample	*CL2
08/17/96	2	3	Possum	*CL3
10/17/96	2	1	DayinLife	*CL1
10/27/96	8	2	Life Mars	*CL2
11/03/96	4	2	Possum	*CL2
11/18/96	10	2	HelloBaby	Llama
11/27/96	5	E	Waste	*CLE
12/01/96	3	2	Steep	Johnny B.
12/31/96	7	1	Sample	*CL1
02/16/97	3	2	Lovin Cup	*CL2
02/20/97	3	1	Bowie	*CL1
03/02/97	8	2	Slave	*CL2
08/02/97	29	2	Lovin Cup	*CL2
08/17/97	10	E	Circus	*CLE
11/22/97	7	E	Bouncing	*CLE
11/26/97	2	2	PoorHeart	*CL2
12/06/97	7	2	Sl Monkey	*CL2
12/12/97	4	2	Izabella	*CL2
12/31/97	5	E	New York	*CLE
>> 12/31/97	**0**			

TWIST AROUND
Inspiration: Part of the batch of new songs in summer 1997.
Musical History and Evolution: The band took to the jam in Twist Around fairly quickly, stretching it out in early performances including 7/29/97 Phoenix, AZ, and 8/3/97 George, WA. Though the song hasn't changed much in its first few months, its jam gives signs that it might become something special.
Rotation History: Appeared eleven times in 1997, including three on the fall tour.
Discography: Has not yet appeared on a Phish album.

Twist Around [11] [Twist]
By Anastasio/Marshall

Date	Gap	Set	Before	After
06/14/97	[905]	2	*OP2	Piper
06/20/97	3	2	Cavern	Bouncing
06/21/97	1	1a	Chalkdust	Cavern
06/24/97	2	2	NICU	Piper
07/05/97	7	1a	Caspian	Piper
07/29/97	10	2	Wading	Taste
08/03/97	4	1	My Mind	Jesus
08/06/97	1	1	Beauty	Also Sprac
11/14/97	10	2	Piper	Jam
11/23/97	6	1	Sparkle	Stash
12/06/97	8	2	Izabella	Piper
>> 12/31/97	**9**			

UNION FEDERAL
Inspiration: This one-time-only jam was recorded during one of Phish's marathon Oh Kee Pa Ceremonies in 1989. As a fully improvisational piece of music, it appears in no show setlists.
Musical History and Evolution: None.
Rotation History: None.
Discography: Appears on the Elektra rerelease of *Junta* (1992) as a bonus live track.

VIBRATION OF LIFE
Inspiration: An effect created by Trey and Mike that seeks to tap the natural vibration of the universe, seven beats per second. Trey says that creating the vibration in concert helps recharge the crowd and the band.
Musical History and Evolution: Not really a song at all, the Vibration of Life is identified in the nitty-gritty notes of *Almanac* setlists only when directly identified by Trey. It's often included in the spacey opening segment of YEM.
Rotation History: First seen on fall tour 1992, the initial appearance came on 11/23/92 in Binghamton, NY. Since then, Trey has announced it at random to various crowds, though not in 1997 (most recently on fall tour 1996 on 11/16/96 in Omaha, NE).
Discography: Has yet to appear on a Phish album.

VULTURES
Inspiration: One of the new songs debuted on summer tour 1997.
Musical History and Evolution: As a lyrically complex new song, featuring overlapping vocals, Vultures immediately captured fans' affections on summer tour 1997, though versions differed little from one another. But then the band only played it once the rest of the year, on 12/13/97 in Albany, NY.
Rotation History: Played ten times in 1997.
Discography: Has yet to appear on a Phish album.

Vultures [10] [Vultures]
By Anastasio/Marshall

Date	Gap	Set	Before	After
06/13/97	[904]	2	Water	Slave
06/19/97	3	1	Waste	RunJim
06/24/97	4	1	Dogs Stole	Guelah
07/02/97	5	1	Ginseng	Water
07/22/97	8	1	Bouncing	Bye Bye
07/31/97	6	2	Circus	McGrupp
08/03/97	2	1	Dirt	My Mind
08/11/97	5	2	Piper	My Soul
08/17/97	5	1	Dogs Stole	Water
12/13/97	21	1	Sample	Tube
>> 12/31/97	**4**			

WADING IN THE VELVET SEA
Inspiration: One of the new songs debuted on summer tour 1997.
Musical History and Evolution: This slow ballad has the potential to be jammed out in the same fashion as Lifeboy or perhaps Prince Caspian, with a somewhat open-ended jam in the latter half of the song. However, most of the initial versions in summer 1997 were similarly tame.
Rotation History: A favorite choice on the first half of the 1997 summer tour, in Europe, Wading disappeared after 8/2/97, with only three American performances completed.
Discography: Has yet to appear on a Phish album.

Wading in the Velvet Sea [10] [Wading]
By Anastasio/Marshall

Date	Gap	Set	Before	After
06/13/97	[904]	1	Wolfman's	Taste
06/16/97	2	2	Reba	Dirt
06/19/97	1	2	Saw It	Piper
06/24/97	4	2	Piper	Ghost
06/25/97	1	1	Theme	Saw It
07/02/97	4	2	Wormtown	*CL2
07/10/97	5	1	Llama	Lizards
07/21/97	2	2	Bowie	Theme
07/29/97	5	1	Antelope	Twist
08/02/97	3	2	Sparkle	Lovin Cup
>> 12/31/97	**35**			

WALFREDO
Inspiration: For their tour of smaller European venues in February and

March 1997, the band composed two rotation/instrument-switching songs, Rocka William and Walfredo. Walfredo apparently takes its name from Walfredo Reyes, one of the Santana band percussionists, and recounts memories from Phish's tour as opening act for Santana on summer tour 1992.

Musical History and Evolution: As a rotation song, the music is composed, and the few performances differed little from one another.

Rotation History: Appeared four times on the winter Europe tour in February 1997, but not since 2/22/97 in Rome, Italy.

Discography: Has yet to appear on a Phish album.

Walfredo [4] [Walfredo]

By Phish

02/13/97	[889]	1	Stash	Taste
02/14/97	1	2	Reba	RockaW
02/18/97	3	1	Waste	CharZero
02/22/97	3	1	*OP1	Also Sprac
>> 12/31/97	70			

WASTE

Inspiration: One of the batch of slower songs with more thoughtful lyrics written for the *Billy Breathes* sessions, Waste is a lament in the form of a plea.

Musical History and Evolution: Little to speak of, as the song is generally short and sweet—like its album counterpart—in concert. During its debut performance on 6/6/96 at the Joyous Lake Club in Woodstock, VT, it was dubbed "no ending" because the band had yet to write an ending for it. Two months later, they played it three times on the acoustic mini-stage (8/5/96, 8/13/96, and 8/16/96), and by fall tour 1996, were playing electric versions of it.

Rotation History: Appeared regularly in concert in 1996 and 1997.

Discography: Appears on *Billy Breathes* (1996).

Waste [30] [Waste]

By Anastasio/Marshall

06/06/96	[820]	2	Stash	CharZero
07/10/96	13	1a	Split&Melt	Bowie
07/19/96	5	1a	Adeline	Sqirm Coil
08/05/96	10	2	Therm	Talk
08/13/96	5	2	Therm	Train Song
08/16/96	2	2	Sqirm Coil	Talk
10/16/96	2	E	*OPE	*CLE
10/18/96	2	2	Reba	Harry
10/21/96	2	1	Stash	Possum
10/26/96	4	2	McGrupp	Antelope
11/02/96	4	2	Antelope	Harry
11/07/96	3	1	Stash	Guyute
11/11/96	3	E	*OPE	Cavern
11/18/96	5	E	*OPE	Johnny B.
11/23/96	3	2	Catapult	AmGrace
11/27/96	2	E	*OPE	TweezRep
11/29/96	1	2	YEM	Harry
02/13/97	10	1	Taste	PoorHeart
02/16/97	2	1	Tweeze	Cavern
02/18/97	2	1	Stash	Walfredo
02/21/97	2	2	Reba	Caspian
02/25/97	3	1	Stash	Taste
02/28/97	2	2	Axilla	Julius
03/02/97	2	2	PYITE	CharZero
03/18/97	1	2	Love Me	Chalkdust
06/14/97	2	2	Dogs Stole	Bowie
06/19/97	2	1	Maze	Vultures
07/06/97	12	2	YEM	Rocky Top
07/26/97	8	2	Free	Johnny B.
12/11/97	33	E	*OPE	*CLE
>> 12/31/97	6			

WATER IN THE SKY

Inspiration: This new bluegrass-tinged original's lyrics are fairly vague, though the general connotation of the song is positive.

Musical History and Evolution: New on summer tour 1997, Water in the Sky is a short, composed piece that has varied little thus far.

Rotation History: Played sixteen times in 1997, but only two of those came after the summer tour.

Discography: Has not yet appeared on a Phish album.

Water in the Sky [16] [Water]

By Anastasio/Marshall

06/13/97	[904]	2	Maze	Vultures
06/16/97	2	1	Taste	Sample
06/19/97	1	1	PYITE	Waste
06/22/97	3	1a	Taste	Stash
07/02/97	6	1	Vultures	Weekapaug
07/22/97	8	1	My Soul	Stash
07/23/97	1	1	Ginseng	Limb
07/25/97	1	1	Maze	Bathtub
07/30/97	3	1	Chalkdust	Weigh
08/02/97	2	1	Wolfman's	Split&Melt
08/08/97	3	1	It's Ice	CharZero
08/11/97	3	1	Maze	Guyute
08/13/97	1	1	PoorHeart	Gumbo
08/17/97	3	1	Vultures	Maze
11/29/97	11	1	Horn	Bowie
12/30/97	13	1	Taste	PYITE
>> 12/31/97	1			

THE WEDGE

Inspiration: The lyrics speak of taking "the highway to the great divide," but are otherwise just a typical Phish flight of fancy.

Musical History and Evolution: This song was a late addition to *Rift*, and unlike all the other songs on the album it was recorded at the band's mixing studio (the Castle in Nashville, TN). For the album version, all the instruments were recorded separately, and drum overdubs by Fishman were included, making the song impossible to perform live exactly as on the album. Debuting the song on spring tour 1993 with performances which the fans enjoyed more than the band did, the boys tinkered with it for the next few months before abandoning it. They gave it another go, this time with a reworked intro and a bit of a different pace, at Red Rocks on 8/20/93, then let it rest almost two years until summer tour 1995, when the band gave it a go in shorter, tighter, and seemingly more successful form. The two performances in 1997 were slower versions, and the band seemed to struggle trying to find the song's groove.

Rotation History: With less than twenty total performances, there's not much here. Wedge was common only in February 1993 and June 1995, but since 6/30/95 it's been a rarity, surfacing that fall on 10/25/95 and 11/14/95, once in 1996 on 10/29/96, and twice in 1997, on 8/17/97 and 11/29/97.

Discography: Appears on *Rift* (1993).

The Wedge [19] [Wedge]

By Anastasio/Marshall

02/03/93	[505]	1	Llama	Divided
02/04/93	1	2	Chalkdust	Mike's
02/06/93	2	1	Lawn Boy	Bouncing
02/09/93	2	1	Rift	Chalkdust
02/12/93	3	1	Esther	Chalkdust
02/15/93	2	2	Weekapaug	PoorHeart
02/23/93	7	1	Chalkdust	Paul&Silas
03/25/93	20	2	Mockbird	Mike's
08/20/93	63	1	It's Ice	Ginseng
06/07/95	134	1	Scent	FunkBitch
06/09/95	2	2	Split&Melt	Scent
06/15/95	4	1	Taste	Stash
06/23/95	6	2	Lizards	Antelope
06/30/95	6	1	Taste	Lizards
10/25/95	25	1	Divided	Scent
11/14/95	9	E	*OPE	Rocky Top
10/29/96	70	2	Weekapaug	CharZero
08/17/97	81	1	*OP1	Beauty
11/29/97	11	1	*OP1	Foam
>> 12/31/97	11			

WEEKAPAUG GROOVE

Inspiration: After playing a show at the yacht club of a friend of Trey's in the small seacoast town of Weekapaug, RI, in the mid 1980s, the band was driving back to Boston to crash at Mike Gordon's house when the old 1970s song "Oh, What a Night" came on the van's radio. As Mike recalled it at the time of the release of *Slip Stitch and Pass*, he started playing with the words in the song, creating the meaningless phrase, "Trying to make a woman that you move/Sharing in the Weekapaug groove." He later formulated it into a song.

Musical History and Evolution: Always linked in some way with Mike's Song (there has yet to be a show with Weekapaug but without Mike's Song since the Mike's > Hydrogen > Weekapaug trio came together in 1988) Weekapaug has been stretched out in much the same way as Mike's Song. The jam in the middle of the song is anchored on both sides by the Weekapaug chorus; in special circumstances, the final Weekapaug chorus becomes more like a vocal jam (see 11/19/92 and 12/30/93 for examples of this). Many best-version recommendations of Mike's Groove are listed under the Mike's Song entry, but a few special Weekapaugs that stand out include 11/8/91 Tuscaloosa, AL, with alternate "bucket of lard" lyrics; 12/28/94 Philadelphia, PA, glorious version with "Little Drummer Boy" jamming; 12/7/95 Niagara Falls, NY, with a jam out of Weekapaug; 12/31/95 New York, NY, an incredibly melodious jam into Sea and Sand; 10/22/96, with circus troupe onstage at Madison Square Garden, drawn-out jam with no return to lyrics; and 12/6/96 Las Vegas, NV, with the first instance of start-stop jamming that became commonplace in 1997. Also, jams on the Rolling Stones' "Can't You Hear Me Knocking" are common in Weekapaugs, especially from fall tour 1994 and throughout 1996 and 1997—listen for it at the end of Weekapaug on *Slip Stitch and Pass* from 3/1/97 in Hamburg, Germany, an unfinished version that never comes back around to the final Weekapaug refrain (not an uncommon occurance).

Rotation History: Not played as often as Mike's Song, because there are numerous instances of a show with Mike's but with no Weekapaug, but no exceptions the other way around. Perhaps the closest the band has come to playing Weekapaug without Mike's came on 11/29/97 in Worcester, MA, when the band locked into Weekapaug in the midst of a long Runaway Jim jam, but never sang the lyrics. Though by no means as common as it was in the late 1980s and early 1990s, however, Weekapaug still surfaces as part of the Mike's Groove suite at least ten times a year (eleven, actually, in 1997).

Discography: Appears on *Slip Stitch And Pass* (1997).

Weekapaug Groove [274] [Weekapaug]

By Gordon

07/23/88	[46]	1	I am H2	Lizards
07/24/88	1	1	I am H2	Bold
07/25/88	1	2	I am H2	Bold
10/12/88	7	1	I am H2	Wilson
11/05/88	3	2	I am H2	IDK
11/11/88	1	2	I am H2	Jazz
02/07/89	6	1	I am H2	Golgi
03/03/89	4	2	I am H2	Fee
03/04/89	1	1	I am H2	Fee
03/30/89	2	2	I am H2	YEM
04/14/89	6	2	I am H2	Esther
04/15/89	1	1	I am H2	Esther
04/20/89	2	2	I am H2	Love You
05/06/89	9	1	I am H2	Esther
05/09/89	3	1	I am H2	Sloth

Long VERSIONS

Is bigger better? Some phans seem to think so, as they seek to amass collections of some of Phish's longest performances of jam songs. The list below is a collection of many of the 25-minute-plus performances Phish has pulled out in recent years, omitting some from 1997 because of the increased frequency of long jams. But beware—not all are must-hear listening, though they are all interesting in their own ways. *Almanac* editor recommendations are marked with an asterisk.

Antelope: 8/14/93 Tinley Park, IL (25+ minutes, but comprising several other complete songs besides Antelope).*

Bathtub Gin: 11/7/96 Lexington, KY (25 minutes).*

Bowie: 11/26/94 Minneapolis, MN (30+ minutes);* 12/29/94 Providence, RI (30+ minutes).*

DWD: 12/12/95 Providence, RI (35 minutes).

Free: 11/22/95 Landover, MD (30 minutes).

Ghost: 7/3/97 Nuremburg, Germany (30 minutes); 7/23/97 Atlanta, GA (27 minutes).*

Harpua: 12/6/96 Las Vegas, NV (30 minutes, but includes lots of other stuff).*

Mike's Song/Weekapaug Groove: Though many versions of the Mike's Groove suite stretch on for 30 or 40 minutes, no individual performances of Mike's or Weekapaug have achieved this length on their own.

Runaway Jim: 6/16/95 Raleigh, NC (30 minutes);* 11/29/97 Worcester, MA (60 minutes, including Harry Hood and Weekapaug jams).*

Simple: 11/16/94 Ann Arbor, MI (25+ minutes, out of Mike's Song).*

Stash: 11/14/95 Orlando, FL (30+ minutes, including Manteca and an a cappella Dog Faced Boy in the middle);* 7/2/97 Amsterdam (30+ minutes, including a funky improvisational jam that eventually segues into Llama).*

05/20/89	7	2	I am H2	Foam
05/21/89	1	1	I am H2	Split&Melt
05/26/89	1	1	I am H2	Sanity
05/27/89	1	1	I am H2	FunkBitch
05/28/89	1	2	I am H2	Bathtub
06/23/89	5	1	I am H2	Lizards
06/30/89	2	2	I am H2	*CL2
08/17/89	5	1	I am H2	*CL1
08/19/89	2	1	I am H2	*CL1
10/06/89	8	1a	I am H2	Sloth
10/07/89	1	1	I am H2	Suzie
10/21/89	5	2	I am H2	*CL2
10/26/89	2	1	I am H2	*CL1
11/02/89	3	1	I am H2	Fee
11/09/89	3	2	I am H2	*CL2
11/10/89	1	1	I am H2	*CL1
11/16/89	2	1	I am H2	Bathtub
12/07/89	6	1	I am H2	Alumni
12/09/89	2	2	I am H2	Contact
12/16/89	2	1a	I am H2	Lizards
12/29/89	1	1	I am H2	*CL1
12/31/89	2	2	I am H2	Ya Mar
01/20/90	1	1	I am H2	Harry
01/27/90	3	1	I am H2	*CL1
01/28/90	1	2	I am H2	*CL2
02/09/90	7	1	I am H2	Carolina
02/10/90	1	2	I am H2	*CL2
02/15/90	1	1	I am H2	*CL1
02/17/90	2	1a	I am H2	Split&Melt
02/23/90	2	2	I am H2	HwayHell
03/01/90	3	2	I am H2	*CL2
03/03/90	2	1	I am H2	MSO
03/07/90	1	2	I am H2	*CL2
03/08/90	1	2	I am H2	Curtis
03/28/90	4	2	I am H2	Jesus
04/04/90	1	2	I am H2	Lizards
04/05/90	1	2	I am H2	Brain
04/07/90	2	1	I am H2	Bowie
04/08/90	1	2	I am H2	Fee
04/18/90	5	1	I am H2	Uncle Pen
04/20/90	2	2	I am H2	La Grange
04/22/90	2	1	I am H2	*CL1
04/25/90	1	2	I am H2	*CL2
04/26/90	1	2	I am H2	*CL2
04/28/90	1	2	I am H2	*CL2
05/04/90	3	2	I am H2	Caravan
05/06/90	1	1	I am H2	*CL1
05/11/90	2	1	I am H2	Uncle Pen
05/13/90	2	2	I am H2	Foam
05/23/90	3	2	I am H2	*CL2
06/05/90	4	1	I am H2	Ya Mar
06/07/90	1	2	I am H2	*CL2
06/08/90	1	1	I am H2	Foam
06/09/90	1	1	I am H2	*CL1
06/16/90	1	3	I am H2	*CL3
09/13/90	1	2	I am H2	Magilla
09/16/90	3	1a	I am H2	Magilla
10/05/90	7	1	I am H2	MSO
10/07/90	2	1	I am H2	A-Train
10/12/90	2	2	I am H2	*CL2
10/30/90	2	2	I am H2	Magilla
10/31/90	1	2	I am H2	*CL2
11/02/90	1	1	I am H2	Esther
11/03/90	1	2	I am H2	Paul&Silas
11/04/90	1	2	I am H2	Manteca
11/08/90	1	1	I am H2	*CL1
11/10/90	1	1	I am H2	*CL1
11/16/90	1	2	I am H2	Lawn Boy
11/17/90	1	2	I am H2	Esther
11/24/90	1	1	I am H2	Sqirm Coil
11/26/90	1	2	I am H2	*CL2
11/30/90	1	1	I am H2	Esther
12/07/90	3	2	I am H2	Donna
12/08/90	1	1	I am H2	*CL1
12/28/90	1	1	I am H2	Golgi
12/31/90	2	1	I am H2	Auld
02/08/91	5	2	I am H2	Horn
02/14/91	2	2	I am H2	Foam
02/16/91	2	1	I am H2	*CL1
02/21/91	3	1	I am H2	*CL1
02/26/91	4	2	I am H2	*CL2
02/28/91	2	1	I am H2	Cavern
03/01/91	1	1	I am H2	*CL1
03/07/91	3	2	I am H2	Guelah
03/15/91	4	1	I am H2	*CL1
03/17/91	2	1	I am H2	Foam
03/22/91	2	2	I am H2	*CL2
04/05/91	8	1	I am H2	*CL1
04/11/91	2	2	I am H2	*CL2
04/15/91	3	2	I am H2	Horn
04/19/91	3	1	I am H2	Adeline
04/21/91	2	1	I am H2	Adeline
04/27/91	4	2	I am H2	Fluffhead
05/04/91	3	1	I am H2	*CL1
05/10/91	2	2	I am H2	*CL2
05/12/91	2	2	I am H2	Sqirm Coil
05/17/91	2	1	I am H2	A-Train
07/11/91	3	2	I am H2	Touch Me
07/12/91	1	2	I am H2	Touch Me
07/14/91	2	3	I am H2	Touch Me
07/15/91	1	1a	I am H2	Flat Fee
07/18/91	1	1	I am H2	*CL1
07/21/91	3	1	I am H2	*CL1
07/23/91	1	1	I am H2	*CL1
07/25/91	2	2	I am H2	*CL2
07/27/91	2	1a	I am H2	*CL1
09/26/91	3	2	I am H2	Lawn Boy
09/28/91	2	2	I am H2	*CL2
10/03/91	3	2	I am H2	Esther
10/04/91	1	2	I am H2	*CL2
10/10/91	3	2	I am H2	*CL2
10/13/91	3	1	I am H2	*CL2
10/18/91	3	2	I am H2	IDK
10/24/91	3	2	I am H2	Lizards
10/27/91	2	2	I am H2	Tela
11/01/91	4	2	I am H2	A-Train
11/08/91	4	2	I am H2	Jesus
11/12/91	3	2	I am H2	Guelah
11/15/91	3	2	I am H2	Eliza
11/19/91	2	2	I am H2	Mango
11/21/91	2	1	I am H2	*CL1
11/23/91	2	2	I am H2	Horn
12/04/91	3	2	I am H2	Sparkle
12/05/91	1	2	I am H2	Fee
12/31/91	3	3	I am H2	*CL3
03/07/92	2	2	I am H2	Rosie
03/14/92	4	1	I am H2	*CL1
03/17/92	1	2	I am H2	Love You
03/20/92	2	2	I am H2	Sanity
03/24/92	2	2	I am H2	Guelah
03/27/92	3	2	I am H2	Horse
03/31/92	3	2	I am H2	Fee
04/04/92	3	2	I am H2	Glide
04/06/92	2	2	I am H2	NICU
04/09/92	2	2	I am H2	Horse
04/13/92	2	2	I am H2	Magilla
04/16/92	2	2	I am H2	Horn
04/19/92	3	2	I am H2	Horse
04/21/92	1	2	I am H2	Weigh
04/23/92	2	2	I am H2	Lizards
04/24/92	1	2	I am H2	Mango
04/29/92	2	2	I am H2	Love You
05/01/92	2	2	I am H2	Mound
05/03/92	2	2	I am H2	Mango
05/05/92	1	2	I am H2	Horse
05/07/92	2	2	I am H2	Fee
05/14/92	5	2	I am H2	McGrupp
05/18/92	4	2	I am H2	Fee
07/16/92	15	2	I am H2	*CL2
08/17/92	18	2	I am H2	Horn
11/19/92	11	2	I am H2	Bouncing
11/21/92	2	2	I am H2	Horse
11/23/92	2	2	I am H2	Lngthwise
11/28/92	3	1	I am H2	*CL1
12/01/92	2	1	I am H2	*CL1
12/03/92	2	2	I am H2	Lawn Boy
12/05/92	2	2	I am H2	WhipPost
12/08/92	3	2	I am H2	Horse
12/11/92	2	2	I am H2	Esther
12/29/92	4	2	I am H2	Bayou
12/31/92	2	3	Auld	Harpua
02/04/93	2	2	TMWSIY	Lawn Boy
02/06/93	2	2	I am H2	Life Boy
02/09/93	2	2	I am H2	Weigh
02/11/93	2	2	I am H2	Mound
02/15/93	3	2	I am H2	Wedge
02/18/93	2	2	I am H2	Mound
02/20/93	2	2	I am H2	FEFY
02/23/93	3	2	I am H2	Terrapin
02/27/93	3	2	I am H2	Terrapin
03/03/93	2	2	I am H2	Glide
03/05/93	1	2	I am H2	Jesus
03/09/93	3	2	I am H2	Horse
03/13/93	2	2	I am H2	FEFY
03/17/93	3	2	I am H2	Horse
03/19/93	2	2	I am H2	Love You
03/22/93	2	2	I am H2	*CL2
03/25/93	2	2	I am H2	Golgi
03/27/93	2	2	I am H2	Rosie
03/30/93	2	2	I am H2	Horse
04/02/93	3	2	I am H2	Lizards
04/10/93	4	2	Great Gig	FunkBitch
04/13/93	2	2	I am H2	Brain
04/16/93	2	2	I am H2	Horse
04/21/93	4	2	Great Gig	Gumbo
04/23/93	2	2	I am H2	Lngthwise
04/25/93	2	2	I am H2	Fee
04/29/93	2	2	I am H2	Terrapin
05/01/93	2	2	Great Gig	Cavern
05/08/93	6	2	I am H2	AmGrace
07/17/93	5	2	Leprech	Faht
07/24/93	5	2	YSZahov	PurplRain
07/31/93	6	2	Leprech	PurplRain
08/02/93	1	2	Sqirm Coil	Bike
08/11/93	6	2	Great Gig	Esther
08/16/93	5	2	Faht	Mound
08/24/93	4	2	Ginseng	Wilson
12/30/93	6	2	McGrupp	PurplRain
04/06/94	4	2	Life Boy	Sqirm Coil
04/09/94	2	2	I am H2	Tela
04/21/94	10	2	I am H2	Scent
04/29/94	6	2	I am H2	BeLikeYou
05/14/94	11	2	I am H2	TMWSIY
05/19/94	3	2	I am H2	Lizards
06/09/94	10	2	I am H2	Golgi
06/13/94	3	2	I am H2	Esther
06/17/94	3	2	I am H2	Harpua
06/22/94	4	2	I am H2	TMWSIY
07/02/94	8	2	I am H2	McGrupp
07/10/94	6	2	I am H2	Bouncing
10/08/94	6	2	I am H2	Fluffhead
10/13/94	4	2	YSZahov	Foreplay
10/21/94	6	2	I am H2	Sl Monkey
10/25/94	3	2	Mango	YSZahov
11/04/94	8	2	Tela	Ya Mar
11/25/94	11	2	Harpua	Mango
12/06/94	8	2	Mango	Bike
12/10/94	4	2	I am H2	DoInRoad
12/28/94	1	2	Mango	Contact
12/31/94	3	2	YSZahov	AmGrace
06/10/95	5	2	I am H2	AmGrace
06/20/95	7	2	Contact	Rosie
06/25/95	4	2	DoInRoad	AmGrace
06/30/95	4	2	Contact	AmGrace
09/30/95	7	2	Keyboard	Suspicious
10/11/95	7	2	McGrupp	Llama
10/19/95	5	2	I am H2	Lawn Boy
10/25/95	5	2	Sparkle	Suzie
11/11/95	7	1	PoorHeart	Horse
11/15/95	3	2	Life Mars	Fee
11/25/95	7	2	Str Design	Harry
12/01/95	4	2	Mike's	Mango
12/07/95	4	2	Mike's	AmGrace
12/16/95	7	2	Simple	Sqirm Coil
12/31/95	5	2	Auld	Sea&Sand
07/23/96	18	2	I am H2	Bike
08/05/96	5	2	I am H2	*CL2
08/13/96	5	2	Life Boy	Therm
08/16/96	2	2	Contact	*CL2
10/22/96	7	2	Steep	*CL2
10/29/96	5	2	Silent	Wedge
11/06/96	4	2	Steep	Scent
11/08/96	2	2	SSB	*CL2
11/15/96	5	2	Mustard	*CL2
11/23/96	5	2	Axilla	Catapult
12/04/96	7	2	Lawn Boy	*CL2
12/06/96	1	2	Harry	Adeline
12/28/96	1	2	Str Design	SSB
03/01/97	16	2	Lawn Boy	Mango
07/02/97	15	1	Water	*CL1
07/22/97	8	2	I am H2	HelloBaby
07/31/97	6	2	I am H2	*CL2
08/09/97	5	2	Slave	*CL2
11/13/97	7	2	I am H2	*CL2
11/22/97	6	1	I am H2	Harry
12/02/97	6	2	Ya Mar	Bouncing
12/09/97	5	1	I am H2	Dogs Stole
12/13/97	3	2	Circus	Harry
12/31/97	4	2	Roses	*CL2
>> 12/31/97	**0**			

WEIGH

Inspiration: Though Mike has said that he wrote the lyrics for Weigh after watching the Martin Scorsese movie *After Hours*, there's no apparent connection between the two, unless you count sheer strangeness.

Musical History and Evolution: Not much to speak of, as the band has performed Weigh much like its debut performance on 3/7/92 in Portsmouth, NH, ever since then.

Rotation History: Usually appears just a few times each year since its peak of fourteen times played in

1993, but in 1997, the band harvested a bumper crop of three Weighs.
Discography: Appears on *Rift* (1993) and on *Slip Stitch and Pass* (1997).

Weigh [33] [Weigh]
By Gordon

03/07/92	[385]	2	Sqirm Coil	Chalkdust
03/12/92	2	E	Adeline	TweezRep
03/21/92	6	2	Bowie	Rosie
03/30/92	6	2	Sqirm Coil	Chalkdust
04/03/92	3	2	Possum	YEM
04/05/92	2	2	Maze	Landlady
04/21/92	11	2	Weekapaug	Catapult
04/25/92	4	2	Harry	*CL2
07/16/92	32	2	RunJim	Landlady
07/26/92	8	1a	Divided	Split&Melt
11/23/92	25	2	Llama	Mike's
02/09/93	26	2	Weekapaug	MSO
02/17/93	6	1	Possum	All Things
02/20/93	3	1	Possum	All Things
03/22/93	21	1	Rift	Reba
03/30/93	6	2	BBJ	Mike's
04/10/93	7	1	RunJim	Sparkle
04/20/93	7	1	RunJim	Sparkle
04/23/93	3	1	RunJim	Sparkle
05/03/93	8	1	Rift	Chalkdust
05/05/93	1	2	PoorHeart	BBJ
07/29/93	17	1	Divided	Rift
08/11/93	9	1	RunJim	It's Ice
08/17/93	6	1	Divided	Maze
12/30/93	9	1	Bowie	Curtain
05/20/94	37	2	Antelope	Axilla 2
06/07/95	89	1	Possum	Taste
10/22/95	40	1	RunJim	NICU
08/13/96	66	1	Chalkdust	It's Ice
11/07/96	20	1	Chalkdust	Rift
03/01/97	36	1	DWD	Beauty
07/30/97	28	1	Stash	Piper
08/17/97	12	3	NICU	Guyute
>> 12/31/97		**25**		

WILSON

Inspiration: A Gamehendge song, Wilson is sung from the perspective of Errand Woolfe, the leader of the revolutionaries, who despises Wilson's mistreatment of the Lizards, as the song's lyrics make clear.
Musical History and Evolution: The song started as another Trey, Tom, and Aaron composition, with Trey reworking the lyrics to fit the emerging Gamehendge theme in 1987–88. Since then, the song has remained relatively unchanged, though starting on spring tour 1994, the audience usurped the opening "Wilson" chants from the band, as heard on *A Live One*. Also, in the 1980s (and more recently on 11/3/94), the band sometimes cut Wilson short before the final jam and jumped into Peaches En Regalia, creating a cool segue. And on two occasions, Trey used the intro to Wilson to trigger electronic noise-maker devices: 12/31/91 Worcester, MA, with swear words, and 12/9/95 Albany, NY, with Beavis & Butt-head sounds. Then there's the wierdest Wilson of them all, the 7/13/94 Patterson, NY performance which was bookended by the beginning and end of Cavern.
Rotation History: If you graphed Wilson's play history in the 1990s, it would look like a near-perfect bell curve, with 1994 representing the apex with twenty-seven plays, and 1990 and 1997 holding down the sides (with six and seven plays, respectively). Many of those appearances were as show or set openers, a frequent place to find Wilson.
Discography: Appears on *A Live One* (1995), as a version recorded on 12/30/94 in New York, NY.

Wilson [145] [Wilson]
By Anastasio/Marshall/Woolfe

10/15/86	[8]	1a	*OP1	Slave
03/06/87	3	2	FWorld	*CL2
08/10/87	7	1	Golgi	Quinn
08/21/87	1	1	Shaggy	CamlWalk
09/12/87	4	1	FunkBitch	Reagan
01/30/88	4	2	*OP2	Slave
02/08/88	2	2	Fluffhead	Peaches
03/11/88	1	1	YEM	Golgi
03/12/88	1	1a	Tela	ACDCBag
03/31/88	2	2	YEM	*CL2
05/15/88	3	1a	McGrupp	Peaches
06/15/88	3	1	YEM	Rocky Top
06/20/88	2	1	Halley's	Ya Mar
07/23/88	4	2	Curtain	Terrapin
09/24/88	8	1	YEM	Peaches
10/12/88	1	1	Weekapaug	Forbin's
10/29/88	1	3	IDK	Peaches
11/05/88	2	2	*OP2	Peaches
01/26/89	3	1a	GTBT	Fluffhead
02/06/89	3	1	Curtain	Peaches
02/18/89	3	1a	Golgi	Peaches
03/03/89	2	1	*OP1	McGrupp
04/15/89	10	1	YEM	Peaches
04/30/89	7	1	Divided	Peaches
05/09/89	7	1	*OP1	Peaches
05/20/89	7	1	Lizards	Divided
06/23/89	9	1	YEM	Peaches
09/09/89	15	1	PYITE	MSO
10/01/89	1	1	Harry	Foam
10/26/89	9	1	IDK	Lizards
10/31/89	2	2	Bowie	Reba
01/27/90	24	1	Bouncing	Reba
01/28/90	1	2	*OP2	Antelope
02/09/90	7	2	Reba	A-Train
06/16/90	53	1	Divided	Reba
09/22/90	7	1	Magilla	Landlady
11/26/90	20	2	Mockbird	Mike's
02/15/91	16	1	Curtain	Divided
03/01/91	11	1	*OP1	Foam
04/21/91	29	1	Rocky Top	Divided
05/10/91	9	2	Harry	PoorHeart
08/03/91	21	1	*OP1	Foam
10/13/91	14	1	RunJim	Reba
10/18/91	3	1	Reba	Llama
10/28/91	6	2	Divided	Dinner
11/14/91	12	1	*OP1	Uncle Pen
11/16/91	2	1	Uncle Pen	RunJim
11/19/91	1	1	Love You	Divided
11/21/91	2	2	*OP2	Harry
12/07/91	8	1	*OP1	RunJim
12/31/91	1	3	*OP3	Sqirm Coil
03/13/92	5	2	*OP2	Brother
03/20/92	4	1	*OP1	Reba
03/25/92	3	1	*OP1	Sparkle
03/31/92	5	1	*OP1	Divided
04/05/92	4	1	Divided	PoorHeart
04/18/92	9	1	*OP1	Divided
04/22/92	3	2	Rift	YEM
05/01/92	6	2	BurAlive	All Things
05/08/92	6	2	*OP2	MSO
07/16/92	23	1	Sparkle	Dinner
08/17/92	18	1	Rift	All Things
11/27/92	17	1	Rift	Divided
12/02/92	4	2	*OP2	Possum
12/08/92	6	1	Rift	Llama
12/13/92	4	1	BurAlive	Divided
12/29/92	2	1	Divided	Uncle Pen
12/31/92	2	1	Rift	Divided
02/06/93	4	1	Foam	My Friend
02/11/93	4	2	Landlady	Uncle Pen
02/13/93	2	2	RunJim	Uncle Pen
02/20/93	5	2	*OP2	Reba
02/25/93	4	2	Sparkle	YEM
03/13/93	10	1	Llama	Antelope
03/22/93	7	2	Tela	ACDCBag
03/26/93	3	2	*OP2	RunJim
04/17/93	15	2	*OP2	Reba
04/25/93	7	2	*OP2	Curtain
04/30/93	3	2	*OP2	Sparkle
07/25/93	18	1	*OP1	Foam
07/31/93	5	2	*OP2	RunJim
08/08/93	5	2	Harry	It's Ice
08/17/93	8	1	*OP1	Llama
08/24/93	3	2	Weekapaug	Rift
12/29/93	5	1	Divided	Sparkle
04/09/94	7	1	Magilla	Rift
04/15/94	5	1	Harry	Chalkdust
04/23/94	7	2	*OP2	Antelope
04/30/94	5	2	*OP2	Bowie
05/10/94	7	2	Maze	Julius
05/14/94	3	1	Llama	DWD
05/23/94	7	2	*OP2	Antelope
05/27/94	3	1	*OP1	RunJim
05/29/94	2	E	*OPE	Golgi
06/11/94	3	1	*OP1	Chalkdust
06/18/94	5	1	*OP1	Rift
06/24/94	5	1	Divided	It's Ice
06/26/94	2	1	Tela	ACDCBag
06/30/94	2	2	*OP2	Maze
07/08/94	6	1	Tela	ACDCBag
07/13/94	3	2	Cavern	Cavern
10/07/94	4	2	Reba	Scent
10/15/94	7	1	*OP1	Sparkle
10/22/94	5	2	Tweezer	Reba
10/27/94	4	1	*OP1	Sparkle
11/03/94	5	1	Divided	Peaches
11/13/94	3	1	*OP1	Sparkle
11/17/94	3	1	Bouncing	Divided
11/23/94	5	1	*OP1	Sparkle
12/03/94	7	1	*OP1	Divided
12/09/94	5	2	*OP2	PoorHeart
12/30/94	4	1	*OP1	Rift
06/17/95	11	2	*OP2	Maze
07/01/95	11	2	*OP2	Maze
10/02/95	7	2	*OP2	CTB
10/07/95	4	1	AArmy	Antelope
10/13/95	3	2	Theme	Antelope
10/21/95	6	1	Reba	CTB
10/31/95	7	1	Divided	Ya Mar
11/15/95	6	2	*OP2	Theme
11/22/95	5	1	CTB	Antelope
12/01/95	6	2	Mango	Suspicious
12/09/95	6	2	Timber Ho	Gumbo
12/15/95	4	1	Harry	Maze
12/28/95	3	2	Theme	BurAlive
07/12/96	13	1	*OP1	Divided
08/05/96	13	1	*OP1	PoorHeart
08/10/96	3	2	*OP2	DWD
08/14/96	3	1	*OP1	DWD
08/17/96	2	3	*OP3	Frankstein
10/16/96	1	1	DWD	BurAlive
10/21/96	4	2	*OP2	Chalkdust
11/06/96	10	2	*OP2	Curtain
11/15/96	7	1	*OP1	Divided
11/29/96	8	2	*OP2	Simple
12/06/96	5	1	*OP1	Peaches
12/31/96	4	2	Chalkdust	Sparkle
02/17/97	4	1	Divided	My Soul
02/21/97	3	2	Antelope	Oh Kee
06/27/97	18	1a	*OP1	Chalkdust
08/09/97	22	2	*OP2	Foam
08/13/97	3	1	Crosseyed	Adeline
11/16/97	6	2	Simple	Harry
12/05/97	12	1	Ghost	FunkBitch
>> 12/31/97		**10**		

WOLFMAN'S BROTHER

Inspiration: Part of the group of songs written in-studio for inclusion on *Hoist*, Wolfman's was a collaborative effort by the band, with lyrics supplied by Tom Marshall, and a "Shirley Temple" utterance supplied by Fishman.
Musical History and Evolution: Because it was recorded for *Hoist* with horns, the band had to rework it slightly for live performances. Though they played it much less frequently in 1994 than other new album songs, the song didn't seem to suffer for lack of the horns; in fact, the funky groove emerged in a longer form than was possible on the album. (Fish's "Shirley Temple" is missing from all live performances of the song, though.) The band had a breakthrough on this song in 1997, though, beginning on 3/1/97 in Hamburg, Germany, when the band took the Wolfman's jam out into a funky realm and wandered for a while, then without ever directly returning to the Wolfman's theme, segued into Jesus Left Chicago. This pairing is preserved on *Slip Stitch and Pass*, with Wolfman's being one of the main reasons that show was selected as Phish's second live album. Throughout the summer and fall of 1997, Wolfman's continued to be a jam paradise, with a 30-minute version coming on 11/30/97 in Worcester, MA, complete with shouted Sanity lyrics and a heavy-metal jam.
Rotation History: After being ignored for a long period (it wasn't played from the "GameHoist" show on 6/26/94 until the fall tour 1995 opener on 9/27/95) Wolfman's has increased in frequency in the past few years, appearing eighteen times in 1997 as the band became infatuated with its funk jam.
Discography: Appears on *Hoist* (1994) and on *Slip Stitch And Pass* (1997).

Long VERSIONS

Tweezer: 5/7/94 Dallas, TX (67 minutes, but most is not specifically Tweezer);* 11/2/94 Bangor, ME (30 minutes, as heard on *A Live One)*;* 11/28/94 Bozeman, MT (45 minutes, the source for Montana on *A Live One)*;* 6/14/95 Memphis, TN (45 minutes), and 6/22/95 Canandaigua, NY (50+ minutes, including My Generation jam).
Wolfman's Brother: 11/30/97 Worcester, MA (30 minutes, with Sanity and Esther lyrics shouted and a heavy-metal jam).*
You Enjoy Myself: Quite a few versions of YEM in recent years have hovered around the 30-minute mark, but none has yet approached 10/31/95 Chicago, IL (45 minutes).*

Wolfman's Brother [43] [Wolfman's]

By Phish/Marshall

04/04/94	[615]	2	Split&Melt	BeLikeYou
04/06/94	2	2	DWD	Sparkle
04/15/94	7	2	Julius	Alumni
04/17/94	2	2	Bowie	Uncle Pen
04/30/94	10	2	Bowie	Peaches
05/04/94	3	2	Julius	Magilla
05/20/94	11	2	Axilla 2	Rift
06/13/94	12	1	Divided	Dinner
06/26/94	11	2	Sample	Scent
09/27/95	88	1	*OP1	Rift
10/02/95	4	1	PoorHeart	Rift
10/08/95	5	1	Sparkle	Reba
10/24/95	10	1	Maze	AArmy
11/25/95	18	1	Rift	RunJim
12/01/95	4	1	PoorHeart	Chalkdust
04/26/96	16	1a	YEM	Scent
08/05/96	22	1	Divided	Foam
10/16/96	9	2	*OP2	Taste
10/21/96	4	2	Chalkdust	Reba
10/26/96	4	1	CTB	Reba
11/03/96	5	2	Divided	Sparkle
11/14/96	7	1	Uncle Pen	CTB
11/22/96	5	1	RunJim	Taste
12/02/96	7	2	Divided	Taste
12/28/96	3	1	NICU	It's Ice
02/13/97	4	1	Chalkdust	Also Sprac
02/18/97	4	2	Maze	Reba
03/01/97	8	1	Beauty	Jesus
06/13/97	3	1	Limb	Wading
06/16/97	2	1	Chalkdust	Oblivious
06/24/97	5	2	*OP2	Reba
07/11/97	11	1a	Beauty	Johnny B.
07/21/97	1	2	*OP2	Magilla
07/25/97	3	1	Beauty	Maze
07/30/97	3	1	NICU	Chalkdust
08/02/97	2	1	Divided	Water
08/08/97	3	2	*OP2	Free
08/16/97	6	2	*OP2	Simple
11/14/97	3	2	*OP2	Piper
11/19/97	3	2	Also Sprac	Makisupa
11/30/97	7	1	FunkBitch	Love Me
12/07/97	5	2	Timber	Boogie
12/31/97	8	1	Beauty	Limb
>> 12/31/97		**0**		

YOU ENJOY MYSELF

Inspiration: In the summer of 1985, Fish and Trey set off on a trip across Europe, during which time Trey wrote YEM and the music to Harry Hood, among other classic Phish tunes. The main lyric in the song, "Wash-a Uffizi, drive me to Firenze," refers to the world-famous Uffizi art gallery in Firenze (Florence), Italy, and the title of the song stems from a phrase an Italian man said in broken English to Fish and Trey, complimenting them on their musical acumen. Lengthy and tiresome debate ensued both on and off the Phish.Net over "WATSIYEM?" ("What are they saying in 'You Enjoy Myself?'"). Mike published letters asking the question many times in the Phish newsletter in 1992 and 1993, and published the correct answer three times, mixed in with numerous incorrect answers. But in concert the band members don't necessarily sing the "real" line; Page has said that he has no idea what they're saying most of the time. The closest approximation might be "Wash Uffizi, drive me to Firenze," dropping the "a" from the written version of the lyric, though early on spring tour 1993, at the height of the debate, they sang, "Water your team in a beehive, I'm-a sent you," just to mess with people's minds a bit.

Musical History and Evolution: Perhaps the most popular Phish song of them all, YEM's history stretches on almost as long as Phish's history. The musical complexity of the song broke new ground for Trey as a songwriter, and his decision to have Phish perform the song played a part in Jeff Holdsworth's separation from the band in the mid 1980s, as he decided he had no interest in performing this kind of music. The song's structure became increasingly complex throughout the 1980s, with the intricate five-or-so-minute opening sequence developing a spacey well and a series of sharp peaks. After the first lyric sequence follows the trampoline segment (YEM is currently the only song the band uses trampolines on, having dropped them from Mike's Song), then an improvisational jam, before a bass-and-drum solo leads to a vocal jam that begins with a return to the "Wash Uffizi" phrase and then into vocal improvisation. In the summer of 1997, though, the band remade the end of the song, abandoning the traditional bass-and-drums solo and long vocal jam, and instead finishing YEMs with different segues into a shorter vocal jam, or no vocal jam at all. Happily, the versions continue to be as good as ever.

Though fans can name hundreds of favorite versions (this is, after all, the most-played Phish song in the band's history by a wide margin), some very favorite versions include: 5/28/89 Hebron, NY, "Poop!"; 7/25/92 Stowe, VT, with Carlos Santana; 5/5/93 Albany, NY, long jam with Col. Bruce, the Dude of Life, and the Aquarium Rescue Unit; 6/11/94 Morrison, CO, just beautiful; 11/23/94 St. Louis, MO, spacey and cool; 10/31/95 Chicago, IL, forty-five minutes long, very experimental; 12/9/95 Albany, NY, silent jam and two incredible improv sections; and 11/19/96 Kansas City, MO, a nice long version with "Groove Is in Your Heart" jam.

Rotation History: Played only one in every four shows in 1997, its worst showing ever. YEM is easily the most-played Phish song of them all, and often appeared as often as every other show, or at least every third show, for most of the 1980s and 1990s.

Discography: Appears on *Junta* (1989) and on *A Live One* (1995), as a live version taken from 12/8/94 San Diego, CA. A snippet also appears on their "White Album."

You Enjoy Myself [382] [YEM]

By Anastasio

04/15/86	[7]	1a	Possum	Anarchy
12/06/86	3	1a	Bowie	Dog Log
03/11/87	2	1a	Flat Fee	Lushngton
03/23/87	1	1	Alumni	Sparks
04/24/87	1	1a	Fluffhead	Dave's
05/11/87	2	1a	LTJP	Possum
08/09/87	1	2	Bowie	Ya Mar
08/10/87	1	2	Sally	La Grange
09/12/87	5	1	Possum	Curtain
10/14/87	2	1	A-Train	Golgi
11/19/87	2	1	FunkBitch	Sally
01/30/88	1	2	Curtis	Sloth
03/11/88	3	1	A-Train	Wilson
03/31/88	3	2	Fire	Wilson
05/14/88	2	2	Light Up	Lizards
05/15/88	1	1a	Golgi	Suzie
05/23/88	1	1a	Golgi	Rocky Top
06/15/88	2	1	Alumni	Wilson
06/18/88	1	1	Emma	GTBT
06/20/88	1	1	Peaches	Fluffhead
07/12/88	3	1	Peaches	IDK
07/23/88	4	3	*OP3	Contact
08/03/88	3	2	IKALittle	Jesus
08/06/88	1	1	La Grange	Cities
08/27/88	1	1a	Satin Doll	FunkBitch
09/08/88	1	2	Possum	Cities
09/24/88	2	1	Alumni	Wilson
10/12/88	1	2	Alumni	Contact
10/29/88	1	3	GTBT	Possum
11/05/88	2	1	Fire	Possum
11/11/88	1	1	Divided	Slave
12/02/88	1	1	Contact	*CL1
01/26/89	1	1a	Alumni	Lizards
02/05/89	1	1a	La Grange	*CL1
02/06/89	1	1	La Grange	All Blues
02/17/89	2	1a	ACDCBag	Fee
02/18/89	1	1a	Peaches	La Grange
02/24/89	1	2	ACDCBag	CamlWalk
03/03/89	1	1	McGrupp	Foam
03/30/89	3	1	Weekapaug	You're NG
04/14/89	6	1	*OP1	Bold
04/15/89	1	1	Esther	Wilson
04/20/89	2	2	WalkAway	Split&Melt
04/30/89	5	1	IDK	McGrupp
05/05/89	3	1	Golgi	Ya Mar
05/06/89	1	1	*OP1	IDK
05/09/89	3	2	*OP2	La Grange
05/13/89	3	1	Alumni	Golgi
05/20/89	4	1	Alumni	Lizards
05/21/89	1	1	Sloth	Ya Mar
05/26/89	1	1	Sloth	*CL1
05/27/89	1	1	Fee	A-Train
05/28/89	1	1	Suzie	*CL1
06/23/89	5	1	ACDCBag	Wilson
06/30/89	2	1	FunkBitch	McGrupp
08/12/89	3	1a	IDK	Possum
08/17/89	2	2	Fee	Lizards
08/23/89	1	2	Ya Mar	ACDCBag
08/26/89	1	1	Divided	Possum
09/09/89	4	2	Ya Mar	Alumni
10/01/89	1	2	Possum	Brain
10/07/89	2	E	*OPE	*CLE
10/14/89	3	1	Alumni	Makisupa
10/20/89	1	1	Mockbird	Oh Kee
10/22/89	2	1	Mockbird	Oh Kee
10/26/89	1	1	Golgi	Fee
10/31/89	2	2	*OP2	Bowie
11/02/89	1	2	Golgi	Kung
11/03/89	1	1	BundleJoy	PYITE
11/09/89	2	1	Bathtub	A-Train
11/10/89	1	1	MSO	My Girl
11/11/89	1	1a	MSO	Brain
11/16/89	1	1	Reba	Frankstein
12/07/89	6	1	IDK	A-Train
12/08/89	1	2	IDK	Possum
12/31/89	6	1	IDK	Oh Kee
01/27/90	4	2	Caravan	Sqirm Coil
01/28/90	1	2	Sqirm Coil	Bathtub
02/09/90	7	1	Suzie	WalkAway
02/10/90	1	1	Suzie	Bathtub
02/23/90	5	1	Alumni	Possum
02/24/90	1	1	Carolina	Golgi
03/01/90	2	1	IDK	Possum
03/03/90	2	1	Rocky Top	Possum
03/08/90	2	1	Dinner	Ya Mar
03/09/90	1	2	HwayHell	La Grange
03/17/89	2	2	Foam	*CL2
03/28/90	1	1	RunJim	GTBT
04/04/90	1	1	Golgi	WalkAway
04/05/90	1	1	Suzie	Lizards
04/06/90	1	1	Cavern	Uncle Pen
04/07/90	1	2	Foam	Bike
04/08/90	1	1	FunkBitch	Brain
04/12/90	3	1	Possum	A-Train
04/13/90	1	2	Alumni	Curtis
04/18/90	3	1	Foam	MSO
04/20/90	2	2	Jesus	*CL2
04/22/90	2	2	Bouncing	Fluffhead
04/25/90	1	2	Ya Mar	Esther
04/26/90	1	1	Foam	Uncle Pen
04/28/90	1	1	Possum	Rift
04/29/90	1	1a	Ya Mar	Dinner
05/04/90	2	1	MSO	Lizards
05/06/90	1	2	Jaeger	*CL2
05/19/90	6	1	La Grange	Lizards
05/23/90	1	1	Ya Mar	Brain
05/24/90	1	1	Reba	Oh Kee
05/31/90	1	1a	Possum	Dinner
06/01/90	1	1a	Bouncing	Divided
06/05/90	1	2	Lizards	Curtis
06/07/90	2	1	Reba	Lizards
06/08/90	1	1	Bouncing	Divided
06/16/90	2	2	Bathtub	Lizards
09/15/90	3	E	Commun	*CLE
09/28/90	5	2	Dinner	Divided
10/06/90	4	1a	Foam	Oh Kee
10/08/90	2	1	MSO	Oh Kee
10/12/90	1	1	Suzie	Dinner
10/31/90	3	1	Bouncing	Asse Fest
11/02/90	1	2	Foam	Lizards
11/03/90	1	1	RunJim	GTBT
11/04/90	1	2	Jesus	*CL2
11/08/90	1	2	Bouncing	BBFCM
11/10/90	1	2	Suzie	Asse Fest
11/16/90	1	1	Foam	Magilla
11/17/90	1	1	Bouncing	Cavern
11/24/90	1	2	RunJim	Love You
11/26/90	1	1	BurAlive	Paul&Silas
12/01/90	2	1	MSO	RunJim
12/07/90	2	1	Landlady	Asse Fest
12/08/90	1	2	No Good	FunkBitch
12/29/90	2	1	Llama	Esther
12/31/90	1	2	Magilla	Rocky Top
02/02/91	2	1	Destiny	Chalkdust
02/07/91	2	2	Destiny	*CL2
02/27/91	13	1	Landlady	Fee
03/06/91	4	1	Golgi	Landlady
03/13/91	4	1	Landlady	Cavern
03/16/91	2	2	Cavern	*CL2
03/22/91	3	1	Llama	Landlady
03/28/91	2	1a	Bouncing	Guelah
04/04/91	5	1	Suzie	Sqirm Coil
04/06/91	2	1	Llama	Bathtub
04/11/91	1	1	Carolina	Sqirm Coil
04/12/91	1	2	JIm	Fluffhead
04/16/91	3	1	Golgi	Paul&Silas
04/20/91	3	1	Bouncing	SettingSail
04/26/91	4	1	Foam	Llama
05/03/91	3	2	Tela	Harpua
05/11/91	4	2	Chalkdust	PoorHeart
05/16/91	2	1	Chalkdust	Magilla
05/18/91	2	1	Chalkdust	Paul&Silas
05/25/91	1	1a	Bouncing	Cavern
07/13/91	3	2	Brain	*CL2
07/19/91	4	1	Sqirm Coil	Gumbo
07/20/91	1	2	TMWSIY	Rocky Top
07/24/91	3	1	Tela	*CL1
07/26/91	2	2	Dinner	Flat Fee
08/03/91	2	2	IDK	Rocky Top
09/25/91	1	2	RunJim	Chalkdust
09/27/91	2	2	Suzie	TweezRep
09/29/91	2	1	Landlady	Oh Kee
10/02/91	1	2	Landlady	MSO
10/11/91	6	1	Chalkdust	Lizards
10/15/91	3	1	Destiny	Rocky Top
10/17/91	1	2	Fluffhead	Love You
10/19/91	2	2	PoorHeart	Oh Kee
10/28/91	5	2	Bathtub	Sqirm Coil
10/31/91	2	1	Paul&Silas	RunJim
11/02/91	2	2	RunJim	*CL2
11/07/91	2	1	It's Ice	Landlady
11/09/91	2	1	Tube	Horn
11/13/91	3	1	Terrapin	*CL1
11/14/91	1	E2	*OPE2	*CLE2

11/16/91	2	2	Brother	Horn
11/20/91	2	1	Llama	*CL1
11/22/91	2	2	Lizards	*CL2
11/24/91	2	2	A-Train	Golgi
11/30/91	1	1	Guelah	*CL1
12/06/91	3	2	Sparkle	Horn
03/12/92	6	1	Llama	*CL1
03/19/92	4	2	Rosie	*CL2
03/21/92	2	2	Rosie	*CL2
03/25/92	2	2	Sqirm Coil	Horn
03/30/92	4	2	Mound	BBFCM
04/01/92	2	2	Llama	Horse
04/03/92	1	2	Weigh	Mango
04/05/92	2	2	All Things	Horse
04/07/92	2	2	Eliza	My Friend
04/12/92	2	2	Rift	Lawn Boy
04/15/92	2	2	Chalkdust	Reba
04/17/92	2	2	Brother	Fluffhead
04/22/92	4	2	Wilson	PoorHeart
04/25/92	3	2	Bathtub	Horse
04/30/92	2	2	My Mind	Horse
05/02/92	2	2	Foam	Chalkdust
05/06/92	3	2	Sqirm Coil	All Things
05/08/92	2	2	Maze	Horse
05/10/92	2	1a	IDK	Possum
05/12/92	1	2	Bathtub	Guelah
05/15/92	2	1a	Chalkdust	Adeline
05/16/92	1	2	Sqirm Coil	Horse
06/19/92	3	1a	Cavern	*CL1
06/30/92	5	1a	Adeline	*CL1
07/11/92	5	1a	Cavern	Suzie
07/14/92	2	2	Paul&Silas	A-Train
07/24/92	8	1a	Sqirm Coil	TweezRep
07/25/92	1	1a	Rift	Llama
07/31/92	5	1a	Oh Kee	GTBT
08/13/92	3	1a	Foam	*CL1
08/19/92	4	1a	Guelah	Uncle Pen
08/24/92	3	1a	Reba	*CL1
08/27/92	2	1a	Sparkle	Llama
08/29/92	2	1a	Maze	*CL1
10/30/92	2	1a	Adeline	*CL1
11/20/92	2	2	Tube	FEFY
11/22/92	2	2	Tela	Faht
11/25/92	2	2	FEFY	Lizards
11/30/92	3	2	Uncle Pen	Sqirm Coil
12/02/92	2	1	Horn	*CL1
12/04/92	2	2	Faht	*CL2
12/06/92	2	2	Bathtub	TMWSIY
12/07/92	1	1	Bouncing	*CL1
12/10/92	2	2	Maze	Love You
12/12/92	2	2	Guelah	Brain
12/28/92	2	2	Sloth	Lizards
12/30/92	2	2	Bathtub	TMWSIY
02/03/93	2	2	Sparkle	Life Boy
02/05/93	2	2	It's Ice	Love You
02/07/93	2	2	Glide	BBJ
02/10/93	2	2	Sparkle	Horse
02/12/93	2	2	FEFY	Ya Mar
02/13/93	1	2	Llama	BBJ
02/17/93	2	2	Horn	Lngthwise
02/19/93	2	2	Paul&Silas	Ya Mar
02/22/93	3	2	Glide	Oh Kee
02/25/93	2	2	Wilson	Uncle Pen
02/26/93	1	2	BBJ	Lngthwise
03/02/93	2	2	Llama	Love You
03/06/93	3	2	FEFY	Rosie
03/08/93	1	2	Kung	Lizards
03/12/93	2	2	Sparkle	Mound
03/14/93	2	2	Curtis	Life Boy
03/16/93	1	2	Chalkdust	Bike
03/18/93	2	2	Tela	Uncle Pen
03/21/93	2	2	Llama	MSO
03/24/93	2	2	FEFY	Horse
03/26/93	2	2	Silent	BBJ
03/28/93	2	2	Bathtub	Paul&Silas
03/31/93	2	2	It's Ice	Harpua
04/03/93	3	2	Sloth	Jesus
04/05/93	1	2	Glide	Rosie
04/09/93	1	2	My Friend	MSO
04/12/93	2	2	BBJ	Terrapin
04/14/93	2	2	BBJ	Harpua
04/17/93	2	2	Halley's	Life Boy
04/20/93	2	2	Llama	WhipPost
04/22/93	2	2	BBJ	Uncle Pen
04/24/93	2	2	BBJ	Bike
04/27/93	2	2	BBJ	Horse
04/30/93	2	2	Brain	Golgi
05/02/93	2	2	PYITE	Lizards
05/05/93	2	2	Ya Mar	Jam
05/07/93	2	2	BBJ	Great Gig
05/29/93	2	1a	BBJ	RunJim
07/16/93	3	2	Bouncing	PoorHeart
07/18/93	2	2	Fee	PurplRain
07/23/93	3	2	BBJ	BBFCM
07/27/93	3	1a	PurplRain	*CL1
07/29/93	2	2	Sparkle	PurplRain
08/03/93	4	2	It's Ice	Lizards
08/06/93	1	2	Uncle Pen	Halley's
08/09/93	3	2	My Mind	Contact
08/14/93	4	2	Daniel	PurplRain
08/17/93	3	2	Suzie	PurplRain
08/20/93	1	2	Chalkdust	PurplRain
08/25/93	3	2	Paul&Silas	Bats&Mice
08/28/93	2	2	PurplRain	Contact
12/28/93	1	2	Sample	My Friend
12/31/93	3	2	Lawn Boy	*CL2
04/05/94	2	2	If I Could	BeLikeYou
04/11/94	5	2	BBJ	AmGrace
04/14/94	2	2	Scent	Nellie
04/16/94	2	2	Bouncing	Sqirm Coil
04/20/94	3	2	Fee	Rainbow
04/23/94	3	2	Ginseng	Who Fire
04/29/94	4	1	Halley's	FEFY
05/04/94	4	2	Bouncing	Landlady
05/08/94	3	2	Cavern	Halley's
05/13/94	3	2	Scent	PurplRain
05/16/94	2	2	Julius	BBFCM
05/20/94	3	2	Rift	*CL2
05/23/94	3	2	PYITE	Possum
05/26/94	2	2	Dog Faced	AmGrace
05/28/94	2	2	Llama	Jam
06/11/94	4	1	Chalkdust	Rift
06/14/94	2	2	Sparkle	Bike
06/18/94	3	2	Life Boy	Chalkdust
06/25/94	6	2	Axilla 2	Rosie
06/30/94	3	2	Maze	Sparkle
07/05/94	4	2	Cities	Great Gig
07/08/94	2	2	Stash	Julius
07/14/94	4	2	Uncle Pen	Sparkle
10/09/94	5	2	Scent	AmGrace
10/12/94	2	2	Scent	Nellie
10/15/94	3	2	Scent	AmGrace
10/23/94	6	2	Halley's	DWD
10/26/94	2	2	Axilla 2	Catapult
10/29/94	3	2	Uncle Pen	Bike
11/03/94	3	2	Julius	BBFCM
11/14/94	4	2	Adeline	*CL2
11/17/94	2	2	Sparkle	Love You
11/19/94	2	2	Sparkle	Rosie
11/23/94	3	2	Life Boy	TweezRep
12/04/94	8	2	Axilla 2	PurplRain
12/07/94	2	2	AmGrace	*CL2
12/09/94	2	2	Rosie	Suzie
12/30/94	4	2	I'm Blue	PurplRain
05/16/95	2	1a	Glide 2	Adeline
06/10/95	4	1	Rift	LCBill
06/16/95	4	2	Carolina	Sqirm Coil
06/19/95	2	2	Sparkle	AArmy
06/23/95	3	1	Taste	*CL1
06/26/95	3	2	PoorHeart	Str Design
06/29/95	2	2	Str Design	AArmy
09/29/95	7	1	CTB	Adeline
10/03/95	3	1	Simple	*CL1
10/08/95	4	2	Sample	Suspicious
10/14/95	3	2	Rift	HelloBaby
10/21/95	5	2	Sparkle	PurplRain
10/24/95	2	2	Bouncing	Sl Monkey
10/28/95	3	2	Scent	Str Design
10/31/95	2	3	*OP3	Jesus
11/10/95	2	2	Scent	Str Design
11/14/95	3	2	Str Design	*CL2
11/18/95	3	2	I'mSoTired	Contact
11/22/95	3	2	Bouncing	Str Design
11/29/95	4	2	Possum	Fog
12/04/95	4	2	CTB	Sample
12/09/95	4	2	Gumbo	Lawn Boy
12/31/95	10	3	Sea&Sand	Sanity
04/26/96	1	1a	CTB	Wolfman's
06/06/96	1	2	ACDCBag	Chalkdust
07/05/96	2	1a	ACDCBag	Scent
07/11/96	5	2	Terrapin	HelloBaby
07/13/96	2	1a	Chalkdust	*CL1
07/18/96	3	1a	It's Ice	*CL1
07/22/96	3	1a	DayinLife	*CL1
07/24/96	2	1a	Julius	Golgi
08/07/96	6	2	Life Mars	HelloBaby
08/14/96	4	2	RunJim	Horse
10/18/96	5	2	Maze	Reba
10/22/96	3	1	Free	*CL1
10/26/96	3	2	DWD	Sparkle
10/31/96	3	1	DWD	Caspian
11/07/96	4	2	Bike	*CL2
11/09/96	2	2	DayinLife	Taste
11/13/96	2	2	Caspian	Theme
11/19/96	5	2	Bathtub	SSB
11/24/96	3	2	DayinLife	Lovin Cup
11/29/96	2	2	Steep	Waste
12/02/96	3	1	Bouncing	IDK
12/06/96	2	1	Llama	CTB
12/29/96	2	2	Lizards	Rotation
02/14/97	4	1	NICU	Adeline
02/21/97	5	1	Crosseyed	*CL1
02/26/97	4	2	Ha Ha Ha	Kung
03/02/97	3	E	*OPE	*CLE
06/29/97	12	1a	*OP1	Taste
07/06/97	5	2	Free	Waste
07/09/97	1	2	CTB	Ghost
07/11/97	2	1a	Johnny B.	*CL1
07/23/97	3	2	Sample	RMWay
07/26/97	2	1	Dirt	Isabella
07/31/97	3	1	Saw It	*CL1
08/06/97	3	1	Ya Mar	*CL1
08/11/97	4	2	My Soul	CharZero
08/16/97	3	1	Ginseng	Train Song
11/13/97	2	1	My Soul	CharZero
11/17/97	3	2	Circus	*CL2
11/28/97	6	1	Curtain	IDK
12/03/97	4	1	Also Sprac	*CL1
12/29/97	9	2	Tube	*CL2
>> 12/31/97	**2**			

UNFINISHED Versions

WHAT DOES IT MEAN for a Phish song to be unfinished? That depends on which song you're talking about.

Phish jam songs come in two loose sorts—those with different beginnings, middles, and ends, and those with thematic endings that often reflect the beginnings. When the band veers off in the midst of an Antelope jam and never gets around to singing the lyrics, or leaves Harry Hood behind without telling the crowd to feel good about Hood, those are obviously unfinished versions. But in a song like DWD, Stash, Bathtub Gin, or Weekapaug, when the band doesn't come back around to the final refrain or theme, it doesn't always seem as notable an omission—in fact, that's practically standard on most 1997 editions of those songs.

Before 1997, fans made more of an effort to keep track of unfinished versions. There are unfinished Antelopes from 11/30/94 Olympia, WA, and 7/12/96 Amsterdam (on a night when almost every song was unfinished), but then on their winter tour in Europe in early 1997, every Antelope the band played was unfinished! Similarly, the DWD played on 6/26/95 in Saratoga Springs, NY, segues into Free with no return to the DWD theme, just as Bathtub Gin on 8/13/93 in Indianapolis, IN, segues into Ya Mar with no return to the Bathtub Gin theme. Those are "unfinished" in a sense, but they are not as fretted about as unfinished Antelopes or Hoods are.

Speaking of Hood, the fall tour 1995 brought a rash of unfinished Hoods at the start of the tour, including the great version on 10/7/95 in Spokane, WA, the last of that unfinished group. But the band still leaves some Hoods unfinished, as they did in Austin, TX, on 7/26/97 when they took off into Free and never sang the final Hood verse. Even the great 12/30/97 version from Madison Square Garden, in all its glowstick war glory, never actually found its ending notes.

• Cover Songs •

All Along the Watchtower [2] [Watchtower]

By Bob Dylan

04/21/93	[629]	E	Jam	*CLE
10/22/96	226	E	*OPE	*CLE
>> 12/31/97	**111**			

Also Sprach Zarathustra (2001) [98] [Also Sprac]

By Deodato, after Richard Strauss

07/16/93	[579]	2	*OP2	Split&Melt
07/17/93	1	2	*OP2	Tweezer
07/18/93	1	2	*OP2	PoorHeart
07/21/93	1	1	*OP1	Split&Melt
07/22/93	1	2	*OP2	Tweezer
07/23/93	1	2	*OP2	PoorHeart
07/24/93	1	2	*OP2	Split&Melt
07/25/93	1	2	*OP2	Suzie
07/27/93	1	1	*OP1	Rift
07/28/93	1	2	*OP2	Axilla
07/30/93	2	2	*OP2	Tweezer
08/02/93	2	2	*OP2	Mike's
08/07/93	3	2	*OP2	Mike's
08/08/93	1	2	*OP2	Rift
08/12/93	3	2	*OP2	Landlady
08/14/93	2	2	*OP2	Antelope
08/17/93	3	2	*OP2	Bowie
08/20/93	1	2	*OP2	Slave
08/26/93	4	2	*OP2	Bowie
08/28/93	1	2	*OP2	Rift
12/30/93	3	2	*OP2	Mike's
04/11/94	8	2	*OP2	Maze
04/14/94	2	2	*OP2	Antelope
04/18/94	4	2	*OP2	Sample
04/21/94	2	2	*OP2	Maze
05/08/94	13	2	*OP2	Antelope
05/12/94	2	2	*OP2	Antelope
05/16/94	3	2	*OP2	Antelope
05/20/94	3	2	*OP2	Antelope
05/26/94	5	2	*OP2	Antelope
06/11/94	6	2	*OP2	Antelope
06/17/94	4	2	*OP2	Sample
06/22/94	4	2	*OP2	Mike's
07/02/94	8	2	*OP2	Mike's
07/05/94	2	2	*OP2	PYITE
07/09/94	3	2	*OP2	Split&Melt
07/14/94	3	2	*OP2	Sample
07/16/94	2	2	Harpua	Harpua

10/08/94	2	2	*OP2	Sample
10/15/94	6	2	*OP2	RunJim
10/21/94	4	2	*OP2	Mike's
10/28/94	6	2	*OP2	Bowie
11/03/94	4	2	*OP2	Simple
11/17/94	6	2	*OP2	Bowie
11/20/94	3	2	*OP2	Bowie
11/25/94	3	2	*OP2	Mike's
11/28/94	2	1	Chalkdust	Scent
12/02/94	3	1	PoorHeart	Sparkle
12/06/94	3	2	Sample	PoorHeart
12/10/94	4	2	Guyute	Mike's
12/31/94	4	3	MSO	NewYear's
06/14/95	7	2	*OP2	PoorHeart
06/24/95	8	2	*OP2	Halley's
06/30/95	5	2	*OP2	Possum
09/29/95	6	2	*OP2	Maze
10/05/95	5	2	*OP2	RunJim
10/13/95	5	1	Ya Mar	Maze
10/21/95	6	2	*OP2	Bowie
10/27/95	4	2	*OP2	Bowie
11/11/95	6	2	*OP2	Bowie
11/19/95	6	2	Theme	Curtain
11/28/95	5	2	*OP2	Maze
12/02/95	4	2	*OP2	Maze
12/08/95	4	2	*OP2	Tweezer
12/15/95	5	2	Rotation	Bowie
12/17/95	2	2	Free	Harry
12/30/95	3	1	Caspian	Suzie
04/26/96	2	1a	Scent	Harry
07/06/96	4	1a	*OP1	Reba
07/11/96	4	2	Bouncing	Maze
07/23/96	9	2	*OP2	RunJim
08/05/96	5	2	*OP2	DWD
08/16/96	7	3	Makisupa	DWD
10/17/96	3	1	*OP1	FunkBitch
10/22/96	4	2	*OP2	DWD
10/31/96	6	3	Brother	Maze
11/08/96	5	2	*OP2	Maze
11/13/96	3	2	*OP2	Suzie
11/18/96	4	2	*OP2	Simple
11/24/96	4	2	*OP2	Sparkle
11/30/96	3	2	Contact	Timber Ho
12/06/96	4	1	PoorHeart	Llama
12/31/96	4	3	*OP3	Auld Lang
02/13/97	1	1	Wolfman's	Stash
02/18/97	4	2	Peaches	My Soul
02/22/97	3	1	Walfredo	FunkBitch
03/02/97	6	2	*OP2	Maze
06/21/97	7	1a	Sample	PoorHeart
07/10/97	12	2	*OP2	Julius
08/06/97	12	1	Twist	ACDCBag
08/17/97	3	2	Uncle Pen	Art Jam
11/14/97	2	1	FEFY	FunkBitch
11/19/97	3	2	*OP2	Wolfman's
11/26/97	4	2	CharZero	Cities
12/03/97	5	1	Gumbo	YEM
12/12/97	6	1	FunkBitch	CamlWalk
12/31/97	5	3	*OP3	Auld Lang
>> 12/31/97		0		

Amazing Grace [107] [AmGrace]

By John Newton

02/03/93		E	*OPE	TweezRep
02/04/93	1	E	*OPE	GTBT
02/05/93	1	E	*OPE	Lovin Cup
02/07/93	2	E	*OPE	Contact
02/09/93	1	2	Bike	*CL2
02/10/93	1	E	Adeline	TweezRep
02/11/93	1	E	Bold	*CLE
02/12/93	1	E	*OPE	GTBT
02/13/93	1	E	*OPE	TweezRep
02/15/93	1	1	*OP1	Suzie
02/18/93	2	2	Mound	Adeline
02/19/93	1	2	Llama	*CL2
02/22/93	3	E	*OPE	Fire
02/25/93	2	E	*OPE	GTBT
02/27/93	2	E	Sl Monkey	Rocky Top
03/02/93	1	2	Harry	*CL2
03/05/93	2	2	Sqirm Coil	*CL2
03/08/93	2	2	Lizards	*CL2
03/09/93	1	E	*OPE	Rocky Top
03/13/93	2	E	MSO	BBFCM
03/16/93	2	2	Llama	*CL2
03/17/93	1	1	Stash	Paul&Silas
03/19/93	2	E	*OPE	Chalkdust
03/22/93	2	E	*OPE	Fire
03/24/93	1	1	Sample	Cavern
03/26/93	2	E	*OPE	Rocky Top
03/30/93	3	E	MSO	*CLE
04/02/93	3	E	*OPE	Rocky Top
04/10/93	4	E	*OPE	GTBT
04/12/93	1	E	*OPE	HwayHell
04/16/93	3	E	Gumbo	*CLE
04/18/93	2	E	*OPE	Rocky Top
04/20/93	1	E	FunkBitch	*CLE
04/22/93	2	E	ACDCBag	*CLE
04/24/93	2	E	*OPE	GTBT
04/27/93	2	E	*OPE	*CLE
04/30/93	2	E	SWMB	TweezRep
05/02/93	2	E	Sl Monkey	*CLE
05/03/93	1	E	Memories	HwayHell
05/05/93	1	E	*OPE	Cavern
05/07/93	2	E	*OPE	Golgi
05/08/93	1	2	Weekapaug	AGJam
05/29/93	1	1	RunJim	*CL1
07/17/93	4	E	*OPE	Daniel
07/23/93	4	E	*OPE	Daniel
07/30/93	6	E	WalkAway	*CLE
08/02/93	2	E	Sl Monkey	*CLE
08/06/93	2	E	*OPE	*CLE
08/13/93	6	2	Suzie	*CL2
08/16/93	3	E	*OPE	Rocky Top
08/21/93	3	E	*OPE	Nellie
08/25/93	2	1	Nellie	Stash
08/28/93	2	E	Daniel	*CLE
12/31/93	4	E	Golgi	*CLE
04/05/94	2	2	Chalkdust	*CL2
04/09/94	3	E	*OPE	HwayHell
04/11/94	2	2	YEM	Oh Kee
04/15/94	3	E	Magilla	*CLE
04/21/94	5	2	Possum	*CL2
04/25/94	4	E	*OPE	Bold
05/07/94	8	E	*OPE	Sample
05/12/94	3	E	*OPE	Rocky Top
05/16/94	3	2	BBFCM	BBFCM
05/21/94	4	2	Harry	*CL2
05/23/94	2	E	Ginseng	HwayHell
05/26/94	2	2	YEM	*CL2
06/16/94	9	E	Ginseng	GTBT
06/21/94	4	E	*OPE	*CLE
06/26/94	5	E	Old Home	Tube
07/05/94	6	2	MSO	Golgi
10/09/94	11	2	YEM	Julius
10/13/94	3	2	It's Ice	Mike's
10/15/94	2	2	YEM	Foreplay
10/18/94	2	1	Divided	*CL1
10/22/94	3	2	Reba	ACDCBag
10/26/94	3	E	Long Time	*CLE
10/31/94	4	E	*OPE	Costume
11/03/94	2	E	Nellie	HwayHell
11/13/94	3	2	BBFCM	Sqirm Coil
11/16/94	2	E	*OPE	Suzie
11/19/94	3	2	Harry	GTBT
11/23/94	3	1	Divided	*CL1
11/30/94	4	E	Silent	*CLE
12/07/94	6	2	LongJourn	YEM
12/31/94	7	2	Weekapaug	*CL2
06/10/95	5	2	Weekapaug	Sample
06/14/95	2	2	All Things	Horse
06/20/95	5	E	Slave	*CLE
06/25/95	4	2	Weekapaug	Cavern
06/30/95	4	2	Weekapaug	Sqirm Coil
07/03/95	3	E	Simple	*CLE
09/28/95	2	2	Keyboard	Sample
09/30/95	2	E	*OPE	GTBT
10/05/95	3	2	Lifeboy	*CL2
10/17/95	8	1	Str Design	*CL1
10/20/95	2	1	HelloBaby	AGJam
10/29/95	7	2	Lifeboy	*CL2
11/11/95	4	1	Stash	Fee
11/16/95	4	2	Brain	Possum
11/30/95	9	2	Str Design	*CL2
12/07/95	5	2	Weekapaug	*CL2

One-Timers

Cover songs that Phish has played only once (excepting Dude of Life songs, Fishman tunes, and Halloween albums). An asterisk after the song name indicates the song was performed with special guest(s).

Song	Date	Original Artist
All Blues	02/06/89	Miles Davis
Amoreena	08/13/97	Elton John/B. Taupin
Anarchy in the U.K.	10/14/89	Sex Pistols
Big Leg Emma	06/18/88	Frank Zappa
Blue Bossa	07/23/88	Kenny Dorham
Blue Sky	08/12/89	Allman Brothers
Bluegrass Breakdown*	11/16/94	Bill Monroe
Bohemian Rhapsody*	12/31/96	Queen
Brown Eyed Girl*	11/16/95	Van Morrison
Cecilia	6/25/97	Simon & Garfunkle
Choo Choo Ch'Boogie*	03/02/93	Louis Jordan
Come Together	12/08/95	The Beatles
Diamond Girl*	12/31/92	Seals and Croft
Doin' My Time*	08/07/96	Johnny Cash
Don't Want You No More	12/01/84	Spencer Davis
Dooley*	11/20/94	The Dillards
Fire on the Mountain	12/01/84	Hart/Hunter
Gloria	05/16/95	Them
Golden Lady	10/20/94	Stevie Wonder
Got My Mojo Workin'*	02/25/97	Preston/Foster
Help Me*	04/10/93	S. Williamson/Leake
Help on the Way	04/01/86	Garcia/Hunter
Hi-Heel Sneakers*	04/23/93	Robert Higgenbotham
I'll Come Running	05/16/95	Brian Eno
It's My Life*	03/02/93	The Animals
La Bamba	08/21/87	Los Lobos
Little Red Rooster*	02/25/97	Willie Dixon
Lively Up Yourself	04/21/92	Bob Marley
Love Me Like a Man*	03/18/97	Unknown
Low Rider	08/21/87	War
Luke-a-Roo*	03/02/93	Unknown
The Maker*	10/15/94	Daniel Lanois
Mean Mr. Mustard*	11/15/96	The Beatles
Messin' with the Kid*	08/08/97	Mel London/Wells
Moose the Mooche*	07/12/91	Charlie Parker
My Generation	10/31/95	The Who
New York, New York	12/31/97	Frank Sinatra
99 Years*	08/07/96	Unknown
Not Fade Away*	04/01/86	Hardin/Petty
Ode to a Dream*	08/07/96	Unknown
One Meatball*	02/25/97	Ry Cooder
Phase Dance	09/27/87	Pat Metheny
The Price of Love	03/30/89	Everly Brothers
Psycho Killer	12/07/97	Talking Heads
Reconsider Baby*	03/18/97	Lowell Fulson
Revival	10/30/85	Allman Brothers
Rock and Roll All Night	02/20/93	Kiss
Rocky Mountain Way	07/23/97	Joe Walsh
Roll in My Sweet Baby's Arms*	11/18/94	Flatt/Scruggs
Slipknot!	04/01/86	Jerry Garcia
Spanish Flea	12/01/84	Herb Alpert
Stand	06/13/97	Sly & Family Stone
That's All Right (Mama)*	05/06/93	Arthur Crudup
Them Changes	11/30/97	Buddy Miles
Three Little Birds*	06/17/95	Bob Marley
We're an American Band	11/16/96	Grand Funk Railroad
Why Don't You Love Me	03/23/87	Red Hot Chili Peppers
Why You Been Gone So Long*	05/06/93	Traditional
Wild Child	09/08/88	Lou Reed
You're No Good	03/30/89	Carole King

08/05/96 35 2 Str Design Mike's
08/16/96 7 E *OPE *CLE
11/16/96 24 2 Suzie *CL2
11/23/96 4 2 Waste Harry
11/30/96 4 2 FunkBitch Grace Jam
12/31/96 8 E *OPE *CLE
>> 12/31/97 78

Auld Lang Syne [8] [Auld]

By Robert Burns

12/31/90 [256] 1 Weekapaug BurAlive
12/31/91 127 2 BurAlive RunJim
12/31/92 121 3 Mike's Weekapaug
12/31/93 110 3 *OP3 DWD
12/31/94 123 3 Also Sprach TropicalHDN
12/31/95 81 3 *OP3 Weekapaug
12/31/96 80 3 Also Sprach DWD
12/31/97 77 3 Also Sprach Tweezer
>> 12/31/97 0

Avenu Malkenu [59] [Avenu]

Traditional

03/11/87 [12] 1a TMWSIY TMWSIY
05/11/87 4 1a TMWSIY TMWSIY
08/29/87 5 1 TMWSIY TMWSIY
09/12/87 2 1 TMWSIY TMWSIY
02/08/88 7 2 TMWSIY TMWSIY
07/24/88 17 3 TMWSIY TMWSIY
09/12/88 6 1a TMWSIY TMWSIY
02/24/89 15 1 TMWSIY TMWSIY
08/19/89 50 1 TMWSIY TMWSIY
08/26/89 2 3 TMWSIY TMWSIY
03/09/90 62 1 TMWSIY TMWSIY
05/04/90 23 1 TMWSIY TMWSIY
06/09/90 15 2 TMWSIY TMWSIY
02/07/91 40 2 TMWSIY TMWSIY
02/09/91 2 1 TMWSIY TMWSIY
02/28/91 12 1 TMWSIY TMWSIY
03/16/91 9 1 TMWSIY TMWSIY
04/11/91 13 2 TMWSIY TMWSIY
04/20/91 7 2 TMWSIY TMWSIY
04/27/91 5 2 TMWSIY TMWSIY
05/03/91 2 1 TMWSIY TMWSIY
05/17/91 7 1 TMWSIY TMWSIY
07/11/91 3 2 TMWSIY TMWSIY
07/13/91 2 1 TMWSIY TMWSIY
07/20/91 5 2 TMWSIY TMWSIY
07/26/91 5 1 TMWSIY TMWSIY
07/27/91 1 1 TMWSIY TMWSIY
10/24/91 21 1 TMWSIY TMWSIY
11/02/91 7 2 TMWSIY TMWSIY
11/21/91 13 2 TMWSIY TMWSIY
03/26/92 22 2 TMWSIY TMWSIY
04/09/92 11 2 TMWSIY TMWSIY
04/18/92 6 2 TMWSIY TMWSIY
05/18/92 23 2 TMWSIY TMWSIY
07/16/92 15 2 TMWSIY TMWSIY
11/28/92 36 2 TMWSIY Maze
12/06/92 7 2 TMWSIY TMWSIY
12/13/92 6 2 TMWSIY TMWSIY
12/30/92 3 2 TMWSIY TMWSIY
02/04/93 3 2 TMWSIY TMWSIY
03/27/93 38 2 TMWSIY TMWSIY
04/20/93 16 2 TMWSIY TMWSIY
07/22/93 23 2 TMWSIY Rocky Top
08/07/93 12 2 TMWSIY Sloth
04/18/94 32 2 TMWSIY TMWSIY
05/14/94 19 2 TMWSIY TMWSIY
06/22/94 23 2 TMWSIY TMWSIY
07/01/94 7 2 TMWSIY TMWSIY
07/14/94 9 1 TMWSIY TMWSIY
10/16/94 11 1 TMWSIY TMWSIY
10/29/94 10 2 TMWSIY TMWSIY
11/19/94 11 1 TMWSIY Antelope
06/30/95 40 2 TMWSIY Mike's
10/03/95 9 1 TMWSIY TMWSIY
11/09/95 20 2 TMWSIY TMWSIY
12/30/95 31 1 TMWSIY TMWSIY
10/25/96 40 2 TMWSIY TMWSIY
11/15/96 14 2 TMWSIY My Mind
12/28/96 14 2 TMWSIY Mike's
11/29/97 67 1 TMWSIY TMWISY
>> 12/31/97 14

Back in the USSR [2] [USSR]

By The Beatles

10/31/94 [707] 2 *OP2 Prudence
12/06/94 22 E *OPE *CLE
>> 12/31/97 237

Bats and Mice [2] [Bats & Mice]

By Baby Gramps

08/25/93 [608] 2 YEM Sqirm Coil
08/26/93 1 2 Lizards Chalkdust
>> 12/31/97 357

Beaumont Rag [2] [Beaumont]

Traditional

10/14/94 [694] 2 Nellie Foreplay
10/18/94 3 2 Old Home Nellie
>> 12/31/97 269

Beauty of My Dreams [21] [Beauty]

By Del McCoury

02/16/97 [891] 1 *OP1 Split&Melt
02/18/97 2 1 *OP1 Cavern
02/25/97 5 2 *OP2 Sample
03/01/97 3 1 Weigh Wolfman's
03/18/97 2 1 My Soul Harry
06/13/97 1 1 Dogs Stole Billy
06/16/97 2 1 Sample Theme
06/19/97 1 E *OPE CharZero
06/24/97 4 1 Split&Melt Dogs Stole
06/29/97 3 1a Bouncing Chalkdust
07/03/97 3 1 Divided Taste
07/11/97 5 1a Stash Wolfman's
07/25/97 4 1 *OP1 Wolfman's
07/29/97 2 1 Theme Gumbo
08/06/97 5 1 Stash Twist
08/13/97 5 1 Silent C&P
08/17/97 3 1 Wedge Dogs Stole
11/13/97 1 1 Split My Soul
11/21/97 5 1 Split&Melt Dogs Stole
12/09/97 12 1 Dogs Stole Horn
12/31/97 7 1 MSO Wolfman's
>> 12/31/97 0

Bike [25] [Bike]

By Syd Barrett

11/19/87 [27] 3 La Grange Slave
01/30/88 1 3 Golgi BBFCM
04/07/90 161 2 YEM Harpua
05/15/90 22 1 Harry Caravan
11/10/90 33 2 Divided Possum
05/17/91 73 2 Cavern BBFCM
11/20/91 56 2 Landlady Cavern
04/07/92 33 2 Maze My Mind
05/07/92 21 2 Fee Sqirm Coil
12/28/92 74 2 Lizards Harry
02/09/93 9 2 Lizards AmGrace
02/15/93 5 2 BBJ Fee
03/16/93 20 2 Lngthwise Lawn Boy
04/02/93 14 2 BBJ Chalkdust
04/16/93 8 2 BBJ HwayHell
04/24/93 7 2 YEM Harry
08/02/93 28 2 Weekapaug Antelope
05/06/94 48 2 Julius Bowie
05/21/94 11 2 Julius Harry
06/14/94 12 2 YEM Possum
10/29/94 43 2 YEM Antelope
12/06/94 23 2 Weekapaug I'm Blue
11/24/95 68 2 AArmy Fee
07/23/96 39 2 Weekapaug Slave
11/07/96 29 2 Bathtub YEM
>> 12/31/97 101

Won't You Come Home Bill Bailey [3] [BBailey]

Traditional

07/28/93 [588] E F/S Boogie *CLE
04/22/94 42 E F/S Boogie *CLE
11/18/95 163 E *OPE *CLE
>> 12/31/97 173

Blackbird [2] [Blackbird]

By The Beatles

10/31/94 [707] 2 So Tired Piggies
11/22/94 12 2 Curtain RunJim
>> 08/17/97 247

Blue Bayou [2] [BBayou]

By Roy Orbison

07/16/92 [451] E *OPE Sqirm Coil
12/29/92 51 2 Terrapin Sqirm Coil
>> 08/17/97 464

Bold as Love [52] [Bold]

By Jimi Hendrix

07/11/88 [44] 1 Fire Forbin's
07/23/88 2 1 WalkAway No Dogs
07/24/88 1 1 Weekapaug *CL1
07/25/88 1 2 Weekapaug Light Up
09/08/88 4 1 Mockbird *CL1
09/12/88 1 1a Fee Timber Ho
09/24/88 1 1 Divided *CL1
10/29/88 2 1 Golgi La Grange
11/03/88 1 2 Contact A-Train
11/05/88 1 2 Peaches Lizards
11/11/88 1 2 Fee Timber Ho
12/02/88 1 1 Golgi A-Train
03/30/89 12 1 *OP1 McGrupp
04/14/89 6 1 YEM Lizards
05/06/89 12 1 Possum ACDCBag
05/09/89 3 2 Lizards Harpua
05/13/89 3 2 Suzie Lizards
05/20/89 4 2 *OP2 Mike's
05/26/89 2 1 *OP1 ACDCBag
08/17/89 14 3 Oh Kee PYITE
08/19/89 2 1 Rocky Top Mango
08/26/89 2 2 *OP2 Ya Mar
10/06/89 6 1a Golgi Dinner
03/17/90 58 2 Jam Oh Kee
04/07/90 5 2 A-Train Fee
04/18/90 6 2 Oh Kee Lawn Boy
11/19/92 285 E *OPE *CLE
11/22/92 3 E *OPE Carolina
11/27/92 3 E *OPE *CLE
12/03/92 5 E *OPE *CLE
12/10/92 6 E *OPE Carolina
02/11/93 15 E *OPE AmGrace
02/26/93 12 E *OPE Adeline
04/13/93 31 E *OPE Adeline
08/11/93 43 E Adeline *CLE
08/25/93 10 E *OPE Rocky Top
04/17/94 18 E Rosie *CLE
04/25/94 7 E AmGrace *CLE
05/14/94 13 E *OPE *CLE
05/21/94 5 E *OPE *CLE
12/28/94 33 E *OPE *CLE
06/16/95 12 E *OPE *CLE
06/24/95 6 E *OPE *CLE
10/13/95 20 E *OPE *CLE
12/02/95 31 E *OPE *CLE
12/14/95 8 E *OPE *CLE
11/27/96 67 1 Theme *CL1
02/18/97 15 E *OPE *CLE
11/14/97 50 E *OPE *CLE
11/23/97 6 2 DWD *CL2
12/05/97 7 E *OPE *CLE
12/28/97 7 E *OPE *CLE
>> 12/31/97

Boogie on Reggae Woman [3] [Boogie]

By Stevie Wonder

04/29/87 [15] 3 Antelope Timber Ho
03/21/88 18 1a Divided Timber Ho
12/07/97 925 2 Wolfman's Reba
>> 12/31/97 8

Butter Them Biscuits [4] [Butter]

By Jeff Mosier

11/18/94 [716] 1 Split&Melt Old Home
11/19/94 1 1 I'm Blue LongJourn
11/20/94 1 1 If I Could LongJourn
11/22/94 1 2 I'm Blue LongJourn
>> 12/31/97 246

Caravan [37] [Caravan]

By Duke Ellington

01/20/90 [157] 1a Sqirm Coil *CL1
01/27/90 3 2 Breakdown YEM
01/28/90 1 2 Bouncing Sqirm Coil
02/15/90 9 1 Dinner Bathtub
02/17/90 2 1a Dinner Bathtub
02/24/90 3 E Lizards *CLE
03/03/90 4 2 Dinner Fluffhead
03/08/90 2 2 ACDCBag IDK
03/09/90 1 1 TMWISY Ya Mar
04/06/90 6 2 Harry Reba
04/13/90 6 2 Harry Possum
04/20/90 3 2 *OP2 Mike's
04/28/90 5 2 Harry IDK
05/04/90 3 2 Weekapaug Brain
05/10/90 2 2 Harry Reba
05/15/90 4 1 Bike BBFCM
05/31/90 4 1 Bouncing Esther
06/05/90 2 2 Divided Dinner
06/16/90 4 3 Rocky Top Brain
11/30/90 28 E *OPE Oh Kee
12/07/90 3 2 Donna Tweezer
02/15/91 12 E *OPE BBFCM
07/14/91 59 2 Suzie Divided
07/15/91 1 E *OPE Contact
07/20/91 3 2 Reba Dinner
07/23/91 2 E *OPE Golgi
09/25/91 6 1 Landlady Reba
04/05/93 216 2 PoorHeart PYITE
04/13/93 4 1 Guelah Cavern
04/24/93 9 1 Rift SWMB
05/07/93 10 1 Sparkle Lizards
07/23/93 10 1 Rift Nellie
04/11/94 37 1 *OP1 PoorHeart
04/23/94 10 1 DWD Hi-Heel
05/04/94 8 E *OPE *CLE
12/02/94 87 2 Gumbo Suzie
12/29/96 160 1 PoorHeart Cavern
>> 12/31/97 80

Carolina [61] [Carolina]

By Donaldson/Kahn

01/20/90 [158] 1a Harry Sqirm Coil
01/27/90 3 1 *OP1 Bathtub
01/28/90 1 1 La Grange Forbin's
02/09/90 7 1 Weekapaug *CL1
02/10/90 1 1 Possum Contact
02/15/90 1 1 *OP1 Oh Kee
02/23/90 4 1 Foam Rocky Top
02/24/90 1 1 *OP1 YEM
03/01/90 2 E *OPE Slave
03/03/90 2 2 FunkBitch Divided
03/08/90 2 1 Foam Oh Kee
03/11/90 2 2 *OP2 Antelope
03/28/90 2 2 *OP2 Adeline
04/04/90 1 1 Divided *CL1
04/05/90 1 1 Bowie Oh Kee
04/06/90 1 2 *OP2 La Grange
04/08/90 2 E *OPE Fire
04/29/90 13 1a *OP1 Possum
10/06/90 30 1a Bowie *CL1
10/12/90 3 E *OPE GTBT
11/04/90 6 1 *OP1 ACDCBag
03/17/91 42 1 *OP1 Bouncing
04/04/91 9 1 Possum Golgi
04/11/91 3 1 Foam YEM
04/16/91 4 2 RunJim TweezRep
10/13/91 48 E2 *OPE2 *CLE2
10/28/91 9 1 Bowie *CL1
03/11/92 29 E Memories Sl Monkey
03/28/92 12 2 Memories IDK
04/01/92 3 1 Bowie *CL1
04/16/92 10 2 Terrapin Memories
04/30/92 10 E *OPE Cavern
05/06/92 5 E *OPE GTBT
11/21/92 56 2 *OP2 Curtain
11/22/92 1 E Bold TweezRep
11/25/92 2 E Harry *CLE
12/04/92 7 2 Sqirm Coil Harry
12/06/92 2 2 Lengthwise Cavern
12/08/92 2 E *OPE Fire
12/10/92 1 E Bold TweezRep
12/29/92 5 E *OPE Rocky Top
12/31/92 2 E *OPE Fire
02/17/93 12 E *OPE GTBT
03/12/93 16 E Adeline Rocky Top
03/24/93 9 E *OPE Sqirm Coil
03/27/93 3 E Sqirm Coil *CLE
04/01/93 4 E *OPE TweezRep
04/05/93 3 E *OPE Fire

04/25/93 14 E SWMB Rocky Top
05/01/93 4 E *OPE Rocky Top
08/07/93 26 E *OPE La Grange
05/20/94 55 1 Dog Faced ACDCBag
06/22/94 19 E *OPE Cavern
06/24/94 2 2 Cavern DWD
07/06/94 9 1 My Mind Bowie
10/28/94 25 1 Sample *CL1
06/16/95 41 2 Free YEM
06/29/95 10 1 Split&Melt *CL1
11/21/95 39 2 Suspicious DayinLife
10/27/96 64 E Possum *CLE
08/17/97 82 1 Taste *CL1
>> 12/31/97 25

Cinnamon Girl [2] [CinnGirl]
By Neil Young

03/18/97 [903] 1 *OP1 NICU
07/31/97 27 E *OPE *CLE
>> 12/31/97 36

Cities [18] [Cities]
By Talking Heads

12/01/84 [0] 1a Don't Want Skippy
12/06/86 10 1a Skin It *CL1
04/29/87 5 1 Skin It Fuck Face
06/18/88 26 1 GTBT *CL1
07/12/88 4 2 *OP2 Lizards
07/24/88 2 2 OYWD Bowie
08/06/88 3 1 YEM Dave's
09/08/88 2 2 YEM GTBT
07/05/94 627 2 Lifeboy YEM
03/01/97 222 1 *OP1 Oh Kee
06/16/97 5 E *OPE PoorHeart
06/20/97 2 1 Taste Horn
07/01/97 7 2 Bathtub Jam
07/30/97 14 2 Bowie Bowie
08/10/97 7 2 *OP2 Jam
08/16/97 4 3 Halley's Llama
11/26/97 10 2 Also Sprac Ya Mar
12/28/97 13 1 Julius Curtain
>> 12/31/97 3

Communication Breakdown [3] [Commun]
By Led Zeppelin

01/27/90 [160] 2 *OP2 Caravan
01/28/90 1 1 Mockbird *CL1
09/15/90 63 E *OPE YEM
>> 12/31/97 742

Corrina [12] [Corrina]
By Bo Carter

Phish's Version based on that by Taj Mahal

03/06/87 [11] 1 GTBT Golgi
03/11/87 1 1 *OP1 Golgi
03/23/87 1 2 Crimson WDYLM
05/11/87 3 1a Golgi LTJP
08/09/87 1 2 McGrupp *CL2
11/19/87 10 2 Fee Alumni
01/30/88 1 2 Slave Fire
03/11/88 3 1 Flat Fee Lizards
05/25/88 8 3 BBFCM Harpua
06/18/88 2 2 Mike's Rocky Top
02/05/89 22 1 WhipPost Bowie
02/06/89 1 2 WhipPost *CL2
>> 12/31/97 902

Cracklin' Rosie [46] [Rosie]
By Syd Barrett

03/07/92 [385]
03/12/92 2 2 Weekapaug TweezRep
03/14/92 2 2 Bowie MSO
03/19/92 2 2 Harry Possum
03/21/92 2 2 Weigh YEM
03/25/92 2 2 Chalkdust Golgi
03/26/92 1 2 Cavern Possum
03/30/92 3 2 Chalkdust Bouncing
04/01/92 2 2 Chalkdust Sqirm Coil
04/04/92 2 2 Sqirm Coil My Friend
04/06/92 2 2 Stash Uncle Pen
04/12/92 3 2 NICU Harry
04/15/92 2 2 NICU MSO
04/17/92 2 2 Uncle Pen TweezRep
04/22/92 4 2 PoorHeart Harpua
04/23/92 1 2 Maze Golgi
04/30/92 4 2 Chalkdust Harry
05/02/92 2 2 Chalkdust Cavern
05/03/92 1 2 Mango Dinner
05/09/92 5 2 Llama Golgi
05/14/92 3 2 Stash Possum
05/16/92 2 2 ACDCBag PoorHeart
11/25/92 51 2 Tweezer MSO
12/03/92 6 2 BBJ A-Train
12/13/92 9 2 BBJ Harry
02/10/93 11 2 Silent Possum
02/21/93 9 2 Bathtub Sqirm Coil
03/06/93 9 2 YEM BBFCM
03/21/93 10 2 BBJ Harry
03/27/93 5 2 Weekapaug PoorHeart
04/05/93 7 2 YEM TweezRep
05/02/93 19 2 Antelope BBFCM
05/06/93 3 2 Rocky Top Mama
08/06/93 21 2 Slave TweezRep
08/24/93 13 2 Rift Antelope
12/31/93 7 3 Suzie Harry
04/17/94 12 E *OPE Bold
06/25/94 46 2 YEM Harry
10/26/94 31 2 Catapult Bowie
11/19/94 14 2 YEM Harry
12/09/94 15 2 BBJ YEM
12/29/94 3 2 Lizards GTBT
06/20/95 14 2 Weekapaug HwayHell
06/30/95 8 E *OPE Golgi
11/12/95 32 2 Slave Possum
08/14/96 58 2 Theme Sample
>> 12/31/97 119

Crosseyed and Painless [5] [Crosseyed]
By Talking Heads

10/31/96 [861] 2 Punches GCurve
11/02/96 1 2 *OP2 Antelope
02/16/97 29 1 Bouncing Guelah
02/21/97 4 1 Lizards YEM
08/13/97 43 1 Beauty Wilson
>> 12/31/97 29

Crossroads [8] [Crossroads]
By Robert Johnson

05/08/93 [575] 2 Mike's Mike's
10/11/95 196 2 Suzie HelloBaby
10/25/95 10 2 Suzie *CL2
11/10/95 6 2 YEM YEM
12/09/95 21 2 Slave Adeline
08/09/97 127 1 Lawn Boy *CL1
12/03/97 20 E *OPE *CLE
12/29/97 9 1 Golgi CTB
>> 12/31/97 2

Cry Baby Cry [3] [Cry Baby]
By The Beatles

10/31/94 [707] 2 Savoy Revol 9
11/22/94 12 2 YSZahav Curtain
06/16/95 27 1 Ya Mar It's Ice
>> 12/31/97 220

Battle of Curtis Lowe [22] [Curtis]
By Lynyrd Skynyrd

04/29/87 [16] 3 McGrupp Good Times
08/29/87 6 1 Alumni Sally
09/12/87 2 2 Dog Log Antelope
11/19/87 4 3 Dinner WhipPost
01/30/88 1 2 Divided YEM
03/11/88 3 2 Harry Harpua
06/20/88 11 2 A-Train Bowie
07/23/88 4 3 Slave GTBT
10/29/88 10 2 Divided Mike's
02/05/89 7 1 BBFCM Forbin's
02/06/89 1 2 BBFCM Icculus
05/26/89 38 3 FunkBitch Possum
08/19/89 16 2 FunkBitch Bowie
02/09/90 50 2 Foam Bowie
03/08/90 13 2 Weekapaug Golgi
04/13/90 13 2 Alumni Sloth
04/26/90 7 2 Adeline Mike's
06/05/90 16 2 YEM GTBT
10/30/90 21 2 Llama Fluffhead
03/14/93 296 2 Bowie YEM
04/23/93 29 2 Maze It's Ice
08/02/93 29 2 Sparks Rift
>> 12/31/97 374

Daniel (Saw the Stone) [15] [Daniel]
Traditional

07/15/93 [578] 2 WalkAway *CL2
07/16/93 1 1 *OP1 Golgi
07/17/93 1 E AmGrace TweezRep
07/21/93 2 1 PurplRain *CL1
07/23/93 2 E AmGrace *CLE
07/24/93 1 2 PurplRain GTBT
07/29/93 4 2 PurplRain GTBT
07/31/93 2 2 PurplRain HwayHell
08/08/93 5 2 Love You GTBT
08/14/93 5 2 Sqirm Coil YEM
08/17/93 3 1 FEFY *CL1
08/21/93 2 2 Harry *CL2
08/25/93 2 1 ACDCBag Sample
08/28/93 2 E *OPE AmGrace
02/23/97 287 2 *OP2 Suzie
>> 12/31/97 69

A Day in the Life [43] [DayinLife]
By The Beatles

06/10/95 [742] E *OPE *CLE
06/19/95 6 E *OPE *CLE
06/23/95 3 E *OPE *CLE
06/29/95 5 2 AArmy *CL2
07/03/95 4 2 BBFCM Possum
09/27/95 1 2 HelloBaby *CL2
09/29/95 2 2 Cryin *CL2
10/02/95 2 E *OPE *CLE
10/06/95 3 E HelloBaby *CLE
10/11/95 3 2 HelloBaby *CL2
10/14/95 2 E *OPE *CLE
10/19/95 3 E *OPE *CLE
10/24/95 4 E *OPE *CLE
10/31/95 5 2 Jesus Suzie
11/11/95 3 1 Mike's PoorHeart
11/16/95 4 2 *OP2 Bowie
11/21/95 3 2 Carolina *CL2
11/25/95 3 1 PoorHeart Bowie
11/29/95 2 E *OPE *CLE
12/02/95 3 2 Tweezer Golgi
12/08/95 4 E CTogether *CLE
12/17/95 7 1 PoorHeart Antelope
12/30/95 3 E *OPE *CLE
04/26/96 2 1a Sample Bowie
07/06/96 4 1a PoorHeart Maze
07/11/96 4 E *OPE *CLE
07/22/96 8 1a Stash YEM
08/06/96 7 2 Caspian BBFCM
08/10/96 2 2 Harry *CL2
08/17/96 5 3 Tweezer Possum
10/17/96 2 1 CharZero TweezRep
11/02/96 11 2 Harry Adeline
11/09/96 5 2 Bowie YEM
11/14/96 3 2 Antelope *CL2
11/19/96 4 2 Bowie Bathtub
11/24/96 3 2 Bowie YEM
12/01/96 4 2 Simple Reba
12/29/96 5 2 Bowie Bathtub
02/14/97 4 2 Scent *CL2
02/20/97 4 2 Steep RunJim
02/28/97 6 E *OPE *CLE
12/07/97 58 E *OPE *CLE
12/30/97 7 1 Chalkdust *CL1
>> 12/31/97 1

Donna Lee [20] [Donna]
By Duke Ellington

10/29/88 [56] 3 Slave Antelope
11/11/88 3 E FunkBitch *CLE
05/06/89 31 2 *OP2 Suzie
06/23/89 19 1 Peaches Fee
06/30/89 2 1 Possum Fluffhead
08/26/89 9 2 ACDCBag FunkBitch
10/20/89 11 2 ACDCBag Split&Melt
02/10/90 38 2 Rocky Top Fee
03/09/90 13 1 Possum Antelope
04/05/90 5 2 ACDCBag Tweezer
05/13/90 23 2 Foam Tweezer
05/24/90 4 1 Tweezer Reba
06/07/90 4 1 Suzie Possum
10/30/90 20 1 Bouncing Asse Fest
11/17/90 8 2 Rocky Top GTBT
11/26/90 2 1 Paul&Silas Bowie
12/07/90 4 2 Weekapaug Caravan
12/29/90 3 E *OPE ACDCBag
04/26/91 52 E *OPE Fire
07/12/91 14 1 Bathtub ACDCBag
>> 12/31/97 645

Don't You Wanna Go [5] [Wanna Go]
By the Missionary Sisters

05/16/95 [738] 1a *OP1 Ha Ha Ha
06/08/95 2 1 *OP1 Ha Ha Ha
06/14/95 4 1 *OP1 Gumbo
06/26/95 10 1 My Friend Bathtub
09/28/95 8 2 PoorHeart Tweezer
>> 12/31/97 204

Drowned [7] [Drowned]
By The Who

10/31/95 [786] 2 Sea&Sand Bell Boy
12/31/95 33 2 *OP2 Lizards
02/28/97 82 2 Taste Caspian
03/18/97 3 2 Taste Caspian
12/03/97 52 1 My Soul Old Home
12/11/97 5 2 *OP2 Roses
12/28/97 3 2 Ghost Scent
>> 12/31/97 3

Emotional Rescue [2] [EmRescue]
By the Rolling Stones

11/21/97 [947] 1 *OP1 Split&Melt
12/31/97 19 1 *OP1 Ya Mar
>> 12/31/97 0

Eyes of the World [2] [Eyes]
By Garcia/Hunter

Originally Performed by the Grateful Dead

12/01/84 [0] E *OPE *CLE
05/03/85 2 1a Scarlet WhipPost
>> 12/31/97 964

Fire [95] [Fire]
By Jimi Hendrix

12/01/84 [0] 1a Scarlet FOTM
04/29/87 15 1 SwingLow Skin It
08/10/87 3 1 GTBT ACDCBag
09/12/87 5 2 Makisupa Terrapin
09/27/87 1 2 Fluffhead Fee
11/19/87 3 1 Harry *CL1
01/30/88 1 2 Corrina Fluffhead
02/07/88 1 1a *OP1 McGrupp
03/21/88 4 1a Lizards ACDCBag
03/31/88 1 2 A-Train YEM
05/14/88 2 2 *OP2 IDK
05/25/88 3 2 Suzie *CL1
06/21/88 4 1 Mockbird *CL1
07/11/88 1 1 FunkBitch Bold
07/23/88 2 2 Sloth Curtain
08/06/88 4 1 Dinner *CL1
10/29/88 6 2 A-Train *CL2
11/03/88 1 1 *OP1 Golgi
11/05/88 1 2 TLAH YEM
01/26/89 3 1a BBFCM Fire
02/07/89 4 E *OPE *CLE
04/20/89 16 1 Fluffhead Esther
05/06/89 9 2 Contact Harry
05/13/89 6 E *OPE WhipPost
05/28/89 8 2 *OP2 Mike's
12/08/89 46 2 Lawn Boy *CL2
03/01/90 27 E2 *OPE2 *CLE2
04/05/90 10 1 Lizards *CL1
04/08/90 3 E Carolina *CL2

04/13/90 4 1 Reba *CL1
04/22/90 5 2 Harry *CL2
04/29/90 4 1a Lizards *CL1
09/14/90 20 2 Destiny *CL2
11/03/90 18 E Fluffhead *CLE
11/08/90 2 E Jesus *CLE
11/16/90 2 E Contact *CLE
11/26/90 3 E *OPE Contact
02/16/91 17 E Lawn Boy *CLE
02/27/91 8 1 Bouncing *CL1
03/22/91 13 1 Reba *CL1
03/28/91 2 E Lawn Boy *CLE
04/15/91 11 2 Magilla *CL2
04/26/91 8 E Donna Lee *CL2
05/12/91 8 E Antelope *CLE
10/10/91 30 E Sqirm Coil *CLE
11/07/91 18 E2 Lawn Boy *CLE2
03/13/92 25 E Contact *CLE
03/20/92 4 E Lawn Boy *CLE
03/24/92 2 E Lawn Boy *CLE
04/13/92 15 E Memories *CLE
11/30/92 79 E Fee *CLE
12/08/92 8 E Carolina *CLE
12/28/92 5 E Memories *CLE
12/31/92 3 E Carolina *CLE
02/06/93 4 E *OPE *CLE
02/15/93 7 E Contact *CLE
02/22/93 6 E AmGrace *CLE
03/03/93 6 E *OPE *CLE
03/22/93 13 E AmGrace *CLE
04/05/93 11 E Carolina *CLE
04/23/93 12 E *OPE *CLE
08/12/93 36 E *OPE Freebird
08/17/93 5 E Memories *CLE
04/16/94 21 E *OPE *CLE
04/29/94 10 E *OPE *CLE
05/03/94 3 E Nellie *CLE
05/19/94 11 E Adeline *CLE
05/27/94 7 E *OPE *CLE
06/21/94 12 2 *OP2 PoorHeart
06/26/94 5 E Tube *CLE
07/03/94 5 E *OPE *CLE
10/13/94 15 E *OPE *CLE
11/20/94 25 E2 *OPE2 *CLE2
09/28/95 44 E *OPE *CLE
10/07/95 7 E *OPE *CLE
10/25/95 12 E *OPE *CLE
11/12/95 8 E *OPE *CLE
11/25/95 9 E *OPE *CLE
11/30/95 3 1 Lizards *CL1
12/12/95 9 E *OPE *CLE
12/16/95 3 E *OPE *CLE
12/29/95 3 2 Bouncing *CL2
06/06/96 4 E Ya Mar *CLE
07/13/96 9 1a Split&Melt FunkBitch
08/10/96 15 E Contact *CLE
10/26/96 14 E *OPE *CLE
11/03/96 5 E *OPE *CLE
11/19/96 11 2 SSB *CL2
11/27/96 4 2 SSB *CL2
12/02/96 4 E *OPE *CLE
07/30/97 47 2 Caspian *CLE
11/17/97 16 1 Ghost *CL1
11/29/97 7 E Moby Dick *CLE
12/09/97 7 E *OPE *CLE
12/31/97 7 1 Sloth *CL1
>> 12/31/97 0

Fixin' to Die [2] [Fixin']

By Booker White

11/17/94 [715] E LongJourn *CLE
11/30/94 9 2 Antelope Ya Mar
>> 12/31/97 242

Foreplay > Long Time [16] [Foreplay]/[Long Time]

By Boston

10/07/94 [688] E *OPE Cavern
10/08/94 1 E *OPE Rocky Top
10/10/94 2 E *OPE TweezRep
10/12/94 1 2 Nellie Harry
10/13/94 1 2 Weekapaug Cavern
10/14/94 1 2 Beaumont Sqirm Coil
10/15/94 1 2 AmGrace Bouncing
10/20/94 3 2 Nellie Chalkdust
10/21/94 1 E Adeline Cavern
10/25/94 3 E *OPE Golgi
10/26/94 1 E Nellie AmGrace
10/28/94 2 2 Nellie *CL2
11/02/94 3 E Old Home TweezRep
11/12/94 3 2 Nellie Harry
12/06/94 18 2 I'm Blue Antelope
12/09/94 3 E I'm Blue TweezRep
>> 12/31/97 234

Frankenstein [48] [Frankstein]

By Edgar Winters Group

11/11/89 [142] 1a Brain *CL1
11/16/89 1 1 YEM *CL1
11/30/89 2 1 Lawn Boy *CL1
12/03/90 106 1 Lawn Boy *CL1
07/11/91 69 2 Touch Me *CL2
07/12/91 1 E Adeline Fee
07/13/91 1 1 Bouncing *CL1
07/15/91 2 1 Sqirm Coil *CL1
07/24/91 6 2 IDK Suzie
07/26/91 2 E Lawn Boy Split&Melt
06/11/94 329 2 Contact *CL2
06/14/94 2 2 *OP2 Demand
06/17/94 2 2 Julius *CL2
06/23/94 5 2 *OP2 Bowie
06/30/94 5 1 Bouncing *CL1
07/08/94 6 2 YEM YEM
10/31/94 26 1 *OP1 Sparkle
11/30/94 17 1 *OP1 PoorHeart
12/03/94 3 2 *OP2 Suzie
12/07/94 3 2 Rift Divided
12/30/94 6 E *OPE *CLE
06/15/95 9 E Bouncing *CLE
10/07/95 24 2 Contact Harry
10/19/95 7 2 *OP2 PoorHeart
10/28/95 7 2 Str Design Chalkdust
11/11/95 5 2 Sl Monkey Suspicious
11/22/95 8 E PoorHeart *CLE
12/04/95 8 2 Sample *CL2
12/14/95 7 1 MSO *CL1
12/31/95 7 3 Sanity *CL3
08/17/96 31 3 Wilson Scent
10/19/96 4 1 Caspian *CL1
10/31/96 8 E *OPE *CLE
11/07/96 4 E *OPE *CLE
11/16/96 7 1 Sparkle *CL1
11/29/96 7 1 *OP1 NICU
12/06/96 5 1 DWD *CL1
12/28/96 1 1 Mango *CL1
02/13/97 4 2 Harry *CL2
02/18/97 4 2 Harry *CL2
02/23/97 4 1 Fluffhead Bowie
02/28/97 3 2 Caspian Bowie
07/23/97 25 E *OPE *CLE
08/03/97 7 2 HelloBaby *CL2
08/13/97 6 2 Golgi *CL2
11/22/97 10 1 Billy Izabella
12/03/97 7 2 Caspian Harry
12/30/97 10 E Sally *CLE
>> 12/31/97 1

Freebird [20] [Freebird]

By Lynyrd Skynyrd

03/06/87* [11] 2 *OP2 Harry
07/15/93 [578] E Chalkdust *CLE
07/16/93 1 E Llama *CLE
07/18/93 2 E Rocky Top *CLE
07/22/93 2 E *OPE *CLE
07/24/93 2 E Golgi *CLE
07/29/93 4 E Rocky Top *CLE
07/31/93 2 E ACDCBag *CLE
08/03/93 2 E PoorHeart *CLE
08/08/93 3 E MSO *CLE
08/12/93 3 E Fire *CLE
08/15/93 3 2 Nellie *CL2
08/20/93 3 E Mango *CLE
08/26/93 4 E *OPE *CLE
12/30/93 4 1 Bathtub *CL1
04/23/94 18 E *OPE *CLE
05/06/94 9 E Ginseng *CLE
05/13/94 5 E *OPE *CLE
05/29/94 13 2 Antelope *CL2
06/19/94 9 E *OPE *CLE
>> 12/31/97 299
*** Performed electric; all others a cappella**

Funky Bitch [91] [FunkBitch]

By Son Seals

03/06/87 [11] 1 *OP2 GTBT
03/23/87 2 1 *OP1 Mike's
08/21/87 6 1 Divided Harry
09/12/87 4 1 Slave Wilson
09/27/87 1 1 Bowie Golgi
11/19/87 3 1 Sparks YEM
01/30/88 1 1 *OP1 Mustang
03/11/88 3 1 Chicken Sally
05/25/88 8 1 Rocky Top Alumni
06/18/88 2 1 Curtain Possum
07/11/88 3 1 Curtain Fire
07/24/88 3 1 Golgi Forbin's
08/03/88 2 2 Satin Doll WalkAway
08/06/88 1 1 A-Train Dinner
08/27/88 1 1a YEM WalkAway
10/29/88 5 3 Peaches *CL3
11/11/88 3 E Peaches Donna
04/15/89 20 2 *OP2 Golgi
05/26/89 23 3 Slave Curtis
05/27/89 1 1 Weekapaug Fee
05/28/89 1 3 *OP3 La Grange
06/30/89 7 1 *OP1 YEM
08/19/89 7 2 Bathtub Curtis
08/26/89 2 2 Donna Foam
12/15/89 32 1a Antelope Jesus
01/27/90 8 1 Reba Mike's
02/25/90 16 1 Mockbird Sqirm Coil
03/03/90 3 2 Esther Carolina
03/28/90 6 2 WhipPost Mike's
04/07/90 4 2 Mockbird A-Train
04/08/90 1 1 Divided YEM
04/09/90 1 2 *OP2 Esther
04/13/90 3 1 *OP1 Dinner
04/18/90 1 2 Sloth Reba
05/10/90 12 2 *OP2 RunJim
05/13/90 3 2 Reba Adeline
11/04/90 32 1 Harry Asse Fest
12/03/90 9 1 Bathtub Ya Mar
12/08/90 2 2 YEM *CL2
12/28/90 1 2 Don't Get *CL2
04/19/91 48 1 *OP1 Dinner
07/24/91 28 2 Bouncing IDK
07/26/91 2 2 Flat Fee Sqirm Coil
07/25/92 126 1a Llama *CL1
12/29/92 44 1 *OP1 RunJim
02/19/93 16 2 Lawn Boy MSO
03/13/93 15 1 Landlady Bouncing
03/28/93 12 1 Landlady Sparkle
04/10/93 8 2 Weekapaug Help Me
04/20/93 7 E *OPE AmGrace
07/29/93 29 1 *OP1 Divided
04/23/94 42 1 *OP1 Rift
07/06/94 49 E Memories *CLE
11/13/94 32 E *OPE TweezRep
11/22/94 7 2 *OP2 Jam
12/31/94 18 1 Divided *CL1
06/07/95 2 1 Wedge Slave
07/01/95 19 E *OPE *CLE
10/15/95 16 E *OPE *CLE
10/29/95 10 E *OPE *CLE
11/16/95 8 1 Guyute *CL1
11/28/95 7 2 BBFCM *CL2
12/11/95 10 2 Suspicious *CL2
06/06/96 11 1 RunJim Theme
07/05/96 2 1a *OP1 Chalkdust
07/12/96 5 1 Ya Mar Taste
07/13/96 1 1a Fire Chalkdust
07/17/96 2 1a Ya Mar *CL1
08/04/96 9 1 Chalkdust Guyute
10/17/96 11 1 AlsoSprac Sparkle
10/21/96 3 E *OPE *CLE
11/02/96 8 E *OPE *CLE
11/06/96 2 2 Sample *CL2
11/15/96 7 E *OPE *CLE
11/23/96 5 1 Rift *CL1
11/30/96 4 2 Taste AmGrace
12/30/96 7 1 Talk Theme
02/14/97 3 2 DWD Reba
02/22/97 6 1 AlsoSprac Theme
03/18/97 7 E HelloBaby *CLE
07/06/97 16 2 Rocky Top *CL2
07/10/97 2 E *OPE *CLE
07/21/97 2 2 Jam Slave
08/14/97 16 1 Ya Mar Fluffhead
08/16/97 1 3 Limb *CL3
11/14/97 2 1 Also Sprac Guyute
11/19/97 3 1 Limb Theme
11/30/97 7 1 Guyute Wolfman's
12/05/97 3 1 Wilson BE Katy
12/12/97 5 1 *OP1 Also Sprac
12/28/97 2 1 Farmhouse FunkBitch
>> 12/31/97 3

■

Funny as It Seems [3] [Funny]

By J.J. Cale

06/20/97 [908] 1 Horn Limb
07/01/97 7 1 Limb Saw It
08/09/97 20 2 Mike's Simple
>> 12/31/97 31

Ginseng Sullivan [51] [Ginseng]

By Norman Blake

08/11/93 [598] 1 It's Ice My Friend
08/13/93 2 1 Stash Fluffhead
08/15/93 2 2 Adeline Nellie
08/20/93 3 1 Wedge Rift
08/24/93 2 2 Mike's Weekapaug
08/25/93 1 1 Foam Nellie
08/28/93 2 1 Foam Maze
12/31/93 4 1 Stash Reba
04/06/94 3 E *OPE Nellie
04/10/94 3 2 Fluffhead BeLikeYou
04/13/94 2 1 Julius Divided
04/23/94 9 2 Spark Harry
04/25/94 2 1 DWD Dog Faced
04/30/94 3 1 Rift Adeline
05/06/94 4 E *OPE Freebird
05/10/94 3 2 Harry Dog Faced
05/14/94 3 1 MSO Bowie
05/17/94 2 1 Scent Dog Faced
05/19/94 1 E *OPE Nellie
05/22/94 3 1 MSO Dog Faced
05/23/94 1 E *OPE AmGrace
05/26/94 2 2 Mound Dog Faced
06/09/94 4 2 Scent Mike's
06/13/94 3 1 Stash Julius
06/16/94 2 E *OPE AmGrace
06/21/94 4 2 BBFCM BBFCM
07/05/94 11 2 Great Gig MSO
10/10/94 12 1 Old Home Nellie
06/20/95 58 1 Spock's Foam
06/23/95 2 1 Reba Free
10/21/96 103 1 CharZero Stash
11/15/96 17 1 Caspian Train Song
11/18/96 2 1 Guelah Reba
11/22/96 2 1 Taste Sample
11/24/96 2 E *OPE Cavern
12/28/96 8 1 Billy Split&Melt
02/16/97 6 1 Guelah Tweezer
06/20/97 17 2 Bye Bye Cavern
07/02/97 8 1 Str Design Vultures
07/09/97 3 1 Caspian Split&Melt
07/10/97 1 1 Limb Bathtub
07/21/97 2 1 Dirt Bathtub
07/23/97 2 1 Dogs Stole Water
08/02/97 6 1 Theme Ghost
08/10/97 5 1 Bye Bye Harry
08/16/97 4 1 Ghost YEM
11/19/97 6 1 Theme Fee
11/29/97 6 1 Sloth Saw It
12/02/97 2 E *OPE Sample
12/05/97 2 1 My Friend Limb
12/13/97 6 1 Theme Str Design
>> 12/31/97 4

Going Down Slow [2] [Going Down]

By the Allman Brothers

09/13/90 [222] 2 Stash Oh Kee
09/14/90 1 E *OPE *CLE
>> 12/31/97 743

Good Times Bad Times [138] [GTBT]

By Led Zeppelin

12/06/86 [10] 1a McGrupp Skin It
03/06/87 1 1 FunkBitch Corrina
04/29/87 4 3 Fluffhead Anarchy
08/10/87 3 1 Divided Fire
09/12/87 5 2 Alumni Rocky Top
09/27/87 1 1 Phase Skin It
01/30/88 4 1 A-Train *CL1
05/15/88 9 1a Suzie Fluffhead
05/23/88 1 1a Possum *CL1
06/15/88 2 2 A-Train WhipPost
06/18/88 1 1 YEM Cities
06/21/88 2 2 Jesus Contact

07/12/88 2 2 Sally Peaches
07/23/88 1 3 Curtis *CL3
09/08/88 6 2 Cities OYWD
09/24/88 2 3 *OP3 Fluffhead
10/12/88 1 2 Possum *CL3
10/29/88 1 3 Fluffhead YEM
11/03/88 1 1 Alumni TLAH
11/05/88 1 2 IDK *CL2
12/02/88 2 2 IDK Alumni
01/26/89 1 1a Fee Wilson
02/05/89 2 1 *OP1 WalkAway
02/06/89 1 2 *OP2 WalkAway
02/18/89 3 1a Possum Golgi
03/03/89 2 1 Alumni *CL1
03/04/89 1 1 Golgi *CL1
04/15/89 9 E *OPE *CLE
05/05/89 10 2 A-Train *CL2
05/20/89 11 E *OPE *CLE
05/27/89 3 1 Bathtub *CL1
06/23/89 6 E Contact *CLE
08/23/89 10 2 Foam *CL2
10/06/89 7 E *OPE *CLE
10/07/89 1 1 Alumni *CL1
10/14/89 3 1 Makisupa *CL1
10/22/89 3 1 IDK *CL1
11/02/89 4 1 Esther *CL1
11/09/89 3 1 A-Train *CL1
02/23/90 34 E IDK *CLE
03/01/90 3 2 Lizards Foam
03/08/90 4 E Contact *CLE
03/17/90 3 E *OPE *CLE
03/28/90 1 1 YEM *CL1
04/04/90 1 2 IDK *CL2
04/06/90 2 2 Alumni *CL2
04/12/90 5 1 Divided *CL1
05/10/90 14 2 ACDCBag *CL2
05/11/90 1 2 Love You *CL2
05/19/90 4 2 Jesus *CL2
05/24/90 2 E *OPE *CLE
05/31/90 1 E *OPE *CLE
06/05/90 2 2 Curtis *CL2
06/07/90 1 1 Lizards *CL1
06/09/90 2 2 *OP2 Harry
10/05/90 12 E *OPE *CLE
10/07/90 2 2 Lizards Golgi
10/12/90 2 E Carolina *CLE
10/30/90 2 E Lizards Contact
11/03/90 3 1 YEM *CL1
11/17/90 5 2 Donna *CL2
11/24/90 1 2 Love You BBFCM
02/26/91 25 E Love You *CLE
03/07/91 6 2 MSO *CL2
04/05/91 16 2 MSO *CL2
04/12/91 3 2 MSO *CL2
04/16/91 3 E Brain *CLE
04/27/91 8 E Bouncing *CLE
05/16/91 8 2 Lizards *CL2
10/19/91 36 E *OPE *CLE
11/14/91 17 E Bouncing *CLE
03/14/92 20 E Sl Monkey *CLE
04/01/92 12 E Lawn Boy *CLE
05/01/92 21 E Lawn Boy *CLE
05/06/92 4 E Carolina *CLE
05/17/92 9 E Lawn Boy *CLE
06/27/92 6 E IDK *CLE
07/31/92 22 1a YEM *CL1
11/20/92 18 E2 Adeline *CLE2
12/01/92 8 E *OPE *CLE
12/05/92 4 E Memories *CLE
12/11/92 5 E Contact *CLE
12/31/92 6 2 Glide *CL2
02/04/93 2 E AmGrace *CLE
02/12/93 7 E AmGrace *CLE
02/17/93 3 E Carolina *CLE
02/21/93 4 E Adeline Paul&Silas
02/25/93 3 E AmGrace *CLE
03/05/93 5 E *OPE *CLE
03/18/93 9 E *OPE *CLE
03/24/93 4 2 Terrapin *CL2
04/03/93 9 E *OPE *CLE
04/10/93 3 E AmGrace *CLE
04/24/93 11 E AmGrace *CLE
05/29/93 12 E *OPE *CLE
07/17/93 4 2 Rift *CL2
07/24/93 5 2 Daniel *CL2
07/29/93 4 2 Daniel *CL2
08/08/93 7 2 Daniel *CL2
08/16/93 7 2 A-Train *CL2
08/25/93 5 2 Sqirm Coil *CL2
12/30/93 5 E Rocky Top *CLE
04/13/94 9 E Adeline *CLE
04/18/94 5 E *OPE *CLE
04/24/94 5 2 Contact *CL2
04/28/94 2 1a Julius *CL1
05/08/94 8 2 Halley's *CL2
05/13/94 3 2 PurplRain *CL2
05/26/94 10 E *OPE *CLE
05/29/94 3 E2 Harry *CLE2
06/16/94 6 E AmGrace *CLE
07/05/94 15 E *OPE *CLE
10/12/94 13 E *OPE *CLE
10/23/94 9 2 Fee *CL2
11/19/94 16 2 AmGrace *CL2
11/25/94 4 E *OPE *CLE
12/04/94 7 2 PurplRain *CL2
12/10/94 5 E """Crew""" *CLE
12/29/94 2 2 Rosie *CL2
06/08/95 5 E *OPE *CLE
06/23/95 11 2 Llama *CL2
09/30/95 13 E AmGrace *CLE
10/21/95 14 1 AArmy TweezRep
11/11/95 10 E AArmy *CLE
11/21/95 7 E *OPE *CLE
12/08/95 12 1 Caspian *CL1
12/15/95 5 E *OPE TweezRep
07/10/96 14 1a HelloBaby *CL1
10/29/96 34 E *OPE *CLE
11/13/96 9 E *OPE *CLE
11/23/96 7 E *OPE *CLE
12/06/96 8 2 Adeline *CL2
12/30/96 3 1 Theme *CL1
02/23/97 10 2 DoInRoad *CL2
07/05/97 21 1a CharZero *CL2
08/10/97 18 2 Jam Rotation
12/13/97 26 1 Tube *CL1
12/29/97 2 E *OPE *CLE
>> 12/31/97 2

Great Gig in the Sky [11] [Great Gig]
By Pink Floyd

03/14/93 [534] 2 BBJ Sqirm Coil
03/17/93 2 2 Silent Golgi
03/26/93 7 2 Suzie TweezRep
04/10/93 10 2 Mike's Weekapaug
04/21/93 8 2 Mike's Weekapaug
05/01/93 8 2 Mike's Weekapaug
05/07/93 5 2 YEM Harry
07/28/93 14 2 Harry Chalkdust
08/11/93 10 2 Mike's Weekapaug
05/02/94 39 1 *OP1 Split&Melt
07/05/94 42 2 YEM Ginseng
>> 12/31/97 287

Have Mercy [8] [Mercy]
By the Mighty Diamonds

04/01/86 [6] 1 Quinn Harry
04/15/86 1 1a Makisupa Dog Log
10/15/86 1 1a Mike's Harry
10/31/86 1 2 Bowie Harry
02/20/93 510 2 Weekapaug All Night
05/08/93 56 2 Weekapaug Bowie
08/14/93 26 2 WalkAway Antelope
11/12/94 110 2 DWD DWD
>> 12/31/97 255

Hello My Baby [42] [HelloBaby]
By Howard/Singer/Emerson

09/27/95 [761]
10/02/95 4 2 Harry DayinLife
10/06/95 3 2 Slave Lizards
10/11/95 3 2 Crossroads DayinLife
10/14/95 2 2 YEM Scent
10/20/95 4 1 Free AmGrace
11/09/95 9 2 Life Mars Sqirm Coil
11/12/95 3 1 Split&Melt *CL1
11/19/95 5 1 It's Ice Julius
11/25/95 4 2 Harry PoorHeart
11/28/95 1 1 Guyute Sample
12/04/95 5 1 Silent Guitar
12/07/95 2 1 Possum *CL1
12/17/95 8 E *OPE RunJim
12/31/95 4 2 Str Design Mike's
04/26/96 1 E *OPE Cavern
07/10/96 7 1a Bowie GTBT
07/11/96 1 2 YEM *CL2
07/12/96 1 3 Free *CL3
07/18/96 4 1a Stash It's Ice
07/23/96 4 1 Stash *CL1
08/02/96 3 1 Tweezer Possum
08/07/96 4 2 YEM *CL2
08/12/96 2 2 Antelope Golgi
08/14/96 2 1 Stash *CL1
08/16/96 1 2 Str Design Mike's
10/19/96 5 2 Antelope *CL2
10/23/96 3 1 Foam CharZero
10/29/96 4 2 Slave *CL2
11/14/96 10 E Stash *CLE
11/18/96 3 2 Tweezer TweezRep
11/22/96 2 2 Slave *CL2
02/22/97 21 2 Free *CL2
03/01/97 5 1 Reba Possum
03/02/97 1 1 Chalkdust *CL1
03/18/97 1 E *OPE FunkBitch
06/19/97 4 E CharZero *CLE
06/22/97 3 1a Theme Ghost
07/09/97 10 E *OPE *CLE
07/22/97 4 2 Weekapaug *CL2
08/03/97 8 2 Taste Frankstein
11/16/97 12 1 Taste *CL1
>> 12/31/97 22

Helter Skelter [2] [Helter]
By The Beatles

10/31/94 [707] 2 Sadie Long Long
11/17/94 8 1 *OP1 Scent
>> 12/31/97 251

Highway to Hell [61] [Hell]
By AC/DC

10/01/89 [125] E *OPE *CLE
10/06/89 1 1a Possum BBFCM
10/07/89 1 2 Contact *CL2
10/14/89 3 2 AnarchUK Possum
10/31/89 6 2 Lizards *CL2
11/02/89 1 E *OPE *CLE
11/09/89 3 E *OPE *CLE
11/10/89 1 2 Harpua A-Train
12/31/89 15 1 Satin Doll *CL1
02/10/90 13 E IDK *CLE
02/17/90 3 1a Foam *CL1
02/23/90 2 2 Weekapaug *CL2
03/09/90 8 2 Slave YEM
03/28/90 3 2 Cavern *CL2
04/04/90 1 E Contact *CLE
04/06/90 2 E Jesus *CLE
04/13/90 6 2 Possum *CL2
04/26/90 7 E *OPE *CLE
05/04/90 4 2 Brain Antelope
05/11/90 3 1 Reba *CL1
05/19/90 4 1 Lizards *CL1
05/24/90 2 2 Harry Contact
11/04/90 28 E Contact *CLE
11/26/90 6 E Contact *CLE
12/08/90 5 E Contact *CLE
12/28/90 1 E Bouncing *CLE
04/04/91 39 2 Magilla *CL2
04/22/91 12 2 Lizards *CL2
05/10/91 8 E A-Train *CLE
10/28/91 44 2 WhipPost *CL2
11/15/91 13 E *OPE Suzie
04/12/93 184 E AmGrace *CLE
04/16/93 3 2 Bike *CL2
04/23/93 6 2 Sqirm Coil *CL2
05/03/93 8 E AmGrace *CLE
05/07/93 3 2 Harpua *CL2
07/23/93 10 2 Chalkdust *CL2
07/31/93 7 2 Daniel *CL2
08/13/93 9 E *OPE *CLE
12/28/93 11 2 Harry *CL2
04/09/94 8 E AmGrace *CLE
04/20/94 9 E *OPE *CLE
04/30/94 8 E Sl Monkey *CLE
05/17/94 12 E *OPE *CLE
05/23/94 5 E AmGrace *CLE
06/09/94 6 E *OPE *CLE
06/19/94 8 2 MSO *CL2
06/25/94 5 E *OPE *CLE
07/02/94 5 2 Slave *CL2
07/14/94 8 2 Harry *CL2
10/16/94 11 E *OPE *CLE
10/22/94 4 2 ACDCBag *CL2
10/28/94 5 E Fee *CLE
11/03/94 4 E AmGrace *CLE
11/22/94 10 2 Harry *CL2
06/20/95 30 2 Rosie *CL2
10/21/95 29 E *OPE *CLE
06/06/96 42 2 Scent *CL1
10/31/96 41 1 Sanity DWD
12/01/96 20 E *OPE *CLE
02/26/97 18 E *OPE *CLE
>> 12/31/97 67

How High the Moon [3] [How High]
By Morgan Lewis

04/22/90 [199] 2 Fluffhead Esther
04/26/90 2 2 *OP2 Esther
03/08/93 329 1 Forbin's Mockbird
>> 12/31/97 436

Hoochie Coochie Man [2] [Hoochie]
By Willie Dixon

04/10/93 [553] 2 Help Me Cavern
08/08/97 381 E *OPE Messing
>> 12/31/97 32

I Know a Little [4] [IKAL]
By Lynyrd Skynyrd

08/10/87 [18] 2 *OP2 Mustang
05/25/88 21 3 Fee BBFCM
06/18/88 2 2 Antelope Mike's
08/03/88 8 1 *OP1 YEM
>> 12/31/97 917

I Walk the Line [10] [Walk Line]
By Johnny Cash

11/19/92 [480] 2 It's Ice Tweezer
11/20/92 1 1 Memories Bowie
11/23/92 3 2 Sqirm Coil Llama
11/27/92 2 2 McGrupp Bowie
12/02/92 4 2 Sqirm Coil RunJim
12/05/92 2 2 Reba Reba
12/10/92 4 2 Love You Oh Kee
12/30/92 6 1 Reba Reba
02/10/93 8 2 Tweezer Sparkle
03/09/93 20 2 Love You Sqirm Coil
>> 12/31/97 435

I Wanna Be Like You [9] [BeLikeYou]
From Disney's *Jungle Book*

04/04/94 [615] 2 Wolfman's Oh Kee
04/05/94 1 2 YEM Chalkdust
04/10/94 3 2 Ginseng Harry
04/15/94 4 2 Alumni Cavern
04/18/94 3 2 DWD Cavern
04/22/94 3 2 RunJim Sqirm Coil
04/29/94 5 2 Weekapaug Cavern
05/03/94 3 2 Chalkdust Slave
06/10/94 22 2 Possum Harry
>> 12/31/97 306

If I Only Had a Brain [30] [Brain]
From *The Wizard of Oz*

04/14/89 [78] 2 *OP2 Mike's
05/13/89 18 2 Harry Contact
10/01/89 29 2 YEM Contact
11/10/89 16 2 Lizards Possum
11/11/89 1 1a YEM Frankstein
04/05/90 45 2 Weekapaug Contact
04/08/90 3 1 YEM Oh Kee
04/25/90 10 1 *OP1 Divided
05/04/90 5 2 Caravan HwayHell
05/23/90 8 1 YEM Oh Kee
06/16/90 8 3 Caravan Mike's
10/06/90 12 1a Possum Bowie
12/31/90 23 2 Rocky Top Antelope
04/16/91 44 E *OPE GTBT
07/13/91 22 2 Stash YEM
10/12/91 25 1 Brother Harry
11/14/91 22 2 A-Train Lizards
04/19/92 45 2 Lawn Boy RunJim
06/23/92 25 1a BBFCM Golgi
12/12/92 60 2 YEM Sqirm Coil
02/07/93 10 2 Sqirm Coil TweezRep
02/25/93 14 2 FEFY Golgi
03/18/93 14 2 BBJ Sqirm Coil
03/30/93 9 2 Silent TweezRep

04/13/93	9	2	Weekapaug	Sqirm Coil
04/30/93	13	2	Harry	YEM
08/21/93	38	2	Bowie	Harry
12/29/93	6	2	BBJ	Adeline
10/25/94	90	2	BBJ	Possum
11/16/95	90	2	Harry	AmGrace
>> 12/31/97	**174**			

I'm Blue I'm Lonesome [27] [I'm Blue]

By James B. Smith

11/16/94	[714]	2	Simple	LongJourn
11/17/94	1	E	*OPE	Nellie
11/19/94	2	1	Antelope	Butter
11/22/94	2	2	BBFCM	Butter
11/30/94	5	1	Bouncing	LongJourn
12/06/94	5	2	Bike	Foreplay
12/07/94	1	2	Julius	LongJourn
12/09/94	2	E	*OPE	Foreplay
12/30/94	4	2	Tweezer	YEM
09/30/95	28	1	Antelope	Sample
10/03/95	2	1	FEFY	Free
10/06/95	2	1	Reba	Rift
10/08/95	2	1	Reba	Caspian
10/13/95	2	1	Billy	Caspian
10/15/95	2	1	Str Design	Bowie
10/17/95	1	E	LongJourn	*CLE
10/20/95	2	2	LongJourn	Bouncing
10/22/95	2	1	Sample	Stash
10/25/95	2	1	LongJourn	Chalkdust
11/14/95	9	1	Julius	Cavern
11/18/95	3	1	Slave	Sample
11/21/95	2	1	LongJourn	Guyute
11/24/95	2	1	Tela	Maze
11/25/95	1	1	LongJourn	Str Design
11/29/95	2	2	PoorHeart	LongJourn
12/05/95	5	1	Bowie	*CL1
12/12/95	5	1	Antelope	Sqirm Coil
>> 12/31/97	**156**			

I'm So Tired [2] [I'm Tired]

By The Beatles

10/31/94	[707]	2	Martha	Blackbird
11/18/95	86	2	Free	YEM
>> 12/31/97	**173**			

It's No Good Trying [3] [No Good]

By Syd Barrett

12/07/90	[252]	2	Suzie	Bowie
12/08/90	1	2	Golgi	YEM
12/28/90	1	2	Divided	Don't Get
>> 12/31/97	**712**			

Izabella [8] [Izabella]

By Jimi Hendrix

06/13/97	[904]	E	Stand	*CLE
07/26/97	23	1	YEM	*CL1
08/13/97	11	2	Ghost	Sl Monkey
11/16/97	6	2	Harry	*CL2
11/22/97	4	1	Frankstein	*CL1
12/06/97	9	2	Tweezer	Twist
12/12/97	4	2	Caspian	TweezRep
12/30/97	4	2	Harpua	Harry
>> 12/31/97	**1**			

Jesus Just Left Chicago [51] [Jesus]

By ZZ Top

08/10/87	[18]	2	Bowie	WhipPost
01/30/88	10	1	Possum	Sally
05/14/88	8	2	BBFCM	Fluffhead
05/25/88	3	2	*OP2	Fluffhead
06/18/88	2	2	McGrupp	*CL2
06/21/88	2	2	Alumni	GTBT
07/12/88	2	1	Fluffhead	Makisupa
07/24/88	2	3	Peaches	McGrupp
08/03/88	2	1	YEM	*CL1
05/28/89	55	3	Ya Mar	Split&Melt
12/15/89	48	1a	FunkBitch	Contact
02/23/90	22	2	Bathtub	Tela
03/28/90	11	2	Weekapaug	Lizards
04/05/90	2	2	Uncle Pen	ACDCBag
04/06/90	1	E	*OPE	HwayHell
04/09/90	3	2	Harry	Divided
04/12/90	2	1	Cavern	Divided
04/20/90	4	2	ACDCBag	YEM
05/19/90	15	2	Rift	GTBT
11/04/90	30	2	Suzie	YEM
11/08/90	1	E	*OPE	Fire
12/29/90	12	2	Stash	Dinner
02/03/91	4	E	*OPE	BBFCM
03/06/91	18	E	*OPE	*CLE
04/06/91	18	1	Possum	Alumni
07/24/91	35	2	Bowie	MSO
07/25/91	1	2	PoorHeart	Lizards
09/25/91	4	2	Cavern	RunJim
10/13/91	13	2	MSO	Bouncing
11/08/91	16	2	Weekapaug	Self
11/23/91	12	E	*OPE	BBFCM
03/05/93	152	2	Weekapaug	MSO
03/17/93	8	2	Reba	Mound
04/03/93	14	2	YEM	MSO
08/11/93	48	2	Rift	MSO
08/26/93	11	2	Rift	Lizards
06/13/94	53	2	Reba	Scent
06/22/94	7	2	BBJ	Sample
10/25/94	33	2	Axilla 2	BBJ
12/01/94	23	2	Tweezer	Harry
12/06/94	4	1	Fluffhead	Sparkle
10/31/95	56	3	YEM	DayinLife
10/31/96	76	3	Steep	Suzie
11/27/96	17	2	DWD	Scent
12/04/96	5	E	*OPE	*CLE
02/22/97	13	2	Simple	Harry
03/01/97	5	1	Wolfman's	Reba
06/19/97	6	2	Piper	Caspian
08/03/97	25	1	Twist	Limb
11/17/97	13	2	Johnny B.	Circus
12/07/97	13	1	Psycho	My Mind
>> 12/31/97	**8**			

Johnny B. Goode [22] [Johnny B.]

By Chuck Berry

06/17/95	[747]	2	Tweezer	Tweezer
07/03/95	13	2	Bowie	Bowie
12/31/95	58	E	*OPE	*CLE
07/12/96	10	E	Bathtub	*CLE
07/21/96	6	1	Timber Ho	*CL1
08/06/96	8	E	*OPE	*CLE
10/16/96	8	2	Sqirm Coil	*CL2
10/25/96	7	E	*OPE	*CLE
11/02/96	5	1	Free	*CL1
11/18/96	11	E	Waste	*CLE
12/01/96	8	2	TweezRep	Slave
12/28/96	4	E	*OPE	*CLE
02/13/97	4	E	Caspian	*CLE
02/16/97	2	E	Theme	*CLE
02/22/97	5	E	*OPE	*CLE
03/02/97	6	1	*OP1	Uncle Pen
07/11/97	20	1a	Wolfman's	YEM
07/26/97	5	2	Waste	*CL2
08/02/97	4	2	DWD	Sparkle
11/17/97	14	2	Oblivious	Jesus
11/28/97	6	2	Ghost	*CL2
12/11/97	9	2	DWD	*CL2
>> 12/31/97	**6**			

Jump Monk [2] [JumpMonk]

By Charles Mingus

03/12/88	[32]	1a	*OP1	McGrupp
04/24/94	600	1	Bathtub	Bathtub
>> 12/31/97	**334**			

La Grange [57] [La Grange]

By ZZ Top

08/10/87	[18]	2	YEM	Icculus
09/12/87	5	2	Terrapin	Fluffhead
11/19/87	4	3	CamlWalk	Bike
05/25/88	12	3	One Love	Fee
06/15/88	1	1	Golgi	Fee
06/18/88	1	1	Golgi	Suzie
07/23/88	5	2	BlueBossa	Alumni
07/24/88	1	2	Fluffhead	Lizards
08/06/88	3	1	*OP1	YEM
09/24/88	4	1	Peaches	A-Train
10/29/88	2	1	Bold	Contact
02/05/89	7	1	Bowie	YEM
02/06/89	1	1	Fee	YEM
02/18/89	3	1a	YEM	Contact
03/30/89	5	2	Undone	Golgi
05/09/89	21	2	YEM	If I Don't
05/13/89	3	1	Golgi	Fluffhead
05/28/89	3	3	FunkBitch	Sloth
08/26/89	16	E	Lizards	*CLE
10/07/89	7	1	Fee	Makisupa
10/20/89	4	E	*OPE	Slave
10/22/89	2	1	*OP1	Forbin's
11/10/89	8	2	My Girl	Harry
12/09/89	10	1	Dinner	Lizards
01/20/90	6	1a	Tela	Lawn Boy
01/27/90	3	E	*OPE	*CLE
01/28/90	1	1	Fluffhead	Carolina
02/10/90	8	2	*OP2	Esther
02/24/90	6	2	Sqirm Coil	Bathtub
03/09/90	7	2	YEM	Contact
03/28/90	3	2	Contact	Rift
04/06/90	3	2	Carolina	Esther
04/09/90	3	2	Uncle Pen	Foam
04/13/90	3	1	Esther	Oh Kee
04/18/90	1	2	*OP2	Fee
04/20/90	2	2	Weekapaug	Rift
04/25/90	3	2	Esther	Dinner
05/13/90	10	2	Adeline	Foam
05/19/90	2	1	Adeline	YEM
05/23/90	1	2	Lizards	McGrupp
06/09/90	7	2	TMWSIY	Fee
06/16/90	1	3	*OP3	Ya Mar
09/13/90	1	E	Lizards	*CLE
10/07/90	12	1	A-Train	*CL1
11/02/90	6	E	Lawn Boy	*CLE
02/08/91	21	E	Landlady	*CLE
02/14/91	2	E	Uncle Pen	*CLE
02/26/91	9	1	Golgi	*CL1
03/17/91	12	E	Lawn Boy	*CLE
08/02/93	308	1	Dog Log	*CL1
08/07/93	3	E	Carolina	*CLE
08/14/93	6	E	*OPE	*CLE
12/29/95	215	2	Bass Jam	Bouncing
11/16/96	56	2	*OP2	RunJim
11/30/96	8	2	*OP2	It's Ice
12/29/96	6	1	Sqirm Coil	*CL1
02/25/97	12	2	Caspian	Adeline
>> 12/31/97	**68**			

Life on Mars [19] [Life Mars]

By David Bowie

10/13/95	[772]	1	Fluffhead	*CL1
10/22/95	7	2	BBFCM	Uncle Pen
10/25/95	2	2	Reba	CTB
10/27/95	1	E	*OPE	*CLE
11/09/95	4	2	TMWSIY	HelloBaby
11/15/95	5	2	Mike's	Weekapaug
11/19/95	3	E	*OPE	TweezRep
11/24/95	3	E	*OPE	Rocky Top
07/21/96	37	2	Reba	Free
07/25/96	4	1a	Antelope	Harry
08/07/96	5	2	Possum	YEM
08/16/96	5	3	NICU	Harry
10/21/96	6	2	Maze	Simple
10/27/96	5	2	Fluffhead	TweezRep
11/03/96	4	2	Tweezer	Possum
11/14/96	7	2	Scent	Demand
11/29/96	9	1	Bathtub	Maze
12/04/96	4	2	PYITE	Reba
03/02/97	19	1	Catapult	Chalkdust
>> 12/31/97	**64**			

Light Up or Leave Me Alone [5] [Light Up]

By Traffic

08/21/87	[19]	1	Curtain	Shaggy
05/14/88	17	2	Halley's	YEM
05/23/88	2	1	Rocky Top	IDK
07/24/88	9	2	*OP2	Fluffhead
07/25/88	1	2	Bold	Fluffhead
>> 12/31/97	**918**			

Lonesome Cowboy Bill [3] [LCBill]

By Velvet Underground

05/16/95	[738]	1a	Theme	Free
06/07/95	1	2	Theme	AArmy
06/10/95	3	1	YEM	Suzie
>> 12/31/97	**224**			

Long Journey Home [15] [LongJourn]

Traditional

11/16/94	[714]	2	I'm Blue	Chalkdust
11/17/94	1	E	Nellie	Fixin'
11/18/94	1	1	Old Home	*CL1
11/19/94	1	1	Butter	*CL1
11/20/94	1	1	Butter	Dooley
11/22/94	1	2	Butter	Harry
11/30/94	5	1	I'm Blue	*CL1
12/07/94	6	2	I'm Blue	AmGrace
12/29/94	5	E	*OPE	Sl Monkey
10/17/95	40	E	*OPE	I'm Blue
10/20/95	2	2	Guitar	I'm Blue
10/25/95	4	1	Str Design	I'm Blue
11/21/95	14	1	Divided	I'm Blue
11/25/95	3	2	Mike's	I'm Blue
11/29/95	2	2	I'm Blue	Slave
>> 12/31/97	**166**			

Long Time [16] [LongTime]

By Boston

See Foreplay

Love Me [7] [Love Me]

By Leiber/Stoller

Originally performed by Elvis Presley

02/13/97	[889]	1	Peaches	Bowie
02/20/97	5	1	Chalkdust	Taste
02/23/97	3	1	Sloth	Rift
02/28/97	3	2	Bowie	Axilla
03/18/97	3	2	Bowie	Reconsider
08/14/97	36	2	Chalkdust	Sparkle
11/30/97	14	1	Wolfman's	Sqirm Coil
>> 12/31/97	**13**			

Love You [74] [Love You]

By Syd Barrett

04/20/89	[81]	2	Weekapaug	Harpua
04/09/90	110	2	Divided	Tweezer
04/29/90	12	1a	WalkAway	Lizards
05/11/90	5	2	Ya Mar	GTBT
06/07/90	10	2	Divided	Mike's
10/31/90	21	2	Suzie	Mike's
11/03/90	2	2	Possum	Antelope
11/17/90	5	2	Esther	Possum
11/24/90	1	2	YEM	GTBT
02/07/91	13	2	Cavern	Lizards
02/09/91	2	2	Cavern	Sqirm Coil
02/16/91	3	2	Rocky Top	Golgi
02/26/91	7	E	*OPE	GTBT
02/27/91	1	2	Sloth	Possum
03/01/91	2	2	Possum	Bowie
03/06/91	2	1	Divided	MSO
04/04/91	16	2	Divided	BBFCM
05/10/91	20	2	Chalkdust	Mike's
10/04/91	29	E	Rocky Top	Llama
10/13/91	6	2	Bouncing	Bowie
10/15/91	1	2	Suzie	Ya Mar
10/17/91	1	2	YEM	Possum
11/01/91	10	E	*OPE	Stash
11/07/91	3	2	A-Train	Possum
11/12/91	4	2	Cavern	Antelope
11/15/91	3	2	Harry	Bouncing
11/19/91	2	1	Chalkdust	Wilson
11/23/91	4	2	Fee	MSO
12/04/91	3	2	Chalkdust	Golgi
03/13/92	9	2	Rift	Possum
03/17/92	2	2	Weekapaug	Llama
03/27/92	7	2	Harry	Golgi
03/31/92	3	2	MSO	Possum
04/05/92	4	2	Bowie	A-Train
04/13/92	5	2	Sqirm Coil	Possum
04/18/92	4	2	Harry	Rocky Top
04/24/92	5	2	Horn	Glide
04/29/92	2	2	Weekapaug	Golgi
05/05/92	5	2	Llama	Sqirm Coil
05/15/92	8	1a	Bouncing	Chalkdust
05/17/92	2	2	Sanity	Sparkle
05/18/92	1	2	Cavern	RunJim

After ZARATHUSTRA

Since its debut in summer '93, these songs have followed Also Sprach the most number of times.

1) Antelope 11
2) Maze 10
3) David Bowie 9
4) Mike's Song 8
5) Poor Heart 5

06/20/92	2	1a	Horn	Llama
11/21/92	44	2	Sqirm Coil	A-Train
11/28/92	5	2	Sqirm Coil	Harpua
12/01/92	2	2	Llama	Dinner
12/07/92	6	2	Bowie	Sqirm Coil
12/10/92	2	2	YEM	Walk Line
12/30/92	6	2	BBJ	A-Train
02/05/93	4	2	YEM	Sqirm Coil
02/11/93	5	2	Bouncing	Lizards
02/19/93	6	2	MSO	Llama
02/22/93	3	2	Llama	Sqirm Coil
03/02/93	5	2	YEM	My Life
03/05/93	2	2	BBJ	Sqirm Coil
03/09/93	3	2	BBJ	Walk Line
03/13/93	2	2	FEFY	TweezRep
03/19/93	5	2	Weekapaug	Golgi
03/28/93	7	2	BBJ	Possum
04/03/93	5	2	MSO	Cavern
04/09/93	2	2	MSO	Possum
04/18/93	7	2	WalkAway	TweezRep
04/22/93	3	2	Uncle Pen	TweezRep
04/27/93	4	2	Silent	Cavern
05/03/93	5	2	BBJ	MSO
08/08/93	25	2	BBJ	Daniel
05/12/94	48	2	Possum	Contact
05/17/94	4	2	Sample	Slave
06/30/94	27	2	Antelope	Chalkdust
10/10/94	16	2	DWD	Slave
11/17/94	24	2	YEM	Slave
12/28/94	19	2	Llama	Sqirm Coil
12/08/95	73	2	Tweezer	Sqirm Coil
07/05/97	111	1a	Harry	PoorHeart
>> 08/17/97	48			

Most Frequent COVERS

Phish's favorite covers, listed by order of total number of times played.

1) Uncle Pen 176
2) Sweet Adeline 159
3) Rocky Top 151
4) Ya Mar 140
5) GTBT 138
6) Amazing Grace 109
7) Also Sprach 98
8) Fire 95
9) Funky Bitch 91
10) Take the A-Train 83
11) Love You 75
12) Paul and Silas 72
13) Carolina 61
13) Highway to Hell 61
15) Peaches 60
16) Avenu Malkenu 59
17) La Grange 57
18) Bold as Love 52
19) Ginseng Sullivan 51
19) Jesus Left Chicago 51
20) Frankenstein 48
20) Terrapin 48
21) Cracklin' Rosie 46
22) Timber Ho 45
23) Walk Away 44

Loving Cup [38] [Lovin Cup]
By the Rolling Stones

02/03/93	[505]	1	*OP1	Rift
02/05/93	2	E	AmGrace	*CLE
02/10/93	4	1	*OP1	Foam
02/19/93	7	1	*OP1	Rift
02/26/93	6	2	*OP2	Paul&Silas
03/14/93	10	1	*OP1	Foam
03/21/93	5	2	*OP2	My Friend
03/30/93	7	2	*OP2	Rift
08/08/93	50	1	Foam	RunJim
04/17/94	30	1	*OP1	Foam
05/07/94	15	2	*OP2	Sparkle
11/04/94	69	E	*OPE	Rocky Top
06/19/95	38	2	Mango	Sparkle
07/03/95	12	1	Antelope	Sparkle
11/09/95	26	E	*OPE	*CLE
12/09/95	22	E	*OPE	*CLE
07/15/96	22	2	Maze	Makisupa
07/23/96	6	2	RunJim	Sparkle
08/04/96	4	1	Maze	*CL1
11/08/96	26	2	Simple	Mike's
11/19/96	8	1	Taste	*CL1
11/24/96	3	2	YEM	Suzie
02/16/97	14	2	Bowie	TweezRep
02/25/97	7	1	Taste	*CL1
06/24/97	13	E	*OPE	*CLE
07/01/97	4	2	Cities	Slave
07/21/97	8	E	*OPE	*CLE
07/29/97	5	1	Steep	*CL1
08/02/97	3	2	Wading	TweezRep
08/08/97	3	2	Limb	Caspian
08/16/97	6	E	Contact	*CLE
11/13/97	2	E	*OPE	*CLE
11/21/97	5	2	Slave	*CL2
11/30/97	6	1	Sqirm Coil	*CL1
12/05/97	3	2	Lizards	Chalkdust
12/09/97	3	1	Horn	*CL1
12/11/97	1	1	Limb	Rocky Top
12/31/97	6	3	Caspian	*CL3
>> 12/31/97	0			

Manteca [9] [Manteca]
By Duke Ellington

11/04/90	[242]	2	Weekapaug	RunJim
12/28/90	12	2	Tweezer	Tweezer
03/16/91	29	E	*OPE	Possum
04/18/92	130	2	Rift	Bathtub
02/21/93	107	2	Stash	Stash
05/03/93	51	2	Tweezer	Tweezer
05/05/93	1	2	My Friend	My Friend
10/28/94	133	2	Bowie	Bowie
11/14/95	85	2	Stash	Stash
>> 12/31/97	176			

Melt the Guns [2] [Melt Guns]
By XTC

10/31/86	[9]	1	Slave	Dave's
04/29/87	6	2	Dog Log	Dave's
>> 12/31/97	951			

Memories [37] [Memories]
Traditional

11/17/90	[246]	E	*OPE	Adeline
09/26/91	90	E	*OPE	PoorHeart
09/28/91	2	1	Golgi	*CL1
10/03/91	3	2	Tweezer	*CL2
10/04/91	1	1	*OP1	Chalkdust
10/15/91	7	E	*OPE	Harry
10/17/91	1	1	*OP1	Landlady
10/24/91	4	E	*OPE	Adeline
10/31/91	5	1	*OP1	Brother
11/07/91	4	1	*OP1	Chalkdust
11/12/91	4	E2	Split&Melt	*CLE2
11/21/91	7	E	*OPE	Adeline
12/06/91	7	1	*OP1	Foam
03/11/92	5	E	Sanity	Carolina
03/17/92	4	E	*OPE	Adeline
03/27/92	7	E	*OPE	Adeline
03/28/92	1	2	*OP2	Carolina
04/13/92	11	E	*OPE	Fire
04/15/92	1	E	*OPE	Adeline
04/16/92	1	2	Carolina	Adeline
04/21/92	4	2	Maze	*CL2
05/03/92	9	E	*OPE	Adeline
05/08/92	4	1	Bowie	*CL1
08/30/92	50	1a	Llama	Antelope
11/20/92	3	1	Lizards	Walk Line
11/23/92	3	1	Bouncing	Bowie
11/27/92	2	1	Mound	RunJim
12/05/92	7	E	*OPE	GTBT
12/11/92	5	E	My Friend	Bowie
12/28/92	3	E	*OPE	Fire
02/18/93	16	2	AmGrace	Adeline
03/14/93	17	E	*OPE	Adeline
05/03/93	37	E	*OPE	AmGrace
08/09/93	26	1	Divided	Sqirm Coil
08/17/93	7	E	*OPE	Fire
12/28/93	7	E	*OPE	Golgi
07/06/94	69	E	Nellie	FunkBitch
>> 12/31/97	286			

Minute by Minute [2] [Minute]
By the Doobie Brothers

09/13/90	[222]	1	Antelope	BurAlive
09/15/90	2	2	Foam	Harry
>> 12/31/97	742			

Mustang Sally [6] [Mustang]
By Wilson Pickett

10/15/86	[8]	1a	Shaggy	Fluffhead
10/31/86	1	1	*OP1	CamlWalk
08/10/87	9	2	IKAL	YEM
08/29/87	3	1	Suzie	Ya Mar
01/30/88	7	1	FunkBitch	ACDCBag
06/21/88	15	1	Rocky Top	Suzie
>> 12/31/97	923			

My Mind's Got a Mind of Its Own [28] [My Mind]
By Jimmy Dale Gilmore

03/07/92	[385]	1	Brother	Foam
03/11/92	1	2	Bathtub	Brother
03/13/92	2	2	Lizards	Sloth
04/07/92	18	2	Bike	Golgi
04/30/92	15	2	Sqirm Coil	YEM
05/06/92	5	1	Foam	Maze
02/07/93	83	2	FEFY	Reba
07/15/93	69	1	IDK	Leprech
07/17/93	2	1	Sample	Stash
07/22/93	3	1	Horn	Sample
07/25/93	3	1	Sloth	IDK
07/29/93	3	1	FEFY	Forbin's
08/02/93	3	1	Makisupa	Dog Log
08/09/93	5	2	My Friend	YEM
08/13/93	3	1	Fluffhead	Horn
04/25/94	33	2	Sample	Antelope
04/29/94	2	1	Sanity	Llama
05/27/94	21	2	Nellie	Mike's
07/06/94	24	1	Axilla 2	Carolina
12/08/94	51	2	Possum	Axilla 2
06/16/95	15	1	It's Ice	Dog Faced
06/26/95	8	1	Sloth	It's Ice
10/22/95	25	1	ACDCBag	Sloth
12/04/95	25	1	Stash	Axilla 2
07/21/96	30	1	If I Could	Split&Melt
11/15/96	37	2	Avenu	Mike's
08/03/97	61	1	Vultures	Twist
12/07/97	26	1	Jesus	It's Ice
>> 12/31/97	8			

My Soul [30] [My Soul]
By Clifton Chenier

02/13/97	[889]	2	CTB	PYITE
02/17/97	3	1	Wilson	Guyute
02/18/97	1	2	Also Sprach	Maze
02/21/97	2	1	*OP1	Foam
02/25/97	3	1	RunJim	Meatball
02/26/97	1	1	Harry	Tube
02/28/97	1	1	Paul&Silas	CTB
03/02/97	2	1	Guyute	RunJim
03/18/97	1	1	PYITE	Beauty
06/14/97	2	1	Talk	CTB
06/21/97	4	E	*OPE	*CLE
06/25/97	3	1	Limb	*CL1
06/29/97	2	E	*OPE	*CLE
07/03/97	3	1	Piper	Divided
07/06/97	2	E	*OPE	*CLE
07/09/97	1	2	DWD	CTB
07/22/97	4	1	RunJim	Water
07/30/97	5	E	*OPE	*CLE
08/06/97	4	2	RunJim	Ghost
08/11/97	4	2	Vultures	YEM
08/16/97	3	2	Simple	Jam
11/13/97	2	1	Beauty	YEM
11/16/97	2	1	NICU	BE Katy
11/23/97	5	1	*OP1	Theme
11/26/97	1	1	Gumbo	McGrupp
11/28/97	1	E	*OPE	*CLE
12/03/97	4	1	PYITE	Drowned
12/09/97	4	1	Chalkdust	Stash
12/13/97	3	E	*OPE	Sqirm Coil
12/30/97	3	2	Harry	Sl Monkey
>> 12/31/97	1			

Nellie Cane [41] [Nellie]
Traditional

02/23/93	[522]	2	Weekapaug	Weekapaug
07/16/93	57	1	All Things	Horn
07/23/93	5	1	Caravan	Maze
07/24/93	1	1	Horn	Divided
07/28/93	3	1	Foam	Split&Melt
07/31/93	3	1	Foam	Divided
08/03/93	2	1	RunJim	Foam
08/06/93	1	1	Divided	Chalkdust
08/09/93	3	1	Glide	Divided
08/12/93	2	1	Guelah	Split&Melt
08/15/93	3	2	Ginseng	Freebird
08/21/93	4	E	AmGrace	*CLE
08/24/93	1	1	It's Ice	Split&Melt
08/25/93	1	1	Ginseng	AmGrace
12/29/93	4	E	*OPE	Cavern
04/05/94	4	E	*OPE	Golgi
04/06/94	1	E	Ginseng	Adeline
04/09/94	2	1	Bathtub	Julius
04/14/94	4	2	YEM	Dog Faced
04/16/94	2	1	Fluffhead	Antelope
04/22/94	5	1	All Things	Divided
05/03/94	8	E	*OPE	Fire
05/10/94	5	2	Dog Faced	Bowie
05/19/94	6	E	Ginseng	Adeline
05/27/94	7	2	Julius	Mind
05/29/94	2	2	*OP2	Split&Melt
06/10/94	2	1	Sample	Demand
07/06/94	20	E	Old Home	Memories
07/08/94	1	E	*OPE	Cavern
10/10/94	10	1	Ginseng	Chalkdust
10/12/94	1	2	YEM	Foreplay
10/14/94	2	2	Chalkdust	Beaumont
10/18/94	3	2	Beaumont	Llama
10/20/94	1	2	Harry	Foreplay
10/26/94	5	E	*OPE	Foreplay
10/28/94	2	2	Old Home	Foreplay
11/03/94	4	E	MSO	AmGrace
11/12/94	2	2	Old Home	Foreplay
11/14/94	2	2	Old Home	Adeline
11/17/94	2	E	I'm Blue	LongJourn
12/08/94	16	2	Reba	Adeline
>> 12/31/97	235			

The Old Home Place [27] [Old Home]
By the Dillards

06/26/94	[673]	E	*OPE	AmGrace
07/03/94	5	1	Horn	Reba
07/06/94	2	E	*OPE	Nellie
10/10/94	11	1	Guyute	Ginseng
10/13/94	2	2	*OP2	Antelope
10/18/94	4	2	Lifeboy	Beaumont
10/21/94	2	1	Mango	Stash
10/28/94	6	2	Chalkdust	Nellie
11/02/94	3	E	*OPE	Foreplay
11/12/94	3	2	Rift	Nellie
11/14/94	2	2	Julius	Nellie
11/18/94	4	1	Butter	LongJourn
12/31/94	21	2	*OP2	Maze
06/15/95	8	1	ACDCBag	Taste
10/11/95	26	1	Stash	Cavern

11/10/95	16	1	Fog	It's Ice
12/07/95	19	1	*OP1	Curtain
08/13/96	40	1	FEFY	PYITE
08/17/96	3	1	*OP1	PYITE
10/18/96	3	1	Guelah	CTB
11/16/96	20	1	Free	Bowie
11/30/96	8	1	Fluffhead	Uncle Pen
06/25/97	32	1	ACDCBag	Theme
07/06/97	7	1	RunJim	Dogs Stole
11/16/97	25	1	Farmhouse	Billy
12/03/97	11	1	Drowned	Gumbo
12/28/97	8	1	Sample	RunJim
>> 12/31/97	**3**			

On Your Way Down [9] [OYWD]

By Little Feat

07/23/88	[46]	1	Lizards	ACDCBag
07/24/88	1	2	Alumni	Cities
09/08/88	5	2	GTBT	WhipPost
09/24/88	2	1	Golgi	Alumni
02/06/89	10	1	Divided	IDK
02/24/89	4	1	Antelope	*CL1
03/30/89	4	1	PriceLove	Ya Mar
04/15/89	8	1	Peaches	Alumni
08/12/89	35	1a	Rocky Top	Wonderful
>> 12/31/97	**852**			

Paul and Silas [72] [Paul&Silas]

By Earl Scruggs

09/13/90	[222]	1	BurAlive	Bouncing
09/14/90	1	1	Reba	Stash
09/15/90	1	1	Divided	Landlady
09/16/90	1	1a	Tweezer	Mike's
09/28/90	4	E	*OPE	*CLE
10/12/90	7	2	Divided	Magilla
10/30/90	2	3	*OP3	Lizards
11/03/90	3	2	Weekapaug	Stash
11/16/90	4	2	Tube	Lizards
11/26/90	3	1	YEM	Donna
03/15/91	34	2	Horn	Cavern
03/22/91	4	2	Foam	Stash
04/11/91	10	1	Cavern	Tweezer
04/16/91	4	1	YEM	Cavern
04/18/91	1	2	Sloth	Horn
04/19/91	1	E	*OPE	BBFCM
04/20/91	1	2	Sqirm Coil	Cavern
05/03/91	7	1	Fee	Tweezer
05/18/91	8	1	YEM	Foam
07/13/91	4	2	Flat Fee	Lizards
09/27/91	15	1	Tweezer	It's Ice
10/03/91	4	2	*OP2	Mike's
10/10/91	4	1	Foam	Split&Melt
10/18/91	6	1	Foam	Reba
10/28/91	6	2	Stash	Bathtub
10/31/91	2	1	Bathtub	YEM
11/02/91	2	1	Reba	Foam
11/12/91	6	2	Sqirm Coil	Mike's
11/14/91	2	2	Fee	It's Ice
11/20/91	4	1	Stash	Bathtub
11/24/91	4	1	Sloth	Stash
11/30/91	1	1	Brother	Guelah
12/05/91	2	1	Golgi	Split&Melt
03/11/92	6	1	My Friend	Reba
03/27/92	11	1	Reba	Sloth
04/06/92	8	2	Bathtub	Mike's
04/19/92	9	1	Stash	My Friend
04/25/92	5	1	My Friend	Reba
05/16/92	15	2	It's Ice	Tweezer
07/14/92	15	2	Sqirm Coil	YEM
07/16/92	2	2	Glide	Mike's
11/28/92	36	2	Suzie	Tweezer
12/06/92	7	2	Stash	BBJ
12/11/92	4	2	Bouncing	BBJ
12/30/92	5	1	Fluffhead	Reba
02/05/93	4	2	Silent	It's Ice
02/19/93	11	2	It's Ice	YEM
02/21/93	2	E	GTBT	PiginPen
02/23/93	2	1	Wedge	Antelope
02/26/93	2	2	Lovin Cup	Tweezer
03/03/93	3	1	Guelah	Sample
03/06/93	2	2	Reba	BBJ
03/14/93	5	1	Stash	Sample
03/17/93	2	1	AmGrace	It's Ice
03/28/93	9	2	YEM	BBJ
04/01/93	3	1	My Friend	Fluffhead
04/05/93	3	1	Fluffhead	Stash
04/12/93	3	2	Fee	It's Ice
04/23/93	9	2	It's Ice	BBJ
05/01/93	6	2	Halley's	Mike's
07/22/93	14	2	Possum	TMWSIY
08/08/93	13	1	FEFY	IDK
08/15/93	6	1	Fee	Stash
08/25/93	6	2	My Friend	YEM
12/30/93	5	1	Sample	Forbin's
04/15/94	11	1	Guelah	Harry
04/20/94	4	2	Magilla	BBJ
04/24/94	4	1	Dog Faced	It's Ice
06/24/94	39	1	All Things	Horn
11/19/94	46	1	Axilla 2	TMWSIY
10/24/95	63	1	My Friend	Fog
02/28/97	120	1	Carini	My Soul
>> 12/31/97	**66**			

Peaches En Regalia [60] [Peaches]

By Frank Zappa

10/15/86	[8]	1a	Harry	Golgi
10/31/86	1	2	SwingLow	Bowie
03/23/87	4	1	Peaches	Ride Capt.
04/29/87	2	3	*OP3	Fluffhead
05/11/87	1	1a	Clod	TMWSIY
08/10/87	2	1	*OP1	Alumni
08/21/87	1	1	Dog Log	Divided
09/27/87	5	1	Golgi	A-Train
10/14/87	1	1	*OP1	A-Train
02/07/88	4	1a	Alumni	Reagan
02/08/88	1	2	Wilson	Divided
05/15/88	7	1a	Wilson	IDK
05/23/88	1	1	IDK	Possum
05/25/88	1	1	Alumni	Golgi
06/20/88	3	1	Slave	YEM
06/21/88	1	2	Contact	Golgi
07/12/88	2	2	GTBT	*CL2
07/23/88	1	2	Alumni	*CL2
07/24/88	1	3	TMWSIY	Jesus
08/03/88	2	2	*OP2	Mike's
09/08/88	3	1	*OP1	WalkAway
09/24/88	2	1	Wilson	La Grange
10/29/88	2	3	Wilson	FunkBitch
11/05/88	2	2	Wilson	Bold
11/11/88	1	E	*OPE	FunkBitch
02/06/89	5	1	Wilson	Fee
02/18/89	3	1a	Wilson	YEM
03/30/89	5	3	*OP3	Foam
04/15/89	7	1	Wilson	OYWD
04/30/89	7	1a	Wilson	Antelope
05/09/89	7	1	Wilson	Ya Mar
05/28/89	11	2	Ride Capt.	A-Train
06/23/89	5	1	Wilson	Donna
12/28/93	502	1	*OP1	PoorHeart
12/29/93	1	1	RunJim	Foam
12/31/93	2	1	Reba	IDK
04/05/94	2	2	*OP2	Ya Mar
04/09/94	3	2	Reba	BBJ
04/23/94	12	2	Fee	PoorHeart
04/30/94	5	2	Wolfman's	Harry
05/13/94	9	2	McGrupp	Scent
05/27/94	11	2	Suzie	My Friend
06/18/94	10	2	*OP2	MLB Jam
07/10/94	17	1	Horn	Rift
10/12/94	9	2	*OP2	Bowie
10/22/94	8	2	*OP2	Bowie
11/03/94	9	1	Wilson	Glide
11/14/94	4	2	*OP2	Bowie
12/01/94	12	2	*OP2	Mound
12/07/94	5	1	*OP1	RunJim
12/31/94	7	1	Mound	Divided
12/01/96	144	1	*OP1	PoorHeart
12/06/96	3	1	Wilson	PoorHeart
12/31/96	4	1	Axilla	PYITE
02/13/97	1	1	CharZero	Love Me
02/18/97	4	2	*OP2	AlsoSprac
02/23/97	4	2	Silent	Mike's
02/28/97	3	1	CTB	Stash
>> 12/31/97	**66**			

Pig in a Pen [2] [PiginPen]

Traditional

02/21/93	[520]	E	Paul&Silas	*CLE
11/16/94	194	1	Stash	TnWaltz
>> 12/31/97	**252**			

Purple Rain [30] [PurplRain]

By Prince

07/16/93	[579]	2	PoorHeart	Harry
07/18/93	2	2	YEM	Golgi
07/21/93	1	1a	BBJ	Daniel
07/24/93	3	2	Weekapaug	Daniel
07/25/93	1	2	Lizards	Harpua
07/27/93	1	1a	It's Ice	YEM
07/29/93	2	2	YEM	Daniel
07/31/93	2	2	Weekapaug	Daniel
08/03/93	2	2	Spark	Golgi
08/07/93	2	2	McGrupp	Antelope
08/14/93	6	2	YEM	Golgi
08/17/93	3	2	YEM	MSO
08/20/93	1	2	YEM	Cavern
08/28/93	5	2	BBJ	YEM
12/30/93	3	2	Weekapaug	Slave
04/13/94	9	2	Bowie	ACDCBag
04/30/94	14	2	Possum	BBFCM
05/07/94	5	2	Cb Jam	HYHU Jam
05/13/94	4	2	YEM	GTBT
05/25/94	9	2	Julius	Sqirm Coil
06/16/94	10	2	BBFCM	Golgi
10/08/94	25	2	Fluffhead	Harry
10/23/94	12	2	DWD	Harry
11/25/94	20	2	Mango	Antelope
12/04/94	7	2	YEM	GTBT
12/30/94	9	2	YEM	Harry
10/21/95	43	2	YEM	Harry
07/12/96	50	2	Antelope	NICU
07/15/96	2	2	Julius	Uncle Pen
08/06/96	12	2	BBFCM	Harry
>> 12/31/97	**124**			

Quinn the Eskimo [6] [Quinn]

By Bob Dylan

04/01/86	[6]	1	*OP1	HaveMercy
04/15/86	1	1a	PrepHipp	Slave
10/15/86	1	1a	Slave	Mike's
03/06/87	3	1	Golgi	Sally
04/29/87	4	2	Halley's	Quinn
08/10/87	3	1	Wilson	Divided
>> 12/31/97	**948**			

The Real Me [2] [Real Me]

By The Who

10/31/95	[785]	2	I am Sea	Quadrop
12/29/95	31	2	Bathtub	Bathtub
>> 12/31/97	**150**			

Ride Captain Ride [4] [Ride Capt.]

By Blues Image

03/23/87	[13]	1	Peaches	*CL1
05/28/89	91	2	Sanity	Peaches
12/12/92	395	E	*OPE	TweezRep
12/30/92	4	E	*OPE	Adeline
>> 12/31/97	**463**			

Rocky Top [151] [Rocky Top]

By Bordleaux/Felice

09/12/87	[23]	2	GTBT	Sally
05/23/88	15	1	YEM	Light Up
05/25/88	1	1	Curtain	FunkBitch
06/15/88	1	1	Wilson	McGrupp
06/18/88	1	2	Corrina	McGrupp
06/21/88	2	1	Fluffhead	Mustang
03/30/89	29	3	Satin Doll	*CL3
08/12/89	42	1a	Ya Mar	OYWD
08/17/89	2	1	Sloth	Harry
08/19/89	2	1	PYITE	Bold
10/22/89	15	1	Foam	Split&Melt
12/07/89	16	2	Suzie	Ya Mar
12/09/89	2	1	In a Hole	Bowie
02/10/90	18	2	ACDCBag	Donna
02/23/90	5	1	Carolina	Dinner
03/03/90	5	1	Reba	YEM
06/16/90	42	3	Fee	Caravan
11/04/90	21	2	Golgi	Llama
11/17/90	4	2	Lawn Boy	Donna
12/29/90	9	1	Lawn Boy	Horn
12/31/90	1	2	YEM	Brain
02/09/91	6	E2	Contact	*CLE2
02/16/91	3	2	Fluffhead	Love You
02/27/91	8	E	*OPE	*CLE
03/16/91	10	1	Curtain	Forbin's
03/23/91	4	1	Mockbird	*CL1
04/05/91	7	2	*OP2	Stash
04/12/91	3	1	Stash	Golgi
04/15/91	2	E	Sqirm Coil	*CLE
04/19/91	3	1	IDK	Mike's
04/21/91	2	1	Golgi	Wilson
04/22/91	1	E	Lawn Boy	*CLE
05/02/91	4	1	*OP1	Drums
05/04/91	2	2	Horn	Possum
05/12/91	4	2	ACDCBag	*CL2
05/17/91	2	2	Guelah	Landlady
07/12/91	4	1	ACDCBag	Cavern
07/20/91	6	2	YEM	*CL2
08/03/91	7	2	YEM	*CL2
09/27/91	3	E	Glide	*CLE
10/02/91	3	E	IDK	*CLE
10/04/91	2	E	Golgi	Love You
10/06/91	2	2	Sqirm Coil	*CL2
10/12/91	3	1	Lawn Boy	Contact

The Dude of Life ONSTAGE

When Phish took the stage for the first time at Nectar's, the Dude of Life joined them to sing the lyrics to Fluffhead, which he wrote. He recorded an album, *Crimes of the Mind*, with Phish in 1991, and he's shown up with Phish to share his songs. Performances by the Dude of Life in the 1990s include 9/13/90 New York City; 5/12/91 Burlington (vocals on Mike's); 8/3/91 Amy's Farm; 11/8/91 Tuscaloosa, AL; 11/20/92 Albany; 12/31/92 Boston (lead vocals on Diamond Girl); 5/6/93 (vocals in jam with ARU); 8/9/93 Toronto, ON; 8/28/93 Berkeley, CA; and 7/10/94 Saratoga, NY. The band seemed to be calling him onstage at the 12/13/97 show in Albany, but the Dude, who was in the audience, did not make an appearance.

Dude of Life Original	#P	Debut Date
Crimes of the Mind	5	08/03/91
Dahlia	1	09/13/90
Family Picture	1	11/08/91
Life Is a TV Show	1	11/08/91
The Revolution's Over	1	09/13/90
Self	4	09/13/90
She's Bitching Again	1	08/03/91

10/15/91	2	1	YEM	*CL1
10/17/91	1	E	Magilla	*CLE
10/24/91	4	E	Adeline	*CLE
10/28/91	3	E	Horn	*CLE
10/31/91	2	E	Glide	*CLE
11/07/91	4	E	Fee	*CLE
11/16/91	8	E	Glide	*CLE
11/19/91	1	E	Glide	*CLE
11/22/91	3	1	Stash	*CL1
11/24/91	2	E	Adeline	*CLE
11/30/91	1	E	Contact	*CLE
12/06/91	3	E	Lawn Boy	*CLE
12/31/91	2	E	Lawn Boy	TweezRep
03/11/92	3	2	Harry	*CL2
03/19/92	5	E	Sl Monkey	*CLE
03/21/92	2	E	Bouncing	*CLE
04/01/92	8	2	Contact	*CL2
04/03/92	1	E	*OPE	*CLE
04/05/92	2	E	Lawn Boy	*CLE
04/09/92	3	E	Sl Monkey	*CLE
04/12/92	1	E	Adeline	*CLE
04/15/92	2	E	Adeline	*CLE
04/18/92	3	2	Love You	*CL2
04/22/92	3	E	A-Train	*CLE
04/29/92	4	E	Horn	*CLE
05/01/92	2	E2	*CLE2	*CLE2
05/05/92	3	E	Contact	*CLE
05/07/92	2	E	Sl Monkey	*CLE
05/14/92	5	E	Sl Monkey	*CLE
05/15/92	1	1a	Adeline	*CL1
05/18/92	3	E	*OPE	*CLE
06/24/92	4	1a	Cavern	*CL1
07/01/92	3	1a	Adeline	*CL1
07/09/92	2	E	*OPE	*CLE
07/27/92	15	E	*OPE	*CLE
08/02/92	5	1a	Cavern	*CL1
08/28/92	11	1a	RunJim	*CL1
11/23/92	8	E	Sl Monkey	*CLE
12/02/92	6	E	Golgi	*CLE
12/04/92	2	E	Fee	*CLE
12/13/92	8	E	Adeline	*CLE
12/29/92	2	E	Carolina	*CLE
02/09/93	8	E	Cavern	*CLE
02/18/93	7	2	Adeline	*CL2
02/27/93	8	E	AmGrace	*CLE
03/09/93	6	E	AmGrace	*CLE
03/12/93	1	E	Carolina	*CLE
03/17/93	4	E	Adeline	*CLE
03/26/93	7	E	AmGrace	*CLE
04/02/93	6	E	AmGrace	*CLE
04/12/93	5	E2	*OPE2	*CLE2
04/18/93	5	E	AmGrace	*CLE
04/25/93	6	E	Carolina	*CLE
05/01/93	4	E	Carolina	*CLE
05/06/93	4	2	Jam	Rosie
07/18/93	8	E	*OPE	Freebird
07/22/93	2	2	Avenu	*CL2
07/29/93	6	E	*OPE	Freebird
08/09/93	8	E	*OPE	*CLE
08/16/93	6	E	AmGrace	*CLE
08/25/93	5	E	Bold	*CLE
12/30/93	5	E	*OPE	GTBT
04/14/94	10	E	*OPE	*CLE
05/12/94	21	E	AmGrace	*CLE
05/16/94	3	E	Fee	*CLE
05/29/94	11	E	Golgi	*CLE
06/10/94	2	E	Sl Monkey	*CLE
06/17/94	5	E	Sl Monkey	*CLE
06/24/94	6	E	*OPE	*CLE
07/01/94	5	E	*OPE	*CLE
07/10/94	7	E	Golgi	*CLE
07/15/94	3	E	Sl Monkey	*CLE
10/08/94	3	E	Long Time	*CLE
11/04/94	21	E	Lovin Cup	*CLE
11/26/94	12	E	*OPE	*CLE
12/04/94	6	E	Sl Monkey	*CLE
12/08/94	3	E	Silent	*CLE
06/14/95	13	E	Simple	TweezRep
06/26/95	10	E	Sl Monkey	*CLE
10/03/95	12	E	*OPE	*CLE
10/08/95	4	E	Bouncing	*CLE
10/20/95	7	E	Sl Monkey	*CLE
11/14/95	13	E	Wedge	*CLE
11/24/95	7	E	Life Mars	*CLE
12/04/95	7	E	Bouncing	*CLE
07/23/96	32	E	*OPE	*CLE
08/04/96	4	E	*OPE	*CLE
08/13/96	6	E	Sl Monkey	*CLE
10/19/96	7	E	Fee	*CLE
11/06/96	11	E	*OPE	*CLE
12/02/96	18	1	*OP1	ACDCBag
12/29/96	4	E	*OPE	*CLE
02/17/97	6	E	Sl Monkey	*CLE
02/23/97	5	E	Billy	*CLE
06/14/97	8	E	Circus	*CLE
06/20/97	3	E	Circus	*CLE
06/24/97	3	1	Caspian	*CL1
07/03/97	6	1	Theme	*CL1
07/06/97	2	2	Waste	FunkBitch
07/29/97	9	2	Sample	Sqirm Coil
08/09/97	7	E	Circus	*CLE
08/14/97	4	E	Bouncing	*CLE
08/16/97	1	2	Slave	Julius
11/28/97	11	1	Theme	*CL1
12/06/97	6	E	*OPE	*CLE
12/11/97	3	1	Lovin Cup	*CL1
12/28/97	3	2	Slave	Cavern
>> 08/17/97	**3**			

Roses Are Free [2] [Roses]

By Ween

12/11/97	[960]2		Drowned	BBFCM
12/31/97	6	2	Circus	Weekapaug
>> 12/31/97	**0**			

Satin Doll [12] [Satin Doll]

By Duke Ellington

06/20/88	[42]	2	Golgi	A-Train
07/11/88	2	1	*OP1	Suzie
07/23/88	2	2	Antelope	BlueBossa
08/03/88	3	2	Harry	FunkBitch
08/06/88	1	2	ACDCBag	Sanity
08/27/88	1	1	*OP1	YEM
09/12/88	2	1a	Timber Ho	Lizards
03/30/89	19	3	BBFCM	Rocky Top
12/31/89	84	1	Lizards	HwayHell
02/25/90	20	1	Bowie	Rift
04/12/93	378	1	Llama	Antelope
05/08/93	21	1	Reba	Cavern
>> 12/31/97	**391**			

Scarlet Begonias [2] [Scarlet]

By Jerry Garcia/Robert Hunter

12/01/84	[0]	1a	*OP1	Fire
05/03/85	2	1a	*OP1	Eyes
>> 12/31/97	**964**			

Sea and Sand [2] [Sea Sand]

By The Who

10/31/95	[785]2		5:15	Drowned
12/31/95	33	3	Weekapaug	YEM
>> 12/31/97	**148**			

Shaggy Dog [8] [Shaggy]

By Lightning Hopkins

10/15/86	[8]	1a	CamlWalk	Sally
10/31/86	1	1	Creek Jam	Fluffhead
08/21/87	10	1	Light Up	Wilson
02/07/88	10	1a	McGrupp	Golgi
05/15/88	8	1a	Fluffhead	Lizards
09/12/88	16	1a	*OP1	A-Train
11/03/88	4	1	Lizards	Foam
10/29/95	727	2	It's Ice	Possum
>> 12/31/97	**240**			

Soul Shakedown Party [2] [SSP]

By Bob Marley

02/17/97	[892]1		*OP1	Divided
02/20/97	2	1	Tweezer	Chalkdust
>> 12/31/97	**72**			

She Caught the Katy [2] [Katy]

By Taj Mahal

12/06/86	[10]	1a	WhipPost	ACDCBag
04/29/87	5	1	*OP1	Alumni
>> 12/31/97	**949**			

Skin It Back [6] [Skin It]

By Little Feat

10/31/86	9	2	Sanity	Icculus
12/06/86	1	1a	GTBT	Cities
04/29/87	5	1	Fire	Cities
08/21/87	4	1	Fee	Low Rider
09/27/87	5	1	GTBT	*CL1
07/25/88	24	3	*OP3	Harpua
>> 12/31/97	**915**			

Sneaking Sally Through the Alley [19] [Sally]

By Robert Palmer

10/30/85	[4]	1a	Slave	I Wish
10/15/86	4	1a	Fluffhead	*CL1
10/31/86	1	1	Dave's	Halley's
12/06/86	1	1a	Tush	PrepHipp
03/06/87	1	1	Quinn	*CL1
05/11/87	5	1a	Slave	Clod
08/29/87	5	1	Curtis	Makisupa
09/12/87	2	2	Rocky Top	Fee
11/19/87	4	1	YEM	Harry
01/30/88	1	1	Jesus	Alumni
03/11/88	3	1	FunkBitch	A-Train
03/21/88	2	1a	McGrupp	Divided
05/15/88	4	1a	Lizards	A-Train
05/25/88	2	1	Golgi	Suzie
06/20/88	3	2	Jam	Tela
07/12/88	3	2	Lizards	GTBT

FishmanSongs

Though rarer these days than the early '90s, "Fishman tunes"—during which Jon Fishman moves to center stage as Trey takes over on drums for a song—still surface. Fishman songs are often preceded and followed by a brief jam built around Argent's super-cheesy '80s hit Hold Your Head Up (HYHU), chosen because Fishman despises the song. For most of spring '92, the band segued into and out of Fishman songs with Cold as Ice by Foreigner. (#P is total number of times played by Phish.)

Song	#P	Debut	Last	Original Artist
Baby Lemonade	1	03/11/92	03/11/92	Syd Barrett
Bike	25	11/19/87	11/07/96	Syd Barrett
Cracklin' Rosie	46	03/07/92	08/14/96	Neil Diamond
Cecilia	1	06/25/97	06/25/97	Simon & Garfunkle
Cryin'	1	09/29/95	09/29/95	Aerosmith
Faht	12	11/23/92	12/02/95	Fishman
Great Gig in the Sky	11	03/14/93	07/05/94	Pink Floyd
If I Only Had a Brain	30	04/14/89	11/16/95	*The Wizard of Oz*
I Wanna Be Like You	9	04/04/94	06/10/94	*Jungle Book*
It's No Good Trying	3	12/07/90	12/28/90	Syd Barrett
Lengthwise	22	11/19/92	10/20/94	Fishman
Lonesome Cowboy Bill	3	05/16/95	06/10/95	Velvet Underground
Love You	75	04/20/89	07/05/97	Syd Barrett
Minute by Minute	2	09/13/90	09/15/90	Doobie Brothers
Purple Rain	30	07/16/93	08/06/96	Prince
Suspicious Minds	10	09/30/95	12/06/96	Elvis Presley
Terrapin	48	09/12/87	07/11/96	Syd Barrett
Touch Me	9	07/11/91	12/02/94	The Doors
Why Don't We Do It in the Road	4	10/31/94	02/23/97	The Beatles
Wind Beneath My Wings	1	11/28/95	11/28/95	Bette Midler

Note: Whipping Post, though sometimes a Fishman song, is not included here.

07/24/88 2 1 Mockbird Mike's
05/28/89 57 3 Sloth Jam
12/30/97 861 1 *OP1 Taste
>> 12/31/97 1

Something's Wrong with My Baby [3] [SWMB]

By Sam & Dave

04/24/93 [564]1 Caravan Sparkle
04/25/93 1 E *OPE Carolina
04/30/93 3 E *OPE AmGrace
>> 12/31/97 398

Somewhere over the Rainbow [2] [Rainbow]

From *The Wizard of Oz*

08/17/92 [469]2 A-Train Cavern
04/20/93 159 2 YEM *CL2
>> 12/31/97 338

Soul Shakedown Party [2] [Shakedown]

By Bob Marley

02/17/97 [892] OPI Divided Sky
02/20/97 Tweezer Chalkdust
>> 12/31/97 74

Sparks [13] [Sparks]

By The Who

03/23/87 [13] 1 YEM Fluffhead
04/29/87 2 2 Slave Jam
08/21/87 4 2 Golgi Flat Fee
11/19/87 8 1 McGrupp FunkBitch
09/24/88 27 2 Fee WhipPost
11/05/88 4 E Suzie Divided
09/13/90 164 2 A-Train Reba
08/02/93 370 2 Mike's Curtis
08/07/93 3 2 Mike's Kung
08/14/93 6 2 Antelope WalkAway
05/07/94 40 2 Tweezer Makisupa
10/29/94 65 2 TMWSIY Uncle Pen
11/29/96 173 2 Simple Sparkle
>> 12/31/97 87

Star Spangled Banner [9] [SSB]

By Francis Scott Key

10/17/96 [851]2 Lizards Bowie
10/21/96 3 1 *OP1 Sample
10/25/96 3 2 Cavern *CL2
10/31/96 4 1 CharZero *CL1
11/08/96 5 2 Mike's Weekapaug
11/19/96 8 2 YEM Fire
11/27/96 4 2 DWD Fire
12/28/96 7 2 Weekapaug *CL2
12/02/97 69 1 Taste *CL1
>> 08/17/97 12

Suspicious Minds [13] [Suspicious]

By Mark James

Originally Performed by Elvis Presley

09/30/95 [764]2 Weekapaug Cavern
10/06/95 4 2 Keyboard Slave
10/08/95 2 2 YEM Dog Faced
10/15/95 4 2 Sample Harry
10/19/95 2 2 Kung Possum
10/27/95 6 1 Fee *CL1
11/11/95 6 2 Frankstein Antelope
11/21/95 7 2 Keyboard Carolina
12/01/95 7 2 Wilson Bowie
12/11/95 7 2 Harry FunkBitch
12/15/95 3 1 Ha Ha Ha CTB
10/29/96 48 2 CharZero Slave
12/06/96 24 E Harpua Harpua
>> 12/31/97 82

Sweet Adeline [160] [Adeline]

By Richard H. Gerard

03/28/90 [185]2 Carolina WhipPost
04/25/90 15 2 Foam Reba
04/26/90 1 2 Cavern Curtis
04/28/90 1 1 *OP1 Oh Kee
05/04/90 3 1 WhipPost TMWSIY
05/13/90 5 2 FunkBitch La Grange
05/19/90 2 1 Alumni La Grange
05/23/90 1 1 Possum *CL1
06/05/90 4 2 *OP2 Divided
11/17/90 29 E Memories *CLE
04/19/91 56 1 Weekapaug *CL1
04/20/91 1 2 Suzie *CL2
04/21/91 1 1 Weekapaug *CL1
04/27/91 4 1 *OP1 Asse Fest
05/02/91 1 1 Bowie *CL1
05/03/91 1 1 Lizards *CL1
05/16/91 6 E *OPE *CLE
07/12/91 5 E *OPE Frankstein
07/23/91 8 2 Tweezer Dinner
07/25/91 2 1 ACDCBag Cavern
07/26/91 1 2 Tweezer Lizards
09/26/91 4 E PoorHeart *CLE
10/04/91 6 E *OPE Golgi
10/06/91 2 E *OPE Possum
10/11/91 2 E *OPE BBFCM
10/18/91 5 1 Lizards Antelope
10/24/91 3 E Memories Rocky Top
11/01/91 6 1 Divided *CL1
11/09/91 5 1 Brother *CL1
11/13/91 3 E MSO *CLE
11/21/91 6 E Memories Golgi
11/24/91 3 E *OPE Rocky Top
12/04/91 2 E *OPE Suzie
12/07/91 3 E *OPE Golgi
03/07/92 3 E *OPE Golgi
03/12/92 2 E *OPE Weigh
03/17/92 3 E Memories *CLE
03/19/92 1 E2 *OPE2 *CLE2
03/27/92 6 E Memories *CLE
03/28/92 1 2 IDK *CL2
03/31/92 2 E *OPE *CLE
04/05/92 4 1 Possum *CL1
04/12/92 4 E *OPE Rocky Top
04/15/92 2 E Memories Rocky Top
04/16/92 1 2 Memories Suzie
04/21/92 4 E *OPE Cavern
05/03/92 9 E Memories TweezRep
05/07/92 3 E *OPE Sl Monkey
05/15/92 6 1a YEM Rocky Top
05/16/92 1 E *OPE Suzie
06/23/92 5 1a Maze Uncle Pen
06/24/92 1 1a Llama Uncle Pen
06/30/92 2 1a Possum YEM
07/01/92 1 1a Split&Melt Rocky Top
07/12/92 5 1a *OP1 Chalkdust
07/19/92 6 1a Bowie *CL1
07/27/92 6 1a Llama *CL1
08/14/92 7 1a Llama *CL1
08/20/92 4 1a Bowie *CL1
08/25/92 3 1a Llama *CL1
08/28/92 2 1a Stash Sqirm Coil
08/30/92 2 1a Antelope *CL1
10/30/92 1 1a Stash YEM
11/20/92 2 E2 *OPE2 GTBT
11/22/92 2 1 Bathtub Antelope
11/25/92 2 1 Cavern Cavern
12/01/92 4 1 Maze Mike's
12/03/92 2 1 Reba Antelope
12/05/92 2 1 Divided Uncle Pen
12/07/92 2 2 Sqirm Coil *CL2
12/08/92 1 1 Mound Stash
12/10/92 1 1 Reba Cavern
12/13/92 3 E *OPE Rocky Top
12/28/92 1 1 Golgi Antelope
12/30/92 2 E Ride Capt *CLE
02/06/93 5 2 Stash All Things
02/10/93 3 E *OPE AmGrace
02/18/93 6 2 Memories Rocky Top
02/21/93 3 E *OPE GTBT
02/23/93 2 E *OPE PoorHeart
02/26/93 2 E Bold *CLE
03/03/93 3 2 Sqirm Coil *CL2
03/06/93 2 E *OPE PoorHeart
03/12/93 2 E *OPE Carolina
03/14/93 2 E Memories Golgi
03/16/93 1 1 *OP1 BurAlive
03/17/93 1 E *OPE Rocky Top
03/21/93 3 E Sl Monkey TweezRep
03/25/93 3 E BBJ *CLE
03/31/93 5 E ACDCBag *CLE
04/09/93 5 E *OPE Golgi
04/13/93 3 E Bold *CLE
04/17/93 3 E *OPE BBFCM
04/21/93 3 E *OPE Cavern
04/29/93 6 E My Friend *CLE
05/06/93 6 E *OPE Contact
08/11/93 25 E *OPE Bold
08/15/93 4 2 Glide Ginseng
08/24/93 5 E PoorHeart *CLE
12/29/93 5 2 Brain Chalkdust
04/06/94 5 E Nellie *CLE
04/13/94 5 E *OPE GTBT
04/24/94 10 E *OPE *CLE
04/30/94 4 1 Ginseng *CL1
05/03/94 2 1 Sample *CL1
05/08/94 4 E *OPE Golgi
05/16/94 5 1 Stash *CL1
05/19/94 2 E Nellie Fire
05/25/94 5 1 MSO Chalkdust
06/14/94 9 1 Guelah Guelah
06/21/94 5 2 Dog Faced Julius
06/24/94 3 1 Reba Sample
07/05/94 8 1 DWD *CL1
10/12/94 13 1 Julius *CL1
10/14/94 2 1 Bathtub Rift
10/16/94 2 2 Dog Faced Sample
10/21/94 3 E *OPE Foreplay
10/27/94 5 2 DWD *CL2
11/14/94 9 2 Nellie YEM
11/22/94 6 1 DWD *CL1
11/26/94 3 2 Bowie Lizards
11/28/94 1 1 Divided *CL1
12/01/94 2 1 Split&Melt *CL1
12/04/94 3 1 Mound Possum
12/08/94 3 2 Nellie Bowie
05/16/95 7 1a YEM Sample
06/09/95 3 2 AArmy Slave
06/13/95 2 E *OPE Julius
06/17/95 4 2 AArmy Harry
06/22/95 3 1 Cavern *CL1
06/24/95 2 2 AArmy Golgi
06/28/95 3 E *OPE Guitar
09/29/95 8 1 YEM Suzie
10/03/95 3 2 Faht Split&Melt
10/07/95 3 2 Harry *CL2
10/13/95 3 2 Guitar Sqirm Coil
10/22/95 7 E *OPE Sqirm Coil
10/29/95 5 1 Slave *CL1
11/10/95 3 2 ACDCBag *CL2
11/15/95 4 1 Split&Melt Sqirm Coil
11/22/95 5 1 Sample *CL1
12/05/95 9 E Theme *CLE
12/09/95 3 2 Crossroads *CL2
12/15/95 4 2 Bowie *CL2
12/29/95 4 1 Llama *CL1
07/05/96 6 E *OPE *CLE
07/07/96 2 1a Tweezer Uncle Pen
07/19/96 9 1a Foam Waste
08/04/96 7 2 Bowie Slave
08/13/96 6 2 Str Design Bowie
11/02/96 16 2 DayinLife *CL2
11/13/96 7 1 CharZero *CL1
12/02/96 13 2 Harry *CL2
12/06/96 2 2 Weekapaug GTBT
02/14/97 5 1 YEM Axilla
02/20/97 4 2 RunJim *CL2
02/25/97 4 2 La Grange *CL2
03/01/97 3 E Taste *CLE
07/09/97 19 1 Taste Harry
08/13/97 18 1 Wilson *CL1
>> 12/31/97 28

Swing Low Sweet Chariot [9] [SwingLow]

Traditional

10/15/86 [8] 1a Golgi CamlWalk
10/31/86 1 2 ACDCBag Peaches
03/23/87 4 2 Golgi *CL2
04/29/87 2 1 Golgi Fire
08/21/87 4 3 Sanity *CL3
08/29/87 2 2 Slave Curtain
06/18/88 20 2 BBFCM Antelope
10/20/89 90 2 Harry In a Hole
11/16/94 583 1 Bluegrass *CL1
>> 12/31/97 252

Take the A-Train [83] [A-Train]

By Duke Ellington

04/29/87 [15] 2 Dave's Halley's
09/27/87 9 1 Peaches Possum
10/14/87 1 1 Peaches YEM
11/19/87 2 3 LTJP CamlWalk
01/30/88 1 1 Alumni GTBT
03/11/88 3 1 Sally YEM
03/31/88 3 2 Mockbird Fire
05/14/88 2 2 Alumni *CL2
05/15/88 1 1a Sally Curtain
05/23/88 1 1a *OP1 Golgi
06/15/88 2 2 Dinner GTBT
06/20/88 2 2 Satin Doll Curtis
07/12/88 3 1 *OP1 Timber Ho
08/06/88 5 1 Cities FunkBitch
08/27/88 1 1a Mike's Golgi
09/12/88 2 1a Shaggy Fee
09/24/88 1 1 La Grange Divided
10/29/88 2 2 Mike's Fire
11/03/88 1 2 Bold Antelope
11/05/88 1 2 Possum Golgi
12/02/88 2 1 Bold Divided
01/26/89 1 1a Lizards Divided
02/06/89 3 1 Sanity Golgi
02/17/89 2 1a Golgi Alumni
03/03/89 3 2 Split&Melt Bowie
03/04/89 1 1 *OP1 IDK
05/05/89 19 2 IDK GTBT
05/13/89 7 1 WalkAway Split&Melt
05/20/89 4 2 Contact Bowie
05/27/89 3 1a YEM Fluffhead
05/28/89 1 2 Peaches Possum
08/19/89 14 2 Split&Melt Divided
11/09/89 22 1 YEM GTBT
11/10/89 1 2 HwayHell Antelope
11/30/89 4 2 Split&Melt Suzie
12/07/89 4 1 YEM ACDCBag
12/09/89 2 2 *OP2 Fluffhead
02/09/90 17 2 Wilson Alumni
02/24/90 7 1 IDK Antelope
03/07/90 5 1 Esther Lizards
03/08/90 1 1 Suzie Antelope
03/11/90 2 2 Dinner Sloth
03/28/90 2 1 Suzie RunJim
04/04/90 1 1 WalkAway Possum
04/07/90 3 2 FunkBitch Bold
04/12/90 4 1 YEM Cavern
04/18/90 2 1 MSO Possum
04/20/90 2 1 *OP1 Divided
05/23/90 16 2 McGrupp Antelope
06/05/90 4 1 Suzie Bowie
09/13/90 5 2 BurAlive Sparks
10/07/90 12 1 Weekapaug La Grange
02/16/91 31 1 Cavern Landlady
03/13/91 16 E *OPE BBFCM
03/23/91 6 E *OPE BBFCM
04/19/91 15 2 Sqirm Coil Antelope
05/03/91 8 E *OPE BBFCM
05/10/91 3 E *OPE HwayHell
05/17/91 4 1 Weekapaug *CL1
07/18/91 8 1 Stash Cavern
10/12/91 22 1 Chalkdust Dinner
10/27/91 9 2 Destiny Antelope
11/01/91 4 2 Weekapaug Tela
11/07/91 3 2 Bowie Love You
11/14/91 6 2 Tweezer Brain
11/24/91 8 2 Chalkdust YEM
03/14/92 12 1 Chalkdust Mike's
03/21/92 4 2 Suzie My Friend
04/05/92 11 2 Love You RunJim
04/13/92 5 1 Foam Bowie
04/22/92 7 E *OPE Rocky Top
04/29/92 4 1 Bouncing Bowie
05/06/92 6 2 Terrapin Golgi
07/14/92 23 2 YEM TweezRep
08/17/92 20 2 Terrapin Rainbow
11/21/92 13 2 Love You Llama
11/27/92 4 2 Faht Cavern
12/03/92 5 2 Rosie Cavern
12/30/92 12 2 Love You Llama
02/12/93 10 1 IDK Antelope
05/05/93 59 E Cavern Cavern
08/16/93 31 2 BBJ GTBT
04/13/94 19 2 Fee Bowie
>> 12/31/97 344

Take Me to the River [2] [River]

By Al Green

11/21/95 [795]2 Bowie Bowie
07/10/97 126 2 Ghost *CL2
>> 12/31/97 45

Tennessee Waltz [2] [TnWaltz]
By Patti Page

05/06/93 [573] 1 Been Gone FastTrain
11/16/94 141 1 PiginPen Bluegrass
>> 12/31/97 252

Terrapin [50] [Terrapin]
By Sid Barrett

09/12/87 [24] 2 Fire La Grange
07/23/88 23 2 Wilson Antelope
10/29/88 10 3 Foam BBFCM
04/30/89 30 1a Antelope Fluffhead
01/27/90 74 2 Antelope Divided
05/06/90 46 2 Bowie Jaeger
06/09/90 14 2 Antelope Harpua
10/12/90 16 2 Landlady Divided
10/30/90 2 2 Fluffhead BurAlive
02/15/91 26 2 Harry Chalkdust
03/13/91 17 2 Tweezer Oh Kee
03/22/91 5 2 Guelah Mike's
05/04/91 25 E *OPE RunJim
05/18/91 7 2 Bowie Lizards
10/03/91 23 E *OPE TweezRep
10/06/91 3 1 Brother Golgi
10/19/91 8 2 Oh Kee Harry
10/24/91 2 2 Bouncing Possum
11/09/91 11 2 Landlady MSO
11/13/91 3 1 IDK YEM
11/16/91 3 2 Chalkdust Llama
12/07/91 11 2 Lizards Harpua
03/20/92 10 2 Harry Possum
04/09/92 15 2 Chalkdust Cavern
04/16/92 4 2 PoorHeart Carolina
04/25/92 8 E *OPE PoorHeart
05/01/92 3 2 Llama Golgi
05/06/92 4 2 Chalkdust A-Train
05/08/92 2 2 Chalkdust Harry
05/12/92 3 2 Chalkdust PoorHeart
08/17/92 38 2 Horn A-Train
11/20/92 12 2 Harry Lengthwise
11/30/92 7 2 Sqirm Coil Cavern
12/29/92 14 2 Weekapaug Bayou
02/03/93 3 2 Lifeboy BBJ
02/12/93 8 2 Ya Mar Harry
02/20/93 6 2 BBJ Harry
02/23/93 3 2 Weekapaug Possum
02/27/93 3 2 Weekapaug Fee
03/03/93 2 2 FEFY Adeline
03/08/93 3 E *OPE Chalkdust
03/24/93 11 2 Silent GTBT
04/01/93 7 2 BBJ Cavern
04/12/93 6 2 YEM TweezRep
04/29/93 13 2 Weekapaug Sqirm Coil
06/13/94 95 2 BBJ Slave
07/01/94 14 2 Possum Harry
11/20/94 42 2 Rift Julius
06/13/95 25 1 Reba Sparkle
07/11/96 84 2 Lizards YEM
>> 12/31/97 139

Timber Ho [45] [Timber Ho]
By Josh White

04/29/87 [16] 3 Boogie Slave
08/29/87 6 2 Harry ACDCBag
11/19/87 6 2 *OP2 Fluffhead
02/07/88 2 1a ACDCBag *CL1
03/21/88 4 1a Boogie Lizards
06/15/88 7 1 Fee IDK
07/12/88 5 1 A-Train Fluffhead
09/12/88 8 1a Bold Satin Doll
10/29/88 3 3 BBFCM Slave
11/11/88 3 2 Bold Lizards
02/07/89 6 2 Lizards Contact
10/06/89 61 1a *OP1 Mike's
12/08/89 24 2 Tela Slave
06/16/90 71 1 Bouncing Lawn Boy
12/30/92 282 1 Bowie Bowie
07/03/95 257 2 *OP2 Bowie
10/03/95 6 2 *OP2 It's Ice
10/08/95 4 2 CTB Ya Mar
10/20/95 7 2 *OP2 Scent
10/28/95 6 1 Mound Uncle Pen
11/16/95 9 1 Simple Guyute
11/25/95 6 2 *OP2 Kung
11/29/95 2 2 *OP2 Sparkle
12/04/95 4 2 *OP2 Sparkle
12/09/95 4 2 *OP2 Wilson
12/14/95 3 2 Tweezer Tweezer
12/28/95 4 2 *OP2 Theme
07/21/96 19 1 Fee Johnny B.
08/12/96 11 2 *OP2 Sparkle
10/25/96 12 2 Caspian TMWSIY
11/03/96 6 2 *OP2 Divided
11/11/96 5 2 *OP2 Divided
11/18/96 5 1 CTB Poor Heart
11/30/96 7 2 Also Sprac Taste
12/04/96 3 1 Uncle Pen Sample
12/30/96 4 2 *OP2 Uncle Pen
02/17/97 5 1 Guyute Billy
07/01/97 23 2 Jam Bathtub
07/26/97 12 2 *OP2 Bowie
08/11/97 10 2 *OP2 Piper
11/16/97 7 2 *OP2 Simple
11/28/97 7 2 *OP2 Limb
12/07/97 7 2 *OP2 Wolfman's
12/09/97 1 2 Simple Contact
12/31/97 7 2 *OP2 Mike's
>> 12/31/97 0

Time Loves a Hero [3] [TLAH]
By Little Feat

10/29/88 [56] 1 Lizards Golgi
11/03/88 1 1 GTBT WalkAway
11/05/88 1 1 Slave Fire
>> 12/31/97 908

Touch Me [9] [Touch Me]
By The Doors

07/11/91 [320] 2 Weekapaug Frankstein
07/12/91 1 2 Weekapaug Oh Kee
07/14/91 2 3 Weekapaug Harry
07/19/91 3 1 Gumbo *CL1
07/21/91 2 E Gumbo *CLE
07/23/91 1 2 Gumbo *CL2
07/25/91 2 2 Gumbo Magilla
07/27/91 2 E *OPE Contact
12/03/94 394 2 Slave Julius
>> 12/31/97 239

Tush [2] [Tush]
By ZZ Top

12/06/86 [10] 1a Dog Log Sally
08/10/87 8 2 Anarchy Reagan
>> 12/31/97 948

Uncle Pen [176] [Uncle Pen]
By Bill Monroe

03/28/90 [185] 1 Tweezer Oh Kee
04/04/90 1 2 Lizards Sloth
04/05/90 1 2 Reba Jesus
04/06/90 1 1 YEM Divided
04/08/90 2 1 Suzie Possum
04/09/90 1 2 Esther La Grange
04/12/90 2 1 WalkAway Possum
04/18/90 2 1 Weekapaug Curtain
04/22/90 4 1 Divided Oh Kee
04/26/90 2 1 YEM Dinner
04/28/90 1 1 Suzie Dinner
04/29/90 1 1a Bouncing Divided
05/04/90 2 2 Sloth Tweezer
05/06/90 1 1 Bouncing Reba
05/10/90 1 1 Suzie Bouncing
05/11/90 1 1 Weekapaug Bouncing
05/13/90 2 1 RunJim Divided
05/23/90 3 1 Suzie Bouncing
05/31/90 2 1a IDK Divided
06/05/90 2 1 Sqirm Coil Mike's
06/07/90 1 2 Tweezer Divided
06/09/90 2 1 Tweezer Mike's
06/16/90 1 1 Horn Bouncing
09/22/90 7 2 Fee Bouncing
10/04/90 3 1 Sloth Bowie
10/05/90 1 2 Alumni Split&Melt
10/07/90 2 1 Divided Stash
10/12/90 2 1 Bouncing Cavern
10/30/90 2 1 Suzie Cavern
10/31/90 1 E *OPE BBFCM
11/03/90 2 2 Fee Reba
11/08/90 2 1 Foam Llama
11/26/90 5 2 *OP2 Forbin's
02/07/91 12 2 Guelah Cavern
02/14/91 3 E *OPE La Grange
02/21/91 5 2 Guelah Bowie
03/17/91 16 1 Fluffhead Stash
03/23/91 3 2 Lizards Cavern
04/04/91 6 E Contact *CLE
04/12/91 4 1 Llama Divided
04/16/91 3 2 BurAlive Tweezer
04/21/91 4 2 Llama Harry
04/22/91 1 2 Bathtub Landlady
04/26/91 2 2 *OP2 Split&Melt
10/03/91 34 1 Foam It's Ice
10/12/91 6 1 Tweezer Fluffhead
10/13/91 1 E Eliza *CLE
10/18/91 3 2 Brother Guelah
10/24/91 3 2 Lizards Tube
11/01/91 6 1 Fluffhead Tube
11/12/91 7 1 Golgi Brother
11/14/91 2 1 Wilson Llama
11/16/91 2 1 Landlady Wilson
11/19/91 1 1 *OP1 Foam
11/21/91 2 2 Mango Tweezer
11/23/91 2 1 Chalkdust Brother
11/30/91 2 2 Chalkdust Harry
12/06/91 3 1 Reba Sqirm Coil
03/12/92 6 2 Sqirm Coil Bowie
03/20/92 5 2 Cavern Harry
03/24/92 2 2 Brother IDK
03/26/92 2 1 Fluffhead NICU
03/30/92 3 2 Golgi Tweezer
04/01/92 2 2 Silent Tweezer
04/04/92 2 1 Reba Chalkdust
04/06/92 2 2 Rosie Cavern
04/09/92 2 1 Reba Stash
04/13/92 2 1 Golgi Stash
04/15/92 1 1 Stash Cavern
04/17/92 2 2 Tweezer Rosie
04/21/92 3 1 Suzie Split&Melt
04/23/92 2 1 Split&Melt Guelah
04/24/92 1 1 Mockbird Sloth
04/30/92 3 1 Reba Stash
05/03/92 3 1 It's Ice Fee
05/06/92 2 2 Bouncing Chalkdust
05/08/92 2 1 Reba It's Ice
05/10/92 2 1a Stash Cavern
05/12/92 1 1 BurAlive Horn
06/23/92 8 1a Adeline BBFCM
06/24/92 1 1a Adeline Guelah
06/27/92 1 1a Bouncing Bowie
07/12/92 7 1a Fluffhead Maze
07/15/92 2 1 My Friend Split&Melt
07/28/92 11 1a Bouncing Sqirm Coil
08/19/92 9 1a YEM Llama
08/30/92 8 1a *OP1 Landlady
11/21/92 4 2 Silent Guelah
11/30/92 6 2 Glide YEM
12/01/92 1 2 All Things Llama
12/03/92 2 1 Bouncing Chalkdust
12/05/92 2 1 Adeline Golgi
12/08/92 3 1 Mockbird Guelah
12/11/92 2 1 It's Ice Stash
12/13/92 2 1 Fee Stash
12/29/92 2 1 Wilson Stash
02/04/93 4 2 Lawn Boy BBJ
02/06/93 2 2 Lifeboy BBJ
02/11/93 4 2 Wilson Mike's
02/13/93 2 2 Wilson Tweezer
02/21/93 6 1 PYITE Horn
02/22/93 1 2 It's Ice Tweezer
02/25/93 2 2 YEM BBJ
03/02/93 3 2 My Friend Tweezer
03/05/93 2 2 Guelah Mike's
03/08/93 2 2 Cavern Stash
03/13/93 3 2 Glide BBJ
03/18/93 4 2 YEM BBJ
03/19/93 1 2 It's Ice Sample
03/22/93 2 1 Guelah Stash
03/25/93 2 2 Sample Forbin's
03/27/93 2 1 My Friend Sample
03/31/93 3 2 Bouncing Harry
04/02/93 2 2 Sample Llama
04/10/93 4 1 My Friend Chalkdust
04/13/93 2 2 Sloth FEFY
04/16/93 2 2 Silent BBJ
04/20/93 3 1 Glide Lawn Boy
04/22/93 2 2 YEM Love You
04/25/93 3 2 Contact BBJ
04/29/93 2 1 Split&Melt Sloth
05/02/93 3 2 BBJ Bouncing
05/06/93 3 2 Tela BBJ
07/18/93 8 1 Divided Cavern
07/23/93 3 2 My Friend BBJ
07/30/93 6 1 Llama Stash
08/06/93 4 2 Sqirm Coil YEM
08/21/93 12 2 Horn Fee
08/24/93 1 1 Silent Maze
12/28/93 4 2 FEFY Harry
04/11/94 10 2 Mockbird Sample
04/17/94 5 2 Wolfman's Sloth
04/22/94 4 1 Horn PYITE
04/29/94 5 2 Fee Mike's
05/06/94 5 2 Golgi Sample
05/12/94 4 2 Silent Fluffhead
05/17/94 4 2 Lifeboy BBJ
05/25/94 6 1 Sample Stash
06/14/94 9 1 My Friend IDK
06/23/94 7 2 Axilla 2 Tweezer
07/05/94 9 1 If I Could Stash
07/14/94 6 2 If I Could YEM
10/22/94 15 E *OPE TweezRep
10/29/94 6 2 Sparks YEM
12/01/94 19 1 Sample FEFY
12/29/94 10 1 Silent IDK
06/10/95 7 2 Fee Mike's
06/17/95 5 1 Fee Julius
06/20/95 2 1 Caspian Mike's
07/01/95 9 2 Theme Stash
09/30/95 6 1 Reba Horn
10/08/95 6 1 Caspian Free
10/13/95 2 2 Tube Theme
10/17/95 3 1 Stash ACDCBag
10/22/95 4 2 Life Mars Slave
10/28/95 4 1 Timber Ho Sample
11/11/95 5 2 Suzie Fluffhead
11/16/95 4 2 Lifeboy Ha Ha Ha
11/22/95 4 1 Fluffhead Cavern
11/28/95 3 2 Suzie Free
12/07/95 7 E *OPE *CLE
12/28/95 9 2 IDK Slave
07/07/96 9 1a Adeline Cavern
07/15/96 6 2 PurplRain Antelope
11/14/96 40 1 ACDCBag Wolfman's
11/27/96 8 1 Sloth Free
11/30/96 2 1 Old Home Caspian
12/04/96 3 1 Horn Timber Ho
12/30/96 4 2 Timber Ho ACDCBag
02/14/97 3 1 Billy Antelope
02/20/97 4 2 CharZero Stash
03/02/97 8 1 Johnny B. Sample
06/22/97 8 1a Dirt CharZero
07/05/97 8 1a Bouncing Sample
07/30/97 11 2 Bouncing Caspian
08/17/97 12 2 Bathtub Also Sprac
>> 12/31/97 25

Undone [5] [Undone]
By The Guess Who

03/30/89 [72] 2 No Good La Grange
08/19/89 2 2 Bowie Alumni
10/22/89 15 E *OPE *CLE
11/30/89 12 2 Mockbird Fee
12/07/89 4 2 Possum *CL2
>> 12/31/97 817

Walk Away [44] [WalkAway]
By the James Gang

07/23/88 [46] 1 Possum Bold
07/24/88 1 1 *OP1 Golgi
08/03/88 2 2 FunkBitch *CL2
08/27/88 2 1a FunkBitch Fluffhead
09/08/88 1 1 Peaches Slave
09/24/88 2 2 Lizards Possum
10/29/88 2 2 Alumni Divided
11/03/88 1 1 TLAH Lizards
11/05/88 1 1 Golgi Fluffhead
02/05/89 5 1 GTBT Harry
02/06/89 1 2 GTBT Harry
02/18/89 3 1a Lizards Possum
03/03/89 2 2 Possum Forbin's
04/20/89 12 2 Divided YEM
05/13/89 15 1 Foam A-Train
06/30/89 15 2 *OP2 ACDCBag
08/17/89 5 2 *OP2 ACDCBag
09/09/89 8 2 Harry Possum
10/20/89 7 2 No Dogs Dinner
10/26/89 3 2 Reba Bathtub
10/31/89 2 1 Fee Bathtub
12/07/89 13 2 Ya Mar Lizards
02/09/90 19 1 YEM Bouncing
02/23/90 6 1 Ya Mar Bouncing
03/28/90 11 1 Fee Tweezer
04/04/90 1 1 YEM A-Train
04/07/90 3 1 Landlady *CL1
04/08/90 1 2 Golgi Lizards
04/12/90 3 1 Ya Mar Uncle Pen
04/18/90 2 2 Reba Oh Kee

Doin' It A Cappella

Phish's small crop of a cappella songs seems to grow at the rate of roughly one a year, with 1996's addition being the Star Spangled Banner (Phish has also performed it four times before NBA and NHL games). Below is a list of Phish's a cappella choices, including total number of times played, the debut date and most recent performance, and the original artist or composer.

Song	#P	Debut	Last	Original Artist
Amazing Grace	109	02/03/93	12/31/96	John Newton
Carolina	61	01/20/90	08/17/97	Donaldson/Kahn
Freebird	19	07/15/93	06/19/94	Lynyrd Skynyrd
Hello My Baby	42	09/27/95	11/16/97	Howard/Singer/Emerson
Memories	37	11/17/90	07/06/94	Traditional
Star Spangled Banner	9	10/17/96	12/02/97	Francis Scott Key
Sweet Adeline	159	03/28/90	08/13/97	Richard H. Gerard
Who by Fire	1	04/23/93	04/23/93	Leonard Cohen

04/29/90 8 1a Bouncing Divided
05/24/90 11 2 Fee Harry
10/18/91 137 E Sparkle Sqirm Coil
11/02/91 10 2 Guelah Landlady
02/20/93 158 2 Tweezer Tweezer
03/28/93 26 2 *OP2 RunJim
04/18/93 14 2 Ya Mar Love You
04/30/93 9 2 Tweezer Mound
07/15/93 10 2 Lizards Daniel
07/22/93 5 2 Tweezer Sparkle
07/30/93 7 E *OPE AmGrace
08/14/93 11 2 Sparks Have Mercy
12/29/93 11 2 BBFCM BBJ
05/07/94 29 2 SE Jam Jam
>> 12/31/97 325

When the Circus Comes [15] [Circus]

By Los Lobos

02/13/97 [889]2 Slave Maze
02/16/97 2 2 Simple Swept
02/20/97 3 1 Gumbo Bowie
02/22/97 2 1 NICU Talk
06/14/97 9 E *OPE Rocky Top
06/20/97 3 E *OPE Rocky Top
07/01/97 7 E *OPE *CLE
07/22/97 9 E *OPE Harry
07/31/97 6 2 RunJim Vultures
08/09/97 5 E *OPE Rocky Top
08/17/97 6 E *OPE TweezRep
11/17/97 4 2 Jesus YEM
11/30/97 8 2 Piper Antelope
12/13/97 9 2 Llama Weekapaug
12/31/97 4 2 Piper Roses
>> 12/31/97 0

While My Guitar Gently Weeps [16] [Guitar]

By The Beatles

10/31/94 [707]2 Bungalow WarmGun
11/02/94 1 1 Scent *CL1
12/08/94 23 1 Lizards *CL1
06/07/95 8 E *OPE *CLE
06/14/95 5 2 AArmy *CL2
06/22/95 6 E AArmy *CLE
06/28/95 5 E Adeline *CLE
07/02/95 4 1 Rift *CL1
10/05/95 8 E *OPE *CLE
10/13/95 5 2 Lizards Adeline
10/20/95 5 2 Gumbo LongJourn
10/28/95 6 E *OPE *CLE
11/15/95 8 2 Fee *CL2
12/04/95 13 1 HelloBaby *CL1
12/11/95 5 E *OPE *CLE
02/26/97 90 1 Dog Log *CL1
>> 12/31/97 67

Whipping Post [31] [WhipPost]

By the Allman Brothers Band

05/03/85 [2] 1a Eyes McGrupp
11/23/85 3 1a Mike's Antelope
12/06/86 5 1a LDB Jam Katy
08/10/87 8 2 Jesus Anarchy
11/19/87 9 3 Curtis LTJP
01/30/88 1 2 Sloth *CL2
05/15/88 9 1a Flat Fee ACDCBag
05/25/88 2 2 Fluffhead *CL2
06/15/88 1 2 GTBT Reagan
09/08/88 12 2 OYWD *CL2
09/24/88 2 2 Sparks *CL2
10/29/88 2 2 Halley's Fee
11/03/88 1 2 *OP2 Contact
11/11/88 2 2 Lizards *CL2
02/05/89 4 1 Mockbird Corrina
02/06/89 1 2 Icculus Corrina
02/07/89 1 3 Slave *CL3
05/09/89 28 2 Harpua *CL2
05/13/89 3 E Fire *CLE
03/07/90 84 E *OPE *CLE
03/09/90 2 E *OPE *CLE
03/28/90 3 2 Adeline FunkBitch
04/09/90 6 2 Tweezer *CL2
05/04/90 14 1 *OP1 Adeline
05/10/90 2 E *OPE *CLE
06/05/90 10 E *OPE Golgi
10/28/91 140 2 Harpua HwayHell
12/06/91 24 2 Llama Possum
12/05/92 112 2 Weekapaug TweezRep
04/20/93 67 2 YEM Golgi
08/10/96 284 2 Fluffhead Harry
>> 12/31/97 122

Why Don't We Do It in the Road [4] [DoInRoad]

By The Beatles

10/31/94 [707]2 Don'tPass I Will
12/10/94 26 2 Weekapaug PoorHeart
06/25/95 20 2 Mike's Weekapaug
02/23/97 144 2 Mike's GTBT
>> 12/31/97 69

Wipeout [2] [Wipeout]

By The Ventures

04/15/91 [299]2 *OP2 Mike's
04/27/91 9 2 Sqirm Coil TweezRep
>> 12/31/97 658

Ya Mar [140] [Ya Mar]

By the Mustangs

05/11/87 [16] 1a Makisupa *CL1
08/09/87 1 2 YEM Divided
08/29/87 4 1 Mustang TMWSIY
05/25/88 18 3 IDK One Love
06/20/88 3 1 Wilson *CL1
03/30/89 30 1 OYWD Fluffhead
05/05/89 17 1 YEM Fluffhead
05/09/89 4 1 Peaches Mike's
05/21/89 8 1a YEM ACDCBag
05/28/89 3 3 Jam Jesus
06/23/89 5 2 Harry Split&Melt
08/12/89 5 1a ACDCBag Rocky Top
08/17/89 2 1 *OP1 Suzie
08/23/89 3 2 Mockbird YEM
08/26/89 1 2 Bold Slave
09/09/89 4 2 *OP2 YEM
10/01/89 1 1 Foam Oh Kee
10/07/89 2 1 Golgi Mike's
10/14/89 3 1 Golgi Split&Melt
10/21/89 2 1 Fee In A Hole
10/22/89 1 1 Suzie Foam
11/09/89 7 1 Golgi Curtain
11/30/89 5 1 Divided Oh Kee
12/07/89 4 2 Rocky Top WalkAway
12/08/89 1 1 Split&Melt Reba
12/29/89 4 1 Divided Oh Kee
12/31/89 2 2 Weekapaug Split&Melt
01/27/90 4 1 Bathtub Oh Kee
02/09/90 8 2 Dinner Reba
02/23/90 6 1 Dinner WalkAway
03/01/90 3 1 Golgi Divided
03/08/90 4 1 Possum Foam
03/09/90 1 1 Caravan Bouncing
03/11/90 1 2 Sloth Split&Melt
03/28/90 2 1 Possum Fee
04/05/90 2 1 Possum Bowie
04/06/90 1 1 Divided Dinner
04/12/90 5 1 Golgi WalkAway
04/20/90 4 1 Alumni Cavern
04/25/90 3 2 Reba YEM
04/29/90 3 1a Possum YEM
05/11/90 5 2 Tweezer Love You
05/19/90 4 1 Golgi Alumni
05/23/90 1 1 Divided YEM
06/05/90 4 1 Weekapaug Oh Kee
06/16/90 4 3 La Grange Foam
09/16/90 4 1a Reba Tube
10/05/90 7 2 Curtain Alumni
02/15/91 32 2 Bathtub Guelah
04/15/91 35 1 Sloth Foam
04/20/91 4 2 Sloth Split&Melt
05/10/91 10 1 Cavern Dinner
08/03/91 21 3 Stash Fluffhead
10/15/91 15 2 Love You Golgi
10/24/91 5 1 Stash Divided
10/31/91 5 1 Brother Sloth
11/12/91 8 E *OPE BBFCM
11/16/91 4 1 Stash Cavern
12/05/91 9 1 Split&Melt Fluffhead
04/13/92 29 2 Magilla Sqirm Coil
04/24/92 9 2 Cavern Foam
02/12/93 95 2 YEM Terrapin
02/19/93 5 2 YEM BBJ
02/27/93 7 2 BBJ Mike's
03/21/93 14 2 Tweezer Llama
04/01/93 9 2 Fee Tweezer
04/18/93 11 2 Mike's WalkAway
04/29/93 8 2 It's Ice Mound
05/05/93 5 2 BBJ YEM
05/30/93 5 1a Foam Silent
07/16/93 2 1 My Friend BurAlive
07/22/93 4 1 Mound PoorHeart
07/28/93 5 1 RunJim Sample
07/31/93 3 1 Sample Split&Melt
08/03/93 2 1 Silent Llama
08/13/93 7 2 Bathtub Mike's
08/24/93 7 2 Horn Mike's
12/28/93 6 1 Suzie It's Ice
04/05/94 5 2 Peaches Tweezer
04/10/94 4 2 My Friend Antelope
04/18/94 7 2 BBJ Mike's
04/24/94 5 1 My Friend Axilla 2
05/06/94 8 1 My Friend Stash
06/29/94 34 E *OPE TweezRep
07/10/94 9 2 Glide Mike's
10/14/94 11 E *OPE Cavern
10/27/94 10 2 Julius Tweezer
11/04/94 6 2 Weekapaug Golgi
11/30/94 14 2 Fixin' Mike's
12/07/94 6 1 Sloth Split&Melt
06/16/95 16 1 Esther Cry Baby
06/25/95 7 1 *OP1 ACDCBag
07/01/95 5 1 *OP1 Llama
09/29/95 5 2 Free Split&Melt
10/06/95 5 1 *OP1 Stash
10/08/95 2 2 Timber Ho Sample
10/13/95 2 1 *OP1 Also Sprac
10/20/95 5 1 My Friend Ha Ha Ha
10/25/95 4 1 *OP1 Sample
10/31/95 4 1 Wilson Sparkle
11/11/95 3 1 Silent Stash
11/16/95 4 1 Mound Simple
11/21/95 3 2 Glide Mike's
11/29/95 5 1 ACDCBag Reba
12/04/95 4 2 Sparkle Antelope
12/12/95 6 1 *OP1 Sample
12/16/95 3 1 Fog Sloth
12/30/95 4 2 *OP2 Free
04/26/96 2 1a *OP1 ACDCBag
06/06/96 1 E *OPE Fire
07/10/96 4 1a Chalkdust Split&Melt
07/12/96 2 1 Split&Melt FunkBitch
07/17/96 3 1a Bowie FunkBitch
07/24/96 6 1a Chalkdust Julius
08/02/96 2 1 *OP1 DWD
08/07/96 4 1 Stash Gumbo
08/12/96 2 1 *OP1 Split&Melt
08/16/96 3 1 Bathtub ACDCBag
10/17/96 3 2 *OP2 Chalkdust
10/23/96 5 2 Brother Tweezer
10/27/96 3 2 Caspian Tweezer
11/02/96 3 1 *OP1 Julius
11/13/96 7 1 It's Ice Taste
11/19/96 5 2 *OP1 ACDCBag
11/27/96 4 1 My Friend Chalkdust
12/02/96 4 2 *OP2 Divided
12/30/96 5 1 *OP1 Sloth
02/14/97 3 2 ACDCBag DWD
02/21/97 5 2 *OP2 Antelope
02/28/97 5 1 Steep CharZero
07/01/97 15 1 Horn Limb
07/10/97 6 2 Magilla Ghost
07/25/97 5 2 Taste Drums
07/31/97 4 1 Ghost Dogs Stole
08/06/97 3 1 ACDCBag YEM
08/14/97 6 1 *OP1 FunkBitch
11/26/97 11 2 Cities PYITE
12/02/97 4 2 Dog Faced Weekapaug
12/13/97 8 1 *OP1 Axilla
12/31/97 4 1 EmRescue MSO
>> 12/31/97 0

Yerushalayim Schel Zahav [12] [YSZahav]

By N. Scheimer-Sapir

07/16/93 [579]2 YEM YEM
07/24/93 6 2 Mike's Weekapaug
06/26/94 88 2 S&M Jam *CL2
06/30/94 2 2 YEM YEM
07/02/94 2 2 Mike's I am H2
07/08/94 4 2 Reba It's Ice
07/15/94 5 2 It's Ice Dog Faced
10/13/94 7 2 Mike's Weekapaug
10/25/94 9 2 Weekapaug Glide
11/14/94 11 2 Bowie Slave
11/22/94 6 2 Jam Cry Baby
12/31/94 18 2 Mike's Weekapaug
>> 12/31/97 229

• Cover Song Chart •

The following is a list of all cover songs performed by Phish at least twice, not including Fishman cover songs, Dude of Life songs, or a cappella songs [see elsewhere]. Total number of times played (#P) are calculated through 12/31/97.

Note: "Original Artist" refers either to the artist who first wrote/recorded the song or the artist who popularized it.

Song	#P	Debut	Last	Original Artist
All Along the Watchtower	2	04/21/94	10/22/96	Bob Dylan
Also Sprach Zarathustra	98	07/16/93	12/31/97	Deodato, after Strauss
Auld Lang Syne	8	12/31/90	12/31/97	Robert Burns
Avenu Malkenu	59	05/11/87	11/29/97	Traditional
Back in the USSR	2	10/31/94	12/06/94	The Beatles
Ballad of Curtis Lowe	22	04/29/87	08/02/93	Lynyrd Skynyrd
Bats and Mice	2	08/25/93	08/26/93	Baby Gramps
Beaumont Rag	2	10/14/94	10/18/94	Traditional
Beauty of My Dreams	21	02/16/97	12/31/97	Del McCoury
Bill Bailey	3	07/28/93	11/18/95	Traditional
Blackbird	2	10/31/94	11/22/94	The Beatles
Blue Bayou	2	07/14/92	12/29/92	Roy Orbison
Bold as Love	52	07/11/88	12/28/97	Jimi Hendrix
Butter Them Biscuits	4	11/18/94	11/22/94	Jeff Mosier
Caravan	37	01/20/90	12/29/96	Duke Ellington
Cinnamon Girl	2	03/18/97	07/31/97	Neil Young
Cities	18	12/01/84	12/28/97	Talking Heads
Communication Breakdown	3	01/27/90	09/15/90	Led Zeppelin
Corrina Corrina	11	03/06/87	02/06/89	Bo Carter/Taj Mahal
Crosseyed and Painless	5	10/31/96	08/13/97	Talking Heads
Crossroads	8	05/08/93	12/29/97	Robert Johnson
Cry Baby Cry	3	10/31/94	06/16/95	The Beatles
Daniel (Saw the Stone)	15	07/15/93	02/23/97	Traditional
Day in the Life	43	06/10/95	12/30/97	The Beatles
Donna Lee	20	11/11/87	07/12/91	Duke Ellington
Don't You Wanna Go	5	05/16/95	09/28/95	Missionary Sisters
Drowned	7	10/31/95	12/28/97	The Who
Emotional Rescue	2	11/21/97	12/31/97	Rolling Stones
Eyes of the World	2	12/01/94	05/03/85	Garcia/Hunter
Fire	95	12/01/84	12/31/97	Jimi Hendrix
Fixin' to Die	2	11/17/94	11/30/94	Booker White
Foreplay	16	10/07/94	12/09/94	Boston
Frankenstein	48	11/11/89	12/30/97	Edgar Winters Group
Funky Bitch	91	03/06/87	12/28/97	Son Seals
Funny as It Seems	3	06/20/97	08/09/97	J.J. Cale
Ginseng Sullivan	51	08/11/93	12/13/97	Norman Blake
Going Down Slow	2	09/13/90	09/14/90	Allman Brothers
Good Times Bad Times	138	12/06/86	12/29/97	Led Zeppelin
Hall and Solace	72	09/13/90	02/28/97	Earl Scruggs
Have Mercy	8	04/01/86	11/14/94	Mighty Diamonds
Helter Skelter	2	10/31/94	11/19/94	The Beatles
Highway to Hell	61	10/01/89	02/26/97	AC/DC
How High the Moon	3	04/22/90	03/08/93	Morgan Lewis
Hoochie Coochie Man	2	04/10/93	08/08/97	Muddy Waters
I'm Blue I'm Lonesome	30	11/16/94	12/12/95	James B. Smith
I'm So Tired	2	10/31/94	11/18/95	The Beatles
I Know a Little	4	08/10/87	08/03/88	Lynyrd Skynyrd
Izabella	8	06/13/97	12/30/97	Jimi Hendrix
I Walk the Line	9	11/19/92	03/09/93	Johnny Cash
Jesus Just Left Chicago	51	08/10/87	12/07/97	ZZ Top
Johnny B. Goode	22	06/17/95	12/11/97	Chuck Berry
Jump Monk	2	03/12/88	04/24/94	Charles Mingus
La Grange	57	08/10/87	02/25/97	ZZ Top
Life on Mars?	19	10/11/95	03/02/97	David Bowie
Light Up or Leave Me Alone	5	08/21/87	07/25/88	Traffic
Long Journey Home	15	11/17/94	11/29/95	Traditional
Long Time	16	10/07/94	12/09/94	Boston
Love Me	7	02/13/97	11/30/97	Leiber/Stoller for Elvis Presley
Loving Cup	38	02/03/93	12/31/97	Rolling Stones
Manteca	9	11/04/90	11/14/95	Duke Ellington
Melt the Guns	2	10/31/86	04/29/87	XTC
Mustang Sally	6	10/15/86	06/21/88	Wilson Pickett
My Mind's Got a Mind of Its Own	28	03/07/92	12/07/97	Jimmy Dale Gilmore
My Soul	30	02/13/97	12/30/97	Clifton Chenier
Nellie Cane	41	02/23/93	12/08/94	Traditional
On Your Way Down	9	07/23/88	08/12/89	Allen Toussaint
Peaches En Regalia	60	10/15/86	02/28/97	Frank Zappa
Pig in a Pen	2	02/21/93	11/16/94	Traditional
Quinn the Eskimo	7	04/01/86	08/10/87	Bob Dylan
The Real Me	2	10/31/95	12/29/95	The Who
Ride Captain Ride	4	03/23/87	12/30/92	Blues Image
Rocky Top	151	09/12/87	12/28/97	Bordleaux/Felice
Roses Are Free	2	12/11/97	12/31/97	Ween
Satin Doll	12	06/20/88	05/08/93	Duke Ellington
Scarlet Begonias	2	12/01/84	05/03/85	Garcia/Hunter
Sea and Sand	2	10/31/95	12/31/95	The Who
Shaggy Dog	8	10/15/86	10/29/95	Lightnin' Hopkins
Soul Shakedown Party	2	02/17/97	02/20/97	Bob Marley
She Caught the Katy	2	12/06/86	04/29/87	Taj Mahal
Skin It Back	6	10/31/86	07/25/88	Little Feat
Sneaking Sally through the Alley	20	10/30/85	12/30/97	Allen Toussaint
Something's Wrong with My Baby	3	04/23/93	04/30/93	Sam and Dave
Somewhere over the Rainbow	2	08/17/92	04/20/93	Wizard of Oz
Sparks	13	03/23/87	11/29/96	The Who
Swing Low Sweet Chariot	9	10/15/86	11/16/94	Traditional
Take the A-Train	78	10/15/86	04/13/94	Duke Elllington
Take Me to the River	2	11/21/95	07/10/97	Al Green
Tennessee Waltz	2	05/06/93	11/16/94	Patti Page
The Old Home Place	27	06/26/94	12/28/97	The Dillards
Timber (Jerry) [Timber Ho]	45	04/29/87	12/31/97	Josh White
Time Loves a Hero	4	10/29/88	11/05/88	Little Feat
Tush	2	12/06/86	08/10/87	ZZ Top
Uncle Pen	176	03/28/90	07/15/96	Bill Monroe
Undone	5	03/30/89	12/07/89	The Guess Who
Walk Away	44	07/23/88	05/07/94	James Gang
When the Circus Comes	15	02/13/97	12/31/97	Los Lobos
While My Guitar Gently Weeps	16	10/31/94	02/26/97	The Beatles
Whipping Post	31	05/03/85	08/10/96	Allman Brothers
Wipeout	2	04/15/91	04/27/91	The Ventures
Ya Mar	140	05/11/87	12/31/97	The Mustangs
Yerushalayim Schel Zahav	11	07/16/93	12/31/94	N. Scheimer-Sapir

Appendix

READERS' SURVEY

Here they are, the results of the latest *Pharmer's Almanac* readers survey. Since we began distributing surveys in 1995, we have received about 1,000 responses! Included here are results from surveys received in the second half of 1997 and early 1998. This is a fresh new batch of respondents, an entirely different group from those whose responses appeared in volume 4. Interestingly, the last three sets of results have dubbed three different songs as the most popular Phish tune: Mike's Song, YEM, and now, Harry Hood. The most popular shows attended also have changed dramatically, reflecting more recent performances. Please note that there is a new survey on page 323 of the *Almanac*. Fill it out and send it on in!

Survey STATS

Your age
Average: 21.4
Median: 20
Youngest: 13
Oldest: 50

Your first Phish show
Median: 10/2/95
Earliest: 11/19/87

Phavorite Phish songs
1) Harry Hood
2) YEM
3) Mike's Song
4) Guyute
5) Divided Sky
6) Antelope
7) PYITE
8) Weekapaug
9) Lizards
10) AC/DC Bag

Least phavorite Phish songs
1) Bouncing
2) Sample
3) Sparkle
4) Tweezer
5) Fee
6) Esther
7) Golgi
8) Simple
9) It's Ice
10) BBFCM

Phish songs whose lyrics you like most
1) Waste
2) Chalkdust
3) Reba
4) Lizards
5) Strange Design
6) Free
7) Theme
8) PYITE
9) Fluffhead
10) Esther

Songs Phish should experiment with more
1) Guyute
2) Free
3) 2001
4) Halley's Comet
5) Bouncing
6) Ha Ha Ha
7) Simple
8) Sample
9) Cars Trucks Buses
10) Theme

Songs Phish should play more often
1) Guyute
2) Harpua
3) Tube
4) Halley's Comet
5) Mango
6) Fluffhead
7) The Wedge
8) Brother
9) Funky Bitch
10) Esther

Songs Phish should play less often
1) Bouncing
2) Sample
3) Sparkle
4) Character Zero
5) Chalkdust
6) Maze
7) DWD
8) Julius
9) Fee
10) Tweezer

continued

More Survey STATS

How many Phish shows you have on tape
Average: 62
Most: 430

How many hours of Phish you have on tape
Average: 177
Most: 1,220

Three bands besides Phish that you enjoy
1) Grateful Dead
2) moe.
3) Allman Brothers Band
4) Medeski Martin & Wood
5) Dave Matthews Band
6) Widespread Panic
7) Leftover Salmon
8) Santana
9) The Beatles
10) P-Funk

The band member you would spend an hour with, if you could
1) Trey
2) Fishman
3) Mike
4) Page
5) Mimi Fishman (1 vote)

Your favorite Phish album
1) *Junta*
2) *A Live One*
3) *A Picture of Nectar*
4) *Rift*
5) *Slip Stitch and Pass*
6) *Billy Breathes*
7) *Hoist*
8) *Lawn Boy*

Your favorite venue to see Phish
1) Deer Creek, Noblesville, IN
2) Red Rocks, Morrison, CO
3) Anywhere
4) Great Woods, Mansfield, MA
5) Madison Square Garden, New York, NY
6) Alpine Valley, East Troy, WI
7) Hampton Coliseum, Hampton, VA
8) The Gorge, George, WA
9) The Centrum, Worcester, MA
10) Sugarbush, Fayston, VT

Your least favorite venue to see Phish
1) Rosemont Horizon, Chicago, IL
2) Waterloo Village, Stanhope, NJ
3) Hersheypark Arena, Hershey, PA
4) CoreStates Spectrum, Philadelphia, PA
5) Bryce Jordan Center, State College, PA
6) The Palace, Auburn Hills, MI
7) Hartford Civic Center, Hartford, CT
8) Alpine Valley, East Troy, WI
9) Madison Square Garden, New York, NY
10) The Centrum, Worcester, MA

The best Phish shows you've seen
1) 8/16/96 Clifford Ball, Plattsburgh, NY
2) 12/31/96 FleetCenter, Boston, MA
3) 10/31/94 Civic Center, Glens Falls, NY
4) 8/17/96 Clifford Ball, Plattsburgh, NY
5) 12/30/96 FleetCenter, Boston, MA
6) 12/29/96 CoreStates Spectrum, Philadelphia, PA
7) 8/10/96 Alpine Valley, East Troy, WI
8) 10/31/96 The Omni, Atlanta, GA
9) 8/13/96 Deer Creek, Noblesville, IN
10) 12/1/95 Hersheypark, Hershey, PA

How many Phish shows you have seen
Average: 16
Median: 12
Least: 0
Most: 100

the best Phish sticker you ever saw

• I Went • Antelope X-ing • Give a man some fish and he can eat for a day, give a man some Phish and he can groove for a lifetime • Feelin' good about Hood • Thanks Trey • We Went • Wilson sucks • Icculus 3:16 • Phishagonia • I brake for Possum • Forbin's • Phisholicious. • Laugh and laughing fall apart • I brake for Antelope • See the city, see the zoo, traffic light won't let me through • Weekapaugruven • Phishisgruven • Phunkingruvin • Enoughegnugen! • Surrender to the Phlow • Got dank? • Follow me to Gamehendge • Gamehendge State • Trey Bien • Nothing Runs Like an Antelope (with John Deere turned into "High Geere") • My other car is a flying hot dog! • Icculus Saves • This car climbed Mt. Icculus • Page fans are people too • Was it for this my life I sought? • The Phish logo (can't beat it) •

if you could ask any question of the band, what it would be

• Who are you, really? • Could you please stay for more than 1 or 2 shows? • What's your favorite book? • Could I write up one of your setlists? • Why weigh on a sunny day? • What the hell is Trey thinking when he makes those faces while he's jamming? • Why doesn't Trey get some decent clothes? • Will they ever play a Dead song? • Why do they play Bouncin' as an encore? • Who opened on 12/13/97? Was that a real band? • Why didn't you make all of those damn people happy at Red Rocks and play Destiny Unbound? • How do you decide on a setlist? • Where do you come up with the basis for your music? • Where did the name Phish come from? • What was it like to play on "Letterman" and "Conan"? • Do you think that fans read too much into your songs and setlists? • Do you think you might ever want to stop what you're doing? • Why don't you want his autograph? Is it really because he looks too much like Dave or do you have other reasons? • How do you do it? • How often do you guys jam? • Are you human? • Why doesn't the Dude of Life come onstage anymore? • How did you guys ever get to be this good? • What is your favorite song to play? • Can I become a roadie for you guys? • What's your favorite movie? • When do you most feel the music coming through you, not from you? • Have you ever noticed me? • Why no Burlington Memorial Aud. shows? • How do you think up such crazy ideas and lyrics? • What's the real story behind Penn State '86? • Why do you retire certain songs for years at a time? • Do you know when it's a hot show? • Are the fans' favorite songs your favorites too? • If there was no money in it, would you still play? • Who is the musician you admire most? • If you couldn't play music, what would you do? • How do you guys know what the other one is going to do? • How on earth could you be a Flyers phan? [for Trey] • Is the light setup supposed to look like Darth Vader? • Who would win in a fight, Trey or Mike? • Do you know how happy you make people? • What do you have against Destiny Unbound? • If Budweiser offered you $50 million to sponsor a tour, would you drink any of that swill? • Does Tom Marshall write just lyrics, or some of the melodies too? • Does Trey ever get on your nerves, being so bossy and all? • What movies do you watch on the bus? • What do you think of bands like moe., The Disco Biscuits, etc. • Does Kuroda play a role in the jamming? Do you follow his cues? • Where did you get that phunk? • Will you stay together forever? • What are you saying in YEM? • What would you do if you ate my daddy's shoes?

the best Phish T-shirt you have ever seen

• The Nike NICU shirt. • Vermont's Phinest. • Mike's Song Star Wars shirt. • Fishman playing the vacuum with his Lawn Boy beard, goggles, and long hair with Funky Bitch on the back. • YEM shirt with pics of God, Man, shit, and boy on the back. • Clifford Ball shirt. • Maxell NO2. • Air Gordon. • Gamehendge University. • Weekapaugruven. • Gone Phishin'—be back around 4:20. • The shirt with a toilet, microphone, a plate, and an open book (Jon, Mike, Trey, and Page) and "What is a band?" on the back. • The Llama L. L. Bean shirt. • The Reba done like Sega logo. • Runaway shirt that looks like Subway. • Phish—the taste that kids love. • Phuck Yeah. • Chief Wiggum, Makisupa Policeman. • The blue '95 tour shirt. • Gone Phishin' (green). • Shirts with the Phish logo. • Funky Bitch with Marge Simpson. • Calvin and Hobbes "Sharin' the Groove." • Camel Walk shirt that looks like a pack of Camels. • Rift shirt that looks like Jiff. • Glide. • Buried Alive shirt that looks like Burger King. • The shirt with two lesbians with the words "Smells like Phish" (Don't know who made them or who would actually buy one, but you have to respect the creativity). • Mound (like the candy bar). • The Punch You in the Eye that looks like Hawaiian Punch. • A shirt with a beautiful drawing of Trey.

the wackiest, most unexpected thing to ever happen to you at a Phish show

On the Roads: • On the way to Maine a woman walked in front of our van and put her hand up to stop us so her friend could cross, and then she flashed us! • The muffler on the bus in front of us fell off and slid under my car on the way to Plattsburgh. • Driving on Highway 420 on the way to Auburn Hills. We celebrated! • On the way to Deer Creek I pulled up behind a truck that had a large llama on it that said, "Add a llama to your life."• Almost hit a cow on the way to Va. Beach 7/21/97, then when I got there I bought a ticket from someone I had met in moving traffic.• Getting searched from Canada to the States on the way to the Went, only to realize that we had forgotten a ticket, so we were searched again on the way back to Canada and then again on the way back in! • When I blew out a tire in northern Maine. I had already cleared Customs and found a glass piece in the spare tire compartment. • On the way to Limestone I was pulled over while smoking a bowl with beers in plain view, trooper gives me a warning and tells me to have a good show. • On the way to the Palace in '96, we slid off the road during a blizzard. Cops pulled us out, gave us directions, and didn't ask any questions. • I caravaned to Plattsburgh in two cars and I ended up with my friend Melissa and a kid we dubbed "drug lord."He had a conspiracy theory on hemp and the government and took more acid than I ever thought possible. • Car broke down so we hitched a ride. Cops pulled us over, stripped the car, and arrested four out of six of us. • When I left my lights on while I was at school before the Portland show and needed a new battery, which I didn't get until 5:00.

Inside the Show: • We managed to enter the concert area at the Went a half hour early. We walked right past security, through the gates, and up to the stage! • Ate too much acid and shit my pants during a Bathtub Gin opener at Deer Creek. • Gel caps at Hara Arena in '94. Gives new meaning to "Bouncing around the Room!" • 6/19/94 my boyfriend and I wanted to hear Fast Enough figuring that it was unlikely. It was the only *Rift* tune they played! • Champagne Supernova 12/29/96. • Glowstick war, Albany 12/13/97. • Getting blindsided by a twirler at the Spectrum. • I opened my eyes in the middle of a jam at Worcester to see a glowstick heading right for me. I threw up my left hand and caught it! • Some guy at the Clifford Ball passed out on one of my friends and broke his nose. • I closed my eyes during Maze and saw the concert. When I opened them it wasn't so fun, so I closed them. • 11/27/92 I was ticketless and security pulled us into the show during intermission. At the end, I rolled a cigarette and some lady security person pulled me out by the hair. I walked past the bus and saw Mike Gordon. I told him what had happened and he said, "Yeah, we need to start playing bigger places."• Running into a chick and talking, then losing my shit and seeing a chick I worked with, then needing water really badly and while drinking from a sink seeing a friend who was lost too . . . then it was all chill. • My friend passed out at the end of the first set at 11/8/96 because of the heat. • There was a guy on campus who my friends kept mistaking for me. I found out his name and wanted to meet him. At the 12/1/95 Hershey show, I sat down next to some friends and he just happened to be sitting next to me! My friends thought that he was me at first! • At Hartford '96 I was walking to my seat when this guy walks past me and just hands me a backstage pass! One in a million! • My first Phish show, Sample was the first song, and I got goosebumps. It was the first time that I had felt that way since I had last seen the Dead. • Me and my girlfriend were walking to a booth to get some water. I saw this guy and said, "Hey, is that Page?" Page turned around and said, "Yeah, it is." I was spellbound. Couldn't talk, and then someone else went and talked to him. • Thunderstorm in Raleigh '97. • That my brother Sean started the glowstick war at the Great Went. • Getting soaked during the 7/22/97 show. I felt like a Phish swimming through the sea. • At Red Rocks, I met Benjy Eisen of the Phish.Net while I was tripping and I asked him what he thought of the show. "It sucks," he said, "but I'll sell you one of those giant red rocks over there, no money down!" He was joking, but because I was tripping I took him seriously and ran around saying "no money down" until I came down.

Overall: • A scalper giving me $100 to get change amongst 15,000 people. • The first night of the Went, back at the campsite, when I realized that I was at peace with myself and the universe and Phish helped get me there. • Getting thrown up against a wall by Boston police before the 12/31/96 show for my bag of cloves. Spent two hours trying to figure it out. I missed half of the first set. • Seeing a beer cart run into a fan at my first show on 10/18/96. • No toilet paper in Maine! • My wife trying to kidnap my kid from my parents' place while I was at a show. Apparently during an awesome Theme > Black Eyed Katy. She got busted. • Summer '96 tour, five of us and no tent. It sucked! • I drank a bottle of Boone's and smoked some dank with my high school English teacher. • Talking to the band members at every show. • Getting smuggled into the Went with six other people in a U-Haul, hidden in blankets and sweaters with bongs and bowls and drums. • Made Fishman Frock T-shirts and nobody bought them. • I was painting the car in Town Square at the Went when security informed us that we weren't supposed to be painting it! OOPS! • Seeing nearly everyone from my town at the Went, not together, in all of those people. • Friend gets caught sneaking one ounce of weed into a show. The cop dumps it out into the trash, then says, "enjoy the show."• $10 parking! • Trey giving me a ticket in Lexington. • Mike giving me a ticket for 4/22/94. • Entering Gamehendge. • At Pine Lakes campground (Deer Creek) I saw someone pull in catfish over 100 pounds! • 12/31/96 Ran away from home and drove seven hours south to Boston. I told my folks where I was from a pay phone outside of the FleetCenter. • I saw Chinese New Year kung fu performers at First Night, Boston, on chilly night on the way to see Phish for New Year's Eve. • In Morrison, CO '94, my friends and I got back to our campsite after the second show to find all of our gear gone! • Having police steal our tickets for peeing in some bushes near the lot. • Hampton, Oct. '96 I got lost with these two girls from Va. Beach in the lot. Ate a hundred cheese sandwiches and paid $70 for a cab home. • This guy walked by and gave me a fifty-dollar bill with his number and a piece of paper. One of them bumped into me and said, "Excuse me." It was Mike Gordon.

your first Phish experience

• When I first got to the lot for my first show. I was all smiles! • Hearing Sanity. • Riding in the car with my brother and asking him what this "bag it, tag it" song was about. • Waiting for three hours to get into the lot, and rushing in to the show to the sounds of Mike busting into Wilson. • Heard a tape of 5/1/92 in a friend's car and argued as to whether Trey was better than Jimmy Page. I was wrong. Trey is better. • My brother making me listen, thank God. • 7/25/92, fourth-row center stage. Santana smiled at me! • Mann Music Center. I went to one show and it changed my life. • Listening to my brother's *A Live One* and not liking it until I heard it a million times. • Charleston Coliseum on 11/18/95. • Hearing DWD on the radio. • Sitting in a friend's basement listening to Weigh. • Hearing Reba in my friend's dorm room and thinking that it was the shittiest thing ever. Now it's my favorite. • Deer Creek '95. • Listening to *A Picture of Nectar* in my buddy's car and thinking how goofy the lyrics were. • Listening to *Junta* over and over and over again. • *Rift*. • Sitting in a "communal" house with kind strangers getting high. Replacing Zappa with *Rift*. Weigh sold me! • Having a friend explain to me that Phish had very little in common with Fishbone. • Tripping for the second time in my life in my friend's car, *Rift* was playing, and Lengthwise went through my head all night. • Listening to Lizards at work. • Hearing *Rift* when I was eleven and not liking it until a year later. • 11/24/95, first time I heard the vacuum and Suzy! • 12/30/96 was such a blast! • ALS > DWD Jan. '94 and being blown away by Trey's ability. • After the Lake Placid show in '95. • Seeing them play Chalkdust on "Letterman." • In Philly with the most spectacular light show during 2001. I couldn't believe what I was seeing. • A friend threw in a show one night and the next thing I knew I was dancing. I had to wait until the Clifford Ball to catch a show though. • A friend of mine had a bootleg of 7/21/91 and I fell in love. • '93 New Year's show. • Pouring rain at Stowe 7/22/93. • Clifford Ball!!! • I was ten when I heard Tweezer coming from my camp counselor's boom box. I was hooked. The year before I had written to my parents about this great new band called the Grateful Dead. • When my friend gave me *Lawn Boy* and I thought, "what the phuck is this shit?" • Thinking how crazy it was that they were laughing hysterically in Oh Kee Pah. • Hearing Maze and thinking that I had to see them live. • Hearing Divided Sky while in Tortola in the British V.I. • Listening to Bowie at a friend's house while we ate eggrolls. • 11/9/89, just taking it all in. • Noticing how different the scene was as compared to the Dead scene. Not as out of hand. • Dorm room bootleg sessions. My buddy was singing Weigh a lot, so I asked him what was up. • Hearing Oh Kee Pah and wondering who was playing guitar. • Seeing a Phish ticket in a friend's coffin. • Getting way too fucked up for the Boston Garden NYE show. • Two hits of acid, a Walkman, set I of 10/31/90 in a snowstorm. • Hearing *Rift* in a jeep with the top down in the seventh grade. • Some friends were listening in their dorm room and I was like, "What the hell is this?" I borrowed some tapes to listen to and after hearing Reba I was hooked. • Omaha 11/16/96 with a snow/ice storm going on outside. • World Trade Center, Boston, on New Year's Eve '90. One thousand phans dressed like it was Halloween. • Listening to a Nectar's tape. • Gamehendge at Great Woods. • A teammate let me borrow a tape for a road trip. Sparkle got me hooked. • Hearing Fee. • A girlphriend told me about them; I bought an album and was hooked. • The first time I heard *Rift* I was taken for a ride that I'll never forget. • I was a newcomer to the scene, fourteen years old, at 6/13/95. What a great first show! • My cousin gave me a tape with Sparkle on it. The next day I went out and bought *Rift*. • My friends and I turned sixteen so we ran away from home in Maine to see Phish at Deer Creek. • Listening to Phish at a friend's party in high school and seeing them in Atlanta the next day. • I walked into Hunt's during encore 11/87 and saw them play BBFCM with less than ten people in the bar.

if you could make any request of the band, what it would be

• Come hang out with us and see what we do when we're not at a show. • Score my movies in about ten years. • RED ROCKS!!! • Give me a job where I can tour with the band. • Destiny Unbound (I'll jump on the bandwagon!). • Play PYITE more often. • Quit the long, pointless jams and sing more. • More show for the price. Some of the ticket prices are outrageous for the sets. • Never stop playing. • Surprise shows at small clubs and bars. • Don't ever break up! • Don't write any more short, catchy songs. • Let me play with you. • GAMEHENDGE. • Send me a crystal-clear board tape of every show. • More Phunk! • Play Guyute at every show. • More chess games. • Keep up the Halloween shows and festivals. • Play forever. • Cover a hip-hop tune. • Keep having fun. • Play at my house on my birthday. • Talk to the audience more often, like you used to. • A secret show at Nectar's . . . and I get a ticket! • Do not continue to promote drug use through the lyrics to Makisupa. • Play at Tupper Lake, NY, at the park. • Let Fishman sing more. • No European tours. • BIG BALL JAM!!! • More long stands at cool venues. • To love me! • Encore Mango more often. • Cut back on Bouncin'. • More long jams. • Play at Quonset Air Force Base in Rhode Island. • New England fall tour. • Play a show at Peabody's in Hamilton, NY. • Come over and chill. • Play with the Black Crowes. • Give me a job. • Allow vending and let me play with them sometime. • To meet them. • Never sell out! • More jazz. • More surprise guests. • Don't change a thing. • More time between announcement of tour dates and mail-order deadline. • Live from the Mars Hotel on Halloween. • More East Coast summer shows. • Let the Dude sing!!! • Smaller venues, but if they must play larger ones, play Buckeye Lake! • Don't give up Jewish songs. • Bring back some old-school songs and drop It's Ice, Scent of a Mule, and Fee. • Stop playing the Billy Breathes crap. • Open up merchandising rights. • Play in Athens, Georgia. • Play in Minnesota more. • Kick that funky beat for an eternity! • Let me play Sample with them. • Small venues. • Give in and play a Dead tune already!!! • Play the boathouse in Norfolk, Va. as long as I could get a ticket. • For Fishman to keep wearing the dress. • Allow cameras. • Pump up the volume a little. • Let me make out the setlist one night. • Bring the Dude of Life on tour. • Play my basement. • If they play Antelope in Michigan, please say "Tony Bommarito" instead of "Marco Esquandolas." We would go nuts! • Write a song about me and my dog, Roo. • Practice more. You're getting sloppy!

your favorite Phish musical moment

Show-Specific: • At the Went when Trey started talking about art and passed the band's piece through the crowd. • At Champaign '97 when during an insane Makisupa jam, the music stopped and Trey counted 1-2-3 with his fingers and launched back into Makisupa. • At the Went on the second day during Hood when everyone started throwing the glow rods [7]. • Raleigh 7/22/97. Thunderstorms dumped on us and the band and crowd jammed out to Taste like never before. Even though both sets were cut short, I have never been so satisfied with a performance.• Darien Lake with Uncle Sam and the Bozos. Awesome! [4] • The multi-instrument playing at the 7/21/97 show. They were just doin' it without a care. It was freedom! • When Trey ran laps around the stage at Rochester during BBFCM (12/11/97). The light show was intense!!! • Bohemian Rhapsody at New Year's in Boston. • The 100-proof Bathtub Gin at Rupp Arena on 11/7/96. • Mike's Song to open the Hampton 11/22/97 show. • Mudsliding during intermission at Raleigh 7/22/97 followed by an impromptu drum circle. • Bit of Axilla I in the middle of Hood 12/6/96. • Rotation Jam 12/29/96. • Sitting on the top of a U-Haul, tripping, listening to YEM in the distance, watching the sun set at the Went. • Auld Lang Syne > DWD NYE. '93. • When they opened with My Friend My Friend at my first show (Spac '95). • Tweezer 2/20/93. • Trey playing with Claypool. • 12/8/95 Cleveland!!! Tweezer > Kung > Tweezer > Love You! Come Together encore for Lennon. • 12/31/93. I reached an ecstasy I never dreamed of! • Tweezer > Mango at Bangor, ME, 11/2/94. • Bathtub Gin at the Went. • Piano solo on Squirming Coil 8/16/96. • Divided Sky at Plattsburgh. First time I ever shroomed and my favorite song hit at the height of my trip. Cathartic! • The YEM switch jam on 12/29/96 leading into Mike's piano solo with "Sixteen Candles." • Jazzfest. • The lightning 8/6/96. • Second set, 8/10/96. • Whipping Post, 8/10/96. • Meeting Mike and Page at the Lowell show, 5/16/95. • Warren Haynes at Portland. What a sight, Trey and Warren Haynes. • Tweezer 4/22/94. • Antelope 7/16/94. This night was my birthday, my fiftieth show, and my last show before starting a real job. • When the lights and the music seemed to control the wind during Split Open and Melt at Mud Island, 6/14/95. • Divided Sky, 12/31/96, when they first hit the lyrics and the white lights hit. Incredible. • 2001 12/31/96. • Second set at the Roxy, 2/20/93. Mike's > Kung > Hydrogen > Weekapaug > Have Mercy > Rock and Roll All Night Jam > Weekapaug > FEFY and all the other shit they threw in there. • 2/23/90. • Contact 8/10/96. • Theme 8/13/97. • 10/2/95. • 7/13/94, Cavern > Wilson > Cavern. • When they weaved into the Makisupa jam with Page on the theremin at the end of Antelope on 7/6/97. • Slave, 8/4/96 Red Rocks. I thought that Trey's guitar had fallen to pieces because he was playing the shit out of it! • Fish blowing up his drums, 10/31/95. • The GameHoist show, 6/26/94. • 5/19/85, Eyes of the World. • 8/9/97. • Antelope 12/31/93. • DWD with all of the balloons, 12/31/96. • Sugar Blue playing with Phish 4/10/93. • First set, Deer Creek 8/10/97. • Gamehendge at Great Woods '94. • REBA 12/31/93!!

Non-Show-Specific: • All of them!!!!! • Whenever Trey hits that chord during Antelope that changes it from a happy song into something powerful. •At the beginning of YEM after Mike does his thing, and Trey comes in gradually until they break back into the song. • Mid-Stash as the notes flow and repeat again and again. • Any YEM phunk jam! • The part in Guyute at the end just before the lyrics start and they shine the white lights so bright. • When I lose myself during Free. I'll forget that I'm dancing. I get so high that I've nearly fallen down!!! • Antelope!!! • Anytime I feel Phishtacy. You feel this "thing" from your soul to the bottom of your toes. Makes you just want to explode! • Watching Kuroda's fantastic light show!!! • The part in Slave when Page breaks out into what sort of sounds like the theme song to Taxi. • Getting to yell BOYYY!!!! • Everything after Agghhh . . . BOY . . . in YEM. • That indescribable moment when your feet forget what your hands are doing and the music takes you away. • Bass solo at the beginning of Weekapaug. • Transition from Mike's > Simple and Hydrogen > Weekapaug. Amazing!!! • Phish jamming with Popper. • The day *Billy Breathes* came out! • Everytime Trey makes one of those faces. Looks like he's in pain, but he's just so into it. • Page's solos. • YEM vocal jam. • BIG BALL JAM. • The first time I heard Bouncing, the crowd was bouncing, the band was bouncing. It was great! • GAMEHENDGE! • You can feel good about Hood! • Runaway Jim when Mike is playing his soft bass part and then Trey comes in . . . Wah!Wah!Wah! . . . Wah!Wah!Wah!

the most annoying person you have ever met at a Phish show

In the Lots: • People asking for a miracle [8]. • Scammers at shows who try to rip people off and sell fake acid and tickets. • T-shirt people. • The guy who pretends to be an undercover cop and is really just a guy with a walkie-talkie selling stickers. • People who look down on spare changers and miracle seekers. • The people who say that you are under arrest when you're tokin' up and then try to sell you a sticker.

Phan Types: • Bouncin' fans and "whitehats" (drunken college students who don't even like Phish). • The ones always asking for cigarettes or a beer. • The freak with the UFO fliers on summer tour '97. EVERYTHING was symbolic of something else. • A.G.—Complete Ganker!!!!! • Spare changers, people who constantly rag on Phish and insist the Dead is where it's at, and people who don't dance. • People who try to persuade one's emotions inside a venue by messing with them. • People who sit down or are too messed up to enjoy a phat jam. Get up and DANCE!!! • People who keep asking, "What song is this?" • Phish know-it-alls! • Posers. • Those who feel that drugs/touring are the only way to be a phan. • The jerks that go for the drugs and the image and not the music. • A tour dog named Harpua who wouldn't stop sniffing my butt. • Frat boys. • Sorority girls. • Phish fans who preach peace and love and then rank on people in fraternities and sororities. • Snobby hippies. • Phish fans who claim they hate the Grateful Dead. • Saw a fan combing lice out of his hair.

Phriends???: • All the people with no money who suddenly become your friends after they see you buy that bag of dank. • My friend Saul, who feels the need to predict the opening song of every show he goes to. • I saw Mike and then the people I went to the show with saw him and abandoned me coatless and in freezing rain. • Kid from my high school who hit on my girlfriend for a whole set.

Those Wacky Teenagers: • Little kids at a show who are just there to smoke or fall asleep. • Little girls that go nuts when they play Bouncin'. • Little kids who jump up and down during Bouncin'. • These twelve-year-old kids who were throwing food off the balcony. • The twelve-year-old kids who ask you for drugs. • This young kid who said he had twenty shots of vodka. I was sitting in the hall waiting for my friend who was in the bathroom. I had to wait there for her and had to listen to him yell lewd remarks to every woman that walked by. I asked him to stop but he said no. And he ate all of my popcorn.

Teenager's Revenge: • People who think that just because you are young you don't know anything about Phish. • People who think that they can take advantage of me because I'm a kid.

Altered Experiences: • This one kid at a Philly show, holiday '96, who was tripping and kept smacking me until I finally told him to get lost. • Dude at the Went who was freaking out on something. He was mumbling to himself in some made-up language and kept jumping around and yelling at people. • People who drink too much and need help to stand up. • A drunk guy next to me during set break. • This guy, Brian, at Albany 12/13/97. He was drinking and on Valiums and had to be the most annoying drunk ever, and I had to sit next to him! • The girl who threw up all over herself and my stuff. • Some heroin addicts in the Las Vegas parking lots. • People who go to the shows only to get fucked up. • This lady who was tripping and vomited on the hill at Alpine. Most of us were gagging through the second set. • This drunk who pissed on the seat next to me while yelling, "Trey, you make me float upon the waves! Trey, I'm floating!"

In the Show: • Guy in front of me in a Hawaiian shirt and a bad haircut at Deer Creek who was jumping so high I couldn't see. • This asshole who crowded in up front because he "had to meet Trey." After about a half hour of verbally abusing him he disappeared. • Two kids on 12/30/96 who were smoking cigars. • The five middle-aged guys behind me at 12/31/97. They kept complaining to their friend (the only phan in the group) that Phish sucked and they wanted to leave. • When looking for my brother's seat on the floor in Philly, I couldn't find it because his stuff was under it. I was asking people and this guy in the row behind me taped his seat number to his head and kept saying, "seat 9, seat 9, seat 9, seat 9." • Some dude that was falling over every two minutes in front of me. • Someone asked me three times what song they were playing. Harpua, Harpua, and Harpua. • This guy in front of me yelling, "The spaghetti's on my head," during an awesome Sloth. • The asshole at Darien who stepped on my foot. When I gave him a look he said, "Hey, man, it's a Phish show. Anything goes!" What a tool. • The wankers who had a hot dog fight behind us at 12/29/96 and got mustard on my friend. • Guys in front of me in Auburn Hills talking about how many times they had seen Ozzy and Motley Crüe at the Palace. • This girl screaming during a cappella, "I can do anything I want!" • This guy who kept saying during Sleeping Monkey how bad the song sucked. • This ugly naked guy who danced the whole show naked next to me. • This guy in Lincoln, Nebraska, who kept asking me to "fix his pipe." Seven times he asked, and I had no dope!

Talkers, Singers, and Spewers: • This guy from Chicago who kept telling me how awesome the Bulls and Bears were. • Anyone who feels the need to yell in the Divided Sky space! • People who talk all show. • The person behind me singing louder than Trey.

Security/Police: • Security guard at Champaign that began macing the crowd when a kid collapsed. • People trying to bust the vendors. Get a life! • Most security folks. • The security at Richmond's Classic Amphitheater. For some reason, perhaps the color of my skin, I was the only one out of my group of friends asked to leave for trying to bring in beer. This was the last time that I drank at a show. • Security at Bryce Jordan. • The bald security guard in Spokane, WA, who hassled everyone inside and outside of the venue. • POLICE. • M.S.G. security.

Happy Thoughts: • I've never met nicer people!!!!!

The Pharmer's Almanac Volume 5 Survey Form

Welcome to our fifth readers' survey. Please send us your thoughts on this page, a photocopy of this page, or separate sheets of paper as needed. All submissions become property of *The Pharmer's Almanac*. Have fun!

PHISH'S MUSIC

What three Phish songs do you...

Most enjoy? __________

Least enjoy? __________

Most like the lyrics to? __________

What three songs would you like to see the band...

Play more often? __________

Play less often? __________

Experiment with more? __________

What song would you like to see the band...

Revive? __________

Start covering? __________

What is your favorite Phish musical moment? __________

ON TOUR

How many Phish shows have you seen? __________

When did you see your first show? __________

What are the three best Phish shows you've seen (in order)? __________

Where is your favorite venue to see Phish? __________

Where is your least favorite venue to see Phish? __________

On your way to or at a Phish show, what's... __________

The most intense, wacky, or unexpected thing that's happened to you? __________

The most annoying person (or people) you've met? __________

The best Phish t-shirt and bumper sticker you've seen? __________

What was your first Phish experience? __________

If you could make one request of the band, what would it be? __________

If you could ask one question of the band, what would it be? __________

If you could spend an hour with one band member, who would you choose? __________

ON TAPES

How many Phish shows do you have on tape? __________

How many hours of Phish do you have on tape? __________

What are your three favorite live Phish tapes (in order)? __________

What makes your favorite tape so great? __________

What's your favorite Phish album? __________

What are three musical acts besides Phish you enjoy? __________

If you have a tape list, please include it with your survey responses. (See Note below for more information.)

THE PHARMER'S ALMANAC

Where did you get your copy of the Almanac? __________

Which features of the Almanac*...*

Do you most enjoy? __________

Do you least enjoy? __________

What's missing from the Almanac *that should be added?* __________

Any other thoughts or ideas? What did we miss? What else should we be asking? __________

ABOUT YOU...

Name: __________

Address: __________

City/State/Zip: __________

Phone: __________

E-mail: __________

Age: __________ Sex: F M

I grant permission to The Pharmer's Almanac *to use my submissions.*

(signature) __________ *(date)* __________

Important Note: In the future, The Pharmer's Almanac might send out information about upcoming editions of the book or new products to people on our mailing list. If you would prefer NOT to receive information from us by [ ] U.S. mail or [ ] e-mail, please check the appropriate box(es). Also, as part of the *Almanac*'s ongoing research project to track down missing setlists and update currently erroneous setlists, we might phone or e-mail people based on tapelists they submit to us and ask them about the contents of tapes which appear on their lists. If you would prefer NOT to be contacted by us by [ ] phone or by [ ] e-mail as part of our research project, please check the appropriate box(es). Thanks.

• Acknowledgments •

When four of us set out to create *The Pharmer's Almanac*, we envisioned it as a community project, one which would capture the collective voice of Phish fans, not just our own. In the three years that have passed since we first conceived the idea of the *Almanac*, it has been our pleasure, and thrill, to meet and share knowledge with so many of the people who help form the Phish world.

We have also come to admire and respect many in the online world who were the first to begin compiling Phish's history, especially as it relates to setlists. Without their tireless efforts this work could not exist, especially as most of the setlists contained in the *Almanac* can be traced back to, or were sourced directly from, their compilations and the Phish.Net archive.

Some of the active online historians who deserve mention are, from the early years, Dan Shoop, Shelly Culberston, Lee Silverman, and Ellis Godard, and more recently, Andrew Gadiel, Dan Schar, and Pat Johnson.

We are also equally indebted to many journalists and rock music critics who have published interviews with the band or unearthed various snippets of Phish history. Many of their contributions are noted throughout the book when quotes from the band are sourced directly from their articles, but we would also like to make special mention of the folks at *Relix, Dupree's Diamond News, Unbroken Chain,* and *Pollstar*, as well as Richard Gehr and Paul Robicheau. All of their works in covering Phish are unparalleled.

We also wish to acknowledge Dave Thompson and his book *Go Phish!* (St. Martin's, 1997) and make special mention of Dean Budnick and *The Phishing Manual* (Hyperion, 1996). *The Phishing Manual* in particular raised standard for levels of detail in unearthing band history—Dean and his book are worthy of the highest praise.

Our expanding base of photographers also has our gratitude.

And then there is the long list of those who lent a helping hand to us in other ways over the last three years. They include: Chris DiLeo, Tom Baggot, Gary Perkinson, Tara Chasnoff, Joanne Bernstein, Keri Lee Marino, Matt Monaco, everyone at SGB and the Brown *Daily Herald*, Les Kippel, Ken Hays, Lee Crompton, Leigh Gallagher, Chris Woody, Pete Shapiro, Chis Zahn, Adam Levine, Peter Dunn, Mom Glass, Don Kantor, Matt Bush, Howie Kopman, Marty Zimmerman, Michelle Gross, John Dindus, Bruce Burgess, and many others.

We also wish to thank our wonderful editorial contributors, artists, and those who were interviewed by us. Without all of you, there would be no *Almanac*.

Editorial Contributors

Jesse Appleman, Jay Archibald, Julie Beck, William Bengle, B. P., John Boeheim, Marco Burgio, James Cabot, Caroline Carillo, Tina Campbell, Jagjit Chadha, Paige Clemm, David Clement, Bob Colby, Joey Conroy, Dan Corbin, Michael Davidoff, Jeremy Davis, Benjy Eisen, Dan Gibson, Chris De Gieson, Dom DeLuca, Michael & Rebecca Dougherty, Sean Ferris, John Fitch, Mark Fields, A. J. Fucile, Pete Gershon, Daniel Gladman, Nancy Grossman, Todd Haggle, Peter Hancock, Ric Hanna, Jason Hedrington, Kevin Hogan, Christine Holbrook, Mike Indgin, Justin Jeromon, Lane Jost, Jordan Kahn, Russell Kahn, Jon Katz, Charlie Lazarus, Adam Levine, Alyssa Litoff, George Lyons, Linda Mahdesian, Robert McArty, Shawn McFarland, Jon Mohr, Matt Monaco, Dan O'Brien, Monique O'Connell, Steve Paolini, Gary Perkinson, Tom Pinnick, James Pollin, David Porter, Josh Porter, Todd Prusin, Rebecca Quate, Mike Railey, Mike Ricci, Emily Rigmont, Jason Roberts, Michael Rotkowitz, Greg M. Schwartz, Jonathan Schwartz, Kirsti Scutt, Greg Shanken, Andy Shirey, Steve Silberman, Katie Silver, Andrew Smith, Ed Smith, Steve Spott, Ali Tariq, Mike Thomas, Scott Thornburg, Steve Tremblay, Jeff Trinco, Josh Valentine, Steve Wallace, Butch Weiss, Shep Williams, Thomas Zerkowski.

Consultants

Dan Archer, Tom Baggot, Rob Dasaro, Rob Florence, Chad Garland, Pete Gershon, Mike Graff, John Greene, Dave Grippo, Gordon Hookailo, Jamie Janover, Greg Kelly, Jamie Masefield, Katie McConnell, Brendan McKenna, Steve Pollak, Michael Ray, Ken Schneiderman, Rich Seaberg, Charlene Smith, Patrick Smith, Gordon Stone, Stacey Starkweather.

Artists

Keri Lee Marino, Jeremy Sheely, Brian Smith.

Photographers

Jay Archibald, Marco Burglio, Jong Chan Cho, David Clement, Randy Austin-Cordova, Emily Barrett, Anthony Buchla, Jessica Fausty, Jason Gleasony, Christine Holbrook, Russel Kahn, Jessica Kamens, George Lyons, Lucas Nataly, Allison Offerman, Kelley Thomas.

The Pharmer's Market

U.S. MAIL
The Pharmer's Almanac
328 Flatbush Ave.
Suite 122
Brooklyn, NY 11238

PHONE: (718) 398-4442
ask for Andy or Larry

FAX: (718) 398-0127

EMAIL: apharmers@aol.com

Inevitable Plastic Presence: We accept all major credit cards.

THE PHARMER'S MARKET E-Z ORDER FORM

Description of Fabulous Item	*Price*	*Qty.*	*Total Item Price*
The Pharmer's Almanac, Volume 5 *The current edition. 336 pages.*	**$17.95**		
The Pharmer's Almanac, Volume 4 *November 1997. 276 pages.*	**$15.95**		
The Pharmer's Almanac, Volume 3 *November, 1996. 224 pages.*	**$13.95**		
The Pharmer's Almanac, Volume 2 *July, 1996. 176 pages.* *Limited supply—call to check availability.*	**$13.95**		
The Pharmer's Almanac, Volume 1 *February, 1996. 100 pages.*	**$13.95**		
Almanac T-Shirt *Features the Almanac logo (seen above) in white on red or blue 100% cotton shirt.*	**$10.00**		
Almanac Volume 2 Cover Poster *Individually signed and numbered by rock artist Chris Di Leo. 20"x27".* *100 available—call to check availability.*	**$10.00**		
Almanac Sticker *Features the Almanac logo. Free with back issue or multiple book orders.*	**$1.00**		

Item Subtotal	
Shipping *See column at right for shipping costs.*	
NY Sales Tax *NY residents add 8%.*	
GRAND TOTAL	

METHOD OF PAYMENT

___ *Personal check enclosed.*

___ *U.S. Postal money order enclosed.*

___ *Bill my credit card: (circle one)*

Visa Mastercard Discover Amex

*Account Number:*___________________

*Expiration Date:*___________________

Shipping Expenses:

- All copies of the Almanac, *postage included.*
- T-shirts, add $3 per shirt ordered.
- Posters, add $3 for any number ordered.
- Stickers, postage free.

NOTE: If you are ordering three or more items, just add a total of $5 for postage and we'll pick up the rest.

Ordering Info:

- Make checks payable to "The Pharmer's Almanac."
- Do not send cash.
- Please keep a copy of your order form for your records.
- Orders should be sent to The Pharmer's Almanac, 328 Flatbush Ave., Suite 122, Brooklyn, NY 11238, or faxed to **(718) 398-0127**. You can also order from us by phone by calling **(718) 398-4442**.
- Please allow up to four weeks for delivery.

Name: ___________________ Phone: ___________________

Address: ___________________ Email: ___________________

City/State/Zip ___________________

Please see note on reverse side.